DATE DUE

			PRINTED IN U.S.A.

TWENTIETH-CENTURY ROMANCE AND GOTHIC WRITERS

PREFACE

KAY MUSSELL

EDITOR

JAMES VINSON

ASSOCIATE EDITOR

D.L. KIRKPATRICK

GALE RESEARCH COMPANY
BOOK TOWER • DETROIT, MICHIGAN 48226

CONTENTS

PREFACE

The roots of gothic and romance fiction lie in the origins of the novel form itself. In the 18th and early 19th centuries, the two most prominent types of fiction—the seduction story and the gothic tale of terror—were the predecessors of today's romance fiction, and for two centuries writers on both sides of the Atlantic have written stories of romantic adventure that appealed to a largely middle-class audience. But as the novel form matured, the gothic and romantic subject matter was left behind, becoming the province of popular writers who continued to write such tales while more serious authors examined topics of a more universal character. Critics of early fiction often noted the high percentage of female readers for gothic and romance; but most serious novelists were male, addressing themselves to an audience that was not sex-specific.

Romances, however, continued to flourish even in eclipse. Although these novels received little critical attention, publishers and readers kept them alive. The books were written, published, read, and enjoyed whether or not the literary establishment took notice of them and despite the disrepute into which they had fallen.

In the 20th century, gothic and romance novels have had a steady popularity, although only a handful of authors prior to 1960 enjoyed significant public attention, usually through the repeated production of best-sellers or by writing a single block-buster novel with romantic overtones. Writers like Mary Roberts Rinehart, for example, who wrote both romantic mysteries and straight romances, were occasionally so prolific and so successful that they achieved public prominence over a long period of time. Alternatively, a writer such as Margaret Mitchell, author of one exceptionally popular historical romance, might influence scores of lesser writers who never achieved her audience.

For the most part, however, writers of gothic and romantic novels have worked in relative obscurity, attracting a largely female audience of readers who were in on the secret. Both gothics and romances have been categorized by critics and scholars as "mere" love stories or as unrealistic emotional adventures unworthy of serious consideration. Nevertheless, in the early 1980's two of the five best-selling authors in the world—Barbara Cartland and Janet Dailey— were writers of romance.

Gothic and romantic novels are closely related forms of fiction, although within the range of plot conventions there is significant variation in both form and quality. Like other narrative formulas, these books share a common set of interests and take place in similar fictional worlds. Detective and mystery novels, for example, share a fascination with the mythology of crime. Horror novels and science fiction are always interested in the "what-if," the speculation about alien conditions that might impinge upon the rational world. Westerns are concerned with the grand adventure of settling new territory and building a civilization in the wilderness. Spy stories involve the clash of nations and the dirty business of espionage. Romances and gothics take place in a world in which love and domesticity are central to the protagonists' value system and in which conventional conflicts are often centered around the family, however adventurous a novel's plot may be. Suspense may derive from the exciting historical adventure of living in an age of turmoil; it may come from the titillation of the outrageous and horrifying; or it may result from the exquisite conflict between potential lovers. But whatever the ingredients of the individual plot or formula, gothic and romantic novels share a concern with the details of women's personal lives, of mate selection and family formation, of problems between lovers, and of the impact of events upon domestic affairs. Writers of gothics and romances delineate the effect of extreme situations upon men and women in the realm of their conventional domestic concerns; and these novels often—although not always—portray a woman at the center of the action.

Gothic and romantic novels are best seen as parts of a continuum, with books having more or less domestic orientation while still maintaining a commitment to the adventure that can be found within the framework of love and human relationships. The novels of the softcover romance series focus upon the private, intimate relationships between lovers, charting the course of the couple's developing feelings until they make a lifetime commitment to each other. These romances are relatively short and resemble each other to a remarkable degree. Even in series novels, however, there is variation in quality and inventiveness. On the opposite end of the spectrum are the more adventurous gothic romances and some historical romances, books in which the characters are threatened not by their personal difficulties but by forces from the world outside. In gothics, potential lovers are kept apart by the machinations of the villain; in historical romances, by the momentous events of the setting in the past.

Series romances aim at an audience that is almost totally female, and the adventure of such novels rarely transcends the issue of the love story; on the other hand, historical romances and family saga romances paint a picture on a wider canvas, with the family rather than an individual woman at the center. The very essence of romance and gothic, however, remains personal, interior, concerned with motivation and action that brings a story to a kind of domestic stasis. The lovers may be separated or united, the family may be intact or disrupted, but the stories are always told against a domestic value system in which characters are rewarded or punished according to conventional moral norms.

The past two decades have seen a dramatic resurgence in the romantic genres. New authors have achieved great success and reprints of older novels have found wide circulation. Romance series have proliferated. In these twenty years, several stages of development in romances have occurred, and although some predict the market will soon collapse, it shows no sign of doing so at present.

In the early 1960's, the most popular type of fiction in the gothic/romance genre was the novel of romantic suspense, called conveniently by publishers "gothic romance." British writers were most prominent, but their American colleagues were also active. The modern popularity of the gothic romance can probably be most accurately dated from the publication in 1960 of *Mistress of Mellyn* by Eleanor Burford Hibbert (writing as Victoria Holt). The novel showed its derivation from the Brontës and Daphne du Maurier on almost every page, but it captured the imaginations of readers and writers alike and sparked an upsurge in novels of domestic adventure with sprightly heroines who solved mysteries, protected families and children (not necessarily their own), and won the love of the hero by the final page. For most of that decade, the output of gothic romances remained high, led by Holt, Dorothy Eden, Mary Stewart, and Phyllis Whitney, who were imitated by a host of other writers. As the popularity of the gothic romance grew, other romantic formulas also achieved wider distribution. Historical fiction became more prevalent as publishers searched for new authors while also reprinting older works by such writers as Georgette Heyer and Barbara Cartland. In the latter part of the decade and throughout the 1970's, Regency romances, inspired by Heyer, achieved great success.

Although the gothic and historical romance formulas were the best known, other related types of women's fiction continued to sell. Various series of romantic love stories were popular in Britain, although their distribution in the United States was only a fraction of its current level. The United States was more an audience for romances than a major producer until the first of the erotic romances (or "bodice-rippers") by such American authors as Kathleen Woodiwiss and Rosemary Rogers. The new American romance formula of the 1970's differed from its predecessors in one significant way: the books were much more sexually explicit, featuring heroines whose sexual encounters (in or out of marriage) were more graphically described than in other romances. Before this change, premarital sex had always been a sign that a character was a "fallen woman," similar to the heroine of Kathleen Winsor's *Forever Amber*, and therefore unworthy of a lasting marriage. By the middle of the decade, however, the erotic romances with either historical or contemporary settings were at center stage, with gothics and straight romances flourishing at a lesser level.

The United States is currently experiencing a high-level competition among publishers of series romances. Toward the end of the decade, the distribution of series romances increased rapidly as the alliance between Mills and Boon in Britain and Harlequin in Canada moved to dominance in the American market. Both those firms had exceptionally effective marketing strategies, selling books by mail order and subscription as well as in retail outlets. As American publishers recognized the success of the Mills and Boon/Harlequin strategy, competition ignited. Simon and Schuster, formerly Harlequin's American distributor, inaugurated the Silhouette Romance series to compete for a share of the lucrative market. In a period of slightly more than two years (1980-82) Silhouette had proliferated into four distinct series of romances, including a line for teenagers, a growing segment of the market. Silhouette also lured Mills and Boon authors with some success and began aggressive marketing abroad.

In the same two years, other American publishers followed suit. Dell redesigned its romance series and inaugurated a new line called Candlelight Ecstasy Romances, featuring a more sophisticated and explicit portrayal of sexuality. Jove began its Second Chance at Love series, with heroines who had failed the first time around and now, older and wiser, were ready for a more adult relationship. Bantam, working with the British publishing firm of Robert Hale, started its Circle of Love series, a more restrained and traditional romance formula than most of the other new lines. Ballantine began a series entitled Life and Love, using older heroines and deriving from the more sophisticated novels of such romance writers as Danielle Steel and Helen Van Slyke.

Each of these new series emphasized the company's product through packaging, formula control enforced by author's "tipsheets," and advertising to promote an image of the series' quality and diversity within a narrow range of predictable plots. The formula control of these publishers relies upon extensive market research aimed at discovering what women want to read so that editors can tailor the product to particular segments of the market. Such publisher control is relatively new in popular fiction. To be sure, series of novels were published in the 19th century, and certain publishing houses have long been known for issuing particular kinds of genre fiction, but the production and marketing of series romance novels represents a more complex development in popular entertainment, comparable to the way television programs are developed, packaged, and sold.

Institutional support for romances has also increased. The Romantic Writers of America was established to provide services to American authors similar to those offered British writers by the older Romantic Novelists Association. Newsletters for fans of romances are proliferating, and conventions for romance readers and authors have been held. Romance is big business today, and the book establishment has had to take notice.

The current situation, however, is probably an aberration, one of those historical moments when the gothic and romance formulas are particularly appealing to a wide audience. Over the past two centuries, these formulas have experienced intermittent waves of prominence that eventually waned, although their production has never entirely disappeared. The novels of especially popular authors remain in print for generations of readers while the more ephemeral works are forgotten.

Only recently, under the influence of the emerging fields of popular culture and women's studies, have scholars begun to look systematically and seriously at gothic and romance writers and readers. Because the area of study is so new, it is hampered by a paucity of bibliographical and critical materials. A reference book like this volume should make basic information available for further scholarly consideration.

—Kay Mussell

READING LIST

Abartis, Caesarea, "The Ugly-Pretty, Dull-Bright, Weak-Strong Girl in the Gothic Mansion," in *Journal of Popular Culture* (Bowling Green, Ohio), Fall 1979.

Allen, Richard O., "If You Have Tears: Sentimentalism as Soft Romanticism," in *Genre* (Plattsburgh, New York), June 1975.

Anderson, Rachel, *The Purple Heart Throbs: The Sub-Literature of Love*. London, Hodder and Stoughton, 1974.

Bailey, Margaret, "The Women's Magazine Short-Story Heroine in 1957 and 1967," in *Journalism Quarterly* (Minneapolis), 1969.

Bayer-Berenbaum, Linda, *The Gothic Imagination: Expansion in Gothic Literature and Art*. Rutherford, New Jersey, Fairleigh Dickinson University Press, 1982.

Berman, Phyllis, "They Call Us Illegitimate," in *Forbes* (New York), 6 March 1978.

Britton, Anne, and Marion Collin, *Romantic Fiction*. London, Boardman, 1960.

Cawelti, John G., *Adventure, Mystery, and Romance: Formula Stories as Art and Popular Culture*. Chicago, University of Chicago Press, 1976.

Cecil, Mirabel, *Heroines in Love 1750-1974*. London, Joseph, 1974.

Cornillon, Susan Koppelman, editor, *Images of Women in Fiction: Feminist Perspective*. Bowling Green, Ohio, Popular Press, 1972.

Douglas, Ann, "Soft-Porn Culture," in *New Republic* (Washington, D.C.), 30 August 1980.

Drake, Robert Y., Jr., "Tara Twenty Years After," in *Georgia Review* (Athens), Summer 1958.

Franzwa, Helen, "Female Roles in Women's Magazine Fiction 1940-1970," in *Woman: Dependent or Independent Variable?*, edited by Rhoda Kesler Unger and Florence L. Denmark. New York, Psychological Dimensions, 1975.

Greenfeld, Beth, and Juliann E. Fleenor, editors, *The Female Gothic*. St. Albans, Vermont, Eden Press, 1982.

Hackett, Alice Payne, and James Henry Burke, *Eighty Years of Best Sellers*. New York, Bowker, 1977.

Harlequin 30th Anniversary 1949-1979: The First 30 Years of the World's Best Romance Fiction. Toronto, Harlequin, 1979.

Hart, James D., *The Popular Book: A History of America's Literary Taste*. New York, Oxford University Press, 1950.

Harvey, Brett, "Boy Crazy," in *Village Voice* (New York), 10 February 1982.

Hoekstra, Ellen, "The Pedestal Myth Reinforced: Women's Magazine Fiction 1900-1920," in *New Dimensions in Popular Culture*, edited by Russel B. Nye. Bowling Green, Ohio, Popular Press, 1972.

Hofstadter, Beatrice, "Popular Culture and the Romantic Heroine," in *American Scholar* (Washington, D.C.), Winter 1960-61.

Inge, M. Thomas, editor, *Handbook of American Popular Culture 1-2* (includes sections on gothic fiction and romantic fiction). Westport, Connecticut, Greenwood Press, 2 vols., 1979-80.

Mann, Peter H., *The Romantic Novel: A Survey of Reading Habits*, and *A New Survey: The Facts about Romantic Fiction*. London, Mills and Boon, 2 vols., 1969-74.

Minundri, Regina, "From Jane to Germaine, with Love," in *Library Journal* (New York), 15 February 1973.

Moers, Ellen, *Literary Women*. New York, Doubleday, 1976; London, W.H. Allen, 1977.

Mussell, Kay, "Beautiful and Damned: The Sexual Woman in Modern Gothic Fiction," in *Journal of Popular Culture* (Bowling Green, Ohio), Summer 1975.

Mussell, Kay, *Women's Gothic and Romantic Fiction: A Reference Guide*. Westport, Connecticut, Greenwood Press, 1981.

Nye, Russell B., editor, *New Dimensions in Popular Culture*.   Bowling Green, Ohio, Popular Press, 1972.

Nye, Russel B., *The Unembarrassed Muse: The Popular Arts in America*.   New York, Dial Press, 1970.

O'Toole, Patricia, "Paperback Virgins," in *Human Behavior* (Los Angeles), February 1979.

Radcliffe, Elsa J., *Gothic Novels of the Twentieth Century: An Annotated Bibliography*. Metuchen, New Jersey, Scarecrow Press, 1979.

Radway, Janice, "The Utopian Impulse in Popular Literature: Gothic Romances and 'Feminist' Protest," in *American Quarterly* (Philadelphia), Summer 1981.

Regan, Nancy, "A Home of One's Own: Women's Bodies in Recent Women's Fiction," in *Journal of Popular Culture* (Bowling Green, Ohio), Spring 1978.

Ritchie, Claire, *Writing the Romantic Novel*.   London, Bond Street, 1962.

Robinson, Lillian S., "On Reading Trash," in *Sex, Class, and Culture*.   Bloomington, Indiana University Press, 1978.

"Romance Fiction: A PW Special Report" edited by Daisy Maryles and Robert Dahlin, in *Publishers Weekly* (New York), 13 November 1981.

Ruggiero, Josephine A., and Louise C. Weston, "Pulp Feminists," in *Human Behavior* (Los Angeles), February 1978.

Russ, Joanna, "What Can a Heroine Do? or, Why Women Can't Write," in *Images of Women in Fiction: Feminist Perspectives*, edited by Susan Koppelman Cornillon.   Bowling Green, Ohio, Popular Press, 1972.

Smith, Herbert F., *The Popular American Novel 1865-1920*.   Boston, Twayne, 1980.

Walsh, Mary Roth, "Images of Women Doctors in Popular Fiction," in *Journal of Popular Culture* (Bowling Green, Ohio), Summer 1978.

EDITOR'S NOTE

The selection of writers included in this book is based upon the recommendations of the advisers listed on page xv.

The entry for each writer consists of a biography, a bibliography, and a signed critical essay. Living authors were invited to add a comment on their work. The bibliographies list writings according to the categories of romance and gothic fiction and other publications, and is further sub-divided under pseudonyms. Series characters are indicated for novels. Original British and United States editions of all books have been listed; other editions are listed only if they were the first editions, though an exception has been made to include publications of Harlequin Books (Toronto). As a rule all uncollected short stories published since the entrant's last collection have been listed.

Entries include notations of available bibliographies, manuscript collections, and critical studies. Other critical materials appear in the Reading List of secondary works on the genre.

We would like to thank the entrants and contributors for their patience and cooperation in helping us to compile this book.

ADVISERS

Rachel Anderson
Mary Cadogan
Barbara Cartland
Warren French

Kay Mussell
Victor Neuberg
Elsa J. Radcliffe
Janice Radway

CONTRIBUTORS

Patricia Altner
Rachel Anderson
Jane S. Bakerman
Earl F. Bargainnier
Melvyn Barnes
Susan B. Berneis
E.F. Bleiler
Marylaine Block
Wendy Bousfield
Susan Branch
Jean Buchanan
Mary Cadogan
Jennifer Cargill
Tessa Rose Chester
Pamela Cleaver
Warren French
Marcia G. Fuchs
Jane Gottschalk
Elizabeth Grey
Marion Hanscom
Marion R. Harris
Barrie Hayne
Joanne Harack Hayne
Michael Held
Allayne C. Heyduk
Joan Hinkemeyer
Louis James
Margaret Jensen
Barbara Kemp
Larry N. Landrum
Lornie Leete-Hodge

Marilyn Lockhart
George C. Longest
Mary C. Lynn
Gina Macdonald
Joan McGrath
Sally Allen McNall
P.R. Meldrum
Arlene Moore
Marilynn Motteler
Kay Mussell
Necia A. Musser
Kim Paynter
Kathy Piehl
Nancy H. Pogel
Janice Radway
Nancy Regan
Bette B. Roberts
Karen Robertson
Lucy Rogers
Josephine A. Ruggiero
Geoffrey A. Sadler
Anne M. Shields
Andrea Lee Shuey
Katherine Staples
Judith Summers
Thomas R. Tietze
W.M. von Zharen
George Walsh
Louise C. Weston
Peggy York
Paula M. Zieselman

TWENTIETH-CENTURY ROMANCE AND GOTHIC WRITERS

Alice Abbott
Joan Aiken
Patricia Ainsworth
Madame Albanesi
Hervey Allen
Lucilla Andrews
Evelyn Anthony
Jane Arbor
Michael Arlen
Charlotte Armstrong
Elizabeth Ashton
Nan Asquith
Ruby M. Ayres

Faith Baldwin
Florence L. Barclay
Countess Barcynska
Susan Barrie
Betty Beaty
Helen Beauclerk
Lily Adams Beck
Pamela Bennetts
Evelyn Berckman
Elisabeth Beresford
Anne Betteridge
Gloria Bevan
Laura Black
Jane Blackmore
Charity Blackstock
Kathryn Blair
Stephanie Blake
Ursula Bloom
Marjorie Bowen
Madeleine Brent
Ann Bridge
Katrina Britt
Louis Bromfield
Iris Bromige
D.K. Broster
Nancy Buckingham
Mary Burchell
Lolah Burford
Rose Burghley
G.B. Burgin
Gwendoline Butler

Elizabeth Cadell
Hall Caine
Janet Caird
Taylor Caldwell
Robyn Carr
Barbara Cartland
David Case
Isobel Chace
Hester W. Chapman
Mollie Chappell
Theresa Charles
Brian Cleeve

Sophie Cleugh
Marian Cockrell
Virginia Coffman
Marion Collin
Catherine Cookson
Jilly Cooper
Marie Corelli
Thomas B. Costain
Juanita Coulson
Caroline Courtney
Frances Cowen
Mary Francis Craig
Cecily Crowe

Janet Dailey
Iris Danbury
Dorothy Daniels
Clare Darcy
Marcia Davenport
Dorothy Salisbury Davis
Warwick Deeping
E.M. Delafield
Mazo de la Roche
R.F. Delderfield
Ethel M. Dell
Viña Delmar
Joyce Dingwell
Maud Diver
Anne Duffield
Daphne du Maurier
Dorothy Dunnett
Alice Dwyer-Joyce
Juliet Dymoke

Suzanne Ebel
Mignon G. Eberhart
Dorothy Eden
May Edginton
Anne Edwards
Mary Elgin
Anne Eliot
Elizabeth
Rosemary Ellerbeck
Hebe Elsna
Clare Emsley
Audrey Erskine-Lindop
Susan Ertz

Eleanor Farnes
Jeffery Farnol
Catherine Fellows
Edna Ferber
Rachel Field
Glenna Finley
Julia Fitzgerald
Valerie Fitzgerald
Gilbert Frankau
Rose Franken

Cynthia Freeman

Patricia Gallagher
Charles Garvice
Catherine Gaskin
Catherine Gavin
Roberta Gellis
Mary Ann Gibbs
Anna Gilbert
Janice Holt Giles
Constance Gluyas
Elinor Glyn
Rumer Godden
Ethel Edison Gordon
Elizabeth Goudge
Maysie Greig
Hettie Grimstead
Mabel Barnes Grundy

H. Rider Haggard
Pamela Haines
Anne Hampson
Mollie Hardwick
W.G. Hardy
Marilyn Harris
Rosemary Harris
Elizabeth Harrison
Phyllis Hastings
Constance Heaven
Georgette Heyer
Robert Hichens
Grace Livingston Hill
Pamela Hill
Naomi A. Hintze
Jane Aiken Hodge
Isabelle Holland
Victoria Holt
Anthony Hope
Lance Horner
Mary Howard
Susan Howatch
Elizabeth Hoy
Susan Hufford
E.M. Hull
Fannie Hurst
Baroness von Hutten

Susan Inglis
Margaret Irwin

Shirley Jackson
Naomi Jacob
Barbara Ferry Johnson
Mary Johnston
Velda Johnston

Margaret Kennedy
Barbara Kevern

Frances Parkinson Keyes
Flora Kidd
Katheryn Kimbrough
Russell Kirk
Alanna Knight

Rosalind Laker
Charlotte Lamb
Roumelia Lane
Jacqueline La Tourrette
Elsie Lee
Doris Leslie
Maynah Lewis
Marjorie Lewty
Alice Chetwynd Ley
Rachel Lindsay
Norah Lofts
Laura London
Emilie Loring
Claire Lorrimer
Dorothy Mackie Low
Marie Belloc Lowndes
Margaret Lynn

Dorothy Macardle
Mrs. Patrick MacGill
Leila Mackinlay
Charlotte MacLeod
Jean S. MacLeod
Margaret Maddocks
Audrie Manley-Tucker
Jean Marsh
Edison Marshall
Rosamond Marshall
Rhona Martin
Anne Mather
Patricia Matthews
Wynne May
Anne Maybury
Laurie McBain
George Barr McCutcheon
Adeline McElfresh
Marjorie McEvoy
Barbara Michaels
Lady Miles
Margaret Millar
Marlys Millhiser
Margaret Mitchell
L.M. Montgomery
Doris Langley Moore
Annette Motley
Frances Murray
Netta Muskett

Betty Neels
Sarah Neilan
Christopher Nicole
Kathleen Norris

Kate Norway

Elisabeth Ogilvie
Rohan O'Grady
Kyle Onstott
Baroness Orczy

Edith Pargeter
Margaret Pargeter
Barbara Anne Pauley
Lilian Peake
Margaret Pedler
Elizabeth O. Peter
Maureen Peters
Natasha Peters
Rosamunde Pilcher
Bentz Plagemann
D.A. Ponsonby
Eleanor H. Porter
Gene Stratton Porter
Ivy Preston
Evadne Price

Florence Engel Randall
Rona Randall
Claire Rayner
Henrietta Reid
Elizabeth Renier
Barbara Riefe
Mary Roberts Rinehart
Claire Ritchie
Irene Roberts
Janet Louise Roberts
Willo Davis Roberts
Denise Robins
Mary Linn Roby
Rosemary Rogers
Margaret Rome
Berta Ruck
Anne Rundle

Rafael Sabatini
Mabel St. John
Nicole St. John
Carola Salisbury
Petra Sawley
Sara Seale
Elizabeth Seifert
Anya Seton
Samuel Shellabarger
Olga Sinclair

Frank G. Slaughter
Doris E. Smith
Lady Eleanor Smith
Joan Smith
Danielle Steel
Marguerite Steen
Anne Stevenson
D.E. Stevenson
Florence Stevenson
Mary Stewart
Jessica Stirling
Rebecca Stratton
Jean Stubbs
Essie Summers
Annie S. Swan

Jill Tattersall
Elswyth Thane
Kay Thorpe
Sylvia Thorpe
Nigel Tranter
Joanna Trollope

Mrs. George de Horne Vaizey
Helen Van Slyke
Patricia Veryan

Jennifer Wade
Lucy Walker
Sheila Walsh
Margaret Way
Jean Francis Webb
Jean Webster
Mary Westmacott
Gwen Westwood
Phyllis A. Whitney
Claudette Williams
C.N. and A.M. Williamson
Kathleen Winsor
Violet Winspear
Daoma Winston
Kathleen E. Woodiwiss
Anne Worboys
P.C. Wren
Esther Wyndham
May Wynne

Chelsea Quinn Yarbro
Dornford Yates
Frank Yerby

ABBOTT, Alice.   Pseudonym for Kathryn Borland, née Kilby, and Helen Ross Speicher, née Smith. Also write as Jane Land, and Jane and Ross Land.   **BORLAND, Kathryn**.   American.   Born in Pullman, Michigan, 14 August 1916. Educated at Butler University, Indianapolis, B.S. 1937. Married James Borland in 1942; one son and one daughter. Editor, *North Side Topics* weekly newspaper, Indianapolis, 1939-42. Agent: Jay Garon-Brooke Associates, 415 Central Park West, 17D, New York, New York 10025. Address: R.R. 3, South Maish Road, Frankfort, Indiana 46041, U.S.A.   **SPEICHER, Helen Ross**.   American.   Born in Indianapolis, Indiana, 14 September 1915. Educated at Butler University, Indianapolis, B.A. in journalism (magna cum laude) 1937. Married Kenneth E. Speicher in 1941; three sons and one daughter. Editor, International Typographical Union, Indianapolis, 1937-41; editor of plant magazine, International Harvester, Indianapolis, 1942-44. Address: R.R. 2, Box 490, Indianapolis, Indiana 42680, U.S.A.

ROMANCE AND GOTHIC PUBLICATIONS

Novels

> *The Third Tower*.   New York, Ace, 1974.
> *Good-bye, Julie Scott*.   New York, Ace, 1975.

OTHER PUBLICATIONS

Novel

> *Stranger in the Land* (as Jane Land), edited by Sharon Jarvis.   New York, Ballantine, 1974.

Other (juvenile)

> *Southern Yankees*.   Indianapolis, Bobbs Merrill, 1960.
> *Allan Pinkerton, Young Detective*.   Indianapolis, Bobbs Merrill, 1962.
> *Miles and the Big Black Hat* (as Jane and Ross Land).   Indianapolis, Seale, 1963.
> *Everybody Laughed and Laughed*.   Indianapolis, Seale, 1964.
> *Eugene Field, Young Poet*.   Indianapolis, Bobbs Merrill, 1964.
> *Phillis Wheatley, Young Colonial Poet*.   Indianapolis, Bobbs Merrill, 1968.
> *Harry Houdini, Young Magician*.   Indianapolis, Bobbs Merrill, 1969.
> *Clocks, From Shadow to Atom*.   Chicago, Follett, 1969; Kingswood, Surrey, World's Work, 1970.
> *Good-by to Stony Crick*.   New York, McGraw Hill, 1974.

*   *   *

Alice Abbott writes about vulnerable young women trapped by bewildering circumstances wherein the familiar turns frightening and the trusted proves dangerous. They are isolated in large, rambling houses from which escape seems impossible, on an island in *The Third Tower*, amid heavy snow in *Good-bye, Julie Scott*.

The Third Tower is a chilling story of obsessive hatred that transforms a seemingly benign woman into a vindictive fiend. The heroine, Ruth Hood, hired as a companion-teacher to a blind child, finds she must fight not only the obvious obstacles of the child's sense of helplessness and the adults' disgust with her untrained physical habits, but also the unexpected problems of a housekeeper who seeks to thwart her progress, a father who is alienated from his daughter, a lovely rival who uses the child to compete for the rich father's love, and, most horrifying, a hypnotic midnight voice urging the child to acts of violence, threatening her with

7

abuse and terror. Despite her acrophobia, Ruth must battle an enraged maniac on the roof to save herself and her protégé and to protect the man she loves from the truth about his first wife's infidelity.

In *Good-bye, Julie Scott*, from the moment she receives word of her sizeable inheritance, Julie Scott is beset by troubles—a young woman dressed like her killed near her apartment, a lawyer claiming her inheritance is valueless, ESP visions at odds with her seeming reality, a dilapidated ruin in place of her grandfather's mansion, surly servants who hold her a virtual prisoner without telephone or transportation, and a boyfriend who proves part of a devious plot to defraud her of her fortune. When her identification is replaced by that of a dead woman, she runs for her life, pursued through snow, captured and recaptured. Only a real lawyer's suspicions and her own ESP powers can save her from a slow, lingering death.

In each of these books Alice Abbott depicts the hidden strengths and resources of the young and afflicted when faced with betrayal, greed and madness.

—Gina Macdonald

AIKEN, Joan (Delano).   British.   Born in Rye, Sussex, 4 September 1924; daughter of the poet Conrad Aiken; sister of Jane Aiken Hodge, *q.v.* Educated at Wychwood School, Oxford, 1936-40. Married 1) Ronald George Brown in 1945 (died, 1955), one son and one daughter; 2) Julius Goldstein in 1976. Worked for the BBC, 1942-43; Librarian, United Nations Information Centre, London, 1943-49; Sub-Editor and Features Editor, *Argosy*, London, 1955-60; Copywriter, J. Walter Thompson, London, 1960-61. Recipient: *Guardian* Award, 1969; Mystery Writers of America Edgar Allan Poe Award, 1972. Agent: A.M. Heath, 40-42 William IV Street, London WC2N 4DD; or, Brandt and Brandt, 1501 Broadway, New York, New York 10036, U.S.A. Address: The Hermitage, East Street, Petworth, West Sussex GU28 0AB, England.

ROMANCE AND GOTHIC PUBLICATIONS

Novels

> *The Silence of Herondale.*   New York, Doubleday, 1964; London, Gollancz, 1965.
> *The Fortune Hunters.*   New York, Doubleday, 1965.
> *Trouble with Product X.*   London, Gollancz, 1966; as *Beware of the Banquet*, New York, Doubleday, 1966.
> *Hate Begins at Home.*   London, Gollancz, 1967; as *Dark Interval*, New York, Doubleday, 1967.
> *The Ribs of Death.*   London, Gollancz, 1967; as *The Crystal Crow*, New York, Doubleday, 1968.
> *The Embroidered Sunset.*   London, Gollancz, and New York, Doubleday, 1970.
> *Died on a Rainy Sunday.*   London, Gollancz, and New York, Holt Rinehart, 1972.
> *The Butterfly Picnic.*   London, Gollancz, 1972; as *A Cluster of Separate Sparks*, New York, Doubleday, 1972.
> *Voices in an Empty House.*   London, Gollancz, and New York, Doubleday, 1975.
> *Castle Barebane.*   London, Gollancz, and New York, Viking Press, 1976.
> *Last Movement.*   London, Gollancz, and New York, Doubleday, 1977.
> *The Five-Minute Marriage.*   London, Gollancz, 1977; New York, Doubleday, 1978.

The Smile of the Stranger. London, Gollancz, and New York, Doubleday, 1978.
The Lightning Tree. London, Gollancz, 1980; as *The Weeping Ash*, New York, Doubleday, 1980.
The Young Lady from Paris. London, Gollancz, 1982; as *The Girl from Paris*, New York, Doubleday, 1982.

Short Stories

The Windscreen Weepers and Other Tales of Horror and Suspense. London, Gollancz, 1969.

OTHER PUBLICATIONS (for children)

Fiction

All You've Ever Wanted and Other Stories. London, Cape, 1953.
More Than You Bargained For and Other Stories. London, Cape, 1955; New York, Abelard Schuman, 1957.
The Kingdom and the Cave. London, Abelard Schuman, 1960; New York, Doubleday, 1974.
The Wolves of Willoughby Chase. London, Cape, 1962; New York, Doubleday, 1963.
Black Hearts in Battersea. New York, Doubleday, 1964; London, Cape, 1965.
Nightbirds on Nantucket. London, Cape, and New York, Doubleday, 1966.
The Whispering Mountain. London, Cape, 1968; New York, Doubleday, 1969.
A Necklace of Raindrops and Other Stories. London, Cape, and New York, Doubleday, 1968.
Armitage, Armitage, Fly Away Home. New York, Doubleday, 1968.
A Small Pinch of Weather and Other Stories. London, Cape, 1969.
Night Fall. London, Macmillan, 1969; New York, Holt Rinehart, 1971.
Smoke from Cromwell's Time and Other Stories. New York, Doubleday, 1970.
The Green Flash and Other Tales of Horror, Suspense and Fantasy. New York, Holt Rinehart, 1971.
All and More. London, Cape, 1971.
The Cuckoo Tree. London, Cape, and New York, Doubleday, 1971.
The Kingdom under the Sea and Other Stories. London, Cape, 1971.
A Harp of Fishbones and Other Stories. London, Cape, 1972.
Arabel's Raven. London, BBC Publications, 1972; New York, Doubleday, 1974.
The Escaped Black Mamba. London, BBC Publications, 1973.
All But a Few. London, Penguin, 1974.
The Bread Bin. London, BBC Publications, 1974.
Midnight Is a Place. London, Cape, and New York, Viking Press, 1974.
Not What You Expected: A Collection of Short Stories. New York, Doubleday, 1974.
Mortimer's Tie. London, BBC Publications, 1976.
A Bundle of Nerves. London, Gollancz, 1976.
The Faithless Lollybird and Other Stories. London, Cape, 1977; New York, Doubleday, 1978.
The Far Forests: Tales of Romance, Fantasy, and Suspense. New York, Viking Press, 1977.
Go Saddle the Sea. New York, Doubleday, 1977; London, Cape, 1978.
Tale of a One-Way Street and Other Stories. London, Cape, 1978; New York, Doubleday, 1979.
Mice and Mendelson. London, Cape, 1978.
Mortimer and the Sword Excalibur. London, BBC Publications, 1979.
The Spiral Stair. London, BBC Publications, 1979.
A Touch of Chill (stories). London, Gollancz, 1979; New York, Delacorte Press, 1980.
Arabel and Mortimer. London, Cape, 1980; New York, Doubleday, 1981.

The Shadow Guests.   London, Cape, and New York, Delacorte Press, 1980.
Mortimer's Portrait on Glass.   London, BBC Publications, 1980.
Mr. Jones's Disappearing Taxi.   London, BBC Publications, 1980.
The Stolen Lake.   London, Cape, and New York, Delacorte Press, 1981.
A Whisper in the Night.   London, Gollancz, 1982.

Plays

Winterthing, music by John Sebastian Brown (produced Albany, New York, 1977).   New
    York, Holt Rinehart, 1972; included in *Winterthing, and The Mooncusser's Daughter*,
    1973.
Winterthing and The Mooncusser's Daughter.   London, Cape, 1973; *The Mooncusser's
    Daughter* published separately, New York, Viking Press, 1974.
Street, music by John Sebastian Brown (produced London, 1977).   New York, Viking
    Press, 1978.
Moon Mill (produced London, 1982).

Television Plays: *The Dark Streets of Kimballs Green*, 1976; *Mortimer's Tie*, 1976; *The
    Apple of Trouble*, 1977; *Midnight Is a Place* (serial), from her own novel, 1977; *The Rose
    of Puddle Fratrum*, 1978; *Armitage, Armitage, Fly Away Home*, from her own novel,
    1978.

Verse

The Skin Spinners.   New York, Viking Press, 1976.

Other

The Way to Write for Children (for adults).   London, Hamish Hamilton, 1982.

Translator, *The Angel Inn*, by Contessa de Ségur.   London, Cape, 1976; Owings Mills,
    Maryland, Stemmer House, 1978.

Joan Aiken comments:

I first began reading romantic and gothic fiction professionally in the 1950's when I was
working for an English publishing firm, Amalgamated Press, which in its various magazines
(*Woman's Journal, Argosy, Suspense, Woman & Home*) used a number of writers such as
Charlotte Armstrong, Dorothy Eden, Mary Stewart, Mignon G. Eberhart. I became interested
in the gothic/suspense form and, encouraged by my agent, Jean LeRoy (who wrote a useful
little manual *Sell Them a Story*, in which, among other things, she urged would-be gothic
writers to study *Jane Eyre* as a model), I decided to try my hand at the genre. My first attempt,
House of Shadows, never got finished (that title has been used several times since, though) but
my next, *Hit and Run*, was used serially in *Suspense*, and several others appeared serially in
Everywoman. At this time a children's book of mine had been sold to the American publishers,
Doubleday, whose Crime Club editor, Isabelle Taylor, asked if I had any adult fiction. I
showed her my serialised stories and she encouraged me to extend them into full-length novels,
which were published as *Hate Begins at Home, The Silence of Herondale*, etc. As the gothic
market then began to be somewhat saturated I tried my hand at Regency romances, but I still
prefer the classic gothic and wish it had not been so over-used. However as this is the case I
propose to stick to Domestic Suspense for my next books.

*   *   *

The very fecundity of her ideas makes Joan Aiken's books difficult to summarize, or indeed to categorize. One of those authors who writes both contemporary gothics and historical romances, Aiken ornaments her conceits with more purely literary skill than many other romance/gothic writers. Yet at some point in almost all of her books she seems to skirt, or even fall over, the edge of absurdity. This willingness to take risks, if that is what it is to be called, is one of the most characteristic elements of the Aiken style. For instance, in *Last Movement* Mike Meiklejohn learns the terrible secret about her missing father: following a sex change operation, (s)he is now a prominent Irish soprano. This element of the fantastically improbable, as opposed to the merely unearthly fantastic (forebodings, dreams that foretell the future, haunted houses occur in Aiken's novels—*The Weeping Ash*, for one—as well as in books by many other authors of gothics), makes Mike laugh when she first hears it; a purely nervous reaction, she claims. But may not the reader, too, laugh? Aiken's fantasies for children are full of this kind of improbability, which is what gives them their air of light-hearted charm. It does not always blend as successfully with the more serious, terrifying, and, sometimes, erotic matter of her adult books.

Aiken's technical virtuosity also shows in her unwillingness to be bound to a simple narrative formula. Several books—*Last Movement*, *The Weeping Ash*—alternate chapters from different viewpoints. An encounter will be described, perhaps, in a third-person narrative focusing on one character's feelings; then a first-person account shows the episode from a different point of view. In *The Weeping Ash* the story goes back and forth between two sets of characters in different continents whose lives are connected as they gradually approach the moment when their paths will converge and the conflicts that exist among them will be settled. In *Voices in an Empty House*, which is possibly more a straight novel than a romance/gothic, this technique is overlaid with multiple flashbacks that explore the relationships between a man, his ex-wife, her dead first husband, and her son, as the man desperately tries to find his step-son to persuade him to undergo crucial heart surgery.

There is nothing unusual in one of Aiken's characters needing surgery: a strong element in her style is her intense interest in physical illness. From Lucy's heart condition in *The Embroidered Sunset* to Mrs. Carteret's frailness and invalidism in *The Five-Minute Marriage*, there is always someone with a serious ailment. This is not mere soap opera. The conditions and consequences of disease play a significant role in the novels. More specifically, many of the ailments involve periods of amnesia. Thomas in *Voices in an Empty House*, Annette in *The Fortune Hunters*, and Caroline in *Hate Begins at Home* are all inconvenienced to some extent and even endangered by their frustrating bouts of amnesia. Scylla in *The Weeping Ash* is semi-conscious for long periods; her brother Cal has epilepsy; their cousin by marriage Fanny has spells that she cannot explain to her domineering and brutal husband.

The Weeping Ash is also an example of Aiken's use of recurrent characters. The benefactor of Fanny's husband is the same Juliana who escaped from the French Revolution by a daring balloon flight in *The Smile of the Stranger*. Juliana herself does not appear in the second book, but some of the other characters from *The Smile of the Stranger* do. Mike Meiklejohn's wooer in *Last Movement* is the ebullient Dr. Adnan who had loved and lost Lucy in *The Embroidered Sunset*.

Children bring out a tenderness in Aiken; even a young infant in *Trouble with Product X* can win hearts. But she can also sacrifice them to the exigencies of her plot; two children die in *Hate Begins at Home*. So the threat to a young child and her infant brother keeps nerves taut in *Died on a Rainy Sunday*. Aside from young children, warm family relationships are almost nonexistent. Only peripheral characters are allowed normal families. The heroines are confined to mothers who are neglectful (*The Ribs of Death*), malignant (*The Smile of the Stranger*), or, at best, dead at an early age (*Died on a Rainy Sunday*). Siblings are usually equally hostile, although the twins Scylla and Cal in *The Weeping Ash* are a rare exception.

Another notable facet of Aiken's style is her sense of place: the isle of Dendros in *Last Movement*, the island of Manhattan in *Voices in an Empty House*, India in *The Weeping Ash* are all actual presences in the stories, seeming at times to come alive as characters in their own right.

Although Aiken has ambitions beyond the gothic, her own wayward imagination keeps the novels at genre level. Her spiky, independent heroines, capable in their careers, nonetheless fall helplessly in love with the wrong person and only free themselves after bizarre struggles, sometimes to find happiness, sometimes just to find the endurance to continue the struggle

(*The Ribs of Death*, for example, has an inconclusive ending). Yet her gripping, sensitive style transcends formulas; her well-rounded characters and strong plots carry the reader with her.

—Susan Branch

AINSWORTH, Harriet.   *See* **CADELL, Elizabeth**.

AINSWORTH, Patricia.   Pseudonym for Patricia Nina Bigg.   Australian.   Born in 1932. Address: 5A Way Avenue, Myrtle Bank, South Australia 5064, Australia.

ROMANCE AND GOTHIC PUBLICATIONS

Novels

The Flickering Candle.   London, Hale, 1968.
The Candle Rekindled.   London, Hale, 1969.
Steady Burns the Candle.   London, Hale, 1970.
The Devil's Hole.   London, Hale, 1971.
Portrait in Gold.   London, Hale, 1971.
A String of Silver Beads.   London, Hale, 1972.
The Bridal Lamp.   London, Hale, 1975.
The Enchanted Cup.   London, Hale, 1980.

*   *   *

The first three novels by Patricia Ainsworth are set in 17th-century England, following the fortunes of the owners of two country estates. In *The Flickering Candle* the main protagonists are Frances Faraday and the Earl of Debenham, and the story describes the growth of their relationship against the background of the outbreak of the Civil War. *The Candle Rekindled* takes up the story 12 years later during the Protectorate, and *Steady Burns the Candle* is set another five years later at the start of the reign of Charles II; some of the characters reappear 15 years on in *The Enchanted Cup*. The novels are light-weight in construction, with no real substance to the characters, and lack a strong story-line. Ainsworth's handling of the historical period involved is also shaky, with details that obtrude rather than blending in. *The Devil's Hole* is more successful, possibly because it is set in the author's native Australia. The background of the early colonial days around 1877 is well described, with feeling for the beauties of the Australian coast, but despite tighter construction, more rounded characters, and more realistic dialogue, the pace again is slow and the dramatic sequences not handled quite as well as they could be. *Portrait in Gold* is also set in the Australian colony of Victoria, and the fevered days of the gold-rush are depicted with an authentic period flavour. With *A String of Silver Beads* and *The Bridal Lamp*, the author returns to historical England. The former book is set in the year of the Armada, and tells the story of Crispin Wynwood's reluctance to take up his inheritance, and his troubled romance with Felice Averil: the narrative is better controlled, although the final denouement is a little too far-fetched. In *The Bridal Lamp*, again set in Charles II's reign, drama of a different kind is introduced when Carey suspects her husband of trying to kill her.

Although details of setting and historical period are based on research and create a colourful background, particularly to the later books, Ainsworth cannot quite control her narrative well enough to sustain the dramatic pace and keep up suspense: the development of her characters also suffers from weak handling and many of her protagonists do not mature sufficiently to gain credibility as individuals.

—Tessa Rose Chester

AIRLIE, Catherine.   *See* **MacLEOD, Jean S**.

ALBANESI, Madame (Effie Adelaide Maria Albanesi, née Henderson). Also wrote as Effie Rowlands.   British.   Born in 1859. Married Le Chevalier Carlo Albanesi (died, 1926); one daughter. *Died 16 October 1936.*

ROMANCE AND GOTHIC PUBLICATIONS

Novels

> *Margery Daw* (published anonymously).   London, Stevens, and New York, Munro, 1886.
> *The Blunder of an Innocent*.   London, Sands, 1899.
> *Peter, A Parasite*.   London, Sands, 1901.
> *Brave Barbara*.   New York, Street and Smith, 1901.
> *Love and Louisa*.   London, Sands, and Philadelphia, Lippincott, 1902.
> *Susannah and One Elder*.   London, Methuen, 1903; as *Susannah and One Other*, Methuen, and New York, McClure, 1904.
> *Capricious Caroline*.   London, Methuen, 1904.
> *Marian Sax*.   London, Hurst and Blackett, 1905.
> *The Brown Eyes of Mary*.   London, Methuen, 1905.
> *Sweet William*.   London, Hodder and Stoughton, 1906.

I Know a Maiden. London, Methuen, 1906.
A Little Brown Mouse. London, Hodder and Stoughton, 1906.
A Young Man from the Country. London, Hurst and Blackett, 1906.
Love-in-a-Mist. London, Hodder and Stoughton, 1907.
The Strongest of All Things. London, Hurst and Blackett, 1907.
Simple Simon. London, Newnes, 1907.
Sister Anne. London, Hodder and Stoughton, 1908.
The Rose of Yesterday. London, Hodder and Stoughton, 1908.
Drusilla's Point of View. London, Hurst and Blackett, 1908.
Pretty Polly Pennington. London, Collins, 1908; as *Sweet and Lovely*, 1933.
The Forbidden Road. New York, Cupples and Leon, 1908.
The Laughter of Life. New York, Cupples and Leon, 1908.
The Invincible Amelia; or, The Polite Adventuress. London, Methuen, 1909.
A Question of Quality. London, Hurst and Blackett, 1909.
Envious Eliza. London, Nash, 1909.
The Marriage of Margaret. London, Pearson, 1909.
The Glad Heart. London, Methuen, 1910.
For Love of Anne Lambert. London, Pearson, 1910.
Maisie's Romance. London, Pearson, 1910.
A Wonder of Love. London, Stanley Paul, 1911.
Poppies in the Corn. London, Hutchinson, 1911.
Heart of His Heart. London, Stanley Paul, 1911.
Olivia Mary. London, Methuen, 1912.
The Beloved Enemy. London, Methuen, 1913.
One of the Crowd. London, Chapman and Hall, 1913.
Cissy. London, Collins, 1913.
The Cap of Youth. London, Hutchinson, 1914.
The Sunlit Hills. London, Hutchinson, 1914.
Hearts and Sweethearts. London, Hutchinson, 1916.
When Michael Came to Town. London, Hutchinson, 1917.
Truant Happiness. London, Ward Lock, 1918.
Diana Falls in Love. London, Ward Lock, 1919.
Tony's Wife. London, Holden and Hardingham, 1919; as *Punch and Judy*, London, Hardingham, 1919.
Patricia and Life. London, Ward Lock, 1920.
The House That Jane Built. London, Ward Lock, 1921.
Roseanne. London, Collins, 1922.
Truth in a Circle. London, Collins, 1922.
A Bird in a Storm. London, Collins, 1924.
Sally in Her Alley. London, Collins, 1925.
The Shadow Wife. London, Stanley Paul, 1925.
Sally Gets Married. London, Collins, 1927.
The Green Country. London, Ward Lock, 1927.
The Moon Through Glass. London, Collins, 1928.
Claire and Circumstances. London, Collins, 1928; as *In Love with Claire*, 1932.
Gold in the Dust. London, Ward Lock, 1929.
A Heart for Sale. London, Ward Lock, 1929.
The Clear Stream. London, Ward Lock, 1930.
Loyalty. London, Collins, 1930.
The Courage of Love. London, Ward Lock, 1930.
White Flame. London, Ward Lock, 1930.
Coloured Lights. London, Ward Lock, 1931.
All's Well with the World. London, Ward Lock, 1932.
The Moon of Romance. London, Ward Lock, 1932.
Snow in Summer. London, Ward Lock, 1932.
A Star in the Dark. London, Ward Lock, 1933.
White Branches. London, Ward Lock, 1933.
Through the Mist. London, Ward Lock, 1934.

The Half Open Door. London, Ward Lock, 1934.
An Unframed Portrait. London, Nicholson and Watson, 1935.
As a Man Loves. London, Ward Lock, 1936.
The Hidden Gift. London, Nicholson and Watson, 1936.
A Leaf Turned Down. London, Ward Lock, 1936.
The Little Lady. London, Ward Lock, 1937.
The Love That Lives. London, Mellifont Press, 1937.
The One Who Counted. London, Ward Lock, 1937.

Novels as Effie Rowlands

The Spell of Ursula. Philadelphia, Lippincott, 1894.
The Woman Who Came Between. London, Pearson, 1895; New York, Street and
    Smith, n.d.
At Great Cost. New York, Bonner, 1895.
Little Kit. New York, Bonner, 1895.
A Faithful Traitor. London, Stevens, and Philadelphia, Lippincott, 1896.
The Fault of One. London, Kegan Paul, and Philadelphia, Lippincott, 1897.
The Kingdom of a Heart. London and New York, Routledge, 1899.
They Laugh That Win. London and New York, Routledge, 1899.
A Woman Scorned. New York, Street and Smith, 1899.
A King and a Coward. New York, Street and Smith, 1899; London, Hodder and
    Stoughton, 1912.
Little Lady Charles. New York, Street and Smith, 1899; London, Stanley Paul, 1910.
The Heart of Hetta. Chicago, Laird and Lee, 1900.
Husband and Foe. New York, Street and Smith, 1900; London, Hutchinson, 1911.
Beneath a Spell. New York, Street and Smith, 1900; London, Stanley Paul, 1910.
A Charity Girl. New York, Street and Smith, 1900; London, Stanley Paul, 1911.
The Man She Loved. New York, Street and Smith, 1900; London, Ward Lock, 1911.
One Man's Evil. New York, Street and Smith, 1900; London, Newnes, 1910.
For Ever True. New York, Street and Smith, 1904; London, Hodder and Stoughton,
    1910.
A Love Almost Lost. London, Henderson, 1905.
Angel of Evil. New York, Street and Smith, 1905.
Her Husband and Her Love. New York, Street and Smith, 1905.
So Like a Man. New York, Street and Smith, 1905.
The Splendid Man. New York, Street and Smith, 1905.
The Wiles of a Siren. New York, Street and Smith, 1906.
The End Crowns All. New York, Street and Smith, 1906; London, Hutchinson, 1910.
A Shadowed Happiness. New York, Street and Smith, 1906; London, Newnes, 1910.
For Love of Sigrid. New York, Street and Smith, 1906.
Love's Greatest Gift. New York, Street and Smith, 1906; as *The White in the Black* (as
    Madame Albanesi), London, Collins, 1926.
My Lady of Dreadwood. New York, Street and Smith, 1906.
A Wife's Triumph. New York, Street and Smith, 1906.
Pretty Penelope. London, Cassell, 1907.
Her Punishment. London, Hurst and Blackett, 1910.
The Man She Married. London, Stanley Paul, 1910.
After Many Days. London, Newnes, 1910.
Contrary Mary. London, Hodder and Stoughton, 1910.
A Dangerous Woman. London, Ward Lock, 1910.
For Love of Speranza. London, Hodder and Stoughton, 1910.
The Game of Life. London, Ward Lock, 1910.
Her Heart's Longing. London, Hurst and Blackett, 1910.
Her Kingdom. London, Amalgamated Press, 1910.
John Galbraith's Wife. London, Hodder and Stoughton, 1910.
Love for Love. London, Hodder and Stoughton, 1910.

A Loyal Man's Love. London, Newnes, 1910.
The Master of Lynch Towers. London, Hodder and Stoughton, 1910.
The Mistress of the Farm. London, Newnes, 1910.
Bitter Sweet. London, Newnes, 1910.
A Splendid Destiny. London, Stanley Paul, 1910.
Barbara's Love Story. London, Hodder and Stoughton, 1911.
Brave Heart. London, Amalgamated Press, 1911.
Carlton's Wife. London, Ward Lock, 1911.
Dare and Do. London, Stanley Paul, 1911.
False Faith. London, Amalgamated Press, 1911.
For Ever and a Day. London, Amalgamated Press, 1911.
A Girl with a Heart. London, Ward Lock, 1911.
Her Mistake. London, Amalgamated Press, 1911.
Leila Vane's Burden. London, Amalgamated Press, 1911.
A Life's Love. London, Hodder and Stoughton, 1911.
Love's Harvest. London, Amalgamated Press, 1911.
The Madness of Love. London, Hodder and Stoughton, 1911.
The Man at the Gate. London, Amalgamated Press, 1911.
The One Woman. London, Hodder and Stoughton, 1911.
The Power of Love. London, Amalgamated Press, 1911.
Splendid Love. London, Amalgamated Press, 1911.
White Abbey. London, Stanley Paul, 1911.
A Wild Rose. London, Amalgamated Press, 1911.
A Woman Worth Winning. London, Amalgamated Press, 1911.
A Woman's Heart. London, Hodder and Stoughton, 1911.
The Young Wife. London, Hodder and Stoughton, 1911.
Love's Fire. London, Hutchinson, 1911.
The Triumph of Love. London, Pearson, 1911.
On the Wings of Fate. New York, Street and Smith, n.d.; London, Newnes, 1916.
Andrew Leicester's Love. New York, Street and Smith, n.d.
Carla. New York, Street and Smith, n.d.
Change of Heart. New York, Street and Smith, n.d.
False and True. New York, Street and Smith, n.d.
For Love and Honor. New York, Street and Smith, n.d.
The Girl's Kingdom. New York, Street and Smith, n.d.
Interloper. Chicago, Donohue, n.d.
Kinsman's Sin. New York, Street and Smith, n.d.
Love's Cruel Whim. New York, Street and Smith, n.d.
Selina's Love Story. New York, Street and Smith, n.d.
Siren's Heart. New York, Street and Smith, n.d.
Spurned Proposal. New York, Street and Smith, n.d.
Temptation of Mary Barr. New York, Street and Smith, n.d.
Tempted by Love. New York, Street and Smith, n.d.
With Heart So True. New York, Street and Smith, n.d.
Woman Against Her. New York, Street and Smith, n.d.
Woman Against Woman. New York, Street and Smith, n.d.
Woman Scorned. New York, Street and Smith, n.d.
A Golden Dawn. London, Hodder and Stoughton, 1912.
A Heart's Triumph. London, Hodder and Stoughton, 1912; New York, Street and Smith, n.d.
Hester Trefusis. London, Hurst and Blackett, 1912.
The House of Sunshine. London, Stanley Paul, 1912.
In Love's Land. London, Ward Lock, 1912.
A Love Match. London, Amalgamated Press, 1912.
The Love of His Life. London, Stanley Paul, 1912.
The Rose of Life. London, Ward Lock, 1912.
Temptation. London, Newnes, 1912.
To Love and to Cherish. London, Everett, 1912.

The Wooing of Rose. London, Stanley Paul, 1912.
His One Love. London, Hurst and Blackett, 1912.
Lavender's Love Story. London, Hurst and Blackett, 1912.
Love Wins. London, Hurst and Blackett, 1912.
A Modern Witch. London, Hurst and Blackett, 1912.
Beth Mason. London, Hodder and Stoughton, 1913.
Elsie Brant's Romance. London, Cassell, 1913.
Hearts at War. London, Hurst and Blackett, 1913.
The Joy of Life. London, Cassell, 1913.
Lady Patricia's Faith. London, Hodder and Stoughton, 1913.
Love's Mask. London, Stanley Paul, 1913.
Margaret Dent. London, Cassell, 1913.
Ruth's Romance. London, Hodder and Stoughton, 1913.
Stranger Than Truth. London, Hodder and Stoughton, 1913.
The Surest Bond. London, Cassell, 1913.
Through Weal and Through Woe. London, Ward Lock, 1913.
In Daffodil Time. London, Pearson, 1913.
The Heart of a Woman. London, Pearson, 1913.
Judged by Fate. London, Hurst and Blackett, 1913.
The Hand of Fate. London, Hodder and Stoughton, 1914.
Her Husband. London, Chatto and Windus, 1914.
An Irish Lover. London, Hodder and Stoughton, 1914.
Money or Wife? London, Ward Lock, 1914.
On the High Road. London, Hurst and Blackett, 1914.
Two Waifs. London, Hodder and Stoughton, 1914.
At Her Mercy. London, Pearson, 1914.
The Price Paid. London, Chatto and Windus, 1914.
Prudence Langford's Ordeal. London, Pearson, 1914.
Love's Young Dream. London, Ward Lock, 1914.
Above All Things. London, Newnes, 1915.
Sunset and Dawn. London, Ward Lock, 1915.
The Woman's Fault. London, Hurst and Blackett, 1915.
The Girl Who Was Brave. London, Pearson, 1916.
The Splendid Friend. London, Hutchinson, 1917.
The Heart of Angela Brent. London, Pearson, 1917.
A Strange Love Story. London, Hurst and Blackett, 1919.
John Helsby's Wife. London, Hurst and Blackett, 1920.
Mary Dunbar's Love. London, Pearson, 1921.
Against the World. London, Pearson, 1923.
The Flame of Love. London, Ward Lock, 1923.
The Garland of Youth. London, Ward Lock, 1923.
Young Hearts. London, Ward Lock, 1924.
The Life Line. London, Hodder and Stoughton, 1924.
Real Gold. London, Hodder and Stoughton, 1924.
Out of a Clear Sky. London, Ward Lock, 1925.
The Way of Youth. London, Hodder and Stoughton, 1925.
Brave Love. London, Ward Lock, 1926.
A Bunch of Blue Ribbons. London, Ward Lock, 1926.
Lady Feo's Daughter. London, Hodder and Stoughton, 1926.
The Gates of Happiness. London, Ward Lock, 1927.
A Man from the West. London, Ward Lock, 1927.
Fateful Promise. New York, Street and Smith, n.d.
Her Golden Secret. New York, Street and Smith, n.d.
Hero for Love's Sake. New York, Street and Smith, n.d.
Unhappy Bargain. New York, Street and Smith, n.d.
Fine Feathers. London, Ward Lock, 1928.
Lights and Shadows. London, Ward Lock, 1928.
Spring in the Heart. London, Ward Lock, 1929.

While Faith Endures.   London, Ward Lock, 1929.
Coulton's Wife.   London, Ward Lock, 1930.
Dorinda's Lovers.   London, Wright and Brown, 1930.
The Fighting Spirit.   London, Ward Lock, 1930.
Sunlight Beyond.   London, Ward Lock, 1930.
Wings of Chance.   London, Ward Lock, 1931.
Princess Charming.   London, Wright and Brown, 1931.
Green Valleys.   London, Wright and Brown, 1932.
The Laughter of Life.   London, Ward Lock, 1932; New York, Cupples and Leon, n.d.
A Loyal Defence.   London, Ward Lock, 1932.
A Ministering Angel.   London, Ward Lock, 1933.
Frances Fights for Herself.   London, Ward Lock, 1934.
A School for Hearts.   London, Ward Lock, 1934.
A World of Dreams.   London, Ward Lock, 1935.
The One Who Paid.   London, Ward Lock, 1935.
The Heart Line.   London, Ward Lock, 1936.
The Lamp of Friendship.   London, Ward Lock, 1936.
Her Father's Wish.   London, Ward Lock, 1937.
The Top of the Tree.   London, Ward Lock, 1937.

OTHER PUBLICATIONS

Other

Meggie Albanesi.   London, Hodder and Stoughton, 1928.

*   *   *

The upper-class Edwardian's concern for physical comfort and material value is well illustrated by Madame Albanesi's *Temptation* (published under the name Effie Rowlands), in which a young orphaned girl, destitute and starving, is offered a life of ease if she succumbs to the temptation of impersonating a missing heiress, and thus eventually securing for herself marriage to the local squire. The moral, far from suggesting that love brings its own rewards, or that girls who sell their souls risk their lives for material gain will endure a fate worse than death, seems to be the reverse: that ill-gotten gains bring you "all the luxury of appointment that is so necessary and so very ordinary to the very rich."

Albanesi's style is marked by lavish use of the exclamation mark, and the repetition of key words: "Alone in the world! Alone! With only seventeen years of life behind her! She, poor little soul, was alone! Quite-quite alone!" Heroes are sometimes "stained with shame," a blot on their character which can only be lifted by the true love of a good lady (not woman).

During her long career, Albanesi produced over 200 novels, all variations on true-love-with-complications, though none with any marked note of religious, political, or moral quest. There is more than a suggestion that the state of being in love brings in its wake not only mortal happiness but material good fortune too. If a girl's love is true, she will marry the right man, and continue to be rich and happy for the rest of her life. Although many of her titles contain "Love"—*Love's Harvest, Love for Love, Brave Love, The Love of His Life, A Flame of Love, The Man She Loved*, etc.—there is surprisingly very little kissing. Some of her heroines avoid the kiss by fainting. Others faint anyway: "She gave a low cry, and stretched out her hands. She reeled forward, struggled a little, and then, catching impotently at a chair as she fell, she sank huddled and unconscious."

Albanesi would have shared with a publisher's reader of the time a thorough appreciation of the "eternal importance of love in the financial and popular success of a novel." However, occasionally she branched out from love. *The Clear Stream*, for example, is a family saga, about Marcella Dolamore and her many children; and *An Irish Lover*, although not strictly a hospital romance, contains some details about nurses in the home (circa 1914), and curious notes about home-nursing methods of those days. For instance, that one important item towards helping save the life of Henry is to keep the sound of passing traffic deadened by having straw placed on the street. The ensuing silence, combined with nurse Rachel's miraculous (though unexplained) nursing power, restores his health.

What is most astonishing about Madame Albanesi is how she managed to produce over 200 novels during her career, at a time when the electric tape-recorder had not yet been invented.

—Rachel Anderson

ALLARDYCE, Paula. *See* **BLACKSTOCK, Charity.**

ALLEN, (William) Hervey (Jr.). American. Born in Pittsburgh, Pennsylvania, 8 December 1889. Educated at Shady Side Academy; United States Naval Academy, Annapolis, Maryland, 1910-11; University of Pittsburgh, B.Sc. 1915 (Phi Beta Kappa); Harvard University, Cambridge, Massachusetts, 1920-22. Served in the Pennsylvania National Guard, 1916, and in the United States infantry in France, 1917-18; served with the War Manpower Commission during World War II. Married Ann Hyde Andrew in 1927; two daughters and one son. Worked for Bell Telephone Company, 1915; English teacher, Porter Military Academy, Charleston, South Carolina, 1920-21, and Charleston High School, 1922-24; lecturer at Columbia University, New York, 1924-25, Vassar College, Poughkeepsie, New York, 1926-27, and Bread Loaf School, Vermont, 1930-31. Staff member, *Saturday Review*, New York. Litt.D.: University of Pittsburgh, 1934; Washington and Jefferson College, Washington, Pennsylvania, 1947. Member of the Board of Governors, St. John's College, Annapolis; Trustee, University of Miami. Member, American Academy, and Royal Society of Arts. *Died 28 December 1949.*

ROMANCE AND GOTHIC PUBLICATIONS

Novels

> *Anthony Adverse.* New York, Farrar and Rinehart, and London, Gollancz, 1933.
> *Action at Aquila.* New York, Farrar and Rinehart, and London, Gollancz, 1938.
> *The City in the Dawn.* New York, Rinehart, 1950.
> > *The Forest and the Fort.* New York, Farrar and Rinehart, and London, Heinemann, 1943.
> *Bedford Village.* New York, Farrar and Rinehart, and London, Heinemann, 1944.
> *Toward the Morning.* New York, Rinehart, 1948.

Short Stories

It Was Like This: Two Stories of the Great War.   New York, Farrar and Rinehart, 1940.

Uncollected Short Stories

"Blood Lust," in *New Stories for Men*, edited by Charles Grayson.   New York, Doubleday, 1941.
"The Shenandoah," in *Fighting American*, edited by Van Wyck Mason.   New York, Reynal, 1943.

OTHER PUBLICATIONS

Verse

Ballads of the Border.   Privately printed, 1916.
Wampum and Old Gold.   New Haven, Connecticut, Yale University Press, 1921.
Carolina Chansons: Legends of the Low Country, with Du Bose Heyward.   New York, Macmillan, 1922.
The Bride of Huitzil: An Aztec Legend.   New York, Drake, 1922.
Christmas Epithalamium.   Privately printed, 1923.
Earth Moods and Other Poems.   New York, Harper, 1925.
New Legends.   New York, Farrar and Rinehart, 1929.
Sarah Simon, Character Atlantean.   New York, Doubleday, 1929.
Songs for Annette.   New York, Rudge, 1929.

Other

Israfel: The Life and Times of Edgar Allan Poe.   New York, Doran, 1926; London, Gollancz, 1935.
Toward the Flame: A War Diary.   New York, Doran, 1926; London, Gollancz, 1934.
Du Bose Heyward: A Critical and Biographical Sketch.   New York, Doran, 1927.

Editor, with others, *Year Book of the Poetry Society of South Carolina 1921-23.*   Privately printed, 3 vols., 1921-23.
Editor, with Thomas Ollive Mabbott, *Poe's Brother: The Poems of William Henry Leonard Poe.*   New York, Doran, 1926.
Editor, *The Works of Edgar Allan Poe.*   New York, Black, 1927.
Editor, *The Best Known Works of Edgar Allan Poe.*   New York, Blue Ribbon, 1931.

*   *   *

Before the sprawling historical novel had become a best-selling commonplace, Hervey Allen's *Anthony Adverse* seemed a revolutionary creation. One huge work, it contained three volumes: each volume made up of three books, and, after all, an epilogue: it was of a breadth unheard of since the palmy days of the Victorian three-decker, and all to tell the story of a single adventurous life.

Hervey Allen was a storyteller who assumed the indulgence as well as the interest of a patient audience. He digressed to offer tendentious opinions, to discourse upon the scenery of Europe, Africa, and the New World, to say nothing of the open seas; to wax lyrical, toss in snippets of poems, epitaphs culled from tombstones, proverbs, and trivia of all sorts. The continuity of his story is tenuous at best, and the hero's character does not so much develop as alter with chameleon rapidity from one episode to the next. From the opening chapters in which Anthony's ill-starred parents Maria and Denis have their brief, glorious affair and provoke the undying vengence of Maria's cuckolded husband Don Luis, to the end of the marathon story, Anthony careens from destitution to enormous wealth and back again. He has at least three great loves in his life, as well as numerous passing interludes; he becomes embroiled in several hideous tragedies, in the loathsome slave trade, in the Napoleonic campaigns, in financial dealings with the Rothschilds, in a lazar house-cum-prison, and in this fashion, practically ad infinitum, the story of the romantic foundling plunges and lurches along, from one unlikely coincidence to the next.

Into this one fictional lifetime are crammed enough events and exploits to furnish several novels of ordinary length with plot and to spare. There is a certain fascination in the long-drawn-out odyssey, but throughout the reader is uneasily conscious of prodigious stage management. If ever a novel demanded of its readers "a willing suspension of disbelief," that novel was *Anthony Adverse*. Once committed to this Niagara of improbability, one is swept into a world where no loose ends are ever left to dangle, where parted lovers always meet again, where revenge never falters or fails, and where nemesis stalks the hero as the crocodile stalked Captain Hook. There are a few very affecting scenes, as well as a great deal of material that is totally unnecessary; in that respect, at least, the novel closely resembles life.

Allen went on to write other novels, planning indeed to conjure up a panoramic picture of colonial America, but died before completing the gigantic task. His name was made by and will be remembered for his tremendously successful fictional offspring, Anthony, the nameless waif born under "adverse conditions" to embody a life of epic adventure.

—Joan McGrath

AMES, Jennifer.   *See* GREIG, Maysie.

ANDREWS, Lucilla (Mathew).   Also writes as Diana Gordon; Joanna Marcus.   British. Trained as a nurse at St. Thomas's Hospital, London, during World War II. Married a doctor in 1947 (died, 1954); one daughter. Lives in Edinburgh. Address: c/o Heinemann, 10 Upper Grosvenor Street, London W1X 9PA, England.

ROMANCE AND GOTHIC PUBLICATIONS

Novels

    The Print Petticoat.   London, Harrap, 1954.
    The Secret Armour.   London, Harrap, 1955.
    The Quiet Wards.   London, Harrap, 1956.

The First Year. London, Harrap, 1957.
A Hospital Summer. London, Harrap, 1958.
My Friend the Professor. London, Harrap, 1960.
Nurse Errant. London, Harrap, 1961.
The Young Doctors Downstairs. London, Harrap, 1963.
Flowers for the Doctor. London, Harrap, 1963.
The New Sister Theatre. London, Harrap, 1964.
The Light in the Ward. London, Harrap, 1965.
A House for Sister Mary. London, Harrap, 1966.
Hospital Circles. London, Harrap, 1967.
A Few Days in Endel (as Diana Gordon). London, Corgi, 1968.
Highland Interlude. London, Harrap, 1968.
The Healing Time. London, Harrap, 1969.
Edinburgh Excursion. London, Harrap, 1970.
Ring o' Roses. London, Harrap, 1972.
Silent Song. London, Harrap, 1973.
In Storm and in Calm. London, Harrap, 1975.
The Crystal Gull. London, Harrap, 1978.
One Night in London. London, Heinemann, 1979.
Marsh Blood (as Joanna Marcus). London, Hutchinson, 1980.
A Weekend in the Garden. London, Heinemann, 1981.

OTHER PUBLICATIONS

Other

No Time for Romance: An Autobiographical Account of a Few Moments in British and Personal History. London, Harrap, 1977.

*   *   *

Lucilla Andrews may, or may not, have "invented" the hospital romance, but she certainly set a pattern which has been followed by innumerable other authors in much the same way as Georgette Heyer begat the Regency novels.

Like most who write this kind of story, she trained as a nurse, in London during World War II, and her grim experiences there have left a lasting impression on the style and content of her novels. She pulls no punches; readers' noses are positively rubbed in medical fact—often gruesome. (A week after she described the results of a motor-bike accident in *Woman's Weekly* the sale of skid-lids soared.) Her war-time experiences, described in her autobiography, ironically titled *No Time for Romance*, make it clear that everything she writes is either based on personal experience, or the result of scrupulous inquiry into the latest medical methods, discoveries, and treatments.

Her stories are not always (though often) set in big teaching hospitals. She likes to introduce remote or unusual backgrounds which, apart from adding colour and excitement to her story, demonstrate the different environments in which nursing (and romance!) occur, and the difficulties under which medical practice must sometimes be undertaken.

A good example of every aspect of her imaginative and ingenious use of her theme, and her topicality, is to be found in *In Storm and in Calm*, which takes its relief-nurse heroine to an isolated Shetland island at the time when the North Sea oil rigs were first coming into use. Charlotte quickly learns that instead of the quiet cottage hospital she expected, Thessa General, though tiny, is ultra modern, staffed and equipped to deal with all kinds of medical and surgical emergencies which come from the islands', and the world's, fishing fleets, and the new oil rigs. Patients arrive by trawler, tanker, lifeboat, helicopter, and ambulance, at all hours, in all seasons. There is, of course, a love story. The author patiently (perhaps a little wearily?) reiterates the fact that nurses and doctors are much given to marrying each other if only because they are too busy to meet anyone else. (She herself married a doctor.)

Anyone who has ever been in hospital, or even visited one, will know that there exists there an enclosed, almost hot-house, atmosphere which heightens the emotions of everyone—be they patient or part of the medical team. This is, perhaps, what makes hospital novels so popular: the romance has an authenticity and an inevitability which give it both credibility and an extra edge, set as it is against the background of emergency. Lucilla Andrews exploits this situation with great skill; but what really sets her apart is the variety she introduces, and her refusal to prettify the reason why her characters are where they are. She isn't afraid to grind axes, either. One of her *bêtes noirs* is the drunken driver. Her descriptions of the aftermath of drinking and driving are enough to put anyone off alcohol for life!

—Elizabeth Grey

ANTHONY, Evelyn. Pseudonym for Evelyn Bridget Patricia Ward-Thomas, née Stephens. British. Born in London, 3 July 1928. Educated at Convent of the Sacred Heart, Roehampton, to 1944, and privately. Married Michael Ward-Thomas in 1955; two daughters and four sons. Recipient: *Yorkshire Post* award, 1973. Agent: A.P. Watt Ltd., 26-28 Bedford Row, London WC1R 4HL, England. Address: Castlesize, Sallins, Co. Kildare, Ireland.

ROMANCE AND GOTHIC PUBLICATIONS

Novels

> *Imperial Highness.* London, Museum Press, 1953; as *Rebel Princess*, New York, Crowell, 1953.
> *Curse Not the King.* London, Museum Press, 1954; as *Royal Intrigue*, New York, Crowell, 1954.
> *Far Flies the Eagle.* New York, Crowell, 1955.
> *Anne Boleyn.* London, Museum Press, and New York, Crowell, 1957.
> *Victoria and Albert.* London, Crowell, 1958; as *Victoria*, London, Museum Press, 1959.
> *Elizabeth.* London, Museum Press, 1960; as *All the Queen's Men*, New York, Crowell, 1960.
> *Charles the King.* London, Museum Press, and New York, Doubleday, 1961.
> *Clandara.* London, Hurst and Blackett, and New York, Doubleday, 1963.
> *The Heiress.* London, Hurst and Blackett, and New York, Doubleday, 1964.
> *The French Bride.* New York, Doubleday, 1964; London, Arrow, 1966.
> *Valentina.* London, Hurst and Blackett, and New York, Doubleday, 1966.
> *The Rendezvous.* London, Hutchinson, 1967; New York, Coward McCann, 1968.
> *Anne of Austria.* London, Hurst and Blackett, 1968; as *The Cardinal and the Queen*, New York, Coward McCann, 1968.
> *The Legend.* London, Hutchinson, and New York, Coward McCann, 1969.
> *The Assassin.* London, Hutchinson, and New York, Coward McCann, 1970.
> *The Tamarind Seed.* London, Hutchinson, and New York, Coward McCann, 1971.
> *The Poellenberg Inheritance.* London, Hutchinson, and New York, Coward McCann, 1972.
> *The Occupying Power.* London, Hutchinson, 1973; as *Stranger at the Gates*, New York, Coward McCann, 1973.

The Malaspiga Exit.   London, Hutchinson, 1974; as *Mission to Malaspiga*, New York, Coward McCann, 1974.

The Persian Ransom.   London, Hutchinson, 1975; as *The Persian Price*, New York, Coward McCann, 1975.

The Silver Falcon.   London, Hutchinson, and New York, Coward McCann, 1977.

The Return.   London, Hutchinson, and New York, Coward McCann, 1978.

The Grave of Truth.   London, Hutchinson, 1979.

The Janus Imperative.   New York, Coward McCann, 1980.

The Defector.   London, Hutchinson, 1980; New York, Coward McCann, 1981.

The Avenue of the Dead.   London, Hutchinson, 1981.

*   *   *

The heroines of Evelyn Anthony's many stories of intrigue and danger are almost interchangeable. They are invariably impeccably ladylike, even if circumstance or inclination has forced them to bend one or another of the commandments. They tend to fragility in appearance, coupled somehow with an almost irresistible sexual attractiveness; they are slight, with long narrow hands and feet, which appear to advantage in the elegant and expensive hand-sewn leather they favour; none of these ladies is obliged to count pennies.

The Anthony lady is often masochistic to a degree which normal persons would find distinctly neurotic; she is capable of astonishing devotion, and she loves only once, forever, although sometimes before she discovers *true* love her heart may have misled her into settling for less, in or out of marriage. But no matter—it cannot last. *Somewhere*, perhaps under an alias, or hiding out in Mexico, or lying in wait for the target he has been engaged to assassinate, is the only man for Louise, or Anna, or Elizabeth, or Judith, or....

Friendly mockery of Evelyn Anthony's predictable heroines, however, does not mean that her stories are at all laughable. They are taut, gripping, often explosive in their resolutions, such as the holocaust in *The Tamarind Seed* which must be the hero's death pyre; the last-minute, heartbreaking gun battle in *The Legend*, in which their happiness is snatched from the fleeting lovers in the very moment of success; or the shattering passage in *The Occupying Power* in which S.S. reprisal for Allied wartime sabotage threatens the lives of all the children of a tiny French town, and their desperate parents, untrained in the use of arms, struggle to rescue them at the brink of the mass grave dug ready to receive their bodies: these are scenes that can hold their own with the best in suspense fiction.

Though her characters may be almost indistinguishable one from another, her plots are masterful. Once caught up in the skulduggery behind the scenes in the spymaster's hidden headquarters, the slums of Beirut, or the gilded haunts of the Beautiful People, the reader is trapped. These are tales of the sort that once begun must be finished—and readers of Anthony's thrillers know they have little chance of outguessing this ingenious writer.

Oddly enough, considering that her suspense stories revolve around the misadventures of helpless ladies who are pawns in the hands of great powers they do not even try to understand, Anthony also creates romantic fiction often based on the lives of the most powerful and formidable women who ever lived. Elizabeth Tudor, probably the most written-about of all English monarchs, has never been more believably portrayed in all her regal and dangerous unpredictability than by Evelyn Anthony, who convincingly interprets the ways in which the great queen's extraordinary childhood, and the self-seeking men who surrounded her throughout her adult life, shaped a woman whose career still fascinates. More like Anthony's own fictional heroines, the ill-fated Mary Stuart is treated with greater sympathy than most of Elizabeth's biographers accord her. The life of another less glamorous, but equally intriguing English monarch, Victoria, is the subject of a biographical novel dealing with the period between her accession to the throne as an 18-year-old and the fateful day of the Prince Consort's death. Surely Anthony comes as close as anyone can to discovering the character of the incredibly self-willed and stubborn young autocrat who became the Widow of Windsor.

Less familiar to English-speaking readers than the British monarchy are the Russian Tsars, subjects of a fascinating trilogy which deals with the lives of Catherine the Great, her son Paul, whose eccentricities won him the sobriquet of The Death's Head Tsar, and his son Alexander. She casts new light on a blood-soaked dynasty whose exploits do much to explain the revolution that was to come. In these and other costume romances, she brings to life some of history's most brilliant and dramatic personages.

Happily Evelyn Anthony is a prolific writer, both of suspense and of romantic fiction; happily, because there is an army of devoted readers anxious for the "good read" of which her name on a title page is a certain guarantee.

—Joan McGrath

ARBOR, Jane.   British.   Widow.   Owner of a book shop and circulating library, then free-lance writer. Address: c/o Mills and Boon Ltd., 15-16 Brooks Mews, London W1A 1DR, England.

ROMANCE AND GOTHIC PUBLICATIONS

Novels

This Second Spring.   London, Mills and Boon, 1948.
Each Song Twice Over.   London, Mills and Boon, 1948.
Ladder of Understanding.   London, Mills and Boon, 1949.
Strange Loyalties.   London, Mills and Boon, 1949; Toronto, Harlequin, 1962; as *Doctor's Love*, Harlequin, n.d.
By Yet Another Door.   London, Mills and Boon, 1950.
No Lease for Love.   London, Mills and Boon, 1950; Toronto, Harlequin, 1964; as *My Surgeon Neighbour*, Harlequin, n.d.
The Heart Expects Adventure.   London, Mills and Boon, 1951.
Eternal Circle.   London, Mills and Boon, 1952; Toronto, Harlequin, 1958; as *Nurse Atholl Returns*, Harlequin, n.d.
Memory Serves My Love.   London, Mills and Boon, 1952.
Flower of the Nettle.   London, Mills and Boon, 1953.
Such Frail Armour.   London, Mills and Boon, 1953; Toronto, Harlequin, 1959.
Jess Mawney, Queen's Nurse.   London, Mills and Boon, 1954.
Dear Intruder.   London, Mills and Boon, 1955; Toronto, Harlequin, 1965.
Folly of the Heart.   London, Mills and Boon, 1955.
Towards the Dawn.   London, Mills and Boon, 1956; Toronto, Harlequin, 1959.
City Nurse.   London, Mills and Boon, 1956; as *Nurse Greve*, Toronto, Harlequin, n.d.
Yesterday's Magic.   London, Mills and Boon, 1957; Toronto, Harlequin, 1967.
Far Sanctuary.   London, Mills and Boon, 1958; Toronto, Harlequin, 1960.
Nurse Harlowe.   Toronto, Harlequin, 1959.
Sandflower.   London, Mills and Boon, 1959; Toronto, Harlequin, 1961.
Consulting Surgeon.   Toronto, Harlequin, 1959.
No Silver Spoon.   London, Mills and Boon, 1959; Toronto, Harlequin, 1964.
Queen's Nurse.   Toronto, Harlequin, 1960.
A Girl Named Smith.   London, Mills and Boon, 1960; Toronto, Harlequin, 1966.
Nurse of All Work.   London, Mills and Boon, and Toronto, Harlequin, 1962.
Nurse in Waiting.   London, Mills and Boon, and Toronto, Harlequin, 1962.
Desert Nurse.   London, Mills and Boon, 1963; Toronto, Harlequin, 1964.
Jasmine Harvest.   London, Mills and Boon, and Toronto, Harlequin, 1963.

Lake of Shadows. London, Mills and Boon, 1964; Toronto, Harlequin, 1965.
Kingfisher Tide. London, Mills and Boon, and Toronto, Harlequin, 1965.
High Master of Clere. London, Mills and Boon, and Toronto, Harlequin, 1966.
Summer Every Day. London, Mills and Boon, 1966; Toronto, Harlequin, 1967.
Golden Apple Island. London, Mills and Boon, 1967; Toronto, Harlequin, 1968.
Stranger's Trespass. London, Mills and Boon, 1968; Toronto, Harlequin, 1969.
The Cypress Garden. London, Mills and Boon, and Toronto, Harlequin, 1969.
The Feathered Shaft. London, Mills and Boon, and Toronto, Harlequin, 1970.
Walk into the Wind. London, Mills and Boon, and Toronto, Harlequin, 1970.
The Other Miss Donne. London, Mills and Boon, and Toronto, Harlequin, 1971.
The Linden Leaf. London, Mills and Boon, and Toronto, Harlequin, 1971.
The Flower on the Rock. London, Mills and Boon, 1972; Toronto, Harlequin, 1973.
Wildfire Quest. London, Mills and Boon, and Toronto, Harlequin, 1972.
Roman Summer. London, Mills and Boon, and Toronto, Harlequin, 1973.
The Velvet Spur. London, Mills and Boon, and Toronto, Harlequin, 1974.
Meet the Sun Halfway. London, Mills and Boon, and Toronto, Harlequin, 1974.
The Wide Fields of Home. London, Mills and Boon, and Toronto, Harlequin, 1975.
Tree of Paradise. London, Mills and Boon, 1976; Toronto, Harlequin, 1977.
Smoke into Flame. Toronto, Harlequin, 1976.
Flash of Emerald. London, Mills and Boon, 1977.
Two Pins in a Fountain. London, Mills and Boon, and Toronto, Harlequin, 1977.
A Growing Moon. London, Mills and Boon, 1977; Toronto, Harlequin, 1978.
Late Rapture. London, Mills and Boon, 1978; Toronto, Harlequin, 1979.
Return to Silbersee. London, Mills and Boon, 1978; Toronto, Harlequin, 1979.
Pact Without Desire. London, Mills and Boon, 1979.
The Devil Drives. London, Mills and Boon, 1979; Toronto, Harlequin, 1980.
One Brief Sweet Hour. London, Mills and Boon, 1980; Toronto, Harlequin, 1981.
Where the Wolf Leads. London, Mills and Boon, 1980; Toronto, Harlequin, 1981.

*   *   *

Jane Arbor is an English writer who spent her early years owning a book shop and circulating library. This experience proved to be of great value to her, for she gained exceptional knowledge about romance readers. She knows just what they expect and what kinds of romance stories have the greatest appeal.

In a short autobiographical sketch, she used the phrase, "acceptable storyteller." In any discussion of her as a writer, it is a telling phrase, for that is just what she is: a storyteller of great originality and sensitivity. She is a craftsman of the art as she tangles her skein of characters and background into a many-hued tapestry of love and happiness.

She displays a most enviable discipline for work, for she has published over 50 novels. Her early apprenticeship years produced numerous doctor/nurse stories that yet make enjoyable reading, although later she developed the more typical story that is so familiar to her readers. She, herself, admits that character motivation is the element that she prefers to start with when beginning to develop a new novel, although background has been the initial factor in some of her works. In making her observation, she noted the amount of research she carries out in creating the proper setting for a novel. She uses Morocco, Venice, the Greek Islands, Amsterdam, and the Pacific Islands for settings, to mention but a few. She choses detail carefully and weaves description in so that there is a gradual awareness of the setting. Perhaps this is because of her meticulousness in developing her backgrounds that make them seem so authentic. Arbor avoids the too innocent image in developing her female characters; the girls in her stories are often well-educated and have responsible jobs.

Gillian Harlowe in *Folly of the Heart* is a trained staff nurse in a hospital. Dinah Fleming in *A Growing Moon* travels to Venice to take over a tourist office for her company, while Alice Martin in *Meet the Sun Halfway* has been trained in domestic science so she has the experience and ability to take over a children's convalescent home in Morocco.

For all of their experience and surface sophistication, each makes the mistake of falling in love with a man out of their reach. It is here that Arbor shows particular ability in defining her characters as each girl faces the fact that they can never hope to have their love returned.

Gillian succumbs to a brillant surgeon, Adrian Pilgrim; Dinah befriends the young cousins of Cesare Visdal, an Italian nobleman; while Alice loses her heart to Karim Ibn Charles, a very wealthy and influential Moroccan, who happens to own the home that the children are in.

Generally, action in the story is interwoven with the typical activities that the characters are involved with and against the background of the growing awareness and tension between the men and women. In this context Arbor makes use of the triangular plot quite effectively.

Arbor often relies heavily on secondary characters to confound the simplicity of love. There are frequent misunderstandings and an undercurrent of jealousy as each assumes that the other loves someone else. Just as frequently, Arbor includes a potential rival in the form of an old girl-friend or a female colleague who, though not really in love with the hero, is determined to have him anyway. Only at the very end of the story does the heroine begin to realize that she might have won the hero's love after all, although certain incidents throughout the story have left her confused and hopeful, as he seems to offer her faint gestures of encouragement.

Jane Arbor's novels always end on that satisfying note of love's inevitable victory. Her readers have the same satisfying feeling as they reluctantly put down a finished novel.

—Arlene Moore

ARLEN, Leslie. *See* **NICOLE, Christopher**.

ARLEN, Michael. British. Born Dikran Kouyoumdjian in Rustchuk, Bulgaria, 16 November 1895; emigrated to England, 1901; naturalized as Michael Arlen in 1922. Educated at Malvern College, Worcestershire; studied medicine at the University of Edinburgh, 1913. Served as Civil Defense Public Relations Officer in the West Midlands, 1940-41. Married Atalanta, daughter of Count Mercati, in 1928; one son and one daughter. Staff member, *Ararat: A Searchlight on Armenia*, London, 1916, and columnist, *The Tatler*, London, 1939-40; lived in Cannes, 1928-39, and in New York City after 1945. *Died 23 June 1956.*

ROMANCE AND GOTHIC PUBLICATIONS

Novels

    The London Venture. London, Heinemann, and New York, Dodd Mead, 1920.

Piracy: A Romantic Chronicle of These Days. London, Collins, 1922; New York, Doran, 1923.

The Green Hat: A Romance for a Few People. London, Collins, and New York, Doran, 1924.

Young Men in Love. London, Hutchinson, and New York, Doran, 1927.

Lily Christine. New York, Doubleday, 1928; London, Hutchinson, 1929.

Men Dislike Women: A Romance. London, Heinemann, and New York, Doubleday, 1931.

Man's Mortality. London, Heinemann, and New York, Doubleday, 1933.

Hell! Said the Duchess: A Bed-Time Story. London, Heinemann, and New York, Doubleday, 1934.

Flying Dutchman. London, Heinemann, and New York, Doubleday, 1939.

Short Stories

The Romantic Lady. London, Collins, and New York, Dodd Mead, 1921.

These Charming People. London, Collins, 1923; New York, Doran, 1924; selection, as *The Man with the Broken Nose and Other Stories*, Collins, 1927.

May Fair, in Which Are Told the Last Adventures of These Charming People. London, Collins, and New York, Doran, 1925; selection, as *The Ace of Cads and Other Stories*, Collins, 1927.

Ghost Stories. London, Collins, 1927; New York, Arno Press, 1976.

Babes in the Wood. London, Hutchinson, and New York, Doubleday, 1929.

The Ancient Sin and Other Stories. London, Collins, 1930.

A Young Man Comes to London. Privately printed, 1931.

The Short Stories. London, Collins, 1933.

The Crooked Coronet and Other Misrepresentations of the Real Facts of Life. London, Heinemann, and New York, Doubleday, 1937.

Uncollected Short Stories

"The Dead Half-Hour," in *English Review* (London), January 1920.

"The Fall of Lady Toni," in *English Review* (London), April 1920.

"Tea at the Ritz," in *Smart Set* (New York), December 1921.

"Lark among Crows," in *Everybody's* (London), January 1924.

"Punctilious Parbald," in *Everybody's* (London), March 1924.

"The Sheik of Alabam," in *Everybody's* (London), April 1924.

"Salute Mr. Lancelot," in *Redbook* (Dayton, Ohio), December 1924.

"One Gold Coin," in *Bookman* (London), January, February 1925.

"The Legend of Isolde," in *Redbook* (Dayton, Ohio), March 1925.

"The Hand and the Flower," in *Redbook* (Dayton, Ohio), May 1925.

"The Knife Thrower," in *Redbook* (Dayton, Ohio), July 1925.

"Portrait of a Lady with Grey Eyes on Fifth Avenue," in *Liberty* (New York), 16 January 1926.

"Portrait of a Girl on Hollywood Boulevard," in *Liberty* (New York), 20 February 1926.

"Why Men Join Clubs," in *Redbook* (Dayton, Ohio), August 1926.

"Eyes of the Blind," in *Redbook* (Dayton, Ohio), September 1926.

"Love in Eternity," in *Redbook* (Dayton, Ohio), January 1928.

"The Great Emerald Mystery," in *Redbook* (Dayton, Ohio), February 1928.

"First Love," in *Liberty* (New York), 20 April 1929.

"O Chivalry!," in *Liberty* (New York), 20 July 1929.

"An Affair of the Heart," in *Cosmopolitan* (New York), October 1929.

"Transatlantic," in *Liberty* (New York), 16 May 1931.

"Gay Falcon," in *To the Queen's Taste*, edited by Ellery Queen. Boston, Little Brown, 1946; London, Faber, 1949.

OTHER PUBLICATIONS

Plays

> *Dear Father* (produced London, 1924; revised version, as *These Charming People*, produced New York, 1925).
> *Why Shelmerdene Was Late for Dinner*, adaptation of his story "The Real Reason Why Shelmerdene Was Late for Dinner" (produced London, 1924).
> *The Green Hat*, adaptation of his own novel (produced Detroit, London, and New York, 1925). New York, Doran, 1925.
> *The Zoo*, with Winchell Smith (produced Southsea and Pittsburgh, 1927). New York and London, French, 1927.
> *Good Losers*, with Walter Hackett (produced London, 1931). London, French, 1933.

Screenplay: *The Heavenly Body*, with others, 1943.

Critical Study: *Michael Arlen* by Harry Keyishian, New York, Twayne, 1975.

*   *   *

"To be as improbable as life will be is as far beyond the honest novelist's courage as it must be against the temper of his craft...." Michael Arlen said this, but his own story reads like the most far-fetched romance: unknown young Armenian with an unpronounceable name offers his first novel to a world-famous London publisher, and is accepted. Following his publisher's advice, he changes his name to Michael Arlen, goes on to write *The Green Hat*, and takes the world by storm. (Literally, for his heroine Iris Storm proved the truth of Oscar Wilde's contention that Nature copies Art. The world did its best to copy Iris.) The impact of this single novel is now difficult to comprehend. In these television-dominated days, it is impossible to recapture the atmosphere of a time before even radio had taken firm hold; a time when *everyone* read, not just the few, and not only read but discussed the latest releases as a matter of some significance.

The First World War had recently rocked the firm foundation of the universe, and suddenly the unthinkable had become the possible. The audience of *The Green Hat* had just come through the war to end all wars, but which instead ended all peace. Old rules and beliefs were crumbling. The young people fortunate enough to have escaped the holocaust were disillusioned and jaded. They were the Bright Young Things; they frightened and disturbed the older generation who did not, *could* not, understand them. These were the young people who recognized, or thought they recognized, themselves as the characters of Michael Arlen's novels, and they made *The Green Hat* in particular one of the greatest best sellers of all time.

Today it is a period piece. Even in his lifetime, Michael Arlen was left behind, while time and fashion remorselessly forged ahead, and he could not. He was a writer who could do but one thing, and was fortunate enough to do it at exactly the propitious moment. Even his quirky brand of idiosyncratic English was forgiven him then, as it would not have been at another time.

And what, after all, was the furor about? *The Green Hat* is the muddled story of Iris, a troubled young woman with a "past" and a dissolute present. She wears two wedding rings—for two husbands now dead: she carries a smouldering torch for the one true love of her life, her girlhood sweetheart, from whom she was parted by his father's interference, and who is but newly married to a fluttering ingenue named Venice.

Iris does a great deal of restless rushing to and fro in her huge yellow Hispano-Suiza, which to Arlen seemed to typify the spirit of the entire era. She is regarded by all her acquaintance as a depraved character, yet aside from her free-love life-style, she behaves throughout with self-sacrificing nobility. Much evil is hinted at, little is explicit, but it becomes plain as the action lumbers clumsily along that there were dark doings at the time of Iris's tragic first marriage, and that her husband, idolized by everyone but his young bride, was not the hero he seemed to be. The spectre of syphilis, hitherto unmentionable, is raised; it was a daring stroke for a novelist of the 1920's. For young women, though not young men, were expected to behave with a certain decorum and restraint, which Iris did not. The story ends with the great yellow Hispano-Suiza in flames, and Iris's green hat, worn "pour le sport," lying in the grass by the roadside. One last time, the déclassé lady has sacrificed herself for her true love.

Iris and her set represented for Arlen a distinct race of English that he believed could not survive the crassness of the 20th century, belonging as they did to a time of different standards and ideals. "They of the superior nerves had failed, they died that slow white death which is reserved for privilege in defeat."

—Joan McGrath

ARMSTRONG, Charlotte. Also wrote as Jo Valentine. American. Born in Vulcan, Michigan, in 1905. Educated at the University of Wisconsin, Madison; Barnard College, New York, B.A. 1925. Married Jack Lewi; one daughter and two sons. Worked in the *New York Times* advertising department, as a fashion reporter for *Breath of the Avenue* (a buyer's guide), and in an accounting firm. Recipient: Mystery Writers of America Edgar Allan Poe Award, 1956. *Died 18 July 1969.*

ROMANCE AND GOTHIC PUBLICATIONS

Novels (series: MacDougal Duff)

> *Lay On, MacDuff!* (Duff).   New York, Coward McCann, 1942; London, Gifford, 1943.
> *The Case of the Weird Sisters* (Duff).   New York, Coward McCann, and London, Gifford, 1943.
> *The Innocent Flower* (Duff).   New York, Coward McCann, 1945; as *Death Filled the Glass*, London, Cherry Tree Books, 1945.
> *The Unsuspected.*   New York, Coward McCann, 1946; London, Harrap, 1947.
> *The Chocolate Cobweb.*   New York, Coward McCann, 1948; London, Davies, 1952.
> *Mischief.*   New York, Coward McCann, 1950; London, Davies, 1951.
> *The Black-Eyed Stranger.*   New York, Coward McCann, 1951; London, Davies, 1952.
> *Catch-as-Catch-Can.*   New York, Coward McCann, 1952; London, Davies, 1953; as *Walk Out on Death*, New York, Pocket Books, 1954.
> *The Trouble in Thor* (as Jo Valentine).   New York, Coward McCann, and London, Davies, 1953; as *And Sometimes Death*, New York, Pocket Books, 1954.
> *The Better to Eat You.*   New York, Coward McCann, and London, Davies, 1954; as *Murder's Nest*, New York, Pocket Books, 1954.
> *The Dream Walker.*   New York, Coward McCann, and London, Davies, 1955; as *Alibi for Murder*, New York, Pocket Books, 1956.
> *A Dram of Poison.*   New York, Coward McCann, and London, Davies, 1956.
> *Mask of Evil.*   New York, Fawcett, 1958.
> *The Seventeen Widows of Sans Souci.*   New York, Coward McCann, and London, Davies, 1959.
> *Duo: The Girl with a Secret, Incident at a Corner.*   New York, Coward McCann, 1959; London, Davies, 1960.
> *Something Blue.*   New York, Ace, 1962.
> *Who's Been Sitting in My Chair?*   New York, Ace, 1962.
> *Then Came Two Women.*   New York, Ace, 1962.

A Little Less Than Kind. New York, Coward McCann, 1963; London, Collins, 1964.
The Mark of the Hand. New York, Ace, 1963.
The One-Faced Girl. New York, Ace, 1963.
The Witch's House. New York, Coward McCann, 1963; London, Collins, 1964.
The Turret Room. New York, Coward McCann, and London, Collins, 1965.
Dream of Fair Woman. New York, Coward McCann, and London, Collins, 1966.
The Gift Shop. New York, Coward McCann, and London, Collins, 1967.
Lemon in the Basket. New York, Coward McCann, 1967; London, Collins, 1968.
The Balloon Man. New York, Coward McCann, and London, Collins, 1968.
Seven Seats to the Moon. New York, Coward McCann, and London, Collins, 1969.
The Protégé. New York, Coward McCann, and London, Collins, 1970.

Short Stories

The Albatross. New York, Coward McCann, 1957; London, Davies, 1958.
I See You. New York, Coward McCann, 1966.

OTHER PUBLICATIONS

Plays

The Happiest Days (produced New York, 1939).
Ring Around Elizabeth (produced New York, 1940).   New York, French, 1942.

Screenplays: *The Unsuspected*, 1947; *Don't Bother to Knock*, 1952.

Manuscript Collection: Mugar Memorial Library, Boston University.

*   *   *

"But it's peanut reading," a character in *The Dream Walker* says of his supply of thrillers. "You can't stop till they're all gone." A story by Charlotte Armstrong is peanut reading; you can't put it down until it's finished. And it's wholesome.

MacDougal Duff solved detective puzzles in *Lay On, Mac Duff, The Case of the Weird Sisters*, and *The Innocent Flower*, but in the last he falls in love with Mary Moriarity, and her with seven children. His proposal ended detecting. Thereafter, Armstrong concentrated on suspense. The most marked characteristic of her novels and short stories is a sense of family. Romantic love can be a by-product but is not the main action.

Frequently the evil force is known early on, presented without formula and with great variety in structure, setting, and tone. *The Unsuspected*, the earliest suspense success, features a smooth-talking manipulator, opposed by a cousin and fiancé of his first victim. In *The Dream Walker* the narrator helps her cousin to thwart a revenge plot to discredit their uncle, a statesman of good repute; the plot involves seeming bi-location. *The Witch's House* imprisons a missing college professor whose wife presses the search. A plucky mother's fight for custody of her 4-year-old involves the drug scene (*The Balloon Man*). Good but not best battles against known villains are *The Chocolate Cobweb, The Better to Eat You*, and *Something Blue*.

Mental cases? A young psychotic baby-sitter in a New York hotel stars in *Mischief*. *A Little Less Than Kind* offers the added appeal of *Hamlet* parallels and non-parallels, but the son is not putting on the antics of madness. *The Turret Room* hides an ex-husband, discharged from a mental hospital, the victim of the family's protection of another. *Dream of Fair Woman* has a complex identity problem in a young woman who cannot be awakened from sleep.

The hero of *The Black-Eyed Stranger* risks his life to foil the kidnap plan of caricatured criminals—grimly tense. However, when a detective leaves a dying message in a piggy bank (*The Gift Shop*), he begins a fairy-tale spoof of hard-boiled thrillers, and Harry Fairchild leads

31

the chase to find a 7-year-old girl. Equally amusing is *The One-Faced Girl*, about a girl unwittingly involved with criminals.

Lemon in the Basket mixes international intrigue with a family of famous parents, the second son the title character. Caught between rival political factions and family problems, J. Middleton Little celebrates his name in *Seven Seats to the Moon*. It is the most satisfying of the novels that add comment on life to the action. Among the latter, different complications provide different turns and twists of plot in *The Seventeen Widows of Sans Souci* and *The Protégé*.

The Edgar-winning *A Dram of Poison* has compassion and humor. A sister's gross misunderstanding of psychology and his new marriage tempt a 55-year-old professor to suicide, but he loses the bottle of poison. A merry hunt is on, like the tale of the Golden Goose, and eccentrics discuss philosophies as miles and time conclude the cliff hanger.

As Jo Valentine, Armstrong wrote *The Trouble in Thor* about a summer in the 1920's in the fictional shaft-mining town of Thor, in Michigan's Upper Peninsula. After a labored beginning, all narrative threads work toward the attempt to rescue five miners trapped by a collapsed pillar.

The qualities of her best novels are also in her consistently good short stories. Armstrong fans gobble her goobers.

—Jane Gottschalk

ARNETT, Caroline.   *See* ELIOT, Anne.

ASHTON, Ann.   *See* KIMBROUGH, Katheryn.

ASHTON, Elizabeth.   Address: c/o Mills and Boon Ltd., 15-16 Brooks Mews, London W1A 1DR, England.

ROMANCE AND GOTHIC PUBLICATIONS

Novels

> *The Pied Tulip*. London, Mills and Boon, 1969; Toronto, Harlequin, 1970.
> *The Benevolent Despot*. London, Mills and Boon, and Toronto, Harlequin, 1970.
> *Parisian Adventure*. London, Mills and Boon, and Toronto, Harlequin, 1970.
> *Cousin Mark*. London, Mills and Boon, and Toronto, Harlequin, 1971.
> *The Enchanted Wood*. London, Mills and Boon, 1971.
> *Sweet Simplicity*. London, Mills and Boon, 1971.
> *Flutter of White Wings*. London, Mills and Boon, and Toronto, Harlequin, 1972.
> *A Parade of Peacocks*. London, Mills and Boon, 1972; Toronto, Harlequin, 1973.
> *Scorched Wings*. London, Mills and Boon, 1972; Toronto, Harlequin, 1975.
> *The Rocks of Arachenza*. London, Mills and Boon, 1973; Toronto, Harlequin, 1974.
> *Sigh No More*. London, Mills and Boon, 1973; Toronto, Harlequin, 1974.
> *The Bells of Bruges*. London, Mills and Boon, 1973.
> *Alpine Rhapsody*. Toronto, Harlequin, 1973.
> *Errant Bride*. London, Mills and Boon, 1973; Toronto, Harlequin, 1974.
> *Moorland Magic*. London, Mills and Boon, and Toronto, Harlequin, 1973.
> *Dark Angel*. London, Mills and Boon, and Toronto, Harlequin, 1974.
> *The House of the Eagles*. London, Mills and Boon, 1974; Toronto, Harlequin, 1975.
> *Dangerous to Know*. London, Mills and Boon, 1974.
> *The Road to the Border*. London, Mills and Boon, 1974; Toronto, Harlequin, 1975.
> *The Scent of Sandalwood*. London, Mills and Boon, 1974.
> *Miss Nobody from Nowhere*. London, Mills and Boon, and Toronto, Harlequin, 1975.
> *The Willing Hostage*. London, Mills and Boon, 1975.
> *Crown of Willow*. London, Mills and Boon, 1975; Toronto, Harlequin, 1976.
> *The Player King*. London, Mills and Boon, and Toronto, Harlequin, 1975.
> *Sanctuary in the Desert*. London, Mills and Boon, 1976; Toronto, Harlequin, 1977.
> *My Lady Disdain*. London, Mills and Boon, and Toronto, Harlequin, 1976.
> *Mountain Heritage*. London, Mills and Boon, 1976; Toronto, Harlequin, 1977.
> *Lady in the Limelight*. Toronto, Harlequin, 1976.
> *Aegean Quest*. Toronto, Harlequin, 1977.
> *Voyage of Enchantment*. Toronto, Harlequin, 1977.
> *Green Harvest*. Toronto, Harlequin, 1977.
> *Breeze from the Bosphorus*. Toronto, Harlequin, 1978.
> *The Garden of the Gods*. London, Mills and Boon, 1978.
> *The Golden Girl*. London, Mills and Boon, and Toronto, Harlequin, 1978.
> *The Questing Heart*. London, Mills and Boon, and Toronto, Harlequin, 1978.
> *Rendezvous in Venice*. London, Mills and Boon, and Toronto, Harlequin, 1978.
> *The Joyous Adventure*. London, Mills and Boon, 1979.
> *Moonlight on the Nile*. London, Mills and Boon, and Toronto, Harlequin, 1979.
> *Reluctant Partnership*. London, Mills and Boon, 1979; Toronto, Harlequin, 1981.
> *Borrowed Plumes*. London, Mills and Boon, 1980; Toronto, Harlequin, 1981.
> *The Rekindled Flame*. London, Mills and Boon, and Toronto, Harlequin, 1980.
> *Sicilian Summer*. London, Mills and Boon, 1980; Toronto, Harlequin, 1981.
> *Silver Arrow*. London, Mills and Boon, 1980; Toronto, Harlequin, 1981.
> *Rebel Against Love*. London, Mills and Boon, and Toronto, Harlequin, 1981.

*   *   *

Elizabeth Ashton has been a published writer since the late 1960's when her first novel *The Pied Tulip* appeared. Since then, she has regularly produced fascinating novels for her many readers. To date, she has written over 40 novels.

Although well within the early guidelines of romance writing, she is one of the "new" romance writers who are becoming increasingly popular. Her style is much more dramatic and forceful. Emotion is heightened in her stories and often the reader is caught in a web of suspense that is nearly over-powering. The fact that the denouement in her novels comes within pages, even paragraphs, of the ending makes her readers' reaction even more intense.

Generally, her heroines are more aware than is usual in romances; that is, they have a surface sophistication and are often exposed to wealthy people and adult situations. Rachel Reed in *The Garden of the Gods* has had an expensive finishing school education. Averil Avon in *Lady in the Limelight*, although from a small village, becomes a leading stage actress, while Renee Thorton in *Parisian Adventure* is an English fashion model.

Although her heroes are experienced men of the world, they tend to display a contempt and cynical attitude towards women in general. However, they are not ones to miss an opportunity in making use of a woman for their own purposes. Leon Sabastian is a well-known couturier who sees Renee and wants to use her as one of his models. Cass Dakers is a famous writer who rescues Rachel as she tries to swim from a yacht off of the island of Corfu. In *Lady in the Limelight* Philip Conway is an important actor and director who is determined to groom Averil to stardom regardless of her own wishes. All are dominating, ruthless, sensual men who fall in love in spite of their determination not to.

Again Elizabeth Ashton is one of those writers who obviously work hard at creating believable backgrounds. Her use of Paris and the world of fashion is fascinating, as are her descriptions of Italy, Corfu, and other areas of France. In using her backgrounds, she skillfully lets the heroines' movement and actions give her impression of her physical surroundings. Since the heroines' reactions are frequently enthusiastic and extremely appreciative, the descriptions are naturally colorful and evocative.

In at least one of her novels, she re-introduces characters from a previous story. Renee and Leon in *Parisian Adventure* become secondary characters in *A Paradise of Peacocks*. In this novel, Charmian meets Alex Dimitriou, a wealthy Greek business man.

In each of her novels, Elizabeth Ashton extends the plot complications and adds a certain element of irresolution in such a way that readers feel the heroine's pathetic situation. Typical of the kinds of complications is that of Francesca in *Dark Angel* who marries Angelo Vittorini. She is going to have his child, but he does not know it when he writes and asks for a permanent separation. She returns to England and eventually has a daughter. He does not learn about it until the end of the story when he visits her to discuss a divorce.

Despondency, heightened passion, and emotional reactions all play dominant parts in Elizabeth Ashton's writing as the heroine faces the failure of her love. Readers may find the heightened suspense overpowering at times, but it does not seem to diminish her audience.

—Arlene Moore

ASQUITH, Nan. Pseudonym for Nancy Evelyn Pattinson. British. Born in Barnsley, Yorkshire. Educated at St. Winifred's school, Broadstairs, Kent; Wintersthorpe, Birkdale, Lancashire. Married to Denis F.C. Pattinson. Has worked as advertising copywriter. Address: c/o Mills and Boon Ltd., 15-16 Brooks Mews, London W1A 1DR, England.

Novels

> *My Dream Is Yours.*   London, Mills and Boon, 1954; as *Doctor Robert Comes Around*,
> Toronto, Harlequin, 1965.
> *With All My Heart.*   London, Mills and Boon, 1954; Toronto, Harlequin, 1968.
> *Believe in To-morrow.*   London, Mills and Boon, 1955; Toronto, Harlequin, 1971.
> *Only My Heart to Give.*   London, Mills and Boon, 1955; Toronto, Harlequin, 1969.
> *The Certain Spring.*   London, Mills and Boon, 1956; Toronto, Harlequin, 1968.
> *Honey Island.*   London, Mills and Boon, 1957.
> *The House on Brinden Water.*   London, Mills and Boon, 1958; as *The Doctor Is
> Engaged*, Toronto, Harlequin, 1962.
> *The Time for Happiness.*   London, Mills and Boon, 1959.
> *Time May Change.*   London, Mills and Boon, 1961; Toronto, Harlequin, 1974.
> *The Way the Wind Blows.*   London, Mills and Boon, 1963.
> *The Quest.*   London, Mills and Boon, 1964.
> *The Summer at San Milo.*   London, Mills and Boon, 1965.
> *Dangerous Yesterday.*   London, Mills and Boon, 1967.
> *The Garden of Persephone.*   London, Mills and Boon, 1967; Toronto, Harlequin, 1978.
> *The Admiral's House.*   London, Mills and Boon, 1969.
> *Turn the Page.*   London, Mills and Boon, and Toronto, Harlequin, 1970.
> *Beyond the Mountain.*   London, Mills and Boon, 1970.
> *Carnival at San Cristobal.*   London, Mills and Boon, 1971.
> *Out of the Dark.*   London, Mills and Boon, 1972.
> *The Girl from Rome.*   London, Mills and Boon, and Toronto, Harlequin, 1973.
> *The Sun in the Morning.*   London, Mills and Boon, 1974.

*   *   *

Nan Asquith was one of the more traditional romance writers of the 1950's and 1960's. Ten of her novels appeared in the Harlequin Romances beginning in 1962 with the publication of *The House on Brinden Water*. Her charming stories and attractive heroines gained her a wide reading audience during this period. Although some of her novels were written over 20 years ago, there is a dateless quality in her novels that makes her just as readable today as then.

Despite the fact that they are traditional in formula, there is nothing simplistic about her novels. Complexity of character and well-thought-out plots show Asquith's talent as a romance writer. In her novels she pays close attention to developing her heroines by showing their inner growth. Jane Roper in *The Girl from Rome* falls in love with a young Italian, Gino, only to realize that he has no intention of marrying her. She has just completed the tourist season in Rome as a tour guide and had planned on remaining there, expecting his proposal. Her own moral standards and the realization that she has placed herself in a difficult position eventually force her to leave.

Rowan Langham in *Time May Change* meets Blake Hobart again after several years. She had been engaged to him, but did not have the maturity to make her own decision; consequently, her family influenced her to break the engagement. Since then, Rowan's father has died and she has had to grow up and assume more responsibility. Because of her added maturity, she is able to see Blake and her love in a more adult perspective.

Asquith is able to show the heroines' dilemma in such a way that their actions are well motivated and logical given their background and personality. She provides sufficient depth of character to make them believable by permitting frequent bouts of indecision and "might-have-been" regrets.

Her plots tend to be slower paced and less complicated than those in more recent novels. She makes use of foreign settings and unusual activities such as a Mediterranean cruise, but the focus of her stories remains on her characters.

In developing the personalities of her heroes, Asquith again tends to keep them low key and approachable. They are human with touching lapses of weakness that makes them more realistic. Vance Morley takes Jane with him as his fiancée because he had once been engaged to Anthea, his sister-in-law. He is not sure of his feelings toward her and feels the need of protection, so that his brother will not be upset. Blake Hobart pretends to continue his racing career in order to learn if Rowan really is willing to acknowledge their love regardless of his occupation, for she had originally wanted him to give it up and join her father's company.

Both men show sensitive needs to protect themselves and it adds a further dimension to their characters. They are portrayed as vulnerable people trying to cope with life just as others must. In a sense, it is their masculine outlook and an awareness of their responsibilities that cause them to act as they do. Blake must know that Rowan's sense of love and loyalty will withstand pressures of time and circumstances, a test she had failed once before. Vance, aware of his sister-in-law's tendency to see things only as she wishes to, tries to protect his brother the best way he can.

In a way, Nan Asquith is a subtle writer. On the surface, her novels seem light and frothy. Yet hidden beneath the surface is a delicate blending of love and people. Her readers were constantly exposed to ideals that surround the relationships of men and women. Step by step, she lets her characters realize their own needs and the needs of their loved ones so that the ending is a satisfying blend of suspense and certainty, both for her characters and her readers alike.

—Arlene Moore

AYRES, Ruby M(ildred).   British.   Born in January 1883. Married Reginald William Pocock in 1909. Regular contributor to the *Daily Chronicle* and *Daily Mirror*. *Died 14 November 1955.*

ROMANCE AND GOTHIC PUBLICATIONS

Novels

  Richard Chatterton, V.C. London, Hodder and Stoughton, 1915; New York, Watt, 1919.
  The Long Lane to Happiness. London, Hodder and Stoughton, 1915.
  The Making of a Man. London, Newnes, 1915.
  The Road That Bends. London, Hodder and Stoughton, 1916.
  Paper Roses. London, Hodder and Stoughton, 1916.
  A Man of His Word. London, Hodder and Stoughton, 1916.
  The Year After. London, Newnes, 1916.
  The Littl'st Lover. London, Hodder and Stoughton, 1917; New York, Doran, 1925.
  The Black Sheep. London, Hodder and Stoughton, 1917.
  The Winds of the World. London, Hodder and Stoughton, 1918; New York, Watt, 1921.
  The Remembered Kiss. London, Hodder and Stoughton, 1918.
  For Love. London, Hodder and Stoughton, 1918.
  The Second Honeymoon. London, Hodder and Stoughton, 1918; New York, Watt, 1921.
  Invalided Out. London, Hodder and Stoughton, 1918.
  The Phantom Lover. London, Hodder and Stoughton, 1919; New York, Watt, 1921.
  The Girl Next Door. London, Hodder and Stoughton, 1919.

The One Who Forgot. London, Hodder and Stoughton, 1919.

The Scar. London, Hodder and Stoughton, 1920; New York, Watt, 1921.

A Bachelor Husband. London, Hodder and Stoughton, and New York, Watt, 1920.

The Master Man. London, Hodder and Stoughton, 1920.

The Woman Hater. London, Hodder and Stoughton, 1920.

The Marriage of Barry Wicklow. London, Hodder and Stoughton, 1920; New York, Watt, 1921.

The Beggar Man. London, Hodder and Stoughton, 1920.

The Dancing Master. London, Hodder and Stoughton, 1920.

The Uphill Road. New York, Watt, 1921.

The Waif's Wedding. London, Hodder and Stoughton, 1921.

The Fortune Hunter. London, Hodder and Stoughton, 1921.

Her Way and His. London, Hodder and Stoughton, 1921.

The Highest Bidder. London, Hodder and Stoughton, 1921.

His Word of Honour. London, Hodder and Stoughton, 1921.

The Love of Robert Dennison. London, Hodder and Stoughton, 1921.

Brown Sugar. London, Hodder and Stoughton, 1921.

A Loveless Marriage. London, Hodder and Stoughton, 1921.

The Making of a Lover. London, Hodder and Stoughton, 1921.

The Man's Way. London, Hodder and Stoughton, 1921.

Nobody's Lovers. London, Hodder and Stoughton, 1921.

The One Unwanted. London, Hodder and Stoughton, 1921.

The Street Below. London, Hodder and Stoughton, 1922; New York, Doran, n.d.

A Gamble with Love. London, Hodder and Stoughton, 1922.

The Little Lady in Lodgings. London, Hodder and Stoughton, 1922.

The Lover Who Died. London, Hodder and Stoughton, 1922.

The Matherson Marriage. London, Hodder and Stoughton, 1922; New York, Doran, 1923.

The Romance of a Rogue. London, Hodder and Stoughton, and New York, Doran, 1923.

Love and a Lie. London, Hodder and Stoughton, 1923.

The Man Without a Heart. London, Hodder and Stoughton, 1923; New York, Doran, 1924.

The One Who Stood By. London, Hodder and Stoughton, 1923.

The Eager Search. London, Hodder and Stoughton, 1923.

Candle Light. London, Hodder and Stoughton, and New York, Doran, 1924.

Ribbons and Laces. London, Hodder and Stoughton, 1924.

Paul in Possession. London, Hodder and Stoughton, 1924.

The Man the Women Loved. London, Hodder and Stoughton, 1925; New York, Doran, 1926.

The Marriage Handicap. London, Hodder and Stoughton, 1925.

Overheard. London, Hodder and Stoughton, 1925; New York, Doran, 1926.

Charity's Chosen. London, Hodder and Stoughton, and New York, Doran, 1926.

Spoilt Music. London, Hodder and Stoughton, and New York, Doran, 1926.

The Faint Heart. London, Hodder and Stoughton, 1926.

The Planter and the Tree. London, Hodder and Stoughton, 1926; New York, Doran, 1927.

Wynne of Windwhistle. London, Hodder and Stoughton, 1926.

By the Gate of Pity. New York, Street and Smith, 1927.

The Luckiest Lady. London, Hodder and Stoughton, and New York, Doran, 1927.

Life Steps In. London, Hodder and Stoughton, 1928; New York, Doubleday, 1929.

The Family. London, Hodder and Stoughton, 1928.

Broken. London, Hodder and Stoughton, and New York, Doubleday, 1928.

Lovers. London, Hodder and Stoughton, and New York, Doubleday, 1929.

The Heartbreak Marriage. London, Hodder and Stoughton, 1929.

One Month at Sea, Together with George Who Believed in Allah. London, Hodder and Stoughton, 1929.

In the Day's March. London, Hodder and Stoughton, and New York, Doubleday,

1930.

Giving Him Up. London, Hodder and Stoughton, 1930.

My Old Love Came. London, Hodder and Stoughton, 1930.

One Summer. London, Hodder and Stoughton, and New York, Doubleday, 1930.

The Big Fellah. London, Hodder and Stoughton, and New York, Doubleday, 1931; as *Love Comes to Mary*, New York, Grosset and Dunlap, 1932.

Men Made the Town. London, Hodder and Stoughton, and New York, Doubleday, 1931.

The Little Man. London, Hodder and Stoughton, 1931; as *Winner Take All*, New York, Doubleday, 1937.

The Princess Passes. London, Hodder and Stoughton, 1931.

By the World Forgot. London, Hodder and Stoughton, 1932; New York, Doubleday, 1933.

So Many Miles. New York, Doubleday, 1932; London, Hodder and Stoughton, 1933.

Changing Pilots. London, Hodder and Stoughton, and New York, Doubleday, 1932.

Look to the Spring. London, Hodder and Stoughton, 1932; New York, Doubleday, 1933.

Always Tomorrow. London, Hodder and Stoughton, 1933; New York, Doubleday, 1934.

Come to My Wedding. London, Hodder and Stoughton, and New York, Doubleday, 1933.

Love Is So Blind. London, Hodder and Stoughton, 1933; New York, Doubleday, 1934.

All Over Again. New York, Doubleday, 1934; London, Hodder and Stoughton, 1935.

From This Day Forward. London, Hodder and Stoughton, and New York, Doubleday, 1934.

Much-Loved. London, Hodder and Stoughton, and New York, Doubleday, 1934.

Than This World Dreams Of. London, Hodder and Stoughton, 1934; New York, Doubleday, 1935.

Between You and Me. London, Hodder and Stoughton, 1935.

Feather. New York, Doubleday, 1935; London, Hodder and Stoughton, 1936.

The Man in Her Life. London, Hodder and Stoughton, and New York, Doubleday, 1935.

Some Day. London, Hodder and Stoughton, and New York, Doubleday, 1935.

The Sun and the Sea. London, Hodder and Stoughton, and New York, Doubleday, 1935.

Compromise. London, Hodder and Stoughton, and New York, Doubleday, 1936.

After-Glow. London, Hodder and Stoughton, and New York, Doubleday, 1936.

Follow the Shadow. London, Hodder and Stoughton, 1936; New York, Doubleday, 1937.

High Noon. London, Hodder and Stoughton, 1936; New York, Doubleday, 1937.

Somebody Else. New York, Doubleday, 1936; London, Hodder and Stoughton, 1937.

Too Much Together. London, Hodder and Stoughton, and New York, Doubleday, 1936.

Living Apart. New York, Doubleday, 1937; London, Hodder and Stoughton, 1938.

Owner Gone Abroad. London, Hodder and Stoughton, and New York, Doubleday, 1937.

Silver Wedding. London, Hodder and Stoughton, 1937.

Unofficial Wife. New York, Doubleday, 1937; London, Hodder and Stoughton, 1938.

The Tree Drops a Leaf. London, Hodder and Stoughton, and New York, Doubleday, 1938.

Return Journey. New York, Doubleday, 1938; London, Hodder and Stoughton, 1939.

And Still They Dream. New York, Doubleday, 1938; London, Hodder and Stoughton, 1939.

One to Live With. London, Hodder and Stoughton, and New York, Doubleday, 1938.

There Was Another. London, Hodder and Stoughton, and New York, Doubleday, 1938.

Big Ben. New York, Doubleday, 1939.

The Moon in the Water. New York, Doubleday, 1939.

The Thousandth Man. London, Hodder and Stoughton, and New York, Doubleday, 1939.

Week-End Woman. London, Hodder and Stoughton, and New York, Doubleday, 1939.

Little and Good. London, Hodder and Stoughton, and New York, Doubleday, 1940.

The Little Sinner. London, Hodder and Stoughton, and New York, Doubleday, 1940.

Wallflower. London, Hodder and Stoughton, and New York, Doubleday, 1940.

Sometimes Spring Is Late. London, Hodder and Stoughton, 1941.

Sunrise for Georgie. London, Hodder and Stoughton, 1941.

Still Waters. London, Hodder and Stoughton, and New York, Doubleday, 1941.

The Constant Heart. New York, Doubleday, 1941.

Rosemary—For Forgetting. London, Hodder and Stoughton, 1941.

Young Is My Love. New York, Doubleday, 1941; as *The Young at Heart*, London, Hodder and Stoughton, 1942.

Nothing Lovelier. London, Hodder and Stoughton, 1942.

Lost Property. New York, Doubleday, 1943.

Man Friday. London, Hodder and Stoughton, 1943.

Love Comes Unseen. New York, Doubleday, 1943; as *One Woman Too Many*, London, Hodder and Stoughton, 1952.

Starless Night. London, Hodder and Stoughton, 1943.

The Lady from London. London, Hodder and Stoughton, 1944.

The Dreamer Wakes. London, Hodder and Stoughton, 1945.

April's Day. London, Macdonald, 1945.

Where Are You Going? London, Hodder and Stoughton, 1946.

Salt of the Earth. London, Macdonald, 1946.

Young Shoulders. London, Hodder and Stoughton, 1947.

Missing the Tide. London, Hodder and Stoughton, 1948.

The Story of John Willie. London, Macdonald, 1948.

Steering by a Star. London, Hodder and Stoughton, 1949.

The Day Comes Round. London, Hodder and Stoughton, 1949; New York, Arcadia House, 1950.

The Man from Ceylon. London, Hodder and Stoughton, 1950.

The Man Who Lived Alone. London, Macdonald, 1950.

The Story of Fish and Chips. London, Macdonald, 1951; as *Bright Destiny*, New York, Arcadia House, 1952.

Twice a Boy. London, Hodder and Stoughton, 1951.

The Youngest Aunt. London, Hodder and Stoughton, 1952.

One Sees Stars. London, Hodder and Stoughton, 1952.

Love Without Wings. London, Hodder and Stoughton, 1953; New York, Arcadia House, 1954.

Dark Gentleman. London, Hodder and Stoughton, 1953.

Old-Fashioned Heart. New York, Arcadia House, 1953.

Short Stories

The Shadow Man and Other Stories. London, Hutchinson, 1919.

Our Avenue and Other Stories. London, Pearson, 1922; New York, Arcadia House, 1936.

Happy Endings. London, Jarrolds, 1935.

Autumn Fires: Two Love Stories. London, Hodder and Stoughton, 1951.

OTHER PUBLICATIONS

Other

Castles in Spain: The Chronicles of an April Month. London, Cassell, 1912.

*   *   *

Ruby M. Ayres's first novel (of some 150) was published in the 1910's. Most of them were made of a bland and jokey mixture which proved to be almost timeless. Consequently, many were still selling under the guise of new novels well into the 1960's and 1970's.

Publishers are naturally reluctant to relinquish a steady-selling commercial name. If, by misfortune, a publisher's best-selling author runs out of steam, dies, or cannot keep up with the insatiable appetite of her readers, demand for her works can be fulfilled by re-issuing the novels, just as they are, or as a new novel with an up-to-date dust jacket, or in a modified version. Ayres's novels were eminently suitable for this treatment. *Week-End Woman*, for example, made its first appearance in 1939. Some 30 years later it reappeared with a newly designed jacket, but only minor alterations to the text. In 1939 Slane the shady suitor is, for example, said to be "a man on leave from India." In 1969 he has become "a man on leave from the Middle East oil company in which he had a good job." In 1939 Mariette, "heroine with an angel's face," wears hats when she goes out to lunch. In the less constricting 1960's, she must lunch hatless. In 1939 her rich husband's imperious treatment of restaurant waiters is demanding and aggressive: "Here waiter, keep this stuff hot till I come back," he orders. Then, "Where's my dinner?" and "Come and light the fire some of you fellows—don't just stand there gaping." In the 1969 text the publisher's editor had realised that such treatment of minions is no longer socially acceptable. The stereotype of the ideal man remains quite unchanged. In both versions, he has "grey eyes, dark brows, dark hair and a certain ruthlessness about the mouth and chin, good-looking in a manly, rather severe way."

The slightly suggestive title and blurb might lead one to expect some titillation, or at least a hint of illicit sexual activity: "Wealth alone could not compensate for the lack of any real affection. And so she turned to other men. One affair followed another in quick succession as she sought vainly for something real to cling to." This blurb is misleading. Mariette's behaviour may seem plain daft, but is never adulterous, for, as she repeatedly wails to one of her admirers: "I can't—I'm afraid. Yes, of course I love you—but I can't face it—I'm not made that way. I hate scandal—I'm afraid." She has little to be afraid of. We read how the man "ran his hands over her shoulders and slim body" (1939). By 1969, even this innocuous move has been omitted, and he does not lay a finger on her. The book's principal concern, in both versions, is upholding the reputation of the heroine. As society became more permissive, Ayres's stories were re-created to seem more strait-laced.

Rosemary—For Forgetting, similarly, was a successful re-issue. It is the tale of a rich girl who falls irrevocably in love with an "unsuitable person." The rich father has him sent away; the engagement is broken off. Rosemary spends the rest of the book trying to forget her childhood sweetheart until, on the penultimate page, her father now being dead, the lovers are re-united. Although first published in 1941, the novel is so totally lacking in topicality that it could be successfully re-issued in 1966 with only minor changes to the text. Indeed, the one careless point is the publishers' choice of illustration. Rosemary is said to live in a large country house a few hours from Paddington Station. She has "fair hair, and her eyes were as blue as forget-me-nots; her tiny hands and feet were perfect, and when she laughed one corner of her mouth lifted itself a little higher than the other corner in an oddly fascinating manner." In the 1966 jacket, although no doubt still oddly fascinating, she is shown as having raven-black hair, coal-dark eyes, and thick symmetrical lips. While being kissed on the ear by a man in a lime-green sports shirt, she is standing in front of what is clearly no wealthy Home Counties residence, but a North American log-chalet. This kind of carelessness in presentation can have done little to raise the prestige of romantic fiction, then at a low ebb.

The cheap re-issues of popular fiction have always been seen as a threat to the more serious novelist. E.H. Lacon Watson, a journalist lecturing in the 1930's, said that they were actually destroying the livelihood of the less well selling writers. "In recent years, every change that has been made in the world of publishing and bookselling has been in favour of the few big sellers and against the author with a small, if select, audience." In fact, the readership of these two types of fiction was different. Ayres herself described, with a touch of self-mockery, the kind of girl who might be reading her own novels. There is "a kind-eyed, sentimental under house-maid," in *The Master Man* (1920), "who was young and romantic and devoured every novel she could get hold of."

By "every novel" Ayres clearly does not mean the highbrow heavy weights, but novels such as her own. Hers are fantasy-spinning, harmless escapism, jauntily written, with convoluted plots, and an excess of metaphors piled one on the other. If she had been out to expound some profound message, these many varied metaphors might well have obscured the meaning. But she was not. She was out to entertain. Just occasionally, there is a heroine, such as Marlene (*Where Are You Going?*) who not only starts out confused and upset, but ends up with second best too. "She asked herself the question, 'Where are you going?' and failed to find an answer." Luckily, she ends up with a partner equally unsure where he is going, a tired-looking, discharged soldier "with a slight limp."

She had her craft in perspective, and was quite aware of where *she* was going.

> Do you believe really believe in the romance you've written so much about? Do you believe it lasts? I'm frequently asked the question by people who are kind enough to enjoy reading my books and I can imagine it would be very disillusioning if I were to reply—"No, I don't believe in it. I just write love stories because they sell." That wouldn't be true either. I must certainly believe in romance and know that it can and does last providing it is mixed with two most important ingredients—tolerance and a sense of humour.... I'm not pretending to be original when I say that more marriages have been ruined by a nagging wife than there can ever be by an atomic bomb. I firmly believe that romance can be lively even when the strawberry season is over and there is only bread and cheese in the larder and no matter whether you agree with me or not, I'll go on writing love stories with happy endings.

—Rachel Anderson

BALDWIN, Faith. American. Born in New Rochelle, New York, 1 October 1893. Attended Packer School; Miss Fuller School; Briarcliff School. Married Hugh H. Cuthrell in 1920 (died, 1953); two sons and two daughters. Free-lance writer: faculty member, Famous Writers School, Westport, Connecticut. *Died 18 March 1978.*

ROMANCE AND GOTHIC PUBLICATIONS

Novels

> *Mavis of Green Hill.*   Boston, Small Maynard, and London, Hodder and Stoughton, 1921.
> *Laurel of Stonystream.*   Boston, Small Maynard, 1923; as *The Maid of Stonystream*, London, Sampson Low, 1924.
> *Magic and Mary Rose.*   Boston, Small Maynard, 1924.
> *Thresholds.*   Boston, Small Maynard, 1925; London, Sampson Low, 1926.
> *Those Difficult Years.*   Boston, Small Maynard, 1925; London, Sampson Low, 1926.
> *Three Women.*   New York, Dodd Mead, 1926; London, Sampson Low, 1927.
> *Departing Wings.*   New York, Dodd Mead, 1927; London, Sampson Low, 1928.
> *Rosalie's Career.*   New York, Clode, 1928.
> *Betty.*   New York, Clode, and London, Sampson Low, 1928.
> *Alimony.*   New York, Dodd Mead, 1928; London, Sampson Low, 1929.
> *The Incredible Year.*   New York, Dodd Mead, 1929; London, Sampson Low, 1930.
> *Garden Oats.*   New York, Dodd Mead, and London, Sampson Low, 1929.

Broadway Interlude, with Achmed Abdullah. New York, Payson and Clark, 1929; London, Selwyn and Blount, 1930.

Make-Believe. New York, Dodd Mead, 1930; London, Sampson Low, 1931.

The Office Wife. New York, Dodd Mead, and London, Sampson Low, 1930.

Skyscraper. New York, Cosmopolitan, 1931; London, Sampson Low, 1932; as *Sky-scraper Souls*, New York, Grosset and Dunlap, 1932.

Today's Virtue. New York, Dodd Mead, 1931.

Self-Made Woman. New York, Farrar and Rinehart, 1932; London, Sampson Low, 1933.

Week-End Marriage. New York, Farrar and Rinehart, and London, Sampson Low, 1932.

Girl on the Make, with Achmed Abdullah. New York, Long and Smith, and London, Selwyn and Blount, 1932.

District Nurse. New York, Farrar and Rinehart, 1932; London, Sampson Low, 1933.

White-Collar Girl. New York, Farrar and Rinehart, 1933; London, Sampson Low, 1934.

Beauty. New York, Farrar and Rinehart, and London, Sampson Low, 1933.

Love's a Puzzle. New York, Farrar and Rinehart, 1933; London, Sampson Low, 1934.

Innocent Bystander. New York, Farrar and Rinehart, 1934; London, Sampson Low, 1935.

Within a Year. New York, Farrar and Rinehart, and London, Sampson Low, 1934.

Honor Bound. New York, Farrar and Rinehart, 1934; London, Sampson Low, 1936.

American Family. New York, Farrar and Rinehart, 1935; as *Conflict*, London, Sampson Low, 1935.

The Puritan Strain. New York, Farrar and Rinehart, and London, Sampson Low, 1935.

The Moon's Our Home. New York, Farrar and Rinehart, 1936; London, Sampson Low, 1937.

Men Are Such Fools! New York, Farrar and Rinehart, 1936; London, Sampson Low, 1937.

Private Duty. New York, Farrar and Rinehart, 1936; London, Sampson Low, 1938.

That Man Is Mine! London, Sampson Low, 1936; New York, Farrar and Rinehart, 1937.

The Heart Has Wings. New York, Farrar and Rinehart, 1937; London, Sampson Low, 1938.

Twenty-Four Hours a Day. New York, Farrar and Rinehart, 1937; London, Sampson Low, 1939.

Manhattan Nights. New York, Farrar and Rinehart, 1937.

Hotel Hostess. New York, Farrar and Rinehart, 1938; London, Sampson Low, 1940.

Enchanted Oasis. New York, Farrar and Rinehart, 1938; London, Sampson Low, 1940.

Rich Girl, Poor Girl. New York, Farrar and Rinehart, 1938; London, Sampson Low, 1939.

White Magic. New York, Farrar and Rinehart, 1939; London, Sampson Low, 1945.

Station Wagon Set. New York, Farrar and Rinehart, 1939; London, Hale, 1945.

The High Road. New York, Farrar and Rinehart, 1939; London, Sampson Low, 1944.

Career by Proxy. New York, Farrar and Rinehart, 1939; London, Sampson Low, 1943.

Letty and the Law. New York, Farrar and Rinehart, 1940; London, Hale, 1946.

Medical Center. New York, Farrar and Rinehart, 1940; London, Hale, 1946.

Rehearsal for Love. New York, Farrar and Rinehart, 1940; London, Hale, 1946.

Something Special. New York, Farrar and Rinehart, 1940.

Temporary Address: Reno. New York, Farrar and Rinehart, 1941.

And New Stars Burn. New York, Farrar and Rinehart, 1941; London, Hale, 1948.

The Heart Remembers. New York, Farrar and Rinehart, 1941.

Blue Horizons. New York, Farrar and Rinehart, 1942; London, Hale, 1951.

Breath of Life. New York, Farrar and Rinehart, 1942; London, Hale, 1953.

The Rest of My Life with You. New York, Farrar and Rinehart, 1942; London, Hale, 1947.

You Can't Escape. New York, Farrar and Rinehart, 1943; London, Hale, 1952.

Washington, U.S.A. New York, Farrar and Rinehart, 1943.
Change of Heart. New York, Farrar and Rinehart, 1944; London, Hale, 1949.
He Married a Doctor. New York, Farrar and Rinehart, 1944; London, Hale, 1953.
A Job for Jenny. New York, Farrar and Rinehart, 1945; as *Tell Me My Heart*, 1950.
Arizona Star. New York, Farrar and Rinehart, 1945; London, Hale, 1949.
No Private Heaven. New York, Farrar and Rinehart, 1946; London, Hale, 1954.
Woman on Her Own. New York, Rinehart, 1946; London, Hale, 1954.
Give Love the Air. New York, Rinehart, 1947; London, Hale, 1955.
Sleeping Beauty. New York, Rinehart, 1947; London, Hale, 1954.
Marry for Money. New York, Rinehart, 1948; London, Hale, 1955.
The Golden Shoestring. New York, Rinehart, 1949; London, Hale, 1956.
Look Out for Liza. New York, Rinehart, 1950; London, Hale, 1956.
The Whole Armor. New York, Rinehart, 1951; London, Hale, 1956.
The Juniper Tree. New York, Rinehart, 1952; London, Hale, 1957.
Three Faces of Love. New York, Rinehart, 1957; London, Hale, 1958.
Blaze of Sunlight. New York, Rinehart, 1959; London, Hale, 1960.
Testament of Trust. New York, Holt Rinehart, 1960.
Harvest of Hope. New York, Holt Rinehart, 1962.
The West Wind. New York, Holt Rinehart, 1962; London, Hale, 1963.
The Lonely Man. New York, Holt Rinehart, 1964; as *The Lonely Doctor*, London, Hale, 1964; as *Echoes of Another Spring*, New York, Dell, 1965.
There Is a Season. New York, Holt Rinehart, and London, Hale, 1966.
Evening Star. New York, Holt Rinehart, 1966.
The Velvet Hammer. New York, Holt Rinehart, and London, Hale, 1969.
Take What You Want. New York, Holt Rinehart, 1970; London, Hale, 1971.
Any Village. New York, Holt Rinehart, 1971; London, Hale, 1972.
One More Time. New York, Holt Rinehart, 1972; London, Hale, 1974.
No Bed of Roses. New York, Holt Rinehart, 1973; London, Hale, 1975.
Time and the Hour. New York, Holt Rinehart, 1974; London, Hale, 1975.
New Girl in Town. New York, Holt Rinehart, 1975.
Thursday's Child. New York, Holt Rinehart, 1976; London, Hale, 1977.
Hold On to Your Heart. London, Hale, 1976.
Adam's Eden. New York, Holt Rinehart, 1977; London, Hale, 1978.

Short Stories

Wife vs. Secretary. New York, Grosset and Dunlap, 1934.
Five Women (includes *Star on Her Shoulder, Detour, Let's Do the Town*). New York, Farrar and Rinehart, 1942; London, Hale, 1946.
They Who Love. New York, Rinehart, 1948.

Uncollected Short Stories

"Sitter for Mother," in *Collier's* (Springfield, Ohio), 30 April 1949.
"I'm Not for You," in *American* (Springfield, Ohio), September 1949.
"White Elephant," in *American* (Springfield, Ohio), November 1949.
"Urge," in *Good Housekeeping* (New York), December 1949.
"Night of the Execution," in *American* (Springfield, Ohio), February 1950.
"Man from Santa," in *Good Housekeeping* (New York), December 1950.
"Mrs. Anderson's Daughter Gets Married," in *Good Housekeeping* (New York), August 1951.
"Susan Emery," in *American* (Springfield, Ohio), October 1951.
"Silent the Song," in *Woman's Home Companion* (Springfield, Ohio), April 1952.
"Steadfast Heart," in *Good Housekeeping* (New York), April 1952.
"Tomorrow's Bride," in *Woman's Home Companion* (Springfield, Ohio), September 1952.

"Someone They Used to Know," in *McCall's* (Dayton, Ohio), April 1953.
"Christmas Heart," in *American* (Springfield, Ohio), December 1953.
"Man She Never Knew," in *Cosmopolitan* (New York), January 1955.
"Sheer Enchantment," in *Anthology of Best Short Stories 7*, edited by Robert Oberfirst. New York, Fell, 1959.
"The Gossamer World," in *A Diamond of Years: The Best of the Woman's Home Companion*, edited by Helen Otis Lamont. New York, Doubleday, 1961.
"Sleight of Hand," in *Good Housekeeping* (Des Moines, Iowa), October 1963.

OTHER PUBLICATIONS

Play

Screenplay: *Portia on Trial*, with Samuel Ornitz and E.E. Paramore, Jr., 1937.

Verse

Sign Posts. Boston, Small Maynard, 1924.
Widow's Walk: Variations on a Theme. New York, Rinehart, 1954.

Other

Judy: A Story of Divine Corners (juvenile). New York, Dodd Mead, 1930.
Babs: A Story of Divine Corners (juvenile). New York, Dodd Mead, and London, Sampson Low, 1931.
Mary Lou: A Story of Divine Corners (juvenile). New York, Dodd Mead, 1931.
Myra: A Story of Divine Corners (juvenile). New York, Dodd Mead, 1932.
Face Toward the Spring. New York, Rinehart, 1956; London, Davies, 1957.
Many Windows: Seasons of the Heart. New York, Rinehart, 1958; London, Davies, 1959.
Living by Faith. New York, Holt Rinehart, 1964.

*   *   *

Unlike most popular romances, Faith Baldwin's novels are neither predatory nor manipulative. In that sense, they are old-fashioned. Most contemporary romances prey on their readers' needs and insecurities, perhaps on their need for insecurity, their mostly unconscious desire to prolong adolescence, that uncertain, indeterminate state where—despite probability—one might indeed turn out to be beautiful, to be wildly loved. Baldwin's books appeal to the obverse of this romantic fantasy, to the need for stability, lifelong sharing, patient familiarity. There is a bit of adolescence to them, particularly to her earlier books, but it is the cozy adolescent fantasy of proximity and protection, as when the young heroines of *The Heart Has Wings* and *Enchanted Oasis* are compelled by "accidents" to spend innocent nights with the men of their dreams. Baldwin's novels are less romances than comedies: ripe, full of sunlight, crowded with people making do with each other. Comedies in the classical sense, her books are pledges of our willingness to live life with others no better than they might be and certainly no better than ourselves.

The folk who populate these novels are usually rich, solid (if sometimes troubled), and almost never dull. They are, fancifully, the burghers of Dutch painting come out of their dark countinghouses into sunlit American suburbs. Ministers, country doctors, district nurses, lawyers (both urban and suburban), booksellers, aviators, real estate agents, and, occasionally—earlier in Baldwin's half-century career—a movie star, the idle rich: this is the litany of Baldwin's saints. Remarkably, she makes them come to life, and sometimes brilliantly. Baldwin seems able to do this out of her own generosity of spirit, her willingness to see characters as they are, not (in the unspoken imperative of romance fiction) as they should—but dare not—be. The aptly titled *Blaze of Sunlight*, to my mind Baldwin's richest novel, illustrates her tolerant generosity. Rose Holmes, the widowed heroine, ought to be an exemplar of romance fiction: passionately, almost single-mindedly devoted to her man, during his life and after his death. Yet Baldwin shows that this devotion has enriched Rose by impoverishing her children, and, by inference, the community around her, for it has deprived them of her gifts. This is the lesson Rose must learn. If, unlike classical comedy, *Blaze of Sunlight* does not end with a marriage, it does culminate in Rose's re-attachment: Rose walks out of the dark tunnel of her grief into the sunlit community where actions, even private emotions, have consequence.

Baldwin's tunnel metaphor suits both this character and her work as a whole. For, although her books are love stories, Baldwin is always stretching the radically tight focus of romance fiction and the tunnel-vision it imposes. Children and neighbors are frequent in her books and rarely serve as stage-props: rather they seem about to live busy lives of their own. In a multi-generation novel like *American Family* we get to see those lives intertwine. Moreover, Baldwin's protagonists—almost as often male as female, another departure from standard romance—have careers, again believably, not just as props. Like as not these careers encourage and express human connectedness—lawyers, doctors, teachers, ministers—and, equally likely, Baldwin's characters are immersed in the dailiness of their occupations, not in the moments of high drama each affords.

There are occasional false notes, of course. *Take What You Want*, a late novel, is tonally dissonant, sounding like a standard off-the-rack romance: girl swept off her feet by a rich older man and disapproved of by his family. Or, earlier, the falsely countrified speech of *Make-Believe* where Baldwin's gift for dialogue fails her. Yet Baldwin's is a remarkable 50-year, 60-plus novel career of comfort and progress. Her books are not quite real: there's no landedness to them, no root. Yet they are real as the mind is real, inhabiting problems; living, not without trouble, but with good humor and companionship.

—Nancy Regan

BARCLAY, Ann. *See* **GREIG, Maysie**.

BARCLAY, Florence L(ouisa, née Charlesworth). Also wrote as Brandon Roy. British. Born in Limpsfield, Surrey, 2 December 1862. Married Charles W. Barclay in 1881; two sons and six daughters. *Died 10 March 1921.*

R OMANCE AND G OTHIC P UBLICATIONS

Novels

Guy Mervyn (as Brandon Roy).   London, Blackett, 3 vols., 1891; edition revised by one
of her daughters, New York and London, Putnam, 1932.
A Notable Prisoner.   London, Marshall, 1905.
The Wheels of Time.   New York, Crowell, 1908; London, Putnam, 1910.
The Rosary.   New York and London, Putnam, 1909.
The Mistress of Shenstone.   New York and London, Putnam, 1910.
The Following of the Star.   New York and London, Putnam, 1911.
Through the Postern Gate.   New York and London, Putnam, 1912.
The Upas Tree.   London and New York, Putnam, 1912.
The Broken Halo.   London and New York, Putnam, 1913.
The Wall of Partition.   London and New York, Putnam, 1914.
My Heart's Right There.   London and New York, Putnam, 1914.
The White Ladies of Worcester.   London and New York, Putnam, 1917.
Returned Empty.   London and New York, Putnam, 1920.

O THER P UBLICATIONS

Other

The Golden Censer.   London, Hodder and Stoughton, and New York, Doran, 1914.
In Hoc + Vince: The Story of a Red Cross Flag.   London and New York, Putnam, 1915.

Critical Study: *The Life of Florence L. Barclay: A Study in Personality* by One of Her
Daughters, London and New York, Putnam, 1921.

*   *   *

Florence L. Barclay was not as prolific as most of her contemporaries in the field. She did not
need to be. *The Rosary*, published in 1909, roughly halfway through her literary career, secured
her an ample readership, for, as the *Publisher's Circular* had already pronounced: "Of all forms
of fiction, the semi-religious is the most popular." Within 9 months *The Rosary* sold 150,000
hardback copies; it was still a best seller 20 years later, and in 1928 was being serialised in
Woman's World, "the favourite paper of a Million Homes." One admirer of her work assessed
that, within two years of publication, *The Rosary* had been "read and wept over by threequar-
ters of the housemaids in Great Britain" (though this generous statistic must be tempered by
another popular novelist's judgement that "the tears of the uneducated are proverbially near
their eyes").

The predominant theme of all her novels—as befits the work of a parson's wife—concerns
the Christian conversion of one or other of the partners in love. Mortal love cannot be wholly
real, wholly acceptable, until he, or she, has also found the love of God, this state of grace being
described in a succession of metaphors: "Come home to the Father's House," "had his broken
halo restored," "until her heart beats in unison with the heart of the Virgin Mother in
Bethlehem's starlit stable." The revelation of true earthly love and of true heavenly love is often
simultaneous, the one acting as a catalyst on the other.

A recurring subsidiary theme is of the younger man in love with the much older woman,
which Barclay first, delicately, touched on in *Guy Mervyn*. This was her first novel, but it made
little impact when it originally appeared, chiefly because the publishing firm went bankrupt and
only a few copies were distributed. *The Rosary*, too, appeared originally in another form, as a
short story or (as she herself preferred it to be known) a *novella*, under the title *Wheels of
Fortune*. Unlike some romantic novelists who prided themselves in never changing a line once

written, Barclay saw the need for rewriting, reworking, and polishing. No amount of rewriting would diminish her main message:

> My aim is: Never to write a line which could introduce the taint of sin or the shadow of shame into any home. Never to draw a character which would tend to lower the ideals of those who, by means of my pen, make intimate acquaintance with a man or a woman of my own creating. There is enough sin in the world without an author's powers of imagination being used in order to add even fictitious sin to the amount. Too many bad, mean, morbid characters already, alas! walk this earth. Why should writers add to their numbers and risk introducing them into beautiful homes, where such people in actual life would never for one moment be tolerated? A great French writer and savant has said: "The only excuse for fiction is that it should be more beautiful than fact."

The result of writing only on subjects which are more beautiful than fact is that there can be no villains in her plots, and the denouements must be brought about by some highly improbable act of fate or natural disaster. *The Rosary* has, probably, the silliest plot of all, its motive force, its suspense, being maintained by the "masquerade device," a technique always popular with romantic novelists in which the heroine poses as maid/titled lady/nurse/secretary in order to be near the one she loves. But only when her true identity is revealed can true love flourish.

The religious atmosphere of the books, the tone of spiritual reverence, is conveyed by enthusiastic use of capital letters, both for the personal pronouns of the members of the trinity and for abstractions of anything which sounds remotely mystical—the Unseen, The Great Chance, Love, Life, The Little White Lady. There is a frequent repetition of emotive adverbs and adjectives—thrill, throb, tender, soul, gentle, and strange and sweet, this last one being a compound adjective, like sweet and sour, or his and hers. The religion is chiefly one of nostalgia, for reader as well as the characters. Christmas carols, well-known hymns, and long quotations from the better-known scriptures bring about strange emotional feelings in the players. Searing remembrances of lost childhood result in Christian conversion, and it is in shared emotional-cum-religious experiences that the lovers find their true unity, rather than in any explicit sexual activity. Whenever possible, the desire or opportunity for physical union is postponed, or made impossible by the intricacies of plot. Thus in *The Broken Halo* the elderly wife has a weak heart, and so her youthful husband must keep himself in a separate bedroom and endure an unconsummated marriage. On the night that he finally realizes his true, deep burning love for her, she dies of a heart attack, thus putting off till the Great Forever any possible consummation.

Similarly, in *The Following of the Star* the alliance between rich heiress and poor missionary is entirely a *marriage de convenance*, enabling her to give money for his excellent work in the typhoid-ridden swamps of Central Africa. Immediately after their marriage, he departs forever. Unknown to them, but abundantly clear to the reader, they are desperately in love. An impossible courtship, riddled with crossed letters and misunderstandings, ensues. When at last they are re-united, and a normal relationship for two healthy people would seem feasible, the author's religious imagination prevents them going about it in the normal way. Instead, they enjoy an unusual life-giving intercourse through the arms. The missionary (temporarily indisposed) lies in bed while the heiress kneels at his side in what she admits to be an exceedingly uncomfortable position, clutches his head against her breast and, it being Christmas Eve (note the novel's title), croons "Hark the Herald Angels Sing" to him, knowing that this is the one thing which will save his life. "Every moment of contact with your vital force is vitalizing him," announces a bystander to the scene. "It is like pouring blood into empty veins, only a more subtle and mysterious process, and more wonderful in its result." It was not physiological ignorance which caused Barclay to write so often about marital union in this way. (She herself was happily married, and produced eight children.) As one of her daughters wrote: "She was out to supply her fellow men with joy, refreshment, inspiration. She was not out to make art for art's sake, or to perform a literary tour de force. [Her readers] ask merely to be pleased, rested, interested, amused, inspired to a more living faith in the beauty of human affection and the goodness of God."

The mystical euphoria of her novels gave genuine spiritual comfort to many, for, as the novelist-hero in one of her books explains: "The thing of first importance is to uplift your readers; to raise their ideals; to leave them with a sense of hopefulness, which shall arouse within them a brave optimism such as inspired Browning's oft-quoted noble lines." Even today, there are readers who recall being moved and uplifted by *The Rosary*. A fellow novelist of the time paid Florence Barclay this tribute: "*The Rosary* will probably live, because its power is very uncommon—as uncommon, on its lower plane, as the power of *Wuthering Heights*.... Mrs. Barclay...was undoubtedly a great writer on her plane—Shakespeare of the servants' hall. Her power is terrific—at any rate in *The Rosary*. I had infinitely rather have written *The Rosary* than *The Forsyte Saga*."

—Rachel Anderson

BARCYNSKA, Countess (Hélène). Pseudonym for Marguerite Florence Jervis; also wrote as Marguerite Barclay; Oliver Sandys. British. Born in Henzada, Burma, in 1894; grew up in India. Educated at schools in Herne Bay, Kent, Crouch End, London, and near Radlett, Hertfordshire; Academy of Dramatic Art, London. Married 1) Armiger Barclay (Count Barcynsky); 2) Caradoc Evans in 1933 (died, 1945), one son. Journalist for *Sievier's Monthly, World*, and *Answers*, all in London; managed the Rogues and Vagabonds Repertory Players in Wales, and a theatre in Broadstairs, Kent. *Died 10 March 1964.*

ROMANCE AND GOTHIC PUBLICATIONS

Novels

> *The Honey Pot: A Story of the Stage.* London, Hurst and Blackett, and New York, Dutton, 1916.
> *If Wishes Were Horses.* London, Hurst and Blackett, and New York, Dutton, 1917.
> *Love Maggy.* London, Hurst and Blackett, 1918.
> *Sanity Jane.* London, Hurst and Blackett, 1919.
> *Love's Last Reward.* London, Hurst and Blackett, 1920.
> *Pretty Dear: A Romance.* London, Hurst and Blackett, 1920; as *Rose o' the Sea*, Boston, Houghton Mifflin, 1920.
> *Jackie.* London, Hurst and Blackett, and Boston, Houghton Mifflin, 1921.
> *Ships Come Home.* London, Hurst and Blackett, 1922.
> *Webs.* London, Hurst and Blackett, 1922.
> *Tesha, A Plaything of Destiny.* London, Hurst and Blackett, 1923.
> *We Women!* London, Hurst and Blackett, 1923.
> *The Russet Jacket: A Story of the Turf.* London, Hurst and Blackett, 1924.
> *Back to the Honey-Pot: A Story of the Stage.* London, Hurst and Blackett, 1925.
> *Hand Painted.* London, Hurst and Blackett, 1925.
> *Decameron Cocktails.* London, Hurst and Blackett, 1926.
> *Mint Walk.* London, Hurst and Blackett, 1927.
> *A Certified Bride.* London, Hurst and Blackett, 1928.
> *Milly Comes to Town.* London, Chapman and Hall, 1928.
> *He Married His Parlourmaid.* London, Chapman and Hall, 1929.
> *Fantoccini.* London, Chapman and Hall, 1930.

The Joy Shop. London, Chapman and Hall, 1931.
A Woman of Experience. London, Hurst and Blackett, 1931.
I Loved a Fairy. London, Hurst and Blackett, 1933.
Under the Big Top. London, Hurst and Blackett, 1933.
Exit Renee. London, Hurst and Blackett, 1934.
Publicity Baby. London, Hurst and Blackett, 1935.
Pick Up and Smile. London, Hutchinson, 1936.
God and Mr. Aaronson. London, Hutchinson, 1937.
Keep Cheery. London, Hutchinson, 1937.
Hearts for Gold. London, Hutchinson, 1938.
Sweetbriar Lane. London, Hutchinson, 1938.
Writing Man. London, Hutchinson, 1939.
That Trouble Piece! London, Rich and Cowan, 1939.
Let the Storm Burst. London, Rich and Cowan, 1941.
Black-Out Symphony. London, Rich and Cowan, 1942.
The Wood Is My Pulpit. London, Rich and Cowan, 1942.
Joy Comes After. London, Rich and Cowan, 1943.
Love Never Dies. London, Rich and Cowan, 1943.
Astrologer. London, Rich and Cowan, 1944.
The Tears of Peace. London, Rich and Cowan, 1944.
Love Is a Lady. London, Rich and Cowan, 1945.
We Lost Our Way. London, Rich and Cowan, 1948.
Gorgeous Brute. London, Rich and Cowan, 1949.
Conjuror. London, Rich and Cowan, 1950.
Bubble over Thorn. London, Rich and Cowan, 1951.
Those Dominant Hills. London, Rich and Cowan, 1951.
Beloved Burden. London, Rich and Cowan, 1954.
Miss Venus of Aberdovey. London, Rich and Cowan, 1956.
Angel's Eyes. London, Hurst and Blackett, 1957.
The Jackpot. London, Hurst and Blackett, 1957.
Two Faces of Love. London, Hurst and Blackett, 1958.
Prince's Story. London, Hurst and Blackett, 1959.
Black Harvest. London, Hurst and Blackett, 1960.
These Changing Years. London, Hurst and Blackett, 1961.
I Was Shown Heaven. London, Hurst and Blackett, 1962.
Smile in the Mirror. London, Hurst and Blackett, 1963.

Novels as Oliver Sandys

The Woman in the Firelight. London, Long, 1911.
Chicane. London, Long, 1912.
The Garment of Gold. London, Hurst and Blackett, 1921.
Chappy—That's All. London, Hurst and Blackett, 1922.
The Green Caravan. London, Hurst and Blackett, 1922.
Old Roses. London, Hurst and Blackett, 1923.
The Pleasure Garden. London, Hurst and Blackett, 1923.
Sally Serene. London, Hurst and Blackett, 1924.
Tilly-Make-Haste. London, Hurst and Blackett, 1924.
Blinkeyes. London, Hurst and Blackett, 1925.
Mr. Anthony. London, Hurst and Blackett, 1925.
The Curled Hands. London, Hurst and Blackett, 1926.
The Ginger-Jar. London, Hurst and Blackett, 1926.
The Crimson Ramblers. London, Hurst and Blackett, 1927.
The Sorcerers. London, Hurst and Blackett, 1927.
Mops. London, Hurst and Blackett, 1928.
Vista, The Dancer. London, Hurst and Blackett, 1928.
Cherry. London, Hurst and Blackett, 1929.

The Champagne Kiss. London, Hurst and Blackett, 1929.
Bad Lad. London, Hurst and Blackett, 1930.
Mr. Scribbles. London, Hurst and Blackett, 1930.
Sally of Sloper's. London, Hurst and Blackett, 1930.
Jinks. London, Hurst and Blackett, 1931.
Misty Angel. London, Hurst and Blackett, 1931.
Butterflies. London, Hurst and Blackett, 1932.
Squire. London, Hurst and Blackett, 1932.
Just Lil. London, Hurst and Blackett, 1933.
Sir Boxer. London, Hurst and Blackett, 1933.
Happy Day. London, Hurst and Blackett, 1934.
Spangles. London, Hurst and Blackett, 1934.
Tiptoes. London, Hurst and Blackett, 1935.
The Curtain Will Go Up. London, Hutchinson, 1936.
The Show Must Go On. London, Hutchinson, 1936.
Angel's Kiss. London, Hutchinson, 1937.
The Happy Mummers. London, Hutchinson, 1937.
Prince Charming. London, Hutchinson, 1937.
Crinklenose. London, Hutchinson, 1938.
Love Is a Flower. London, Hurst and Blackett, 1938.
Mud on My Stockings. London, Hurst and Blackett, 1938.
Hollywood Honeymoon. London, Hurst and Blackett, 1939.
Old Hat. London, Hurst and Blackett, 1939.
Whatagirl. London, Hurst and Blackett, 1939.
Calm Waters. London, Hurst and Blackett, 1940.
Singing Uphill. London, Hurst and Blackett, 1940.
Jack Be Nimble. London, Hurst and Blackett, 1941.
Wellington Wendy. London, Hurst and Blackett, 1941.
Lame Daddy. London, Hurst and Blackett, 1942.
Meadowsweet. London, Hurst and Blackett, 1942.
Swell Fellows. London, Hurst and Blackett, 1942.
Merrily All the Way. London, Hurst and Blackett, 1943.
No Faint Heart. London, Hurst and Blackett, 1943.
Miss Paraffin. London, Hurst and Blackett, 1944.
Poppet & Co. London, Hurst and Blackett, 1944.
Deputy Pet. London, Hurst and Blackett, 1945.
Learn to Laugh Again. London, Hurst and Blackett, 1947.
The Constant Rabbit. London, Hurst and Blackett, 1949.
Dot on the Spot. London, Hurst and Blackett, 1949.
Shining Failure. London, Hurst and Blackett, 1950.
Bachelor's Tonic. London, Hurst and Blackett, 1951.
Kiss the Moon. London, Hurst and Blackett, 1951.
Let's All Be Happy. London, Hurst and Blackett, 1952.
Quaint Place. London, Hurst and Blackett, 1952.
Shine My Wings. London, Hurst and Blackett, 1954.
Suffer to Sing. London, Hurst and Blackett, 1955.
The Happiness Stone. London, Hurst and Blackett, 1956.
A New Day. London, Hurst and Blackett, 1957.
Dear Mr. Dean. London, Hurst and Blackett, 1957.
Butterflies in the Rain. London, Hurst and Blackett, 1958.
Cherrystones. London, Hurst and Blackett, 1959.
The Tinsel and the Gold. London, Hurst and Blackett, 1959.
The Wise and the Steadfast. London, Hurst and Blackett, 1961.
The Golden Flame. London, Ward Lock, 1961.
The Poppy and the Rose. London, Hurst and Blackett, 1962.
The Happy Hearts. London, Ward Lock, 1962.
Laughter and Love Remain. London, Ward Lock, 1962.
Madame Adastra. London, Hurst and Blackett, 1964.

Novels as Marguerite Barclay

The Activities of Lavie Jutt, with Armiger Barclay.　London, Stanley Paul, 1911.
Letters from Fleet Street, with Armiger Barclay.　London, Palmer, 1912.
Where There Are Women, with Armiger Barclay.　London, Unwin, 1915; revised edition, as *The Five-Hooded Cobra* (as Oliver Sandys), London, Hurst and Blackett, 1932.
Peter Day-by-Day, with Armiger Barclay.　London, Simpkin Marshall, 1916.
Yesterday Is Tomorrow.　London, Rich and Cowan, 1950.
Sunset Is Dawn.　London, Rich and Cowan, 1953.
The Miracle Stone of Wales.　London, Rider, 1957.

Short Stories

Twenty-One.　London, Hurst and Blackett, 1924.
The Golden Snail and Other Stories.　London, Hurst and Blackett, 1927.
S.O.S. Queenie and Other Stories (as Oliver Sandys).　London, Hurst and Blackett, 1928.
Running Free and Other Stories.　London, Chapman and Hall, 1929.

OTHER PUBLICATIONS

Other as Oliver Sandys

Full and Frank: The Private Life of a Woman Novelist.　London, Hurst and Blackett, 1941.
Caradoc Evans.　London, Hurst and Blackett, 1946.
Unbroken Thread: An Intimate Journal.　London, Rider, 1948.

Editor, *The Little Mother Who Sits at Home* (as Countess Barcynska).　London, Jack, and New York, Dutton, 1915.

*　　　*　　　*

Despite a prolific output of novels, published over a span of more than 50 years, Countess Barcynska nevertheless managed to maintain great popularity, beginning with her first full-length novel, *The Honey Pot*, through to her final works in the 1960's. This achievement was due to a high degree of ingenuity in characterization and plot, combined with the consistent ability to produce a gripping story.

The writer's use of two pseudonyms, Countess Barcynska and Oliver Sandys, was due more to the circumstances in which she found herself than to any real dichotomy in style or subject matter of the novels. Fortunately these vicissitudes of her life (described in her autobiography *Full and Frank*) seem to have provided her with a wealth of experience in life and love, enabling her to portray a wide variety of situations and relationships most convincingly.

The experience of running a repertory company herself led to a preoccupation with the theatre in many of her novels, e.g., *The Curtain Will Go Up* and *The Happy Mummers* as Oliver Sandys and *I Was Shown Heaven, Smile in the Mirror, The Honey Pot*, and *Back to the Honey-Pot*, as Countess Barcynska. In the "honey pot" novels, for example, the insecurity, frustrations, and glamour of the theatre are clearly witnessed through the story of Maggie Oliver—at first the leading light in her company but later returning under a false name to experience the life of a chorus girl.

Another feature common to many of the novels is the description of various "spiritual experiences" felt by the characters. The schoolboy Peter in *Joy Comes After* "sees" his dead mother in the attic, and Martin Leffley from *If Wishes Were Horses* is "moved" in an unusual way while listening to a simple sermon in a country church to pray for forgiveness for the wrong he did his servant Ada. However, such experiences, where they occur, are not frightening to the characters concerned or to the reader, and indeed the writer took comfort from such experiences in her own life.

To find a weak man such as Martin Leffley in these novels is not unusual, for it was into developing her female characters that Countess Barcynska seems to have channelled most of her energies. When the detail of the plots have long faded, it is the women—the indomitable Aunt Polly in *If Wishes Were Horses*, the gypsy Molly Yetta in *Astrologer*, or the actress Phyllis Clun in *I Was Shown Heaven*—who remain strong in one's memory. Indeed it is in such characterization that the writer's strength lies, for one will look in vain for detailed scenic descriptions or great subtleties of plot. Many of the plots place great reliance on coincidence, as in *Black Harvest* where the two children of the heroine (one adopted, one not), fall in love and wish to marry, but in fact turn out to be half-brother and sister, an occurrence caused by an extremely unusual set of coincidences!

The "happy-ever-after" ending is also a marked feature of these novels. However many tragedies happen in the course of the books, they always seem to end on a happy note. In *Writing Man*, for example, Dick's wife and baby have both died separately in tragic circumstances but the novel ends with him beginning to write another book, inspired by an awareness of his wife's "presence." Perhaps the authoress Daisy Bell, also in *Writing Man*, expresses Countess Barcynska's own feeling when she says "It's very consoling to make one's characters happy at the end of one's books and it makes people who read them happy too—especially the ones who are sad."

Countess Barcynska took great pains to show, through the fates of various characters, the inevitable consequences of wrong-doing. In her earlier novels the moralistic aphorisms can become rather tiresome. However, in later novels, the morals are less overt and are often centred around the problems of love and human relationships. The penalties of marrying for the wrong reasons came to Evan Evans in *Astrologer*, who married out of chivalry, and to Martin Leffley in *If Wishes Were Horses* for marrying his deceased landlady's daughter almost for convenience.

Despite showing some of the characteristics of an earlier age in her writings, Countess Barcynska was a writer of great ability who, as she said herself, knew how "to make people laugh and smile and weep." In all, her stories have a certain elusive combination which makes for very compelling reading.

—Kim F. Paynter

BARRIE, Susan.   Also writes as Anita Charles; Pamela Kent. Address: c/o Mills and Boon Ltd., 15-16 Brooks Mews, London W1A 1DR, England.

ROMANCE AND GOTHIC PUBLICATIONS

Novels

  Mistress of Brown Furrows.   London, Mills and Boon, 1952; Toronto, Harlequin, 1963.
  The Gates of Dawn.   London, Mills and Boon, 1954; Toronto, Harlequin, 1964.
  Marry a Stranger.   London, Mills and Boon, 1954; Toronto, Harlequin, 1966.
  Carpet of Dreams.   London, Mills and Boon, 1955; Toronto, Harlequin, 1967.
  Hotel Stardust.   London, Mills and Boon, 1955.

Dear Tiberius.   London, Mills and Boon, 1956.
The House of the Laird.   London, Mills and Boon, 1956; Toronto, Harlequin, 1961.
So Dear to My Heart.   London, Mills and Boon, 1956; Toronto, Harlequin, 1961.
Air Ticket.   London, Mills and Boon, 1957.
Four Roads to Windrush.   London, Mills and Boon, 1957; Toronto, Harlequin, 1962.
Heart Specialist.   London, Mills and Boon, 1958; Toronto, Harlequin, 1961.
The Stars of San Cecilio.   London, Mills and Boon, 1958; Toronto, Harlequin, 1963.
The Wings of the Morning.   London, Mills and Boon, 1960; Toronto, Harlequin, 1965.
Nurse Nolan.   Toronto, Harlequin, 1961.
Bride in Waiting.   London, Mills and Boon, 1961; Toronto, Harlequin, 1971.
Moon at the Full.   London, Mills and Boon, 1961; Toronto, Harlequin, 1965.
Royal Purple.   London, Mills and Boon, 1962; Toronto, Harlequin, 1967.
A Case of Heart Trouble.   London, Mills and Boon, and Toronto, Harlequin, 1963.
Mountain Magic.   London, Mills and Boon, 1964; Toronto, Harlequin, 1965.
Hotel at Treloan.   Toronto, Harlequin, 1964.
Castle Thunderbird.   London, Mills and Boon, 1965; Toronto, Harlequin, 1966.
No Just Cause.   London, Mills and Boon, 1965; Toronto, Harlequin, 1966.
Master of Melincourt.   London, Mills and Boon, 1966; Toronto, Harlequin, 1968.
The Quiet Heart.   London, Mills and Boon, 1966; Toronto, Harlequin, 1967.
Rose in the Bud.   London, Mills and Boon, 1966; Toronto, Harlequin, 1967.
Accidental Bride.   London, Mills and Boon, 1967; Toronto, Harlequin, 1968.
Victoria and the Nightingale.   London, Mills and Boon, 1967.
The Marriage Wheel.   London, Mills and Boon, 1968; Toronto, Harlequin, 1969.
Wild Sonata.   London, Mills and Boon, and Toronto, Harlequin, 1968.
Return to Tremarth.   Toronto, Harlequin, 1969.
Night of the Singing Birds.   London, Mills and Boon, and Toronto, Harlequin, 1970.

Novels as Pamela Kent

Moon over Africa.   London, Mills and Boon, 1955; Toronto, Harlequin, 1966.
Desert Doorway.   London, Mills and Boon, 1956; Toronto, Harlequin, 1965.
City of Palms.   London, Mills and Boon, 1957; Toronto, Harlequin, 1964.
Sweet Barbary.   London, Mills and Boon, 1957; Toronto, Harlequin, 1964.
Meet Me in Istanbul.   London, Mills and Boon, 1958; Toronto, Harlequin, 1966.
Flight to the Stars.   London, Mills and Boon, 1959; Toronto, Harlequin, 1961.
The Chateau of Fire.   London, Mills and Boon, 1961.
Dawn on the High Mountain.   London, Mills and Boon, 1961.
Journey in the Dark.   London, Mills and Boon, 1962.
Bladon's Rock.   London, Mills and Boon, 1963; Toronto, Harlequin, 1964.
The Dawning Splendour.   London, Mills and Boon, 1963.
Enemy Lover.   London, Mills and Boon, 1964; Toronto, Harlequin, 1965.
The Gardenia Tree.   London, Mills and Boon, 1965.
Gideon Faber's Choice.   London, Mills and Boon, 1965; Toronto, Harlequin, 1966.
Star Creek.   London, Mills and Boon, 1965; Toronto, Harlequin, 1966.
Cuckoo in the Night.   London, Mills and Boon, 1966; Toronto, Harlequin, 1967.
White Heat.   London, Mills and Boon, 1966.
Beloved Enemies.   London, Mills and Boon, 1967; Toronto, Harlequin, 1970.
The Man Who Came Back.   London, Mills and Boon, and Toronto, Harlequin, 1967.
Desert Gold.   London, Mills and Boon, and Toronto, Harlequin, 1968.
Man from the Sea.   London, Mills and Boon, 1968; Toronto, Harlequin, 1969.
Nile Dusk.   London, Mills and Boon, 1972; Toronto, Harlequin, 1974.

Novels as Anita Charles

The Black Benedicts.   London, Wright and Brown, 1956; Toronto, Harlequin, 1966.
My Heart at Your Feet.   London, Wright and Brown, 1957.

One Coin in the Fountain. London, Wright and Brown, 1957; Toronto, Harlequin, 1966.
Interlude for Love. London, Wright and Brown, 1958.
The Moon and Bride's Hill. London, Wright and Brown, 1958.
Autumn Wedding. London, Wright and Brown, 1963.
The King of the Castle. London, Wright and Brown, 1963; Toronto, Harlequin, 1969.
White Rose of Love. London, Wright and Brown, 1963; Toronto, Harlequin, 1968.

*   *   *

Susan Barrie, who also writes as Pamela Kent and Anita Charles, writes the best kind of romances; they are sweet, tender, slightly improbable, and totally loving. In truth her name is Susan Barrie and she began writing in the mid-1950's. Like so many of the writers who wrote then, she took her turn writing doctor/nurse romances and later broadened to the traditional romance that is so popular today.

Her heroines are touchingly innocent and immediately awaken the masculine urge to protect. Their sturdy attempt at independence merely strengthens this urge until marriage is the only weapon to enforce male infallibility. In fact, the typcial conclusion of a romance goes like this: "whether you like it or not, I *am* going to marry you!" Such resolution in the face of willing compliance is sufficent for her readers to enjoy her novels over and over again.

Susan Barrie seems to have a special fondness for young innocence as she sets a story moving by having her heroine faced with an immediate problem or new set of circumstances that are very strange to her. Frederica Wells in *The Marriage Wheel* (Susan Barrie) must find a new job, now that her former employer has died. Since she acted as a chauffeur to an elderly lady, Frederica sees no reason why she can't continue in the same occupation; a conclusion that Humphrey Lestrode, her next employer, is quick to dispute. The fact that she has a flighty mother and a helplessly feminine sister merely adds to her worries of being independent and self-sufficient. In *Beloved Enemies* (Pamela Kent) Caprice Vaughan inherits a manor house from a great-uncle. It comes complete with furniture, housekeeper, and an irascible tenant who insists on sharing the house with her.

Surprisingly, the novels that she writes under the name of Anita Charles are quite different. These take on an intensity that has sharp emotional overtones that are far from sweet and tender. Stephanie Wayne goes to Portugal to visit her brother Tim. He is an artist, while she is a sculptress. Circumstances bring them into contact with Dom Manoel de Romeirio and his fiancée Madelena Almedia. Love springs up between Stephanie and Dom Manoel, but his sense of honor refuses to let him break his engagement. The torment of unfulfilled love is unbearable for Stephanie until two events occur; a boat wreck, and Madelena's declaration of love for Tim. The title of this novel is *White Rose of Love.*

Dominating, cynical, ruthless men attempt to deal with Susan Barrie's heroines and it is not surprising that they have unexpected difficulties throughout the stories. They have their own ideas of women and it is not particularly flattering. However, the heroines' inexplicable ability to confound their beliefs defeats them in the end. They find that one can't argue with wide-eyed goodness, sweet honesty, and soft hearts.

Romance readers find Susan Barrie's novels more than delightful nonsense. She has a wonderful sense of story, balanced by charmingly developed characters. She is one of those writers who has that special touch in telling her stories so that it makes her readers return over and over again to a favorite story. Her plots may not be particularly complicated, and the mood of the story may not always be intense or dramatic, but she insures her readers of more than a pleasant hour of reading as she spins her storytelling web about them.

—Arlene Moore

BARRINGTON, E.   *See* **BECK, L. Adams**.

BEATY Betty (née Smith).   Also writes as Karen Campbell; Catherine Ross.   British. Born in Farsley, Yorkshire. Educated at Bradford Girls Grammar School; Leeds University, diploma in social science and public administration. Served in the Women's Auxiliary Air Force. Married the writer David Beaty in 1948; three children. Worked as airline hostess and medical social worker in a London hospital. Agent: A.P. Watt Ltd., 26-28 Bedford Row, London WC1R 4HL. Address: Woodside, Hever, Edenbridge, Kent, England.

ROMANCE AND GOTHIC PUBLICATIONS

Novels

> *South to the Sun*.   London, Mills and Boon, 1956; Toronto, Harlequin, 1964.
> *Maiden Flight*.   London, Mills and Boon, 1956; Toronto, Harlequin, 1963.
> *Amber Five*.   London, Mills and Boon, 1958; Toronto, Harlequin, 1964.
> *The Butternut Tree*.   London, Mills and Boon, 1958.
> *The Top of the Climb*.   London, Collins, 1962.
> *The Path of the Moonfish*.   London, Mills and Boon, 1964; Toronto, Harlequin, 1966.
> *The Atlantic Sky*.   London, Mills and Boon, 1967.
> *Miss Miranda's Walk*.   London, Mills and Boon, and Toronto, Harlequin, 1967.
> *The Swallows of San Fedora*.   London, Mills and Boon, 1970.
> *Love and the Kentish Maid*.   London, Mills and Boon, 1971; Toronto, Harlequin, 1976.
> *Head of Chancery*.   London, Mills and Boon, 1972; Toronto, Harlequin, 1976.
> *Master at Arms*.   London, Mills and Boon, 1973; Toronto, Harlequin, 1977.
> *Fly Away, Love*.   London, Mills and Boon, 1975; Toronto, Harlequin, 1977.
> *Exchange of Hearts*.   London, Mills and Boon, 1980.
> *Wings of the Morning*, with David Beaty.   New York, Coward McCann, and London, Macmillan, 1982.

Novels as Catherine Ross

> *From This Day Forward*.   London, Cape, 1959.
> *The Colours of the Night*.   London, Joseph, 1962.
> *The Trysting Tower*.   London, Joseph, 1966.
> *Battle Dress*.   London, Eyre Methuen, 1979.

Novels as Karen Campbell

> *Suddenly, In the Air*.   London, Collins, 1969.
> *Thunder on Sunday*.   London, Collins, 1972.
> *Wheel Fortune*.   London, Collins, 1973.
> *Death Descending*.   London, Collins, 1976; New York, Stein and Day, 1977.
> *The Bells of St. Martin*.   London, Eyre Methuen, 1979.

*   *   *

Betty Beaty writes novels under three names. The one thing all have in common is that they are love stories, and the emotional content is convincing because it comes genuinely and directly from the author's own heart. She believes in "real love," and it shows.

As Betty Beaty she has written thirteen "straight" Mills and Boon romances, most based on her own experiences as an airline hostess and a medical social worker in a London hosptial; or from travelling abroad with her husband, the novelist David Beaty, during a period of seven years he spent as a diplomatic representative of the British Foreign Office—or their joint holidays, often spent big-ship cruising, which provides glamorous settings for shipboard romance. From her flying experience came such books as *Maiden Flight* and *South to the Sun*, which ingeniously combine the love interest with behind-the-scenes glimpses of life as an air-stewardess. Her medical training led to books such as *The Path of the Moonfish*, and from a diplomatic visit to South America came *Head of Chancery*.

Beaty's close connection with flying—directly, and indirectly through her husband (who was one of the first post-war commercial transatlantic pilots)—led her to write five slightly tougher novels in the name of Karen Campbell. Outstanding among them is *Suddenly, In the Air*, the story of a sky-jack, in which she slowly and expertly increases the tension until, very near the end of the story, there is an explosion of action and violence which almost lifts the reader off her chair. An added piquancy arises from the story's being told from the standpoint of the only girl-member of the crew: the stewardess.

The Catherine Ross books are longer and more deeply analytical of character and situation. Two are based on war-time experiences in the Women's Royal Air Force, and are the only novels I have encountered which truly capture the spirit and atmosphere of that time from the service-*women's* point of view. *The Colours of the Night* and *Battle Dress* (the first set on an English bomber station, the second on a fighter station in Orkney) are full of domestic detail as well as the excitement and heartache of a moment in history which changed the lives and outlook of many a hitherto-sheltered middle-class girl, catapulting her into harsh reality, physical danger, and self-reliance; presenting her, often for the first time, with deep emotional challenges at a moment when the man, or men, in her life were at their most vulnerable. These two novels are very much "real-life" love stories, born of the author's immediate experience, at a time in her own life when she too was most exposed to the deepest and most memorable emotional disturbances. (When, in fact, she herself met the man to whom she has been happily married ever since.)

Betty and David Beaty have recently completed their first long, joint, novel: *Wings of the Morning*, a love-story set in the early days of flying.

—Elizabeth Grey

BEAUCLERK, Helen (de Vere).   Pseudonym for Helen Mary Dorothea Bellingham.   British.   Born in Cambridge, 20 September 1892. Studied music in Paris. Translator and secretary in London, 1914-18; staff member, London *Evening Standard* and Birmingham *Post*. *Died in 1969.*

Novels

The Green Lacquer Pavilion.   London, Collins, and New York, Doran, 1926.
The Love of the Foolish Angel.   London, Collins, and New York, Cosmopolitan, 1929.
The Mountain and the Tree.   London, Collins, 1935; New York, Coward McCann, 1936.
So Frail a Thing: Love Scenes of the Twentieth Century.   London, Gollancz, 1940.
Shadows on a Wall.   London, Gollancz, 1941.
Where the Treasure Is.   London, Gollancz, 1944.
There Were Three Men.   London, Gollancz, 1949.

OTHER PUBLICATIONS

Other

Translator, *The Tale of Igor.*   London, Beaumont, 1918.
Translator, *War Nursing,* by Charles Richet.   London, Heinemann, 1918.
Translator, with Nadia Evrenov, *Thamar Karsavina,* by Valerien Svetlov.   London, Beaumont, 1922.
Translator, with Violet Macdonald, *Journey Through Life,* by Amedée Ozenfant.   London, Gollancz, 1939.
Translator, *The Beggars,* by L.R. des Forêts.   London, Dobson, 1949.
Translator, *Philippine,* by Danielle Hunebelle.   London, Secker and Warburg, 1955.
Translator, *My Apprenticeship,* by Colette.   London, Secker and Warburg, 1957.
Translator, *Honeymoon round the World,* by Dominique Lapierre.   London, Secker and Warburg, 1957.
Translator, *Earthly Paradise,* by Colette.   London, Secker and Warburg, 1966.

*   *   *

The novels of Helen Beauclerk fall into two groups: those which were produced before the Second World War and set in much earlier times (*The Green Lacquer Pavilion, The Love of the Foolish Angel,* and *The Mountain and the Tree*), and those which appeared during and after the War, had 20th-century settings, and frequently dealt with the War and its effects on men and women (*So Frail a Thing, Shadows on a Wall, Where the Treasure Is,* and *There Were Three Men*).

The Green Lacquer Pavilion caused quite a stir when it first appeared, and it was well received. Illustrated and decorated by Edmund Dulac, it is a romantic fantasy set in the early 18th century in the country house of Sir John and Lady Taveridge, where the host and hostess and a group of guests suddenly find themselves within the landscape depicted on a green and gold lacquer screen (one of Lady Taveridge's "newly imported Eastern styles") next to a little pavilion the colour of green jade. They have various adventures in this mysterious eastern land and eventually return to their own place and time. Beauclerk conveys splendidly an 18th-century feeling in this novel as regards dialogue, narrative style, details of life and fashion, and the pastiche dedication.

Her next novel, *The Love of the Foolish Angel,* is possibly her most perfect. The *Times Literary Supplement* called it "a creation of an almost flawless loveliness," and it was the first choice of the then newly formed Book Society. Set in Biblical lands in early Christian days, it is the story of Tamael, an angel mistakenly cast out of Heaven along with Lucifer and his crew. Now black and hideous, Tamael proves a very ineffective devil and is sent by his masters to Earth, to tempt the maiden Basilea. To do this he takes the form of a golden haired man (not unlike an angel), falls in love with Basilea, and attempts to protect her from evil, suffering much on her behalf. In the end, the two of them achieve a kind of redemption. The tale is told in a simple, lucid, almost pellucid style, with the strength and directness of a legend.

Legend, mythology, and folk beliefs form the basis of her third book, *The Mountain and the Tree*, which is written in four parts, ambitiously set in a span of times and religions from primitive pagan (nature worship of Mother Earth) to Greek to early Christian. There are four stories, connected by theme as they examine the ancient status of man (Tree) and woman (Mountain) and their relationship against the religion of the time, and there is more than a suggestion that the coming of Christianity removed much of the power and status anciently ascribed to woman. The writing in *The Mountain and the Tree* is very strong and flowing, as though the author is carried along by the power of her sources (*The Golden Bough*, etc., as freely acknowledged in the foreword).

The novels which Beauclerk set in her own time seem rather pale by comparison, although they are written with comparable skill and ease. The effects of the War and people's attitudes and reactions to it loom understandably large: in *Shadows on a Wall* the experiences during the first 12 months of the War of two childhood friends, Jane and Adèle, one in England, one in France, are contrasted; *Where the Treasure Is* is the story of a badly matched husband and wife in wartime. The two remaining novels, *So Frail a Thing* and *There Were Three Men*, deal with the interconnected lives of three people from the century's early years to the beginning of the Second World War.

—Jean Buchanan

BECK, L(ily) Adams (née Moresby).   Also wrote as E. Barrington; Louis Moresby.   British. Grew up in Asia; settled in Victoria, British Columbia, after World War 1. *Died 3 January 1931.*

Romance and Gothic Publications

Novels

 The Key of Dreams.   New York, Dodd Mead, 1922; London, Constable, 1923.
 The Treasure of Ho.   New York, Dodd Mead, 1924; London, Collins, 1925.
 The Way of Stars: A Romance of Reincarnation.   New York, Dodd Mead, 1925; London, Collins, 1926.
 The House of Fulfilment.   New York, Cosmopolitan, and London, Unwin, 1927.
 The Garden of Vision.   New York, Cosmopolitan, 1929; London, Benn, 1933.
 The Joyous Story of Astrid.   New York, Cosmopolitan, 1931.

Novels as E. Barrington

 The Chaste Diana.   New York, Dodd Mead, and London, Lane, 1923.
 The Gallants.   Boston, Little Brown, 1924; London, Harrap, 1927.
 The Divine Lady.   New York, Dodd Mead, 1924; London, Harrap, 1925.
 Glorious Apollo.   New York, Dodd Mead, 1925; London, Harrap, 1926.
 The Exquisite Perdita.   New York, Dodd Mead, and London, Harrap, 1926.
 The Thunderer.   New York, Dodd Mead, and London, Harrap, 1927.
 The Empress of Hearts.   New York, Dodd Mead, and London, Harrap, 1928.

The Laughing Queen: A Romance of Cleopatra.   New York, Dodd Mead, and London, Harrap, 1929; as *Cleopatra*, New York, Grosset and Dunlap, 1934.
The Duel of Queens.   New York, Doubleday, and London, Cassell, 1930.
The Irish Beauties   New York, Doubleday, and London, Cassell, 1931.
Anne Boleyn.   New York, Doubleday, and London, Cassell, 1932.
The Great Romantic.   New York, Doubleday, and London, Cassell, 1933.
The Wooing of the Queens.   London, Cassell, 1934.
The Graces.   London, Cassell, 1934.
The Crowned Lovers.   London, Cassell, 1935.

Novels as Louis Moresby

The Glory of Egypt.   New York, Doran, and London, Nelson, 1926.
Rubies.   New York, Doran, 1927; as Lily Adams Beck, London, Harrap, 1927.
Captain Java.   New York, Doubleday, and London, Harrap, 1928.

Short Stories

The Ninth Vibration and Other Stories.   New York, Dodd Mead, 1922; London, Unwin, 1929.
The Ladies: A Shining Constellation of Wit and Beauty (as E. Barrington).   Boston, Little Brown, and London, Unwin, 1922.
The Perfume of the Rainbow and Other Stories.   New York, Dodd Mead, 1923; London, Benn, 1931.
Dreams and Delights.   New York, Dodd Mead, 1926; London, Benn, 1932.
The Openers of the Gate: Stories of the Occult.   New York, Cosmopolitan, 1930.
Dream Tea.   London, Benn, 1934.

OTHER PUBLICATIONS

Other

The Splendour of Asia: The Story and Teaching of the Buddha.   New York, Dodd Mead, 1926; London, Collins, 1927; as *The Life of the Buddha*, Collins, 1939.
The Story of Oriental Philosophy.   New York, Cosmopolitan, 1928.
The Way of Power: Studies in the Occult.   New York, Cosmopolitan, 1928.
The Ghost Plays of Japan.   New York, Japan Society, 1933.
A Beginner's Book of Yoga, edited by David Merrill Bramble.   New York, Farrar and Rinehart, 1937.

Translator, with S. Yamabe, *Buddhist Psalms*.   New York, Dutton, and London, Murray, 1921.

*   *   *

The fiction of Lily Adams Beck falls into two main groupings, historical romances published under the pseudonym E. Barrington, and occult and Oriental fiction issued as by L. Adams Beck. A third grouping, adventure novels printed under the name Louis Moresby, is much less important.

E. Barrington's costume romances focus mostly on famous women of history. They embody some sympathy for the woman's role in certain notorious situations, not without a certain amount of sentimentalization and manipulation of history. Typical is *The Divine Lady* (1924), the author's best-known work. This is based on the life of Lady Emma Hamilton, in origin a country girl of great beauty, whose ladder of mistress-ship carried her to Sir William Hamilton, ambassador to the court of Naples, who eventually married her. During the Napoleonic Wars Emma became the mistress of Horatio Nelson in an affair that was notorious in its day and has since been used many times in fiction. Beck expands key moments in Emma's life in an episodic story frequently interrupted by authorial reflections. While opinions of Emma have varied, Beck tries to show her as primarily a simple, devoted, passionate woman, a rather thoughtless pawn of fate, a characterization that does not jell. Nor is the author successful in portraying the complex characters of Hamilton and Nelson. Beck considered historical accuracy important, but managed to overlook the fact that Emma had lost her beauty and was fat and nearly 40 when she met Nelson. In a similar vein of shallow, simplistic sympathy are *Glorious Apollo*, about Lord and Lady Byron; *The Empress of Hearts*, about Marie Antoinette and the Diamond Necklace; and *The Duel of Queens*, about Mary Queen of Scots.

More interesting, perhaps because they are based on a personal commitment, are Beck's occult and Oriental romances. Among these are a short story collection, *The Ninth Vibration*; *The Way of Stars*, a thriller about world peril, war, and romance; *The House of Fulfilment*, a mystical novel; and *The Openers of the Gate*, the cases of a British occult psychologist. Mostly set in the Orient and based on Oriental philosophy and religions, as mediated through Theosophy, these stories deal with such topics as reincarnation and love, karma, hidden teachings, mahatmas, paranormal abilities, and psychic advancement. Sometimes sexuality is important, but at other times sexuality is renounced in favor of a higher call to asceticism. Related to these supernatural fictions is *The Treasure of Ho*, which deals with adventure and romance in China during the reign of the Dowager Empress.

In these occult and Oriental stories the level of craftsmanship is higher than in the sentimental historical novels. The author's knowledge of the Orient and Oriental thought, however, has been characterized as superficial and glib. A nonfiction work in this area, *The Story of Oriental Philosophy*, coordinates the ideas behind much of the author's life and work.

—E.F. Bleiler

BENNETTS, Pamela (née James). Also writes as Margaret James. British. Born in Hampstead, London, 23 July 1922. Educated at Emmanuel Church School, Hampstead; St. Marylebone School for Girls, London. Married William George Bennetts in 1942; one daughter. Staff member, London Diocesan Fund, 1938-80: retired as Deputy Secretary, 1980. Address: 24 Flower Lane, Mill Hill, London NW7 2JE, England.

ROMANCE AND GOTHIC PUBLICATIONS

Novels

> *The Borgia Prince.* London, Hale, 1968; New York, St. Martin's Press, 1975.
> *The Borgia Bull.* London, Hale, 1968.
> *The Venetian.* London, Hale, 1968.
> *The Suzerain.* London, Hale, 1968.
> *The Adversaries.* London, Hale, 1969.
> *The Black Plantagenet.* London, Hale, 1969.
> *Envoy from Elizabeth.* London, Hale, 1970; New York, St. Martin's Press, 1973.
> *Richard and the Knights of God.* London, Hale, 1970; New York, St. Martin's Press, 1973.

The Tudor Ghosts. London, Hale, 1971.
Royal Sword at Agincourt. London, Hale, and New York, St. Martin's Press, 1971.
A Crown for Normandy London, Hale, 1971.
Bright Son of York. London, Hale, 1971.
The Third Richard. London, Hale, 1972.
The Angevin King. London, Hale, 1972.
The de Montfort Legacy. London, Hale, and New York, St. Martin's Press, 1973.
The Lords of Lancaster. London, Hale, and New York, St. Martin's Press, 1973.
The Barons of Runnymede. London, Hale, and New York, St. Martin's Press, 1974.
A Dragon for Edward. London, Hale, and New York, St. Martin's Press, 1975.
My Dear Lover England. London, Hale, and New York, St. Martin's Press, 1975.
The She-Wolf. London, Hale, 1975; New York, St. Martin's Press, 1976.
Death of the Red King. London, Hale, and New York, St. Martin's Press, 1976.
Stephen and the Sleeping Saints. London, Hale, and New York, St. Martin's Press, 1977.
The House in Candle Square. London, Hale, 1977; as *The Haunting of Sara Lessingham* (as Margaret James), New York, St. Martin's Press, 1978.
Don Pedro's Captain. London, Hale, and New York, St. Martin's Press, 1978.
Ring the Bell Softly. London, Hale, 1978; as Margaret James, New York, St. Martin's Press, 1978.
One Dark Night. London, Hale, 1978.
Footsteps in the Fog. London, Hale, 1979; as Margaret James, New York, St. Martin's Press, 1979.
Marionette. London, Hale, 1979; as Margaret James, New York, St. Martin's Press, 1979.
A Voice in the Darkness. London, Hale, 1979; as Margaret James, New York, St. Martin's Press, 1979.
Amberstone. London, Hale, 1980; as Margaret James, New York, St. Martin's Press, 1980.
The Quick and the Dead. London, Hale, 1980; as Margaret James, New York, St. Martin's Press, 1980.
Lucy's Cottage. London, Hale, 1981; as Margaret James, New York, St. Martin's Press, 1981.
Beau Barron's Lady. London, Hale, 1981.
The Marquis and Miss Jones. London, Hale, 1981.
Regency Rogue. London, Hale, 1981.
The Michaelmas Tree. London, Hale, 1982.

Pamela Bennetts comments:

I had always wanted to write, but kept telling myself that I hadn't got time, having a full-time job, plus a home to run. In 1966 I decided to try: now or never! My intention was, and still is, to entertain my readers. My books, whether historical romances, gothic thrillers, or Georgian romances, are intended as a means of escape from the trials and tribulations of everyday modern life. I want people who are kind enough to read them to enjoy them and forget the H-bomb and the kitchen sink. However, I am always extremely careful to do my research carefully, for I would never knowingly cheat my readers by including inaccurate facts. Being human, I'm sure I fail sometimes, but I do my very best. I hope I can go on writing for many years yet, as I'm only happy when I'm working on a work, and like a lost soul in between novels.

*   *   *

Pamela Bennetts takes the story of England's turbulent past and breathes life into the characters of that distant era. Most of her novels are set in England's middle ages although at least two of them take place during the time of Elizabeth I. Each story focuses on a prominent historical event in the reign of England's rulers. In the Holy Land the Crusader king, Richard the Lionheart, fights the infidel Saladin (*Richard and the Knights of God*). Richard's brother

King John reluctantly acknowledges the rights of his nobles in *The Barons of Runnymede*. After initial defeat Henry III and his son, the future Edward I, overcome the enigmatic Simon de Montfort (*The de Montfort Legacy*). The glory of Edward's own reign is captured in the novel *A Dragon for Edward*. All of the stories are well researched and often contain a bibliography for any reader wishing to pursue the subject.

Although the major historical figures are convincingly portrayed in a Bennetts novel, it is the development of the minor characters that gives substance to the stories. Their private lives and loves thread through the plots and keep the novels from becoming mere fictionalized popular history. There is always a romance and it often centers on a love/hate relationship which keeps the lovers at odds until almost the very end.

Bennetts is a born storyteller. Her alternating historical narrative with dramatic scenarios is well handled. She conveys a vivid sense of what life was like in those distant times and lightly weaves descriptions of dress, manners, foods, and furnishings into the story.

Writing in the USA under the pseudonym Margaret James, Bennetts introduces her readers to chilling tales of frightening events which take over the lives of the innocent. Through vignettes of action, thought, or dialogue, in short mysteries teeming with characters, James creates a cast of suspicious rogues, any one of whom could be the perpetrator of some horror. In the novel *Footsteps in the Fog*, terror reigns in Victorian London. An ax murderer is on the loose, but nowhere is the fear more intense than in the house of prostitution run by Thea Podulski. Two of her girls have been hidiously murdered by decapitation and several rather suspicious men had patronized the establishment at the times in question.

False clues and innuendo abound in a Margaret James tale so that a characteristic novel teases the reader and keeps her guessing all the way to the end. The denouement always surprises since often vital information leading to the culprit's identity is withheld. For the female protagonist there is usually a hint of romance as in *A Voice in the Darkness*. At one point young governess Harriet can no longer doubt that her handsome employer (whom she secretly loves) is guilty of the murder and mayhem which beset the village. Of course, he is really innocent. The author has an excellent ear for dialogue and her use of colloquial speech is superb. This British writer's mysteries have proven to be quite popular imports for US readers.

—Patricia Altner

BERCKMAN, Evelyn (Domenica). American. Born in Philadelphia, Pennsylvania, 18 October 1900. Educated at Columbia University, New York. Concert pianist and composer: compositions include the ballets *From the Odyssey* and *County Fair* and other works. Lived in London after 1960. *Died 18 September 1978.*

ROMANCE AND GOTHIC PUBLICATIONS

Novels

The Evil of Time.   New York, Dodd Mead, 1954; London, Eyre and Spottiswoode, 1955.
The Beckoning Dream.   New York, Dodd Mead, 1955; London, Eyre and Spottiswoode, 1956; as *Worse Than Murder*, New York, Dell, 1957.
The Strange Bedfellow.   New York, Dodd Mead, 1956; London, Eyre and Spottiswoode, 1957; as *Jewel of Death*, New York, Pyramid, 1968.

The Blind Villain. New York, Dodd Mead, and London, Eyre and Spottiswoode, 1957; as *House of Terror*, New York, Dell, 1960.

The Hovering Darkness. New York, Dodd Mead, 1957; London, Eyre and Spottiswoode, 1958.

No Known Grave. New York, Dodd Mead, 1958; London, Eyre and Spottiswoode, 1959.

Lament for Four Brides. New York, Dodd Mead, 1959; London, Eyre and Spottiswoode, 1960.

Do You Know This Voice? New York, Dodd Mead, 1960; London, Eyre and Spottiswoode, 1961.

Blind-Girl's-Buff. New York, Dodd Mead, and London, Eyre and Spottiswoode, 1962.

A Thing That Happens to You. New York, Dodd Mead, 1964; as *Keys from a Window*, London, Eyre and Spottiswoode, 1965.

A Simple Case of Ill-Will. London, Eyre and Spottiswoode, 1964; New York, Dodd Mead, 1965.

Stalemate. London, Eyre and Spottiswoode, and New York, Doubleday, 1966.

A Case in Nullity. London, Eyre and Spottiswoode, 1967; New York, Doubleday, 1968.

The Heir of Starvelings. New York, Doubleday, 1967; London, Eyre and Spottiswoode, 1968.

The Long Arm of the Prince. London, Hale, 1968.

She Asked for It. New York, Doubleday, 1969; London, Hamish Hamilton, 1970.

The Voice of Air. New York, Doubleday, 1970; London, Hale, 1971.

A Finger to Her Lips. London, Hale, and New York, Doubleday, 1971.

The Stake in the Game. London, Hamish Hamilton, 1971; New York, Doubleday, 1973.

The Fourth Man on the Rope. London, Hamish Hamilton, and New York, Doubleday, 1972.

The Victorian Album. London, Hamish Hamilton, and New York, Doubleday, 1973.

Wait. London, Hamish Hamilton, 1973; as *Wait, Just You Wait*, New York, Doubleday, 1973.

Indecent Exposure. London, Hamish Hamilton, 1975; as *The Nightmare Chase*, New York, Doubleday, 1975.

The Blessed Plot. London, Hamish Hamilton, 1976.

The Crown Estate. New York, Doubleday, 1976.

Be All and End All. London, Hamish Hamilton, 1976.

Journey's End. New York, Doubleday, 1977.

OTHER PUBLICATIONS

Other

Nelson's Dear Lord: A Portrait of St. Vincent. London, Macmillan, 1962.

The Hidden Navy. London, Hamish Hamilton, 1973.

Creators and Destroyers of the English Navy. London, Hamish Hamilton, 1974.

Victims of Piracy: The Admiralty Court 1575-1678. London, Hamish Hamilton, 1979.

Manuscript Collection: Mugar Memorial Library, Boston University.

*　　　*　　　*

Although often categorised as a crime writer, Evelyn Berckman produced multi-faceted work and it is virtually impossible to pin a label upon her. Most of her books have the element of mystery, many can be described as psychological thrillers, some have historical settings or make impressive use of long-term flashback techniques, while others are pure gothic; the interesting thing is that she had the ability to fuse several or all of these elements in a single novel, and invariably with commendable attention to detail and literary craftsmanship.

A keen interest in art, history, and archaeology is evident in many of her stories, combining authenticity with an atmosphere of menace in which her women protagonists are more than equal to the occasion. *The Evil of Time, The Strange Bedfellow,* and *Lament for Four Brides* are accomplished examples from the early period of her career.

Her forays into history, and particularly those stories in which she presents a modern mystery and traces it back to its historical roots, display a masterly technique in a difficult field. *The Victorian Album,* strange and eerie, shows us the innermost thoughts of a latent medium who is impelled by an old album to delve back into a Victorian murder. Berckman's skilled hand shows her heroine's initial curiosity developing into the inexorable pursuit of truth and fulfilment, and a strong line of suspense leads to a disturbing climax. In *The Blessed Plot* she weaves an ingenious connection between events of 1975 and 1214, while *Be All and End All* presents a tantalising mixture of historical bibliography, complex relationships, a menacing chateau near Paris, and an appalling secret finally revealed. All of these novels embody romance/gothic elements and mystery rather than detection, but she could also produce the highly competent romantic historical novel without complications—as witness *The Long Arm of the Prince,* a most literate and enthralling Elizabethan mystery.

With *The Heir of Starvelings* Berckman made her principal contribution to the truly gothic field. This Victorian tale is replete with foreboding, as genteel Davina Milne occupies her mind following her fiancé's death by taking the post of nursemaid-teacher at a grim old house. "The entire place," she is told, "is a sort of nightmare." With a deft touch, Berckman shows this to be an understatement.

"Miss Berckman," said Violet Grant in the *Daily Telegraph*, "is extremely good at drawing flawed women so perceptively that one cannot but sympathise with them." This is undeniable, and is but one facet of her ability to present credible characters and emotions. We must recognise also her many touches of romance without sentimentality, her superb plotting, her innate sense of history, her excellent use of the English language, and her great versatility; taken together, such qualities should rightfully have placed this remarkable and sadly unsung talent in the front rank of popular novelists.

—Melvyn Barnes

BERESFORD, Elisabeth. British. Born in Paris, France. Educated at St. Mary's Hall, Brighton; St. Catherines, Bramley; Ditchling Dame School, Sussex; Brighton and Hove High School. Served as a radio operator in the Women's Naval Service during World War II. Married Max Robertson in 1949; one daughter and one son. Since 1948, free-lance journalist. Agent: A.M. Heath Ltd., 40-42 William IV Street, London WC2N 4DD; or, David Higham Associates, 5-8 Lower John Street, London W1R 4HA, England.

ROMANCE AND GOTHIC PUBLICATIONS

Novels

Paradise Island. London, Hale, 1963.
Escape to Happiness. London, Hale, 1964; New York, Nordon, 1980.
Roses round the Door. London, Hale, and New York, Paperback Library, 1965.
Island of Shadows. London, Hale, 1966; New York, Dale, 1980.
Veronica. London, Hale, 1967; New York, Nordon, 1980.
A Tropical Affair. London, Hale, 1967; as *Tropical Affairs,* New York, Dell, 1978.

Saturday's Child.   London, Hale, 1968; as *Echoes of Love*, New York, Dell, 1979.
Love Remembered.   London, Hale, 1970; New York, Dale, 1978.
Love and the S.S. Beatrice.   London, Hale, 1972; as *Thunder of Her Heart*, New York, Dale, 1978.
Pandora.   London, Hale, 1974.
The Steadfast Lover.   London, Hale, 1980.
The Silver Chain.   London, Hale, 1980.
The Restless Heart.   New York, Valueback, 1982.

OTHER PUBLICATIONS (for children)

Fiction

The Television Mystery.   London, Parrish, 1957.
The Flying Doctor Mystery.   London, Parrish, 1958.
Trouble at Tullington Castle.   London, Parrish, 1958.
Cocky and the Missing Castle.   London, Constable, 1959.
Gappy Goes West.   London, Parrish, 1959.
The Tullington Film-Makers.   London, Parrish, 1960.
Two Gold Dolphins.   London, Constable, 1961; Indianapolis, Bobbs Merrill, 1964.
Danger on the Old Pull 'n Push.   London, Parrish, 1962.
Strange Hiding Place.   London, Parrish, 1962.
Diana in Television.   London, Collins, 1963.
The Missing Formula Mystery.   London, Parrish, 1963.
The Mulberry Street Team.   Penshurst, Kent, Friday Press, 1963.
Awkward Magic.   London, Hart Davis, 1964; as *The Magic World*, Indianapolis, Bobbs Merrill, 1965.
The Flying Doctor to the Rescue.   London, Parrish, 1964.
Holiday for Slippy.   Penshurst, Kent, Friday Press, 1964.
Game, Set, and Match.   London, Parrish, 1965.
Knights of the Cardboard Castle.   London, Methuen, 1965.
Travelling Magic.   London, Hart Davis, 1965; as *The Vanishing Garden*, New York, Funk and Wagnalls, 1967.
The Hidden Mill.   London, Benn, 1965; New York, Meredith Press, 1967.
Peter Climbs a Tree.   London, Benn, 1966.
Fashion Girl.   London, Collins, 1967.
The Black Mountain Mystery.   London, Parrish, 1967.
Looking for a Friend.   London, Benn, 1967.
The Island Bus.   London, Methuen, 1968.
Sea-Green Magic.   London, Hart Davis, 1968.
The Wombles.   London, Benn, 1968; New York, Meredith Press, 1969.
David Goes Fishing.   London, Benn, 1969.
Gordon's Go-Kart.   London, Benn, 1970.
Stephen and the Shaggy Dog.   London, Methuen, 1970.
Vanishing Magic.   London, Hart Davis, 1970.
The Wandering Wombles.   London, Benn, 1970.
Dangerous Magic.   London, Hart Davis, 1972.
The Invisible Womble and Other Stories.   London, Benn, 1973.
The Secret Railway.   London, Methuen, 1973.
The Wombles in Danger.   London, Benn, 1973.
The Wombles at Work.   London, Benn, 1973.
Invisible Magic.   London, Hart Davis, 1974.
The Wombles Go to the Seaside.   London, World Distributors, 1974.
The Wombles Gift Book.   London, Benn, 1975.
The Snow Womble.   London, Benn, 1975.
Snuffle to the Rescue.   London, Kestrel, 1975.

Tomsk and the Tired Tree. London, Benn, 1975.
Wellington and the Blue Balloon. London, Benn, 1975.
Orinoco Runs Away. London, Benn, 1975.
The Wombles Make a Clean Sweep. London, Benn, 1975.
The Wombles to the Rescue. London, Benn, 1975.
The MacWombles's Pipe Band. London, Benn, 1976.
Madame Cholet's Picnic Party. London, Benn, 1976.
Bungo Knows Best. London, Benn, 1976.
Tobermory's Big Surprise. London, Benn, 1976.
The Wombles Go round the World. London, Benn, 1976.
The World of the Wombles. London, World Distributors, 1976.
Wombling Free. London, Benn, 1978.
Toby's Luck. London, Methuen, 1978.
Secret Magic. London, Hart Davis, 1978.
The Happy Ghost. London, Methuen, 1979.
The Treasure Hunters. London, Methuen, and New York, Elsevier Nelson, 1980.
Curious Magic. London, Granada, and New York, Elsevier Nelson, 1980.
The Four of Us. London, Hutchinson, 1981.
The Animals Nobody Wanted. London, Methuen, 1982.

Plays

The Wombles, adaptation of her own stories (produced London, 1974).
Road to Albutal (for adults), with Nick Renton (produced Edinburgh, 1976).

Screenplay: *The Wombles*, 1977.

Television Plays: more than 60 scripts.

Other

The Wombles Annual 1975-1978. London, World Distributors, 4 vols., 1974-77.

Elisabeth Beresford comments:

In some of my romantic novels, I have based the plot on a mystery including crime and espionage. I try to give all my characters believable personalities, and there's always an occasional touch of humour.

*   *   *

Elisabeth Beresford is an experienced writer whose romances, though on the whole light-weight with little depth to them, are nevertheless fluently written and display a convincing awareness of the transformations love can bring about. All of her work so far has a contemporary background except for *Veronica*, but the surroundings vary from the exotic locations of Trinidad and Greece, to the Australian bush, and back home to London. The characters in her first book, *Paradise Island*, verge on stereotypes, and the plot has a predictable outcome, but in *Escape to Happiness*, the story of an English girl who takes a job on an Australian sheep farm to get away from her emotional problems, the characters have more individuality, and the author gradually suggests the feel of the loneliness of outback life in both description and dialogue, although the narrative still has its implausible aspects. In *Island of Shadows* a more dramatic note is introduced, and the climax is well handled. *Veronica* is altogether a stronger novel, held together by the personality of the main character backed up by a lively and sympathetic view of life in the early 1900's for a young girl on her own in London.

In her later novels, Beresford begins to handle her characters with far more depth and skill, particularly in *A Tropical Affair* and *Saturday's Child*, where the relationships between the main protagonists are touched with wry humour and insight. In *Love Remembered* Beresford again brings in a dramatic hint of danger to the life of luxury led by Achilles Vidal, but the promise of suspense is unfulfilled and the story tails off towards the end. *The Steadfast Lover*, however, is a more sustained and lasting novel, with a touch of the supernatural, and centres round the sad and tragic figure of Emma Smith, escaping to her wild island home from a broken love affair and ruined career. Beresford writes with a verbal facility and an increasing ability to imbue her characters with distinct personalities through smoothly controlled narrative and natural, lively dialogue.

—Tessa Rose Chester

BETTERIDGE, Anne. Pseudonym for Margaret Edith Potter, née Newman; also writes as Anne Melville; Margaret Newman; Margaret Potter. British. Born in Harrow, Middlesex, 21 June 1926. Educated at Harrow County School for Girls, 1937-44; St. Hugh's College, Oxford (Major Scholar), 1944-47, B.A. 1947, M.A. 1952. Married Jeremy Potter in 1950; two children. Teacher in England and Egypt, 1947-50; Editor, *The King's Messenger* children's magazine, London, 1950-55; Adviser, Citizens' Advice Bureau, Twickenham, 1962-70. Recipient: Romantic Novelists Association Major Award, 1966. Agent: A.D. Peters, 10 Buckingham Street, London WC2N 6BU, England.

ROMANCE AND GOTHIC PUBLICATIONS

Novels

The Foreign Girl. London, Hurst and Blackett, 1960.
The Young Widow. London, Hurst and Blackett, 1961.
Spring in Morocco. London, Hurst and Blackett, 1962; New York, Beagle, 1973.
The Long Dance of Love. London, Hurst and Blackett, 1963.
The Younger Sister. London, Hurst and Blackett, 1964.
Return to Delphi. London, Hurst and Blackett, 1964.
Single to New York. London, Hurst and Blackett, 1965; New York, Beagle, 1973.
The Chains of Love. London, Hurst and Blackett, 1965; New York, Beagle, 1973.
The Truth Game. London, Hurst and Blackett, 1966; New York, Beagle, 1973.
A Portuguese Affair. London, Hurst and Blackett, 1966; New York, Beagle, 1973.
A Little Bit of Luck. London, Hurst and Blackett, 1967; New York, Beagle, 1973.
Shooting Star. London, Hurst and Blackett, 1968.
Love in a Rainy Country. London, Hurst and Blackett, 1969.
Sirocco. London, Hurst and Blackett, 1970; New York, Beagle, 1973.
The Girl Outside. London, Hurst and Blackett, 1971; New York, Beagle, 1973.
Journey from a Foreign Land. London, Hurst and Blackett, 1972.
The Sacrifice. London, Hurst and Blackett, 1973.
The Stranger on the Beach. London, Hurst and Blackett, 1974.
The Temp. London, Hurst and Blackett, 1976.
The Tiger and the Goat. London, Hurst and Blackett, 1978.

Novels as Anne Melville (series: Lorimers)

The Lorimer Line.   London, Heinemann, and New York, Doubleday, 1977.
The Lorimer Legacy.   London, Heinemann, 1979; as *Alexa*, New York, Doubleday, 1979.
Lorimers at War.   London, Heinemann, 1980.
Lorimers in Love.   London, Heinemann, 1981.
Blaize (includes *Lorimers at War* and *Lorimers in Love*).   New York, Doubleday, 1981.

Short Stories

A Time of Their Lives.   London, Hurst and Blackett, 1974.
A Place for Everyone.   London, Hurst and Blackett, 1977.

Uncollected Short Stories

"Souvenir of the Party," in *Homes and Gardens* (London), 1969.
"Silver Stars," in *Hers* (London), 1969.
"A Castle in the Air," in *Woman's World* (Australia).
"Christmas Box," in *My Home and Family* (London), 1970.
"Net Curtains," in *Homes and Gardens* (London), 1975.
"A Greener Shade of Green," in *Homes and Gardens* (London), 1975.
"Live as Family," in *Fair Lady* (Cape Town), 1978.
"The Boy on the Bus" (as Margaret Potter), in *Daily Telegraph Magazine* (London), 1979.

OTHER PUBLICATIONS

Novel as Margaret Newman

Murder to Music.   London, Long, 1959.

Other (juvenile) as Margaret Potter

The Touch-and-Go Year.   London, Dobson, 1968; New York, Meredith Press, 1969.
The Blow-and-Grow Year.   London, Dobson, 1969.
Sandy's Safari.   London, Dobson, 1971.
The Story of the Stolen Necklace.   London, Dobson, 1974.
Trouble on Sunday.   London, Methuen, 1974.
Smoke over Shap.   London, BBC Publications, 1975.
The Motorway Mob.   London, Methuen, 1976.
Tony's Special Place.   London, Bodley Head, 1977.

*   *   *

Anne Betteridge prefers to describe her novels as "domestic" rather than romantic, and it is true that they are mainly rooted in everyday life. But the early ones, in particular, do have a central, and romantic, love-theme. In fact she won the 1966 Romantic Novelists Association Major Award for *The Truth Game*, and served for some years on the Association's Committee. She withdrew after a time, feeling that her books were moving further and further away from pure romance. But she is always concerned with personal relationships and the interaction of emotions between men and women.

Several years ago she turned away altogether from the fairly short, relatively simple, stories of her early writing years and began a major undertaking, using the pseudonym Anne Melville.

Her development as a "domestic" writer reaches its culmination in a long family chronicle beginning in the 1870's and running through to the present day: the saga of the Lorimer family. The original idea for the story was based on a factual bank crash in Glasgow late in the 19th century; but the setting for Anne Melville's story is Bristol, a city she knows well and to which she travels frequently to gather atmosphere, background, and colour.

At the centre of the story is the family whose ruin came through the folly and shady dealing of the (fictional) Bristol bank's owner, John Junius Lorimer. Margaret, his daughter, is the main character in the first volume, *The Lorimer Line*. Though the failure of the bank brings her hardship, and lost love, it also makes possible her emancipation from the restrictions of upper-middle-class Victorian life. Margaret has always wanted to be a doctor, and though her new poverty places many handicaps in her way (and there are others, intrinsic to Victorian England) it gives her the spur to break loose and fight for her personal and professional rights. The book closes on a note of optimism, and with the hook firmly embedded in the reader, who is left waiting to find out "what happened next."

What happened next were three more volumes *The Lorimer Legacy*, *Lorimers at War*, and *Lorimers in Love*—which bring the story, so far, up to 1947. Anne Melville handles this much bigger canvas with confidence, authority, and obvious enjoyment, like an athlete stretching her muscles and reaching towards the outer limits of her ability. She comes from a writing background and has all the versatility, application and skill of a "born" novelist. She succeeds in all her intentions, whether it is to write a simple love-story, a complex narrative like the Lorimer saga, or a crime story (as Margaret Newman she wrote just one, *Murder to Music*), or (as Margaret Potter) a series of highly successful children's books.

Everything she writes is enjoyable in the best sense, and her many-faceted talent adds freshness and flavour to each new book, or type of book, or subject. I have the feeling that in the Lorimer series she has found her true métier.

—Elizabeth Grey

BEVAN, Gloria. Australian. Born in Kalgoorlie, Western Australia; emigrated to New Zealand as a child. Married; three daughters. Lives in Onehunga, Auckland. Address: c/o Mills and Boon Ltd., 15-16 Brooks Mews, London W1A 1DR, England.

ROMANCE AND GOTHIC PUBLICATIONS

Novels

The Distant Trap. London, Mills and Boon, 1969; Toronto, Harlequin, 1970.
The Hills of Maketu. London, Mills and Boon, and Toronto, Harlequin, 1969.
Beyond the Ranges. London, Mills and Boon, 1970; Toronto, Harlequin, 1971.
Make Way for Tomorrow. London, Mills and Boon, and Toronto, Harlequin, 1971.
It Began in Te Rangi. London, Mills and Boon, 1971; Toronto, Harlequin, 1972.
Vineyard in a Valley. London, Mills and Boon, and Toronto, Harlequin, 1972.
Flame in Fiji. London, Mills and Boon, and Toronto, Harlequin, 1973.
The Frost and the Fire. London, Mills and Boon, and Toronto, Harlequin, 1973.
Connelly's Castle. London, Mills and Boon, and Toronto, Harlequin, 1974.
High-Country Wife. London, Mills and Boon, 1974; Toronto, Harlequin, 1975.
Always a Rainbow. London, Mills and Boon, and Toronto, Harlequin, 1975.

Dolphin Bay.   London, Mills and Boon, and Toronto, Harlequin, 1976.
Bachelor Territory.   London, Mills and Boon, and Toronto, Harlequin, 1977.
Plantation Moon.   London, Mills and Boon, 1977; Toronto, Harlequin, 1978.
Fringe of Heaven.   London, Mills and Boon, and Toronto, Harlequin, 1978.
Kowhai Country.   London, Mills and Boon, 1979.
Half a World Away.   London, Mills and Boon, 1980; Toronto, Harlequin, 1981.
Master of Mahia.   London, Mills and Boon, and Toronto, Harlequin, 1981.

*   *   *

Although born in Australia, Gloria Bevan considers herself a New Zealander. Her obvious love of her country and her particular talent for weaving interesting background information into her novels makes her one of the more popular romance writers today. Although concentrating on New Zealand background, she does not limit herself to this area.

In *Flame in Fiji* Robyn Carlisle meets David Kinnear who is in the process of re-building and re-decorating a guest house that she and her brother own. As the story unfolds, the heroine experiences events that are unique to the island. She has a sight-seeing tour of noted coral reefs early in the story. She also takes part in a "Makiti," an island feast and entertainment. Later in the story she has a chance to see and learn about the "Firewalkers," that is, warriors who walk on white-hot stones. These are but three of the many elements in the story that make it so enjoyable, for Gloria Bevan has included an amazing amount of information in a way that readers find acceptable. Her care for detail, her ability to chose just the right element or incident to develop the story line, gives her an added edge in making her novels so entertaining.

In *Bachelor Territory* Gloria Bevan uses her own country as background, especially the area about Daragaville. Here she depends on two elements in furthering her story, the fact that this part of the country has a large concentration of Yugoslavian settlers and that it was also part of the early Maori area of the country. Again she is able to weave accurate information into her story by having one character engaged in writing a book of original Maori proverbs. Some of these are skillfully used throughout the novel to give an added spark of interest. Because of her fondness of detail and for providing such interesting touches, her novels have an added dimension that her readers enjoy immensely.

At the same time, her characters and plots are particularly effective as she works out her stories. Her heroines are sensitive, caring girls who find themselves with unexpected problems to handle and unexpected decisions to make. In *Flame in Fiji* Robyn clings to memories of an unhappy childhood and the special love she has for her brother. The fact that her brother is reckless and seemingly irresponsible makes it that much harder for her to fall in love with David, for he seems to know only the worse side of her brother, Johnny.

Her heroes are more subtly drawn than usual in romances. They are not the "larger than life" figure, but well balanced and masculine in their actions and beliefs. There is a more realistic portrayal of her men in the sense that they all have some sort of profession or occupation that they really work at. David Kinnear is an architect while Craig Carter in *Bachelor Territory* is a sheep farmer. Movement in the story makes use of this fact so that day-to-day activities that would be normal for them are carefully used to further the plot.

Gloria Bevan balances character and plot in such a way that her novels are exciting, as she frequently awakens a sense of adventure in her readers. The fact that she makes use of such special backgrounds and adds unusual glimpses of other people and places makes her particularly enjoyable to read. This ability is quite special, for many readers look forward to finding writers who have this particular quality in their writing. The exotic and far-away are brought closer so that the reader has a sense of familiarity with these places and events. In fact, more than one reader has concluded that it is the next best thing to being there, after they have spent a pleasant few hours of reading one of Gloria Bevan's stories.

—Arlene Moore

BLACK, Laura.   Address: c/o St. Martin's Press, 175 Fifth Avenue, New York, New York 10010, U.S.A.

<small>ROMANCE AND GOTHIC PUBLICATIONS</small>

Novels

> *Glendraco*.   New York, St. Martin's Press, and London, Hamish Hamilton, 1977.
> *Ravenburn*.   New York, St. Martin's Press, 1978; as *Castle Raven*, London, Hamish Hamilton, 1978.
> *Wild Cat*.   New York, St. Martin's Press, and London, Hamish Hamilton, 1979.
> *Strathgallant*   New York, St. Martin's Press, and London, Hamish Hamilton, 1981.

*   *   *

Laura Black's novels are reminiscent of morality plays, with vice punished and virtue rewarded in the end. What comes before the expected conclusion is more like old-fashioned melodrama. The villain is unredeemably villainous, the heroine utterly pure, and the hero as perfect as the romantic imagination can construct him.

These novels read like pure froth, but they are threaded with a sophisticated good humor that parodies the very style that it copies. There seems to be no middle ground in Black's work. Her heroines are impossibly beautiful, impossibly spirited, and impossibly capable. At the same time the characters are almost irresistible to the reader, perhaps because there is no common ground between any reader and these literary paragons. The heroes are alluring for much the same reason; they are superhuman creations endowed with every virtue and advantage. The villains are personifications of vice, and yet they manage to show remorse or to die with great style by the end of the books. This is not to say, however, that any of the characters are less than believable. Their greatest charm is their naturalness in the face of such positive and negative perfection.

The plots of Black's novels are difficult to characterize as they contain elements of the pure romance, the gothic, the historical romance, and the novel of romantic suspense. Each style seems to be represented by a sub-plot in each book. No single style takes constant precedence; all are blended into a surprisingly cohesive whole. The books are more frankly sexual than most examples of the genres represented, save the historical romance. The sex goes beyond mere bodice-ripping; incest is a major theme in *Ravenburn*. The resolution of this sexual dilemma is not at all unexpected, but it is certainly pleasing.

All of Black's work to date deals with the rather closed society of upper-class Victorian Scotland. The relative smallness of the social circle represented leads to one of the intriguing facets of the novels. The hero and heroine of each book appear again in the following book, making the novels feel more like a unit than like single works.

Black has a genuine ear for both dialogue and dialect. Many of the secondary characters speak Scots dialect, which she makes almost audible to the reader. She also manages to solve the problem of an unfamiliar dialect vocabulary by defining words in context without becoming didactic. The descriptive passages are also worthy of note. They are highly detailed yet fluid, so that the reader feels that she knows the smallest facet of the lives and surroundings of the heroines.

Laura Black's work could be called florid, but it is evocative of a florid world that no longer exists—if it ever did. She has created romantic fantasies with a tenuous base in reality, but spun so attractively that a reader can hardly refuse to be drawn within.

—Susan Quinn Berneis

BLACK, Veronica.   *See* **PETERS, Maureen**.

BLACKMORE, Jane.   Address: c/o Piatkus Books, 17 Brook Road, Loughton, Essex IG10 1BW, England.

Romance and Gothic Publications

Novels

> *Towards Tomorrow*.   London, Collins, 1941.
> *They Carry a Torch*.   London, Collins, 1943.
> *It Happened to Susan*.   London, Collins, 1944; New York, Dell, 1973.
> *Snow in June*.   London, Collins, 1947.
> *The Square of Many Colours*.   London, Collins, 1948; New York, Ace, 1975.
> *So Dark the Mirror*.   London, Collins, 1949.
> *The Nine Commandments*.   London, Collins, 1950.
> *The Bridge of Strange Music*.   London, Collins, 1952; New York, Ace, 1974.
> *Beloved Stranger*.   London, Collins, 1953; New York, Dell, 1973.
> *Perilous Waters*.   London, Collins, 1954; New York, Dell, 1973.
> *Three Letters to Pan*.   London, Collins, 1955; New York, Ace, 1971.
> *The Closing Door*.   London, Collins, 1955.
> *Bitter Love*.   London, Collins, 1956; New York, Ace, 1973.
> *Storm in the Family*.   London, Collins, 1956.
> *A Woman on Her Own*.   London, Collins, 1957; New York, Ace, 1971.
> *The Lonely House*.   London, Collins, 1957.
> *Beware the Night*.   London, Collins, 1958; New York, Ace, 1968.
> *Dangerous Love*.   London, Collins, 1958.
> *Tears in Paradise*.   London, Collins, 1959; New York, Ace, 1973.
> *The Missing Hour*.   London, Collins, 1959; New York, Ace, 1975.
> *Bitter Honey*.   London, Collins, 1960.
> *A Trap for Lovers*.   London, Collins, 1960.
> *The Night of the Stranger*.   London, Collins, 1961; New York, Ace, 1967.
> *The Dark Between the Stars*.   London, Collins, 1961; New York, Ace, 1967.
> *Two in Shadow*.   London, Collins, 1962.
> *It Couldn't Happen to Me*.   London, Collins, 1962; New York, Dell, 1972.
> *Joanna*.   London, Collins, 1963; New York, Dell, 1972.
> *That Night*.   London, Collins, 1963; New York, Lancer, 1969.
> *Flight into Love*.   London, Collins, 1964; New York, Paperback Library, 1966.
> *Return to Love*.   London, Collins, 1964; as *Stephanie*, New York, Ace, 1972.
> *Girl Alone*.   London, Collins, 1965.
> *Man of Power*.   London, Collins, 1966.
> *Miranda*.   London, Collins, 1966; New York, Dell, 1973.
> *Gold for My Girl*.   London, Collins, 1967; as *Deed of Innocence*, New York, Ace, 1969.
> *Raw Summer*.   London, Collins, 1967; New York, Dell, 1972.
> *The Other Room*.   London, Collins, 1968; as *A Love Forbidden*, London, Coronet, 1974.
> *The Velvet Trap*.   New York, Ace, 1969.

The Lilac Is for Sharing.   London, Collins, 1969.
Lonely Night.   London, Collins, 1969.
Broomstick in the Hall.   New York, Ace, 1970; London, Collins, 1971.
Dance on a Hornet's Nest.   London, Collins, 1970.
Hunter's Mate.   London, Collins, 1971.
The Room in the Tower.   London, Collins, 1972; New York, Ace, 1973.
The Deep Pool.   London, Collins, and New York, Ace, 1972.
My Sister Erica.   London, Collins, 1973; New York, Ace, 1975.
The Cresselly Inheritance.   London, Collins, 1973; New York, Ace, 1974.
Angel's Tear.   New York, Ace, 1974.
Night of the Bonfire.   London, Collins, and New York, Ace, 1974.
And Then There Was Georgia.   London, Collins, and New York, Ace, 1975.
Lord of the Manor.   London, Collins, 1975.
Ravenden.   London, Collins, 1976.
Hawkridge.   New York, Ace, 1976.
Silver Unicorn.   London, Collins, 1977.
Of Wind and Fire.   Loughton, Essex, Piatkus, 1980.
Wildfire Love.   Loughton, Essex, Piatkus, 1980.

*   *   *

The macabre, primitive mystical past, dreams, evil, witches, ghosts, immortality, twilight groves, the occult, telepathy—these are the paraphernalia which Jane Blackmore brings to her writing and which allows her to come tantalizingly close to being a gothic/romance writer. The mysticism, playing with the dim consciousness of the beyond, interweaving forebodings, suspicion, and trepidation with a love triangle and/or an inheritance squabble set a mercurial pace. Because terror and catastrophe are potent ingredients for the reader, Blackmore has the potentiality to write exciting novels.

In *The Deep Pool* the combination is an ancestral estate, a governess, and evil. *The Cresselly Inheritance* formula is similar. Murder is the background for *The Missing Hour.* A variant on these themes is found in *Angel's Tear.* This novel is concerned with the jet-set attempting to find the primal energy through occult worship. A heroine becomes entangled through no fault of her own, finding herself with vague feelings of inferiority and in love with the melancholy, attractive hero who is striving to partake of the elixir of life. Like many of her novels, it has intervals of gloomy expectation, crescendos of emotion amidst wealth and splendor, and conspiratory villains and villainesses, placing the unknowing victim at the mercy of capriciousness. However, in Blackmore's quest to update her gothic romance, allowing spells and enchantments to be produced through LSD, she commits several errors in this and in other novels. Capitulation into ephemeral vocabulary causes the novel to flag, detracting from the pace of the plot's development. In *The Deep Pool* and, to a lesser extent in other novels, the ending fails miserably. There is also a degree of implausibility surrounding too many circumstances; for example, a heroine has just enough wine to be subdued but not enough to prevent her overhearing the discussion of her fate. In *The Cresselly Inheritance* the unity of exposition falters. Often the heroines are improbably desensitized into acquiescence to the terror which is about to befall them.

The gothic romance novel is there in its embryonic stage. It never quite comes to maturation.

—W.M. von Zharen

BLACKSTOCK, Charity. Pseudonym for Ursula Torday; also writes as Paula Allardyce; Lee Blackstock; Charlotte Keppel. British. Born in London. Educated at Kensington High School, London; Lady Margaret Hall, Oxford, B.A. in English; London School of Economics, social science certificate. Worked as a typist at the National Central Library, London. Recipient: Romantic Novelists Association Major Award, 1961. Agent: Christine Green, John Johnson, 45-47 Clerkenwell Green, London EC1R 0HT. Address: 23 Montagu Mansions, London W1H 1LD, England.

ROMANCE AND GOTHIC PUBLICATIONS

Novels

Dewey Death. London, Heinemann, 1956; with *The Foggy, Foggy Dew*, New York, British Book Centre, 1959.

Miss Fenny. London, Hodder and Stoughton, 1957; as *The Woman in the Woods* (as Lee Blackstock), New York, Doubleday, 1958.

The Foggy, Foggy Dew. London, Hodder and Stoughton, 1958; with *Dewey Death*, New York, British Book Centre, 1959.

All Men Are Murderers. New York, Doubleday, 1958; as *The Shadow of Murder*, London, Hodder and Stoughton, 1959.

The Bitter Conquest. London, Hodder and Stoughton, 1959; New York, Ballantine, 1964.

The Briar Patch. London, Hodder and Stoughton, 1960; as *Young Lucifer*, Philadelphia, Lippincott, 1960.

The Exorcism. London, Hodder and Stoughton, 1961; as *A House Possessed*, Philadelphia, Lippincott, 1962.

The Gallant. London, Hodder and Stoughton, 1962; New York, Ballantine, 1966.

Mr. Christopoulos. London, Hodder and Stoughton, 1963; New York, British Book Centre, 1964.

The Factor's Wife. London, Hodder and Stoughton, 1964; as *The English Wife*, New York, Coward McCann, 1964.

When the Sun Goes Down. London, Hodder and Stoughton, 1965; as *Monkey on a Chain*, New York, Coward McCann, 1965.

The Knock at Midnight. London, Hodder and Stoughton, 1966; New York, Coward McCann, 1967.

Party in Dolly Creek. London, Hodder and Stoughton, 1967; as *The Widow*, New York, Coward McCann, 1967.

The Melon in the Cornfield. London, Hodder and Stoughton, 1969; as *The Lemmings*, New York, Coward McCann, 1969.

The Daughter. New York, Coward McCann, 1970; London, Hodder and Stoughton, 1971.

The Encounter. New York, Coward McCann, 1971; Loughton, Essex, Piatkus, 1981.

The Jungle. London, Hodder and Stoughton, and New York, Coward McCann, 1972.

The Lonely Strangers. New York, Coward McCann, 1972; London, Hodder and Stoughton, 1973.

People in Glass Houses. London, Hodder and Stoughton, and New York, Coward McCann, 1975.

Ghost Town. London, Hodder and Stoughton, and New York, Coward McCann, 1976.

I Met Murder on the Way. London, Hodder and Stoughton, 1977; as *The Shirt Front*, New York, Coward McCann, 1977.

Miss Charley. London, Hodder and Stoughton, 1979.

With Fondest Thoughts. London, Hodder and Stoughton, 1980.

Dream Towers. London, Hodder and Stoughton, 1981.

Novels as Ursula Torday

The Ballad-Maker of Paris. London, Allan, 1935.
No Peace for the Wicked. London, Nelson, 1937.
The Mirror of the Sun. London, Nelson, 1938.

Novels as Paula Allardyce

After the Lady. London, Ward Lock, 1954.
The Doctor's Daughter. London, Ward Lock, 1955.
A Game of Hazard. London, Ward Lock, 1955.
Adam and Evelina. London, Ward Lock, 1956.
The Man of Wrath. London, Ward Lock, 1956.
The Lady and the Pirate. London, Ward Lock, 1957.
Southarn Folly. London, Ward Lock, 1957.
Beloved Enemy. London, Ward Lock, 1958.
My Dear Miss Emma. London, Ward Lock, 1958; Chicago, Playboy Press, 1980.
Death My Lover. London, Ward Lock, 1959.
A Marriage Has Been Arranged. London, Ward Lock, 1959.
Johnny Danger. London, Ward Lock, 1960; as *The Rebel Lover*, Chicago, Playboy Press, 1979.
Witches' Sabbath. London, Ward Lock, 1961; New York, Macmillan, 1962.
The Gentle Highwayman. London, Ward Lock, 1961.
Adam's Rib. London, Hodder and Stoughton, 1963; as *Legacy of Pride*, New York, Dell, 1975.
The Respectable Miss Parkington-Smith. London, Hodder and Stoughton, 1964; as *Paradise Row*, New York, Dell, 1976.
Octavia; or, The Trials of a Romantic Novelist. London, Hodder and Stoughton, 1965; New York, Dell, 1977.
The Moonlighters. London, Hodder and Stoughton, 1966; as *Gentleman Rogue*, New York, Dell, 1975.
Six Passengers for the "Sweet Bird." London, Hodder and Stoughton, 1967.
Waiting at the Church. London, Hodder and Stoughton, 1968; as *Emily*, New York, Dell, 1976.
The Ghost of Archie Gilroy. London, Hodder and Stoughton, 1970; as *Shadowed Love*, New York, Dell, 1977.
Miss Jonas's Boy. London, Hodder and Stoughton, 1972; as *Eliza*, New York, Dell, 1975.
The Gentle Sex. London, Hodder and Stoughton, 1974; as *The Carradine Affair*, New York, Pocket Books, 1976.
Miss Philadelphia Smith. London, Hodder and Stoughton, 1977.
Haunting Me. London, Hodder and Stoughton, 1978; New York, St. Martin's Press, 1979.
The Rogue's Lady. Chicago, Playboy Press, 1979.
The Vixen's Revenge. Chicago, Playboy Press, 1980.

Novels as Charlotte Keppel

Madam, You Must Die. London, Hodder and Stoughton, 1974; as *Loving Sands, Deadly Sands*, New York, Delacorte Press, 1975.
My Name Is Clary Brown. New York, Random House, 1976; as *When I Say Goodbye, I'm Clary Brown*, London, Hodder and Stoughton, 1977.
I Could Be Good to You. London, Hutchinson, and New York, St. Martin's Press, 1980.
The Villains. Loughton, Essex, Piatkus, 1980; New York, St. Martin's Press, 1982.
The Ghosts of Fontenoy. Loughton, Essex, Piatkus, 1981.

Other

The Children. Boston, Little Brown, 1966; as Wednesday's Children, London, Hutchinson, 1967.

*   *   *

A wide-ranging and fertile imagination, tempered by common sense, is a rare quality in a writer of romantic fiction, yet this is a quality that Charity Blackstock possesses. From the beginning of her career her fiction has spanned countries and eras with confident skill.

Two early novels display this diversity and reveal literary techniques that can be observed to develop steadily. The Bitter Conquest, a historical novel set in the Scotland of 1750, has as its central character a somewhat reluctant hero, Adams. He is an English soldier bitterly disillusioned by futile bloodletting for a cause in which he has no conviction. The romantic element is introduced early, and develops in careful counterpoint to Adam's exploration of his own and his country's motives. There are gothic elements in the novel as well, including macabre descriptions of the bleak moors around Culloden—and even a severed head. By contrast, The Briar Patch is set in Paris four years after World War II, and the protagonists are two teenagers: Deirdre is Irish, attending a finishing school, and Max is a Jewish survivor of Nazi-occupied Poland. Though the portrayal of their developing intimacy is clouded by hopeless pessimism, the novel holds the reader's interest by its sensitive characterisation and a plot packed with exciting incident.

Blackstock returned to a similar period in The Knock at Midnight, but switched to modern-day Australia for Party in Dolly Creek. This book introduces the theme of soul-searching that pervades many of Blackstock's subsequent novels.

Perhaps the least successful of Blackstock's works is The Melon in the Cornfield, mainly because the characters involved in this tale of racial conflict in a West London technical college never come to life. Blackstock, like many other romantic novelists, does not contrive to avoid a patronising tone when dealing with a primarily political subject. The Lonely Strangers, however, shows Blackstock at full strength; in it she returns to the mid-18th century and to the people of Scotland, this time a group of exiles in Paris whose spirits are broken by defeat but whose characters are alive with emotion.

The majority of Blackstock's more recent works have a contemporary setting and rely for their interest and success upon a realistic presentation of modern-day crises. A good example is Ghost Town whose main character, Elizabeth Walters, is a former journalist, past middle age, with several unsuccessful relationships behind her. Her mental journey to self-realisation is presented by flashbacks that juxtapose past and present experiences. Mrs. Walters's own views on literature form another aspect of the novel. In Dream Towers Barbara Wyatt leaves her unfaithful husband to retreat to their country cottage. The working out of her true feelings toward Ben is linked metaphorically with her curiosity about the occupant of a mysterious mansion—and the laying to the village's "ghost" enables Barbara to lay her own "ghosts" to rest.

Charity Blackstock's consistently realistic characters, whose reactions can be readily related to common experience, have contributed to her success in the field of romantic fiction. Hers is not remote, high-flown romanticism but has at its base "heart and sincerity" without which, as Elizabeth Walters proposed in Ghost Town, writing is "no use at all."

—Anne M. Shields

BLAIR, Kathryn. Also writes as Rosalind Brett; Celine Conway. Address: c/o Mills and Boon Ltd., 15-16 Brooks Mews, London W1A 1DR, England.

ROMANCE AND GOTHIC PUBLICATIONS

Novels

Bewildered Heart. London, Mills and Boon, 1950; Toronto, Harlequin, 1964.
The House at Tegwani. London, Mills and Boon, 1950; Toronto, Harlequin, 1963.
No Other Haven. London, Mills and Boon, 1950; Toronto, Harlequin, 1966.
Dearest Enemy. London, Mills and Boon, 1951; Toronto, Harlequin, 1967.
Flowering Wilderness. London, Mills and Boon, 1951; Toronto, Harlequin, 1967.
Mayenga Farm. London, Mills and Boon, 1951; Toronto, Harlequin, 1965.
The Enchanting Island. London, Mills and Boon, 1952; Toronto, Harlequin, 1963.
The Fair Invader. London, Mills and Boon, 1952; as *Plantation Doctor*, Toronto, Harlequin, 1962.
The White Oleander. London, Mills and Boon, 1953; as *Nurse Laurie*, Toronto, Harlequin, 1962.
Dear Adversary. London, Mills and Boon, 1953; Toronto, Harlequin, 1964.
Barbary Moon. London, Mills and Boon, 1954; Toronto, Harlequin, 1965.
Sweet Deceiver. London, Mills and Boon, 1955; Toronto, Harlequin, 1965.
Tamarisk Bay. London, Mills and Boon, 1956; Toronto, Harlequin, 1962.
Wild Crocus. London, Mills and Boon, 1956; Toronto, Harlequin, 1963.
Valley of Flowers. London, Mills and Boon, 1957.
The Tulip Tree. London, Mills and Boon, 1958; Toronto, Harlequin, 1966.
Love This Enemy. London, Mills and Boon, 1958; Toronto, Harlequin, 1964.
The Golden Rose. London, Mills and Boon, 1959; Toronto, Harlequin, 1962.
The Man at Mulera. London, Mills and Boon, 1959; Toronto, Harlequin, 1965.
A Summer at Barbazon. London, Mills and Boon, 1960; as *A Nurse at Barbazon*, Toronto, Harlequin, 1964.
The Primrose Bride. London, Mills and Boon, 1961; Toronto, Harlequin, 1966.
Children's Nurse. Toronto, Harlequin, 1961.
Battle of Love. London, Mills and Boon, 1961; Toronto, Harlequin, 1966.
The Affair in Tangier. London, Mills and Boon, 1962.
They Met in Zanzibar. London, Mills and Boon, 1962; Toronto, Harlequin, 1967.
The Surgeon's Marriage. London, Mills and Boon, 1963; Toronto, Harlequin, 1964.
The Dangerous Kind of Love. London, Mills and Boon, 1964.
This Kind of Love. Toronto, Harlequin, 1964.
Doctor Westland. Toronto, Harlequin, 1965.

Novels as Rosalind Brett

Green Leaves. Hanley, Staffordshire, Locker, 1947.
Pagan Interlude. Hanley, Staffordshire, Locker, 1947.
Secret Marriage. Hanley, Staffordshire, Locker, 1947.
And No Regrets. London, Rich and Cowan, 1948; Toronto, Harlequin, 1974.
Winds of Enchantment. London, Rich and Cowan, 1949; Toronto, Harlequin, 1968.
They Came to Valeira. London, Rich and Cowan, 1950; Toronto, Harlequin, 1974.
Brittle Bondage. London, Rich and Cowan, 1951; Toronto, Harlequin, 1969.
Love This Stranger. London, Rich and Cowan, 1951; Toronto, Harlequin, 1974.
Stormy Haven. London, Mills and Boon, 1952; Toronto, Harlequin, 1962.
Fair Horizon. London, Mills and Boon, 1952; Toronto, Harlequin, 1963.
Towards the Sun. London, Mills and Boon, 1953; Toronto, Harlequin, 1962.
Whispering Palms. London, Mills and Boon, 1954; Toronto, Harlequin, 1963.
Winds in the Wilderness. London, Mills and Boon, 1954; Toronto, Harlequin, 1963.

Sweet Waters. London, Mills and Boon, 1955; Toronto, Harlequin, 1964.
A Cottage in Spain. London, Mills and Boon, 1955; Toronto, Harlequin, 1975.
Portrait of Susan. London, Mills and Boon, 1956; Toronto, Harlequin, 1963.
Quiet Holiday. London, Mills and Boon, 1957; as *Nurse on Holiday*, Toronto, Harlequin, 1963.
Tangle in Sunshine. London, Mills and Boon, 1957; Toronto, Harlequin, 1964.
Young Tracy. London, Mills and Boon, 1958; Toronto, Harlequin, 1964.
Too Young to Marry. London, Mills and Boon, 1958; Toronto, Harlequin, 1964.
The Reluctant Guest. London, Mills and Boon, 1959; Toronto, Harlequin, 1964.
Hotel Mirador. London, Mills and Boon, 1959; Toronto, Harlequin, 1966.
Dangerous Waters. London, Mills and Boon, 1960; Toronto, Harlequin, 1964.
The Bolambo Affair. London, Mills and Boon, 1961; Toronto, Harlequin, 1967.
Spring at the Villa. London, Mills and Boon, 1961; as *Elizabeth Browne, Children's Nurse*, Toronto, Harlequin, 1965.
The Girl at White Drift. London, Mills and Boon, 1962; Toronto, Harlequin, 1967.
For My Sins. London, Mills and Boon, 1966.

Novels as Celine Conway

Return of Simon. London, Mills and Boon, 1953; Toronto, Harlequin, 1965.
The Blue Caribbean. London, Mills and Boon, 1954; Toronto, Harlequin, 1964.
Flowers in the Wind. London, Mills and Boon, 1954; as *Doctor's Assistant*, Toronto, Harlequin, 1964.
Full Tide. London, Mills and Boon, 1954; Toronto, Harlequin, 1964.
Three Women. London, Mills and Boon, 1955; Toronto, Harlequin, 1966.
The Tall Pines. London, Mills and Boon, 1956; Toronto, Harlequin, 1963.
The Rustle of Bamboo. London, Mills and Boon, 1957.
Wide Pastures. London, Mills and Boon, 1957; Toronto, Harlequin, 1962.
At the Villa Massina. London, Mills and Boon, 1958; Toronto, Harlequin, 1965.
My Dear Cousin. London, Mills and Boon, 1959; Toronto, Harlequin, 1965.
Came a Stranger. London, Mills and Boon, 1960; Toronto, Harlequin, 1965.
Flower of the Morning. London, Mills and Boon, 1960; Toronto, Harlequin, 1966.
Perchance to Marry. London, Mills and Boon, 1961; Toronto, Harlequin, 1966.
White Doctor. Toronto, Harlequin, 1961.
The Rancher Needs a Wife. London, Mills and Boon, 1962; Toronto, Harlequin, 1963.
Ship's Surgeon. London, Mills and Boon, 1962; Toronto, Harlequin, 1963.

*   *   *

Kathryn Blair's writing began in the late 1940's and she published numerous novels through the 1960's. She is also a writer who preferred to use a pseudonym, and for years her novels appeared under the names of Rosalind Brett and Celine Conway. In fact, she wrote and published under all three names for some time during the 1950's and 1960's.

Her style of writing is surprising, however, for one does not find the usual limitations in plot or characters that seem to typify romances of those years. In fact, she is quite modern and could easily be mistaken for a contemporary writer. She uses strong characterization, emotional and dramatic involvement, and exotic backgrounds to tell her stories. Many take place in Africa and Europe. Underlying psychological difficulties also seem to play a part in her motivation, as characters fight circumstances and their own hidden fears and desires.

In *Young Tracy* (Rosalind Brett) the heroine, Maggie Tracy, finds herself left in charge of a supply store deep in the wilds of Africa while her parents return on a trip to England. Nick Heward arrives to set up a construction base for a projected bridge in the area. He seeks to establish the store as a base for supplies and encounters Maggie. Another complication in the novel is Don Caldwell and his mother. Don falls in love with Maggie, but she can only think of him as a friend. Gradually Nick and Maggie fall in love, but events constantly set them at odds, until Mrs. Caldwell's growing psychological difficulties bring things to a head. Maggie's youthfulness, her unawareness, and, most of all, her stubborn idealistic need to help her parents all bring out the anger and frustration that Nick feels as he seeks to protect Maggie. The story line centers on several layers of conflict as the heroine and hero finally cut through the many elements of disagreement and confusion.

The Man at Mulera (Kathryn Blair) is no less complex as Lou Prentice arrives in Africa to take charge of her cousin's little boy, Keith. She is disturbed and later horrified to learn that the will making her a guardian of the child also stipulates that she and Ross Gilmore act as joint guardians, even to the extent that neither can marry without the other's permission. Lou finds herself forced to remain in Africa and slowly she becomes involved with Ross on questions of care and discipline for the boy. In this novel Blair makes full use of her creative ability as she draws numerous threads of conflict together in a seemingly impossible situation. Secondary characters such as Greg Allwyn, Ross Gilmore's new manager, and Paula Craddock, the District Commissioner's sister, add their strands to the various sub-plots and conflicts. Greg is a weak, spineless person who plays on Lou's sympathies. Paula is determined to become Ross's wife, regardless of his inclinations. Again Blair's use of psychological overtones raises the suspense and adds tremendously to character motivation.

One may not dismiss Kathryn Blair as simply another romance writer. She shows unusual talent in developing complex characters and in letting them write their own stories. Her heroines are far from the simple peaches-and-cream caricatures that one thinks of in romances, neither are her heroes so predictable and stereotyped. A timeless quality in her writings makes her one of those rare writers who has something to say to any generation reading her, a fact that modern readers appreciate as they often re-read one of her well-written novels.

—Arlene Moore

BLAKE, Stephanie.

ROMANCE AND GOTHIC PUBLICATIONS

Novels

Flowers of Fire.   Chicago, Playboy Press, 1977; Feltham, Middlesex, Hamlyn, 1978.
Daughter of Destiny.   Chicago, Playboy Press, 1977; Feltham, Middlesex, Hamlyn, 1978.
Blazon of Passion.   Chicago, Playboy Press, 1978; Feltham, Middlesex, Hamlyn, 1979.
So Wicked My Desire.   Chicago, Playboy Press, and Feltham, Middlesex, Hamlyn, 1979.
Secret Sins.   Chicago, Playboy Press, 1980.
Wicked Is My Flesh.   Chicago, Playboy Press, 1980.
Scarlet Kisses.   Chicago, Playboy Press, 1981.
Unholy Desires.   Chicago, Playboy Press, 1981.

*   *   *

Sin, passion, and alliteration mark the titles of Stephanie Blake's novels: *Scarlet Kisses, Flowers of Fire, Daughter of Destiny, Blaze of Passion, So Wicked My Desire, Secret Sins, Wicked Is My Flesh*, and *Unholy Desires*. Incredible coincidences, lifted-from-the textbook history (running in long, itemized passages), trite literary allusions, and stereotyped characters (who speak, like the author, in clichés), together with a contemporary faddishness and vulgarity of speech dilute the sin and dull the passion. Still, the fast-moving stories hypnotize like flaming fires, and the passion-filled pages keep the reader's fingers yearning, burning, turning for more. It is easy to understand Blake's blazing popularity.

Flowers of Fire spans the Irish Revolution, the American Civil War, the California Gold Rush, and the early West (with Custer's Last Stand, Chief Crazy Horse, and Butch Cassidy), as it follows Ravena Wilding, a stunningly beautiful woman torn between the twin O'Neil brothers: Roger, "the treacherous, twisted brother who, through lies and deception, takes lovely Ravena for his own," and Brian, "the rogue, who said, 'Hate me or love me, but never forget me,' and captured Ravena's heart for all time." Jefferson Davis and other historical figures appear as characters in the appropriate places, along with characters from other fictions: Scarlett O'Hara (" 'I tell you,' says Jefferson Davis, "the last time I set eyes on a beauty such as yours was in Savannah, Georgia. Come to think of it, she was of Irish extraction, too. Scarlett O'Hara is her name. Lovely. Reminds me very much of you, Miss Ravena. Except for the eyes. And to tell the truth, she was a trifle skinny for my tastes.' "), as does Rhett Butler's new-found brother, Dan, who carries on a love affair with the insatiable Ravena. Ravena is given to quoting John Donne ("No man is an island") and Alfred Lord Tennyson ("Into the valley of death,/ Rode the Six Hundred") at critical moments.

In *Daughter of Destiny*, the sweeping continuation of the O'Neil saga, Ravena's daughter, Sabrina, voyages from violent Ireland and England (where her mother had a meeting with Queen Victoria, who "looked like a stouter version of *Whistler's Mother*") to violent India (and the cult of "Thuggee"), and back to Britain, where she rejects the advances of a rude Winston Churchill. Dan Butler reappears, and Colette, the casual *amour* of Glenn Blake, Sabrina's *fiancé*, sees him at a church wedding and speculates: "Dan Butler...Hmmm...I'll bet he's good in bed." *Daughter of Destiny* concludes with this touching scene between mother Sabrina and sons Fitz and Hugh:

> "Mother, did we make you cry? Hugh's voice trembled. "We're sorry, mom. Honestly we are." Fitz got up and came around the table. He put his arms around her neck and pressed his face to her head.
> Self-consciously Hugh came around too and stood at the side of her chair with a hesitant hand on her shoulder.
> "Yes, mother, we love you."
> She looked up, from one to the other, and her smile was like the sun breaking through a spring shower.
> "And I love you." She held on to them tightly and looked lovingly at her husband.
> "I love all of you so very much. Truly my cup runneth over."

Blaze of Passion tracks another fiery woman from 19th-century England to a penal colony in the Australian jungle. *Secret Sins* details the adventures of three generations of Tate women "from the watery wreckage of the Titanic to the bottomless maelstrom of the Bermuda Triangle." *Wicked Is My Flesh* conglomerates the eruption of Mauna Loa, the San Francisco Fire, and a Swiss avalanche. It concludes: "He [Luke Callahan] smiled at his two loves [his wife and his daughter] and said, 'I could not dream of a world more wonderful or more complete than the world I share with you.' " Amen.

—Marcia G. Fuchs

BLOOM, Ursula (Harvey). Also writes as Sheila Burns; Mary Essex; Rachel Harvey; Deborah Mann; Lozania Prole; Sara Sloane. British. Born in Chelmsford, Essex. Married 1) Arthur Brownlow Denham-Cookes in 1916 (died, 1918), one son; 2) Charles Gower Robinson in 1925. Journalist: Beauty Editor, *Woman's Own*; staff member, *Sunday Pictorial*. Has exhibited her needlework. Fellow, Royal Historical Society. Address: 191 Cranmer Court, London S.W.3, England.

ROMANCE AND GOTHIC PUBLICATIONS

Novels

The Great Beginning. London, Hutchinson, 1924.
Vagabond Harvest. London, Hutchinson, 1925.
The Driving of Destiny. London, Hutchinson, 1925.
Our Lady of Marble. London, Hutchinson, 1926.
The Judge of Jerusalem. London, Harrap, 1926.
Spilled Salt: The Story of a Spy. London, Hutchinson, 1927.
Candleshades: The Story of a Soul. London, Hutchinson, 1927; New York, Watt, 1928.
Base Metal: The Story of a Man. London, Hutchinson, 1928; as *Veneer*, New York, Watt, 1929.
An April After. London, Hutchinson, 1928.
To-morrow for Apricots London, Hutchinson, 1929; as *The Eternal Tomorrow*, New York, Watt, 1929.
Tarnish. London, Hutchinson, 1929.
The Secret Lover. London, Hutchinson, 1930; New York, Dutton, 1931.
The Passionate Heart. London, Hutchinson, 1930; Canoga Park, California, Major, 1978.
The Gossamer Dream. London, Hutchinson, 1931.
Pack Mule. London, Hutchinson, 1931; New York, Dutton, 1932.
Trackless Way. London, Hurst and Blackett, 1931.
Fruit on the Bough: The Story of a Brother and Sister. London, Hutchinson, 1931; as *Flood of Passion*, New York, Dutton, 1932.
The Pilgrim Soul. London, Hutchinson, 1932.
Breadwinners. London, Hutchinson, 1932.
The Cypresses Grow Dark. London, Hutchinson, 1932.
Love's Playthings. London, Hutchinson, 1932.
The Log of a Naval Officer's Wife. London, Hurst and Blackett, 1932.
Rose Sweetman. London, Hutchinson, 1933.
Spread Wings. London, Hutchinson, 1933.
Better to Marry. New York, Dutton, 1933.
Wonder Cruise. London, Hutchinson, 1933; New York, Dutton, 1934.
Enchanted Journey. London, Hutchinson, 1933.
Love Is Everything. London, Hutchinson, 1933; as *Love, Old and New*, New York, Dutton, 1933.
Mediterranean Madness. London, Hutchinson, 1934.
The Questing Trout. London, Hutchinson, 1934.
Pastoral. London, Hutchinson, 1934.
Young Parent. London, Hutchinson, 1934.
This Is Marriage. London, Hutchinson, 1935.
Harvest of a House. London, Hutchinson, 1935.
The Gipsy Vans Come Through. London, Hutchinson, 1936.
The Laughing Lady. London, Collins, 1936.
Laughter in Cheyne Walk. London, Collins, 1936; Philadelphia, Lippincott, 1937.
Marriage of Pierrot. London, Cherry Tree, 1936.
Three Cedars. London, Collins, 1937.
Leaves Before the Storm. London, Rich and Cowan, 1937.

The Golden Venture.   London, Rich and Cowan, 1938.
Lily-of-the-Valley.   London, Rich and Cowan, 1938.
The Brittle Shadow.   London, Readers Library, 1938.
Beloved Creditor.   London, Cassell, 1939.
These Roots Go Deep.   London, Cassell, 1939.
Trailing Glory.   London, Hale, 1940.
The Woman Who Was To-morrow.   London, Cassell, 1940.
The Flying Swans.   London, Cassell, 1940.
Spring in September.   London, Hale, 1941.
Silver Orchids.   London, Hale, 1941.
The Virgin Thorn.   London, Cassell, 1941.
Dinah's Husband.   London, Cassell, 1941.
The Golden Flame.   London, Hale, 1941.
Age Cannot Wither.   London, Cassell, 1942.
Lovely Shadow.   London, Cassell, 1942.
No Lady Buys a Cot.   London, Chapman and Hall, 1943.
Marriage in Heaven.   London, Hale, 1943.
A Robin in a Cage.   London, Cassell, 1943.
Nightshade at Morning.   London, Mellifont Press, 1944.
No Lady in Bed.   London, Chapman and Hall, 1944.
The Fourth Cedar.   London, Cassell, 1944.
The Painted Lady.   London, Macdonald, 1945.
The Faithless Dove.   London, Cassell, 1945.
Three Sons.   London, Macdonald, 1946.
A Garden for My Child.   London, Gifford, 1946.
No Lady with a Pen.   London, Chapman and Hall, 1947.
Adam's Daughters.   London, Macdonald, 1947.
Alien Corn.   London, Hamish Hamilton, 1947.
Facade.   London, Macdonald, 1948.
Next Tuesday.   London, Macdonald, 1949.
No Lady in the Cart.   London, Convoy, 1949.
Gipsy Flower.   London, Hale, 1949.
The King's Wife.   London, Hutchinson, 1950; Canoga Park, California, Major, 1979.
Eleanor Jowitt, Antiques.   London, Macdonald, 1950.
The Song of Philomel.   London, Macdonald, 1950.
How Dark, My Lady! A Novel Concerning the Life of William Shakespeare.   London,
   Hutchinson, 1951.
Pavilion.   London, Hutchinson, 1951.
Nine Lives.   London, Macdonald, 1951.
Orange Blossom for Sandra.   London, Hale, 1951.
The Sentimental Family.   London, Macdonald, 1951.
As Bends the Bough.   London, Macdonald, 1952.
Twilight of a Tudor.   London, Hutchinson, 1952.
Moon Song.   London, Hale, 1953.
Sea Fret.   London, Hutchinson, 1953.
Marriage of Leonora.   London, Hale, 1953.
The First Elizabeth.   London, Hutchinson, 1953.
Matthew, Mark, Luke, and John.   London, Hutchinson, 1954.
Daughters of the Rectory.   London, Hutchinson, 1955.
The Gracious Lady.   London, Hutchinson, 1955.
The Girl Who Loved Crippen.   London, Hutchinson, 1955.
The Silver Ring.   London, Hutchinson, 1955.
The Tides of Spring Flow Fast.   London, Hutchinson, 1956.
Brief Springtime.   London, Hutchinson, 1957.
The Abiding City.   London, Hutchinson, 1958.
Monkey Tree in a Flower Pot.   London, Hutchinson, 1958.
Undarkening Green.   London, Hutchinson, 1959.
The Romance of Charles Dickens.   London, Hale, 1960.

The Thieving Magpie.   London, Hutchinson, 1960.
The Cactus Has Courage.   London, Hutchinson, 1961.
Prelude to Yesterday.   London, Hutchinson, 1961; Los Angeles, Pinnacle, 1978.
Harvest-Home Come Sunday.   London, Hutchinson, 1962.
Ship in a Bottle.   London, Hutchinson, 1962.
The Gated Road.   London, Hutchinson, 1963.
The Ring Tree.   London, Hutchinson, 1964.
The House That Died Alone.   London, Hutchinson, 1964.
The Quiet Village.   London, Hutchinson, 1965.
The Ugly Head.   London, Hutchinson, 1965.
The Dandelion Clock.   London, Hutchinson, 1966.
The Old Adam.   London, Hutchinson, 1967.
Two Pools in a Field.   London, Hutchinson, 1967.
Yesterday's Tomorrow.   London, Hutchinson, 1968; Canoga Park, California, Major, 1978.
The Dragonfly.   London, Hutchinson, 1968.
The Flight of the Falcon.   London, Hutchinson, 1969.
The Hunter's Moon.   London, Hutchinson, 1969.
The Tune of Time.   London, Hutchinson, 1970.
Perchance to Dream.   London, Hutchinson, 1971.
The Caravan of Chance.   London, Hutchinson, 1971.
Edwardian Day-Dream.   London, Hutchinson, 1972.
The Cheval Glass.   London, Hutchinson, 1973.
The Old Rectory.   London, Hutchinson, 1973.
Mirage on the Horizon.   London, Hutchinson, 1974; Canoga Park, California, Major, 1979.
The Old Elm Tree.   London, Hutchinson, 1974.
The Twisted Road.   London, Hutchinson, 1975.
The Turn of Life's Tide.   London, Hutchinson, 1976.
The House on the Hill.   London, Hutchinson, 1977.
The Fire and the Rose.   Canoga Park, California, Major, 1977.
The Woman Doctor.   London, Hutchinson, 1978.
Bittersweet.   Canoga Park, California, Major, 1978.
Born for Love.   Canoga Park, California, Major, 1978.
Mirage of Love.   Canoga Park, California, Major, 1978.
Sunday Love.   Canoga Park, California, Major, 1978.
A Change of Heart.   Canoga Park, California, Major, 1979.
Forever Autumn.   Canoga Park, California, Major, 1979.
Gypsy Flame.   Canoga Park, California, Major, 1979.
Honor's Price.   Canoga Park, California, Major, 1979.
The Queen's Affair.   Canoga Park, California, Major, 1979.
Sweet Spring of April.   Canoga Park, California, Major, 1979.

Novels as Sheila Burns

The Passionate Adventure.   London, Cassell, 1936.
Dream Awhile.   London, Cassell, 1937.
Take a Chance.   London, Cassell, 1937.
Honeymoon Island.   London, Cassell, 1938.
Lady! This Is Love!   London, Cassell, 1938.
Week-end Bride.   London, Cassell, 1939.
Wonder Trip.   London, Cassell, 1939.
Adventurous Heart.   London, Cassell, 1940.
Meet Love on Holiday.   London, Cassell, 1940.
Romance Is Mine.   London, Cassell, 1941.
The Stronger Passion.   London, Cassell, 1941.
Bridal Sweet.   London, Cassell, 1942; as *Bride Alone*, New York, Arcadia House, 1943.

Thy Bride Am I. London, Cassell, 1942.
Romantic Fugitive. London, Cassell, 1943; New York, Arcadia House, 1944.
Romance of Jenny W.R.E.N. London, Cassell, 1944; as *Jenny W.R.E.N.*, New York, Arcadia House, 1945.
Vagrant Lover. London, Macdonald, 1945.
Hold Hard, My Heart. London, Macdonald, 1946.
Bride—Maybe. London, Macdonald, 1946.
Desire Is Not Dead. London, Macdonald, 1947.
The Chance Romance. London, Eldon Press, 1948.
Air Liner. London, Eldon Press, 1948.
To-morrow Is Eternal. London, Macdonald, 1948.
Faint with Pursuit. London, Eldon Press, 1949.
No Trespassers in Love. London, Macdonald, 1949.
The Cuckoo Never Weds. London, Eldon Press, 1950.
Primula and Hyacinth. New York, Arcadia House, 1950.
Not Free to Love. London, Eldon Press, 1950; as *Heaven Lies Ahead* (as Sara Sloane), New York, Arcadia House, 1951.
Hold Back the Heart. New York, Arcadia House, 1951.
Rosebud and Stardust. London, Eldon Press, 1951.
Live Happily—Love Song. London, Eldon Press, 1952.
Love Me To-morrow. London, Eldon Press, 1952.
Romantic Intruder. London, Hutchinson, 1952.
Tomorrow We Marry. London, Hutchinson, 1953.
Beloved and Unforgettable. London, Hutchinson, 1953.
Please Burn after Reading. London, Hutchinson, 1954.
How Dear Is My Delight! London, Hutchinson, 1955.
Adventure in Romance. London, Hutchinson, 1955.
Romantic Summer Sea. London, Hutchinson, 1956.
The Sweet Impulse. London, Hutchinson, 1956.
How Rich Is Love? London, Hurst and Blackett, 1957.
The Beloved Man. London, Hurst and Blackett, 1957.
This Dragon of Desire. London, Hurst and Blackett, 1958.
The Storm Bird. London, Hurst and Blackett, 1959.
The Lasting Lover. London, Hurst and Blackett, 1960.
Doctor Gregory's Partner. London, Hurst and Blackett, 1960.
Doctor to the Rescue. London, Hurst and Blackett, 1961.
The Dishearted Doctor. London, Hale, 1961.
Dr. Irresistible, M.D. London, Hale, 1962.
The Eyes of Doctor Karl. London, Hale, 1962.
Heartbreak Surgeon. London, Hale, 1963.
Theatre Sister in Love. London, Hale, 1963.
When Doctors Love. London, Hale, 1964.
Doctor's Distress. London, Digit, 1964.
Doctor Delightful. London, Hale, 1964.
Doctor Called David. London, Hale, 1966.
Doctor Divine. London, Hale, 1966.
A Surgeon's Sweetheart. London, Hale, 1966.
The Beauty Surgeon. London, Hale, 1967.
The Flying Nurse. London, Hale, 1967.
Romantic Cottage Hospital. London, Hale, 1967.
The Dark-eyed Sister. London, Hale, 1968.
Casualty Ward. London, Hale, 1968.
Acting Sister. London, Hale, 1968.
Surgeon at Sea. London, Hale, 1969.
The Nurse Who Shocked the Matron. London, Hale, 1970.
Sister Loving Heart. London, Hale, 1971.
Cornish Rhapsody. London, Hale, 1972.
Romance and Nurse Margaret. London, Hale, 1972.

The Bells Still Ring. London, Hale, 1976.

Novels as Mary Essex

Haircut for Samson. London, Chapman and Hall, 1940.
Nesting Cats. London, Chapman and Hall, 1941.
Eve Didn't Care. London, Chapman and Hall, 1941.
Marry to Taste. London, Chapman and Hall, 1942.
Freddy for Fun. London, Chapman and Hall, 1943.
The Amorous Bicycle. London, Chapman and Hall, 1944.
Divorce? Of Course. London, Chapman and Hall, 1945.
Young Kangaroos Prefer Riding. London, Chapman and Hall, 1947.
Domestic Blister. London, Chapman and Hall, 1948.
Six Fools and a Fairy. London, Jenkins, 1948.
Full Fruit Flavour. London, Jenkins, 1949.
The Herring's Nest. London, Jenkins, 1949.
An Apple for the Doctor. London, Jenkins, 1950.
Tea Is So Intoxicating. London, Jenkins, 1950.
Dark Gentleman, Fair Lady. London, Jenkins, 1951.
A Gentleman Called James. London, Jenkins, 1951.
She Had What It Takes. London, Jenkins, 1952.
Forty Is Beginning. London, Jenkins, 1952.
Danielle, My Darling. London, Dakers, 1954.
The Passionate Springtime. London, Hale, 1956.
Forbidden Fiancé. London, Hale, 1957.
The Dark Lover. London, Hale, 1957.
A Nightingale Once Sang. London, Hale, 1958.
It's Spring, My Heart! London, Hale, 1958.
Romance of Summer. London, Hale, 1959.
This Man Is Not for Marrying. London, Hale, 1959.
The Fugitive Romantic. London, Hale, 1960.
The Love Story of Dr. Duke. London, Hale, 1960.
A Sailor's Love. London, Hale, 1961.
Doctor on Call. London, Hale, 1961.
Date with a Doctor. London, Hale, 1962.
Dr. Guardian of the Gate. London, Hale, 1962.
Nurse from Killarney. London, Hale, 1963.
A Strange Patient for Sister Smith. London, Hale, 1963.
The Sangor Hospital Story. London, Hale, 1963.
The Hard-Hearted Doctor. London, Hale, 1964.
Doctor and Lover. London, Hale, 1964.
Dare-Devil Doctor. London, Hale, 1965.
Romantic Theatre Sister. London, Hale, 1965.
Hospital of the Heart. London, Hale, 1966.
The Little Nurse. London, Hale, 1967.
The Romance of Dr. Dinah. London, Hale, 1967.
Assistant Matron. London, Hale, 1967.
The Adorable Doctor. London, Hale, 1968.
The Ghost of Fiddler's Hill. London, Hale, 1968.
The Sympathetic Surgeon. London, Hale, 1968.
Doctor on Duty Bound. London, Hale, 1969.
When a Woman Doctor Loves. London, Hale, 1969.
The Dangerous Doctor. London, Hale, 1970.
Heart Surgeon. London, Hale, 1971.
The Fascinating Doctor. London, Hale, 1972.
The Nurse Who Fell in Love. London, Hale, 1972.
A Nurse Called Liza. London, Hale, 1973.

The Dark Farm. London, Hale, 1974.
A Doctor's Love. London, Hale, 1974.

Novels as Lozania Prole

Our Dearest Emma. London, Museum Press, 1949; as *The Magnificent Courtesan*, New York, McBride, 1950; as *Emma Hart*, Toronto, Harlequin, 1951.
Pretty, Witty Nell! London, Hale, and New York, McGraw Hill, 1953; as *The Fabulous Nell Gwynne*, Toronto, Harlequin, 1954; as *Sweet Nell*, London, Corgi, 1965.
To-night, Josephine! London, Hale, and New York, McGraw Hill, 1954.
The King's Pleasure. London, Hale, and New York, McGraw Hill, 1954.
The Enchanting Courtesan. London, Hale, 1955; New York, Pocket Books, 1975.
My Wanton Tudor Rose: The Love Story of Lady Katheryn Howard. London, Hale, 1956.
The Little Victoria. London, Hale, 1957.
A Queen for England. London, Hale, 1957.
Harry's Last Love. London, Hale, 1958.
The Stuart Sisters. London, Hale, 1958.
Consort to the Queen. London, Hale, 1959.
The Little Wig-Maker of Bread Street. London, Hale, 1959.
For Love of the King. London, Hale, 1960.
The Tudor Boy. London, Hale, 1960.
The Queen's Midwife. London, Hale, 1961.
My! My Little Queen! London, Hale, 1961.
A King's Plaything. London, Hale, 1962.
Queen Guillotine. London, Hale, 1962.
The Ghost That Haunted a King. London, Hale, 1963.
The Wild Daughter. London, Hale, 1963.
Daughter of the Devil. London, Hale, 1963; New York, Pocket Books, 1974.
Henry's Golden Queen. London, Hale, 1964.
The Three Passionate Queens. London, Hale, 1964.
Marlborough's Unfair Lady. London, Hale, 1965.
The Haunted Headsman. London, Hale, 1965.
The Dangerous Husband. London, Hale, 1966.
Nelson's Love. London, Hale, 1966.
The Dark-Eyed Queen. London, Hale, 1967; New York, Pocket Books, 1976.
King Henry's Sweetheart. London, Hale, 1967.
The Queen Who Was a Nun. London, Hale, 1967.
The Greatest Nurse of Them All. London, Hale, 1968.
Prince Philanderer. London, Hale, 1968.
The Loves of a Virgin Princess. London, Hale, 1968.
Sweet Marie-Antoinette. London, Hale, 1969; New York, Pocket Books, 1973.
The Boutique of the Singing Clocks. London, Hale, 1969.
The Enchanting Princess. London, Hale, 1970.
The Last Tsarina. London, Hale, 1970.
Judas Iscariot—Traitor! London, Hale, 1971.
A Queen for the Regent. London, Hale, 1971.
The Two Queen Annes. London, Hale, 1971; New York, Pocket Books, 1973.
The Ten-Day Queen. London, Hale, 1972.
Taj Mahal, Shrine of Desire. London, Hale, 1972.
The Queen's Daughters. London, Hale, 1973.
Albert the Beloved. London, Hale, 1974.
The Last Love of a King. London, Hale, 1974.
The Lass a King Loved. London, Hale, 1975.
The King's Daughter. London, Hale, 1975.
When Paris Fell. London, Hale, 1976.

Novels as Deborah Mann

The Woman Called Mary. London, Hale, 1960; as *A Woman Called Mary*, London, Corgi, 1966.
Now Barrabas Was a Robber. London, Corgi, 1968.
The Song of Salome. London, Corgi, 1969.
Pilate's Wife. London, Corgi, 1976.

Novels as Rachel Harvey

The Village Nurse. London, Hurst and Blackett, 1967.
Dearest Doctor. London, Hurst and Blackett, 1968.
Weep Not for Dreams. London, Hale, 1968.
The Little Matron of the Cottage Hospital. London, Hale, 1969.
Darling District Nurse. London, Hale, 1970.
Nurse on Bodmin Moor. London, Hale, 1970.
Doctor Called Harry. London, Hale, 1971.
Sister to a Stranger. London, Hale, 1971.
Love Has No Secrets. London, Hale, 1972.
The Gipsy Lover. London, Hale, 1973.
The Doctor Who Fell in Love. London, Hale, 1974.
The Love Story of Nurse Julie. London, Hale, 1975.

Short Stories

Tiger. Privately printed, 1903 (?).
Winifred. Privately printed, 1903.
Girlie. Privately printed, 1904.
The Cherry Hat. Privately printed, 1904.
Crazy Quilt: A Volume of Stories. London, Hutchinson, 1933.
Wartime Beauty. London, Todd, 1943.

OTHER PUBLICATIONS

Plays

A Paymaster in Every Family. London, French, 1943.
One Wedding, Two Brides. London, French, 1943.
What's in a Name? A Nativity Play. London, French, 1947.
Displaced Person. London, French, 1948.

Radio Plays: *Dog Collar* series, 1961, 1963; *Way Through the Wilderness*, 1962; *The Mother*, 1964; *Jean Meadows, Vet* series, 1964; *Green Finger*, 1965; and others.

Other

A Lamp in the Darkness: A Series of Essays on Religion. London, Hutchinson, 1930; Los Corwin, 1978.
Mistress of None (autobiography). London, Hutchinson, 1933.
Holiday Mood. London, Hutchinson, 1934.
Without Make-Up. London, Joseph, 1938.
The ABC of Authorship. London, Blackie, 1938; Philadelphia, Westminster, 1973.
A Cad's Guide to Cruising. London, Rich and Cowan, 1938.

Letters to My Son. London, Cassell, 1939.

The Log of No Lady, Being the Story of a London Woman Evacuated Before the Outbreak of War. London, Chapman and Hall, 1940.

The Housewife's Beauty Book. London, Hale, 1941.

Time, Tide and I. London, Chapman and Hall, 1942.

Me—After the War: A Book for Girls Considering the Future. London, Gifford, 1944.

The Changed Village. London, Chapman and Hall, 1945.

The Little Fir Tree (juvenile). London, Hutchinson, 1945.

Rude Forefathers. London, Macdonald, 1945.

Questions Answered about Knitting [Beauty]. London, Jordan, 2 vols., 1945-46.

Ursula's Cook Book for the Woman Who Has No Time to Spare. London, Gifford, 1946.

You and Your Holiday [Child, Home, Dog, Looks, Life, Fun, Needle]. London, Gifford, 8 vols., 1946-50.

No Lady Meets No Gentleman. London, Low, 1947.

Pumpkin the Pup (juvenile). London, Hutchinson, 1947.

Smugglers Cave (juvenile). London, Riddle, 1947.

Caravan for Three (juvenile). London, University of London Press, 1947.

Cookery. London, Foyle, 1949.

Three Girls Come to Town (juvenile). London, Macdonald, 1950.

Mum's Girl Was No Lady. London, Convoy, 1951.

New World round the Corner. London, British Rubber Development Board, 1951.

For the Bride. London, Museum Press, 1952.

Trilogy (autobiography). London, Hutchinson, 1954.

Curtain Call for the Guv'nor: A Biography of George Edwardes. London, Hutchinson, 1954.

The Girls' Book of Popular Hobbies. London, Burke, 1954; New York, Roy, 1956 (?).

Hitler's Eva. London, Hutchinson, 1954.

No Lady Has a Dog's Day: A Casual Book of Reminiscences. London, Hutchinson, 1956.

Victorian Vinaigrette. London, Hutchinson, 1956.

The Elegant Edwardians. London, Hutchinson, 1957.

Down to the Sea in Ships. London, Hutchinson, 1958.

He Lit the Lamp: A Biography of Professor A.M. Low. London, Burke, 1958.

Wanting to Write: A Complete Guide for Would-Be Writers. London, Stanley Paul, 1958.

The Inspired Needle. London, Hurst and Blackett, 1959.

Youth at the Gate. London, Hutchinson, 1959.

Sixty Years of Home. London, Hurst and Blackett, 1960.

War Isn't Wonderful. London, Hutchinson, 1961.

Mrs. Bunthorpe's Respects: A Chronicle of Cooks. London, Hutchinson, 1963.

Parson Extraordinary. London, Hale, 1963.

The Rose of Norfolk. London, Hale, 1964.

Price above Rubies. London, Hutchinson, 1965.

Rosemary for Stratford-on-Avon. London, Hale, 1966.

The Mightier Sword. London, Hale, 1966.

A Roof and Four Walls. London, Hale, 1967.

The House of Kent. London, Hale, 1969.

Rosemary for Frinton. London, Hale, 1970.

The Great Tomorrow. London, Hale, 1971; New York, Zebra, 1978.

Rosemary for Chelsea. London, Hale, 1971.

The Duke of Windsor. London, Hale, 1972.

Requesting the Pleasure. London, Hale, 1973.

Princesses in Love. London, Hale, 1973.

The Royal Baby. London, Hale, 1975.

Life Is No Fairy Tale. London, Hale, 1976.

The Great Queen Consort. London, Hale, 1976.

Edward and Victoria. London, Hale, 1977.

Editor, *Woman's Annual 1951*.   London, Elek, 1950.

*   *   *

Ursula Bloom is a woman of rare quality, a great professional, whose writing career spans many decades. From childhood she wanted to write and began with a children's story, *Tiger*, privately printed when she was seven years old. Marie Corelli helped her, and one of her stories was given to Prince Edward and his sister, Princess Mary. Always keenly interested in people, she was a natural reporter, though women were frowned on in that profession in the years after the First World War. She covered the Crippen murder story which was later used as part of one of her books, as was her coverage of the Ruth Ellis case.

One of the most prolific authors in the country, Bloom is listed in the *Guinness Book of Records* credited with 500 full-length titles by 1975. Her first novel, appropriately called *The Great Beginning*, and a best seller, told of a young "slip of a girl who passionately desired motherhood," but whose scheming mother married her to a man whose ancestry, filled with a dread disease, denied her children. But in true romantic fiction style she finds love and there is a happy ending. This success was followed with many romances with a simple boy meets girl theme. Bloom has drawn on her own experience for many of her characters and settings: time spent in hospitals, for instance, was used in her popular hospital tales.

Romantic novels with memorable titles (*An April After*—after what?) soon filled the shelves. She was proud of her family, especially her gypsy forebear (*The Rose of Norfolk*), and this gave her much accurate background when writing about gypsies in stories such as *Gypsy Flower* and *Caravan of Chance*.

Always an adventurous and energetic writer, Ursula Bloom would tackle any hurdle. She wrote stories, articles, beauty counselling, plays, biographies of her family, autobiographies, and works on the Royal Family. There were books of memory on places such as Stratford-on-Avon where much of her childhood was spent, and she always retained her knowledge and love of the works of Shakespeare. Chelsea took on a new look under her penmanship, and she wrote cookery books and others. Sheila Burns, Mary Essex, Deborah Mann were among the pseudonyms she used for her romances, Burns for the hospital stories, Essex for modern romances, and Mann for historical tales, though at first she used her own name for romances.

In all her books she wrote with a transparent honesty that shines through her lines, setting down life as she experienced it, without varnish. In many ways, her personal life was unusual, tinged with sadness, pain and suffering, grief and pleasure, and she could write with ease about all of those experiences. Maybe her upbringing in a vicarage had an effect, for her heroines were always chaste, though to be fair so were most heroines of the period. She was ever helpful to others—again her "parish" caring background—and was an agony columnist and wrote much on religion, God, and death for a Sunday paper, collecting material from all over the country, indulging herself in reporting. Bloom could write movingly on conditions in the Welsh coal valleys where lack of work created social problems.

Her book *The Secret Lover* was a new departure, a diary telling of an old bachelor hermit who had been an old roué with a secret love in his imagination. The idea of the Editor of the former *Sunday Dispatch* for her to write a historical novel, to be first serialised in the paper, was the forerunner of much success. It was decided that a book on Lady Hamilton would launch the series, and *Our Dearest Emma* was the result. It tells the story of one of the country's most notorious, most forgiven women, and Bloom's simple style of telling that tale without lurid details makes it a historical classic to this day. *Our Dearest Emma* was written under a new pseudonym, Lozania Prole, and began a long series of historical novels. She chose to write many biographical novels of famous women, Nell Gwynn, Florence Nightingale, Mrs. Fitzherbert, Hitler's Eva, Ethel Le Neve; the French Revolution and Regency Brighton formed the background for many of these stirring, robust books.

A resourceful worker, Bloom devoted her life to keeping the wheels of authorship turning with hospital life, light romances, historical novels, and biographies of herself and others. When writing of her own life, her family, her mother (one of her most moving books, *Price above Rubies*), she spared nothing, and the reader joined her when buying a house, living in the country or with the Edwardians. Essentially honest, she never held back from her readers, and they lived again with her the days of poverty, selling possessions, finding a bargain, and the problems of a struggling writer. She had a deep sense of awareness of religion. This is often hid, as with so many children of the vicarage, though she wrote of religious characters, often unusual ones—Judas Iscariot, Barabbas—and a moving story of the Taj Mahal revealing a depth of sensitivity not often revealed in light romances.

Ursula Bloom's work lives on, popular today with all ages. This remarkable woman can look back with pride on her books.

—Lornie Leete-Hodge

BOWEN, Marjorie. Pseudonym for Gabrielle Margaret Vere Campbell; also wrote as Robert Paye; George Preedy; Joseph Shearing; John Winch. British. Born on Hayling Island, Hampshire, 29 October 1886. Married 1) Zeffrino Emilio Costanzo in 1912 (died, 1916), one son; 2) Arthur L. Long in 1917, two sons. *Died 23 December 1952.*

Romance and Gothic Publications

Novels

The Viper of Milan. London, Alston Rivers, and New York, McClure Phillips, 1906.
The Glen o' Weeping. London, Alston Rivers, 1907; as The Master of Stair, New York, McClure Phillips, 1907.
The Sword Decides! London, Alston Rivers, and New York, McClure, 1908.
Black Magic: A Tale of the Rise and Fall of Antichrist. London, Alston Rivers, 1909.
The Leopard and the Lily. New York, Doubleday, 1909; London, Methuen, 1920.
William III Trilogy:
 I Will Maintain. London, Methuen, 1910; New York, Dutton, 1911; revised edition, London, Penguin, 1943.
 Defender of the Faith. London, Methuen, and New York, Dutton, 1911.
 God and the King. London, Methuen, 1911; New York, Dutton, 1912.
Lovers' Knots. London, Everett, 1912.
The Quest of Glory. London, Methuen, and New York, Dutton, 1912.
The Rake's Progress. London, Rider, 1912.
The Soldier from Virginia. New York, Appleton, 1912; as Mister Washington, London, Methuen, 1915.
The Governor of England. London, Methuen, 1913; New York, Dutton, 1914.
A Knight of Spain. London, Methuen, 1913.
The Two Carnations. London, Cassell, and New York, Reynolds, 1913.
Prince and Heretic. London, Methuen, 1914; New York, Dutton, 1915.
Because of These Things.... London, Methuen, 1915.
The Carnival of Florence. London, Methuen, and New York, Dutton, 1915.
William, By the Grace of God—. London, Methuen, 1916; New York, Dutton, 1917; abridged edition, Methuen, 1928.
The Third Estate. London, Methuen, 1917; New York, Dutton, 1918; revised edition, as Eugénie, London, Fontana, 1971.
The Burning Glass. London, Collins, 1918; New York, Dutton, 1919.
Kings-at-Arms. London, Methuen, 1918; New York, Dutton, 1919.
Mr. Misfortunate. London, Collins, 1919.
The Cheats. London, Collins, 1920.

The Haunted Vintage. London, Odhams Press, 1921.
Rococo. London, Odhams Press, 1921.
The Jest. London, Odhams Press, 1922.
Affairs of Men (selections from novels). London, Cranton, 1922.
Stinging Nettles. London, Ward Lock, and Boston, Small Maynard, 1923.
The Presence and the Power. London, Ward Lock, 1924.
Five People. London, Ward Lock, 1925.
Boundless Water. London, Ward Lock, 1926.
Nell Gwyn: A Decoration. London, Hodder and Stoughton, 1926; as *Mistress Nell Gwyn*, New York, Appleton, 1926; London, Mellifont Press, 1949.
Five Winds. London, Hodder and Stoughton, 1927.
The Pagoda: Le Pagode de Chanteloup. London, Hodder and Stoughton, 1927.
The Countess Fanny. London, Hodder and Stoughton, 1928.
Renaissance Trilogy:
  The Golden Roof. London, Hodder and Stoughton, 1928.
  The Triumphant Beast. London, Lane, 1934.
  Trumpets at Rome. London, Hutchinson, 1936.
Dickon. London, Hodder and Stoughton, 1929.
The English Paragon. London, Hodder and Stoughton, 1930.
The Devil's Jig (as Robert Paye). London, Lane, 1930.
Brave Employments. London, Collins, 1931.
Withering Fires. London, Collins, 1931.
The Shadow on Mockways. London, Collins, 1932.
Dark Rosaleen. London, Collins, 1932; Boston, Houghton Mifflin, 1933.
Passion Flower. London, Collins, 1932; as *Beneath the Passion Flower* (as George Preedy), New York, McBride, 1932.
Idlers' Gate (as John Winch). London, Collins, and New York, Morrow, 1932.
Julia Roseingrave (as Robert Paye). London, Benn, 1933.
I Dwelt in High Places. London, Collins, 1933.
Set with Green Herbs. London, Benn, 1933.
The Stolen Bride. London, Lovat Dickson, 1933; abridged edition, London, Mellifont Press, 1946.
The Veil'd Delight. London, Odhams Press, 1933.
A Giant in Chains: Prelude to Revolution—France 1775-1791. London, Hutchinson, 1938.
Trilogy:
  God and the Wedding Dress. London, Hutchinson, 1938.
  Mr. Tyler's Saints. London, Hutchinson, 1939.
  The Circle in the Water. London, Hutchinson, 1939.
Exchange Royal. London, Hutchinson, 1940.
Today Is Mine. London, Hutchinson, 1941.
The Man with the Scales. London, Hutchinson, 1954.

Novels as George Preedy

General Crack. London, Lane, and New York, Dodd Mead, 1928.
The Rocklitz. London, Lane, 1930; as *The Prince's Darling*, New York, Dodd Mead, 1930.
Tumult in the North. London, Lane, and New York, Dodd Mead, 1931.
The Pavilion of Honour. London, Lane, 1932.
Violante: Circe and Ermine. London, Cassell, 1932.
The Devil Snar'd. London, Benn, 1932.
Dr. Chaos, and The Devil Snar'd. London, Cassell, 1933.
Double Dallilay. London, Cassell, 1933; as *Queen's Caprice*, New York, King, 1934.
The Autobiography of Cornelius Blake, 1773-1810, of Ditton See, Cambridgeshire. London, Cassell, 1934.
Laurell'd Captains. London, Hutchinson, 1935.

The Poisoners. London, Hutchinson, 1936.
My Tattered Loving. London, Jenkins, 1937; as *The King's Favourite* (as Marjorie Bowen), London, Fontana, 1971.
Painted Angel. London, Jenkins, 1938.
The Fair Young Widow. London, Jenkins, 1939.
Dove in the Mulberry Tree. London, Jenkins, 1939.
Primula. London, Hodder and Stoughton, 1940.
Black Man—White Maiden. London, Hodder and Stoughton, 1941.
Findernes' Flowers. London, Hodder and Stoughton, 1941.
Lyndley Waters. London, Hodder and Stoughton, 1942.
Lady in a Veil. London, Hodder and Stoughton, 1943.
The Fourth Chamber. London, Hodder and Stoughton, 1944.
Nightcap and Plume. London, Hodder and Stoughton, 1945.
No Way Home. London, Hodder and Stoughton, 1947.
The Sacked City. London, Hodder and Stoughton, 1949.
Julia Ballantyne. London, Hodder and Stoughton, 1952.

Novels as Joseph Shearing

Forget-Me-Not. London, Heinemann, 1932; as *Lucile Cléry*, New York, Harper, 1932; as *The Strange Case of Lucile Cléry*, Harper, 1941.
Album Leaf. London, Heinemann, 1933; as *The Spider in the Cup*, New York, Smith and Haas, 1934.
Moss Rose. London, Heinemann, 1934; New York, Smith and Haas, 1935.
The Golden Violet: The Story of a Lady Novelist. London, Heinemann, 1936; New York, Smith and Durrell, 1941; as *Night's Dark Secret* (as Margaret Campbell), New York, New American Library, 1975.
Blanche Fury; or, Fury's Ape. London, Heinemann, and New York, Harrison Hilton, 1939.
Aunt Beardie. London, Hutchinson, and New York, Harrison Hilton, 1940.
Laura Sarelle. London, Hutchinson, 1940; as *The Crime of Laura Sarelle*, New York, Smith and Durrell, 1941.
The Fetch. London, Hutchinson, 1942; as *The Spectral Bride*, New York, Smith and Durrell, 1942.
Airing in a Closed Carriage. London, Hutchinson, and New York, Harper, 1943.
The Abode of Love. London, Hutchinson, 1945.
For Her to See. London, Hutchinson, 1947; as *So Evil My Love*, New York, Harper, 1947.
Mignonette. New York, Harper, 1948; London, Heinemann, 1949.
Within the Bubble. London, Heinemann, 1950; as *The Heiress of Frascati*, New York, Berkley, 1966.
To Bed at Noon. London, Heinemann, 1951.

Short Stories

God's Playthings. London, Smith Elder, 1912; New York, Dutton, 1913.
Shadows of Yesterday: Stories from an Old Catalogue. London, Smith Elder, and New York, Dutton, 1916.
Curious Happenings. London, Mills and Boon, 1917.
Crimes of Old London. London, Odhams Press, 1919.
The Pleasant Husband and Other Stories. London, Hurst and Blackett, 1921.
Seeing Life! and Other Stories. London, Hurst and Blackett, 1923.
The Seven Deadly Sins. London, Hurst and Blackett, 1926.
Dark Ann and Other Stories. London, Lane, 1927.
The Gorgeous Lover and Other Tales. London, Lane, 1929.

Sheep's-Head and Babylon, and Other Stories of Yesterday and Today.   London, Lane, 1929.

Old Patch's Medley; or, A London Miscellany.   London, Selwyn and Blount, 1930.

Bagatelle and Some Other Diversions (as George Preedy).   London, Lane, 1930; New York, Dodd Mead, 1931.

Grace Latouche and the Warringtons: Some Nineteenth-Century Pieces, Mostly Victorian.   London, Selwyn and Blount, 1931.

Fond Fancy and Other Stories.   London, Selwyn and Blount, 1932.

The Last Bouquet: Some Twilight Tales.   London, Lane, 1932.

The Knot Garden: Some Old Fancies Re-Set (as George Preedy).   London, Lane, 1933.

Orange Blossoms (as Joseph Shearing).   London, Heinemann, 1938.

The Bishop of Hell and Other Stories.   London, Lane, 1949.

OTHER PUBLICATIONS

Plays as George Preedy

Captain Banner (produced London, 1929).   London, Lane, 1930.

A Family Comedy, 1840 (as Marjorie Bowen).   London, French, 1930.

The Question.   London, French, 1931.

The Rocklitz (produced London, 1931).

Rose Giralda (produced London, 1933).

Court Cards (produced London, 1934).

Royal Command (produced Wimbledon, Surrey, 1952).

Screenplay: *The Black Tulip* (as Marjorie Bowen), 1921.

Other

Luctor et Emergo, Being an Historical Essay on the State of England at the Peace of Rsywyck.   Newcastle upon Tyne, Northumberland Press, 1925.

The Netherlands Display'd; or, The Delights of the Low Countries.   London, Lane, 1926; New York, Dodd Mead, 1927.

Holland, Being a General Survey of the Netherlands.   London, Harrap, 1928; New York, Doubleday, 1929.

The Winged Trees (juvenile).   Oxford, Blackwell, 1928.

The Story of the Temple and Its Associations.   London, Griffin Press, 1928.

Sundry Great Gentlemen: Some Essays in Historical Biography.   London, Lane, and New York, Dodd Mead, 1928.

William, Prince of Orange, Afterwards King of England, Being an Account of His Early Life.   London, Lane, and New York, Dodd Mead, 1928.

The Lady's Prisoner (juvenile).   Oxford, Blackwell, 1929.

Mademoiselle Maria Gloria (juvenile).   Oxford, Blackwell, 1929.

The Third Mary Stuart, Being a Character Study with Memoirs and Letters of Queen Mary II of England 1662-1694.   London, Lane, 1929.

Exits and Farewells, Being Some Account of the Last Days of Certain Historical Characters.   London, Selwyn and Blount, 1930.

Mary, Queen of Scots, Daughter of Debate.   London, Lane, 1934; New York, Putnam, 1935.

The Scandal of Sophie Dawes.   London, Lane, 1934; New York, Appleton Century, 1935.

Patriotic Lady: A Study of Emma, Lady Hamilton, and the Neapolitan Revolution of 1799.   London, Lane, 1935; New York, Appleton Century, 1936.

The Angel of Assassination: Marie-Charlotte de Corday d'Armont, Jean-Paul Marat,

Jean-Adam Lux: Three Disciples of Rousseau (as Joseph Shearing). London, Heinemann, and New York, Smith and Haas, 1935.

Peter Porcupine: A Study of William Cobbett, 1762-1835. London, Longman, 1935; New York, Longman, 1936.

William Hogarth, The Cockney's Mirror. London, Methuen, and New York, Appleton Century, 1936.

Crowns and Sceptres: The Romance and Pageantry of Coronations. London, Long, 1937.

The Lady and the Arsenic: The Life and Death of a Romantic, Marie Cappelle, Madame Lafarge (as Joseph Shearing). London, Heinemann, 1937; New York, A.S. Barnes, 1944.

This Shining Woman: Mary Wollstonecraft Godwin 1759-1797 (as George Preedy). London, Collins, and New York, Appleton Century, 1937.

Wrestling Jacob: A Study of the Life of John Wesley and Some Members of His Family. London, Heinemann, 1937; abridged edition, London, Watts, 1948.

World's Wonder and Other Essays. London, Hutchinson, 1938.

The Trumpet and the Swan: An Adventure of the Civil War (juvenile). London, Pitman, 1938.

The Debate Continues, Being the Autobiography of Marjorie Bowen, by Margaret Campbell. London, Heinemann, 1939.

Ethics in Modern Art (lecture). London, Watts, 1939.

Child of Chequer'd Fortune: The Life, Loves, and Battles of Maurice de Saxe, Maréchal de France (as George Preedy). London, Jenkins, 1939.

Strangers to Freedom (juvenile). London, Dent, 1940.

The Life of John Knox (as George Preedy). London, Jenkins, 1940.

The Life of Rear-Admiral John Paul Jones, 1747-1792 (as George Preedy). London, Jenkins, 1940.

The Courtly Charlatan: The Enigmatic Comte de St. Germain (as George Preedy). London, Jenkins, 1942.

The Church and Social Progress: An Exposition of Rationalism and Reaction. London, Watts, 1945.

In the Steps of Mary, Queen of Scots. London, Rich and Cowan, 1952.

Editor, *Great Tales of Horror.* London, Lane, 1933.
Editor, *More Great Tales of Horror.* London, Lane, 1935.
Editor, *Some Famous Love Letters.* London, Jenkins, 1937.

*   *   *

Most of Margaret Campbell's books, under whichever pseudonym she wrote, are historical novels about real people or romances set in the past. Many of her crime novels either use period settings or are imaginative reconstructions of historical crimes. *My Tattered Loving* (*The King's Favourite*), for instance, is a fictionalised account of the celebrated 17th-century Overbury murder.

Her historical novels as Marjorie Bowen are usually fictional biographies, and strongly partisan. She portrays Richard III in *Dickon* as a perfect medieval knight, *sans peur, sans reproche* (but let us not forget he was a contemporary of the Borgias). Her Richard could never have killed his brother Clarence or Henry VI, much less the Princes in the Tower, although the book shys away from this last issue. Her Richard is physically attractive—no mention of a withered arm or humpback here. In *The Governor of England* she portrays Cromwell as a compassionate private man who nevertheless believes that he has a divine mission and so reluctantly concludes that the king's death is necessary. Indeed Bowen seems to have held low opinions of all the Stuarts bar one. She draws a harsh portrait of James I slobbering and fawning in *The King's Favourite*, she refers to Charles II as a man who would but for his birth "have spent his life as a tavern idler buying his indulgences with his quips," and James II she castigates as "a pompous doll bigot—vain, sensuous and arrogant and to a curious degree cruel." Her great hero is William III, one of our dullest kings, little loved by his English subjects and who had little liking for England. Even her partisan writing fails to hide the fact that

William only accepted the English crown as a means of vanquishing Louis XIV. Her trilogy on William's life, *I Will Maintain*, *Defender of the Faith*, and *God and the King*, shows this clearly. The first book covers his early years up to the Dutch Revolution of 1672 when he became Stadtholder; the second relates how he reluctantly married his cousin, the English princess Mary, fought Louis, and drew Holland together. The third book is about his time as King of England and shows his frustrations dealing with the English who disliked him. Bowen is above all William's apologist—she even tries to absolve him of any guilt for the Massacre of Glencoe in *The Glen o' Weeping*, but hardly convinces this reader. So fond was she of William and of Holland that, besides several non-fiction books on the subject, she also wrote about William III's ancestor William the Silent in *Prince and Heretic* and *William by the Grace of God—*.

Bowen often featured revolution in her books. *A Giant in Chains* is about the causes of the French revolution of 1789; *Forget-Me-Not* (as Joseph Shearing) concerns France in 1848 in the last days of Louis Philippe. *Dark Rosaleen* tells of the ill-fated Irish uprising of 1798; in it she draws a sympathetic portrait of Edward Fitzgerald, the idealistic younger son of one of Ireland's most important families who, influenced by the French revolution, was anxious to set Ireland free from English oppression. Because he was too noble and selfless to see or expect treachery, he died—not untypically for a Bowen book, for she dearly loved a doom-laden plot—seldom for her the happy ending. In her romances she created unhappy people and loaded the dice against them. *The Viper of Milan*, her first and probably most famous book (written when she was 17), is set in her version of 14th-century Italy. The chief character (one can hardly call one so infamous "hero") is the cruel, ruthless Visconti, ruler of Milan who kills or maims every member of his family, betrays his allies, and even kills his own true love. *Findernes' Flowers* (as George Preedy) and *The Rake's Progress* are typical of her light romances: both are set in the 18th century and tell of doomed families and star-crossed lovers; both have sad endings heavy with wasted lives.

Her historical backgrounds are full of well-researched details with rich descriptions of period clothes, but her style is too florid for today's taste and her dialogue is the most serious stumbling block for the modern reader, being full of "fair sirs" beseeching, t'were, and wert. Immensely popular in her own day, her books are rather neglected nowadays, for modern readers prefer faster moving stories and a lighter touch. Her characterisation lacks depth, and the thoughts and motives attributed to her characters (especially in the romances) are a little superficial, although her historical judgements are usually sound when she is not gripped by bias.

—Pamela Cleaver

BRAMWELL, Charlotte. *See* **KIMBROUGH, Katheryn**.

BRANDON, Sheila. *See* **RAYNER, Claire**.

BRENT, Madeleine. A pseudonym. Recipient: Romantic Novelists Association Major Award, 1978.

Novels

Tregaron's Daughter. London, Souvenir Press, and New York, Doubleday, 1971.
Moonraker's Bride. London, Souvenir Press, and New York, Doubleday, 1973.
Kirkby's Changeling. London, Souvenir Press, 1975; as *Stranger at Wildings*, New York, Doubleday, 1976.
Merlin's Keep. London, Souvenir Press, 1977; New York, Doubleday, 1978.
The Capricorn Stone. London, Souvenir Press, 1979; New York, Doubleday, 1980.
The Long Masquerade. London, Souvenir Press, 1981; New York, Doubleday, 1982.

Uncollected Short Stories

"Winds of the Morning," in *Good Housekeeping* (Des Moines, Iowa), November 1977.
"Call Home the Heart," in *Good Housekeeping* (Des Moines, Iowa), April 1978.

*   *   *

Madeleine Brent creates heroines who claim to be ordinary but who are really far from average females. While none of them has any pretensions toward feminism each has qualities usually associated in romantic novels with male characters. They are strong, resourceful, determined, and persistent; in addition they pursue unusual careers. The last is an even more interesting detail as the novels are set in Victorian England, a combination of period and location not often associated with women serving in capacities other than menial. Instead of the mundane activites of governess or housemaid, Brent's heroines are trapeze artists or music-hall clowns. Even the heroines who do not follow careers could hardly be called common: Jani, in *Merlin's Keep*, is an orphan raised in Tibet who turns out to be a deposed Indian princess.

The locations in Brent's works are as out-of-the-ordinary as the women. England is a sort of home base in each book, but much of the action takes place in places as diverse and exotic as Tibet, the Dordogne, China, and Italy. Whether the setting is a fisherman's cottage in Cornwall or a mission in China, however, the descriptions ring true, for Brent has the ability to sketch surroundings with words. In fact, the strength of her descriptions lies in her ability to assume the reader's familiarity with the scene that she portrays. She does not backtrack into a wealth of detail but touches upon salient features as if reminding a friend of a well-known spot.

The men in these novels are more realistically drawn than in many romances. The secondary male characters are quite unusual by being older men: Sembur and Mr. Lambert in *Merlin's Keep* and Sir Robert in *Kirkby's Changeling* are treated sympathetically and at great length. Brent also makes hero look like villain and villain like hero very successfully, as in *Moonraker's Bride* where the reader is made as uncertain as the heroine about which man to trust.

The heroes as well as the heroines prove to be unusual. Again like the heroines the men are neither paragons nor prigs but merely larger-than-life mortals who live dramatic lives.

The plots of these novels are complex with strong elements of mystery. Each book is also bipartite; it almost seems that the works are divided down the middle into compartments in the heroine's life. Neither compartment is complete without the other but the line of division is strongly marked, often by a geographical shift.

The combination of naturalistic dialogue and deft description makes these rather long romances move very swiftly. Even if the plots were weaker than they are, however, the characterization alone would make them stand above most gothics.

—Susan Quinn Berneis

BRETT, Rosalind.   *See* **BLAIR, Kathryn.**

BRIDGE, Ann.   Pseudonym for Lady Mary Dolling O'Malley, née Sanders.   British. Born in Shenley, Hertfordshire, 11 September 1889. Educated at the London School of Economics, diploma 1913. Married Sir Owen St.Clair O'Malley in 1913; two daughters and one son. Secretary, Charity Organization Society, London, 1911-13; British Red Cross representative in Hungary, 1940-41; worked with the Polish Red Cross, 1944-45, and did relief work in France after World War II. Fellow, Society of Antiquaries in Scotland. *Died 9 March 1974.*

ROMANCE AND GOTHIC PUBLICATIONS

Novels (series: Julia Probyn in *The Lighthearted Quest* and all books thereafter)

Peking Picnic.   London, Chatto and Windus, and Boston, Little Brown, 1932.
The Ginger Griffin.   London, Chatto and Windus, and Boston, Little Brown, 1934.
Illyrian Spring.   London, Chatto and Windus, and Boston, Little Brown, 1935.
Enchanter's Nightshade.   London, Chatto and Windus, and Boston, Little Brown, 1937.
Four-Part Setting.   London, Chatto and Windus, and Boston, Little Brown, 1939.
Frontier Passage.   London, Chatto and Windus, and Boston, Little Brown, 1942.
Singing Waters.   London, Chatto and Windus, 1945; New York, Macmillan, 1946.
And Then You Came.   London, Chatto and Windus, 1948; New York, Macmillan, 1949.
The Dark Moment.   London, Chatto and Windus, 1951; New York, Macmillan, 1952.
A Place to Stand.   London, Chatto and Windus, and New York, Macmillan, 1953.
The Lighthearted Quest.   London, Chatto and Windus, and New York, Macmillan, 1956.
The Portuguese Escape.   London, Chatto and Windus, and New York, Macmillan, 1958.

The Numbered Account, with Susan Lowndes.   London, Chatto and Windus, and New York, McGraw Hill, 1960.
Julia Involved (omnibus).   New York, McGraw Hill, 1962.
The Tightening String.   London, Chatto and Windus, and New York, McGraw Hill, 1962.
The Dangerous Islands.   New York, McGraw Hill, 1963; London, Chatto and Windus, 1964.
Emergency in the Pyrenees.   London, Chatto and Windus, and New York, McGraw Hill, 1965.
The Episode at Toledo.   New York, McGraw Hill, 1966; London, Chatto and Windus, 1967.
The Malady in Madeira.   New York, McGraw Hill, 1969; London, Chatto and Windus, 1970.
Julia in Ireland.   New York, McGraw Hill, 1973.

Short Stories

The Song in the House.   London, Chatto and Windus, 1936.

OTHER PUBLICATIONS

Other

The Selective Traveller in Portugal, with Susan Lowndes.   London, Evans, 1949; New York, Knopf, 1952; revised edition, London, Chatto and Windus, 1958, 1967; New York, McGraw Hill, 1961.
The House at Kilmartin (juvenile).   London, Evans, 1951.
Portrait of My Mother.   London, Chatto and Windus, 1955; as *A Family of Two Worlds*, New York, Macmillan, 1955.
Facts and Fictions: Some Literary Recollections.   London, Chatto and Windus, and New York, McGraw Hill, 1968.
Moments of Knowing: Some Personal Experiences Beyond Normal Knowledge.   London, Hodder and Stoughton, and New York, McGraw Hill, 1970.
Permission to Resign: Goings-On in the Corridors of Power.   London, Sidgwick and Jackson, 1971.

*   *   *

In one of her novels Ann Bridge wrote, "is there any human pleasure much keener than the return after absence to a well-loved place, a place long familiar, full of associations of happiness?" This is the key to her writing, because in each of her books, besides setting in motion believable characters and exploring a human situation, she uses a place as the mainspring of her work. Her experiences as a diplomatic wife in China gave her the background for *Peking Picnic*, *The Ginger Griffin*, *Four-Part Setting* and her best short story "The Buick Saloon." Her experiences and the places she visited while *en poste* with her husband are used in *Frontier Passage*, a novel about the Spanish civil war, and *A Place to Stand* and *The Tightening String*, about Hungary in the 1940's. These three are semi-documentaries, blending historical and imaginary happenings. Another "modern historical novel" is *The Dark Moment*, about the part played by women in Kemal Ataturk's revolution in Turkey. While she was in Turkey she researched it by talking to women who actually took part in the events. *Illyrian Spring*, a story set in Yugoslavia, actually popularised tourism there, a fact she laughs at, caricaturing herself as Susan Glanfield, the authoress who achieved this in *Singing Waters*, a novel about Albania which is otherwise a dull, tiresome read with unsympathetic characters.

Usually her characterisation is good. She mostly writes about well-bred, upper-class people with money and servants—apart from the occasional highland laird who is terribly poor but so well connected that it does not matter (Glasdeir's well-married daughter in *And Then You Came*, for instance, provides new cars and cattle gates with the wave of the fairy godmother's wand). In most of her books there is a charming middle-aged woman in whom the younger heroine can confide—the middle-aged lady is often the nicest character in the book, and is, one feels, probably based on herself. She usually has several aristocratic men about the place— either strong and silent or sensitive and articulate, and always very capable. Her plots centre on happy and unhappy love affairs set against marvellous descriptions of her beloved places. Her characters are not only concerned about marriage but about making the right sort of marriage, and there is a snobbish preoccupation with money and breeding which was probably acceptable in the 1930's and 1940's when she wrote but which jars a little today.

Bridge's writing has a leisurely pace and a certain coolness. If occasionally she runs to a purple passage when her characters' emotions are aroused she soon brings them down to earth by sending them into the village to fetch the fish or down to the market to collect flowers to decorate their charming houses. Nothing really nasty ever happens in a Bridge book, although she often puts an illness into the story to give it tension and does not shy away from death but treats it rather sentimentally. Details of her research are sometimes used too fully with an almost teacherly eagerness, but her plots are well thought out and her characters well rounded.

Ann Bridge's later books are a series of romantic thrillers using a basic cast of the same characters centred on her heroine, Julia Probyn (a cool, beautiful journalist who looks dumb but is not), and Julia's charming middle-aged godmother, Mrs. Hathaway, who do amateur sleuthing in exotic places among delightful, well-connected people—the strain of snobbery is stronger than ever in this series. *The Lighthearted Quest* has Morocco for its setting and smuggling for its plot, *The Episode at Toledo* and *Emergency in the Pyrenees* are set in Spain and Portugal, *The Numbered Account* takes place in Switzerland and contrasts banking and diplomacy, and *Dangerous Islands* (like her interesting fantasy book *And Then You Came*) uses the West Highlands of Scotland and archaeology.

All Bridge's books (with the exception of *Singing Waters*) have a great deal of charm, many acute observations on life and people, and are very satisfying to read.

—Pamela Cleaver

BRISCO, Patty. *See* **MATTHEWS, Patricia**.

BRITT, Katrina.   Address: c/o Mills and Boon Ltd., 15-16 Brooks Mews, London W1A 1DR, England.

ROMANCE AND GOTHIC PUBLICATIONS

Novels

A Kiss in a Gondola.   London, Mills and Boon, 1968; Toronto, Harlequin, 1969.
Healer of Hearts.   London, Mills and Boon, 1969; Toronto, Harlequin, 1970.
A Fine Romance.   London, Mills and Boon, 1969.
The Fabulous Island.   London, Mills and Boon, 1970; Toronto, Harlequin, 1971.
The Masculine Touch.   London, Mills and Boon, 1970.
The Unknown Quest.   London, Mills and Boon, and Toronto, Harlequin, 1971.
The Gentle Flame.   London, Mills and Boon, 1971; Toronto, Harlequin, 1973.
A Spray of Edelweiss.   London, Mills and Boon, and Toronto, Harlequin, 1972.
Strange Bewilderment.   London, Mills and Boon, and Toronto, Harlequin, 1973.
Reluctant Voyager.   London, Mills and Boon, and Toronto, Harlequin, 1973.
The Guarded Gates.   London, Mills and Boon, 1973; Toronto, Harlequin, 1974.
Famous Island.   Toronto, Harlequin, n.d.
The Greater Happiness.   London, Mills and Boon, 1974; Toronto, Harlequin, 1975.
The House Called Sakura.   London, Mills and Boon, 1974; Toronto, Harlequin, 1975.
The King of Spades.   London, Mills and Boon, and Toronto, Harlequin, 1974.
The Cruiser in the Bay.   London, Mills and Boon, 1975.
Take Back Your Love.   London, Mills and Boon, and Toronto, Harlequin, 1975.
The Spanish Grandee.   London, Mills and Boon, 1975; Toronto, Harlequin, 1976.
The Emerald Garden.   London, Mills and Boon, and Toronto, Harlequin, 1976.
Girl in Blue.   London, Mills and Boon, 1976; Toronto, Harlequin, 1977.
If Today Be Sweet.   London, Mills and Boon, 1976; Toronto, Harlequin, 1977.
The Villa Faustina.   Toronto, Harlequin, 1977.
The Faithful Heart.   London, Mills and Boon, and Toronto, Harlequin, 1977.
The Silver Tree.   London, Mills and Boon, 1977; Toronto, Harlequin, 1978.
The Enchanted Woods.   London, Mills and Boon, and Toronto, Harlequin, 1978.
The Hills Beyond.   London, Mills and Boon, 1978.
Open Not the Door.   London, Mills and Boon, and Toronto, Harlequin, 1978.
The Man on the Peak.   London, Mills and Boon, 1979.
Flowers for My Love.   London, Mills and Boon, 1979; Toronto, Harlequin, 1980.
The Midnight Sun.   London, Mills and Boon, 1979.
The Wrong Man.   London, Mills and Boon, 1980; Toronto, Harlequin, 1981.
A Girl Called Tegi.   London, Mills and Boon, 1980.
Island for Dreams.   London, Mills and Boon, and Toronto, Harlequin, 1980.
Hotel Jacarandas.   London, Mills and Boon, 1980.
Another Time, Another Place.   London, Mills and Boon, 1981.
Man at Key West.   London, Mills and Boon, 1982.

*   *   *

Katrina Britt is a Mills and Boon author, reprinted by Harlequin, whose contemporary romances make good reading, partly because she employs a greater variety of plots than the usual romanticist, but mainly because she has a good, clear prose style. While this is formula fiction with heroines "drowning in a pool of bliss," and heroes whose "eyes twinkle devilishly," or whose "lips thin with anger," Britt has the gift of describing romantic feelings well without excessive cloying. Her stories are frequently set in Venice or Spain, but she has also used Nice, Switzerland, the Canary Islands, England, and Tokyo. One theme used frequently is the idea of different worlds or clash of cultures, with her English heroines displaying a cool Saxon strain versus the high-bred passionate Spaniard (*The Guarded Gates* and *The Villa Faustina*). She puts the theme of the villainess sister to good use in *The Spanish Grandee* and *The Emerald Garden*, good stories despite their heroines' long-suffering nobility in refusing to unmask their sisters.

In other novels Britt employs more contemporary themes. The sub-plot in *Take Back Your Love*, set in Tokyo, concerns a hippy pop-singing group, one of whose members dies from drug taking. However, the use of modern themes produces a somewhat spurious effect, since the main plot invariably concerns a dreamy-eyed heroine in love with a masterful, commanding man. The heroine of *The Guarded Gates* even defends her anti-women's rights feelings on several occasions.

In another departure, in *Girl in Blue* Britt seems to attempt to write a story with greater depth and seriousness, but doesn't quite succeed. Felicity marries Curt, a brilliant young lawyer, experiences the death of her mother and brother in an auto accident, believes her husband to be involved with another woman, leaves him, bears his child, of which he knows nothing, and is eventually reunited with him. All this is much too heavy going for a writer who should stay with the lighter romantic story, which she does so well.

—Necia A. Musser

BROMFIELD, Louis.   American.   Born in Mansfield, Ohio, 27 December 1896. Educated at Cornell University Agricultural College, Ithaca, New York, 1914-15; School of Journalism, Columbia University, New York, 1916, honorary war degree 1920. Served in the American Ambulance Corps, with the 34th and 168th divisions of the French Army, 1917-19: Croix de Guerre. Married Mary Appleton Wood in 1921 (died, 1952); three daughters. Reporter, City News Service and Associated Press, New York, 1920-22; Editor and/or Critic for *Musical America*, *The Bookman*, and *Time*, also worked as an assistant to a theatrical producer and as Advertising Manager of Putnam's, publishers, all New York, 1922-25; lived in Senlis, France, 1925-38; settled on a farm in Richland County, Ohio, 1939, and lived there until his death. President, Emergency Committee for the American Wounded in Spain, 1938. Director, United States Chamber of Commerce. Recipient: Pulitzer Prize, 1927. LL.D: Marshall College, Huntington, West Virginia; Parsons College, Fairfield, Iowa; Litt.D.: Ohio Northern University, Ada. Chevalier, Legion of Honor, 1939. Member, National Institute of Arts and Letters. *Died 18 March 1956.*

ROMANCE AND GOTHIC PUBLICATIONS

Novels

The Green Bay Tree.   New York, Stokes, and London, Unwin, 1924.
Possession.   New York, Stokes, 1925; as *Lilli Barr*, London, Unwin, 1926.
Early Autumn.   New York, Stokes, and London, Cape, 1926.
A Good Woman.   New York, Stokes, and London, Cape, 1927.
The Strange Case of Miss Annie Spragg.   New York, Stokes, and London, Cape, 1928.
Twenty-Four Hours.   New York, Stokes, and London, Cassell, 1930.
A Modern Hero.   New York, Stokes, and London, Cassell, 1932.
The Farm.   New York, Harper, and London, Cassell, 1933.
The Man Who Had Everything.   New York, Harper, and London, Cassell, 1935.
It Had to Happen.   London, Cassell, 1936.

The Rains Came: A Novel of Modern India.   New York, Harper, and London, Cassell, 1937.
Night in Bombay.   New York, Harper, and London, Cassell, 1940.
Wild Is the River.   New York, Harper, 1941; London, Cassell, 1942.
Until the Day Break.   New York, Harper, 1942; London, Consul, 1962.
Mrs. Parkington.   New York, Harper, 1943; London, Cassell, 1944.
What Became of Anna Bolton.   New York, Harper, 1944; London, Cassell, 1945.
Colorado.   New York, Harper, 1947; London, Cassell, 1950.
The Wild Country.   New York, Harper, 1948; London, Cassell, 1950.
Mr. Smith.   New York, Harper, 1951; London, Cassell, 1952.

Short Stories

Awake and Rehearse.   New York, Stokes, and London, Cape, 1929.
Tabloid.   New York, Random House, 1930.
Here Today and Gone Tomorrow: Four Short Novels.   New York, Harper, and London, Cassell, 1934.
It Takes All Kinds.   New York, Harper, and London, Cassell, 1939; *Bitter Lotus* published separately, Cleveland, World, 1944; selection as *Five Long Short Stories*, New York, Avon, 1945; *McLeod's Folly* published separately, Cleveland, World, 1948; selection as *You Get What You Give*, London, Cassell, 1951.
The World We Live In: Stories.   New York, Harper, 1944; London, Cassell 1946.
Kenny.   New York, Harper, 1947; London, Cassell, 1949.

Uncollected Short Stories

"We Are Not in Georgia," in *Good Housekeeping* (New York), January 1941.
"Crime Passionel," in *New Yorker*, 25 March 1944.
"Les Demoiselles," in *New Yorker*, 26 May 1945.

OTHER PUBLICATIONS

Plays

The House of Women, adaptation of his novel *The Green Bay Tree* (produced New York, 1927; London, 1928).
De Luxe, with John Gearon (produced New York, 1935).
Times Have Changed, adaptation of a play by Edouard Bourdet (produced New York, 1935).

Screenplay: *Brigham Young—Frontiersman*, with Lamar Trotti, 1940.

Other

The Work of Robert Nathan.   Indianapolis, Bobbs Merrill, 1927.
England, A Dying Oligarchy.   New York, Harper, 1939.
Pleasant Valley.   New York, Harper, 1945; London, Cassell, 1946.
A Few Brass Tacks.   New York, Harper, 1946.
Malabar Farm.   New York, Harper, 1948; London, Cassell, 1949.
The Works (Malabar Edition).   London, Cassell, 15 vols., 1949-54.
Out of the Earth.   New York, Harper, 1950; London, Cassell, 1951.
The Wealth of the Soil.   Detroit, Ferguson, 1952.
A New Pattern for a Tired World.   New York, Harper, and London, Cassell, 1954.

From My Experience: The Pleasures and Miseries of Life on a Farm. New York, Harper, 1955; London, Cassell, 1956.
Animals and Other People. New York, Harper, 1955; London, Cassell, 1956.
Walt Disney's Vanishing Prairie. New York, Simon and Schuster, and London, Harrap, 1956.

Critical Studies: *Louis Bromfield and His Books: An Evaluation* by Morrison Brown, London, Cassell, 1956; *The Heritage: A Daughter's Memories of Louis Bromfield* by Ellen Bromfield Geld, New York, Harper, 1962; *Louis Bromfield* by David D. Anderson, New York, Twayne, 1964.

*   *   *

Louis Bromfield is a neglected author who in his own day was very popular and much respected—indeed, he won the Pulitzer Prize for literature with *Early Autumn*, the third book of an inter-related series in which he set out to present a pageant of the changing American scene in the early years of this century while at the same time exploring the idea of escape from convention. The first book of this saga was *The Green Bay Tree*, set in a small town in Ohio at the time when it was changing from a farming community to an industrial town. He shows us different aspects of the community's life by portraying several different families, but the main focus is Lily, a "new woman"—very attractive to men with opportunites to marry, all of which she rejects fearing to be tied down, preferring to have her child outside wedlock. *Possession* is the next book which runs parallel in time and place to the first, but shows us another set of families and glimpses of some of the people from the first book. A new woman is at the centre of this book too: she makes her bid for freedom by rejecting family life for the concert platform. *Early Autumn* is connected with the previous books when the daughter of the family at the centre of this book marries Lily's illegitimate son. This portrait of an old New England family is almost an American Forsyte saga, for it has the same emphasis on money and property and it is the heroine's devotion to duty that triumphs over her longing to escape convention. The fourth book is *A Good Woman*, an ironic title, since the woman arranges her son's life to such a degree that she manouvres not only his call to the mission field but also his marriage, and in so doing she ruins three lives while thinking herself good and righteous. The good woman's daughter-in-law can only find escape through death.

Bromfield would have pleased his fans had he gone on with his richly plotted, intricate panoramas but he was ready for another format. *The Strange Case of Miss Annie Spragg* is a loosely connected set of short stories making up a novel. Each chapter tells the tale of one of the several witnesses to a miracle in Italy. The stories are skilfully told, cleverly meshed with superbly drawn characters. *Twenty-Four Hours* was another book of the same type: each of the people attending a dinner one night relates what happens to him or her between dinner and teatime the next day. The whole makes a surprisingly complete book.

The Rains Came is Bromfield's most famous book—perhaps because it became a much-acclaimed film, but also because it was an excellent book. He visited India in 1932 and it took him four years to digest the experience and process it into a novel. Ranchipur, where the story is set, is based on Baroda, one of the most up-to-date Indian states at that time. The destinies of a large number of people are worked out against the tension of the dry season and the bursting of the dam that comes with the monsoon. Bromfield symbolizes the decadence of Europe in the character of Ransome, America through Aunt Phoebe, and contrasts it with awakening India symbolized by the Maharajah. *Night in Bombay*, his other Indian novel, was not nearly as successful; nevertheless, the characters are interesting and the descriptions evocative of the sights, sounds, smells, and the feel of India.

Bromfield could write other kinds of books too. *Wild Is the River* is a romantic historical novel about the American Civil War set against the background of the occupation of New Orleans by the Yankees; *Until the Day Breaks*, a melodramatic spy story, is set against occupied Paris in the 1940's. *Colorado* is a send-up of the Western, and *The Wild Country* is a strangely beautiful story of a boy growing up in his grandfather's farm observing the people round him.

In all Bromfield's books there is good solid characterization, strong plotting, lush romance, and the exploration of a socially significant theme against beautiful descriptions. It is high time some of his books were brought to the attention of a new generation to whom they would have a great deal to say.

—Pamela Cleaver

BROMIGE, Iris (Amy Edna).   British.   Born in London, in 1910. Educated at the Clapham County Secondary School, London. Married to Alan Frank Bromige. Address: c/o Hodder and Stoughton Ltd., Mill Road, Dunton Green, Sevenoaks, Kent TN13 2YA, England.

ROMANCE AND GOTHIC PUBLICATIONS

Novels

The Traceys.   London, Longman, 1946; New York, Beagle, 1974.
Stay But till Tomorrow.   London, Longman, 1946; New York, Ballantine, 1975.
Checquered Pattern.   London, Longman, 1947; as A Chance for Love, New York, Ballantine, 1975.
Tangled Roots.   London, Longman, 1948; New York, Ballantine, 1975.
Marchwood.   London, Hodder and Stoughton, 1949; New York, Beagle, 1974.
The Golden Cage.   London, Hodder and Stoughton, 1950; New York, Ballantine, 1974.
April Wooing.   London, Hodder and Stoughton, 1951; New York, Beagle, 1973.
Laurian Vale.   London, Hodder and Stoughton, 1952; New York, Ballantine, 1975.
The House of Conflict.   London, Hodder and Stoughton, 1953; as Shall Love Be Lost?, New York, Beagle, 1974.
Gay Intruder.   London, Hodder and Stoughton, 1954; New York, Ballantine, 1973.
Diana Comes Home.   London, Hodder and Stoughton, 1955; New York, Beagle, 1974.
The New Owner.   London, Hodder and Stoughton, 1956; New York, Ballantine, 1973.
The Enchanted Garden.   London, Hodder and Stoughton, 1956; New York, Beagle, 1972.
A New Life for Joanna.   London, Hodder and Stoughton, 1957; New York, Beagle, 1973.
Family Group.   London, Hodder and Stoughton, 1958; New York, Ballantine, 1975.
The Conway Touch.   London, Hodder and Stoughton, 1958; New York, Ballantine, 1974.
The Flowering Year.   London, Hodder and Stoughton, 1959; New York, Beagle, 1973.
The Second Mrs. Rivers.   London, Hodder and Stoughton, 1960; New York, Beagle, 1973.
Fair Prisoner.   London, Hodder and Stoughton, 1960; New York, Beagle, 1974.
Alex and the Raynhams.   London, Hodder and Stoughton, 1961; New York, Pocket Books, 1972.
Come Love, Come Hope.   London, Hodder and Stoughton, 1962; New York, Beagle, 1972.
Rosevean.   London, Hodder and Stoughton, 1962; Philadelphia, Chilton, 1963.
The Family Web.   London, Hodder and Stoughton, 1963; New York, Beagle, 1972.
A House Without Love.   London, Hodder and Stoughton, 1964; New York, Beagle, 1973.

The Young Romantic. London, Hodder and Stoughton, 1964; New York, Ballantine, 1975.

The Challenge of Spring. London, Hodder and Stoughton, 1965; New York, Beagle, 1972.

The Lydian Inheritance. London, Hodder and Stoughton, 1966; New York, Beagle, 1972.

The Stepdaughter. London, Hodder and Stoughton, 1966.

The Quiet Hills. London, Hodder and Stoughton, 1967; New York, Beagle, 1974.

An April Girl. London, Hodder and Stoughton, 1967; New York, Beagle, 1971.

Only Our Love. London, Hodder and Stoughton, 1968; New York, Beagle, 1974.

The Master of Heronsbridge. London, Hodder and Stoughton, 1969; New York, Beagle, 1974.

The Tangled Wood. London, Hodder and Stoughton, 1969; New York, Beagle, 1971.

Encounter at Alpenrose. London, Hodder and Stoughton, 1970; New York, Beagle, 1973.

A Sheltering Tree. London, Hodder and Stoughton, 1970; New York, Beagle, 1973.

A Magic Place. London, Hodder and Stoughton, 1971; New York, Beagle, 1973.

Rough Weather. London, Hodder and Stoughton, 1972; New York, Pinnacle, 1981.

Golden Summer. London, Hodder and Stoughton, 1972; New York, Beagle, 1973.

The Broken Bough. London, Hodder and Stoughton, 1973.

The Night of the Party. London, Hodder and Stoughton, 1974.

The Bend in the River. London, Hodder and Stoughton, 1975.

A Haunted Landscape. London, Hodder and Stoughton, 1976.

A Distant Song. London, Hodder and Stoughton, 1977; New York, Pinnacle, 1980.

The Happy Fortress. London, Hodder and Stoughton, 1978.

The Paths of Summer. London, Hodder and Stoughton, 1979.

One Day, My Love. London, Hodder and Stoughton, 1980.

*   *   *

The quality of Iris Bromige's work has remained remarkably consistent over the past 30 years. Many of her books follow the fortunes of various members of the Rainwood clan, presided over by the matriarchal Mirabel, and usually centre on one of her many grand-children; other members flit in and out as the plot requires, but the Rainwood family as a whole is so scattered and detached that knowledge of previous Rainwood novels does not spoil the reader's appreciation of specific works, and the family as an institution infiltrates most of her work, Rainwood or not.

The plots follow a pattern that seldom varies: the heroine, in her mid-twenties, has reached a turning-point in her life—the death of a parent, as in *Only Our Love*, or the sour end to an unsatisfactory relationship, as in *Come Love, Come Hope*, necessitating a reappraisal of her position. In *Rosevean*, as an example of a typical situation, Ann joins the Pendine family as secretary-companion to the rich ruling head, facing an unpredictable and challenging future among a cast of differing personalities. The Bromige heroines are resourceful, honest, truthful, and incurable romantics, though they work hard and responsibly at their various jobs. The main male character is usually in his early thirties, the self-possessed and seemingly arrogant type, often determined through past bitter experience not to be drawn into a close relationship. Then follows the gradual breakdown of barriers between the two protagonists, through hostile and gentle encounters, through easy banter and serious discussion, to the heart-searching necessary to all true romance, with misunderstandings brought in just at the thawing stage to heighten the tension. The lovers at last accept their capitulation, and all doubts are resolved in the final obligatory reconciliation scene.

The narrative shape is well handled, despite some early spasmodic weaknesses, as in *Alex and the Raynhams*, which also tends to rely too heavily on dialogue; later novels gain a better balance between dialogue, description, and action. Pauses from the drama are admirably filled by descriptions of the countryside (either the West Country or Northumberland) in its natural beauty, seasonal touches tending to reflect the bitter-sweet pangs of falling in and out of love.

Bromige gives little concession to the loosening of family ties and increased freedom for youth in the last two decades, her books being based on solid middle- and upper-middle-class family values: however old-fashioned and unworldly this seems at times, it gives her work a secure and warm foundation. Her interest in both major and minor characters centres on them not as distinct personalities, but more on the way that the different kinds of relationships experienced by them contrast with the headiness of the passing flirtation and the depth of feeling that goes to make the lasting love necessary for a successful marriage.

—Tessa Rose Chester

BRONTE, Louisa. *See* **ROBERTS, Janet Louise**.

BROSTER, D(orothy) K(athleen). British. Born in 1877. Educated at Cheltenham Ladies' College; St. Hilda's College, Oxford, M.A. *Died 7 February 1950.*

ROMANCE AND GOTHIC PUBLICATIONS

Novels

> *Chantemerle*, with Gertrude Winifred Taylor. London, Murray, and New York, Brentano's, 1911.
> *The Vision Splendid*, with Gertrude Winifred Taylor. London, Murray, 1913; New York, Brentano's, 1914.
> *Sir Isumbras at the Ford.* London, Murray, 1918.
> *The Yellow Poppy.* London, Duckworth, 1920; New York, McBride, 1922.
> *The Wounded Name.* London, Murray, 1922; New York, Doubleday, 1923.
> *Mr. Rowl.* London, Heinemann, and New York, Doubleday, 1924.
> *The Flight of the Heron.* London, Heinemann, 1925; New York, Dodd Mead, 1926.
> *The Gleam in the North.* London, Heinemann, 1927; New York, Coward McCann, 1931.
> *The Dark Mile.* London, Heinemann, 1929; New York, Coward McCann, 1934.
> *Ships in the Bay!* London, Heinemann, and New York, Coward McCann, 1931.
> *Almond, Wild Almond.* London, Heinemann, 1933.
> *World under Snow*, with G. Forester. London, Heinemann, 1935.
> *Child Royal.* London, Heinemann, 1937.
> *The Sea Without a Haven.* London, Heinemann, 1941.
> *The Captain's Lady.* London, Heinemann, 1947.

Short Stories

A Fire of Driftwood. London, Heinemann, 1932.
Couching at the Door. London, Heinemann, 1942.

OTHER PUBLICATIONS

Verse

The Short Voyage and Other Verses. Privately printed, 1950.

Other

The Happy Warrior. London, Cayme Press, 1926.

*   *   *

D.K. Broster's first two novels, *Chantemerle* and *The Vision Splendid*, were written in collaboration with Miss G.W. Taylor. Although they were not as polished as Broster's later work, they established a writing pattern: carefully constructed historical settings; intelligent presentation, with some consideration of historical ideas behind action; and clear characterizations. Romance per se is central in *Chantemerle*, but in general in Broster's work is secondary to period political matters. All in all, the general model for Broster's work would seem to be Robert Louis Stevenson.

The author's most important work is usually considered to be her Jacobite trilogy, *The Flight of the Heron*, *The Gleam in the North*, and *The Dark Mile*. Set in Scotland from 1745 to 1755, they are essentially concerned with the psychological concomitants and aftermaths of the uprising. In *The Flight of the Heron*, when Prince Charles is being hunted by English troops, the focus of the story is on the odd friendship that arises between Ewen Cameron, one of the prince's supporters, and Captain Windham, the leader of the English troops. *The Gleam in the North*, set several years later, centers around the historical capture and execution of Dr. Archibald Cameron, an agent of Prince Charles's. The Scottish feeling that Cameron was being treated harshly in being executed without trial (on the basis of an earlier judgment) is contrasted with the English feeling that Cameron was a dangerous agitator who had done much harm and would do more. The story is told via Ewen Cameron. *The Dark Mile*, set in the Highlands, examines the psychological damage done by the rebellion. Young lovers, one related to Ewen Cameron, discover that family loyalty is stronger than love. Olivia's father had commanded troops that killed Ian's brother in battle, and this can never be forgiven, even though it was only the fortune of war. (The obstacle to love is removed, unfortunately, by a device unworthy of the author.) Moving in the background of the last two books is a fictional version of Pickle the spy. Broster follows Andrew Lang's identification of Pickle. All three volumes are well plotted and carry conviction.

Other historical novels include *Sir Isumbras at the Ford*, set in Scotland and France in the 1790's; *The Wounded Name*, France just before Napoleon's return from Elba; and *Ships in the Bay!*, Wales, 1796, with Irish rebels and French Revolutionaries.

Broster's best-known story is the short story "Couching at the Door," from the collection of the same name. Often anthologized and highly regarded, it is based on the personalities of Oscar Wilde (mingled a little with Aleister Crowley) and Aubrey Beardsley. It describes a unique punishment for having attended a Black Mass.

—E.F. Bleiler

BUCKINGHAM, Nancy. Pseudonym for John and Nancy Sawyer; also writes as Nancy John; Erica Quest. British. **SAWYER, Nancy (Buckingham)**: born in Bristol, 10 August 1924. Married John Sawyer in 1949; one son and one daughter. Worked as medical social worker. **SAWYER, John**: born in London, 4 October 1919. Director of a London advertising firm. Both are now full-time writers. Agent: A.M. Heath, 40-42 William IV Street, London WC2N 4DD, England; or, Brandt and Brandt, 1501 Broadway, New York, New York 10036, U.S.A.

ROMANCE AND GOTHIC PUBLICATIONS

Novels

> *Victim of Love*.   London, Hale, 1967; as *The Hour Before Moonrise*, New York, Ace, 1967.
> *Cloud over Malverton*.   New York, Ace, 1967; London, Hale, 1970.
> *Heart of Marble*.   London, Hale, 1967; as *Storm in the Mountains*, New York, Ace, 1967.
> *Romantic Journey*.   London, Hale, 1968; as *The Legend of Baverstock Manor*, New York, Ace, 1968.
> *The Dark Summer*.   London, Hale, and New York, Ace, 1968.
> *Call of Glengarron*.   London, Ace, 1968; New York, Hale, 1969.
> *Kiss of Hot Sun*.   London, Hale, 1969.
> *The Secret of the Ghostly Shroud*.   New York, Lancer, 1969; as *Shroud of Silence*, London, Hale, 1970.
> *The House Called Edenhythe*.   London, Hale, 1970; New York, Hawthorn, 1972.
> *Return to Vienna*.   New York, Dell, 1971; London, Hale, 1973.
> *Quest for Alexis*.   New York, Hawthorn, 1973; London, Hale, 1974.
> *Valley of the Ravens*.   New York, Hawthorn, 1973; London, Hale, 1975.
> *The Jade Dragon*.   New York, Hawthorn, 1974; London, Hale, 1976.
> *The Other Cathy*.   London, Eyre Methuen, 1978; South Yarmouth, Massachusetts, Curley, 1981.
> *Vienna Summer*.   London, Eyre Methuen, and New York, St. Martin's Press, 1979.
> *Marianna*.   London, Eyre Methuen, 1981.

Novels as Erica Quest

> *The Silver Castle*.   New York, Doubleday, 1978.
> *The October Cabaret*.   New York, Doubleday, 1979.
> *Design for Murder*.   New York, Doubleday, 1981.

Novels as Nancy John

> *The Spanish House*.   New York, Pocket Books, and London, Hodder and Stoughton, 1981.
> *Tormenting Flame*.   New York, Pocket Books, and London, Hodder and Stoughton, 1981.
> *To Trust Tomorrow*.   New York, Pocket Books, 1981.
> *Prisoner of Passion*.   New York, Pocket Books, 1981.
> *A Man for Always*.   New York, Pocket Books, 1981.
> *So Many Tomorrows*.   New York, Pocket Books, 1982.
> *Web of Passion*.   New York, Pocket Books, 1982.

*   *   *

The husband and wife team of John Sawyer and Nancy Buckingham is prolific both as to the number of books published as well as to the type of book written. As Nancy Buckingham, they write both gothic and romantic suspense, as Nancy John, "category" romance, and as Erica Quest, romantic suspense and mystery.

Most of Buckingham's early books are more romantic suspense (à la Mary Stewart) than gothic. *Call of Glengarron* has the brooding castle and haunting woods of Scotland as backdrop, but the time is contemporary and the mood is that of a true mystery. In a word, it is pedestrian. *Cloud over Malverton, The Dark Summer*, and *Heart of Marble* are similar, the writing, if anything, more juvenile. *Romantic Journey* is a true modern dress gothic—strange house, weird characters, secret passages, etc. In this book for the first time characters are well drawn and the plot moves well, centered as it is on a double identity. The best of these early works is *Victim of Love*. In this novel of romantic suspense the characterization is full and real. The plot moves quickly and the ending is unusual and far from storybook. *Quest for Alexis* could have been the script for a 1950's "B" movie. The muddled love affairs interfere with the plot. With *Valley of the Ravens, The House Called Edenhythe*, and *The Jade Dragon* Buckingham succeeds better. These gothics have Victorian settings with suitable fog, terrain, and characters, though the result is still somewhat lackluster.

As Nancy John and Erica Quest the Sawyers have found their métier. *Tormenting Flame*, and other Nancy John novels are all formula romances written to the specifications of the publishers, but the books are better written than any of their predecessors. Their characters are real and vibrant, and the reader cares what happens to them. Settings are glowingly and accurately described, be they in Australia, Spain, or England. The plots move swiftly; the action is believable. *The Silver Castle*, their first book as Erica Quest, is romantic suspense and could have been written as Nancy Buckingham. It is a "crossover" book. The remaining Quest titles have emerged as pure mystery story.

The Sawyers display amazing versatility. Nancy Buckingham, while not the greatest of the gothic/romantic suspense authors, is far from the worst. Erica Quest could become one of the top flight mystery writers. Nancy John is one of the best of the formula/category romance writers. They are a formidable combination.

—Paula M. Zieselman

BURCHELL, Mary. Pseudonym for Ida Cook. British. Born in Sunderland, County Durham. Educated at the Duchess' School, Alnwick, Northumberland. Former President, Romantic Novelists Association. Address: c/o Mills and Boon Ltd., 15-16 Brooks Mews, London W1A 1DR, England.

ROMANCE AND GOTHIC PUBLICATIONS

Novels

> *Wife to Christopher.* London, Mills and Boon, 1936.
> *Nobody Asked Me.* London, Mills and Boon, 1937; Toronto, Harlequin, 1976.
> *Except My Love.* London, Mills and Boon, 1937; Toronto, Harlequin, 1973.
> *Call—And I'll Come.* London, Mills and Boon, 1937; Toronto, Harlequin, 1973.
> *But Not for Me.* London, Mills and Boon, 1938; Toronto, Harlequin, 1971.

Other Lips Have Loved You. London, Mills and Boon, 1938; as *Two Loves Have I*, 1976.
With All My Worldly Goods. London, Mills and Boon, 1938; Toronto, Harlequin, 1961.
Yet Love Remains. London, Mills and Boon, 1938; Toronto, Harlequin, 1975.
After Office Hours. London, Mills and Boon, 1939.
Little Sister. London, Mills and Boon, 1939; New York, Arcadia House, 1947.
One of the Family. London, Mills and Boon, 1939.
Such Is Love. London, Mills and Boon, 1939; Toronto, Harlequin, 1975.
Yours with Love. London, Mills and Boon, 1940.
Pay Me Tomorrow. London, Mills and Boon, 1940; Toronto, Harlequin, 1974.
One Man's Heart. London, Mills and Boon, 1940; Toronto, Harlequin, 1972.
I'll Go with You. London, Mills and Boon, 1940.
Accompanied by His Wife. London, Mills and Boon, 1941; Toronto, Harlequin, 1974.
Always Yours. London, Mills and Boon, 1941.
Just a Nice Girl. London, Mills and Boon, 1941; Toronto, Harlequin, 1975.
Strangers May Marry. London, Mills and Boon, 1941; Toronto, Harlequin, 1974.
Where Shall I Wander? London, Mills and Boon, 1942.
Thine Is My Heart. London, Mills and Boon, 1942.
Love Made the Choice. London, Mills and Boon, 1942; Toronto, Harlequin, 1975.
Dare I Be Happy? London, Mills and Boon, 1943; Toronto, Harlequin, 1975.
My Old Love Came. London, Mills and Boon, 1943.
Thanks to Elizabeth. London, Mills and Boon, 1944.
Take Me with You. London, Mills and Boon, 1944; Toronto, Harlequin, 1965.
Dearly Beloved. London, Mills and Boon, 1944; Toronto, Harlequin, 1967.
Away Went Love. London, Mills and Boon, 1945; Toronto, Harlequin, 1964.
Cinderella after Midnight. London, Mills and Boon, 1945; Toronto, Harlequin, 1967.
Meant for Each Other. London, Mills and Boon, 1945; Toronto, Harlequin, 1966.
Wife by Arrangement. London, Mills and Boon, 1946; Toronto, Harlequin, 1960.
It's Rumoured in the Village. London, Mills and Boon, 1946; Toronto, Harlequin, 1973.
First Love—Last Love. London, Mills and Boon, 1946.
Find Out the Way. London, Mills and Boon, 1946.
Not Without You. London, Mills and Boon, 1947.
Under Joint Management. London, Mills and Boon, 1947.
Ward of Lucifer. London, Mills and Boon, 1947; Toronto, Harlequin, 1967.
The Brave in Heart. London, Mills and Boon, 1948; Toronto, Harlequin, 1975.
If You Care. London, Mills and Boon, 1948.
Then Come Kiss Me. London, Mills and Boon, 1948; Toronto, Harlequin, 1958.
Wish on the Moon. London, Mills and Boon, 1949.
If This Were All. London, Mills and Boon, 1949.
I Will Love You Still. London, Mills and Boon, 1949.
Choose Which You Will. London, Mills and Boon, 1949; Toronto, Harlequin, 1966.
At First Sight. London, Mills and Boon, 1950.
A Letter for Don. London, Mills and Boon, 1950.
Love Him or Leave Him. London, Mills and Boon, 1950; Toronto, Harlequin, 1961.
Tell Me My Fortune. London, Mills and Boon, 1951; Toronto, Harlequin, 1975.
Mine for a Day. London, Mills and Boon, 1951.
Here I Belong. London, Mills and Boon, 1951.
Over the Blue Mountains. London, Mills and Boon, 1952; Toronto, Harlequin, 1960.
Stolen Heart. London, Mills and Boon, 1952; Toronto, Harlequin, 1962.
Sweet Adventure. London, Mills and Boon, 1952; Toronto, Harlequin, 1968.
A Ring on Her Finger. London, Mills and Boon, 1953.
No Real Relation. London, Mills and Boon, 1953.
The Heart Must Choose. London, Mills and Boon, 1953.
The Heart Cannot Forget. London, Mills and Boon, 1953; Toronto, Harlequin, 1966.
Meet Me Again. London, Mills and Boon, 1954; as *Nurse Alison's Trust*, Toronto, Harlequin, 1964.

When Love's Beginning. London, Mills and Boon, 1954; Toronto, Harlequin, 1969.
Under the Stars of Paris. London, Mills and Boon, 1954; Toronto, Harlequin, 1976.
Yours to Command. London, Mills and Boon, 1955; Toronto, Harlequin, 1964.
The Prettiest Girl. London, Mills and Boon, 1955.
Hospital Corridors. London, Mills and Boon, 1955; Toronto, Harlequin, 1958.
For Ever and Ever. London, Mills and Boon, 1956; Toronto, Harlequin, 1959.
Loving Is Giving. London, Mills and Boon, 1956; Toronto, Harlequin, 1967.
On the Air. London, Mills and Boon, 1956; Toronto, Harlequin, 1960.
To Journey Together. London, Mills and Boon, 1956; Toronto, Harlequin, 1970.
Loyal in All. London, Mills and Boon, 1957; as *Nurse Marika, Loyal in All*, Toronto, Harlequin, 1963.
Love Is My Reason. London, Mills and Boon, 1957; Toronto, Harlequin, 1959.
Joanna at the Grange. London, Mills and Boon, 1957.
And Falsely Pledge My Love. London, Mills and Boon, 1957; Toronto, Harlequin, 1965.
Dear Sir. London, Mills and Boon, 1958; Toronto, Harlequin, 1961.
Dear Trustee. London, Mills and Boon, 1958; Toronto, Harlequin, 1959.
The Girl in the Blue Dress. London, Mills and Boon, 1958; Toronto, Harlequin, 1976.
Star Quality. London, Mills and Boon, 1959; as *Surgeon of Distinction*, Toronto, Harlequin, 1959.
Honey. London, Mills and Boon, 1959; Toronto, Harlequin, 1977.
Corner House. London, Mills and Boon, 1959.
Across the Counter. London, Mills and Boon, 1960; Toronto, Harlequin, 1961.
Choose the One You'll Marry. London, Mills and Boon, and Toronto, Harlequin, 1960.
Paris—And My Love. London, Mills and Boon, 1960; Toronto, Harlequin, 1961.
My Sister Celia. London, Mills and Boon, 1961; Toronto, Harlequin, 1971.
Reluctant Relation. London, Mills and Boon, 1961; Toronto, Harlequin, 1962.
The Wedding Dress. London, Mills and Boon, 1962; Toronto, Harlequin, 1964.
House of Conflict. London, Mills and Boon, 1962; Toronto, Harlequin, 1963.
Inherit My Heart. London, Mills and Boon, 1962; Toronto, Harlequin, 1963.
Dangerous Loving. London, Mills and Boon, 1963.
Sweet Meadows. London, Mills and Boon, 1963.
Do Not Go, My Love. London, Mills and Boon, 1964; Toronto, Harlequin, 1972.
The Strange Quest of Anne Weston. London, Mills and Boon, 1964; as *The Strange Quest of Nurse Anne*, Toronto, Harlequin, 1965.
Girl with a Challenge. London, Mills and Boon, 1965; Toronto, Harlequin, 1970.
Her Sister's Children. London, Mills and Boon, 1965.
A Song Begins. London, Mills and Boon, 1965; Toronto, Harlequin, 1966.
The Other Linding Girl. London, Mills and Boon, 1966; Toronto, Harlequin, 1970.
The Broken Wing. London, Mills and Boon, 1966; Toronto, Harlequin, 1967; as *Damaged Angel*, Mills and Boon, 1967.
When Love Is Blind. London, Mills and Boon, 1967; Toronto, Harlequin, 1968.
Though Worlds Apart. London, Mills and Boon, 1967; Toronto, Harlequin, 1969.
The Marshall Family. London, Mills and Boon, 1967; Toronto, Harlequin, 1968.
A Home for Joy. London, Mills and Boon, 1968; Toronto, Harlequin, 1969.
Missing from Home. London, Mills and Boon, 1968; Toronto, Harlequin, 1969.
The Curtain Rises. London, Mills and Boon, 1969; Toronto, Harlequin, 1970.
The Rosewood Box. London, Mills and Boon, 1970.
Child of Music. London, Mills and Boon, 1970; Toronto, Harlequin, 1971.
Second Marriage. London, Mills and Boon, 1971.
Music of the Heart. London, Mills and Boon, and Toronto, Harlequin, 1972.
Design for Loving. London, Mills and Boon, 1972.
Unbidden Melody. London, Mills and Boon, 1973; Toronto, Harlequin, 1974.
Song Cycle. London, Mills and Boon, and Toronto, Harlequin, 1974.
Remembered Serenade. London, Mills and Boon, and Toronto, Harlequin, 1975.
Elusive Harmony. London, Mills and Boon, 1976; Toronto, Harlequin, 1977.
Nightingales. London, Mills and Boon, and Toronto, Harlequin, 1980.

OTHER PUBLICATIONS

Other as Ida Cook

We Followed Our Stars (on opera singers). London, Hamish Hamilton, and New York, Morrow, 1950.
My Life, with Tito Gobbi. London, Macdonald and Jane's, 1979.

*   *   *

Mary Burchell's favorite setting for her contemporary romances is the world of opera. An avid fan herself, Burchell realistically describes the hard work and discipline required from opera singers who must fiercely compete for prize roles at the same time that she lovingly portrays the excitement and glamour that result from the creation of beautiful music by talented, temperamental stars. Burchell's world of opera is a proverbial "small world," for these romances either revolve around or at least mention the same cast of characters. In fact, a number of the romances have been grouped together as "The Warrender Saga" after one of the main characters, Sir Oscar Warrender, a conductor. His romance with and marriage to a young girl whom he trains to be a singer are told in *A Song Begins*. He and his wife play an essential but supporting role in the other romances. Other musical characters who reappear include Conrad Schreiner, another teacher and conductor, and his mistress, Manora Venescu, a singer. Florian, a fashion designer, is also alluded to in several novels. Thus, once Burchell develops a character she is fond of, she carried him or her over into other novels. This is an interesting, effective technique for involving readers.

Burchell experiments in other ways as well. For example, in one novel *Call—And I'll Come*, the first three chapters and the last chapter are written from the perspective of the hero while the middle of the novel is written from the heroine's perspective, an unusual arrangement for a formula romance. In other Burchell romances the reader is aware that she is being told a story by a narrator who occasionally draws back to make editorial comments on the characters and their behaviour, although the narrator is usually telling the story from the heroine's perspective.

Burchell is not a dramatic writer with a taste for flamboyant, impossible characters and fast-paced, violent action. Most of the characters in her romances, even the rival suitors, are nice but flawed human beings. There are very few arch villains. The heroines are quiet, serious, maternal young women who have sufficient flashes of humor and temper to make them intriguing to the heroes who are basically unromantic but loyal and thoughtful, vitally alive men who are dedicated to their work. Most of the "action" consists of the heroes and heroines maturing. The heroines develop their occupational and social skills and become increasingly self-confident while the heroes are shaken from their rather oblivious confidence that they will get their way in all things. This growth takes place over weeks or even months, and much of that time is spent apart from each other. In the end, of course, they are united, both wiser than before.

Mary Burchell is a romance writer whose approach to romance has changed very little over the last 20 years. She does not dwell on passion; she does not describe fiery love-making between the hero and heroine. These traits may make her romances seem rather tame for modern tastes but what they lack in passion they make up for in sincerity and a certain charm, particularly the novels that deal with opera.

—Margaret Jensen

BURFORD, Eleanor. *See* **HOLT, Victoria.**

BURFORD, Lolah. American. Born in 1931. Educated at Bryn Mawr College, Pennsylvania, degree. Address: c/o Macmillan, 866 Third Avenue, New York, New York 10022, U.S.A.

ROMANCE AND GOTHIC PUBLICATIONS

Novels

Vice Avenged: A Moral Tale. New York, Macmillan, and London, Macmillan, 1971.
The Vision of Stephen: An Elegy. New York, Macmillan, 1972; London, Cassell, 1973.
Edward, Edward. New York, Macmillan, 1973; London, Cassell, 1974.
MacLyon. New York, Macmillan, 1974; London, Weidenfeld and Nicolson, 1975.
Alyx. New York, Macmillan, 1977.
Seacage. New York, Macmillan, 1979.

*   *   *

Lolah Burford's novels are neither for the meek nor the militant, the little old lady or the strident feminist. Raw sex is the major element of each novel—sex of every variety, from rape to incest, sadism, homosexuality, and other gross perversions. Though cloaked in velvet prose, Burford's "polite pornography" is explicit and pervasive.

The typical Burford novel begins with an act of sexual violence. *Vice Avenged: A Moral Tale*, Burford's first novel, set in 18th-century London, opens with a round of cards; the winner must "ravish" a "virgin of good family" and return with the bloody proof of his deed. Young Marquis Bysshe Gore is the rakish victor in this cruel and dangerous game. Cressida, daughter of the Duke of Salisbury, is the innocent victim whom the players have chosen by lot. The rape occurs: Gore is violent and merciless; Cressida frightened and submissive, but (according to Burford) she gradually enjoys being taken and falls in love with Gore. *Alyx*, a more recent Burford effusion, set on an 18th-century Caribbean sugar plantation, begins with Smith, the "plantation stud," taking by force an inexperienced young slave girl. Alyx, too, falls in love with the rapacious villain. But villain turns out to be hero when "Smith" turns out to be Simon, the kidnapped Sixth Earl of Halford. As if to justify these fictional reactions, Burford quotes Alexander Pope: "Ev'ry woman is at heart a rake."

Diverging from her standard plot devices, Burford, in *The Vision of Stephen*, combines the 7th century with the 19th. Young Margery discovers behind her piano a grate through which 7th-century Stephen enters her world—the England of 1822—and magically disappears and re-appears to live out a 1200-year time-shuttle. To establish validity for her deft contraposition of time sequences, Burford studied Bede's *Ecclesiastical History of the English Nation*. Rather pretentiously, Burford concludes her novel with Alfred's preface to the translation of *The Pastoral Care* (AD 894), in Old English—a bit difficult for those who are not medievalists.

Burford's plots are fast-paced, full of action and intrigue. The well-researched, historically correct settings (Burford is a Bryn Mawr graduate) are various: 18th-century London (*Vice Avenged*); the 7th-century Anglo-Saxon kingdom of Northumbria (*The Vision of Stephen*); the 19th-century pre-Regency unrest in England, Napoleonic Wars, and flowering of Vienna (*Edward, Edward*); the 18th-century Protestant Rebellion in Scotland (*MacLyon*); the 18th-century Caribbean sugar plantation (*Alyx*); and "Another Time" in an unnamed land (*Seacage*). Burford's prose style is sophisticated, and consists mostly of dialogue, spoken with the formality and grandiloquence of times past, and few descriptive passages.

—Marcia G. Fuchs

BURGHLEY, Rose.   Address: c/o Mills and Boon Ltd., 15-16 Brooks Mews, London W1A 1DR, England.

ROMANCE AND GOTHIC PUBLICATIONS

Novels

And Be Thy Love.   London, Mills and Boon, 1958; Toronto, Harlequin, 1961.
Love in the Afternoon.   London, Mills and Boon, 1959.
The Sweet Surrender.   London, Mills and Boon, 1959; Toronto, Harlequin, 1966.
Bride by Arrangement.   London, Mills and Boon, 1960.
A Moment in Paris.   London, Mills and Boon, 1961.
Highland Mist.   London, Mills and Boon, 1962; Toronto, Harlequin, 1967.
The Garden of Don José.   London, Mills and Boon, 1964; Toronto, Harlequin, 1965.
Man of Destiny.   London, Mills and Boon, and Toronto, Harlequin, 1965.
A Quality of Magic.   London, Mills and Boon, 1966; Toronto, Harlequin, 1967.
The Afterglow.   London, Mills and Boon, 1966; as *Alpine Doctor*, Toronto, Harlequin, 1970.
Bride of Alaine.   London, Mills and Boon, and Toronto, Harlequin, 1966.
Folly of the Heart.   London, Mills and Boon, 1967.
The Bay of Moonlight.   London, Mills and Boon, and Toronto, Harlequin, 1968.
Return to Tremarth.   London, Mills and Boon, 1969.

*   *   *

Between 1958 and 1969, Rose Burghley wrote fewer than 15 novels, yet her romances remain as some of the most charming and well-written novels of those years. She, as other romance writers of that period, seemed to have delighted in telling tender stories of love and happiness. Her novels followed a standard pattern and her characters had typical characteristics. However, these facts do not detract from the overall effect of her stories. For that matter, it may have been one of the elements that helped to make her a popular writer. Her readers knew the kind of novel she wrote and they knew that each new novel would be just as entertaining. Generally, her novels centered on sweet, young girls who suddenly find themselves in unusual circumstances which eventually led to them falling in love. Actually, Burghley's novels could be modern adaptions of the "Beggar Maid Story," for in each example of her writings one finds the heroine completely out of her depth and struggling to cope with new and unexpected situations and emotions.

Her story of Lois Tarrant, in the novel *The Garden of Don José*, is perhaps her most delightful, for it satisfies every romantic dream imaginable. Lois has been sent by a London fashion house to deliver a trousseau to a a a young girl in Spain. Just as Lois is about to return home, she learns that Doña Inez's intended husband has been critically hurt in a car accident.

Ruthlessly, her guardian, Don José, insists that Lois stay to support Doña Inez during those terrifying hours. Her sympathy and compassion are instantly played upon through the rest of the novel as she is skillfuly manipulated by Don José. Her efforts to remember "her place," to avoid falling in love with Don José, come to nothing as he forces her to admit her love.

In another novel Burghley uses a different approach. In *Bride of Alaine* Amanda Wells and her wealthy friend, Judy Macrae, are stranded on a Scottish island after Judy insists on viewing the large tower dwelling that dominates the island. When Amanda has to go for help for Judy because she has hurt her ankle, she is greeted by a servant with the words, "I'll tell the master the Bride of Alaine is here!" Later, Amanda understands that he referred to a local superstition where a young heiress would come to the island to restore wealth to the family. Complications develop as Judy becomes fascinated by Alaine Urquhart, the owner of the island. Amanda feels she must stay in the background and watch her seemingly successful pursuit of Alaine, not realizing that local legend can not be disregarded.

The typical elements of romance in these stories should have made them trite. Rose Burghley's sympathetic handling of her heroines' dilemmas, her truly outstanding ability to convey the tentative dawning of love, make her novels unexpectedly touching. Her creative use of plot complication and skillful character development all help her to tell tender, endearing stories that can not be dismissed so lightly. In fact, this is the basis for her well-earned reputation as a romance writer.

—Arlene Moore

BURGIN, G(eorge) B(rown). British. Born in Croydon, Surrey, 15 January 1856. Educated at Totteridge Park Public School. Married Georgina Benington in 1893 (died, 1940). Private Secretary to Baker Pasha and accompanied him to Asia Minor in the 1880's; journalist: Sub-Editor, *The Idler*, to 1899; General Editor, New Vagabond Library, 1896-97. Secretary, Authors' Club, 1905-08. Fellow, Institute of Journalists. *Died 20 June 1944.*

ROMANCE AND GOTHIC PUBLICATIONS

Novels

> *The Dance at the Four Corners.* Bristol, Arrowsmith, 1894.
> *Tuxter's Little Maid.* London, Cassell, 1895; as *At Tuxter's,* New York, Putnam, 1895.
> *Gascoigne's Ghost.* London, Beeman, and New York, Harper, 1896.
> *The Judge of the Four Corners.* London, Innes, 1896.
> *Tomalyn's Quest.* London, Innes, and New York, Harper, 1896.
> *Fortune's Footballs.* London, Pearson, and New York, Appleton, 1897.
> *"Old Man's" Marriage.* London, Richards, 1897.
> *The Cattle Man.* Londn, Richards, 1898.
> *Settled Out of Court.* London, Pearson, 1898.
> *The Bread of Tears.* London, Long, 1899.
> *The Hermits of Gray's Inn.* London, Pearson, 1899.
> *The Tiger's Claw.* London, Pearson, 1900.
> *The Person in the House.* London, Hurst and Blackett, 1900.
> *The Way Out.* London, Long, 1900.
> *A Goddess of Gray's Inn.* London, Pearson, 1901.

A Son of Mammon. London, Long, 1901.
A Wilful Woman. London, Long, 1902.
The Man Who Died. London, Everett, 1903.
The Ladies of the Manor. London, Richards, 1903; New York, Smart Set, 1904.
The Hermit of Bonneville. London, Richards, 1904.
The Land of Silence. London, Nash, 1904.
The Devil's Due. London, Hutchinson, 1905.
The Marble City. London, Hutchinson, 1905.
The Belles of Vaudroy. London, Hutchinson, 1906.
The Only World. London, Richards, 1906.
Peggy the Pilgrim. London, Richards, 1907.
Which Woman?. London, Nash, 1907.
Fanuela. London, Hutchinson, 1907.
Flowers of Fire. London, Nash, 1908.
Galahad's Garden. London, Nash, 1908.
A Woman's Way. London, Hutchinson, 1908.
Simple Savage. London, Hutchinson, 1909.
The Slaves of Allah. London, Hutchinson, 1909.
The Trickster. London, Stanley Paul, 1909.
Diana of Dreams. London, Hutchinson, 1910.
The King of Four Corners. London, Hutchinson, 1910.
This Son of Adam. London, Hutchinson, 1910.
The Belle of Santiago. London, Hutchinson, 1911.
A Lady of Spain. London, Hutchinson, 1911.
The Vision of Balmaine. London, Hutchinson, 1911.
Dickie Dilver. London, Hutchinson, 1912.
Varick's Legacy. London, Hutchinson, 1912.
The Love That Lasts. London, Hodder and Stoughton, 1913.
The "Second-Sighter's" Daughter. London, Hutchinson, 1913.
The Duke's Twins. London, Hutchinson, 1914.
Within the Gates. London, Hutchinson, 1914.
A Game of Hearts. London, Hutchinson, 1915.
The Herb of Healing. London, Hutchinson, 1915.
The Girl Who Got Out. London, Hutchinson, 1916.
The Hut by the River. London, Hutchinson, 1916.
The Greater Gain. London, Hutchinson, 1917.
The Puller of Strings: An Ottawa Valley Romance. London, Hutchinson, 1917.
Lady Mary's Money. London, Hutchinson, 1918.
The Throw-Back. London, Hutchinson, 1918.
A Gentle Despot. London, Hutchinson, 1919.
A Rubber Princess. London, Hutchinson, 1919.
Pilgrims of Circumstance. London, Hutchinson, 1920.
Uncle Jeremy. London, Hutchinson, 1920.
The Faithful Fool. London, Books, 1921.
The Man from Turkey. London, Hutchinson, 1921.
Cyrilla Seeks Herself. London, Hutchinson, 1922.
Love and the Locusts. London, Hutchinson, 1922.
Manetta's Marriage. London, Hutchinson, 1922.
The Man Behind. London, Hutchinson, 1923.
Sally's Sweetheart. London, Hutchinson, 1923.
The Kiss. London, Hutchinson, 1924.
The Lord of Little Langton. London, Hutchinson, 1924.
The Spending of the Pile. London, Hutchinson, 1924.
The Young Labelle. London, Hutchinson, 1924.
Fleurette of Four Corners. London, Hutchinson, 1925.
The Hate That Lasts. London, Hutchinson, 1925.
Mariette's Lovers. London, Hutchinson, 1925.
The Forest Lure. London, Hutchinson, 1926.

Young Deloraine. London, Hutchinson, 1926.
The Dale of Dreams. London, Hutchinson, 1927.
The Hundredth Man. London, Hutchinson, 1927.
The House of Fiske. London, Hutchinson, 1927.
Allandale's Daughters. London, Hutchinson, 1928.
The Final Test. London, Hutchinson, 1928.
Nitana. London, Hutchinson, 1928.
All Things Come Round. London, Hutchinson, 1929.
Out of the Swim. London, Wright and Brown, 1930.
The Woman Without a Heart. London, Alexander Ouseley, 1930.
The Duke's Strategem. London, Wright and Brown, 1931.
One Traveller Returns. London, Wright and Brown, 1931.
Eternal Justice. London, Wright and Brown, 1932.
When Dreams Come True. London, Wright and Brown, 1932.
The Wrong Woman. London, Wright and Brown, 1932.
The Wheels of Fate. London, Wright and Brown, 1933.
A Poor Millionaire. London, Wright and Brown, 1933.
A Fateful Fraud. London, Wright and Brown, 1934.
The Honour of Four Corners. London, Wright and Brown, 1934.
Pierrepont's Daughters. London, Wright and Brown, 1935.
Who Loses Pays. London, Wright and Brown, 1935.
Slaves of the Ring. London, Hutchinson, 1936.
Uncle Patterley's Money. London, Wright and Brown, 1936.
The Golden Penny. London, Wright and Brown, 1937.
The Ills Men Do. London, Wright and Brown, 1937.
A Pious Fraud. London, Wright and Brown, 1938.
The Man in the Corner. London, Wright and Brown, 1939.

Short Stories

His Lordship, and Others. London, Henry, 1893.

OTHER PUBLICATIONS

Other

Memoirs of a Clubman. London, Hutchinson, 1921; New York, Dutton, 1922.
More Memoirs (and Some Travels). London, Hutchinson, and New York, Dutton, 1922.
Many Memories. London, Hutchinson, 1922; New York, Dutton, 1923.
Some More Memoirs. London, Hutchinson, 1924.

Editor, *The Vagabond's Annual.* Bristol, Arrowsmith, 1893.

*   *   *

Behind the initials of G.B. Burgin lurks that rarity among romantic novelists—the male writer. Working from the late 1890's until the mid-1930's, Burgin produced roughly 80 novels. Other male novelists of the period, such as P.C. Wren and Rafael Sabatini, mixed up the love element with a fair amount of adventure, escapism, travel, and excitement, rather than concentrating only on matters of the heart. G.B. Burgin is openly sentimental about love, and keeps his heroines firmly on their pedestals. Suitors declare their love with vigorous, straight-forward ardour: "Cyrilla, you are divinely, most exquisitely beautiful. You are so beautiful that I am afraid of you. You hurt me.... Don't you see, Cyrilla, don't you know, that you are the embodiment of all that is sweetest and dearest in the world to me? You're heaven's explanation on earth. You know what I mean?" The heroine wanted to be swept off her feet, held tightly in strong arms, and perhaps even to be very slightly maltreated. "Frankly, she liked men and their society. There was...an unconscious brutality with most of them, which gave a girl something to think about."

The sentimental nonsense of tales like *The Kiss* or *Cyrilla* is harmless daydreaming; however the dissemination of the belief that some girls actually *like* being brutalised is more questionable.

—Rachel Anderson

BURNS, Sheila. *See* **BLOOM, Ursula.**

BUTLER, Gwendoline (née Williams). Also writes as Jennie Melville. British. Born in London. Educated at Haberdashers' Aske's Hatcham Girls' School, London, 1939-42; Lady Margaret Hall, Oxford, 1944-49, B.A. in modern history 1949. Married Lionel Butler in 1949 (died, 1981); one daughter. Taught at two Oxford colleges for a short time. Recipient: Crime Writers Association Silver Dagger, 1973; Romantic Novelists Association Major Award, 1981. Agent: John Farquharson Ltd., 8 Bell Yard, London WC2A 2JU. Address: 32 Harvest Road, Englefield Green, Surrey, England.

ROMANCE AND GOTHIC PUBLICATIONS

Novels (series: Inspector John Coffin)

> *Receipt for Murder.* London, Bles, 1956.
> *Dead in a Row* (Coffin). London, Bles, 1957.
> *The Dull Dead.* London, Bles, 1958; New York, Walker, 1962.
> *The Murdering Kind.* London, Bles, 1958; New York, Roy, 1964.
> *The Interloper.* London, Bles, 1959.
> *Death Lives Next Door* (Coffin). London, Bles, 1960; as *Dine and Be Dead*, New York, Macmillan, 1960.
> *Make Me a Murderer* (Coffin). London, Bles, 1961.
> *Coffin in Oxford.* London, Bles, 1962.
> *Coffin for Baby.* London, Bles, and New York, Walker, 1963.
> *Coffin Waiting.* London, Bles, 1963; New York, Walker, 1965.
> *Coffin in Malta.* London, Bles, 1964; New York, Walker, 1965.
> *A Nameless Coffin.* London, Bles, 1966; New York, Walker, 1967.
> *Coffin Following.* London, Bles, 1968.
> *Coffin's Dark Number.* London, Bles, 1969.

A Coffin from the Past. London, Bles, 1970.

A Coffin for Pandora. London, Macmillan, 1973; as *Olivia*, New York, Coward McCann, 1974.

A Coffin for the Canary. London, Macmillan, 1974; as *Sarsen Place*, New York, Coward McCann, 1974.

The Vesey Inheritance. New York, Coward McCann, 1975; London, Macmillan, 1976.

The Brides of Friedberg. London, Macmillan, 1977; as *Meadowsweet*, New York, Coward McCann, 1977.

The Red Staircase. New York, Coward McCann, 1979; London, Collins, 1980.

Novels as Jennie Melville (series: Charmian Daniels)

Come Home and Be Killed (Daniels). London, Joseph, 1962; New York, British Book Centre, 1964.

Burning Is a Substitute for Loving (Daniels). London, Joseph, 1963; New York, British Book Centre, 1964.

Murderers' Houses (Daniels). London, Joseph, 1964.

There Lies Your Love (Daniels). London, Joseph, 1965.

Nell Alone. London, Joseph, 1966.

A Different Kind of Summer. London, Joseph, 1967.

The Hunter in the Shadows. London, Hodder and Stoughton, 1969; New York, McKay, 1970.

A New Kind of Killer, An Old Kind of Death. London, Hodder and Stoughton, 1970; as *A New Kind of Killer*, New York, McKay, 1971.

Ironwood. London, Hodder and Stoughton, and New York McKay, 1972.

Nun's Castle. New York, McKay, 1973; London, Hodder and Stoughton, 1974.

Raven's Forge. London, Macmillan, and New York, McKay, 1975.

Dragon's Eye. New York, Simon and Schuster, 1976; London, Macmillan, 1977.

Axwater. London, Macmillan, 1978; as *Tarot's Tower*, New York, Simon and Schuster, 1978.

Murder Has a Pretty Face (Daniels). London, Macmillan,   1981.

OTHER PUBLICATIONS

Play

Radio Play: *Nell Alone*, from her own novel, 1968.

*   *   *

Edmund Crispin once wrote in *The Sunday Times*: "Miss Melville is as satisfying as Miss Gwendoline Butler, whom in some important respects she resembles." It could have been tongue-in-cheek on the part of that witty reviewer, but the fact remains that for some time the crime novels of Gwendoline Butler and Jennie Melville enjoyed separate identities; later they became more obviously products of the one deft hand, particularly when they developed into the romantic/gothic field.

The high point for Gwendoline Butler occurred with *A Coffin for Pandora*, a feast of suspense in 19th-century Oxford. A tale of kidnapping and mysterious death, with a rather independent young governess in danger, it is not only superbly plotted but marvellously evocative of the period with its upstairs and downstairs contrasts between rich and poor. This skill in conveying an atmosphere of haunting menace against an authentic social background is also evident in later books. *The Vesey Inheritance* is a substantial novel set in Victorian London, involving an innocent 19-year-old heroine up from the country who senses something mysterious in her family history and fears that her half-brother means to harm her. *The Brides of Friedberg* stays in period, but switches location to Germany and follows the fortunes of two girls from an English upper-class family; it is a tale of poison, again portraying the social scene from the rich in their palaces to the poor and exploited to complement the main storyline.

Gwendoline Butler was praised by Patrick Cosgrave in *The Spectator* for her writing, characterisation, and touch; indeed, he called her "the Jane Austen of the crime story." If this is applied specifically to her beguiling mysteries in the gothic tradition, it must be noted that her work in this field has been mainly under the Melville pseudonym. As Melville she is one of the foremost exponents of stories featuring young women caught up in lonely buildings permeated with an air of evil and corruption.

Melville's settings are diverse—a remote mansion, an old observatory, a redundant iron foundry—and yet they share the common aura of "something wicked this way comes." The narrator-heroine is confused about the source of her mortal danger, and on the brink of fatally misguided choices between apparent friends and enemies. Romance plays a key part, but handsome and charming men are not always what they seem and the ruthless and masterful male is not easily identifiable by the heroine as lover or villain and may well be both. In spite of these common features, however, Melville's novels are by no means formulistic. While such books as *Ironwood*, *Raven's Forge*, *Dragon's Eye*, and *Axwater* are uniform in displaying gripping readability, an intimate style, blended perceptiveness and ironic humor, and, above all, an ability to squeeze every sinister nuance from a character or situation, they also show her versatility as a superlative plotter.

—Melvyn Barnes

BUTTERWORTH, Michael.   *See* **SALISBURY, Carola**.

CADELL, (Violet) Elizabeth (née Vandyke).   Also writes as Harriet Ainsworth.   British. Born in Calcutta, India, 10 November 1903. Married H.D.R.M. Cadell in 1928 (died); one son and one daughter. Address: c/o Hodder and Stoughton, Mill Road, Dunton Green, Sevenoaks, Kent TN13 2YA, England.

ROMANCE AND GOTHIC PUBLICATIONS

Novels

> *My Dear Aunt Flora*.   London, Hale, 1946.
> *Last Straw for Harriet*.   New York, Morrow, 1947; as *Fishy, Said the Admiral*,   London, Hale, 1948.

River Lodge. London, Hale, 1948.

Gay Pursuit. New York, Morrow, 1948; London, Hale, 1950; as *Family Gathering*, Hale, 1979.

Iris in Winter. New York, Morrow, 1949; London, Hale, 1951.

Brimstone in the Garden. New York, Morrow, 1950.

The Greenwood Shady. London, Hodder and Stoughton, 1951.

Enter Mrs. Belchamber. New York, Morrow, 1951; as *The Frenchman and the Lady*, London, Hodder and Stoughton, 1952.

Men and Angels. London, Hodder and Stoughton, 1952.

Crystal Clear. New York, Morrow, 1953; as *Journey's Eve*, London, Hodder and Stoughton, 1953.

Spring Green. London, Hodder and Stoughton, 1953.

The Cuckoo in Spring. New York, Morrow, and London, Hodder and Stoughton, 1954.

Around the Rugged Rock. New York, Morrow, 1954; as *The Gentlemen Go By*, London, Hodder and Stoughton, 1954.

The Lark Shall Sing. New York, Morrow, and London, Hodder and Stoughton, 1955; as *The Singing Heart*, New York, Berkley, 1959.

The Blue Sky of Spring. London, Hodder and Stoughton, 1956.

I Love a Lass. New York, Morrow, 1956.

Bridal Array. London, Hodder and Stoughton, 1957; Toronto, Harlequin, 1959.

The Green Empress. London, Hodder and Stoughton, 1958.

Sugar Candy Cottage. London, Hodder and Stoughton, 1958.

Alice, Where Art Thou? London, Hodder and Stoughton, 1959.

The Yellow Brick Road. London, Hodder and Stoughton, and New York, Morrow, 1960.

Honey for Tea. London, Hodder and Stoughton, 1961; New York, Morrow, 1962.

Six Impossible Things. London, Hodder and Stoughton, and New York, Morrow, 1961.

Language of the Heart. London, Hodder and Stoughton, 1962; as *The Toy Sword*, New York, Morrow, 1962.

Letter to My Love. London, Hodder and Stoughton, 1963.

Mixed Marriage: The Diary of a Portuguese Bride. London, Hodder and Stoughton, 1963.

Be My Guest. London, Hodder and Stoughton, 1964; as *Come Be My Guest*, New York, Morrow, 1964.

Canary Yellow. London, Hodder and Stoughton, and New York, Morrow, 1965.

The Fox from His Lair. London, Hodder and Stoughton, 1965; New York, Morrow, 1966.

The Corner Shop. London, Hodder and Stoughton, 1966; New York, Morrow, 1967.

The Stratton Story. London, Hodder and Stoughton, 1967.

Mrs. Westerby Changes Course. New York, Morrow, 1968.

The Golden Collar. London, Hodder and Stoughton, and New York, Morrow, 1969.

The Friendly Air. London, Hodder and Stoughton, 1970; New York, Morrow, 1971.

The Past Tense of Love. London, Hodder and Stoughton, and New York, Morrow, 1970.

Home for the Wedding. London, Hodder and Stoughton, 1971; New York, Morrow, 1972.

The Haymaker. London, Hodder and Stoughton, 1972.

Royal Summons. New York, Morrow, 1973.

Deck with Flowers. London, Hodder and Stoughton, 1973; New York, Morrow, 1974.

The Fledgling. London, Hodder and Stoughton, and New York, Morrow, 1975.

Game in Diamonds. London, Hodder and Stoughton, and New York, Morrow, 1976.

Parson's House. London, Hodder and Stoughton, and New York, Morrow, 1977.

Round Dozen. London, Hodder and Stoughton, and New York, Morrow, 1978.

Return Match. London, Hodder and Stoughton, and New York, Morrow, 1979.

The Marrying Kind. London, Hodder and Stoughton, and New York, Morrow, 1980.

Any Two Can Play. New York, Morrow, 1981.

A Lion in the Way. London, Hodder and Stoughton, and New York, Morrow, 1982.

Novels as Harriet Ainsworth

Consider the Lilies. London, Hodder and Stoughton, 1956.
Shadows on the Water. London, Hodder and Stoughton, 1958; as Elizabeth Cadell, New York, Morrow, 1958.
Death among Friends. London, Hodder and Stoughton, 1964.

OTHER PUBLICATIONS

Other

Sun in the Morning (juvenile). New York, Morrow, 1950; London, Hodder and Stoughton, 1951.

*   *   *

Normality is the essence of Elizabeth Cadell's popular novels. Her heroines are usually intelligent, practical, efficient, their faults the result of impulsiveness and warm-heartedness. Sometimes their suitors will chafe as this impulsiveness brings in its wake a stream of young nephews, eccentric old ladies, and lovable animals to interfere with their courtship. But even imperious suitors accept this, ultimately, or are replaced by more understanding young men.

Beyond this, the novels are substantially middle class, or perhaps middle class plus. There are few Cinderellas swept away by titled millionaires. Alexandra (*The Cuckoo in Spring*) is one of Cadell's most humbly circumstanced heroines, yet she is self-supporting, a secretary with a firm of solicitors. On some level, the Cadell hero and heroine must meet as equals, since her basic plot shows two people of the same class finding each other and overcoming obstacles that are mildly amusing, to the reader if not to the protagonists.

Often giving her books a Spanish or Portuguese setting, Cadell provides a good read, a piece of escapism where the crucial phone call does not go unanswered and even the rejected suitor is not too crushed by his rejection. Like another prolific writer of romances, D. E. Stevenson, Cadell has a limpid charm of writing that, with the many bizarre subsidiary characters, turns the best of her romances, like *Honey for Tea*, into comedies of manners. And this comic tone allows Cadell to be more realistic than similar authors in areas where her characters are less than perfect. Lucille in *The Lark Shall Sing* is frankly bossy; her beautiful sister tends to ineffectual tears. Kerry's long-lost mother has spent 20 years as mistress to a series of successful men in *The Past Tense of Love*.

Another example of Cadell's realistic streak in the midst of romantic fantasy is her clear-eyed portrayal of children. The three youngest Waynes in *The Lark Shall Sing* are individualized, charming to read about, but possibly less than charming to have to live with. The epitome of the objective portrayal of the child is Tory Brooke in *The Fledgling*. Eponymous heroine though she may be, Tory's determination to recast her circumstances to suit herself shows her as too deliberate and calculating to be altogether attractive. As she waits for her widowed father and the woman of his, and her, choice to announce the happy ending she has contrived for them all, she can be seen, whether or not Cadell intends it, as too cold-blooded for comfort.

At the other end of the scale, particularly in some of her earlier books, Cadell shows an attractive middle-aged woman involved in romantic or family problems. In *Last Straw for Harriet* it is Harriet who holds stage center, not the romantic young people. The eye that Cadell turns on the aged, like the eye she turns on the young, is sympathetic but not sentimental.

Mrs. Westerby Changes Course and *Canary Yellow* may veer in the direction of the suspense story; *Brimstone in the Garden* has a supernatural slant; but Cadell's real genre is clearly romance in perhaps its safest, most wholesome form. If "life isn't like that," it is clearly life's fault, not Cadell's.

—Susan Branch

CAINE, (Thomas Henry) Hall. British. Born in Runcorn, Cheshire, 14 May 1858. Educated at schools on the Isle of Man and in Liverpool. Married Mary Chandler in 1882; two sons. Worked as an architect's clerk, schoolmaster, then a journalist: leader-writer, Liverpool *Mercury*; companion-secretary to D.G. Rossetti, in London until Rossetti's death, 1882, then lived in the Isle of Man. Lecturer, Royal Institution, 1892; Justice of the Peace, and member of the House of Keys, Isle of Man. Freeman of Douglas, Isle of Man, 1928. Officer of the Order of Leopold, Belgium; Companion of Honour, 1922. Knighted, 1918. *Died 31 August 1931.*

ROMANCE AND GOTHIC PUBLICATIONS

Novels

> *The Shadow of a Crime.* London, Chatto and Windus, 3 vols., and New York, Harper, 3 vols., 1885.
> *She's All the World to Me.* New York, Harper, 1885.
> *The Deemster.* London, Chatto and Windus, 3 vols., 1887; New York, Appleton, 1 vol., 1888.
> *A Son of Hagar.* London, Chatto and Windus, 1887; New York, Fenno, 1895.
> *The Bondman: A New Saga.* New York, Lovell, 1889; London, Heinemann, 3 vols., 1890.
> *The Scapegoat.* London, Heinemann, 2 vols., 1891; New York, Lovell, 1 vol., 1891.
> *The Manxman.* London, Heinemann, and New York, Appleton, 1894.
> *The Mahdi; or, Love and Race.* New York, Appleton, and London, Clarke, 1894.
> *The Christian.* London, Heinemann, and New York, Appleton, 1897.
> *The Eternal City.* London, Heinemann, and New York, Appleton, 1901.
> *The Prodigal Son.* London, Heinemann, and New York, Appleton, 1904.
> *Drink: A Love Story on a Great Question.* London, Newnes, 1906; New York, Appleton, 1907.
> *The White Prophet.* London, Heinemann, 2 vols., 1909; New York, Appleton, 1 vol., 1909; revised edition, Heinemann, 1 vol., 1911.
> *The Woman Thou Gavest Me.* London, Heinemann, and Philadelphia, Lippincott, 1913.
> *The Master of Man.* London, Heinemann, and Philadelphia, Lippincott, 1921.
> *The Woman of Knockaloe: A Parable.* London, Cassell, and New York, Dodd Mead, 1923.

Short Stories

> *Capt'n Davy's Honeymoon, The Last Confession, The Blind Mother.* London, Heinemann, 1892; *Capt'n Davy's Honeymoon* published New York, Appleton, 1892; *The Last Confession, The Blind Mother* published New York, Tait, 1892.

OTHER PUBLICATIONS

Plays

> *The Ben-my-Chree*, with Wilson Barrett (produced London, 1888).
> *The Good Old Times*, with Wilson Barrett (produced London, 1889).
> *The Bondman* (produced Bolton, Lancashire, 1892; London, 1906). London, Daily Mail, 1906.
> *Yan, The Icelander; or, Home Sweet Home* (produced Hartlepool, 1900; as *The Quality of Mercy*, produced Manchester, 1911). Privately printed, 1896.

The Christian, adaptation of his own novel (produced Liverpool and London, 1899; revised version, produced London, 1907). London, Collier, 1907.

The Eternal City, adaptation of his own novel (produced London and New York, 1902). Privately printed, 1902.

The Prodigal Son, adaptation of his own novel (produced London and New York, 1905). Privately printed, 1905.

Pete, with Louis N. Parker, adaptation of the novel *The Manxman* by Caine (produced London, 1908). London, Collier, 1908.

The Fatal Error (produced London, 1908).

The Bishop's Son, adaptation of his novel *The Deemster* (produced London, 1910). Privately printed, 1910.

The Eternal Question, adaptation of his novel *The Eternal City* (produced London, 1910). Privately printed, 1910.

The Prime Minister (produced Atlantic City, 1916; as *Margaret Schiller*, produced New York, 1916; as *The Prime Minister*, produced London, 1918). Privately printed, 1918.

The Iron Hand (produced London, 1916).

The Woman Thou Gavest Me, adaptation of his own novel (produced Boston, 1917).

Screenplays: *Victory and Peace*, 1918; *Darby and Joan*, 1919.

Other

Richard III and Macbeth...: A Dramatic Study. London, Simpkin Marshall, 1877.

Recollections of Dante Gabriel Rossetti. London, Stock, 1882; Boston, Roberts, 1883; revised edition, London, Cassell, 1928.

Cobwebs of Criticism. London, Stock, 1883; New York, Dutton, 1908.

Life of Samuel Taylor Coleridge. London, Scott, 1887; New York, Scribner, n.d.

The Prophet: A Parable. London, Heinemann, 1890.

The Little Manx Nation. London, Heinemann, and New York, United States Book Company, 1891.

Mary Magdalene: The New Apocrypha. Privately printed, 1891.

The Little Man Island: Scenes and Specimen Days in the Isle-of-Man. Douglas, Steam Packet Company, 1894.

My Story. London, Heinemann, 1908; New York, Appleton, 1909.

Why I Wrote "The White Prophet." Privately printed, 1909.

King Edward: A Prince and a Great Man. London, Collier, 1910.

The Drama of Three Hundred Sixty Five Days: Scenes in the Great War. London, Heinemann, and Philadelphia, Lippincott, 1915.

Our Girls: Their Work for the War. London, Hutchinson, 1916.

Life of Christ, edited by Sir Derwent Hall Caine. London, Collins, and New York, Doubleday, 1938.

Editor, *Sonnets of Three Centuries*. London, Stock, 1882; Boston, Clarke, 1883.

Editor, *King Albert's Book: A Tribute to the Belgian King and People*. London, Daily Telegraph, 1914.

*   *   *

Hall Caine was one of the great names of popular fiction at the turn of the century and continued to be so for three decades afterwards. He mingled with the great, was championed by other writers and poets of the time, fought vociferously for the cause of the one-volume (as against the cumbersome three-volume) novel in order that cheaper and more manageable fiction, including his own, could reach a wider public. Thus, his enthusiastic readership included not only the highly literate, but the great uneducated masses. He wrote with moral passion on great and noble subjects and saw himself as "the Shakespeare of the novel." With the decline of religious authority, it seemed necessary for writers such as he to take on themselves the mammoth task of maintaining among the reading masses the moral standards which he felt to be lacking. Today, 50 years after his death, his name is almost forgotten. What is astonishing is that a writer who was so pretentious, so self-important, and whose skill was so inadequate for the task he set himself should have ever been taken seriously in the first place.

The most popular of his 20th-century novels was *The Woman of Knockaloe*, set, like many, on the Isle of Man. He was a pacifist for most of his life, and this romance, written shortly after the end of the First World War telling of the forbidden and unacceptable love between a Manxwoman and a German prisoner-of-war, is an impassioned anti-war cry. As Claud Cockburn pointed out in *Best Seller*, the Great War, for all its horror, provided excellent literary food for the popular writers. It was "a gift, a natural, manna from heaven. It furnished him with a range of fictional and dramatic equipment such as had been ready to hand in the workshops of the Greek classical dramatists."

The noble intentions of the author of *The Woman of Knockaloe*, the fine motives of his driving force, the proper care to try to end all future war by the power of his pen, contrast strongly with the banality of treatment. The love between Mona and Oskar is necessarily furtive, but utterly pure. Their affair is hopelessly doomed from the start, for the rest of the world is against them. They are driven to a mutual suicide pact. At dawn, they climb a heather-clad mountain to make their love leap from the top, to the "heaving and singing" sea below. They agree that their leap must be simultaneous, so, as in some ludicrous charade, they solemnly strap themselves together with Oskar's long coat belt. "They are now eye to eye, breast to breast, heart to heart."

Hall Caine's lifelong enemy was the equally popular romantic novelist, Marie Corelli, whose own first novel he had turned down for publication. She, too, believed herself to be a Shakespeare of the prose form. They had much in common. Q.D. Leavis, in *Fiction and the Reading Public*, said that their novels "make play with the key words of the emotional vocabulary which provoke the vague warm surges of feeling associated with religion and religion substitutes—e.g., life, death, love, good, evil, sin, home, mother, noble, gallant, purity, honour. These responses can be touched off with a dangerous ease."

—Rachel Anderson

CAIRD, Janet (Hinshaw). British. Born in Livingstonia, Malawi, 24 April 1913. Educated at Dollar Academy, Clackmannan; Edinburgh University, 1931-35, M.A. (honours) in English literature 1935; University of Grenoble and the Sorbonne, Paris (Stevenson Exchange Scholar), 1935-36; St. George's Training College, Edinburgh, 1936-37. Married James Bowman Caird in 1938; two daughters. English and Latin teacher, Park School for Girls, Glasgow, 1937-38, Royal High School, Edinburgh, 1940-41, and Dollar Academy, 1941-43. Agent: A.M. Heath & Co. Ltd., 40-42 William IV Street, London WC2N 4DD, England. Address: 1 Drummond Crescent, Inverness IV2 4QW, Scotland.

ROMANCE AND GOTHIC PUBLICATIONS

Novels

    Murder Reflected. London, Bles, 1965; as *In a Glass Darkly*, New York, Morrow, 1966.
    Perturbing Spirit. London, Bles, and New York, Doubleday, 1966.
    Murder Scholastic. London, Bles, 1967; New York, Doubleday, 1968.
    The Loch. London, Bles, 1968; New York, Doubleday, 1969.

Murder Remote. New York, Doubleday, 1973; as *The Shrouded Way*, New York, New
American Library, 1973.
The Umbrella-Maker's Daughter. London, Macmillan, and New York, St. Martin's
Press, 1980.

OTHER PUBLICATIONS

Verse

Some Walk a Narrow Path. Edinburgh, Ramsay Head Press, 1977.

Other

Angus the Tartan Partan (juvenile). London, Nelson, 1961.

Manuscript Collection: Mugar Memorial Library, Boston University.

*   *   *

Janet Caird's particular gift is for creating an atmosphere of menace. Her stories are set in
small towns in Scotland, and the intense, inbred relationships of village life are minutely
observed.

In her first mystery, *Murder Reflected*, the heroine, looking through the town's camera
obscura, observes murder being done. As she is unable to keep this fact secret, several other
murders follow, and her own life is endangered. The heroine is unnecessarily silly, but the other
characters are both interesting and well-developed. *Murder Scholastic* involves blackmail and
murder at a Scottish academy. There's an especially brilliant, nightmarish scene in which weird
masked figures skate in flickering firelight, the villain and heroine among them in a cat-and-
mouse chase. In *Perturbing Spirit* Caird's gift for the eerie and theatrical shows itself again as a
village festival is taken over by a mysterious stranger who invests it with the trappings of
ancient, sacrificial religions while he attempts to use it for his own sinister purposes. In *The
Loch* the lake itself has always been an object of superstitious awe for the villagers of Lochie, an
awe which increases when the loch floods the town and then recedes into nothing, exposing
caves tenanted by a pre-Celtic people. Tragedy is inevitable from the moment rumors circulate
of treasure hidden in the cave. In *Murder Remote* unscrupulous men in search of treasure
commit murder and hold an entire isolated village hostage. *The Umbrella-Maker's Daughter* is
by far her best book, and is in fact genuine literature. The umbrella-maker's daughter is an
outsider in a community normally suspicious of outsiders. But when disaster hits the town,
normal standards of behavior lapse, and unfocused feelings of rage and despair find a vicious
outlet.

Romance is present in all these novels, but it is the least satisfactory element because Caird's
heroes and heroines fail to involve the reader; subsidiary characters are often fascinating, but
her heroines are boring. One reads Caird less for the romance than for the gothic atmosphere
she draws so well.

—Marylaine Block

CALDWELL, (Janet Miriam) Taylor (Holland).   Also writes as Max Reiner.   American.
Born in Prestwich, Manchester, England, 7 September 1900. Educated at the University of
Buffalo, now State University of New York, A.B. 1931. Served in the United States Naval
Reserve, 1918-19. Married 1) William Fairfax Combs in 1919 (divorced, 1931), one daughter;
2) Marcus Reback in 1931 (died, 1970), one daughter; 3) William E. Stancell in 1972 (divorced,
1973); 4) William Robert Prestie in 1978. Court Reporter, New York State Department of
Labor, Buffalo, 1923-24; Member of the Board of Special Inquiry, Department of Justice,
Buffalo, 1924-31. Recipient: Buffalo *Evening News* award, 1949; Grand Prix Chatrain, 1956.
D.Litt.: D'Youville College, Buffalo, 1964; St. Bonaventure College, New York, 1977. Address:
Ivanhoe Lane, Greenwich, Connecticut 06830, U.S.A.

ROMANCE AND GOTHIC PUBLICATIONS

Novels

> *Dynasty of Death.*   New York, Scribner, 1938; London, Collins, 1939.
> *The Eagles Gather.*   New York, Scribner, and London, Collins, 1940.
> *Time No Longer* (as Max Reiner).   New York, Scribner, 1941.
> *The Earth Is the Lord's.*   New York, Scribner, and London, Collins, 1941.
> *The Strong City.*   New York, Scribner, and London, Collins, 1942.
> *The Arm and the Darkness.*   New York, Scribner, and London, Collins, 1943.
> *The Turnbulls.*   New York, Scribner, 1943; London, Collins, 1944.
> *The Final Hour.*   New York, Scribner, 1944; London, Collins, 1945.
> *The Wide House.*   New York, Scribner, 1945; London, Collins, 1946.
> *This Side of Innocence.*   New York, Scribner, 1946; London, Collins, 1947.
> *There Was a Time.*   New York, Scribner, 1947; London, Collins, 1948.
> *Melissa.*   New York, Scribner, 1948; London, Collins, 1949.
> *Let Love Come Last.*   New York, Scribner, 1948; London, Collins, 1950.
> *The Balance Wheel.*   New York, Scribner, 1951; as *The Beautiful Is Vanished*, London,
>   Collins, 1951.
> *The Devil's Advocate.*   New York, Crown, 1952.
> *Maggie, Her Marriage.*   New York, Fawcett, 1953; London, Muller, 1954.
> *Never Victorious, Never Defeated.*   New York, McGraw Hill, and London, Collins,
>   1954.
> *Your Sins and Mine.*   New York, Fawcett, 1955; London, Muller, 1956.
> *Tender Victory.*   New York, McGraw Hill, and London, Collins, 1956.
> *The Sound of Thunder.*   New York, Doubleday, 1957; London, Collins, 1958.
> *Dear and Glorious Physician.*   New York, Doubleday, and London, Collins, 1959.
> *The Listener.*   New York, Doubleday, 1960; as *The Man Who Listens*, London, Collins,
>   1961.
> *A Prologue to Love.*   New York, Doubleday, 1961; London, Collins, 1962.
> *Grandmother and the Priests.*   New York, Doubleday, 1963; as *To See the Glory*,
>   London, Collins, 1963.
> *The Late Clare Beame.*   New York, Doubleday, 1963; London, Collins, 1964.
> *A Pillar of Iron.*   New York, Doubleday, 1965; London, Collins, 1966.
> *Wicked Angel.*   New York, Fawcett, 1965; London, Coronet, 1966.
> *No One Hears But Him.*   New York, Doubleday, and London, Collins, 1966.
> *Testimony of Two Men.*   New York, Doubleday, 1968; London, Collins, 1969.
> *Great Lion of God.*   New York, Doubleday, and London, Collins, 1970.
> *Captains and the Kings.*   New York, Doubleday, 1972; London, Collins, 1973.
> *Glory and the Lightning.*   New York, Doubleday, 1974; London, Collins, 1975.
> *To Look and Pass.*   London, White Lion, 1974.
> *The Romance of Atlantis*, with Jess Stearn.   New York, Morrow, 1975; London, Fon-
>   tana, 1976.
> *Ceremony of the Innocent.*   New York, Doubleday, 1976; London, Collins, 1977.

I, Judas, with Jess Stearn.   New York, Atheneum, 1977; London, New English Library, 1978.
Bright Flows the River.   New York, Doubleday, 1978; London, Collins, 1979.
Answer As a Man.   New York, Putnam, and London, Collins, 1981.

OTHER PUBLICATIONS

Other

Dialogues with the Devil.   New York, Doubleday, 1967; London, Collins, 1968.
On Growing Up Tough.   Old Greenwich, Connecticut, Devin Adair, 1971; as *Growing Up Tough*, London, Stacey, 1971.

Critical Study: *In Search of Taylor Caldwell* by Jess Stearn, New York, Stein and Day, 1981.

*   *   *

Taylor Caldwell's long list of successes as a popular author began only in 1938 with the wide acceptance of her first published novel. However, her interest in writing has been life-long; she completed her first novel at 12. Caldwell's published works reflect her views and wide-ranging interests. They include historical novels in settings as disparate as ancient Greece and Rome and Richelieu's France; Biblical novels interpreting the events and figures of the Gospels; one detective tale; and novels which discuss the author's religious views. However, Caldwell's most characteristic works, best selling and critically acclaimed, are her epic novels about the growth and influence of American political and industrial dynasties and the lives and loves of the families that comprise them. The continuing appeal of these long, complex, and often didactic works lies in their evaluation of the American Dream in terms of domestic and moral values. In over 20 novels of monumental scope and length, Caldwell demonstrates that the glamor, prestige, and beauty of the social elite must be governed by the moral values of the home if it is to be a meaningful or happy world for the people who inhabit it. In Caldwell's fiction, women's love as wives and mothers provides the basis for the moral continuity her industrialist heroes too often ignore or reject.

Caldwell's first novel, *Dynasty of Death*, and its two sequels, *The Eagles Gather* and *The Final Hour*, develop the saga of two French-American families, the Barbours and the Bouchards, whose power in the armaments industry can shape world policy and economics, elect and defeat presidents, and begin and end world wars in the interests of family wealth and influence. The marriages between the 52 members of the Barbour and Bouchard clan become political alliances, often loveless, often betrayed, and producing an increasingly refined line of American aristocrats, absorbed in their own superiority and power. The absolute power of the Barbour/Bouchard dynasty ends as the last scion admits, however grudgingly, the merits of democracy, forces the members of his clan to support the American effort against Nazi Germany, and marries for love, amid plots, counterplots, adultery, heartbreak, and scandal.

Caldwell's powerful industrialists are typically self-made men of pronounced ethnic background; the heroes of *The Strong City* and *The Balance Wheel*, for example, are German immigrants. In addition, Caldwell's novels tend to trace the fortunes of the families they discuss through more than one generation, like the Irish political dynasty of *Captains and the Kings*. Favorite Caldwell themes are ethnic, religious, and personal intolerance (*The Wide House*), the failure of parental discipline (*Let Love Come Last*), and the conflict between the desire for power and money and the humane values of love, marital love, parental love, and Christian *caritas* (*Melissa, A Prologue to Love, Bright Flows the River, Answer As a Man*). The victories Caldwell grants love and virtue over greed, self-indulgence, and decadence are few and reserved. She parallels the conflict between power and action to love and contemplation in ancient times to the same conflict in the 19th and 20th centuries: the Post-Industrial Age is inevitably the moral loser. Caldwell's good and generous women suffer; her self-made men are consumed morally and spiritually by selfish delusions, blighting the larger world they themselves consume.

Despite her gloomy themes, wordy and often platitudinous prose, and stylised characterisation, Caldwell is an expert storyteller who plays on themes popular with readers, especially with women readers, since the popularity of the domestic novel of the 19th century. In Caldwell's fiction, women represent the good, even if they must suffer for it; sexuality and sexual purity represent personal power; money, the root of all evil, is a masculine addition; harmonious relations between the generations are the duty and the reward of mothers; and powerful dynasties must be based on convoluted conspiracies and moral seduction. Caldwell adapts her formula to a variety of painstakingly researched American settings and periods, and her novels, despite their slow development, carefully evoke time and place. Most important, and most fascinating to Caldwell's mass audience, she presents the equally glamorous and repellent world of the American Dream, a world in which women are, although not politically powerful without men, at least moral victors in their own right.

—Katherine Staples

CAMPBELL, Karen. *See* **BEATY, Betty.**

CARR, Philippa. *See* **HOLT, Victoria.**

CARR, Roberta. *See* **ROBERTS, Irene.**

CARR, Robyn.   American.   Born in St. Paul, Minnesota. Married; two children. Address: c/o Little, Brown and Company, 34 Beacon Street, Boston, Massachusetts 02106, U.S.A.

ROMANCE AND GOTHIC PUBLICATIONS

Novels

    Chelynne.   Boston, Little Brown, 1980.
    The Blue Falcon.   Boston, Little Brown, 1981.
    The Bellerose Bargain.   Boston, Little Brown, 1982.

*   *   *

A relative newcomer to the field of historical romances, Robyn Carr is still difficult to assess. Her two novels *Chelynne* and *The Blue Falcon* vary widely in many aspects including the success of the final results.

Chelynne, set in Restoration England, offers a rather intricate plot and well-developed, likeable characters. Chelynne, a young innocent, marries Chadwick Hawthorne as arranged by her uncle. Ready to love her husband, she is instead rejected by him, and the marriage remains unconsummated. This unhappy state of affairs is exacerbated by a mystery from Chad's past, Chelynne's possible relationship with King Charles II, and various minor characters who keep the waters of the plot well stirred and muddied.

In *The Blue Falcon* Carr turns to the England of King Richard and the Crusaders to tell the story of two lovers, Conan and Chandra, and three families driven apart and manipulated by the scheming of Conan's mother, Lady Udele. Again Carr has created many characters to people her story, but she is much less successful in developing them and in keeping their various stories intertwined. The characters are stiff and their dialogue is stilted, as if Carr is not truly at home in this period of history. The narrative is not smooth and much of the story is devoted to scenes and speeches of renunciation by Conan and Chandra. Things do pick up when Lady Udele is plotting and causing trouble and when Conan finally returns from the Crusades, but all in all the pace is rather slow. Even the inclusion of a hint of the occult in the person of the clairvoyant Giselle does not succeed. Carr cannot seem to make up her mind to believe in her own creation here and fails fully to exploit the possibilities.

Robyn Carr clearly has the potentiality to develop into one of the better writers of historical romances. Yet until she has produced more works upon which to base a judgement, her significance in the field will remain minor.

—Barbara Kemp

CARTLAND, Barbara (Hamilton).   Also wrote as Barbara McCorquodale.   British.   Educated at Malvern Girls' College; Abbey House, Netley Abbey, Hampshire. Married 1) Alexander George McCorquodale in 1927 (divorced, 1933), one daughter; 2) Hugh McCorquodale in 1936 (died, 1963), two sons. Free-lance writer since 1925. Honorary Junior Commander, Auxiliary Territorial Service, and Bedfordshire Welfare Officer and Librarian, 1941-49; Bedfordshire Cadet Officer, St. John Ambulance Brigade, 1943-47, and County Vice-President Cadets, 1948-50; Hertfordshire Vice-President, Nursing Cadets, 1951; Hertfordshire Chairman, St. John Council; County Councillor, Hertfordshire, 1955-64; President, Hertfordshire branch of Royal College of Midwives, 1957. Editor, Library of Love series. Vice-President, Romantic Novelists Association and Oxfam; President, National Association of Health, 1966. Certificate of Merit, Eastern Command, 1946; Dame of Grace, St. John of Jerusalem. Address: Camfield Place, Hatfield, Hertfordshire, England.

ROMANCE AND GOTHIC PUBLICATIONS

Novels

> *Jig-Saw.* London, Duckworth, 1925.
> *Sawdust.* London, Duckworth, 1926.
> *If the Tree Is Saved.* London, Duckworth, 1929.
> *For What?* London, Hutchinson, 1930.
> *Sweet Punishment.* London, Hutchinson, 1931; New York Pyramid, 1973.
> *A Virgin in Mayfair.* London, Hutchinson, 1932.
> *Just Off Piccadilly.* London, Hutchinson, 1933.
> *Not Love Alone.* London, Hutchinson, 1933.
> *A Beggar Wished....* London, Hutchinson, 1934.
> *Passionate Attachment.* London, Hutchinson, 1935.
> *First Class, Lady?* London, Hutchinson, 1935.
> *Dangerous Experiment.* London, Hutchinson, 1936; as *Search for Love*, New York, Greenberg, 1937.
> *Desperate Defiance.* London, Hutchinson, 1936.
> *The Forgotten City.* London, Hutchinson, 1936.
> *Saga at Forty.* London, Hutchinson, 1937.
> *But Never Free.* London, Hutchinson, 1937; as *The Adventurer*, London, Arrow, 1977.
> *Broken Barriers.* London, Hutchinson, 1938.
> *Bitter Winds.* London, Hutchinson, 1938.
> *The Gods Forget.* London, Hutchinson, 1939.
> *The Black Panther.* London, Rich and Cowan, 1939.
> *Stolen Halo.* London, Rich and Cowan, 1940; New York, Pyramid, 1973.
> *Now Rough—Now Smooth.* London, Hutchinson, 1941.
> *Open Wings.* London, Hutchinson, 1942.
> *The Leaping Flame.* •London, Hale, 1942.
> *The Dark Stream.* London, Hutchinson, 1944.
> *After the Night.* London, Hutchinson, 1944; as *Towards the Stars*, London, Arrow, 1971.
> *Yet She Follows.* London, Hale, 1944; as *A Heart Is Broken*, 1972.
> *Escape from Passion.* London, Hale, 1945.
> *Armour Against Love.* London, Hutchinson, 1945; New York, Pyramid, 1974.
> *Out of Reach.* London, Hutchinson, 1945.
> *The Hidden Heart.* London, Hutchinson, 1946; New York, Pyramid, 1970.
> *Against the Stream.* London, Hutchinson, 1946.
> *The Dream Within.* London, Hutchinson, 1947.
> *If We Will.* London, Hutchinson, 1947; as *Where Is Love?*, London, Arrow, 1971.
> *Against This Rapture.* London, Hutchinson, 1947.
> *No Heart Is Free.* London, Rich and Cowan, 1948.
> *A Hazard of Hearts.* London, Rich and Cowan, 1949; New York, Pyramid, 1969.
> *The Enchanted Moment.* London, Rich and Cowan, 1949.
> *A Duel of Hearts.* London, Rich and Cowan, 1949; New York, Pyramid, 1970.
> *The Knave of Hearts.* London, Rich and Cowan, 1950; New York, Pyramid, 1971.
> *The Little Pretender.* London, Rich and Cowan, 1951; New York, Pyramid, 1971.
> *Love Is an Eagle.* London, Rich and Cowan, 1951.
> *A Ghost in Monte Carlo.* London, Rich and Cowan, 1951.
> *Love Is the Enemy.* London, Rich and Cowan, 1952; New York, Pyramid, 1970.
> *Cupid Rides Pillion.* London, Hutchinson, 1952.

Elizabethan Lover. London, Hutchinson, 1953; New York, Pyramid, 1971.
Love Me for Ever. London, Hutchinson, 1953; as *Love Me Forever*, New York, Pyramid, 1970.
Desire of the Heart. London, Hutchinson, 1954; New York, Pyramid, 1969.
The Enchanted Waltz. London, Hutchinson, 1955; New York, Pyramid, 1971.
The Kiss of the Devil. London, Hutchinson, 1955.
The Captive Heart. London, Hutchinson, 1956; New York, Pyramid, 1970.
The Coin of Love. London, Hutchinson, 1956; New York, Pyramid, 1969.
Sweet Adventure. London, Hutchinson, 1957; New York, Pyramid, 1970.
Stars in My Heart. London, Hutchinson, 1957; New York, Pyramid, 1971.
The Golden Gondola. London, Hutchinson, 1958; New York, Pyramid, 1971.
Love in Hiding. London, Hutchinson, 1959; New York, Pyramid, 1969.
The Smuggled Heart. London, Hutchinson, 1959.
Love under Fire. London, Hutchinson, 1960.
Messenger of Love. London, Hutchinson, 1961; New York, Pyramid, 1971.
The Wings of Love. London, Hutchinson, 1962; New York, Pyramid, 1971.
The Hidden Evil. London, Hutchinson, 1963; New York, Pyramid, 1971.
The Fire of Love. London, Hutchinson, 1964; New York, Avon, 1970.
The Unpredictable Bride. London, Hutchinson, 1964; New York, Pyramid, 1969.
Love Holds the Cards. London, Hutchinson, 1965; New York, Pyramid, 1970.
A Virgin in Paris. London, Hutchinson, 1966; New York, Pyramid, 1971.
Love to the Rescue. London, Hutchinson, 1967; New York, Pyramid, 1970.
Love Is Contraband. London, Hutchinson, 1968; New York, Pyramid, 1970.
The Enchanting Evil. London, Hutchinson, 1968; New York, Pyramid, 1969.
The Unknown Heart. London, Hutchinson, 1969; New York, Pyramid, 1971.
Debt of Honor. New York, Pyramid, 1970.
Innocent Heiress. New York, Pyramid, 1970.
Lost Love. New York, Pyramid, 1970.
The Reluctant Bride. London, Hutchinson, 1970.
The Royal Pledge. New York, Pyramid, 1970.
The Secret Fear. London, Hutchinson, 1970; New York, Pyramid, 1971.
The Secret Heart. New York, Pyramid, 1970.
The Pretty Horse-Breakers. London, Hutchinson, 1971.
The Queen's Messenger. New York, Pyramid, 1971.
Stars in Her Eyes. New York, Pyramid, 1971.
Innocent in Paris. New York, Pyramid, 1971.
The Audacious Adventuress. London, Hutchinson, 1971; New York, Pyramid, 1972.
A Halo for the Dead. London, Arrow, 1972.
The Irresistible Buck. London, Arrow, 1972.
The Complacent Wife. London, Hutchinson, 1972.
Lost Enchantment. London, Hutchinson, 1972; New York, Pyramid, 1973.
The Odious Duke. London, Arrow, 1973.
The Little Adventure. London, Hutchinson, 1973; New York, Bantam, 1974.
The Daring Deception. London, Arrow, 1973.
The Wicked Marquis. London, Hutchinson, 1973; New York, Bantam, 1974.
No Darkness for Love. London, Hutchinson, and New York, Bantam, 1974.
The Ruthless Rake. London, Pan, and New York, Bantam, 1974.
The Glittering Lights. New York, Bantam, 1974; London, Corgi, 1975.
A Sword to the Heart. New York, Bantam, 1974; London, Corgi, 1975.
The Penniless Peer. London, Pan, and New York, Bantam, 1974.
The Magnificent Marriage. London, Corgi, 1974; New York, Bantam, 1975.
Lessons in Love. London, Arrow, and New York, Bantam, 1974.
The Karma of Love. London, Corgi, 1974; New York, Bantam, 1975.
The Bored Bridegroom. London, Pan, and New York, Bantam, 1974.
The Castle of Fear. London, Pan, and New York, Bantam, 1974.
The Cruel Count. London, Pan, 1974; New York, Bantam, 1975.
The Dangerous Dandy. London, Pan, and New York, Bantam, 1974.
Journey to Paradise. London, Arrow, and New York, Bantam, 1974.

Call of the Heart. London, Pan, and New York, Bantam, 1975.
Love Is Innocent. London, Hutchinson, and New York, Bantam, 1975.
Shadow of Sin. London, Corgi, 1975.
Bewitched. London, Corgi, and New York, Bantam, 1975.
The Devil in Love. London, Corgi, and New York, Bantam, 1975.
Fire on the Snow. London, Hutchinson, 1975; New York, Bantam, 1976.
The Flame Is Love. London, Pan, 1975.
Food for Love. London, Corgi, 1975.
The Frightened Bride. London, Pan, and New York, Bantam, 1975.
The Impetuous Duchess. London, Corgi, and New York, Bantam, 1975.
The Mask of Love. London, Corgi, and New York, Bantam, 1975.
The Tears of Love. London, Corgi, and New York, Bantam, 1975.
A Very Naughty Angel. London, Pan, and New York, Bantam, 1975.
An Arrow of Love. London, Pan, 1975; New York, Bantam, 1976.
As Eagles Fly. London, Pan, and New York, Bantam, 1975.
A Frame of Dreams. London, Pan, 1975; New York, Bantam, 1976.
A Gamble with Hearts. London, Pan, 1975; New York, Bantam, 1976.
A Kiss for the King. London, Pan, 1975; New York, Bantam, 1976.
Say Yes, Samantha. London, Pan, and New York, Bantam, 1975.
The Elusive Earl. London, Hutchinson, and New York, Bantam, 1976.
The Blue-Eyed Witch. London, Hutchinson, 1976.
An Angel in Hell. London, Pan, 1976.
The Bitter Winds of Love. London, Arrow, 1976; New York, Jove, 1978.
A Dream from the Night. London, Corgi, and New York, Bantam, 1976.
Fragrant Flower. London, Pan, and New York, Bantam, 1976.
The Golden Illusion. London, Pan, and New York, Bantam, 1976.
The Heart Triumphant. London, Corgi, 1976.
Hungry for Love. London, Corgi, 1976.
The Husband Hunters. London, Pan, and New York, Bantam, 1976.
The Incredible Honeymoon. London, Pan, and New York, Bantam, 1976.
Love and Linda. London, Arrow, 1976.
Moon over Eden. London, Pan, and New York, Bantam, 1976.
Never Laugh at Love. London, Corgi, 1976.
No Time for Love. London, Pan, and New York, Bantam, 1976.
Passions in the Sand. London, Pan, and New York, Bantam, 1976.
The Proud Princess. London, Corgi, 1976.
A Rainbow to Heaven. London, Arrow, 1976.
The Secret of the Glen. London, Corgi, 1976.
The Slaves of Love. London, Pan, 1976.
The Wild Cry of Love. London, Pan, 1976.
The Disgraceful Duke. London, Corgi, 1976.
The Mysterious Maid-Servant. London, Hutchinson, 1977.
The Dragon and the Pearl. London, Hutchinson, and Williamsport, Pennsylvania, Duron, 1977.
Conquered by Love. London, Pan, 1977.
The Curse of the Clan. London, Pan, and Williamsport, Pennsylvania, Duron, 1977.
Dance on My Heart. London, Arrow, 1977.
The Dream and the Glory. London, Pan, 1977.
A Duel with Destiny. London, Corgi, 1977.
Kiss the Moonlight. London, Pan, 1977.
Look, Listen, and Love. London, Pan, and Williamsport, Pennsylvania, Duron, 1977.
Love at Forty. London, Arrow, 1977.
Love in Pity. London, Arrow, 1977.
Love Locked In. London, Pan, and New York, Dutton, 1977.
The Magic of Love. London, Pan, 1977.
The Marquis Who Hated Women. London, Pan, and Williamsport, Pennsylvania, Duron, 1977.
The Outrageous Lady. London, Pan, and Williamsport, Pennsylvania, Duron, 1977.

The Sign of Love. Williamsport, Pennsylvania, Duron, 1977; London, Pan, 1978.
A Rhapsody of Love. London, Pan, 1977.
The Taming of Lady Lorinda. London, Pan, 1977.
This Time It's Love. London, Arrow, 1977; New York, Jove, 1979.
Vote for Love. London, Corgi, 1977.
The Wild, Unwilling Wife. London, Pan, and New York, Dutton, 1977.
The Love Pirate. Williamsport, Pennsylvania, Duron, 1977; London, Corgi, 1978.
Punishment of a Vixen. Williamsport, Pennsylvania, Duron, and London, Corgi, 1977.
A Touch of Love. Williamsport, Pennsylvania, Duron, 1977; London, Corgi, 1978.
The Temptation of Torilla. Williamsport, Pennsylvania, Duron, 1977; London, Corgi, 1978.
Love and the Loathsome Leopard. Williamsport, Pennsylvania, Duron, 1977; London, Corgi, 1978.
The Hell-Cat and the King. Williamsport, Pennsylvania, Duron, 1977; London, Pan, 1978.
No Escape from Love. Williamsport, Pennsylvania, Duron, 1977; London, Corgi, 1978.
The Saint and the Sinner. Williamsport, Pennsylvania, Duron, 1977; London, Corgi, 1978.
The Naked Battle. Williamsport, Pennsylvania, Duron, 1977; London, Hutchinson, 1978.
Love Leaves at Midnight. London, Hutchinson, and Williamsport, Pennsylvania, Duron, 1978.
The Passion and the Flower. London, Pan, and New York, Dutton, 1978.
Love, Lords, and Lady-Birds. London, Pan, and New York, Dutton, 1978.
A Fugitive from Love. London, Pan, and Williamsport, Pennsylvania, Duron, 1978.
The Problems of Love. London, Corgi, and Williamsport, Pennsylvania, Duron, 1978.
The Twists and Turns of Love. London, Arrow, and Williamsport, Pennsylvania, Duron, 1978.
Magic or Mirage. London, Corgi, and Williamsport, Pennsylvania, Duron, 1978.
The Ghost Who Fell in Love. London, Pan, and New York, Dutton, 1978.
The Chieftain Without a Heart. London, Corgi, and New York, Dutton, 1978.
Lord Ravenscar's Revenge. London, Corgi, and Williamsport, Pennsylvania, Duron, 1978.
A Runaway Star. London, Pan, and Williamsport, Pennsylvania, Duron, 1978.
A Princess in Distress. London, Pan, and Williamsport, Pennsylvania, Duron, 1978.
The Judgement of Love. Williamsport, Pennsylvania, Duron, 1978; London, Hutchinson, 1979.
Lovers in Paradise. Williamsport, Pennsylvania, Duron, 1978; London, Pan, 1979.
The Race for Love. Williamsport, Pennsylvania, Duron, 1978; London, Corgi, 1979.
Flowers for the God of Love. London, Pan, 1978; New York, Dutton, 1979.
The Irresistible Force. London, Arrow, and Williamsport, Pennsylvania, Duron, 1978.
Alone in Paris. London, Arrow, 1978; Williamsport, Pennsylvania, Duron, 1979.
Love in the Dark. London, Hutchinson, and Williamsport, Pennsylvania, Duron, 1979.
The Duke and the Preacher's Daughter. London, Corgi, and Williamsport, Pennsylvania, Duron, 1979.
The Drums of Love. London, Pan, and Williamsport, Pennsylvania, Duron, 1979.
The Prince and the Pekingese. London, Pan, and Williamsport, Pennsylvania, Duron, 1979.
A Serpent of Satan. London, Pan, and Williamsport, Pennsylvania, Duron, 1979.
Love in the Clouds. London, Corgi, and New York, Dutton, 1979.
The Treasure Is Love. London, Arrow, and Williamsport, Pennsylvania, Duron, 1979.
Imperial Splendour. London, Pan, and New York, Dutton, 1979.
Light of the Moon. London, Pan, and Williamsport, Pennsylvania, Duron, 1979.
The Prisoner of Love. London, Arrow, and Williamsport, Pennsylvania, Duron, 1979.
The Duchess Disappeared. London, Pan, and Williamsport, Pennsylvania, Duron, 1979.
Love Climbs In. London, Corgi, and Williamsport, Pennsylvania, Duron, 1979.
A Nightingale Sang. London, Corgi, and Williamsport, Pennsylvania, Duron, 1979.

Terror in the Sun. London, Pan, and New York, Bantam, 1979.
Who Can Deny Love? London, Corgi, and Williamsport, Pennsylvania, Duron, 1979.
Bride to the King. London, Corgi, 1979; New York, Dutton, 1980.
Only Love. London, Arrow, 1979; New York, Bantam, 1980.
The Dawn of Love. London, Corgi, 1979; New York, Dutton, 1980.
Love Has His Way. London, Corgi, 1979; New York, Dutton, 1980.
A Gentleman in Love. London, Pan, 1979.
Women Have Hearts. London, Pan, 1979; New York, Bantam, 1980.
The Explosion of Love. London, Hutchinson, 1980.
A Heart Is Stolen. London, Corgi, 1980.
The Power and the Prince. London, Pan, 1980.
Free From Fear. London, Pan, and New York, Bantam, 1980.
A Song of Love. London, Pan, and New York, Jove, 1980.
Love for Sale. London, Corgi, and New York, Dutton, 1980.
Little White Doves of Love. London, Pan, and New York, Bantam, 1980.
The Perfection of Love. London, Corgi, and New York, Bantam, 1980.
Lost Laughter. London, Pan, and New York, Dutton, 1980.
Punished with Love. London, Pan, and New York, Bantam, 1980.
Lucifer and the Angel. London, Hutchinson, 1980.
Ola and the Sea Wolf. London, Arrow, and New York, Bantam, 1980.
The Prude and the Prodigal. London, Pan, and New York, Bantam, 1980.
The Goddess and the Gaiety Girl. London, Pan, and New York, Bantam, 1980.
Signpost to Love. London, Corgi, 1980; New York, Bantam, 1981.
Money, Magic, and Marriage. London, Arrow, 1980.
Love in the Moon. London, New English Library, 1980.
Pride and the Poor Princess. London, Corgi, 1980.
The Waltz of Hearts. London, Pan, 1980.
From Hell to Heaven. New York, Bantam, 1981.
The Kiss of Life. London, Hutchinson, 1981.
Afraid. London, Arrow, 1981.
Dreams Do Come True. London, Pan, 1981.
In the Arms of Love. London, Hutchinson, 1981.
For All Eternity. New York, Jove, 1981.
Pure and Untouched. New York, Everest House, 1981.
Count the Stars. London, New English Library, 1981.

Novels as Barbara McCorquodale

Sleeping Swords. London, Hale, 1942.
Love Is Mine. London, Rich and Cowan, 1952; as Barbara Cartland, New York, Pyramid, 1972.
The Passionate Pilgrim. London, Rich and Cowan, 1952.
Blue Heather. London, Rich and Cowan, 1953.
Wings on My Heart. London, Rich and Cowan, 1954.
The Kiss of Paris. London, Rich and Cowan, 1956.
The Thief of Love. London, Jenkins, 1957.
Love Forbidden. London, Rich and Cowan, 1957.
Lights of Love. London, Jenkins, 1958; as Barbara Cartland, New York, Pyramid, 1973.
Sweet Enchantress. London, Jenkins, 1958.
A Kiss of Silk. London, Jenkins, 1959.
The Price Is Love. London, Jenkins, 1960.
The Runaway Heart. London, Jenkins, 1961.
A Light to the Heart. London, Ward Lock, 1962.
Love Is Dangerous. London, Ward Lock, 1963.
Danger by the Nile. London, Ward Lock, 1964.
Love on the Run. London, Ward Lock, 1965; as Barbara Cartland, New York, Pyramid, 1973.

Theft of the Heart.   London, Ward Lock, 1966.

OTHER PUBLICATIONS

Plays

Blood Money (produced London, 1925).
French Dressing, with Bruce Woodhouse (produced London, 1943).

Radio Plays: *The Rose and the Violet*, music by Mark Lubbock, 1942; *The Caged Bird*, 1957.

Verse

Lines on Life and Love.   London, Hutchinson, 1972.

Other

Touch the Stars: A Clue to Happiness.   London, Rider, 1935.
Ronald Cartland.   London, Collins, 1942; as *My Brother, Ronald*, London, Sheldon Press, 1980.
The Isthmus Years 1919-1939 (autobiography).   London, Hutchinson, 1943.
You—in the Home.   London, Standard Art, 1946.
The Years of Opportunity 1939-1945 (autobiography).   London, Hutchinson, 1948.
The Fascinating Forties: A Book for the Over-Forties.   London, Jenkins, 1954; revised edition, London, Corgi, 1973.
Marriage for Moderns.   London, Jenkins, 1955.
Bewitching Women.   London, Muller, 1955.
The Outrageous Queen: A Biography of Christina of Sweden.   London, Muller, 1956.
Polly—My Wonderful Mother.   London, Jenkins, 1956.
Be Vivid, Be Vital.   London, Jenkins, 1956.
Love, Life, and Sex.   London, Jenkins, 1957; revised edition, London, Corgi, 1973.
The Scandalous Life of King Carol.   London, Muller, 1957.
The Private Life of Charles II: The Women He Loved.   London, Muller, 1958.
Look Lovely, Be Lovely.   London, Jenkins, 1958.
Vitamins for Vitality.   London, Foyle, 1959.
The Private Life of Elizabeth, Empress of Austria.   London, Muller, 1959.
Husbands and Wives.   London, Barker, 1961; revised edition, as *Love and Marriage*, London, Thorsons, 1971.
Josephine, Empress of France.   London, Hutchinson, 1961.
Diane de Poitiers.   London, Hutchinson, 1962.
Etiquette Handbook.   London, Hamlyn, 1963; revised edition, as *Book of Etiquette*, London, Hutchinson, 1972.
The Many Facets of Love.   London, W.H. Allen, 1963.
Metternich, The Passionate Diplomat.   London, Hutchinson, 1964.
Sex and the Teenager.   London, Muller, 1964.
Living Together.   London, Muller, 1965.
The Pan Book of Charm.   London, Pan, 1965.
Woman: The Enigma.   London, Frewin, 1965.
I Search for the Rainbow 1946-1966 (autobiography).   London, Hutchinson, 1967.
The Youth Secret.   London, Corgi, 1968.
The Magic of Honey.   London, Corgi, 1970; revised edition, 1976.
We Danced All Night 1919-1929 (autobiography).   London, Hutchinson, 1970.
Health Food Cookery Book.   London, Hodder and Stoughton, 1971.

Book of Beauty and Health.   London, Hodder and Stoughton, 1972.
Men Are Wonderful.   London, Corgi, 1973.
Food for Love.   London, Corgi, 1975.
The Magic of Honey Cookbook.   London, Corgi, 1976.
Recipes for Lovers, with Nigel Gordon.   London, Corgi, 1977.
Book of Useless Information.   London, Corgi, 1977.
I Seek the Miraculous.   London, Sheldon Press, and New York, Dutton, 1978.
Book of Love and Lovers.   London, Joseph, 1978.
Love at the Helm (Mountbatten Memorial Trust volume).   London, Weidenfeld and
   Nicolson, 1980; New York, Everest House, 1981.
Romantic Royal Marriages.   New York, Beaufort, 1981.
Keep Young and Beautiful (selections), with Elinor Glyn.   London, Duckworth, 1982.

Editor, *The Common Problem*, by Ronald Cartland.   London, Hutchinson, 1943.
Editor, *The Light of Love: A Thought for Every Day*.   London, Sheldon Press, and New
   York, Elsevier Nelson, 1979.

Critical Study: *Barbara Cartland, Crusader in Pink* by Henry Cloud, London, Weidenfeld and
Nicolson, 1979.

*   *   *

It is a daunting task to assess the work of Barbara Cartland, whose prodigious output of
almost three hundred books, vast sales of over 100 million copies, and reputation as the Queen
of the Genre are overwhelming. Each branch of 20th-century English light fiction has its
phenomenon—and the achievements of Barbara Cartland are to romantic fiction what those of
Charles Hamilton ("Frank Richards") are to the school story, or those of Agatha Christie are to
detective fiction.

Her reputation as an unsurpassed contributor to the genre became established by the end of
the 1960's; since then she has gone from strength to strength and there seems no slackening in
the pace of her production of romantic stories. Still the innocent but exotically named
heroines—the Deloras, Magnolias, Darcias, and Udelas—flare into vivid and passionate life,
fresh from the Cartland typewriter or dictating-machine, and still they are avidly received by
millions of readers all over the world. The books, though one might have thought them a
peculiarly English caprice, have been translated into many languages. They are flagrantly
escapist and unconcerned with social issues; they are class-ridden and anti-feminist—the
apotheosis, in fact, of attitudes that are today condemned by trendy critics—but their success
speaks for itself. Barbara Cartland provides for her millions of loyal readers the confirmation
that romance is alive and well, even in our materialistic society, and that the individual is still
important, in this age of group-causes and group-lobbying and group-consciousness. Her
confidence in her beliefs is magnificent; her passion for the quintessential English gentleman or
aristocrat is idealistic but engaging; and her feelings for innocence, for the feminine aspects of
life, and for simple decency are deep-rooted and sincere.

In literary terms, of course, one can find flaws in the Cartland canon. Inevitably, in a writing
career that has spanned over half a century, she has established a formula on which she falls
back with increasing dependence. The more recent books have a facile quality, a carelessness,
which is not evident in her early works. The novels now are slim, and often issued immediately
in paper-back. They are unlikely to be preserved for posterity in the collections of public or
university libraries, although these institutions will almost certainly retain many of her earlier,
more substantial hard-backed novels. Her heroines, despite their distinctive and gloriously
feminine, romantic names, are, in fact, interchangeable and without individualization. Similarly, her heroes are now symbolic embodiments of masculine strength, magnetism, and
charisma rather than real human beings.

It is an intriguing exercise, however, to look back at Barbara Cartland's early novels, and to
savour their freshness, incisive and occasionally acerbic comments, and sheer storytelling skill.
One hopes that the author might one day pause in the production line of 20-plus novels every
year to read once again her own early books, and to create, from the vitality of these and the

light of her later expertise and experience of life one or two romances that will become Cartland classics for posterity.

Her first novel, *Jig-Saw*, has charm and conviction as well as an appropriate freshness. It starts on a spring day, with "excitements, sensations—all palpitating to be discovered," with "a poignancy in the atmosphere as a catch of breath before a tremendously thrilling experience...." *And* it is Paris, which abounds in the *gaité de coeur* for which the city is celebrated. Mona Vivien, as English as they come despite her "strikingly beautiful" resemblance to the "type beloved of Botticelli," is packing up after her last day as a pupil at a St. Cloud convent-school to return to London. She is on the tremulous threshold of young womanhood, which Cartland conveys so well. Back in Belgrave Square, life is "a fairy cinematograph...of hectic sensations," a cultural and social round which thrills Mona, and, of course, produces for her the young Marquis who turns out to be her true and upright love—despite the rival claims of his mysterious, fascinating and worldly half-brother, who one day whisks her off unchaperoned "to see the sunrise in a fairyland of silver birches." This turns out, rather prosaically perhaps to those who know its much-trodden picnic-littered paths, to be Wimbledon Common at dawn. But Barbara Cartland acknowledges the elusive quality of such magically romantic excursions when Mona reflects, on her return to Belgrave Square and disillusioning daytime brightness, that "Romance, criticised with the hideous sanity of breakfast-time, droops its wings and slinks away."

Nevertheless this, like the other early novels, has a reflective and lyrical quality that has sadly disappeared from the recent books. In *Jig-Saw*, for example, Mona's love of London, of poetry, and her joy and eagerness in new experiences come across with sensitivity and conviction. Innocence in the stories of the 1920's and 1930's was filled out and made persuasive by passionate questioning of the darker areas of life. Her heroines then were distinctive personalities who were, in a sympathetic and believable way, awakened to broader and deeper areas of experience, passion, and wonder by the heroes.

A look at the recent books shows that although this awakening through romance still continues for the leading Cartland ladies, it has settled firmly into a pattern. The dialogue at the end of each book is, one feels, interchangeable with that of any of the others. When Seldon, the handsome, aristocratic and arrogant Duke of Otterburn, and the American heiress Magnolia Vandevilt acknowledge their love, after a lot of time and languishing looks, at the end of *Dollars for the Duke* (1981), their final clinch predictably carries them "on waves of ecstasy into the starlit sky." At the end of *Love for Sale* (1980), another worldly-wise Duke and his innocent teenage beloved share a kiss which, she felt, "carried her up towards the stars that were now shining in the sky outside." And the heroines share the same tremulous, breathless, and ecstatic manner of speech: "I have...always wanted to...have your...children," says Darcia in a whisper at the end of *The Perfection of Love* (1980), while Udela husks in *Love for Sale*, "...when I have been awake in the darkness I have...pretended that you were...kissing me"; Magnolia caps it all in *Dollars for the Duke* by her whispered and wondering affirmation of passion: "I love...you and everything you do...will be perfect and...also...Divine."

Really, perhaps, it is greedy to ask more from Barbara Cartland than this superb romanticism—but one feels that she is capable of something very much more searching, sympathetic "and...also..." real.

—Mary Cadogan

CASE, David.   American.   Married. Full-time writer: has published some 300 works under pseudonyms. Has lived in England since 1960. Agent: Richard Curtis Associates Inc., 156 East 52nd Street, New York, New York, 10022, U.S.A. Address: 5 Slieu Curn, Kirk Michael, Isle of Man, United Kingdom.

ROMANCE AND GOTHIC PUBLICATIONS

Novels

    Fengriffen: A Chilling Tale.   New York, Hill and Wang, 1970.
    The Third Grave.   Sauk City, Wisconsin, Arkham House, 1981.

Short Stories

    The Cell: Three Tales of Horror.   New York, Hill and Wang, 1969; as *The Cell and Other Tales of Horror*, London, Macdonald, 1969.
    Fengriffin and Other Stories.   London, Macdonald, 1971; as *And Now the Screaming Starts*, London, Pan, 1973.
    Among the Wolves and Other Tales.   Sauk City, Wisconsin, Arkham House, 1982.

OTHER PUBLICATIONS

Novels

    Plumb Drillin'.   New York, Stein and Day, 1975; London, W.H. Allen, 1976; as *Gold Fever*, New York, Belmont, 1982.
    The Fighting Breed.   New York, Zebra, 1980.
    Wolf Tracks.   New York, Belmont, 1980.
    Guns of Valentine.   New York, Ace, 1982.

*   *   *

My first impression of Fengriffen House was skeletal. I saw it from the carriage, rising against a stormy sundown like the blackened bones of some monstrous beast—not the fragile, bleached bones of decaying man, but the massive, arched columns of a primordial saurian who had wandered to this desolate moor and there lay down and died, perhaps of loneliness, long ages before. The spires and towers loomed up in sharp silhouette and the structure squatted beneath, sunken but not cowed, crouched ready to spring, so that the house seemed to exist on two planes at the same time—massive and slender, bulky and light, gross and fragile. It was a building that had aged through a series of architectural blunders, and it was awesome....as I gazed upon this remarkable construction, I sensed a pervading evil, an adumbration of unholy darkness.... The wind was in the trees, playing a leitmotif behind the horses' clattering hooves. Perhaps it was the chill in the air that caused me to shiver....

The mood of David Case's *Fengriffen: A Chilling Tale* is set in this opening scene. Loneliness pervades. Leitmotives hover. Adumbrations loom. Readers shiver, caught up in such drama as one might expect from an experienced writer. Readers must be impressed also with the rococo overlay of profuse prose squatting on the classic Gothic plot.
    Fengriffen (marsh-monster?) tells the story of a beautiful young woman, Catherine Fen-

griffen. Her husband, Charles Fengriffen, has called in Doctor Pope, a young psychologist (psychology is the new field of scientific inquiry) to talk to Catherine and to determine the cause of her recent strange behavior. A man of science and hence a skeptic, Doctor Pope—who tells the tale—uncovers the Fengriffen Curse, a horrible superstition—or terrible truth?—that, like some "primordial saurian" holds Catherine—as it does all Fengriffen brides—in its chelate death grip. When her baby is born with the mark of the beast, Catherine leaps with the child from one of Fengriffen Manor's prisonous towers to the rocks below.

The "Three Tales of Horror" that comprise *The Cell*, Case's first work of Gothic fiction, are similarly adorned and equally chilling. "The Hunter," lurking in the dark moor of Dartmoor, is a monstrous creature who preys on solitary travelers and takes off—and takes off with—their heads. The title story, "The Cell," is another chiller, this time of lycanthropy (according to the *Oxford English Dictionary*, a kind of insanity in which the patient, imagining himself a wolf, exhibits all a wolf's instincts and propensities). The sombre theme of the final story, "The Dead End," is, as one may surmise, the end of the world.

Fengriffen, written in 1970, seems to mark the end of Case's Gothic world. Five years later, with *Plumb Drillin'*, and then in *The Fighting Breed* and *Wolf Tracks*, Case turns to the Wild West for inspiration and, possibly, relief. The settings change, as does the dialogue (" 'Kee-rist!' Dalton snorted."), but the winds over the desert—as Case so skillfully evokes them—are as chilling as the winds over his moors and fens.

—Marcia G. Fuchs

CASS, Zoe. *See* **LOW, Dorothy Mackie**.

CHACE, Isobel. Pseudonym for Elizabeth (Mary Teresa) Hunter. Born in 1934. Address: c/o Mills and Boon Ltd., 15-16 Brooks Mews, London W1A 1DR, England.

ROMANCE AND GOTHIC PUBLICATIONS

Novels

The African Mountain. London, Mills and Boon, 1960.
The Japanese Lantern. London, Mills and Boon, 1960; Toronto, Harlequin, 1966.
Flamingoes on the Lake. London, Mills and Boon, 1961; Toronto, Harlequin, 1965.
The Song and the Sea. London, Mills and Boon, 1962; Toronto, Harlequin, 1963.
The Hospital of Fatima. London, Mills and Boon, 1963; Toronto, Harlequin, 1975.
The Wild Land. London, Mills and Boon, 1963; Toronto, Harlequin, 1964.
A House for Sharing. London, Mills and Boon, 1964; Toronto, Harlequin, 1965.
The Rhythm of Flamenco. London, Mills and Boon, and Toronto, Harlequin, 1966.

The Spider's Web. London, Mills and Boon, 1966; as *The Secret Marriage*, 1966.
The Land of the Lotus-Eaters. London, Mills and Boon, 1966; Toronto, Harlequin, 1971.
A Garland of Marigolds. London, Mills and Boon, and Toronto, Harlequin, 1967.
Brittany Blue. London, Mills and Boon, 1967.
Oranges and Lemons. London, Mills and Boon, 1967; Toronto, Harlequin, 1968.
The Saffron Sky. London, Mills and Boon, and Toronto, Harlequin, 1968.
The Damask Rose. London, Mills and Boon, 1968; Toronto, Harlequin, 1969.
A Handful of Silver. London, Mills and Boon, 1968; Toronto, Harlequin, 1969.
The Legend of Katmandu. London, Mills and Boon, 1969.
Flower of Ethiopia. London, Mills and Boon, 1969.
Sugar in the Morning. London, Mills and Boon, 1969; Toronto, Harlequin, 1970.
The Day That the Rain Came Down. London, Mills and Boon, and Toronto, Harlequin, 1970.
The Flowering Cactus. London, Mills and Boon, 1970; Toronto, Harlequin, 1971.
To Marry a Tiger. London, Mills and Boon, 1971; Toronto, Harlequin, 1972.
The Wealth of the Islands. London, Mills and Boon, 1971; Toronto, Harlequin, 1972.
Home Is Goodbye. London, Mills and Boon, 1971; Toronto, Harlequin, 1972.
The Flamboyant Tree. London, Mills and Boon, 1972; Toronto, Harlequin, 1973.
The English Daughter. London, Mills and Boon, 1972.
Cadence of Portugal. London, Mills and Boon, 1972; Toronto, Harlequin, 1973.
A Pride of Lions. London, Mills and Boon, 1972; Toronto, Harlequin, 1973.
The Tartan Touch. London, Mills and Boon, 1972; Toronto, Harlequin, 1973.
The House of Scissors. London, Mills and Boon, 1972; Toronto, Harlequin, 1974.
The Dragon's Cave. London, Mills and Boon, 1972; Toronto, Harlequin, 1974.
The Edge of Beyond. London, Mills and Boon, 1973; Toronto, Harlequin, 1974.
A Man of Kent. London, Mills and Boon, 1973; Toronto, Harlequin, 1974.
The Cornish Hearth. London, Mills and Boon, and Toronto, Harlequin, 1975.
A Canopy of Rose Leaves. London, Mills and Boon, 1976; Toronto, Harlequin, 1977.
The Clouded Veil. London, Mills and Boon, and Toronto, Harlequin, 1976.
The Desert Castle. Toronto, Harlequin, 1976.
Singing in the Wilderness. London, Mills and Boon, and Toronto, Harlequin, 1976.
The Whistling Thorn. Toronto, Harlequin, 1977.
The Mouth of Truth. Toronto, Harlequin, 1977.
Second Best Wife. Toronto, Harlequin, 1978.

Novels as Elizabeth Hunter

Cherry-Blossom Clinic. London, Mills and Boon, 1961; Toronto, Harlequin, 1962.
Spiced with Cloves. London, Mills and Boon, 1962; Toronto, Harlequin, 1966.
Watch the Wall My Darling. London, Mills and Boon, 1963.
No Sooner Met. London, Mills and Boon, 1965.
There Were Nine Castles. London, Mills and Boon, 1967.
The Crescent Moon. London, Mills and Boon, 1973; Toronto, Harlequin, 1974.
The Tree of Idleness. London, Mills and Boon, 1973; Toronto, Harlequin, 1974.
The Tower of the Winds. London, Mills and Boon, 1973; Toronto, Harlequin, 1974.
The Beads of Nemesis. London, Mills and Boon, 1974; Toronto, Harlequin, 1975.
The Bride Price. London, Mills and Boon, 1974; Toronto, Harlequin, 1976.
The Bonds of Matrimony. London, Mills and Boon, and Toronto, Harlequin, 1975.
The Spanish Inheritance. London, Mills and Boon, and Toronto, Harlequin, 1975.
The Voice in the Thunder. London, Mills and Boon, and Toronto, Harlequin, 1975.
The Sycamore Song. London, Mills and Boon, 1975; Toronto, Harlequin, 1976.
The Realms of Gold. London, Mills and Boon, 1976; Toronto, Harlequin, 1977.
Pride of Madeira. Toronto, Harlequin, 1977.
Bride in the Sun. New York and London, Silhouette, 1980.
The Lion's Shadow. New York and London, Silhouette, 1980.
A Touch of Magic. New York and London, Silhouette, 1981.

*   *   *

Isobel Chace has long been a popular romance writer with a particularly individual style of writing that is quite distinctive, although she also writes under the name of Elizabeth Hunter.

She enjoys taking an improbable situation and making her readers believe it. She must—for she is a past master at "once upon a time" beginnings and "they lived happily ever after" endings. Her novels are "happy novels" regardless of the trials and suspense the heroine must encounter before she finds that strongest of havens, her loved one's arms.

In *The Bonds of Matrimony* Hero Kaufman needs to gain British nationality in order to migrate to Britain. To achieve it, she offers her farm in the drought-struck part of Kenya to Benedict Carmichael in exchange for a wedding ring. Morag Grant meets Pericles Holmes and his two children in *The Beads of Nemesis* while she is on a walking holiday in Greece. He takes her in charge so that she can mind the children, but, with true Greek thoroughness, he marries her out of hand before she really knows what is going on. These are typical of the stories that she writes as Elizabeth Hunter.

Writing under the name of Isobel Chace, she devises plots equally daring. *To Marry a Tiger* finds Ruth Arnold trying to protect her flighty sister and ending by being forced into marriage by Mario Verdecchio, a Sicilian. Although the encounter was innocent enough, she still had stayed the night in his home without a chaperon. Finally, Kirsty MacTaggart in *The Tartan Touch* finds herself married to Andrew Fraser, a stranger, within days of her father's death. He has come to Scotland from Australia to research family records, and, once he finds what he is looking for, he seems to sweep Kirsty along with him.

In each of these novels, the writer develops strong motivation, believable characters, and an added touch of romance. She has a special knack of describing the backgrounds that she portrays in her novels as she uses Scotland, the Mediterranean countries, and Australia as locales. She also includes special scenes and descriptions of each country in such a way that the reader has a sense of authenticity in the things she mentions. Certainly she depends heavily on various customs in these countries to help her make the story work. For instance, Ruth in *To Marry a Tiger* is unaware of the Sicilian concept of honor so that, when the marriage takes place, she believes it is solely because of the antiquated beliefs of the people and not because Mario is attracted to her.

Improbable as some of her plots seem, it is impossible for the reader not to become absorbed in the story almost immediately. Her characters emerge quite naturally as they move and speak against the background of the unfolding plot. Perhaps it is this element of characterization that makes her novels work, for she has a delicacy of touch in this facet of writing that few romance writers can match. She is able to make her heroines come alive in the nicest way as they meet and fall in love with the man in the story. Depth of character is woven lightly but effectively through her novels as both the girl and man react to the situation they find themselves in.

Plausibility is perhaps another key to her writing, for no matter how bizarre or outlandish the situation is, she is able to provide solid, logical motivation for the actions of her characters. Regardless of the name she writes under, Isobel Chace holds a special place in the hearts of romance readers. Somehow she adds a special sense wonder to her stories that makes each one seem especially right.

—Arlene Moore

CHANDOS, Fay. *See* **CHARLES, Theresa**.

CHAPMAN, Hester W(olferstan, née Pellatt). British. Born in London, 26 November 1899. Educated privately. Worked for the American Red Cross during World War II. Married 1) N.K. Chapman in 1926 (died); 2) R.L. Griffin in 1938 (died). Worked as a model in Paris and a telephone operator, secretary, governess, and schoolmistress in London. *Died 6 April 1976.*

ROMANCE AND GOTHIC PUBLICATIONS

Novels

She Saw Them Go By. London, Gollancz, and Boston, Houghton Mifflin, 1933.
To Be a King: A Tale of Adventure. London, Gollancz, 1934.
Long Division. London, Secker and Warburg, 1943.
I Will Be Good. London, Secker and Warburg, 1945; Boston, Houghton Mifflin, 1946.
Worlds Apart. London, Secker and Warburg, 1946.
Ivor Novello's King's Rhapsody (novelization of stage play). London, Harrap, 1950; Boston, Houghton Mifflin, 1951.
Ever Thine. London, Cape, 1951.
Falling Stream. London, Cape, 1954.
The Stone Lily. London, Cape, 1957.
Eugenie. London, Cape, and Boston, Little Brown, 1961.
Lucy. London, Cape, 1965; New York, Reynal, 1966.
Fear No More. London, Cape, and New York, Reynal, 1968.
Limmerston Hall. London, Cape, 1972; New York, Coward McCann, 1973.

OTHER PUBLICATIONS

Other

Great Villiers: A Study of George Villiers, Second Duke of Buckingham. London, Secker and Warburg, 1949.
Mary II, Queen of England. London, Cape, 1953; Westport, Connecticut, Greenwood Press, 1976.
Queen Anne's Son: A Memoir of William Henry, Duke of Gloucester. London, Deutsch, 1954.
The Last Tudor King: A Study of Edward VI. London, Cape, 1958; New York, Macmillan, 1959.
Two Tudor Portraits: Henry Howard, Earl of Surrey, and Lady Katherine Grey. London, Cape, 1960; Boston, Little Brown, 1963.
Lady Jane Grey. London, Cape, 1962; Boston, Little Brown, 1963.
The Tragedy of Charles II in the Years 1630-1660. London, Cape, and Boston, Little Brown, 1964.
Privileged Persons: Four Seventeenth-Century Studies. London, Cape, and New York, Reynal, 1966.
The Sisters of Henry VIII: Margaret Tudor, Queen of Scotland...Mary Tudor, Queen of France and Duchess of Suffolk. London, Cape, 1969; as *The Thistle and the Rose*, New York, Coward McCann, 1971.
Caroline Matilda, Queen of Denmark. London, Cape, 1971; New York, Coward McCann, 1972.
Anne Boleyn. London, Cape, 1974; as *The Challenge of Anne Boleyn*, New York, Coward McCann, 1974.
Four Fine Gentlemen. London, Constable, and Lincoln, University of Nebraska Press, 1977.

Editor, with Princess Romanovsky-Pavlovsky, *Diversion.* London, Collins, 1946.

*   *   *

Although at first sight Hester Chapman's books are very different each from the other (historical novels, costume romances, old-fashioned gothic, modern comedies of manners), they are in fact a homogenous whole because each of them explores in a different way the effect of a strong, overpowering woman on the people round her. To my mind her best books are her historical novels, and the best of all is *Fear No More*. This is a book of quite extraordinary power which stays in the mind long after it is finished. It is the story of the downfall of the French monarchy and all the events that led up to the revolution, but it is seen entirely through the eyes of the little Dauphin. Everything is described in the strange half-comprehending way that things appear to a child with little things magnified and big things trivialised. The total picture that emerges thus amazes. The strong woman of this book is, of course, Marie Antoinette who is always seen obliquely.

Another historical novel is *Lucy*, set in 17th-century London. It is mainly about the effect of Lucy's devastating personality on the people round her, but because these people are all actors and courtiers it is also the story of the Restoration theatre. *The Stone Lily* is about the revolution in Sicily in 1848, a subject which appealed to Chapman for she wrote two more books about revolution—*To Be a King* and *She Saw Them Go By*—but she created imaginary countries and situations for these books and used English point-of-view characters to enable her to comment on the decadence and pretension of old ruling families. She also wrote a novelised version of Ivor Novello's romantic musical *King's Rhapsody*.

All these books have her strange, strong women, but her strangest female characters are those reserved for her gothic novels. In *Ever Thine*, set in a boy's prep school, there is Victoire, a woman who ruins the lives of two men and two children through her wilfulness. The heroine of *Limmerston Hall*, a Victorian gothic piece, behaves with almost decorous impropriety in her unrequited passion for the man who she believes may have killed her sister and may, even as she tries to attract him, be attempting to kill her nephew and niece. But although this book promises much with its hints and foreshadowing, it delivers little. *I Will Be Good* is a book of almost stupefying dullness even though it should be interesting, being about a murderess and her motives. *Falling Stream* is a surprising modern novel, lightly written, but featuring a strong wilful woman masquerading as a weak invalid and spoiling the lives of everyone with whom she comes into contact—a delightful light read.

An air of sadness hangs over all Hester Chapman's books; "how splendid things might have been," they seem to say, but the strongly drawn, overpowering women are there to put a stop to that. Her style changes to fit the period portrayed. Her pace is perhaps a little leisurely for today's taste, except for the exquisite *Fear No More*—that has an air of timelessness and the power to haunt.

—Pamela Cleaver

CHAPPELL, Mollie.   British.   Agent: Curtis Brown Ltd., 1 Craven Hill, London W2 3EP, England.

ROMANCE AND GOTHIC PUBLICATIONS

Novels

> *The Widow Jones.* London, Collins, 1956.
> *Endearing Young Charms.* London, Collins, 1957.
> *Bachelor Heaven.* London, Collins, 1958.
> *A Wreath of Holly.* London, Collins, 1959.
> *One Little Room.* London, Collins, 1960.
> *A Lesson in Loving.* London, Collins, 1961; New York, Fawcett, 1975.
> *The Measure of Love.* London, Collins, 1961.
> *Caroline.* London, Collins, 1962; New York, Fawcett, 1975.
> *Come by Chance.* London, Collins, 1963.
> *The Garden Room.* London, Collins, 1964.
> *The Ladies of Lark.* London, Collins, 1965.
> *Bright Promise.* London, Collins, 1966.
> *Bid Me Live.* London, Collins, 1967.
> *Since Summer.* London, Collins, 1967.
> *The Wind in the Green Trees.* London, Collins, 1969.
> *The Hasting Day.* London, Collins, 1970.
> *Summer Story.* London, Collins, 1972.
> *Valley of Lilacs.* London, Collins, 1972.
> *Family Portrait.* London, Collins, 1973.
> *Cressy.* London, Collins, 1973.
> *Five Farthings.* London, Collins, 1974.
> *A Letter from Lydia.* London, Collins, 1974.
> *Seton's Wife.* London, Collins, 1975.
> *In Search of Mr. Rochester.* London, Collins, 1976.
> *The Loving Heart.* London, Collins, 1977; New York, Fawcett, 1979.
> *Country Air.* London, Collins, 1977.
> *The Romantic Widow.* London, Collins, 1978; New York, Fawcett, 1979.
> *Wintersweet.* London, Collins, 1978.
> *Serena.* London, Hale, 1980.
> *Dearest Neighbour.* London, Hale, 1981.

OTHER PUBLICATIONS

Other (juvenile)

> *Little Tom Sparrow.* Leeds, E.J. Arnold, 1950.
> *Tusker Tales.* Leeds, E.J. Arnold, 1950.
> *Rhodesian Adventure.* London, Collins, 1950.
> *The Gentle Giant.* Leeds, E.J. Arnold, 1951.
> *The House on the Kopje.* London, Collins, 1951.
> *The Sugar and Spice.* London, Collins, 1952.
> *St. Simon Square.* London, Nelson, 1952.
> *The Fortunes of Frisk.* London, Collins, 1953.
> *Cat with No Fiddle.* London, Collins, 1954.
> *The Mystery of the Silver Circle.* London, Collins, 1955.
> *Kit and the Mystery Man.* London, Collins, 1955.

*   *   *

Mollie Chappell has evolved from being a writer of short stories for children, as in *Tusker Tales*, and for young girls, as in *Rhodesia Adventure* (both with African settings) via the light comedy of *Bachelor Heaven* to being a writer of romantic novels suitable for mature women.

Chappell's novels form a distinct species in the romantic class and, in their rather whimsical way, go against the general run. Romance in her novels is very controlled and chaste, and is seen vicariously rather than experienced in the first person. The world of her books is the world of comfortably off middle-aged womanhood in Southern England in the present, though some of the novels are set in mid-19th-century England. Her stories do not contain much action and plots are modest. The stories are, however, overburdened with characters, many dead or unmet, but ranging from the occasional odd and seedy type, such as Jacko in *The Hasting Day*, to the more common cool and crisp young woman, such as Lucy in *Summer Story*. Most characters are somewhat ordinary and there is often little opportunity for them to be developed.

In *Country Air* one sees the variations between brothers in their life achievements with careful gradation. This book contains many of the elements to be found in Chappell's other works: a setting in the English country towns of Clout and Carvel, careful assessment of strangers and relatives, including their clothes. On a rather deeper level is the presence of orphans who have lost both parents, as also occurs in *In Search of Mr. Rochester, Serena*, and *Dearest Neighbour*.

Settings are predictable, being either a rather vague and wearisome London and pretty villages such as Wintersweet (*Wintersweet*) as well as the frequently occurring Clout and Carvel. Family relationships are often complex and difficult to work out exactly, and involve distantly related members of the same family. Other relationships often include not-so-close friends and also those with a special closeness such as secretaries and housekeepers.

Chappell has recently written historical romances, such as *Serena* and *Dearest Neighbour*, and the well-established themes of orphaned children are dealt with at length. The setting of a genteel mid-Victorian England helps to add to the pathos and sentimentality of the treatment. While in *Dearest Neighbour* there is a setting of rectories and solid country houses, there is nevertheless a controlled amount of melodrama and tragedy. It is largely a feminine world of daughters "coming out," and ends in a chaste pledging of love between the hero and heroine. True to the Chappell style there is an approving eye cast on these proceedings by the girl's former governess. In *Serena* a stronger moral attitude (similar to that in *Seton's Wife*) is developed when the courage of the heroine is combined with love to defeat despair when the girl achieves the serenity befitting her name.

A serenity does, in fact, pervade most of Chappell's work through the detached posture of the narrators. The essence of the main characters is that they look out on life from on observing viewpoint rather than from actual experience. Many of the minor characters are very shallow indeed; gossip rather than passion rules. The style of writing is often flat and simple. While it is almost naive, at times it also has the effect of producing a "stream of consciousness" type of prose fitting the very internalised thoughts and action.

—P.R. Meldrum

CHARLES, Anita. *See* **BARRIE, Susan.**

CHARLES, Theresa.   Pseudonym for Irene Maude Swatridge, née Mossop; also writes as Fay Chandos; Leslie Lance; Virginia Storm; Jan Tempest.   British.   Born in Woking, Surrey.   Educated privately.   Married Charles John Swatridge in 1934. Agent: Curtis Brown Ltd., 1 Craven Hill, London W2 3EP. Address: Middlecombe, Beeson, Kingsbridge, Devon TQ7 2EW, England.

<small>ROMANCE AND GOTHIC PUBLICATIONS</small>

Novels (with Charles Swatridge)

The Distant Drum.   London, Longman, 1940.
My Enemy and I.   London, Longman, 1941.
To Save My Life.   London, Longman, 1946.
Happy Now I Go.   London, Longman, 1947; as *Dark Legacy*, New York, Dell, 1968.
Man-Made Miracle.   London, Longman, 1949.
The Ugly Prince (as Virginia Storm).   New York, Arcadia House, 1950.
At a Touch I Yield.   London, Cassell, 1952.
Fairer Than She.   London, Cassell, 1953; New York, Dell, 1968.
My Only Love.   London, Cassell, 1954.
The Kinder Love.   London, Cassell, 1955.
The Burning Beacon.   London, Cassell, 1956; New York, Lancer, 1966.
The Ultimate Surrender.   London, Cassell, 1958.
A Girl Called Evelyn.   London, Hale, 1959.
No Through Road.   London, Hale, 1960.
House on the Rocks.   London, Hale, 1962; New York, Paperback Library, 1966.
Ring for Nurse Raine.   London, Hale, 1962.
Widower's Wife.   London, Hale, 1963; as *Return to Terror*, New York, Paperback Library, 1966.
Patient in Love.   London, Hale, 1963.
Nurse Alice in Love.   London, Hale, 1964; as *Lady in the Mist*, New York, Ace, 1966.
The Man for Me.   London, Hale, 1965; as *The Shrouded Tower*, New York, Ace, 1966.
How Much You Mean to Me.   London, Hale, 1966.
Proud Citadel.   London, Hale, and New York, Dell, 1967.
The Way Men Love.   London, Hale, 1967.
The Shadowy Third.   London, Hale, 1968.
From Fairest Flowers.   London, Hale, 1969.
Wayward as the Swallow.   London, Hale, 1970.
Second Honeymoon.   London, Hale, 1970.
My True Love.   London, Hale, 1971.
Therefore Must Be Loved.   London, Hale, 1972.
Castle Kelpiesloch.   London, Hale, 1973.
Nurse by Accident.   London, Hale, 1974.
The Flower and the Nettle.   London, Hale, 1975.
Trust Me, My Love.   London, Hale, 1975.
One Who Remembers.   London, Hale, 1976.
Rainbow after Rain.   London, Hale, 1977.
Crisis at St. Chad's.   London, Hale, 1977.
Just for One Weekend.   London, Hale, 1978.
Surgeon's Reputation.   London, Hale, 1979.
With Somebody Else.   London, Hale, 1981.
Surgeon's Sweetheart.   London, Hale, 1981.

Novels as Jan Tempest

Stepmother of Five.   London, Mills and Boon, 1936.

Someone New to Love. London, Mills and Boon, 1936.
Be Still, My Heart! London, Mills and Boon, 1936.
Kiss—and Forget. London, Mills and Boon, 1936.
Believe Me, Beloved—. London, Mills and Boon, 1936.
All This I Gave. London, Mills and Boon, 1937.
If I Love Again. London, Mills and Boon, 1937.
No Other Man—. London, Mills and Boon, 1937.
Grow Up, Little Lady! London, Mills and Boon, 1937.
Carey, Come Back! London, Mills and Boon, 1937.
Face the Music—for Love. London, Mills and Boon, 1938.
Man—and Waif. London, Mills and Boon, 1938.
Because My Love Is Come. London, Mills and Boon, 1938; as *Because My Love Is Coming*, 1958.
When First I Loved.... London, Mills and Boon, 1938.
Hilary in His Heart. London, Mills and Boon, 1938.
Say You're Sorry. London, Mills and Boon, 1939.
My Only Love. London, Mills and Boon, 1939.
Uninvited Guest. London, Mills and Boon, 1939.
I'll Try Anything Once. London, Mills and Boon, 1939.
Top of the Beanstalk. London, Mills and Boon, 1940.
The Broken Gate. London, Mills and Boon, 1940.
Why Wouldn't He Wait? London, Mills and Boon, 1940.
Little Brown Girl. London, Mills and Boon, 1940.
Always Another Man. London, Mills and Boon, 1941.
The Moment I Saw You. London, Mills and Boon, 1941.
The Unknown Joy. London, Mills and Boon, 1941.
Ghost of June. London, Mills and Boon, 1941.
No Time for a Man. London, Mills and Boon, 1942.
Romance on Ice. London, Mills and Boon, 1942.
If You'll Marry Me. London, Mills and Boon, 1942.
A Prince for Portia. London, Mills and Boon, 1943.
Wife after Work. London, Mills and Boon, 1943.
The Long Way Home. London, Mills and Boon, 1943.
"Never Again!" Said Nicola. London, Mills and Boon, 1944.
The One Thing I Wanted. London, Mills and Boon, 1944.
Utility Husband. London, Mills and Boon, 1944.
Westward to My Love. London, Mills and Boon, 1944.
Love While You Wait. London, Mills and Boon, 1944.
Not for This Alone. London, Mills and Boon, 1945.
To Be a Bride. London, Mills and Boon, 1945.
The Orange Blossom Shop. London, Mills and Boon, 1946.
Happy with Either. London, Mills and Boon, 1946.
House of the Pines. London, Mills and Boon, 1946; New York, Ace, 1967; as *House of Pines*, Ace, 1975.
Bachelor's Bride. London, Mills and Boon, 1946.
Lovely, Though Late. London, Mills and Boon, 1946.
Close Your Eyes. London, Mills and Boon, 1947.
Teach Me to Love. London, Mills and Boon, 1947.
How Can I Forget? London, Mills and Boon, 1948; as *First I Must Forget* (as Virginia Storm), New York, Arcadia House, 1951.
Cinderella Had Two Sisters. London, Mills and Boon, 1948; as *Virginia Storm*, New York, Arcadia House, 1950.
Short-Cut to the Stars. London, Mills and Boon, 1949.
Never Another Love. London, Mills and Boon, 1949; New York, Arcadia House, 1950.
Promise of Paradise. New York, Gramercy, 1949.
Nobody Else—Ever. London, Mills and Boon, 1950.
A Match Is Made. London, Mills and Boon, 1950.
Now and Always. New York, Arcadia House, 1950.

Until I Find Her.   New York, Arcadia House, 1950; London, Mills and Boon, 1951.
Two Loves for Tamara.   London, Mills and Boon, 1951.
Open the Door to Love.   London, Mills and Boon, 1952.
Without a Honeymoon.   London, Mills and Boon, 1952.
Happy Is the Wooing.   London, Mills and Boon, 1952.
Meet Me by Moonlight.   London, Mills and Boon, 1953.
Give Her Gardenias.   London, Mills and Boon, 1953.
Enchanted Valley.   London, Mills and Boon, 1954.
First-Time of Asking.   London, Mills and Boon, 1954.
Ask Me Again.   London, Mills and Boon, 1955.
Where the Heart Is.   London, Mills and Boon, 1955.
For Those in Love.   London, Mills and Boon, 1956.
Wedding Bells for Willow.   London, Mills and Boon, 1956.
Craddock's Kingdom.   London, Mills and Boon, 1957.
...Will Not Now Take Place.   London, Mills and Boon, 1957.
The Youngest Sister.   London, Mills and Boon, 1958.
Because There Is Hope.   London, Mills and Boon, 1958.
Romance for Rose.   London, Mills and Boon, 1959.
Stranger to Love.   London, Mills and Boon, 1960.
Mistress of Castlemount.   London, Mills and Boon, 1961.
The Turning Point.   London, Mills and Boon, 1961.
That Nice Nurse Nevin.   London, Mills and Boon, and Toronto, Harlequin, 1963.
The Madderleys Married.   London, Mills and Boon, 1963.
The Flower and the Fruit.   London, Mills and Boon, 1964.
Nurse Willow's Ward.   Toronto, Harlequin, 1965.
The Way We Used to Be.   London, Mills and Boon, 1965.
Jubilee Hospital.   Toronto, Harlequin, 1966.
The Lonesome Road.   London, Mills and Boon, 1966.
Meant to Meet.   London, Mills and Boon, 1967.
Lyra, My Love.   Chicago, Moody Press, 1969.

Novels as Fay Chandos

No Limit to Love.   London, Mills and Boon, 1937.
No Escape from Love.   London, Mills and Boon, 1937.
Man of My Dreams.   London, Mills and Boon, 1937.
Before I Make You Mine.   London, Mills and Boon, 1938.
Wife for a Wager.   London, Mills and Boon, 1938.
Gay Knight I Love.   London, Mills and Boon, 1938.
All I Ask.   London, Mills and Boon, 1939.
Another Woman's Shoes.   London, Mills and Boon, 1939.
When Three Walk Together.   London, Mills and Boon, 1939.
The Man Who Wasn't Mac.   London, Mills and Boon, 1939.
Husband for Hire.   London, Mills and Boon, 1940.
You Should Have Warned Me.   London, Mills and Boon, 1940.
When We Two Parted.   London, Mills and Boon, 1940.
Substitute for Sherry.   London, Mills and Boon, 1940.
Women Are So Simple.   London, Mills and Boon, 1941.
Only a Touch.   London, Mills and Boon, 1941.
Awake, My Love!   London, Mills and Boon, 1942.
A Letter to My Love.   London, Mills and Boon, 1942.
Eve and I.   London, Mills and Boon, 1943.
A Man to Follow.   London, Mills and Boon, 1943.
Away from Each Other.   London, Mills and Boon, 1944.
Made to Marry.   London, Mills and Boon, 1944.
Just a Little Longer.   London, Mills and Boon, 1944.
Last Year's Roses.   London, Mills and Boon, 1945.

A Man for Margaret.   London, Mills and Boon, 1945.
Three Roads to Romance.   London, Mills and Boon, 1945.
When Time Stands Still.   London, Mills and Boon, 1946.
Home Is the Hero.   London, Mills and Boon, 1946.
Because I Wear Your Ring.   London, Mills and Boon, 1947.
Cousins May Kiss.   London, Mills and Boon, 1947.
Lost Summer.   London, Mills and Boon, 1948.
Since First We Met.   London, Mills and Boon, 1948.
June in Her Eyes.   London, Mills and Boon, 1949.
For a Dream's Sake.   London, Mills and Boon, 1949.
Fugitive from Love.   London, Mills and Boon, 1950.
There Is a Tide....   London, Mills and Boon, 1950.
This Time It's Love.   London, Mills and Boon, 1951.
First and Favourite Wife.   London, Mills and Boon, 1952.
Families Are Such Fun.   London, Mills and Boon, 1952.
Leave It to Nancy.   London, Mills and Boon, 1953.
The Other One.   London, Mills and Boon, 1953.
Find Another Eden.   London, Mills and Boon, 1953.
Just Before the Wedding.   London, Mills and Boon, 1954.
Doctors Are Different.   London, Mills and Boon, 1954.
Husbands at Home.   London, Mills and Boon, 1955.
Hibiscus House.   London, Mills and Boon, 1955; as *Nurse Incognito*, Toronto, Harle-
   quin, 1964.
So Nearly Married.   London, Mills and Boon, 1956.
The Romantic Touch.   London, Mills and Boon, 1957.
Partners Are a Problem.   London, Mills and Boon, 1957.
Model Girl's Farm.   London, Mills and Boon, 1958.
Nan—and the New Owner.   London, Mills and Boon, 1959.
Wild Violets.   London, Mills and Boon, 1959.
When Four Ways Meet.   London, Mills and Boon, 1961.
Sister Sylvan.   London, Mills and Boon, 1962.
Two Other People.   London, Mills and Boon, 1964.
Don't Give Your Heart Away.   London, Mills and Boon, 1966.
Stranger in Love.   London, Mills and Boon, 1966.
Farm by the Sea.   London, Mills and Boon, 1967.
The Three of Us.   London, Mills and Boon, 1970.
Sweet Rosemary.   London, Mills and Boon, 1972.

Novels as Leslie Lance

Alice, Where Are You?   London, Hodder and Stoughton, 1940.
Take a Chance.   London, Hodder and Stoughton, 1940.
The Dark Stranger.   London, Sampson Low, 1946.
Man of the Family.   London, Hurst and Blackett, 1952.
Spun by the Moon.   London, Ward Lock, 1960.
Sisters in Love.   London, Ward Lock, 1960.
A Summer's Grace.   London, Ward Lock, 1961.
Springtime for Sally.   London, Ward Lock, 1962.
Spreading Sails.   London, Ward Lock, 1963.
The Young Curmudgeon.   London, Ward Lock, 1964.
I'll Ride Beside You.   London, Ward Lock, 1965.
Bright Winter.   London, Ward Lock, 1965.
No Summer Beauty.   London, Ward Lock, 1967.
Return to King's Mere.   London, Hale, 1967.
Bride of Emersham.   New York, Pyramid, 1967.
Nurse in the Woods.   London, Hale, 1969.
The Summer People.   London, Hale, 1969.

Nurse Verena in Weirwater.   London, Hale, 1970.
No Laggard in Love.   London, Hale, 1971.
The New Lord Whinbridge.   London, Hale, 1973.
Now I Can Forget.   London, Hale, 1973.
The Love That Lasts.   London, Hale, 1974.
The Maverton Heiress.   London, Hale, 1975.
The Return of the Cuckoo.   London, Hale, 1976.
Romance at Wrecker's End.   London, Hale, 1976.
Island House.   London, Hale, 1976.
Cousins by Courtesy.   London, Hale, 1977.
The Family at the Farm.   London, Hale, 1978.
Orchid Girl.   London, Hale, 1978.
The Girl in the Mauve Mini.   London, Hale, 1979.
The Rose Princess.   London, Hale, 1979.
Doctor in the Snow.   London, Hale, 1980.
The House in the Woods.   New York, Ace, 1980.
Hawk's Head.   London, Hale, 1981.
Someone Who Cares.   London, Hale, 1982.

OTHER PUBLICATIONS as Irene Mossop

Other (juvenile)

Well Played, Juliana!   London, Sampson Low, 1928.
Prunella Plays the Game.   London, Sampson Low, 1929.
Freesia's Feud.   London, Warne, 1930.
The Luck of the Oakleighs.   London, Warne, 1930.
Chris in Command.   London, Sampson Low, 1930.
Sylvia Sways the School.   London, Sampson Low, 1930.
Theresa's First Term.   London, Nisbet, 1930.
Vivien of St. Val's.   London, Shaw, 1931.
Charm's Last Chance.   London, Nisbet, 1931.
Nicky—New Girl.   London, Sampson Low, 1931.
Rona's Rival.   London, Warne, 1931.
A Rebel at "Rowans."   London, Sampson Low, 1932.
Barbara Black-Sheep.   London, Warne, 1932.
Una Wins Through.   London, Warne, 1932.
Feud in the Fifth.   London, Sampson Low, 1933.
Hilary Leads the Way.   London, Warne, 1933.
The Taming of Pickles.   London, Shaw, 1933.
The Fifth at Cliff House.   London, Warne, 1934.
The Four V's.   London, Warne, 1934.
The Fourth at St. Faith's.   London, Shaw, 1934.
Play Up, Pine House!   London, Sampson Low, 1934.
Theresa on Trial.   London, Warne, 1935.
Theda Marsh.   London, Shaw, 1935.
The Gay Adventure.   London, Warne, 1937.

*   *   *

Irene Mossop began writing at the end of the 1920's and has produced some 240 novels. However, her books, mostly romantic stories, have managed to retain their sense of crisp inventiveness. Her pen names—particularly Virginia Storm and Jan Tempest—are well chosen and appropriate for the exciting and atmospheric moods of many of her romantic adventures. The titles also endorse the flavour of the books—*No Limit to Love, Husband for Hire, Meant to Meet*, etc.

Several of the author's heroines start out in a rather calculating way, going to the lengths of participating in forced or fake marriages in order to improve their circumstances, or those of someone dear to them. But, by the final pages of each novel, these phoney marriages have generally focussed satisfyingly into liaisons of true love.

There are also accounts of steady and happy marriages that begin to misfire because the heroine becomes insensitive to her spouse's psychological needs. In *The Way We Used to Be*, for instance, Leonie's parents suddenly make a lot of money, and Leonie fails to recognize that the resultant parental subsidy is damaging her hard-working veterinary-surgeon husband's masculine pride—and, of course, their marriage. But happily she comes to her senses, and a realistic appraisal of the illogical qualities of married interdependence just in time to salvage her romantic relationship with her husband.

Variations on these married and romantic themes are deftly handled in the flow of novels by this writer. She is also skilled at manipulating the romantic thriller story, as in *The Girl in the Mauve Mini*, for example. (Her juvenile stories, written as Irene Mossop, are also rich in excitement and suspense.)

She writes as Theresa Charles in collaboration with her husband, Charles John Swatridge, and as co-authors in the romantic genre they have the briskness and colour that remind one of the flavour of stories by the earlier husband and wife partnership of C.N. and A.M. Williamson. *Nurse by Accident* introduces an intriguing new angle on romance—that of the accident-prone heroine whose love life, as well as her career, is threatened by her habit of unintentionally making things go cockeyed. Nurse Nicola Warren falls in love in this accident-prone way—always with the wrong man, of course—until she meets an almost-too-charming-to-be-true solicitor, who knows that the solution to her problem is for him to gather her into his arms with the unoriginal but, in this case, extremely apt comment: "You need a husband to keep an eye on you...."

—Mary Cadogan

CHESTERTON, Denise. *See* **ROBINS, Denise**.

CHRISTIE, Agatha. *See* **WESTMACOTT, Mary**.

CLEEVE, Brian (Talbot). Irish. Born in Thorpe Bay, Essex, England, 22 November 1921. Educated at Selwyn House, Broadstairs, Kent, 1930-35; St. Edward's School, Oxford, 1935-38; University of South Africa, Pretoria, 1951-53, B.A. 1953; National University of Ireland, Dublin, 1954-56, Ph.D. 1956. Served in the British Merchant Navy, 1939-45. Married Veronica McAdie in 1945; two daughters. Free-lance journalist in South Africa, 1948-54, and in Ireland since 1954. Broadcaster, Radio Telefis Eireann, Dublin, 1962-72. Address: 60 Heytesbury Lane, Ballsbridge, Dublin 4, Ireland.

ROMANCE AND GOTHIC PUBLICATIONS

Novels

Sara. London, Cassell, and New York, Coward McCann, 1976.
Kate. London, Cassell, and New York, Coward McCann, 1977.
Judith. London, Cassell, and New York, Coward McCann, 1978.
Hester. London, Cassell, 1979; New York, Coward McCann, 1980.

OTHER PUBLICATIONS

Novels

The Far Hills. London, Jarrolds, 1952.
Portrait of My City. London, Jarrolds, 1952.
Birth of a Dark Soul. London, Jarrolds, 1953; as *The Night Winds*, Boston, Houghton Mifflin, 1954.
Assignment to Vengeance. London, Hammond, 1961.
Death of a Painted Lady. London, Hammond, 1962; New York, Random House, 1963.
Death of a Wicked Servant. London, Hammond, 1963; New York, Random House, 1964.
Vote X for Treason. London, Collins, 1964; New York, Random House, 1965; as *Counterspy*, New York, Lancer, 1966.
Dark Blood, Dark Terror. New York, Random House, 1965; London, Hammond, 1966.
The Judas Goat. London, Hammond, 1966; as *Vice Isn't Private*, New York, Random House, 1966.
Violent Death of a Bitter Englishman. New York, Random House, 1967; London, Corgi, 1969.
You Must Never Go Back. New York, Random House, 1968.
Exit from Prague. London, Corgi, 1970; as *Escape from Prague*, New York, Pinnacle, 1973.
Cry of Morning. London, Joseph, 1971; as *The Triumph of O'Rourke*, New York, Doubleday, 1972.
Tread Softly in This Place. London, Cassell, and New York, Day, 1972.
The Dark Side of the Sun. London, Cassell, 1973.
A Question of Inheritance. London, Cassell, 1974; as *For Love of Crannagh Castle*, New York, Dutton, 1975.

Short Stories

The Horse Thieves of Ballysaggert and Other Stories. Cork, Mercier Press, 1966.

Other

Colonial Policies in Africa. Johannesburg, St. Benedict's House, 1954.
Dictionary of Irish Writers. Cork, Mercier Press, 3 vols., 1967-71.
The House on the Rock. London, Watkins, 1980.
The Seven Mansions. London, Watkins, 1980.

Editor, *W.B. Yeats and the Designing of Ireland's Coinage.* Dublin, Dolmen Press, 1972.

Manuscript Collection: Mugar Memorial Library, Boston University.

Brian Cleeve comments:

I began writing romantic fiction by mistake. I meant to write a historical family saga covering the 19th century, beginning with a Spanish gypsy orphan in the Peninsular War. She took over the book and the whole novel became her story, as *Sara*. People liked the book, and I wrote three more, with vaguely similar themes, and young heroines in extravagant, romantic, yet historically accurate (I hope) situations. I thought of them as historical novels rather than as romances. I wanted to explore the idea of young women striving for personal liberation at a period when this was becoming even more difficult to achieve than it had been a hundred years earlier.

*   *   *

Brian Cleeve's Regency romances (*Sarah, Kate, Judith, Hester*) focus on the suffering and maturation of young women who, through their shocking experiences with war, revolution, poverty, prison, and crime, shed the naivety of youth, taste freedom, and learn the responsibilities it entails. They are usually attracted to tough, forceful men with values alien to their own. Often they are swept along by history, and must learn to deal with human cruelty, prejudice, hypocrisy, and greed. Their histories are a tangled web of love and intrigue, class conflicts, and sexual battles as they learn to trust instinct and to reassess old values.

While an overprotected Judith and Hester are shocked by the unjust demands of adulthood, Sarah and Kate grow up amid chaos and turmoil—Sarah as a witness to her parents' slaughter by Bonaparte's soldiers in Spain and as a long-suffering guerrilla fighter with her adopted soldier-father, Kate as a member of a troupe of actors and as the sole survivor of a political massacre. Both Sarah and Kate barely escape the London white slave market; both drift into the criminal underworld, Sarah by working in a disreputable gambling house, Kate by acquiescing in smuggling operations. Judith, too, though a proper young lady, ultimately consorts with smugglers because of her father's illness and the resultant financial necessity. Only Hester, caught up in the monstrosities of the French Revolution and the injustices of Marat and Robespierre, acts on principles, not necessity; she learns to ride and fight and kill like a man, and to accept discomfort and daily knowledge of possible death, while retaining her feminine allures and self-respect.

Kate and Judith are both weak women, unsure of their values, fearful of their sexuality, guilt-ridden, naive, torn between a sense of propriety and of expediency. But while it is Kate's weakness and fragility that help her find security and success despite the criminal prosecution of herself and her lover and the public persecution of her outcast friends, it is Judith's kindness and strength of heart that enable her to overcome the unforeseen results of her moral slip: stoning by neighbors, pursuit by rich relatives, torture in an insane asylum, and beggary on London streets; ultimately she expiates her past through charitable works among the poor and criminal classes and through shocking exposés aimed at redefining man's obligations to fellow man. In so doing, she regains her sense of self as well as her lost lover.

Hester and Sarah, in contrast, are strong-willed young women, whose major problem is deciding where their true allegiances lie and how best to attain their goals. Sarah learns to use virtuous resistance and special intuitive and visionary powers learned from a fellow outcast to achieve her destiny: rejection of prim hypocrisy and acceptance of hard-nosed humanitarian-ism that lead her to reject an aristocratic suitor, console a dying man, reform a young thief, and use a newly gained fortune to provide a home for orphans. Hester's decisions are more straightforward, for she must choose between the high-sounding rhetoric of freedom and the values of her birth and heritage, between idealistic theory and practical reality, between a man who pampers her femininity and another who demands action as partner and equal, between safety in England and death in France.

Against a background of danger and social disapproval, Cleeve's romantic heroines reveal the strength, the passion, and the worth that make men fight for them, hypocrites fear them, and fellow orphans trust them. Cleeve vividly depicts the horrors of early 19th-century life and the helplessness of all but a privileged few, while involving his reader through twists of plot and dramatic action which never allow a predictable conclusion.

—Virginia Macdonald

CLEUGH, Sophia.   Married to Dennis Cleugh.

ROMANCE AND GOTHIC PUBLICATIONS

Novels

> *Matilda, Governess of the English*.   New York, Macmillan, 1924; London, Butterworth, 1925.
> *Ernestine Sophie*.   New York, Macmillan, 1925; London, Butterworth, 1926.
> *Jeanne Margot*.   New York, Macmillan, and London, Butterworth, 1927.
> *A Common Cheat*.   New York, Macmillan, and London, Butterworth, 1928.
> *Spring*.   New York, Macmillan, and London, Hodder and Stoughton, 1929.
> *Song Bird*.   Boston, Houghton Mifflin, and London, Hodder and Stoughton, 1930.
> *Enchanting Clementina*.   London, Hodder and Stoughton, 1930; Boston, Houghton Mifflin, 1931.
> *The Daisy Boy*.   London, Hodder and Stoughton, 1931; as *Young Jonathan*, Boston, Houghton Mifflin, 1932.
> *Loyal Lady*.   London, Hodder and Stoughton, 1932; as *Anne Marguerite*, Boston, Houghton Mifflin, 1932.
> *The Hazards of Belinda*.   London, Hodder and Stoughton, and Boston, Houghton Mifflin, 1933.
> *Lindy Lou*.   London, Hodder and Stoughton, 1934.
> *The Angel Who Couldn't Sing*.   London, Hodder and Stoughton, and New York, Doubleday, 1935.
> *Wind Which Moved a Ship*.   London, Newnes, and New York, Doubleday, 1936.

*   *   *

Sophia Cleugh, a romance writer of the 1920's and 1930's plunges the modern reader into another world. Few things can reveal the changes that have occurred in gothic romances as vividly as actually reading material written over half a century ago. Two aspects disturb the modern reader. Cleugh's persistent habit of alternating lengthy involved and often convoluted sentences with sentence fragments is particularly jarring. Frequent re-reading for sentence sense is essential for the reader unfamiliar with this style. Also disturbing to most modern readers are the lengthy descriptive passages as well as detailed discussions of the most minute details of daily life accompanied by thorough relating of all accompanying emotional responses.

In *Young Jonathan* numerous pages are devoted to desultory descriptions and idle chatter during an afternoon tea while Jonathan is assiduously digging daisies from the lawn. An even greater impasse to the plot is apparent in *Matilda, Governess of the English* during numerous exchanges between the Duchess and her maid, Mrs. Kincaid. In *Spring* the initial descriptions and the languorous pace of the novel recall another more leisurely time and place when the reader could luxuriate in a novel that was much ado about little.

Yet, while Cleugh's plots move at the same pace as do those of Henry James, her fine wit more than compensates for the absence of fast-paced action or heady romance, or even great mystery. A multitude of aphorisms and clichés only serves to add a special charm and authenticity to these early works ("But, as we have heard time and again, tread on the veriest worm too often, and the creature will turn").

Romantic names such as Sweet William, Gilliflower, Larkspur, Nina, and various titles of nobility abound in Cleugh's novels. She also shows a rather 19th-century interest in children. Children of various ages figure prominently in all of her books, and they are not just property and appendages of their parents but complete personages in their own rights and often described with great wit and clarity.

Although reading aloud is no longer in vogue, were it a habit to which we might someday return, Cleugh, with her often clever turning of a phrase, should be read aloud. While the plot lines—of young maidens seeking a romance not guided by their Mamas or poor young people making good—are not original, a novel which treats language as if it were a treasure has lasting value. In addition, Sophia Cleugh's novels remain as representative novels of manners of another time and place.

—Joan Hinkemeyer

COATES, Sheila. *See* **LAMB, Charlotte**.

COCKRELL, Marian (née Brown). American. Born in Birmingham, Alabama, 15 March 1909. Educated at Sophie Newcomb College, New Orleans, 1926-29; Metropolitan Art School, New York, 1929-30. Married Francis Marion Cockrell in 1931; one daughter. Agent: Oliver G. Swan, Collier Associates, 280 Madison Avenue, New York, New York 10016. Address: 910 El Paseo, Ojai, California 93023, U.S.A.

ROMANCE AND GOTHIC PUBLICATIONS

Novels

Yesterday's Madness.   New York, Harper, 1943.
Lillian Harley.   New York, Harper, 1943.
Dark Waters, with Frank Cockrell.   Cleveland, World, 1944.
Something Between.   New York, Harper, 1946.
The Revolt of Sarah Perkins.   New York, McKay, 1965; London, Hurst and Blackett,
   1966.
Mixed Blessings.   New York, Times Books, 1978.
The Misadventures of Bethany Price.   New York, Times Books, 1979.
Mixed Company.   New York, Popular Library, 1979.

Uncollected Short Stories

"For the Debts of My Wife," in *Pictorial Review* (New York), January 1938.
"The Girl Who Asked Too Much," in *Good Housekeeping* (New York), April 1939.
"Big Operator," in *Saturday Evening Post Stories of 1940*, edited by Wesley Stout.   New
   York, Random House, 1940.
"Amateur," in *Good Housekeeping* (New York), March and April 1946.

OTHER PUBLICATIONS

Plays

Screenplay: *Dark Waters*, with Joan Harrison, 1945.

Television Plays: for *Alfred Hitchcock* series.

Other

Shadow Castle (juvenile).   New York, McGraw Hill, 1945.

Manuscript Collection: Mugar Memorial Library, Boston University.

Marian Cockrell comments:

I enjoy writing. I write to interest and entertain, with characters that are life-like, and amusing conversation. The protagonists are all women, and tend to develop a sense of independence in trying to solve their problems in their time and circumstances. I now prefer to write about the past—early 1900's or 1870's. There is always a love story, but the books are not *about* the love story, but about the difficulties of the heroine, of which the love story is a part.

*   *   *

The chief flaw, for me, in much romantic fiction, is the emotional vacuum in which the heroines live. They have few, if any, friends and relatives, and are totally dependent on the men they love for emotional warmth. This is why I find Marian Cockrell's books unusually appealing. Her characters are all part of a small community; her people know everything about each other, gossip about each other, and care about each other. Her characters are richly varied and entirely believable, ranging from normal and kindly characters, through mild eccentrics, full-blown lunatics, and self-righteous, malicious gossips.

Her novels from the 1940's are set in the 1940's, and they now seem dated, though likable. *Something Between*, which brings three pleasant romances to fruition, is nevertheless primarily about a confused adolescent boy trying to prevent his mother's remarriage. Her historical romances work much better. *The Revolt of Sarah Perkins* tells of a small Colorado town during the 1860's which sets out to find a schoolteacher too plain to get married and too beaten-down to give them any trouble. What they get instead is a woman of intelligence, spirit, and humor, who shakes up the town by demanding not only decent facilities, but also that those facilities be shared with all children, including the daughter of a prostitute, and a child who is half-Indian. Cockrell herself says that her book is about the women of the west, "their strengths and weaknesses, gentleness and compassion, bigotry and intolerance." *Mixed Blessings*, set in a small Southern town in the early 1900's, tells of the tribulations of a young woman trying to support herself and her brother by running a boarding house inhabited by a certifiable looney, two warring women, and their offspring. The heroine is warm and loving, and cheerfully accepts the burdens of those she loves. It takes a while for her to find a man who can live up to her. *The Misadventures of Bethany Price* has a 16-year-old heroine who, faced with a middle-aged husband she dislikes and a stepson who rapes her, runs away. She finds friends in a small pioneer community, but she also arouses public hostility by her unconventional behavior and uncompromising honesty and fairness.

The world Cockrell creates is not only believable; it is also entertaining. Her perceptions of the world are acute and amusing. While her chief strength lies in the reality of her characters, her plots are briskly paced and funny.

—Marylaine Block

COFFMAN, Virginia (Edith). Also writes as Victor Cross; Jeanne Duval; Virginia C. DuVaul; Anne Stanfield. American. Born in San Francisco, California, 30 July 1914. Educated at schools in San Francisco and Long Beach, California; University of California, Berkeley, 1933-38, A.B. 1938. Secretary in fan mail and publicity departments, David O. Selznick Studios, Culver City, California, 1944, Monogram Studios, Hollywood, 1945-50, RKO-Howard Hughes Studios, Hollywood, 1951-52, Columbia Studios, Hollywood, 1952-53, and Hal Roach Television, Culver City, 1953-56; secretary, H.F. Bennett, realtors, Reno, Nevada, 1965-66. Agent: Jay Garon-Brooke Associates, 415 Central Park West, New York, New York 10025. Address: 1106 Imperial Plaza, 200 North Third Street, Boise, Idaho 83702, U.S.A.

ROMANCE AND GOTHIC PUBLICATIONS

Novels (series: Lucifer Cove; Moura)

Moura. New York, Crown, 1959.
The Affair at Alkali. New York, Arcadia House, 1960; as *Nevada Gunslinger*, London, Gresham, 1962.
The Beckoning. New York, Ace, 1965; as *The Beckoning from Moura*, 1977.
Curse of the Island Pool. New York, Lancer, 1965.
Castle Barra. New York, Paperback Library, 1966.

The Secret of Shower Tree. New York, Lancer, 1966; as *Strange Secrets*, New York, New American Library, 1976.
Black Heather. New York, Lancer, 1966.
The High Terrace. New York, Lancer, 1966; as *To Love a Dark Stranger*, London, Hale, 1969.
Castle at Witches' Coven. New York, Lancer, 1966.
A Haunted Place. New York, Lancer, 1966; Aylesbury, Buckinghamshire, Milton House, 1975.
The Demon Tower. New York, New American Library, 1966.
The Devil Vicar. New York, Ace, 1966; revised edition, as *Vicar of Moura*, 1972.
The Shadow Box. New York, Lancer, 1966.
Blood Sport (as Victor Cross). New York, Award, 1966; London, Tandem, 1967.
The Small Tawny Cat. New York, Lancer, 1967; as *The Stalking Terror*, New York, New American Library, 1977.
Richest Girl in the World. New York, Lancer, 1967.
The Chinese Door. New York, Lancer, 1967; London, Hale, 1971.
The Rest Is Silence. New York, Lancer, 1967.
A Few Fiends to Tea. New York, Belmont, 1967.
The Hounds of Hell. New York, Belmont, 1967.
One Man Too Many. New York, Lancer, 1968.
The Villa Fountains. New York, Belmont, 1968.
The Mist at Darkness. New York, New American Library, 1968.
Call of the Flesh. New York, Lancer, 1968.
The Candidate's Wife. New York, Lancer, 1968.
The Dark Gondola. New York, Ace, 1968; as *The Dark Beyond Moura*, 1977.
Of Love and Intrigue. New York, New American Library, 1969.
Lucifer Cove:
  1. *The Devil's Mistress*. New York, Lancer, 1969.
  2. *Priestess of the Damned*. New York, Lancer, 1970.
  3. *The Devil's Virgin*. New York, Lancer, 1970.
  4. *Masque of Satan*. New York, Lancer, 1971.
  5. *Chalet Diabolique*. New York, Lancer, 1971.
  6. *From Satan, With Love*. New York, Lancer, 1972.
Isle of the Undead. New York, Lancer, 1969; as *Voodoo Widow*, London, Hale, 1970.
The Beach House. New York, New American Library, 1970; Loughton, Essex, Piatkus, 1982.
Masque by Gaslight. New York, Ace, 1970; (as Virginia C. DuVaul) London, Hale, 1971.
The Vampyre of Moura. New York, Ace, 1970.
The Master of Blue Mire. New York, Dell, 1971; Aylesbury, Buckinghamshire, Milton House, 1975.
Night at Sea Abbey. New York, Lancer, 1972; Loughton, Essex, Piatkus, 1981.
The House on the Moat. New York, Lancer, 1972.
Mistress Devon. New York, Arbor House, 1972.
The Cliffs of Dread. New York, Lancer, 1972; Loughton, Essex, Piatkus, 1981.
The Dark Palazzo. New York, Arbor House, 1973; Loughton, Essex, Piatkus, 1980.
Garden of Shadows. New York, Lancer, 1973.
A Fear of Heights. New York, Lancer, 1973; as *Legacy of Fear*, New York, New American Library, 1979.
The Evil at Queens Priory. New York, Lancer, 1973; Loughton, Essex, Piatkus, 1980.
Survivor of Darkness. New York, Lancer, 1973.
The House at Sandalwood. New York, Arbor House, 1974; Aylesbury, Buckinghamshire, Milton House, 1975.
Hyde Place. New York, Arbor House, 1974.
The Ice Forest. New York, Dell, 1975.
Veronique. New York, Arbor House, 1975; London, Souvenir Press, 1978.
Marsanne. New York, Arbor House, 1976; London, Souvenir Press, 1979.
The Alpine Coach. New York, Dell, 1976; London, Souvenir Press, 1980.

Careen. New York, Dell, 1977.
Enemy of Love. New York, Dell, 1977.
Fire Dawn. New York, Arbor House, 1977; Loughton, Essex, Piatkus, 1979.
The Gaynor Women. New York, Arbor House, 1978; London, Souvenir Press, 1981.
Looking-Glass. New York, Dell, 1979.
Dinah Faire. New York, Arbor House, 1979; London, Souvenir Press, 1982.
Pacific Cavalcade. New York, Arbor House, 1980.
The Golden Marguerite (as Anne Stanfield). New York, Fawcett, 1981.
The Lombard Cavalcade. New York, Arbor House, 1982.

Novels as Jeanne Duval

The Lady Serena. New York, New American Library, 1979.
The Ravishers. New York, New American Library, 1980.

Virginia Coffman comments:

Even a writer's poorest work often takes long, agonizing hours. One's best work occasionally turns out to be a breeze. The work of romance writers certainly deserves as much respect as dead-blonde-in-the-alley novels and those repetitive, boring tales about children possessed of the devil, which have proliferated lately. Yet these types receive genuine critical attention, though most of them are carbon copies quite as unreal as any gothic.

My books for the last ten years have been historical romances and romantic sagas, the latter dealing with the period I have personally witnessed (1914 to the present).

However, I haven't forgotten those wonderful years after I introduced the first genuine Brontë-Le Fanu-type gothic in 1959 (*Moura*). This occurred following a 50-year period gothic drought. For the next six years I wrote about the gothic atmosphere and horrors that had always intrigued me. My interest in the Le Fanu-type novel began in my childhood in San Francisco when I made up gothic mysteries for my school friends. My stories always dealt with weird, haunted, terrifying houses and landscapes (with logical explanations). When I travel in Europe of the U.S.A., or on shipboard, I am not too observant of people—so I'll never be a great writer. But I feel that few writers can be as observant as I when it comes to the atmosphere of places, streets, rooms, halls, alleys. I believe the one special thing the reader will get out of my books is the atmosphere.

I am not ashamed of this. Some writers can't even boast of *one* outstanding quality.

                              *   *   *

Virginia Coffman, who has some 60 novels to her credit, combines elements of several genres in her works: the apparently supernatural threat of the gothic novel, the crime-solving of detective fiction, and the period atmosphere of the historical romance. Writing in the first person or using an omniscient narrative voice, she typically focuses upon suspenseful action and intrigue rather than psychological and philosophical exploration. She resolves her plots at the end by defeating the corrupt forces and by elaborately explaining their mysteries.

Although she does use the gothic convention of the innocent heroine pursued by evil, as is the case with 18-year-old Climene Beauhan who purchases on her own an estate in *Castle at Witches' Coven*, Coffman also presents more individualized female protagonists who depart from the romantic stereotype and complete their fates without happy marriages: Kay Aronson, a thrice-married widow of 35 who seeks the answers to her husband's death in *Chalet Diabolique* (No. 5 of the *Lucifer Cove* series); Judith Cameron, a 33-year-old parolee from a prison, whose attraction for Stephen Giles remains unfulfilled in *The House at Sandalwood*; Veronique, from the novel of the same name, who must go on through life to raise her daughter without her dead love, Gilles Marsan. Two examples whose outcomes in love are conventionally fortunate are still unique as gothic heroines: Anne Killian of *The Mist at Darkness* is a widow; Lady Leslie Fisher is unhappily married and then widowed in *Isle of the Undead*. These women tend to have an experience and an understated realism atypical of their counterparts in other romances, along with a modern sensual quality and desire unsuitable for the traditional innocent heroine.

Romantic interest is thus secondary to gothic effects of terror and suspense in Coffman's fiction, with her protagonists confronting a variety of seemingly supernatural powers, such as witches, voodoo artists, zombies, tribal curses, and ghosts, in dark, forbidding places. We gradually learn that these threats are created by human corruption—greedy relatives, smugglers, or opportunists, jilted lovers, mad aristocrats—but for a time they are described in convincing atmospheres that bewilder and scare the reader, as well as the heroine. In her Radcliffean *The Mist at Darkness*, for instance, "The creature loomed in the darkness as an enormous, evil bird. Its wrappings, like wings, threatened to engulf the very walls in its pursuit of me." Whether in 19th-century European countrysides or contemporary California, Hawaii, and Caribbean landscapes, the settings of her novels convey the obscurity and remoteness appropriate for supernatural terror.

Appealing especially to female readers of gothic romances, Virginia Coffman's books offer light entertainment with occasionally substantial heroines.

—Bette B. Roberts

COLLIN, Marion (née Cripps).   British.   Born in Aylesbury, Buckinghamshire, 12 May 1928. Married to John W. Collin; one daughter. Student nurse, Isle of Wight, 1945-48; medical secretary, London, 1948-52; secretary, 10th International Congress of Dermatologists, London; fiction editor, *Woman's Own*, London, 1952-56. Agent: Elaine Greene Ltd., 31 Newington Green, London N16 9PU. Address: 41 Clifton Road, Heaton Moor, Stockport, Cheshire, England.

ROMANCE AND GOTHIC PUBLICATIONS

Novels

Nurse Maria.   London, Mills and Boon, 1963.
Nurse at the Top.   London, Mills and Boon, and Toronto, Harlequin, 1964.
Doctors Three.   London, Mills and Boon, 1964; Toronto, Harlequin, 1965.
Nurse in the Dark.   London, Mills and Boon, 1965.
The Doctor's Delusion.   London, Mills and Boon, 1967; Toronto, Harlequin, 1968.
The Shadow of the Court.   London, Mills and Boon, 1967.
The Man on the Island.   London, Mills and Boon, 1968.
Sun on the Mountain.   London, Mills and Boon, 1969.
Nurse on an Island.   London, Mills and Boon, 1970.
Calling Dr. Savage.   London, Mills and Boon, 1970.
House of Dreams.   London, Mills and Boon, 1971.
Sawdust and Spangles.   London, Mills and Boon, 1972.

Other

Romantic Fiction, with Anne Britton.   London, Boardman, 1960.

*   *   *

In *Romantic Fiction* (1960) Marion Collin and Anne Britton presented their formula for the successful love story: *girl meets boy, girl gets boy, girl loses boy, girl gets boy*. Having arrived at her formula, Collin used it for her first novel, *Nurse Maria*, and thereafter rang the changes upon it. Her principal medium is the doctor/nurse romance (recognisable by title), with the splendid variant of the doctor/doctor romance in which the heroine is also a doctor (*Doctors Three* and *The Doctor's Delusion*). The atmosphere of the hospital, even of the operating theatre, pervades these books. The descriptions of disease, treatments, and surgery are convincing, and are frequently not for the faint-hearted ("The rotting appendix reared up easily, and... she severed it from the bowel"—*The Doctor's Delusion*). The smaller details of hospital life are there too—nurses chatting in the sluice, the eternal bedpan, etc. There is a certain incongruity, no doubt occurring in real life, about Love and the Hospital ("She could never rid herself of guilt when he kissed her in uniform." "She had created love out of a dream. The real thing had been under her nose up on Men's Surgical"—*Nurse at the Top*). We have to assume that as hospitals can produce medically dramatic situations endlessly they can also produce romantically dramatic situations in considerable profusion (while still functioning perfectly).

All of Collin's novels except one are set in modern times (*The Shadow of the Court* is set in the Crimean War). Locations range from an industrial English city (notably St. Luke's Infirmary, later General Hospital, in Manchester), to exotic islands in the Caribbean, to tea-plantations in Ceylon. Some later novels have non-medical settings and non-medical heroines: Jo in *House of Dreams* is a model, Kate in *Sawdust and Spangles* is Girl Friday in a circus, and Jan in *Sun on the Mountain* is P.A. in her father's tea company. But the lure of the stethoscope is strong and the characters in these novels are never too far from medicine: Jo suffers from a burst appendix, accidents happen in the circus, and in Ceylon Jan meets a glamorous woman doctor and her widowed father takes up with a lapsed nurse.

The heroines of Collin's novels are capable, honest, serious young women who are conscious of their responsibilities. Her medical heroines are dedicated, competent professionals, sometimes almost cases of Lamp Fever; they always put their patients first, even when their private lives are turmoils of emotion (which they are most of the time, until a happy conclusion is reached). If Collin's heroines do have a fault, it is their naivety which, helped along by their dedication to medicine and other responsibilites, makes them unaware of their physical attractiveness. The heroine is frequently contrasted with some predatory pussycattish *femme fatale* who wreaks havoc in her romantic life. But this is all part of the growing-up process which accompanies each heroine's progress towards true love as she resists or sees through the attractions of some spurious (or merely less earnest) charmer who temporarily impedes her path to the worthier man. Collin is particularly good at providing male red herrings, so that the reader is as much in two minds about possible husbands as the heroine.

—Jean Buchanan

CONWAY, Celine.   *See* **BLAIR, Kathryn**.

CONWAY, Laura.   *See* **ELSNA, Hebe**.

COOKSON, Catherine (Ann, née McMullen).   Also wrote as Catherine Marchant.   British. Born in Tyne Dock, County Durham, 20 June 1906. Married Thomas H. Cookson in 1940. Recipient: Royal Society of Literature Winifred Holtby Prize, 1968. Agent: Anthony Sheil Associates Ltd., 2 Morwell Street, London WC1B 3AR. Address: Bristol Lodge, Langley on Tyne, Hexham, Northumberland NE47 5LA, England.

ROMANCE AND GOTHIC PUBLICATIONS

Novels (series: Mallen; Mary Ann; Tilly Trotter)

Kate Hannigan.   London, Macdonald, 1950; New York, Bantam, 1972.
The Fifteen Streets.   London, Macdonald, 1952; New York, Bantam, 1973.
Colour Blind.   London, Macdonald, 1953; New York, New American Library, 1977.
A Grand Man.   London, Macdonald, 1954; New York, Macmillan, 1955.
Maggie Rowan.   London, Macdonald, 1954; New York, New American Library, 1975.
The Lord and Mary Ann.   London, Macdonald, 1956; New York, Morrow, 1975.
Rooney.   London, Macdonald, 1957; New York, Bantam, 1976.
The Devil and Mary Ann.   London, Macdonald, 1958; New York, Morrow, 1976.
The Menagerie.   London, Macdonald, 1958; New York, Bantam, 1975.
Slinky Jane.   London, Macdonald, 1959; New York, New American Library, 1976.
Fanny McBride.   London, Macdonald, 1959; New York, Bantam, 1976.
Fenwick Houses.   London, Macdonald, 1960; New York, Bantam, 1973.
Love and Mary Ann.   London, Macdonald, 1961; New York, Morrow, 1976.
The Garment.   London, Macdonald, 1962; New York, New American Library, 1974.
Life and Mary Ann.   London, Macdonald, 1962; New York, Morrow, 1977.
The Blind Miller.   London, Macdonald, 1963; New York, New American Library, 1974.
Marriage and Mary Ann.   London, Macdonald, 1964; New York, Morrow, 1978.
Hannah Massey.   London, Macdonald, 1964; New York, New American Library, 1973.
Mary Ann's Angels.   London, Macdonald, 1965; New York, Morrow, 1978.
The Long Corridor.   London, Macdonald, 1965; New York, New American Library, 1976.
The Unbaited Trap.   London, Macdonald, 1966; New York, New American Library, 1974.
Mary Ann and Bill.   London, Macdonald, 1967; New York, Morrow, 1979.

Katie Mulholland. London, Macdonald, and Indianapolis, Bobbs Merrill, 1967.
The Round Tower. London, Macdonald, 1968; New York, New American Library, 1975.
The Glass Virgin. Indianapolis, Bobbs Merrill, 1969; London, Macdonald, 1970.
The Nice Bloke. London, Macdonald, 1969; as *The Husband*, New York, New American Library, 1976.
The Invitation. London, Macdonald, 1970; New York, New American Library, 1974.
The Dwelling Place. London, Macdonald, and Indianapolis, Bobbs Merrill, 1971.
Feathers in the Fire. London, Macdonald, 1971; Indianapolis, Bobbs Merrill, 1972.
Pure as the Lily. London, Macdonald, 1972; Indianapolis, Bobbs Merrill, 1973.
The Mallen Novels. London, Heinemann, 1979.
  The Mallen Girl. New York, Dutton, 1973; London, Heinemann, 1974.
  The Mallen Streak. London, Heinemann, and New York, Dutton, 1973.
  The Mallen Lot. New York, Dutton, 1974; as *The Mallen Litter*, London, Heinemann, 1974.
The Invisible Cord. London, Heinemann, and New York, Dutton, 1975.
The Gambling Man. London, Heinemann, and New York, Morrow, 1975.
The Tide of Life. London, Heinemann, and New York, Morrow, 1976.
The Girl. London, Heinemann, and New York, Morrow, 1977.
The Cinder Path. London, Heinemann, and New York, Morrow, 1978.
The Man Who Cried. London, Heinemann, and New York, Morrow, 1979.
Tilly Trotter. London, Heinemann, 1980; as *Tilly*, New York, Morrow, 1980.
Tilly Trotter Wed. London, Heinemann, 1981; as *Tilly Wed*, New York, Morrow, 1981.
Tilly Trotter Widowed. London, Heinemann, 1982; as *Tilly Alone*, New York, Morrow, 1982.

Novels as Catherine Marchant

Heritage of Folly. London, Macdonald, 1962; New York, Lancer, 1965.
The Fen Tiger. London, Macdonald, 1963; as *The House on the Fens*, New York, Lancer, 1965.
House of Men. London, Macdonald, 1963; New York, Lancer, 1965.
The Mists of Memory. New York, Lancer, 1965.
Evil at Roger's Cross. New York, Lancer, 1966; as *The Iron Facade*, London, Heinemann, 1976.
Miss Martha Mary Crawford. London, Heinemann, 1975; New York, Morrow, 1976.
The Slow Awakening. London, Heinemann, 1976; New York, Morrow, 1977.

OTHER PUBLICATIONS

Play

Screenplay: *Jacqueline*, with others, 1956.

Other

Matty Doolin (juvenile). London, Macdonald, 1965; New York, New American Library, 1976.
Joe and the Gladiator (juvenile). London, Macdonald, 1968; New York, New American Library, 1977.
Our Kate: An Autobiography. London, Macdonald, 1969; Indianapolis, Bobbs Merrill, 1971; revised edition, Macdonald, 1982.
The Nipper (juvenile). London, Macdonald, and Indianapolis, Bobbs Merrill, 1970.
Blue Baccy (juvenile). London, Macdonald, 1972; Indianapolis, Bobbs Merrill, 1973.

Our John Willy (juvenile).   London, Macdonald, and Indianapolis, Bobbs Merrill, 1974.
Mrs. Flannagan's Trumpet (juvenile).   London, Macdonald and Jane's, 1976; New
    York, Lothrop, 1980.
Go Tell It to Mrs. Golightly (juvenile).   London, Macdonald and Jane's, 1977; New
    York, Lothrop, 1980.
Lanky Jones (juvenile).   London, Macdonald, and New York, Lothrop, 1981.

Manuscript Collection: Boston University.

*   *   *

Jarrow, Shields, Tyneside, towns of northern, industrialized England—towns drawn in
Dickensian darkness with wasted men, women, and children marching away from dawn to the
darkness of the coal pits or the stultifying noise and danger of the mill—this is Catherine
Cookson's country, alive with evil. The evil is that of exploitation, whether by rich of the poor,
the powerful of the weak, men of women, or the reverse. As the heath is a living presence in
Hardy's novels, so too is the northern landscape of Cookson's England at any time from the
early 1800's through the 1970's. *Pure as the Lily* is prefaced by a poem in which Cookson
explores her personal feeling for this area:

> I view you not, Jarrow, through
> the misty, nostalgic glow of love:
>
>
>   .   .   .   .
>
>
> but as I walk
> your new broad shining streets
> I see them with no joy,
> only as a facade
> covering the men and women
> of my time;
> for they are in my marrow.
> They whom the new generation
> would forget,
> they are my Jarrow.

From these intense memories Cookson has published over 40 books which have been translated
into eight languages. Over the years she has evolved a distinctly personal type of romantic
fiction involving the people—lower, middle, and upper class—of "her" area of England.
    Cookson's novels literally span whole lifetimes, and, while the protagonist is usually femi-
nine, such as Katie Mulholland, or Mary Walton, Tilly Trotter, or Cissie Brodie, Cookson has
also used men as protagonists, such as Edward MacFell in *The Cinder Path* or Abel Mason in
The Man Who Cried. Usually these good people try to do what is moral in a world gone mad to
deny morality of any kind. Theirs is the goodness and charity that live in the darkness of evil;
theirs is the giving when they have literally nothing left to give. All desire to be clean, honest, to
love and be loved and to work honorably for their wage; however, the obstacles to this dream
are many and include economics, the demands of those weaker than they for whom they are
responsible, their own emotions, and many violent happenings. The usual Cookson story
begins in tragedy. Abel ("the man who cried") is on his way to the funeral of his beloved Mrs.
Alice, who has been tortured and killed by her husband (buckshot first in feet, then in stomach,
then in face) because of a nasty letter Abel's wife wrote to Alice's husband. Cissie Brodie of *The
Dwelling Place* watches the bodies of her parents, both dead of the fever. She is 15 and left
responsible for no less than nine brothers and sisters. Tragedy stalks Cookson characters with
violent and oftentimes bloody ease whether male or female. Herein lies the Cookson plot.
    Cissie, for example, keeps the family together after eviction from the family cottage with the
help of the wheelwright Matt Turnbull. She sets up housekeeping in a cave on the common
land. Two younger brothers, aged nine and eleven, go down the mine in order to earn money.

Graphic descriptions of brutality sufferd by these boys and the rape of Cissie by the young Lord-to-be Clive Fischel in front of Cissie's younger sister Sarah are more standard Cookson fare. Matt marries the miller's daughter in spite of being in love with Cissie so the boys can be employed at the mill. Cissie is forced to give up her child, the result of the rape, to the present Lord Fischel, who desires a grandson. Only after Matt's wife freezes to death and he subsequently marries Cissie and after her brothers and sisters are grown and settled, does it turn out that Cissie loves Clive Fischel! Certainly one of the more startling plot twists in any literature. Cissie's sister Sarah remarks that Cissie "had been nobody's except this man's from the day she had watched him mate her." Cookson's plots twist and turn almost incestuously. Tilly Trotter is mistress to one man and marries his oldest son by his wife. Emily (*The Tide of Life*) finds happiness only with the first husband of the evil wife of the man whose mistress Emily becomes out of pity. Mary Walton is seduced by the man whom she has seen her mother try unsuccessfully to seduce.

Of course these twists are often brought about through the machinations of the evil person in the story. In Cissie's case, the person who is most evil is Clive Fischel's sister who urged him to rape Cissie and then stands and watches. In the end Mary Walton cannot forgive her mother for baiting her father until he attacks and disfigures the man, Ben, and for burning down the house where Mary's brother Jimmy and the woman he loves are sleeping, killing her and condemning him to insanity and an eventual alcoholic death. The punishment for the truly evil person present in every Cookson story is to die alone, unloved and unmourned. (The Apache torture death of the evil uncle in *Tilly Trotter Weds* must be the ultimate in horror even for Cookson.)

The critique of the Cookson canon would not be complete without a mention of her series, most recently the Mallen Trilogy and the Tilly Trotter series. The Mallen Trilogy is billed as "a dark tale of passion" and follows the fortunes of the family of Thomas Mallen through the eyes and experiences of Anna Brigmore, a lady of reduced circumstances who comes to Highbanks Hall as governess and who becomes through three successive volumes 1) mistress to Thomas, 2) adopted mother to the children from his rape of his niece by marriage (Barbara Mallen), 3) governess to Harry Bensham's children at Highbanks Hall in order to support Barbara, 4) Harry Bensham's wife, and 5) sole mistress of Highbanks Hall. The evil in this particular tale is softened somewhat by sympathy for the sufferings of the persons who do the evil. The reader cannot help liking Thomas Mallen, or feeling dreadfully sorry for Barbara, even though both cause much violence.

In *Tilly Trotter* Cookson deals with witchcraft and local superstition. But in the second of the proposed trilogy, *Tilly Trotter Wed*, the wedding of Tilly to her old master's son Matthew takes Tilly to Texas. The Texas setting is a departure for Cookson and she prefaces the story with an apologetic note ending, "after all I am merely a teller of tales." Cookson's Texas is as harsh, violent, and deceptively beautiful as her own Jarrow/Shields area. However, Cookson's Texas is an uncomfortable place, and never attains the emotional realism of her native corner of England. The sloth attributed to Mexicans and the unmitigated ferocity of the Indian attackers lack the balance and justification that Cookson gives her more familiar characters. It was with great relief I watched Tilly sail back to England at the close of this second volume in her continuing story.

Passion, violence, courage, and responsibility make up a Cookson story, though there is little of happiness for the protagonist until the end of the book. Plots are tangled and tinged with hopelessness but always resolved in the end. Characters are searching for love and economic stability. Evil and violence, and with less motivation than usual for romance gothic stories, are Cookson hallmarks. And always in the background are the mines and mills which mold the lives of the people to whom Cookson has succeeded in paying lasting tribute in her stories: the "lost youth/clumping through bone-chilling dawns/.../spent cinders spilling/from their barrows/on their way back/to Jarrow, dead Jarrow."

—Marilynn Motteler

COOPER, Henry St. John. *See* **ST. JOHN, Mabel**.

COOPER, Jilly (née Sallitt). British. Born 21 February 1937. Educated at Godolphin School, Salisbury. Married Leo Cooper in 1961; one son and one daughter. Reporter, *Middlesex Independent*, Brentford, 1957-59; worked as account executive, copywriter, publishers reader, receptionist, puppy fat model, and typist. Since 1969, Columnist, *Sunday Times*, London. Address: c/o Sunday Times, 200 Gray's Inn Road, London WC1X 8EZ, England.

ROMANCE AND GOTHIC PUBLICATIONS

Novels

> *Emily*. London, Arlington, 1975.
> *Bella*. London, Arlington, 1976.
> *Harriet*. London, Arlington, 1976.
> *Octavia*. London, Arlington, 1977.
> *Imogen*. London, Arlington, 1978.
> *Prudence*. London, Arlington, 1978.

OTHER PUBLICATIONS

Other

> *How to Stay Married*. London, Methuen, 1969; New York, Taplinger, 1970.
> *How to Survive from Nine to Five*. London, Methuen, 1970.
> *Jolly Super*. London, Methuen, 1971.
> *Men and Super Men*. London, Eyre Methuen, 1972.
> *Jolly Super Too*. London, Eyre Methuen, 1973.
> *Women and Super Women*. London, Eyre Methuen, 1974.
> *Jolly Superlative*. London, Eyre Methuen, 1975.
> *Super Men and Super Women* (omnibus). London, Eyre Methuen, 1976.
> *Work and Wedlock* (omnibus). London, Magnum, 1977.
> *Superjilly*. London, Eyre Methuen, 1977.
> *Class: A View from Middle England*. London, Eyre Methuen, 1979.
> *Supercooper*. London, Eyre Methuen, 1980.
> *Little Mabel* (juvenile). London, Granada, 1980.
> *Little Mabel's Great Escape* (juvenile). London, Granada, 1981.
> *Love and Other Heartaches*. London, Arlington, 1981.

> Editor, with Tom Hartman, *Violets and Vinegar: An Anthology of Women's Writings and Sayings*. London, Allen and Unwin, 1980.
> Editor, *The British in Love*. London, Arlington, 1980.

*   *   *

The discernment and observation that have sharpened many of the love stories of the last decade have reached an apex in Jilly Cooper's accounts of heroines who are romantically inclined but also wry, gutsy, earthy, and at times anarchic. Her stories are at the far end of the spectrum from, say, those of Barbara Cartland which are in the classic and sentimental mould. Jilly Cooper (like Mabel St. John in 1908) gives the romantic novel a fresh, invigorating, and frequently funny slant. With her stories, one feels that the genre is on the brink of a breakthrough into an exciting and still uncharted new lease of life.

She has her own highly individual style and method of packaging her novels, of course. The title of each book is the name of its heroine, and possibly every heroine reflects certain aspects of her author. (It is the representation of Jilly Cooper's own face—in many moods—that provides cover illustrations for the stories and no other picture would seem more relevant to the different plots.) Sometimes rueful, sometimes racy, but always romantically persuasive, the narratives are at their most stylish when in the first person (*Emily, Prudence,* and *Octavia,* for example). Her novels are extremely inventive and occasionally outrageous. They present a glittering mosaic of misunderstandings and changing partners, idealism and disillusionment, glamour and good nature, in settings as varied as colleges, canal barges, and haunted Highland castles.

—Mary Cadogan

CORELLI, Marie.   Pseudonym for Mary Mackay.   British.   Born in Bayswater, London, 1 May 1855. Educated privately; studied music and made debut as a pianist, London, 1884. Writer from 1885; settled in Stratford-on-Avon, 1901. *Died 21 April 1924.*

ROMANCE AND GOTHIC PUBLICATIONS

Novels

> *A Romance of Two Worlds.*   London, Bentley, 2 vols., 1886; New York, Ivers, 1 vol., n.d.
> *Vendetta; or, The Story of One Forgotten.*   London, Bentley, 3 vols., 1886; New York, Ivers, 1 vol., n.d.
> *Thelma: A Society Novel.*   London, Bentley, 3 vols., 1887; New York, Ivers, 1 vol., n.d.
> *Ardath: The Story of a Dead Self.*   London, Bentley, 3 vols., 1889; New York, Ivers, 1 vol., n.d.
> *My Wonderful Wife: A Study in Smoke.*   London, White, 1889; New York, Ivers, 1890.
> *Wormwood: A Drama of Paris.*   London, Bentley, 3 vols., 1890; New York, Munro, 1 vol., 1890.
> *The Soul of Lilith.*   London, Bentley, 3 vols., 1892; New York, Lovell, 1 vol., 1892.
> *Barabbas: A Dream of the World's Tragedy.*   London, Methuen, 3 vols., 1893; Philadelphia, Lippincott, 1 vol., 1893.
> *The Sorrows of Satan; or, The Strange Experiences of One Geoffrey Tempest, Millionaire: A Romance.*   London, Methuen, 3 vols., 1895; Philadelphia, Lippincott, 1 vol., 1896.
> *The Murder of Delicia.*   London, Skeffington, and Philadelphia, Lippincott, 1896; as *Delicia,* London, Constable, 1917.
> *The Mighty Atom.*   London, Hutchinson, and Philadelphia, Lippincott, 1896.
> *Ziska.*   Bristol, Arrowsmith, and Chicago, Stone and Kimball, 1897.

Jane: A Social Incident.   London, Hutchinson, and Philadelphia, Lippincott, 1897.

Boy.   London, Hutchinson, and Philadelphia, Lippincott, 1900.

The Master-Christian.   London, Methuen, and New York, Dodd Mead, 1900.

Temporal Power: A Study in Supremacy.   London, Methuen, and New York, Dodd Mead, 1902.

God's Good Man: A Simple Love Story.   London, Methuen, and New York, Dodd Mead, 1904.

The Strange Visitation of Josiah McNason: A Christmas Ghost Story.   London, Newnes, 1904; as *The Strange Visitation,* London, Hodder and Stoughton, 1912.

The Treasure of Heaven: A Romance of Riches.   London, Constable, and New York, Dodd Mead, 1906.

Holy Orders.   London, Methuen, and New York, Stokes, 1908.

The Devil's Motor.   London, Hodder and Stoughton, and New York, Doran, 1910.

The Life Everlasting: A Reality of Romance.   London, Methuen, and New York, Doran, 1911.

Innocent: Her Fancy and His Fact.   London, Hodder and Stoughton, and New York, Doran, 1914.

The Young Diana: An Experience of the Future.   London, Hutchinson, and New York, Doran, 1918.

My "Little Bit."   London, Collins, and New York, Doran, 1919.

The Secret Power.   London, Methuen, and New York, Doubleday, 1921.

Love—and the Philosopher: A Study in Sentiment.   London, Methuen, and New York, Doran, 1923.

Short Stories

The Hired Baby and Other Stories and Social Sketches.   Leipzig, Tauchnitz, 1891; New York, Optimus, 1894.

Three Wise Men of Gotham.   Philadelphia, Lippincott, 1896.

Cameos.   London, Hutchinson, and Philadelphia, Lippincott, 1896.

The Song of Miriam and Other Stories.   New York, Munro, 1898.

The Love of Long Ago and Other Stories.   London, Methuen, 1920; New York, Doubleday, 1921.

OTHER PUBLICATIONS

Verse

Poems, edited by Bertha Vyver.   London, Hutchinson, 1925; New York, Doran, 1926.

Other

The Silver Domino; or, Side-Whispers, Social and Literary.   London, Lamley, 1892.

Patriotism or Self-Advertisement? A Social Note on the War.   London, Greening, and Philadelphia, Lippincott, 1900.

The Greatest Queen in the World: A Tribute to the Majesty of England 1837-1900.   London, Skeffington, 1900.

An Open Letter to His Eminence Cardinal Vaughan.   London, Lamley, 1900.

A Christmas Greeting of Various Thoughts, Verses, and Fancies.   London, Methuen, 1901; New York, Dodd Mead, 1902.

The Passing of the Great Queen.   London, Methuen, and New York, Dodd Mead, 1901.

The Vanishing Gift: An Address on the Decay of the Imagination.   Edinburgh, Philosophical Institution, 1902.

The Plain Truth of the Stratford-upon-Avon Controversy.   London, Methuen, 1903.

Free Opinions Freely Expressed on Certain Phases of Modern Social Life and Conduct.
London, Constable, and New York, Dodd Mead, 1905.
Woman or Suffragette? A Question of National Choice. London, Pearson, 1907.
Is All Well with England? London, Jarrolds, 1917.
Eyes of the Sea (on the Grand Fleet). London, Marshall, 1917.
Praise and Prayer: A Simple Home Service. London, Methuen, 1923.
Open Confession to a Man from a Woman. London, Hutchinson, 1924; New York,
    Doran, 1925.
Harvard House Guide Book, with Percy S. Brentnall and Bertha Vyver. Privately
    printed, 1931.

Critical Studies: *Marie Corelli: The Life and Death of a Best-Seller* by George Bullock,
London, Constable, 1940; *Marie Corelli: The Woman and the Legend* by Eileen Bigland,
London, Jarrolds, 1953; *Marie Corelli: The Story of a Friendship* by William Stuart Scott,
London, Hutchinson, 1955; *Now Barabbas Was a Rotter: The Extraordinary Life of Marie
Corelli* by Brian Masters, London, Hamish Hamilton, 1978.

                         *   *   *

   Marie Corelli has been claimed as the first modern "bestseller" author for the reading public
expanded by Forster's 1870 Education Act. At the time of her death *The Sorrows of Satan* and
Thelma had gone through 60 and 56 editions respectively. In the face of mainly hostile
reception from the literary establishment, she refused after 1893 to send out review copies, but
this did nothing to lessen her popularity: Richard Hoggart has noted that his aunts in
working-class Leeds considered *The Sorrows of Satan* "a classic"; it was also praised by Queen
Victoria. The huge popularity of her novels makes her of social interest, but her writing itself
has the fascination of an intense, emotive imagination almost totally uninhibited by considera-
tions of style, taste, or factual reality.
   Her life itself was an elaborately cultivated fantasy. Almost certainly born in London, May 1,
1855, the illegitimate daughter of Charles Mackay, songwriter, and Ellen Mills, she claimed to
be born in 1854 of aristocratic Italian blood. In 1884 she made a well-received debut as an
improvatrice pianist in London—a character to emerge, thinly disguised, as the heroine of her
first novel, *A Romance of Two Worlds*, who, on the verge of a nervous breakdown, was
released through the help of a Paris scientist Heliobas to discover her "personal electricity" and
so explore the spiritual realm. This curious blend of mysticism and pseudo-science was to
become one hallmark of her writing. It gave comforting assurance to those disturbed by the
impact of science—in particular Darwinism—on the thought and life of the period. Wireless
telegraphy and light-rays, she informed readers of *The Life Everlasting*, were known to
Egyptian priests and the Hermetic Brethren "ages before the coming of Christ," and the mystic
Heliobas, who appears in several of her works, was a Chaldean descended from the Wise Men
from the East.
   The Soul of Lilith combines the myths of Frankenstein and Pygmalion. El-Râmi, an
Egyptian sage, uses a chemical elixir to bring to life a child who grows up as Lilith. Controlling
her body, he wishes to possess her soul, considering a female soul a minor entity. Although
warned of his error by Heliobas, he professes to Lilith his love for her, and she dissolves to dust.
The horror of a scientific view of life was even more sensationally attacked in *The Mighty
Atom*, which owes a possible debt to J.S. Mill's *Autobiography* (1873). The 11-year-old Lionel
Valliscourt is told by his materialist teacher, Professor Cadman-Gore, that the basis of all
existence is the atom. Lionel pertly out-argues his mentor; nevertheless when his child love
Jessamine, daughter of the local sexton, dies, he determines to find out whether there is life after
death and hangs himself. (Combe-Martin, the setting for the story, became a minor place of
pilgrimage due to the popularity of the novel.)
   In *Barabbas* she pioneered the Biblical epic. Spiced with a subplot showing Judas Escariot to
have betrayed Christ under the prompting of his sister Judith Escariot, who is a lover of
Caiaphas, and with accounts of the Crucifixion that in emotionalism border on the porno-
graphic, the book could be attacked but not ignored. *The Master-Christian* is a more subdued
work. It tells how Christ returned to earth as Manuel, a street urchin discovered outside the

Cathedral in Rouen. Rejected by the Roman Catholic Church, Manuel is taken in by Cardinal Felix Bonport who, in a sensational scene, is received up into heaven.

Throughout her work she savagely attacked both the established churches and the society of the day whose attentions she in private life courted with paranoic intensity. *Thelma* concerns a pure and mystic Norwegian girl discovered on a visit to that country by Sir Philip Bruce-Errington, and brought back to England to be his wife. She is more than a match in debate for the sensual, hypocritical Anglican clergyman Charles Dyceworthy, but when the evil Lady Winsleigh has her husband suspect her of unchastity, she retires to Norway, finally to be recovered by the penitent Sir Philip. Apart from the account of corrupt London society life, the novel is remarkable for its evocation of the wild Norse landscape and religion that is set against it. Although Marie Corelli had never been to Norway, guides were soon showing visitors Thelma's rock.

Corelli is, however, most likely to be remembered by *The Sorrows of Satan*. The hero, Geoffrey Tempest, is mysteriously left five million pounds by an uncle, and is befriended by Prince Lucio Ramañez. It is soon clear that the Prince is Satan, after Tempest's soul. The contest is complicated by the two women in his life, the wicked Lady Sibyl Elton and the brilliant, spiritual Mavis Clare, author, who as critics were quick to point out, had the same initials as her creator. The originality of this Faust story is that Prince Lucio himself hopes for Tempest's salvation—forced to expiate his fall from heaven, when man ceases to worship him, he will be free to return to grace. A strong story line and the melodramatic life of the main characters made it deservedly her most popular work.

Corelli saw herself as fulfilling a mission to assert "the underlying spiritual quality of life as it really is," and her work was widely quoted by both fashionable and popular preachers. Her success points to an undoubted thirst for religious literature. She also made it comfortable: the only evil was that willed by man, and every reader had the power for spiritual growth towards total goodness. She embodied this message in fiction that is vulgar in the fullest sense, clichéd, melodramatic, uninformed; yet with an imaginative flair, theatricality, and self-conviction that ultimately defies criticism by literary conventions.

—Louis James

COSTAIN, Thomas B(ertram). American. Born in Brantford, Ontario, Canada, 8 May 1885. Attended schools in Brantford. Married Ida Randolph Spragge in 1910; two daughters. Reporter, Brantford *Courier*; Editor, Guelph *Daily Mercury*, Ontario, 1908-10, and *Maclean's*, Toronto, 1910-12; Chief Associate Editor, *Saturday Evening Post*, Philadelphia, 1920-34; story editor, Twentieth Century-Fox, 1934-36; Advisory Editor, Doubleday, publishers, New York, 1939-46. Founding Editor, *American Cavalcade* magazine, 1937. D.Litt.: University of Western Ontario, London. *Died 8 October 1965.*

ROMANCE AND GOTHIC PUBLICATIONS

Novels

> *For My Great Folly.* New York, Putnam, 1942.
> *Ride with Me.* New York, Doubleday, 1944.
> *The Black Rose.* New York, Doubleday, 1945; London, Staples Press, 1947.
> *The Moneyman.* New York, Doubleday, 1947; London, Staples Press, 1948.

High Towers. New York, Doubleday, and London, Staples Press, 1949.
Son of a Hundred Kings. New York, Doubleday, 1950.
The Silver Chalice. New York, Doubleday, 1952; London, Hodder and Stoughton, 1953.
The Tontine. New York, Doubleday, 2 vols., 1955; London, Collins, 1956.
Below the Salt. New York, Doubleday, 1957; London, Collins, 1958.
The Darkness and the Dawn. New York, Doubleday, 1959; London, Collins, 1960.
The Last Love. New York, Doubleday, 1963; London, W.H. Allen, 1964.

OTHER PUBLICATIONS

Other

Joshua, Leader of a United People, with Rogers MacVeagh. New York, MacVeagh, 1943.
A History of the Plantagenets:
  The Conquerors. New York, Doubleday, 1949; as *The Conquering Family,* 1962.
  The Magnificent Century. New York, Doubleday, 1951.
  The Three Edwards. New York, Doubleday, 1958. .
  The Last Plantagenets. New York, Doubleday, 1962.
The White and the Gold: The French Regime in Canada. New York, Doubleday, 1954; London, Collins, 1957.
The Mississippi (juvenile). New York, Random House, 1955.
William the Conqueror (juvenile). New York, Random House, 1959; as *All about William the Conqueror,* London, W.H. Allen, 1961.
The Chord of Steel: The Story of the Invention of the Telephone. New York, Doubleday, 1960.

Editor, with John Beecroft, *Stories [More Stories, 30 Stories] to Remember.* New York, Doubleday, 5 vols., 1956-61.
Editor, *Twelve Short Novels.* New York, Doubleday, 1961.
Editor, *Read with Me.* New York, Doubleday, 1965.

*   *   *

Thomas B. Costain's historical romances combine a fascination with historical minutiae with a deep-seated desire to expose tyranny in all its facets and to promote democracy as the only truly humanistic form of government. At their best (*The Black Rose, Below the Salt, For My Great Folly*) his novels integrate historical events of great moment with the romantic frustrations of a young couple, usually separated by rank and family. The historical events range from Attila the Hun's final assault on Rome to Genghis Khan's invasion of China, from the Norman Conquest to the Magna Carta, from the founding of New Orleans to the final days of Napoleon. At their weakest, history is superimposed on romance to produce digressions and references inexplicable in terms of plot and character (*Son of a Hundred Kings, The Last Love, High Towers*). Costain's favorite digressions trace linguistic origins of words like "rubbernecking," relate the personal history of obscure associates of famous personalities, or expostulate on democratic theories. Costain's historical evaluations are always in terms of modern American democratic values and perspectives rather than historical necessities, expectations, and sensibilities. The result is, despite the wealth of fact, ancients who talk like moderns, adolescents who could be your neighbors, and past cultures and conflicts that seem to foreshadow present democratic concepts.

His Plantagenet tetralogy is vital to understanding the virtues and vices of his historical romances. A moving pageant of history, rich in humanizing details and anecdotes ordinary histories so often ignore, it is marred by disrupted chronology necessitating repetition and by an all too modern interpretation of historical actions and relationships; Costain tries to right the record and show how even the best of kings is but a tyrant, his good acts undercut by cruelty and indifference, and how, even in medieval times, the democratic spirit was at work as peasants rebelled for more rights, freedom, and privilege. Such a stance leads to his justifying even their destructive acts, deploring the nobility that punished them, eulogizing the Wat Tylers and John Balls of the past. In a way this historical account verges on romance, for it pays special tribute to Richard II's love for Isabel, Henry V's for Katherine, Richard III's for Anne. Its panoramic sweep and plethora of characters and events, its attempts to reinterpret the past from a modern perspective are typical of Costain's fictive technique.

Often his heroes are men out of time who have come to view their culture—its customs, politics, and values—with disdain or disgust. Frequently they meet a visionary who looks forward to an age of democracy, fairness, and scientific advancement (Roger Bacon, Galileo, St. Peter). Occasionally there are anachronisms: an awe-struck 17th-century youth musing over "the elevated conversations, the universal truths," propounded by Shakespeare, Jonson, Dekker, and Sly in the Mermaid Tavern, or the first Christians talking like 20th-century protestants. These heroes take pride in the competitive skills of their culture, and eventually match them against experts, proving they can make the longest shot, produce the fastest horse, or make a chalice worthy of Christ's last cup. They break bad laws in the name of justice and suffer long journeys and separation as self-made outcasts.

The scene frequently moves back and forth from the steppes to Rome, from Jerusalem to Antioch, from London to Peking, from Montreal to New Orleans. Ultimately these men find their destiny in a noble woman, sometimes met on journeys (*The Black Rose, Ride with Me, The Silver Chalice*), but more often a rich neighbor, loved since childhood (*Son of a Hundred Kings, For My Great Folly, High Towers, Darkness and Dawn, Below the Salt*). Romance thrives despite differences of race, culture, loyalty, or creed: Christian loves pagan; Norman, Saxon; orphaned factory worker, wealthy heiress. The man, always lower ranked, achieves position through courage, industry, and initiative; the factory worker turns star reporter, the lowly Saxon gains knighthood and wealth, the waif turns architectural genius.

Costain strives to integrate historical pageant with the trials and tribulations of his lovers. *The Darkness and the Dawn* traces the last years of Attila the Hun, particularly his final unsuccessful assault on Rome, to contrast the effete decadence of Roman culture with the hearty practicality of Mongolian hordes, to emphasize the dehumanizing effects of both extremes, and to eulogize the rebelliousness of spirited plainsmen who must toy with tyranny ultimately to be free—play Rome against Hun for their own advantage. To win his Norman lady's hand in *The Black Rose*, a Saxon noble, his fortune lost to Norman invaders, seeks fame and fortune in a daring trip to China where he meets, rescues, and falls in love with the captive daughter of a Saxon crusader. To save her, he must outwit slave traders and Mongols alike, and put his trust in a Chinese legend about pale visitors who foretell the will of gods. In *Below the Salt*, a novel mix of modern and medieval, an American Senator employs a young writer to help him write his biography, trace the Plantagenet line in Ireland, uncover a Saxon document that inspired the Magna Carta, and confirm his Saxon past and 20th-century present. The story moves from the sadistic tortures, dank cells, and limited horizons that Costain always associates with tyrannies to a modern romance involving descendants of the ghost who walks their hills. *For My Great Folly* is a convincing portrait of the Free Rovers, brave and lusty English sea captains like John Ward, who, despite James I's opposition, modelled their seamanship on Sir Walter Raleigh and fought to keep the lanes open for English ships—attacking Spanish vessels, freeing slaves, and taking rich booty. The tale sweeps through the Mediterranean and captures the grim horrors of sea life (rickets, scurvy, death-in-a-basket, becalmed seas) as well as the pride in seamanship and craftsmanship that made English sailors great. Its central character spurns court posturing for the romance and patriotism of the high seas, and acts with courage to force a foolish king to act for England's honor and safety. *Ride with Me* follows the romantic adventures of a lame newspaper man, who uses his paper to goad the government into decisive action against Napoleon; who initiates use of carrier pigeons, war correspondents, "special" editions, and the power press to improve news service; and who pursues his vivacious French mistress, a Royalist turned Bonapartist, through the major steps in the Napoleonic saga: Spain, Russia, escape from Elba, defeat at Waterloo, and bloody reprisal therafter. Doubtful of his prowess and ability, the hero discovers his strengths as, separated by distance, by scandal, by political conviction, he seeks his beloved. As is clear from each of these books, it is the amalgam of beautiful women, idealistic men, and tyrannical threats that most interests Costain. Too often, however, in an attempt to make a political point, Costain makes his heroes and heroines sacrificial idealists, his villains self-centered sadists.

Several of Costain's books involve the history of important merchant families. The *Money-man* focuses on the influence of wealthy merchant Jacques Coeur and his family on trade and politics during the reign of Charles VII; *The Tontine* involves two families entangled in an annuity-lottery-insurance scheme; *High Towers* traces the LeMoyne family's willing sacrifice of individual members for a greater cause—conquering the wilderness and building an empire for France; their success in driving out hostile Indians, frustrating greedy countrymen, and manipulating a hesitant king to found New Orleans and control the Mississippi seems to justify this stance. *Son of a Hundred Kings* deals with one of Costain's many orphans who seek their heritage, but its main thrust is the conflicts, competitions, and hatreds of a wealthy, turn-of-the-century Canadian family that rose to fame and wealth through investments in journalism and motorcars.

When Costain is content to focus on plot and character and to discuss historical events only as they relate to his central focus, his books have a compelling force that commands interest, but when he lets his fascination with detail lead him to wander from the plot, his novels degenerate into a disconnected patchwork of anecdotes. *The Last Love* is typical of his attempts to do too much, for it tries to recreate Napolean's drive, power, triumph, and genius; humanize him; characterize those important figures around him, including past loves; summarize his significant acts and battles; and follow the metamorphosis of his final, would-be mistress from childhood to womanhood. Thus Costain must be evaluated in terms of how well he reconciles his different but ambitious goals, the extremes of depicting detailed history, creating exciting plot, indulging in sentimental romance, and defending democratic idealism.

—Gina Macdonald

COULSON, Juanita (née Wellons). American. Born in Anderson, Indiana, 12 February 1933. Educated at Ball State University, Muncie, Indiana, B.S. 1954, M.A. 1961. Married the writer Robert Coulson in 1954; one son. Elementary school teacher, Huntington, Indiana, 1954-55; collator, Heckman Book Bindery, North Manchester, Indiana, 1955-57; publisher, *SFWA Forum,* for two years. Since 1953, Editor, with Robert Coulson, *Yandro* fan magazine; since 1963, free-lance writer. Recipient: Hugo Award, for editing, 1965. Guest of Honor, World Science Fiction Convention, 1972. Agent: James Allen, Box 278, Milford, Pennsylvania 18337. Address: Route 3, Hartford City, Indiana 47348, U.S.A.

ROMANCE AND GOTHIC PUBLICATIONS

Novels

The Secret of Seven Oaks. New York, Berkley, 1972.
Door into Terror. New York, Berkley, 1972.
Stone of Blood. New York, Ballantine, 1975.
Fear Stalks the Bayou. New York, Ballantine, and Skirden, Lancashire, Magna, 1976.
Dark Priestess. New York, Ballantine, 1977.
Fire of the Andes. New York, Ballantine, 1979.

OTHER PUBLICATIONS

Novels

> Crisis on Cheiron.   New York, Ace, 1967.
> The Singing Stones.   New York, Ace, 1968.
> Unto the Last Generation.   Toronto, Laser, 1975.
> Space Trap.   Toronto, Laser, 1976.
> The Web of Wizardry.   New York, Ballantine, 1978.
> The Death God's Citadel.   New York, Ballantine, 1980.
> Children of the Stars:
> 1. Tomorrow's Heritage.   New York, Ballantine, 1981.
> 2. Outward Bound.   New York, Ballantine, 1982.

Juanita Coulson comments:

In my romance and gothic novels I always try to include an element of fantasy, sometimes partially explained at the conclusion—offering an alternate, "rational" reason for some of the mysterious events of the story. But in the instance of Dark Priestess the form and time-set of the novel allowed me to dispense with all modern rationalizations. A romance, by its very nature, calls for suspension of disbelief. And if the protagonist—heroine—genuinely believes in the supernatural element affecting her life and the lives of others within the story, I feel the characters should respond accordingly. In modern times, perhaps not all events are explainable by hard, cold logic. The most outrageous things may someday be proved true. For a very long time, science disdained the theory of the German meteorologist Wegener, who suggested that certain peculiarities of the globe could be explained by means of drifting continents. It took a very long time for the experts to realize he was right after all. So it may not be wise to dismiss intuition, hunches, and other paraphysical phenomena—such as I've employed in telling my romances and gothics. Maybe it's all nonsense. And maybe some if it contains a kernal of truth. Time may tell. And thus I provide, in most cases, a choice: solid reason and the heroine's inner feelings.

                          *   *   *

Juanita Coulson's books try to fit modern liberated career women into the traditional gothic style without offending anyone's sensibilities. In other words, the women must not be too capable, too sexually free, in the last analysis, too modern. Some authors have successfully done this—Barbara Mertz, especially in her books under the name Elizabeth Peters, is one example. But when Coulson tries to force her characters into the gothic mold, their independence will not fit. When danger threatens, the feisty heroine turns around and starts looking for a man to get her out of her predicament. This not only undercuts Coulson's thrust, but also makes the heroines rather less interesting than they might otherwise be. The male characters also exemplify stereotypes all too familiar in gothics: for instance, the wild brother who is really reliable; the solid brother who is really a villain.

Coulson's failure in characterization is especially surprising when one compares her gothics to her science-fiction books, where she does portray a fairly wide array of independent women characters (the two sisters in The Death God's Citadel, for instance, are different in many ways, but even the timorous Ilissa has her own strength). Eileen, in Fear Stalks the Bayou, on the other hand, is little more than a woman who bites off more than she can chew and wants help as soon as she realizes it.

Fear Stalks the Bayou is one of a series of "Zodiac Gothics": the characters' astrological signs are given and after the denouement a "note" explains how an astrological analysis made everyone's actions and motives apparent, if not inevitable, from the first. This format is perhaps responsible for some of the woodenness in the plotting in the book, as well as the strain on Coulson's writing, never more than workmanlike, as she tries to insert birthdates inconspicuously in the text.

The contemporary real-estate development motive and the heroines' interest in modern art contrast with the more old-fashioned mildly exotic background of a clannish family in Creole New Orleans. So even in the incidentals of this story can be seen the conflict that plagues Coulson—a conflict between the traditional elements of the gothic romance and the more current type of romantic suspense story.

—Susan Branch

COURTNEY, Caroline.

ROMANCE AND GOTHIC PUBLICATIONS

Novels

Duchess in Disguise. New York, Warner, and London, Arlington, 1979.
A Wager for Love. New York, Warner, and London, Arlington, 1979.
Love Unmasked. New York, Warner, and London, Arlington, 1979.
Guardian of the Heart. New York, Warner, 1979; London, Arlington, 1980.
Dangerous Engagement. New York, Warner, 1979; London, Arlington, 1980.
The Fortunes of Love. New York, Warner, and London, Arlington, 1980.
Forbidden Love. New York, Warner, 1980.
Love Triumphant. New York, Warner, 1980.
The Romantic Rivals. New York, Warner, 1980.
Love's Masquerade. London, Arlington, 1981.
Heart of Honour. London, Arlington, 1982.
Libertine in Love. London, Arlington, 1982.

*   *   *

Of all the contemporary romance novelists, Caroline Courtney is the most likely to succeed Barbara Cartland as the grande dame of the formula romance. Her characters and style recall the early Cartland at her best, before her heroines became too breathless or incoherent to speak in complete sentences. The plots are simplistic and focus on the heroine and her emotions. The innocent heroines and stalwart heroes are likeable people who display all the requisite virtues, such as sensitivity, fidelity, tenderness, and self-sacrifice. Even the names are right: Clorinda, Davinia, Candida, Serenity, Valeria; Julian, Gilles, Justin, Greville, Auberon. Whatever the names, however, the hero and heroine are clearly meant for each other from the moment they meet, although there are always problems to overcome before they can be united and love triumph over all.

One of her earliest novels, *Duchess in Disguise*, exhibits the general characteristics and themes found in her other books. Clorinda, a pure, young country miss, weds a notorious rake, the Duke of Westhampton. Dismissed to one of his country estates, she resolves to seek revenge. She disguises herself and poses as yet another virginal innocent, and in this guise she wins his love. He learns the value of true love and is ready to sacrifice his reputation to pursue this ideal. Mutual love is revealed and everyone lives happily ever after.

The idea of the masquerade or disguise appears in about half of Courtney's novels, and is directly reflected in several titles. Similarly the theme of the disillusioned rake redeemed by pure love occurs frequently (*A Wager for Love, Guardian of the Heart, Forbidden Love,*

Libertine in Love). Obviously none of this is particularly original. Fans of Barbara Cartland and Georgette Heyer will undoubtedly recognize many of the elements in Courtney's plots. However, Caroline Courtney has polished the romance formula to a fine sheen. For sheer escapist, romantic fantasy, she is hard to beat.

—Barbara Kemp

COWEN, Frances. Also writes an Eleanor Hyde. British. Born in Oxford, 27 December 1915. Educated at Ursuline Convent, Oxford, 1920-28; Milham Ford School, Oxford, 1928-35. Married George Heinrich Munthe in 1938 (died, 1941); one daughter. Worked for Blackwell, publishers, Oxford 1938-39; member of Air Raid Precautions staff, Dartmouth, 1940-44; Assistant Secretary, Royal Literary Fund, London, 1955-66. Agent: Hughes Massie Ltd., 69 Great Russell Street, London WC1B 3DH. Address: Flat One, 13 Thornton Hill, Wimbledon, London S.W. 19, England.

Romance and Gothic Publications

Novels

The Little Heiress. London, Gresham, 1961.
The Balcony. London, Gresham, 1962.
A Step in the Dark. London, Gresham, 1962.
The Desperate Holiday. London, Gresham, 1962.
The Elusive Quest. London, Gresham, 1965.
The Bitter Reason. London, Gresham, 1966.
Scented Danger. London, Gresham, 1966.
The One Between. London, Hale, 1967.
The Gentle Obsession. London, Hale, 1968.
The Fractured Silence. London, Hale, 1969.
The Daylight Fear. London, Hale, 1969; New York, Ace, 1973.
The Shadow of Polperro. London, Hale, 1969; New York, Ace, 1973.
Edge of Terror. London, Hale, 1970.
The Hounds of Carvello. London, Hale, 1970; New York, Ace, 1973.
The Nightmare Ends. London, Hale, 1970; New York, Ace, 1972.
The Lake of Darkness. London, Hale, 1971; New York, Ace, 1974.
The Unforgiving Moment. London, Hale, 1971.
The Curse of the Clodaghs. London, Hale, 1973; New York, Ace, 1974.
Shadow of Theale. London, Hale, and New York, Ace, 1974.
The Village of Fear. New York, Ace, 1974; London, Hale, 1975.
The Secret of Weir House. London, Hale, 1975.
The Dangerous Child. London, Hale, 1975.
The Haunting of Helen Farley. London, Hale, 1976.
The Medusa Connection. London, Hale, 1976.
Sinister Melody. London, Hale, 1976.
The Silent Pool. London, Hale, 1977.
The Lost One. London, Hale, 1977.
Gateway to Nowhere. London, Hale, 1978.

The House Without a Heart. London, Hale, 1978.
House of Larne. London, Hale, 1980.
Wait for Night. London, Hale, 1980.
The Elusive Lover. London, Hale, 1981.

Novels as Eleanor Hyde

Tudor Maid. London, Hale, 1972.
Tudor Masquerade. London, Hale, 1972.
Tudor Mayhem. London, Hale, 1973.
Tudor Mystery. London, Hale, 1974.
Tudor Myth. London, Hale, 1976.
Tudor Mausoleum. London, Hale, 1977.
Tudor Murder. London, Hale, 1977.
Tudor Mansion. London, Hale, 1978.
Tudor Malice. London, Hale, 1979.
The Princess Passes. London, Hale, 1979.

OTHER PUBLICATIONS

Other (juvenile)

In the Clutch of the Green Hand. London, Nelson, 1929.
The Wings That Failed. London, Collins, 1931; abridged, as *The Plot That Failed*, 1933.
The Milhurst Mystery. London, Blackie, 1933.
The Conspiracy of Silence. London, Sheldon Press, 1935.
The Perilous Adventure. London, Queensway Press, 1936.
Children's Book of Pantomimes. London, Cassell, 1936.
Laddie's Way: The Adventures of a Fox Terrier. London, Lutterworth Press, 1939.
The Girl Who Knew Too Much. London, Lutterworth Press, 1940.
Mystery Tower. London, Lutterworth Press, 1945.
Honor Bound. London, Lutterworth Press, 1946.
Castle in Wales. Huddersfield, Schofield and Sims, 1947.
The Secret of Arrivol. Huddersfield, Schofield and Sims, 1947.
Mystery at the Walled House. London, Lutterworth Press, 1951.
The Little Countess. London, Thames, 1954.
The Riddle of the Rocks. London, Lutterworth Press, 1956.
Clover Cottage. London, Blackie, 1958.
The Secret of Grange Farm. London, Children's Press, 1961.
The Secret of the Loch. London, Children's Press, 1963.

*   *   *

Frances Cowen is adept at producing emotional suspense stories—for juveniles in full-length books and tales published in the *Girl's Own Paper* and in adult detective fiction and thriller romances. She has been writing for five decades but her feeling for the romantic Gothic mood is as intense as ever. *The Secret of Weir House* combines the flavours of Edwardian and modern life with English and American interest. Gisele—from the USA—inherits a Thames-side Victorian house from a remote English relative, but when she arrives to claim her property, it is not only occupied by squatters but overhung with a ghostly mystery that is linked to the death by drowning of a great aunt just before the first world war. Stephen, a London social worker, however, not only helps Gisele to unravel the mystery but, of course, to find love.

Cowen is most strongly associated with romance when she writes historical novels as Eleanor Hyde. There are nine of these books in the "Tudor" series, with vivid conveyance of the period by discerning use of historical trappings, ritual pageantry and splendours. There are the sights and sounds of viol, lute, and recorder playing in the musicians' gallery of great houses; the herb garden of a country manor; the "chaotic medley" of men-at-arms, ladies-in-waiting, and courtiers attending "Gloriana" on one of her journeys—and so on. Events in the first of these novels (*Tudor Maid*) clearly illustrate the dramatic and romantic nature of the series. Ann de Chaubriez, the illegitimate daughter of a French marquis and an English mother, is brought up in France. Eventually, orphaned abruptly by her father's murder, and unprovided for, she is taken to England to work ostensibly as a governess in the home of an unscrupulous plotter against the Queen. (He tries to use Ann's auburn-haired, pale-faced resemblance to the Queen in a scheme to overthrow her.)

Ann undergoes some hair-raising adventures before being rescued from these intrigues by Richard Davenant—a young Englishman who not only clears her reputation but marries her. Similar themes recur in the books. In the last novel of the series, *Tudor Malice*, there is another orphaned heroine, Isobelle, who finds herself exposed to black magic as well as court intrigues. In her case too, romantic love—in the shape of a miller's son, Matthew Holborn—lifts her out of the hazards of association with magic and majesty.

—Mary Cadogan

CRAIG, Alisa.   *See* **MacLEOD, Charlotte**.

CRAIG, Mary Francis (née Young).   Also writes as M.S. Craig; Alexis Hill; Mary Francis Shura.   American.   Born in Pratt, Kansas, 27 February 1923. Attended Maryville State College, Missouri, 1940-43. Married 1) Daniel C. Shura in 1943 (died, 1959), two daughters and one son; 2) Raymond Craig in 1961, one daughter. Public Relations Director, Girl Scouts of America, 1960-61; Director and Vice-President, Young Brothers Cattle Corp.; book reviewer, San Rafael *Independent Journal*, California, 1973-77. Recipient: Central Missouri State University award, 1974; New York Poetry Forum Lillian Steinhauer Award, 1976. Agent: McIntosh and Otis, 475 Fifth Avenue, New York, New York 10017. Address: 301 Hinsdale Drive, No. 112, Clarendon Hills, Illinois 60514, U.S.A.

ROMANCE AND GOTHIC PUBLICATIONS

Novels

> *The Shop on Threnody Street* (as Mary Francis Shura).   New York, Grosset and Dunlap, 1972.
> *A Candle for the Dragon.*   New York, Dell, 1973.

Ten Thousand Several Doors. New York, Hawthorn, 1973; as *Mistress of Lost River*, New York, Manor, 1976.
The Cranes of Ibycus. New York, Hawthorn, 1974; as *Shadows of the Past*, New York, Manor, 1976.
Were He a Stranger. New York, Dodd Mead, 1978; London, Collins, 1979.
Passion's Slave (as Alexis Hill). New York, Jove, 1979.
The Untamed Heart (as Alexis Hill). New York, Jove, 1980.
The Chicagoans: Dust to Diamonds (as M.S. Craig). New York, Jove, 1981.

OTHER PUBLICATIONS

Other (juvenile) as Mary Francis Shura

Simple Spigott. New York, Knopf, 1960; London, Hamish Hamilton, 1967.
The Garret of Greta McGraw. New York, Knopf, 1961.
Mary's Marvelous Mouse. New York, Knopf, 1962; London, Hamish Hamilton, 1965.
The Nearsighted Knight. New York, Knopf, 1964.
Run Away Home. New York, Knopf, 1965.
Shoe Full of Shamrock. New York, Atheneum, 1965.
A Tale of Middle Length. New York, Atheneum, 1966.
Backwards for Luck. New York, Knopf, 1967.
Pornada. New York, Atheneum, 1968.
The Valley of the Frost Giants. New York, Lothrop, 1971.
The Seven Stone. New York, Holiday House, 1972.
Topcat of Tam. New York, Holiday House, 1972.
The Riddle of Raven's Gulch. New York, Dodd Mead, 1964; as *The Riddle of Raven's Hollow*, New York, Scholastic, 1976.
The Season of Silence. New York, Atheneum, 1976.
The Gray Ghosts of Taylor Ridge. New York, Dodd Mead, 1978.
Mister Wolf and Me. New York, Dodd Mead, 1979.
The Barkley Street Six-Pack. New York, Dodd Mead, 1979.
Chester. New York, Dodd Mead, 1980.
Happles and Cinnamunger. New York, Dodd Mead, 1981.

Manuscript Collection: University of Oregon, Eugene.

Mary Francis Craig comments:

There is a dreadful tendency on the part of non-writers, knowing nothing else to say, to ask, "What are you working on...the Great American Novel?" I have learned to reply that I will attempt such a work when there is only one America in the United States. Having lived in many different parts of this nation, I am persuaded that there are more different "Americas" than many people know of.

This comes to mind in the introduction of my work. I am a writer and an American and an adult. Like the earth we walk on, I have become these things through time and the layering of experience. Therefore, even as with my nation, I find myself an untidy collection of different personalities, different people. It has made sense to me to separate the work of these different people under different names.

I am that twentieth-century rarity, a person whose childhood, while not without adversity, was happy and stimulating. That is the world of my children's books, a world of animals and good things to eat and problems that can be solved by the child himself and the commitment of learning the kinds of love he will need as an adult.

My adult books come from other, sometimes darker streams. It is a good and satisfying way to work and live.

*   *   *

Mary Craig is better known as Mary Francis Shura, a writer of juvenile fiction. Her reputation has yet to be made in the world of adult romantic suspense.

Her first effort, *The Shop on Threnody Street*, marked a promising debut. *Ten Thousand Several Doors*, a gothic suspense tale, relates the efforts of Lorelei Wells to settle her father's estate. Murder, mistaken identity, and intrigue along with plenty of young men for the heroine to choose from provide an average story that is not especially remarkable. In *The Cranes of Ibycus* Chryselis Clement determines to fulfill her grandfather's deathbed wish to deliver a package to Mathew Martin whose whereabouts are unknown. Her search naturally leads to murder, intrigue, suspense, and romance. All three of these novels are competently written and contain all the proper ingredients for the romantic suspense genre, but somehow they don't succeed—they are neither brilliant nor particularly memorable.

Were He A Stranger takes place in southern California where a young woman's husband has been thrown over a cliff while jogging. Although she is suspected of the dirty deed, she is allowed to help with the investigation along with an attractive lawyer. Double identity, murder, and large sum of money move the plot creakingly to Atlanta and Chicago. Again, this is average fare.

Craig's latest novel is a large scale saga, *The Chicagoans: Dust to Diamonds*. Perhaps the change in genre will be profitable, since, in the field of romantic suspense, Mary Craig is still only a very minor light.

—Marilyn Lockhart

CROWE, Cecily (née Teague).   American.   Born in New York City. Educated at St. Agatha School, New York; Columbia University, New York. Married 1) Richard H. Crowe (died), one daughter; 2) James A. Bentley in 1975. Agent: Harold Ober Associates, 40 East 49th Street, New York, New York 10017. Address: Brick House, Mirror Lake, New Hampshire 03853, U.S.A.

ROMANCE AND GOTHIC PUBLICATIONS

Novels

    Miss Spring.   New York, Random House, 1953.
    The Tower of Kilraven.   New York, Holt Rinehart, 1965.
    Northwater.   New York, Holt Rinehart, 1968.
    The Twice-Born.   New York, Random House, 1972.
    Abbeygate.   New York, Coward McCann, 1977.
    The Talisman.   New York, St. Martin's Press, 1979.

Manuscript Collection: Boston University Library.

*   *   *

It is obvious that Cecily Crowe honed her novelistic skills by writing short stories. Her prose style is exquisitely crafted and tight as befits the short story which must reveal much in a confined space. Crowe's novels burst with highly detailed, almost practiced descriptive passages. One feels that she knows every secret of the lives of even her minor characters.

While these novels fall into the category of romantic suspense their true emphasis is on romance, in the sense that both the characters and the reader are transported to a world remote from ordinary life. The heroines are as a rule rather unglamorous women, often older than the average romantic heroine. For the most part they are widows or in some manner losers at love. When these women are tranplanted into exotic environments like castles and brought into contact with traditionally brooding Gothic heroes their adventures are escapist entertainment of the highest order. Crowe's sense of humor saves her work from being merely frothy. There is a tongue-in-cheek feeling about much of her work that seems lovingly to parody the style that she has chosen. Her humor is evident in *The Tower of Kilraven* when she first describes the frankly sexual allure of one of the heroes and then describes him as mounted upon a "tall, self-centered-looking horse." Flashes of such humor and mockery as this run through most of her work.

The characters in Cecily Crowe's writing are so painstakingly delineated that they stand out against the rich backgrounds like beautifully detailed miniatures. Even children, who often get very short shrift in romances, are treated as full characters rather than plot devices. Thomas, Maggie, and Anne in *Abbeygate* are memorable for their complete naturalness. They are neither perfect creatures nor monsters, but believably troubled children. The secondary characters in all the novels are drawn with somewhat broader strokes, like Dottie in *The Talisman*, whose passion for costumes like a Hawaiian print skirt, shocking pink sweater, and Tartan shawl is a metaphor for her personality. The heroes are perhaps the least realistic of all the characters since they are made in the Heathcliff-Mr. Rochester mold. Nevertheless, they are human and attractive in their flaws so that the reader can hardly fail to respond to their charms.

Crowe's training in the short story emerges again in the endings of her books. She avoids the over-writing and the sensation of winding down that is often found in romances. In *The Tower of Kilraven* the love story is left hanging as the heroine leaves the castle without having made a choice between two prospective lovers. A less confident author might have written this ending to death. The crispness and finality of these denouements leave the reader satisfied rather than sated.

—Susan Quinn Berneis

CURTIS, Peter. *See* **LOFTS, Norah**.

DAILEY, Janet.   American.   Born in Storm Lake, Iowa, 21 May 1944. Educated at Independence High School, Iowa, graduated 1962. Married William Dailey; two stepchildren. Secretary, Omaha, Nebraska, 1963-74. Recipient: Romance Writers of America Golden Heart

Award, 1981. Agent: William Dailey, Star Route 4, Box 2197, Branson, Missouri 65616, U.S.A.

Novels

No Quarter Asked.   London, Mills and Boon, 1974; Toronto, Harlequin, 1976.
Savage Land.   London, Mills and Boon, 1974; Toronto, Harlequin, 1976.
Something Extra.   London, Mills and Boon, 1975; Toronto, Harlequin, 1978.
Fire and Ice.   London, Mills and Boon, 1975; Toronto, Harlequin, 1976.
Boss Man from Ogallala.   London, Mills and Boon, 1975; Toronto, Harlequin, 1976.
After the Storm.   London, Mills and Boon, 1975; Toronto, Harlequin, 1976.
Land of Enchantment.   London, Mills and Boon, 1975; Toronto, Harlequin, 1976.
Sweet Promise.   London, Mills and Boon, 1976; Toronto, Harlequin, 1979.
The Homeplace.   London, Mills and Boon, and Toronto, Harlequin, 1976.
Dangerous Masquerade.   London, Mills and Boon, 1976; Toronto, Harlequin, 1977.
Show Me.   London, Mills and Boon, 1976; Toronto, Harlequin, 1977.
Valley of the Vapours.   London, Mills and Boon, 1976; Toronto, Harlequin, 1977.
The Night of the Cotillion.   London, Mills and Boon, 1976; Toronto, Harlequin, 1977.
Fiesta San Antonio.   London, Mills and Boon, and Toronto, Harlequin, 1977.
Bluegrass King.   London, Mills and Boon, and Toronto, Harlequin, 1977.
A Lyon's Share.   London, Mills and Boon, and Toronto, Harlequin, 1977.
The Widow and the Wastrel.   London, Mills and Boon, and Toronto, Harlequin, 1977.
The Ivory Cane.   London, Mills and Boon, 1977; Toronto, Harlequin, 1978.
Six White Horses.   London, Mills and Boon, 1977; Toronto, Harlequin, 1979.
To Tell the Truth.   London, Mills and Boon, 1977; Toronto, Harlequin, 1978.
The Master Fiddler.   London, Mills and Boon, 1977; Toronto, Harlequin, 1978.
Giant of Medabi.   London, Mills and Boon, and Toronto, Harlequin, 1978.
Beware of the Stranger.   London, Mills and Boon, and Toronto, Harlequin, 1978.
Darling Jenny.   London, Mills and Boon, and Toronto, Harlequin, 1978.
The Indy Man.   London, Mills and Boon, and Toronto, Harlequin, 1978.
Reilly's Woman.   London, Mills and Boon, and Toronto, Harlequin, 1978.
For Bitter or Worse.   London, Mills and Boon, 1978; Toronto, Harlequin, 1979.
Tidewater Lover.   London, Mills and Boon, 1978; Toronto, Harlequin, 1979.
The Bride of the Delta Queen.   London, Mills and Boon, 1978; Toronto, Harlequin, 1979.
Green Mountain Man.   London, Mills and Boon, 1978; Toronto, Harlequin, 1979.
Sonora Sundown.   London, Mills and Boon, and Toronto, Harlequin, 1978.
Summer Mahogany.   London, Mills and Boon, 1978; Toronto, Harlequin, 1979.
The Matchmakers.   London, Mills and Boon, and Toronto, Harlequin, 1978.
Big Sky Country.   London, Mills and Boon, and Toronto, Harlequin, 1978.
Low Country Liar.   London, Mills and Boon, and Toronto, Harlequin, 1979.
Strange Bedfellow.   London, Mills and Boon, and Toronto, Harlequin, 1979.
For Mike's Sake.   London, Mills and Boon, and Toronto, Harlequin, 1979.
Sentimental Journey.   London, Mills and Boon, and Toronto, Harlequin, 1979.
Sweet Promise.   London, Mills and Boon, and Toronto, Harlequin, 1979.
Bed of Grass.   London, Mills and Boon, 1979; Toronto, Harlequin, 1980.
That Boston Man.   London, Mills and Boon, 1979; Toronto, Harlequin, 1980.
Kona Winds.   London, Mills and Boon, 1979; Toronto, Harlequin, 1980.
A Land Called Deseret.   London, Mills and Boon, and Toronto, Harlequin, 1979.
Touch the Wind.   New York, Pocket Books, 1979; London, Fontana, 1980.
Difficult Decision.   London, Mills and Boon, and Toronto, Harlequin, 1980.
Enemy in Camp.   London, Mills and Boon, and Toronto, Harlequin, 1980.
Heart of Stone.   London, Mills and Boon, and Toronto, Harlequin, 1980.
Lord of the High Lonesome.   London, Mills and Boon, and Toronto, Harlequin, 1980.

The Mating Season. London, Mills and Boon, and Toronto, Harlequin, 1980.
Southern Nights. London, Mills and Boon, and Toronto, Harlequin, 1980.
The Thawing of Mara. London, Mills and Boon, and Toronto, Harlequin, 1980.
One of the Boys. London, Mills and Boon, and Toronto, Harlequin, 1980.
The Rogue. New York, Pocket Books, and London, Fontana, 1980.
Wild and Wonderful. London, Mills and Boon, 1980; Toronto, Harlequin, 1981.
Ride the Thunder. New York, Pocket Books, and London, Fontana, 1981.
A Tradition of Pride. London, Mills and Boon, and Toronto, Harlequin, 1981.
The Travelling Kind. London, Mills and Boon, and Toronto, Harlequin, 1981.
Dakota Dreamin'. London, Mills and Boon, and Toronto, Harlequin, 1981.
The Hostage Bride. New York, Silhouette, 1981; London, Silhouette, 1982.
Night Way. New York, Pocket Books, 1981.
Calder:
   This Calder Sky. New York, Pocket Books, 1981.
   This Calder Range. New York, Pocket Books, 1982.
   Stands a Calder Man. New York, Pocket Books, 1982.
Lancaster Men. New York, Silhouette, 1981.
For the Love of God. New York, Silhouette, 1981.
Northern Magic. London, Mills and Boon, and Toronto Harlequin, 1982.
With a Little Luck. London, Mills and Boon, and Toronto, Harlequin, 1982.
That Carolina Summer. London, Mills and Boon, and Toronto, Harlequin, 1982.
Terms of Surrender. New York, Silhouette, 1982.
Wildcatter's Woman. New York, Silhouette, 1982.

Uncollected Short Story

"The Eye of the Beholder," in *Family Circle* (New York), 1981.

Janet Dailey comments:

I consider myself to be a teller of stories about the inter-relationships of people whether it be in the multi-character form of my major novels published by Pocket Books, or the one-on-one, man/woman relationships of my romance stories. To me, it is extremely important that each story be uniquely different, even if they retain common elements such as conflicts that are resolved to "happy endings." I write my stories to entertain. That is their purpose for being. It's very rewarding for an author artistically to learn of the hours of enjoyment people have derived from reading his or her works. I know it's been true for me.

*   *   *

Every afternoon American television dramatizes in soap opera after soap opera the story of a passionate, successful man desperately in love with a beautiful, partially rejecting woman. Because soap operas, like other folklore, weave their spells through stretching and repetition, these heroically devoted men conceive affections that last literally for years, through marriages, divorces, remarriages, even through casting changes. What they can never outlast, it seems, is their audience's patient attention to a tale of diligent pursuit, or rather, of what it is like to be diligently pursued. These are women's stories, after all; a permanently smitten man is necessary, but women's stories still tell the tale of the pursued. From such a point of view, a strong man is not diminished by his hopelessly undying passion, even if he is made to whimper occasionally. Rather, he increases in importance and attractiveness because he manifests emotional vulnerability. Whatever else they give their audiences, American soap operas provide women with embodiment of this fantasy. You are beautiful, they insinuate; you are hesitatingly passionate, you are desperately loved.

The novels of Janet Dailey tell this insistent story, too, though in fore-shortened versions. Hers are not leisurely tales like the incrementally repeated afternoon soaps. Rather, Dailey writes urgent novels of rapid, briefly thwarted pursuit, often in hurried prose, especially in those done to the ten-chapter tune of her trademark romances, Harlequin and Silhouette. These brief romances are indeed "silhouettes"—one-dimensional portraits of single-minded characters; they are bare-bones books, which pay little attention to secondary characters, personal histories, temporal settings (other than a vague "now"), or even to place. In fact, though the back covers of Dailey's Harlequins reiterate her intention to set a romance in each of the 50 states, place has little resonance in her novels. Janet Dailey's shorter novels are Rest-Stop Romances, replete with a fleeting mention of each state's highlights, but lacking the leisure and warmth of long acquaintance with any.

When we enter Dailey's fictional world we trade "leisure," "warmth," and "long acquaintance" for haste, ardent fires, and instant recognition. The "ardent fires" and "instant recognition" take place, of course, between the two principals, whose often denied but utterly undeniable attraction for each other sparks each book. Dailey is a canny writer and varies the circumstances of each fateful attraction without ever altering the supra-rational impetus behind it. "Physical chemistry" is the way the heroine of *Touch the Wind* "rationalizes" this passion—in her case a puzzling ardor for the Mexican outlaw who has kidnapped her. Other heroines explain in different but equally fatal terms the myth that underlies Dailey's world: "It was always you," Kit pronounces at the end of *Lord of the High Lonesome*, "There was never anyone else but you." For Dailey's women this is inevitably true. Even if they have had previous lovers or husbands, they have not been really *touched* before. In *Dakota Dreamin'* Edie's late husband has never moved her the way her truculent new neighbor has; in *Green Mountain Men* the dead husband is fictitious; in *Show Me* even the heroine's prior sexual encounter with the hero has been fabricated to protect a child. In this sense, each Dailey heroine is chaste; even if experienced she is essentially untouched until the grand passion depicted in each book awakens her.

This awakening, of course, is disturbing, because in true romance fashion Dailey's heroines find themselves devastatingly aroused by men they initially dislike and don't entirely trust. The fearsomeness of this arousal leaves the heroine in a prolonged state of semi-surrender, as Dailey treats hero and reader alike to continual, teasing *romantus interruptus*, punctuated by the heroine's frantic, belated cries of "No!" Given the radically tight focus of romance fiction, I am surprised to find that Dailey's love and sex scenes are often the most poorly written parts of her books. Stock phrases show up in novel after novel: each hero has "muscular thighs," impresses upon each heroine his "hard male shape" (as genitally explicit as Dailey gets), and "forays upon the slopes" of her breasts. The woman, meanwhile, is responsible but resistant until the man's insistent kiss has "parted her lips"; she then finds "flames leaping within her" at the "searing fire in his kiss," or, alternatively, finds herself "drowning in his kisses" and seeks "the lifeline of his mouth." This writing about the heart is itself without heart, cliché-ridden, hasty and dispirited. It may be typical of romance, but it is not indicative of what Dailey is able to do, for elsewhere she shows herself capable of better, more compelling prose. Generally, her longer books are superior pieces of workmanship, not simply padded Harlequins. In *Touch the Wind, The Rogue, Ride the Thunder,* and *Night Way* Dailey tackles more ambitious subjects and her writing perks up. It is as if in writing about outlaws and Indians, ranching and riding she comes much closer to her own emotional center of gravity, either because these are activities she knows or because they spring from her personal fantasy life. *Night Way*, to my mind her best book, shows what Dailey can do when she is controlling her romance formula rather than letting it take over her books. In this novel she develops several characters, historically and emotionally, shifts point of view and setting, lovingly details place and local culture, and sustains the narrative with greater skill. In no way does Dailey sacrifice her strong-man-loves-somewhat-unwilling-woman formula in *Night Way* and the other longer books; she simply fleshes out her silhouettes.

The contrast between Dailey's improbably urgent short romances and her longer, better written romantic novels suggests in some ways that there are two Janet Dailey's available to romance readers. The trademark romances have won Dailey her audience and made her fortune, but they have not elicited her best work. Her announced intention to write a four-volume Calder saga, as well as her recent promotion of Silhouette's "longer editions" suggest that Dailey herself is aware of this and chooses to move on. Though her trailer may continue around the Interstates, it seems possible that Dailey is ready to add to her formulaic strong-man-in-pursuit novels that other staple of romance fiction, devotion to place.

—Nancy Regan

DANBURY, Iris. British. Married. Worked as typist and secretary; owner of a typing business; then full-time writer. Address: c/o Mills and Boon Ltd., 15-16 Brooks Mews, London W1A 1DR, England.

ROMANCE AND GOTHIC PUBLICATIONS

Novels

The Gentle Invader. London, Mills and Boon, 1957.
My Heart a Traitor. London, Mills and Boon, 1958.
One Enchanted Summer. London, Mills and Boon, 1958.
Feather in the Wind. London, Mills and Boon, 1959.
The Rose-Walled Castle. London, Mills and Boon, 1959.
The Rainbow Shell. London, Mills and Boon, 1960.
The Silent Nightingale. London, Mills and Boon, 1961.
Hotel Belvedere. London, Mills and Boon, 1961; Toronto, Harlequin, 1969.
Bride of Kylsaig. London, Mills and Boon, 1963; Toronto, Harlequin, 1968.
Story de Luxe. London, Mills and Boon, 1963.
Home from the Sky. London, Mills and Boon, 1964.
The Marble Mountain. London, Mills and Boon, 1964.
Bonfire in the Dusk. London, Mills and Boon, 1965.
Illyrian Summer. London, Mills and Boon, 1965.
Doctor at Drumlochan. London, Mills and Boon, 1966; Toronto, Harlequin, 1967.
The Eagle of Segarra. London, Mills and Boon, 1966.
Doctor at Villa Ronda. London, Mills and Boon, 1967; Toronto, Harlequin, 1968.
Rendezvous in Lisbon. London, Mills and Boon, 1967; Toronto, Harlequin, 1968.
Feast of the Candles. London, Mills and Boon, 1968; Toronto, Harlequin, 1970.
Hotel by the Loch. London, Mills and Boon, 1968; Toronto, Harlequin, 1969.
Chateau of Pines. London, Mills and Boon, and New York, Golden Press, 1969.
Isle of Pomegranates. London, Mills and Boon, 1969; Toronto, Harlequin, 1970.
Island of Mermaids. London, Mills and Boon, 1970; Toronto, Harlequin, 1971.
Serenade at Santa Rosa. London, Mills and Boon, and Toronto, Harlequin, 1970.
The Legend of Roscano. London, Mills and Boon, 1971; Toronto, Harlequin, 1972.
Summer Comes to Albarosa. London, Mills and Boon, and Toronto, Harlequin, 1971.
Jacaranda Island. London, Mills and Boon, and Toronto, Harlequin, 1972.
Mandolins of Mantori. London, Mills and Boon, and Toronto, Harlequin, 1973.
The Silver Stallion. London, Mills and Boon, 1973; Toronto, Harlequin, 1974.
The Fires of Torretta. London, Mills and Boon, and Toronto, Harlequin, 1974.
The Amethyst Meadows. London, Mills and Boon, and Toronto, Harlequin, 1974.
A Pavement of Pearl. Toronto, Harlequin, 1975.
The Scented Island. London, Mills and Boon, 1976; Toronto, Harlequin, 1977.
The Windmill of Kalakos. London, Mills and Boon, and Toronto, Harlequin, 1976.

The Painted Palace.   Toronto, Harlequin, 1977.

*   *   *

Iris Danbury, a Mills and Boon author reprinted by Harlequin Books, writes contemporary romances. She has a particular affinity for island locales as well as other foreign settings. After a few shaky earlier novels, such as *Hotel Belvedere*, Danbury hit her stride in *Isle of Pomegranates* and *Island of Mermaids*. The formula she evolves here and follows in her later novels includes first, the heroine who travels to some Mediterranean area; second, the hero, an intriguing man seemingly indifferent to the heroine; third, various alternative men who are romantic possibilities; fourth, various women who serve to arouse the heroine's jealousy; and last, a resolution when hero and heroine finally break through the misconceptions that have kept them apart. Her men and women are types, used over again in novel after novel. The heroines are spunky, resourceful, independent, and determined not to be duped or to reveal their love. The heroes are usually engineers or geologists, with occupations appropriate to their being stationed in the foreign locale and to their being reluctant to form permanent attachments. They may appear brusque, arrogant, and overbearing, but underneath it all they are true-blue English types, with all the proper feelings. Their rivals are often local Spanish dons or Italian signors, who fascinate but do not win the heroine.

Since Danbury's plots are so similar, much of the interest in her stories is provided by the background, which ranges from the Lamini Islands of Italy to Capri, the Canary Islands, Sicily, Rhodes, Corsica, Portugal, and Spain. The author is obviously familiar with these locales, and describes the local scenery and tourist spots. Local foods, festivals (as in *The Fires of Torretta*), and living conditions liven her plots. However, the setting remains a backdrop for the romance, and there is no real involvement with the people. The matter of finding a poor family a home in *Summer Comes to Albarosa*, one of Danbury's better books, is about as serious as her stories ever get. The author's chief limitation is a repetitious and prolix style which rather quickly induces boredom. However, her novels are cheerful and pleasant, and certainly in the middle rank within the genre.

—Necia A. Musser

DANIELS, Dorothy (née Smith).   Also writes as Danielle Dorsett; Angela Gray; Cynthia Kavanaugh; Helaine Ross; Suzanne Somers; Geraldine Thayer; Helen Gray Weston.   American.   Born in Waterbury, Connecticut, 1 July 1915. Educated at Central Connecticut State College, New Britain. Married to Norman A. Daniels. Formerly, actress and school teacher. Agent: Robert P. Mills Ltd., 333 Fifth Avenue, New York, New York 10016. Address: 6107 Village 6, Camarillo, California 93010, U.S.A.

ROMANCE AND GOTHIC PUBLICATIONS

Novels

The Dark Rider (as Geraldine Thayer).   New York, Avalon, 1961.
Jennifer James, R.N.   New York, Fawcett, 1962.
No Tears Tomorrow (as Helaine Ross).   New York, Avalon, 1962.
Eve Originals.   New York, Lancer, 1962.

Cruise Ship Nurse. New York, Paperback Library, 1963.
Country Nurse. New York, Berkley, 1963.
World's Fair Nurse. New York, Paperback Library, 1964.
Island Nurse. New York, Paperback Library, 1964.
The Tower Room. New York, Lancer, 1965.
The Leland Legacy. New York, Pyramid, 1965.
Shadow Glen. New York, Paperback Library, 1965.
Marriott Hall. New York, Paperback Library, 1965.
Darkhaven. New York, Paperback Library, 1965.
The Unguarded. New York, Lancer, 1965.
The Mistress of Falcon Hill. New York, Pyramid, 1965.
Dance in Darkness. New York, Lancer, 1965.
Cliffside Castle. New York, Lancer, 1965.
The Lily Pond. New York, Paperback Library, 1965.
Marble Leaf. New York, Lancer, 1966; as *The Marble Angel*, 1970.
Midday Moon. New York, Lancer, 1966.
Knight in Red Armor. New York, Lancer, 1966.
Nurse at Danger Mansion. New York, Lancer, 1966; as *Danger Mansion*, n.d.
Dark Villa. New York, Lancer, 1966.
Bride of Lenore (as Cynthia Kavanaugh). New York, Pyramid, 1966.
The Deception (as Cynthia Kavanaugh). New York, Pyramid, 1966.
Mystic Manor (as Helen Gray Weston). New York, Paperback Library, 1966.
The Templeton Memoirs. New York, Lancer, 1966.
This Ancient Evil. New York, Lancer, 1966.
The Last of the Mansions. New York, Lancer, 1966; as *Survivors of Darkness*, 1969.
House of False Faces (as Helen Gray Weston). New York, Paperback Library, 1967.
House of Stolen Memories. New York, Lancer, 1967; as *Mansion of Lost Memories*, 1969.
The Sevier Secrets. New York, Lancer, 1967.
Screen Test for Laurel. New York, Avon, 1967.
Traitor's Road. New York, Lancer, 1967.
House of Seven Courts. New York, Lancer, 1967.
The Eagle's Nest. New York, Lancer, 1967.
Mostly by Moonlight. New York, Lancer, 1968.
Blue Devil Suite. New York, Belmont, 1968.
Affair at Marrakesh. New York, Pyramid, 1968.
Candle in the Sun. New York, Lancer, 1968.
Lady of the Shadows. New York, Paperback Library, 1968.
Duet. New York, Lancer, 1968.
Strange Paradise. New York, Paperback Library, 1969.
Affair in Hong Kong. New York, Pyramid, 1969.
Voice on the Wind. New York, Paperback Library, 1969.
The Carson Inheritance. New York, Paperback Library, 1969.
The Tormented. New York, Paperback Library, 1969.
The Curse of Mallory Hall. New York, Fawcett, 1970; New York, Coronet, 1972.
The Man from Yesterday. New York, Paperback Library, 1970.
The Dark Stage. New York, Paperback Library, 1970.
Emerald Hill. New York, Paperback Library, 1970.
Willow Weep. New York, Pyramid, 1970.
Island of Evil (novelization of TV series). New York, Paperback Library, 1970.
Raxl, Voodoo Princess (novelization of TV series). New York, Paperback Library, 1970.
The Raging Waters. New York, Pyramid, 1970.
The Attic Rope. New York, Lancer, 1970.
The Unearthly. New York, Lancer, 1970.
Journey into Terror. New York, Pyramid, 1971.
Key Diablo. New York, Paperback Library, 1971.
The House of Many Doors. New York, Paperback Library, 1971.

The Bell. New York, Paperback Library, 1971.
Diablo Manor. New York, Paperback Library, 1971; London, Star, 1977.
Witch's Castle. New York, Paperback Library, 1971.
The Beaumont Tradition. New York, Paperback Library, 1971.
The Lattimer Legend. New York, Lancer, 1971.
Shadows of Tomorrow. New York, Paperback Library, 1971.
Dueling Oaks (as Danielle Dorsett). New York, Pinnacle, 1972.
The Spanish Chapel. New York, Belmont, 1972.
Conover's Folly. New York, Paperback Library, 1972.
The House of Broken Dolls. New York, Paperback Library, 1972.
The Lanier Riddle. New York, Paperback Library, 1972.
Castle Morvant. New York, Paperback Library, 1972.
Maya Temple. New York, Paperback Library, 1972.
The Larrabee Heiress. New York, Paperback Library, 1972.
Shadows from the Past. New York, Paperback Library, 1972.
The House on Circus Hill. New York, Paperback Library, 1972.
Dark Island. New York, Paperback Library, 1972.
Witch's Island. New York, Paperback Library, 1972.
The Stone House. New York, Paperback Library, 1973.
The Duncan Dynasty. New York, Paperback Library, 1973.
The Silent Halls of Ashenden. New York, Paperback Library, 1973.
The Possession of Tracy Corbin. New York, Paperback Library, 1973.
Hills of Fire. New York, Paperback Library, 1973.
The Prisoner of Malville Hall. New York, Paperback Library, 1973.
Jade Green. New York, Paperback Library, 1973.
The Caldwell Shadow. New York, Paperback Library, 1973.
Image of a Ghost. New York, Paperback Library, 1973.
The Apollo Fountain. New York, Warner, 1974.
Island of Bitter Memories. New York, Warner, 1974.
Child of Darkness. New York, Pocket Books, 1974.
Ghost Song. New York, Pocket Books, 1974.
The Two Worlds of Peggy Scott. New York, Pocket Books, 1974; Bolton-by-Bowland,
    Lancashire, Magna, 1977.
The Exorcism of Jenny Slade. New York, Pocket Books, 1974.
A Web of Peril. New York, Pyramid, 1974.
Illusion at Haven's Edge. New York, Pocket Books, 1975; Bolton-by-Bowland, Lanca-
    shire, Magna, 1977.
The Possessed. New York, Pocket Books, 1975.
The Guardian of Willow House. New York, Pocket Books, 1975; Bolton-by-Bowland,
    Lancashire, Magna, 1977.
The Unlamented. New York, Pocket Books, 1975.
The Tide Mill. New York, Popular Library, 1975.
Shadow of a Man. New York, Popular Library, 1975.
Marble Hills. New York, Warner, 1975.
Blackthorn. New York, Pocket Books, 1975.
Whistle in the Wind. New York, Pocket Books, 1976.
Night Shade. New York, Pocket Books, 1976.
The Vineyard Chapel. New York, Pocket Books, 1976.
Circle of Guilt. New York, Pocket Books, 1976.
Juniper Hill. New York, Pocket Books, 1976.
Portrait of a Witch. New York, Pocket Books, 1976.
The Summer House. New York, Warner, 1976.
Terror of the Twin. New York, Berkley, 1976.
Dark Heritage. New York, New American Library, 1976.
Twilight at the Elms. New York, New American Library, 1976.
Poison Flower. New York, Pocket Books, 1977.
Nightfall. New York, Pocket Books, 1977.
Wines of Cyprien. New York, Pyramid, 1977.

A Woman in Silk and Shadows. New York, New American Library, 1977.
In the Shadows. New York, New American Library, 1978.
The Lonely Place. New York, New American Library, 1978.
Hermitage Hill. New York, New American Library, 1978.
Perrine. New York, Warner, 1978.
The Magic Ring. New York, Warner, 1978.
Meg. New York, New American Library, 1979.
The Cormac Legend. New York, New American Library, 1979.
Yesterday's Evil. New York, New American Library, 1979.
Veil of Treachery. New York, New American Library, 1979.
The Purple and the Gold. New York, New American Library, 1980.
Legend of Death. New York, New American Library, 1980.
Valley of the Shadows. New York, New American Library, 1980.
Bridal Black. New York, New American Library, 1980.
House of Silence. New York, New American Library, 1980.
Nicola. New York, Belmont, 1980.
Sisters of Valcour. New York, Warner, 1981.
Saratoga. New York, Belmont, 1981.
Monte Carlo. New York, Belmont, 1981.

Novels as Suzanne Somers

The Caduceus Tree. New York, Avalon, 1961; as *A Nurse for Doctor Keith* (as Dorothy
    Daniels), New York, Paperback Library, 1962.
House of Eve. New York, Avalon, 1962.
Image of Truth. New York, Avalon, 1963.
The Mists of Mourning. New York, Belmont, 1966.
The Romany Curse. New York, Belmont, 1971.
The House on Thunder Hill. New York, Curtis, 1973.
Touch Me. Los Angeles, Nash, 1973.
Until Death. New York, Curtis, 1973.

Novels as Angela Gray

The Ghost Dancers. New York, Lancer, 1971.
The Golden Packet. New York, Lancer, 1971.
The Lattimore Arch. New York, Lancer, 1971.
Blackwell's Ghost. New York, Lancer, 1972.
Ashes of Falconwyck. New York, Lancer, 1973.
The Watcher in the Dark. New York, Ballantine, 1973.
Nightmare at Riverview. New York, Lancer, 1973.
Ravenswood Hall. New York, Lancer, 1973.
The Warlock's Daughter. New York, Lancer, 1973.
The Love of the Lion. New York, Pocket Books, 1980.

Manuscript Collection: Bowling Green State University, Ohio.

*   *   *

Dorothy Daniels's publications include some 35 stories and 150 novels written since the early
1940's. Offering gothic fare, her works typically present an innocent and unprotected heroine
pursued by a murderous villain in a remote setting. This bewildered yet courageous protagonist, who moves from one life-threatening incident to the next, finally triumphs over her trials
to marry a suitable young man at the end of the novel, when all mysteries and motives are
elaborately explained. Avoiding the actual supernatural and the psychological complexity of

evil, the author mingles elements of romantic and detective fiction in her works, as falling in love and finding the right clues lighten scenes of terror.

As the titles of her novels indicate, Daniels relies heavily upon setting to create Gothic effects. Although she makes no serious effort to develop her historical or geographical material, her scenes are as vivid as they are varied in evoking fear. All manner of ominous mansions, estates, castles, and chapels with mysterious rooms are described: a chamber of horrors in the secluded mansion on the jungle of a Florida Key; a secret room for restraining insane family members in the Beaudin estate on Long Island; a labyrinthine Virginian forest hiding a killer at Mallory Hall; a remote chapel with a secret entry at Mystic Manor near the Hudson River. Though seemingly the abodes of witches, voodoo artists, and ghosts, these settings house human villainy. In *The Eagle's Nest* members of a new Nazi movement rather than Nazi ghosts walk the castle grounds; in *Castle Morvant* the writer of the ballet rather than a supernatural counterpart sabotages the performance. Moving away from the Gothic in her most recent works (*Saratoga* and *Monte Carlo*, 1981), Daniels discards the apparent supernatural for portraits of ruthless, moneyed criminals.

To endure and outwit these evil forces, the female protagonist must be courageous and determined, as well as young and beautiful. Despite the variety of careers Daniels assigns to her heroines—companion, governess, social secretary, hotel manager, nurse, reporter, scientist, ballet dancer—the ultimate goals are survival and a successful marriage. Daniels's books attract the female reader interested in the entertainment provided by a combination of gothic terror, mystery, and love story in fiction.

—Bette B. Roberts

DANTON, Rebecca. *See* **ROBERTS, Janet Louise**.

DARBY, Catherine. *See* **PETERS, Maureen.**

DARCY, Clare. American. Address: c/o Walker, 720 Fifth Avenue, New York, New York 10019, U.S.A.

ROMANCE AND GOTHIC PUBLICATIONS

Novels

Georgina.   New York, Walker, 1971; London, Wingate, 1974.
Cecily; or, A Young Lady of Quality.   New York, Walker, 1972; London, Wingate, 1975.
Lydia; or, Love in Town.   New York, Walker, 1973; London, Wingate, 1976.
Victoire.   New York, Walker, 1974; London, Wingate, 1976.
Allegra.   New York, Walker, 1975; London, Wingate, 1976.
Lady Pamela.   New York, Walker, 1975; London, Wingate, 1977.
Regina.   New York, Walker, 1976; London, Raven, 1977.
Elyza.   New York, Walker, 1976; London, Raven-Macdonald and Jane's, 1977.
Cressida.   New York, Walker, 1977; London, Raven, 1978.
Eugenia.   New York, Walker, 1977; London, Raven, 1978.
Gwendolen.   New York, Walker, 1978; London, Raven, 1979.
Rolande.   New York, Walker, 1978; London, Raven, 1979.
Letty.   New York, Walker, and London, Futura, 1980.
Caroline and Julia.   New York, Walker, 1982.

Uncollected Short Story

"Love's Own Promise," in *Good Housekeeping* (Des Moines, Iowa), August 1977.

*   *   *

Clare Darcy's lively and entertaining tales are set in the Regency period described so well in the novels of Georgette Heyer. Like Heyer, Darcy writes comedies of manners with the obligatory happy endings. Unlike many others who have followed in Heyer's footsteps, Darcy takes some pains over her historical accuracy. The manners and customs of high society, the elegant dress of both men and women, the geography of the fashionable world from Brighton to London to Vienna, even the vocabulary of her characters are all portrayed with careful attention to detail and authenticity. The historical characters who appear amid the fictional creations are also depicted convincingly, from Wellington to Lady Jersey. Thus the novels, each of which bears the name of its spirited heroine, have a depth and a substance unusual in the genre. This is particularly true of Darcy's early efforts; in recent years the pressures of success seem to have taken their toll and her work adheres much more closely to established formulae.

Darcy's heroines are invariably orphans, adrift in the world, and they make their way towards their happy endings aided by their own wits and their sense of adventure. Most, although of good family, are penniless, unprotected by family or friends; some (as in *Elyza* and *Letty*) are runaways. A few (*Lady Pamela*, *Cressida*) are wealthy, and past their girlhood, but they too lack love and a sense of belonging. While clearly virtuous and innocent, Darcy heroines are decidedly unconventional and a bit reckless. The threats of social scandal and financial disaster dismay them only temporarily, for they are unquenchingly optimistic about their futures, with good reason. Each one ends up in the arms of an older and more experienced hero, wealthy, and titled, who has until that moment thought himself immune to love. Sometimes, the hero and heroine have been involved in an earlier, blighted, romance (*Allegra* and *Cressida*); they always quarrel before true love conquers all. To each other they are at once infuriating and irresistible. Although her characters follow a set pattern, they are not cardboard figures; Darcy endows them with flaws as well as virtues, and most have a believable vitality.

The plots of Darcy's novels are simple and predictable. The fatherless heroine sets out in the world fleeing grasping guardians or trying to solve another's problems (frequently a brother or friend, rarely her own). She meets the hero, a notorious rake, and is drawn to him, but does not admit her attraction, as they immediately quarrel. Rather comical villains threaten to thwart the heroine's plans, but she, ever valiant, perseveres in her journey through the perils of the fashionable world. In the end, all misunderstandings and coincidences are cleared up, and the hero and heroine admit their love for each other. The heroine's future is assured, and clearly a happy one.

Clare Darcy's vignettes of Regency London are entertaining fare. Her strong-willed heroines appeal to 20th-century readers, while her darkly attractive heroes are tamed by love in a thoroughly satisfying, albeit anachronistic way. Darcy's reviewers have designated her as Georgette Heyer's successor with some justice, for she describes the same imaginary world with the same light touch.

—Mary C. Lynn

D'ARCY, Pamela. *See* **ROBY, Mary Linn**.

DAVENPORT, Marcia (née Gluck). American. Born in New York City, 9 June 1903; daughter of the singer Alma Gluck. Educated at Shipley School, Philadelphia; Wellesley College, Massachusetts, 1921-22; University of Grenoble, Summer 1922. Married Russell Davenport in 1929 (divorced), one daughter; also one daughter from first marriage. Copywriter in Philadelphia, 1924-27; staff member, *New Yorker*, 1927-30; music critic for Theatre Guild newsletter, later called *Stage*, 1930-38; commentator for Salzburg and Metropolitan opera broadcasts, 1936-37. Agent: Brandt and Brandt, 1501 Broadway, New York, New York 10036, U.S.A.

ROMANCE AND GOTHIC PUBLICATIONS

Novels

Of Lena Geyer. New York, Scribner, and London, Heinemann, 1936; as *Lena Geyer*, London, Collins, 1949.
The Valley of Decision. New York, Scribner, 1942; London, Collins, 1944.
East Side, West Side. New York, Scribner, 1947; London, Collins, 1948.
My Brother's Keeper. New York, Scribner, and London, Collins, 1954.
The Constant Image. New York, Scribner, and London, Collins, 1960.

Uncollected Short Story

"Stars Go Down," in *Good Housekeeping* (New York), November 1932.

OTHER PUBLICATIONS

Other

> Mozart. New York, Scribner, 1932; London, Heinemann, 1933; revised edition, Scribner, 1956.
> Garibaldi, Father of Modern Italy (juvenile). New York, Random House, 1957.
> Too Strong for Fantasy (autobiography). New York, Scribner, 1967; London, Collins, 1968.

*   *   *

Marcia Davenport seems obsessed with the theme of unhealthy self-denial. In *Of Lena Geyer* the diva of the title resolutely denies herself the consolation of love, starving a naturally passionate nature, because she is convinced that any satisfaction of carnal desire will be detrimental to the music to which she has devoted her life. Not until her voice seems irretrievably lost, at the end of her long career, does she behave like a normal human being; and her eccentricities infect those who surround her and dance attendance upon her. Another Davenport heroine, Jessie Bourne of *East Side, West Side*, wilfully imprisons herself in a sterile charade of marriage, preferring a life of empty elegance over any attempt to escape into real life. Even more perverse is the behaviour of Mary Rafferty in *The Valley of Decision*. Having refused to marry the man she loves with all her heart, for what seem insufficient and unconvincing reasons, she then proceeds to egg him into a disastrous marriage, while she becomes housekeeper in his home, presiding over the desolation she has created. Generations of her unlucky lover's descendants puzzle over the curious relationship—and small wonder. It *is* a puzzle.

Most bizarre, yet strangely the most likeable of all the Davenport menagerie of odd characters, are Seymour and Randall Holt, of *My Brother's Keeper*. Warped in their formative years by the tyranny of an evil, power-mad grandmother, the brothers become in time caricatures of the very person they so hated; miserly, reclusive, life-denying, they live and die miserably in the crumbling, rubbish-choked brownstone that has become their mausoleum even during their dismal lifetimes.

Least attractive, on the other hand, are the romantic pair whose story is the subject of *The Constant Image*. Having embarked in a completely cold-blooded fashion upon an adulterous affair—apparently simply because that is what the "beautiful people" are doing this season—Harriet Piers is dismayed to discover that the amusing interlude has taken on an unexpected dimension. She has unintentionally fallen desparately in love with Carlo, and he with her. Everyone in their cosmopolitan circle sees this as an excellent opportunity for Carlo's long-suffering wife to behave nobly yet again; and when this time she fails to do so, her false friend and faithless husband magically become the injured parties, in both their own and the author's estimation. The self-denial in this particular story happens along a little after the fact, but happen it does. There is peculiar taint about *The Constant Image*, as of a moral code spoiled and left rotting.

Davenport's people are unpleasant creatures, concerned with appearance and the conventions more than with reality. For all their misadventures, most of them are well-cushioned against the rudeness of a crude world: only the well-to-do play significant roles upon her stage. Popular in their day, Davenport's novels now seem shallow and unrealistic. Seekers after sensation ensnared by paperback editions with torrid jacket illustrations will suffer one more disappointment: no hot blood flows through these flaccid veins.

—Joan McGrath

DAVIS, Dorothy Salisbury. American. Born in Chicago, Illinois, 26 April 1916. Educated at Holy Child High School, Waukegan, Illinois; Barat College, Lake Forest, Illinois, A.B. 1938. Married Harry Davis in 1946. Past President, Mystery Writers of America. Agent: McIntosh and Otis Inc., 475 Fifth Avenue, New York, New York 10017. Address: Snedens Landing, Palisades, New York 10964, U.S.A.

ROMANCE AND GOTHIC PUBLICATIONS

Novels (series: Julie Hayes; Mrs. Norris and Jasper Tully)

The Judas Cat. New York, Scribner, 1949; London, Corgi, 1952.
The Clay Hand. New York, Scribner, 1950; London, Corgi, 1952.
A Gentle Murderer. New York, Scribner, 1951; London, Corgi, 1953.
A Town of Masks. New York, Scribner, 1952.
Death of an Old Sinner (Norris and Tully). New York, Scribner, 1957; London, Secker and Warburg, 1958.
A Gentleman Called (Norris and Tully). New York, Scribner, and London, Secker and Warburg, 1958.
Old Sinners Never Die (Norris). New York, Scribner, 1959; London, Secker and Warburg, 1960.
Black Sheep, White Lamb. New York, Scribner, 1963; London, Boardman, 1964.
The Pale Betrayer. New York, Scribner, 1965; London, Hodder and Stoughton, 1967.
Enemy and Brother. New York, Scribner, 1966; London, Hodder and Stoughton, 1967.
God Speed the Night, with Jerome Ross. New York, Scribner, 1968; London, Hodder and Stoughton, 1969.
Where the Dark Streets Go. New York, Scribner, 1969; London, Hodder and Stoughton, 1970.
Shock Wave. New York, Scribner, 1972; London, Hodder and Stoughton, 1974.
The Little Brothers. New York, Scribner, 1973; London, Barker, 1974.
A Death in the Life (Hayes). New York, Scribner, 1976; London, Gollancz, 1977.
Scarlet Night (Hayes). New York, Scribner, 1980; London, Gollancz, 1981.

OTHER PUBLICATIONS

Novels

Men of No Property. New York, Scribner, 1956.
The Evening of the Good Samaritan. New York, Scribner, 1961.

Other

Editor, *A Choice of Murders*. New York, Scribner, 1958; London, Macdonald, 1960.
Editor, *Crime Without Murder*. New York, Scribner, 1970.

Manuscript Collection: Brooklyn College Library, City University of New York.

*   *   *

The work of Dorothy Salisbury Davis indicates her keen perception as a student of human nature. A distinguishing feature of her writings—ironic, perhaps, in one so opposed to physical violence—is the preoccupation with crime and criminal psychology. Following the early success of *The Clay Hand* and *The Judas Cat*, this interest became apparent in such works as *A*

Gentle Murderer, with its sympathetic portrayal of a killer who must be found in order to avert further tragedy. Davis's explorations of the criminal mind are far from morbid. Rather she seeks for the minor flaws of character, the unforeseen shifts of circumstance, that lead certain human beings to break the confines of the law, and the often disastrous consequences of their actions. The theme is central to one of her most celebrated books, *Death of an Old Sinner*, where a retired general finds himself drawn into blackmail and eventually pays with his life. So intrigued was the author by the character she had created that the lovable rogue is revisited in a "prequel," *Old Sinners Never Die*. Much of the interest of the Davis novel stems from the battle of wits between hunter and hunted, with close parallels often being drawn between the detective and his prey. *The Pale Betrayer* is a good example, its "criminal" a college lecturer who finds himself involved in an act of espionage which gets out of hand and results in the death of a friend. In the ensuing course of the detection, where Mather at last atones by the sacrifice of his own life, he and the detective Marks come to a close understanding of each other's innermost nature. Similar themes pervade the excellent *Enemy and Brother* and *Where the Dark Streets Go*. *God Speed the Night*, written with Jerome Ross, is set in occupied France. A Jewish refugee is helped by a nun who disguises herself as his wife after the latter dies in the local convent. The two are pursued in a duel of wits by the dissolute, hen-pecked Vichy police chief, whose power as a hunter of criminals is his only claim to self-respect. As always, the subtle workings of the human mind are set down in the clean unadorned style which is Davis's hallmark.

An excellent writer of short stories, Davis's skill and psychological penetration serve her well in the shorter forms of fiction. Some of her later works might be described as "straightforward" detective stories, with the difference that her probing intelligence gives them a depth denied to most. Marks, the detective, returns in *The Little Brothers*, a fast-paced thriller involving a teenage gang, murder, and drug trafficking. *Shock Wave* investigates a similar crime against a backcloth of racial unrest in the Deep South. Most recently, she has produced two fine novels starring the female sleuth Julie Hayes. *A Death in the Life* has her tracking down a murderer in the red light district, while art theft is the theme of *Scarlet Night*. Julie Hayes is a lively and credible—if unorthodox—detective, and a tribute to the subtle skills of her creator.

—Geoffrey Sadler

DEEPING, (George) Warwick. British. Born in Southend, Essex, 28 May 1877. Educated at Merchant Taylors' School, London; Trinity College, Cambridge, B.A., M.A., M.B.; studied medicine at Middlesex Hospital, London, and practiced as a doctor for one year. Served in the Royal Army Medical Corps, 1915-18. Married Maude Phyllis Merrill. *Died 20 April 1950.*

ROMANCE AND GOTHIC PUBLICATIONS

Novels

Uther and Igraine. London, Richards, and New York, Outlook, 1903.
Love among the Ruins. London, Richards, and New York, Macmillan, 1904.
The Seven Streams. London, Nash, 1905; New York, Fenno, 1909.
The Slanderers. New York, Harper, 1905; London, Cassell, 1907.
Bess of the Woods. London and New York, Harper, 1906.

A Woman's War. London and New York, Harper, 1907.
Bertrand of Brittany. London and New York, Harper, 1908.
Mad Barbara. London, Cassell, 1908; New York, Harper, 1909.
The Red Saint. London, Cassell, 1909; New York, McBride, 1940.
The Return of the Petticoat. London and New York, Harper, 1909; revised edition, London, Cassell, 1913.
The Lame Englishman. London, Cassell, 1910.
The Rust of Rome. London, Cassell, 1910.
Fox Farm. London, Cassell, 1911; as *The Eyes of Love,* New York, McBride, 1933.
Joan of the Tower. London, Cassell, 1911; New York, McBride, 1941.
Sincerity. London, Cassell, 1912; as *The Strong Hand,* 1912; as *The Challenge of Love,* New York, McBride, 1932.
The House of Spies. London and New York, Cassell, 1913.
The White Gate. London, Cassell, 1913; New York, McBride, 1914.
The King Behind the King. London, Cassell, and New York, McBride, 1914.
The Pride of Eve. London, Cassell, 1914.
Marriage by Conquest. London, Cassell, and New York, McBride, 1915.
Unrest. London, Cassell, 1916; as *Bridge of Desire,* New York, McBride, 1916.
Martin Valliant. London, Cassell, and New York, McBride, 1917.
Valour. London, Cassell, 1918; New York, McBride, 1934.
Second Youth. London, Cassell, 1919; New York, Grosset and Dunlap, 1932.
The Prophetic Marriage. London, Cassell, 1920; New York, Grosset and Dunlap, 1932.
The House of Adventure. London, Cassell, 1921; New York, Macmillan, 1922.
Lantern Lane. London, Cassell, 1921.
Orchards. London, Cassell, 1922; as *The Captive Wife,* New York, Grosset and Dunlap, 1933.
Apples of Gold. London, Cassell, 1923.
The Secret Sanctuary; or, The Saving of John Stretton. London, Cassell, 1923.
Suvla John. London, Cassell, 1924.
Three Rooms. London, Cassell, 1924.
Sorrell and Son. London, Cassell, 1925; New York, Knopf, 1926.
Doomsday. London, Cassell, and New York, Knopf, 1927.
Kitty. London, Cassell, and New York, Knopf, 1927.
Old Pybus. London, Cassell, and New York, Knopf, 1928.
Roper's Row. London, Cassell, and New York, Knopf, 1929.
Exiles. London, Cassell, 1930; as *Exile,* New York, Knopf, 1930.
The Road. London, Cassell, 1931; as *The Ten Commandments,* New York, Knopf, 1931.
Old Wine and New. London, Cassell, and New York, Knopf, 1932.
Smith. London, Cassell, and New York, Knopf, 1932.
Two Black Sheep. London, Cassell, and New York, Knopf, 1933.
The Man on the White Horse. London, Cassell, and New York, Knopf, 1934.
Seven Men Came Back. London, Cassell, and New York, Knopf, 1934.
Sackcloth into Silk. London, Cassell, 1935; as *The Golden Cord,* New York, Knopf, 1935.
No Hero—This. London, Cassell, and New York, Knopf, 1936.
Blind Man's Year. London, Cassell, and New York, Knopf, 1937.
These White Hands. New York, McBride, 1937.
The Woman at the Door. London, Cassell, and New York, Knopf, 1937.
The Malice of Men. London, Cassell, and New York, Knopf, 1938.
Fantasia. London, Cassell, 1939; as *Bluewater,* New York, Knopf, 1939.
Shabby Summer. London, Cassell, 1939; as *Folly Island,* New York, Knopf, 1939.
The Man Who Went Back. London, Cassell, and New York, Knopf, 1940.
The Shield of Love. London, Cassell, and New York, McBride, 1940.
Corn in Egypt. London, Cassell, 1941; New York, Knopf, 1942.
The Dark House. London, Cassell, and New York, Knopf, 1941.
I Live Again. London, Cassell, and New York, Knopf, 1942.
Slade. London, Cassell, and New York, Dial Press, 1943.

Mr. Gurney and Mr. Slade. London, Cassell, 1944; as *The Cleric's Secret*, New York, Dial Press, 1944.

Reprieve. London, Cassell, and New York, Dial Press, 1945.

The Impudence of Youth. London, Cassell, and New York, Dial Press, 1946.

Laughing House. London, Cassell, 1946; New York, Dial Press, 1947.

Portrait of a Playboy. London, Cassell, 1947; as *The Playboy*, New York, Dial Press, 1948.

Paradise Place. London, Cassell, 1949.

Old Mischief. London, Cassell, 1950.

Time to Heal. London, Cassell, 1952.

Man in Chains. London, Cassell, 1953.

The Old World Dies. London, Cassell, 1954.

Caroline Terrace. London, Cassell, 1955.

The Serpent's Tooth. London, Cassell, 1956.

The Sword and the Cross. London, Cassell, 1957.

Short Stories

Countess Glika and Other Stories. London, Cassell, 1919.

Martyrdom, with *The House Behind the Judas Tree* by Gilbert Frankau and *Forbidden Music* by Ethel Mannin. London, Readers Library, 1929; as *Three Stories of Romance*, 1936.

The Short Stories of Warwick Deeping. London, Cassell, 1930.

Stories of Love, Courage, and Compassion. New York, Knopf, 1930.

Two in a Train and Other Stories. London, Cassell, 1935.

*   *   *

Traditionalist Warwick Deeping turned out 70 novels in an effort to keep alive the pastoral vision of Edwardian England in the years after World War I; but only his early *Sorrell and Son* (1925) became a mass audience favorite in the United States as well as the British Empire. This harrowing tale of an aristocratic World War I veteran's returning to find himself destitute and deserted by his wife recounts Stephen Sorrell's successful struggle to emerge from a demeaning position to regain dignity and wealth, while continuing to command the loyalty of his son. Throughout his travails, Sorrell's obsession is to remain a gentleman and have his son educated as befits a gentleman. The reviewer for *The New Statesman* complained that "it is difficult to understand how a man so wisely determined when he reaches bottom could have fallen so low" (31 October 1925); but the criticism misses the source of the novel's enduring popularity. *Sorrell and Son* is no Samuel Smiles success story, but rather a secularized allegory in the tradition of *Pilgrim's Progress*. The author arbitrarily reduces Sorrell to a Job-like state so that he can describe the sort of person who can rehabilitate himself in a fictional reincarnation of the "stiff upper lip" tradition that kept Britons going through demoralizing times. His son, Christopher, even becomes a doctor, not just because the position is properly genteel, but so that in a heart-rending conclusion he can administer an overdose of morphine that ends his father's physical sufferings after this man has triumphed over moral defeats the world has administered to him. *Sorrell and Son* appeared the same year as *The Great Gatsby*; and it can be read as an unintended reply to Fitzgerald's cynical, ironic tale of father-son relationships destroyed in a squalid world. Deeping's tribute to the triumph of the old verities was enormously more popular than Fitzgerald's novel at the time of their publication; but Deeping never again found the formula to shape his nostalgic vision into a popular myth.

—Warren French

DELAFIELD, E.M.   Pseudonym for Edmée Elizabeth Monica De la Pasture.   British.   Born in Sussex, 9 June 1890; daughter of the writer Mrs. Henry De la Pasture. Served in the Voluntary Aid Detachment, 1914-17, then with the Ministry of National Services, Bristol, 1917-18. Married Arthur Paul Dashwood in 1919; one son and one daughter. Journalist: regular contributor to *Time and Tide* and *Punch*. Justice of the Peace, Cullompton, Devon. *Died 2 December 1943*.

ROMANCE AND GOTHIC PUBLICATIONS

Novels

Zella Sees Herself.   London, Heinemann, and New York, Knopf, 1917.
The War-Workers.   London, Heinemann, and New York, Knopf, 1918.
The Pelicans.   London, Heinemann, 1918; New York, Knopf, 1919.
Consequences.   London, Hodder and Stoughton, and New York, Knopf, 1919.
Tension.   London, Hutchinson, and New York, Macmillan, 1920.
The Heel of Achilles.   London, Hutchinson, and New York, Macmillan, 1921.
Humbug.   London, Hutchinson, 1921; New York, Macmillan, 1922.
The Optimist.   London, Hutchinson, and New York, Macmillan, 1922.
A Reversion to Type.   London, Hutchinson, and New York, Macmillan, 1923.
Mrs. Harter.   London, Hutchinson, 1924; New York, Harper, 1925.
Messalina of the Suburbs (includes story and play).   London, Hutchinson, 1924.
The Chip and the Block.   London, Hutchinson, 1925; New York, Harper, 1926.
Jill.   London, Hutchinson, 1926; New York, Harper, 1927.
The Way Things Are.   London, Hutchinson, 1927; New York, Harper, 1928.
The Suburban Young Man.   London, Hutchinson, 1928.
What Is Love?   London, Macmillan, 1928; as *First Love*, New York, Harper, 1929.
Turn Back the Leaves.   London, Macmillan, and New York, Harper, 1930.
Diary of a Provincial Lady.   London, Macmillan, 1930; New York, Harper, 1931.
Challenge to Clarissa.   London, Macmillan, 1931; as *House Party*, New York, Harper, 1931.
Thank Heaven Fasting.   London, Macmillan, 1932.
A Good Man's Love.   New York, Harper, 1932.
The Provincial Lady Goes Further.   London, Macmillan, 1932; as *The Provincial Lady in London*, New York, Harper, 1933.
Gay Life.   London, Macmillan, and New York, Harper, 1933.
The Provincial Lady in America.   London, Macmillan, and New York, Harper, 1934.
The Bazalgettes: A Tale (published anonymously).   London, Hamish Hamilton, 1935.
Faster! Faster!   London, Macmillan, and New York, Harper, 1936.
Nothing Is Safe.   London, Macmillan, and New York, Harper, 1937.
The Provincial Lady in War-Time.   London, Macmillan, and New York, Harper, 1940.
No One Now Will Know.   London, Macmillan, and New York, Harper, 1941.
Late and Soon.   London, Macmillan, and New York, Harper, 1943.

Short Stories

The Entertainment.   London, Hutchinson, and New York, Harper, 1927.
Women Are Like That: Short Stories.   London, Macmillan, 1929; New York, Harper, 1930.
When Women Love.   New York, Harper, 1938; as *Three Marriages*, London, Macmillan, 1939.
Love Has No Resurrection and Other Stories.   London, Macmillan, 1939.

OTHER PUBLICATIONS

Plays

To See Ourselves: A Domestic Comedy (produced London, 1930; New York, 1935).
London and New York, French, 1932.
The Glass Wall (produced London, 1933). London, Gollancz, 1933.

Screenplays: Crime on the Hill, with others, 1933; Moonlight Sonata (The Charmer), with
Edward Knoblock and Hans Rameau, 1937.

Other

General Impressions. London, Macmillan, 1933.
Ladies and Gentlemen in Victorian Fiction. London, Hogarth Press, and New York,
Harper, 1937.
As Others Hear Us: A Miscellany. London, Macmillan, 1937.
Straw Without Bricks: I Visit Soviet Russia. London, Macmillan, 1937; as I Visit the
Soviets: The Provincial Lady Looks at Russia, New York, Harper, 1937.
People You Love. London, Collins, 1940.
This War We Wage. New York, Emerson, 1941.

Editor, The Time and Tide Album. London, Hamish Hamilton, 1932.
Editor, The Brontës: Their Lives Recorded by Their Contemporaries. London, Hogarth
Press, 1935; Westport, Connecticut, Meckler, 1980.

Bibliography: in Ten Contemporaries, 2nd series by John Gawsworth, London, Benn, 1933.

*   *   *

A prolific writer whose work spans three decades, E.M. Delafield explores the human
capacity for self-deception and self-love, often revealed in affairs of the heart. These aspects are
present in her first novel—appropriately titled Zella Sees Herself—and recur constantly in later
books. Nowadays Delafield is best known for her superb comic masterpiece The Diary of a
Provincial Lady, a work justly famous for its sardonic wit and shrewd insights into human
nature. Its popularity led to a number of sequels, all of which are amusing without matching the
excellence of their original. Unfortunately the fame of the "Provincial Lady" has tended to
detract from other novels of a different kind, where the humor is muted, and the author
approaches various facets of life and love in a witty but serious manner.

Delafield's best novel in this style is generally thought to be Thank Heaven Fasting, where the
heroine experiences and rejects romantic passion for the staid affections of a reliable middle-
aged suitor. The pressures of upper-class society, where marriage is regarded as all-important
and spinsterhood a fate worse than death, is admirably portrayed. So, too, is the heroine's
ability to think herself in love at each encounter. This, though, is to give too cynical an
interpretation of Delafield's motives. Though gothic elements are occasional and slight—her
study of a female criminal in Messalina of the Suburbs, and parts of When Women Love
(Three Marriages) are exceptions—romance figures largely in her work. Delafield is no
stranger to passion, though her recounting of it is often dispassionate. The early novel The Heel
of Achilles concentrates on the possessive self-love of Lydia Raymond, who throughout her life
ruthlessly claims the centre of the stage for herself under the guise of caring for others. Lydia,
who marries without love, is brought to her downfall by her daughter Jennie, the one person for
whom she cares. Her selfishness and hypocrisy are laid bare at last in her vain struggle to usurp
the life experience of Jennie for herself. Though the ending has rather too much of the sermon
about it, its character studies go deeper than those of Thank Heaven Fasting. Like many of
Delafield's novels, it is unjustly neglected.

Turn Back the Leaves centres on the growth to womanhood of Stella, child of an illicit liaison, who is brought up as a "cousin" in the household of the wronged husband. Delafield describes her impact on the family, and its eventual break-up. The story is interesting, but an uneasy shift of focus from Stella to her "cousins" near the end weakens the book as a whole. More effective is *When Women Love*, which views three different relationships in 1857, 1897, and 1937 respectively. The first, "The Wedding of Rose Barlow," deals with the young bride in a marriage of convenience who falls in love with her French cousin, and is finally reunited with him after surviving the horrors of the Cawnpore massacre, where her husband dies. "A Girl of the Period" looks satirically at a "modern" girl of 1897, who is engaged without being in love, and openly scorns sentiment. When her fiancé falls for someone else she strikes a noble pose in "releasing" him, but when she herself becomes infatuated by the rakish Courtenay, promised to her friend, Violet fights viciously with her rival rather than give him up. "We Meant to Be Happy" describes an ill-fated extra-marital affair where disillusion sets in, and the husband's illness serves to blackmail the erring wife into submission. The three stories are skilfully related, the tone varied in each case.

In *No One Now Will Know* the author explores Rosalie Meredith's love for the Creole Lucian Lempriere, her illicit passion for his brother Fred, and her violent death. This central theme—described in retrospect over three generations—is paralleled by Rosalie's friend Kate, and her unrequited love for Lucian. There is an ironic echo a generation later, when Rosalie's daughter Callie loses her own lover to her best friend, Elisabeth. The tangle of relationships is adroitly presented, the author refraining from comment to let the reader draw his own conclusions.

Late and Soon is Delafield's last novel, and ranks among her best. The story takes place over a winter weekend in 1942, at the country home of Valentine, Lady Arbell. A group of soldiers are billeted there, and Valentine recognizes their Colonel—Rory Lonergan—as the young Irish artist with whom she fell in love as a girl, but was prevented from marrying. Now he re-enters her life as the lover of her worldly daughter, Primrose. The re-awakening of their love and its traumatic resolution are brilliantly depicted by Delafield, who eyes her characters with a wry affection. *Late and Soon* is a worthy conclusion to her career, marred as it was by her premature death.

Delafield's work extends beyond the novel. She produced three collections of short stories, which display all her familiar talents. *Love Has No Resurrection* is typical, with tales ranging from the tragic to the comic and mundane, often touching on the deluding power of passion and its consequences. Other works include plays, socio-political commentaries, and literary criticism. Her articles for *Punch* and *Time and Tide*, many of them masterly examples of humorous dialogue, are collected in *As Others Hear Us*. Delafield's vision is broad as it is deep, her analyses of human character at once sharp and sympathetic. Her writing reveals a natural warmth, a wary fondness for the human heart, no matter how often it deceives.

—Geoffrey Sadler

---

de la ROCHE, Mazo (Louise). Canadian. Born in Newmarket, Ontario, 15 January 1879. Educated at schools in Galt, Ontario, and Toronto; Parkdale Collegiate Institute, Toronto; University of Toronto. Had two adopted daughters. Full-time writer from childhood; lived in Windsor, England, 1929–39; thereafter lived in Toronto. Recipient: Lorne Pierce Medal, 1938; University of Alberta National Award Medal, 1951. Litt.D.: University of Toronto, 1954. *Died 12 July 1961.*

Novels (series: Jalna)

Possession.   New York and London, Macmillan, 1923.
Delight.   New York and London, Macmillan, 1926.
Jalna.   Boston, Little Brown, and London, Hodder and Stoughton, 1927.
Whiteoaks of Jalna.   Boston, Little Brown, 1929; as *Whiteoaks*, London, Macmillan, 1929.
Finch's Fortune (Jalna).   Boston, Little Brown, and London, Macmillan, 1931.
Lark Ascending.   Boston, Little Brown, and London, Macmillan, 1932.
The Thunder of New Wings, in *Chatelaine* (Toronto), June-December 1932.
The Master of Jalna.   Boston, Little Brown, and London, Macmillan, 1933.
Beside a Norman Tower.   Boston, Little Brown, and London, Macmillan, 1934.
Young Renny (Jalna—1906).   Boston, Little Brown, and London, Macmillan, 1935.
Whiteoak Harvest (Jalna).   Boston, Little Brown, and London, Macmillan, 1936.
The Very House.   Boston, Little Brown, and London, Macmillan, 1937.
Growth of a Man.   Boston, Little Brown, and London, Macmillan, 1938.
Whiteoak Heritage (Jalna).   Boston, Little Brown, and London, Macmillan, 1940.
Wakefield's Course.   Boston, Little Brown, 1941; London, Macmillan, 1942.
The Two Saplings.   London, Macmillan, 1942.
The Building of Jalna.   Boston, Little Brown, 1944; London, Macmillan, 1945.
Return to Jalna.   Boston, Little Brown, 1946; London, Macmillan, 1948.
Mary Wakefield.   Boston, Little Brown, and London, Macmillan, 1949.
Renny's Daughter (Jalna).   Boston, Little Brown, and London, Macmillan, 1951.
The Whiteoak Brothers: Jalna—1923.   Boston, Little Brown, and London, Macmillan, 1953.
Variable Winds at Jalna.   Boston, Little Brown, 1954; London, Macmillan, 1955.
Centenary at Jalna.   Boston, Little Brown, and London, Macmillan, 1958.
Morning at Jalna.   Boston, Little Brown, and London, Macmillan, 1960.

Short Stories

Explorers of the Dawn.   New York, Knopf, and London, Cassell, 1922.
The Sacred Bullock and Other Stories of Animals.   Boston, Little Brown, and London, Macmillan, 1939.
A Boy in the House and Other Stories.   Boston, Little Brown, and London, Macmillan, 1952.

Plays

Low Life (produced Montreal, 1925).   Toronto, Macmillan, 1925; in *Low Life and Other Plays*, 1929.
Come True (produced Toronto, 1927).   Toronto, Macmillan, 1927; in *Low Life and Other Plays*, 1929.
The Return of the Emigrant (produced Toronto, 1928).   Included in *Low Life and Other Plays*, 1929.
Low Life and Other Plays (includes *Come True* and *The Return of the Emigrant*).   Toronto, Macmillan, and Boston, Little Brown, 1929.
Whiteoaks, adaptation of her own novel (produced London, 1936; New York, 1938).   Boston, Little Brown, and London, Macmillan, 1936.
The Mistress of Jalna (produced London, 1952).

Other

> *Portrait of a Dog.*   Boston, Little Brown, and London, Macmillan, 1930.
> *Quebec, Historic Seaport.*   New York, Doubleday, 1944; London, Macmillan, 1946.
> *The Song of Lambert* (juvenile).   Boston, Little Brown, and London, Macmillan, 1955.
> *Ringing the Changes: An Autobiography.*   Boston, Little Brown, and New York, Macmillan, 1957.
> *Bill and Coo* (juvenile).   Boston, Little Brown, and London, Macmillan, 1958.

Critical Studies: *Mazo de la Roche of Jalna* by Ronald Hambleton, New York, Hawthorn, 1966; *Mazo de la Roche* by George Hendrick, New York, Twayne, 1970.

*   *   *

The Whiteoaks of Jalna are among the most famous families in the popular fiction of the 20th century; they have been favourably compared with Galsworthy's Forsytes for their enduring ability to fascinate. Through some 15 titles the Whiteoaks held their course; neither wealthy nor particularly distinguished, having no social pretensions, indeed, completely self-absorbed. They lived in fairy-tale British Colonial style in and around the rambling Southern Ontario mansion from which the series takes its title. Old Adelaide, the family autocrat whose 100th birthday celebrations provided one of the highpoints of the saga, is the most powerful figure in this matriarchal society. For years she keeps her family in line by holding the secret of her mysterious will over their heads like a liontamer's whip, for she owns all the family fortune. Even after she has finally left the scene her influence pervades the action, and she is apparently reincarnated in the person of her great granddaughter Adelaide in the later stories.

The Whiteoaks are no average family. Several generations live under the roof of Jalna, and seldom amicably. Passions flare in an extraordinary fashion—the Jalna countryside is dotted, figuratively speaking, with illegitimate Whiteoak offspring. Elopements, jiltings, and various forms of interfamilial chicanery and double dealing are practically a matter of routine; incest by mistake is but narrowly avoided. Renny, the master of Jalna, eschews subtlety, and darkly suspects the artistic talent of his half-brothers as a sign of fundamental weakness and undependability, but he is a father figure to all, except when occupied by falling in or out of love with their womenfolk. The brothers seduce or run off with their sisters-in-law or the au pair; bicker and squabble viciously among themselves; enter or leave a monastery with complete sang-froid; and present a united front to the world, no matter what may be happening behind the family facade.

Obviously, any attempt to summarize a Jalna plot will suggest sensationalism comparable with that of a soap opera; but this does less than justice to de la Roche's magical ability to create larger-than-life characters in whom wild eccentricities seem only what might be expected. Her stories sweep along at such a pace that the reader is caught up and carried away, unprotesting. Jalna was a never-never land that became more real than reality to generations of de la Roche's devoted readers all over the world, who could scarcely believe that with her death the Whiteoak saga came, unresolved, to its ending. A long, well-filled shelf of *Jalna* stories was not enough for the devotees who now will never know for certain whether Renny's wilful daughter, young Adelaide, could have filled the place of the formidable Gran she so closely resembled.

Mazo de la Roche wrote of other subjects through the years, and with some success, but only the Jalna series lives on. It was not, and never claimed to be, great literature; but it was no small achievement to create, as Mazo de la Roche created, a fictional empire so full of life, vigour, and personality, that it has survived its author and her times to become a minor tradition.

—Joan McGrath

DELDERFIELD, R(onald) F(rederick).   British.   Born in Greenwich, London, 12 February 1912. Attended West Buckland School, Devon. Served in the Royal Air Force, 1940-45: Public Relations Officer, 1944-45. Married May Evans in 1936; one son and one daughter. Reporter, Sub-Editor, and Editor, *Exmouth Chronicle*, 1929-39, 1945-47, then free-lance writer. *Died 24 June 1972.*

ROMANCE AND GOTHIC PUBLICATIONS

Novels

> *All over the Town.*   London, Bles, 1947; New York, Simon and Schuster, 1977.
> *Seven Men of Gascony.*   London, Laurie, and Indianapolis, Bobbs Merrill, 1949.
> *Farewell the Tranquil Mind.*   London, Laurie, 1950; as *Farewell the Tranquil*, New York, Dutton, 1950.
> *The Avenue Story.*   London, Hodder and Stoughton, 1964; as *The Avenue*, New York, Simon and Schuster, 1969.
>> *The Dreaming Suburb.*   London, Hodder and Stoughton, 1958.
>> *The Avenue Goes to War.*   London, Hodder and Stoughton, 1958.
> *There Was a Fair Maid Dwelling.*   London, Hodder and Stoughton, 1960; as *Diana*, New York, Putnam, 1960.
> *Stop at a Winner.*   London, Hodder and Stoughton, 1961; New York, Simon and Schuster, 1978.
> *The Unjust Skies.*   London, Hodder and Stoughton, 1962.
> *The Spring Madness of Mr. Sermon.*   London, Hodder and Stoughton, 1963; as *Mr. Sermon*, New York, Simon and Schuster, 1970.
> *Too Few for Drums.*   London, Hodder and Stoughton, 1964; New York, Simon and Schuster, 1971.
> *A Horseman Riding By.*   London, Hodder and Stoughton, 1966; New York, Simon and Schuster, 1967.
> *Cheap Day Return.*   London, Hodder and Stoughton, 1967; as *Return Journey*, New York, Simon and Schuster, 1974.
> *The Green Gauntlet.*   London, Hodder and Stoughton, and New York, Simon and Schuster, 1968.
> *Come Home Charlie and Face Them.*   London, Hodder and Stoughton, 1969; as *Charlie Come Home*, New York, Simon and Schuster, 1976.
> *God Is an Englishman.*   London, Hodder and Stoughton, and New York, Simon and Schuster, 1970.
> *Theirs Was the Kingdom.*   London, Hodder and Stoughton, and New York, Simon and Schuster, 1971.
> *To Serve Them All My Days.*   London, Hodder and Stoughton, and New York, Simon and Schuster, 1972.
> *Give Us This Day.*   London, Hodder and Stoughton, and New York, Simon and Schuster, 1973.
> *Post of Honor.*   New York, Ballantine, 1974.
> *Long Summer Days.*   New York, Pocket Books, 1974.

OTHER PUBLICATIONS

Plays

> *Spark in Judaea* (produced London, 1937).   Boston, Baker, 1951; London, de Wolfe and Stone, 1953.
> *Twilight Call* (produced Birmingham, 1939).
> *Printer's Devil* (produced London, 1939).

This Is My Life, with Basil Thomas (as *Matron*, produced Wolverhampton, 1942). London, Fox, 1944.
Worm's Eye View (produced London, 1945).   Published in *Embassy Successes 1*, London, Sampson Low, 1946; New York, French, 1948.
The Spinster of South Street (produced London, 1945).
Peace Comes to Peckham(produced London, 1946).   London, French, 1948.
All over the Town, adaptation of his own novel (produced London, 1947).   London, French, 1948.
The Queen Came By (produced London, 1948).   London, Deane, and Boston, Baker, 1949.
Sailors Beware: An Elizabethan Improbability.   London, Deane, 1950.
The Elephant's Graveyard (produced Chesterfield, 1951).
Waggonload o' Monkeys: Further Adventures of Porter and Taffy (produced London, 1951).   London, Deane, 1952.
Golden Rain (produced Windsor, 1952).   London, French, 1953.
Miaow! Miaow!   London, French, 1952.
The Old Lady of Cheadle.   London, Deane, 1952.
Made to Measure (broadcast, 1953).   London, French, 1952.
The Bride Wore an Opal Ring (broadcast, 1954).   London, French, 1952.
Follow the Plough (produced Leatherhead, Surrey, and London, 1953).
The Testimonial (broadcast, 1953).   London, French, 1953.
Glad Tidings (produced 1953).
The Offending Hand (produced Northampton, 1953).   London, Deane, 1955.
The Orchard Walls (produced Aldershot, Hampshire, and London, 1953).   London, French, 1954.
Absent Lover: A Plantagenet Improbability.   London, French, 1953.
Smoke in the Valley (broadcast, 1954).   London, French, 1953.
The Guinea-Pigs.   London, Deane, 1954.
Home Is the Hunted.   London, French, 1954.
Musical Switch.   London, de Wolfe and Stone, 1954.
The Rounderlay Tradition.   London, Deane, 1954.
Ten till Five.   London, de Wolfe and Stone, 1954.
Where There's a Will.   London, French, 1954.
And Then There Were None (broadcast, 1955).   London, French, 1954.
Uncle's Little Lapse.   London, de Wolfe and Stone, 1955.
The Mayerling Affair (produced Pitlochry, 1957).   London, French, 1958.
Duty and the Beast, adaptation of a work by Hans Keuls (produced Worthing, Sussex, 1957).
Flashpoint.   London, French, 1958.
Once Aboard a Lugger.   London, French, 1962.
Wild Mink.   London, French, 1962.
My Dearest Angel (produced Pitlochry, 1963).

Screenplays: *All over Town*, with others, 1949; *Worm's Eye View*, with Jack Marks, 1951; *Value for Money*, with William Fairchild, 1955; *Where There's a Will*, 1955; *Now and Forever*, with Michael Pertwee, 1956; *Keep It Clean*, with Carl Nystrom, 1956; *Home and Away*, with Vernon Sewell, 1956; *On the Fiddle*, with Harold Buchman, 1961.

Radio Plays: *The Cocklemouth Cornet*, 1938; *The Comet Covers a Wedding*, 1939; *Made to Measure*, 1953; *The Testimonial*, 1953; *The Bride Wore an Opal Ring*, 1954; *Smoke in the Valley*, 1954; *And Then There Were None*, 1955; *This Happy Brood*, 1956; *Midal· Beach*, 1960; *Napoleon in Love*, 1960; *The Avenue Goes to War*, from his own novel, 1961; *The Dreaming Suburb*, from his own novel, 1962; *A Horseman Riding By*, from his own novel, 1967.

Television Plays: *The Day of the Sputnik*, 1963; *Jezebel*, 1963 (USA).

Other

These Clicks Made History: The Stories of Stanley ("Glorious") Devon, Fleet Street Photographer. Exmouth, Devon, Raleigh Press, 1946.
Nobody Shouted Author (autobiography). London, Laurie, 1951.
Bird's Eye View: An Autobiography. London, Constable, 1954.
The Adventures of Ben Gunn. London, Hodder and Stoughton, 1956; Indianapolis, Bobbs Merrill, 1957.
Napoleon in Love. London, Hodder and Stoughton, 1959; Boston, Little Brown, 1960.
The March of the Twenty-Six: The Story of Napoleon's Marshals. London, Hodder and Stoughton, 1962; as *Napoleon's Marshals*, Philadelphia, Chilton, 1966.
Under an English Sky. London, Hodder and Stoughton, 1964.
The Golden Millstones: Napoleon's Brothers and Sisters. London, Weidenfeld and Nicolson, 1964; New York, Harper, 1965.
The Retreat from Moscow. London, Hodder and Stoughton, and New York, Atheneum, 1967.
Imperial Sunset: The Fall of Napoleon 1813-1814. Philadelphia, Chilton, 1968; London, Hodder and Stoughton, 1969.
For My Own Amusement (autobiography). London, Hodder and Stoughton, 1968; New York, Simon and Schuster, 1972.
Overture for Beginners (autobiography). London, Hodder and Stoughton, 1970.

Editor, *Tales Out of School: An Anthology of West Buckland Reminiscences 1895-1963.* St. Austell, Cornwall, H.E. Warne, 1963.

*   *   *

R.F. Delderfield's novels are not so much classic love stories as family sagas punctuated by strong romantic impulses. In *The Avenue Goes to War*, for instance, the hard-bitten, self-seeking Elaine abandons affluence and security with a rich lover to live with the impoverished and disgraced Archie. In *God Is an Englishman* Adam Swan makes a sudden and surprising decision to marry the fiercely independent but terribly vulnerable 18-year-old Henrietta. Broader canvases of the English country or suburban scene, and astute socio-political comment add realism and drama to Delderfield's romantic relationships, which are basically straight-forward and described strictly from a masculine stance—something that is unusual in the general run of romantic novels. There is none of the tremulous, long-winded lead up and final-scene-only clinch that forms the love story pattern when the narrative viewpoint is that of the traditional heroine of the genre. Delderfield's emphasis is on married love and mutuality, not only of passion but of various levels of experience. In *God Is an Englishman* Adam's and Henrietta's relationship only really begins to flower when, after seven years of marriage, Henrietta is forced to become actively involved in her husband's work commitments. David Powlett-Jones, the boarding-school headmaster hero of *To Serve Them All My Days*, far from wanting a merely ornamental or domesticated wife, encourages Chris in her career ambitions. She is his second wife, as David marries once in his youth and again in middle-age.

Romantic relationships in Delderfield's books are in fact often of the second-time-around, middle-aged, or even elderly variety. In *The Dreaming Suburb* Jim Carver loses his first wife almost as soon as he returns home from the trenches at the end of the first World War. He does not marry his second wife, Edith—a spinster neighbour he has known for over 25 years—until the end of World War II (in the closing pages of *The Avenue Goes to War*, the sequel to *The Dreaming Suburb*). Edith and Jim are in their sixties; they have suffered bombing and bereavement, and each is sustained by the friendship of the other and by the helpfulness of neighbours. (There is always a strong community feeling in Delderfield's novels, even when his heroes and heroines go against the tide of popular opinion.) Their late marriage is a satisfying one. Even though love is often expressed by the brewing of pots of tea and the filling of hot water bottles for each other rather than by acts of passion, theirs is nevertheless a romantic story.

Second or late marriages, of course, add variety to any novel, and particularly to those of the family saga type which the author handled so well. (At least three of the leading male characters in *The Avenue Goes to War* marry twice.) Although Delderfield's emphasis is on very much-married love, there is, however, always a place in his novels for the realistic extra-marital affair. In *The Dreaming Suburb* Archie Carver as, a teenage errand boy during the first World War, engages in grocery black-marketeering which brings him, as well as a great deal of extra cash, a satisfying sexual initiation with the lovely and full-blooded wife of an officer who is away at the front. Archie is a go-getter, and so—in the sequel—is Elaine Frith. Delderfield is at his best when writing of non-conformist characters of a complex disposition, and particularly about their romantic involvements. Elaine quickly discards the claustrophobic morality of her narrow-minded upbringing, and as a very young girl begins to exploit her sexual power over men. Later on, she purposefully harnesses this to further her clearly defined material ambitions, and she is untroubled by the strictures of neighbours on her activities: "Marvellous what some women'll do nowadays for a pound of granulated and a tin of pineapple chunks, isn't it?" (The provider of wartime black market goodies is once again Archie Carver.)

Generally speaking, however, in Delderfield's novels the brief affair or sexual encounter, whatever its intensity, is prevented by its tucked away nature from having deep significance in the hero's life. He cannot achieve with a mistress the mutuality at all levels of experience that he might (hopefully) know with a wife.

Love and war are inextricably intertwined in these several-generational sagas in a way that is inevitable when the influence of the two world wars plays such an important part in the author's assessment of life. Delderfield's most poignant vignette of a romantic encounter in a war setting occurs in *A Horseman Riding By*. Paul Craddock, an Army Officer at the Western Front in 1915, has a chance meeting on the road to Messines with his ex-wife, Grace, who is serving as an ambulance driver. They meet again by mutual consent, and amid the mud and carnage and disillusionment they communicate with a completeness that they never managed to achieve in their once comfortable life in England. The residual bitterness of his breakup with Grace is wiped away for Paul—and the encounter helps him to understand aspects of his present marriage to Claire, a much younger woman. But his new found and comradely closeness to Grace is soon shattered. She is killed by the blast of an enemy bomb on one of her ambulance runs. In the hands of a less skilful storyteller, this encounter could have been embarrassing or banal—but it works, in the unsentimental and robust manner in which all Delderfield's fictional romantic situations do.

—Mary Cadogan

DELL, Ethel M(ary).   British.   Born in Streatham, London, 2 August 1881. Educated at Streatham College for Girls, 1893-98. Married Gerald Tahourdin Savage in 1922. *Died 19 September 1939.*

ROMANCE AND GOTHIC PUBLICATIONS

Novels

> *The Way of an Eagle*.   New York, Putnam, 1911; London, Unwin, 1912.
> *The Knave of Diamonds*.   London, Unwin, and New York, Putnam, 1913.
> *The Rocks of Valpré*.   New York, Putnam, 1913; London, Unwin, 1914.
> *The Desire of His Life* (includes "Her Compensation").   London, Holden and Hardingham, 1914; New York, Burt, 1927.

The Keeper of the Door.   London, Unwin, and New York, Putnam, 1915.
The Bars of Iron.   London, Hutchinson, and New York, Putnam, 1916.
The Hundredth Chance.   London, Hutchinson, and New York, Putnam, 1917.
The Rose of Dawn.   New York, Putnam, 1917.
Greatheart.   London, Unwin, and New York, Putnam, 1918.
The Lamp in the Desert.   London, Hutchinson, and New York, Putnam, 1919.
The Top of the World.   London, Cassell, and New York, Putnam, 1920.
The Princess's Game.   London, Hardingham, 1920.
The Lucky Number.   New York, Putnam, 1920.
The Obstacle Race.   London, Cassell, and New York, Putnam, 1921.
Charles Rex.   London, Hutchinson, and New York, Putnam, 1922.
Tetherstones.   London, Hutchinson, and New York, Putnam, 1923.
The Unknown Quantity.   London, Hutchinson, and New York, Putnam, 1924.
A Man under Authority.   London, Cassell, 1925; New York, Putnam, 1926.
The Black Knight.   London, Cassell, and New York, Putnam, 1926.
By Request.   London, Unwin, 1927; as *Peggy by Request*, New York, Putnam, 1928.
The Gate Marked "Private."   London, Cassell, and New York, Putnam, 1928.
The Altar of Honour.   London, Hutchinson, 1929; New York, Putnam, 1930.
Storm Drift.   London, Hutchinson, 1930; New York, Putnam, 1931.
Pullman (omnibus).   London, Benn, 1930.
The Silver Wedding.   London, Hutchinson, 1932; as *The Silver Bride*, New York, Putnam, 1932.
The Prison Wall.   London, Cassell, 1932; New York, Putnam, 1933.
Dona Celestis.   London, Benn, and New York, Putnam, 1933.
The Electric Torch.   London, Cassell, and New York, Putnam, 1934.
Where Three Roads Meet.   London, Cassell, 1935; New York, Putnam, 1936.
Honeyball Farm.   London, Hutchinson, and New York, Putnam, 1937.
The Juice of the Pomegranate.   London, Cassell, and New York, Doubleday, 1938.
The Serpent in the Garden.   London, Cassell, and New York, Doubleday, 1938.
Sown among Thorns.   London, Cassell, and New York, Doubleday, 1939.

Short Stories

The Swindler and Other Stories.   London, Unwin, and New York, Putnam, 1914.
The Safety-Curtain and Other Stories.   London, Unwin, and New York, Putnam, 1917.
The Tidal Wave and Other Stories.   London, Cassell, 1919; New York, Putnam, 1920.
Rosa Mundi and Other Stories.   London, Cassell, and New York, Putnam, 1921.
The Odds and Other Stories.   London, Cassell, and New York, Putnam, 1922.
The Passerby and Other Stories.   London, Hutchinson, and New York, Putnam, 1925.
The House of Happiness and Other Stories.   London, Cassell, and New York, Putnam, 1927.
The Live Bait and Other Stories.   London, Benn, and New York, Putnam, 1932.

OTHER PUBLICATIONS

Verse

Verses.   London, Hutchinson, and New York, Putnam, 1923.

Critical Study: *Nettie and Sissie: The Biography of Ethel M. Dell and Her Sister Ella* by Penelope Dell, London, Hamish Hamilton, 1977.

*   *   *

Absurd though they may at first seem, the novels of Ethel M. Dell have nonetheless a boisterous power, an irresistible quality about them, defined by Queenie Leavis as sheer luxuriant vitality: "Even the most critical reader who brings only an ironical appreciation to their work cannot avoid noticing a certain power, the secret of their success with the majority. Bad writing, false sentiment, sheer silliness, and a preposterous narrative are all carried along by the magnificent vitality of the author, as they are in *Jane Eyre*."

Such gripping tales as *The Way of an Eagle, The Lamp in the Desert, The Hundredth Chance, The Black Knight*, and *The Knave of Diamonds* are a highly readable mixture which combines quasi-religious themes with drama, action, and full-blooded adventure. Dashing officer heroes with murky pasts, exercising gallantry and bravery, are reminiscent of some of the 19th-century heroes of a Ouida or a Rhoda Broughton novel. The heroines, sensitive and virginal, strong but innocent, are no longer tormented by urgent doctrinal doubt, misgivings about the 39 Articles or the meaning of the original sin. For, as interest in orthodox Christianity gradually waned, it was replaced, in popular romantic fiction, by a new, less clearly defined spiritual quest. The heroines are driven by passions which are simultaneously of an earthly and a heavenly nature. Their vague, mystical uncertainty runs a parallel course to their difficulties and sufferings of mortal love. Thus, for example, Ann Carfax is tormented by the need for a prayerful life, but, in her darkest hour finds total inability to pray: "Powerless, she sank upon her knees by the open window, striving painfully, piteously, vainly, to pray. But no words came to her, no prayer rose from her wrung heart. It was as though she knelt in outer darkness before a locked door." (This is from *The Knave of Diamonds*, the title referring to the ambiguous, but probably sinful, nature of the hero.) Stella, similarly, in *The Way of an Eagle*, is beset by intense inner doubts and fears, not specifically religious, but rather, spiritually worthy "feelings": "And again, very deep down in her soul there stirred that blind, unconscious entity, of the existence of which she herself had so vague a knowledge, feeling upwards, groping outwards, to the light."

Ill-defined though such feelings may be, the implication is that they have a worth, a value, which is as good, if not better, than orthodox religion. Heroines (less often heroes) grapple with their doubt for a couple of hundred pages, before the ultimate discovery of some symbol in their lives which represents for them a renewal and refreshment of the spirit. In *The Lamp in the Desert* that symbol is clear. Christ is the lamp, which lights up the Desert of the World: "Her halting feet were now guided by God's Lamp. She had come to realise that the wanderers in the wilderness are ever His especial care, and that she would come at last into the Presence of God Himself." Her acceptance of her Creator, after such a prolonged period of confusion, occurs at the same time as her rediscovery of her love for her long-lost husband.

In *The Way of an Eagle* that symbolic bird refers less to our Lord, more to the primeval, bird-like nature of the fierce husband whom she both fears, and dreams of longingly. He is the eagle who will gather her up, and bear her swiftly through wide spaces to his eyrie in the mountains. The eagle-hero is not without his acknowledgement of one greater than he. When hero and heroine, thwarted pair, uncover their mutual passion while communing with nature at the top of the mountain, it is the man who decides that prayer would be appropriate: "Do you know what we are going to do as soon as we are married, sweetheart? We are going to climb the highest mountain in the world, to see the sun rise, and to thank God."

The searing, or burning, or scorching, kiss became one of the hallmarks of romance; and E.M. Dell was an early perfectionist at hot literary embraces. "His quick breath scorched her face, and in a moment almost before she knew what was happening, his lips were on her own. He kissed her as she had never been kissed before—a single fiery kiss that sent all the blood in tumult to her heart." Or "There was sheer unshackled savagery in the holding of his arms, and dismay thrilled her through and through." And "Again his lips pressed hers, and again from head to foot she felt as if a flame had scorched her." Today, Barbara Cartland may declare that what readers want is innocence and chastity. In the 1930's what they wanted was hot kissing and unbridled passion. Ray Smith's Twopenny Library reported in 1933 that the three women authors most in demand were Ethel M. Dell, Elinor Glyn, and Marie Corelli, in that order.

Despite the "religious" content, the novels are full of blood, guts, and thunder. Dell included tempests, infant deaths, runaway horses, wife-beating, men going violently mad, fine young lovers crippled for life, an electric storm, falling meteors, and a mutiny at the Northwest frontier. During times of chaos, men are aware of the importance of risking life to protect the honour of the heroine. This bravery results in a number of hand-to-hand fights to the death: "So long as his heart should beat he would defend that one precious possession that yet remained—the honour of the woman who loved him and whom he loved as only the few knew how to love."

Dell did not have the pretensions of some other popular novelists of her era. She was not seeking literary glory; nor did she continually complain, as did Marie Corelli or Elinor Glyn, that her work was misunderstood by the critics. She did not hold herself out as some female latter-day Shakespeare like Ouida or Hall Caine. The loyalty of her readers was the reward she sought and enjoyed. She repaid them by dedicating to them one of her novels, *By Request*, a gesture which signals the importance, for popular writers, of a close reader/writer relationship. Those who do not have it, aspire to it; those who do, rightly nurture it.

—Rachel Anderson

DELMAR, Viña (née Croter). American. Born in New York City, 29 January 1905. Attended public schools in New York. Married Eugene Delmar in 1921; one child. Worked as typist, switchboard operator, usher, actress, and theatre manager, then free-lance writer. Address: c/o Harcourt Brace Jovanovich, 757 Third Avenue, New York, New York 10017, U.S.A.

ROMANCE AND GOTHIC PUBLICATIONS

Novels

    Bad Girl. New York, Harcourt Brace, 1928; London, Allan, 1929.
    Kept Woman. New York, Harcourt Brace, 1929; as *The Other Woman*, London, Allan, 1930.
    Women Live Too Long. New York, Harcourt Brace, and London, Allan, 1932; as *The Restless Passion*, New York, Avon, 1947.
    The Marriage Racket. New York, Harcourt Brace, and London, Allan, 1933.
    Mystery at Little Heaven. Los Angeles, Times Mirror Press, 1933.
    The End of the World. New York, International Magazine Company, 1934.
    The Love Trap. New York, Avon, 1949.
    New Orleans Lady. New York, Avon, 1949.
    About Mrs. Leslie. New York, Harcourt Brace, 1950; London, Hale, 1952.
    Strangers in Love. New York, Dell, 1951.
    The Marcaboth Women. New York, Harcourt Brace, 1951; London, Hale, 1953.
    The Laughing Stranger. New York, Harcourt Brace, 1953; London, Hale, 1954.
    Ruby. New York, Pocket Books, 1953.
    Beloved. New York, Harcourt Brace, 1956; London, Hale, 1957.
    The Breeze from Camelot. New York, Harcourt Brace, 1959; London, Davies, 1960.
    The Big Family. New York, Harcourt Brace, 1961.
    The Enchanted. New York, Harcourt Brace, 1965.
    Grandmère. New York, Harcourt Brace, 1967.
    The Freeways. New York, Harcourt Brace, 1971.
    A Time for Titans. New York, Harcourt Brace, 1974.
    McKeever. New York, Harcourt Brace, 1976.

Short Stories

> *Loose Ladies.* New York, Harcourt Brace, 1929; as *Women Who Pass By*, London, Allan, 1929.

Uncollected Short Stories

> "Pick Up," in *World's Best Short Stories of the Year 1929*, edited by Paul Palmer. New York, Minton Balch, 1929.
> "Forces," in *Saturday Evening Post* (Philadelphia), 27 September 1930.
> "Year and Forever," in *Best American Love Stories of the Year*, edited by Margaret Widdemer. New York, Day, 1932.
> "Day Never Came," in *Delineator* (New York), January-March 1935.
> "Secret," in *Pictorial Review* (New York), November 1936.
> "Two Lovely Ladies," in *Ladies Home Journal* (Philadelphia), November 1939.
> "Phantom Shore," in *Ladies Home Journal* (Philadelphia), July 1940.
> "What Husbands Don't Know," in *Ladies Home Journal* (Philadelphia), August 1941.
> "Where Is Kay Tonight?," in *Good Housekeeping* (New York), January 1942.
> "If We Could Be Alone," in *Ladies Home Journal* (Philadelphia), March 1942.
> "Lily Hunter and the U.S.A.," in *Good Housekeeping* (New York), April 1942.
> "Do You Take These Women?," in *Good Housekeeping* (New York), June, July 1942.
> "Never Too Late," in *Good Housekeeping* (New York), October 1942.
> "Family Affair," in *Ladies Home Journal* (Philadelphia), November 1942.
> "Outsider," in *Good Housekeeping* (New York), August 1943.
> "Mousie," in *Ladies Home Journal* (Philadelphia), September 1943.
> "Someday I'll Dance with You," in *Good Housekeeping* (New York), November 1943.
> "I Promised," in *Good Housekeeping* (New York), December 1943.
> "Coming Home," in *Good Housekeeping* (New York), March 1944.
> "Time of Her Life," in *Woman's Home Companion* (Springfield, Ohio), September 1944.
> "Magic Cottage," in *Good Housekeeping* (New York), October 1944.
> "You'll Marry Me at Noon," in *Ladies Home Journal* (Philadelphia), January 1945.
> "Man in Her Room," in *Good Housekeeping* (New York), June 1945.
> "Where Were You?," in *Woman's Home Companion* (Springfield, Ohio), August 1946.
> "Letter to a Lady," in *American Magazine* (Springfield, Ohio), December 1946.
> "Ballad for a Fish Fry," in *Ladies Home Journal* (Philadelphia), December 1952.
> "Half-Guilty Wife," in *Woman's Home Companion* (Springfield, Ohio), April 1953.
> "Something for the Heart," in *Woman's Home Companion* (Springfield, Ohio), October 1953.
> "She Glittered When She Walked," in *Ladies Home Journal* (Philadelphia), September 1954.
> "Midnight of a Bridesmaid," in *Ladies Home Journal* (Philadelphia), March 1955.
> "Honeymoon," in *Woman's Home Companion* (Springfield, Ohio), January 1956.
> "The Second Mrs. Thorpe," in *Saturday Evening Post Stories 1957*. New York, Random House, 1957.
> "Too Lovely to Last," in *Good Housekeeping* (New York), August 1957.
> "Lady with a Secret," in *Good Housekeeping* (New York), March 1961.
> "Devil to Pay," in *Good Housekeeping* (New York), February 1962.

OTHER PUBLICATIONS

Plays

> *Bad Girl*, with Brian Marlowe, adaptation of the novel by Delmar (produced New York, 1930).
> *The Rich, Full Life* (produced New York, 1945). New York, French, 1945.

Mid-Summer (produced New York, 1953). New York, French, 1954.

Warm Wednesday. New York, French, 1959.

The Rest Is Silence, adaptation of her screenplay *Make Way for Tomorrow* (produced Moscow, 1970).

Screenplays: *A Soldier's Plaything*, with Perry Vikroff, 1930; *The Awful Truth*, with Dwight Taylor, 1937; *Make Way for Tomorrow*, 1937.

Other

The Becker Scandal: A Time Remembered (autobiography). New York, Harcourt Brace, 1968.

*   *   *

Viña Delmar is essentially a formulator of character studies. Her early novels recount the experiences of lower-middle-class women typical of their times. In later creations she describes persons of a higher social and educational milieu. Her works range from light fiction to deeper historical novels. Most involve romance to some degree, but love is not the prevailing theme in all her stories.

Delmar's entertaining first novel, *Bad Girl*, tells the story of the meeting and hasty wedding of a very young couple and the birth of their child. They have never learned the principles of communication, and each hopes the other will automatically know his wants and feelings. A major misunderstanding occurs when each thinks the other does not truly want the baby which, in reality, both are excited about. After the birth, they shyly reveal their pleasure to each other, but there is little hope for increased communication despite this experience. Both characters are clearly delineated and alive.

Ruby's birthday is the signal in *The Marcaboth Women* for the women to review their own lives and accomplishments. Each of the Marcaboth wives has a problem to deal with when her husband insists she drop everything to buy and deliver a birthday gift to the new wife of the oldest brother. Ruby is 20 years old, selfish, and, by her existence, capable of changing the lives of the other family members. Even the clan matriarch recognizes the impending alteration of her family dominence. The characters are deftly drawn with a few strokes of the pen and neatly interwoven with each other. This skillfully painted family portrait entices the reader to the end.

With *Beloved* Delmar delves into historical biography. Her subject is Judah Benjamin, Governor of Louisiana and Confederate Secretary of State and an attorney of great accomplishment. Benjamin marries a beautiful Creole incapable of remaining faithful to one man and, by his understanding of her character, earns her love and the appellation "Beloved" in her letters to him. It is a tale of tenderness surrounded by doubt, prejudice, and war. The story is carefully developed and the characters seem to mature naturally. Some of the novelist's assumptions about the Civil War could cause debate among historical purists, but the book is recommended for lovers of the genre.

The John Slidell family is the subject of *The Big Family*, members of whom were important in early American history. Delmar has faithfully adhered to historical fact. There is an amplitude of romantic detail and exciting events, but since the novel covers three generations there is little depth. The reader gets a more complete picture of the New Orleanean Slidell in *Beloved* than is available in this work. It is, nevertheless, an interesting and masterful example of Delmar's abilities as an historical novelist.

Delmar is an author of distinction, and her works have been popular and widely reviewed. Her skill in character development and dialogue has increased over the years and hers is an important name in romantic and historical fiction.

—Andrea Lee Shuey

DINGWELL, Joyce. Australian. Address: c/o Mills and Boon Ltd., 15-16 Brooks Mews, London W1A 1DR, England.

ROMANCE AND GOTHIC PUBLICATIONS

Novels

Australian Hospital. London, Mills and Boon, 1955; Toronto, Harlequin, 1960.
Greenfingers Farm. London, Mills and Boon, 1955; Toronto, Harlequin, 1966.
Second Chance. London, Mills and Boon, 1956.
Wednesday's Children. London, Mills and Boon, 1957; as *Nurse Trent's Children*, Toronto, Harlequin, 1961.
Will You Surrender? London, Mills and Boon, 1957; Toronto, Harlequin, 1968.
The Coral Tree. London, Mills and Boon, 1958; Toronto, Harlequin, 1961.
If Love You Hold. London, Mills and Boon, 1958; as *Doctor Benedict*, Toronto, Harlequin, 1962; as *Love and Doctor Benedict*, Toronto, Harlequin, 1978.
The Girl at Snowy River. London, Mills and Boon, 1959; Toronto, Harlequin, 1964.
The House in the Timberwoods. London, Mills and Boon, 1959; Toronto, Harlequin, 1963.
Nurse Jess. London, Mills and Boon, and Toronto, Harlequin, 1959.
Tender Conquest. London, Mills and Boon, 1960; Toronto, Harlequin, 1964.
The Third in the House. London, Mills and Boon, 1961; Toronto, Harlequin, 1965.
The Wind and the Spray. London, Mills and Boon, 1961; Toronto, Harlequin, 1969.
The Boomerang Girl. London, Mills and Boon, 1962; Toronto, Harlequin, 1967.
River Nurse. London, Mills and Boon, 1962; Toronto, Harlequin, 1963.
The New Zealander. London, Mills and Boon, 1963; Toronto, Harlequin, 1967.
The Timber Man. London, Mills and Boon, 1964; Toronto, Harlequin, 1965.
The English Boss. London, Mills and Boon, 1964.
The Kindly Giant. London, Mills and Boon, 1964.
The Man from the Valley. London, Mills and Boon, and Toronto, Harlequin, 1966.
The Feel of Silk. London, Mills and Boon, 1967; Toronto, Harlequin, 1969.
I and My Heart. London, Mills and Boon, 1967; Toronto, Harlequin, 1970.
Clove Orange. London, Mills and Boon, 1967; Toronto, Harlequin, 1971.
A Taste for Love. London, Mills and Boon, 1967; Toronto, Harlequin, 1968.
Hotel Southerly. London, Mills and Boon, 1968; Toronto, Harlequin, 1970.
Venice Affair. London, Mills and Boon, and Toronto, Harlequin, 1968.
Nurse Smith, Cook. London, Mills and Boon, 1968; as *No Females Wanted*, Toronto, Harlequin, 1970.
The Drummer and the Song. London, Mills and Boon, and New York, Golden Press, 1969.
One String for Nurse Bow. London, Mills and Boon, 1969; as *One String for Her Bow*, Toronto, Harlequin, 1970.
Spanish Lace. London, Mills and Boon, and Toronto, Harlequin, 1969.
Crown of Flowers. London, Mills and Boon, 1969; Toronto, Harlequin, 1971.
Demi-Semi Nurse. London, Mills and Boon, 1969.
September Street. London, Mills and Boon, 1969; Toronto, Harlequin, 1972.
West of the River. London, Mills and Boon, 1970; as *Guardian Nurse*, Toronto, Harlequin, 1970.
Pool of Pink Lilies. London, Mills and Boon, 1970; Toronto, Harlequin, 1973.
Mr. Victoria. London, Mills and Boon, 1970.
Nickel Wife. London, Mills and Boon, 1970; Toronto, Harlequin, 1972.
Sister Pussycat. London, Mills and Boon, 1971; Toronto, Harlequin, 1974.
A Thousand Candles. London, Mills and Boon, 1971; Toronto, Harlequin, 1972.
Red Ginger Blossom. London, Mills and Boon, and Toronto, Harlequin, 1972.
Wife to Sim. London, Mills and Boon, 1972; Toronto, Harlequin, 1973.
Friday's Laughter. London, Mills and Boon, 1972.

There Were Three Princes. London, Mills and Boon, 1972; Toronto, Harlequin, 1974.
The Mutual Look. London, Mills and Boon, and Toronto, Harlequin, 1973.
The Cattleman. London, Mills and Boon, 1974; Toronto, Harlequin, 1975.
The New Broom. London, Mills and Boon, 1974; Toronto, Harlequin, 1976.
Flamingo Flying South. London, Mills and Boon, 1974; Toronto, Harlequin, 1975.
The Habit of Love. London, Mills and Boon, and Toronto, Harlequin, 1974.
The Kissing Gate. Toronto, Harlequin, 1975.
Cane Music. London, Mills and Boon, and Toronto, Harlequin, 1975.
Love and Lucy Brown. Toronto, Harlequin, 1975.
Corporation Boss. London, Mills and Boon, 1975; Toronto, Harlequin, 1976.
Inland Paradise. London, Mills and Boon, 1976; Toronto, Harlequin, 1977.
Deep in the Forest. Toronto, Harlequin, 1976.
The Road Boss. Toronto, Harlequin, 1976.
A Drift of Jasmine. Toronto, Harlequin, 1977.
The Truth Game. London, Mills and Boon, 1978.
All the Days of Summer. Toronto, Harlequin, 1978.
Remember September. Toronto, Harlequin, 1978.
The Tender Winds of Spring. London, Mills and Boon, 1978.
The Boss's Daughter. London, Mills and Boon, 1978.
Year of the Dragon. Toronto, Harlequin, 1978.
The Angry Man. London, Mills and Boon, 1979.
The All-the-Way Man. London, Mills and Boon, 1980; Toronto, Harlequin, 1981.
Come Back to Love. London, Mills and Boon, 1980; Toronto, Harlequin, 1981.

*   *   *

Joyce Dingwell, an Australian writer, is an author who has adapted herself to the changing demands of the reading public. In the late 1950's and early 1960's, she wrote traditional nurse-doctor romances. However, as the popularity of this type of romance waned, she switched her approach. Her major characters are now in various occupations and the interaction between the hero and heroine is "spicier" or "racier" than before, although her basic plot has remained the same. In fact, in at least one instance she has published the same book twice with only minor revisions. The romance formula and individual patterns of style do not allow for a wide range of variation within romantic fiction as a whole or within the work of a specific author. Nevertheless, one is surprised and disappointed to discover Dingwell repeating herself.

The Angry Man, published in 1979, is an almost identical version of *Greenfingers Farm*, published in 1955. Characters, general plot, concrete situations like an argument about appropriate nightwear on a safari, and even line-for-line dialogue are carried over from the earlier work to the later. This duplication with its slight alterations does serve the purpose of illustrating the changes in Dingwell. A meaningful glance between the hero and the heroine in *Greenfingers Farm* becomes a passsionate embrace which includes the hero unbuttoning the heroine's blouse and touching her breast in *The Angry Man*. The hero's cousin in the earlier work is transformed into an illegitimate brother in the later book, and so on.

Dingwell's main appeal and most distinctive feature is her use of Australian settings, although she occasionally moves her stories to other locales, usually in the South Pacific. In addition, she develops a story line with a fairly large cast of characters. As a result, there are frequently several romances occurring in any one book which may end in multiple marriages. The story line may also typically include elements of danger or sadness. Dingwell's romances are not "stress-free." Heroines, in particular, experience painful losses such as the death of a beloved father. One of the hero's tasks, then, is to break through the heroine's emotional barriers to alleviate her pain with his love. Dingwell's strength, however, lies in her creation of secondary characters and plots rather than in the development of a complex relationship between the hero and heroine.

—Margaret Jensen

DIVER, (Katherine Helen) Maud (née Marshall).　British.　Born in Murree, India, in 1867 (?). Educated in England, but spent early years in India and Ceylon. Married T. Diver in 1896 (died, 1941); one son. Lived in England after 1896: journalist. *Died 14 October 1945.*

ROMANCE AND GOTHIC PUBLICATIONS

Novels

> *The Men of the Frontier Force.*　London, Newnes, 1930.
>> *Capt. Desmond, V.C.*　Edinburgh, Blackwood, 1907; New York, Lane, 1908; revised edition, New York, Putnam, 1914; Blackwood, 1915.
>> *The Great Amulet.*　Edinburgh, Blackwood, and New York, Lane, 1908.
>> *Desmond's Daughter.*　Edinburgh, Blackwood, and New York, Putnam, 1916.
> *Candles in the Wind.*　Edinburgh, Blackwood, and New York, Lane, 1909.
> *Lilamani.*　London, Hutchinson, 1911; as *Awakening*, New York, Lane, 1911.
> *The Hero of Herat.*　London, Constable, 1912; New York, Putnam, 1913.
> *The Judgement of the Sword.*　London, Constable, 1913; New York, Putnam, 1914.
> *Unconquered.*　London, Murray, and New York, Putnam, 1917.
> *Strange Roads.*　London, Constable, 1918.
> *The Strong Hours.*　London, Constable, and Boston, Houghton Mifflin, 1919.
> *Far to Seek.*　Edinburgh, Blackwood, and Boston, Houghton Mifflin, 1921.
> *Lonely Furrow.*　London, Murray, and Boston, Houghton Mifflin, 1923.
> *Coombe St. Mary's.*　Edinburgh, Blackwood, and Boston, Houghton Mifflin, 1925.
> *But Yesterday—.*　London, Murray, and New York, Dodd Mead, 1927.
> *Together.*　London, Newnes, 1928.
> *A Wild Bird.*　London, Murray, and Boston, Houghton Mifflin, 1929.
> *Ships of Youth.*　Edinburgh, Blackwood, and Boston, Houghton Mifflin, 1931.
> *The Singer Passes.*　Edinburgh, Blackwood, and New York, Dodd Mead, 1934.
> *The Dream Prevails.*　London, Murray, and Boston, Houghton Mifflin, 1938.
> *Sylvia Lyndon.*　Edinburgh, Blackwood, and Boston, Houghton Mifflin, 1940.

Short Stories

> *Sunia and Other Stories.*　Edinburgh, Blackwood, and New York, Putnam, 1913.
> *Siege Perilous and Other Stories.*　London, Murray, and Boston, Houghton Mifflin, 1924.

OTHER PUBLICATIONS

Other

> *The Englishwoman in India.*　Edinburgh, Blackwood, 1909.
> *Kabul to Kandahar.*　London, Davies, 1935.
> *Honoria Lawrence: A Fragment of Indian History.*　London, Murray, and Boston, Houghton Mifflin, 1936.
> *Royal India: A Descriptive and Historical Study of India's Fifteen Principal States and Their Rulers.*　London, Hodder and Stoughton, and New York, Appleton Century, 1942.
> *The Unsung: A Record of British Services in India.*　Edinburgh, Blackwood, 1945.

*　　　*　　　*

Maud Diver was born in India and spent her early life there and in Ceylon. This provided her with the background for many of her tales. "I don't know how or why I am so successful in getting the Indian quality of my characters so true. I have really known very few Indians: One didn't know them in my day. It is some sort of sympathetic insight that guides me—and guides me right."

Her first novel, *Capt. Desmond, V.C.*, is set in and around the Punjab cavalry regiment, and at the frontier station of Kohat. With its alluring mixture of exotica, passion, and reassuring confirmation of all the clichés about life, men, love, marriage, and sex, it established her reputation as a popular writer. Diver specialised in marvelously voluptuous overwriting. Even minor descriptive passages which have no bearing on plot, characters, or theme are given full rein, the same weight. Thus, a sunrise: "By now the moon's last rim formed a golden sickle behind a blunt shoulder of rock; while over the eastward levels the topaz-yellow of an Indian dawn rushed at one stride to the zenith of heaven." This is what her readers wanted—that soothing mixture of accepted generalisations, and with a daring, foreign feel. However, lest the background material prove too exotic for her less well-travelled readers, the text is lightly spattered with footnotes explaining the meaning of some less familiar Indian terms (*chuprassee*, a government servant; *chota hazri*, a small breakfast) which add still more to the eastern flavour without confusing. Any obscurity in her novels is caused, less by the foreign setting, more by the luxuriant enthusiasm of her over-written style.

The Hero of Herat was another "frontier biography," and *The Judgement of the Sword* is set in Kabul. At the end of the Great War, she attempted two companion novels, *Strange Roads* and *The Strong Hours*, an ambitious attempt at the family saga story, which tries to show the effects of war on the lives and loves of the Blounts of Avonleigh, "an ancient family dating back to the days of Coeur de Lion." To give the prose more importance, she was partial to the conceit of attaching a literary (and sometimes not so literary) heading or quotation to the start of each brief chapter. These appear to have been selected almost at random, some so trite as to be more like cracker mottos, some popular philosophical tags, others from Emerson, E.M. Forster, Shakespeare, and St. Luke's gospel.

The lack of any sense of proportion is the biggest limitation to many romantic novelists. Most writers get to a point where they realise that there is something that they cannot do in their work. Second-rate novelists such as Maud Diver never reach this point. Nothing is beyond her sublime confidence. She did not relinquish the attempt to ask important moral questions, to tackle impossibly large themes.

—Rachel Anderson

DUFFIELD, Anne (née Tate). American. Born in Orange, New Jersey, 20 November 1893. Educated at a private school in Toronto; the Sorbonne, Paris. Married Edgar Duffield in 1922.

ROMANCE AND GOTHIC PUBLICATIONS

Novels

Miss Mayhew and Ming Yun: A Story of East and West. New York, Stokes, 1928.
The Lacquer Couch. London, Murray, 1928.
Predestined. London, Murray, 1929.
Passionate Interlude. London, Murray, 1931.
Phantasy. London, Cassell, 1932.

Lantern-Light. London, Cassell, 1933; New York, Arcadia House, 1943.

Fleeing Shadows. London, Cassell, 1934; as *Stamboul Love*, New York, Knopf, 1934.

Flaming Felicia. London, Cassell, 1934; New York, Arcadia House, 1941.

Golden Horizons. London, Cassell, 1935; New York, Arcadia House, 1942.

Silver Peaks. London, Cassell, 1935; New York, Arcadia House, 1941.

Wild Memory. London, Cassell, 1935; as *Love's Memory*, New York, Arcadia House, 1936.

Glittering Heights. London, Cassell, 1936.

Moon over Stamboul. London, Cassell, 1936; New York, Arcadia House, 1937.

Paradise. London, Cassell, 1936; as *Brief Rapture*, New York, Arcadia House, 1938.

Bitter Rapture. London, Cassell, 1937.

Enchantment. New York, Curl, 1937.

The House on the Nile. London, Cassell, 1937; as *Gossip*, New York, Curl, 1938.

Gay Fiesta. New York, Arcadia House, 1938; as *The Dragon's Tail*, London, Cassell, 1939.

Grecian Rhapsody. London, Cassell, 1938; as *High Heaven*, 1939.

Desert Moon. London, Cassell, 1939; New York, Arcadia House, 1940.

False Star. New York, Arcadia House, 1939.

Karen's Memory. London, Cassell, and New York, Arcadia House, 1939.

Bubbling Springs. London, Cassell, and New York, Arcadia House, 1940.

The Sweeping Tide. London, Cassell, and New York, Arcadia House, 1940.

The Shadow of the Pines. London, Cassell, 1940; New York, Arcadia House, 1941.

A Bevy of Maids. London, Cassell, 1941; as *Volunteer Nurse*, New York, Arcadia House, 1942.

Old Glory. London, Cassell, 1942; New York, Arcadia House, 1943.

The Inscrutable Nymph. London, Cassell, 1942; as *This Alien Heart*, New York, Arcadia House, 1942.

Sunrise. London, Cassell, 1943; New York, Arcadia House, 1944.

Out of the Shadows. London, Cassell, 1944; as *Turn to the Sun*, New York, Arcadia House, 1944.

Taffy Came to Cairo. London, Cassell, 1944; New York, Arcadia House, 1945.

Repent at Leisure. London, Cassell, 1945; New York, Arcadia House, 1946.

Forever To-morrow. London, Cassell, 1946; New York, Arcadia House, 1951.

Song of the Mocking Bird. London, Cassell, 1946; as *The Lonely Bride*, New York, Arcadia House, 1947.

Wise Is the Heart. New York, Arcadia House, 1947.

Arkady. London, Cassell, 1948.

Dusty Dawn. London, Cassell, 1949; New York, Arcadia House, 1953.

Lovable Stranger. Philadelphia, Macrae Smith, 1949.

Beloved Enemy. London, Cassell, 1950.

Love Deferred. Philadelphia, Macrae Smith, 1951; as *Tomorrow Is Theirs*, London, Cassell, 1952.

Sugar Island. London, Cassell, 1951.

Harbour Lights. London, Cassell, 1953; New York, Arcadia House, 1954.

The Golden Summer. London, Cassell, 1954; New York, Arcadia House, 1955.

The Grand Duchess. London, Cassell, and New York, Arcadia House, 1954.

Come Back, Miranda. London, Cassell, 1955; New York, Berkley, 1974.

Fiametta. London, Cassell, 1956; New York, Arcadia House, 1958.

Castle in Spain. London, Cassell, 1958.

Violetta. London, Cassell, 1960.

*   *   *

Anne Duffield wrote from the 1920's until 1960. The appeal of her books lies in the settings which invariably involve foreign travel on ships. The romance of this world is pretty dated by modern standards and the consistency of the formula which Duffield applies means that her books will have less and less appeal. Duffield belongs to the ocean liner age, and features of that age have disappeared completely, such as the Anglo-Egyptian Community, plantation colonies, and plentiful servants. The romance of being abroad and being in love abroad, however, is a very enduring theme in Duffield's books. Whereas in *Flaming Felicia* (1934) the setting is Egypt, in the novels from the 1950's the settings move closer to home. The mystery of the orient as in *Moon over Stamboul* (1936) gives way to a more conventional holiday setting of Spain in *Castle in Spain* (1958). The traditional mystery settings of romantic novels give way to summer-holiday settings agreeable to conventional young girls. The very foreignness of the men the girls fall in love with, such as Don Eduardo in *Castle in Spain*, makes them that much more attractive. Mixed in with the excitement of foreign settings is an element of danger and mystery, such as the unexpected encounter with snakes in *Bitter Rapture* and *Bubbling' Springs*. Voodoo appears in *Sugar Island*.

The girls in Duffield's books are charmingly flirtatious, attractive, and lively. Yet they are coy about revealing their true feelings for the man they love until they are ready to fall into his arms. Indeed the progression from initial repulsion from a man (for various reasons) to eventual falling in love with him forms the main interest of these novels. Other matters, such as the second man who is also in love with the heroine and the eventual outcome of his relationship with her, are inevitably incidental. The plots are drawn out and slight. They also include rather contrived incidents, such as the use of a car crash or falls from cliffs. Duffield is good at drawing the minutiae of the social relationships of various groups in the middle ranges of society, such as West Indies planter types and the expatriate British. She is very skilful with description of the clothes her heroines and other female characters wear.

Anne Duffield's best attribute is her ability to depict local colour in foreign lands. There is, however, something dated about this as well as the clothes. Even though her 1950's novels were reprinted as late as the 1970's, to the young reader Paris and Spain are no longer romantic in themselves.

—P.R. Meldrum

---

du MAURIER, Daphne. British. Born in London, 13 May 1907; daughter of the actor/manager Sir Gerald du Maurier; granddaughter of the writer George du Maurier. Educated privately and in Paris. Married Lieutenant-General Sir Frederick Browning in 1932 (died, 1965); two daughters and one son. Recipient: Mystery Writers of America Grand Master Award, 1977. Fellow, Royal Society of Literature, 1952. D.B.E. (Dame Commander, Order of the British Empire), 1969. Address: Kilmarth, Par, Cornwall, England.

ROMANCE AND GOTHIC PUBLICATIONS

Novels

The Loving Spirit. London, Heinemann, and New York, Doubleday, 1931.
I'll Never Be Young Again. London, Heinemann, and New York, Doubleday, 1932.
The Progress of Julius. London, Heinemann, and New York, Doubleday, 1933.
Jamaica Inn. London, Gollancz, and New York, Doubleday, 1936.
Rebecca. London, Gollancz, and New York, Doubleday, 1938.
Frenchman's Creek. London, Gollancz, 1941; New York, Doubleday, 1942.
Hungry Hill. London, Gollancz, and New York, Doubleday, 1943.
The King's General. London, Gollancz, and New York, Doubleday, 1946.
The Parasites. London, Gollancz, 1949; New York, Doubleday, 1950.
My Cousin Rachel. London, Gollancz, 1951; New York, Doubleday, 1952.

Mary Anne. London, Gollancz, and New York, Doubleday, 1954.
The Scapegoat. London, Gollancz, and New York, Doubleday, 1957.
Castle Dor, with Arthur Quiller-Couch, completed by du Maurier. London, Dent, and New York, Doubleday, 1962.
The Glass-Blowers. London, Gollancz, and New York, Doubleday, 1963.
The Flight of the Falcon. London, Gollancz, and New York, Doubleday, 1965.
The House on the Strand. London, Gollancz, and New York, Doubleday, 1969.
Rule Britannia. London, Gollancz, 1972; New York, Doubleday, 1973.

Short Stories

Happy Christmas (story). New York, Doubleday, 1940; London, Todd, 1943.
Come Wind, Come Weather. London, Heinemann, 1940; New York, Doubleday, 1941.
Nothing Hurts for Long, and Escort. London, Todd, 1943.
Consider the Lilies (story). London, Todd, 1943.
Spring Picture (story). London, Todd, 1944.
Leading Lady (story). London, Vallancey Press, 1945.
London and Paris (two stories). London, Vallancey Press, 1945.
The Apple Tree: A Short Novel and Some Stories. London, Gollancz, 1952; as *Kiss Me Again, Stranger: A Collection of Eight Stories, Long and Short*, New York, Doubleday, 1953; as *The Birds and Other Stories*, London, Penguin, 1968.
Early Stories. London, Todd, 1954.
The Breaking Point: Eight Stories. London, Gollancz, and New York, Doubleday, 1959; as *The Blue Lenses and Other Stories*, London, Penguin, 1970.
The Treasury of du Maurier Short Stories. London, Gollancz, 1960.
The Lover and Other Stories. London, Ace, 1961.
Not after Midnight and Other Stories. London, Gollancz, 1971; as *Don't Look Now*, New York, Doubleday, 1971.
Echoes from the Macabre: Selected Stories. London, Gollancz, 1976; New York, Doubleday, 1977.
The Rendezvous and Other Stories. London, Gollancz, 1980.

OTHER PUBLICATIONS

Plays

Rebecca, adaptation of her own novel (produced Manchester and London, 1940; New York, 1945). London, Gollancz, 1940; New York, Dramatists Play Service, 1943.
The Years Between (produced Manchester, 1944; London, 1945). London, Gollancz, 1945; New York, Doubleday, 1946.
September Tide (produced Oxford and London, 1948). London, Gollancz, 1949; New York, Doubleday, 1950.

Screenplay: *Hungry Hill*, with Terence Young and Francis Crowdry, 1947.

Television Play: *The Breakthrough*, 1976.

Other

Gerald: A Portrait (on Gerald du Maurier). London, Gollancz, 1934; New York, Doubleday, 1935.
The du Mauriers. London, Gollancz, and New York, Doubleday, 1937.
The Infernal World of Branwell Brontë. London, Gollancz, 1960; New York, Doubleday, 1961.

Vanishing Cornwall, photographs by Christian Browning.   London, Gollancz, and New York, Doubleday, 1967.
Golden Lads: Sir Francis Bacon, Anthony Bacon, and Their Friends.   London, Gollancz, and New York, Doubleday, 1975.
The Winding Stair: Francis Bacon, His Rise and Fall.   London, Gollancz, 1976; New York, Doubleday, 1977.
Growing Pains: The Shaping of a Writer (autobiography).   London, Gollancz, 1977; as *Myself When Young*, New York, Doubleday, 1977.
The Rebecca Notebook and Other Memories (includes short stories).   New York, Doubleday, 1980; London, Gollancz, 1981.

Editor, *The Young George du Maurier: A Selection of His Letters 1860-1867*.   London, Davies, 1951; New York, Doubleday, 1952.
Editor, *Best Stories*, by Phyllis Bottome.   London, Faber, 1963.

*   *   *

A prolific and inventive writer, Daphne du Maurier has never hesitated to experiment with various genres, and she has been widely praised for her short stories, plays, biographies, and autobiographies. It is her novels, however, which have won her the widest fame and a vast following among readers, many of whom consider her to be primarily a consummate writer of love stories.

Certainly a love story is an important facet of almost every du Maurier novel; moreover, there are several other recurring devices—the settings often celebrate her chosen home county, Cornwall, and frequently she depicts some exciting historical period. Furthermore, du Maurier's most successful, most famous novels fall into three general categories: gothics, romances, and family sagas.

Nevertheless, each book is fresh and different from the others because of the ingenuity and variety with which she combines these elements. *The House on the Strand*, for example, is perhaps her most daring blend, a combination of historical novel, science fiction, and crime tale. Here, two very difficult love affairs, one in the 14th century, one in the 20th parallel and complicate each other through the time travels of the protagonist, Richard Young. In *The Scapegoat*, featuring one of du Maurier's most improbable but remarkably persuasive plots (one man's forced impersonation of another), a courtship long since destroyed by ambition and greed remains the source of familial hatred and disruption. The introduction of John, the contemporary hero, to sexual fulfillment parallels and illuminates the older story.

The family sagas *The Loving Spirit* and *Hungry Hill* focus upon history, locale, and personality. The novels depict several members of their central families—the Cornish, seafaring Coombes (*Spirit*) and the Irish, copper-mining Brodricks (*Hill*)—comparing and contrasting the dominant personality in various generations. In these novels the love stories serve primarily to reveal character or to motivate subplot. In *The Flight of the Falcon* and *Rule Britannia*, also family histories though much less panoramic, the love interest is again subordinated, employed as but one of several traditional devices which stimulate the maturations of the protagonists who must confront political oppression, the novels' themes. All four books concern themselves with heritage, with relatives' use of similar and contrasting abilities and traits.

In her gothic novels, however, du Maurier moves the maturation story to center stage, and the love motif becomes the major motivating force. *Jamaica Inn* recounts the adventures of orphaned Mary Yellan who comes to live with her aunt and her uncle, a criminal. Smuggler Joss Merlyn; his outlaw brother, Jem; and Francis Davey, a local vicar, are all attracted to and attract Mary, and she struggles with head, heart, and honor to balance passion, family loyalty, and regard for human life, ultimately opting to follow her heart despite the high cost. Dona St. Columb, the protagonist of *Frenchman's Creek*, a bored, beautiful noblewoman, plays at crime and flirts with infidelity until she takes a daring French pirate as her lover. From him she learns the meaning of responsibility, maturing at last into the woman she was meant to be. Ironically, his lessons in love and duty force her back into the roles of wife and mother, largely in order to free her lover to meet his own destiny. Prisoners of their sex, Mary Yellan accepts and Dona St.

Columb renounces a lover because passion leaves them no choice; maturation means surrender.

For Philip Ashley, protagonist of *My Cousin Rachel*, maturity means torment, for he falls in love with the widow of Ambrose, his cousin and foster father, only to come to suspect Rachel of having poisoned Ambrose. An indecisive youth, Philip finally takes independent, irreversible action (symbol of his delayed maturation), resigning himself to constant future doubt over Rachel's true guilt. In a clever twist, the gothic protagonist here is a young man rather than a girl, and ultimately, Philip opts for kin and heritage rather than for passionate love.

Rebecca, du Maurier's finest and best-known novel, is considered a prototype for the modern gothic. It is the story of a penniless, unnamed girl, a Cinderella figure, who makes an apparently ideal marriage to wealthy Maxim de Winter, a widower. But the heroine's dream of marital happiness and of self-confidence, identity, and maturity as mistress of Manderley, one of Britain's great houses, is quickly banished by the haunting memory of the seemingly perfect, glamorous, beautiful Rebecca, Maxim's first wife. Not until grim secrets about Rebecca are revealed and Maxim's life is consequently threatened can the protagonist take her place as his genuine helpmeet, as a grown woman. Her delayed maturation and happiness are dimmed, however, yielding only subdued, if steadfast, love. This "fairy tale" has a realistic, ironic ending.

Du Maurier's romances are also well laced with irony, a quality which combines with deft characterization to set them above many similar novels. *The King's General* is the story of crippled Honor Harris's lifelong love for Sir Richard Grenvile, the title character. Their fortunes are linked to the history of Menabilly (also partial inspiration for the Manderley of *Rebecca*), and the house stands for the endurance of the leading families amid the conflict between the Royalists and the Parliamentary Armies.

Also bittersweet is the love affair central to *Castle Dor* (begun by Arthur Quiller-Couch and completed by du Maurier), a treatment of the Tristan and Iseult legend set in the 19th century. The doomed romance between Richard, a *Bildungsroman* hero, and Hesta, his first love, is the most memorable section of *I'll Never Be Young Again*, and it is this relationship more than any other which forms Richard's character.

Readers' praise of Daphne du Maurier's ability as a teller of love tales is clearly an appropriate response to her fiction; it should not, however, overshadow appreciation of her equally great skill as an innovator with plot, character, and setting.

—Jane S. Bakerman

DUNNETT, Dorothy (née Halliday). Also writes as Dorothy Halliday. British. Born in Dunfermline, Fife, 25 August 1923. Educated at James Gillespie's High School, Edinburgh; Edinburgh College of Art; Glasgow School of Art. Married Alastair M. Dunnett in 1946; two sons. Worked in the Public Relations Department of the Secretary of State for Scotland, Edinburgh, 1940-46, and the Research Department, Board of Trade, Glasgow, 1946-55. Professional Portrait Painter: has exhibited at the Royal Scottish Academy, Edinburgh, since 1950. Director, Scottish Television Ltd. Recipient: Scottish Arts Council award, 1976. Agent: Curtis Brown Ltd., 1 Craven Hill, London W2 3EP, England. Address: 87 Colinton Road, Edinburgh EH10 5DF, Scotland.

ROMANCE AND GOTHIC PUBLICATIONS

Novels (series: Francis Crawford of Lymond; Johnson Johnson in all Dolly books; Dolly
    books published as Dorothy Halliday in UK)

The Game of Kings (Lymond).   New York, Putnam, 1961; London, Cassell, 1962.
Queens' Play (Lymond).   London, Cassell, and New York, Putnam, 1964.
The Disorderly Knights (Lymond).   London, Cassell, and New York, Putnam, 1966.
Dolly and the Singing Bird.   London, Cassell, 1968; as *The Photogenic Soprano*, Bos-
    ton, Houghton Mifflin, 1968.
Pawn in Frankincense (Lymond).   London, Cassell, and New York, Putnam, 1969.
Dolly and the Cookie Bird.   London, Cassell, 1970; as *Murder in the Round*, Boston,
    Houghton Mifflin, 1970.
The Ringed Castle (Lymond).   London, Cassell, 1971; New York, Putnam, 1972.
Dolly and the Doctor Bird.   London, Cassell, 1971; as *Match for a Murderer*, Boston,
    Houghton Mifflin, 1973.
Dolly and the Starry Bird.   London, Cassell, 1973; as *Murder in Focus*, Boston,
    Houghton Mifflin, 1973.
Checkmate (Lymond).   London, Cassell, and New York, Putnam, 1975.
Dolly and the Nanny Bird.   London, Joseph, 1976.
King Hereafter.   London, Joseph, 1982.

                              *   *   *

Dorothy Dunnett has written six historical romances set in the 16th century which together
cover ten years in the life of her hero, the younger son of an aristocratic Scottish family, Francis
Crawford of Lymond. He has a talent for getting into scrapes and out again, for commanding
men and for charming women. His adventures range across the then known world—the
treacherous Scottish border country during the "Rough Wooing" in *The Game of Kings*;
France and the dissolute court of Henri II in *Queen's Play*; Malta, Tripoli, and Scotland in *The
Disorderly Knights*; the coast and the waters of the Mediterranean with the climax at the
Stamboul court of Suleiman the Magnificent in *Pawn in Frankincense*; Russia and the court of
Ivan the Terrible and the English court of Mary Tudor in *The Ringed Castle*; and finally France
and Scotland again in *Checkmate*. Besides the fascinating Lymond ("a man of wit and crooked
felicities, bred to luxury and heir to a fortune"), we get to know his family, his henchmen, his
enemies, and his friends—especially the Somervilles of Northumberland. It takes young
Phillipa Somerville (an intelligent but stolidly matter-of-fact girl who is ten years old and hates
him in the first book, who is married to him for appearances sake in the fourth book, and who
uncovers all his family secrets against his will in the last two) to redeem him from his arrogant
selfishness, his "detachment dark and icy," and to show him what love is.
    The intricacies of the involved, ingenious, baroque plots are tortuous but fascinating, the
action is violent and exciting, and the mysteries are unravelled satisfyingly. The pace is
spanking and never flags. Dorothy Dunnett writes extremely well, often using words from the
painter's vocabulary to describe scenery; the conversation is witty and urbane, sprinkled with
quotations in several languages. The author relishes unusual words and her use of profuse
detail creates a rich, Brueghel-like effect. Her research is obviously exhaustive, and her period
sense is exact.
    Her modern thrillers written as Dorothy Halliday have the same glitter of sophistication and
inventive unravelling of mysteries as her historical novels. In each of her books of both kinds
there is, over and above the regular spills and thrills, a marvellous, breathtaking set piece or a
wonderful chase. In *Queen's Play*, for instance, it is a reckless, moonlit treasure hunt across the
roofs of Blois undertaken by the young bloods of the court. In *Dolly and the Starry Bird* there is
a nightmare chase in a little van filled with loose balloons any one of which may be the one that
will blow the driver and his companions to bits if it is allowed to burst; in *Dolly and the Nanny
Bird* the heroine has to sail a small boat through unfamiliar waters during a storm at night
surrounded by crooks; in *The Ringed Castle* there is a race on skis and in troikas to beat a

deadly archer. Death is never far away and death when it is met in a Dunnett or a Halliday book is as hideous and messy as it is in reality.

The thrillers all feature Johnson Johnson, a rich painter who wears bifocals and sails his yacht *Dolly* to wonderfully interesting places—the Western Isles in *Dolly and the Singing Bird*, Majorca in *Dolly and the Cookie Bird*, the Caribbean in *Dolly and the Doctor Bird* and the Med. in *Dolly and the Starry Bird* and *Dolly and the Nanny Bird*. Johnson is not nearly such an engaging hero as Lymond, but he is only the common denominator: the emphasis is on the heroines, the birds with unusual jobs who tell the tales in the first person in styles suited to the professions and the lives they lead, all of which are, of course, glamorous. There have been so far an opera singer, a nanny to the rich, a *cordon bleu* cook, a doctor, and an astronomer, all of whom get mixed up in spying and get rescued by Johnson whose playboy-painter life is but a cover of for his real job—master counter-spy. *Dolly and the Singing Bird* is a bit of a cheat in the same way as Agatha Christie's *The Murder of Roger Ackroyd* is; *Dolly and the Doctor Bird* is less fun than usual to read because the Doctor bird is stingy, has no sense of humour, and writes accordingly. But all Dunnett's books, because they are so complex and richly detailed, can be read and read over and over again with undiminished pleasure.

—Pamela Cleaver

DUVAL, Jeanne. *See* **COFFMAN, Virginia**.

DWYER-JOYCE, Alice (Louise, née Myles). British. Born in Birr, Offaly, Ireland, 7 September 1913. Educated at Birr Model School; Alexandra College, Dublin; Royal College of Surgeons, Dublin, medical degree 1936; Richmond Hospital, Dublin. Married Robert Dwyer-Joyce in 1936; one son. In general medical practice with her husband, 1936-78, Histon, Cambridgeshire; Medical Officer, Midfield Children's Home, Oakington, Cambridgeshire, for 20 years. Address: Greystones, Histon, Cambridgeshire CB4 4JE, England.

ROMANCE AND GOTHIC PUBLICATIONS

Novels (series: Dr. Esmond Ross)

> *Price of Inheritance.* London, Hale, 1963.
> *The Silent Lady.* London, Hale, 1964.
> *Dr. Ross of Harton.* London, Hale, 1966.
> *The Story of Doctor Esmond Ross.* London, Hale, 1967.
> *Verdict on Doctor Esmond Ross.* London, Hale, 1968.
> *Dial Emergency for Dr. Ross.* London, Hale, 1969.

Don't Cage Me Wild. London, Hale, 1970.
For I Have Lived Today. London, Hale, 1971.
Message for Doctor Ross. London, Hale, 1971.
Cry the Soft Rain. London, Hale, 1972; New York, St. Martin's Press, 1974.
Reach for the Shadows. London, Hale, 1972; New York, St. Martin's Press, 1973.
The Rainbow Glass. London, Hale, and New York, St. Martin's Press, 1973.
The Brass Islands. London, Hale, 1974.
Prescription for Melissa. London, Hale, 1974.
The Moonlit Way. London, Hale, and New York, St. Martin's Press, 1974.
The Strolling Players. London, Hale, and New York, St. Martin's Press, 1975.
The Diamond Cage. London, Hale, and New York, St. Martin's Press, 1976.
The Master of Jethart. London, Hale, and New York, St. Martin's Press, 1976.
The Gingerbread House. London, Hale, and New York, St. Martin's Press, 1977.
The Banshee Tide. London, Hale, 1977.
The Storm of Wrath. London, Hale, 1977; New York, St. Martin's Press, 1978.
The Glitter-Dust. London, Hale, and New York, St. Martin's Press, 1978.
Lachlan's Woman. London, Hale, and New York, St. Martin's Press, 1979.
Danny Boy. London, Hale, 1979.
The Swiftest Eagle. London, Hale, and New York, St. Martin's Press, 1979.
The House of Jackdaws. London, Hale, and New York, St. Martin's Press, 1980.
The Chieftain. London, Hale, 1980.
The Penny Box. London, Hale, and New York, St. Martin's Press, 1980.
The Glass Heiress. London, Hale, 1981; New York, St. Martin's Press, 1982.
The Cornelian Strand. London, Hale, 1982.

Alice Dwyer-Joyce comments:

I started to write in about 1960, in the midst of a life full of activity, and was glad of it in 1978 when I got increasingly severe arthritis. The authorship has been my escape from the ferocity of disablement.

*   *   *

Alice Dwyer-Joyce brings the stuff of dreams to an everyday world. A touch of magic gilds the remote island communities of her novels, with their ruined castles and half-remembered ancestral ghosts. Elements of folklore and fairytale seem always present—whether the wicked stepmother of *The Gingerbread House*, or the hero of princely lineage who appears in so many of her works. The line between good and evil is sharply drawn—heroes are perfect and unflawed, villains irredeemably wicked. The morality, as in most fairy tales, is Old Testament, with such crimes as adultery and deception punished by death and the wrongdoers irrevocably damned. The shadow of old wrongs remains to haunt later generations, and her books abound with talismans to ward off the unappeased spirits—"The Penny Box," the waterfall in *The Rainbow Glass*, the woolly monkey in *The Master of Jethart*.

A natural prose poet, Dwyer-Joyce is also a qualified doctor, and in many of her works the roles of artist and healer are given an equal emphasis. The early "Dr. Ross" novels which helped to establish her popularity made effective use of her medical knowledge, and the hospital environment serves as background for the novels featuring Dr. Catriona Chisholm—*For I Have Lived Today* and *Prescription for Melissa*. The missionary figure of the doctor martyred in Third World revolution is also a recurrent theme, notably in *Lachlan's Woman*, whose story includes a princely hero betrayed by a faithless wife. There are other works with exotic locations, for example *The Swiftest Eagle*, where action moves from Malaya to Cambodia and its exodus of refugees. Always, though, the author returns to those bleak coastal settings—Ireland or the West Isles—where her atmosphere is strongest, and her Celtic gifts as a storyteller are allowed their fullest expression. Such works as *The Banshee Tide*, with its picture of rural Ireland, or *The Brass Islands* are typical, the highly poeticised speech of the characters in keeping with the landscape they inhabit. More recently *The Chieftain* follows an Irish-American tycoon in search of his roots, evoked by the diary of an ancestor in the 1850's, and

The Glass Heiress explores the theme of a ghostly past. Essentially her message remains the same: the determined heroine struggling against evil or circumstance, fulfilled at last by the love of the noble prince-hero come out of the West, who will help her rebuild the fallen castle and bring back the greatness to their house.

—Geoffrey Sadler

DYMOKE, Juliet. Pseudonym for Juliet Dymoke de Schanschieff. British. Born in Enfield, Middlesex, 28 June 1919. Educated at Chantry Mount School. Married Hugo de Schanschieff in 1942; one daughter. Worked for the Bank of England, London, 1937-42, and for the Canadian Army Medical Records department, London, 1942-44; script reader, Ealing Film Studios, Paramount Films, and Samuel Bronston Productions, 1950-63. Address: Heronswood, Chapel Lane, Forest Row, East Sussex RH18 5BS, England.

ROMANCE AND GOTHIC PUBLICATIONS

Novels (series: Plantagenets)

> *The Orange Sash.* London, Jarrolds, 1958.
> *Born for Victory.* London, Jarrolds, 1960.
> *Treason in November.* London, Jarrolds, 1961.
> *Bend Sinister.* London, Jarrolds, 1962.
> *The Cloisterman.* London, Dobson, 1969.
> *Of the Ring of Earls.* London, Dobson, 1970.
> *Henry of the High Rock.* London, Dobson, 1971.
> *Serpent in Eden.* London, Wingate, 1973.
> *The Lion's Legacy.* London, Dobson, 1974.
> *Shadows on a Throne.* London, Wingate, 1976.
> *A Pride of Kings* (Plantagenets). London, Dobson, 1978.
> *The Royal Griffin* (Plantagenets). London, Dobson, 1978; New York, Ace, 1980.
> *The White Cockade.* London, Dobson, 1979.
> *Lady of the Garter* (Plantagenets). London, Dobson, 1979; New York, Ace, 1980.
> *The Lion of Mortimer* (Plantagenets). London, Dobson, 1979; New York, Ace, 1980.
> *The Lord of Greenwich* (Plantagenets). London, Dobson, 1980.
> *The Sun in Splendour* (Plantagenets). London, Dobson, 1980.
> *A Kind of Warfare.* London, Dobson, 1981.

OTHER PUBLICATIONS

Other (juvenile)

> *The Sons of the Tribune: An Adventure on the Roman Wall.* London, Edward Arnold, 1956.
> *London in the 18th Century.* London, Longman, 1958.
> *Prisoner of Rome.* London, Dobson, 1975.

Juliet Dymoke comments:

My work as an historical novelist naturally includes a great deal of research, and this perhaps is the most exacting as well as a very pleasurable part of my work. I write mainly about England as I know and love England, and I try not to start on a description of a place I do not know without making every effort to see it—it is so easy to be caught out! I am passionately interested in history, European as well as English, but it is the past of these islands that interests me most, and I am fascinated by the lives of our forebears, and how they are similar to and dissimilar from our own. I can trace my own ancestry back to the Norman Conquest and perhaps this was the spur, or the inheritance, that set me on my career. I hope through my work to reach a large number of people, to interest them in the history that has made this country, perhaps in some way to influence them for good—as I myself was influenced by the historical writers I once read.

                              *   *   *

Juliet Dymoke restricts herself neither to a particular historical era nor to a set mode of novel construction: these facts give some idea of her ambitiousness. Realism and authenticity rather than gothic sensationalism or contrived romance are the hallmarks of her style, yet they do not rob her works of excitement.

Dymoke mingles fact and fiction with a satisfying result in her early novel *Treason in November*. She recounts real events with the focus on a central, fictitious, character. Piers Mallory becomes implicated in the Gunpowder Plot of 1605 through a chance acquaintance with one of its instigators, Robert Catesby. There is romance in the novel, but Piers's estrangement from and reunion with his betrothed plays a lesser role than his journey to self-knowledge and the restoring of his good name. In a similar manner, *The Cloisterman* shows Dymoke's own creations existing comfortably alongside historical realities, providing the reader with an insight into the motives of past kings and politicians. *The Cloisterman*, however, relies little on historical facts, as it is the tale of an individual set in a historical milieu, the early reign of Henry VIII, depending for its development on the impulses of its characters. After a clever opening, presenting Sir Thomas More awaiting execution and writing a note of farewell to Julian, the central character, the novel moves in flashback to recount the origin of their acquaintance, exemplifying the author's ingenuity.

For one who has enjoyed Shakespeare's tragedy *Macbeth*, it must be admitted that *Shadows on a Throne* cannot, and does not, inspire an equal feeling of wonder and horror: Dymoke's ability is more successfully employed in her brand of historical fact than in historical legend with all its irrationality, as her series on the Plantagenet dynasty illustrates. Her medieval trilogy gave earlier proof that Dymoke's interest and imagination, once caught, could rise to the most daunting enterprises.

In the Plantagenet series there is further evidence of this author's consistency in attention to detail, character presentation, and narrative style. *A Pride of Kings* covers much ground, both in terms of time and in the number of characters—through a careful linking of chapters the action moves swiftly, even from country to country, without loss of continuity (this can be said of all Dymoke's novels). William Marshall is seen to serve the successive monarchs Henry III, Richard the Lionheart, and John, and meanwhile there is a warm and perceptive portrayal of his marriage, at middle-age, to a 16-year-old girl, which matures into satisfying companionship. In *The Royal Griffin* Eleanor, daughter of King John, marries her first husband for security and her second, Simon de Montfort, on the basis of physical attraction: alongside the subtle comparisons between the two marriages, Simon de Montfort's career from commoner to duke is traced, and it is traced with such skill that his eventual death is truly tragic. Tact and feeling are also employed in the exploration of the relationship between Edward II and Piers Gaveston in *The Lion of Mortimer*, and in this instance Dymoke's achievement stands comparison with Shakespeare's drama. *The Lord of Greenwich* shows the extremes of sensuousness and scholasticism in the personality of Humfrey of Gloucester, the central character, and the reader is taken through the campaigns against France and treated to an accurate account of the Battle of Agincourt.

The enthusiasm which led Juliet Dymoke to write the Plantagenet series has now given rise to a new series, telling of the descendants of the characters in her Scottish novel of the 18th century, *The White Cockade*. Dymoke's energy is unstinting.

—Anne M. Shields

EBEL, Suzanne. Also writes as Suzanne Goodwin; Cecily Shelbourne. British. Born in London. Educated at Roman Catholic schools in England and Belgium. Married John Goodwin in 1948; one daughter and two sons. Recipient: Romantic Novelists Association Major Award, 1964. Agent: Curtis Brown Ltd., 1 Craven Hill, London W2 3EP. Address: 52A Digby Mansions, Hammersmith Bridge Road, London W6 9DF, England.

ROMANCE AND GOTHIC PUBLICATIONS

Novels

> *Love, The Magician.* London, Muller, 1956.
> *Journey from Yesterday.* London, Collins, 1963.
> *The Half-Enchanted.* London, Collins, 1964.
> *The Love Campaign.* London, Collins, 1965
> *The Dangerous Winter.* London, Collins, 1965.
> *A Perfect Stranger.* London, Collins, 1966.
> *A Name in Lights.* London, Collins, 1968; New York, Fawcett, 1975.
> *A Most Auspicious Star.* London, Collins, 1968.
> *Somersault.* London, Collins, 1971.
> *Portrait of Jill.* London, Collins, 1972.
> *Dear Kate.* London, Collins, 1972; New York, Fawcett, 1974.
> *To Seek a Star.* London, Collins, 1973; New York, Fawcett, 1975.
> *The Family Feeling.* London, Collins, 1973; New York, Fawcett, 1975.
> *Girl by the Sea.* London, Collins, 1974; New York, Fawcett, 1976.
> *Music in Winter.* London, Collins, 1975.
> *A Grove of Olives.* London, Collins, 1976.
> *River Voices.* London, Collins, 1976.
> *The Double Rainbow.* London, Collins, 1977.
> *A Rose in Heather.* London, Collins, 1978.
> *Julia's Sister.* London, Severn House, 1982.

Novels as Suzanne Goodwin

> *The Winter Spring.* London, Bodley Head, 1978; as *Stage of Love* (as Cecily Shelbourne), New York, Putnam, 1978.
> *The Winter Sisters.* London, Bodley Head, 1980.
> *Emerald.* London, Magnum, 1980.
> *Love Is My Reason.* London, Hale, 1982.

OTHER PUBLICATIONS

Play

> Radio Play: *Chords and Dischords*, 1975.

Other

> *Explore the Cotswolds by Bicycle*, with Doreen Impey. London, Ward Lock, 1973.
> *London's Riverside, From Hampton Court in the West to Greenwich Palace in the East*, with Doreen Impey. London, Luscombe, 1975; New York, Ballantine, 1976.

*   *   *

Although the backgrounds to Suzanne Ebel's novels, and many of her characters, have for most of us an aura of glamour, she imbues them with an authenticity which springs partly from personal experience, partly from verbal dexterity: from time to time she produces flashing phrases which throw a shaft of dazzling light on to a character or setting which makes the reader see it anew, with startling clarity.

Many of the "glamorous" backgrounds are her own everyday ones. At one time she had three homes: a flat in Hammersmith close to the Thames where she still does her writing; a second, now abandoned, in Stratford-on-Avon (until he moved to the National Theatre, her husband, John Goodwin, was Publicity Director to the Royal Shakespeare Company); and another flat, converted from a granary at the top of an 18th-century house, in the hills above Cannes. She makes good, observant, use of all these settings, and the ambience of the theatre in which her husband moves. For example, *River Voices* is set on a houseboat on the Thames; *A Grove of Olives* has a Provençal background; and *The Double Rainbow* obviously evolved out of her contacts with the theatre world.

The heroine of *The Double Rainbow* is one of her most fully realised heroines, a girl who "grows" convincingly throughout the story from a shy, diffident Oxford undergraduate playing Perdita in *The Tempest* in a scruffy church hall, to an actress of some stature, able to take her place in a company of distinguished players. She is not the only fully realised character. Each member of the Two Rivers Company has been completely conceived. Even the minor ones are real people. Faith's Oxford tutor, Dr. Barrington, is no cut-out-and-stuck-on don: he has his individual quirks which bring him sharply into focus. Mrs. Gratowski, her Polish landlady, could easily have been just a "comic character" but instead she, too, is real person—funny, but with dignity, warmth, and pathos. Even the Director's housekeeper, though only lightly etched in, has mysterious depths. The reader senses much in her that the author does not specifically state. Good character-drawing, again, is at the heart of *A Grove of Olives*, which hinges on the relationship betwen a mother and daughter. Elizabeth, the mother (a sculptor), is especially alive and enchanting. But the setting—a comfortable, rather ramshackle farmhouse in southern France, used by Elizabeth as her studio—is also memorably evoked.

The longer novels, as Suzanne Goodwin, *The Winter Spring* and *The Winter Sisters*, break new ground. While retaining the theatrical theme they are set in the early 19th century, and give an interesting insight into what it was like to act in the wake of Kean and the shadow of Kemble. The Winters are a theatrical family, father Thomas an actor-manager, his wife Ellen the company's costume designer and general dogsbody, daughters Isabella and Lettice actresses. Of the two only Lettice is dedicated to her career. Isabella, a social climber, soon escapes from theatrical "drudgery" into a desirable marriage. There is a slightly deeper and more serious note to these novels than to the average Regency romp. The girls make mistakes, and learn from them painfully. These first (for Suzanne Goodwin) "period" stories catch the atmosphere of the time with precision, without being archly or aggressively "period" in tone. And, as always, the characters are well-rounded people with whom the reader can relate.

—Elizabeth Grey

EBERHART, Mignon G(ood). American. Born in University Place, Nebraska, 6 July 1899. Educated in local schools; Nebraska Wesleyan University, Lincoln, 1917-20. Married 1) John P. Hazen Perry (divorced); 2) Alanson C. Eberhart in 1923. Self-employed writer since 1930. Past President, Mystery Writers of America. Recipient: Scotland Yard Prize, 1931; Mystery Writers of America Grand Master Award, 1970. D.Litt.: Nebraska Wesleyan University, 1935. Agent: Brandt and Brandt, 1501 Broadway, New York, New York 10036. Address: c/o Popular Library, 355 Lexington Avenue, New York, New York 10017, U.S.A.

Novels (series: Sarah Keate and Lance O'Leary)

The Patient in Room 18 (Keate and O'Leary). New York, Doubleday, and London, Heinemann, 1929.

The Mystery of Hunting's End (Keate and O'Leary). New York, Doubleday, 1930; London, Heinemann, 1931.

While the Patient Slept (Keate and O'Leary). New York, Doubleday, and London, Heinemann, 1930.

From This Dark Stairway (Keate and O'Leary). New York, Doubleday, 1931; London, Heinemann, 1932.

Murder by an Aristocrat (Keate and O'Leary). New York, Doubleday, 1932; as *Murder of My Patient*, London, Lane, 1934.

The Dark Garden. New York, Doubleday, 1933; as *Death in the Fog*, London, Lane, 1934.

The White Cockatoo. New York, Doubleday, and London, Falcon Books, 1933.

The House on the Roof. New York, Doubleday, and London, Collins, 1935.

Fair Warning. New York, Doubleday, and London, Collins, 1936.

Danger in the Dark. New York, Doubleday, 1937; as *Hand in Glove*, London, Collins, 1937.

The Pattern. New York, Doubleday, and London, Collins, 1937; as *Pattern of Murder*, New York, Popular Library, 1948.

The Glass Slipper. New York, Doubleday, and London, Collins, 1938.

Hasty Wedding. New York, Doubleday, 1938; London, Collins, 1939.

Brief Return. London, Collins, 1939.

The Chiffon Scarf. New York, Doubleday, 1939; London, Collins, 1940.

The Hangman's Whip. New York, Doubleday, 1940; London, Collins, 1941.

Strangers in Flight. Los Angeles, Bantam, 1941.

Speak No Evil. New York, Random House, and London, Collins, 1941.

With This Ring. New York, Random House, 1941; London, Collins, 1942.

Wolf in Man's Clothing (Keate). New York, Random House, 1942; London, Collins, 1943.

The Man Next Door. New York, Random House, 1943; London, Collins, 1944.

Unidentified Woman. New York, Random House, 1943; London, Collins, 1944.

Escape the Night. New York, Random House, 1944; London, Collins, 1945.

Wings of Fear. New York, Random House, 1945; London, Collins, 1946.

Five Passengers from Lisbon. New York, Random House, and London, Collins, 1946.

The White Dress. New York, Random House, 1946; London, Collins, 1947.

Another Woman's House. New York, Random House, 1947; London, Collins, 1948.

House of Storm. New York, Random House, and London, Collins, 1949.

Hunt with the Hounds. New York, Random House, 1950; London, Collins, 1951.

Never Look Back. New York, Random House, and London, Collins, 1951.

Dead Men's Plans. New York, Random House, 1952; London, Collins, 1953.

The Unknown Quantity. New York, Random House, and London, Collins, 1953.

Man Missing (Keate). New York, Random House, and London, Collins, 1954.

Postmark Murder. New York, Random House, and London, Collins, 1956.

Another Man's Murder. New York, Random House, 1957; London, Collins, 1958.

Melora. New York, Random House, 1959; London, Collins, 1960; as *The Promise of Murder*, New York, Dell, 1961.

Jury of One. New York, Random House, 1960; London, Collins, 1961.

The Cup, The Blade, or the Gun. New York, Random House, 1961; as *The Crime at Honotassa*, London, Collins, 1962.

Enemy in the House. New York, Random House, 1962; London, Collins, 1963.

Run Scared. New York, Random House, 1963; London, Collins, 1964.

Call after Midnight. New York, Random House, 1964; London, Collins, 1965.

R.S.V.P. Murder. New York, Random House, 1965; London, Collins, 1966.

Witness at Large. New York, Random House, 1966; London, Collins, 1967.
Woman on the Roof. New York, Random House, and London, Collins, 1968.
Message from Hong Kong. New York, Random House, and London, Collins, 1969.
El Rancho Rio. New York, Random House, 1970; London, Collins, 1971.
Two Little Rich Girls. New York, Random House, 1972.
The House by the Sea. New York, Pocket Books, 1972.
Murder in Waiting. New York, Random House, 1973; London, Collins, 1974.
Danger Money. New York, Random House, and London, Collins, 1975.
Family Fortune. New York, Random House, 1976; London, Collins, 1977.
Nine O'Clock Tide. New York, Random House, and London, Collins, 1978.
The Bayou Road. New York, Random House, and London, Collins, 1979.
Casa Madrone. New York, Random House, and London, Collins, 1980.
Family Affair. New York, Random House, and London, Collins, 1981.
Next of Kin. New York, Random House, 1982.

Short Stories

The Cases of Susan Dare. New York, Doubleday, 1934; London, Lane, 1935.
Deadly Is the Diamond. New York, Dell, 1942.
*Five of My Best: Deadly Is the Diamond, Bermuda Grapevine, Murder Goes to Market,
Strangers in Flight, Express to Danger*. London, Hammond, 1949.
*Deadly Is the Diamond and Three Other Novelettes of Murder: Bermuda Grapevine, The
Crimson Paw, Murder in Waltz Time*. New York, Random House, 1958; Horn-
church, Essex, Henry, 1981.
The Crimson Paw. London, Hammond, 1959.

OTHER PUBLICATIONS

Plays

320 College Avenue, with Fred Ballard. New York, French, 1938.
Eight O'Clock Tuesday, with Robert Wallsten, adaptation of a novel by Eberhart (produced New York, 1941). New York, French, 1941.

Manuscript Collection: Mugar Memorial Library, Boston University.

*   *   *

Mignon Eberhart is the pre-eminent American woman in the mystery field, but her claim is
even wider. In short, she has consistently produced the hybrid mystery-romance-gothic novel
with a skill very few writers have been able to emulate successfully. With Mignon Eberhart, said
the *New Yorker*, "the ingredients are tested and the cook's hand is remarkably sure."

Her early books gave little indication of the heights she was to reach. In the tradition of Mary
Roberts Rinehart, they featured the middle-aged Nurse Sarah Keate in a succession of
melodramatic situations; the menacing atmosphere of darkened hospital wards or old mansions was there in plenty, with Nurse Keate threatened by shadowy villains and rescued from
mortal danger at the last minute by the masterful male. There were gothic and romantic
touches, the air was suitably eerie, and impending perils were well conveyed, but the heroine left
much to be desired. Later Keate novels, *Wolf in Man's Clothing* and *Man Missing*, deserve
honourable mention nonetheless. Her other series detective, attractive Susan Dare, appeared in
a collection of short stories which are good examples of neat puzzles spiced with romance.

As her career developed, the mystery-romance-gothic combination became more evenly
balanced. Her heroines are not only involved in perilous situations, like the young secretary's
flirtation with espionage in *The Man Next Door*, but are frequently the principal suspects with

the web of circumstances enmeshing them more securely as they struggle. An air of helplessness prevails, sometimes engendered by inability to distinguish between the upright males and the villain who would do her ill. Good examples are *The White Cockatoo, Speak No Evil*, and *With This Ring*; while for sheer psychological suspense, competently blending mystery with terror, among her best are *Fair Warning, Another Man's Murder*, and *Run Scared*.

She is a master of locale. Much travelled herself, she manages invariably to convey the feel and colour of her settings. Sometimes, but not always, these are exotic; she has the perfect gift for putting a plot against just the right background, then skilfully exploiting that background to project mystery and deception and menace. The best gothic romances can extract as much tension and atmosphere from a rambling house or lonely island or street festival, for example, as from a darkly mysterious stranger, and Mignon Eberhart is a superb exponent.

A critic once stated that an Eberhart novel, without need of a mystery plot, would stand on its own as a mirror of the modes and manners of the 20th century. That may well be so, but is perhaps a trifle clinical. The fact that she is literate, plausible, entertaining, and intelligent, and devises stories of compelling readability, is the more likely basis of her considerable popularity with countless readers throughout the world.

—Melvyn Barnes

EDEN, Dorothy.   Also wrote as Mary Paradise.   British.   Born near Christchurch, New Zealand, 3 April 1912. Educated at a village school and a secretarial college. Secretary, 1929-39; lived in London from the 1950's. *Died 4 March 1982*.

Romance and Gothic Publications

Novels

Singing Shadows.   London, Stanley Paul, 1940.
The Laughing Ghost.   London, Macdonald, 1943; New York, Ace, 1968.
We Are for the Dark.   London, Macdonald, 1944.
Summer Sunday.   London, Macdonald, 1946.
Walk into My Parlour.   London, Macdonald, 1947.
The Schoolmaster's Daughters.   London, Macdonald, 1948; as *The Daughters of Ardmore Hall*, New York, Ace, 1968.
Crow Hollow.   London, Macdonald, 1950; New York, Ace, 1967.
The Voice of the Dolls.   London, Macdonald, 1950; New York, Ace, 1971.
Cat's Prey.   London, Macdonald, 1952; New York, Ace, 1967.
Lamb to the Slaughter.   London, Macdonald, 1953; as *The Brooding Lake*, New York, Ace, 1966.
Bride by Candlelight.   London, Macdonald, 1954; New York, Ace, 1972.
Darling Clementine.   London, Macdonald, 1955; as *The Night of the Letter*, New York, Ace, 1967.
Death Is a Red Rose.   London, Macdonald, 1956; New York, Ace, 1970.
The Pretty Ones.   London, Macdonald, 1957; New York, Ace, 1966.
Listen To Danger.   London, Macdonald, 1958; New York, Ace, 1967.
The Deadly Travellers.   London, Macdonald, 1959; New York, Ace, 1966.
The Sleeping Bride.   London, Macdonald, 1959; New York, Ace, 1969.

Samantha. London, Hodder and Stoughton, 1960; as *Lady of Mallow*, New York, Coward McCann, 1962.

Sleep in the Woods. London, Hodder and Stoughton, 1960; New York, Coward McCann, 1961.

Face of an Angel (as Mary Paradise). London, Hale, 1961; New York, Ace, 1966.

Shadow of a Witch (as Mary Paradise). London, Hale, 1962; New York, Ace, 1966.

Whistle for the Crows. London, Hodder and Stoughton, 1962; New York, Ace, 1964.

Afternoon for Lizards. London, Hodder and Stoughton, 1962; as *The Bridge of Fear*, New York, Ace, 1966.

The Bird in the Chimney. London, Hodder and Stoughton, 1963; as *Darkwater*, New York, Coward McCann, 1964.

Bella. London, Hodder and Stoughton, 1964; as *Ravenscroft*, New York, Coward McCann, 1965.

The Marriage Chest. London, Hodder and Stoughton, 1965; as Mary Paradise, New York, Coward McCann, 1966.

Never Call it Loving. London, Hodder and Stoughton, and New York, Coward McCann, 1966.

Siege in the Sun. London, Hodder and Stoughton, and New York, Coward McCann, 1967.

Winterwood. London, Hodder and Stoughton, and New York, Coward McCann, 1967.

The Shadow Wife. London, Hodder and Stoughton, and New York, Coward McCann, 1968.

The Vines of Yarrabee. London, Hodder and Stoughton, and New York, Coward McCann, 1969.

Melbury Square. London, Hodder and Stoughton, 1970; New York, Coward McCann, 1971.

Waiting for Willa. London, Hodder and Stoughton, and New York, Coward McCann, 1970.

Afternoon Walk. London, Hodder and Stoughton, and New York, Coward McCann, 1971.

A Linnet Singing. New York, Pocket Books, 1972.

Speak to Me of Love. London, Hodder and Stoughton, and New York, Coward McCann, 1972.

The Millionaire's Daughter. London, Hodder and Stoughton, and New York, Coward McCann, 1974.

The Time of the Dragon. London, Hodder and Stoughton, and New York, Coward McCann, 1975.

The Salamanca Drum. London, Hodder and Stoughton, and New York, Coward McCann, 1977.

The Storrington Papers. New York, Coward McCann, 1978; London, Hodder and Stoughton, 1979.

Depart in Peace. London, Hodder and Stoughton, 1979.

The American Heiress. London, Hodder and Stoughton, and New York, Coward McCann, 1980.

An Important Family. New York, Morrow, 1982.

Short Stories

Yellow Is for Fear and Other Stories. New York, Ace, 1968; London, Coronet, 1976.

The House on Hay Hill and Other Stories. London, Coronet, and New York, Fawcett, 1976.

Manuscript Collection: Mugar Memorial Library, Boston University.

*   *   *

Dorothy Eden has published steadily since the 1940's. Since 1970 more than five million copies of her books have been sold and she now numbers more than 30 books in print. These figures alone place her as one of the *grande dames* of romance/gothic.

Her plots are traditional in that the heroines must meet the challenge of 1) finding the right mate, 2) being poor and becoming rich or the reverse, and 3) coping with a frontier land. Her typical heroine is content to find and secure her true mate and run his house, mansion, or castle correctly and well. She must be prepared to repel or charm the threatening natives, survive disasters, and protect other women, children, and dependents.

Eden's heroines are usually without family and poor, or they have lost the wealth they once had. Briar in *Sleep in the Woods* was found in a ditch as a baby, clasped in her dead presumed mother's arms. Raised and educated beyond her station by a poor schoolmaster, she goes out as a ladies' maid to New Zealand, facing the untamed frontier and capturing the most eligible bachelor in Wellington. After moving to the bush, she must wrestle with a recalcitrant husband, the man-eating Maori, and her own lies about her non-existent family in England. Briar has a sister in Harriet "Hetty" Brown in *The American Heiress*, published twenty years later in 1980.

Also born on the wrong side of the blanket, Hetty is left on her natural father's doorstep by her poor and dying mother. Her father takes her in but then dies; so the wicked step-mother trains Hetty as her daughter's maid. The trick here is that Hetty is a look-alike for Clemency, her half-sister, so much so that she substitutes for Clemency on dates with her more dull suitors. Therein lies the tale. Hetty, Clemency, and mother sail for England and Clemency's elegant marriage on the *Lusitania*. Briar lies about her non-existent family; Hetty, the lone survivor of this trio, takes Clemency's place, marrying the dashing Major Hugo, Lord Hazzard, heir to one of England's most venerable titles. She, like Briar, must continually struggle with her conscience and wonder when and if she will be found out. For both of them the motivation is, at first, possession of a house/castle and social position. They eventually come to love their husbands, however, but only after trials which reveal their mates' worthiness. Both Hetty and Briar suffer for their lies and both are discovered, though in Hetty's case it takes the next generation to reveal her impersonation. Both characters are saved from triviality by their likeableness and independent spirit. Eden handles the Cinderella story with controlled realism in the areas of sexual implication and setting.

The famous *The Vines of Yarrabee*, perhaps Eden's most widely read novel, tells of the Australian outback, convict labor, and violence mixed with the background of grape-growing and wine-making. In this case, a genteel Eugenia marries Gilbert Massingham and goes to Australia, a most ungenteel place. She, unlike Briar and Hetty, is legitimately of fine English breeding and possesses impeccable social sense, for which quality Gilbert has married her. Eugenia's struggles are concerned with finding her true mate and coping with the frontier. She must adjust to the Australian outback without the prior toughening experiences of Briar and Hetty. Rough times develop character whether rich or poor. Shady financial schemes and love triangles complicate Eugenia's search for her happy ending.

In the Eden canon, *Melbury Square* and *Never Call It Loving* should be singled out as exceptional. In the former, a fashionable portrait artist rules his Kensington Square house, crippling the emotional lives of both his wife and daughter. Maud Lucie, the daughter and protagonist, is a beautiful Edwardian debutante afflicted with a father fixation. Maud carelessly drifts through her youth being her father's favorite model and finds any search on her part for love and happiness thwarted by her dominating father. A selfish and obtuse Maud represents a reality not usually found in gothic/romance heroines. Maud's moment of truth comes only in her crotchety old age when, her father dead, herself tricked, swindled, and poor, she finally finds her independence: "The one left might be old and ugly, but at least she was entirely herself."

Never Call It Loving fictionalizes the real love affair between Charles Stewart Parnell and Katherine O'Shea. In reality their affair ruined Parnell's reputation, which indirectly destroyed the chances for Irish Home Rule and ultimately drove Parnell to an early death. A historical novel *par excellence*, this sensitive recounting proves Eden's ability to write successfully outside the romance/gothic formula.

Eden has been universally praised for her well-researched backgrounds—Australia, Peking, Denmark, New Zealand, Ireland. No country or time period is too remote if it interests the author. There has been some faint carping about unoriginal and artificial plots but for a prolific and successful writer such problems are bound to occur. On the whole, an Eden story is a reliable source of entertainment, well-told and well-researched.

—Marilynn Motteler

EDGAR, Josephine.   *See* **HOWARD, Mary**.

EDGINTON, May (Helen Marion Edginton).   British.   Born in 1883. Married Francis E. Bailey in 1912; one son. *Died 17 June 1957.*

ROMANCE AND GOTHIC PUBLICATIONS

Novels

> *The Weight Carriers*.   London, Everett, 1909.
> *Brass*.   London, Everett, 1910.
> *The Adventures of Napoleon Prince*.   London and New York, Cassell, 1912.
> *The Sin of Eve*.   London, Hodder and Stoughton, 1913; as *A Modern Eve*, New York, Stokes, 1913.
> *Oh! James!*   London, Nash, and Boston, Little Brown, 1914.
> *Married Life; or, The True Romance*.   London, Cassell, 1917; Boston, Small Maynard, 1920.
> *The Street of Gold*.   London, Cassell, 1918.
> *The Man Who Broke the Rule*.   London, Cassell, 1919.
> *Ladies Only*.   London, Duckworth, 1922.
> *The Man Who Dared*.   London, Hodder and Stoughton, 1923.
> *Truimph*.   London, Chapman and Dodd, 1923; New York, Holt, 1924.
> *Trust Emily*.   London, Chapman and Dodd, 1923.
> *Carla Light*.   London, Hutchinson, 1925.
> *The Dream That Happened*.   London, Hutchinson, 1926.
> *The Joy Girl*.   London, Cassell, 1927; Philadelphia, Penn, 1928.
> *The Peach's Progress*.   London, Hutchinson, and Philadelphia, Penn, 1927.
> *The Two Desires*.   London, Hutchinson, 1927.
> *The Woman Who Squandered Men*.   London, Readers Library, 1927; as *Fruit of the Tree*, Philadelphia, Macrae Smith, 1947.
> *The Sunlit Way*.   London, Hutchinson, 1928.
> *My Dear*.   Philadelphia, Penn, 1929.

Life Isn't So Bad. London, Collins, 1929; Philadelphia, Penn, 1930.
Fair Lady. London, Collins, 1929; New York, Macaulay, 1932.
Lamplight. London, Collins, 1930.
Call Her Fannie. London, Collins, and Philadelphia, Penn, 1930; as *Fannie's Fortune*, Collins, 1932.
Money! Money! Money! New York, Macaulay, 1931.
Festival. London, Collins, 1931.
Love-Girl. London, Collins, and New York, Macaulay, 1931.
Tropic Flower. London, Collins, 1932; New York, Macaulay, 1933.
Reckless. New York, Macaulay, 1932.
Dance of Youth. London, Collins, and New York, Macaulay, 1932.
I Like You So Much. New York, Macaulay, 1933.
Holiday. London, Collins, 1933.
The Sun Will Shine. London, Odhams Press, 1933; New York, Macaulay, 1934.
Expensive Lady. London, Collins, and New York, Macaulay, 1934.
Summer Morning. London, Collins, and New York, Macaulay, 1934.
Woman of the Family. London, Collins, 1935; New York, Macaulay, 1936.
Return Journey. London, Collins, 1935.
Favourite Wife. London, Collins, and New York, Macaulay, 1936.
The Child in Their Midst. London, Collins, 1937; New York, Macaulay, 1938.
Emergency Wife. New York, Green Circle, 1937.
Experiment in Love. London, Collins, 1938.
Poor Young People! London, Collins, and New York, Macaulay, 1939.
Wedding Day. London, Collins, 1939; Philadelphia, Penn, 1940.
Once He Was Mine. London, Collins, 1940.
Best Wishes. London, Collins, 1942; as *Stolen Honeymoon*, Philadelphia, Macrae Smith, 1942.
I Promised You. London, Macdonald, 1943.
The Harvest Is Mine. London, Macdonald, 1944.
Invitation to Love. London, Collins, 1944.
The Captain's House. London, Macdonald, 1945; as *Winds of Desire*, Philadelphia, Macrae Smith, 1946.
Expensive. Hanley, Staffordshire, Locker, 1947.
The Soldier and the Ladies. London, Macdonald, 1947.
Surprise. Hanley, Staffordshire, Locker, 1948.
Young Barbara. London, Macdonald, 1948.
The Tall Man. London, Macdonald, 1950.
Ladies' Pleasaunce. London, Macdonald, 1951.
The Richest Man. London, Macdonald, 1952.
Technique. London, Macdonald, 1953.
Two Lost Sheep. London, Macdonald, 1955.

Short Stories

They Were All in Love. London, Collins, 1938.

OTHER PUBLICATIONS

Plays

His Lady Friends, with Frank Mandel (produced Edinburgh, 1918).
The Prude's Fall, with Rudolf Besier (produced London, 1920).
The Ninth Earl, with Rudolf Besier (produced London, 1921).
Secrets, with Rudolf Besier (produced London, 1922). London, French, 1929.
Trust Emily (produced Cambridge and London, 1923).

The Fairy Tale (produced London, 1924).
For Better, For Worse (produced London, 1928).
Deadlock (produced Brighton and London, 1928).

Screenplay: *Lying Lips*, with Bradley King, 1921.

*   *   *

A literary agent, George G. Magnus, explained in *How to Write Serial Fiction* in the 1920's that "Comfortable sentiment is absolutely necessary for popular success." The novels of May Edginton may show this comfortable sentiment, but not much else, lacking the curious zeal or dotty idealism of contemporaries such as Marie Corelli or Florence Barclay. However, the run-of-the-mill escapism is of some interest when put to the good use of morale-raising during the second World War. *The Captain's House* reveals a blatant sybaritic quality, written in a time of lack, with its lavish descriptions of times of plenty. Chauffeurs, cooks, and parlour-maids hover in the background, while the heroine is able to sample an abundance of fresh eggs, cream, and strawberries, and can observe the "softness of the bath towels" and "the luxurious fineness of the soap."

Arnold Bennett, however, said, "I particularly like May Edginton, who has individuality and writes with force." He praised her business-like approach to writing, since it was based on the often-underrated concept of a "cast-iron" plot.

—Rachel Anderson

EDWARDS, Anne.   American.   Born in New York City, 20 August 1927. Educated at the University of California, Los Angeles; Southern Methodist University, Dallas. Married Stephen Citron; one son and one daughter. President, Authors Guild. Agent: Mitch Douglas, International Creative Management, 40 West 57th Street, New York, New York 10019. Address: Blandings Way, Long Mountain Road, R.R. 1, New Milford, Connecticut 06776, U.S.A.

ROMANCE AND GOTHIC PUBLICATIONS

Novels

The Survivors.   New York, Holt Rinehart, and London, W.H. Allen, 1968.
Miklos Alexandrovitch Is Missing.   New York, Coward McCann, 1970; as *Alexandrovitch Is Missing!*, London, Hodder and Stoughton, 1970.
Shadow of a Lion.   New York, Coward McCann, and London, Hodder and Stoughton, 1971.
Haunted Summer.   New York, Coward McCann, 1972; London, Hodder and Stoughton, 1973.
The Hesitant Heart.   New York, Random House, and London, Cassell, 1974.
Child of Night.   New York, Random House, 1975.
Raven Wings.   London, Millington, 1977.

Plays

Screenplays: *Quantez*, with Robert Wright Campbell, 1957; *A Question of Adultery*, 1959.

Other

A Child's Bible.   London, Penguin, 1967; New York, Golden Books, 1970.
Judy Garland: A Biography.   New York, Simon and Schuster, and London, Constable, 1975.
The Inn and Us, with Stephen Citron.   New York, Random House, 1976.
Vivien Leigh: A Biography.   New York, Simon and Schuster, and London, W.H. Allen, 1977.
The Great Houdini (juvenile).   New York, Putnam, 1977.
P.T. Barnum (juvenile).   New York, Putnam, 1977.
Sonya: The Life of Countess Tolstoy.   New York, Simon and Schuster, and London, Hodder and Stoughton, 1981.

Manuscript Collection: University of California, Los Angeles.

*   *   *

One rarely finds an author so gifted and so versatile as to be capable of writing all things well. yet Anne Edwards possesses just such a talent. Not only does the subject matter for her novels vary considerably, but her style is so flexible that it is appropriate to the subject matter and character of each novel. In addition, her characters often transcend the cardboard figures of most novels of this genre.

In *The Survivors*, a novel of modern times, the heroine departs slightly from the formula gothic strong-willed beautiful non-traditional female. Luanne's psyche is a fragile thread as she leaves the refuge of Laurel Groves, the rest home where she retreated after the mass murder of her entire family. Yet in true gothic style Luanne has a handsome male protector. Hans not only enables Luanne to dispel the ghosts of her past, but his unwavering love for her transforms the frightened unworldly girl into an assured confident woman able to confront her ghosts and a murderess all in less than a fortnight. However, the suspense builds so rapidly in this novel that the reader accepts the character incongruities.

Emily Dickinson is the unlikely heroine of *The Hesitant Heart*. Edwards's flexibility shows strongly in this romantic work about the enigmatic recluse of Amherst. Sentence patterns and style blend smoothly with excerpts of poetry and letters of the poet. While the true scholar of Emily Dickinson may shudder at the Emily portrayed here, so many myths surround her that it is fun to suspend our disbelief and play "What if" with Edwards.

Again drawing from history for her characters, Edwards uses some of history's greatest romantics for *Haunted Summer*. Who are better suited to haunt the pages of a gothic romance than Shelley, Lord Byron, and Mary Shelley? Here Edwards creates an aura of horror as she explores the complex relationships between these young people during the summer they spent near the haunted castle of Chillon. The horror mounts through the development of volatile interpersonal relationships and descriptions of the castle until the reader is finally prepared for the ultimate emergence of the monster Frankenstein.

Although previously mentioned novels would lead one to believe that Edwards has her feet firmly planted in some murky past and that she is a writer of only romantic gothic novels, *Shadow of a Lion* reveals her to be equally competent in the modern world when she uses tinselly Hollywood for her setting. This work, which tells the story of film industry personages who were caught in the McCarthy witch hunts of the 1950's, lies realms apart from such books as *The Hesitant Heart*. Yet the same skilled craft of a superb storyteller and analyst of the human character exists here.

With Anne Edwards's interest in the past and with her finely honed writing skills, it's not surprising that *Sonya: The Life of Countess Tolstoy*, a very solid competent biography, reads as smoothly as her lighter novels.

—Joan Hinkemeyer

ELGIN, Mary. Pseudonym for Dorothy Mary Stewart, née Okell.   British.   Born in Douglas, Isle of Man, 7 October 1917. Educated at St. Felix School, Southwold, Suffolk, 1928-34; London University, 1934-35; Mrs. Hoster's Secretarial School, 1938. Married Walter Stewart in 1947; one son and one daughter. Secretary, Short Brothers; manager in an aircraft repair organization, Cambridge, 1940-45; Secretary to the Director, Wellcome Foundation Laboratories, London, 1945-47. Recipient: Romantic Novelists Association award, 1964. *Died 23 March 1965.*

ROMANCE AND GOTHIC PUBLICATIONS

Novels

    Visibility Nil.   London, Hodder and Stoughton, 1963; as *A Man from the Mist*, New York, Mill, 1965.
    Return to Glenshael.   London, Hodder and Stoughton, 1965; as *Highland Masquerade*, New York, Mill, 1966.
    The Wood and the Trees.   London, Hodder and Stoughton, and New York, Mill, 1967.

Manuscript Collection: Boston University Libraries.

*   *   *

Mary Elgin's gothic romances displayed her unique ability to create and use a setting to inform a story. For *Visibility Nil* and *Return to Glenshael* she created a mythical region in the Highlands of northwest Scotland. The country around Anacher and Glenshael is wild and mysterious, but inevitable signs of modernization create tension. Old mansions have been bought by rich newcomers. A massive hydroelectric scheme changes the landscape and creates jobs. A river is dammed, but salmon runs preserve the native fish. One character in both books is clan chief to the neighbors but also a hard-working engineer.

The novels are domestic gothic, relying upon family history, impostures, feuds, and the exoticism of the Highlands for their suspense rather than upon genuine villains or violence. There are mysteries to solve, but they are neither life-threatening nor complex. More important in both is the heroines' emerging sense of self as they learn to live in the changing environment and come to love the heroes.

Elgin's ability to evoke the language of the Highlands was unusually fine; in one novel she describes the regional speech as a derivation of Scots Gaelic rather than a literal translation from it. Her heroines in these first-person novels are lively and strong, speaking in a charming but astringently honest voice.

Because the hero and heroine of one book recur as secondary characters in another, Elgin's works contain a rare picture of a romantic hero and heroine after marriage. The characters have changed and matured, and their relationship is stable; but they are still interesting, acerbic, and witty. Her output may have been meager; but the quality of Elgin's work is consistently high.

—Kay Mussell

ELIOT, Anne. Pseudonym for Lois Dwight Taylor, née Cole; also wrote as Caroline Arnett; Lynn Avery; Nancy Dudley; Allan Dwight; Anne Lattin.   American.   Born in New York City, in 1903. Educated at Smith College, Northampton, Massachusetts, B.A. 1924. Married Turney Allan Taylor (died, 1968); one son and one daughter. Associate Editor, Macmillan, New York; Editor, Whittlesey House and Putnam's Sons, both New York; Senior Editor, William Morrow, and Walker and Company, both New York. *Died 20 July 1979.*

ROMANCE AND GOTHIC PUBLICATIONS

Novels

Return to Aylforth.   New York, Meredith Press, 1967.
Shadows Waiting.   New York, Meredith Press, 1969.
Stranger at Pembroke.   New York, Hawthorn, 1971.
Incident at Villa Rahmana.   New York, Hawthorn, 1972; London, Hale, 1975.
The Dark Beneath the Pines.   New York, Hawthorn, 1974; London, Hale, 1976.

Novels as Caroline Arnett

Melinda.   New York, Fawcett, 1975.
Clarissa.   New York, Fawcett, 1976.
Theodora.   New York, Fawcett, 1977.
Claudia.   New York, Fawcett, 1978.
Stephanie.   New York, Fawcett, 1979.
Christina.   New York, Fawcett, 1980.

OTHER PUBLICATIONS (juvenile)

Novels as Allan Dwight, with Turney Allan Taylor

Spaniards' Mark.   New York, Macmillan, 1933.
Linn Dickson, Confederate.   New York, Macmillan, 1934.
The First Virginians.   New York, Nelson, 1936; London, Nelson, 1938.
Drums in the Forest.   New York, Macmillan, 1936.
Kentucky Cargo.   New York, Macmillan, 1939.
The Silver Dagger.   New York, Macmillan, 1959; London, Collier Macmillan, 1963.
Guns at Quebec.   New York, Macmillan, 1962; London, Collier Macmillan, 1963.
To the Walls of Cartegena.   Williamsburg, Virginia, Colonial Williamsburg, 1967.

Novels as Nancy Dudley

Linda Goes to the Hospital [*Travels Alone, Goes to a TV Studio, Goes on a Cruise*]. New York, Coward McCann, 4 vols., 1953-58.
Linda's First Flight. New York, Coward McCann, 1956.
Cappy and the River (as Lynn Avery). New York, Duell, 1960.
Jorie of Dogtown Common (as Anne Eliot). New York, Abingdon Press, 1962.
The Mystery of the Vanishing Horses (as Lynn Avery). New York, Duell, 1963.

Novels as Anne Lattin

Peter Liked to Draw. Chicago, Wilcox and Follett, 1953.
Peter's Policeman. Chicago, Follett, 1958.
Sparky's Fireman. Chicago, Follett, 1968.

Other

Soldier and Patriot: The Life of General Israel Putnam (as Allan Dwight, with Turney Allan Taylor). New York, Washburn, 1965.

Editor (i.e., adaptor), *Timothy's Shoes and Two Other Stories*, by Mrs. Ewing. New York, Macmillan, 1932.

*   *   *

Lois Dwight Cole began her early writing career with juvenile novels published under the pseudonyms Allan Dwight, Nancy Dudley, and Lynn Avery. She has since entered the field of adult romances, turning out titles in two of its most popular genres—gothic romance and regency romance.

As Anne Eliot, she has written several quite competent and enjoyable novels set in exotic locations and filled with the proper gothic atmosphere. Because the last novel was published in 1974, some of the material is dated, and, when compared to some of today's sexy fare, these can be considered quite tame. Still, it's not always easy to find a well-paced gothic with a plot that isn't obviously predictable—so these novels can be savored for that alone. For example, *Stranger at Pembroke* is a swift-paced gothic tale about a young woman, Tory Ballard, who inherits an old house in Natchez, Mississippi—but only if she can locate the papers of her ancestor Timothy Ballard in three weeks. Two handsome men are eager to aid her in her search, one of them Tory's distant cousin who will become the next heir if her quest fails. The story is skillfully done and the characterizations believable, but the best thing about this novel is the atmosphere of the old South with its Spanish moss and decaying aristocratic mansions.

Incident at Villa Rahmana has a picturesque exotic setting in modern Morocco where Kate Haskell is plunged headlong into a web of intrigue when she comes to help transform the Villa Rahmana into a luxury hotel. Some of the material in the story is now dated, what with the enormous changes in the Arab world in the last ten years, but the book is still an enjoyable read. *The Dark Beneath the Pines* has Andrea Wilmot returning to Five Pines, a camp in the Adirondack Mountains where she had spent her childhood summers. Her uncle, who had run the camp, has mysteriously disappeared along with a large sum of money. Her grandmother has decided to sell the camp to strangers, leaving Andrea no choice but to try to find her uncle and the missing money. Her life is in danger as she tries to discover just who of the several guests and family is behind the entire scheme. The plot is neat and tight, the atmosphere romantically evocative of the slower paced bygone days of private railroad cars and servants.

Cole's latest efforts have constituted a switch from her earlier gothics to the extremely popular regency era romance. Not unexpectedly, as Caroline Arnett, she combines all the ingredients in the right proportions in novels that enchant and delight. These works bring to mind one of the most popular authors in this sub-genre, Clare Darcy. Both novelists use the Regency period to tell the story of the heroine, after whom the book is always named, and her quest for happiness.

One example is *Melinda*, a Regency novel that boasts a strong intelligent heroine. There is a plan afoot to marry her off to a cruel and dishonest man who will surely steal her inheritance and probably rough her up in the bargain. The research has been done well, and the reader is treated to an enchanting tour of rural and urban England. The characters have been shaded in with a fine eye to personality and human foibles, the atmosphere is excellent, and the story is top notch. This is a very pleasant read and guaranteed to satisfy even the most discerning critic of the genre.

Another well-written story is *Clarissa*. This is a from-rags-to-riches and ugly-duckling-to-beautiful-swan tale about a paid companion who is literally plucked from the dinner table to be married to one of society's most eligible bachelors. After she is walked down the aisle and taken to London, she blossoms into a beauty, to the great astonishment of the entire town. As if that weren't enough, she ends by saving her husband's life from Napoleon's spies, winning his love and gaining herself a happy everafter. The reader roots for the heroine the entire way.

—Marilyn Lockhart

ELIZABETH.   Pseudonym for Mary Annette, Countess von Arnim, later Countess Russell, née Beauchamp. Also wrote as Alice Cholmondeley.   British.   Born in Sydney, New South Wales, Australia, 31 August 1866; grew up in Lausanne and London. Educated privately; Blythwood House, London; Miss Summerhayes's School, Ealing, London, 1881-84; Royal College of Music, London. Married 1) Count Henning August von Arnim-Schlagenthin in 1891 (died, 1910), four daughters and one son; 2) Francis Russell, Earl Russell in 1916 (separated, 1919; died, 1931). Lived in Germany, 1891-1908, then in England. *Died 9 February 1941.*

ROMANCE AND GOTHIC PUBLICATIONS

Novels

    The Benefactress.   London and New York, Macmillan, 1901.
    The Ordeal of Elizabeth.   New York, Taylor, 1901.
    The Princess Priscilla's Fortnight.   London, Smith Elder, and New York, Scribner, 1905.
    Fraülein Schmidt and Mr. Anstruther, Being the Letters of an Independent Woman.
        London, Smith Elder, and New York, Scribner, 1907.
    The Caravaners.   London, Smith Elder, and New York, Doubleday, 1909.
    The Pastor's Wife.   London, Smith Elder, and New York, Doubleday, 1914.
    Christine (as Alice Cholmondeley).   London and New York, Macmillan, 1917.
    Christopher and Columbus.   London, Macmillan, and New York, Doubleday, 1919.
    In the Mountains (published anonymously).   London, Macmillan, and New York, Doubleday, 1920
    Vera.   London, Macmillan, and New York, Doubleday, 1921.
    The Enchanted April.   London, Macmillan, 1922; New York, Doubleday, 1923.
    Love.   London, Macmillan, and New York, Doubleday, 1925.
    Introduction to Sally.   London, Macmillan, and New York, Doubleday, 1926.

Expiation. London, Macmillan, and New York, Doubleday, 1929.
Father. London, Macmillan, and New York, Doubleday, 1931.
Jasmine Farm. London, Heinemann, and New York, Doubleday, 1934.
Mr. Skeffington. London, Heinemann, and New York, Doubleday, 1940.

Short Stories

The Pious Pilgrimage. Boston, Badger, 1901.

OTHER PUBLICATIONS

Play

Priscilla Runs Away, adaptation of her novel *The Princess Priscilla's Fortnight* (produced London, 1910).

Other

Elizabeth and Her German Garden.   London and New York, Macmillan, 1898; revised edition, 1900.
The Solitary Summer. London and New York, Macmillan, 1899.
The April Baby's Book of Tunes, with the Story of How They Came to Be Written (juvenile). London and New York, Macmillan, 1900.
The Adventures of Elizabeth in Rügen. London and New York, Macmillan, 1904.
All the Dogs of My Life. London, Heinemann, and New York, Doubleday, 1936.
One Thing in Common (omnibus). New York, Doubleday, 1941.

Critical Study: *Elizabeth of the German Garden: A Biography* by Leslie de Charms, London, Heinemann, 1958.

*   *   *

After reading Virginia Woolf's *To the Lighthouse*, Elizabeth wrote to a friend: "it beats everything anyone else has done hollow. How strident, how vulgar, how coarse *my* stuff for instance seems (and is) after reading that" (quoted in Leslie de Charms's biography). Yet Elizabeth does herself an injustice. She was generally praised by serious critics throughout her long writing career (John Middleton Murry, the husband of her cousin Katherine Mansfield, referred to her novel *Vera* as "a *Wuthering Heights* written by Jane Austen"), and her intelligence and wit are as admirable now as they were when Elizabeth was an internationally known author.

Her first book—*Elizabeth and Her German Garden*, a huge success—was a short autobiographical account of the first year (spring to spring) spent in the country house near Stetten in north Germany of her husband, Count von Arnim. The charm and verbal facility on the surface of the account—of her April, May, and June babies, of the servants who don't know how to account for a (foreign) mistress who won't take regular meals and who prefers roses and hollyhocks to domestic routine, of her husband, the Man of Wrath, who doesn't understand her interest in the seemingly boring landscape, of the friends who fear her husband has exiled her away from the pleasures of Berlin—are undeniable, but we aren't surprised when the dark side of all the charm is revealed in her later books, after her first marriage (to von Arnim), and indeed her second (to Earl Russell), had broken down.

Many of the novels are light and charming, though almost all have a touch of irony about them. *The Benefactress* is an elaborate "opening out" of several motifs of *Elizabeth and Her German Garden*. The socially sophistiated but emotionally naive Anna Estcourt, on inheriting a large estate in north Germany, decides to open the house to women of good family with no means of support. The society friends—both English and German—are given space to reveal themselves ("Trudi's new friends always did think her delightful; and she never had any old ones"); the local middle class is ineffably snobbish and blinkered (the parson "puffing Christianity as though it were a quack medicine"). The Man of Wrath motif is transferred to almost all the men in the book (except her brother, who has become a philosopher and spends his time fishing): even the 20-year-old assistant vicar condescends to Anna, since she is a woman. The English-German theme is solidly used as the basis of the general misunderstandings that run through the book. The actual plot—a rather thin one—centers on her landowning neighbor who aids but disapproves of her charity: when she is finally able to comfort *him* (he is falsely imprisoned), she realizes she loves him. *The Princess Priscilla's Fortnight* and *The Caravaners* reverse the English-Lady-in-Germany theme by bringing a runaway German princess to a small Somerset village in the first, and a pompous German Baron and his party of holiday-makers to Kent in the second. (The German theme is more negatively presented in *Christine*, published during World War I under a pseudonym: what had been a subject of irony and fun in previous works becomes the basis of tragedy in this book.) Sally (*Introduction to Sally*) is a luscious grocer's daughter who marries a Cambridge undergraduate; his snobbish mother drives her away, but Sally's charm is such that a duke and his daughter rescue her, and facilitate a reconciliation. Snobbery figures again in *Jasmine Farm*, where Lady Terence has an affair with her mother's married secretary, Andrew. Since her mother had a rake for a husband, she is very moral; since Andrew's wife's mother is an ex-actress and a social climber, she is willing to compromise—so the two older ladies are able to resolve the dilemma.

Other novels deal with groups of women in differing relationships to each other. *The Enchanted April* shows the effect of the Mediterranean on four women, all of whom are troubled and react to the beauty of the setting in positive ways. *In the Mountains*, set in Switzerland, has a similar theme, though here the three ladies have a more complicated relationship. The narrator (the book is in diary form) is getting away from an intolerable personal situation (never explained), licking her wounds, and the other two are strangers, one ultra conventional, the other a charming, mindless beauty, Dolly, who had kept marrying Germans. The arrival of the narrator's uncle, a Dean ("relieved to find his niece...securely, as it were, embedded in widows") solves all problems, since he promptly falls in love with Dolly. *Expiation* centers on a widow, Millie Bott, forced to live our her widowhood in "correct" form surrounded by female Botts; her old lover of 10 years standing can't help her, though her mother-in-law, the only charming Bott, can.

If *Expiation* is a rather bleak look at love and marriage, several of Elizabeth's other novels are even more revealing. *Love*, which according to Elizabeth's biographer had an autobiographical basis, concerns a 47-year old widow courted by and possibly in love with a 25-year-old man. The climax comes when her priggish son-in-law forces her to marry the young man because they had been forced to stay overnight together. (The theme of the aging beauty is neatly and touchingly told in *Mr. Skeffington*, possibly her best-known work, at least indirectly, since it was made into a movie starring Bette Davis.) But *Fräulein Schmidt and Mr. Anstruther* and *Vera* are probably her bleakest books. The first consists of letters from Fräulein Rose-Marie Schmidt to Roger Anstruther, who had stayed for a year in the Schmidt's house in Jena where he was coached in German by Rose-Marie's father, Professor Schmidt. Reversing the usual progress from coolness to passion, the book begins with Rose-Marie utterly in love with Roger, based on a last-minute avowal before Roger returned to England, and moves haltingly through their break-up, his engagement to an English girl, that engagement's break-up in turn, and Roger's slowly revived interest in Rose-Marie, who by this time regards him only as a friend. Rose-Marie's sensitivity and charm, and her cooling passion, are beautifully revealed (we never read the other side of the correspondence). *Vera* is even more chilling—a convincing portrait of a pure egotist, Everard Wemyss, and a charming woman, Lucy Entwhistle, who becomes involved with him. Wemyss's egotism is revealed to the reader only as Lucy becomes aware of it—she marries him, finds out the ambiguous nature of his previous wife's suicide, and at the end of the book is caught in a position that can lead only to her complete submission to her husband or to an end like his first wife's.

Despite her sometimes bleak views (possibly reflecting her own marriages), what is remembered of Elizabeth's books is their wit and charm. We are often given the chance to see the bully bullied, the egotist defeated, the worm turning—and almost always with a lightness of touch and a verbal felicity that remind us of the numerous comparisons her contemporaries made to Jane Austen.

—George Walsh

ELLERBECK, Rosemary (Anne L'Estrange). Also writes as Anna L'Estrange; Nicola Thorne; Katherine Yorke. British. Born in Cape Town, South Africa. Educated at the London School of Economics, B.A. in sociology. Publishers reader and editor until 1975, then free-lance writer. Address: 96 Townshend Court, Mackennal Street, London N.W. 8, England.

ROMANCE AND GOTHIC PUBLICATIONS

Novels

> *Inclination to Murder.* London, Hodder and Stoughton, 1965.
> *Hammersleigh.* New York, McKay, and London, Hale, 1976.
> *Return to Wuthering Heights* (as Anna L'Estrange). New York, Pinnacle, 1977; London, Corgi, 1978.
> *Rose, Rose, Where Are You?* London, Hale, and New York, Coward McCann, 1978.

Novels as Katherine Yorke

> *The Enchantress.* London, Futura, and New York, Pocket Books, 1979.
> *Falcon Gold.* London, Futura, 1980; New York, Pinnacle, 1981.
> *Lady of the Lakes.* London, Futura, 1981.

Novels as Nicola Thorne

> *The Girls.* London, Heinemann, and New York, Random House, 1967.
> *Bridie Climbing.* London, Mayflower, 1969.
> *In Love.* London, Quartet, 1974.
> *A Woman Like Us.* London, Heinemann, and New York, St. Martin's Press, 1979.
> *The Perfect Wife and Mother.* London, Heinemann, 1980.
> *The Daughters of the House.* London, Granada, and New York, Doubleday, 1981.
> *Where the Rivers Meet.* London, Granada, 1982.

*   *   *

Rosemary Ellerbeck's novels entertain the reader with a good old fashioned yarn often involving history or a real historical character. Ghosts and the English and French settings provide the ingredients for an interesting, dual story—with the present often repeating or paralleling the past.

Hammersleigh is a good example. Set in the Yorkshire countryside, the gothic story revolves around a legend that tells of the forbidden love between a monk and a nun, Agatha, the beautiful Prioress of Hammersleigh Priory over five hundred years ago. Karen Blackwood returns to Hammersleigh village, her childhood home, after the death of her husband. After she meets the reckless and handsome master of the great Hammersleigh Hall, she begins to wonder if her decision to return was her own or somehow involved with the tragic events of the past. This is a good tale of suspense and the world of psychic forces.

Rose, Rose, Where Are You? concerns the past in a different way. Clare Trafford goes to the charming coastal town of Port St. Pierre in order to work on a biography of Joan of Arc. She meets the DeFrigecourts who live in the Chateau de Moulin which is built over the site where Joan was once imprisoned. According to legend, she left a curse on the family, and strange accidents have occurred since then. The Rose of the title is the governess who disappears. At the root of it all is a stolen medieval treasure. This book has mystery in the forefront; romance is secondary, for Clare returns to her estranged husband after his timely appearance near the denouement.

As Nicola Thorne, Ellerbeck writes general category fiction pertaining mostly to a female audience with stories of everyday life and its small trials and tribulations. But Ellerbeck's interest in the past again crops up in *Return to Wuthering Heights*, written as Anna L'Estrange. This is a surprisingly good, quite compelling sequel to Emily Brontë's classic masterpiece, and continues the story of Catherine's daughter, Cathy, after she marries Hareton. Into their lives comes Jack, Heathcliff's natural son, and the hostilities and passions of the past threaten to break loose once again.

—Marilyn Lockhart

ELSNA, Hebe. Pseudonym for Dorothy Phoebe Ansle; also writes as Laura Conway; Vicky Lancaster; Lyndon Snow. Agent: Curtis Brown Ltd., 1 Craven Hill, London W2 3EP, England.

ROMANCE AND GOTHIC PUBLICATIONS

Novels

Child of Passion. London, Hurst and Blackett, 1928.
The Third Wife. London, Hurst and Blackett, 1928.
Sweeter Unpossessed. London, Hurst and Blackett, 1929.
Strait-Jacket. London, Hurst and Blackett, 1930.
Study of Sara. London, Hurst and Blackett, 1930.
We Are the Pilgrims. London, Hurst and Blackett, 1931; as *I Know Not Whither* (as Laura Conway), London, Hale, 1979.
Other People's Fires. London, Hurst and Blackett, 1931.
All Swans. London, Hurst and Blackett, 1932.
Upturned Palms. London, Hurst and Blackett, 1933.
You Never Knew. London, Hurst and Blackett, 1933.
Women Always Forgive. London, Hurst and Blackett, 1934.
Half Sisters. London, Hurst and Blackett, 1934.
Receipt for Hardness. London, Rich and Cowan, 1935.
Uncertain Lover. London, Rich and Cowan, 1935.
Crista Moon. London, Rich and Cowan, 1936.
Brief Heroine. London, Jarrolds, 1937.

People Are So Respectable. London, Jarrolds, 1937.
The Price of Pleasure. London, Amalgamated Press, 1937.
All Visitors Ashore. London, Collins, 1938.
Like Summer Brave. London, Jarrolds, 1938.
This Clay Suburb. London, Jarrolds, 1938; revised edition, as *Bid Time Return*, London, Hale, 1979.
The Wedding Took Place. London, Jarrolds, 1939.
The First Week in September. London, Hutchinson, 1940.
Lady Misjudged. London, Hutchinson, 1941.
Everyone Loves Lorraine. London, Collins, 1941; as *Portrait of Lorraine* (as Laura Conway), 1971.
Our Little Life. London, Collins, 1942; as *Yesterday and Tomorrow* (as Lyndon Snow), 1971.
None Can Return. London, Collins, 1942.
See My Shining Palace. London, Collins, 1942.
Young and Broke. London, Collins, 1943.
No Fields of Amaranth. London, Collins, 1943; revised edition, as Lyndon Snow, 1971.
The Happiest Year. London, Collins, 1944.
I Have Lived Today. London, Collins, 1944; as *The Songless Wood* (as Lyndon Snow), London, Hale, 1979.
Echo from Afar. London, Collins, 1945.
The Gilded Ladder. London, Collins, 1945.
Cafeteria. London, Collins, 1946.
Clemency Page. London, Collins, 1947.
The Dream and the World. London, Collins, 1947; as *A Link in the Chain*, 1975.
Midnight Matinée. London, Collins, 1949.
The Soul of Mary Olivane. London, Collins, 1949; revised edition, as *Mary Olivane*, 1973.
The Door Between. London, Collins, 1950; revised edition, 1971.
No Shallow Stream. London, Collins, 1950; as *The World of Christy Pembroke* (as Lyndon Snow), 1978.
Happy Birthday to You. London, Collins, 1951; as *The Conjurer's Daughter* (as Lyndon Snow), 1979.
The Convert. London, Hale, 1952.
A Day of Grace. London, Hale, 1952.
A Girl Disappears. London, Hale, 1953.
Gail Talbot. London, Hale, 1953; as *If This Be Sin* (as Laura Conway), London, Collins, 1975.
Consider These Women. London, Hale, 1954.
A Shade of Darkness. London, Hale, 1954.
The Season's Greetings. London, Hale, 1954.
The Sweet Lost Years. London, Hale, 1955.
I Bequeath. London, Hale, 1955.
Strange Visitor. London, Hale, 1956; revised edition (as Laura Conway), London, Collins, 1973; New York, Saturday Review Press, 1975.
The Love Match. London, Hale, 1956.
My Dear Lady. London, Hale, 1957.
The Marrying Kind. London, Collins, 1957.
Mrs. Melbourne. London, Hale, 1958; revised edition, 1972.
The Gay Unfortunate. London, Hale, 1958.
The Younger Miss Nightingale. London, Hale, 1959.
Marks upon the Snow. London, Hale, 1960.
Time Is—Time Was. London, Hale, 1960.
The Little Goddess. London, Hale, 1961.
The Lonely Dreamer. London, Hale, 1961; revised edition (as Laura Conway), 1972.
Vicky. London, Hale, 1961; revised edition, as *The Eldest Daughter*, 1974.
Beyond Reasonable Doubt. London, Hale, 1962.
Take Pity upon Youth. London, Hale, 1962.

Minstrel's Court. London, Hale, 1963; revised edition (as Lyndon Snow), London, Collins, 1974.

Lady on the Coin, with Margaret Barnes. London, Macdonald, and Philadelphia, Macrae Smith, 1963.

A House Called Pleasance. London, Hale, 1963; as Laura Conway, New York, Dutton, 1979.

The Undying Past. London, Hale, 1964; as Laura Conway, New York, Dutton, 1980.

Too Well Beloved. London, Hale, 1964; as Laura Conway, New York, Dutton, 1979.

The Brimming Cup. London, Collins, 1965.

The China Princess. London, Collins, 1965.

Saxon's Folly. London, Collins, 1966.

The Queen's Ward. London, Collins, 1967.

The Heir of Garlands. London, Collins, 1968.

The Pursuit of Pleasure. London, Collins, 1969.

The Abbot's House. London, Collins, 1969; as Laura Conway, New York, Saturday Review Press, 1974.

Take Heed of Loving Me. London, Collins, 1970; as Laura Conway, New York, Saturday Review Press, 1976.

Sing for Your Supper. London, Collins, 1970.

The Mask of Comedy. London, Collins, 1970.

The King's Bastard. London, Collins, 1971.

Prelude for Two Queens. London, Collins, 1972.

The Elusive Crown. London, Collins, 1973.

The Cherished One. London, Collins, 1974.

Distant Landscape. London, Collins, 1975.

Cast a Long Shadow. London, Collins, 1976; as Laura Conway, New York, Dutton, 1978.

Heiress Presumptive. London, Hale, 1981.

Red-Headed Bastard. London, Hale, 1981.

Novels as Vicky Lancaster

Gypsy Virtue. London, Mills and Boon, 1936.

Dawn Through the Shutters. London, Mills and Boon, 1937.

Men Are So Strange. London, Mills and Boon, 1937.

Heartbreaker. London, Mills and Boon, 1938.

Masquerade for Love. London, Mills and Boon, 1938.

This Wild Enchantment. London, Mills and Boon, 1938.

Daughter at Home. London, Hurst and Blackett, 1939.

Three Roads to Heaven. London, Mills and Boon, 1939.

Farewell to Veronica. London, Hurst and Blackett, 1940.

Sometimes Spring Returns. London, Hurst and Blackett, 1940.

Must the Dream End. London, Hurst and Blackett, 1941.

Sweet Shipwreck. London, Hale, 1942.

Beggar Girl's Gift. London, Hale, 1943.

The Happy Cinderella. London, Hale, 1943.

Lady—Look Ahead. London, Hale, 1944.

They Loved in Donegal. London, Hale, 1944.

The Sunset Hour. London, Hale, 1946.

Fixed as the Stars. London, Hale, 1946.

So Many Worlds. London, Hale, 1948; revised edition, as *The Sisters* (as Laura Conway), London, Collins, 1971.

All Past Years. London, Hale, 1949.

Perfect Marriage. London, Hale, 1949.

Draw Back the Curtain. London, Hale, 1950.

Short Lease. London, Hale, 1950.

Homecoming. London, Hale, 1951; as *Journey Home* (as Laura Conway), London, Collins, 1978.

They Were Not Divided. London, Hale, 1952; revised edition (as Laura Conway), London, Collins, 1972.

The Career of Stella Merlin. London, Hale, 1953.

Passing Sweet. London, Hale, 1953.

Lover's Staff. London, Hale, 1954.

Many a Human Heart. London, Hale, 1954.

Lovers in Darkness. London, Hale, 1955.

In Search of Love. London, Hale, 1955.

Suspicion. London, Hale, 1955.

The Way of a Man. London, Hale, 1956.

Women in Love. London, Hale, 1957.

Princess in Love. London, Hale, 1957.

Royal Deputy. London, Hale, 1957.

All Our Tomorrows. London, Hale, 1958.

The Amazing Marriage. London, Hale, 1958.

The Unbroken Link. London, Hale, 1959.

The Past Must Die. London, Hale, 1959.

Secret Lives. London, Hale, 1960.

Sweet Wine of Youth. London, Hale, 1960.

The Cobweb Mist. London, Hale, 1961.

Snake in the Grass. London, Hale, 1961.

Doctor in Suspense. London, Hale, 1962.

Love's Second Chance. London, Hale, 1962.

No Good as a Nurse. London, Hale, 1962.

Novels as Lyndon Snow

Young Love Wakes. London, Collins, 1940.

Follow Your Star. London, Collins, 1941.

Second Thoughts. London, Collins, 1941.

But Joy Kissed Me. London, Collins, 1942.

Three Latch Keys. London, Collins, 1943; as *Latchkeys*, 1978.

Dream Daughter. London, Collins, 1944.

Christening Party. London, Collins, 1945.

Dear Yesterday. London, Collins, 1946.

Early Blossom. London, Collins, 1946.

Two Walk Apart. London, Collins, 1948.

The Gift of My Heart. London, Collins, 1948.

Come to My Wedding. London, Collins, 1949.

Golden Future. London, Collins, 1950.

All in the Day's Work. London, Collins, 1950.

A Year of Her Life. London, Collins, 1951.

Poor Butterfly. London, Collins, 1951.

Honoured Guest. London, Collins, 1952.

Made in Heaven. London, Collins, 1952.

Dearest Enemy. London, Collins, 1953; as *The Case Is Closed* (as Laura Conway), London, Hale, 1980.

Wayward Love. London, Collins, 1953.

Always Remember. London, Collins, 1954.

Do Not Forget Me. London, Collins, 1954.

Love Me for Ever. London, Collins, 1955.

Alone with You. London, Collins, 1955.

So Fair My Love. London, Collins, 1956.

To-morrow's Promise. London, Collins, 1956.

For Love Alone. London, Collins, 1957.

Romance Is Always Young. London, Collins, 1957; revised edition, 1975.
Silence Is Golden. London, Collins, 1958.
A Heart to Be Won. London, Collins, 1958.
Moonlight Witchery. London, Collins, 1959.
Stealer of Hearts. London, Collins, 1959.
Happy Event. London, Collins, 1960.
Some Day You'll Love Me. London, Collins, 1960.
The Fabulous Marriage. London, Collins, 1961.
After All. London, Collins, 1961.
Anything Can Happen. London, Collins, 1962.
My Dream Fulfilled. London, Collins, 1962.
Prima Donna. London, Collins, 1963.
Difficult to Love. London, Collins, 1963.
My Brother's Wife. London, Collins, 1964.
The One Who Looked On. London, Collins, 1965.
Bright Face of Honour. London, Collins, 1965.
His Shadow on the Wall. London, Collins, 1965.
My Cousin Lola. London, Collins, 1966.
Spinster of This Parish. London, Collins, 1966.
The Head of the House. London, Collins, 1967.
Poor Relation. London, Collins, 1968.
Moment of Truth. London, Collins, 1968; as Laura Conway, New York, Saturday
   Review Press, 1975.
Francesca. London, Collins, 1970; as Laura Conway, New York, Saturday Review
   Press, 1973.
An Arrow in My Heart. London, Collins, 1972.
Trial and Error. London, Collins, 1973.
Don't Shut Me Out. London, Collins, 1974.
Best Loved Person. London, Collins, 1976.

Novels as Laura Conway

Love Calls Me Home. London, Collins, 1952.
Loving You Always. London, Collins, 1953.
Innocent Enchantress. London, Collins, 1953.
Love's Prisoner. London, Collins, 1954.
So New to Love. London, Collins, 1955.
Enchantment. London, Collins, 1956.
Hard to Win. London, Collins, 1956.
Be True to Me. London, Collins, 1957.
When Next We Meet. London, Collins, 1957.
Wish upon a Dream. London, Collins, 1958; as *Dark Dream*, New York, Dutton, 1976.
No Regrets. London, Collins, 1958.
The Sun Still Shines. London, Collins, 1959.
By Love Transformed. London, Collins, 1959.
Bargain in Love. London, Collins, 1960.
The Turn of the Road. London, Collins, 1960.
Teach Me to Forget. London, Collins, 1961.
Shadow Marriage. London, Collins, 1961.
It's Lonely Without You. London, Collins, 1962.
Lovers in Waiting. London, Collins, 1962.
A Way Through the Maze. London, Collins, 1963.
Safety for My Love. London, Collins, 1963.
Loving Is Different. London, Collins, 1964.
A Butterfly's Hour. London, Collins, 1964; New York, Saturday Review Press, 1973.
Two Fair Daughters. London, Collins, 1965.
Gifted Friend. London, Collins, 1965.

Heiress Apparent. London, Collins, 1966; New York, McCall, 1970.
Five Mrs. Lorrimers. London, Collins, 1966.
For a Dream's Sake. London, Collins, 1967.
The Unforgotten. London, Collins, 1967; New York, Saturday Review Press, 1972.
Dearest Mamma. London, Collins, 1969.
The Night of the Party. London, Collins, 1969; New York, McCall, 1971.
Living with Paula. London, Collins, 1972.
Dark Symmetry. New York, Saturday Review Press, 1973.
Acquittal. London, Collins, 1973.
A Link in the Chain. New York, Dutton, 1975.

Short Stories

The Silver Boy and Other Stories. London, Rich and Cowan, 1936.

OTHER PUBLICATIONS

Plays

The Season's Greetings (produced London, 1953). London, Deane, and Boston, Baker, 1954.
A Shade of Difference, adaptation of her own novel (produced Ventnor, Isle of Wight, 1954).
I Bequeath (produced London, 1954).

Other

Unwanted Wife: A Defence of Mrs. Charles Dickens. London, Jarrolds, 1963.
Catherine of Braganza, Charles II's Queen. London, Hale, 1967.

*   *   *

A prolific author who writes under several pseudonyms, Dorothy Ansle skirts the edge of the gothic tradition. Mysterious forces, reincarnation, occult happenings, and time travel are some of the common, recurring elements which appear in her works. However, the thrills and suspense which can be created by these components are often dulled in Ansle's novels by a heavy emphasis on conversation and the lack of physical action. Although the romantic entanglements end happily enough, the love stories are generally weak. Her interest in her characters seems to be primarily psychological. Consequently there is little emotional involvement for the reader.

In common with many gothic writers, Ansle often uses a house as an actual character in her stories. In *A House Called Pleasance* excessive love for a house creates the motivating force for the actions of the Grenton women. The houses in *The Dream and the World* and *Take Heed of Loving Me* play more sinister roles, in each case acting as a medium through which occult forces are channeled. Houses or estates also figure prominently in *Heiress Apparent, The Night of the Party*, and *The Abbot's House*. Despite its potential, this device is not as fully exploited as it is in the works of some of the topflight gothic authors like Barbara Mertz.

Ansle seems more at home in developing themes of reincarnation and what, for lack of a better term, might be called time travel. In *The Dream and the World* (reprinted as *A Link in the Chain*) the supernatural ties which bind the characters to the past and set them on the path to relive an old tragedy are only gradually revealed. It is this forging of the "chain" which leads to a growing tension for the reader. Parallel worlds in time exist in *Take Heed of Loving Me* and *The Unforgotten*. Characters in these novels have the ability to live in different times and, to a certain extent, to influence events in other eras.

In spite of these modest successes Ansle remains in the shadow of the better gothic novelists. Lack of true suspense and too little emphasis on the development of characters prevent her from joining the ranks of the leaders of the genre.

—Barbara Kemp

EMSLEY, Clare. Pseudonym for Clare (Emsley) Plummer. British. Born in Coventry, Warwickshire, 23 September 1912. Educated privately. Worked for a group of women's magazines; full-time writer from 1955. *Died 12 April 1980.*

ROMANCE AND GOTHIC PUBLICATIONS

Novels

Painted Clay. London, Stanley Paul, 1947.
Keep Thy Heart. London, Stanley Paul, 1949.
The Broken Arcs. London, Stanley Paul, 1951.
The Fatal Gift. London, Stanley Paul, 1951.
Lonely Pinnacle. London, Stanley Paul, 1952.
Unjust Recompense. London, Stanley Paul, 1953,
The True Physician. London, Stanley Paul, 1954.
Flame of Youth. London, Stanley Paul, 1957.
Call Back Yesterday. London, Hurst and Blackett, 1958.
The Long Journey. London, Hurst and Blackett, 1959.
Doctor Michael's Bondage. London, Hurst and Blackett, 1962.
A Nurse's Sacrifice. London, Hurst and Blackett, 1962.
A Surgeon's Folly. London, Hurst and Blackett, 1963.
Doctor at the Crossroads. London, Hurst and Blackett, 1966.
Nurse Catherine's Marriage. London, Hurst and Blackett, 1967.
Sister Rachel's Vigil. London, Hurst and Blackett, 1968.
Doctor Rowland's Daughters. London, Hurst and Blackett, 1970.
A Time to Heal. London, Hurst and Blackett, 1972.
Highway to Fate. London, Hurst and Blackett, 1973.
A Heart's Captivity. London, Hurst and Blackett, 1976.

Novels as Clare Plummer

Unknown Heritage. London, Hale, 1963.
Doctor Adam's Past. London, Hale, 1965.
The Awakening of Nurse Grant. London, Hale, 1967.
An Island for Doctor Phillipa. London, Hale, 1969.
Chris Baynton, S.R.N. London, Hale, 1971.

*   *   *

Clare Plummer, who also writes as Clare Emsley, has produced a large number of romances, many set in a medical context which seems to encourage her imagination to produce varied and convincing stories. However, for Plummer the course of romance is seen very much as a series of choices. Indeed, the basic plot of many of her novels is the choice which has to be made by the protagonist between two prospective partners, who often have markedly different qualities of character. In *Lonely Pinnacle* Richard Flemming's ambition to become a surgeon is hindered by his hesitation between two girls: Jess Oakley, the lovable companion of his childhood, and the rich and beautiful Julie Graham. Although circumstances permit him to marry each in turn, he finds that their different qualities give rise to very different experiences within the relationship.

The reverse situation, where a woman has to make the choice between two men, is found in *A Heart's Captivity*. Here Sister Caroline Grange has a hard time choosing between her star patient, David Armitage, and her former (now "reformed") husband. The story unfolds around the intriguing of a dominant mother who uses Caroline's daughter Jenny as a pawn in her power game.

Very forceful mothers are a common feature of Plummer's novels, and the course of a career or a romance is often dictated by the loyalty or obligation a character feels towards his or her mother. So too, the "price that children pay for broken marriages" (*A Heart's Captivity*) is an oft-made point. The fate of Piero in *Unjust Recompense* is a typical example.

Again and again the same "recipe" of one person and two possible partners (e.g., in *Chris Baynton S.R.N.*, *Unjust Recompense*, and *The Broken Arcs*) is used to produce an interesting and very human story. Although such a pattern could easily lead to a series of predictable plots, the writer has used her creative skills to the full. There is no inevitable choice of "goodie" over "baddie," no trite moral judgements, and few obvious happy endings. For example, in *A Heart's Captivity*, the desire of Elsa Franelli to break free of what she sees as the restrictions caused by a husband and son, is shown to be the only route she can take to find true happiness. Even Julie Graham, the arch villain throughout *Lonely Pinnacle*, finally has a change of heart and returns to her husband, quite contrary to the reader's expectations.

While basically convincing, the plots of these novels are often let down by stilted use of language. Conversation alternates between easy use of natural language and some rather false phraseology. "There was no-one to whom he could explain the feeling of power which was beginning to flow through him in the dissecting room" is one such "gem" which does not ring true, even when encountered in context (in *Lonely Pinnacle*), and Piero's accent and his use of the English language (*Unjust Recompense*) also seem rather unusual for a young boy who has hitherto spent all his life in Italy.

Despite these reservations, Clare Plummer displays a consistent ability to write an enjoyable romance. The medical setting is a successful medium for her characters and plots, and the very human dilemmas she describes are imbued with that touch of reality which is the hallmark of a good story.

—Kim Paynter

ERSKINE-LINDOP, Audrey (Beatrice Noël). British. Born in London, 26 December 1921. Educated at the Convent of Our Lady of Lourdes, Hatch End, Middlesex; Blackdown School, Wellington, Somerset. Married Dudley Gordon Leslie in 1945. Actress with Worthing Repertory Company; then screenwriter in England and Hollywood. Recipient: Prix Roman Policier, 1968. Address: Gray Tiles, Niton Undercliff, Isle of Wight PO38 2NA; or, Kestorway, Chagford, South Devon, England.

Novels

> *Fortune My Foe*. New York, Harper, 1947; as *In Me My Enemy*, London, Harrap, 1948.
>
> *Soldiers' Daughters Never Cry*. New York, Simon and Schuster, 1948; London, Heinemann, 1949.
>
> *The Tall Headlines*. London, Heinemann, and New York, Macmillan, 1950.
>
> *Out of the Whirlwind*. London, Heinemann, 1951; New York, Appleton Century Crofts, 1952.
>
> *The Singer Not the Song*. London, Heinemann, and New York, Appleton Century Crofts, 1953; as *The Bandit and the Priest*, New York, Pocket Books, 1953.
>
> *Details of Jeremy*. London, Heinemann, 1955; as *The Outer Ring*, New York, Appleton Century Crofts, 1955.
>
> *The Judas Figures*. London, Heinemann, and New York, Appleton Century Crofts, 1956.
>
> *Mist over Talla*. New York, Doubleday, 1957; as *I Thank a Fool*, London, Collins, 1958.
>
> *Nicola*. New York, Doubleday, 1959; London, Collins, 1964.
>
> *The Way to the Lantern*. London, Collins, and New York, Doubleday, 1961.
>
> *I Start Counting*. London, Collins, and New York, Doubleday, 1966.
>
> *Sight Unseen*. London, Collins, and New York, Doubleday, 1969.
>
> *Journey into Stone*. New York, Doubleday, 1972; London, Macmillan, 1973.
>
> *The Self-Appointed Saint*. London, Macmillan, and New York, Doubleday, 1975.

OTHER PUBLICATIONS

Plays

> *Let's Talk Turkey*, with Dudley Leslie (produced Windsor, 1954).
> *Beware of Angels*, with Dudley Leslie (produced London, 1959).
>
> Screenplays: *Blanche Fury*, with Hugh Mills and Cecil McGivern, 1948; *Tall Headlines* (*The Frightened Bride*), with Dudley Leslie, 1952; *The Rough and the Smooth* (*Portrait of a Sinner*), with Dudley Leslie, 1959.

Other

> *The Adventures of the Wuffle* (juvenile). London, Methuen, 1966; New York, McGraw Hill, 1968.

*   *   *

"It is the people behind their beliefs that fascinate me far more than what they believe in...." Thus Audrey Erskine-Lindop describes her reasons for writing *The Singer Not the Song*. This statement holds true for her other works as well. In a variety of genres—romantic, historical, sociological—characterization is all important.

The Singer Not the Song is the most obvious example. Father Keogh depicts pure good, and his evil counterpart is Malo. The people of the small Mexican village are pulled first one way and then another between the two men. The battle is to the death over a period of years, and Malo stops at nothing to have his way. The love between the young priest and a romantic child is touching and dangerous for the whole village. The novel is overlong and improbable but tastefully written and intriguing.

Age differences also are important in *I Start Counting*. Wynne at 14 loves George despite the

21 years that separate them. Her love drives her to protect him when she suspects him to be the strangler terrorizing the village. She destroys evidence, withholds information, and tries to make a suicide look like murder to mislead the police. She is partly responsible for her best friend's death and nearly gets herself killed through subterfuge. The killer remains an indistinct person, but Wynne and her family become very real people. The story, finally, is merely diverting.

In *Mist over Talla* an unusual advertisement in the London paper takes Harriet to Shropshire and Ireland as companion to a woman whose husband wants her accompanied every minute. The reasons for this are not explained at first, and Harriet finds understanding her charge very difficult. It is even harder to hide her feelings for Lead Stewart from his wife's eyes. That love would lead to death and the poor prospect for happiness. While not as masterful as her other works, the novel weaves a haunting spell.

The Way to the Lantern is the story of the French Revolution told from the perspective of an English actor who wants to make his fortune but cannot stay away from women. He uses different identities for several woman and finds himself in trouble with each of them as well as with the motley French authorities. This entertaining novel is an unusual and original view of history.

Other novels treat various social problems: irresponsible selfishness in *Out of the Whirlwind*, the effect of a murderer's crime on his own family in *The Tall Headlines*, boredom in *Fortune My Foe*, and homosexuality in *Details of Jeremy*. *Soldiers' Daughters Never Cry* deals with the Nazi takeover of Austria. Some are well done, but others are melodramatic and implausible.

Erskine-Lindop seldom ends her novels happily ever after, but she leaves hope for a brighter future. Each of them is a study of personality and the events that lead to its development. She is a writer of talent, though the quality of her work is uneven.

—Andrea Lee Shuey

ERTZ, Susan. British. Born in Walton-on-Thames, Surrey. Educated privately in England to age 12, and in California to age 18. Married John Ronald McCrindle in 1932 (died, 1977). Fellow, Royal Society of Literature. Agent: Brandt and Brandt, 1501 Broadway, New York, New York 10036, U.S.A. Address: Fir Tree Cottage, Newenden, near Hawkhurst, Kent, England.

ROMANCE AND GOTHIC PUBLICATIONS

Novels

Madame Claire. London, Unwin, and New York, Appleton, 1923.
Nina. London, Unwin, and New York, Appleton, 1924.
After Noon. London, Unwin, and New York, Appleton, 1926.
Now East, Now West. London, Benn, and New York, Appleton, 1927.
The Galaxy. London, Hodder and Stoughton, and New York, Appleton, 1929.
Julian Probert. London, Hodder and Stoughton, 1931; as *The Story of Julian*, New York, Appleton, 1931.
The Proselyte. London, Hodder and Stoughton, and New York, Appleton Century, 1933.

Now We Set Out.   London, Hodder and Stoughton, 1934; New York, Appleton Century, 1935.

Woman Alive.   London, Hodder and Stoughton, 1935; New York, Appleton Century, 1936.

No Hearts to Break.   London, Hodder and Stoughton, and New York, Appleton Century, 1937.

One Fight More.   New York, Appleton Century, 1939; London, Hodder and Stoughton, 1940.

Anger in the Sky.   London, Hodder and Stoughton, and New York, Harper, 1943.

Two Names under the Shore.   London, Hodder and Stoughton, 1947; as *Mary Hallam*, New York, Harper, 1947.

The Prodigal Heart.   London, Hodder and Stoughton, and New York, Harper, 1950.

The Undefended Gate.   London, Hodder and Stoughton, 1953; as *Invitation to Folly*, New York, Harper, 1953.

Charmed Circle.   London, Collins, and New York, Harper, 1956.

In the Cool of the Day.   New York, Harper, 1960; London, Collins, 1961.

Devices and Desires.   London, Collins, 1972; as *Summer's Lease*, New York, Harper, 1972.

The Philosopher's Daughter.   London, Collins, and New York, Harper, 1976.

Short Stories

And Then Face to Face and Other Stories.   London, Unwin, 1927; as *The Wind of Complication*, New York, Appleton, 1927.

Big Frogs and Little Frogs.   London, Hodder and Stoughton, 1938; New York, Harper, 1939.

Uncollected Short Stories

"Someone to Need Him," in *Collier's* (Springfield, Ohio), 24 June 1939.

"Jeopardy of Love," in *Woman's Home Companion* (Springfield, Ohio), October 1939.

OTHER PUBLICATIONS

Other

Black, White, and Caroline (juvenile).   London, Hodder and Stoughton, and New York, Appleton Century, 1938.

*   *   *

Born in England of American parents, Susan Ertz has enjoyed a long and cosmopolitan career as a writer of fiction. Although her novels may be said to fall into the general category of "romance," this description does not really do justice to her range and originality. Her books rarely follow an established formula, though they may contain formulaic elements; the central interest lies not in plot, but rather in the psychology of individual characters. In this respect, her works often strike one as essentially gothic in tone, and, occasionally, as excessively ingenious.

Nina, the story of a woman's hopeless infatuation for an unfaithful husband, exemplifies the author's approach to romantic love. Her novels are filled with examples of romances which end unhappily, or which contain elements of selfishness, manipulation, or cruelty. A recurring theme is the unhealthy influence of families upon their members, and the difficulty experienced by individuals in escaping from what the title of one novel refers to, ironically, as a *Charmed Circle*. The effectiveness of this theme is sometimes blurred, however, by a tendency to present secondary characters as caricatures: *Charmed Circle* is narrated by one son who manages to

255

escape the clutches of his family, who appear to have no redeeming qualities whatever. There is often an element of mystery in the novels, usually associated with an event which occurred in the past. However, as she is essentially unconcerned with plot, this element results in some rather unconvincing convolutions. In *The Philosopher's Daughter*, for example, a girl falls in love with the man she assumes to be her long-lost half-brother. Although generally free from the fascination with exotic locale which characterizes the work of many romance writers, the novels frequently present some version of what might be called the "international theme." *Now East, Now West* presents a contrast between the societies of England and America; *In the Cool of the Day* provides a combination of high romance and travelogue; and *Devices and Desires* is the story of an English woman, unhappily married to a faithless American husband, who is loved by a Frenchman and an American professor, and who, sacrificing herself to her son, loses the love of both. This plot illustrates both the weaknesses and the strengths of the author, who once declared that she preferred "a new idea...to a diamond watch."

—Joanne Harack Hayne

ESSEX, Mary.   *See* **BLOOM, Ursula**.

ESTEVEN, John.   *See* **SHELLABARGER, Samuel**.

EYRE, Annette.   *See* **WORBOYS, Anne**.

FAIRE, Zabrina. *See* **STEVENSON, Florence**.

FARNES, Eleanor. Married; two sons. Address: c/o Mills and Boon Ltd., 15-16 Brooks Mews, London W1A 1DR, England.

ROMANCE AND GOTHIC PUBLICATIONS

Novels

Merry Goes the Time. London, Mills and Boon, 1935.
Tangled Harmonies. London, Mills and Boon, 1936.
Three Happy Pilgrims. London, Mills and Boon, 1937.
Romantic Melody. London, Mills and Boon, 1938.
Hesitation Waltz. London, Mills and Boon, 1939.
The Crystal Spring. London, Mills and Boon, 1940.
I Walk the Mountain Tops. London, Mills and Boon, 1940.
Bloom on the Gorse. London, Mills and Boon, 1941.
Reckless Adventure. London, Mills and Boon, 1942.
Fruits of the Year. London, Mills and Boon, 1942.
The Doctor's Wife. London, Mills and Boon, 1943.
Summer Motley. London, Mills and Boon, 1943.
Brief Excursion. London, Mills and Boon, 1944.
The Quiet Valley. London, Mills and Boon, 1944.
Stormcloud and Sunrise. London, Mills and Boon, 1945.
Journey for Two Travellers. London, Mills and Boon, 1946.
Mistress of the House. London, Mills and Boon, 1946; Toronto, Harlequin, 1966.
The Deep, Wide River. London, Mills and Boon, 1947.
The Opening Flower. London, Mills and Boon, 1948.
The Wayward Stream. London, Mills and Boon, 1949.
The Faithless Friend. London, Mills and Boon, 1949.
Captive Daughter. London, Mills and Boon, 1950.
The Dream and the Dancer. London, Mills and Boon, 1951; Toronto, Harlequin, 1965.
The Golden Peaks. London, Mills and Boon, 1951; Toronto, Harlequin, 1964.
The House by the Lake. London, Mills and Boon, 1952.
Magic Symphony. London, Mills and Boon, 1952; Toronto, Harlequin, 1966.
The Wings of Memory. London, Mills and Boon, 1953; Toronto, Harlequin, 1968.
The Young Intruder. London, Mills and Boon, 1953; Toronto, Harlequin, 1968.
A Home for Jocelyn. London, Mills and Boon, 1953; Toronto, Harlequin, 1967.
Song of Summer. London, Mills and Boon, 1954; as *Doctor's Orders*, Toronto, Harlequin, 1963.
Sister of the Housemaster. London, Mills and Boon, 1954; Toronto, Harlequin, 1965.
The Fortunes of Springfield. London, Mills and Boon, 1955; Toronto, Harlequin, 1967.
The Mist of Morning. London, Mills and Boon, 1955.
Secret Heiress. London, Mills and Boon, 1956; Toronto, Harlequin, 1967.
The Constant Heart. London, Mills and Boon, 1956; Toronto, Harlequin, 1968.
A Season of Enchantment. London, Mills and Boon, 1956.
The Way Through the Forest. London, Mills and Boon, 1957.

The Persistent Lover. London, Mills and Boon, 1957.
The Blessing in Disguise. London, Mills and Boon, 1958.
The Happy Enterprise. London, Mills and Boon, 1958; Toronto, Harlequin, 1959.
The Flight of the Swan. London, Mills and Boon, 1959; Toronto, Harlequin, 1969.
A Stronger Spell. London, Mills and Boon, 1959.
The Painted Ceiling. London, Mills and Boon, 1960.
The Red Cliffs. London, Mills and Boon, 1961; Toronto, Harlequin, 1969.
Lovers' Meeting. London, Mills and Boon, 1962.
A Change of Heart. London, Mills and Boon, 1963; as *Doctor Max*, Toronto, Harlequin, 1963.
The Tangled Web. London, Mills and Boon, 1963.
The Daring Deception. London, Mills and Boon, 1965.
The Pursuit and the Capture. London, Mills and Boon, 1966.
Loving and Giving. London, Mills and Boon, 1968.
The Rose and the Thorn. London, Mills and Boon, 1968.
Rubies for My Love. London, Mills and Boon, 1969.
The Doctor's Circle. London, Mills and Boon, 1970; Toronto, Harlequin, 1971.
The Enchanted Island. London, Mills and Boon, 1970; Toronto, Harlequin, 1971.
A Castle in Spain. London, Mills and Boon, 1971; Toronto, Harlequin, 1972.
A Serpent in Eden. London, Mills and Boon, 1971; Toronto, Harlequin, 1973.
The Valley of the Eagles. London, Mills and Boon, and Toronto, Harlequin, 1972.
The Shadow of Suspicion. London, Mills and Boon, 1972.
The Splendid Legacy. London, Mills and Boon, 1973; Toronto, Harlequin, 1974.
The Runaway Visitors. London, Mills and Boon, 1973; Toronto, Harlequin, 1974.
Homeward Bound. London, Mills and Boon, 1975.
This Golden Estate. London, Mills and Boon, 1975.
The Amaranth Flower. London, Mills and Boon, 1979.

*   *   *

Eleanor Farnes has been writing romance novels since the 1930's and has had over 60 published. Although she is an English writer, she has traveled widely in Europe, South Africa, and North America. She also spends part of each year in Spain where her family has a home.

Her novels reflect her intimate knowledge of the countries she writes about, and she is able to select just the right detail to make that country familiar to her readers. She is another writer who developed her writing skills by beginning with doctor/nurse novels. It was a productive apprenticeship, for she has a sensitive way of developing her characters and telling their stories.

One of her most effective novels is *A Castle in Spain*. Evocative as the title is, it sets the mood of the novel for it is one of her most tender love stories. Venetia Hamilton takes a motoring tour through Spain. She encounters car problems and is aided by Don Andres de Arevado. He arranges for her car to be repaired and also offers her the hospitality of his home. His cousin and her three daughters live there as well, so propriety is maintained.

From this somewhat ordinary start, Eleanor Farnes builds a lovely novel of misunderstood love as conflicting cultures hit head on. Venetia is an independent young woman, who revels in using her mind and abilities. She is not a forward person, but one who was taught from childhood to think for herself and to hold to her own beliefs. Her breezy freshness and strong streak of independence are not qualities that Don Andres wants his cousins exposed to. Almost from her first introduction to the family, she finds herself held up as a bad example, even when she is asked to stay and teach them English.

Eleanor Farnes develops the story from this point by letting Venetia and Don Andres react to each other as each tries to cling to their individual beliefs. Subtly Venetia is allowed to show Don Andres that far from being a disruptive influence, she is actually a warm, capable person with strong depths of feeling and love. Gradually they fall in love despite their cultural differences, and, step by step, Eleanor Farnes shows the changes in attitude of Don Andres as he realizes that he truly loves Venetia. He also realizes that her independence and initiative are qualities he can't help but acknowledge for they have made her into the kind of woman he can love.

In writing this particular story, Eleanor Farnes displays a sensitive understanding of today's young girls as they try to balance their own inner resources against the traditional limits of other people. At the same time, she makes it obvious that love is the strongest force in drawing two people together. The early antagonism between Venetia and Don Andres can only end in love as each grows to understand and respect the other.

In *The Runaway Visitors* Victoria Fenn must take her younger brother and sister to spend the summer with a family friend in Italy. She is a responsive girl who feels the awkwardness of the arrangement for her parents have made it a habit of "dumping" the family on unsuspecting friends and relatives for the summer, while they carry on research activities abroad. Charles Duncan's frequent mention of foundlings being dropped on other people's doorsteps merely adds to her embarrassment and makes her sensitive to other instances of slight.

In developing her heroines, Eleanor Farnes holds to more traditional characterization by having them young, innocent, and often unsure of themselves in an emotional situation. Even Venetia is unawakened to love for all of her abilities and independence. She is still naive in this situation but she does hold true to character by acknowledging the difficulties she must face if she gives into her love for Don Andres.

Her heroes are maturer and again traditional in the sense that they are more sophisticated than the heroine and more experienced in love and love affairs. Yet they have a certain degree of sensitivity to people that is not a standard characteristic in romance novels.

In assessing Eleanor Farnes as a romance writer, one might cite several popular clichés; for instance, she makes her characters live, or she tells a wonderful story. But she does far more than that: her readers not only enjoy her novels the first time around, they can not resist the urge to go back time and time again to re-read them. She is one of those romance writers who remain fresh, exciting and romantic no matter how often one reads her novels.

—Arlene Moore

FARNOL, (John) Jeffery. British. Born in Warwickshire, 10 February 1878. Educated privately; apprenticed briefly to a brass foundry in Birmingham; studied at Westminster School of Art. Married 1) Blanche V.W. Hawley in 1900 (divorced, 1938), one daughter; 2) Phyllis Clarke in 1938, one adopted daughter. Worked in his father's business; lived in the USA, 1902-10: scene painter, Astor Theatre, New York, for two years; lived in England after 1910. *Died 9 August 1952.*

ROMANCE AND GOTHIC PUBLICATIONS

Novels

    My Lady Caprice. London, Stevens and Brown, and New York, Dodd Mead, 1907; as
      The Chronicles of the Imp, London, Sampson Low, 1915.
    The Broad Highway. London, Sampson Low, 1910; Boston, Little Brown, 1911.
    The Money Moon. London, Sampson Low, and Boston, Little Brown, 1911.
    The Oubliette. London, Watt, 1912.
    The Amateur Gentleman. London, Sampson Low, and Boston, Little Brown, 1913.
    The Honourable Mr. Tawnish. London, Sampson Low, and Boston, Little Brown,
      1913.
    Beltane the Smith. London, Sampson Low, and Boston, Little Brown, 1915.
    The Definite Object. London, Sampson Low, and Boston, Little Brown, 1917.

Our Admirable Betty. London, Sampson Low, and Boston, Little Brown, 1918.
The Geste of Duke Jocelyn. London, Sampson Low, 1919; Boston, Little Brown, 1920.
Black Bartlemy's Treasure. London, Sampson Low, and Boston, Little Brown, 1920.
Martin Conisby's Vengeance. London, Sampson Low, and Boston, Little Brown, 1921.
Peregrine's Progress. London, Sampson Low, and Boston, Little Brown, 1922.
Sir John Dering. London, Sampson Low, and Boston, Little Brown, 1923.
The Loring Mystery. London, Sampson Low, and Boston, Little Brown, 1925.
The High Adventure. London, Sampson Low, and Boston, Little Brown, 1926.
The Quest of Youth. London, Sampson Low, and Boston, Little Brown, 1927.
Gyfford of Weare. London, Sampson Low, 1928; as *Guyfford of Weare*, Boston, Little
    Brown, 1928.
Over the Hills. London, Sampson Low, and Boston, Little Brown, 1930.
The Jade of Destiny. London, Sampson Low, 1931; as *A Jade of Destiny*, Boston, Little
    Brown, 1931.
Charmian, Lady Vibart. London, Sampson Low, and Boston, Little Brown, 1932.
The Way Beyond. London, Sampson Low, and Boston, Little Brown, 1933.
Winds of Fortune. London, Sampson Low, 1934; as *Winds of Chance*, Boston, Little
    Brown, 1934.
A Portrait of a Gentleman in Colours: The Romance of Mr. Lewis Berger. London,
    Sampson Low, 1935.
John o' the Green. London, Sampson Low, and Boston, Little Brown, 1935.
A Pageant of Victory. London, Sampson Low, and Boston, Little Brown, 1936.
The Crooked Furrow. London, Sampson Low, 1937; New York, Doubleday, 1938.
The Lonely Road. London, Sampson Low, and New York, Doubleday, 1938.
The Happy Harvest. London, Sampson Low, 1939; New York, Doubleday, 1940.
Adam Penfeather, Buccaneer. London, Sampson Low, 1940; New York, Doubleday,
    1941.
Murder by Nail. London, Sampson Low, 1942; as *Valley of Night*, New York, Double-
    day, 1942.
The King Liveth. London, Sampson Low, 1943; New York, Doubleday, 1944.
The "Piping Times." London, Sampson Low, 1945.
Heritage Perilous. London, Sampson Low, 1946; New York, McBride, 1947.
My Lord of Wrybourne. London, Sampson Low, 1948; as *Most Sacred of All*, New
    York, McBride, 1948.
The Fool Beloved. London, Sampson Low, 1949.
The Ninth Earl. London, Sampson Low, 1950.
The Glad Summer. London, Sampson Low, 1951.
Waif of the River. London, Sampson Low, 1952.
Justice by Midnight, completed by Phyllis Farnol. London, Sampson Low, 1956.

Short Stories

The Shadow and Other Stories. London, Sampson Low, and Boston, Little Brown,
    1929.
Voices from the Dust, Being Romances of Old London. London, Macmillan, and
    Boston, Little Brown, 1932.
A Matter of Business and Other Stories. London, Sampson Low, and Boston, Little
    Brown, 1940.

OTHER PUBLICATIONS

Play

The Honourable Mr. Tawnish, adaptation of his own novel (produced Manchester, 1920;
    London, 1924).

Other

Some War Impressions.   London, Sampson Low, 1918; as *Great Britain at War*, Boston,
    Little Brown, 1918.
Epics of the Fancy.   London, Sampson Low, 1928; as *Famous Prize Fights; or, Epics of
    "The Fancy,"* Boston, Little Brown, 1928.
Hove.   Privately printed, 1937.
A Book [New Book] for Jane (juvenile).   London, Sampson Low, 2 vols., 1937-39.

Critical Studies: *Jeffery Farnol*, Beaminster, Cox, 1964, and *More Memories of My Brother
Jack: Jeffery Farnol*, Beaminster, Cox, 1966, both by E.E. Farnol.

                         *   *   *

Jeffery Farnol provides a link between the major writers of the 19th-century and the
popular romancers of the present. While no one could call him a serious writer like Scott or
Dickens, one can easily note traces of both these writers in his works. The quaint lower-class
characters, the concern for social evils speak of Dickens; the heroes who were "out with the
Jacobites" look back to Scott. Yet the moral purpose of the earlier writers is lacking; the whole
cumbersome plot mechanism merely provides the opportunity to get two young people
together and let them get on with their own business.
    Even the formulas that Farnol uses are not really formulas; they are more like conventions in
which he felt comfortable letting his imagination work. For instance, the hero and heroine are
often disguised when they meet. Either he does not know who she is, so he can unwittingly
disparage her public persona (as in *John o' the Green*, where John tells the girl "Lia" that the
Duchess Ippolita's name " 'tis neigh of horse, 'tis sneeze, 'tis hiccough"); or she fails to recognize
that he is a member of the family of her hereditary enemies (Lady Joan Brandon in *Black
Bartlemy's Treasure*). She is usually quicker than he to realize the truth, however. Farnol's
women are slow only to realize that they are falling in love; other than that, they are
independent, intelligent, and only too likely to try to take control from the heroes when those
gentlemen are moving too slowly. In *The Money Moon*, however, a modern dress version of
Farnol's favorite tale, the hero recognizes what is happening sooner than Anthea; he is also the
one in disguise, and it is not until the end that she discovers he is really at once Prince Charming
and millionaire deus ex machine come to pay off the mortgage.
    What makes all this foolishness pleasant is Farnol's innocent enthusiasm. The whole-
heartedness with which his characters fall into and out of their scrapes and their insistence on
doing what they perceive of as the right thing are curiously endearing. Even the villainous Mr.
Dartry (in *The Lonely Road*) can have a change of heart when Jason reminds him of his
mother. It's sentimental, of course; but it is still reassuring, on some level. Even conventional
romances today do not guarantee quite this level of escapism.
    Farnol's prose may be too rich for the modern reader, but his crazy vehicles of plots do carry
the reader along willy-nilly, dialogues full of ellipses and dashes, fevered but chaste passions,
poetic descriptions of scenery, broadly rendered accents and all. At his best—in *The Crooked
Furrow* and *The Happy Harvest*—Farnol presents genuinely attractive characters in a model of
what a picaresque novel should be. That descendent of the Roundheads, Oliver, and his cousin,
the impulsive "cavalier" Roland, go off at the behest of their stern guardian uncle to find out
how well they can live on a guinea a week in an Arcadian Georgian England, where friendly
gypsies, honorable highwaymen, and faithful servants abound. Oliver, a complete romantic at
heart, adopts an abused child and helps his uncle find the wife he had mistakenly cast off years
before. But the beautiful heroine prefers Roland. Despite his broken heart, Oliver finds
comfort in the fact that he and Roland are finally reconciled, the friends their mothers hoped
they would become. And in the sequel Oliver's virtues find their reward. The little foundling,
grown to be a bewitching young woman, overcomes her fears about her unknown parentage
and Oliver's fears about the difference in their ages and her informal engagement to his other
ward, Robin. Clia redeems her promise at the end of *The Crooked Furrow* to marry Oliver
when she is old enough. Clia is not really one of Farnol's happiest women creations; she is
cloying as a child, and full of imperious wiles as an adult. Yet she's what Oliver wants and for

Oliver, through the third person narration of *The Crooked Furrow* and the rather stuffy first person narration of *The Happy Harvest*, one develops a fondness. Oliver's ward Robin, incidentally, decides that, despite his own love for Clia, the passion that she and Oliver share is so perfect that he cannot sully it with jealousy. Thus Farnol provides an all-round happy ending without the necessity of sketching a second female lead, always a chore for him (the tearful Angela in *Gyfford of Weare* is one example.)

Oliver and Roland find adventures, in both books, in the midst of the crime and poverty of London, which is relieved in part by the work of the ladies of "The Jolly Young Waterman," running the equivalent of a settlement house in a pub in the roughest part of the vast city. London is not present in all Farnol's books, except as an implicit contrast to the idyllic scenes of the southern English countryside. Urban criminals may be misguided louts; rural gypsies, complete with Romany vocabularies, are noble and charming, and cant-spouting highwaymen are helpful to the causes of right.

Farnol's ventures away from his favorite, though vaguely delineated, Regency period are not always happy; that adult fairy-tale without magic, *John o' the Green*, is set mistily "in King Tristan's day"; we are always aware of the disparity between modern life as we know it and the picture presented to us in *The Money Moon*. The linked short stories of *Voices from the Dust* follow the reincarnation of two lovers through English history; they vary from the entertaining ("White Friars") to the absurd ("The White Tower").

Ultimately, what Farnol brings to his chosen genre is the unusual viewpoint of a man writing for women. In Farnol's world women are beautiful but mysterious creatures, the repository of exalted ideals about family and sanctity. But his men never really understand them very well. Women can read his books with bemused condescension at how like children the men in his books are. Men can read his books with fellow feeling, and because there is always a share of fighting and swordplay. Contemporary romances are usually written either by a woman or from a woman's point of view; and they are read almost exclusively by women. Reading Farnol reminds us that this is not the way things have to be, and makes us wonder if something has been lost to us that we used to have.

—Susan Branch

FECHER, Constance.   *See* **HEAVEN, Constance**.

FELLOWS, Catherine.   Recipient: Romantic Novelists Association Netta Muskett Award, 1970. Address: c/o Hodder and Stoughton, Mill Road, Dunton Green, Sevenoaks, Kent TN13 2YA, England.

Novels

Leonora.   London, Hurst and Blackett, 1972; New York, Fawcett, 1974.
The Marriage Masque.   London, Hodder and Stoughton, and New York, Dell, 1974.
The Heywood Inheritance.   London, Hodder and Stoughton, 1975; as *The Love Match*, New York, Dell, 1977.
Vanessa.   New York, Dell, 1978.
Entanglement.   London, Hodder and Stoughton, and New York, Fawcett, 1979.

*   *   *

Catherine Fellows is one of the better imitators of Georgette Heyer. Most of these imitators have no problem creating the farcical elements, frenetic activity, and period trappings Heyer was known for. Fellows and Joan Smith, however, are able to accomplish the more difficult task of creating memorable characters while using stylish, witty, and precisely chosen language.

Leonora is her first novel. Her heroine knows a deep dark secret about the hero and spends a fair amount of time thinking he wants to marry her only to shut her up. The believability is marred by the heroine's unquestioning acceptance of the crime the hero committed. *The Marriage Masque* is excellent. A managing woman reconciles the hero to the daughter he despises, successfully steers her through her youthful romantic follies to a suitable marriage, and then arranges a marriage for herself. It is carried off with great style and humor. In *Vanessa* two sisters end up with desirable husbands after a farcical series of deceptions prompted by the hero's determination to find a woman who wants to marry him, not his wealth and position. *Entanglement* brings off two romances, both exceedingly unlikely, while incidentally thwarting a murderous plot against one of the heroes.

—Marylaine Block

FERBER, Edna.   American.   Born in Kalamazoo, Michigan, 15 August 1887. Educated at Ryan High School, Appleton, Wisconsin. Reporter for the Appleton *Daily Crescent* and, subsequently, for the *Milwaukee Journal* and *Chicago Tribune*, 1904-10; full-time writer from 1910; settled in New York; served as a War Correspondent for the United States Army Air Force during World War II. Recipient: Pulitzer Prize, 1924. Litt.D.: Columbia University, New York; Adelphi College, Garden City, New York. Member, American Academy. *Died 16 April 1968.*

Novels

Dawn O'Hara, The Girl Who Laughed.   New York, Stokes, 1911; London, Methuen, 1925.
Fanny Herself.   New York, Stokes, 1917; London, Methuen, 1923.
The Girls.   New York, Doubleday, 1921; London, Heinemann, 1922.

So Big. New York, Doubleday, and London, Heinemann, 1924.
Show Boat. New York, Doubleday, and London, Heinemann, 1926.
Cimarron. New York, Doubleday, and London, Heinemann, 1930.
American Beauty. New York, Doubleday, and London, Heinemann, 1931.
Come and Get It. New York, Doubleday, and London, Heinemann, 1935.
Nobody's in Town (includes *Trees Die at the Top*). New York, Doubleday, and London, Heinemann, 1938.
Saratoga Trunk. New York, Doubleday, 1941; London, Heinemann, 1942.
Great Son. New York, Doubleday, and London, Heinemann, 1945.
Giant. New York, Doubleday, and London, Gollancz, 1952.
Ice Palace. New York, Doubleday, and London, Gollancz, 1958.

Short Stories

Buttered Side Down. New York, Stokes, 1912; London, Methuen, 1926.
Roast Beef, Medium: The Business Adventures of Emma McChesney and Her Son, Jock. New York, Stokes, 1913; London, Methuen, 1920.
Personality Plus: Some Experiences of Emma McChesney and Her Son, Jock. New York, Stokes, 1914.
Emma McChesney & Co. New York, Stokes, 1915.
Cheerful, By Request. New York, Doubleday, 1918; London, Methuen, 1919.
Half Portions. New York, Doubleday, 1920.
Gigolo. New York, Doubleday, 1920; as *Among Those Present*, London, Nash and Grayson, 1923.
Mother Knows Best. New York, Doubleday, and London, Heinemann, 1927.
They Brought Their Women. New York, Doubleday, and London, Heinemann, 1933.
No Room at the Inn. New York, Doubleday, 1941.
One Basket: Thirty-One Stories. New York, Simon and Schuster, 1947.

OTHER PUBLICATIONS

Plays

Our Mrs. McChesney, with George V. Hobart (produced New York, 1915).
$1200 a Year, with Newman Levy. New York, Doubleday, 1920.
Minick, with George S. Kaufman, adaptation of the story "Old Man Minick" by Ferber (produced New York, 1924). Published as *Old Man Minick: A Short Story...Minick: A Play*, New York, Doubleday, 1924; London, Heinemann, 1925.
The Eldest: A Drama of American Life. New York, Appleton, 1925.
The Royal Family, with George S. Kaufman (produced New York, 1927). New York, Doubleday, 1928; as *Theatre Royal* (produced London, 1935), London, French, 1936.
Dinner at Eight, with George S. Kaufman (produced New York, 1932; London, 1933). New York, Doubleday, 1932; London, Heinemann, 1933.
Stage Door, with George S. Kaufman (produced New York, 1936; London, 1946). New York, Doubleday, 1936; London, Heinemann, 1937.
The Land Is Bright, with George S. Kaufman (produced New York, 1941). New York, Doubleday, 1941.
Bravo!, with George S. Kaufman (produced New York, 1948). New York, Dramatists Play Service, 1949.

Screenplay: *A Gay Old Dog*, 1919.

Other

A *Peculiar Treasure* (autobiography). New York, Doubleday, and London, Heinemann, 1939.
A *Kind of Magic* (autobiography). New York, Doubleday, and London, Gollancz,
1963.

Critical Study: *Women and Success in American Society in the Works of Edna Ferber* by Mary
Rose Shaughnessy, New York, Gordon Press, 1977.

*   *   *

Though she was also a successful short story writer and playwright, Edna Ferber's greatest
literary works are her novels in which she variously combines four major elements: intense and
often difficult love affairs; strong, able female protagonists; dramatic portraits of intriguing
American locales; and serious, if not always profound, examinations of American values. The
American Dream she dissects theoretically includes not only professional success and economic security but also genuine personal fulfillment within a successful marriage and applies to
women as well as to men.

In *Saratoga Trunk* Ferber creates tolerance for her tough, angry heroine, Clio Dulaine, a
stunning beauty of mixed blood, not only through Clio's decision to marry impecunious
gambler Clint Maroon for love but also by distancing Clio's story amid the garish "elegance" of
the racing set of the 1880's. Thus Clio and Clint become acceptable prototypes of Americans
who overcome class bias by exploiting their cleverness and guile, for they achieve the Dream.

But within the Ferber canon, Dream usually differs sharply from the gritty reality which she
depicts and which takes into account racial prejudice, class snobbery, and sexism. Few of her
heroines make happy, lasting marriages; professional success tends to be more attainable
largely because they can achieve it by themselves, by means of personal determination.

At times, Ferber hangs her crowded plots upon exciting historical hooks; *Cimarron* sweeps
from the Land Rush of 1899 into the 1920's attempting to encapsulate Oklahoma history.
Against this background, the marriage of Sabra and Yancey Cravat is both enlarged (they
symbolize divergent responses to frontier life) and diminished (place sometimes briefly overshadows character). *Ice Palace*, a family saga set in Alaska, capitalizes on characters' memories
of such early events as the Gold Rush as well as on the territory's thrust toward statehood, using
heroine Chris Storm's choice of a mate—dashing Outsider or stalwart Alaskan—to reflect
conflicting political and economic impulses. In *Giant* the love between cultured Leslie Benedict
and her brash husband, Bick, is threatened by tension between her more traditional values and
his pragmatic ones. Their personal conflict parallels the struggle between cattle and oil interests
in Texas. These stories are vigorous, brisk, and exciting, though the symbolism is a bit obvious.

Show Boat, Ferber's most famous novel, contrasts the pain in the lives of two pairs of
lovers—Julie and Steve, victims of miscegenation legislation, and Magnolia and Gaylord
Ravenal, victims of conflicting standards—to the glittering, romantic facade of river life.
Similarly, *So Big*, a Pulitzer Prize winner, undercuts the myth of idyllic farm life through the
account of Selina Peake's struggle to earn a living. Both novels touch upon the problems of
single motherhood.

While Ferber clearly depicts the tremendous power of passionate love, she generally demonstrates that romance alone is an inadequate basis for marriage; this theme united with her
examination of the American Dream results in worthy, vivid, compelling fiction.

—Jane S. Bakerman

FIELD, Rachel (Lyman). American. Born in New York City, 19 September 1894. Educated at Springfield High School; Radcliffe College, Cambridge, Massachusetts, 1914-18. Married Arthur Siegfried Pederson in 1935; one adopted daughter. Member of the editorial department, Famous Players-Lasky film company, Hollywood, 1918-23. Recipient: Drama League of America prize, 1918; American Library Association Newbery Medal, for children's book, 1930. *Died 15 March 1942.*

ROMANCE AND GOTHIC PUBLICATIONS

Novels

> *Time Out of Mind.* New York, Macmillan, 1935; London, Macmillan, 1937.
> *To See Ourselves*, with Arthur Pederson. New York, Macmillan, 1937; London, Collins, 1939.
> *All This and Heaven Too.* New York, Macmillan, 1938; London, Collins, 1939.
> *And Now Tomorrow.* New York, Macmillan, 1942; London, Collins, 1943.

Short Story

> *Christmas in London.* Privately printed, 1946.

OTHER PUBLICATIONS

Plays (juvenile)

> *Everygirl*, in *St. Nicholas* (New York), October 1913.
> *Three Pills in a Bottle* (produced Cambridge, Massachusetts, 1917; New York, 1923). Included in *Six Plays*, 1924.
> *Rise Up, Jennie Smith* (produced Cambridge, Massachusetts, 1918). New York, French, 1918.
> *Time Will Tell* (produced Cambridge, Massachusetts, 1920).
> *The Fifteenth Candle.* New York, French, 1921.
> *Six Plays* (includes *Cinderella Married, Three Pills in a Bottle, Columbine in Business, The Patchwork Quilt, Wisdom Teeth, Theories and Thumbs*). New York, Scribner, 1924; *The Patchwork Quilt* published in *One-Act Plays of Today*, edited by J.W. Marriott, London, Gollancz, 1928.
> *The Cross-Stitch Heart and Other Plays* (includes *Greasy Luck, The Nine Days' Queen, The Londonderry Air, At the Junction, Bargains in Cathay*). New York, Scribner, 1927.
> *Patchwork Plays* (includes *Polly Patchwork; Little Square-Toes; Miss Ant, Miss Grasshopper, and Mr. Cricket; Chimney Sweeps' Holiday; The Sentimental Scarecrow*), illustrated by the author. New York, Doubleday, 1930.
> *First Class Matter.* New York, French, 1936.
> *The Bad Penny.* New York, French, 1938.

Verse

> *The Pointed People: Verses and Silhouettes* (juvenile). New Haven, Connecticut, Yale University Press, and London, Oxford University Press, 1924.
> *An Alphabet for Boys and Girls.* New York, Doubleday, and London, Heinemann, 1926.

Taxis and Toadstools: Verses and Decorations (juvenile).   New York, Doubleday, and London, Heinemann, 1926.

A Little Book of Days (juvenile).   New York, Doubleday, and London, Heinemann, 1927.

Points East: Narratives of New England.   New York, Brewer and Warren, 1930.

A Circus Ground.   Washington, D.C., Winter Wheat Press, 1930.

Branches Green.   New York, Macmillan, 1934.

Fear Is the Thorn.   New York, Macmillan, 1936.

Christmas Time (juvenile).   New York, Macmillan, 1941.

Poems (juvenile).   New York, Macmillan, 1957.

Other (fiction for children)

Eliza and the Elves.   New York, Macmillan, 1926.

The Magic Pawnshop: A New Year's Eve Fantasy.   New York, Dutton, 1927; London, Dent, 1928.

Little Dog Toby.   New York, Macmillan, 1928.

Polly Patchwork.   New York, Doubleday, 1928.

Hitty, Her First Hundred Years.   New York, Macmillan, 1929; as *Hitty: The Life and Adventures of a Wooden Doll*, London, Routledge, 1932.

Pocket-Handkerchief Park.   New York, Doubleday, 1929.

Calico Bush.   New York, Macmillan, 1931; London, Collier Macmillan, 1966.

The Yellow Shop.   New York, Doubleday, 1931.

The Bird Began to Sing.   New York, Morrow, 1932.

Hepatica Hawkes.   New York, Macmillan, 1932.

Just Across the Street.   New York, Macmillan, 1933.

Susanna B. and William C.   New York, Morrow, 1934.

The Rachel Field Story Book (includes *The Yellow Shop, Pocket-Handkerchief Park, Polly Patchwork*).   New York, Doubleday, 1958; Kingswood, Surrey, World's Work, 1960.

Other

Fortune's Caravan, from translation by Marian Saunders of a work by Lily Jean-Javal.   New York, Morrow, 1933; London, Oxford University Press, 1935.

God's Pocket: The Story of Captain Samuel Hadlock, Junior, of the Cranberry Isles, Maine.   New York, Macmillan, 1934; London, Macmillan, 1937.

Ave Maria: An Interpretation from Walt Disney's "Fantasia" Inspired by the Music of Franz Schubert.   New York, Random House, 1940.

All Through the Night.   New York, Macmillan, 1940; London, Collins, 1954.

Prayer for a Child.   New York, Macmillan, 1944.

Editor, *The White Cat and Other Old French Fairy Tales*, by Marie Catherine d'Aulnoy.   New York, Macmillan, 1928.

Editor, *American Folk and Fairy Tales.*   New York and London, Scribner, 1929.

Editor, *People from Dickens: A Presentation of Leading Characters from the Books of Charles Dickens.*   New York and London, Scribner, 1935.

*   *   *

In August, 1847, Paris rocked with scandal: the brutal murder of the Duchesse de Praslin was in every headline, on every lip. It was a *cause célèbre* of the juiciest kind, involving as it did a ducal household, a handsome, mysterious governess, identified only as Mlle D., nine orphaned children, and all the titillation bloodied handprints and the Duc's botched suicide by arsenic could provide. Obviously, it was a scandalmonger's delight.

Nearly a century later, the great-niece by marriage of that scarlet lady, Mlle D., told her version of the famous affair in *All This and Heaven Too*, her most successful novel. The almost forgotten players in the 19th-century tragedy are warmed to life by the author's possibly partisan interest in the ancestress on whose tombstone she cracked nuts in her childhood. To Rachel Field, Henriette Deluzy-Desportes was a figure of family legend, not of suggestive headlines. She tells the story of a young governess unfortunate enough to find herself trapped between the unpredictable passions of the half-mad, vindictive Duchesse, and her estranged husband, the blondely Byronic Duc. The truth of the sad story will never now be known, and scarcely matters; but in its day the Praslin murder had an unexpected effect upon the fate of an entire nation, for the scandal helped to topple a shakey monarchy.

Henriette's life took a turn for the better when, hoping to leave notoriety behind, she left Europe to make a new life in America as a schoolmistress. Here she forged her link with the future when she married the novelist's great uncle the Rev. Henry M. Field, and became for her remaining, happier years, a respected if mildly quirky matron. The closing chapters of her life, and her relations with her husband's famous family (brother Cyrus laid the first Trans-Atlantic cable) are not as fascinating as the earlier, unhappy years—but such is life. In this novel, as in none of her others, Rachel Field created a fully rounded, flawed, but sympathetic character in Mlle D. Perhaps she and her great-aunt are each in the other's debt, one for her inspiration, the other for an impassioned defender.

—Joan McGrath

FINLEY, Glenna. American. Born in Puyallup, Washington, 12 June 1925. Educated at Stanford University, California, B.A. (cum laude) 1945; graduate study at University of Washington, Seattle, and Seattle Pacific University, 1957-60. Married Donald MacLeod Witte in 1951; one son. Announcer, KEVR Radio, Seattle, 1941-42; producer, N.B.C. International Division, New York, 1945-47; film librarian, "March of Time" newsreel series, New York, 1947-48; member of the news bureau staff, Time Inc., New York, 1948-49. Since 1957, free-lance writer. Agent: Ann Elmo Agency, 60 East 42nd Street, New York, New York 10017. Address: 2645 34th Avenue West, Seattle, Washington 98199, U.S.A.

ROMANCE AND GOTHIC PUBLICATIONS

Novels

    Death Strikes Out. New York, Arcadia House, 1957.
    Career Wife. New York, Arcadia House, 1964.
    Nurse Pro Tem. New York, Arcadia House, 1967.
    A Tycoon for Ann. New York, Lancer, 1968.
    Journey to Love. New York, New American Library, 1970; London, New English Library, 1977.
    Love's Hidden Fire. New York, New American Library, 1971.
    Treasure of the Heart. New York, New American Library, 1971.
    Love Lies North. New York, New American Library, 1972.
    Bridal Affair. New York, New American Library, 1972; London, New English Library, 1975.
    Kiss a Stranger. New York, New American Library, 1972.
    Love in Danger. New York, New American Library, 1973.

When Love Speaks. New York, New American Library, 1973.
The Romantic Spirit. New York, New American Library, 1973.
Surrender, My Love. New York, New American Library, 1974.
A Promising Affair. New York, New American Library, 1974.
Love's Magic Spell. New York, New American Library, 1974.
The Reluctant Maiden. New York, New American Library, 1975.
The Captured Heart. New York, New American Library, 1975.
Holiday for Love. New York, New American Library, 1976.
Love for a Rogue. New York, New American Library, 1976.
Storm of Desire. New York, New American Library, 1977.
Dare to Love. New York, New American Library, 1977.
To Catch a Bride. New York, New American Library, 1977.
Master of Love. New York, New American Library, 1978.
Beware My Heart. New York, New American Library, 1978.
The Marriage Merger. New York, New American Library, 1978.
Wildfire of Love. New York, New American Library, 1979.
Timed for Love. New York, New American Library, 1979.
Love's Temptation. New York, New American Library, 1979.
Stateroom for Two. New York, New American Library, 1980.
Affairs of Love. New York, New American Library, 1980.
Midnight Encounter. New York, New American Library, 1981.
Return Engagement. New York, New American Library, 1981.
One Way to Love. New York, New American Library, 1982.

Glenna Finley comments:

A good romance novel should contain attractive characters, have a carefully researched locale, and offer a plausible plot—but most of all I think it must be fun to read. In other words, after the reader has paid for the book—all suffering should cease!

*   *   *

Glenna Finley wants to be a romantic writer. Her continual implausible chance incidents, superficial characterizations, and mid-stream alteration of style prevent her from reaching her goal. Infrequently, the reader notices a striving for sustenance with attempts at historical references and psychological descriptions, too minor to be credible amidst the loosely constructed events. Complications stem from obvious improbabilities, aleatory cirumstances. Excitement is secondary to the attire of the heroine and hero.

Even though Finley has worked in business, she displays sparse knowledge of the business woman mentality, covering this inadequacy by depicting the women as mere flesh for a wearing-apparel exhibition. For example, in *Beware My Heart* she attempts to create an energetic, intelligent business woman through the responsiveness of Cristina Kelly, assistant hotel manager and, at least in the opening pages, introduces her with a margin of verve. But this limited formidability is quick-lived and she soon succumbs to the Finley female portraiture, wholly manipulable. The action is halted with exasperating longeurs devoted to detailed descriptions of "camel-colored slacks and matching open-throated silk shirts cut low at the neckline" to complement her figure.

Minor characters are bovine; major ones belong to a world of affluence and power (for who else could purchase the Diors?). Although typically Finley attempts to present characters of contrast, what is illuminated instead is assuredness and haughty egoism versus even more assuredness and haughtier egoism. The point of view, with only a few exceptions, is that of the heroine. In *Dilemma of the Heart*, as with the majority of Finley's novels, the heroine is wealthy or potentially wealthy due to an inheritance; she is matched with a too-good-to-be-true hero. These characters, however, are tedious; they lack depth; their dialogue is mechanical and easily anticipated by the reader. She attempts to inject humor into the monologues of the heroines but it is always ill-placed, a phrase tacked on here and there. Indeed her settings lack individuality:

the chalet in one novel has the same decor as the chalet in another novel. Physical descriptions of characters are often too reminiscent of characters from her other books.

The detractions are too numerous to give stylistic integrity and cohesiveness to her work. Even at her best, Finley never achieves the writing of a solid romance novel for which she strives.

—W.M. von Zharen

FITZGERALD, Julia. Pseudonym for Julia Watson; also writes as Jane de Vere; Julia Hamilton. British. Born in Bangor, North Wales, 18 September 1943. Educated at Elland Grammar School, and Huddersfield College of Art, both Yorkshire. Married and divorced twice; one daughter and one son. Has worked as an artist, jewelry designer, model, and historical adviser to Sphere Books. Address: 4 Lansdowne Grove, Hough Green, Chester, Cheshire CH4 8LD, England.

ROMANCE AND GOTHIC PUBLICATIONS

Novels

The Scarlet Women (as Jane de Vere). London, Corgi, 1969.
Royal Slave. London, Futura, and New York, Ballantine, 1978.
Scarlet Woman. London, Futura, 1979; New York, Nordon, 1981.
Slave Lady. London, Futura, 1980.
Salamander. London, Futura, 1981.
Fallen Woman. London, Futura, 1981.
Venus Rising. London, Futura, 1982.
The Princess and the Pagan. London, Futura, 1982.

Novels as Julia Watson

The Lovechild. London, Hale, 1967; New York, Bantam, 1968.
Medici Mistress. London, Futura, 1968.
The Gentian Trilogy:
   A Mistress for the Valois. London, Hale, 1969.
   The King's Mistress. London, Corgi, 1970.
   The Wolf and the Unicorn. London, Corgi, 1971.
Winter of the Witch. London, Corgi, 1971; New York, Bantam, 1972.
The Tudor Rose. London, Hale, 1972.
Saffron. London, Corgi, 1972.
Love Song. London, Futura, 1981.

Novels as Julia Hamilton

The Last of the Tudors. London, Hale, 1971.

Katherine of Aragon. London, Sphere, and New York, Beagle, 1972; as *Katherine the Tragic Tudor*, London, Hale, 1974.
Anne of Cleves. London, Sphere, and New York, Beagle, 1972.
Son of York. London, Sphere, 1973.
Habsburg series:
The Changeling Queen. London, Hale, 1977.
The Emperor's Daughter. London, Hale, 1978.
The Pearl of the Habsburgs. London, Hale, 1978.
The Snow Queen. London, Hale, 1978.
The Habsburg Inheritance. London, Hale, 1980.

Julia Fitzgerald comments:

"Live dangerously in print" is my motto for today's women readers who are so often tied down by both jobs and families. The passionate, epic love stories that I create are a feast which won't make my readers overweight and which won't have any unpleasant repercussions (unless the dinner's allowed to burn while they're being read). I believe implicitly in love, that it is everything, that it can conquer all, that life would be empty and meaningless without it; and this is also the opinion of my strong-minded, spirited, and undaunted heroines—although my heroes take a little longer to be persuaded! Despite trials and adversities, my heroes and heroines find they can't live without one another, which is exactly the point of love, in my opinion. They are also sensual characters with strong appetites for each other, whose love story is played out against an authentic deeply researched background. Turkey, Venice, London, Dublin and Tipperary, Algiers, Yorkshire, Liverpool, and Greece are just some of the settings featured in my books. Pirates, sultans, pashas, renegades, princes, dukes, kings and queens, magicians, astrologers, and royal intriguers feature among my characters, as do ladies of fashion, courtesans, gypsies, daughters of dukes, and wilful heiresses.

*   *   *

Julia Fitzgerald, though also well-known for the historical romances that she has written under her real name, Julia Watson, and her other pseudonyms, Julia Hamilton and Jane de Vere, is perhaps best known for the Troubadour Historical Romance series that she began in 1978 with the best-selling *Royal Slave*. In these dramatic and colourful novels the heroines are forced to undergo adventure, degradation, and danger—often at the hands of the man they love—from which they emerge, emotionally and physically unscathed, in the end. They are strong-willed and high-spirited women, without any trace of prudery: they are eager to abandon themselves to sexual passion when in love, yet they are determined to preserve their self-pride. Men can crush their stays, but never their integrity. Crush their stays men do: mutual sexual desire and brutish male lust dominate Fitzgerald's novels, allowing her to place her heroines in graphically described situations of overwhelming, almost spiritual passion (Kitty McDonagh's love-making with Carrick in *Venus Rising*) and of utter humiliation (Cassia Morbilly's treatment in the slave-markets of Constantinople in *Royal Slave*).

The need of men to conquer women, be it by love or by force, is strong in Fitzgerald's novels; sado-masochistic leanings permeate even the most tender love-making, where orgasms are described as "cataclysmic," making love as "blissful torture." Time and again, the heroines fall prey to selfish and violent men, intent on satisfying their every sexual impulse. Given the unrelieved unscrupulousness of many of the male characters, it is surprising that the heroines manage to maintain their utter belief in the powers of love. In *Royal Slave*, the 17th-century Cornish Cassia is captured by slave-pirates at the very moment she is being raped by her villainous fiancé. Rescued from being raped yet again, this time by pirates, Cassia proceeds to fall in love with her saviour/captor, the slave-ship's captain, Vincent de Sauvage, and he with her. But Vincent, deeply wounded by previous unhappy emotional involvements, insists on denying his love for her, and on carrying out his plan to sell her to a Sultan's harem. Before he can do so, however, she is kidnapped by Vincent's sexually perverted, scaly-skinned rival, Nathan Dash. When Dash tries to assault her, Cassia strikes out at him with a knife, and she is thrown into the ship's hold with the rest of the women slaves. Sold into a harem, she soon becomes the Sultan's favorite concubine. But after a passionate night spent with Vincent, who bribes his way into the harem to see her, she is tied into a sack and thrown into the Bosphorus at the Sultan's command. On the point of drowning, she is rescued by an English Earl, who imprisons her in his island villa, and plans to use her for his own, diabolic sexual ends. However, at the last minute a reformed Vincent rescues her, and they ride off into the sunset towards marriage and domesticity back home.

Highly dramatic, somewhat titillating plots such as these are offset against detailed historical backgrounds that encompass both the luxury and decadence of the very rich, and the hardships of the destitute. Though one could accuse the author of over-romanticism in her main characters (the women are all young and exceptionally beautiful, the heroes fiery, macho, "god-like" beings), the worlds that they inhabit are nothing if not grim: we are first introduced to 10-year-old Meggie Blunt, the heroine of *Scarlet Woman*, as she crouches in a curtained-off corner of a rat-infested slum where her violent drunken father is raping her ailing mother. After her mother's death, Meggie tries valiantly to make a "respectable" living, but soon discovers that child prostitution is her only means of survival. Similarly, Kitty, the heroine of *Venus Rising*, witnesses the death by famine of her entire family, and is forced into beggary before being adopted by her "Lord Protector" and subsequent lover. Poverty, hunger and hopelessness are all vividly illustrated, as is the invidious position of women forced into prostitution in order to survive in an inhumane world. Fitzgerald is at her strongest when describing scenes such as the brothel in *Slave Lady* or the 19th-century slums of *Scarlet Woman*, at her weakest in writing dialogue for her heroines. However, despite their slightly dated plots, her epic novels are interesting and well-crafted, packed with incidents and anecdotes which, though sometimes not integral to the stories, certainly make for a "good read."

—Judith Summers

FITZGERALD, Valerie.   Brought up in India. Married. Lives in Canada. Recipient: Georgette Heyer Award, 1981. Address: c/o Bodley Head Ltd., 9 Bow Street, London WC2E 7AL, England.

ROMANCE AND GOTHIC PUBLICATIONS

Novel

Zemindar.   London, Bodley Head, 1981.

*   *   *

Valerie Fitzgerald's sprawling but adroitly executed first novel, *Zemindar*, deservedly won the 1981 Georgette Heyer Historical Novel Award. It is a romantic story of unusual discernment, set against the dramatic background of India during the 1857 Mutiny. The plot is a traditional one, with the heroine (Laura) becoming involved in hazardous exploits and, in the process, discovering truths about herself and her feelings for the hero (Oliver).

The novel's strong strand of romance is enhanced by the vivid realism in which this is rooted, and from which it flowers. *Zemindar's* refulgent descriptions of the Indian natural scene and its conveyance of life in the villages and bazaars are authoritative and compelling. They arise from the author's personal memories of growing up in India on a zemindari estate similar to that which is featured in the book, and there is throughout a feeling for the "real India" which so deeply appeals to both Laura and Oliver. As the zemindar (landowner) of a vast estate, Oliver has a passionate sense of responsibility for his land and his people. He is a believable and fleshed-out character, although it is amusing to trace in his contradictory moods of glinting appeal and brooding arrogance a combination of certain characteristics of Heathcliff and Darcy. Valerie Fitzgerald, as an "euthusiastic Austen-ite," acknowledges the possible influence of Jane Austen in her work, if not that of Emily Brontë. Her own heroine is able to demolish social hypocrisies with something of Elizabeth Bennet's wit and economy of style. Laura is both reflective and robust: she reads Marcus Aurelius for pleasure, studies Urdu as part of her effort to understand the real nature of India, but also learns how to handle a revolver to protect herself against the possible "ultimate outrage."

Despite its length of almost 800 pages, *Zemindar* sustains its romantic interest and suspense until the end. In the convention of romantic fiction, the author manages to keep the couple at arm's length until the book's later stages. She does this convincingly by making the first frightening eruptions of the Mutiny curtail Laura's stay at the zemindari estate. It is only after a series of terrifying happenings that Laura, caught up in the five-month siege of Lucknow, discovers the true quality of her feelings for Oliver.

In this satisfying first novel Valerie Fitzgerald illustrates her capacity to present the panoramic as well as an intimate view of events; she knows, too, exactly when to use succinctness in the expression of human emotions, and—most of all—when and how to harness the lusher images of romance.

—Mary Cadogan

FORD, Elbur.   *See* HOLT, Victoria.

FORD, Elizabeth.   *See* GIBBS, Mary Ann.

FRANKAU, Gilbert. British. Born in London, 21 April 1884; son of the writer Julia Davis Frankau (i.e., Frank Danby). Educated at Eton College. Served in the 9th East Surrey Regiment, 1914; transferred to the Royal Field Artillery; Adjutant to the 107th Brigade; invalided out, 1918: Captain; recommissioned in 1939; invalided out, 1941: Squadron Leader. Married 1) Dorothea Frances Black in 1905 (divorced), two daughters, including the writer Pamela Frankau; 2) Aimée de Burgh in 1922 (divorced); 3) Susan Lorna Harris in 1932. Joined his father's wholesale cigar business in 1904: managing director; full-time writer after World War I: Editor, *Britannia*, 1928. *Died 4 November 1952.*

ROMANCE AND GOTHIC PUBLICATIONS

Novels

> *The Woman of the Horizon: A Romance of Nineteen-Thirteen.* London, Chatto and Windus, 1917; New York, Century, 1923.
> *Peter Jackson, Cigar Merchant: A Romance of Married Life.* London, Hutchinson, 1920; as *Peter Jameson: A Modern Romance*, New York, Knopf, 1920.
> *The Seeds of Enchantment.* London, Hutchinson, and New York, Doubleday, 1921.
> *The Love-Story of Aliette Brunton.* London, Hutchinson, and New York, Century, 1922.
> *Gerald Cranston's Lady: A Romance.* London, Hutchinson, and New York, Century, 1924.
> *Life—and Erica: A Romance.* New York, Century, 1924; London, Hutchinson, 1925.
> *Masterson: A Study of an English Gentleman.* London, Hutchinson, and New York, Harper, 1926.
> *So Much Good.* London, Hutchinson, and New York, Harper, 1928.
> *Dance, Little Gentleman!* London, Hutchinson, 1929; New York, Harper, 1930.
> *Martin Make-Believe: A Romance.* London, Hutchinson, 1930; New York, Harper, 1931.
> *Christopher Strong: A Romance.* London, Hutchinson, and New York, Dutton, 1932.
> *The Lonely Man: A Romance of Love and the Secret Service.* London, Hutchinson, 1932; New York, Dutton, 1933.
> *Everywoman.* New York, Dutton, 1933; London, Hutchinson, 1934.
> *Three Englishmen: A Romance of Married Lives.* London, Hutchinson, and New York, Dutton, 1935.
> *Farewell Romance.* London, Hutchinson, and New York, Dutton, 1936.
> *The Dangerous Years: A Trilogy.* London, Hutchinson, 1937; New York, Dutton, 1938.
> *Royal Regiment: A Drama of Contemporary Behaviours.* London, Hutchinson, 1938; New York, Dutton, 1939.
> *Winter of Discontent.* London, Hutchinson, 1941; as *Air Ministry, Room 28*, New York, Dutton, 1942.
> *World Without End.* London, Hutchinson, and New York, Dutton, 1943.
> *Michael's Wife.* London, Macdonald, and New York, Dutton, 1948.
> *Son of the Morning.* London, Macdonald, 1949.
> *Oliver Trenton, K.C.* London, Macdonald, 1951.
> *Unborn Tomorrow: A Last Story.* London, Macdonald, 1953.

Short Stories

> *Men, Maids, and Mustard-Pot: A Collection of Tales.* London, Hutchinson, 1923; New York, Century, 1924.
> *Twelve Tales.* London, Hutchinson, 1927.
> *The House Behind the Judas Tree*, with *Martyrdom* by Warwick Deeping and *Forbidden Music* by Ethel Mannin. London, Readers Library, 1929; as *Three Stories of Romance*, 1936.

Concerning Peter Jackson and Others. London, Hutchinson, 1931.
Wine, Women, and Waiters. London, Hutchinson, 1932.
Secret Services. London, Hutchinson, 1934.
Experiments in Crime and Other Stories. London, Hutchinson, and New York, Dutton, 1937.
Escape to Yesterday: A Miscellany of Tales. London, Hutchinson, 1942.

OTHER PUBLICATIONS

Verse

Eton Echoes: A Volume of Humorous Verse. Eton, G. New, 1901.
The XYZ of Bridge. London, King, 1906.
One of Us: A Novel in Verse. London, Chatto and Windus, 1912; as *Jack—One of Us*, New York, Doran, 1912.
"Tid' apa" (What Does It Matter?). New York, Huebsch, 1914; London, Chatto and Windus, 1915.
The Guns. London, Chatto and Windus, 1916; as *A Song of the Guns*, Boston, Houghton Mifflin, 1916; as *A Song of the Guns in Flanders*, New York, Federal, 1916.
How Rifleman Brown Came to Valhalla. New York, Federal, 1916.
The City of Fear and Other Poems. London, Chatto and Windus, 1917.
One of Them: A Novelette in Verse. London, Hutchinson, 1918.
The Judgement of Valhalla. London, Chatto and Windus, and New York, Federal, 1918.
The Other Side and Other Poems. New York, Knopf, 1918.
The Poetical Works of Gilbert Frankau. London, Chatto and Windus, 2 vols., 1923.
More of Us, Being the Present-Day Adventures of "One of Us": A Novel in Verse. London, Hutchinson, and New York, Dutton, 1937.
Selected Verses. London, Macdonald, 1943.

Other

The Dominant Type of Man. London, Dorland Agency, 1925.
My Unsentimental Journey. London, Hutchinson, 1926.
Gilbert Frankau's Self-Portrait: A Novel of His Own Life. London, Hutchinson, and New York, Dutton, 1940.

Editor, *A Century of Love Stories.* London, Hutchinson, 1935.

*   *   *

The novels of Gilbert Frankau are almost unreadable outside the context of his times. He was deeply concerned with the place in society, still far from being determined, of "the Modern Woman" of the 1920's and 1930's. The reader must constantly readjust contemporary assumptions to the confinements of a day, not so very distant in time, but incredibly so in flavour, in which even persons in circumstances far from affluent had *such* problems with their servants' upstart independent ideas; when for a woman, as now in an odd reversal for a man, cutting or not cutting one's hair was a "statement" of sorts; when it was a daring step for any young woman to attempt to earn a living outside the home or to live apart from her family; and above all, at a time when iron divorce laws could still crush the lives of those unhappy enough to fall afoul of them, as Frankau himself did.

His Bright Young Things, with their snappy conversations, affectations, and nicknames, are all so impossibly dated now that it will require at least another generation before their true charm will begin to reveal itself to the literary researcher's penetratingly anthropological eye. For the present, they are simply too tediously outdated to be readable, not yet antique enough to have attained the period charm of, for example, Regency chit-chat, which was equally as slangy and colloquial.

Above all, Frankau was a product of an age in which the double standard of sexual morality was in fullest flower, and he spends a good deal of time and thought on the exploration of this theme. He appears to accept the premise without question, while deploring the damaging results upon mere fallible human beings unable to uphold unrealistic standards of conduct. Mildly daring in their day, his are the works of a man strictly of his time and milieu—and both have passed.

—Joan McGrath

FRANKEN, Rose (Dorothy, née Lewin). Also writes as Margaret Grant; Franken Meloney. American. Born in Texas, 28 December 1895. Educated at Ethical Culture School, New York. Married 1) S.W.A. Franken in 1914 (died, 1932), three sons; 2) William Brown Meloney in 1937 (died, 1970). Address: 5026 Arlington Avenue, Riverdale, New York, U.S.A.

ROMANCE AND GOTHIC PUBLICATIONS

Novels

> *Pattern.* New York, Scribner, 1925.
> *Twice Born.* New York, Scribner, 1935; London, W.H. Allen, 1969.
> *Call Back Love* (as Margaret Grant, with W.B. Meloney). New York, Farrar and Rinehart, 1937.
> *Of Great Riches.* New York, Longman, 1937; as *Gold Pennies*, London, Constable, 1938.
> *Claudia: The Story of a Marriage.* New York, Farrar and Rinehart, 1939; London, W.H. Allen, 1946.
> *Claudia and David.* New York, Farrar and Rinehart, 1940.
> *Another Claudia.* New York, Farrar and Rinehart, 1943; London, W.H. Allen, 1946.
> *Young Claudia.* New York, Rinehart, 1946; London, W.H. Allen, 1947.
> *The Marriage of Claudia.* New York, Rinehart, and London, W.H. Allen, 1948.
> *From Claudia to David.* London, W.H. Allen, 1949; New York, Harper, 1950.
> *The Fragile Years.* New York, Doubleday, 1952; as *Those Fragile Years*, London, W.H. Allen, 1952; as *The Return of Claudia*, London, W.H. Allen, 1957.
> *Rendezvous.* New York, Doubleday, 1954; as *The Quiet Heart*, London, W.H. Allen, 1954.
> *Intimate Story.* New York, Doubleday, and London, W.H. Allen, 1955.
> *The Antic Years.* New York, Doubleday, 1958.

Novels as Franken Meloney (with W.B. Meloney)

> *Strange Victory.* New York, Farrar and Rinehart, 1939.
> *When Doctors Disagree.* New York, Farrar and Rinehart, 1940.
> *American Bred.* New York, Farrar and Rinehart, 1941.

Uncollected Short Stories

"Beloved Stranger," in *Good Housekeeping* (New York), February 1945.
"What Dreams May Come," in *Good Housekeeping* (New York), April 1945.
"Heaven," in *Lady's Pleasure*.   Philadelphia, Penn, 1946.

OTHER PUBLICATIONS

Plays

Another Language (produced New York and London, 1932).   New York, French, 1932.
Mr. Dooley, Jr. (juvenile), with Jane Lewin.   New York, French, 1932.
Claudia, adaptation of her own novel (produced New York, 1941; London, 1942).   New York, Farrar and Rinehart, 1941.
Outrageous Fortune (produced New York, 1943).   New York, French, 1944.
Doctors Disagree, adaptation of her own novel *When Doctors Disagree* (produced New York, 1943).
Soldier's Wife (produced New York, 1944; London, 1946).   New York, French, 1945.
The Hallams (produced New York, 1948).   New York, French, 1948.

Screenplays: *Alias Mary Dow*, 1935; *Beloved Enemy*, with John Balderston and William Brown Meloney, 1936; *Made for Each Other*, with Jo Swerling, 1939; *Claudia and David*, with William Brown Meloney and Vera Caspary, 1946; *The Secret Heart*, with others, 1946.

Other

When All Is Said and Done (autobiography).   London, W.H. Allen, 1962; New York, Doubleday, 1963.
You're Well Out of Hospital.   London, W.H. Allen, and New York, Doubleday, 1966.

*   *   *

Once upon a time—not all that long ago—a story of young, innocent love won the hearts of a nation. Within the charmed circle of Claudia's wedding ring, it seemed, were contained all the warmth and love, the ideals, hopes, and virtues, of a country in the flower of its youth and promise. Claudia and her David embodied innocence. It was one of Claudia's greatest charms in her husband's eyes, as well as her mother's and (all too obviously) her creator's, that she *was* such an innocent. Married practically out of the schoolroom, to a young man she regarded as being mature and worldly, but who was in fact only twenty-five, the child-bride was launched upon a career of wedded bliss that was to last for nine volumes, in magazine serials, on stage and screen, on radio and television, and in translations all over the world. Plainly the world adored Claudia, through episode after episode. Rose Franken believed that it was a woman's perception of a love story that carried the emotional wallop, and wrote accordingly, on and on and on; apparently the world agreed with her.

Sadly, to return to Claudia's world decades later is to find it a tarnished paradise. The youth of the central characters excuses much, but not all of their smugness, their comfortable wealth that sees itself as straitened circumstances, and their self-consciously "special" carryings-on. It was only to be expected, in Claudia's world, for example, that everyone would adore the young bride, and that domestic servants would gladly set aside their own lives to provide a comfortable background for hers and David's. It is quite impossible now to take seriously this sweetly two-dimensional creation once glowingly described as "one of the classical characters of American literature."

Rose Franken wrote in a style that belonged to the golden era of serialization for magazines with enormous mass circulation—most of them now dead and gone. She wrote prolifically, at great speed, without rereading, let alone rewriting, and it shows. Times and tastes have changed. Even her more "hard-hitting" works, daring in their day (*Twice Born* dared to hint at the existence and problems of homosexuality) have long been overtaken and forgotten. Rose Franken was an author who spoke clearly and compellingly to a particular, specific audience; the lonely service wives of the Second World War, who waited anxiously for their men to return. Their gallantly held ideals of home and fireside, their special war-born reverence for a threatened way of life, lent Franken's work an enormous popularity; but today, *Claudia*, the once so dearly beloved, has faded to a footnote in the history of American popular literature.

—Joan McGrath

FRASER, Jane.   *See* **PILCHER, Rosamunde**.

FREEMAN, Cynthia.   Pseudonym for Bea Feinberg.   American.   Born in New York City. Educated at the University of California, Berkeley. Married; one son and one daughter. Has worked as an interior designer. Address: c/o Arbor House Publishing Company, 235 East 45th Street, New York, New York 10017, U.S.A.

ROMANCE AND GOTHIC PUBLICATIONS

Novels

> *A World Full of Strangers*.   New York, Arbor House, 1975; London, Corgi, 1976.
> *Fairytales*.   New York, Arbor House, 1977; London, Bantam, 1978.
> *The Days of Winter*.   New York, Arbor House, 1978; London, Corgi, 1979.
> *Portraits*.   New York, Arbor House, 1979; Loughton, Essex, Piatkus, 1980.
> *Come Pour the Wine*.   New York, Bantam, and Loughton, Essex, Piatkus, 1981.
> *No Time for Tears*.   New York, Arbor House, 1981.

*   *   *

Romance is always a strong element in Cynthia Freeman's novels, though these fall into the category of the family saga as well as the love story, and their main concerns are with root-seeking and power. However, her most recent novel, *Come Pour the Wine*, is entirely in the romantic tradition.

Freeman's books tend to have the flavour of travelogues through place and time with action ranging through diversely colourful settings (from Polish ghetto to Californian expansiveness, for example, in *Portraits*), as well as through several generations. The author occasionally over-indulges her vivid feeling for place, though often she skilfully harnesses it to accentuate the moods of her characters and the impact of events.

Several of the novels have backgrounds of displacement and disorientation (*A World Full of Strangers*, *Fairytales*, *Portraits*), and immigrant characters who are engaged in seeking social identity and racial roots. Their approach to this is romantic rather than realistic, but nevertheless compelling. It is *Portraits*, her four-generational chronicle of a Jewish immigrant family, that most clearly illustrates Freeman's storytelling skill, through its intense and well-realized relationships, and her characters' convincing struggles to cling to their spiritual heritage in an alien environment.

Perversely, this passionate identification with a specific racial group that gives *Portraits* its vitality produces a serious flaw in her more conventional love story, *Come Pour the Wine*. Allan, a middle-aged Jewish hero, is rather artificially introduced during the book's later stages in order to give heroine Janet the deep and sensitive love that her gentile husband, Bill, lacks the maturity to provide. Bill's inadequacies are carefully rehearsed but—though this is almost certainly not the author's intention—despite his shortcomings he still emerges as a more appealing character than Allan. Janet, however, eventually settles for the duller but more determined of the two men. (Her pairing off with Allan is a literary let-down similar to that produced by Louisa Alcott in *Little Women*, when she made Jo reject lively handsome Laurie for the protective but prosaic Professor Bhaer.)

Apart from this weakness of plot, *Come Pour the Wine* represents the romantic story at its most persuasive. The action unfolds believably from the viewpoint of the intelligent heroine; the "will-he, won't he" themes, although repetitive and lengthy, are enlivened by Freeman's capacity to get beneath the skin of her characters, and to enlist her readers' sympathy for their inadequacies and approbation of their strengths.

—Mary Cadogan

FRENCH, Ashley.   *See* **ROBINS, Denise**.

GALLAGHER, Patricia (née Bienek).   American.   Born in Lockhart, Texas. Attended Trinity University, San Antonio, Texas, 1951. Married James D. Gallagher (died, 1966); one son. Staff member, KTSA Radio, San Antonio, 1950-51. Agent: Scott Meredith Literary Agency, 845 Third Avenue, New York, New York 10022, U.S.A.

Novels

The Sons and the Daughters. New York, Messner, and London, Muller, 1961.
Answer to Heaven. London, Muller, 1962; New York, Avon, 1964.
The Fires of Brimstone. New York, Avon, 1966.
Shannon. New York, Avon, 1967.
Shadows of Passion. New York, Avon, 1971.
Summer of Sighs. New York, Avon, 1971.
The Thicket. New York, Avon, 1973.
Castles in the Air. New York, Avon, 1976.
Mystic Rose. New York, Avon, 1977; Feltham, Middlesex, Hamlyn, 1978.
No Greater Love. New York, Avon, 1979.
All for Love. New York, Avon, 1981.

*   *   *

Patricia Gallagher is a romance novelist who employs the conventions of the genre for unusual goals. This generalization is appropriate to any of her novels (compared to many of her contemporaries she has not written a great deal); it is particularly apt of *Castles in the Air*, her most famous, most popular, work.

Suspend expectation. Devon Marshall, the heroine, does not pursue the hero; he pursues her—and "gets her" within the first 20 pages, in less than exalted circumstances. Devon is a penniless refugee from post-Civil War Virginia, trying to make her way north; she has worked for her father, a newspaper proprietor, before his death; she hopes to get work as a journalist in New York City. Keith, a wealthy Wall Street banker, allows her to stow away in his private railway car, then demands recompense: he rapes her. Ms. Gallagher doesn't mince her scenes. That this one seems credible is a compliment to her powers in conveying the desperation of the times; that she causes both Devon and the reader to subsequently care for, then admire, Keith is a credit to the breadth of her sympathies, her cunning in conveying his own desperation, and her view of the contrariness of human life. Keith loves at first sight, but he is trapped in a hopeless and in some ways despicable marriage by society, his position, and his own conscience. After her initial resistance, Devon and Keith become lovers—passionate, selfless, honorable adulterers; they produce a son, live in the second home that Keith provides for them, then, in the end, after 5 years, part when it becomes apparent that Keith's now half-crazed wife will never release him or conveniently die. They part at Devon's instigation: she agrees to marry a man she does not love, gives up the man and child she does love, and prepares to go live with her new husband half a continent away. A story that begins with a violent passion, then deals with its refinement, ends with its defeat. And lest the reader console himself that Devon may "find happiness" after the last page—that expectation is firmly squelched, as the novel ends, in Devon's dreams, fevered, horrible dreams of the world to which she has exiled herself.

The novel provokes respect. Not only for this vision of the destruction of happy and fulfilling love by society but also for its undoubted expertise as a novel—in its construction, in its handling of time, and in its characterizations. Ms. Gallagher's talent is immediately obvious: the first chapter introduces the main characters, vividly renders Devon's situation in post-war Richmond, establishes the themes that will be developed throughout the book—and does so not in laborious exposition but in a very few seemingly random conversations. Her setting of scene is also admirable: New York City, though its elegance is finely conveyed, is for much of the novel not a world of romance but of seedy rooming houses, dirt, and human greed, poverty and squalor. Most impressive, the love story is not the only story or perhaps even the main one. For "castles in the air" are the dreams of women; and if love, children and family are some of those dreams, so too, and just as important, is the dream of achieving self-hood, of being an entity—as a man may be. Devon's goal is a simple-sounding one: she wishes to be a good journalist; and the main plot of *Castles in the Air* is really of the struggle and hardships such a goal involves—if one is a woman. This quest also ends in defeat.

Devon asks herself early on, trying to make her own way without Keith, whether it is possible for any woman to survive on her own terms "without dissembling and mendacity and guile." Thwarted in her main ambition, she takes a series of servile jobs in order to stay alive, does all of them well, then discovers that she's been given chances because she's physically desirable. Finally, she succumbs to Keith, to the kind of help and comfort his money can provide, and also becomes a protégée of one of Boss Tweed's men, whose influence gains her access to a newspaper. She's successful: she becomes a society reporter (appropriate journalistic work for a woman), excels at her work, eventually becomes known to the best New York society, and earns the right to move from coverage of that society to that of the presidential party in Washington. Still, in any real sense, she never wins. Keith, loving in all other ways, never conceives her work or her aspirations to another kind of reportage as anything other than exercise for exasperatingly attractive high spirits. Her benefactor waits for her to weary. The world—even other women engaged in the same kind of work—fail to take her or (it is implied) each other very seriously.

Early in the story Devon befriends Mally, a poor Irish girl at the rooming house where they both live in less than genteel poverty. Considering Devon's ambitions, Mally says to her: "But you can't marry a dream.... And what else is there for a girl? Marriage and children. That's all there is for us." Devon asks: "But why, Mally? *Why* must it be all there is for us." Mally replies: "Because we're female." Devon sets out to prove Mandy wrong—but in fact proves something else. What separates Mandy from her is not the difference in their ambitions or even in their capacity for vision; the difference is in how well each can survive in a marketplace in which the currency is physical attractiveness. Devon is beautiful; Mally is not; Devon is loved by a rich man and desired by a politically powerful one, they provide her with her opportunities; Mally, conversely, is plain, she has nothing to barter: she never moves from poverty and hopelessness, she falls for the wrong man, her life ends tragically. Mally is not "regarded;" but then neither is Devon, except as an object of love and passion who, in return for inspiring lust, is allowed to "play." The world to which Devon finally gains entrance is described as beautiful because it *is* beautiful—but not for a woman. For if she aspires to being something more than one of the beautiful things, she will be defeated—in the definition of self, in any kind of moral or intellectual fulfillment.

Patricia Gallagher is too good a writer to labor any of these points (indeed, within so obviously feminist a novel, she is scrupulously fair to men: some are rats, some are decent). She presents situation, leaves moral reflection to her readers. And this interest in something beyond a conventional romantic plot, this use of romantic devices to convey her own themes, is common to many of her novels. Yet one puts down any of them with a mild but gnawing dissatisfaction. The problem is language.

Castles in the Air—any of the novels—provides rich examples. The very names of her main characters are risible. And they stare into a "dense opacity." They feel like mice "on a treadmill to oblivion." In conveying information, women sound like a teacher who has presented the same lecture too many times. In being masculine, men reach for the diction and cadences of the King James Bible. If her plots are the antithesis of cliché, her language falls into all the traps.

And yet. The criticism, once made, seems wrong. For every three scenes of bad dialogue, there is one good one. Some of her descriptions are downright embarrassing; some are masterful. She allows some of her "physical" scenes to become mawkish—but, in any of her books, there is sex which is stylishly described, pleasantly torrid. Often—too often—she conveys the emotional relations between people in ways that are, frankly, corny; other times, she invokes feeling with such exactness as to be genuinely affecting and profound. It is as if she is not so much unskillful as lazy with language—or, perhaps, that she devotes such time and effort to "getting it right" in plot, setting, scene, that she has little energy left for words themselves. The result is hit or miss. If she can now refine language as she has perfected the other aspects of her craft, Patricia Gallagher can almost certainly set a standard against which other romance novelists will be measured.

—George Walsh

GARVICE, Charles. Also wrote as Charles Gibson; Caroline Hart. British. Born in 1833. Journalist. County Councillor, Northam, Devon. President, Institute of Lecturers, and Farmers and Landowners Association. Fellow, Royal Society of Literature. *Died 1 March 1920.*

ROMANCE AND GOTHIC PUBLICATIONS

Novels

> *Maurice Durant.* London, Smith, 3 vols., 1875; New York, Ogilvie, n.d.; as *Eyes of Love*, New York, Street and Smith, n.d.
> *On Love's Altar.* New York, Munro, 1892; London, King, 1908; as *A Wasted Love* (as Caroline Hart), Cleveland, Westbrook, n.d.
> *Paid For!* New York, Munro, 1892; London, Hutchinson, 1909.
> *Married at Sight.* New York, Munro, 1894.
> *The Price of Honour* (as Charles Gibson). Cleveland, Westbrook, n.d.
> *His Love So True.* New York, Munro, 1896.
> *The Marquis.* New York, Munro, 1896.
> *Just a Girl.* London, Bowden, 1898; as *An Innocent Girl*, New York, Munro, 1898.
> *She Loved Him.* New York, Street and Smith, 1899; London, Hutchinson, 1909.
> *Claire.* New York, Street and Smith, 1899.
> *Lorrie.* New York, Street and Smith, 1899; London, Hodder and Stoughton, 1910.
> *Modern Juliet.* New York, Street and Smith, 1900; London, Pearson, 1910.
> *Nell of Shorne Mills.* New York, Street and Smith, 1900; London, Hutchinson, 1908.
> *Nance.* London, Sands, 1900.
> *Her Heart's Desire.* London, Sands, 1900; New York, Hurst, 1903.
> *An Outcast of the Family.* London, Sands, 1900.
> *A Coronet of Shame.* London, Sands, 1900; New York, Ogilvie, n.d.
> *Leola Dale's Fortune.* New York, Street and Smith, 1901; London, Hutchinson, 1910.
> *Maida.* New York, Street and Smith, 1901.
> *Only a Girl's Love.* New York, Street and Smith, 1901; London, Hodder and Stoughton, 1911.
> *For Her Only.* New York, Street and Smith, 1902; London, Hodder and Stoughton, 1911.
> *The Lady of Darracourt.* New York, Street and Smith, 1902; London, Hodder and Stoughton, 1911.
> *Jeanne.* New York, Street and Smith, 1902.
> *Heir of Vering.* New York, Street and Smith, 1902; London, Hutchinson, 1910.
> *Woman's Soul.* New York, Street and Smith, 1902.
> *So Nearly Lost.* New York, Street and Smith, 1902; as *The Spring-Time of Love*, London, Hodder and Stoughton, 1910.
> *So Fair, So False.* New York, Street and Smith, 1902.
> *Love's Dilemma.* New York, Street and Smith, 1902; London, Hodder and Stoughton, 1917; as *For an Earldom*, New York, Ogilvie, n.d.
> *Martyred Love.* New York, Street and Smith, 1902.
> *My Lady Pride.* New York, Street and Smith, 1902.
> *Olivia.* New York, Street and Smith, 1902.
> *In Cupid's Chains.* London, Sands, 1902.
> *Woven on Fate's Loom, and The Snowdrift.* New York, Street and Smith, 1903.
> *Staunch of the Heart.* New York, Street and Smith, 1903; as *Adrien Leroy*, London, Newnes, 1912.
> *Her Ransom.* New York, Hurst, 1903.
> *Led by Love.* New York, Street and Smith, 1903.
> *Staunch as a Woman.* New York, Street and Smith, 1903; London, Hodder and Stoughton, 1910.
> *A Jest of Fate.* New York, Munro, 1904; London, Newnes, 1909.

Her Humble Lover.   Cleveland, Westbrook, 1904; as *The Usurper*, Chicago, Donohue, n.d.
Love Decides.   London, Hutchinson, 1904.
Linked by Fate.   London, Hutchinson, 1905.
Love, The Tyrant.   London, Hutchinson, 1905.
Edna's Secret Marriage.   New York, Street and Smith, 1905.
The Other Woman.   New York, Street and Smith, 1905.
When Love Meets Love.   New York, Street and Smith, 1906.
A Girl of Spirit.   London, Hutchinson, 1906; New York, Street and Smith, n.d.
Diana and Destiny.   London, Hodder and Stoughton, 1906; as *Diana's Destiny*, New York, Burt, n.d.
Where Love Leads.   London, Hutchinson, 1907.
The Gold in the Gutter.   London, Hutchinson, 1907.
Sacrifice to Art.   Chicago, Stein, 1908.
Sample of Prejudice.   Chicago, Stein, 1908.
Slave of the Lake.   Chicago, Stein, 1908.
Taming of Princess Olga.   Chicago, Stein, 1908.
Woman Decides.   Chicago, Stein, 1908.
My Lady of Snow.   Chicago, Stein, 1908.
Linnie.   Chicago, Stein, 1908.
Olivia and Others.   London, Hutchinson, 1908.
A Love Comedy.   Chicago, Stein, 1908; London, Hodder and Stoughton, 1912.
Marcia Drayton.   London, Newnes, 1908.
Female Editor.   Chicago, Stein, 1908.
Leave Love to Itself.   Chicago, Stein, 1908.
First and Last.   Chicago, Stein, 1908.
In the Matter of a Letter.   Chicago, Stein, 1908.
Farmer Holt's Daughter.   Chicago, Stein, 1908.
Story of a Passion.   London, Hutchinson, 1908; New York, Burt, n.d.
Kyra's Fate.   London, Hutchinson, 1908; New York, Burt, n.d.
The Rugged Path.   London, Hodder and Stoughton, 1908.
In Wolf's Clothing.   London, Hodder and Stoughton, 1908.
Queen Kate.   London, Hodder and Stoughton, 1909.
The Scribblers' Club.   London, Hodder and Stoughton, 1909.
The Fatal Ruby.   London, Hodder and Stoughton, and New York, Doran, 1909.
By Dangerous Ways.   London, Amalgamated Press, 1909; New York, Burt, n.d.
A Fair Imposter.   London, Newnes, 1909.
A Heritage of Hate.   London, Amalgamated Press, 1909.
The Mistress of Court Regina.   London, Hutchinson, 1909; Philadelphia, Royal, n.d.
At Love's Cost.   London, Hutchinson, 1909; New York, Burt, n.d.
Ashes of Love.   New York, Ogilvie, 1910.
Barriers Between.   London, Hodder and Stoughton, 1910.
The Beauty of the Season.   London, Hodder and Stoughton, 1910.
Better Than Life.   London, Hodder and Stoughton, 1910.
Dulcie.   London, Hodder and Stoughton, 1910.
The Earl's Daughter.   London, Hodder and Stoughton, 1910; as *The Earl's Heir*, Chicago, Donohue, n.d.
A Girl from the South.   London, Cassell, 1910.
The Heart of a Maid.   London, Hodder and Stoughton, 1910.
Once in a Life.   London, Hodder and Stoughton, 1910.
Only One Love.   London, Hodder and Stoughton, 1910; New York, Street and Smith, n.d.
A Passion Flower.   London, Hodder and Stoughton, 1910; New York, Street and Smith, n.d.
With All Her Heart.   London, Newnes, 1910.
Floris.   London, Hutchinson, 1910.
Signa's Sweetheart.   London, Hutchinson, 1910.
Sweet as a Rose.   London, Hutchinson, 1910.

Leslie's Loyalty. London, Hodder and Stoughton, 1911; New York, Street and Smith, n.d.; as *Her Love So True*, Philadelphia, Royal, n.d.

Miss Estcourt. London, Hutchinson, 1911.

My Love Kitty. London, Hutchinson, 1911.

That Strange Girl. London, Hutchinson, 1911.

Violet. London, Hutchinson, 1911.

Doris. London, Newnes, 1911.

Elaine. London, Newnes, 1911; New York, Street and Smith, n.d.

He Loves Me, He Loves Me Not. London, Hodder and Stoughton, 1911; New York, Street and Smith, n.d.

His Guardian Angel. London, Newnes, 1911; New York, Street and Smith, n.d.

Lord of Himself. London, Hodder and Stoughton, 1911.

The Other Girl. London, Hodder and Stoughton, 1911.

Sweet Cymbeline. London, Newnes, 1911; New York, Street and Smith, n.d.

A Wilful Maid. London, Newnes, 1911; New York, Street and Smith, n.d.; as *Phillippa*, Chicago, Donohue, n.d.

The Woman in It. London, Hodder and Stoughton, 1911.

Wounded Heart. New York, Ogilvie, 1911.

Breta's Double. New York, Street and Smith, n.d.

His Perfect Trust. Philadelphia, Royal, n.d.

Imogene. New York, Street and Smith, n.d.

Love of a Life Time. Philadelphia, Royal, n.d.

Lucille. Chicago, Donohue, n.d.

Out of the Past. New York, Street and Smith, n.d.

Price of Honor. Philadelphia, Royal, n.d.

Pride of Her Life. New York, Street and Smith, n.d.

Royal Signet. Philadelphia, Royal, n.d.

The Spider and the Fly. New York, Street and Smith, n.d.

Sydney. New York, Street and Smith, n.d.

'Twix Smile and Tear. New York, Street and Smith, n.d.

Wasted Love. New York, Street and Smith, n.d.

Love in a Snare. London, Hodder and Stoughton, 1912.

Fate. London, Newnes, 1912; New York, Ogilvie, 1913.

Fickle Fortune. London, Newnes, 1912.

In Fine Feathers. London, Hodder and Stoughton, 1912.

Stella's Fortune. London, Hodder and Stoughton, 1912; New York, Street and Smith, n.d.; as *Sculptor's Wooing*, New York, Ogilvie, n.d.

Two Maids and a Man. London, Hodder and Stoughton, 1912; as *Two Girls and a Man*, London, Wright and Brown, 1937.

The Verdict of the Heart. London, Newnes, 1912.

Country Love. London, Hutchinson, 1912.

Reuben. London, Hutchinson, 1912.

Nellie. London, Hutchinson, 1913; as Caroline Hart, Cleveland, Westbrook, n.d.

The Loom of Fate. London, Newnes, 1913.

The Woman's Way. London, Hodder and Stoughton, 1914.

Iris. London, Newnes, 1914.

The Call of the Heart. London, Hodder and Stoughton, 1914.

In Exchange for Love. London, Hodder and Stoughton, 1914.

The One Girl in the World. London, Hodder and Stoughton, 1915.

Love, The Adventurous. London, Hodder and Stoughton, 1917.

Creatures of Destiny. New York, Burt, n.d.

Heart for Heart. New York, Burt, n.d.

Love and a Lie. New York, Burt, n.d.

Shadow of Her Life. New York, Burt, n.d.

'Twas Love's Fault. New York, Burt, n.d.

When Love Is Young. New York, Burt, n.d.

The Waster. London, Lloyds, 1918.

The Girl in Love. London, Skeffington, 1919.

Wicked Sir Dare.   London, Hutchinson, 1938.

Novels as Caroline Hart

A Hidden Terror.   Cleveland, Westbrook, 1910.
Angela's Lover.   Cleveland, Westbrook, n.d.
For Love or Honor.   Cleveland, Westbrook, n.d.
From Want to Wealth.   Cleveland, Westbrook, n.d.
From Worse Than Death.   Cleveland, Westbrook, n.d.
Game of Love.   Cleveland, Westbrook, n.d.
Haunted Life.   Cleveland, Westbrook, n.d.
Hearts of Fire.   Cleveland, Westbrook, n.d.
Her Right to Love.   Cleveland, Westbrook, n.d.
Lil, The Dancing Girl.   Cleveland, Westbrook, n.d.
Lillian's Vow.   Cleveland, Westbrook, n.d.
Little Princess.   Cleveland, Westbrook, n.d.
Love's Rugged Path.   Cleveland, Westbrook, n.d.
Madness of Love.   Cleveland, Westbrook, n.d.
Nameless Bess.   Cleveland, Westbrook, n.d.
Nobody's Wife.   Cleveland, Westbrook, n.d.
Redeemed by Love.   Cleveland, Westbrook, n.d.
Rival Heiresses.   Cleveland, Westbrook, n.d.
She Loved Not Wisely.   Cleveland, Westbrook, n.d.
Strange Marriage.   Cleveland, Westbrook, n.d.
That Awful Scar.   Cleveland, Westbrook, n.d.
Vengeance of Love.   Cleveland, Westbrook, n.d.
Women Who Came Between.   Cleveland, Westbrook, n.d.
Woman Wronged.   Cleveland, Westbrook, n.d.
Working Girl's Honor.   Cleveland, Westbrook, n.d.

Short Stories

The Girl Without a Heart and Other Stories.   London, Newnes, 1912.
A Relenting Fate and Other Stories.   London, Newnes, 1912.
All Is Not Fair in Love and Other Stories.   London, Newnes, 1913.
The Tessacott Tragedy and Other Stories.   London, Newnes, 1913.
The Girl in the 'bacca Shop.   London, Skeffington, 1920.
Miss Smith's Fortune and Other Stories.   London, Skeffington, 1920.

OTHER PUBLICATIONS

Plays

The Fisherman's Daughter (produced London, 1881).
A Life's Mistake.   London, Hutchinson, 1910.
Marigold, with Allan F. Abbott (produced Glasgow, 1914).

Verse

Eve and Other Verses.   Privately printed, 1873.

Other

A Farm in Creamland: A Book of the Devon Countryside. London, Hodder and
Stoughton, 1911; New York, Doran, 1912.

Editor, The Red Budget of Stories. London, Hodder and Stoughton, 1912.

*   *   *

Charles Garvice was an English writer of the early 1900's. His novels actually became
popular in the mid-1890's and were so well received by American readers that many of his
works were printed by American publishers in pirated editions even after the 1891 international
copyright agreement.

Garvice's style and his frequent diversions into social commentary would tend to put modern
readers off from fully enjoying his works today. Often his stories began by drawing comparisons between his developing characters and the common people of the poorer sections of
London. Frequently his characters display a deep and unusual social consciousness that make
them aware of economic and labor changes of the day that worked to the detriment of the
working classes. In fact, this theme of helping the working classes or of accepting people as
people remains a solid underlying force throughout many of his novels. On another level is his
consistent emphasis on natural, instinctive qualities within the lower classes that make these
people just as socially acceptable as those from the upper ranks. Often the reader finds phrases
such as "He had the instincts of a gentleman" or "She moved and spoke in the manner born"
applied to characters from the working classes. The fact that these qualities could be found in
the lower classes made that person even more exceptional and valued. From this element in his
novels alone, one can understand why they appealed so greatly to American readers.

That is not, however, the major cause of his popularity. For Garvice had an unusual ability to
weave fast-paced and intricate and believable plots that did not need to rely on coincidence to
succeed. Missing jewels or treasures were combined with missing or lost heiresses. His plots
usually centered on the hero of the story, and the action is told from his viewpoint. He is usually
from a titled family and he usually succeeds to the title or is reinstated into his father's good
graces. In The Gold in the Gutter Clive Harvey is the third son of a family of notable rakes and
spendthrifts who becomes a radical thinker and wins a seat in the House of Commons.
Basically, the development of Garvice's stories rests on the hero's ability to overcome obstacles
and in the process, of course, to win the girl who has captured his heart. If any major flaw
emerges in Garvice's writing, it is his tendency to draw his characters larger than life; even the
hero's faults assume a virtuous glow so that one does not come to grips with the real person
Garvice is attempting to characterize. He is too good, too virtuous, too everything to be readily
acceptable to today's readers. In spite of this drawback, one must conclude that his writings fall
very definitely into the romance genre. Actually Garvice is within the traditional guidelines of
the misunderstood hero who faces all sorts of trials before he succeeds in achieving his goal.

Dialogue is often cleverly used to round out a character. It is sharp, and frequently colorful
and rich, adding to the speaker's overall character. Description is not always kept as short as
one would like, but from the period in which he was writing, that cannot be considered a fault.
Certainly he mastered the technique of telling a good, moving story that kept readers waiting
for the next chapter.

His writing apparently appealed to men as well as women, for some of his works actually
could be classified as adventure stories rather than straight romances. For example, in The
Rugged Path Jack, the son of Sir William Morton, leaves home after disagreeing with his
father. He is literally cut off from his father and any money his father would leave him. The
prospect certainly does not upset him, for he sails to Australia and undertakes a whole new life
for himself. The Australian scenes are quite well presented by Garvice, indicating careful
research to lend accuracy to his works. The scene shifts back to England, with the death of his
father and the arrival of the villain in the person of his cousin, Hesketh Carton. Contested wills,
fetching girls of the new breed, and the hero's own queer sense of honor add to an intriguing
story and eventual happiness.

It is difficult to summarize Garvice as a romance writer. Barring stylistic elements that
certainly date his work, he still can be enjoyably read by anyone. In fact, careful editing and the

presentation of his works as historical novels might make them appealing even now. Yet, he was not an outstanding writer. He may not have had that special spark that would allow for such liberties to be taken. Perhaps it would make no difference, for romance writers tend to want to tell a good story and to make people experience, just for a moment, someone else's life and happiness. The fact that Garvice wrote well over 150 novels indicates that he may have achieved his purpose and did not particularly care for lasting fame.

—Arlene Moore

GASKIN, Catherine. Irish. Born in Dundalk, County Louth, 2 April 1929. Educated at Holy Cross College, Sydney, Australia. Married Sol Cornberg in 1955. Lived in London, 1948-55, and in New York, 1955-67. Address: White Rigg, East Ballaterson, Maughold, Isle of Man, United Kingdom.

ROMANCE AND GOTHIC PUBLICATIONS

Novels

This Other Eden.   London, Collins, 1947.
With Every Year.   London, Collins, 1949.
Dust in the Sunlight.   London, Collins, 1950.
All Else Is Folly.   London, Collins, and New York, Harper, 1951.
Daughter of the House.   London, Collins, 1952; New York, Harper, 1953.
Sara Dane.   London, Collins, 1954; Philadelphia, Lippincott, 1955.
Blake's Reach.   London, Collins, and Philadelphia, Lippincott, 1958.
Corporation Wife.   London, Collins, and New York, Doubleday, 1960.
I Know My Love.   London, Collins, and New York, Doubleday, 1962.
The Tilsit Inheritance.   London, Collins, and New York, Doubleday, 1963.
The File on Devlin.   London, Collins, and New York, Doubleday, 1965.
Edge of Glass.   London, Collins, and New York, Doubleday, 1967.
Fiona.   London, Collins, and New York, Doubleday, 1970.
A Falcon for a Queen.   London, Collins, and New York, Doubleday, 1972.
The Property of a Gentleman.   London, Collins, and New York, Doubleday, 1974.
The Lynmara Legacy.   London, Collins, 1975; New York, Doubleday, 1976.
The Summer of the Spanish Woman.   London, Collins, and New York, Doubleday, 1977.
Family Affairs.   London, Collins, and New York, Doubleday, 1980.
Promises.   London, Collins, 1982.

*   *   *

Catherine Gaskin has created her own niche in the world of the romantic novel. Her works contain the familiar gothic elements—disputed inheritance, forbidden love, mysterious strangers, ancestral homes and their hidden skeletons, the culminating act of violence. What sets her apart is her ability to integrate these elements into the fabric of a modern world so convincingly drawn as to anchor the fantastic firmly to earth. *This Other Eden*, the first novel she later rewrote as *The Lynmara Legacy*, reveals the talent as already fully formed. Its theme, of an American girl's succession to an English inheritance, is basically the same in both versions, and displays her skill in the blending of realism and romance.

Since then, her writing is roughly divisible into two main streams: the modern stories with gothic ingredients, and the entirely historical romances. The latter tend to be longer, and sometimes more ambitious. Viewed critically, they are often less satisfying. Though immensely popular, *Sara Dane* lacks that sure sense of solid reality that marks even the earliest of Gaskin's contemporary novels. Without the social background so ably provided in the modern works, its events seem unneccesarily theatrical and shorn of conviction. The story—of a transported servant girl who rises to wealth and power in colonial Australia—moves uncertainly from one crisis to another, with the arrivals and departures of Sara's prospective lovers rendered improbably convenient. The characters lack the authentic feeling of life encountered in the heroines of *All Else Is Folly* or *Daughter of the House*, quieter present-day works which absorb their wilder elements without strain. Susan Taite, the sophisticated and sensual fashion editor of *All Else Is Folly*, comes over more strongly than Sara as a person. Sara, one feels, is a character in a book; Susan, a living woman evoked by words. *Blake's Reach*, a story of smuggling adventure off the Romney Marshes in the 18th century, and *I Know My Love* with its historical Australian setting, to some extent suffer from the same defects. Exciting period adventures, they do not possess the depth of penetration seen in other works. Measured beside Gaskin's best productions, the romances impress mainly as costume dramas rather than portrayals of life.

Corporation Wife, one of her most satisfying books, explores the lives of four women in a small town taken over by an industrial company. Gaskin studies the women—two executive wives and two "natives"—in terms of their loves and ambitions, and the different way in which each adapts to the pressures of the corporation in her life. Her touch is sure, romance and tragedy made part of a convincing social scene, the characters perfectly and subtly realized. Equally skilled are *The Tilsit Inheritance*, where a pottery concern provides the background for a disputed legacy and love for a dark stranger, and the imaginative spy mystery *The File on Devlin*. Gaskin shows a keen awareness of various crafts and their commercial applications, and this knowledge is utilised in most of her works. Examples include the mechanics of glass design in *Edge of Glass*, fashion in *All Else Is Folly*, viticulture in *The Summer of the Spanish Woman*, and distilling whiskey in *A Falcon for a Queen*. Presentation of her characters at work is a major factor in the authenticity of Gaskin's best novels.

The Property of a Gentleman displays the aspects of the Gaskin novel in perfect balance. Against a background of art auctioneering, the heroine falls in love with the heir to a mansion in the Lake District. Action revolves around the discovery of a skeleton and related art treasures, and the book has a violent denouement. This novel shares another factor with many of Gaskin's works, the emphasis on the family and the ancestral home. This forms the core of *The Lynmara Legacy*, whose self-reliant and determined heroine Nicole Rainard is typical of the "Gaskin woman" in other novels. It is a significant aspect of later books, longer involved family chronicles which to some extent overlap the historical romances. *A Falcon for a Queen* blends the two in a story of Victorian Scotland, its theme the inheritance of a distilling business. The plot flares to a Brontë-esque climax with a holocaust destroying the distillery. The strongly drawn background gives the book a credibility denied to earlier romances, its characters and events given a greater depth. *The Summer of the Spanish Woman* and *Family Affairs*, two recent ambitious works, have some excellent scenes but lack overall unity. *Family Affairs* is in many ways reminiscent of *The Lynmara Legacy*, with the heroine providing a stabilising element in an English landed family. The writing is strong but uneven, an early surge of action followed by a sedate middle section against which the dramatic closing stages jar uneasily.

Catherine Gaskin has produced an impressive body of work, unique of its kind. More than most, she has brought a modern dimension to the gothic romance.

—Geoffrey Sadler

GAVIN, Catherine (Irvine). British. Born in Aberdeen, Scotland, in 1907. Educated at the University of Aberdeen, M.A. (honours) 1928, Ph.D. 1931. Married John Ashcraft in 1948. Lecturer in History, University of Aberdeen, 1932-34, 1941-43, and the University of Glasgow, 1934-36; editorial writer, European bureau chief, and war correspondent, Kemsley Newspapers, 1943-45; correspondent in the Middle East and Ethiopia, *Daily Express*, London, 1945-47; staff member, *Time*, New York, 1950-52. Active in Scottish politics in the 1930's: conservative candidate for parliament twice. Address: c/o Hodder and Stoughton Ltd., Mill Road, Dunton Green, Sevenoaks, Kent TN13 2YA, England.

ROMANCE AND GOTHIC PUBLICATIONS

Novels

    Clyde Valley. London, Barker, 1938.
    The Hostile Shore. London, Methuen, 1940.
    The Black Milestone. London, Methuen, 1941.
    The Mountain of Light. London, Methuen, 1944.
    Second Empire Quartet:
        Madeleine. New York, St. Martin's Press, 1957; London, Macmillan, 1958.
        The Cactus and the Crown. London, Hodder and Stoughton, and New York, Doubleday, 1962.
        The Fortress. London, Hodder and Stoughton, and New York, Doubleday, 1964.
        The Moon into Blood. London, Hodder and Stoughton, 1966.
    The Devil in Harbour. London, Hodder and Stoughton, and New York, Morrow, 1968.
    The House of War. London, Hodder and Stoughton, and New York, Morrow, 1970.
    Give Me the Daggers. London, Hodder and Stoughton, and New York, Morrow, 1972.
    The Snow Mountain. London, Hodder and Stoughton, 1973; New York, Pantheon, 1974.
    Second World War trilogy:
        Traitors' Gate. London, Hodder and Stoughton, and New York, St. Martin's Press, 1976.
        None Dare Call It Treason. London, Hodder and Stoughton, and New York, St. Martin's Press, 1978.
        How Sleep the Brave. London, Hodder and Stoughton, and New York, St. Martin's Press, 1980.

OTHER PUBLICATIONS

Other

    Louis Philippe, King of the French. London, Methuen, 1933.
    Britain and France: A Study of Twentieth Century Relations, The Entente Cordiale. London, Cape, 1941.
    Edward the Seventh: A Biography. London, Cape, 1941.
    Liberated France. London, Cape, and New York, St. Martin's Press, 1955.

*   *   *

The closer a historical novelist sets her books to the present day, the more she puts her scholarship on the line and invites criticism, for many readers will remember the events and will be quick enough to say "this did not happen" or "this did happen but not for that reason" if she is wrong. Catherine Gavin passes this test with flying colours in what she calls her "war novels"—four about World War I and a trilogy about World War II—all of which will have readers who lived through the events portrayed. They will agree that not only does she get her history right but that she has a masterly way of evoking the atmosphere of a given place at a precise moment in time. Thus having found her accounts of times we are competent to judge trustworthy, we feel she must be right, too, when she tells us about earlier periods of history.

Her "Second Empire Quartet" is a series of books set in the 19th century and loosely connected by their theme: they set out to explore various revolutionary struggles, mixing fictional characters with historical personalities. *The Fortress* tells of the naval campaign in the Baltic in 1885 through the eyes of an American in the Royal Navy and adumbrates Finland's struggles through his Finnish wife; *The Moon into Blood* is about the Risorgimento in Italy with a fictional American hero who works with Cavour and Garibaldi; *Madeleine* is about the Second Empire in France, and *The Cactus and the Crown* the ill-fated Hapsburg intervention in Mexico. The Mexican countryside is the real star of this book and the American characters are more royalist than revolutionary, although Gavin lets her heroine have her cake and eat it too.

The World War I novels are concerned with the pressures of war, the way such pressures distort behaviour, and the way change may grow out of it. *The Devil in Harbour* is about spying and divided loyalties and the battle of Jutland. *The Snow Mountain*, about the fall of the Romanovs, is a poignant recreation of that sad story; Gavin's interpretations of the Czar and Czarina's motives are excellent, and the fictitious American consul, the Russian officer, and the revolutionary girl who share the story are extremely believable. *Give Me the Daggers* is about General Mannerheim's fight for Finnish independence in 1918, but also about a young man coming to terms with a disfiguring wound and a spoiled young girl learning unselfishness. *The House of War* is about Kemal Ataturk's struggle for Turkish freedom in 1922 but also about the break up of a marriage. The history in all these books is accurate and well integrated into the fiction, the descriptions of places is excellent and the characterisation of factual and fictional people is so good you cannot "see the join." A felicitous touch which adds verity is the way a character who plays a major part in one novel gets a walk-on part in another—descendants of people in *The Fortress* turn up in *Give Me the Dangers* and Joe Calvert the consul in *The Snow Mountain* appears as godfather to the heroine of *None Dare Call It Treason*, one of the World War II novels.

This remarkable trilogy is about France's struggle. *Traitors' Gate*, set in London and Brazil, evokes the atmosphere and emotions of 1940 quite amazingly; *None Dare Call It Treason* takes place in the unoccupied zone of France, mainly in Nice and Menton, and explores different kinds of loyalty and betrayal. *How Sleep the Brave* takes the story through the liberation to the end of the war, and includes an understated yet unforgettably horrific description of the massacre at Oradour-sur-Glane. Throughout the trilogy hardly anyone has a good word to say for de Gaulle, and the reader will probably never be able to think of him in quite the same way again.

Catherine Gavin is extremely skilful at blending fact and fiction, and if occasionally readers feel she is giving us too big a chunk of history it is because the romance is so entertaining that we are impatient to know what will happen next.

—Pamela Cleaver

GELLIS, Roberta (Leah, née Jacobs). Also writes as Max Daniels; Priscilla Hamilton; Leah Jacobs. American. Born in New York City, 27 September 1927. Educated at Hunter College, New York, 1943-47, B.A. 1947; Brooklyn Polytechnic Institute, 1949-52, M.A. 1952; New York University, 1953-58, M.A. Married Charles Gellis in 1947; one son. Chemist, Foster D. Snell Inc., New York, 1947-53; Editor, McGraw-Hill Book Company, New York, 1953-56; then free-lance editor, for Macmillan Company, New York, 1956-58 and since 1971, and for

Academic Press, New York, 1956-70. Agent: Lyle Kenyon Engel, BCI, Schillings Crossing Road, Canaan, New York 12029. Address: 119 Princeton Street, Roslyn Heights, New York 11577, U.S.A.

ROMANCE AND GOTHIC PUBLICATIONS

Novels

> *Knight's Honor.*   New York, Doubleday, 1964; London, Mayflower, 1979.
> *Bond of Blood.*   New York, Doubleday, 1965; London, Mayflower, 1979.
> *The Psychiatrist's Wife* (as Leah Jacobs).   New York, New American Library, 1966.
> *Sing Witch, Sing Death.*   New York, Bantam, 1975.
> *The Sword and the Swan.*   Chicago, Playboy Press, 1977; London, Mayflower, 1979.
> *The Roselynde Chronicles*:
>> 1. *Roselynde.*   Chicago, Playboy Press, 1978; Feltham, Middlesex, Hamlyn, 1979.
>> 2. *Alinor.*   Chicago, Playboy Press, 1978; Feltham, Middlesex, Hamlyn, 1979.
>> 3. *Joanna.*   Chicago, Playboy Press, 1978; Feltham, Middlesex, Hamlyn, 1979.
>> 4. *Gilliane.*   Chicago, Playboy Press, and Feltham, Middlesex, Hamlyn, 1979.
>> 5. *Rhiannon.*   Chicago, Playboy Press, 1982.
> *Love Token* (as Priscilla Hamilton).   Chicago, Playboy Press, 1979.
> *Heiress Series*:
>> *The English Heiress.*   New York, Dell, 1980.
>> *The Cornish Heiress.*   New York, Dell, 1981.
> *Siren Song.*   Chicago, Playboy Press, 1981.

OTHER PUBLICATIONS

Novels as Max Daniels

> *Space Guardian.*   New York, Pocket Books, 1978.
> *Offworld!*   New York, Pocket Books, 1979.

Roberta Gellis comments:

Perhaps in reaction against the cynical attitudes and impersonal horrors perpetrated by humankind on humankind, I have always been fascinated by the past. In medieval times, there was a passionate belief in honor, truth, courage, and loyalty. This is not to say that I think men and women at that time were different or better; they were not. However, when they diverged from the path, when they were dishonorable or cowardly, they knew they had done wrong; they did not tell themselves that "everybody does it." And, although cruelty and slaughter were as rife then as now, one at least had to face one's victim; there were no bombs that killed faceless thousands impersonally.

The combination of these high standards and my awareness that people are people in any place or time has led me to attempt to present the social and political history of the medieval period, especially medieval England, in human terms. In any time the two great desires of human beings are for love and power. Thus, I try to weave together a strong love story and the political events, showing the latter through the eyes of the people affected. Most of my books are in continuing series, which permits me to give a chronological history not only of the nation but also of a family.

The Roselynde Chronicles, for example, begin with the young heiress, Alinor of Roselynde, and detail, through her two marriages, the reign of Richard the Lionhearted and the early years of King John. In *Joanna* I deal with the marriage of Alinor's daughter and the last four years of John's reign, showing how Joanna's marriage increased both the power and the responsibilities of the family. The spread of influence of the Roselynde clan is increased still further in Volume 4 of the Chronicles, when Alinor's eldest son marries another heiress, twice widowed. Through all the books I attempt to show the conditions, both physical and social, in which these people lived. Moreover, I try to present events as *these* people saw and felt them by the use of chronicles written at the time rather than by the use of modern history books, although I also consult modern texts. Historical events and historical personages are presented as accurately as possible, although the central characters of my books are almost always fictional.

However, I do not want any reader to believe that I am writing historical texts. To my characters, as to any human being, their own personal affairs are of essential importance, of far greater importance than any political event—unless that political event effects them directly. It is, thus, the love story in each book that is the central theme, not political and social history. To each man and woman personal need and desire are not only of overriding importance, but these emotions color all other events. So I emphasize the personal element, for in real life that is how we frail humans perceive our world, and that is how my characters perceived theirs.

*   *   *

When one reads a Roberta Gellis novel, one should be prepared to enter a historical world of great vitality. Her stories are carefully researched and are loaded with details of life and manners of the period. Historical figures wander easily into the narrative or may even take center stage, as does Henry VII, the central figure in *The Dragon and the Rose*. At first glance the wealth of detail might appear overwhelming, but Gellis creates such real characters that they bring all the facts into focus and make history a living thing rather than a collection of dry dates and events. The underlying love stories serve to point out how historical events affect individuals.

Gellis's most prolific output has been devoted to the medieval period. The popular series, the Roselynde Chronicles, takes the reader through one of the most tumultuous eras of English history. Action in the first two volumes, *Roselynde* and *Alinor*, moves to the Crusades and into the rebellion against King John. Later volumes involve the characters in events leading to the Magna Carta, war with France, and later rebellions against Henry III. Gellis has recently begun the Heiress Series, set in the more familiar 18th and 19th centuries. No less historically accurate than the Roselynde Chronicles, the two volumes which have appeared so far, *The English Heiress* and *The Cornish Heiress*, do not feature historical personages as characters who appear in the action.

Perhaps the most striking thing about Gellis's creations is the courage, strength, and integrity shown by her female characters. Alinor, first of the exceptional Roselynde women, is not only beautiful and intelligent, but has the almost mystical bond to the land that is usually reserved for males. She may be caught up in great events, but her love for and protection of her land and family remain paramount. Indeed, it is a measure of the importance of women in these stories that the great estate of Roselynde is passed on through the female line. Alinor's daughter, Joanna, proves herself a worthy successor to her mother. Even Alinor's sons, Adam and Simon, search for and find strong, independent women in *Gilliane* and *Rhiannon*. It is to Gellis's credit that she is able to portray such strong women so believably. It would be a mistake, however, to think that these women dominate their male companions. The women may be the central focus, but the men are their equals. They too are fiercely independent, passionate, and devoted to duty and honor. Secure in themselves, they are not threatened by the Roselynde women.

Although the focus shifts somewhat to the male characters in the Heiress Series, the same strength and independence of the men and women come through. It is the view of men and women as individuals who are equal, who are able to maintain their individuality and equality in their male-female relationhips, that is unusual in the historical romance genre.

—Barbara Kemp

GIBBS, Mary Ann. Pseudonym for Marjory Elizabeth Sarah Bidwell, née Lambe; also writes as Elizabeth Ford. British. Born in Seaford, Sussex, Attended secondary schools in Seaford. Married Thomas Edward Palmer Bidwell (died, 1965); one son. Agent: Curtis Brown Ltd., 1 Craven Hill, London W2 3EP, England.

<small>ROMANCE AND GOTHIC PUBLICATIONS</small>

Novels

    A Young Man with Ideas. London, Davies, 1950.
    Enchantment: A Pastoral. London, Davies, 1952.
    A Bit of a Bounder: An Edwardian Trifle. London, Davies, 1952.
    The Guardian. London, Hurst and Blackett, 1958; New York, Beagle, 1974.
    Young Lady with Red Hair. London, Hurst and Blackett, 1959; New York, Beagle, 1974; as *The Penniless Heiress*, London, Coronet, 1975.
    Horatia. London, Hurst and Blackett, 1961; New York, Beagle, 1973.
    The Apothecary's Daughter. London, Hurst and Blackett, 1962; New York, Beagle, 1974.
    Polly Kettle. London, Hurst and Blackett, 1963; New York, Beagle, 1973; as *The Nursery Maid*, London, Coronet, 1975.
    The Amateur Governess. London, Hurst and Blackett, 1964; as *The House of Ravensbourne*, New York, Pyramid, 1965.
    The Sugar Mouse. London, Hurst and Blackett, 1965; New York, Beagle, 1974.
    The Romantic Frenchman. London, Hurst and Blackett, 1967; New York, Beagle, 1973.
    The Sea Urchins. London, Hurst and Blackett, 1968; New York, Beagle, 1973.
    A Parcel of Land. London, Hurst and Blackett, 1969; New York, Beagle, 1973.
    A Lady in Berkshire. London, Hurst and Blackett, 1970; New York, Beagle, 1973.
    The Year of the Pageant. London, Hurst and Blackett, 1971; New York, Beagle, 1973.
    The Moon in a Bucket. London, Hurst and Blackett, 1972; New York, Beagle, 1973.
    The Glass Palace. London, Hurst and Blackett, 1973; New York, Mason Charter, 1975.
    A Wife for the Admiral. London, Hurst and Blackett, 1974; as *The Admiral's Lady*, New York, Mason Charter, 1975.
    A Most Romantic City. London, Hurst and Blackett, and New York, Mason Charter, 1976.
    The Tempestuous Petticoat. London, Hurst and Blackett, and New York, Mason Charter, 1977.
    A Young Lady of Fashion. London, Hurst and Blackett, 1978; New York, Fawcett, 1979.
    The Tulip Tree. London, Hurst and Blackett, and New York, Fawcett, 1979.
    Dinah. Loughton, Essex, Piatkus, and New York, Fawcett, 1981.
    The Milliner's Shop. Loughton, Essex, Piatkus, 1981; as *Renegade Girl*, New York, Fawcett, 1981.
    The Marquess. Loughton, Essex, Piatkus, 1982.

Novels as Elizabeth Ford

    Fog. London, Chapman and Hall, 1933.
    The House with the Myrtle Trees. London, Lutterworth Press, 1942.
    The Blue Cockade: A Romantic Novel of 1780. London, Lutterworth Press, 1943.
    Queen's Harbour. London, Hurst and Blackett, 1944.
    The Young Ladies' Room. London, Hurst and Blackett, 1945.
    The Irresponsibles. London, Hurst and Blackett, 1946.
    Mountford Show. London, Hurst and Blackett, 1948.
    Spring Comes to the Crescent. London, Hurst and Blackett, 1949.
    So Deep Suspicion. London, Hurst and Blackett, 1950.

Four Days in June.   London, Hurst and Blackett, 1951.
Just Around the Corner.   London, Hurst and Blackett, 1952.
English Rose.   London, Hurst and Blackett, 1953.
One Fine Day.   London, Hurst and Blackett, 1954.
Meeting in the Spring.   London, Hurst and Blackett, 1954.
Outrageous Fortune.   London, Hurst and Blackett, 1955.
That Summer at Bacclesea.   London, Hurst and Blackett, 1956.
The Empty Heart.   London, Hurst and Blackett, 1957.
The Cottage at Drimble.   London, Hurst and Blackett, 1957.
Butter Market House.   London, Hurst and Blackett, 1958.
Heron's Nest.   London, Hurst and Blackett, 1960.
A Week by the Sea.   London, Hurst and Blackett, 1962.
A Holiday Engagement: A Maplechester Novel.   London, Hurst and Blackett, 1963.
No Room for Joanna: A Maplechester Novel.   London, Hurst and Blackett, 1964.
A Country Holiday.   London, Hurst and Blackett, 1966; as *Dangerous Holiday*, New
    York, Ace, 1967.
The Turbulent Messiters.   London, Hurst and Blackett, 1967.
Limelight for Jane.   London, Hurst and Blackett, 1970.
The Day of the Storm.   London, Hurst and Blackett, 1971.
The Green Beetle.   London, Hurst and Blackett, 1972.
The Belvedere.   London, Hurst and Blackett, 1973.
Young Ann.   London, Hurst and Blackett, 1973.
A Charming Couple.   London, Hurst and Blackett, 1975.
The Amber Cat.   London, Hurst and Blackett, 1976.
Open Day at the Manor.   London, Hurst and Blackett, 1977.

OTHER PUBLICATIONS

Other

The Years of the Nannies.   London, Hutchinson, 1960.

Mary Ann Gibbs comments:

I am meticulous as to research and always do my own. I find that only by reading journals, diaries, letters, guides, and fiction of the era in which my books are set, and by studying minutely dress, jewellery, maps, transport, etc., can I recreate the atmosphere of the time. I never use what I call "gadsookery" in dialogue, as I have often found that many of the expressions used today were used as a matter of course at the beginning of the last century, and a word here and there will be enough to bring the reader back to the years in which the books are set. I never dictate my books. I do not think I could even use a dictaphone. I type them out as a first draft, which is then scribbled over and re-typed several times before I embark on the final typing, and even then I change phrases and sometimes characters, as I go. In other words I live in and with the book while I am writing.

*   *   *

A plucky girl with a zest for life and a refusal to let its adversities overwhelm her characterize the type of heroine always present in a Mary Ann Gibbs romance. The fact that the girl is usually not a stunning beauty and might even be considered plain does not prevent her from winning one of society's more desirable bachelors. She lives in a place and time (19th-century England) where morals and manners are applied rigidly. A Gibbs heroine often finds it necessary to abandon conventional manners in order to survive catastrophe while still remaining a lady and keeping a sense of self-worth. In *The Apothecary's Daughter* Susanna becomes the recipient of expensive gifts from Lord Vigilant, a much older man with a rakish past. That she is his long lost illegitimate daughter is kept secret at the insistence of her foster father, the apothecary. The scandal threatens to ruin Susanna's good name forever, but in the end the truth comes out. Meanwhile a man of position, Hugo Vigilant, the Lord's cousin and heir, has come to love her and finally wins her hand.

Often the young ladies of Gibbs's romances are left destitute by a negligent father and must give up the dream of marrying an eligible man of society, their impoverishment making them no longer acceptable. In *The Amateur Governess* (US title *The House of Ravensbourne*) Catherine finds herself penniless after the sudden death of a father from whom she inherits nothing but debts. Taking the job of governess to the young daughter of a wealthy tradesman, Catherine solves the mystery of the child's mistreatment by a cruel aunt and wins the love of the little girl's father. Similarly, Vicky Langford of *The Milliner's Shop* (US title *Renegade Girl*) must make her own way when her father leaves the country, the charge of fraud following in his wake. She provides for herself and her brother by taking a job as a clerk in a milliner's shop; she does not feel sorry for herself when all of her proper society friends cross her permanently off their lists. All, that is, except for a very few, one of whom is Sebastian, whose love for this young lady knows no bounds.

A novel by Mary Ann Gibbs tells of old-fashioned romance in which love has a special tenderness. There often exists an element of mystery—in fact Gibbs writes suspense novels as Elizabeth Ford—but the stories mainly center on the many obstacles the lovers must overcome in order to live happily ever after.

—Patricia Altner

GILBERT, Anna. Pseudonym for Marguerite Lazarus. British. Born in England, 1 May 1916. Educated at Durham University, B.A. (honours) 1937, M.A. 1945. Married Jack Lazarus in 1956. Grammar school English teacher, 1938-73. Recipient: Romantic Novelists Association Major Award, 1976. Agent: Bolt and Watson, 8-12 Old Queen Street, London SW1H 9HP. Address: Oakley Cottage, Swainsea Lane, Pickering, North Yorkshire, England.

ROMANCE AND GOTHIC PUBLICATIONS

Novels

Images of Rose. London, Hodder and Stoughton, and New York, Delacorte Press, 1974.
The Look of Innocence. London, Hodder and Stoughton, and New York, St. Martin's Press, 1975.
A Family Likeness. London, Hodder and Stoughton, 1977; New York, St. Martin's Press, 1978.
Remembering Louise. London, Hodder and Stoughton, and New York, St. Martin's Press, 1978.
The Leavetaking. London, Hodder and Stoughton, 1979; New York, St. Martin's Press, 1980.
Flowers for Lilian. London, Hodder and Stoughton, 1980; New York, St. Martin's Press, 1981.
Miss Bede Is Staying. Loughton, Essex, Piatkus, 1982.

Anna Gilbert comments:

My books are romantic in atmosphere in so far as romanticism implies a selection of the pleasing and picturesque aspects of reality, rather than the squalid. My aim is to charm and intrigue the reader, and to create tension by other means than the use of sensational material. I hope to appeal to women who want the reassurance of traditional values in stories which involve convincing characters in experiences of universal interest: love, loss, sadness, fear, forgiveness resolving into happiness, though the ultimate happiness is not always unalloyed.

The stories depend upon a strong plot and are set in Victorian England: a society near enough in time to be well documented but far enough away to offer escape from the complications of contemporary life. I choose close-knit, claustrophobic situations and relationships. Tension arises from some element of mystery and the gradual accumulation of significant detail leading to its disclosure: secrecy, deception, illusion—created and dispelled. I am particularly interested in the way innocence and generosity are exploited by selfishness and greed.

My favourite setting is the English countryside: remote hamlets and villages, woods and moors, small market towns: a country in itself mysterious, beautiful, and menacing, and for me constantly interfused with haunting glimpses of the ideal.

*   *   *

Anna Gilbert's first book, *Images of Rose*, was shortlisted for the 1974 Romantic Novelists Association Major Award. In 1975 she won the Award with her second book, *The Look of Innocence*. She writes Victorian stories with a strong element of mystery—classics of their kind.

Her plots are intricate and subtle. Her favourite theme is the quiet but relentless manipulation of people by each other, and the helplessness of the good and innocent in the face of ruthless egotism and jealousy. The manner, as much as the matter, is important. Her work is stylish and elegant. She writes with fastidious care, making every word count (not for nothing has she taught English to a high level), and she is past mistress at the art of heightening tension by placing a gentle finger on the reader's nerves.

In *Remembering Louise*, for example, the story begins in a deceptively low key, carefully setting the scene and filling in the heroine's background with loving detail, with no more than a hint of underlying unease. Character, place, and small, apparently trivial, incidents dominate the early pages and absorb the attention. Even when Hesther, the narrator, becomes involved in a shockingly violent incident, it at first seems peripheral to the story. Hesther is the daughter of a jeweller and watchmaker in the small north-country town of Wickborough. She is overjoyed when her pretty sister who has lived for many years in Scotland comes home unexpectedly. But from the moment she arrives Louise, sweet, docile and housewifely though she is, has a disrupting influence. Without lifting a finger, or her eyes, she manages, apparently unwittingly, to destroy not only Hesther's present contentment, but her lovingly planned future too. But Hesther continues to love her, and as her world crumbles around her she worries about the mysterious stranger in black whose life she might have saved, but didn't.

Gilbert returns again and again (notably in *Flowers for Lilian*) to this theme of a relationship in which one person, usually a woman, remorselessly dominates and takes advantage of another in order to get her own way. The plots differ and the stories are far from repetitious, but Gilbert's pre-occupation with the subject is a continuing thread throughout her work.

Her understanding of the period about which she writes, and the countryside in which her stories are set, the northeast of England, are inherent in everything she writes. She brings the landscape to life graphically and memorably. Her insight into rural life in that part of the world in the 19th century is in some measure explained by her deep interest in the literature, history, diaries, memoirs, letters, and biographies of the time, which results in minute, almost "eye-witness" descriptions of everyday dress and household objects, as well as the daily routine of those who lived in small, often remote, communities in those days. The vividness with which she conveys their lives and surroundings draws the reader inexorably into the atmosphere of her novels.

—Elizabeth Grey

GILES, Janice Holt. American. Born in Altus, Arkansas. Attended the University of Arkansas, Fayetteville; Transylvania University, Lexington, Kentucky. Married 1) Otto Moore (divorced, 1939), one daughter; 2) Henry Giles in 1945. Assistant to the Dean, Presbyterian Seminary, Louisville, 1941-50; then free-lance writer. *Died in 1979.*

ROMANCE AND GOTHIC PUBLICATIONS

Novels

The Enduring Hills.   Philadelphia, Westminster Press, 1950.
Miss Willie.   Philadelphia, Westminster Press, 1951.
Tara's Healing.   Philadelphia, Westminster Press, 1951.
Harbin's Ridge, with Henry Giles.   Boston, Houghton Mifflin, 1951.
40 Acres and No Mule.   Philadelphia, Westminster Press, 1952.
The Kentuckians.   Boston, Houghton Mifflin, 1953.
The Plum Thicket.   Boston, Houghton Mifflin, 1954.
Hannah Fowler.   Boston, Houghton Mifflin, 1956.
The Believers.   Boston, Houghton Mifflin, 1957.
The Land Beyond the Mountains.   Boston, Houghton Mifflin, 1958.
Johnny Osage.   Boston, Houghton Mifflin, 1960.
Savanna.   Boston, Houghton Mifflin, 1961.
Voyage to Santa Fe.   Boston, Houghton Mifflin, 1962.
Find Me a River.   Boston, Houghton Mifflin, 1964.
Time of Glory.   Boston, Houghton Mifflin, 1966.
Special Breed.   Boston, Houghton Mifflin, 1966.
The Great Adventure.   Boston, Houghton Mifflin, 1966.
Shady Grove.   Boston, Houghton Mifflin, 1968.
Six-Horse Hitch.   Boston, Houghton Mifflin, 1969.

Short Stories

Wellspring.   Boston, Houghton Mifflin, 1975.

OTHER PUBLICATIONS

Other

A Little Better Than Plumb: The Biography of a House, with Henry Giles.   Boston,
    Houghton Mifflin, 1963.
The Damned Engineers.   Boston, Houghton Mifflin, 1970.
Around Our House, with Henry Giles.   Boston, Houghton Mifflin, 1971.
The Kinta Years (autobiography).   Boston, Houghton Mifflin, 1973.

Editor, *The G.I. Journal of Sergeant Giles*, by Henry Giles.   Boston, Houghton Mifflin,
    1965.

*   *   *

It is impossible to think of Janice Holt Giles's work without envisioning her own particular part of the world. A regional writer in the best sense, her novels project the spirit of the pioneers who first tamed the rugged forest country of Kentucky and the westward wilderness. Her best tales unfold the continuing saga of a pioneering family, the Fowlers, through several generations, beginning with her most truly memorable fictional heroine, Hannah Fowler. Hannah is a true child of the new world. Born and raised among the hills by a restlessly wandering father, she dimly remembers a town-bred mother who tried out but could not learn to love the new life Hannah needs if she is to thrive. Where her mother pined for company of her own kind. Hannah shies from it like any forest creature; her ideal home is a cabin in a clearing, out of sight of the nearest neighbour folk, for she holds with the old frontier saying that "If you can see their smoke, they're too close." Alone in the world after her father's death, which is as hard and lonely as the life he has chosen to lead, Hannah is fairly forced to marry, against her independent inclinations. Women are scarce and sought-after, here at the back of the beyond, and men need strong and capable wives who will give them the children the country life requires. Hannah can have her pick of the single men of the fort, for all come courting in the abrupt and unromantic fashion of the time and place—but Hannah has chosen her own mate, Tice, and the matter is soon settled.

In Giles's hands this oddly arranged marriage of convenience becomes one of the deepest and most touching, if most understated, love stories of the frontier. Two less articulate people would be hard to find, but speech is scarcely necessary to Hannah and Tice; they completely understand one another. Through the vicissitudes of a very hard life, they become steadily more devoted, and from their strength and understanding grow new generations of the Fowler family, the subjects of further adventures as the country continues to open westward.

Giles is a writer who knows her subject and her setting absolutely. The day-to-day detail of her peoples' lives is as fascinating as their encounters with marauding Indians, ferocious weather, and the incredible privations that were a part of life at the outermost edge of civilization. It is humbling for a city-bred 20th-century reader to realize the proud self-sufficiency of these people of the not-so-long-ago, who could survive in the trackless forest equipped only with a knife and a flintlock gun; make a home and raise a family, and see the accomplishment as nothing remarkable. They had an independence that their remote descendants have long since exchanged for comforts and luxuries undreamt of by Hannah. How heartily she would have despised so poor an example of horse trading: a birthright frittered away for a mess of inferior pottage.

—Joan McGrath

GILLEN, Lucy. *See* **STRATTON, Rebecca.**

GLUYAS, Constance.   Born in England, in 1920. Served in the British Women's Auxiliary Air Force during World War II. Married Donald Gluyas in 1944. Lives in California. Address: c/o Teresa Kralik, New American Library, 1633 Broadway, New York, New York 10019, U.S.A.

Novels

The King's Brat. Englewood Cliffs, New Jersey, Prentice Hall, 1972; London, Hale, 1974.
Born to Be King. Englewood Cliffs, New Jersey, Prentice Hall, 1974; London, Hale, 1976.
My Lady Benbrook. Englewood Cliffs, New Jersey, Prentice Hall, 1975.
Brief Is the Glory. New York, McKay, 1975.
The House on Twyford Street. New York, McKay, 1976; London, Magnum, 1978.
My Lord Foxe. New York, McKay, 1976; London, Magnum, 1980.
Savage Eden. New York, New American Library, 1976; London, Sphere, 1978.
Rogue's Mistress. New York, New American Library, 1977; London, Sphere, 1978.
Woman of Fury. New York, New American Library, 1978; London, Hale, 1980.
Flame of the South. New York, New American Library, 1979; London, Sphere, 1981.
Madame Tudor. New York, New American Library, 1979.
Lord Sin. New York, New American Library, 1980.
The Passionate Savage. New York, New American Library, 1980.
The Bridge to Yesterday. New York, New American Library, 1981.

*   *   *

Constance Gluyas depicts a universe of romantic violence. Her novels have historical settings, and are notable for the turbulent passions of their heroines and the torture and humiliation to which they are subjected. Whether struggling for a crust in the gutters of Restoration London, or slaving on a tobacco plantation, Gluyas's ladies undergo brutal punishment, and display a breath-taking sexual vigour. Strong in endurance, they challenge all that a cruel world flings at them. It follows that the man of their choice must be even stronger and more masterful.

The King's Brat is typical, its urchin heroine imprisoned in Newgate for theft. Freed by Charles II, the intrepid Angel quickly works her way into society. Sought after by the King, she herself chooses the artist Nicholas Tavington. Though the course of their love is marred, they survive the horrors of the Great Plague to find wedded bliss. *The King's Brat* is a touch long-winded (verbosity is a familiar Gluyas failing), but the story is lively and the action full-blooded, the author dwelling equally on the delights of love and the squalor of poverty and prison in the 1660's.

Born to Be King is set during the 1745 Jacobite rebellion, with Elizabeth Drummond disguising herself as a man to join the rebels. The novel centres on her love-affair with the Englishman Moncrieff, who intends to betray the Prince but is later won over to his cause. The fortunes of the Jacobites are followed to Culloden, and final exile. Faster-moving than *The King's Brat*, *Born to Be King* contains the usual ingredients—wilful heroine, dark satanic hero, and their fierce love-hate relationship—that recur constantly in Gluyas's work.

Woman of Fury, with its witch-finder villain, is closer to fantasy than most. The perverted lustful Matthew Lorne, who covets his adopted daughter and kills wife and son with casual brutality, is so incredibly evil he teeters on the edge of absurdity. Some of the coincidences, too, are scarcely to be believed. But Gluyas's creations do not inhabit the real world. Theirs is the fevered kingdom of the imagination, where subtleties of character and plot give way to the garish visions of nightmare and dream. This accepted, the fast and furious action helps to suspend disbelief.

Among the most famous Gluyas novels are *Savage Eden* and *Rogue's Mistress*, with their central characters of Justin "Rogue" Lawrence and Caroline Fane. The works follow Lawrence and Caroline in their adventures as robbers in England, and later as convict settlers in the United States. The ferocity of love and hate is continually present. Like other Gluyas heroes and heroines, Justin and Caroline quarrel frequently, and their very lovemaking partakes of violence. The more recent *Flame of the South* deals with similar leading characters who combine passion with their efforts to free black slaves from the Southern plantations. The action is swift and savage as ever, the appetites as unquenchable.

Gluyas's creations, with their fiery heroines and formidable heroes, are of a world other than our own. Though a far from satisfactory stylist—sometimes prolix, at other times cramming the action into too short a compass—her writing drives home the one unvarying theme: the clash of strong woman with stronger man, and their physical union. The battle of the sexes becomes tedious, but on its own gothic grounds it remains valid. Gluyas writes with animal vigour, and shows herself fully aware of the beast beneath the skin.

—Geoffrey Sadler

GLYN, Elinor (née Sutherland).   British.   Born in Jersey, Channel Islands, 17 October 1864, of Canadian parents; grew up in Ontario and Jersey. Educated privately. Married Clayton Glyn in 1892 (died, 1915); two daughters. Canteen worker and war correspondent during World War I. Lived in the USA, 1920-29: film producer, writer, and director. *Died 23 September 1943.*

ROMANCE AND GOTHIC PUBLICATIONS

Novels

> *The Visits of Elizabeth.*   London, Duckworth, 1900; New York, Lane, 1901.
> *The Reflections of Ambrosine.*   London, Duckworth, and New York, Harper, 1902; as *The Seventh Commandment,* New York, Macaulay, n.d.
> *The Damsel and the Sage.*   London, Duckworth, and New York, Harper, 1903.
> *The Vicissitudes of Evangeline.*   London, Duckworth, and New York, Harper, 1905; as *Red Hair,* New York, Macaulay, n.d.
> *Beyond the Rocks.*   London, Duckworth, and New York, Harper, 1906.
> *Three Weeks.*   London, Duckworth, and New York, Business, 1907.
> *Elizabeth Visits America.*   London, Duckworth, and New York, Duffield, 1909.
> *His Hour.*   London, Duckworth, and New York, Appleton, 1910; as *When His Hour Came,* London, Newnes, 1915.
> *The Reason Why.*   London, Duckworth, and New York, Appleton, 1911.
> *Halcyone.*   London, Duckworth, and New York, Appleton, 1912; as *Love Itself,* New York, Author's Press, 1924 (?).
> *The Sequence 1905-1912.*   London, Duckworth, 1913; as *Guinevere's Lover,* New York, Appleton, 1913.
> *The Man and the Moment.*   New York, Appleton, 1914; London, Duckworth, 1915.
> *The Career of Katherine Bush.*   New York, Appleton, 1916; London, Duckworth, 1917.
> *The Price of Things.*   London, Duckworth, 1919; as *Family,* New York, Appleton, 1919.
> *Man and Maid—Renaissance.*   London, Duckworth, 1922; as *Man and Maid,* Philadelphia, Lippincott, 1922.
> *The Great Moment.*   London, Duckworth, and Philadelphia, Lippincott, 1923.
> *Six Days.*   London, Duckworth, and Philadelphia, Lippincott, 1924.
> *This Passion Called Love.*   London, Duckworth, and Auburn, New York, Author's Press, 1925.

Love's Blindness. London, Duckworth, and Auburn, New York, Author's Press, 1926.
The Flirt and the Flapper. London, Duckworth, 1930.
Love's Hour. London, Duckworth, and New York, Macaulay, 1932.
Glorious Flames (novelization of screenplay). London, Benn, 1932; New York, Macaulay, 1933.
Sooner or Later. London, Rich and Cowan, 1933; New York, Macaulay, 1935.
Did She? London, Rich and Cowan, 1934.
The Third Eye. London, Long, 1940.

Short Stories

The Contract and Other Stories. London, Duckworth, 1913; *The Point of View* published separately, New York, Appleton, 1913.
It and Other Stories. London, Duckworth, and New York, Macaulay, 1927.
Saint or Satyr? and Other Stories. London, Duckworth, 1933; as *Such Men Are Dangerous*, New York, Macaulay, 1933.

Uncollected Novel

"Elizabeth's Daughter," in *Novel Magazine* (London), February-May 1919.

OTHER PUBLICATIONS

Plays

Three Weeks, adaptation of her own novel (produced London, 1908).

Screenplays: *The Great Moment*, with Monte M. Katterjohn, 1921; *The World's a Stage*, with Colin Campbell and George Bertholon, 1922; *His Hour*, with King Vidor and Maude Fulton, 1924; *Three Weeks (The Romance of a Queen)*, with Carey Wilson, 1924; *How to Educate a Wife*, with Douglas Z. Doty and Grant Carpenter, 1924; *Man and Maid*, 1925; *The Only Thing*, 1925; *Love's Blindness*, 1926; *Ritzy*, with others, 1927; *It*, with others, 1927; *Three Week-Ends*, with others, 1928; *The Man and the Moment*, with Agnes Christine Johnston and Paul Perez, 1929; *Such Men Are Dangerous*, with Ernst Vajda, 1930; *Knowing Men*, with Edward Knoblock, 1930.

Other

The Sayings of Grandmama and Others. London, Duckworth, and New York, Duffield, 1908.
Letters to Caroline. London, Duckworth, 1914; as *Your Affectionate Godmother*, New York, Appleton, 1914.
Three Things. London, Duckworth, and New York, Hearst, 1915.
Destruction. London, Duckworth, 1918.
Points of View. London, Duckworth, 1920.
The Philosophy of Love. London, Duckworth, 1920.
The Elinor Glyn System of Writing. Auburn, New York, Author's Press, 4 vols., 1922.
The Philosophy of Love (different book from above). Auburn, New York, Author's Press, 1923; as *Love—What I Think of It*, London, Readers Library, 1928.
Letters from Spain. London, Duckworth, 1924.
The Wrinkle Book; or, How to Keep Looking Young. London, Duckworth, 1927; as *Eternal Youth*, New York, Macmillan, 1928.

Romantic Adventure (autobiography).   London, Nicholson and Watson, 1936; New
   York, Dutton, 1937.
Keep Young and Beautiful (selections), with Barbara Cartland.   London, Duckworth,
   1982.

Theatrical Activities:

   Director: **Films** — *Knowing Men*, 1930; *The Price of Things*, 1930.

   Actress: **Play** — The Queen, in *Three Weeks*, London, 1908.

Critical Study: *Elinor Glyn: A Biography* by Anthony Glyn, London, Hutchinson, 1955;
revised edition, 1968.

                              *   *   *

Elinor Glyn always felt that writing should stress feeling rather than ideas. Perhaps this
explains why, when she addressed the 1931 International P.E.N. Congress as a best-selling
author of 30 years' standing, she described herself as "A society person of no particular brains
or talents." She added, "I can't think why my books sell and make so much money." Glyn's
loyal readers found both intelligence and appeal in her romances, and the fantasy world of
rank, beauty, breeding, passion, and heroic self-restraint these works created.

Glyn's first novel, *The Visits of Elizabeth*, is a naughty epistolary romance featuring a pert,
charming ingenue narrator who observes the eccentricities and extra-marital adventures of
French and English nobility at a series of house-parties she attends. The novel created a great
stir among Glyn's society acquaintances, on whom it was based. The tone, form, and malicious
good humor appeared in two other novels, *Elizabeth Visits America* and *Elizabeth's Daughter*.
The three Elizabeth novels all reflect Glyn's views, travels, and preoccupation with good
breeding and physical beauty.

A second romance formula appears in a series of novels based on mismatches, marriages
between sensitive, beautiful aristocrats and unfeeling, unmannered newly rich. *The Reflections
of Ambrosine*, *The Vicissitudes of Evangeline*, and *Beyond the Rocks* are representative. The
titled half of the pair finds a true soulmate in a handsome and titled suitor. However sorely
tempted by adulterous passion, the heroines of these tales resist until their moneyed louts die
and they are free to marry again. These novels reflect a mistrust of money and a snobbish
insistence on rank difficult for the modern reader to accept.

Glyn's greatest success, the one work which best displays her style, her characters, and her
favorite themes of elegant snobbery and spiritual/sexual attraction is *Three Weeks*—a purple
prose hymn to aristocratic soul passion. Roughly inspired by the assassination of Queen Draga
of Serbia, *Three Weeks* describes the spiritual and sensual awakening of a handsome young
English noble, Paul, by an unnamed, dark, wilful Slavic beauty of noble rank—the Lady. After
their meeting in Switzerland, Paul presents the Lady with a gift that he feels reflects her
untamed and splendid spirit: a tigerskin. When he next calls on the Lady, he sees:

   a bright fire burnt in the grate, and some palest mauve curtains were drawn....And
   loveliest sight of all, in front of the fire, stretched at full length, was his tiger—and on
   him—also at full length—reclined his lady, garbed in some strange clinging garment
   of heavy purple crepe, one white arm resting on the beast's head, her back supported
   by a pile of velvet cusions and a heap of rarely bound books at her side, while between
   her lips was a rose not redder than they—an almost scarlet rose.

The relationship between Paul and the Lady soon blossoms into a short but intense affair that
takes them to Venice, where they part, never to meet again. The Lady, however, has conceived a
son who will some day inherit the throne of Russia.

Despite its heady mixture of eroticism and exoticism, *Three Weeks* remains remarkably
moral in tone. The adulterous love of Paul and the Lady is based on a mutually lofty

recognition of beauty and nobility; their physical union represents a small portion of their spiritual experience. Denied each other by Fate, the lovers are punished for their adultery by the Lady's brutal murder at the hands of her degenerate husband. Critical response to *Three Weeks* was favorable but guarded; popular response was spectacular. Elinor Glyn became a household word and all of her works best-sellers. Moral objection was voiced largely in America, where the novel was banned in several states. However, readers on both sides of the Atlantic were drawn by the image of passion blazing beyond sexuality in *Three Weeks*; "It," sexuality and attraction, was delineated, but never so vividly, in Glyn's later films and fiction.

Elinor Glyn's travels in the United States and her work in the developing American film industry modified her rigid early views on noble blood and gentle breeding. Her later works, notably *The Career of Katherine Bush*, show that independent, handsome, disciplined men and women can train themselves for social standing. This theme demonstrates that character can triumph over circumstances to allow a hero or heroine to find ennobling love.

The shortcomings of Elinor Glyn's 25 romances—the defense of snobbery, the equation of character with physical beauty, the remarkable combination of bourgeois prudishness and aristocratic passion—are the very elements that made her romances so appealing to her readers. Glyn herself described romance as "spiritual disguise created by the imagination with which to envelop material happenings with desires and thus bring them into greater harmony with the soul." Glyn's novels created a romance world which her readers could otherwise never know. With her and through her work, generations of readers lived this fantasy of romance.

—Katherine Staples

GODDEN, (Margaret) Rumer. British. Born in Sussex, 10 December 1907. Educated privately and at Moira House, Eastbourne, Sussex. Married 1) Laurence Sinclair Foster in 1934, two daughters; 2) James Lesley Haynes Dixon in 1949 (died, 1973). Former director of a children's ballet school, Calcutta. Recipient: Whitbread Award, for children's book, 1973. Agent: Curtis Brown Ltd., 1 Craven Hill, London W2 3EP, England. Address: The Small House, Tundergarth, Lockerbie, Dumfriesshire DG11 2PU, Scotland.

ROMANCE AND GOTHIC PUBLICATIONS

Novels

Chinese Puzzle. London, Davies, 1936.
The Lady and the Unicorn. London, Davies, 1937.
Black Narcissus. London, Davies, and Boston, Little Brown, 1939.
Gypsy, Gypsy. London, Davies, and Boston, Little Brown, 1940.
Breakfast with the Nikolides. London, Davies, and Boston, Little Brown, 1942.
A Fugue in Time. London, Joseph, 1945; as *Take Three Tenses: A Fugue in Time*, Boston, Little Brown, 1945.
The River. London, Joseph, and Boston, Little Brown, 1946.
A Candle for St. Jude. London, Joseph, and New York, Viking Press, 1948.
A Breath of Air. London, Joseph, 1950; New York, Viking Press, 1951.
Kingfishers Catch Fire. London, Macmillan, and New York, Viking Press, 1953.
An Episode of Sparrows. New York, Viking Press, 1955; London, Macmillan, 1956.
The Greengage Summer. London, Macmillan, and New York, Viking Press, 1958.

China Court: The Hours of a Country House. London, Macmillan, and New York, Viking Press, 1961.
The Battle of the Villa Fiorita. London, Macmillan, and New York, Viking Press, 1963.
In This House of Brede. London, Macmillan, and New York, Viking Press, 1969.
The Peacock Spring. London, Macmillan, 1975; New York, Viking Press, 1976.
Five for Sorrow, Ten for Joy. London, Macmillan, and New York, Viking Press, 1979.
The Dark Horse. London, Macmillan, 1981; New York; Viking Press, 1982.

Short Stories

Mooltiki and Other Stories and Poems of India. London, Macmillan, and New York, Viking Press, 1957.
Swans and Turtles: Stories. London, Macmillan, 1968; as *Gone: A Thread of Stories*, New York, Viking Press, 1968.

OTHER PUBLICATIONS

Plays

Screenplays: *The River*, with Jean Renoir, 1951; *Innocent Sinners*, with Neil Patterson, 1958.

Verse (juvenile)

In Noah's Ark. London, Joseph, and New York, Viking Press, 1949.
St. Jerome and the Lion. London, Macmillan, and New York, Viking Press, 1961.

Other

Rungli-Rungliot (Thus Far and No Further). London, Davies, 1943; as *Rungli-Rungliot Means in Paharia, Thus Far and No Further*, Boston, Little Brown, 1946; as *Thus Far and No Further*, London, Macmillan, 1961.
Bengal Journey: A Story of the Part Played by Women in the Province 1939-1945. London, Longman, 1945.
The Doll's House (juvenile). London, Joseph, 1947; New York, Viking Press, 1948.
The Mousewife (juvenile). London, Macmillan, and New York, Viking Press, 1951.
Impunity Jane: The Story of a Pocket Doll (juvenile). New York, Viking Press, 1954; London, Macmillan, 1955.
Hans Christian Andersen: A Great Life in Brief. London, Hutchinson, and New York, Knopf, 1955.
The Fairy Doll (juvenile). London, Macmillan, and New York, Viking Press, 1956.
Mouse House (juvenile). New York, Viking Press, 1957; London, Macmillan, 1958.
The Story of Holly and Ivy (juvenile). London, Macmillan, and New York, Viking Press, 1958.
Candy Floss (juvenile). London, Macmillan, and New York, Viking Press, 1960.
Miss Happiness and Miss Flower (juvenile). London, Macmillan, and New York, Viking Press, 1961.
Little Plum (juvenile). London, Macmillan, and New York, Viking Press, 1963.
Home Is the Sailor (juvenile). London, Macmillan, and New York, Viking Press, 1964.
Two under the Indian Sun (autobiography), with Jon Godden. London, Macmillan, and New York, Knopf, 1966.
The Kitchen Madonna (juvenile). London, Macmillan, and New York, Viking Press, 1969.

Operation Sippacik (juvenile).   London, Macmillan, and New York, Viking Press, 1969.

The Tale of the Tales: The Beatrix Potter Ballet.   London, Warne, 1971.

Shiva's Pigeons: An Experience of India, with Jon Godden.   London, Chatto and Windus, and New York, Viking Press, 1972.

The Old Woman Who Lived in a Vinegar Bottle (juvenile).   London, Macmillan, and New York, Viking Press, 1972.

The Diddakoi (juvenile).   London, Macmillan, and New York, Viking Press, 1972.

Mr. McFadden's Hallowe'en (juvenile).   London, Macmillan, and New York, Viking Press, 1975.

The Rocking Horse Secret (juvenile).   London, Macmillan, 1977; New York, Viking Press, 1978.

The Butterfly Lions: The Story of the Pekingese in History, Legend and Art.   London, Macmillan, 1977; New York, Viking Press, 1978.

A Kindle of Kittens (juvenile).   London, Macmillan, 1978; New York, Viking Press, 1979.

Gulbadan: Portrait of a Rose Princess at the Mughal Court.   London, Macmillan, 1980; New York, Viking Press, 1981.

The Dragon of Og (juvenile).   London, Macmillan, and New York, Viking Press, 1981.

Editor, *Round the Day, Round the Year, The World Around: Poetry Programmes for Classroom or Library.*   London, Macmillan, 6 vols., 1966-67.

Editor, *A Letter to the World: Poems for Young Readers*, by Emily Dickinson.   London, Bodley Head, 1968; New York, Macmillan, 1969.

Editor, *Mrs. Manders' Cookbook*, by Olga Manders.   London, Macmillan, and New York, Viking Press, 1968.

Editor, *The Raphael Bible.*   London, Macmillan, and New York, Viking Press, 1970.

Translator, *Prayers from the Ark* (verse), by Carmen de Gasztold.   New York, Viking Press, 1962; London, Macmillan, 1963.

Translator, *The Creatures' Choir* (verse), by Carmen de Gasztold.   New York, Viking Press, 1965; as *The Beasts' Choir*, London, Macmillan, 1967.

Critical Study: *Rumer Godden* by Hassell A. Simpson, New York, Twayne, 1973.

*   *   *

Although many of Rumer Godden's novels might fit into the broad category of romance, they rarely concentrate on an individual's solitary search for love and happiness. Instead, her characters always exist as part of larger entities from which they cannot escape.

First, a person is part of his culture. This fact is most clear in the novels set in India. Europeans can never change or become part of the Indian world. The nuns in *Black Narcissus* discover this in the Himalayas. Instead of changing the local people by bringing them modern education and medicine, the sisters' own discipline breaks down as rules are bent to accommodate the foreign life. After one sister goes mad, the nuns are forced to leave, realizing that their stay will have made no impact and will be quickly forgotten. Just as the Indians will not change to conform to European ways, neither can an English person become an Indian. Despite Sophie Ward's desire to live like the peasants in Kashmir in *Kingfishers Catch Fire*, she cannot understand village ways. Her blindness to local customs puts her children in danger. After her daughter is badly beaten, Sophie must leave.

Secondly, people are bound by their religion. The submission of the individual to religion is most apparent in *Black Narcissus, In This House of Brede*, and *Five for Sorrow, Ten for Joy*, which concern women in religious communities. But the presence of the Divine is felt in other works as well. For example, in *A Candle for St. Jude* Miss Ilse is convinced that disaster at her sister-in-law's ballet school is averted because of her prayers to St. Jude, patron of impossible causes.

Above all, an individual is part of a family. As young Harriet discovers in *The River*, within a family one learns fundamental lessons about life, love, birth, and death during the passage from childhood to adulthood. Fanny Clavering (*The Battle of the Villa Fiorita*) discovers that family ties cannot be broken. When she runs away to Italy with her lover, her children follow, and a saddened and subdued Fanny returns with them to England. The continuity of family is most apparent in *A Fugue in Time* and *China Court*, both of which are set in houses that have been part of a family for generations. In *China Court* Mrs. Quin wills the estate to her granddaughter on the condition that she marry a man she has never met but whom Mrs. Quin admires because he has restored her farm. This arranged marriage is the antithesis of the modern idea of romance, but Peter and Tracy agree. These two books employ one of Godden's most successful devices, the parallel inclusion of past, present, and future time. Layers on layers of family sayings fill *China Court*, and their meanings become clear only as the history of the house is revealed.

The juxtaposition of past, present, and future events enriches some of her best books, *In This House of Brede* and *Five for Sorrow, Ten for Joy*. Godden maintains reader interest in details of the nuns' present life, and the characters gradually assume more depth as their former lives are revealed through flashbacks.

Godden's fine handling of time shifts is one of the techniques that enrich her writing. Another is her evocation of place. Her descriptive skill is especially apparent in her Indian novels, notably *The River*.

Although her books do not demand rereading or in-depth study to be understood, they reveal Godden's careful attention to the craft of writing. As Virgilia Peterson said, "If it can be objected that Miss Godden's reach never exceeds her grasp, it can also be argued that perfection, on any scale, does not need to be justified."

—Kathy Piehl

GOODWIN, Suzanne. *See* **EBEL, Suzanne.**

GORDON, Ethel Edison. American. Born in New York City, 5 May 1915. Educated at Washington Square College of New York University, B.A. (cum laude) 1936 (Phi Beta Kappa). Married Herman Gordon in 1936; one son. Agent: John Schaffner Associates, 425 East 51st Street, New York, New York 10022. Address: 105 Lake Drive, Hewlett Harbor, New York 11557, U.S.A.

Novels

    Freer's Cove.   New York, Coward McCann, 1972.
    The Chaperone.   New York, Coward McCann, 1973; London, Barker, 1974.
    The Birdwatcher.   New York, McKay, 1974; London, Barker, 1975.
    The Freebody Heiress.   New York, McKay, and London, Barker, 1974.
    The French Husband.   New York, Crowell, 1977.
    The Venetian Lover.   New York, Dell, 1982.

Uncollected Short Stories

    "Hat for My Wife," in *Woman's Home Companion* (Springfield, Ohio), May 1947.
    "His Wife's Sister," in *Woman's Home Companion* (Springfield, Ohio), December 1948.
    "Change of Heart," in *Collier's* (New York), 24 September 1949.
    "Time for Innocence," in *Collier's* (New York), 28 October 1950.
    "Mainly about Caroline," in *Collier's* (New York), 23 January 1951.
    "Blue Coast," in *Collier's* (New York), 8 November 1952.
    "Markham's Girl," in *Collier's* (New York), 28 March 1953.
    "Rose in Her Hair," in *Collier's* (New York), 23 May 1953.
    "Fault of Love," in *Cosmopolitan* (New York), June 1953.
    "Deception," in *Ladies Home Journal* (Philadelphia), February 1957.
    "Child Lost," in *Ladies Home Journal* (Philadelphia), June 1958.
    "Quiet Baby," in *Cosmopolitan* (New York), October 1959.
    "Love Me, Love My Mother," in *Cosmopolitan* (New York), January 1960.
    "No Time Like Yesterday," in *Cosmopolitan* (New York), June 1960.
    "Love Incognito," in *Ladies Home Journal* (Philadelphia), April 1961.
    "For All My Family, With Love," in *Redbook* (Dayton, Ohio), August 1961.
    "Safe, Sure Place," in *Redbook* (Dayton, Ohio), July 1962.
    "Long Dream," in *Redbook* (Dayton, Ohio), September 1962.
    "Remember," in *Redbook* (Dayton, Ohio), March 1963.
    "Small Cause for Alarm," in *Redbook* (Dayton, Ohio), June 1963.
    "Holiday Dance," in *Redbook* (Dayton, Ohio), December 1963.
    "Someone to Share," in *Redbook* (Dayton, Ohio), June 1964.
    "Summer Husband," in *Redbook* (Dayton, Ohio), January 1965.
    "New Neighbors," in *Redbook* (Dayton, Ohio), November 1965.
    "My Enemy," in *Redbook* (Dayton, Ohio), January 1966.
    "Legacy," in *McCall's* (Dayton, Ohio), April 1966.
    "Make Me No Match" in *McCall's* (Dayton, Ohio), May 1967.
    "House by the Water," in *Redbook* (Dayton, Ohio), October 1969.
    "Mrs. Marvel's Magic Carpet," in *Ladies Home Journal* (Philadelphia), May 1970.
    "Well-Loved Wife," in *Redbook* (Dayton, Ohio), June 1971.

OTHER PUBLICATIONS

Novels (juvenile)

    Where Does the Summer Go.   New York, Crowell, 1967.
    So Far from Home.   New York, Crowell, 1968.

Ethel Edison Gordon comments:

I have always enjoyed using an interesting foreign locale—foreign to me in America, that is—as a background for my fiction. Usually an American girl finds herself in a suspenseful situation in an environment that is different from her own. She moves from one continent to the other, to unravel the romantic but hostile predicament. This gives me a chance to re-visit the places I've enjoyed through fiction—from the Shetland Isles to the mountains of France to the lagoons of Venice.

*   *   *

In the 1970's, Ethel Edison Gordon turned to writing gothic romance after having published two novels for young people and numerous romantic short stories. All of her work has a modern and relevant theme.

In her first novel, *Where Does the Summer Go*, 15-year-old Freddie learns to accept adult imperfections and loses much of her idealism as she forges new relationships with her boyfriend and family. The book is written with perception and realism and is satisfying for young adult readers, but the next novel, *So Far From Home*, suffers from awkward time changes. Orphaned at 13, Miranda clings to an idealized past, and, at 18, recognizes that people and events probably were not as she remembers them.

Freer's Cove is Gordon's only gothic novel set entirely in the United States. Pregnant, Daisy becomes a companion to the expectant wife of Amos Freer. She snoops into family affairs and attempts to solve the mystery of the death of Ernest Freer's wife. She finds herself in grave danger after her son is born. To dip into this book is to be committed to the end.

In *The Chaperone* Carrie Belding, a teacher, accompanies a student on a trip to France and must assess the love between Maria and an American hotelier. When death threatens and then occurs, Carrie wonders if the killer is the man with whom she has reluctantly fallen in love. The story is entertaining and easy to read.

The Birdwatcher involves some missing top-secret research notes. A visit to the Shetland Isles is designed to help Lisette forget the missing papers and her dead fiancé, but it offers attempts on her life instead. She cannot understand her cousin's demented behavior or her husband's apparently callous reactions. The novel is packed with red herrings which keep the reader turning pages steadily.

The Freebody Heiress begins in New England when a young college professor rents an unused gatehouse from an overprotected and extremely shy heiress. Iris falls in love with Sexton as he teaches her independence, but she cannot trust him and flees to France where Sexton finds and marries her. Honeymooning in Switzerland, Iris's life is threatened. The twists and turns are expected, but the writing is professional and well done.

In *The French Husband* Luc has been disinherited from his family's vineyards and is obsessed with getting reinstated. Emily follows him to France and becomes involved in the family history as well as with her husband's brother. Hatred and revenge almost get her killed as Luc loses grip on reality. An obvious plot has some interesting turns, and the setting is lovely and vividly described.

Readers can relate to Gordon's writings and to her main characters because they are contemporary and real. What she began in her short stories, she expanded in her novels, often using the same themes and character types. Short stories and novels alike reveal a talented and professional writer who offers her readers well-thought-out entertainment.

—Andrea Lee Shuey

GOUDGE, Elizabeth (de Beauchamp). British. Born in Wells, Somerset, 24 April 1900. Educated at Grassendale School, Southbourne, Hampshire; Reading University School of Art. Recipient: Library Association Carnegie Medal, 1947. Fellow, Royal Society of Literature, 1946. Agent: David Higham Associates Ltd., 5-8 Lower John Street, London WIR 4HA. Address: Rose Cottage, Peppard Common, Henley-on-Thames, Oxfordshire, England.

ROMANCE AND GOTHIC PUBLICATIONS

Novels

Island Magic. London, Duckworth, and New York, Coward McCann, 1934.
The Middle Window. London, Duckworth, 1935; New York, Coward McCann, 1939.
A City of Bells. London, Duckworth, and New York, Coward McCann, 1936.
Towers in the Mist. London, Duckworth, and New York, Coward McCann, 1938.
The Bird in the Tree. London, Duckworth, and New York, Coward McCann, 1940.
The Castle on the Hill. London, Duckworth, and New York, Coward McCann, 1941.
Green Dolphin Country. London, Hodder and Stoughton, 1944; as *Green Dolphin Street*, New York, Coward McCann, 1944.
The Herb of Grace. London, Hodder and Stoughton, 1948; as *Pilgrim's Inn*, New York, Coward McCann, 1948.
Gentian Hill. London, Hodder and Stoughton, and New York, Coward McCann, 1949.
The Heart of the Family. London, Hodder and Stoughton, and New York, Coward McCann, 1953.
The Rosemary Tree. London, Hodder and Stoughton, and New York, Coward McCann, 1956.
The White Witch. London, Hodder and Stoughton, and New York, Coward McCann, 1958.
The Dean's Watch. London, Hodder and Stoughton, and New York, Coward McCann, 1960.
The Scent of Water. London, Hodder and Stoughton, and New York, Coward McCann, 1963.
The Child from the Sea. London, Hodder and Stoughton, and New York, Coward McCann, 1970.

Short Stories

The Fairies' Baby and Other Stories. London, Foyle, 1919.
A Pedlar's Pack and Other Stories. London, Duckworth, and New York, Coward McCann, 1937.
The Golden Skylark and Other Stories. London, Duckworth, and New York, Coward McCann, 1941.
The Ikon on the Wall and Other Stories. London, Duckworth, 1943.
The Reward of Faith and Other Stories. London, Duckworth, 1950; New York, Coward McCann, 1951.
White Wings: Collected Short Stories. London, Duckworth, 1952.
The Lost Angel. London, Hodder and Stoughton, and New York, Coward McCann, 1971.

OTHER PUBLICATIONS

Fiction (for children)

Sister of the Angels: A Christmas Story. London, Duckworth, and New York, Coward McCann, 1939.
Smoky-House. London, Duckworth, and New York, Coward McCann, 1940.
The Well of the Star. New York, Coward McCann, 1941.
Henrietta's House. London, University of London Press-Hodder and Stoughton, 1942; as *The Blue Hills*, New York, Coward McCann, 1942.
The Little White Horse. London, University of London Press, 1946; New York, Coward McCann, 1947.
Make-Believe. London, Duckworth, 1949; Boston, Bentley, 1953.
The Valley of Song. London, University of London Press, 1951; New York, Coward McCann, 1952.
Linnets and Valerians. Leicester, Brockhampton Press, and New York, Coward McCann, 1964.
I Saw Three Ships. Leicester, Brockhampton Press, and New York, Coward McCann, 1969.

Plays

Joy Will Come Back (produced London, 1937).
Suomi (produced London, 1938). Included in *Three Plays*, 1939.
Three Plays: Suomi, The Brontës of Haworth, and Fanny Burney. London, Duckworth, 1939.
Fanny Burney (produced Oldham, Lancashire, 1949). Included in *Three Plays*, 1939.

Verse

Songs and Verses. London, Duckworth, 1947; New York, Coward McCann, 1948.

Other

The Elizabeth Goudge Reader, edited by Rose Dobbs. New York, Coward McCann, 1946; as *At the Sign of the Dolphin: An Elizabeth Goudge Anthlogy*, London, Hodder and Stoughton, 1947.
God So Loved the World: A Life of Christ (juvenile). London, Hodder and Stoughton, and New York, Coward McCann, 1951.
Saint Francis of Assisi. London, Duckworth, 1959; as *My God and My All: The Life of St. Francis of Assisi*, New York, Coward McCann, 1959.
The Chapel of the Blessed Virgin Mary, Buckler's Hard, Beaulieu. Privately printed, 1966.
A Christmas Book (anthology). London, Hodder and Stoughton, and New York, Coward McCann, 1967.
The Ten Gifts (anthology), edited by Mary Baldwin. London, Hodder and Stoughton, and New York, Coward McCann, 1969.
The Joy of the Snow: An Autobiography. London, Hodder and Stoughton, and New York, Coward McCann, 1974.
Pattern of People: An Elizabeth Goudge Anthology, edited by Muriel Grainger. London, Hodder and Stoughton, 1978; New York, Coward McCann, 1979.

Editor, *A Book of Comfort: An Anthology.* London, Joseph, and New York, Coward McCann, 1964.

Editor, *A Diary of Prayer*.   London, Hodder and Stoughton, and New York, Coward
   McCann, 1966.
Editor, *A Book of Peace: An Anthology*.   London, Joseph, 1967; New York, Coward
   McCann, 1968.
Editor, *A Book of Faith*.   London, Hodder and Stoughton, and New York, Coward
   McCann, 1976.

*   *   *

Elizabeth Goudge's sun-warmed world is not one of unruffled serenity—but it is one of deep underlying peace and certainty. Troubles and grief will certainly come to her people, but they are made bearable by the faith that they will in time, like the grain of sand that chafes the oyster, be transmuted into pearls.

Her own religious convictions provide a bedrock for the roster of stories which have for so many years charmed and enchanted huge audiences. Charmed, for they are charming as Dresden figurines or filigree music boxes are charming: not the hard gritty stuff of real life, nor ever pretending to be so; prettier and finer textured than the world they scarcely resemble. Enchanted, as well, for these stories are magical in the fairy tale sense. Goudge's stories for younger readers, like the notably successful *The Little White Horse*, are indeed fairy tales of unicorns and enchanted castles, and the magical aura remains in her stories for adult readers, those loyal souls who boldly keep faith with the creed of "happily ever after."

Goudge's romances seem especially concerned with two categories of lovers who seldom play prominent roles in such tales, the very young, too young even to become engaged, and the very old, still devoted after long years of marriage, or reunited after a lifetime of separation. Her best-loved work, which triumphantly combined both of these perspectives, is *Green Dolphin Country* (*Green Dolphin Street*). In this long tale of three interwoven life stories, the trio of young lovers, Marianne, Marguerite, and William, meet as children, far too young, it would seem, for them to form any lasting attachments, too young indeed to think of any such matters. But these are not ordinary children, they are *Goudge* children, and they meet on a day of enchantment. They do learn to love—forever.

But there are three of them, and alas, one man can marry only one sister, not two. When the trio are grown, and William has made his way to the other side of the world and won his fortune, he, the beloved of both sisters, must choose one to be his bride. Marguerite has always been his true love, although he has a sharp admiration for the spirited elder sister, Marianne. In the letter proposing marriage to the one woman he longs for, William's hand betrays his heart—he addresses the letter to the wrong sister, and is accepted. A true gentleman, William resolves to live and die with his mistake locked in his memory, never to hurt the woman he has married so reluctantly. No one shall ever know...and indeed, William and Marianne make a life for themselves, though not the life either had dreamed of, while Marguerite becomes a nun, and fills an empty life with prayer and eventual peace. Suddenly, long years later, in a fit of anger with his wife, William lets slip the truth that their life together has been based upon a lie and a sham; that he married Marianne out of pity, not for love. Marianne is shocked, both by what has been hidden from her, and that William has made this lifelong gallant gesture to save her pride. Bravely she tells Marguerite of William's old mistake. It is all a tale of long ago, but Marguerite's life is illumined with joy that she had not been mistaken in William's devotion, and that it remains true. And Marianne has her reward; by telling her sister the secret, as William would not have done out of loyalty to her, she wins his admiring love after all. This story, with its panoramic sweep of action from the Channel Islands to New Zealand, and its strongly contrasted characterization, captured the fancy of an admiring public, and is as readable today as ever.

It has worn better, perhaps, than others of her stories, most of them set in the peaceful English cathedral towns she loves so well. Placid exteriors may sometimes conceal highly coloured drama, but Goudge's quiet, sunny cities of church towers and bells provide settings for gentle, wistful romances in which true love never goes unrequited, and hearts, though broken, always mend in time.

Roly-poly loveable vicars are endlessly understanding; deans may appear formidable, but are melted butter beneath the stern facade; young men desert families or sweethearts, have returned broken and aimless from the wars, or have fled the brutal life of midshipmen: they must inevitably meet glowing young women who will make all well. A young actress, for instance, who longs to lay aside her laurels for a life of placid domesticity, adores to work in an unlikely little book store and longs to live in a cottage—or, more unlikely still, who contrives to combine this life with one of amazing success on the West End stage.

Goudge's children are not like those who burden and glorify the lives of ordinary folk. There is in her work a fairly definite division between youngsters of two sorts, typified by the children of *A City of Bells* (and other titles), Hugh Anthony and Henrietta. The boy is a thoughtless, healthily selfish freckled ball of endless energy, who will almost always do the right thing if it is only explained to him in a tactful way: the girl is a sensitive wisp, prey to storms of emotion, given to moments of transcendent joy of the world, who forgives her feckless father for his neglect, and adores her bumptious step-brother.

In varied guises—for occasionally it is the boy who is introspective and super-sensitive—these children appear and reappear, and are recognizable still in most of her adult characters. It is easy to trace the source of the angel child who sees the world's beauty with thankful joy: she must closely resemble her literary mother, who describes scenes of beauty so vividly that they are spread before the readers' eyes in colours that live.

Elizabeth Goudge is a writer for a clearly defined audience; for readers who know what they like, and who happily read it over and over again, preferring only minor variations on the theme; who deplore horrid surprises or harsh truths, and who like nice people living in nice places to have stories that end nicely. There is little here of passion, but a great deal of enduring love. For those who prefer the steadily burning candle to the fitful blaze, Elizabeth Goudge's books are quiet, dependable beacons across the stormy seas of ordinary life.

—Joan McGrath

GRANGE, Peter. *See* **NICOLE, Christopher**.

GRAY, Angela. *See* **DANIELS, Dorothy**.

GRAY, Harriet. *See* **ROBINS, Denise**.

GREIG, Maysie. Pseudonym for Jennifer Greig-Smith; also wrote as Jennifer Ames; Ann Barclay; Mary Douglas Warre; Mary Douglas Warren. Australian. Born in Sydney, New South Wales, in 1902. Educated at Presbyterian Ladies' College, Pymble, New South Wales. Married 1) Delano Ames; 2) Maxwell Murray in 1937 (died, 1956); 3) Jan Sopoushek in 1959. Journalist: staff member of Sydney *Sun* before coming to London: contributor to *Westminster Gazette, Daily Sketch*, and *Mirror*; also worked in New York and Boston. Vice-President, New South Wales P.E.N. *Died 10 June 1971*.

ROMANCE AND GOTHIC PUBLICATIONS

Novels

Peggy of Beacon Hill. Boston, Small Maynard, 1924; London, Jenkins, 1926.
The Luxury Husband. London, Long, and New York, Dial Press, 1928.
Ragamuffin. London, Long, 1929.
Satin Straps. London, Long, and New York, Dial Press, 1929.
Jasmine—Take Care! or, A Girl Must Marry. London, Benn, 1930; as *A Girl Must Marry*, New York, Dial Press, 1931.
Lovely Clay. London, Benn, 1930; New York, Doubleday, 1933.
A Nice Girl Comes to Town. London, Long, and New York, Dial Press, 1930.
The Man She Bought. New York, Dial Press, 1930.
This Way to Happiness. London, Long, 1931; New York, Dial Press, 1932; as *Janice*, Cleveland, World, 1947.
One-Man Girl. London, Benn, and New York, Dial Press, 1931.
The Women Money Buys. New York, Dial Press, 1931.
Faint Heart, Fair Lady. London, Long, 1932.
Laughing Cavalier. London, Long, 1932.
Little Sisters Don't Count. London, Benn, 1932; New York, Doubleday, 1934.
Cake Without Icing. London, Benn, and New York, Dial Press, 1932; revised edition, as *Marriage Without a Ring*, London, Collins, 1972.
Professional Lover. London, Benn, and New York, Doubleday, 1933; as *Screen Lover*, London, Collins, 1969.
Parents Are a Problem. London, Hodder and Stoughton, 1933; as *Love, Honour, and Obey*, New York, Doubleday, 1933.
A Bad Girl Leaves Town. New York, Doubleday, 1933.
Men Act That Way. New York, Doubleday, 1933.
Heart Appeal. London, Hodder and Stoughton, 1934; New York, Doubleday, 1935.
She Walked into His Parlour. London, Hodder and Stoughton, 1934.
Ten Cent Love. New York, Doubleday, 1934.
I Lost My Heart. London, Hodder and Stoughton, 1935; New York, Doubleday, 1936; as *The Sinister Island* (as Jennifer Ames), London, Collins, 1968.
Love and Let Me Go. New York, Doubleday, 1935; London, Hodder and Stoughton, 1936; as *Love Me*, London, Collins, 1971.
Marry in Haste. London, Hodder and Stoughton, and New York, Doubleday, 1935.

Rich Man, Poor Girl.   London, Hodder and Stoughton, and New York, Doubleday, 1935.

Challenge to Happiness.   London, Hodder and Stoughton, 1936; New York, Doubleday, 1937.

The Girl from Nowhere.   Hanley, Staffordshire, Locker, 1936; New York, Doubleday, 1942; as *The Girl Who Wasn't Welcome*, London, Collins, 1969.

Odds on Love.   London, Hodder and Stoughton, and New York, Doubleday, 1936.

Workaday Lady.   London, Hodder and Stoughton, and New York, Doubleday, 1936.

Touching the Clouds.   New York, Doubleday, 1936.

New Moon Through a Window.   London, Hodder and Stoughton, and New York, Doubleday, 1937.

Retreat from Love.   London, Hodder and Stoughton, 1937; as Jennifer Ames, New York, Doubleday, 1937.

The Pretty One.   London, Hodder and Stoughton, 1937; as Jennifer Ames, New York, Doubleday, 1937.

The Girl Men Talked About.   London, Hodder and Stoughton, 1938; as *Stopover in Paradise*, New York, Doubleday, 1938; as *The Golden Garden*, London, Collins, 1968.

Young Man Without Money.   London, Hodder and Stoughton, 1938; as *Debutante in Uniform*, New York, Doubleday, 1938.

Stepping under Ladders.   London, Hodder and Stoughton, 1938; New York, Doubleday, 1939; as *Girl in Jeopardy*, London, Collins, 1967.

Other Women's Beauty.   London, Hodder and Stoughton, 1938.

Strange Beauty.   New York, Doubleday, 1938.

Ask the Parlourmaid.   London, Hodder and Stoughton, 1939; as *Unmarried Couple*, New York, Doubleday, 1940.

Girl on His Hands.   London, Hodder and Stoughton, and New York, Doubleday, 1939.

A Man to Protect You.   London, Hodder and Stoughton, and New York, Doubleday, 1939.

Grand Relations.   London, Hodder and Stoughton, 1940; as *A Fortune in Romance*, New York, Doubleday, 1940; as *A Girl and Her Money*, London, Collins, 1971.

The Man Is Always Right.   London, Hodder and Stoughton, and New York, Doubleday, 1940.

Rich Twin, Poor Twin.   London, Hodder and Stoughton, and New York, Doubleday, 1940.

Girl Without Credit.   New York, Doubleday, 1941; London, Hodder and Stoughton, 1942.

This Desirable Bachelor.   London, Hodder and Stoughton, and New York, Doubleday, 1941.

Heaven Isn't Here.   New York, Doubleday, 1941.

No Retreat from Love.   New York, Doubleday, 1942; Hanley, Staffordshire, Locker, 1947.

Salute Me Darling.   London, Hodder and Stoughton, 1942; as *Heartbreak for Two*, New York, Doubleday, 1942.

The Wishing Star.   New York, Doubleday, 1942; as Mary Douglas Warre, London, Hutchinson, 1943.

Pathway to Paradise.   New York, Doubleday, 1942; London, Collins, 1943.

Professional Hero.   London, Collins, and New York, Doubleday, 1943.

I've Always Loved You.   New York, Doubleday, 1943.

Reluctant Millionaire.   London, Collins, 1944; New York, Random House, 1945.

One Room for His Highness.   London, Collins, 1944.

Girl with a Million.   London, Collins, 1945.

I Loved Her Yesterday.   London, Collins, 1945.

Darling Clementine.   London, Collins, 1946; as *Candidate for Love*, New York, Random House, 1947.

Table for Two.   London, Collins, and New York, Random House, 1946.

Castle in the Air.   London, Collins, 1947.

The Thirteenth Girl.   Hanley, Staffordshire, Locker, 1947.

Take This Man.   London, Collins, 1947.

I Met Him Again. London, Collins, 1948.

Yours Forever. London, Collins, and New York, Random House, 1948.

Whispers in the Sun. London, Collins, and New York, Random House, 1949; as *The Reluctant Cinderella* (as Jennifer Ames), New York, Avalon, and Collins, 1952.

Dark Carnival. New York, Random House, 1950; as Jennifer Ames, London, Collins, 1951.

My Heart's Down Under. London, Collins, 1951; as Jennifer Ames, New York, Avalon, 1951.

It Happened One Flight. London, Collins, 1951; New York, Macfadden, 1966.

London, Here I Come. London, Collins, 1951; as *Assignment to Love* (as Jennifer Ames), New York, Avalon, 1953.

Wagon to a Star. London, Collins, 1952; as Jennifer Ames, New York, Avalon, 1953.

Lovers under the Sun. London, Collins, 1954; as *Passport to Happiness*, New York, Avalon, 1955; as *Ship's Doctor*, Collins, 1966.

That Girl in Nice. London, Collins, 1954; as *Love Is a Gamble* (as Jennifer Ames), New York, Avalon, 1954.

Cloak and Dagger Lover. London, Collins, 1955; as *Moon over the Water* (as Mary Douglas Warren), New York, Arcadia House, 1956.

Kiss in Sunlight. London, Collins, 1956; New York, Avalon, 1957.

Girl Without Money. London, Collins, 1957.

No Dowry for Jennifer. New York, Avalon, 1957.

Love Is a Gambler. London, Collins, 1958.

Love Is a Thief. London, Collins, 1959; New York, Macfadden, 1966.

Send for Miss Marshall. London, Collins, 1959.

Follow Your Love. New York, Avalon, 1959.

Doctor in Exile. London, Collins, 1960; New York, Avalon, 1961.

Catch Up to Love. New York, Avalon, 1960.

Kiss of Promise. New York, Avalon, 1960.

Cherry Blossom Love. London, Collins, 1961; New York, Macfadden, 1967.

Every Woman's Man. London, Collins, 1961; New York, Macfadden, 1966.

The Doctor Is a Lady. London, Collins, 1962.

Nurse at St. Catherine's. London, Collins, 1963.

French Girl in Love. London, Collins, 1963.

Every Woman's Doctor. London, Collins, 1964.

Married Quarters. London, Collins, 1964; New York, Macfadden, 1966.

Nurse in Danger. London, Collins, 1964.

The Doctor and the Dancer. London, Collins, 1965.

Doctor on Wings. London, Collins, 1966.

Never the Same. London, Collins, 1970.

Novels as Jennifer Ames

Pandora Lifts the Veil. New York, Dial Press, 1932; London, Hodder and Stoughton, 1933.

Anything But Love. London, Hodder and Stoughton, 1933.

Cruise. London, Hodder and Stoughton, 1934; as *Romance on a Cruise* (as Maysie Greig), New York, Doubleday, 1935.

Good Sport. London, Hodder and Stoughton, 1934; as Maysie Greig, New York, Doubleday, 1934; as *Love Will Win*, London, Fontana, 1969.

Romance for Sale. London, Hodder and Stoughton, 1934; as Maysie Greig, New York, Doubleday, 1934.

I'll Get over It. London, Hodder and Stoughton, 1935; as Maysie Greig, New York, Doubleday, 1936; as *Jilted* (as Jennifer Ames), London, Collins, 1968.

Sweet Peril. London, Hodder and Stoughton, 1935; as *Sweet Danger* (as Maysie Greig), New York, Doubleday, 1935.

I Seek My Love. London, Hodder and Stoughton, 1936; as *Dreams Get You Nowhere* (as Maysie Greig), New York, Doubleday, 1937.

Tinted Dream. London, Hodder and Stoughton, 1936; as *Doctor's Wife* (as Maysie Greig), New York, Doubleday, 1937; as *Doctor Brad's Nurse*, London, Collins, 1966.

Her World of Men. London, Hodder and Stoughton, 1937; as Maysie Greig, New York, Doubleday, 1938.

Elder Sister. London, Hodder and Stoughton, 1938; New York, Doubleday, 1939.

Stranger Sweetheart. London, Hodder and Stoughton, 1938; as *Honeymoons Arranged* (as Maysie Greig), New York, Doubleday, 1938.

Bury the Past. London, Hodder and Stoughton, 1939; as Maysie Greig, New York, Doubleday, 1939.

Dangerous Holiday. London, Hodder and Stoughton, 1939; as *Dangerous Cruise* (as Maysie Greig), New York, Doubleday, 1940.

Not One of Us. London, Hodder and Stoughton, 1939; as Maysie Greig, New York, Doubleday, 1939.

Make the Man Notice You. London, Hodder and Stoughton, 1940; as Maysie Greig, New York, Doubleday, 1940.

Honeymoon Alone. London, Hodder and Stoughton, 1940; as Maysie Greig, New York, Doubleday, 1941; as *Honeymoon for One*, London, Collins, 1971.

Ring Without Romance. London, Hodder and Stoughton, 1940; as Maysie Greig, New York, Doubleday, 1941.

Too Many Women. London, Hodder and Stoughton, 1941; as Maysie Greig, New York, Doubleday, 1941.

Diplomatic Honeymoon. London, Collins, 1942; as Maysie Greig, New York, Doubleday, 1942.

Dark Sunlight. London, Collins, 1943.

The Impossible Marriage. London, Collins, 1943.

At the Same Time Tomorrow. London, Collins, 1944; as Maysie Greig, New York, Doubleday, 1944.

Restless Beauty. London, Collins, 1944.

I Married Mr. Richardson. London, Collins, 1945.

Journey in the Dark. London, Collins, 1945.

Lovers in the Dark. London, Collins, 1946.

Take Your Choice, Lady. London, Collins, 1946.

Fear Kissed My Lips. London, Collins, 1947.

Heart in Darkness. New York, Arcadia House, 1947.

Shadow Across My Heart. London, Collins, 1948; as Mary Douglas Warren, New York, Arcadia House, 1952.

She'll Take the High Road. London, Collins, 1948.

Danger Wakes My Heart. London, Collins, 1949; as *Danger in Eden*, New York, Avalon, 1950.

Lips for a Stranger. London, Collins, 1949.

Too Much Alone. London, Collins, 1950.

Flight to Happiness. New York, Avalon, 1950.

After Tomorrow. New York, Avalon, 1951; as *Overseas Nurse*, New York, Ace, 1961.

The Frightened Heart. London, Collins, 1952; as *Date with Danger* (as Maysie Greig), New York, Random House, 1952.

The Fearful Paradise. London, Collins, 1953; as *This Fearful Paradise* (as Maysie Greig), New York, Random House, 1953.

Flight into Fear. London, Collins, and New York, Avalon, 1954.

Shadows Across the Sun. London, Collins, 1955; as *Shadow over the Island* (as Mary Douglas Warren), New York, Arcadia House, 1955.

Rough Seas to Sunrise. London, Collins, 1956; as *Winds of Fear* (as Maysie Greig), New York, Avalon, 1956.

Night of Carnival. London, Collins, 1956.

Love on Dark Wings. London, Collins, 1957.

Follow Your Dream. New York, Avalon, 1957.

Beloved Knight. London, Collins, 1958; New York, Avalon, 1959.

Doctor's Nurse. London, Collins, 1959.
Love in a Far Country. London, Collins, 1960; New York, Avalon, 1965.
Love in the East. London, Collins, 1960.
Perilous Quest. New York, Avalon, 1960.
Her Heart's Desire. New York, Avalon, 1961.
Diana Goes to Tokyo. London, Collins, 1961.
It Started in Hongkong. London, Collins, 1961.
The Timid Cleopatra. London, Collins, 1962.
Honeymoon in Manila. London, Collins, 1962.
Geisha in the House. London, Collins, 1963.
Sinners in Paradise. London, Collins, 1963.
The Two of Us. London, Collins, 1964.
Happy Island. London, Collins, 1964.
Nurse's Holiday. London, Collins, 1965.
Nurse's Story. London, Collins, 1965.
Doctor Ted's Clinic. London, Collins, 1967.
The Doctor Takes a Holiday. London, Collins, 1969.
Write from the Heart. London, Hale, 1972.

Novels as Ann Barclay

Other Men's Arms. London, Collins, 1936.
Swing High, Swing Low. London, Collins, 1936.
Men as Her Stepping Stones. London, Collins, 1937; as Maysie Greig, New York, Doubleday, 1938.

Novels as Mary Douglas Warren

Reunion in Reno. New York, Carlton House, 1941.
The Rich Are Not Proud. New York, Carlton House, 1942.
Southern Star. New York, Arcadia House, 1950.
The Manor Farm. New York, Arcadia House, 1951.
The Sunny Island. New York, Arcadia House, 1952.
Salt Harbor. New York, Arcadia House, 1953.
The High Road. New York, Arcadia House, 1954.
The Doctor Decides. London, Collins, 1963.

*   *   *

Maysie Greig, writing prolifically under several names, favoured a heroine who was pert and petite rather than philosophical and introspective. Unlike the romantic heroines of only a very few years earlier, Greig's do not believe in a personal God, nor are they stirred by Christian doubt or reflection, although some of the activities usually associated with belief in a deity are practised by hero or heroine, particularly at times of great stress or sexual tension. Thus, for example, in *Love and Let Me Go* we see Sally and Red, an unreliable wandering artist, rush into a marriage against the wishes of Sally's beastly family who believe in "duty above love." Sally's dad won't let them sleep together even after marriage. Having originally met on a camping holiday (hiking, cycling, walking, and the great outdoors were much in vogue in the mid-1930's), Sally and Red finally manage to consummate that marriage while camping in the Lake District. As Red carries his girlish bride into their honeymoon tent, he is moved to pray to an un-named deity. " 'I'm not a religious man but I feel like going down on my knees right now and praying that our love will always be as glorious as it is now.' She nodded slowly." This camping scene is not typical. On the whole, Greig liked her heroines to be sophisticated, elegant, languid, fascinated by good clothes and firm men. While it used to be a girl's soul that counted for so much, now it is her clothes and make-up. Greig's girls spend a great deal of time getting ready to go out, wondering what to wear to suit the surroundings: "I'll wear it tonight when he takes me out to dinner somewhere swish." While being courted, a girl liked to be taken out to dine in Soho or Knightsbridge, followed by a show or a visit to a nightclub. Occasionally, beneath her desire for would-be glamorous outings with urban lustre, a girl showed a wide-eyed, breathless spirit, questing for adventure, which could be absorbed by a variation on background. Greig tried out various settings—the hospital romance, travel, a forest fire, a romance set in "Jamaica's fashionable Montego Bay," and even a political romance, *Rich Twin, Poor Twin*.

Although some of the girls hold down jobs—Jennifer Prudence in *Anything But Love* is a successful magazine illustrator, Annette in *Kiss in Sunlight* a restless nurse, while the occupation of the heroine of *The Lady Is a Doctor* is self-explanatory—the chief occupation of these girls is to preserve reputation and to find a man, preferably as described in the title *A Man to Protect You*. Such chaps are lean and hard: "Jason, lean, dark-skinned, was very distinctive in full dress kit. Jenny felt all the other women in the dining room must be envying her. Or if they weren't they should be!" Nigel, we read, looked very attractive in his well-cut dark blue suit. And on another occasion, we see how the cut accentuated his height and powerful shoulders. But despite many jutting jaws and powerful shoulders, the heroes conform to an ideal of middle-class gentility and prim pleasantness. The ideal man is a soft-centred savage in city clothes.

In the 1920's and 1930's new ideas on sexual freedom, on allowing the biological urge to follow its natural course, were being advocated by more serious writers and philosophers, while practical advice was being offered by Marie Stopes. Despite alluringly daring titles like *Too Many Women, Anything But Love, Professional Lover*, or *Fear Kissed My Lips*, sexual freedom (either before or after marriage) was not sought by a Greig girl. There was still one man for one woman. Chastity was a much prized virtue, and virginity, although not openly named as such, was "something very precious." It was, as a heroine who has narrowly avoided seduction, observes: "Something which she had kept locked inside her for years. Something which, once broken, could never be repaired. Something he probably didn't know about, couldn't even guess at."

Any critique of Maysie Greig's approach to her craft, is best summed up in her own resumé of her philosophy.

> I write happy love stories because I believe happiness is the greatest virtue in the world and misery the greatest sin. You can so infect people with your own misery that you can make them miserable when they were quite happy and contented before. To be happy is as though you opened every window in your mind and let in strong, clean sunlight. That is why I think everyone should try to be happy, and read stories that make one happy, rather than those that increase one's sense of futility and despair. If I tried to write a really miserable story I think I should end up by committing suicide!

This happiness was only to be found in the discovery of a true and lasting love. That love, once established, carried a sanctity. One must revere happy love. Her own beliefs were echoed by her characters.

> "Happiness is the most important thing," he said quietly, "and love. Not only love of a woman, but love of the whole world you are living in. Why waste time scrambling for worldly goods when but to live happily and simply gives one such an intense pleasure?...Do you think that God intended any of us to lead a life of miserable self-sacrifice for the sake of others? Do you think He would have given us the power of love if He meant us to deny that love when it came to us? No, your first duty lies to our love, because that's the most important thing in the world."

Medieval courtly love may have held that true love was only possible through a passion created by suffering, continual partings and re-unions, and an ultimate separation. Maysie Greig, however, held that true love could, and should, be happy love, and that this happiness was a beginning and an end in itself. This was not only what she believed, but what her reading public wanted. She gave it to them, and "won the affection of a great and admiring public," who shared her view that "Love is the most fascinating, inspiring, complete emotion in the world.

Happiness is the greatest virtue, and misery the greatest sin in the world." Shallow, vacuous statements to some, but indisputable and convincing dogma to her and her readership.

—Rachel Anderson

GREY, Belinda. *See* **PETERS, Maureen**.

GREY, Brenda. *See* **MACKINLAY, Leila**.

GREY, Georgina. *See* **ROBY, Mary Linn**.

GRIMSTEAD, Hettie. Also writes as Marsha Manning. British. Born in Manchester, Lancashire. Educated privately. Overseas Press Officer, ENSA, during World War II. Journalist: staff member, United Press International, for 25 years. Agent: Curtis Brown Ltd., 1 Craven Hill, London W2 3EP, England.

ROMANCE AND GOTHIC PUBLICATIONS

Novels

Painted Virgin.   London, Daniel, 1931.

The Journey Home. London, Mills and Boon, 1950.
Navy Blue Lady. London, Mills and Boon, 1951.
The Twisted Road. London, Mills and Boon, 1951.
The Captured Heart. London, Mills and Boon, 1952.
Strangers May Kiss. London, Mills and Boon, 1952.
The Passionate Summer. London, Mills and Boon, 1953.
Song of Surrender. London, Mills and Boon, 1953.
Candles for Love. London, Mills and Boon, 1954.
Winds of Desire. London, Mills and Boon, 1954.
Enchanted August. London, Mills and Boon, 1955.
The Tender Pilgrim. London, Mills and Boon, 1955.
The Burning Flame. London, Mills and Boon, 1956.
Escape to Paradise. London, Mills and Boon, 1956.
The Reluctant Bride. London, Mills and Boon, 1957.
Scales of Love. London, Mills and Boon, 1957.
The Unknown Heart. London, Mills and Boon, 1958.
Tinsel Kisses. London, Mills and Boon, 1958.
Dream Street. London, Mills and Boon, 1959.
A Kiss in the Sun. London, Mills and Boon, 1959; New York, Paperback Library, 1966.
The Path to Love. London, Mills and Boon, 1960.
Sweet Prisoner. London, Mills and Boon, 1961.
The Golden Moment. London, Mills and Boon, 1962.
Love Has Two Faces. London, Mills and Boon, 1962.
Wedding for Three. London, Mills and Boon, 1963.
Whisper to the Stars. London, Mills and Boon, 1963; Toronto, Harlequin, 1970.
When April Sings. London, Mills and Boon, 1964.
The Door of the Heart. London, Mills and Boon, 1965.
Once upon a Kiss. London, Mills and Boon, 1965.
Shake Down the Moon. London, Mills and Boon, 1966.
The Sweetheart Tree. London, Mills and Boon, 1966.
Orchids for the Bride. London, Mills and Boon, 1967.
The Tender Chord. London, Mills and Boon, 1967.
Chase a Rainbow. London, Mills and Boon, 1968.
Portrait of Paula. London, Mills and Boon, 1968; New York, Fawcett, 1975.
September's Girl. London, Mills and Boon, 1969; New York, Fawcett, 1975.
The Lovely Day. London, Mills and Boon, 1970.
Roses for Breakfast. London, Mills and Boon, 1970; New York, Fawcett, 1975.
Island Affair. London, Mills and Boon, 1971; New York, Fawcett, 1975.
The Winter Rose. London, Mills and Boon, 1972; New York, Fawcett, 1975.
Fires of Spring. London, Mills and Boon, 1973; New York, Fawcett, 1975.
Tuesday's Child. London, Mills and Boon, 1973; New York, Fawcett, 1975.
The Tender Vine. London, Mills and Boon, 1974; New York, Fawcett 1976.
Sister Rose's Holiday. London, Mills and Boon, 1975.

Novels as Marsha Manning

Kisses for Three. London, Ward Lock, 1958; New York, Paperback Library, 1966.
Passport to Love. London, Ward Lock, 1958.
The Heart Alone. London, Ward Lock, 1959.
Skyscraper Hotel. London, Ward Lock, 1959.
Because You're Mine. London, Ward Lock, 1960.
Magic of the Moon. London, Ward Lock, 1961.
Star of Desire. London, Ward Lock, 1961.
Circle of Dreams. London, Ward Lock, 1962.
Roses for the Bride. London, Ward Lock, 1962.
Flower of the Heart. London, Ward Lock, 1963.
Lucy in London. London, Ward Lock, 1964.

Our Miss Penny. London, Ward Lock, 1964.
Sister Marion's Summer. London, Ward Lock, 1965.
Lover Come Lonely. London, Ward Lock, 1965; New York, Arcadia House, 1967.
Full Summer's Kiss. London, Ward Lock, 1966.
The Proud Lover. London, Ward Lock, 1966; New York, Fawcett, 1975.
Four of Hearts. London, Ward Lock, and New York, Arcadia House, 1967.
Dreams in the Sun. London, Ward Lock, 1967; New York, Bantam, 1971.
Friend of the Bride. London, Ward Lock, 1968.
Some Day My Love. London, Ward Lock, 1968.
Yesterday's Lover. London, Mills and Boon, 1969.
Holiday Affair. London, Mills and Boon, 1969.
To Catch a Dream. London, Mills and Boon, 1970; New York, Fawcett, 1974.
Summer Song. London, Mills and Boon, 1971; New York, Fawcett, 1975.
The Smiling Moon. London, Mills and Boon, 1972; New York, Fawcett, 1974.
Sweet Friday. London, Mills and Boon, 1972; New York, Fawcett, 1974.
The Magic City. London, Mills and Boon, 1973; New York, Fawcett, 1976.
Dance of Summer. London, Mills and Boon, 1974; New York, Fawcett, 1976.
Wedding of the Year. London, Mills and Boon, 1974; New York, Fawcett, 1976.
Chance Encounter. London, Mills and Boon, 1975.
Day of Roses. London, Mills and Boon, 1976.
The Passionate Rivals. London, Hale, 1978.

*   *   *

Hettie Grimstead has had a long career as a romantic novelist beginning with *Painted Virgin* of 1931, a classic story of the girl going from rags to riches via the stage and giving it up for love. There are period colour and social observation in the book.

After something of a gap, Grimstead returned to a successful romantic writing formula which involves classic romantic situations, such as the shipboard romance of *The Captured Heart*. There the romantic situations are seen through the eyes of a young heroine, and are predictable and kept fairly simple. There is often glamour added by a foreign setting. The emotions displayed are healthy and conventional and do not transgress safe bounds. Romantic attraction often occurs as a disturbing but unspecified effect.

The plots of Grimstead's novels revolve about the theme of unusually sensible, attractive, but colourless young women who, on entering a new career, are confronted with the dilemma of choosing between two young men, one of whom is a steady reliable suitor, the other a dashing Don Juan. The different novels present variations upon that basically triangular theme: thus in *Roses for Breakfast* the dashing male really does love her and, in the dramatic turn, where she only discovers his love at the very end of the novel, she gives up her steady fiancé who loves her to go off and marry the other. In *Chase a Rainbow* there are two Don Juan types, one perfidious and the other awakening too late to his true feeling for her, but the heroine chooses steady love over both of these. In *The Lovely Day* the Don Juan is unmasked as a gold digger and the heroine is then able to appreciate the steady one who loves her.

There is not much character or emotional development in Grimstead's novels. Love is based on proven immediate physical attraction by the first kiss the hero and heroine share: thus the heroine in *Chase a Rainbow* could say, "when you kissed me, that was the proof I needed. Now I am sure of your love." The heroines are uncomplicated and trusting, believing in a happy ever after love and marriage.

Another way in which Grimstead achieves variety in her many novels is by changing the career of the heroine and her environment. She chooses careers such as office girl, student au-pair, and actress which have wide and varying degrees of appeal to the young reading public. Within this apparently realistic context her heroines unrealistically find themselves pursued by rich, handsome, eligible bachelors who are head over heels in love with them. Usually the heroine doesn't seem worthy of such devotion. This type of romance would appeal to previous generations of young inexperienced women, but the love displayed is almost too chaste by modern standards.

This style of writing, even though it dates from the 1950's to the 1970's, is fixed in an earlier tradition, and, with its rather simple titles, naive attitudes, and brittle glamour, would be considered very dated to a much more cynical generation.

—P.R. Meldrum

GRUNDY, (Mrs.) Mabel (Sarah) Barnes.

ROMANCE AND GOTHIC PUBLICATIONS

Novels

A Thames Camp.   Bristol, Arrowsmith, 1902; as *Two in a Tent—and Jane*, 1913.
The Vacillations of Hazel.   Bristol, Arrowsmith, 1905.
Marguerite's Wonderful Year.   Bristol, Arrowsmith, 1906.
Hazel of Heatherland.   New York, Baker and Taylor, 1906.
Dimbie and I—and Amelia.   New York, Baker and Taylor, 1907.
Hilary on Her Own.   New York, Baker and Taylor, and London, Hutchinson, 1908.
Gwenda.   New York, Baker and Taylor, 1910; as *Two Men and Gwenda*, 1910.
The Third Miss Wenderby.   New York, Baker and Taylor, and London, Hutchinson, 1911.
Patricia Plays a Part.   London, Hutchinson, 1913; New York, Dodd Mead, 1914.
Candytuft—I Mean Veronica.   London, Hutchinson, 1914.
An Undressed Heroine.   London, Hutchinson, 1916.
Her Mad Month.   London, Hutchinson, 1917.
A Girl for Sale.   London, Hutchinson, 1920.
The Great Husband Hunt.   London, Hutchinson, 1922.
The Mating of Marcus.   London, Hutchinson, 1923.
Sleeping Dogs.   London, Hodder and Stoughton, 1924; New York, Stokes, 1926.
Three People.   London, Hodder and Stoughton, 1926.
The Strategy of Suzanne.   London, Hutchinson, 1929.
Pippa.   London, Hutchinson, 1932.
Sally in a Service Flat.   London, Hutchinson, 1934.
Private Hotel—Anywhere.   London, Hutchinson, 1937.
Paying Pests.   London, Hutchinson, 1941.
Mary Ann and Jane.   London, Hutchinson, 1944.
The Two Miss Speckles.   London, Hutchinson, 1946.

*   *   *

A novel by Mabel Barnes Grundy reads like a breath of fresh air. This author, whose 25 books were published between 1902 and 1946, writes with verve, enthusiasm, and energy in a distinctive style which is characterised by its ease and wit. Grundy's novels are mostly of the "roads to matrimony" type. They move along at a brisk pace with plenty of action and ingenious plots. Their atmosphere is gently romantic rather than loaded with emotion. Their heroines are charming, enterprising, high-spirited, independent-minded, witty, modern enough to smoke and drink cocktails (in the 1920's and 1930's), but ultimately traditionalist in that they marry solid, reliable, *nice* men whom they will allow to take care of them. The personality of the heroine is strongly established, particularly in those novels in which the heroine is narrator, as Peronelle, the heroine/narrator of *The Great Husband Hunt*, and Sally of *Sally in a Service Flat*, who describes one morning's post thus: "*July 7* Another repulsive Income Tax paper has arrived and of the same sticky hue. I suppose those who perpetuate these abominable documents imagine that we will be reminded of sunshine when we catch sight of their yellow envelopes, but nothing of the sort, jaundice or yellow-fever is nearer the mark."

Grundy's characters are endearing, good-humoured people, sometimes benignly eccentric (and consequently good at helping the plot along) as, for instance, the uncle in *The Great Husband Hunt* who offers £1,000 and a substantial dowry to the first of his four dependent nieces to get engaged. The dialogue is consistently light-hearted and amusing, as this exchange between Hazel and her pompous, over-aesthetic fiancé, Eustace: "There is a little book on monistic and genetic philosophy I want to read to you," he said. "I think it will help you to feel happier." "Is it about monasteries?" I inquired (*The Vacillations of Hazel*; Eustace later asks to be released from their engagement, and Hazel marries nice, comfortable Mr. Ickworth, her devoted admirer for many years).

The wit with which Grundy habitually treats her plots, characters, and dialogue extends also to the titles of her novels, which are alliterative, eyecatching, and intriguing. Sometimes they may even appear rather risqué, though of course they prove to be entirely respectable. The *Undressed Heroine* is simply a dowdily dressed young woman whose romantic prospects improve no end when she is provided with artistic and beautiful clothes by Mrs. Clinton Tomkins, an eccentric well-wisher. *Her Mad Month* is the time spent in Harrogate by an independent-minded heroine who runs away in her stern grandmother's absence and incidentally "meets her fate." The heroine of *A Girl for Sale* is the enterprising and modern Whiff Woffran who finds herself without a job after the Armistice and in desperation advertises in the newspaper for a new employer (whom she marries).

Mabel Barnes Grundy's delightful novels brought her many admirers, including *Times Literary Supplement* reviewers, and although they would today be regarded as period pieces it is a shame that they are so difficult to come by.

—Jean Buchanan

HAGGARD, H(enry) Rider. British. Born in Bradenham, Norfolk, 22 June 1856. Educated at Ipswich Grammar School, Suffolk; Lincoln's Inn, London, 1881-85: called to the Bar, 1885. Married Louisa Mariana Margitson in 1880; one son and three daughters. Lived in South Africa, as Secretary to Sir Henry Bulwer, Lieutenant-Governor of Natal, 1875-77, member of the staff of Sir Theophilus Shepstone, Special Commissioner in the Transvaal, 1877, and Master and Registrar of the High Court of the Transvaal, 1877-79; returned to England, 1879; managed his wife's estate in Norfolk, from 1880; worked in chambers of Henry Bargave Deane, 1885-87; Unionist and Agricultural candidate for East Norfolk, 1895; Co-Editor, *African Review*, 1898; travelled throughout England investigating condition of agriculture and the rural population, 1901-02; British Government Special Commissioner to report on Salvation Army settlements in the United States, 1905; Chairman, Reclamation and Unemployed Labour Committee, Royal Commission on Coast Erosion and Afforestation, 1906-11; travelled around the world as a Member of the Dominions Royal Commission, 1912-17. Chairman of the Committee, Society of Authors, 1896-98; Vice-President, Royal Colonial Institute, 1917. Knighted, 1912; K.B.E. (Knight Commander, Order of the British Empire), 1919. *Died 14 May 1925.*

Novels (series: Allan Quatermain; She)

Dawn.   London, Hurst and Blackett, 3 vols., 1884; New York, Appleton, 1 vol., 1887.
The Witch's Head.   London, Hurst and Blackett, 3 vols., 1884; New York, Appleton, 1 vol., 1885.
King Solomon's Mines (Quatermain).   London and New York, Cassell, 1885.
She: A History of Adventure.   New York, Harper, 1886; London, Longman, 1887.
Allan Quatermain.   London, Longman, and New York, Harper, 1887.
Jess.   London, Smith Elder, and New York, Harper, 1887.
A Tale of Three Lions, and On Going Back.   New York, Munro, 1887.
Mr. Meeson's Will.   New York, Harper, and London, Spencer Blackett, 1888.
Maiwa's Revenge.   New York, Harper, and London, Longman, 1888.
My Fellow Laborer (includes "The Wreck of the 'Copeland'").   New York, Munro, 1888.
Colonel Quaritch, V.C.   New York, Lovell, 1888; London, Longman, 3 vols., 1888.
Cleopatra.   London, Longman, and New York, Harper, 1889.
Beatrice.   London, Longman, and New York, Harper, 1890.
The World's Desire, with Andrew Lang.   London, Longman, and New York, Harper, 1890.
Eric Brighteyes.   London, Longman, and New York, United States Book Company, 1891.
Nada the Lily.   New York and London, Longman, 1892.
Montezuma's Daughter.   New York and London, Longman, 1893.
The People of the Mist.   London and New York, Longman, 1894.
Heart of the World.   New York, Longman, 1895; London, Longman, 1896.
Joan Haste.   London and New York, Longman, 1895.
The Wizard.   Bristol, Arrowsmith, and New York, Longman, 1896.
Doctor Therne.   London and New York, Longman, 1898.
Swallow.   New York and London, Longman, 1899.
The Spring of a Lion.   New York, Neeley, 1899.
Lysbeth.   New York and London, Longman, 1901.
Pearl-Maiden.   London and New York, Longman, 1903.
The Brethren.   London, Cassell, and New York, Doubleday, 1904.
Stella Fregelius: A Tale of Three Destinies.   London and New York, Longman, 1904.
Ayesha: The Return of She.   London, Ward Lock, and New York, Doubleday, 1905.
Benita: An African Romance.   London, Cassell, 1906; as *The Spirit of Bambatse,* New York, Longman, 1906.
The Way of the Spirit.   London, Hutchinson, 1906.
Fair Margaret.   London, Hutchinson, 1907; as *Margaret,* New York, Longman, 1907.
The Lady of the Heavens.   New York, Authors and Newspapers Association, 1908; as *The Ghost Kings,* London, Cassell, 1908.
The Yellow God.   New York, Cupples and Leon, 1908; London, Cassell, 1909.
The Lady of Blossholme.   London, Hodder and Stoughton, 1909.
Morning Star.   London, Cassell, and New York, Longman, 1910.
Queen Sheba's Ring.   London, Nash, and New York, Doubleday, 1910.
The Mahatma and the Hare: A Dream Story.   London, Longman, and New York, Holt, 1911.
Red Eve.   London, Hodder and Stoughton, and New York, Doubleday, 1911.
Marie.   London, Cassell, and New York, Longman, 1912.
Child of Storm.   London, Cassell, and New York, Longman, 1913.
The Wanderer's Necklace.   London, Cassell, and New York, Longman, 1914.
The Holy Flower.   London, Ward Lock, 1915; as *Allan and the Holy Flower,* New York, Longman, 1915.
The Ivory Child.   London, Cassell, and New York, Longman, 1916.
Finished.   London, Ward Lock, and New York, Longman, 1917.
Moon of Israel.   London, Murray, and New York, Longman, 1918.

Love Eternal. London, Cassell, and New York, Longman, 1918.
When the World Shook. London, Cassell, and New York, Longman, 1919.
The Ancient Allan. London, Cassell, and New York, Longman, 1920.
She and Allan. New York, Longman, and London, Hutchinson, 1921.
The Virgin of the Sun. London, Cassell, and New York, Doubleday, 1922.
Wisdom's Daughter. London, Hutchinson, and New York, Doubleday, 1923.
Heu-Heu; or, The Monster (Quatermain). London, Hutchinson, and New York, Doubleday, 1924.
Queen of the Dawn. New York, Doubleday, and London, Hutchinson, 1925.
The Treasure of the Lake. New York, Doubleday, and London, Hutchinson, 1926.
Allan and the Ice-Gods. London, Hutchinson, and New York, Doubleday, 1927.
Mary of Marion Isle. London, Hutchinson, and New York, Doubleday, 1929.
Belshazzar. London, Paul, and New York, Doubleday, 1930.

Short Stories

Allan's Wife and Other Tales. London, Blackett, and New York, Harper, 1889.
Black Heart and White Heart, and Other Stories. London, Longman, 1900; as *Elissa, and Black Heart and White Heart*, New York, Longman, 1900.
Smith and the Pharaohs and Other Tales. Bristol, Arrowsmith, 1920; New York, Longman, 1921.
The Best Short Stories of Rider Haggard, edited by Peter Haining. London, Joseph, 1981.

OTHER PUBLICATIONS

Other

Cetywayo and His White Neighbours; or, Remarks on Recent Events in Zululand, Natal, and the Transvaal. London, Trübner, 1882; revised edition, 1888; reprinted in part, as *The Last Boer War*, London, Kegan Paul, 1899; as *A History of the Transvaal*, New York, New Amsterdam, 1899.
Church and the State: An Appeal to the Laity. Privately printed, 1895.
A Farmer's Year, Being His Commonplace Book for 1898. London and New York, Longman, 1899.
The New South Africa. London, Pearson, 1900.
A Winter Pilgrimage:... Travels Through Palestine, Italy, and the Island of Cyprus. London and New York, Longman, 1901.
Rural England. London and New York, Longman, 2 vols., 1902.
A Gardener's Year. London and New York, Longman, 1905.
Report on the Salvation Army Colonies. London, His Majesty's Stationery Office, 1905; as *The Poor and the Land*, London and New York, Longman, 1905.
Regeneration, Being an Account of the Social Work of the Salvation Army in Great Britain. London, Longman, 1910; New York, Longman, 1911.
Rural Denmark and Its Lessons. London and New York, Longman, 1911.
A Call to Arms to the Men of East Anglia. Privately printed, 1914.
The After-War Settlement and the Employment of Ex-Service Men in the Oversea Dominions. London, Saint Catherine Press, 1916.
The Days of My Life: An Autobiography, edited by C.J. Longman. London and New York, Longman, 2 vols., 1926.
The Private Diaries of Sir H. Rider Haggard 1914-1925, edited by D.S. Higgins. London, Cassell, and New York, Stein and Day, 1980.

Bibliography: *A Bibliography of the Writings of Sir Henry Rider Haggard* by J.E. Scott, London, Elkin Mathews, 1947.

Critical Studies: *Rider Haggard: His Life and Works* by Morton N. Cohen, London, Hutchinson, 1960, New York, Walker, 1961, revised edition, London, Macmillan, 1968; *H. Rider Haggard: A Voice from the Infinite* by Peter Berresford Ellis, London, Routledge, 1978; *Rider Haggard, The Great Storyteller* by D.S. Higgins, London, Cassell, 1981, New York, Stein and Day, 1982.

*   *   *

Rider Haggard was above all a spinner of yarns, a teller of tales. That most of them were tall tales does not matter in the least, for in his books, through the power of his writing, the wildly impossible is made to seem not only possible but convincingly true. He is probably best known for his books set in Africa which he knew well, and he had a great fondness for and sympathy with its native peoples. The Zulu nation in particular appealed to him, and in *Nada the Lily* (which was his own favourite among his many books) he told the story of the Zulu king Chaka through the eyes of Mopo, Chaka's witch doctor. In the romances *Marie, Child of Storm* and *Finished* he completed the history of the Zulus down to his own time.

From time to time Haggard has been criticised because his attitude to war and his descriptions of battles make him seem to relish bloodshed. This is not necessarily his own attitude but his interpretation of the Zulu philosophy which can be summed up in the words he puts in the mouth of Umslopogas in *Allan Quatermain*—"man is born to kill. He who kills not when his blood is hot is a woman and no man." Nor must we forget the very different atmosphere of his jingoistic era.

Besides historical novels, Haggard wrote romances pure and simple often with an African background. The best known are *King Solomon's Mines* with its classic treasure motif and *She* and its sequel *Ayesha*, two books that are wonderfully erotic without the sex being in any way explicit, and also to some degree feminist without any sacrifice of the traditional "Boys' Own" adventure motif. Also set in Africa is *Swallow* which charts the great trek of the Boers; in *The People of the Mist* he gives us his version of Africa's pre-history.

Haggard was master of description; he had the ability to bring a vivid picture of the countryside he was describing immediately before the reader's eyes. His characterization varied—he was especially good at Africans like the unforgettable Umslopogas, the Zulu prince who often accompanied Allan Quatermain on his adventures; Allan, the archetypal great white hunter, was also a well-drawn character, being based partly on himself and partly on a friend. But in some of his historical novels his characters are rather two-dimensional—perhaps because the stories run on at such a pace and action is all. For instance, in *Red Eve*, a stirring tale set at the time of Crécy dealing with the eternal triangle and the battle between the powers of good and evil, the hero, heroine, and villain are all stock characters. The incidents, however—battles, narrow escapes, brushes with the Plague, appearance at the court of the Doge of Venice—keep one reading until the end. *Eric Brighteyes*, set in ancient Iceland, is more satisfying because the characters are better drawn; and there is a wonderful atmosphere with saga overtones in this doom laden tale. Haggard's fertile imagination roamed far and wide in many different periods of history. *Pearl-Maiden* is about early Christian martyrs, *The Brethren* is about the Crusades, and *Lysbeth* is set in the days of William the Silent.

Rider Haggard was immensely successful in his own lifetime; his books were best sellers, and much admired by fellow writers like Rudyard Kipling and Andrew Lang. Many of his books are little known today (although *King Solomon's Mines* and *She* are undying classics), but Rider Haggard never wrote a dull book and many of his other stories repay attention and can still be enjoyed by lovers of the imaginative romance and the ripping yarn.

—Pamela Cleaver

HAINES, Pamela. British. Born in Harrogate, Yorkshire, 4 November 1929. Educated at St. Joseph's Convent, Tamworth, Staffordshire, 1938; Newnham College, Cambridge, 1949-52, M.A. in English. Married Tony Haines in 1955; three daughters and two sons. Recipient: *Spectator* New Writing Prize, 1971; Yorkshire Art Award, 1975. Agent: A.D. Peters, 10 Buckingham Street, London WC2N 6BU. Address: c/o Collins, 14 St. James's Place, London SW1A 1PS, England.

ROMANCE AND GOTHIC PUBLICATIONS

Novels

> *Tea at Gunter's*. London, Heinemann, 1974.
> *A Kind of War*. London, Heinemann, 1976.
> *Men on White Horses*. London, Collins, 1978.
> *The Kissing Gate*. London, Collins, and New York, Doubleday, 1981.

*   *   *

The novels of Pamela Haines share a nucleus of common themes. All portray the growth of a young girl to womanhood, the fight for independence from the smothering shadow of the past, the idealized love for the flawed love object. All are pervaded by a strong tragic sense and the lurking threat of violence. From the first there are indications that the early balanced precision will be forsaken in favour of a growing breadth of vision, a wider compass. It seems inevitable that their author should eventually come to the full-scale family saga of *The Kissing Gate*.

Tea at Gunter's focuses on the heroine's attempts at self-realization, which are threatened by the pervasive dream-world of her mother, still living in a romanticised past of love for her effete step-brother Gervase. When Lucy herself falls in love with the scion of a related family, the ghost of Gervase overshadows them, and final freedom is achieved only at a terrible cost. A poised, subtle work, *Tea at Gunter's* is the most perfect of Pamela Haines's creations, the author displaying a mastery of tone and considerable psychological penetration. *A Kind of War* explores the minds of three women, each of a different generation, whose lives are lacking for the want of one fulfilling individual. Skilfully the novel traces each through her past and present life, moving toward the concluding tragedy in a clean underplayed style which reveals the nature of the differing characters, the grief tinged with welcome touches of humour. Already in *A Kind of War* one senses a movement outward from the confines of the work, a yearning for larger forms.

Men on White Horses describes Edwina's growth from childhood to maturity in Edwardian Yorkshire. Beginning with a brilliant portrayal of her early years, the author indicates the threat to her selfhood posed by her pretty mother with her obsessive love for a homosexual brother, and later by a domineering schoolfriend. Physically and spiritually scarred by life, her one secret love tragically killed, Edwina finds fulfilment in her music and its related symbol, the sea. When at the last she feels life return in waves in her pianist's hands, the reader knows that her spirit remains unconquered by its suffering. Measured beside the opening part of the book, some of the later chapters are less satisfying, but the novel as a whole is a remarkable achievement.

The Kissing Gate, which combines gothic romance with the psychological subtlety of previous novels, is the most ambitious of Pamela Haines's works, and follows the Rawson family through three generations of the last century. The kissing gate of the title—symbol of love and death—is central to the novel. Here Sarah Rawson rescues the squire's son, and begins the involvement between the Rawsons and the aristocratic Inghams which spans the course of the book. The story is continued in Sarah's children—John the medical student, and the artistic Ned—and ends with her grand-daughter, another Sarah, leaving the kissing gate for a new life. Most of the action, though, is dominated by two Catherines—both outsiders brought to Downham by John. Catriona Drummond, who marries him, and Kate the Irish girl he saves from the Great Famine and starvation. Catriona, dogged by family disgrace and unfulfilled love, remains a stranger; Kate becomes the focus for the lives of the rest, her selfless love rewarded after a succession of tragedies. Their personalities overshadow the plot, and give the work direction. Violence flares most fiercely in this novel—the brutal lecher Charles Ingham and his fearful death, the massacre of Ned's family by the psychopathic Greaves, Sarah's rape and miscarriage. The railway runs a dark thread through the story, instrument of disgrace and death. A huge epic novel, *The Kissing Gate* lacks the perfect balance of earlier works. There are flaws in the fabric—too many unhappy marriages, unfortunate accidents, fortuitous deaths. None of them matters, however, since interest is sustained to such an extent that they are scarcely noticed. In its vast scale and sureness of character insights, this is the most impressive of Pamela Haines's novels.

Haines's writings show an excellent period sense. Whether the contemporary setting of her first two novels, or the Victorian age of her last, the feel of the time is splendidly caught. Her grasp of character is sure, her dialogue superb. Her books present the essence of life, its tragedy leavened by sharp flashes of humour. With a clear but sympathetic eye she depicts the transient joys, the harrowing griefs, the slow poignant awakening of love.

—Geoffrey Sadler

HALLIDAY, Dorothy.   *See* **DUNNETT, Dorothy**.

HAMILL, Ethel.   *See* **WEBB, Jean Francis**.

HAMILTON, Julia.   *See* **FITZGERALD, Julia**.

HAMPSON, Anne. British. Left school at age 14; later attended Manchester College of Education, teaching certificate. Married for 14 years. Cafe owner, sewing factory worker, and operated a milk route; teacher for four years, then full-time writer. Address: c/o Mills and Boon Ltd., 15-16 Brooks Mews, London W1A 1DR, England.

<small>ROMANCE AND GOTHIC PUBLICATIONS</small>

Novels

Eternal Summer. London, Mills and Boon, 1969; Toronto, Harlequin, 1970.
Precious Waif. London, Mills and Boon, 1969; Toronto, Harlequin, 1970.
Unwary Heart. London, Mills and Boon, 1969; Toronto, Harlequin, 1970.
The Autocrat of Melhurst. London, Mills and Boon, 1969; Toronto, Harlequin, 1970.
Gates of Steel. London, Mills and Boon, 1970; Toronto, Harlequin, 1973.
By Fountains Wild. London, Mills and Boon, 1970; Toronto, Harlequin, 1973.
Heaven Is High. London, Mills and Boon, 1970; Toronto, Harlequin, 1972.
Love Hath an Island. London, Mills and Boon, 1970; Toronto, Harlequin, 1971.
The Hawk and the Dove. London, Mills and Boon, 1970; Toronto, Harlequin, 1973.
Beyond the Sweet Waters. London, Mills and Boon, 1970; Toronto, Harlequin, 1971.
When the Bough Breaks. London, Mills and Boon, 1970; Toronto, Harlequin, 1971.
An Eagle Swooped. London, Mills and Boon, 1970; Toronto, Harlequin, 1974.
Isle of the Rainbows. London, Mills and Boon, 1970; Toronto, Harlequin, 1972.
Dark Hills Rising. London, Mills and Boon, 1971; Toronto, Harlequin, 1975.
The Rebel Bride. London, Mills and Boon, 1971; Toronto, Harlequin, 1973.
Stars of Spring. London, Mills and Boon, and Toronto, Harlequin, 1971.
Wings of the Night. London, Mills and Boon, 1971; Toronto, Harlequin, 1973.
Follow a Shadow. London, Mills and Boon, 1971; Toronto, Harlequin, 1977.
Gold Is the Sunrise. London, Mills and Boon, 1971; Toronto, Harlequin, 1972.
Petals Drifting. London, Mills and Boon, 1971; Toronto, Harlequin, 1974.
South of Mandraki. London, Mills and Boon, 1971; Toronto, Harlequin, 1973.
Waves of Fire. London, Mills and Boon, 1971; Toronto, Harlequin, 1973.
The Fair Island. London, Mills and Boon, 1972; Toronto, Harlequin, 1975.
Enchanted Dawn. London, Mills and Boon, 1972; Toronto, Harlequin, 1976.
Beloved Rake. London, Mills and Boon, 1972; Toronto, Harlequin, 1974.
The Plantation Boss. London, Mills and Boon, 1972; Toronto, Harlequin, 1973.
There Came a Tyrant. London, Mills and Boon, and Toronto, Harlequin, 1972.
Dark Avenger. London, Mills and Boon, 1972; Toronto, Harlequin, 1973.
Wife for a Penny. London, Mills and Boon, 1972; Toronto, Harlequin, 1974.
Hunter of the East. London, Mills and Boon, 1973; Toronto, Harlequin, 1974.
Boss of Bali Creek. London, Mills and Boon, 1973; Toronto, Harlequin, 1977.
Blue Hills of Sintra. London, Mills and Boon, 1973; Toronto, Harlequin, 1974.
Dear Stranger. London, Mills and Boon, and Toronto, Harlequin, 1973.
Stormy the Way. London, Mills and Boon, 1973; Toronto, Harlequin, 1974.
When Clouds Part. London, Mills and Boon, 1973; Toronto, Harlequin, 1974.
Master of Moonrock. Toronto, Harlequin, 1973.
Windward Crest. London, Mills and Boon, 1973.
A Kiss from Satan. Toronto, Harlequin, 1973.
The Black Eagle. London, Mills and Boon, 1973; Toronto, Harlequin, 1975.
Dear Plutocrat. London, Mills and Boon, 1973; Toronto, Harlequin, 1976.
After Sundown. Toronto, Harlequin, 1974.
Stars over Sarawak. London, Mills and Boon, and Toronto, Harlequin, 1974.
Fetters of Hate. London, Mills and Boon, 1974; Toronto, Harlequin, 1975.
Pride and Power. London, Mills and Boon, 1974; Toronto, Harlequin, 1975.
The Way of a Tyrant. London, Mills and Boon, and Toronto, Harlequin, 1974.
Moon Without Stars. London, Mills and Boon, 1974; Toronto, Harlequin, 1977.
Not Far from Heaven. London, Mills and Boon, 1974.

Two of a Kind. London, Mills and Boon, 1974.
Autumn Twilight. London, Mills and Boon, 1975; Toronto, Harlequin, 1976.
Flame of Fate. London, Mills and Boon, 1975.
Jonty in Love. London, Mills and Boon, 1975.
Reap the Whirlwind. London, Mills and Boon, 1975.
South of Capricorn. London, Mills and Boon, 1975.
Sunset Cloud. London, Mills and Boon, 1976; New York, Oxford University Press, 1979.
Song of the Waves. London, Mills and Boon, 1976; Toronto, Harlequin, 1977.
Dangerous Friendship. Toronto, Harlequin, 1976.
Satan and the Nymph. London, Mills and Boon, 1976.
A Man to Be Feared. London, Mills and Boon, and Toronto, Harlequin, 1976.
Isle at the Rainbow's End. London, Mills and Boon, 1976; Toronto, Harlequin, 1977.
Hills of Kalamata. London, Mills and Boon, 1976; Toronto, Harlequin, 1977.
Fire Meets Fire. London, Mills and Boon, 1976.
Dear Benefactor. London, Mills and Boon, 1976.
Call of the Outback. London, Mills and Boon, 1976; Toronto, Harlequin, 1977.
Call of the Veld. London, Mills and Boon, 1977; Toronto, Harlequin, 1978.
Harbour of Love. London, Mills and Boon, 1977; Toronto, Harlequin, 1979.
The Shadow Between. London, Mills and Boon, 1977; Toronto, Harlequin, 1978.
Sweet Is the Web. London, Mills and Boon, 1977; Toronto, Harlequin, 1978.
Moon Dragon. London, Mills and Boon, 1978.
To Tame a Vixen. London, Mills and Boon, 1978.
Master of Forrestmead. London, Mills and Boon, 1978.
Under Moonglow. London, Mills and Boon, and Toronto, Harlequin, 1978.
For Love of a Pagan. London, Mills and Boon, 1978.
Leaf in the Storm. London, Mills and Boon, and Toronto, Harlequin, 1978.
Above Rubies. Toronto, Harlequin, 1978.
Fly Beyond the Sunset. Toronto, Harlequin, 1978.
Isle of Desire. Toronto, Harlequin, 1978.
South of the Moon. Toronto, Harlequin, 1979.
Bride for a Night. London, Mills and Boon, 1979; Toronto, Harlequin, 1981.
Chateau in the Palms. London, Mills and Boon, 1979.
Coolibah Creek. London, Mills and Boon, 1979.
A Rose from Lucifer. London, Mills and Boon, 1979.
Temple of Dawn. London, Mills and Boon, 1979.
Call of the Heathen. London, Mills and Boon, 1980.
The Laird of Locharrun. London, Mills and Boon, 1980.
Pagan Lover. London, Mills and Boon, 1980.
The Dawn Steals Softly. New York and London, Silhouette, 1980.
Stormy Masquerade. New York and London, Silhouette, 1980.
Second Tomorrow. London, Silhouette, 1980.
Man of the Outback. New York, Silhouette, 1980; London, Silhouette, 1981.
Where Eagles Nest. New York, Silhouette, 1980.
Payment in Full. New York and London, Silhouette, 1980.
Beloved Vagabond. Toronto, Harlequin, 1981.
Man Without a Heart. New York, Silhouette, 1981.
Shadow of Apollo. New York, Silhouette, 1981.

*   *   *

Anne Hampson's version of the romantic formula focuses primarily upon intense, frequently physically violent interaction between an unfathomable hero and a transparent heroine. This emphasis is well chosen because it articulates in pleasant fantasy some of the personal concerns and experiences of women in reality. The story is told from the heroine's perspective so the reader identifies with her and her feelings of vulnerability. The heroine feels dangerously exposed to the dominant male hero: "The black eyes, marble-hard, were fixed upon her in a searching scrutiny which seemed to be absorbing every single thing about her...even what went on in the secret places of her mind" (*Leaf in the Storm*). In contrast, the hero is impenetrable, seemingly invulnerable. The same novel describes the heroine's struggles to understand him: "His eyes held the most odd expression; nothing she could read was there, yet she felt that if she could have read the expression it would have been revealing in a way that was totally unexpected." This portrayal is appealing since, traditionally, men have been socialized to repress their feelings, particularly loving ones. Compared to women, they disclose little of themselves. Women, therefore, are often left feeling exposed in a one-sided exhange of emotions while men remain enigmas. Hampson incorporates this emotionally charged state of affairs in her romances.

The heroine's distance from the hero is further stressed by Hampson's frequent use of forced marriages or marriages of convenience, or "pretend" engagements and marriages as a plot device. In these situations, the hero and heroine are bound by the most intimate of ties yet they are strangers. The heroine of *For Love of a Pagan* agonizes over her lack of knowledge about men in general and her husband specifically: "The doubts hurt, since she would rather feel she had full trust in her husband. Mingling with the doubts was a return of her fear of him, of the uncertainty as to how he would eventually turn out. She knew so little about him, about his inner nature...."

The relationship is not only baffling to her but also frightening. Encounters are often violent, ranging from spankings and shakings to rapes (within the bonds of marriage). Many critics have condemned writers like Hampson for glamorizing sexual violence but I think that, in this case, they have underestimated the intent of the writer and the sophistication of the readers. In these violent episodes, the heroine is usually sexually responsive so the "rape" is not entirely against her will. In fact, she would not be resisting at all but she does not want him to make love to her if he does not love her. It is at this point that the reader and the heroine temporarily part company for the astute reader knows the hero would not be attempting to overcome her resistance if he did not love her already. The violence is an expression of the emotion that the heroine is afraid the hero does not feel and that he has hidden so successfully. Hampson gives the readers clues to guide their interpretation in this direction: "This was a side of him she had suspected but never expected to see, for usually he was so calm and self-possessed, more than able to control his passions. But not now..." (*Temple of the Dawn*). This emotional break-through is a relief because the hero is no longer so remote. Savagery eventually gives way to tenderness. The message is clear to the reader who knows that the happy ending means that the violence between the hero and heroine is over because now they can express their love directly. Hampson is explicit about getting this point across: " 'I will never frighten you again, my darling,' he promised and she knew without any doubt at all that he spoke the truth" (*For Love of a Pagan*).

Hampson also devotes attention to the settings of her stories. Two of her favorite settings seem to be South Africa and Greece and the Greek Islands. Her affectionate descriptions of the flora, fauna, topography, and customs of these places also add to the appeal of her romances.

—Margaret Jensen

HARDWICK, Mollie (née Greenhalgh). Also writes as Mary Atkinson; John Drinkrow. British. Born in Manchester. Educated at Manchester High School for Girls. Married the writer Michael Hardwick in 1961; one son. Announcer, Manchester, 1940-45, and drama script editor and producer, London, 1946-62, BBC Radio; then free-lance writer. Recipient: Romantic Novelists Association Major Award, 1977. Fellow, Royal Society of Arts. Agent: London Management Ltd., 235 Regent Street, London W1A 2JT. Address: Barton Cottage, The Street, Kennington, Ashford, Kent TN24 9HB, England.

ROMANCE AND GOTHIC PUBLICATIONS

Novels

Upstairs, Downstairs series:
  Sarah's Story. London, Sphere, 1973; New York, Pocket Books, 1975.
  The Years of Change. London, Sphere, and New York, Dell, 1974.
  Mrs. Bridges' Story. London, Sphere, 1975.
  The War to End Wars. London, Sphere, and New York, Dell, 1975.
  Thomas and Sarah. London, Sphere, 1978.
The Duchess of Duke Street. London, Panther, 3 vols., 1976; New York, Holt Rinehart,
  1 vol., 1977.
Beauty's Daughter: The Story of Lady Hamilton's "Lost" Daughter. London, Eyre
  Methuen, 1976; New York, Coward McCann, 1977.
Charlie Is My Darling. London, Eyre Methuen, and New York, Coward McCann, 1977.
The Atkinson Heritage:
  The Atkinson Heritage. London, Futura, 1978.
  Sisters in Love. London, Futura, 1979.
  Dove's Nest. London, Futura, 1980.
Lovers Meeting. London, Eyre Methuen, and New York, St. Martin's Press, 1979.
Willowwood. London, Eyre Methuen, and New York, St. Martin's Press, 1980.
Monday's Child. London, Macdonald, 1981; New York, St. Martin's Press, 1982.

OTHER PUBLICATIONS

Novels

The Private Life of Sherlock Holmes (novelization of screenplay), with Michael Hard-
  wick. London, Mayflower, 1970; New York, Bantam, 1971.
The Gaslight Boys (novelization of TV series), with Michael Hardwick. London, Wei-
  denfeld and Nicolson, 1976.
Juliet Bravo. London, Pan, 1980.
Calling Juliet Bravo. London, BBC Publications, 1981.
Juliet Bravo 2. London, Severn House, 1981.

Plays

Four [and *Four More*] *Sherlock Holmes Plays*, with Michael Hardwick. London,
  Murray, 2 vols., 1964-73; New York, French, 2 vols., 1964-74.
The Game's Afoot: Sherlock Holmes Plays, with Michael Hardwick. London, Murray,
  1969; New York, French, 1970.
Plays from Dickens, with Michael Hardwick. London, Murray, and New York, French,
  1970.
Alice in Wonderland, adaptation of the story by Lewis Carroll. London, Davis Poynter,
  1974.
A Christmas Carol, adaptation of the story by Dickens. London, Davis Poynter, 1974.

Radio Plays: *The Corpse in the Case*, 1962; *Going Concern*, 1963; *The Prisoner's Friend*,
from a work by Andrew Garve, 1964; *A Shadow of Doubt*, 1964; *Mrs. Thompson*, 1965;
Sarah Churchill, 1966; *Dear Miss Prior*, from a story by Thackeray, 1970; *The French
Lieutenant's Woman*, from the novel by John Fowles, 1974; and others.

Television Plays: *A Question of Values*, with Michael Hardwick, 1976; *The Cedar Tree*;
The Dickens of a Christmas; *Charles Dickens, Storyteller Extraordinary*; and others.

Other with Michael Hardwick

The Jolly Toper.   London, Jenkins, 1961; New York, State Mutual, 1978.
The Sherlock Holmes Companion.   London, Murray, 1962; New York, Doubleday, 1963.
Sherlock Holmes Investigates.   New York, Lothrop, 1963.
The Man Who Was Sherlock Holmes.   London, Murray, and New York, Doubleday, 1964.
The Charles Dickens Companion.   London, Murray, 1965; New York, Holt Rinehart, 1966.
The Plague and the Fire of London.   London, Parrish, 1966.
Writers' Houses: A Literary Journey in England.   London, Phoenix House, 1968; as *A Literary Journey*, South Brunswick, New Jersey, A.S. Barnes, 1970.
Alfred Deller: A Singularity of Voice.   London, Cassell, 1968; New York, Praeger, 1969.
Dickens's England.   London, Dent, and South Brunswick, New Jersey, A.S. Barnes, 1970.
Charles Dickens...As They Saw Him.   London, Harrap, 1970.
The Vintage Operetta Book (as John Drinkrow).   London, Osprey, 1972.
The Charles Dickens Encyclopedia.   London, Osprey, and New York, Scribner, 1973.
The Bernard Shaw Companion.   London, Murray, 1973; New York, St. Martin's Press, 1974.
The Vintage Musical Comedy Book (as John Drinkrow).   London, Osprey, 1974.
The Charles Dickens Quiz Book.   London, Luscombe, and New York, Larousse, 1974.

Editor, *The World's Greatest Sea Mysteries.*   London, Odhams Press, 1967.

Other

Emma, Lady Hamilton.   London, Cassell, 1969; New York, Holt Rinehart, 1970.
Mrs. Dizzy: The Life of Mary Ann Disraeli.   London, Cassell, and New York, St. Martin's Press, 1972.
The Thames-Side Book (as Mary Atkinson).   London, Osprey, 1973.
The World of Upstairs, Downstairs.   Newton Abbot, David and Charles, and New York, Holt Rinehart, 1976.

Editor, *Stories from Dickens.*   London, Arnold, 1968.

Mollie Hardwick comments:

I would describe myself as an historical, rather than a romantic/gothic novelist. My novels grew out of my non-fiction works (i.e., *Emma, Lady Hamilton*), by way of a request from Sphere Books to write an original novel based on the character of Sarah the housemaid from *Upstairs, Downstairs*. I write, in general, out of my personal enthusiasms (the age of Nelson, the Jacobite Rising of 1745, the Regency theatre, cricket, etc.). In general I stick to the 18th century and the early 19th, disliking Victoriana as such; though *Monday's Child* is set in the 1880's. My next novel, in preparation for Macdonald, is set much farther back in time, beginning during the Wars of the Roses. I might one day write a gothic novel, with a strong supernormal element—who knows? My motivation in writing fiction is to tell a story that will entertain my readers (and incidentally myself) and perhaps provide them with a temporary escape from everyday life.

*   *   *

Mollie Hardwick is one of the most prolific and versatile British writers in the field of light fiction. This does not mean that she writes carelessly. Far from it. She writes with thoughtful precision, and where important historical fact is concerned her accuracy is never in doubt. But she also has the facility for combining fact with fiction in a manner which adds verisimilitude to her period stories. In other words, she knows the rules so well that she knows when she can break them.

Her full range extends from best-selling novels to standard literary studies, biographies and anthologies (especially of Dickens and Conan Doyle), from television, stage, and radio plays to feature series in women's magazines. She sometimes writes in collaboration with her husband Michael, but more and more often, as their literary interests expand, they diverge in different directions.

Hardwick now finds herself concentrating more on the writing of novels, mainly set in the 19th century. This side of her work began when she was asked to compose "background" stories to the *Upstairs, Downstairs* television series, explaining and expanding the lives of the characters before they joined the Bellamy household. There was little on which to base her stories, so she had to invent a "past" for each character. This experience led her to write more fiction, based in part on real historical events and people.

Beauty's Daughter was the first of her period novels in which fact and fiction are closely interwoven. The "Beauty" of the story is Emma Hamilton, Nelson's love, and the "daughter" Emily Hart, Emma's first child. Hardwick herself has had a long love-affair with Nelson and Lady Hamilton, and her affection for, and knowledge of, their entwined lives are reflected in the easy and convincing narration of this facet of Emma's life. *Beauty's Daughter* was followed by *Charlie Is My Darling*, in which the "real" character is the Bonnie Prince, and the fictional heroine a sort of composite of all those anonymous women who fell victim to his charms. *Lovers Meeting*, with its unusual setting of life in the Regency theatre, and the illustrious clown Grimaldi as one of its characters; and *Willowwood* introduced the Pre-Raphaelite painters.

In every case the introduction of these real people is done with a sureness of touch which leaves the intrigued reader uncertain where fact ends and fiction begins. There is no fanfare when a real person slips into the story. In her latest novel, *Monday's Child*, Edward Prince of Wales flits briefly across the pages—and the beautiful young heroine has the temerity to reject his advances!

My personal favourites among her novels are to be found in the Atkinson trilogy, based on the history of Mollie's own maternal ancestors who lived in and around Lancaster and Kendal, where she spent her own childhood holidays, and where she first heard the stories on which the books are based "from very old ladies" of the family. The result is one of the best of family sagas, written with all the integrity and literary skill of which the author is so notably capable.

—Elizabeth Grey

HARDY, Laura. *See* **LAMB, Charlotte.**

HARDY, W(illiam) G(eorge). Canadian. Born in Oakwood, Ontario, 3 February 1895. Educated at the University of Toronto, B.A. 1917, M.A. 1920; University of Chicago, Ph.D. 1922. Married Llewella May Sonley in 1919 (died), two daughters and one son. Lecturer in

Classics, University of Toronto, 1918-20; Lecturer, 1920-22, Assistant Professor, 1922-28, Associate Professor, 1928-33, and Professor of Classics, 1933-65, University of Alberta, Edmonton. President, 1930, and play producer, Edmonton Little Theatre. President, Canadian Authors Association, 1950-52; Member of the Council, Classical Association of Canada. Recipient: University of Alberta National Award in Letters, 1962. Agent: Constance Smith Associates, 18 East 41st Street, New York, New York, 10017, U.S.A. Address: 10828 79th Avenue, Edmonton, Alberta, Canada.

ROMANCE AND GOTHIC PUBLICATIONS

Novels

> Abraham, Prince of Ur.   New York, Dodd Mead, 1935; as Father Abraham, London, Lovat Dickson, 1935.
> Turn Back the River.   New York, Dodd Mead, and London, Lovat Dickson, 1938.
> All the Trumpets Sounded.   New York, Coward McCann, 1942; London, Macdonald, 1946.
> The Unfulfilled.   Toronto, McClelland and Stewart, 1951; New York, Appleton Century Crofts, 1952.
> The City of Libertines.   Toronto, McClelland and Stewart, and New York, Appleton Century Crofts, 1957; London, Heinemann, 1959.
> The Scarlet Mantle: A Novel of Julius Caesar.   Toronto, Macmillan, 1978.
> The Bloodied Toga: A Novel of Julius Caesar.   Toronto, Macmillan, 1979.

OTHER PUBLICATIONS

Other

> Education in Alberta.   Calgary, Calgary Herald, 1946.
> From Sea unto Sea: Canada 1850-1920: The Road to Nationhood.   New York, Doubleday, 1960.
> The Greek and Roman World: Ten Radio Talks.   Toronto, Canadian Broadcasting Corporation, 1960; revised edition, Cambridge, Massachusetts, Schenkman, 1962, 1970.
> Our Heritage from the Past.   Toronto, McClelland and Stewart, 1964.
> Journey into the Past, with J.W.R. Gwyne-Timothy.   Toronto, McClelland and Stewart, 1965.
> Origins and Ordeals of the Western World.   Cambridge, Massachusetts, Schenkman, 1968.

> Editor, The Alberta Golden Jubilee Anthology.   Toronto, McClelland and Stewart, 1955.
> Editor, Alberta: A Natural History.   Edmonton, Hurtig, 1967.

*   *   *

The early works of W.G. Hardy were based upon social commentary on the Canada of the day: The Unfulfilled examined Canadian/British Canadian/American relations. These novels were flavoured by what was for the day a surprising emphasis on explicitly sexual carryings-on; but even so, Hardy's first few books made relatively little stir. His fame rests in large part upon his Roman trilogy, three massive volumes which are not precisely a series, since they are readable as self-sufficient works, but sharing certain elements, most notably the presence of Julius Caesar.

City of Libertines examines the politics and decadence of Roman life in the latter days of the

Republic. The plot hinges upon the destructive adoration of the poet Catullus for his faithless "Lesbia." She was in real life Clodia Pulcher, sister of that Clodius Pulcher who created the scandal of a scandalous era by profaning the sacred rites of the Good Goddess, a religious ceremony forbidden to men. The uproar caused by his blasphemous act, and the subsequent manipulation of the Roman population by the self-seeking libertines of the title, provide a jolting comparison with the political manipulation of peoples of the 20th century. Although not the central figure in this novel, Caesar plays a significant role as a presence on the periphery, watchfully prepared to seize any opportunity the fates may afford him.

The Scarlet Mantle covers the mid-period of the life of Julius Caesar. Here is the warrior, the renegade who led his troops, more loyal to himself than to Rome, across the Rubicon, thus casting his personal challenge in the teeth of the Republic. Parallel with Caesar's story runs another thread, that of the life of a humble soldier, Fadius, a fictional character whose changing life and perceptions reflect the effects of Caesar's career upon his times and countrymen.

The Roman trilogy concludes with The Bloodied Toga, telling of the climax of Caesar's life and reign, and of his relations with the voluptuous Egyptian queen Cleopatra.

Hardy certainly was comfortably familiar with the historic accounts that provide a basis for his Roman stories, and included the facts as a comprehensible and coherent chain of events in a convincing fashion, but the baldly contemporary language of his Romans is obtrusive and tends to undercut the effect of his ease and familiarity with the intricacies of ancient history.

Apparently jealous of the commercial success of the "slick" novels of the era, some of which his writer persona scornfully lists in The Unfulfilled, Hardy seems to have resolved to conquer cheap fiction from within. His obsessive emphasis on sexual relations, in particular sex as a manipulative weapon especially though not exclusively of women, becomes tiresomely repetitive and predictable. Let any man and woman occupy adjacent space in any of his Roman titles, and inevitably their clothing will shortly slither to the floor to the accompaniment of a good deal of embarrassingly adolescent bedroom badinage. Though his work would have benefitted by the attentions of a ruthless editor, Hardy's later novels won for him an extensive public who may, at intervals, have learned something about ancient Rome backstage.

—Joan McGrath

HARLE, Elizabeth.   *See* **ROBERTS, Irene.**

HARRIS, Marilyn.   American.   Born in Oklahoma City, Oklahoma, 4 June 1931. Educated at Cottey College, 1949-51; University of Oklahoma, Norman, B.A. 1953, M.A. 1955. Married Edgar V. Springer, Jr., in 1953; one son and one daughter. Address: 1846 Rolling Hills, Norman, Oklahoma 73069, U.S.A.

Novels (series: Eden)

Bledding Sorrow. New York, Putnam, 1976.
This Other Eden. New York, Putnam, 1977.
The Prince of Eden. New York, Putnam, 1978; London, Futura, 1980.
The Eden Passion. New York, Putnam, 1979; London, Macdonald, 1981.
The Women of Eden. New York, Putnam, 1980.
Eden Rising. New York, Putnam, 1982.

OTHER PUBLICATIONS

Novels

In the Midst of Earth. New York, Doubleday, 1969.
Hatter Fox. New York, Random House, 1973; London, Gollancz, 1974.
The Conjurers. New York, Random House, 1974; London, Panther, 1977.

Short Stories

King's Ex. New York, Doubleday, and London, Gollancz, 1967.

Other (juvenile)

The Peppersalt Land. New York, Four Winds Press, 1970.
The Runaway's Diary. New York, Four Winds Press, 1971.

*   *   *

In Marilyn Harris's first gothic romance, *Bledding Sorrow*, a three-century old drama of imprisonment, madness, adultery, mutilation, and murder slowly and plausibly repeats itself in the present. In her masterpiece of historical romance, the Eden novels, Harris also sounds, believably, the rest of the painful notes in the scale of passion: abandonment, exile, bastardy, betrayal, incest, rape, and sado-masochism. *This Other Eden*, set in the 1790's, begins when Thomas Eden has his servant girl, Marianne, stripped and flogged for insubordination. The book chronicles his attacks of remorse and his attempts to possess her, which include persuading her sister to abet a kidnapping, and also a sham marriage. They finally plunge together into "the whole ecstatic process of domination and submission." But when a child, Edward, is born, Thomas suffers another personality change and rejects them both. In order to get Marianne back this time, he has *himself* flogged. She nurses him back to health, they marry, and a legitimate son, James, is born. Harris turns history to good account with frequent and bizarre appearances by Beckford (author and builder, of an early gothic novel and castle) and by Lord Nelson's mistress Emma Hamilton, who gains social acceptance for Marianne.

The Prince of Eden, however, is less love story than tragedy of circumstance. The "Prince," Edward, as a result of his parents' marriage settlement, owns Eden. He is selling it off piecemeal to finance various rescue operations among the poor and criminal classes of London in the 1830's. Opium addiction (learned from De Quincey, practised with Branwell Brontë) and a grand passion for his brother's intended bride, Harriet, drive Edward farther outside the bounds of bourgeois respectability. Harriet refuses to run off with Edward. Unfortunately, she is pregnant and must feign a long illness before her wedding; fortunately, Edward learns of this in time to rescue his son, John.

Edward's revulsion from the charade of respectability is further underlined by his involvement with the radical causes of the day. When he proposes to use half the Eden estate on a friend's system of Ragged Schools, James sues for the right to the property. He loses, but Edward, in a typical act of self-immolation, gives it up. He is subsequently killed in an industrial accident, leaving John with nothing but the dream of Eden.

In *The Eden Passion* John realizes this dream, but ironically at the cost of rejecting all his father's beliefs. With this novel, in fact, Harris begins to undermine the conventions of her genre: she creates no more romantic heroes. John, bastard of a bastard, returns to Eden and has for the first and only love of his life his own mother, Harriet, and the rest of the Eden novels chart the pathology of his exile from this love. Although this is gothic romance at its source, Harris's increased attention to themes of social injustice and crimes of imperialism ultimately debunks the myth of the Great Family Estate. When the doomed lovers learn the truth, Harriet blinds and imprisons herself, while John flees to commerce in the City, in the Crimea (where his war wounds are tended by Florence Nightingale), and to India, in search of fortune. He returns to England with an Indian woman who has had her tongue cut out while rescuing him during the 1857 mutiny in Delhi. With Dhari's and Harriet's mutilation, Harris says more than "Passion is dangerous." While John, in his pain, amasses a great fortune, marries, and acquires Eden at last, his women have no consolation but that of being among his valued acquisitions.

In *The Women of Eden* Harris develops this theme. The title is that of a painting of John's wife Lila, Dhari, Harriett's daughter Mary, and Elizabeth, the former prostitute who raised him. An observer says they look sick to their stomachs. Certainly John's behavior becomes increasingly sickening. His wife is repeatedly subjected to marital rape and dies in grotesque agony of a neglected uterine cancer. Dhari is brutalized. Mary is at first a wretched prisoner of his idea of her as a pure maiden; when he sees her in her American lover's embrace, he arranges to have her raped by a gang of thugs. John hates women (especially suffragettes—Elizabeth, by the way, is one), radicals, the poor, Americans, and those he terms Sodomites, whom he also plots to victimize. John's frustrated desire for social acceptance is, he thinks, blocked by a newspaper columnist's attack: "Eden present[s] a contradiction of material splendor and moral bankruptcy, though unwittingly he serve[s] as the most polished mirror ever held to English society in recent times." Eden is denied revenge upon the writer, who is Mary's lover. They escape to America, Dhari and John's lawyer marry and leave for Canada, and Elizabeth joins the French feminists. So much for the Women of Eden and for English society in 1870. Harris has ended the Eden series by accusing a society of providing gothic materials.

—Sally Allen McNall

HARRIS, Rosemary (Jeanne). British. Born in London, 20 February 1923. Educated at Thorneloe School, Weymouth; St. Martin's, Central, and Chelsea schools of art, London; Department of Technology, Courtauld Institute, London. Served in the Red Cross Nursing Auxiliary, Westminster Division, London, 1941-45. Picture Restorer, 1949; Reader, Metro-Goldwyn-Mayer, 1951-52; Children's Book Reviewer, *The Times*, London, 1970-73. Recipient: Library Association Carnegie Medal, 1969; Arts Council grant 1971. Agent: Michael Horniman, A.P. Watt and Son, 26/28 Bedford Row, London WC1R 4HL. Address: 33 Cheyne Court, Flood Street, London SW3 5TR, England.

ROMANCE AND GOTHIC PUBLICATIONS

Novels

The Summer-House. London, Hamish Hamilton, 1956.
Voyage to Cythera. London, Bodley Head, 1958.
Venus with Sparrows. London, Faber, 1961.
All My Enemies. London, Faber, 1967; New York, Simon and Schuster, 1973.
The Nice Girl's Story. London, Faber, 1968; as *Nor Evil Dreams*, New York, Simon and
    Schuster, 1974.
A Wicked Pack of Cards. London, Faber, 1969; New York, Walker, 1970.
The Double Snare. London, Faber, 1974; New York, Simon and Schuster, 1975.
Three Candles for the Dark. London, Faber, 1976.

OTHER PUBLICATIONS (for children)

Fiction

The Moon in the Cloud. London, Faber, 1968; New York, Macmillan, 1969.
The Shadow on the Sun. London, Faber, and New York, Macmillan, 1970.
The Seal-Singing. London, Faber, and New York, Macmillan, 1971.
The Child in the Bamboo Grove. London, Faber, 1971; New York, S.G. Phillips, 1972.
The Bright and Morning Star. London, Faber, and New York, Macmillan, 1972.
The King's White Elephant. London, Faber, 1973.
The Flying Ship. London, Faber, 1975.
The Little Dog of Fo. London, Faber, 1976.
I Want to Be a Fish. London, Kestrel, 1977.
A Quest for Orion. London, Faber, 1978.
Green Finger House. London, Eel Pie, 1980.
Tower of the Stars. London, Faber, 1980.
The Enchanted Horse. London, Kestrel, 1981.

Plays

Television Plays: *Peronik*, 1976; *The Unknown Enchantment*, 1982.

Other

The Lotus and the Grail: Legends from East to West. London, Faber, 1974; abridged
    edition, as *Sea Magic and Other Stories of Enchantment*, New York, Macmillan, 1974.
Beauty and the Beast. London, Faber, 1979; New York, Doubleday, 1980.

Rosemary Harris comments:

My fiction for adults grew primarily out of a thwarted desire to produce plays for the
theatre—and I hope some of what I learned about drama, dialogue, and character in action was
a help when it came to novel-writing. I still believe that a strong plot combined with character
development is the truly important basis on which most fiction or dramatic writers need to lean.
Look, for instance, at Shaffer's play *Amadeus* which has all the traditional elements, combined
with a truly modern approach of his own. If I could do something half as good as that in a novel
or play, I should be more than delighted.

*   *   *

Rosemary Harris's first novel, *The Summer-House*, is different from her later books although it has some of the ingredients of the later Harrises—the smooth urbane style with a sophisticated sparkle, a heroine who has two chaps to choose between (lucky girl), and close-knit, tangled family relationships and friendships. But the main difference between this book and its successors is that it is a straightforward tale without terror whereas all the other books are modern gothics—intensely feminine stories of fear and romance. What makes them all the more frightening and claustrophobic is that the menace usually comes from someone who is beloved and should be above suspicion. *All My Enemies* tells of a twin sister who murders the heroine's husband and tries to pretend that her sister is mad as well as bad; *A Wicked Pack of Cards* throws suspicion on both of the heroine's suitors and is laden with red herrings as well as literary allusions. In *The Nice Girl's Story* the villain has to be either the heroine's step-son or her husband—but which? *The Double Snare* has an amnesiac heroine who does not know whom she should love or whom she should fear, and who suspects everyone, even her own previous persona. In *Three Candles for the Dark*, however, Harris has gone over the top with her gothic ingredients which include a scarred heroine, a lonely house, a mad woman, incest, a pyromaniac, killer dogs, a helpless child to hamper the heroine and tug at her heart strings, a sadist, and a double-cross. How's that for Grand Guignol?

Harris is excellent at character drawing; she is a distinguished children's writer and, as one would expect, she produces lively, believable child characters too. *A Wicked Pack of Cards* (my favourite of her gothics) features a whole family of well-drawn and sharply differentiated children, especially Culbertson (so-called because she was taken out to bridge-parties while in her carry cot), the ten-year-old balletomane who is the lynch-pin of the plot. Joss, the imprisoned boy in *Three Candles for the Dark*, is the most believable character in the book. All her thrillers are written in the first person by the heroine, and Harris finds a different style and tone for each one in keeping with her profession (teacher, actress, journalist, and novelist) and, what is much more difficult, manages to convey her heroine's faults within this framework. The other thing that Harris does well is convey a sense of place. It is more than giving us evocative descriptions, it is dozens of well-chosen little details which make you feel as if you are actually there: Paris in *The Summer-House*, Italy in *The Double Snare*, a suburban comprehensive school with all its inwardness in *The Nice Girl's Story*, London and Alexandria in *All My Enemies*, an English seaside town in *A Wicked Pack of Cards* and the Vermont countryside in *Three Candles for the Dark*.

Rosemary Harris's books are always a pleasure to read and deserve to be better known.

—Pamela Cleaver

HARRISON, (Edith) Elizabeth (Tatchell).

ROMANCE AND GOTHIC PUBLICATIONS

Novels

    Coffee at Dobree's.   London, Ward Lock, 1965.
    The Physicians.   London, Ward Lock, 1966.
    The Ravelston Affair.   London, Ward Lock, 1967.

Emergency Call.   London, Hurst and Blackett, 1970.
Accident Call.   London, Hurst and Blackett, 1971.
Ambulance Call.   London, Hurst and Blackett, 1972.
Surgeon's Call.   London, Hurst and Blackett, 1973.
On Call.   London, Hurst and Blackett, 1974.
Hospital Call.   London, Hurst and Blackett, 1975.
Dangerous Call.   London, Hurst and Blackett, 1976.
To Mend a Heart.   London, Hurst and Blackett, 1977.
Young Doctor Goddard.   London, Hurst and Blackett, 1978.
A Doctor Called Caroline.   London, Hurst and Blackett, 1979.

*   *   *

Unlike most "hospital" novelists, Elizabeth Harrison has never nursed, though for most of her working life she has been closely connected with the medical profession, mainly in an administrative and research capacity. This, I think, has been to her (and the reader's) advantage. Hers are not the conventional doctor-nurse romances. She rarely writes about nurses. Her central characters are usually doctors, and it is from their point of view that we see life. She sees doctors not as little tin gods, though, but as all-too-human, often arrogant on the upper slopes, prone to human frailty at every level.

Her novels are almost all set in the fictional Central London Hospital. This gives her scope to develop character from story to story, which she does. Sons and daughters follow eminent fathers into the profession through "their" hospital. The reader comes to know them, and their foibles.

One of her most interesting and complex characters is Leo Rosenstein, an outstanding young surgeon, over-conscious of his lowly (East End) origins compared to his colleagues, all of whom have the "right" accent, clothes, school, and family backgrounds—a fact which drives Leo to hide his sensitivity and sharp intelligence behind an exaggerated lack of "couth."

The exploration of personality, as much as the medical detail and the love-interest, obviously fascinates Harrison. The high-and-mighty Ravelstons, for example: "No heart—all brain, the lot of them; supercilious too, and moneyed," is how one embittered colleague sums them up. But one of them is riding for a fall in *The Ravelston Affair*, which leads to his being "struck off," the worst, and most humiliating, punishment a doctor can suffer. Here, too, is one romantic hospital writer who acknowledges the fact that not all doctors these days are WASPS. There is a touch of racial tension in *The Ravelston Affair*.

In at least two books young doctors get a taste of what it is like to be a patient. *Emergency Call* shows especial insight into the devastating psychological effects on a young man— dominant partner in a happy marriage—of paralysis following a railway accident in which he attempts to rescue a passenger. His young wife's inability to help him back to full life bewilders and frightens her, especially when the pretty nurse assigned to him has more success. The reasons are not the obvious ones. Harrison's subtle and delicate handling of this tricky theme sets the seal, for me, on her shrewd understanding of human nature, in addition to her ability to write dramatic stories and credible dialogue.

Like Lucilla Andrews she keeps up to date in medical matters and the way hospitals are run—and also in contemporary morals. In *Young Doctor Goddard*, for example, the heroine's close friend, another nurse, cheerfully shacks up with one of the doctors (of course they are engaged, and fully intend to marry...). And, to my personal regret, the hospital "politics" which spice the earlier novels are played down in the later ones because, the author explains, that is how it now is in real life.

—Elizabeth Grey

HART, Caroline. *See* **GARVICE, Charles**.

HARTE, Marjorie. *See* **McEVOY, Marjorie**.

HARVEY, Rachel. *See* **BLOOM, Ursula**.

HASTINGS, Phyllis (Dora, née Hodge).   Also writes as John Bedford; Julia Mayfield.   British.   Born in Bristol. Attended the Edgebaston Church of England College for Girls. Married Philip Norman Hastings in 1938; one child. Ballet dancer as a child; later operator of a dairy farm and an antique business. Recipient: Romantic Novelists Association Historical Award, 1973. Address: The Abbot's Cottage, Upper Lake, Battle, East Sussex TN33 0AN, England.

ROMANCE AND GOTHIC PUBLICATIONS

Novels

As Long as You Live.   London, Jenkins, 1951.
Far from Jupiter.   London, Jenkins, 1952.
Crowning Glory.   London, Jenkins, 1952.
Rapture in My Rags.   London, Dent, and New York, Dutton, 1954; as *Scarecrow Lover*, London, Pan, 1960; as *Rapture*, London, Consul, and New York, Popular Library, 1966.
Dust Is My Pillow.   London, Dent, and New York, Dutton, 1955.
The Field of Roses.   London, Dent, 1955; as *Her French Husband*, New York, Dutton, 1956.
The Black Virgin of the Gold Mountain.   London, Dent, 1956.
The Innocent and the Wicked.   New York, Popular Library, 1956.
The Signpost Has Four Arms.   London, Dent, 1957.
The Forest of Stone (as Julia Mayfield).   London, Hale, 1957.
A Time for Pleasure.   New York, Popular Library, 1957.

The Happy Man. London, Hutchinson, 1958.
Golden Apollo. London, Hutchinson, 1958.
The Fountain of Youth. London, Hutchinson, 1959.
Sandals for My Feet. London, Hutchinson, 1960.
Long Barnaby. London, Hodder and Stoughton, 1961; as *Hot Day in High Summer*,
  London, May Fair, 1962.
The Night the Roof Blew Off. London, Hodder and Stoughton, 1962.
Their Flowers Were Always Black. London, Hale, 1967; as *The Harlot's Daughter*,
  London, New English Library, 1967.
The Swan River Story. London, Hale, 1968.
The Sussex Saga:
  All Earth to Love. London, Corgi, 1968.
  Day of the Dancing Sun. London, Corgi, 1971.
An Act of Darkness. London, Hale, 1969; as *The House on Malador Street*, New York,
  Putnam, 1970.
The Stars Are My Children. London, Hale, 1970.
The Temporary Boy. London, Hale, 1971.
When the Gallows Is High. London, Hale, 1971.
The Conservatory. London, Hale, 1973; New York, Pocket Books, 1974.
The Gates of Morning. London, Corgi, 1973.
Bartholomew Fair. London, Hale, 1974.
House of the Twelve Caesars. London, Hale, 1975; New York, Berkley, 1976.
The Image-Maker. London, Hale, 1976.
The Candles of the Night. London, Cassell, 1977.
The Death-Scented Flower. London, Hale, 1977.
Field of the Forty Footsteps. London, Cassell, 1978; New York, St. Martin's Press,
  1979.
The Stratford Affair. London, Hale, 1978.
The Feast of the Peacock. London, Cassell, 1978.
Running Thursday. London, Hale, 1980.
Buttercup Joe. London, Hale, 1980.
Tiger's Heaven. London, Hale, 1981.
The Overlooker. London, Hale, 1982.

OTHER PUBLICATIONS

Other as John Bedford

Looking [and *More Looking*] *in Junk Shops.* London, Parrish, 2 vols., 1961-62.
Talking about Teapots. London, Parrish, 1964.
Collector's Pieces 1-12. London, Cassell, 12 vols., 1964-67.
London's Burning. London, Abelard Schuman, 1966.
Delftware. London, Cassell, 1966.
Still Looking for Junk. London, Macdonald, 1969.

*   *   *

One of Phyllis Hastings's earlier novels, *Rapture in My Rags*, was described in the *New York Times Book Review* (18 July 1954) as "A touching story of a girl's search for affection, her achieving a kind of protective maturity, and her revolt to preserve her new found identity." Many of the author's female characters fit this very description although their personalities and their predicaments vary widely. Endeavoring to overcome loneliness in the midst of coping with peculiar situations is a hallmark of Hastings's heroines. From the confused Anna in *Dust Is My Pillow*, gullible Rose in *The Field of Roses* (US title *Her French Husband*), and responsible Ellie in *The Conservatory* to stalwart Melita in *The Swan River Story*, warped Victoria in *An Act of Darkness* (US title *The House on Malador Street*), and even the indomitable Caroline

Dyke in *The Gates of Morning*, the author relentlessly examines the problems and powers of being female in largely male-dominated situations.

While the trials of women dealing with the men in their lives is the primary focus of romance and gothic fiction, Hastings's style is distinctly her own. She can dispose of years in a sentence or two and describe wide-ranging adventures in understated terms as she does in *The Stars Are My Children*. One delights in the bright bits of humor that crop up sometimes in the most unlikely situations. She distinctively crafts her stories around characters or circumstances that are slightly offbeat, a shade removed from the normal. She has a flair for portraying the neurotic character, such as the obsessed patriarch Isaac Shipton in *Dust Is My Pillow* and religious fanatic Stand Fast Dyke in *The Gates of Morning* as well as the evil sister Margaret in *The Conservatory*. She is also a master at portraying the growing sexual awareness of her heroines. Repressed sexuality accounts for the tension in many of her novels, and she also explores the touchy area of relationships between older women and younger men with humor in *The Stars Are My Children* and sensitivity in *The Gates of Morning*.

Hastings is an insightful student of human nature, always in control of her narrative, often lyrical in her descriptions of country life, but it is her original characters and her taste for the unusual that make her repertoire of stories truly entertaining. A minor character in *The Stars Are My Children* expresses what might well be the author's own philosophy. After Arthur Balmer relates the fantastic tale of his rescue from slavery by a woman who gave him her infant daughter before perishing in a shipwreck and his later 15-year separation from the girl after his impressment, the listener, an old sailor, proclaims, "'Tis a mighty strange story though I have heard stranger. The earth teems with strange stories, it being the dwelling place of such odd creatures as human beings."

—Allayne C. Heyduk

HEATH, Sharon. *See* **RITCHIE, Claire.**

HEAVEN, Constance (née Fecher). Also writes as Constance Fecher; Christina Merlin. British. Born in Enfield, Middlesex, 6 August 1911. Educated at The Convent, Woodford Green, Essex, 1921-28; King's College, London, 1928-31, B.A. (honours) 1931; London College of Music, Licentiate 1931. Married William Heaven in 1939 (died, 1958). Actress, 1939-66: operated theatre companies at Henley-on-Thames with her husband. Chairman, Romantic Novelists Association, 1981. Recipient: Romantic Novelists Association Major Award, 1973. Agent: Carl Routledge, Charles Lavell Ltd., 176 Wardour Street, London W1V 3AA. Address: 37 Teddington Park Road, Teddington, Middlesex TW11 8NB, England.

ROMANCE AND GOTHIC PUBLICATIONS

Novels (series: Kuragin)

The House of Kuragin.   London, Heinemann, and New York, Coward McCann, 1972.
The Astrov Inheritance (Kuragin).   London, Heinemann, 1973; as The Astrov Legacy,
    New York, Coward McCann, 1973.
Castle of Eagles.   London, Heinemann, and New York, Coward McCann, 1974.
The Place of Stones.   London, Heinemann, and New York, Coward McCann, 1975.
The Fires of Glenlochy.   London, Heinemann, and New York, Coward McCann, 1976.
The Queen and the Gypsy.   London, Heinemann, and New York, Coward McCann,
    1977.
Lord of Ravensley.   London, Heinemann, and New York, Coward McCann, 1978.
Heir to Kuragin.   London, Heinemann, 1978; New York, Coward McCann, 1979.
The Wildcliffe Bird.   London, Heinemann, and New York, Coward McCann, 1981.
The Ravensley Touch.   London, Heinemann, and New York, Coward McCann, 1982.

Novels as Constance Fecher

Tudor Trilogy:
    Queen's Delight.   London, Hale, 1966; as Queen's Favorite, New York, Dell, 1974.
    Traitor's Son.   London, Hale, 1967; New York, Dell, 1976.
    King's Legacy.   London, Hale, 1967; New York, Dell, 1976.
Player Queen.   London, Hale, 1968; as The Lovely Wanton, New York, Dell, 1977.
Lion of Trevarrock.   London, Hale, 1969.
The Night of the Wolf.   London, Hale, 1972; New York, Delacorte Press, 1974.

Novels as Christina Merlin

The Spy Concerto.   London, Hale, and New York, St. Martin's Press, 1980.
Sword of Mithras.   London, Hale, 1982.

OTHER PUBLICATIONS

Other (juvenile)

Venture for a Crown.   New York, Farrar Straus, 1968.
Heir to Pendarrow.   New York, Farrar Straus, 1969.
Bright Star: A Portrait of Ellen Terry.   New York, Farrar Straus, 1970; London, Gol-
    lancz, 1971.
The Link Boys.   New York, Farrar Straus, 1971.
The Last Elizabethan: A Portrait of Sir Walter Ralegh.   New York, Farrar Straus, 1972.
The Leopard Dagger.   New York, Farrar Straus, 1973.

Constance Heaven comments:

I came to writing late after some 25 years in the theatre with my husband and then alone after his early death. A lifelong interest in history gave me my first inspiration—a biographical novel about Sir Walter Ralegh which turned into a trilogy covering his son and grandson. From choosing real historical characters I turned to fictional heroes and heroines, and my first true romance was The House of Kuragin set in pre-revolutionary Russia. Quite small incidents often spark off a story: a holiday in the Highlands rich in family feuds, a fascination with the

Camargue in southern France, an abiding interest in the Fen century—and before I know where I am I'm deep in research and inventing a plot to fit the scene. I cannot write to any formula. Plot and people have to come out of the circumstances and often develop in their own way, sometimes against my will. I am of a practical turn of mind so my characters tend to follow suit and I'm not given to the wilder flights of romance. My two recent modern tales (as Christina Merlin) are a relief and contrast to my usual work. Basically I think I write to please myself. It's what I enjoy reading and I hope that others will find the same interest.

*   *   *

The writing of Constance Heaven has strong links with the Brontës. For the most part it inhabits the same 19th century, and uncovers the same dark passions, violence simmering beneath the Victorian respectability. Her heroes are formidable and proud, with a definite streak of ruthlessness. Her governess heroines are spirited, often artistic, their quiet natures masking their inner strength. To this world Heaven brings her own individual voice.

As Constance Fecher she wrote the Tudor trilogy—*Queen's Delight, Traitor's Son, King's Legacy*—where historical characters and events are given a fictional treatment. *Queen's Delight* follows the life of Sir Walter Ralegh from his youth to final execution in the reign of James I. The work is perfectly achieved, the understated style honed to essentials. The author presents the complex nature of Ralegh, his varying fortunes, the triumph and tragedy of his life, without glamour or false dramatics. *Queen's Delight* is a remarkable novel, its restrained skill typical of the trilogy as a whole. *Lion of Trevarrock* and *The Night of the Wolf* are more conventionally gothic stories, well-written though lacking the depth of the Tudor novels. The latter, with its Russian setting, indicates the future course of her work.

The House of Kuragin marks her debut as Constance Heaven, and describes her governess heroine's adventures with the Kuragin family in Tsarist Russia. Her love for the proud Andrei provides the central thread of the story. Quarrels over an inheritance, the sensual Natasha with her murky past, the steward who proves to be the old count's bastard son—all are skillfully interwoven, and the Russian setting beautifully evoked. *The Astrov Inheritance* is an effective sequel.

Castle of Eagles and *The Place of Stones* retain heroes and heroines of the gothic type, the settings respectively Vienna and Napoleonic France. Both are ably written, though they somehow lack the spark of the Kuragin novels. Better is *The Fires of Glenlochy*, set in the Scottish Highlands. The atmosphere is excellently caught, the plot exciting with secret passages and sudden discoveries, the brooding violence erupting in a climax of destruction.

The Queen and the Gypsy is outstanding. A return to Elizabethan history, it presents the tragic figure of Robert Earl of Leicester, torn between ambition and love, for his wife and his queen. Tracking through time, Heaven focuses on the sequence of events that leads to final tragedy. All the old skills are displayed, the characters brought brilliantly to life.

Lord of Ravensley is more ambitious, but less successful. A tangled saga of inheritance and revenge in the Fens, it has good scenes but its length defeats it. More effective is *Heir to Kuragin*, where the second generation of Kuragins are followed to the Caucasus, and which maintains the standard of exotic setting and exciting plot. So, too, does *The Wildcliffe Bird*, imaginatively set in the Staffordshire potteries of the last century. Action is swift, the story skilled, hero and heroine worthy of her best.

—Geoffrey Sadler

HEYER, Georgette.   Also wrote as Stella Martin.   British.   Born 16 August 1902. Educated at seminary schools and Westminster College, London. Married George Ronald Rougier in 1925; one son. Lived in East Africa, 1925-28, and in Yugoslavia, 1928-29. *Died 5 July 1974.*

ROMANCE AND GOTHIC PUBLICATIONS

Novels (series: Superintendent Hannasyde; Inspector Hemingway)

The Black Moth.   London, Constable, and Boston Houghton Mifflin, 1921.
The Great Roxhythe.   London, Hutchinson, 1922; Boston, Small Maynard, 1923.
The Transformation of Philip Jettan (as Stella Martin).   London, Mills and Boon, 1923;
    as *Powder and Patch*, as Georgette Heyer, London, Heinemann, 1930; New York,
    Dutton, 1968.
Instead of the Thorn.   London, Hutchinson, 1923; Boston, Small Maynard, 1924.
Simon the Coldheart.   London, Heinemann, and Boston, Small Maynard, 1925.
These Old Shades.   London, Heinemann, and Boston, Small Maynard, 1926.
Helen.   London and New York, Longman, 1928.
The Masqueraders.   London, Heinemann, 1928; New York, Longman, 1929.
Beauvallet.   London, Heinemann, 1929; New York, Longman, 1930.
Pastel.   London and New York, Longman, 1929.
Barren Corn.   London and New York, Longman, 1930.
The Conqueror.   London, Heinemann, 1931; New York, Dutton, 1966.
Footsteps in the Dark.   London, Longman, 1932.
Why Shoot the Butler?   London, Longman, 1933; New York, Doubleday, 1936.
The Unfinished Clue.   London, Longman, 1934; New York, Doubleday, 1937.
The Convenient Marriage.   London, Heinemann, 1934; New York, Dutton, 1966.
Devil's Cub.   London, Heinemann, 1934; New York, Dutton, 1936.
Regency Buck.   London, Heinemann, 1935; New York, Dutton, 1966.
Death in the Stocks (Hannasyde).   London, Longman, 1935; as *Merely Murder*, New
    York, Doubleday, 1935.
Behold, Here's Poison! (Hannasyde).   London, Hodder and Stoughton, and New York,
    Doubleday, 1936.
The Talisman Ring.   London, Heinemann, 1936; New York, Doubleday, 1937.
An Infamous Army.   London, Heinemann, 1937; New York, Doubleday, 1938.
They Found Him Dead (Hannasyde).   London, Hodder and Stoughton, and New York,
    Doubleday, 1937.
A Blunt Instrument (Hannasyde).   London, Hodder and Stoughton, and New York,
    Doubleday, 1938.
Royal Escape.   London, Heinemann, 1938; New York, Doubleday, 1939.
No Wind of Blame (Hemingway).   London, Hodder and Stoughton, and New York,
    Doubleday, 1939.
The Spanish Bride.   London, Heinemann, and New York, Doubleday, 1940.
The Corinthian.   London, Heinemann, 1940; New York, Dutton, 1966.
Faro's Daughter.   London, Heinemann, 1941; New York, Doubleday, 1942.
Beau Wyndham.   New York, Doubleday, 1941.
Envious Casca (Hemingway).   London, Hodder and Stoughton, and New York,
    Doubleday, 1941.
Penhallow.   London, Heinemann, 1942; New York, Doubleday, 1943.
Friday's Child.   London, Heinemann, 1944; New York, Putnam, 1946.
The Reluctant Widow.   London, Heinemann, and New York, Putnam, 1946.
The Foundling.   London, Heinemann, and New York, Putnam, 1948.
Arabella.   London, Heinemann, and New York, Putnam, 1949.
The Grand Sophy.   London, Heinemann, and New York, Putnam, 1950.
The Quiet Gentleman.   London, Heinemann, 1951; New York, Putnam, 1952.
Duplicate Death (Hemingway).   London, Heinemann, 1951; New York, Dutton, 1969.

Detection Unlimited (Hemingway).   London, Heinemann, 1953; New York, Dutton, 1969.
Cotillion.   London, Heinemann, and New York, Putnam, 1953.
The Toll-Gate.   London, Heinemann, and New York, Putnam, 1954.
Bath Tangle.   London, Heinemann, and New York, Putnam, 1955.
Sprig Muslin.   London, Heinemann, and New York, Putnam, 1956.
April Lady.   London, Heinemann, and New York, Putnam, 1957.
Sylvester; or, The Wicked Uncle.   London, Heinemann, and New York, Putnam, 1957.
Venetia.   London, Heinemann, 1958; New York, Putnam, 1959.
The Unknown Ajax.   London, Heinemann, 1959; New York, Putnam, 1960.
A Civil Contract.   London, Heinemann, 1961; New York, Putnam, 1962.
The Nonesuch.   London, Heinemann, 1962; New York, Dutton, 1963.
False Colours.   London, Bodley Head, 1963; New York, Dutton, 1964.
Frederica.   London, Bodley Head, and New York, Dutton, 1965.
Black Sheep.   London, Bodley Head, 1966; New York, Dutton, 1967.
Cousin Kate.   London, Bodley Head, 1968; New York, Dutton, 1969.
Charity Girl.   London, Bodley Head, and New York, Dutton, 1970.
Lady of Quality.   London, Bodley Head, and New York, Dutton, 1972.
My Lord John.   London, Bodley Head, and New York, Dutton, 1975.

Short Stories

Pistols for Two and Other Stories.   London, Heinemann, 1960; New York, Dutton, 1964.

Other Publications

Play

Radio Play: *The Toll-Gate*, from her own novel, 1974.

*   *   *

Everyone knows—and almost no one enjoys—the kind of historic fiction that has aptly been described as "writing forsoothly," in which modern sentiments are thinly concealed in a contrived form of contemporary speech peppered with "thee" and "thou." That, plus a swirling cape and jack-boots, or, for a female, a fan and red-heeled shoes, is apparently all the author feels is required to establish "period." On the other end of the scale of historic fiction, we find the works of Georgette Heyer. Surely, if by magic she had been transported into the midst of faddish, slangy Regency society, she would have been perfectly in her element, and would never have missed a word or a phrase. Few writers in any field have ever so thoroughly and convincingly immersed themselves in the trivia of their chosen era, until it became as natural to her writing as daily speech. She captured in meticulous detail the ephemeral, so-soon-forgotten catch-phrases and slang that above all give to any time, place, or society its special, inimitable flavour.

Heyer's people are butterflies—the bubbles on the champagne of a favoured way of life lived at the expense of the forgotten ones below: but her books are not tracts, and the dark side of Regency life seldom obtrudes. Her gilded ones toil not, neither do they spin, and they often neglect to pay the bills of those who do the toiling and spinning for them—but never their gambling debts! Their peculiar convictions on the subject of honour are an odd aspect of the times which Heyer fully understands (which is not to say that she approves).

Her menfolk are by modern standards incredibly concerned with their clothing. They spend untold hours with their tailor or bootmaker; hours tying a cravat *just so*. They inflict upon themselves collars so high and stiff that the wearer cannot turn his head, and have their leathers cleaned with champagne in emulation of Mr. Brummell. When at last they are fit to be seen by an admiring public, they wander off for a bare-knuckled boxing match with a professional pug at Jackson's Saloon, risk their own and all bystanders' lives by driving precarious high-perch phaetons "to an inch," with scarcely controllable teams of powerful horses on bad, ill-lit roads, and become involved in duels at the drop of a hat or an eyelash.

Her women lead lives of decorative uselessness, fussing endlessly with the matching of ribbons and reticules, finding the latest novel in the lending library, sending and receiving invitations to this and that, or—horrors!—*not* receiving them, and, always and above all, marrying to advantage. There was, after all, nothing else for a lady to do, except in desperation to accept a post as governess or companion, a fate scarcely better than death.

These, roughly, were the ground rules of a peculiarly individualistic form of society, at once super-refined and heartlessly brutal, and, above all, decorative. It is all so distant now that only a few charming fragments like the Brighton Pavilion remain—except in the pages of the Regency romance. Others have tried, but no one else has succeeded in capturing that mayfly society to the life as Georgette Heyer did. She essayed other periods and settings with mixed success—Tudor, late Mediaeval, even the modern mystery in its heyday of the 1920's—but only in the brief golden time of the disreputable Prinny, the Prince Regent, does she excel all others.

Her plots are slight and their outcome predictable. Two nice people, usually well connected and "possessed of a competency" (although the young lady may have fallen upon difficult times through no fault of her own, victimized perhaps by a profligate brother or wastrel father) meet, fall in love, have difficulties either before or directly after marriage, sort it all out, and the story ends with a certain gleam in the hero's eye, and the heroine murmuring wistfully about the joys of "setting up her nurseries." If plot were all, the popularity of Georgette Heyer's work would be totally inexplicable, but her countless fans could explain that plot has very little to do with it. It is the bubbling good humour, the endlessly complicated social situations, the inspired silliness of the lovely creatures who perform these fantastic courtship rituals, that brings them back time and again for another of her stories.

Her dialogue is extraordinary. Page after page will go by, and the action, such as it is, is not one whit advanced; perhaps one numbskull is trying to enlighten another on a point of philosophy; a pretty young wife is spinning a complicated story to conceal a harmless peccadillo from her apparently stern but generally indulgent husband; a dandy pretends to be a tollgate keeper and exchanges insults with a passing carter; and one reads on and on in fascination. The badinage occupying these pages—and they are her very best pages—might seem to the novice to call for the use of a dictionary of Regency slang, and more than a little background reading in that period: but never mind. As the aficionados say patronizingly "You'll soon catch on," and it's true. You find yourself chuckling as one character "makes a perfect cake of himself" or another asks if "you take me for a flat?" You quite see how important it is for a young lady to have vouchers for Almack's, and that it would never do for her to be seen on St. James's St., under the eyes of the gentlemen's clubs.

Heyer's work is intended to amuse rather than to enlighten, and if there ever was a writer who could brighten a grey day, it was she. She has been criticized for slight historical inaccuracies, for using too much difficult period slang, for slightness and silliness. There may be some truth in the criticism—but no other writer has yet been able to wear her fallen mantle, though many have tried. As Noël Coward once remarked of his own work, he had "a talent to amuse"; Georgette Heyer had that precious talent, and, like the good servant in the parable, she never buried it. She left an astonishing number of gay, happy books, and her grateful readers are indeed amused.

—Joan McGrath

HICHENS, Robert (Smythe). British. Born in Speldhurst, Kent, 14 November 1864. Educated at Clifton College; Royal College of Music, London; London School of Journalism. Journalist: music critic, *The World*. Fellow, Royal Society of Literature, 1926. *Died 20 July 1950.*

ROMANCE AND GOTHIC PUBLICATIONS

Novels

The Green Carnation (published anonymously). London, Heinemann, and New York, Appleton, 1894.

After Tomorrow, and The New Love. New York, Merriam, 1895.

An Imaginative Man. London, Heinemann, and New York, Appleton, 1895.

Flames: A London Phantasy. London, Heinemann, and Chicago, Stone, 1897.

The Londoners: An Absurdity. London, Heinemann, and Chicago, Stone, 1898.

The Daughters of Babylon, with Wilson Barrett. London, Macqueen, and Philadelphia, Lippincott, 1899.

The Slave. London, Heinemann, and Chicago, Stone, 1899.

The Prophet of Berkeley Square: A Tragic Extravaganza. London, Methuen, and New York, Dodd Mead, 1901.

Felix: Three Years of a Life. London, Methuen, 1902; New York, Stokes, 1903.

The Garden of Allah. London, Methuen, and New York, Stokes, 1904.

The Woman with the Fan. London, Methuen, and New York, Stokes, 1904.

The Call of the Blood. London, Methuen, and New York, Harper, 1906.

Barbary Sheep. New York, Harper, 1907; London, Methuen, 1909.

A Spirit in Prison. London, Hutchinson, and New York, Harper, 1908.

Bella Donna. London, Heinemann, and Philadelphia, Lippincott, 1909.

The Knock on the Door. London, Heinemann, and Philadelphia, Lippincott, 1909.

The Dweller on the Threshold. London, Methuen, and New York, Century, 1911.

The Fruitful Vine. London, Unwin, and New York, Stokes, 1911.

The Way of Ambition. London, Methuen, and New York, Stokes, 1913.

In the Wilderness. London, Methuen, and New York, Stokes, 1917.

Mrs. Marden. London, Cassell, and New York, Doran, 1919.

The Spirit of the Time. London, Cassell, and New York, Doubleday, 1921.

December Love. London, Cassell, and New York, Doran, 1922.

After the Verdict. London, Methuen, and New York, Doran, 1924.

The God Within Him. London, Methuen, 1926; as *The Unearthly*, New York, Cosmopolitan, 1926.

The Bacchante and the Nun. London, Methuen, 1927; as *The Bacchante*, New York, Cosmopolitan, 1927.

Dr. Artz. London, Hutchinson, and New York, Cosmopolitan, 1929.

On the Screen. London, Cassell, 1929.

The Bracelet. London, Cassell, and New York, Cosmopolitan, 1930.

The First Lady Brendon. London, Cassell, and New York, Doubleday, 1931.

Mortimer Brice: A Bit of His Life. London, Cassell, and New York, Doubleday, 1932.

The Paradine Case. London, Benn, and New York, Doubleday, 1933.

The Power to Kill. London, Benn, and New York, Doubleday, 1934.

"Susie's" Career. London, Cassell, 1935; as *The Pyramid*, New York, Doubleday, 1936.

The Sixth of October. London, Cassell, and New York, Doubleday, 1936.

Daniel Airlie. London, Cassell, and New York, Doubleday, 1937.

The Journey Up. London, Cassell, and New York, Doubleday, 1938.

Secret Information. London, Hurst and Blackett, and New York, Doubleday, 1938.

That Which Is Hidden. London, Cassell, 1939; New York, Doubleday, 1940.

The Million: An Entertainment. London, Cassell, 1940; New York, Doubleday, 1941.

Married or Unmarried. London, Cassell, 1941.

A New Way of Life. London, Hutchinson, and New York, Doubleday, 1942.

Veils. London, Hutchinson, 1943; as *Young Mrs. Brand*, Philadelphia, Macrae Smith, 1944.
Harps in the Wind. London, Cassell, 1945; as *The Woman in the House*, Philadelphia, Macrae Smith, 1945.
Incognito. London, Hutchinson, 1947; New York, McBride, 1948.
Too Much Love of Living. Philadelphia, Macrae Smith, 1947; London, Cassell, 1948.
Beneath the Magic. London, Hutchinson, 1950; as *Strange Lady*, Philadelphia, Macrae Smith, 1950.
The Mask. London, Hutchinson, 1951.
Nightbound. London, Cassell, 1951.

Short Stories

The Folly of Eustace and Other Stories. London, Heinemann, and New York, Appleton, 1896.
Byeways. London, Methuen, and New York, Dodd Mead, 1897.
Tongues of Conscience. London, Methuen, and New York, Stokes, 1900.
The Black Spaniel and Other Stories. London, Methuen, and New York, Stokes, 1905.
The Hindu. New York, Ainslee, 1917.
Snake-Bite and Other Stories. London, Cassell, and New York, Doran, 1919.
The Last Time and Other Stories. London, Hutchinson, 1923; New York, Doran, 1924.
The Streets and Other Stories. London, Hutchinson, 1928.
The Gates of Paradise and Other Stories. London, Cassell, 1930.
My Desert Friend and Other Stories. London, Cassell, 1931.
The Gardenia and Other Stories. London, Hutchinson, 1934.
The Afterglow and Other Stories. London, Cassell, 1935.
The Man in the Mirror and Other Stories. London, Cassell, 1950.

OTHER PUBLICATIONS

Plays

The Medicine Man, with H.D. Traill (produced London, 1898). New York, De Vinne Press, 1898.
Becky Sharp, with Cosmo Gordon-Lennox, adaptation of the novel *Vanity Fair* by Thackeray (produced London, 1901; as *Vanity Fair*, produced New York, 1911).
The Real Woman (produced London, 1909).
The Garden of Allah, with Mary Anderson, adaptation of his own novel (produced New York, 1911; London, 1920).
The Law of the Sands (produced London, 1916).
Black Magic (produced London, 1917).
Press the Button! (produced London, 1918).
The Voice from the Minaret (produced London 1919; New York, 1922).

Screenplay: *Bella Donna*, with Ouida Bergère, 1923.

Other

The Coastguard's Secret (juvenile). London, Sonnenschein, 1886.
Homes of the Passing Show, with others. London, Savoy Press, 1900.
Egypt and Its Monuments. London, Hodder and Stoughton, and New York, Century, 1908; as *The Spell of Egypt*, Hodder and Stoughton, 1910; Century, 1911.
The Holy Land. London, Hodder and Stoughton, and New York, Century, 1910.

The Near East. London, Hodder and Stoughton, and New York, Century, 1913.
Yesterday: The Autobiography of Robert Hichens. London, Cassell, 1947.

*   *   *

Although Robert Hichens had written earlier material, he first achieved fame with *The Green Carnation*, a very amusing take-off on Oscar Wilde and the Aesthetic Movement, filled with bon mots, strokes of wit, and comic touches. Its intrinsic merit can be seen from the fact that it retained its popularity after the Wilde scandals and is still in print.

A more commercial phenomenon was *The Garden of Allah*, Hichens's best-known work. It sold close to a million copies, was staged, and was filmed at least three times. Although superficially it is a sentimental romance, in substructure (like much of Hichens's other work) it is antisexual, anticipating the earlier versions of *Lady Chatterley's Lover* in its concept of the loathly bridegroom. It is the story of Domini Enfilden, a lonely masculine British spinster who comes to a minor tourist town in North Africa and forces herself upon the only other tourist, the gauche Androvsky. Under the influence of the desert (the garden of Allah) they experience passion and marry. But Androvsky is a runaway monk from a Trappist monastery. He and Domini agree that he must return to his vows, and Domini, after bearing his child, settles in the area without him. The narrative, however, is less significant than the background. Hichens went all out to create North African local color, with the result that for the close reader a remarkable picture emerges of landscape, Arab personality types, and Franco-Arabic social life, all much more interesting than the narrative.

Hichens's next two important works also deal with impermissible love, in this case, adultery. In *The Call of the Blood*, set in Sicily, when Maurice Delarey becomes irritated because his wife has returned to England for a visit, he has an affair with Maddalena, a peasant girl. He is murdered by the girl's father, but his wife never learns what had happened. A sequel, *A Spirit in Prison*, set 16 years later, is concerned with Ruffino, the by blow of Delarey's affair. In both novels Italian local color is applied almost obsessively.

Most of Hichens's other work is romantic fiction of this sort, usually based on a theme of sex gone astray. His stories usually deal with a formalized upper society group, and his treatment of potentially sensational matter always remained restrained and polite. While he outgrew the tendency to fill pages with painterly detail of exotic landscapes and authorial reflections, he substituted for these highly detailed descriptions of events, and his fiction was often overdeveloped and word-choked.

In the 1920's and 1930's Hichens applied himself occasionally to crime situations. Although such fiction was undoubtedly intended to meet the market demand for detective stories, there is little mystery or detection in such stories, but much about the psychological surroundings of crime. *After the Verdict* describes a society man who has been tried and found innocent of murdering his mistress. But, like Androvsky in *The Garden of Allah*, he cannot tolerate his role in marriage and confesses to his wife that he had been an accomplice to suicide. The most important of these crime-romances is *The Paradine Case*, based on a triangle of psychologies: vicious intellect (Justice Horfield), foolish sentiment and emotion (Keane, a barrister), and selfish, ruthless sensuality (Mrs. Paradine). Keane, who is defending Mrs. Paradine in her trial for the murder of her husband, has the misfortune to fall in love with her. His case and his ego both collapse when his thoughtlessness and passion cause him to take the wrong line during the trial. The characters in this novel are better drawn than is usual with Hichens, but it must be admitted that a reader who seen the motion picture made from it may see Horfield as enlarged by Charles Laughton.

Hichens also wrote a fair amount of supernatural and occult fiction. The most important works are: "The Return of the Soul" (*The Folly of Eustace*), dealing with the reincarnation of an abused cat as a vengeful woman; *Flames*, a very long novel about black magic, personality interchange, and redemption by love; *Tongues of Conscience*, short stories in which obsessions are portrayed in terms of fantasy; and *The Dweller on the Threshold*, a novel concerned with psychic research and spiritual vampirism of a sort.

Since little is known about Hichens as a man, it is not possible to say why he failed to realize his early promise. His technical virtuosity, his facility, his remarkable eye for picturesque detail, his originality of thought should have produced better work than overblown society romances. Only a little of the large corpus of his work is still vital: *The Green Carnation*, for its exuberant wit and roman à clef elements; *The Garden of Allah*, for its rich evocation of Africa; and perhaps the motion picture version of *The Paradine Case*.

—E.F. Bleiler

HILL, Grace Livingston.   Also wrote as Marcia Macdonald; some of her works were signed Grace Livingston and Grace Livingston Hill-Lutz. American. Born in Wellsville, New York, 16 April 1865. Educated privately; Cincinnati Art School; Elmira College, New York. Married 1) Thomas Franklin Hill in 1892 (died, 1899); two daughters; 2) Flavius J. Lutz. Wrote a syndicated column for religious newspapers. *Died 23 February 1947.*

ROMANCE AND GOTHIC PUBLICATIONS

Novels

A Chautauqua Idyl.   Boston, Lothrop, 1887.
The Parkerstown Delegate.   Boston, Lothrop, 1892.
In the Way.   Philadelphia, American Baptist Publication Society, 1897.
Lone Point: A Summer Outing.   Philadelphia, American Baptist Publication Society, and London, Baptist Tract and Book Society, 1898.
A Daily Rate.   Philadelphia, Union Press, 1900.
An Unwilling Guest.   Philadelphia, American Baptist Publication Society, 1902.
The Angel of His Presence.   Philadelphia, American Baptist Publication Society, 1902.
The Story of a Whim.   Boston, Golden Rule, 1903.
Because of Stephen.   Boston, Golden Rule, 1904.
The Girl from Montana.   Boston, Golden Rule, 1908.
Marcia Schuyler.   Philadelphia, Lippincott, 1908; as Marcia, London, Hodder and Stoughton, 1921.
Phoebe Dean.   Philadelphia, Lippincott, 1909; London, Hodder and Stoughton, 1921.
Aunt Crete's Emancipation.   Boston, Golden Rule, 1911.
Dawn of the Morning.   Philadelphia, Lippincott, 1911.
The Mystery of Mary.   Philadelphia, Lippincott, 1912.
Lo, Michael!   Philadelphia, Lippincott, 1913; London, Hodder and Stoughton, 1923.
The Man of the Desert.   New York, Revell, 1914.
The Best Man.   Philadelphia, Lippincott, 1914; London, Newnes, 1919.
Miranda.   Philadelphia, Lippincott, 1914; London, Hodder and Stoughton, 1922.
The Obsession of Victoria Gracen.   Philadelphia, Lippincott, 1915.
The Finding of Jasper Holt.   Philadelphia, Lippincott, 1916.
A Voice in the Wilderness.   New York, Harper, 1916.
The Witness.   New York, Harper, 1917.
The Enchanted Barn.   Philadelphia, Lippincott, 1918.
The Search.   Philadelphia, Lippincott, 1919.
The Red Signal.   Philadelphia, Lippincott, 1919.
Cloudy Jewel.   Philadelphia, Lippincott, 1920.
Exit Betty.   Philadelphia, Lippincott, 1920.
The Tryst.   Philadelphia, Lippincott, 1921.
The City of Fire.   Philadelphia, Lippincott, 1922.

Tomorrow about This Time.   Philadelphia, Lippincott, 1923.
The Big Blue Soldier.   Philadelphia, Lippincott, 1923.
Re-Creations.   Philadelphia, Lippincott, 1924.
Ariel Custer.   Philadelphia, Lippincott, 1925.
Not under the Law.   Philadelphia, Lippincott, 1925.
A New Name.   Philadelphia, Lippincott, 1926.
Coming Through the Rye.   Philadelphia, Lippincott, 1926.
Job's Niece.   Philadelphia, Lippincott, 1927.
The White Flower.   Philadelphia, Lippincott, 1927.
Crimson Roses.   Philadelphia, Lippincott, 1928.
Blue Ruin.   Philadelphia, Lippincott, 1928.
Duskin.   Philadelphia, Lippincott, 1929.
The Prodigal Girl.   Philadelphia, Lippincott, 1929.
Ladybird.   Philadelphia, Lippincott, 1930.
The Gold Shoe.   Philadelphia, Lippincott, 1930.
Silver Wings.   Philadelphia, Lippincott, 1931.
The Chance of a Lifetime.   Philadelphia, Lippincott, 1931.
Kerry.   Philadelphia, Lippincott, 1931.
The Challengers.   Philadelphia, Lippincott, 1932.
Happiness Hill.   Philadelphia, Lippincott, 1932.
The Story of the Lost Star.   Philadelphia, Lippincott, 1932.
The Patch of Blue.   Philadelphia, Lippincott, 1932.
The Ransom.   Philadelphia, Lippincott, 1933.
Matched Pearls.   Philadelphia, Lippincott, 1933.
The Beloved Stranger.   Philadelphia, Lippincott, 1933.
Rainbow Cottage.   Philadelphia, Lippincott, 1934.
Amorelle.   Philadelphia, Lippincott, 1934.
The Christmas Bride.   Philadelphia, Lippincott, 1934.
Beauty for Ashes.   Philadelphia, Lippincott, 1935; London, Lane, 1936.
White Orchids.   Philadelphia, Lippincott, 1935.
The Strange Proposal.   Philadelphia, Lippincott, 1935.
April Gold.   Philadelphia, Lippincott, 1936.
Mystery Flowers.   Philadelphia, Lippincott, 1936.
The Substitute Guest.   Philadelphia, Lippincott, 1936.
Sunrise.   Philadelphia, Lippincott, 1937.
Daphne Deane.   Philadelphia, Lippincott, 1937.
Brentwood.   Philadelphia, Lippincott, 1937.
Marigold.   Philadelphia, Lippincott, 1938.
The Minister's Son.   Philadelphia, Lippincott, 1938.
The Divided Battle.   Philadelphia, Lippincott, 1938.
Dwelling.   Philadelphia, Lippincott, 1938.
The Lost Message.   Philadelphia, Lippincott, 1938.
Maris.   Philadelphia, Lippincott, 1938.
Homing.   Philadelphia, Lippincott, 1938.
The Seventh Hour.   Philadelphia, Lippincott, 1939.
Patricia.   Philadelphia, Lippincott, 1939.
Stranger Within the Gates.   Philadelphia, Lippincott, 1939.
Head of the House.   Philadelphia, Lippincott, 1940.
Rose Galbraith.   Philadelphia, Lippincott, 1940.
Partners.   Philadelphia, Lippincott, 1940.
By Way of the Silverthorns.   Philadelphia, Lippincott, 1941.
In Tune with Wedding Bells.   Philadelphia, Lippincott, 1941.
Astra.   Philadelphia, Lippincott, 1941.
The Girl of the Woods.   Philadelphia, Lippincott, 1942.
Crimson Mountain.   Philadelphia, Lippincott, 1942.
The Street of the City.   Philadelphia, Lippincott, 1942.
Spice Box.   Philadelphia, Lippincott, 1943.
The Sound of the Trumpet.   Philadelphia, Lippincott, 1943.

Through These Fires. Philadelphia, Lippincott, 1943.
More Than Conqueror. Philadelphia, Lippincott, 1944.
Time of the Singing of Birds. Philadelphia, Lippincott, 1944.
All Through the Night. Philadelphia, Lippincott, 1945.
A Girl to Come Home To. Philadelphia, Lippincott, 1945.
Bright Arrows. Philadelphia, Lippincott, 1946.
Where Two Ways Met. Philadelphia, Lippincott, 1947.
Mary Arden, completed by Ruth Livingston Hill. Philadelphia, Lippincott, 1948.

Novels as Marcia Macdonald

The Honor Girl. Philadelphia, Lippincott, 1927.
Found Treasure. Philadelphia, Lippincott, 1928.
Out of the Storm. Philadelphia, Lippincott, 1929.
The White Lady. Philadelphia, Lippincott, 1930.

Short Stories

Katharine's Yesterday and Other Christian Endeavor Stories. Boston, Lothrop, 1895.
Beggarman. Philadelphia, Lippincott, 1932.
Her Wedding Garment. Philadelphia, Lippincott, 1932.
The House Across the Hedge. Philadelphia, Lippincott, 1932.
Miss Lavinia's Call and Other Stories. Philadelphia, Lippincott, 1949.
The Short Stories of Grace Livingston Hill, edited by J.E. Clauss. New York, American Reprint Company, 1976.

Other Publications

Plays

A Colonial Girl, with Abbey Sage Richardson (produced New York, 1898).
The Best Birthday: A Christmas Entertainment for Children. Philadelphia, Lippincott, 1938.

Other

Christian Endeavor Hour, with R.G.F. Hill. New York, Revell, 2 vols., 1895-96.
The War Romance of the Salvation Army, with Evangeline Booth. Philadelphia, Lippincott, 1919.

Editor, *Memories of Yesterdays*, by Isabella Alden. Philadelphia, Lippincott, 1931.

*   *   *

"The truth is I never did consciously prepare for my literary career, and furthermore, I have no method at all. Coming from a family of authors, it never came into my mind that preparation was necessary." Grace Livingston Hill remained true to that statement throughout her fecund literary career, preparing little, if any, for the writing of her novels. Although she was surrounded by strong religious background and atmosphere, one finds in her work a myriad of religious contradictions which readily detract from the plot. Hill attempts to simplify complex issues and events by thumbing through the Bible, always with a banal love affair looming around the edges of her evangelical message. This evangelicalism permeates, no, suffocates the reader. Although humility is supposedly the focal point, Hill never fails to allow her characters (whose awareness of the world is characterized by lamentable ignorance) ultimately to luxuriate in affluence; money is the reward for being humble. With frequently prolonged Biblical quotes, expostulations, and interpretations, the pace stagnates.

Hill's works contain no gothic attributes and only hint at a romance. A variant on the typical theme is found in *Head of House*: A college-age girl (Hill refers to the heroines as "girl" and the heroes as "men") valiantly escapes with her six brothers and sisters and hides away for three months to avoid being separated after the death of their parents. This novel is the exception. Other works such as *Happiness Hill* and *Rainbow Cottage* are so sugary, the characters so far removed from even homespun decency, the plot so trite, that the writing is more of an endurance test for the reader; one is almost forced to laugh at the naivety of pitting the "bad, bad guy" against the purity squad. In *Happiness Hill* the characters literally fall over each other trying to outdo the other in meekness. In *Rainbow Cottage* a slap administered by the heroine is enough to provoke a suicide. *All Through the Night* again presents the contradictions of Christianity, allowing the heroine to espouse the virtues of kindness, tolerance, and gentility while the hero, also a "Christian," is "responsible for definitely wiping out as many of the enemy as possible..., setting the world free for peace and quietness." The gratuitous insults and vituperation that the heroine allows from her parsimonious relatives exemplifies her "if-I-were-hanging-by-my-fingers-from-a-cliff, I'd-call-it-climbing-a-mountain" attitude, all adding up to obvious implausibility. The heroine is reduced to a prig.

In addition many references throughout her works are made to the unflappable and supported WASP dominance. There are careless lines of racial slurs and indictments of white superiority in this Christian atmosphere.

Grace Livingston Hill is out of date and out of touch; rather than edifying, her "afflation" forces the reader to succumb to intolerable tedium. She should be classified under religious writers and poor ones, at that, failing piteously as a gothic romance novelist.

—W.M. von Zharen

HILL, Pamela. Also writes as Sharon Fiske. British. Born in Nairobi, Kenya, 26 November 1920. Educated at Hutcheson's Grammar School, Glasgow; Glasgow School of Art, D.A. 1943; Glasgow University. Has worked as a pottery and biology teacher, and as a mink farmer. Agent: Winant Towers, 45-47 Clerkenwell Green, London EC1R 0HT, England. Address: Moorcroft of Glenturk, Newton Stewart DG8 9TH, Scotland.

ROMANCE AND GOTHIC PUBLICATIONS

Novels

Flaming Janet: A Lady of Galloway.   London, Chatto and Windus, 1954; as *The King's Vixen*, New York, Putnam, 1954.
Shadow of Palaces: The Story of Françoise d'Aubigné, Marquise de Maintenon.   London, Chatto and Windus, 1955; as *The Crown and the Shadow*, New York, Putnam, 1955.
Marjorie of Scotland.   London, Chatto and Windus, and New York, Putnam, 1956.
Here Lies Margot.   London, Chatto and Windus, 1957; New York, Putnam, 1958.
Maddalena.   London, Cassell, 1963.

Forget Not Ariadne. London, Cassell, 1965; South Brunswick, New Jersey, A.S. Barnes, 1967.

Julia. London, Cassell, 1967.

The Devil of Aske. London, Hodder and Stoughton, 1972; New York, St. Martin's Press, 1973.

The Malvie Inheritance. London, Hodder and Stoughton, 1973; New York, St. Martin's Press, 1974.

The Incumbent. London, Hodder and Stoughton, 1974; as *The Heatherton Heritage*, New York, St. Martin's Press, 1976.

Whitton's Folly. London, Hodder and Stoughton, and New York, St. Martin's Press, 1975.

Norah Stroyan. London, Hodder and Stoughton, 1976; as *Norah*, New York, St. Martin's Press, 1976.

The Green Salamander. London, Hodder and Stoughton, and New York, St. Martin's Press, 1977.

Tsar's Woman. London, Hale, 1977.

Strangers' Forest. London, Hale, and New York, St. Martin's Press, 1978.

Daneclere. London, Hale, 1978; New York, St. Martin's Press, 1979.

Homage to a Rose. London, Hale, 1979.

Daughter of Midnight. London, Hale, 1979.

Fire Opal. London, Hale, and New York, St. Martin's Press, 1980.

A Place of Ravens. London, Hale, 1980.

Summer Cypress (as Sharon Fiske). London, Hale, 1981.

The House of Cray. London, Hale, and New York, St. Martin's Press, 1982.

*   *   *

Pamela Hill says that she got the idea for her first story—"The One Night," written in 1951—on a bus travelling between Glasgow and Edinburgh. Her imagination—and her pen—have been in the fast lane ever since, as she has written over 20 novels since then.

Hill endows the heroines of her romances with equal stamina. In fact, many of them are practically Amazonian—true daughters of Queen Boadicea, the 1st-century British ruler who led the revolt against the Romans—in their courage, strength, and physical abilities (in Hill, the *heroes* play the supportive roles): *Flaming Janet: A Lady of Galloway* (US title *The King's Vixen*); Françoise d'Aubigné, Marquise of Maintenon (in *Shadow of Palaces*—US title *The Crown and the Shadow*); Marjorie of Scotland; the ruthless and iron-willed Madame of Aske (in *The Devil of Aske*); Livia (*The Malvie Inheritance*), who survives a house of correction to become a guiding force at the Doon estate; the headstrong Primrose Tebb, who at the age of 12 marries Andrew Farquhar (*Strangers' Forest*); the courageous and ambitious Margaret Douglas, mother of Lord Darnley, husband of Mary, Queen of Scots (in *The Green Salamander*); and Fiona/Fiametta (in *Fire Opal*), whose extraordinarily powerful swimming ability saves her from the Turks and helps the Knights of Malta in their defense of Christianity. At least two of Hill's heroines—Françoise d'Aubigné, Marquise of Maintenon and Margaret Douglas— are actual historical figures.

As though she were still looking out the window of that bus, Hill sets her romantic adventures in her native Scotland, with her inner eye seeing the people and places of centuries past (usually, the 17th and 18th). Hill's pen is swift, her characters vividly drawn, and her adventures tight and suspenseful.

—Marcia G. Fuchs

HINTZE, Naomi A(gans). American. Born in Camden, Illinois, 8 July 1909. Attended Maryville College, Tennessee, 1927-29; Ball State Teachers College (now University), Muncie, Indiana, 1929-30. Married Harold Sanborn Hintze in 1930; two sons and one daughter. Member of the Advisory Board, Virginia Center for the Creative Arts. Recipient: Mystery Writers of America Edgar Allan Poe Award, 1970. Agent: McIntosh and Otis Inc., 475 Fifth Avenue, New York, New York 10017. Address: Tyke Hill, Ednam Forest, Charlottesville, Virginia 22901, U.S.A.

ROMANCE AND GOTHIC PUBLICATIONS

Novels

> *You'll Like My Mother.* New York, Putnam, 1969; as *The House with the Watching Eyes*, London, Hale, 1970.
> *The Stone Carnation.* New York, Random House, 1971; London, Hale, 1973.
> *Aloha Means Goodbye.* New York, Random House, 1972; as *Hawaii for Danger*, London, Hale, 1973.
> *Listen, Please Listen.* New York, Random House, 1974; London, Hale, 1975.
> *Cry Witch.* New York, Random House, 1975; London, Collins, 1976.

OTHER PUBLICATIONS

Other

> *Buried Treasure Waits for You.* Indianapolis, Bobbs Merrill, 1962.
> *The Psychic Realm: What Can You Believe?*, with J. Gaither Pratt. New York, Random House, 1975.
> *Time Bomb*, with Peter van der Linde. New York, Doubleday, 1978.

*   *   *

One could describe the novels of Naomi A. Hintze as short and sweet, but for the sting that hides in each one. Her novels are short works of romantic suspense with straightforward and uncomplicated plots. But each novel has a bitter touch to the expected happy ending. Generally the counterpoint to the romance is the death of a character for whom the reader has come to care. In addition, in *The Stone Carnation* and *You'll Like My Mother* the heroines must rebuild ruined lives through new romantic relationships.

Before turning to novels of romantic suspense, Hintze wrote for the juvenile market. This experience seems to color her style in that a number of her works have plots and characters that would hold strong appeal for the late adolescent reader. It is a measure of her skill as a storyteller that this slant does not prevent the books from reaching a broader readership. Her prose is rather simple and the books often contain moments of literary hesitation. The heroines always seem to apply makeup as a means of transition from one scene to another. The dialogue is smooth and natural, however, and makes up for any lack of fluidity in the descriptive passages.

The flawed characters in Hintze's work—the retarded girl in *You'll Like My Mother*, the terminally ill boy in *Aloha Means Goodbye*, the child molester in *Listen, Please Listen*, the old madwoman in *The Stone Carnation*—are drawn with special care. Often they seem more real, more sympathetic than the main characters. This is the means that the author uses to "sting" the reader, for she avoids the flaws in characterization often found in this genre. Her villains are never wholly evil, just as her heroes and heroines are never wholly perfect. Nor is any character too insignificant to escape her notice. The Ginter family in *The Stone Carnation* almost begs to be drawn out into caricatures, but Hintze treats them with a kind of affectionate respect.

The suspense element of these novels carries more weight than the romance, but the two parts would not be as likely to stand alone. The resolution of the mystery in each novel is not totally unexpected, but at the same time is not obvious to the reader far in advance. If there are no surprises, there are also no jarring elements or missing clues to confuse the reader. Despite the bittersweet tone of the endings the novels are satisfying in that all has been said that needs to be said. Perhaps Hintze's novels do not demand very much from the reader, but they consistently deliver tightly plotted and conclusive stories.

—Susan Quinn Berneis

HODGE, Jane Aiken. British. Born in Watertown, Massachusetts, United States, 4 December 1917; daughter of the writer Conrad Aiken, and sister of Joan Aiken, *q.v.* Educated at Hayes Court, Kent, 1929-34; Somerville College, Oxford (Lefevre Fellow), 1935-38, B.A. (honours) 1938; Harvard University, Cambridge, Massachusetts, 1938-39, A.M. 1939. Married Alan Hodge in 1948 (died, 1979); two daughters. Worked for the British Board of Trade, Washington, 1942-44, and the British Supply Council of North America, 1944-45; researcher, Time Inc., New York, 1945-47, and for *Life* magazine, in London, 1947-48; reader for film companies and publishers, and free-lance reviewer, in the 1950's and 1960's. Agent: David Higham Associates, 5-8 Lower John Street, London W1R 4HA. Address: 23 Eastport Lane, Lewes, East Sussex BN7 1TL, England.

ROMANCE AND GOTHIC PUBLICATIONS

Novels

    Maulever Hall. London, Hale, and New York, Doubleday, 1964.
    The Adventurers. New York, Doubleday, 1965; London, Hodder and Stoughton, 1966.
    Watch the Wall, My Darling. New York, Doubleday, 1966; London, Hodder and Stoughton, 1967.
    Here Comes a Candle. London, Hodder and Stoughton, and New York, Doubleday, 1967; as *The Master of Penrose*, New York, Dell, 1968.
    The Winding Stair. London, Hodder and Stoughton, 1968; New York, Doubleday, 1969.
    Marry in Haste. London, Hodder and Stoughton, 1969; New York, Doubleday, 1970.
    Greek Wedding. London, Hodder and Stoughton, and New York, Doubleday, 1970.
    Savannah Purchase. London, Hodder and Stoughton, and New York, Doubleday, 1971.
    Strangers in Company. London, Hodder and Stoughton, and New York, Coward McCann, 1973.
    Shadow of a Lady. New York, Coward McCann, 1973; London, Hodder and Stoughton, 1974.
    One Way to Venice. London, Hodder and Stoughton, 1974; New York, Coward McCann, 1975.
    Rebel Heiress. London, Hodder and Stoughton, and New York, Coward McCann, 1975.
    Runaway Bride. London, Fawcett, 1975; London, Coronet, 1976.
    Judas Flowering. London, Hodder and Stoughton, and New York, Coward McCann, 1976.

Red Sky at Night: Lovers' Delight? New York, Coward McCann, 1977; London, Hodder and Stoughton, 1979.
Last Act. London, Hodder and Stoughton, and New York, Coward McCann, 1979.
Wide Is the Water. London, Hodder and Stoughton, and New York, Coward McCann, 1981.
The Lost Garden. London, Hodder and Stoughton, and New York, Coward McCann, 1982.

OTHER PUBLICATIONS

Other

The Double Life of Jane Austen. London, Hodder and Stoughton, 1972; as *Only a Novel: The Double Life of Jane Austen*, New York, Coward McCann, 1972.

Jane Aiken Hodge comments:

I would rather be called a writer of romance than of gothic. The term gothic now seems to imply a kind of violent horror that I think out of place in books written as entertainment. There is too much violence and horror in real life, and they should be written about seriously, not to titillate. Besides, I prefer the tension of feeling to the spurious kind provided by violence. I hope to keep my reader happily hooked without ever making her (or him) shocked, or sick. This is one reason why I write mainly historical romance, in which it is easier to indulge in moral standards, and a happy ending. A reviewer once said of one of my early books that it was a blend of Jane Austen and the Brontës, and I think this is the comment that has pleased me most in my writing career. I also owe a vast debt to Georgette Heyer, whose impeccable historical accuracy I have always tried to emulate. The background research is part of the pleasure, and so is the tension between historical fact and the vagaries of one's characters. I have, however, also written three novels of modern romantic suspense, enjoyed them very much, and hope to do more. In them, too, I aim for excitement without excessive violence. There seems to be a terrible dearth, just now, of the kind of civilised light reading provided by writers like Dorothy Sayers, Georgette Heyer, or Mary Stewart. It is my immodest ambition to be classed with them.

*   *   *

Jane Aiken Hodge writes some of the best historical fiction now being published. She is prolific and popular without being imprisoned by formula or falling back on predictable, stereotyped characters. Her romances are historical, imbued with a past that has clearly become as real to her as the present is to a writer of contemporary fiction. Hodge's skillful use of historical settings is the key to her success and to the literary quality of her work.

Unlike other practitioners of the genre, Hodge doesn't overwhelm her reader with a mass of historical detail. She masters the history of her period so well that her settings never seem artificial or contrived. Dialogue is often used to set the scene and establish a sense of place, and this is a far more effective technique than the lengthy descriptions of historical settings on which less able writers fall back. Hodge's characters seldom speak in dialect or use period expressions, but they don't use anachronistic metaphors, either. Artifacts, houses, cities, and costume are described only as they are relevant to her plot.

Hodge uses history to add depth to her romantic adventures. Although most of her work is set in the early 19th century (with the exception of two books set in the 1770's), she provides variety by placing the action in several different countries: America, England, Greece, Portugal, France, and Germany. Historical events provide both realism and pace to the stories, which occur in and around the Napoleonic Wars, the Greek struggle for independence, the War of

1812, and the American Revolution. Because we know these conflicts did in fact take place, we are able to see Hodge's stories as more than romantic fantasies, and we can empathize with and experience the conflicts of the hero, heroine, and assorted villains.

In contrast to her historical novels, Hodge's three works of contemporary romance (*Strangers in Company*, *One Way to Venice*, and *Last Act*) are much less effective. While each plot involves suspense as well as romance, the action is slow-moving, the characters rather sketchily described, and their predicaments unbelievable. The three heroines are unfortunately passive: one wrongly believes she is terminally ill, another is a tranquilized and deserted wife and mother, a third is the target of a truly bizarre (and ultimately unconvincing) plot. While all three of these romances entertain, the reader feels pity rather than empathy for the unhappy heroines.

Most of Hodge's women are much more interesting. While her heroines follow the typical pattern of the genre in being orphaned or alone in the world, they are never the passive victims of events beyond their control for long. They confront their villains bravely, and reach out to take the necessary risks. Hodge's heroes are also typical of the genre in being older, capable, usually established in society (but unlucky in love), but the world her heroes move in is the world of affairs, not simply the world of fashion. The typical Hodge hero may be a politician (Mark Maulever in *Maulever Hall*), a secret agent (Lord Leominster in *Marry in Haste*, Charles Vincent in *The Adventurers*, and Gair Varlow in *The Winding Stair*), a businessman (Jonathan Penrose in *Here Comes a Candle*), or a successful planter (Hart Purchis in *Judas Flowering* and *Wide Is the Water*, his grandson Hyde Purchis in *Savannah Purchase*). Hodge's heroines must face not mad monks or jealous rivals, but enemy troops, revolutionary mobs, Barbary pirates, and Greek brigands. Their most impressive asset is their courage, and their independence is firmly asserted. Hodge allows her heroines to enjoy their adventures, and in doing so effectively demolishes the traditional stereotypes about the repressed and delicate ladies of the pre-Victorian era. Mercy Philips (of *Judas Flowering* and *Wide Is the Water*) works as the "Rebel Printer" in British-occupied Savannah; Juana Brett penetrates a Portuguese secret society for a British agent (*The Winding Stair*) and Phyllida Vannick escapes from a Turkish harem (which she prosaically describes as a rather dull all-female society—these books are not melodramas) in *Greek Wedding*. Hodge rarely uses actual historical characters in any but minor and supporting roles, with the successful exception of Emma Hamilton, Lord Nelson's inamorata, who plays a crucial role in *Shadow of a Lady*. Each character has a past, and each is developed well enough so that the reader rather expects them to live on beyond the events of Hodge's story. While her heroes and heroines do follow a common pattern, they are also individuals, with their own characters, occupations (only four of the heroines, for example, are governesses!), and experiences.

Each of Hodge's historical novels has two plots. One is the romance of the hero and heroine, while the other revolves around the suspenseful adventure in which they both participate. Christina Tretton and her cousin Ross Tretteign are involved with smugglers and spies (*Watch the Wall, My Darling*), Kate Croston must rescue Jonathan Penrose's daughter from a kidnapper (*Here Comes a Candle*), Henrietta Marchmont must convince Simon Rivers that she is not a Yankee spy (*Rebel Heiress*), and Kate Warrender, disguised as a man, must expose a radical plot to overthrow the British crown (*Red Sky at Night: Lovers' Delight*). The course of true love is carefully intertwined with the progress of the mystery, while the diverse historical settings provide authenticity. In two of the novels (*The Adventurers* and *Red Sky at Night*) there are two heroines, one maturely beautiful, the other young and innocent (and temporarily passing as a boy). Both pairs of heroines eventually find suitable pairs of heroes.

Without Hodge's skillful use of history, her books would be quite ordinary, with very familiar characters following well-worn plots. Instead, history makes these novels work. Hodge catches her readers up in the past, and we willingly suspend our disbelief to enjoy the suspenseful story. The books are very readable, and the characters interesting enough to sustain our interest until the conclusion. Hodge doesn't lay her history on with a heavy hand, and has described historical novels as "icebergs," for "there is more to them than meets the eye" (in *The Writer*, June 1972). Her own grasp of the period she describes is so sure that the historical details she does provide have the convincing ring of authenticity. We are sure that the rest of the iceberg is there, below the visible surface of the story. Hodge provides just enough of the less romantic and more realistic detail of history (the pain of slavery, the suffering in the lower decks of a British man of war, the hungry citizens of a besieged city) to show us that the past she portrays is the real past, and not a sanitized, museum-pretty version. Her work is believable, entertaining, well-crafted, and very much worth reading.

—Mary C. Lynn

HOLLAND, Isabelle. Also writes as Francesca Hunt. American. Born in Basel, Switzerland, 16 June 1920. Educated at private schools in England; University of Liverpool, 1938-40; Tulane University, New Orleans, B.A. in English 1942. Publicity Director, Lippincott, Dell and Putnam publishing companies, New York, 1960-68. Agent: Jane Wilson, James Brown Associates, 25 West 43rd Street, New York, New York 10036. Address: c/o Rawson Wade Publishers, 630 Third Avenue, New York, New York 10017, U.S.A.

ROMANCE AND GOTHIC PUBLICATIONS

Novels

Kilgaren. New York, Weybright and Talley, 1974; London, Collins, 1975.
Trelawny. New York, Weybright and Talley, 1974; as *Trelawny's Fell*, London, Collins, 1976.
Moncrieff. New York, Weybright and Talley, 1975; as *The Standish Place*, London, Collins, 1976.
Darcourt. New York, Weybright and Talley, 1976; London, Collins, 1977.
Grenelle. New York, Rawson, 1976; London, Collins, 1978.
The de Maury Papers. New York, Rawson, 1977; London, Collins, 1978.
Tower Abbey. New York, Rawson, 1978; London, Collins, 1979.
The Marchington Inheritance. New York, Rawson, 1979; London, Collins, 1980.
Counterpoint. New York, Rawson, 1980; London, Collins, 1981.
The Lost Madonna. New York, Rawson, 1981; London, Collins, 1982.

OTHER PUBLICATIONS (for children)

Fiction

Cecily. Philadelphia, Lippincott, 1967.
Amanda's Choice. Philadelphia, Lippincott, 1970.
The Man Without a Face. Philadelphia, Lippincott, 1972.
The Mystery of Castle Renaldi (as Francesca Hunt). Middletown, Connecticut, American Education Publications, 1972.
Heads You Win, Tails I Lose. Philadelphia, Lippincott, 1973.
Of Love and Death and Other Journeys. Philadelphia, Lippincott, 1975.
Journey for Three. Boston, Houghton Mifflin, 1975; London, Macdonald and Jane's, 1978.
Alan and the Animal Kingdom. Philadelphia, Lippincott, 1977; London, Macdonald and Jane's, 1979.
Hitchhike. Philadelphia, Lippincott, 1977.

Dinah and the Green Fat Kingdom.   Philadelphia, Lippincott, 1978.
Ask No Questions.   London, Macdonald and Jane's, 1978.
Now Is Not Too Late.   New York, Lothrop, 1980.
Summer of My First Love.   New York, Fawcett, 1981.

Manuscript Collection (children's books): Kerlan Collection, University of Minnesota, Minneapolis.

*   *   *

Individually, Isabelle Holland's psychological gothics appear complex, with complicated relationships to be explained as the key to dangers that threaten the heroine. Viewed collectively, however, the books are similar, and the reader will quickly determine the essential ingredients of the basic Holland plot.

Because the story is told by a young woman, and the other characters are seen from her perspective, the reader can never be sure about their motives and is often led astray by the heroine's misconceptions. The Holland devotee soon realizes, though, that the man the heroine dislikes most is the one whom she will eventually love and marry while the man she trusts for most of the book is no good. The heroine usually harbors deep-seated prejudices against her husband-to-be for some real or imagined wrong he has done to her or her family. For example, years ago, Antonia Moncrieff had a one-night fling with a professor who was too drunk to remember the incident (*Moncrieff*). Now she is reluctant to help him edit a book for her publishing company, partly because she never told him about their son.

Usually at least part of the story is set in an old mansion with mysterious passageways, sudden drafts, or strange sound. The locales range from England (*The de Maury Papers*) to the West Indies (*Kilgaren*), but the terror of wandering through unfamiliar settings is about the same. One reason the heroines undertake nocturnal ramblings is their search for straying pets. All Holland's gothics include at least one animal, and her heroines are devoted to their furry companions. Although the animals sometimes lead their owners into trouble, they also help them make important discoveries or warn them of danger.

Children also have a central role in many of the books. In *Grenelle* one child is murdered and another kidnapped by members of a drug ring. In *The Marchington Inheritance* a terrorist group uses a pre-school as a front.

As these incidents indicate, Holland often incorporates topics of current interest in her plots. Exorcism (*Tower Abbey*), Vietnam veterans (*Trelawny*), and political corruption (*The de Maury Papers*) are only some of subjects she uses.

Underlying these topics is one recurring theme: the gulf between classes. Sometimes the heroine dislikes someone rich and powerful and mouths anti-Establishment clichés, but she invariably discovers that the rich are misunderstood. In *Darcourt* the heroine suspects Tristram Darcourt of negotiating deals with the Arabs to control the oil market. In reality, he is cooperating with the government to stop others from doing just that. Tristram asks a properly humbled heroine, "After all...don't the IRA and most other revolutionaries wish to become the Establishment, after, of course, they've unseated the present one?" In other books, such as *Grenelle* and *Trelawny*, the jealousy of a man from the lower class drives him to do anything, even murder, for wealth and power he doesn't deserve.

The long-suffering upper class is but one recurring motif in Holland's novels. Although locales and situations seem exotic for a while, the path through her settings has been well worn.

—Kathy Piehl

HOLLAND, Sheila. *See* **LAMB, Charlotte**.

HOLT, Victoria. Pseudonym for Eleanor Alice Hibbert, née Burford; also writes as Eleanor Burford; Philippa Carr; Elbur Ford; Kathleen Kellow; Jean Plaidy; Ellalice Tate. British. Born in London, in 1906. Educated privately. Married G.P. Hibbert. Agent: A.M. Heath Ltd., 40 William IV Street, London WC2N 4DD, England.

ROMANCE AND GOTHIC PUBLICATIONS

Novels

> *Mistress of Mellyn.* New York, Doubleday, 1960; London, Collins, 1961.
> *Kirkland Revels.* New York, Doubleday, and London, Collins, 1962.
> *Bride of Pendorric.* New York, Doubleday, and London, Collins, 1963.
> *The Legend of the Seventh Virgin.* New York, Doubleday, and London, Collins, 1965.
> *Menfreya in the Morning.* New York, Doubleday, 1966; as *Menfreya*, London, Collins, 1966.
> *The King of the Castle.* New York, Doubleday, and London, Collins, 1967.
> *The Queen's Confession.* New York, Doubleday, and London, Collins, 1968.
> *The Shivering Sands.* New York, Doubleday, and London, Collins, 1969.
> *The Secret Woman.* New York, Doubleday, 1970; London, Collins, 1971.
> *The Shadow of the Lynx.* New York, Doubleday, and London, Collins, 1971.
> *On the Night of the Seventh Moon.* New York, Doubleday, 1972; London, Collins, 1973.
> *The Curse of the Kings.* New York, Doubleday, and London, Collins, 1973.
> *The House of a Thousand Lanterns.* New York, Doubleday, and London, Collins, 1974.
> *Lord of the Far Island.* New York, Doubleday, and London, Collins, 1975.
> *The Pride of the Peacock.* New York, Doubleday, and London, Collins, 1976.
> *The Devil on Horseback.* New York, Doubleday, and London, Collins, 1977.
> *My Enemy the Queen.* New York, Doubleday, and London, Collins, 1978.
> *The Spring of the Tiger.* New York, Doubleday, and London, Collins, 1979.
> *The Mask of the Enchantress.* New York, Doubleday, and London, Collins, 1980.
> *The Judas Kiss.* New York, Doubleday, and London, Collins, 1981.

Novels as Eleanor Burford

> *Daughter of Anna.* London, Jenkins, 1941.
> *Passionate Witness.* London, Jenkins, 1941.
> *The Married Lover.* London, Jenkins, 1942.
> *When All the World Is Young.* London, Jenkins, 1943.
> *So the Dreams Depart.* London, Jenkins, 1944.
> *Not in Our Stars.* London, Jenkins, 1945.
> *Dear Chance.* London, Jenkins, 1947.
> *Alexa.* London, Jenkins, 1948.
> *The House at Cupid's Cross.* London, Jenkins, 1949.
> *Believe the Heart.* London, Jenkins, 1950.

The Love Child. London, Jenkins, 1950.
Saint or Sinner? London, Jenkins, 1951.
Dear Delusion. London, Jenkins, 1952.
Bright Tomorrow. London, Jenkins, 1952.
Leave Me My Love. London, Jenkins, 1953.
When We Are Married. London, Jenkins, 1953.
Castles in Spain. London, Jenkins, 1954.
Heart's Afire. London, Jenkins, 1954.
When Other Hearts. London, Jenkins, 1955.
Two Loves in Her Life. London, Jenkins, 1955.
Begin to Live. London, Mills and Boon, 1956.
Married in Haste. London, Mills and Boon, 1956.
To Meet a Stranger. London, Mills and Boon, 1957.
Pride of the Morning. London, Mills and Boon, 1958.
Blaze of Noon. London, Mills and Boon, 1958.
The Dawn Chorus. London, Mills and Boon, 1959.
Red Sky at Night. London, Mills and Boon, 1959.
Night of Stars. London, Mills and Boon, 1960.
Now That April's Gone. London, Mills and Boon, 1961.
Who's Calling. London, Mills and Boon, 1962.

Novels as Jean Plaidy

Together They Ride. London, Swan, 1945.
Beyond the Blue Montains. New York, Appleton Century, 1947; London, Hale, 1948.
Murder Most Royal. London, Hale, 1949; New York, Putnam, 1972; as *The King's Pleasure*, New York, Appleton Century Crofts, 1949.
The Goldsmith's Wife. London, Hale, and New York, Appleton Century Crofts, 1950; as *The King's Mistress*, New York, Pyramid, 1952.
Catherine de' Medici. London, Hale, 1969.
   Madame Serpent. London, Hale, and New York, Appleton Century Crofts, 1951.
   The Italian Woman. London, Hale, 1952; New York, Putnam, 1975.
   Queen Jezebel. London, Hale, and New York, Appleton Century Crofts, 1953.
Daughter of Satan. London, Hale, 1952; New York, Putnam, 1973; as *The Unholy Woman*, Toronto, Harlequin, 1954.
The Sixth Wife. London, Hale, 1953; New York, Putnam, 1969.
The Spanish Bridegroom. London, Hale, 1954; Philadelphia, Macrae Smith, 1956.
St. Thomas's Eve. London, Hale, 1954; New York, Putnam, 1970.
Gay Lord Robert. London, Hale, 1955; New York, Putnam, 1972.
Royal Road to Fotheringay. London, Hale, 1955; New York, Putnam, 1968.
Charles II. London, Hale, 1972.
   The Wandering Prince. London, Hale, 1956; New York, Putnam, 1971.
   A Health unto His Majesty. London, Hale, 1956; New York, Putnam, 1972.
   Here Lies Our Sovereign Lord. London, Hale, 1957; New York, Putnam, 1973.
Flaunting Extravagant Queen (Marie Antoinette). London, Hale, 1957.
Lucrezia Borgia. London, Hale, 1976.
   Madonna of the Seven Hills. London, Hale, 1958; New York, Putnam, 1974.
   Light on Lucrezia. London, Hale, 1958; New York, Putnam, 1976.
Louis, The Well-Beloved. London, Hale, 1959.
The Road to Compiègne. London, Hale, 1959.
Isabella and Ferdinand. London, Hale, 1970.
   Castile for Isabella. London, Hale, 1960.
   Spain for the Sovereigns. London, Hale, 1960.
   Daughters of Spain. London, Hale, 1961.
Katharine of Aragon. London, Hale, 1968.
   Katharine, The Virgin Widow. London, Hale, 1961.
   The Shadow of the Pomegranate. London, Hale, 1962.

The King's Secret Matter.   London, Hale, 1962.
The Captive Queen of Scots.   London, Hale, 1963; New York, Putnam, 1970.
The Thistle and the Rose.   London, Hale, 1963; New York, Putnam, 1973.
Mary, Queen of France.   London, Hale, 1964.
The Murder in the Tower.   London, Hale, 1964; New York, Putnam, 1974.
Evergreen Gallant.   London, Hale, 1965; New York, Putnam, 1973.
The Last of the Stuarts.   London, Hale, 1977.
  The Three Crowns.   London, Hale, 1965; New York, Putnam, 1977.
  The Haunted Sisters.   London, Hale, 1966; New York, Putnam, 1977.
  The Queen's Favourites.   London, Hale, 1966; New York, Putnam, 1978.
Georgian Saga:
  1. *Queen in Waiting.*   London, Hale, 1967.
  2. *The Princess of Celle.*   London, Hale, 1967.
  3. *The Prince and the Quakeress.*   London, Hale, 1968.
  4. *Caroline, The Queen.*   London, Hale, 1968.
  5. *The Third George.*   London, Hale, 1969.
  6. *Perdita's Prince.*   London, Hale, 1969.
  7. *Sweet Lass of Richmond Hill.*   London, Hale, 1970.
  8. *Indiscretions of the Queen.*   London, Hale, 1970.
  9. *The Regent's Daughter.*   London, Hale, 1971.
  10. *Goddess of the Green Room.*   London, Hale, 1971.
Victorian Saga:
  1. *The Captive of Kensington Palace.*   London, Hale, 1972; New York, Putnam, 1976.
  2. *Victoria in the Wings.*   London, Hale, 1972.
  3. *The Queen and Lord M.*   London, Hale, 1973; New York, Putnam, 1977.
  4. *The Queen's Husband.*   London, Hale, 1973; New York, Putnam, 1978.
  5. *The Widow of Windsor.*   London, Hale, 1974; New York, Putnam, 1978.
Norman Trilogy:
  1. *The Bastard King.*   London, Hale, 1974; New York, Putnam, 1979.
  2. *The Lion of Justice.*   London, Hale, 1975; New York, Putnam, 1979.
  3. *The Passionate Enemies.*   London, Hale, 1976; New York, Putnam, 1979.
Plantagenet Saga:
  1. *The Plantagenet Prelude.*   London, Hale, 1976; New York, Putnam, 1980.
  2. *The Revolt of the Eaglets.*   London, Hale, 1977; New York, Putnam, 1980.
  3. *The Heart of the Lion.*   London, Hale, 1977; New York, Putnam, 1980.
  4. *The Prince of Darkness.*   London, Hale, 1978; New York, Putnam, 1980.
  5. *The Battle of the Queens.*   London, Hale, 1978; New York, Putnam, 1981.
  6. *The Queen from Provence.*   London, Hale, 1979; New York, Putnam, 1981.
  7. *Edward Longshanks.*   London, Hale, 1979.
  8. *The Follies of the King.*   London, Hale, 1980.
  9. *The Vow on the Heron.*   London, Hale, 1980.
  10. *Passage to Pontefract.*   London, Hale, 1981.
  11. *The Star of Lancaster.*   London, Hale, 1981.
  12. *Epitaph for Three Women.*   London, Hale, 1981.
  13. *Red Rose of Anjou.*   London, Hale, 1982.
  14. *The Sun in Splendour.*   London, Hale, 1982.
Hammer of the Scots.   New York, Putnam, 1981.

Novels as Elbur Ford

Poison in Pimlico.   London, Laurie, 1950.
Flesh and the Devil.   London, Laurie, 1950.
The Bed Disturbed.   London, Laurie, 1952.
Such Bitter Business.   London, Heinemann, 1953; as *Evil in the House*, New York, Morrow, 1954.

Novels as Kathleen Kellow

Danse Macabre. London, Hale, 1952.
Rooms at Mrs. Oliver's. London, Hale, 1953.
Lilith. London, Hale, 1954.
It Began in Vauxhall Gardens. London, Hale, 1955.
Call of the Blood. London, Hale, 1956.
Rochester, The Mad Earl. London, Hale, 1957.
Milady Charlotte. London, Hale, 1959.
The World's a Stage. London, Hale, 1960.

Novels as Ellalice Tate

Defenders of the Faith. London, Hodder and Stoughton, 1956.
The Scarlet Cloak. London, Hodder and Stoughton, 1957.
The Queen of Diamonds. London, Hodder and Stoughton, 1958.
Madame du Barry. London, Hodder and Stoughton, 1959.
This Was a Man. London, Hodder and Stoughton, 1961.

Novels as Philippa Carr

The Miracle at St. Bruno's. London, Collins, and New York, Putnam, 1972.
The Lion Triumphant. London, Collins, and New York, Putnam, 1974.
The Witch from the Sea. London, Collins, and New York, Putnam, 1975.
Saraband for Two Sisters. London, Collins, and New York, Putnam, 1976.
Lament for a Lost Lover. London, Collins, and New York, Putnam, 1977.
The Love-Child. London, Collins, and New York, Putnam, 1978.
The Song of the Siren. London, Collins, and New York, Putnam, 1980.
The Drop of the Dice. London, Collins, and New York, Putnam, 1981.
Will You Love Me in September. New York, Putnam, 1981.
The Adultress. London, Collins, 1982.

OTHER PUBLICATIONS

Other as Jean Plaidy

A Triptych of Poisoners. London, Hale, 1958.
The Rise [Growth, End] of the Spanish Inquisition. London, Hale, 3 vols., 1959-61; as
   The Spanish Inquisition: Its Rise, Growth, and End, New York, Citadel Press, 1 vol.,
   1967.
The Young Elizabeth (juvenile). London, Parrish, and New York, Roy, 1961.
Meg Roper, Daughter of Sir Thomas More (juvenile). London, Constable, 1961; New
   York, Roy, 1964.
The Young Mary Queen of Scots (juvenile). London, Parrish, 1962; New York, Roy,
   1963.
Mary, Queen of Scots, The Fair Devil of Scotland. London, Hale, and New York,
   Putnam, 1975.

*   *   *

Writing under various pseudonyms, Eleanor Burford Hibbert has been one of the most
prolific and popular romance writers of the past several decades. Most of her Jean Plaidy
historical romances are based upon the lives of actual women in history; her Victoria Holt

romances sparked a renewed interest in women's gothic; and her Philippa Carr "historical gothics" made her prominent as a writer of family saga romances.

As Jean Plaidy, Hibbert seems to have attempted to describe the lives of prominent European women since the Renaissance. Although they are not uniform in quality, her books all follow a similar pattern. She selects a woman in history—usually connected by birth, marriage, or illicit liaison to a Royal family—whose story she can place at the center of a tale written as though virtually all of the events of the period had had a direct effect on the heroine. Many of the Plaidy books come in sets or series about families: the Plantagenets, the Medicis, the Tudors, the Stuarts, the Georgians, the Victorians, the French Royal Family. The books are popularized history, employing a relatively unsophisticated level of historical analysis, although her knowledge of detail is encyclopedic. She avoids historical controversy by relying upon standard interpretations of character and event and by defining history as it might have appeared to the woman at the center of the story. Some characters who recur in more than one story may seem sympathetic when at the center of the action and unsympathetic when peripheral.

Hibbert's Victoria Holt gothics usually divide into one of three plot types: the "suspicious husband" plot in which the heroine thinks her husband is trying to kill her, the "governess gothic" in which a heroine becomes an employee in a mansion where she discovers terror and danger, and the "adventuress" plot featuring women who engage in impostures and frauds. Holt's villains are crazed members of the mansion's family who use the ancient milieu as a weapon against innocent characters. All her Holt novels are set between the French Revolution and the Edwardian Age and she sometime uses the Pacific Islands or Australia as backgrounds along with her more traditional background of landed estates in England. She is particularly adept at creating terror in a confined space and in imagining interesting motives for her villains. In her gothics, the past always holds the key to the mystery and the heroine must find out the truth before it is too late.

Hibbert's most fully realized gothics include *Mistress of Mellyn* and *Bride of Pendorric*, both set in Cornwall, one of her favorite locales. *Mistress of Mellyn* (1960), the novel that set off the wide popularity of gothic romances in the ensuing decade and a half, has close narrative and thematic similarities to both *Jane Eyre* and *Rebecca*. The governess of the tale solves the mystery of the past, nurtures the hero's troubled daughter, and earns the hero's love by redeeming him from his disillusion about women. Two of her Victoria Holt novels, *My Enemy the Queen* and *The Queen's Confession*, are about actual women in history but the stories are told from the first person as are her other Holt books.

Hibbert's Philippa Carr novels, which she calls "historical gothics," follow the fortunes of a particular family through several generations. The series began with *The Miracle at St. Bruno's*, a novel of the English Reformation. Subsequent books pose two women of a later generation against a background of historical controversy, often involving the religious wars of the period. These books have not been so popular as her Plaidy and Holt novels.

Hibbert is prolific, probably too much so for her own good. Over the past decade, there has been a significant decrease in the complexity and believability of her plots in all three types. Her best work is probably her first five or six Victoria Holt novels when she was setting standards for a host of authors who imitated her formula, although few could match her in the evocation of terror. In recent years, her writing has become tired and dull; her plots, diffuse.

Mistress of Mellyn, however, deserves a place among the most important gothic romances of the century, placing Hibbert (as Holt) near the top of her field as an heiress of Daphne du Maurier, whose *Rebecca* remains the premier gothic romance of our time.

—Kay Mussell

HOPE, Anthony. Pseudonym for Sir Anthony Hope Hawkins. British. Born in London, 9 February 1863. Educated at St. John's Foundation School, London and subsequently in Leatherhead, Surrey; Marlborough School, 1876-81; Balliol College, Oxford (exhibitioner, then scholar), 1881-85, graduated with honours; Middle Temple, London, called to the Bar 1887. Served the government in the Editorial and Public Branch Department, 1914-18. Married Elizabeth Somerville Sheldon in 1903; two sons and one daughter. Practiced law in London, 1887-94, then a full-time writer. Liberal Parliamentary candidate for South Buckinghamshire, 1892. Chairman of the Committee, 1900-03, 1907, and founder of the pension scheme, Authors' Society. Knighted, 1918. *Died 8 July 1933.*

ROMANCE AND GOTHIC PUBLICATIONS

Novels

A Man of Mark.   London, Remington, 1890; New York, Holt, 1895.
Father Stafford.   London and New York, Cassell, 1891.
Mr. Witt's Widow.   London, Innes, and New York, United States Book Company, 1892.
A Change of Air.   London, Methuen, 1893; New York, Holt, 1894.
Half a Hero.   London, Innes, 2 vols., 1893; New York, Harper, 1 vol., 1893.
The Dolly Dialogues.   London, Westminster Gazette, and New York, Holt, 1894.
The God in the Car.   London, Methuen, 2 vols., 1894; New York, Appleton, 1 vol., 1894.
The Indiscretion of the Duchess.   Bristol, Arrowsmith, and New York, Holt, 1894.
The Prisoner of Zenda.   Bristol, Arrowsmith, and New York, Holt, 1894.
The Lady of the Pool.   New York, Appleton, 1894.
The Chronicles of Count Antonio.   London, Methuen, and New York, Appleton, 1895.
Phroso.   London, Methuen, and New York, Stokes, 1897.
Rupert of Hentzau.   Bristol, Arrowsmith, and New York, Holt, 1898.
Simon Dale.   London, Methuen, and New York, Stokes, 1898.
The King's Mirror.   London, Methuen, and New York, Appleton, 1899.
Quisanté.   London, Methuen, and New York, Stokes, 1900.
Captain Dieppe.   New York, Doubleday, 1900; London, Skeffington, 1918.
Tristam of Blent.   London, Murray, and New York, McClure, 1901.
The Intrusions of Peggy.   London, Smith Elder, and New York, Harper, 1902.
Double Harness.   London, Hutchinson, and New York, McClure, 1904.
A Servant of the Public.   London, Methuen, and New York, Stokes, 1905.
Sophy of Kravonia.   Bristol, Arrowsmith, and New York, Harper, 1906.
Tales of Two People.   London, Methuen, 1907.
Helena's Path.   New York, McClure, 1907.
The Great Miss Driver.   London, Methuen, and New York, McClure, 1908.
Second String.   London, Nelson, and New York, Doubleday, 1910.
Mrs. Maxon Protests.   London, Methuen, and New York, Harper, 1911.
A Young Man's Year.   London, Methuen, and New York, Appleton, 1915.
Beaumaroy Home from the Wars.   London, Methuen, 1919; as *The Secret of the Tower*,
     New York, Appleton, 1919.
Lucinda.   London, Hutchinson, and New York, Appleton, 1920.
Little Tiger.   London, Hutchinson, and New York, Doran, 1925.

Short Stories

Sport Royal and Other Stories.   London, Innes, 1893; New York, Holt, 1895.
Lover's Fate, and A Friend's Counsel.   Chicago, Neely, 1894.
Frivolous Cupid.   New York, Platt Bruce, 1895.
Comedies of Courtship.   London, Innes, and New York, Scribner, 1896.
The Heart of Princess Osra and Other Stories.   London, Longman, and New York,
     Stokes, 1896.

A Man and His Model (includes "An Embassy").   New York, Merriam, n.d.
A Cut and a Kiss. Boston, Brown, 1899.
Love's Logic and Other Stories. New York, McClure, 1908.

OTHER PUBLICATIONS

Plays

The Adventure of Lady Ursula (produced New York and London, 1898).   New York,
    Russell, and London, French, 1898.
When a Man's in Love, with Edward Rose (produced London, 1898).
Rupert of Hentzau, adaptation of his own novel (produced Glasgow, 1899; London,
    1900).
English Nell, with Edward Rose, adaptation of the novel *Simon Dale* by Hope (produced
    London, 1900).
Pilkerton's Peerage (produced London, 1902). London, French, 1909.
Captain Dieppe, with Harrison Rhodes (produced New York, 1903; London, 1904).
Helena's Path, with Cosmo Gordon-Lennox (produced London, 1910).
In Account with Mr. Peters, in *Windsor Magazine* (London), December 1914.
Love's Song (produced London, 1916).
The Philosopher in the Apple Orchard: A Pastoral. New York, French, 1936.

Other

Dialogue (address).   Privately printed, 1909.
The New—German—Testament: Some Texts and a Commentary.   London, Methuen,
    1914; New York, Appleton, 1915.
Militarism, German and British. London, Darling, 1915.
Why Italy Is with the Allies. London, Clay, 1917.
Selected Works. London, Harrap, 10 vols., 1925.
Memories and Notes. London, Hutchinson, 1927; New York, Doubleday, 1928.

Critical Studies: *Anthony Hope and His Books* by Charles Mallet, London, Hutchinson, 1935;
"The Prisoner of the Prisoner of Zenda: Hope and the Novel of Society" by S. Gorley Putt, in
Essays in Criticism 6 (Brill, Buckinghamshire), 1956.

*   *   *

Anthony Hope is best known for *The Prisoner of Zenda*, yet he was a man of several parts,
both in his career and in his fiction. The son of a clergyman, he became a Balliol College
Scholar, was elected President of the Oxford Union, and took a First Class degree. He was
called to the Bar in 1887, and faced a brilliant legal career. Interested in politics, he made a
respectable stand as a Liberal against the incumbent Conservative member in 1892. Although
he was to become a prolific novelist with over 30 works of fiction to his credit, he remained
ambivalent to this profession. He called his popular romance *Phroso* "tosh," while taking most
pains over a serious novel such as *Quisanté* which he did not expect the public to notice. In 1918
he was knighted for his war work.
    He began his published writing with social satire and political fiction. *The Dolly Dialogues*,
first published in *The Westminster Review*, received wide attention as a witty and pointed
dramatisation of fashionable foibles. *The God in the Chair*, which still has interest as a sensitive
study of political life, achieved some notoriety for its parallel with the career of Cecil Rhodes.
Willy Rushton, chief founder of the Great Omofaga Company, rides roughshod over his
colleagues and suppresses his own humanity in his quest for power. Maggie Dennison, who
loves him, finally refuses to interpose in his life, recognising this will compromise his real

desires. In *Quisanté* Hope was to portray another odious but brilliant politician who is himself exploited for his popularity, and dies of heart failure after making a speech.

But in 1890, in *A Man of Mark*, a privately printed collection of short stories, he had experimented with adventure set in an imaginary world—in this case the South American state of Aurentland. At the end of 1893, exuberant with winning a legal case, he imagined a tale set in a middle European country, Ruritania, and wrote *The Prisoner of Zenda* in spare moments during four weeks. When it appeared the following year its immediate and overwhelming success made him abandon the law for a full-time writing career—probably to the detriment of his fiction, for he never recaptured the fresh immediacy of this early work.

The appeal of *The Prisoner of Zenda* lies both in its high spirits and in the way in which its world of Ruritania is at once contemporary and antique. A world of feudal ceremony, it can be reached by train (although once there Rassendyll tends to ride on horseback). The castle is half modern residence and half gothic pile with fearful mysteries. In the world of firearms, honour can still be defended in a duel, and political struggles are fought out in romantic adventure. Uniting the two worlds is Rudolph Rassendyll, himself a genetic throwback to a romantic *alliance*, in 1733, of the redheaded Rudolph the Third of Ruritania. He is a modern Cavalier, brave, excellent horseman and swordsman, yet with a hint of self-mockery in his heroism. His narrative voice seduces the reader into willing complicity with the absurd story. The plot itself has some archetypal patterns—double identity, the conflict between Black Michael and Red Ephberg, the love for an unreachable Princess. But any submerged symbolism is contained within the rapidly moving narrative.

Rupert of Hentzau returns to Ruritania some years later. Black Michael is dead, and Rudolph's red hair shows streaks of grey. The danger is now from Rupert, who captures a compromising letter from Queen (earlier Princess) Flavia. Rudolph destroys the letter and saves the Queen's honour—at the cost of his life. The theme of chivalry present in the earlier work here becomes overworked; the basis for the plot is thin, and the narrator is the old retainer Fritz von Tarlehein, who is no substitute for Rudolph. But the narrative pace is still fast, the swashbuckling is exhilarating. Hope wrote other tales of Ruritania, none of them wholly successful. *The Heart of Princess Osra*, for instance, is a series of tales from the country in olden times, in which Osra is educated through five loves—from Stephen the silversmith to the Grand Duke of Mittenheim—into the meanings of the passion. But what the first readers found charming the modern audience is likely to consider heavy-handed and sentimental.

Hope had a weak historical imagination. In *Simon Dale*, for example, he explores his theme of chivalry in 17th-century England. Dale, a country boy, goes to London and enters the employ of Charles I. He offers his pure love to Nell Gwyn against that of the dissolute monarch. Later he leaves the King, respectfully telling him that he pays too high a price for his power. He lives to bring up his own children honorably. By comparison *Sophy of Kravonic* also has an incredible plot. Sophy, an Essex kitchen maid, rises to become for a few days Queen of Kravonic, a Balkan state split into warring parties, and to revenge her dead royal husband. Yet, although Hope had not been to the Balkans, the novel gives a convincing sense of present-day eastern Europe, and it remains one of his most readable novels. It was one of the books that turned Graham Greene to a life of travel.

Anthony Hope was one of the group of adventure story writers that included Robert Louis Stevenson, Rider Haggard and Conan Doyle. But he never achieved a consistent narrative style, and he remains notable for *The Prisoner of Zenda* alone. This introduced "Ruritania" into the English language; it was directly reflected in prose imitations, dramatisations, and film: more remarkably, it entered into the popular consciousness. It established the romantic image of middle Europe for England and America.

—Louis James

HOPE, Margaret. *See* **KNIGHT, Alanna**.

HORNER, Lance, and **Kyle ONSTOTT**. American. **HORNER, Lance**: born in 1903. Worked as advertising copywriter. *Died in 1970.* **ONSTOTT, Kyle**: born in DuQuoin, Illinois, 12 January 1887. Had one son. Licensed by the American Kennel Club as an all-breeds judge, 1921. *Died in 1966.*

ROMANCE AND GOTHIC PUBLICATIONS

Novels by Lance Horner

Falconhurst series:
  Mandingo, with Kyle Onstott. Richmond, Virginia, Denlinger, 1957; London, Longman, 1959.
  Drum. New York, Dial Press, 1962; London, W.H. Allen, 1963.
  Master of Falconhurst. New York, Dial Press, 1964; London, W.H. Allen, 1965.
  Falconhurst Fancy. New York, Fawcett, 1966; London, W.H. Allen, 1967.
  The Mustee. New York, Fawcett, 1967; London, W.H. Allen, 1968.
  Heir to Falconhurst. New York, Fawcett, 1968; London, W.H. Allen, 1969.
  Flight to Falconhurst. New York, Fawcett, 1971; London, W.H. Allen, 1972.
  Mistress of Falconhurst. New York, Fawcett, and London, W.H. Allen, 1973.
The Street of the Sun. New York, Abelard Schuman, 1956.
The Tattooed Road. Middleburg, Virginia, Denlinger, 1960; London, Souvenir Press, 1962; as *Santiago Road*, London, Pan, 1967.
Rogue Roman. New York, Pyramid, 1965; London, W.H. Allen, 1969.
Child of the Sun. London, W.H. Allen, 1966.
The Black Sun. New York, Fawcett, 1967; London, W.H. Allen, 1968.
The Mahound. New York, Fawcett, 1969.
Golden Stud. New York, Fawcett, 1975; as *Six-Fingered Stud*, London, W.H. Allen, 1975.

OTHER PUBLICATIONS by Kyle Onstott

Other

  Your Dog as a Hobby, with Irving C. Ackerman. New York, Harper, 1940.
  Beekeeping as a Hobby. New York, Harper, 1941.
  The Art of Breeding Better Dogs. Washington, D.C., Denlinger, 1946.

*   *   *

As the above bibliography indicates, Lance Horner and Kyle Onstott have to be considered together, for though Onstott wrote only *Mandingo*, his name appears alone on two others and with Horner's on four more in most bibliographies; these six, along with the other eight, are solely by Horner.

Selling in the millions, but dismissed by critics as "trashy," "slimy," or even "regurgitory," Horner and Onstott's novels are formulaic in plot, theme, and character. The plot structure of all the novels is centered upon the system of slavery, whether in the ante-bellum South, the Caribbean, north Africa, or ancient Rome. The effect of slavery upon both masters and slaves is their one theme, and that theme can be summarized in a single phrase: sex, sadism, and miscegenation. Life is presented as being sex-obsessed and filled with violent cruelty resulting from that obsessive sex. The combination of sex and slavery creates a feverish tension among and between blacks and whites, and this tension provides the impetus for the action, which is often lurid. Not only is almost every imaginable form of sex included, but also such extremes of violence as crucifixion, biting through jugular veins, and boiling of human beings. Altogether, sex and violence are pervasive; indeed, they are the essence of Horner and Onstott's fiction.

The eight novels forming the "Falconhurst series" have been the most popular. They present, in discontinuous fashion, the lives of the Maxwell family, their acquaintances, and their slaves at Falconhurst plantation in southwestern Alabama from 1797 to 1887, and they fully illustrate the theme of sex, sadism, and miscegenation. Among the 25 major characters and 50 secondary ones of the eight novels, central is Ham(mond) Maxwell, who appears in all but *Heir to Falconhurst*. He grows up at Falconhurst, which is a slave-breeding plantation, considers it paradise, continually beds the female blacks while believing himself utterly superior to their race, finds sex with white women difficult, and is, whether intended so by the authors, a warped, pathetic bigot. His self-satisfaction is matched by the other white males, who revel in their crude, backward world, exalted by their faith in their superiority to all blacks. The white women, even the capable Dovie Verder of *Falconhurst Fancy* and *Flight to Falconhurst*, seem principally interested in bedding the black male slaves, the result of which is always more violence. Horner and Onstott's presentation of blacks is confused. Sympathy is shown to all. A few are given exceptional qualities, but most have a fear of responsibility and surrender completely to their sexual drives. Slavery is given most of the blame for their weaknesses, but at times they are also presented as being essentially children, savages, or animals. The authors seem uncertain in creating a focused image of blacks; however, sex and callous degradation emerge as the two prime elements of that image and contribute significantly to the total image of the novels. For many readers, novels such as the Falconhurst series provide their only knowledge of the ante-bellum South, just as did earlier romances of "moonlight and magnolias," but whereas those works sentimentalized plantation life, the Falconhurst novels present it as a violent world of inter-racial sex and sadism.

The heroes of the non-Falconhurst novels are similar to Ham Maxwell in their virility, but they are more often slaves, at least for a time, than slaveowners. (However, the heroes of *The Mahound* and *The Black Sun* are respectively a slave trader and a Haitian plantation owner.) *The Tattooed Road*, *The Street of the Sun*, and *Rogue Roman* follow the changes of fortune for their heroes from freeman to slave and back to freedom. This formula is not greatly varied in *Golden Stud*, as well as *Master of Falconhurst*, *The Mustee*, and *Falconhurst Fancy*, by having a black male of light skin pretend to be white, with the ever-present threat of discovery providing suspense and plot twists. All of the non-Falconhurst heroes are in the picaresque tradition, young men attempting to survive, to gain freedom and wealth, and to make love as often as possible by their wit, courage, and looks. Since the novels are so male-dominated, women—black or white, high or low, Southern or Roman—are sex objects. The hero generally has two or three "loves," aside from casual sexual encounters, in the course of a novel before finally winning an idealized woman, previously unattainable because of social differences.

It is easy to ridicule the novels of these two men. There are errors in chronology and anachronisms; the plots are episodic, particularly in the non-Falconhurst novels, and contain massive amounts of coincidence; the characters, both black and white, are stereotypes which are repeated again and again; and sex and violence are so overdone as to become almost parodic. Nevertheless, the novels still sell; the millions in print increase, and since the death of Horner, Harry Whittington (as Ashley Carter) has carried on the line with *Sword of the Golden Stud* (1977) and *Taproots of Falconhurst* (1979). It seems likely that, whatever critics may think of the image the novels present of slavery, that image of sex, sadism, and miscegenation will continue to have popular appeal. *Why* is another question.

—Earl F. Bargainnier

HOWARD, Linden. *See* **MANLEY-TUCKER, Audrie**.

HOWARD, Mary. Pseudonym for Mary Mussi, née Edgar; also writes as Josephine Edgar. British.   Born in London, 27 December 1907. Educated privately. Married Rudolph F. Mussi in 1934; one son and one daughter. Past Chairman, Society of Women Writers and Journalists. Recipient: Romantic Novelists Association Major Award, 1960, 1979, 1980, and Elinor Glyn Award, 1961. Agent: David Higham Associates, 5-8 Lower John Street, London W1R 3PE. Address: 27 Woodfield Avenue, London SW16 1LQ, England.

ROMANCE AND GOTHIC PUBLICATIONS

Novels

Windier Skies.   London, Long, 1930.
Dark Morality.   London, Lane, 1932.
Partners for Playtime.   London, Collins, 1938.
Strangers in Love.   London, Collins, 1939; New York, Doubleday, 1941.
It Was Romance.   London, Collins, 1939.
The Untamed Heart.   London, Collins, 1940.
Far Blue Horizons.   London, Collins, 1940; New York, Doubleday, 1942.
Uncharted Romance.   New York, Doubleday, 1941.
Devil in My Heart.   London, Collins, and New York, Doubleday, 1941.
To-morrow's Hero.   London, Collins, 1941; New York, Doubleday, 1942.
Reef of Dreams.   London, Collins, 1942.
Gay Is Life.   London, Collins, and New York, Doubleday, 1943.
Have Courage, My Heart.   London, Collins, 1943.
Anna Heritage.   London, Collins, 1944; New York, Arcadia House, 1945.
The Wise Forget.   London, Collins, 1944; New York, Arcadia House, 1945.
Family Orchestra.   London, Collins, and New York, Arcadia House, 1945.
The Man from Singapore.   London, Collins, 1946.
Return to Love.   New York, Arcadia House, 1946.
Weave Me Some Wings.   London, Collins, 1947.
The Clouded Moon.   New York, Arcadia House, 1948.
Strange Paths.   London, Collins, 1948.
Star-Crossed.   London, Collins, 1949.
There Will I Follow.   London, Collins, and New York, Arcadia House, 1949.
Two Loves Have I.   London, Collins, 1950; as *Mist on the Hills*, New York, Arcadia House, 1950.
Bow to the Storm.   London, Collins, 1950; as *The Young Lady*, New York, Arcadia House, 1950.
Sixpence in Her Shoe.   London, Collins, 1950; New York, Arcadia House, 1954.
Promise of Delight.   London, Collins, and New York, Arcadia House, 1952.
The Gate Leads Nowhere.   London, Collins, 1953.
Fool's Haven.   London, Collins, 1954; New York, Arcadia House, 1955 (?).
Sew a Fine Seam.   London, Hale, 1954.
Before I Kissed.   London, Collins, 1955.
The Grafton Girls.   London, Collins, 1956.
A Lady Fell in Love.   London, Hale, 1956.

Shadows in the Sun. London, Collins, 1957.
Man of Stone. London, Collins, 1958.
The Intruder. London, Collins, 1959.
The House of Lies. London, Collins, 1960; as *The Crystal Villa*, New York, Lenox Hill Press, 1970.
More Than Friendship. London, Collins, 1960.
Surgeon's Dilemma. London, Collins, 1961.
The Pretenders. London, Collins, 1962.
The Big Man. London, Collins, 1965.
The Interloper. London, Collins, 1967.
The Repeating Pattern. London, Collins, 1968.
The Bachelor Girls. London, Collins, 1968.
The Pleasure Seekers. London, Collins, 1970.
Home to My Country. London, Collins, 1971.
A Right Grand Girl. London, Collins, 1972.
The Cottager's Daughter. New York, 'Dell, 1972.
Soldiers and Lovers. London, Collins, 1973.
Who Knows Sammy Halliday? London, Collins, 1974.
The Young Ones. London, Collins, 1975.
The Spanish Summer. London, Collins, 1977.
Mr. Rodriguez. London, Collins, 1979.

Novels as Josephine Edgar

My Sister Sophie. London, Collins, 1964; New York, Pocket Books, 1974.
The Dark Tower. London, Collins, 1966; New York, Dell, 1969.
The Dancer's Daughter. London, Collins, 1968; New York, Dell, 1970.
Time of Dreaming. London, Collins, 1968; New York, Pocket Books, 1974.
The Devil's Innocents. London, Collins, 1972; New York, Dell, 1975.
The Stranger at the Gate. London, Collins, 1973; New York, Pocket Books, 1975.
The Lady of Wildersley. London, Macdonald and Jane's, 1975; New York, Pocket Books, 1977.
Duchess. London, Macdonald and Jane's, and New York, St. Martin's Press, 1976.
Countess. London, Macdonald and Jane's, and New York, St. Martin's Press, 1978.

Mary Howard comments:

Until 1961 I wrote in the conventional light, popular romantic Style, but with *The Big Man* I began my series of more realistic romantic stories under the Mary Howard name, trying to combine a "good read" with a feeling of contemporary life, and avoiding the clichés of boy meets girl, boy is separated from girl, boy finds girl again/is reconciled after explanations/ happy ending. This series culminated with *The Spanish Summer* and *Mr. Rodriguez*.

I also began the Josephine Edgar books, set in the 19th century, and developed the family saga in *Duchess* and *Countess*, which begin in 1900 and end in the early 1920's.

*   *   *

Mary Howard published her first romantic novels as long ago as the 1930's, but her work has never dated. In 1960 she won the very first Romantic Novelists Association Major Award for the best romantic novel of the year with *More Than Friendship*.

Her most recent novels show all the freshness of a new talent, happily combined with the experience of a mature one. She keeps well in tune with the times, both in theme and outlook. *Soldiers and Lovers*, set in World War II, accurately reflected the feelings and difficulties of that era from the point of view of three women, each different in age, class, and background, brought together in a small country village to battle with ration-cards, blackouts, children, the constant anxiety of the death-dealing enemy in the sky—and other, more personal, agonies of love, tenderness, passion, and parting which only war can bring, and only those who have lived through it can fully understand.

Today she accepts the more liberal attitude towards sexual morals with easy grace, but with due regard for delicate sensibilities. *Mr. Rodriguez*, which won the 1980 Major Award, is a model of its kind. The setting is mildly exotic (Spain), the topic very much up-to-date (a happy extra-marital affair which hurts no one but the participants), the ending sad, but satisfying, and totally lacking in sentimentality. The characters, too, are recognisably of their decade, the 1970's.

Many of her recent novels have been set on the Spanish coast for the very good reason that Howard's artist daughter Susan married a Spanish surgeon and now lives in Barcelona. Howard visits her Spanish family every summer and this gives her plenty of opportunity to absorb the atmosphere of Spain's holiday coast (a useful background for romantic novels) and observe both the Spanish people and English people on holiday. Among other memorable novels with this setting are *A Right Grand Girl* and *The Pleasure Seekers*.

Howard's alter ego, Josephine Edgar, writes period novels set mainly in the 19th century (e.g., the gothic *The Lady of Wildersley*). Outstanding among these are *Duchess*, and its sequel *Countess*—a rags-to-riches story about Viola Corbett, a Victorian working-class girl, the illegitimate offspring of a solid Yorkshire mother and an itinerant Italian acrobat. A girl of instinctive poise, driving ambition, and great natural beauty, she engineers her own transfer from Leeds to London and a job in a fashionable store as a springboard to better things. Needless to say not all the "things" are better, but Viola is a tough and resilient, as well as an enchanting heroine and in the end she gets her deserts.

These two are among the best of the "blockbusters" of the 1970's, coming as they do from the pen of an experienced and accomplished author who knows—and respects—her audience. It was with *Countess* that Josephine Edgar won her third Major Award.

—Elizabeth Grey

HOWATCH, Susan (Elizabeth, née Sturt).   British.   Born in Leatherhead, Surrey, 14 July 1940. Educated at King's College, London, LL.B. 1961. Married Joseph Howatch in 1964; one daughter. Law clerk, Masons of London, 1961-62; secretary, R.C.A. Victor Record Corporation, 1964-65. Agent: Hughes Massie Ltd., 31 Southampton Row, London WC1B 4HL, England.

ROMANCE AND GOTHIC PUBLICATIONS

Novels

    The Dark Shore.   New York, Ace, 1965; London, Hamish Hamilton, 1972.
    The Waiting Sands.   New York, Ace, 1966; London, Hamish Hamilton, 1972.
    Call in the Night.   New York, Ace, 1967; London, Hamish Hamilton, 1972.
    The Shrouded Walls.   New York, Ace, 1968; London, Hamish Hamilton, 1972.
    April's Grave.   New York, Ace, 1969; London, Hamish Hamilton, 1973.
    The Devil on Lammas Night.   New York, Ace, 1970; London, Hamish Hamilton, 1973.
    Penmarric.   New York, Simon and Schuster, and London, Hamish Hamilton, 1971.
    Cashelmara.   New York, Simon and Schuster, and London, Hamish Hamilton, 1974.

The Rich Are Different. New York, Simon and Schuster, and London, Hamish Hamilton, 1977.
Sins of the Fathers. New York, Simon and Schuster, and London, Hamish Hamilton, 1980.

*   *   *

British-born Susan Howatch began writing as a child and started submitting her work for publication as a teenager. Her first novel, *The Dark Shore*, was published when she was in her 20's. Despite her surprise at critics' classification of it as a "modern gothic," *The Dark Shore* launched her career as a writer in this genre. She then produced, in rapid succession, five more modern gothics and two gothic epics or sagas.

Although she's been a US resident since 1964, Howatch's love of England and Scotland, especially Cornwall, is reflected in the British settings of many of her novels. Howatch believes (*The Writer*, May 1974) that settings should provide more than just "scenic glamour"; location should be integral to the story both in terms of plot and atmosphere. So *April's Grave* is set in a remote part of Scotland reachable only by boat; in this novel, and in *The Waiting Sands*, the remoteness itself becomes psychologically unnerving and suspenseful.

Howatch's interest in realism and mystery is also seen in her plots and her characterizations. She shows a fondness for such plot devices as anonymous phone calls, missing characters, shallow graves, surprise murderers, and touches of the occult. Her characters are as three-dimensional as possible, given the constraints of this genre. Howatch says she pays more attention than other gothic writers to her heroes' characterizations, trying to show them as more than just a "splendid facade." Howatch's heroines are spunky, sensible, and risk-taking, as the genre demands, but also can be vulnerable when the occasion arises. Her realistic characters are portrayed with a range of traits—both positive and negative—and interests, including sexual interests and desires. But, they also fit the gothic "formula" enough to move the plot along and provide mystery and suspense as well as romance.

Howatch's six gothics contain all of the above elements, in various mixes and with varying degrees of success. She perceived *The Dark Shore* originally as the story of the hero, for example. Jon was "burdened with loneliness" and his problems were triggered, to some extent, by an anonymous phone call about his dead wife. Howatch tells us, however, that her editor saw this first book as a romantic mystery about a girl in distress at a sinister house by the sea and—"instant gothic."

April's Grave, Call in the Night, and *The Waiting Sands* all offer the reader sexual entanglements along with missing characters and shallow graves to advance the plot. Karen, the heroine of *April's Grave*, is introduced to the hero, an English professor, and turned, "...expecting to see a white-haired, stooping scholar, and had come face to face with all six foot of the charm and grace and frank sexual interest which emanated from Neville Bennett." To get the mystery started, however, is not quite so easy. Not only is April's grave missing but, as one reviewer notes, "April herself has been missing for three years without causing the slightest ripple of concern" (*Best Seller*, 1 March 1974). Eventually, though, April's buried suitcases are accidentally discovered and the web of mystery grows, culminating in another killing and a surprise murderer.

Just as Karen, April's twin, initiated the search for April, so Claire sets off to Europe to find her missing sister, in *Call in the Night*. Here again are shallow graves, broken engagements, and entangled relationships! Claire persists in searching for Gina despite her growing fascination with Garth (the hero) and despite her qualms that he may be not only a murderer, but also a womanizer.

Sexual entanglements also dominate *The Waiting Sands*. Decima invites her oldest friend, Rachel (the heroine), to her 21st birthday party at remote Roshven off the coast of Scotland. But the invitation carries with it a plea for protection from a suspected murder plot by her husband Charles. Decima is due to inherit Roshven on her birthday—if she lives that long! Unusual plot twists involve Charles's sexual liasion with a house guest, gossip and innuendo, suspense, quicksand, and a double murder.

In *The Shrouded Walls* Howatch builds suspense with a surprise heir, a marriage of convenience, murder, and a touch of the occult—a local witch who supplies potions and poisons. She also uses the heroine's persistent curiosity to trigger the plot resolution. This novel, however, is not regarded as one of Howatch's better gothics. One reviewer terms it "strictly a ho-hum affair" (*Best Seller*, 1 December 1971), and a second reviewer credits Howatch with producing interesting characters propelled by believable motives but criticizes her for "sometimes melodramatic prose" (*Library Journal*, 15 January 1972).

Black magic, only a secondary theme in *The Shrouded Walls*, becomes central in *The Devil on Lammas Night*. Howatch's skillful interweaving of realistic characters and complex situations makes a bizarre theme plausible and frightening. The plot involves Nicola and Evan (former lovers) and their possible reconciliation. The action focuses primarily around the sinister Tristan Poole who has leased Colwyn Court (Evan's ancestral home). Poole's Society for the Propagation of Nature Foods is in actuality a witches' coven—and Poole, a warlock. Howatch provides supernatural occurrences convenient "accidental" deaths, and a celebration of Lammas Night featuring a plot to use the heroine in a Satanic wedding.

Despite considerable success with these modern gothic novels, Howatch's reputation as a writer of note was not firmly established until the publication of her best-selling gothic epic or saga *Penmarric* in 1971. It was followed by another highly acclaimed saga, *Cashelmara*. Combined sales have been in the millions. These novels set the style for her recent family sagas (but not gothics), *The Rich Are Different* and *The Sins of the Fathers*. In *Penmarric*, set in Cornwall, and *Cashelmara*, set in Ireland, England, and America, the sprawling and complex tale of several generations of a family is told in turn by each of the characters from their own moral and emotional perspective. It may be that the sagas offer Howatch a more flexible vehicle for pursuing her love of realism. Certainly they allow her more exploration of sexual themes and more complex character development, especially of the male characters who tend to dominate her sagas. Howatch's fans, however, can only hope that she won't abandon the modern gothics and romances that she does so well.

—Josephine A. Ruggiero and Louise C. Weston

HOY, Elizabeth.   Pseudonym for (Alice) Nina Conarain.   Irish.   Born in Dublin. Married. Worked as a nurse and secretary-receptionist; staff member, *Daily News*, London. Address: c/o Mills and Boon Ltd., 15-16 Brooks Mews, London W1A 1DR, England.

ROMANCE AND GOTHIC PUBLICATIONS

Novels

> *Love in Apron Strings*.   London, Hodder and Stoughton, 1933.
> *Roses in the Snow*.   London, Mills and Boon, 1936.
> *Crown for a Lady*.   London, Mills and Boon, 1937.
> *Sally in the Sunshine*.   London, Mills and Boon, 1937.
> *Shadow of the Hills*.   London, Mills and Boon, 1938.
> *Stars over Egypt*.   London, Mills and Boon, 1938.
> *You Belong to Me*.   London, Mills and Boon, 1938.
> *Mirage for Love*.   London, Mills and Boon, 1939.
> *Runaway Bride*.   London, Mills and Boon, 1939.
> *You Took My Heart*.   London, Mills and Boon, 1939; Toronto, Harlequin, 1959.
> *Enchanted Wilderness*.   London, Mills and Boon, 1940.
> *Heart, Take Care!*   London, Mills and Boon, 1940.

It Had to Be You. London, Mills and Boon, 1940.
You Can't Lose Yesterday. London, Mills and Boon, 1940.
I'll Find You Again. London, Mills and Boon, 1941.
Take Love Easy. London, Mills and Boon, 1941.
Come Back My Dream. London, Mills and Boon, 1942; Toronto, Harlequin, 1959.
Hearts at Random. London, Mills and Boon, 1942.
Proud Citadel. London, Mills and Boon, 1942; Toronto, Harlequin, 1975.
Ask Only Love. London, Mills and Boon, 1943.
One Step from Heaven. London, Mills and Boon, 1943.
You Can't Live Alone. London, Mills and Boon, 1944.
Give Me New Wings. London, Mills and Boon, 1944; New York, Arcadia House, 1945.
Sylvia Sorelle. London, Mills and Boon, 1944.
Heart's Haven. London, Mills and Boon, 1945; as *The Heart Remembers*, New York, Arcadia House, 1946.
It's Wise to Forget. London, Mills and Boon, 1945; as *Shatter the Rainbow*, New York, Arcadia House, 1946.
Dear Stranger. London, Mills and Boon, 1946; New York, Arcadia House, 1947.
Sword in the Sun. London, Mills and Boon, 1946.
To Win a Paradise. London, Mills and Boon, 1947; Toronto, Harlequin, 1960.
The Dark Loch. London, Mills and Boon, 1948.
Though I Bid Farewell. London, Mills and Boon, 1948.
Background to Hyacinthe. London, Mills and Boon, 1949.
Immortal Morning. London, Mills and Boon, 1949.
June for Enchantment. London, Mills and Boon, 1949.
The Vanquished Heart. London, Mills and Boon, 1949.
For Love's Sake Only. New York, Arcadia House, 1951.
Silver Maiden. London, Mills and Boon, 1951.
When You Have Found Me. London, Mills and Boon, and New York, Arcadia House, 1951.
White Hunter. London, Mills and Boon, 1951; Toronto, Harlequin, 1961.
The Enchanted. London, Mills and Boon, 1952.
The Web of Love. London, Mills and Boon, 1952.
Fanfare for Lovers. London, Mills and Boon, 1953.
If Love Were Wise. London, Mills and Boon, 1954; Toronto, Harlequin, 1970.
So Loved and So Far. London, Mills and Boon, 1954; Toronto, Harlequin, 1965.
Snare the Wild Heart. London, Mills and Boon, 1955; Toronto, Harlequin, 1966.
Who Loves Believes. London, Mills and Boon, 1955; Toronto, Harlequin, 1965.
Young Doctor Kirkdene. London, Mills and Boon, 1955; Toronto, Harlequin, 1959.
Because of Doctor Danville. London, Mills and Boon, 1956; Toronto, Harlequin, 1958.
My Heart Has Wings. London, Mills and Boon, 1957; Toronto, Harlequin, 1959.
Do Something Dangerous. London, Mills and Boon, 1958; Toronto, Harlequin, 1959.
City of Dreams. London, Mills and Boon, 1959; Toronto, Harlequin, 1960.
Dark Horse, Dark Rider. London, Mills and Boon, 1960; Toronto, Harlequin, 1967.
Dear Fugitive. London, Mills and Boon, and Toronto, Harlequin, 1960.
The Door into the Rose Garden. London, Mills and Boon, 1961.
Heart, Have You No Wisdom? London, Mills and Boon, 1962.
Her Wild Voice Singing. London, Mills and Boon, 1963.
Homeward the Heart. London, Mills and Boon, 1964; Toronto, Harlequin, 1965.
Flowering Desert. London, Mills and Boon, 1965; Toronto, Harlequin, 1966.
The Faithless One. London, Mills and Boon, 1966; Toronto, Harlequin, 1967.
My Secret Love. London, Mills and Boon, 1967.
Honeymoon Holiday. London, Mills and Boon, 1967; Toronto, Harlequin, 1968.
Be More Than Dreams. London, Mills and Boon, 1968; Toronto, Harlequin, 1969.
Music I Hear with You. London, Mills and Boon, 1969; Toronto, Harlequin, 1970.
It Happened in Paris. London, Mills and Boon, 1970; Toronto, Harlequin, 1971.
African Dream. London, Mills and Boon, 1971.
Into a Golden Land. London, Mills and Boon, and Toronto, Harlequin, 1971.
Immortal Flower. London, Mills and Boon, and Toronto, Harlequin, 1972.

That Island Summer.   London, Mills and Boon, and Toronto, Harlequin, 1973.
The Girl in the Green Valley.   London, Mills and Boon, 1973; Toronto, Harlequin, 1974.
Shadows on the Sand.   London, Mills and Boon, and Toronto, Harlequin, 1974.
The Blue Jacaranda.   London, Mills and Boon, and Toronto, Harlequin, 1975.
When the Dream Fades.   London, Mills and Boon, 1980.

OTHER PUBLICATIONS

Other as Nina Conarain

Editor, with Kay Boyle and Laurence Vail, *365 Days*.   New York, Harcourt Brace, and London, Cape, 1936.

*   *   *

Elizabeth Hoy's novels reflect her Irish childhood and her early fondness for writing which later evolved into a journalistic career with the London *Daily News*. From this, it was a short step to writing romance novels which she began publishing in the 1930's. She is one of those writers who feels that she can only write about things she has experienced herself, and that her characters, although imaginary, must have some "foundation in reality." Consequently, her novels often reflect experiences with incidents, background, and people in her life. She spent some time in nurse's training before she had to leave it, but the experiences remained with her, lending a greater degree of authenticity to her early doctor/nurse novels.

A holiday trip to Australia provided her with sufficient material for her to use in her writing and she describes the people and the country with comfortable familiarity. Besides Australia, Hoy uses Ireland, England, and Africa as settings for her other novels.

Because of her own inclination and, perhaps, because of the period she wrote in, Hoy's romances have a more traditional outlook as she describes her heroines and heroes. She also has a touch of the true romantic's ability to make her readers believe the unbelievable. Not, however, without some very genuine soul-searching by the heroine.

The Blue Jacaranda illustrates this and offers a good example of her writing ability. In this novel, Lena Shannon travels from England to Queensland, Australia, to stay with her Uncle Tom. Before her arrival, he dies, leaving a will that thoroughly insures impossible complications. She is to live on his estate for six months with the other inheritor, Rod Carron, and his daughter. By the end of six months, he expects them to marry each other or both lose any inheritance. The fact that Rod has a daughter is an added difficulty, although Lena and she become friends immediately. Both Lena and Rod resent the conditions and are extremely suspicious of each other for they can't feel that such a marriage would work. The estate stands between them as each wonders about the other's willingness to marry for money. Personality clashes and instinctive efforts at self-defense continue to complicate matters until a devastating cyclone strikes the estate. The cyclone is the final touch and shows them the way to resolve their differences.

Shadows on the Sand has an entirely different mood. Alison Gray is sent by a research institution to Cairo to substitute for an elderly secretary. Her arrival instantly brings Scott Crane, her temporary boss, storming down on her as he refuses to let her stay. He is forced to wait for a replacement and he does let her work. Alison's fresh sweetness is not so ingrained that she cannot stand up for herself so that frequent clashes occur between her and Scott. The novel takes place against the background of scientific research, primitive desert country, and the excitement of new archaeological findings. Secondary characters such as other members of the team and an old girl friend play their roles in furthering the plot complications, as do sand storms, antagonistic natives, and unexpected dangers such as falling rocks near the excavation.

Romance readers find Elizabeth Hoy's novels satisfyingly filled with the right mixture of romance, danger, and suspense. Her heroines are well drawn, and not the conventional naive or helpless romance heroine. Her heroes are also a complex assortment; they keep their feet firmly on the ground, their hands and minds in control of every tiniest detail but their hearts, which unaccountably refuse to behave. It is this constant source of amusement which keeps her readers so involved as they wonder just how the "mighty will fall" under Hoy's adept connivance.

—Arlene Moore

HUFFORD, Susan. American. Born in Cincinnati, Ohio, 15 December 1940. Educated at DePauw University, Greencastle, Indiana, B.A. 1960; Temple University, Philadelphia, M.A. 1961. Actress and singer. Agent: Jane Jordan Browne, 410 South Michigan Avenue, Room 828, Chicago, Illinois 60615, U.S.A.

ROMANCE AND GOTHIC PUBLICATIONS

Novels

> *Midnight Sailing.* New York, Popular Library, 1975.
> *The Devil's Sonata.* New York, Popular Library, 1976.
> *A Delicate Deceit.* New York, Popular Library, 1976.
> *Cove's End.* New York, Popular Library, 1977.
> *Satan's Sunset.* New York, Popular Library, 1977.
> *Skin Deep.* New York, Popular Library, 1978.
> *Trial of Innocence.* New York, Popular Library, 1978.
> *Melody of Malice.* New York, Popular Library, 1979.
> *Going All the Way.* New York, New American Library, 1980.

*   *   *

Susan Hufford tells fast-paced stories of beautiful women plunged into frightening situations and familiar, seemingly tranquil surroundings; surface peace is disrupted by evil and death, and even friends and lovers cannot escape suspicion, as heroines seek to come to terms with their family, their past, and their tenuous future.

Her tetralogy, *Midnight Sailing, The Devil's Sonata, A Delicate Deceit*, and *Satan's Sunset*, traces the changing adventures of 25-year-old Hilda Hughes, a petite yet beautiful university professor from Ann Arbor, Michigan, as she deals with terror on romantic cruiseships, amid tropical paradises, and in stunning mansions. Old friends and new acquaintances always seem involved in strange conspiracies that seek to use and abuse her wealth and her psychic sensitivity; handsome psychotic males play power games that end in sadism and death; and her newly discovered sister, Ursula, proves a neurotic, murderous tool of diabolical schemers, both male and female. Her father's sins are visited upon his daughters, who are pursued by vengeful madmen and cultists. The father's adultery endangers both sisters as a psychotic returns from the grave to bring more madness and death in *The Devil's Sonata.* Hilda's love for a crippled but forceful pianist draws her into greater danger in *Satan's Sunset*, wherein a mad artist and a rejected lover plot her demise. Sensitive to threatening atmospheres, but unsure of whom to trust, Hilda usually makes bad judgments, believing the smooth tales of villains and fearing the contradictions and hesitations of friends.

In *Cove's End* New York's top model, a popular jet-setter, escapes to her grandparents' home in Maine, seeking peace and quiet and a new sense of self, only to find a childhood friend murdered, her inheritance a mystery, and her own life threatened. Her lover's acts make him a suspect, despite the absence of motive, and her only relative proves no relative at all.

Hufford's most compelling work, *Trial of Innocence*, set in the 19th century, records the nightmarish experiences of a young girl who leaves a beloved aunt to follow a desperate but cryptic call for aid from her dead sister's husband; but the invitation proves a hoax, and she is left a penniless stranger in a strange land where in-laws believe her a scheming fortune hunter and where, amid Victorian elegance in a rambling Tudor home, an intricate web of lies threatens sanity and life. The naive and innocent heroine must learn to cope with her own unexpected fascination with a cynical, worldly man who both frightens and allures; to compete with a beautiful, catty adventuress whose feminine wiles seem to have already ensnared both love and wealth; and to deal with amoral children whose feigned innocence and make-believe fantasies hide a murderous reality. Here, and throughout Hufford's canon, the secret compulsions of the seeming innocent endanger the truly innocent.

—Gina Macdonald

HULL, E(dith) M(aude).   British.   Married. Lived in Derbyshire.

ROMANCE AND GOTHIC PUBLICATIONS

Novels

> *The Sheik.*   London, Nash, 1919; Boston, Small Maynard, 1921.
> *The Shadow of the East.*   London, Nash, and Boston, Small Maynard, 1921.
> *The Desert Healer.*   London, Nash, and Boston, Small Maynard, 1923.
> *The Sons of the Sheik.*   Boston, Small Maynard, 1925; London, Nash, 1926.
> *The Lion-Tamer.*   London, Nash, and New York, Dodd Mead, 1928.
> *The Captive of Sahara.*   London, Methuen, and New York, Dodd Mead, 1931.
> *The Forest of Terrible Things.*   London, Hutchinson, 1939; as *Jungle Captive*, New York, Dodd Mead, 1939.

OTHER PUBLICATIONS

Other

> *Camping in the Sahara.*   London, Nash, 1926; New York, Dodd Mead, 1927.

*   *   *

Robert Hichens, writing a decade earlier, first made a romantic speciality out of deserts. So, too, Elinor Glyn sent a heroine to consult with a sphinx in the desert (in *His Hour*, 1909). Katharine Rhodes, popular in the 1910's, wrote tales of "the fire and passion of the relentless desert." But it was E.M. Hull who, with *The Sheik* in 1919, first put the desert on the map as a fine place for sexual encounter. The heroine, beautiful but haughty Diana Mayo, pale-skinned but spirited English aristocrat, is the first romantic heroine to be physically assaulted, to learn in the course of 300 pages to enjoy it, and to marry the man who kept on doing it. The morality of whether a man guilty of rape should be ultimately rewarded is highly questionable. Diana's adventures with the Sheik were, possibly, a compensation for E.M. Hull's own lack of amorous excitement, for she was married to a dull pig-breeder called Percy, and, though her real name was Edith Maude, preferred to be called Diana like her ravished heroine.

At the time of writing *The Sheik*, Hull had never set foot in a desert. But this was no disadvantage, for her imagination filled in the background of sunsets, dust, and thirst. The excitement of nightly struggles in the sheik's barbarous yet luxurious tent in the oasis are interspersed with other "eastern" thrills—attacks by rebel Arabs, horse-taming, horse-shooting, servant beating, escapes on horseback into the cruel and inhospitable wastes, the threat of death by vulture or by sandstorm, attempted suicide by the heroine, attempted rape by a rival sheik which proves to be far worse than submission to Diana's own regular assaulter, murder, and many violent deaths of the expendable natives. Erotic passion is linked with fear and pain, and there is a streak of sado-masochism running through the book. The rival rapist is seized by the sheik and throttled to death before Diana's eyes: "With the terrible smile always on his lips, he choked him slowly to death, till the dying man's body arched and writhed in his last agony, till blood burst from his nose and mouth, pouring over the hands that held him like a vice."

The initial rape is distanced, and thus made more discreet, by being reported in the past historic: "She *had* fought until the unequal struggle *had* left her exhausted and helpless in his arms, until her whole body was one agonised ache from the brutal hands that forced her to compliance, until her courageous spirit was crushed by the realization of her own powerlessness." And subsequent struggles are conveyed by constant repetition of crush, kiss, hot, fierce, fire, lips, thrill. In one dialogue between Diana and the sheik, the author finds no less than 11 different variations on "he said" and "she said." Thus, on a single page of text, Diana burst out passionately, and she choked furiously. Then she began desperately. He replied drily. She gasped. He went on evenly. She whispered with dry lips. His reply was given carelessly. She whispered again, but this time jerkily. He continued sarcastically. She murmured faintly.

When she has given up gasping and learned to obey and love, he expresses himself more tenderly. The pinnacle of his passion is a kiss on the upturned palm of her hands. This act of devotion had already been performed in previous romances (e.g., by the blind hero of Florence Barclay's *The Rosary*) but it was in *The Sheik* that it became an established convention, and a gesture which Rudolph Valentino, star of the film version of *The Sheik*, borrowed from the script and used as his trade-mark of passion in other roles.

Diana's relationship with the desert echoes her relationship with the man. The desert both repels and lures her, it tames and brutalises her. "It was the desert at last, the desert that she felt she had been longing for all her life. It was welcoming her softly with the faint rustle of the whispering sand, the mysterious charm of its billowy, shifting surface that seemed beckoning her to penetrate further and further into its unknown obscurities."

Hull followed her highly successful first novel with *The Sons of the Sheik*, but the sons lacked their father's strength and brutality, and the work is sentimental rather than passionate or violent. Hull visited Algeria to produce the non-fiction *Camping in the Sahara* and a small handful of other eastern/desert romance novels, but none had the same impact as her first, which was responsible for sparking off a whole series of sandy romances from other writers, and established the convention of desert passion whose basic elements have remained almost unchanged to the present day. Time and again, never seeming to learn from the experience of others, a spirited girl goes off into the desert and is captured by a mysterious and cruel Arab who tames her. Love blossoms, whereupon it transpires that, for all his foreign ways, he is no arab, but as white-skinned and safely European as herself.

A contemporary, but rival, novelist, Philip Gibbs, wished to make quite clear the distinction between Hull's books, and his own novels, which, while selling well, never reached the peak of *The Sheik*: "My own view is that such freak sales as those of *The Sheik* are not representative of the general reading public of average intelligence—a public which is steadily growing larger and more critical."

—Rachel Anderson

HUNTER, Elizabeth. *See* **CHACE, Isobel**.

HURST, Fannie. American. Born in Hamilton, Ohio, 18 October 1889. Educated at Washington University, St. Louis, B.A. 1909; Columbia University, New York, 1910. Married Jacques S. Danielson in 1915 (died, 1952). Actress in New York before becoming full-time writer. Chairman, Woman's National Housing Commission, 1936-37; Member of the National Advisory Committee to the WPA, 1940-41; U.S. delegate to the U.N. World Health Assembly, Geneva. President, 1936-37, and Vice-President, 1944-46, 1947, Authors League; Trustee, Heckscher Foundation, 1940-60. D.Litt.: Washington University, 1953; Fairleigh Dickinson University, Rutherford, New Jersey. *Died 23 February 1968*.

ROMANCE AND GOTHIC PUBLICATIONS

Novels

Star-Dust: The Story of an American Girl. New York, Harper, 1921.
Lummox. New York, Harper, 1923; London, Cape, 1924.
Appassionata. New York, Knopf, and London, Cape, 1926.
Mannequin. New York, Knopf, 1926.
A President Is Born. New York, Harper, and London, Cape, 1928.
Five and Ten. New York, Harper, and London, Cape, 1929.
Back Street. New York, Cosmopolitan, and London, Cape, 1931.
Imitation of Life. New York, Harper, 1933.
Anitra's Dance. New York, Harper, and London, Cape, 1934.
Great Laughter. New York, Harper, 1936; London, Cape, 1937.
Lonely Parade. New York, Harper, and London, Cape, 1942.
White Christmas. New York, Doubleday, 1942.
Hallelujah. New York, Harper, 1944.
The Hands of Veronica. New York, Harper, and London, Lane, 1947.
Anywoman. New York, Harper, and London, Cape, 1950.
The Name Is Mary. New York, Dell, 1951.
The Man with One Hand. London, Cape, 1953.
Family! New York, Doubleday, 1960.
God Must Be Sad. New York, Doubleday, 1961.
Fool, Be Still. New York, Doubleday, 1964; London, Hale, 1966.

Short Stories

Just Around the Corner: Romance en Casserole. New York, Harper, 1914.
Every Soul Hath Its Song. New York, Harper, 1916.
Gaslight Sonatas. New York, Harper, and London, Hodder and Stoughton, 1918.
Humoresque: A Laugh on Life with a Tear Behind It. New York, Harper, 1919.
The Vertical City. New York, Harper, 1922.
Song of Life. New York, Knopf, and London, Cape, 1927.
Procession. New York, Harper, and London, Cape, 1929.
We Are Ten. New York, Harper, 1937.

Uncollected Short Stories

"Momma and Poppa," in *Saturday Evening Post* (Philadelphia), 19 November 1938.
"Play That Thing," in *Pictorial Review* (New York), March 1939.
"Momma and Her First National Bank," in *Saturday Evening Post* (Philadelphia), 18 March 1939.
"Rosemary for Remembrance," in *Good Housekeeping* (New York), July 1940.
"Sunday Afternoon," in *Woman's Home Companion* (Springfield, Ohio), July 1940.
"What Does Miss Firper Think About?," in *Good Housekeeping* (New York), January 1942.
"Who Is Sylvia?," in *Good Housekeeping* (New York), July 1942.

OTHER PUBLICATIONS

Plays

The Land of the Free, with Harriet Ford (produced New York, 1917).
Back Pay (produced New York, 1921).
Humoresque (produced New York, 1923).
It Is to Laugh (produced New York, 1927).

Screenplays: *The Younger Generation*, with Sonya Levien and Howard J. Green, 1929; *Lummox*, with Elizabeth Meehan, 1930.

Other

No Food with My Meals. New York, Harper, 1935.
Today Is Ladies' Day. New York, Home Institute, 1939.
Anatomy of Me: A Wonderer in Search of Herself. New York, Doubleday, 1958; London, Cape, 1959.

*   *   *

Fannie Hurst may be the worst writer ever to have become an internationally famous best seller. In her heyday, she earned the more-or-less affectionate sobriquet "Queen of the Sob Sisters," but the only aspect of her work likely to inspire tears today would be its truly abysmal style and grammar.

Hurst's stock in trade was the ill-advised golden-hearted woman who gives her all to some unworthy man, and is not thereafter rewarded, in this world at any rate. Of all her many short stories and novels, probably the quintessential Hurst title was *Back Street*, a real tear jerker, later translated into a "three-hankie" moving picture. It is the long-drawn-out, painful story of Ray Schmidt, a flashily attractive young working girl of the turn of the century. Courted and admired by many men, Ray chooses to waste her young womanhood as the guilty secret of an ostensibly respectable married man's life. Her lover, Walter Saxel, is a pillar of the community, blessed with a lovely wife and three adored children. In the "back street" of his life, content to live on stolen bits and scraps of his affection and time, Ray lives a life of seclusion and degradation redeemed only by her lifelong devotion to the man she loves.

Walter loves too, in a selfish and possessive way—but he fails to make any provision for the woman he has kept hidden in a stuffy "love-nest," isolated from the world; and after his untimely death, Ray's declining years are a decrescendo of misery and privation. The moral lesson couldn't be plainer—and could scarcely be wordier, lasting as it does for hundreds of tear-soaked pages.

Fannie Hurst was a product of an age in which the double standards of conduct for men and for women remained for the most part unchallenged; and she well understood the effects upon high spirited youth of censoriousness, continual, critical surveillance, and lack of guidance. If present day readers can still find a lesson worth learning in her writings, it must surely be that of gratitude that they live in a less puritanical era, one in which both men and women have greater freedom to shape their own lives than Fannie Hurst or her creation, Ray Schmidt, ever dreamed of.

—Joan McGrath

HUTTEN, Baroness von.   American.   Born Betsey Riddle in Erie, Pennsylvania, 14 February 1874. Educated in New York. Married Freiherr von Hutten zum Stolzenberg in 1897 (divorced, 1909; regained American nationality in 1938); two sons and two daughters. *Died 26 January 1957.*

ROMANCE AND GOTHIC PUBLICATIONS

Novels

   Miss Carmichael's Conscience: A Study in Fluctuations.   Philadelphia, Lippincott, 1900; London, Pearson, 1902.
   Marr'd in Making.   Phildalephia, Lippincott, and London, Constable, 1901.
   Our Lady of the Beeches.   Boston, Houghton Mifflin, 1902; London, Heinemann, 1907.
   Violett: A Chronicle.   Boston, Houghton Mifflin, 1904.
   Pam.   London, Heinemann, 1904; New York, Dodd Mead, 1905.
   Araby.   New York, Smart Set, 1904.
   He and Hecuba.   New York, Appleton, 1905.
   What Became of Pam.   London, Heinemann, 1906; as *Pam Decides*, New York, Dodd Mead, 1906.
   The One Way Out.   New York, Dodd Mead, 1906.
   The Halo.   New York, Dodd Mead, and London, Methuen, 1907.
   Beechy; or, The Lordship of Love.   New York, Stokes, 1909; as *The Lordship of Love*, London, Hutchinson, 1909.
   Kingsmead.   London, Hutchinson, and New York, Dodd Mead, 1909.
   The Green Patch.   London, Hutchinson, and New York, Stokes, 1910.
   Sharrow.   London, Hutchinson, and New York, Appleton, 1910.
   Mrs. Drummond's Vocation.   London, Heinemann, 1913.
   Maria.   London, Hutchinson, and New York, Appleton, 1914.
   Birds' Fountain.   London, Hutchinson, and New York, Appleton, 1915.
   Mag Pye.   London, Hutchinson, and New York, Appleton, 1917.
   The Bag of Saffron.   London, Hutchinson, 1917; New York, Appleton, 1918.
   Happy House.   London, Hutchinson, 1919; New York, Doran, 1920.
   Mothers-in-Law.   London, Cassell, and New York, Doran, 1922.
   Pam at Fifty.   London, Cassell, and New York, Doran, 1924.
   Julia.   London, Hutchinson, and New York, Doran, 1924.
   Eddy and Edouard.   London, Hutchinson, 1928; New York, Doubleday, 1929.
   The Loves of an Actress.   London, Readers Library, 1929.
   Pam's Own Story.   London, Hutchinson, 1930; Philadelphia, Lippincott, 1931.
   Swan House.   London, Hutchinson, 1930.

Monkey-Puzzle. London, Long, 1932.
Mice for Amusement. London, Hutchinson, 1933; New York, Dutton, 1934.
The Mem. London, Hutchinson, 1934; as *Lives of a Woman*, New York, Dutton, 1935.
Die She Must. London, Hutchinson, 1934; New York, Dutton, 1936.
Cowardly Custard. London, Hutchinson, 1936; as *Gentlemen's Agreement*, New York,
  Dutton, 1936.
The Elgin Marble. London, Hutchinson, 1937; as *Youth Without Glory*, New York,
  Dutton, 1938.
What Happened Is This. London, Hutchinson, 1938; New York, Dutton, 1939.

Short Stories

Helping Hersey. New York, Doran, 1914; London, Skeffington, 1918.
Candy and Other Stories. London, Mills and Boon, 1925.
Flies. London, Mills and Boon, 1927.
The Curate's Egg: A Volume of Stories. London, Mills and Boon, 1930; Freeport, New
  York, Books for Libraries, 1961.
In the Portico and Others. London, Mills and Boon, 1931.
The Notorious Mrs. Gatacre and Other Stories. London, Hutchinson, 1933.

OTHER PUBLICATIONS

Other

The Courtesan: The Life of Cora Pearl. London, Davies, 1933.

Translator, *The Rocket to the Moon*, by Thea von Harbou. New York, World Wide,
  and London, Readers Library, 1930.

*   *   *

Baroness von Hutten produced some 40 novels and collections of short stories, published on both sides of the Atlantic in the first four decades of the century. Her first novel, *Miss Carmichael's Conscience*, was a conventional high-society romance. It was with *Pam* a few years later that resounding success came. *Pam* was immensely popular—it is the story of a society scandal, of the romantic elopement of a beautiful aristocratic English lady and a handsome Italian tenor, who settle in Italy (where people understand about these things and the landscape is romantic); Pam is their illegitimate child, and her story so enthralled readers that Baroness von Hutten produced several sequels, *What Became of Pam, Pam at Fifty*, and *Pam's Own Story*. After *Pam*, Baroness von Hutten's next great success was *Kingsmead* whose charming, wistful young hero, Tommy, Earl of Kingsmead, was much admired.

Baroness von Hutten appeared never to be at a loss for a plot. Her cosmopolitan background allowed her to set her books in Britain, America, and Europe, and her characters came from all levels of society from the highest to the lowest. Some of her settings are very sleazy indeed: Margaret Pye (*Mag Pye*) the daughter of a gentleman fallen on reduced circumstances, is brought up in the Chelsea Workmen's Dwellings, and the central character of *Monkey-Puzzle* is the transparently named Jess Lightfoot, a prostitute who attempts to maintain a respectable front for the sake of her son, the son of a lord. (About the same time as *Monkey-Puzzle*, Baroness von Hutten also produced a biography of Cora Pearl, *The Courtesan*.)

Baroness von Hutten wrote at a great rate, and her writing was frequently praised for its crispness, facility and assurance. Her range as a writer was considerable. Although she made her name as a writer of romantic novels and "family novels" of a fairly melodramatic nature, she also included some psychological portraiture, particularly in *Mothers-in-Law* in which are contrasted the characters of two mothers-in-law (one American, one Italian) of very different upbringing and outlook who meet with the marriage of their children, and in *Eddy and*

Edouard in which the hero, the son of a French aristocrat and her American husband, finds himself torn between two countries and two identities.

With an astute eye to changing tastes in fiction, Baroness von Hutten included in her repertoire from the late 1920's onwards elements of the murder story and the detective story. Most of the short stories in *Flies* are about murders or murderers, whereas the previous volume of short stories, *Candy* was "a collection of pretty and sentimental tales" (*Times Literary Supplement*). *Die She Must* and *What Happened Is This* included elements of the thriller/detective story, though it is characteristic of Baroness von Hutten's capacity to manoeuvre plot and character that neither of these is a straightforward example of its kind.

—Jean Buchanan

HYDE, Eleanor.   *See* **COWEN, Frances**.

INGLIS, Susan.   Pseudonym for Doris Mackie.

ROMANCE AND GOTHIC PUBLICATIONS

Novels

> *Married Man's Girl*.   London, Mills and Boon, 1934.
> *The Marriage of Mary Chard*.   London, Mills and Boon, 1935.
> *She Acted on Impulse*.   London, Mills and Boon, 1936.
> *Uncertain Flame*.   London, Mills and Boon, 1937.
> *Ice Girl*.   London, Mills and Boon, 1938.
> *Tender Only to One*.   London, Mills and Boon, 1938.
> *To Wear Your Ring*.   London, Mills and Boon, 1938.
> *Put Love Aside*.   London, Mills and Boon, 1939.
> *Too Many Men*.   London, Mills and Boon, 1939.
> *Because I Love You*.   London, Mills and Boon, 1940.
> *This Foolish Heart*.   London, Mills and Boon, 1940.
> *Sara Steps In*.   London, Hurst and Blackett, 1947.
> *Dick Heriot's Wife*.   London, Hurst and Blackett, 1947.
> *Jill Takes a Chance*.   London, Hurst and Blackett, 1949.
> *Deb and Destiny*.   London, Hurst and Blackett, 1950.
> *Happiness Can't Wait*.   London, Hurst and Blackett, 1950.
> *Three Men in Her Life*.   London, Hurst and Blackett, 1951.
> *Highland Holiday*.   London, Hurst and Blackett, 1952.

Sister Christine.   London, Hurst and Blackett, 1953.
The Loving Heart.   London, Hurst and Blackett, 1954.
Steven's Wife.   London, Hurst and Blackett, 1958.
The Secret Heart.   London, Hurst and Blackett, 1959.
The Old Hunting Lodge.   London, Hurst and Blackett, 1961.

*   *   *

Susan Inglis is a writer of light contemporary romances set in vague surroundings and peopled by shadowy figures. Most of her books centre round the eternal triangle: the heroine has to choose between a charming but weak and shallow adventurer and a strong, patient, and resourceful hero, to whom she turns in the end, as in *Uncertain Flame, Ice Girl*, and *Deb and Destiny*. Both *The Marriage of Mary Chard* and *Sister Christine* concern marriage for business purposes, in the former, so that Mary can control the wayward daughter of a famous explorer, and in the latter, to satisfy an Indian Rajah that no unmarried woman is nursing his sick son. In both cases the couple's feelings for each other eventually ripen into real love. Other plots deal with the problems of falling for married men (for example, *Married Man's Girl*), or being married to the wrong man (as in *Because I Love You*). *Dick Heriot's Wife* is a slightly stronger story in which a nurse marries a dying man to make him happy, only to find he has left her his estate, which she turns down. Forced to take a job for financial reasons she finds herself nursing the sister of her late husband's cousin, who now owns the estate. Here the characters are more sympathetically realized, and the setting more fully drawn, although the ending, in common with other of her works, is rather too convenient to be credible. *Highland Holiday* also has a more interesting plot, with a varied cast of eight who re-meet each other after a gap of ten years at Allt-na-Culan in the Scottish Highlands.

The majority of Inglis's novels, however, lack variety: her characters are stereotyped, with little depth or individuality, and although the narrative is brisk and set at a determined pace, the themes are slight and insubstantial, set against pale backgrounds that could be anywhere, and written with little involvement and no real suspense. Both style and theme seem to fit the rather conventional "romance" mood of the 1930's and the postwar period.

—Tessa Rose Chester

IRWIN, Margaret (Emma Faith).   British.   Born in London, in 1889. Educated at Clifton School; Oxford University. Married the artist John Robert Monsell in 1929. *Died 11 December 1967*.

ROMANCE AND GOTHIC PUBLICATIONS

Novels

How Many Miles to Babylon?   London, Constable, 1913.
Come Out to Play.   London, Constable, 1914; New York, Doran, 1915.
Out of the House.   London, Constable, and New York, Doran, 1916.
Still She Wished for Company.   Londn, Heinemann, 1924.
Who Will Remember?   New York, Seltzer, 1924.
These Mortals.   London, Heinemann, 1925.

Knock Four Times.   London, Heinemann, and New York, Harcourt Brace, 1927.
Fire Down Below.   London, Heinemann, and New York, Harcourt Brace, 1928.
None So Pretty.   London, Chatto and Windus, and New York, Harcourt Brace, 1930.
Royal Flush: The Story of Minette.   London, Chatto and Windus, and New York, Harcourt Brace, 1932.
The Proud Servant: The Story of Montrose.   London, Chatto and Windus, and New York, Harcourt Brace, 1934.
The Stranger Prince: The Story of Rupert of the Rhine.   London, Chatto and Windus, and New York, Harcourt Brace, 1937.
The Bride: The Story of Louise and Montrose.   London, Chatto and Windus, and New York, Harcourt Brace, 1939.
The Gay Galliard: The Love Story of Mary Queen of Scots.   London, Chatto and Windus, 1941; New York, Harcourt Brace, 1942.
Young Bess.   London, Chatto and Windus, 1944; New York, Harcourt Brace, 1945.
Elizabeth, Captive Princess.   London, Chatto and Windus, and New York, Harcourt Brace, 1948.
Elizabeth and the Prince of Spain.   London, Chatto and Windus, and New York, Harcourt Brace, 1953.

Short Stories

Madame Fears the Dark: Seven Stories and a Play.   London, Chatto and Windus, 1935.
Mrs. Oliver Cromwell and Other Stories.   London, Chatto and Windus, 1940.
Bloodstock and Other Stories.   London, Chatto and Windus, 1953; New York, Harcourt Brace, 1954.

OTHER PUBLICATIONS

Plays

The Happy Man: A Sketch for Acting.   London, Oxford University Press, 1921; Boston, Baker, 1938.
Check to the King of France (juvenile).   London, French, 1933.
Minette (juvenile).   London and New York, French, 1933.
Save the Children (juvenile).   London, French, 1933.
The King's Son, in *Nash's* (London), February 1934.
Madame Fears the Dark (produced London, 1936).   London, Chatto and Windus, 1936.

Other

South Molton Street.   London, Mate, 1927.
The Great Lucifer: A Portrait of Sir Walter Raleigh.   London, Chatto and Windus, and New York, Harcourt Brace, 1960.

*   *   *

The historical novel can be a paraphrase of history with puppet-like characters moving stiffly, it can be a costume drama interspersed with sexual encounters, or it can be an account of what happened illuminated by imaginatively interpreted characters. Margaret Irwin's historical novels are the last kind, and the best known of these is the series about the Stuarts. She began with *Royal Flush* in which the English royal family and the French court are vividly portrayed. Her heroine, Minette, is Charles II's sister who married the horrid Monsieur, perverted brother of Louis XIV. Next came *The Proud Servant* about Montrose the charming Scottish hero, both poet and soldier, who was so badly treated by Charles I of whom she draws a singularly unsympathetic portrait; this is further amplified in *The Stranger Prince*, the story of Rupert of the Rhine, the son of one of England's most popular princesses, Elizabeth Queen of Bohemia. In it Irwin draws lively, fascinating portraits of this branch of the Stuart family and although she is not sympathetic to Charles I she is equally critical of Cromwell, neither of whom did justice to her hero Rupert. One of Rupert's sisters, the tomboy Louise marries Montrose and is heroine of *The Bride*. These books move at a leisurely pace and are full of accurate historical details and delightful revealing touches.

She went back to earlier Stuart history in *The Gay Galliard* which shows us a Mary Queen of Scots probably more sensible and sensitive than she was in real life and makes Bothwell (surely a rogue in reality?) a charming hero. But if her picture of Mary as a romantic, ill-used lady was hard on Elizabeth, Irwin balanced it with a trilogy about the rival queen. *Young Bess, The Captive Princess*, and *Elizabeth and the Prince of Spain* give a vivid, full-length portrait of Elizabeth and are probably her best books. Irwin's interpretation of Elizabeth's thoughts and motives is plausible, and her gift for visualising people brings to life Elizabeth's family, servants, friends, and courtiers.

But Margaret Irwin did not only write historical novels; she had a light hand with fantasy too. *These Mortals*, for instance, is a full-blown fairy tale for adults about an enchanter's daughter who can make herself invisible and uses this gift for clandestine meetings with her imprisoned lover-prince. After a traditional change of the substance for the shadow, the story leads one to draw two equally traditional morals—that looks are not everything and that love conquers all. *Still She Wished for Company* is a ghost story that, Janus-like, faces both ways: a girl in the present is dissatisfied with her life and is looking for her ideal man whose 18th-century portrait she has cherished since she was a schoolgirl. This story is interwoven with that of a young girl in the 18th century whose ex-Hellfire club brother is using her to find his ideal woman, a girl he has glimpsed in dreams since boyhood. The girl in the present sees ghosts of the past and the girl in the past sees into the future with near fatal results.

All these books are written in elegant, lucid prose and although they have an air of sadness, they are a pleasure to read.

—Pamela Cleaver

JACKSON, Shirley (Hardie). American. Born in San Francisco, California, 14 December 1919. Educated at Burlingame High School, California; Brighton High School, Rochester, New York; University of Rochester, 1934-36; Syracuse University, New York, 1937-40, B.A. 1940. Married the writer Stanley Edgar Hyman in 1940; two daughters and two sons. Recipient: Mystery Writers of America Edgar Allan Poe Award, 1961; Syracuse University Arents Medal, 1965. *Died 8 August 1965.*

ROMANCE AND GOTHIC PUBLICATIONS

Novels

    The Road Through the Wall. New York, Farrar Straus, 1948; as *The Other Side of the Street*, New York, Pyramid, 1956.

Hangsaman. New York, Farrar Straus, and London, Gollancz, 1951.
The Bird's Nest. New York, Farrar Straus, 1954; London, Joseph, 1955; as *Lizzie*, New York, New American Library, 1957.
The Sundial. New York, Farrar Straus, and London, Joseph, 1958.
The Haunting of Hill House. New York, Viking Press, 1959; London, Joseph, 1960.
We Have Always Lived in the Castle. New York, Viking Press, 1962; London, Joseph, 1963.

Short Stories

The Lottery; or, The Adventures of James Harris. New York, Farrar Straus, 1949; London, Gollancz, 1950.

OTHER PUBLICATIONS

Plays

The Lottery, adaptation of her own short story, in *Best Television Plays 1950-1951,* edited by William I. Kauffman. New York, Merlin Press, 1952.
The Bad Children: A Play in One Act for Bad Children. Chicago, Dramatic Publishing Company, 1959.

Other

Life among the Savages. New York, Farrar Straus, 1953; London, Joseph, 1954.
The Witchcraft of Salem Village (juvenile). New York, Random House, 1956.
Raising Demons. New York, Farrar Straus, and London, Joseph, 1957.
Special Delivery: A Useful Book for Brand-New Mothers.... Boston, Little Brown, 1960; as *And Baby Makes Three...,* New York, Grosset and Dunlap, 1960.
9 Magic Wishes (juvenile). New York, Crowell Collier, 1963.
Famous Sally (juvenile). New York, Harlin Quist, 1966.
The Magic of Shirley Jackson, edited by Stanley Edgar Hyman. New York, Farrar Straus, 1966.
Come Along with Me: Part of a Novel, Sixteen Stories, and Three Lectures, edited by Stanley Edgar Hyman. New York, Viking Press, 1968.

Critical Study: *Shirley Jackson* by Lenemaja Friedman, Boston, Twayne, 1975.

*   *   *

Shirley Jackson's gothic fiction substitutes decaying mansions for castle ruins; presences, stirrings, and psychotic imaginings for straightforward ghostly sightings; neurotic spinsters, turned inward in despair, for traditional romantic heroines; and evil that grows out of the internal fears and anxieties of individuals and communites for external forces. Yet hers is still a gothic world of dreams and shadows, of sinister threats and nameless fears, of the familiar grown unfamiliar. Reality and nightmare merge in tales of terror, frustration, loneliness, and isolation: a frightening return to childhood in "The Bus," phantom lovers in "The Beautiful Stranger" and "The Daemon Lover," modern daytime ghosts in "The Visit," murderous ghostly hitchikers in "Home," psychic voices in *Come Along with Me,* oldsters who prove witches at heart in "The Little House," "Trial by Combat," "Whistler's Grandmother," and "The Possibility of Evil," and horrifying human cruelty in "The Renegade," "All She Said Was Yes," and·"The Lottery."

Hangsaman, The Bird's Nest, and *We Have Always Lived in the Castle* are more psychological than gothic, given their central focus on the disintegration and fragmentation of personality, but partake of gothic elements, sensibilities, and themes. *Hangsaman* unveils the private world of an ill-adjusted 17-year-old who retreats into Tarot cards, a secret diary, and friendship with an imaginary friend to compensate for being an unpopular outsider. She finally perceives her schizoid condition as dangerous in a late night foray in a dark, wooded area where her friend becomes elusive and unreal, a ghostly, threatening wraith that glides eerily through trees. *The Bird's Nest*, with its shifting points of view, exposes the terror within: conflicting and antagonistic parts of a single self, wherein good and evil are so separated that one persecutes and seeks to discredit the other in unnerving ways, from destruction of property to mud sandwiches to attempted murder. *We Have Always Lived in the Castle* focuses on a lively, likeable young psychotic, Merricat, who poisoned four family members with arsenic and left a fifth crippled. Preoccupied with death and the supernatural, with signs, omens, and hexes to ward off evil, her only friend a cat, she dreams of murder and mayhem, and resorts to pyrotechnics when a greedy, intruding cousin threatens to tempt away her sister. Later the two sisters withdraw into their vine-covered manor, a burned, smashed castle-like ruin, where they live a secret life, nourished by private dreams and the irregular offerings of guilty townspeople.

Like *We Have Always Lived in the Castle*, Jackson's two clearly gothic works, *The Sundial* and *The Haunting of Hill House*, center on a large dark mansion where mysterious and inexplicable events occur. In *The Sundial* it is a 40-room New England mansion, complete with symmetrical architecture, cryptic maxims carved in frontispieces, and formal gardens with maze and lake; but it is marred by a damp grotto, vicious swans, and a misaligned sundial. The story begins with a funeral and hints of foul play, followed by warnings from the dead, voodoo dolls, seances, the mysterious death of a queen figure, and a storm that batters the house and cuts its occupants off from the outside world. Symbolic warnings abound: a snake glides menacingly across the carpet; a glass picture window shatters; statues prove warm; a non-existent gardener appears and disappears; mist shrouds the gardens; a young virgin distinguishes fortune's sign in a hazy mirror. In *The Haunting of Hill House* four intelligent, receptive people meet by prearrangement to record psychic phenomena in Hill House: "a house without kindness," an isolated structure of concentric circles and odd angles, with dangerous towers, dark musty rooms, unfriendly spirits, and a history of "accidental" deaths. The spirits which stir when the gates are locked and night falls take the form of a sub-zero cold spot; hollow knockings, small squeaking sounds, giggles and quiet laughter; turning doorknobs, moving furniture, swaying walls; an unidentified hand in the dark and a small creature darting through the house, writing summons on walls in chalk and blood. The most vulnerable researcher, subject to a stone-throwing poltergeist in her youth and a loveless, frustrated adulthood, tries to identify with her fellow researchers, but, when repelled, begins to hear voices, identify with the house, and seek to become one of its spirits; she claims to obey its summons, for "no one else could satisfy it."

Thus, Shirley Jackson's main contribution to the genre is not her use of updated gothic trappings, but her focus on the "gothic" mind, the psychology of the outsider, the loner, who begins to construct her own reality. For Jackson the real horror is being shut out of the group, being alienated for whatever cause, and, as a result, losing a grasp of what is real and what is not. By carefully controlling point of view, Jackson causes the reader to share in this ambiguity of perception and to vacillate in understanding what is imagination, what reality. Thus she goes beyond the one-dimensional, imposed gothic to deal with the irregular and the imbalanced that arise out of genuine human fears, fears of rejection, of hate, of singularity, of isolation.

—Gina Macdonald

JACOB, Naomi (Ellington). Also wrote as Ellington Gray. British. Born in Ripon, Yorkshire, 1 July 1884. Educated at Middlesborough High School. Teacher in a Middlesborough school; secretary and companion to Marguerite Broadfoot and Eva Moore, music hall entertainers; actress; supervisor in munitions factory during World War I; worked as a Welfare Officer in Overseas Service during World War II. Lived in Sirmione, Italy, after 1930. *Died 26 August 1964.*

ROMANCE AND GOTHIC PUBLICATIONS

Novels

    Jacob Ussher. London, Butterworth, 1925.
    Rock and Sand. London, Butterworth, 1926.
    Power. London, Butterworth, 1927.
    The Plough. London, Butterworth, 1928.
    Saffroned Bridesails (as Ellington Gray). London, Butterworth, 1928.
    The Man Who Found Himself. London, Butterworth, 1929; revised edition, London, Pan, 1952.
    The Beloved Physician. London, Butterworth, 1930.
    Gollantz Saga:
      1. *The Founder of the House.* London, Hutchinson, 1935; New York, Macmillan, 1956.
      2. *That Wild Lie—.* London, Hutchinson, 1930.
      3. *Young Emmanuel.* London, Hutchinson, 1932; New York, New American Library, 1973.
      4. *Four Generations.* London, Hutchinson, and New York, Macmillan, 1934.
      5. *Private Gollantz.* London, Hutchinson, 1943.
      6. *Gollantz: London, Paris, Milan.* London, Hutchinson, 1948.
      7. *Gollantz and Partners.* London, Hutchinson, 1958.
    Tales of the Broad Acres. London, Hutchinson, 1955.
      Roots. London, Hutchinson, 1931.
      The Loaded Stick. London, Hutchinson, 1934; New York, Macmillan, 1935.
      Sally Scarth. London, Hutchinson, 1940.
    Seen Unknown.... London, Hutchinson, 1931.
    Props. London, Hutchinson, 1932.
    Groping. London, Hutchinson, 1933.
    Poor Straws! London, Hutchinson, 1933.
    Honour Comes Back—. London, Hutchinson, and New York, Macmillan, 1935.
    Time Piece. London, Hutchinson, 1936; New York, Macmillan, 1937.
    Barren Metal. London, Hutchinson, and New York, Macmillan, 1936.
    Fade Out. London, Hutchinson, and New York, Macmillan, 1937.
    The Lenient God. London, Hutchinson, 1937; New York, Macmillan, 1938.
    Straws in Amber. London, Hutchinson, 1938; New York, Macmillan, 1939.
    No Easy Way. London, Hutchinson, 1938.
    Full Meridian. London, Hutchinson, 1939; New York, Macmillan, 1940.
    This Porcelain Clay. London, Hutchinson, and New York, Macmillan, 1939.
    They Left the Land. London, Hutchinson, and New York, Macmillan, 1940.
    Under New Management. London, Hutchinson, 1941.
    The Cap of Youth. London, Hutchinson, and New York, Macmillan, 1941.
    Leopards and Spots. London, Hutchinson, 1942.
    White Wool. London, Hutchinson, 1944.
    Susan Crowther. London, Hutchinson, 1945.
    Honour's a Mistress. London, Hutchinson, 1947.
    A Passage Perilous. London, Hutchinson, 1948.
    Mary of Delight. London, Hutchinson, 1949.
    Every Other Gift. London, Hutchinson, 1950.

The Heart of the House. London, Hutchinson, 1951.
A Late Lark Singing. London, Hutchinson, 1952.
The Morning Will Come. London, Hutchinson, 1953.
Antonia. London, Hutchinson, 1954.
Second Harvest. London, Hutchinson, 1954.
The Irish Boy: A Romantic Biography. London, Hutchinson, 1955.
Wind on the Heath. London, Hutchinson, 1956.
What's to Come. London, Hutchinson, 1958.
Search for a Background. London, Hutchinson, 1960.
Three Men and Jennie. London, Hutchinson, 1960.
Strange Beginning. London, Hale, 1961.
Great Black Oxen. London, Hale, 1962.
Yolanda. London, Hale, 1963.
Long Shadows. London, Hale, 1964.
Flavia. London, Hale, 1965.

OTHER PUBLICATIONS

Play

The Dawn (produced Glasgow, 1923).

Other

Me: A Chronicle about Other People. London, Hutchinson, 1933.
Me—in the Kitchen. London, Hutchinson, 1935.
Our Marie: Marie Lloyd: A Biography. London, Hutchinson, 1936.
Me—Again. London, Hutchinson, 1937.
More about Me. London, Hutchinson, 1939.
Shadow Drama, by Nina Abbott, completed by Jacob. London, Duckworth, 1940.
Me—In War-Time. London, Hutchinson, 1940.
Balance Suspended, by Nina Abbott, completed by Jacob. London, Duckworth, 1942.
Me and the Mediterranean. London, Hutchinson, 1945.
Me—Over There. London, Hutchinson, 1947.
Opera in Italy, with James C. Robertson. London, Hutchinson, 1948; Freeport, New
    York, Books for Libraries, 1970.
Me and Mine, 'You and Yours. London, Hutchinson, 1949.
Me—Looking Back. London, Hutchinson, 1950.
Impressions from Italy. London, Hutchinson, 1952.
Robert, Nana, and—Me. London, Hutchinson, 1952.
Just about Us. London, Hutchinson, 1953.
Me—Likes and Dislikes. London, Hutchinson, 1954.
Prince China. London, Hutchinson, 1955.
Me—Yesterday and To-day. London, Kimber, 1957.
Me—and the Stags. London, Kimber, 1962.
Me—and the Swans. London, Kimber, 1963.
Me—Thinking Things Over. London, Kimber, 1964.

Theatrical Activities:

Actress: **Plays** — Julia Cragworthy in *The Young Idea* by Noël Coward, London, 1923; Mrs.
Hackitt in *The Ringer* by Edgar Wallace, London, 1926; Ma Gennochio in *The Nutmeg Tree*
by Margery Sharp, London, 1941; Nurse in *Love for Love* by Congreve, London, 1943.

Critical Study: *Naomi Jacob: The Seven Ages of "Me"* by James Norbury, London, Kimber, 1965.

* * *

The full list of Naomi Jacob's output over the years is staggering. How could any writer have had so much to say? She accomplished her impressive feat by recording the ordinary, but by doing so in a generously florid style that ran to untold pages. She tended to become infatuated with the characters of her own invention—the "good" ones, at any rate. Grudgingly she would sometimes allow some tiny defect or character flaw to one of her pets, such as Emmanuel Gollantz, patriarch of her popular multi-generational family saga, but would hasten to better than redeem it with heaped-up evidence of her dear one's excellence. Her villains, by contrast, are of deepest dye. Julian Gollantz, one of the black sheep, is a near approach to the mustachio-twirling "bad guys" of the early cinema: relentlessly evil, unmotivated in his Iago-like malice, and a foil for the many virtuous Gollantz characters.

For all her broad and sweeping strokes, Naomi Jacob was somehow unable, though infinitely willing, to create a convincingly *important* character. Good or bad (and some of them are indeed quite interesting and/or likeable; one wants to learn their eventual fates), her people do not live up to her own obviously high opinion of them. They remain—ordinary. Like the rest of us, they are earthbound with family concerns of enormous complication and difficulty; though usually quite comfortably fixed, the occasional one must pinch and scrape a little; all are deeply concerned with the mechanics of making a living, with their feet solidly planted on the commerical ground. This does indeed set them apart from the creations of a great many other authors of the romantic novel, whose characters appear to exist like the lilies of the field, neither toiling nor spinning, living only for love.

As well as working, Naomi Jacob's people do love, however. Intensely, burningly, with enormous fervor, self-sacrifice, and dedication: each of them adores—some other ordinary creation. Jacob has a habit of overburdening little characters with giant, heroic emotions that they cannot gracefully sustain. Although this inevitably flattens the sought-after effect of romantic magnificence, it may be that this very quality of "commonplaceness" served to endear her undeniably popular novels to a large, faithful, and "ordinary" public, after all.

—Joan McGrath

JAMES, Margaret. *See* **BENNETTS, Pamela**.

JOHN, Nancy. *See* **BUCKINGHAM, Nancy**.

JOHNSON, Barbara Ferry.   American.   Born in Grosse Pointe, Michigan, 7 July 1923. Educated at Northwestern University, Evanston, Illinois, B.S. 1945; Clemson University, South Carolina, M.A. 1964. Married William David Johnson in 1947; one son and two daughters. Associate Editor, *American Lumberman* magazine, Chicago, 1945-48; high school English teacher, Myrtle Beach, South Carolina, 1960-62. Since 1964, member of the English Department, Columbia College, South Carolina. Agent: Writers House Inc., 21 West 26th Street, New York, New York 10010. Address: Route 1, Box 214, Shallotte, North Carolina 28459, U.S.A.

ROMANCE AND GOTHIC PUBLICATIONS

Novels

> *Lionors*.   New York, Avon, 1975; London, Sphere, 1977.
> *Delta Blood*.   New York, Avon, 1977; London, Sphere, 1978.
> *Tara's Song*.   New York, Avon, 1978; London, Sphere, 1980.
> *Homeward Winds the River*.   New York, Avon, 1979.
> *The Heirs of Love*.   New York, Avon, 1980.

*   *   *

Barbara Ferry Johnson is most interested in the confrontation of men and women from alien cultures and alien backgrounds; she depicts the way love helps them transcend personal prejudices and personal limitations to come to terms with another's values and to learn to see and think with new eyes. In *Tara's Song* an English earl's daughter, taken from a convent in a Viking raid, learns to love a Viking prince and his family, appreciate their values, and fight for their causes. In *Lionors* King Arthur's first love must learn from Merlin and Arthur to see with Nature's eyes and to sacrifice personal need for a nation's vision as her lover is transformed from an orphan of little significance to king of England. In *Delta Blood* and *Homeward Winds the River* a New Orleanean octoroon, Leah, attempts to escape the restrictions imposed by her black blood, but love and war transform her perceptions and lead her to defend Southern values and Southern traditions against Union barbarism and hypocrisy, to work uncomplainingly as a nurse comforting wounded Confederate soldiers, and to help save from death and destruction both them and a plantation (the symbol of the slave tradition which has constricted and limited her life). In *Homeward* she moves North to fulfill her life-long dream—to pass for white, only to learn that each person is trapped in some way, if not by skin color, then by differences in values and ways of life, and that her heritage, though black, is also Southern. The final book in this trilogy, *The Heirs of Love*, traces her children's attempts to come to terms with their white/black heritage and to discover who and what they are and where they truly belong. In each of these books Johnson's heroines must adapt to changing conditions of war and conflict, death, disease, and drudgery, and somehow maintain their spirit and inspire their men to endure seemingly impossible difficulties.

Mystic elements play important roles in these sagas: magic runes embodying ancient secrets in *Tara's Song*, seers and magicians in *Lionors*, and voodoo rites and voodoo princesses in the New Orleans trilogy. Yet each is down-to-earth in its specific detailing of the difficult day-to-day skills women in different ages have had to master, particularly skills vital to the continuation of life and comfort, work born of necessity in hard times—learning to cultivate the land, organize help, preserve and store food, sew, redecorate, rear children, nurse, and even fight. Intrigued by the genetic complexities that reproduce, modify and mold each generation, Johnson examines child-parent conflicts, advocates different approaches for different psychologies, and suggests the difficulty of ever predicting the final results of environment and genes.

But the focus of her books is on the psychology of women's love—Lionors who must hide her love despite her deep romantic yearnings; Tara who fears love's betrayal and learns its selflessness only after suffering slavery, imprisonment, and culture shock in Turkey; and Leah whose emotional and physical needs lead her to become a rich plantation owner's mistress when her deeper longing is to be wife and mother. Each of her heroines is threatened by or endures brutal attack by libidinous males; each finds strength and comfort in a deeply romantic and sexually satisfying love that demands sacrifice and understanding. Each must deal with rivals in love; and each must help her beloved regain his sense of vitality and manhood which injury and humiliation threaten.

Though Barbara Ferry Johnson makes an occasional minor slip in locale and custom, in the main her books conjure up past times with delightful detail, clearly and carefully evoking the hardships and pleasures of by-gone ages to make the alien familiar.

—Gina Macdonald

JOHNSTON, Mary.   American.   Born in Buchanan, Virginia, 21 November 1870. Educated at home. *Died 9 May 1936.*

ОMANCE AND GOTHIC PUBLICATIONS

Novels

The Prisoners of Hope: A Tale of Colonial Virginia.   Boston, Houghton Mifflin, 1898; as *The Old Dominion*, London, Constable, 1899.

To Have and to Hold.   Boston, Houghton Mifflin, 1900; as *By Order of the Company*, London, Constable, 1900.

Audrey.   Boston, Houghton Mifflin, and London, Constable, 1902.

Sir Mortimer.   New York, Harper, and London, Constable, 1904.

Lewis Rand.   Boston, Houghton Mifflin, and London, Constable, 1908.

The Long Roll.   Boston, Houghton Mifflin, 1911.

Cease Firing.   Boston, Houghton Mifflin, and London, Constable, 1912.

Hagar.   Boston, Houghton Mifflin, and London, Constable, 1913.

The Witch.   Boston, Houghton Mifflin, and London, Constable, 1914.

The Fortunes of Garin.   Boston, Houghton Mifflin, and London, Constable, 1915.

Foes.   New York, Harper, 1918; as *The Laird of Glenfernie*, London, Constable, 1919.

Michael Forth.   New York, Harper, 1919; London, Constable, 1920.

Sweet Rocket.   New York, Harper, and London, Constable, 1920.

Silver Cross.   Boston, Little Brown, and London, Butterworth, 1922.

1492.   Boston, Little Brown, 1922; as *Admiral of the Ocean-Sea*, London, Butterworth, 1923.

Croatan.   Boston, Little Brown, 1923; London, Butterworth, 1924.

The Slave Ship.   Boston, Little Brown, 1924; London, Butterworth, 1925.

The Great Valley.   Boston, Little Brown, and London, Butterworth, 1926.

The Exile.   Boston, Little Brown, and London, Butterworth, 1927.

Hunting Shirt.   Boston, Little Brown, 1931; London, Butterworth, 1932.

Miss Delicia Allen.   Boston, Little Brown, and London, Butterworth, 1933.

Drury Randall.   Boston, Little Brown, 1934; London, Butterworth, 1935.

Short Stories

The Wanderers.   Boston, Houghton Mifflin, and London, Constable, 1917.

Uncollected Short Stories

"Nemesis," in *Century* (New York), May 1923.
"Tree," in *Good Housekeeping* (New York), May 1923.
"Buccaneer," in *Ladies Home Journal* (Philadelphia), June 1928.
"Black Lace," in *Ladies Home Journal* (Philadelphia), August 1928.
"Two Business Men," in *Harper's* (New York), September 1928.
"Mockingbird," in *Ladies Home Journal* (Philadelphia), November 1928.
"Elephants Through the Country," in *O. Henry Memorial Award Prize Stories 1929*,
    edited by Blanch C. Williams.   New York, Doubleday, 1929.
"The Angel," in *Ladies Home Journal* (Philadelphia), January 1929.
"The Baptizing," in *Ladies Home Journal* (Philadelphia), April 1929.
"Church Festival," in *Bookman* (New York), September 1929.
"Buried Silver," in *Ladies Home Journal* (Philadelphia), September 1929.
"That Cold," in *Ladies Home Journal* (Philadelphia), November 1929.
"End of the World," in *Ladies Home Journal* (Philadelphia), March 1930.
"After the Storm," in *American Magazine* (Springfield, Ohio), August 1930.
"Lion Loose!," in *Ladies Home Journal* (Philadelphia), October 1930.
"Doctor Barnaby's Vision," in *Pictorial Review* (New York), December 1930.
"The Attic Room," in *Ladies Home Journal* (Philadelphia), December 1935.

OTHER PUBLICATIONS

Play

The Goddess of Reason (produced New York, 1909).   Boston, Houghton Mifflin, and
    London, Constable, 1907.

Other

An Address Read at Vicksburg....   Privately printed, 1907.
The Status of Women.   Richmond, Virginia, Equal Suffrage League of Virginia, 1909.
The Reason Why.   Privately printed, 1910 (?).
To the House of Governors (address).   New York, National American Women Suffrage
    Association, 1912.
Pioneers of the Old South: A Chronicle of English Colonial Beginnings.   New Haven,
    Connecticut, Yale University Press, 1918.

Critical Study: *Three Virginia Writers* by George C. Longest, Boston, Hall, 1978.

*   *   *

For all practical purposes, Mary Johnston's career began in 1898 with publication of *The
Prisoners of Hope*, a romance of colonial Virginia. That initial historical romance acts as a
paradigm of her work in the genre: superior story-telling and romantic sensitivity to landscape
are wedded to an acute interest in colonial Virginia history. Although frequently compared by
early reviewers to Thackeray, Johnston lacked Thackeray's insight into human nature. In the
first romance, her portrait of Sir William Berkeley, for example, is wooden, her dialogue

artificial. Emphasis in her romances clearly falls on action born of quest. Character, at best, is the by-product of quest, or the by-product of a Victorian ideal.

The most successful of her historical romances, however, was *To Have and to Hold*, a considerably more refined romance than *The Prisoners of Hope*, and the number one best-seller for 1900. Grounded in Virginia history, the romance involves the 1622 Indian massacre of Jamestown. It owes its appeal, however, as Ronald Cella has observed, to the love story of Captain Ralph Percy and Lady Jocelyn Smith and the triangle created by her former suitor, the villainous Lord Carnal. The romance, melodramatic though it may be, remains her best-known work.

Audrey, a romance set in colonial Virginia, capitalizes on the vogue created by *To Have and to Hold*. Emphasizing manners, customs, and history, the romance, as *The Independent* observed on 20 November 1902, made a "romantic rainbow of colonial civilization in Virginia." Replacing the traditional forest scene with a colorful town scene, the setting of *Audrey* becomes "illustrative of character" (*New York Times*, 22 February 1902).

Sir Mortimer, set in late 16th-century England; *The Fortunes of Garin*, set in 11th-century France; *Foes*, set in Jacobite Scotland during the 1735 uprising; and *Silver Cross*, set in Tudor England, suggest Johnston's continued exploitation of the genre and her diminishing talent for it. In the European romances the history is superficial and the characterization too frequently "ideal." *Silver Cross*, however, is the most important work in the European corpus. Johnston's mixture of superstition and mysticism in *Silver Cross* creates, as William Rose Benét early perceived, a "telegraphic" style bordering on pointillism (*New York Evening Post*, 18 March 1922). The style, although inappropriate to the romance, does, however, document Johnston's conflicting interests in romance and novel genres.

Croatan, *The Great Valley*, and *Hunting Shirt* mark Johnston's return to her best mode. In all three romances, setting is of major importance, historical event is motivation, character is ideal, and quest suggests the coherence and definition of the plot. *Croatan* achieves a James Fenimore Cooper suspense in its rendering of pursuit and escape. As *The Athenaeum* reviewer observed (17 July 1926), *The Great Valley* owes its success to its depiction of the effect of wilderness on "natures marked out by a poetic mysticism of Celtic birth." Somewhat similarly, *Hunting Shirt* creates a highly successful view of the link between American Indians and Scottish settlers. All these romances are considerably strengthened by the author's familiarity with Virginia setting.

—George C. Longest

JOHNSTON, Velda.   Also writes as Veronica Jason.

ROMANCE AND GOTHIC PUBLICATIONS

Novels

> *Along a Dark Path*. New York, Dodd Mead, 1967; Aylesbury, Buckinghamshire, Milton House, 1974.
> *House above Hollywood*. New York, Dodd Mead, 1968; Aylesbury, Buckinghamshire, Milton House, 1974.
> *A Howling in the Woods*. New York, Dodd Mead, 1968; London, Hale, 1969.

I Came to the Castle. New York, Dodd Mead, 1969; as *Castle Perilous*, London, Hale, 1971.
The Light in the Swamp. New York, Dodd Mead, 1970; London, Hale, 1972.
The Phantom Cottage. New York, Dodd Mead, 1970; London, Hale, 1971.
The Face in the Shadows. New York, Dodd Mead, 1971; London, Hale, 1973.
The People on the Hill. New York, Dodd Mead, 1971; as *Circle of Evil*, London, Hale, 1972.
The Mourning Trees. New York, Dodd Mead, 1972; Aylesbury, Buckinghamshire, Milton House, 1974.
The Late Mrs. Fonsell. New York, Dodd Mead, 1972; Aylesbury, Buckinghamshire, Milton House, 1974.
The White Pavilion. New York, Dodd Mead, 1973; Aylesbury, Buckinghamshire, Milton House, 1974.
Masquerade in Venice. New York, Dodd Mead, 1973; Aylesbury, Buckinghamshire, Milton House, 1974.
I Came to the Highlands. New York, Dodd Mead, 1974; Aylesbury, Buckinghamshire, Milton House, 1975.
The House on the Left Bank. New York, Dodd Mead, 1975.
A Room with Dark Mirrors. New York, Dodd Mead, 1975; London, Prior, 1976.
Deveron Hall. New York, Dodd Mead, 1976; London, Prior, 1977.
The Frenchman. New York, Dodd Mead, and London, Prior, 1976.
The Etruscan Smile. New York, Dodd Mead, 1977; London, W.H. Allen, 1980.
The Hour Before Midnight. New York, Dodd Mead, 1978; London, W.H. Allen, 1981.
The Silver Dolphin. New York, Dodd Mead, 1979.
The People from the Sea. New York, Dodd Mead, 1979.
A Presence in an Empty Room. New York, Dodd Mead, 1980.
The Stone Maiden. New York, Dodd Mead, 1980.
The Fateful Summer. New York, Dodd Mead, 1981.
So Wild a Heart (as Veronica Jason). New York, New American Library, 1981.

Uncollected Short Stories

"Exit Running," in *American Magazine* (Springfield Ohio), March 1950.
"Built-In Smile," in *American Magazine* (Springfield, Ohio), June 1951.
"Those High-Society Blues," in *Saturday Evening Post* (Philadelphia), 24 April 1954.
"Every Minute Counts," in *McCalls* (Dayton, Ohio), April 1957.
"Phantom Cottage," in *Redbook* (Dayton, Ohio), December 1969.
"Strange Welcome," in *Redbook* (Dayton, Ohio), May 1970.

*   *   *

From the prolific pen of Velda Johnston come historical and contemporary romance mysteries in which young ladies find themselves plunged into perilous circumstances where their very lives are endangered. Usually an unsolved murder has taken place and the heroine, sometimes innocently but often because of her own curious nature, becomes the killer's next target. Somewhere close by there is always a man to provide romantic interest, and though the course of this love does not always run smoothly, by the climax of the novel their love has been declared. Often, but not always, it is this man's intervention which saves the lady in distress from the machinations of the villain.

In the historical novel *The Late Mrs. Fonsell* Irene is forced into a marriage with the dark, brooding Jason Fonsell. Many years before, Jason's stepmother had been mysteriously and brutally murdered. Irene, intrigued by this mystery, brings the killer's unwelcome attentions upon herself. Meanwhile, the marriage of convenience to Jason eventually becomes one of love. In the end it is Jason who comes to Irene's rescue as she is stalked by the killer. The more recent novel, *A Presence in an Empty Room*, has an added touch of the supernatural. The evil antagonist whom the newly married Susan Summerslee must overcome is the spirit of her husband's first wife, Irene, who had plotted the death of her husband by paying someone to sabotage his private plane. Instead it is she who dies in the fiery crash. Irene, however, had not counted on the strength of Susan who after much travail effectively exorcises the demon.

What makes Johnston's characters so appealing is their believability. Most of the women are attractive without being overwhelmingly beautiful, and the men, while virile, do not necessarily carry a heavy macho image. Her contemporary heroines are firmly rooted in their middle-class origins and usually have a career, while those of the historical periods belong to the genteel class but with families often skirting the edges of poverty. Almost all of these women have suffered some tragedy or mishap. In *The Frenchman* Joan, an editor for a woman's magazine, contemplates a trip to Europe in order to escape unhappy memories of a disastrous love affair with a married man. Diana (*The People from the Sea*) must take a leave of absence from her job as a children's book editor to recover from a breakdown following divorce. In the historical novel *I Came to the Highlands* Elizabeth, thinking she has lost the love of John, allows herself to succumb to the charms of Charles Stuart, pretender to the English throne, and gives birth to his illegitimate son.

Another attraction of Johnston's novels is the richness of her settings which come from her obvious intimate knowledge of the locations for her stories. Usually the mystery unfolds in an isolated area of wild beauty, often Eastern Long Island or Northern Italy. But her descriptions of cities are equally well done. In the contemporary novel *The Frenchman* and the historical novel *Masquerade in Venice* the reader feels the enchantment of this age-old city of canals.

For all the romance and mystery that are the hallmarks of a Johnston story there is little emphasis on sex (most taking place by innuendo), and there is minimal description of violence. This author is an excellent storyteller. All of her novels are well plotted with neat twists and turns that give an element of drama and excitement all the way through. Still, her stories follow the standard gothic formula and with this in mind the reader can take comfort in the certainty of the heroine's eventual triumph.

—Patricia Altner

KANE, Julia. *See* **ROBINS, Denise.**

KELLOW, Kathleen. *See* **HOLT, Victoria.**

KENNEDY, Margaret. British. Born in London, in 1896. Educated at Cheltenham Ladies College; Somerville College, Oxford, B.A. in history. Married David (later Sir David) Davies in 1925 (died, 1964); one son and two daughters. Fellow, Royal Society of Literature. *Died 31 July 1967.*

ROMANCE AND GOTHIC PUBLICATIONS

Novels

The Ladies of Lyndon. London, Heinemann, 1923; New York, Doubleday, 1925.
The Constant Nymph. London, Heinemann, 1924; New York, Doubleday, 1925.
Red Sky at Morning. London, Heinemann, and New York, Doubleday, 1927.
The Fool of the Family. London, Heinemann, and New York, Doubleday, 1930.
Return I Dare Not. London, Heinemann, and New York, Doubleday, 1931.
A Long Time Ago. London, Heinemann, and New York, Doubleday, 1932.
Together and Apart. London, Cassell, 1936; New York, Random House, 1937.
The Midas Touch. London, Cassell, 1938; New York, Random House, 1939.
The Feast. London, Cassell, and New York, Rinehart, 1950.
Lucy Carmichael. New York, Rinehart, and London, Macmillan, 1951.
Troy Chimneys. New York, Rinehart, 1952; London, Macmillan, 1953.
The Oracles. London, Macmillan, 1955; as *Act of God*, New York, Rinehart, 1955.
The Heroes of Clone. London, Macmillan, 1957; as *The Wild Swan*, New York, Rinehart, 1957.
A Night in Cold Harbour. London, Macmillan, and New York, St. Martin's Press, 1960.
The Forgotten Smile. London, Macmillan, 1961; New York, Macmillan, 1962.
Not in the Calendar. London, Macmillan, and New York, Macmillan, 1964.

Short Stories

A Long Week-End. London, Heinemann, and New York, Doubleday, 1927.
Dewdrops. London, Heinemann, 1928.
The Game and the Candle. London, Heinemann, 1928.
Women at Work. London, Macmillan, 1966.

Uncollected Short Stories

"Pussycat Pennefeather," in *Legion Book*, edited by H.C. Minchin. London, Cassell, 1929.
"Fanny Barnes," in *Mr. Fothergill's Plot*, edited by John Fothergill. London, Oxford University Press, 1931.
"The Gift," in *Good Housekeeping* (New York), September 1931.
"Her Wedding Day," in *Munsey's* (New York), April 1932.
"While There's Life There's Hope," in *Munsey's* (New York), October 1932.
"Brave Men," in *Delineator* (New York), March 1933.
"Blind Man's Holiday," in *Pictorial Review* (New York), February 1935.
"Within Some Heart," in *Pictorial Review* (New York), October 1936.
"Star Song," in *Woman's Home Companion* (Springfield, Ohio), April 1949.
"Never Look Back," in *Ladies Home Journal* (Philadelphia), October-November 1949.

*   *   *

The Constant Nymph was the literary sensation of an era. Everyone read it; everyone was
bowled over. The compulsively readable tale of a sprawling family of genius left its mark
indelibly upon a generation of young writers—but no one ever matched its triumph, not even
Margaret Kennedy herself.

In this famous story, the ill-disciplined brood of an expatriate British composer is notorious
among its victims as "Sanger's Circus." Here and there across Euope, at home everywhere and
nowhere, they lead a straggling, unpredictable life: they were wild, amoral, and dishonest in all
ways but one; to each of them music alone is sacred and apart, not to be treated as lightly as
mere matters of life, love, or death. Suddenly Albert Sanger, the father whose larger-than-life
personality has been the sun around which the wild family circles in orbit, collapses and dies.
What is to become of his uncouth children?

Into their gypsy life, on a mission of mercy, comes respectability in the person of a
determined female cousin with conventional ideas. The rest of the novel, and its sequel, The
Fool of the Family, explores the inevitable clash between self-willed artistic temperament and
law-abiding society. Little Tessa, the nymph whose constancy causes her death, is the pathetic
and unforgettable victim crushed between the irresistible force of her love, and the immovable
object that is her respectable cousin's determination that she shall conform to a code she can
never understand.

The fame of this one stunningly successful book has somewhat obscured the fact that

Kennedy was the author of other novels, one of the most notable being the prize-winning *Troy Chimneys*. The haunting tale of a dual personality, half sensitive, penniless charmer, half self-seeking, conscienceless political climber, is told in a series of brief flashes, as his correspondence is discovered and interpreted years after his untimely death. Miles Lufton, the hero, is a complex creation, slave to the conventions of his age and the ugly necessities of his poverty, but always conscious within himself that he is capable of better things. This tragi-comedy of a man who gained *almost* everything he ever wanted, but found that the price had been too high, and his soul lost in the endeavour, is a beautifully crafted and memorable example of Margaret Kennedy's artistry.

—Joan McGrath

KENT, Pamela. *See* **BARRIE, Susan**.

KEPPEL, Charlotte. *See* **BLACKSTOCK, Charity**.

KEVERN, Barbara. Pseudonym for Donald Lee Shepherd.   American.   Born in Jackson, Michigan, 26 May 1932. Educated at Los Angeles Harbor College, A.A. 1960; California Polytechnic University, Pomona, B.A. 1966. Served in the United States Army, 1952-56. Married Barbara Kevern in 1954; two daughters and one son. Magazine and book editor. Since 1969, owner, Don Shepherd Agency. Address: Don Shepherd Agency, 1680 Vine Street, Suite 1105, Hollywood, California 90028, U.S.A.

ROMANCE AND GOTHIC PUBLICATIONS

Novels

> *Dark Eden*.   New York, Pocket Books, 1973.
> *Darkness Falling*.   New York, Pinnacle, 1974.

The Key. New York, Ballantine, 1974.
The Devil's Vineyard. New York, Pinnacle, 1975.

*   *   *

In Barbara Kevern's tales of gothic horror, seemingly competent young career women find themselves beset by incomprehensible horrors that only they seem to experience and believe: usually knife-wielding ghosts that appear from behind seemingly solid walls. As a result they must face an even greater horror—the question of whether they are drifting into madness or are the victims of some insidious game of psychological torture. The friends or relatives who should support them claim ignorance of murderous sights and sounds, and react with scepticism and statements about nervous breakdowns. Ultimately, however, secret wills, secret passageways, and secret sins make all clear; the heroine is vindicated; and whatever handsome young man is involved understands her suffering and becomes her protector.

Necessary to such plots are monumental, isolated mansions, set amid mist and woods and stone, with winding staircases, precarious balconies, a labyrinth of rooms, ancient crypts, and secret passages to terror. In *The Key* the castle is much like Mont St. Michel, embedded in the cliffs of a rugged island, while the manor in *The Devil's Vineyard* combines old world elegance with a modern California estate to produced hidden corridors for spying on guests, aquariums filled with man-eating sharks, elaborate light shows, and torture chambers for drugged sadists. Occasionally the heroine must balance along slippery ledges to escape the murderous clutches of villainous madmen. Mixed in amid the fake ghosts that haunt such dwellings are the luminescent spirits of the truly dead, spirits that use their energies to guide the heroines from danger and to the secrets that will unlock the motives of their persecutors.

In *Dark Eden* the young heiress suffers the psychological trauma of locks removed by night and replaced by day, tappings from the walls, and a friendly ghost that possesses her body to save her soul. In *The Devil's Vineyard* an old schoolmate lures the heroine to a decadent cultist scene where drug pushers exploit users, and sex and sadism distort reality. *Darkness Falling* focuses on a young woman who leaves the city to escape the guilty memories of a friend's tragic suicide only to find herself dealing with a weird goat woman and her retarded son, fighting off a redneck lynch mob, and protecting a supposed invalid whose goal is murder. As nurse-companion to an eccentric old sea captain in *The Key* the heroine must cope with her sanity being questioned, her employer murdered, and his handsome son suspect. Thus, although Kevern adheres to the same pattern of knife and ghost and will, she lends enough variety of character and scene to make each book unique.

—Gina Macdonald

KEYES, Frances Parkinson (née Wheeler). American. Born in Charlottesville, Virginia, 21 June 1885. Educated privately; Miss Carroll's School and Winsor School, Boston; Mlle. Dardelle's School, Switzerland. Married Henry Wilder Keyes (Governor of New Hampshire, 1917-19, and United States Senator, 1919-31) in 1904 (died, 1938); three sons. Associate Editor, *Good Housekeeping*, New York, 1923-35; Editor, *National Historical Magazine*, 1937-39. Recipient: Siena Medal, 1946; Christopher Medal, 1953. Litt.D.: George Washington University, Washington, D.C., 1921; Bates College, Lewiston, Maine, 1934; L.H.D.: University of New Hampshire, Durham, 1951. Legion of Honor, 1962. *Died 3 July 1970.*

Novels

The Old Gray Homestead. Boston, Houghton Mifflin, and London, Hodder and
Stoughton, 1919; as Sylvia Cary, New York, Paperback Library, 1962.
The Career of David Noble. New York, Stokes, 1921; London, Nash, 1923.
Queen Anne's Lace. New York, Liveright, 1930; London, Eyre and Spottiswoode, 1940.
Lady Blanche Farm: A Romance of the Commonplace. New York, Liveright, 1931;
London, Eyre and Spottiswoode, 1940.
Senator Marlowe's Daughter. New York, Messner, 1933; as Christian Marlowe's
Daughter, London, Eyre and Spottiswoode, 1934.
The Safe Bridge. New York, Messner, 1934; London, Eyre and Spottiswoode, 1935.
Honor Bright. New York, Messner, and London, Eyre and Spottiswoode, 1936.
Parts Unknown. New York, Messner, 1938; as The Ambassadress, London, Eyre and
Spottiswoode, 1938.
The Great Tradition. New York, Messner, and London, Eyre and Spottiswoode, 1939.
Fielding's Folly. New York, Messner, and London, Eyre and Spottiswoode, 1940.
All That Glitters. New York, Messner, and London, Eyre and Spottiswoode, 1941.
Crescent Carnival. New York, Messner, 1942; as If Ever I Cease to Love, London, Eyre
and Spottiswoode, 1943.
Also the Hills. New York, Messner, 1943; London, Eyre and Spottiswoode, 1944.
The River Road. New York, Messner, 1945; as The River Road and Vail d'Alvery,
London, Eyre and Spottiswoode, 2 vols., 1946-47.
Came a Cavalier. New York, Messner, 1947; London, Eyre and Spottiswoode, 1948.
Dinner at Antoine's. New York, Messner, 1948; London, Eyre and Spottiswoode, 1949.
Joy Street. New York, Messner, 1950; London, Eyre and Spottiswoode, 1951.
Steamboat Gothic. New York, Messner, 1952; as Steamboat Gothic and Larry Vincent,
London, Eyre and Spottiswoode, 2 vols., 1952-53.
The Royal Box. New York, Messner, and London, Eyre and Spottiswoode, 1954.
Blue Camellia. New York, Messner, and London, Eyre and Spottiswoode, 1957.
Victorine. New York, Messner, 1958; as The Gold Slippers, London, Eyre and Spottis-
woode, 1958.
Station Wagon in Spain. New York, Farrar Straus, 1959; as The Letter from Spain,
London, Eyre and Spottiswoode, 1959.
The Chess Players. New York, Farrar Straus, 1960; London, Eyre and Spottiswoode,
1961.
Madame Castel's Lodger. New York, Farrar Straus, 1962; London, Eyre and Spottis-
woode, 1963.
The Explorer. New York, McGraw Hill, 1964; London, Eyre and Spottiswoode, 1965.
I, The King. New York, McGraw Hill, and London, Eyre and Spottiswoode, 1966.
The Heritage. New York, McGraw Hill, and London, Eyre and Spottiswoode, 1968.

Short Stories

The Restless Lady and Other Stories. New York, Liveright, 1963; London, Eyre and
Spottiswoode, 1964.

Verse

The Happy Wanderer. New York, Messner, 1935.

Other

Letters from a Senator's Wife. New York, Appleton, 1924.

Silver Seas and Golden Cities: A Joyous Journey Through Latin Lands. New York, Liveright, 1931.

Capital Kaleidoscope: The Story of a Washington Hostess. New York, Harper, 1937.

Written in Heaven: The Life on Earth of the Little Flower of Lisieux. New York, Messner, and London, Eyre and Spottiswoode, 1937; as *Therese, Saint of a Little Way*, Messner, 1950; as *St. Teresa of Lisieux*, Eyre and Spottiswoode, 1950.

Pioneering People in Northern New England: A Series of Early Sketches. Washington, D.C., Judd and Detweiler, 1937.

Along a Little Way. New York, Kenedy, and London, Burns Oates, 1940; revised edition, New York, Hawthorn, 1962.

Bernadette, Maid of Lourdes. New York, Messner, 1940; revised edition, as *The Sublime Shepherdess*, Messner, and London, Burns Oates, 1940; revised edition, as *Bernadette of Lourdes: Shepherdess, Sister, and Saint*, Messner, 1953; London, Hollis and Carter, 1954.

The Grace of Guadalupe. New York, Messner, 1941; London, Burns Oates, 1951.

Once an Esplanade: A Cycle of Two Creole Weddings (juvenile). New York, Dodd Mead, 1947; London, Hollis and Carter, 1949.

All This Is Louisiana. New York, Harper, 1950.

The Cost of a Best Seller (memoirs). New York, Messner, 1950; London, Eyre and Spottiswoode, 1953.

The Frances Parkinson Keyes Cookbook. New York, Doubleday, 1955; London, Muller, 1956.

St. Anne: Grandmother of Our Saviour. New York, Messner, 1955; London, Wingate, 1956; revised edition, New York, Hawthorn, 1962.

Guadelupe to Lourdes (omnibus). St. Paul, Catechetical Guild Educational Society, 1957.

The Land of Stones and Saints (on Spain). New York, Doubleday, 1957; London, Davies, 1958.

Christmas Gift. New York, Hawthorn, 1959; London, Davies, 1960.

Mother Cabrini, Missionary to the World. New York, Farrar Straus, and London, Burns Oates, 1959.

Roses in December (autobiography). New York, Doubleday, and London, Davies, 1960; revised edition, New York, Liveright, 1966.

The Rose and the Lily: The Lives and Times of Two South American Saints. New York, Hawthorn, 1961; London, Davies, 1962.

Three Ways of Love. New York, Hawthorn, 1963; London, Davies, 1964.

Tongues of Fire. New York, Coward McCann, 1966.

All Flags Flying: Reminiscences. New York, McGraw Hill, 1972.

Editor, *A Treasury of Favorite Poems.* New York, Hawthorn, 1963.

Translator, *The Third Mystic: The Self Revelation of María Vela of Avila.* New York, Farrar Straus, and London, Davies, 1960.

*   *   *

Frances Parkinson Keyes, the favorite novelist of many American readers during the middle third of this century, received only a few sympathetic and understanding criticisms during her lifetime. In the most notable of these, "The Queens of Fiction" (*Life*, 6 April 1959), Robert Warnick compared her with Taylor Caldwell and Edna Ferber, noting that then all the fiction of all three was in print. By 1980, the situation had changed; nearly all of Caldwell and Ferber's epics remained available, but almost all of Keyes's had disappeared from print. How could a popular favorite so soon lose her place in readers' affections? The mystery of this "generation gap" poses an important problem in changing tastes, much like the elusive problems that often provide the leisurely momentum for this lady's tales.

One of Warnick's distinctions between these three practitioners of the "big, old-fashioned novel" suggests an answer; he sharply contrasts the "strident world" of Edna Ferber's tales and "the nightmare world" of Taylor Caldwell's with the "gentle and aristocratic world" of Keyes's. As TV epics like *Dallas* and *Dynasty* that are the descendants of the work of these novelists show, the Ferber/Caldwell tradition of violence and nightmare has appropriated an audience that increasingly confuses aristocracy with just being rich.

Although Keyes wrote popular novels about rural New England, Boston, Washington, D.C., and London, among the many places to which her extensive travels had taken her, she discovered the ambiance that best suited her talents and led to her greatest successes when friends lured her to New Orleans in the late 1930's. She lived in a fine old house in the restored French Quarter and elsewhere about Louisiana off and on for the rest of her life, absorbing the unique atmosphere that provided the groundwork for the intricately designed tapestries of her eight tales of traditional Creole society from *Crescent Carnival* to *The Chess Players*. Whether she was creating a tale that spanned three generations (*Crescent Carnival, Steamboat Gothic*) or only a few days that brought to a head years of frustration (*Dinner at Antoine's, Victorine*), whether she was writing nostalgically for children (*Once an Esplanade*) or with more chic for her contemporaries (*The River Road*), whether she moved out of the magic city to the back country (*Blue Camellia*) or to other exotic ports of call around the world (*The Chess Players*), Keyes's legends, to the delight of her lending-library readers and the despair of fashionable reviewers, were richly decorated with the fruits of long and careful research into the culture—in both the artistic and anthropological senses—of the regions that intrigued her.

Reviewers who faulted her indifferent plotting, rambling narratives, flabby style, overindulgence in background material, and long, confidential prefaces sharing her struggles in creating the books and acknowledging the help of those who has befriended her missed altogether the source of her appeal. Reading a novel by Keyes was not a way to pass the time restlessly on idle days, it was rather like a chatty visit from an old and welcome friend who had just returned from fabulous places, brimming over with their quaint lore and exciting gossip.

Since the pattern of all her works—too imprecise to be labeled a formula—is similar, one provides a model for all these local color tales. *Dinner at Antoine's* remains of possibly most interest because of the ever increasing fame of the titular restaurant the characters frequent. Although built around a mysterious murder, it is no detective story, as fans of that genre complained. Too little of the tale concerns the improbable crime and its solution; the event serves simply to hold together a knowing account of the resorts and activities of the glamorous characters as they either adjust to the increasingly commercial society that is destroying their elegant world or simply fade out of the changing picture. The weakness of the novel, like others of the same weave, is that Keyes never quite finds the skill to blend the conventionalized foreground figures into the overpowering background; but this lack of sophisticated technique didn't bother readers who liked to enjoy each page for itself and regretted reaching the drawn-out endings of the meandering tales.

Length and detail alone do not distinguish Keyes's novels from Ferber's and Caldwell's. The reason for the comparative impermanence of Keyes's fabrications is most likely that the societies she portrayed have faded with the passing years. Although neither Keyes nor her readers would probably have thought of themselves as decadent, they were profoundly so; and this fascination with decadence suggests the reason that Creole Louisiana and its hothouse culture provided the ideal vehicle for rewarding their tastes. Mrs. Keyes has since failed to attract readers that still revel in the lusty works of Ferber and Caldwell; but she would not have cared for such vulgarians or their affection. She had the joy of writing for a fastidious class that loved her and whose fantasy world can now only be recaptured through her works.

—Warren French

KIDD, Flora. British. Married; four children. Taught in London. Lives in Canada. Address: c/o Mills and Boon Ltd., 15-16 Brooks Mews, London W1A 1DR, England.

<small>ROMANCE AND GOTHIC PUBLICATIONS</small>

Novels

    Visit to Rowanbank. London, Mills and Boon, 1966.
    Whistle and I'll Come. London, Mills and Boon, 1966; Toronto, Harlequin, 1967.
    Nurse at Rowanbank. Toronto, Harlequin, 1966; London, Mills and Boon, 1967.
    Love Alters Not. London, Mills and Boon, 1967; Toronto, Harlequin, 1968.
    Wind So Gay. London, Mills and Boon, 1968.
    Strange as a Dream. London, Mills and Boon, 1968; Toronto, Harlequin, 1969.
    When Birds Do Sing. London, Mills and Boon, 1970; Toronto, Harlequin, 1971.
    Love Is Fire. London, Mills and Boon, 1971; Toronto, Harlequin, 1972.
    My Heart Remembers. London, Mills and Boon, and Toronto, Harlequin, 1971.
    The Dazzle on the Sea. London, Mills and Boon, and Toronto, Harlequin, 1971.
    If Love Be Love. London, Mills and Boon, and Toronto, Harlequin, 1972.
    Remedy for Love. London, Mills and Boon, and Toronto, Harlequin, 1972.
    The Taming of Lisa. London, Mills and Boon, 1972; Toronto, Harlequin, 1973.
    The Cave of the White Rose. London, Mills and Boon, 1972; Toronto, Harlequin, 1973.
    Beyond the Sunset. London, Mills and Boon, and Toronto, Harlequin, 1973.
    Night on the Mountain. London, Mills and Boon, 1973.
    The Legend of the Swans. Toronto, Harlequin, 1974.
    Gallant's Fancy. London, Mills and Boon, and Toronto, Harlequin, 1974.
    The Paper Marriage. Toronto, Harlequin, 1974.
    Stranger in the Glen. London, Mills and Boon, and Toronto, Harlequin, 1975.
    Enchantment in Blue. London, Mills and Boon, and Toronto, Harlequin, 1975.
    The Bargain Bride. London, Mills and Boon, 1976; Toronto, Harlequin, 1979.
    The Black Knight. London, Mills and Boon, 1976; Toronto, Harlequin, 1977.
    The Dance of Courtship. London, Mills and Boon, and Toronto, Harlequin, 1976.
    The Summer Wife. London, Mills and Boon, and Toronto, Harlequin, 1976.
    Dangerous Pretence. Toronto, Harlequin, 1977.
    Night of the Yellow Moon. London, Mills and Boon, 1977; Toronto, Harlequin, 1978.
    To Play with Fire. London, Mills and Boon, 1977; Toronto, Harlequin, 1978.
    Jungle of Desire. Toronto, Harlequin, 1977.
    Marriage in Mexico. London, Mills and Boon, 1978.
    Castle of Temptation. London, Mills and Boon, 1978.
    Sweet Torment. London, Mills and Boon, and Toronto, Harlequin, 1978.
    Canadian Affair. London, Mills and Boon, 1979.
    Passionate Encounter. London, Mills and Boon, and Toronto, Harlequin, 1979.
    Stay Through the Night. London, Mills and Boon, 1979.
    Tangled Shadows. London, Mills and Boon, 1979; Toronto, Harlequin, 1980.
    Together Again. London, Mills and Boon, and Toronto, Harlequin, 1979.
    The Arranged Marriage. London, Mills and Boon, and Toronto, Harlequin, 1980.
    The Silken Bond. London, Mills and Boon, and Toronto, Harlequin, 1980.
    Wife by Contract. London, Mills and Boon, and Toronto, Harlequin, 1980.
    Beyond Control. London, Mills and Boon, and Toronto, Harlequin, 1981.
    Passionate Stranger. London, Mills and Boon, 1981.
    Personal Affair. London, Mills and Boon, 1981.

*   *   *

Flora Kidd is an English writer who now lives in Canada. The change in country did not occur immediately for she first spent several years living in Scotland. More recently, she has visited several South American countries and later used them as backgrounds for her latest novels. *Sweet Torment* takes place in Colombia, while *Enchantment in Blue* takes place in the Caribbean. For the most part, however, Kidd is most known for her novels with Scottish settings. Here she excels in bringing the country and people to life for her readers.

Sandy Phillips in *The Black Knight* journeys to Scotland to help a cousin. Her trip takes her through many historic places such as Carlisle, Gretna Green, and on into the Galloway part of Scotland. Juliet Grey in *The Cave of the White Rose* is able to travel on into the Highlands and the story is developed against the backgrounds of the moors and mists of Scotland.

Kidd provides a subtle blending that lessens the impact of the physical surroundings and concentrates on the development of character and plot instead. Her heroines tend to be rather young, with a fresh, engaging manner to them. Sandy has just completed a university degree in history and is considering going on for an advanced degree. Juliet, on the other hand, is virtually alone except for relatives who do not care for her. Both have been sheltered, though, and both are unaware of themselves as women. It is this aspect of Kidd's heroines that makes her stories so readable. Slowly and quite cleverly, she lets her heroines grow up and become aware of their capacity to love.

In developing her male characters, she gives them just the right level of experience to help them eventually win their loved ones. They are naturally older and have more experience, but one does not feel that they are too sophisticated and completely out of reach of the heroines.

In a way, it is difficult to catagorize Kidd as a romance writer, for she balances everything so well that glaring differences are not found in her novels. Background stays that way, while character and plot support each other easily. She is intensely creative in developing her characters so that each emerges as a rounded figure.

Her more recent novels, however, are more dramatic and have an added touch of sophistication and maturity in them that her earlier romances lack. Although her heroines are yet naive and unsure of themselves, they face more emotional turmoil throughout the story, and the endings are more suspenseful than in her earlier novels. In these later books the heroine is faced with a hopeless love for a man who is far beyond her reach, and it is not until the very end of the novel that she learns that her love is returned.

The hero is often cynical and hardened. His treatment of the heroine at times borders on cruelty and contempt. The emotional overtones in these novels is heightened and the "despairing" sort of reaction leaves the reader in a turmoil at the end of the novel, for the change of pace is often abrupt.

Flora Kidd is one of the more prolific novelists who publishes in the Harlequin Presents Series. It is this type of novel that dominates this series. It is of particular note that Flora Kidd is able to adapt her style of writing to both kinds of novels, that is, the familiar "sweet" romance and the more modern "sophisticated" ones. Certainly she has developed an avid readership for both types over the last few years.

—Arlene Moore

KIMBROUGH, Katheryn. Pseudonym for John M. Kimbro; also writes as Kym Allyson; Ann Ashton; Charlotte Bramwell; Jean Kimbro. American. Born 12 July 1929. Educated at Pasadena City College, California, 1947-49; California State College (now University), Los Angeles, 1949-51; Institute of Religious Science, 1969-71. Stage director, composer, teacher, masseur, actor. Agent: Oscar Collier, 280 Madison Avenue, New York, New York 10016, U.S.A.

ROMANCE AND GOTHIC PUBLICATIONS

Novels

The House on Windswept Ridge.   New York, Popular Library, 1971; London, Sphere, 1973.
The Twisted Cameo.   New York, Popular Library, 1971; London, Sphere, 1973.
The Children of Houndstooth.   New York, Popular Library, 1972.
Thanesworth House.   New York, Popular Library, 1972.
The Broken Sphinx.   New York, Popular Library, 1972.
Heiress to Wolfskill.   New York, Popular Library, 1973.
The Phantom Flame of Wind House.   New York, Popular Library, 1973.
The Three Sisters of Briarwick.   New York, Popular Library, 1973.
The Specter of Dolphin Cove.   New York, Popular Library, 1973.
Unseen Torment.   New York, Popular Library, 1974.
The Shadow over Pheasant Heath.   New York, Popular Library, 1974.
Phenwick Women:
   1. *Augusta, The First.*   New York, Popular Library, 1975.
   2. *Jane, The Courageous.*   New York, Popular Library, 1975.
   3. *Margaret, The Faithful.*   New York, Popular Library, 1975.
   4. *Patricia, The Beautiful.*   New York, Popular Library, 1975.
   5. *Rachel, The Possessed.*   New York, Popular Library, 1975.
   6. *Susannah, The Righteous.*   New York, Popular Library, 1975.
   7. *Rebecca, The Mysterious.*   New York, Popular Library, 1975.
   8. *Joanne, The Unpredictable.*   New York, Popular Library, 1976.
   9. *Olivia, The Tormented.*   New York, Popular Library, 1976.
  10. *Harriet, The Haunted.*   New York, Popular Library, 1976.
  11. *Nancy, The Daring.*   New York, Popular Library, 1976.
  12. *Marcia, The Innocent.*   New York, Popular Library, 1976.
  13. *Kate, The Curious.*   New York, Popular Library, 1976.
  14. *Ilene, The Superstitious.*   New York, Popular Library, 1977.
  15. *Millijoy, The Determined.*   New York, Popular Library, 1977.
  16. *Barbara, The Valiant.*   New York, Popular Library, 1977.
  17. *Ruth, The Unsuspecting.*   New York, Popular Library, 1977.
  18. *Ophelia, The Anxious.*   New York, Popular Library, 1977.
  19. *Dorothy, The Terrified.*   New York, Popular Library, 1977.
  20. *Ann, The Gentle.*   New York, Popular Library, 1978.
  21. *Nellie, The Obvious.*   New York, Popular Library, 1978.
  22. *Isabelle, The Frantic.*   New York, Popular Library, 1978.
  23. *Evelyn, The Ambitious.*   New York, Popular Library, 1978.
  24. *Louise, The Restless.*   New York, Popular Library, 1978.
  25. *Polly, The Worried.*   New York, Popular Library, 1978.
  26. *Yvonne, The Confident.*   New York, Popular Library, 1979.
  27. *Joyce, The Beloved.*   New York, Popular Library, 1979.
  28. *Augusta, The Second.*   New York, Popular Library, 1979.
  29. *Carol, The Pursued.*   New York, Popular Library, 1979.
  30. *Katherine, The Returned.*   New York, Popular Library, 1980.
  31. *Peggy, The Concerned.*   New York, Popular Library, 1981.
A Shriek in the Midnight Tower.   New York, Popular Library, 1975.
The Moon Shadow (as Kym Allyson).   New York, Berkley, 1976.
Twilight Return: An Astrological Gothic Novel: Cancer (as Jean Kimbro).   New York, Ballantine, 1976.
Night of Tears (as John M. Kimbro).   New York, Ballantine, 1976.

Novels as Charlotte Bramwell

Cousin to Terror. New York, Beagle, 1972.
Stepmother's House. New York, Beagle, 1972.
Brother Sinister. New York, Beagle, 1973.

Novels as Ann Ashton

The Haunted Portrait. New York, Doubleday, 1976.
The Phantom Reflection. New York, Doubleday, 1978; as *Reflection*, New York, Dell, 1979.
Three Cries of Terror. New York, Doubleday, 1980.
Concession. New York, Doubleday, 1981.

OTHER PUBLICATIONS

Plays as Kym Allyson

The Wounded Dove, music by Allyson (produced Hollywood, 1958).
Three Ladies Named Grace (produced Los Angeles, 1958).
Scrooge, music by Allyson, adaptation of the story *A Christmas Carol* by Dickens (produced Monterey Park, California, 1965).
Clown World (produced Monterey Park, California, 1966).

*   *   *

John Kimbro, under the pseudonym of Katheryn Kimbrough, has written many gothic romances. He is essentially a hack writer, who even manages to joke about it. In *A Shriek in the Midnight Tower*, for instance, a character states, "I met a person once whose initials are K.K. who has been writing the things [gothic romances] for years and making a nice living out of it." And in *The Phantom Flame of Wind House* one of the minor characters is a mystery writer named Charlotte Bramwell, also a Kimbro pseudonym.

Kimbro's stories tend to prove that the gothic genre is a difficult one for a man to master. In place of mood and atmosphere, he gives the reader disorganized action and complicated plots, which in some cases even verge on the ridiculous. The perpetrator of a series of murders in *A Shriek in the Midnight Tower* turns out to be a middle-aged midget who through plastic surgery is pretending to be her own 12-year-old niece. Kimbro's characters have absolutely no validity for the reader, and his books give the general impression of being somewhat comic pastiches of the gothic novel.

In 1975 Kimbro began a series of historical novels called the Saga of the Phenwick Women. The series is chiefly remarkable for his having written so many so quickly. The stories are an odd mixture of the historical novel and rambling family saga, laced with violent happenings, and mixed with touches of the supernatural. *Augusta, The First*, set in 1742 in New England, is the first of the series; later volumes carry the Phenwick family through the Revolution and the Civil War. Augusta's spirit, which continues on after her death, appears to the later Phenwick women, and provides one unifying theme throughout the stories. The Phenwick fortune, founded on pirate treasure, provides another, as various caches hidden by Augusta are discovered by later Phenwicks. While the emphasis in the series is on the family saga, the supernatural element sometimes dominates, as in *Rachel, The Possessed*, in which the spirits of two Salem witches fight to possess the heroine. In *Nellie, The Obvious* the idea of reincarnation is introduced. Nellie, living in 1869, believes herself to be the reincarnation of Edward Phenwick, Augusta's son. The series has come full cycle. Intricate as it is, the poor quality of the writing and the artificiality of the characters and plots give the reader to conclude that the whole saga is much ado about nothing.

—Necia A. Musser

KIRK, Russell (Amos).   American.   Born in Plymouth, Michigan, 19 October 1918. Educated at Plymouth High School, graduated 1936; Michigan State University, East Lansing, B.A. 1940; Duke University, Durham, North Carolina, M.A. 1941; St. Andrews University, Scotland, D.Litt. 1952. Served in the United States Army, 1942-46: Staff Sergeant. Married Annette Yvonne Cecile Courtemanche in 1964; four daughters. Assistant Professor of History, Michigan State University, 1946-53; Daly Lecturer, University of Detroit, 1954; Research Professor of Politics, C.W. Post College, 1957-69, and University Professor, Long Island University, 1960-69, Greenvale, New York; Member of the Politics Faculty, New School for Social Research, New York, 1959-61; also visiting professor at several universities. Columnist ("From the Academy"), *National Review*, 1955-80, and for *Los Angeles Times* Syndicate, 1962-75. Since 1960, Editor, *University Bookman*. President, since 1960, Educational Reviewer, and since 1979, Marguerite Eyer Wilbur Foundation; since 1979, Director, Educational Research Council of America Social Science Program. Recipient: American Council of Learned Societies Senior Fellowship, 1949; Guggenheim Fellowship, 1954; Ann Radcliffe Award, 1964; Christopher Award, for non-fiction, 1973. Honorary doctorates: Boston College; St. John's University; Park College, Kansas City; Loyola College, Baltimore; LeMoyne College, Syracuse, New York; Gannon College, Erie, Pennsylvania; Niagara University, New York; Olivet College, Minnesota; Albion College, Minnesota; Central Michigan University, Mt. Pleasant. Agent: Kirby McCauley, 60 East 42nd Street, New York, New York 10017. Address: Piety Hill, Mecosta, Michigan 49332, U.S.A.

ROMANCE AND GOTHIC PUBLICATIONS

Novels

> *Old House of Fear.*   New York, Fleet, 1961; London, Gollancz, 1962.
> *A Creature of the Twilight: His Memorials.*   New York, Fleet, 1966.
> *Lord of the Hollow Dark.*   New York, St. Martin's Press, 1979.

Short Stories

> *The Surly Sullen Bell: Ten Stories and Sketches, Uncanny or Uncomfortable, with a Note on the Ghostly Tale.*   New York, Fleet, 1962; as *Lost Lake*, New York, Paperback Library, 1966.
> *The Princess of All Lands.*   Sauk City, Wisconsin, Arkham House, 1979.

OTHER PUBLICATIONS

Other

    Randolph of Roanoke: A Study in Conservative Thought. Chicago, University of
       Chicago Press, 1951; as *John Randolph of Roanoke,* Chicago, Regnery, 1964.
    The Conservative Mind from Burke to Santayana. Chicago, Regnery, 1953; London,
       Faber, 1954; revised edition, Regnery, 1964.
    St. Andrews. London, Batsford, 1954.
    A Program for Conservatives. Chicago, Regnery, 1954; revised edition, 1962; abridged
       edition, as *Prospects for Conservatives,* 1956.
    Academic Freedom: An Essay in Definition. Chicago, Regnery, 1955.
    Beyond the Dreams of Avarice: Essays of a Social Critic. Chicago, Regnery, 1956.
    The Intelligent Woman's Guide to Conservatism. New York, Devin Adair, 1957.
    The American Cause. Chicago, Regnery, 1957.
    Confessions of a Bohemian Tory: Episodes and Reflections of a Vagrant Career. New
       York, Fleet, 1963.
    The Intemperate Professor and Other Cultural Splenetics. Baton Rouge, Louisiana
       State University Press, 1965.
    Edmund Burke: A Genius Reconsidered. New Rochelle, New York, Arlington House,
       1967.
    The Political Principles of Robert A. Taft, with James McClellan. New York, Fleet,
       1967.
    Enemies of the Permanent Things: Observations of Abnormality in Literature and Poli-
       tics. New Rochelle, New York, Arlington House, 1969.
    Eliot and His Age: T.S. Eliot's Moral Imagination in the Twentieth Century. New York,
       Random House, 1971.
    The Roots of American Order. La Salle, Illinois, Open Court, 1974.
    Decadence and Renewal in the Higher Learning: An Episodic History of American
       University and College since 1953. South Bend, Indiana, Regnery, 1978.

    Editor, *The Scallion Stone,* by Basil A. Smith. Chapel Hill, North Carolina, Whispers
       Press, 1980.
    Editor, *The Portable Conservative Reader.* New York, Viking Press, 1982.

Bibliography: *Russell Kirk: A Bibliography* by Charles Brown, Mt. Pleasant, Michigan,
Clarke Historical Library, 1981.

Manuscript Collection: Clark Historical Library, Central Michigan University, Mt. Pleasant.

Russell Kirk comments:

    My uncanny tales are intended to wake the moral imagination. As Gerald Heard remarked to
me once, good tales of the supernatural must be founded upon theological postulates. (An
admirable example of this is Heard's story "The Chapel of Ease.") According to Heard's
principle, my fiction is concerned with the mysteries of time and circumstance, with evil and
regeneration, mystically delineated. Like W.B. Yeats, I was reared in a family that never
questioned the reality of ghosts and such phenomena—spending my summers, indeed, in an
ancestral house long haunted. Some considerable grains of true narration lie at the core of all
my stories—drawn from my own experiences in Britain or America, or from friends' mischan-
ces. Can Grande della Scala inquired of Dante whether *The Divine Comedy* was to be taken
literally or figuratively. Dante replied that his poem might be applied in either sense. So it is, in
their small way, with my uncanny tales. The characters in them, incidentally, ordinarily are

taken from the life. "Frank Sarsfield," in my tale "A Long, Long Trail a-Windin'," lived in my house for the last six years of his life—and died in a snowdrift, as I had predicted he would.

*   *   *

Best known for his advocacy of conservative philosophy, Russell Kirk writes what he has called "unabashedly Gothic" stories and novels. In present-day settings, Kirk employs such gothic devices as prophetic dreams, ghosts, and ancient houses saturated with the evils of previous inhabitants. Kirk's treatment of the traditionally gothic struggle between agents of good and evil is profoundly religious. Some of Kirk's villains are social reformers, determined to reduce mankind to dreary conformity (Jackman in *The Old House of Fear*, Mr. S.G.W. Barner in "Ex Tenebris"); others are evil spirits who have gained control of human bodies (Mr. Apollinax in *Lord of the Hollow Dark*, Gerontion in "The Peculiar Demesne"). Two characters reappearing in a number of works, Ralph Bain and Manfred Arcane, are powerful guardians of the weak and innocent. In "A Cautionary Note on the Ghostly Tale," Kirk calls for "a return to the ghostly and the Gothic" because "it can touch keenly upon the old reality of evil—and upon injustice and retribution."

One of the pleasures of Kirk's fiction is its allusiveness, lines from Shakespeare, Longfellow, and other poets appearing in surprising contexts. T.S. Eliot is a potent influence. Kirk's characters may find themselves in a "timeless moment," what Eliot calls "the still point of the turning world," in which dead and living interact freely. The damned, like the dead Indian in "The Princess of All Lands," are fixed in time, perpetually acting out some hideous depravity and seeking others to share their suffering. To the saved, timeless moments constitute heaven. As the Canon explains in "Saviourgate," "all the good moments or hours or days that you ever experience are forever present to you, whenever you want them...." For those in a state of sin or despair, timeless moments provide opportunites for redemption. In Kirk's best story, winner of a World Fantasy Award, "There's a Long, Long Trail a-Windin'," a tramp redeems a life of petty thievery by journeying into the past to save children from murderous escaped convicts. Touching upon what Kirk calls "the darkness or the light in souls," his fiction concerns hell, the purgatory of spiritual progress, and salvation—conditions that individuals may experience both before and after they have crossed the border between life and death.

—Wendy Bousfield

KNIGHT, Alanna (née Cleet). Also writes as Margaret Hope. British. Born in County Durham. Educated privately. Married Alexander Harrow Knight in 1951; two sons. Fellow, Society of Antiquaries. Recipient: Romantic Novelists Association Netta Muskett Award, 1968. Agent: Anthony Sheil Associates, 2-3 Morwell Street, London WC1B 3AR, England. Address: 374 Queen's Road, Aberdeen AB1 8DX, Scotland.

ROMANCE AND GOTHIC PUBLICATIONS

Novels

> *Legend of the Loch.* London, Hurst and Blackett, 1969; New York, Lancer, 1970.
> *The October Witch.* London, Hurst and Blackett, and New York, Lancer, 1971.
> *This Outward Angel.* New York, Lancer, 1972.

Castle Clodha.   London, Hurst and Blackett, and New York, Avon, 1972.
Lament for Lost Lovers.   London, Hurst and Blackett, 1972; New York, Avon, 1973.
The White Rose.   London, Hurst and Blackett, 1973; New York, Avon, 1974.
A Stranger Came By.   London, Hurst and Blackett, 1974; New York, Avon, 1975.
The Passionate Kindness.   Aylesbury, Buckinghamshire, Milton House, 1974.
A Drink for the Bridge.   London, Macmillan, 1976.
The Wicked Wynsleys.   New York, Nordon, 1977.
The "Black Duchess."   London, Futura, and New York, Doubleday, 1980.
Castle of Foxes.   New York, Doubleday, 1981.
Colla's Children.   London, Macdonald, 1982.

Novels as Margaret Hope

The Queen's Captain.   New York, Masquerade, 1978.
Hostage Most Royal.   New York, Masquerade, 1979; London, Mills and Boon, 1980.
The Shadow Queen.   New York, Masquerade, 1979; London, Mills and Boon, 1980.

OTHER PUBLICATIONS

Plays

The Private Life of Robert Louis Stevenson, with John Cairney (produced Edinburgh, 1975).
Girl on an Empty Swing (produced Cambridge, 1981).   Macclesfield, New Playwrights Network, 1978.

Radio Documentaries: *Don Roberto: Life of R.B. Cunninghame Graham*, 1975; *Across the Plains*, from a work by Robert Louis Stevenson, 1981.

Other

Editor, *The Robert Louis Stevenson Treasury*.   London, Shepheard Walwyn, 1982.

*   *   *

Scenes of wild beauty that dot that landscape of Scotland become the background of Alanna Knight's eerie gothic tales. A land of tempestuous weather, looming mountains, enchanting lochs, and castles rich with turbulent histories, Scotland is the ideal setting for danger and romance. The female protagonists in Knight's stories are not young ingenues but rather mature women who have either been bitterly disappointed in love or who still wait, wondering if love will ever come. All lead rather dreary lives. Then, suddenly, events turn as each heroine unexpectedly finds herself hurled into a mystery with psychic elements in which their own death looms as a frightening possibility. This new twist in their lives also brings the romance each has sought; the men involved are often cast in the heroic image of Robert the Bruce.

Lucy MacAeden (*This Outward Angel*) has a recurring nightmare of being chased through a strange red desert by some unseen horror. Rescue comes in the guise of the Protector who carries her away from the swiftly pursuing danger. His is a face she recognizes only in dreams, but the pendant of a Thunderbird which he wears has a counterpoint in the real world. Summoned to the side of her former husband's dying uncle, she meets an intriguing young man whom she calls the Barbaric Stranger for his Aztec Indian features. He also wears the Thunderbird. Another novel with a dream motif is *The White Rose*. While the guest of Fraser, the young bachelor laird of Deveron, Candida sees visions of a white rose. In a vivid dream she relives the last moments of this courageous girl who had sacrificed her life in order to help Bonnie Prince Charlie escape from the British soldiers.

The castles that populate the novels of Alanna Knight always have a sinister legend or curse, along with lots of empty wings or turrets to inspire ghostly doings. The turret room of *Castle Clodha* was once the prison of the beautiful witch Rowan, starved to death by an avaricious laird who wanted to marry not this lovely girl carrying his child, but a rich heiress who could bring him much-needed wealth. It takes the modern-day love of May Lachlan and Laird Roderick Malcom MacMhor to dispel the curse of Rowan.

The more recent *Castle of Foxes* has less of a supernatural flavor although ghostly, gothic trappings abound. It is set in the Scottish Highlands during the time of Queen Victoria and Prince Albert. The reader glimpses not only the narrator Tanya's frightening escapades at Devènick Castle but also enchanting scenes of court life at nearby Balmoral.

All of Alanna Knight's stories combine melodic prose and powerful allusion to produce quality gothic adventure with a dash of Scottish nationalism.

—Patricia Altner

LAKER, Rosalind. Pseudonym for Barbara Øvstedal; has written as Barbara Douglas; Barbara Paul. Agent: Laurence Pollinger Ltd., 18 Maddox Street, London W1R OEU, England. Address: c/o Doubleday and Company, 245 Park Avenue, New York, New York 10017, U.S.A.

ROMANCE AND GOTHIC PUBLICATIONS

Novels

> *Sovereign's Key.* London, Hale, 1969.
> *Far Seeks the Heart.* London, Hale, 1970.
> *Sail a Jeweled Ship.* London, Hale, 1971.
> *The Shripney Lady.* London, Hale, 1972.
> *Fair Wind of Love.* London, Hale, 1974; (as Barbara Douglas), New York, Doubleday, 1980.
> *The Smuggler's Bride.* New York, Doubleday, 1975; London, Hale, 1976.
> *Ride the Blue Riband.* New York, Doubleday, 1977; London, Hale, 1978.
> *Warwyck's Woman.* New York, Doubleday, 1978; as *Warwyck's Wife*, London, Eyre Methuen, 1979.
> *Claudine's Daughter.* New York, Doubleday, and London, Eyre Methuen, 1979.
> *Warwyck's Choice.* New York, Doubleday, 1980; as *The Warwycks of Easthampton*, London, Eyre Methuen, 1980.
> *Fly Banners of Silk.* New York, Doubleday, 1981.
> *Gilded Splendour.* New York, Doubleday, 1982.

Novels as Barbara Øvstedal

> *Red Cherry Summer.* London, Hale, 1973.
> *Valley of the Reindeer.* London, Hale, 1973.

Souvenir from Sweden.   London, Hale, 1974.

Novels as Barbara Paul

The Seventeenth Stair.   London, Macdonald and Jane's, and New York, St. Martin's
Press, 1975.
The Curse of Halewood.   London, Macdonald and Jane's, 1976; as *Devil's Fire, Love's
Revenge*, New York, St. Martin's Press, 1976.
The Frenchwoman.   London, Macdonald and Jane's, and New York, St. Martin's Press,
1977.
A Wild Cry of Love.   London, Macdonald and Jane's, 1978.
To Love a Stranger.   New York, St. Martin's Press, 1979.

OTHER PUBLICATIONS

Other

Norway (as Barbara Øvstedal).   London, Batsford, and New York, Hastings House,
1973.

*   *   *

Barbara Øvstedal, writing as Barbara Paul, Rosalind Laker, and Barbara Douglas creates
first-rate romantic suspense novels that are highly recommended to readers.
Her first novel as Barbara Paul was the well-received *The Seventeenth Stair*. Rosella
Eastwood unexpectedly inherits a large chateau in the Loire Valley. The intriguing plot
contains good characterizations, one of Paul's strong points, and many unexpected twists as
strange moans are heard in the night, her maid mysteriously dies, and the neighbors are hostile.
Her romantic interlude with one unhostile neighbor, Phillipe Aubert, is finely done and warms
the pages of this well-written work. The two following Paul novels, *The Curse of Halewood* and
The Frenchwoman, provide entertainment as well. The first involves a young girl, two suitors,
and a mysterious old house. The heroine of *The Frenchwoman*, in actuality only half-French, is
banished by her stepmother to England in a betrothal to a man she doesn't even know and
doesn't trust. Paul's novels all take place in the 19th century giving an added touch of romance
and flavor to her appealing heroines and dashing heroes. They are a real treat for gothic fans.
Rosalind Laker made her debut in the U.S. with *The Smuggler's Bride*, a satisfactory gothic
which follows the trials and tribulations of Harriette Meade as she becomes a governess to an
ill-mannered family, gets herself dismissed, takes on the post of housekeeper to the strange
next-door neighbor, marries him, and, when he dies, inherits his country house complete with
curse. *Ride the Blue Riband* also deals with a young girl and an inherited house, this time in
connection with a race horse who is to run at Epsom Downs. England in 1847 provides the
fascinating background of the caring, training, and racing of thoroughbreds. Next in Laker's
string of successes comes her Warwyck series, a trio of well-received books based in the seaside
town of Easthampton whose blossoming as a resort town is the work of the founder of the
dynasty, Daniel Warwyck, a prize fighter. In an opening scene reminiscent of Hardy's *Mayor of
Casterbridge*, Daniel bids 21 guineas and buys himself a wife in the market place, thereby
changing the future course of his life forever. Together they work to raise themselves to
respectability. The second novel, *Claudine's Daughter*, continues the story of the Warwyck
clan, focusing on one of its illegitimate daughters who returns to Easthampton as a widow. In
Warwyck's Choice the heir to the Warwyck fortunes falls in love with the daughter of a family
who has despised the upstart Warwycks for three generations, until love, in the end, reconciles
them all. Each novel can stand on its own, but the fun is in reading the books in series, following
the generations and noticing the changes in the once slumbering seaside resort.
Finally there is *Fly Banners of Silk*, certainly her most ambitious work to date. Against the
backdrop of Louis Napoleon's Paris, one of the empire's most elegant ages, Louise, a destitute

orphan, drags herself up from the streets of the capital to become involved with one of high fashion's most famous names, Charles Worth. The story of her passionate journey is well told, and the nature of the fashion world is well-researched and enthralling in its detail.

So far, only one title has been published under the pseudonym Barbara Douglas, *Fair Wind of Love*. Sarah Kingsley leaves England to come to Canada in 1812. When she tries to get a job with Bryne Garrett, he wants to marry her instead. Douglas provides an interesting background by presenting the war of 1812 from the Canadian viewpoint. She has a nice touch in the Sarah-Bryne relationship.

Barbara Øvstedal seems to go from strength to strength. Everything she writes has a sure deft touch from the imaginative plotting to the fleshed-out characterizations. All this was evident in her earliest works and has become more so with each new publication.

—Marilyn Lockhart

LAMB, Charlotte.   Pseudonym for Sheila Holland, née Coates; also writes as Sheila Coates; Laura Hardy; Sheila Lancaster.   British.   Born in London, 22 December 1937. Educated at Ursuline Convent, Ilford, Essex. Married Richard Holland in 1959; two sons and three daughters. Secretary, Bank of England, London, 1954-56, and BBC, London, 1956-58. Agent: Caradoc King, A.P. Watt Ltd., 26-28 Bedford Row, London WC1R 4HL, England. Address: Applegate, Port St. Mary, Isle of Man, United Kingdom.

ROMANCE AND GOTHIC PUBLICATIONS

Novels

Follow a Stranger.   London, Mills and Boon, and Toronto, Harlequin, 1973.
Carnival Coast.   London, Mills and Boon, 1973; Toronto, Harlequin, 1974.
A Family Affair.   London, Mills and Boon, and Toronto, Harlequin, 1974.
Star-Crossed.   London, Mills and Boon, 1976; New York, Oxford University Press, 1978.
Sweet Sanctuary.   London, Mills and Boon, and Toronto, Harlequin, 1976.
Festival Summer.   London, Mills and Boon, and Toronto, Harlequin, 1977.
Florentine Spring.   London, Mills and Boon, and Toronto, Harlequin, 1977.
Hawk in a Blue Sky.   London, Mills and Boon, 1977; Toronto, Harlequin, 1978.
Kingfisher Morning.   London, Mills and Boon, 1977.
Master of Comus.   London, Mills and Boon, 1977; Toronto, Harlequin, 1978.
Call Back Yesterday.   London, Mills and Boon, and Toronto, Harlequin, 1978.
Desert Barbarian.   London, Mills and Boon, and Toronto, Harlequin, 1978.
Disturbing Stranger.   London, Mills and Boon, 1978; Toronto, Harlequin, 1979.
Autumn Conquest.   London, Mills and Boon, 1978.
The Long Surrender.   London, Mills and Boon, 1978.
The Cruel Flame.   London, Mills and Boon, 1978; Toronto, Harlequin, 1980.
Duel of Desire.   London, Mills and Boon, 1978.
The Devil's Arms.   London, Mills and Boon, 1978; Toronto, Harlequin, 1979.
Pagan Encounter.   London, Mills and Boon, 1978; Toronto, Harlequin, 1979.
Forbidden Fire.   London, Mills and Boon, 1979.
The Silken Trap.   London, Mills and Boon, 1979; Toronto, Harlequin, 1980.

Dark Dominion.   London, Mills and Boon, 1979.
Fever.   London, Mills and Boon, 1979; Toronto, Harlequin, 1980.
Dark Master.   London, Mills and Boon, 1979.
Temptation.   London, Mills and Boon, and Toronto, Harlequin, 1979.
Twist of Fate.   London, Mills and Boon, 1979; Toronto, Harlequin, 1980.
Possession.   London, Mills and Boon, 1979.
Love Is a Frenzy.   London, Mills and Boon, 1979; Toronto, Harlequin, 1980.
Frustration.   London, Mills and Boon, 1979.
Sensation.   London, Mills and Boon, 1979; Toronto, Harlequin, 1980.
Compulsion.   London, Mills and Boon, 1980; Toronto, Harlequin, 1981.
Crescendo.   London, Mills and Boon, 1980; Toronto, Harlequin, 1981.
Stranger in the Night.   London, Mills and Boon, 1980; Toronto, Harlequin, 1981.
Storm Centre.   London, Mills and Boon, and Toronto, Harlequin, 1980.
Seduction.   London, Mills and Boon, 1980; Toronto, Harlequin, 1981.
Savage Surrender.   London, Mills and Boon, and Toronto, Harlequin, 1980.
A Frozen Fire.   London, Mills and Boon, and Toronto, Harlequin, 1980.
Man's World.   London, Mills and Boon, 1980; Toronto, Harlequin, 1981.
Night Music.   London, Mills and Boon, 1980; Toronto, Harlequin, 1981.
Obsession.   London, Mills and Boon, 1980.
Retribution.   London, Mills and Boon, and Toronto, Harlequin, 1981.
Illusion.   Toronto, Harlequin, 1981.
Heartbreaker.   Toronto, Harlequin, 1981.
Desire.   London, Mills and Boon, and Toronto, Harlequin, 1981.
Dangerous.   London, Mills and Boon, and Toronto, Harlequin, 1981.
Abduction.   London, Mills and Boon, and Toronto, Harlequin, 1981.

Novels as Sheila Holland

Love in a Mist.   London, Hale, 1971.
Prisoner of the Heart.   London, Hale, 1972.
A Lantern in the Night.   London, Hale, 1973.
Falcon on the Hill.   London, Hale, 1974.
Shadows at Dawn.   London, Hale, 1975; Chicago, Playboy Press, 1979.
The Growing Season.   London, Hale, 1975.
The Gold of Apollo.   London, Hale, 1976.
The Caring Kind.   London, Hale, 1976.
The Devil and Miss Hay.   London, Hale, 1977.
Eleanor of Aquitaine.   London, Hale, 1978.
Maiden Castle.   Chicago, Playboy Press, 1978.
Love's Bright Flame.   Chicago, Playboy Press, 1978.
Dancing Hill.   Chicago, Playboy Press, 1978.
Folly by Candlelight.   London, Hale, 1978; Chicago, Playboy Press, 1979; as *The Notorious Gentleman*, Playboy Press, 1980.
Sophia.   Chicago, Playboy Press, 1979.
The Masque.   New York, Zebra, 1979.
The Merchant's Daughter.   Chicago, Playboy Press, 1980.
Miss Charlotte's Fancy.   Chicago, Playboy Press, 1980.
Secrets to Keep.   Chicago, Playboy Press, 1980.

Novels as Sheila Coates

A Crown Usurped.   London, Hale, 1972.
The Queen's Letter.   London, Hale, 1973.
The Flight of the Swan.   London, Hale, 1973.
The Bells of the City.   London, Hale, 1975.

Novels as Sheila Lancaster

Dark Sweet Wanton.   London, Hodder and Stoughton, 1979; New York, Jove, 1980.
The Tilthammer.   London, Hodder and Stoughton, 1980.
Mistress of Fortune.   London, Hodder and Stoughton, 1982.

Novels as Laura Hardy

Burning Memories.   London, Silhouette, 1981.
Playing with Fire.   London, Silhouette, 1981.
Dream Master.   London, Silhouette, 1982.
Tears and Red Roses.   London, Silhouette, 1982.

Charlotte Lamb comments:

I try to write romantic novels which have very real characters and situations, but which never lose sight of the basic truth about romantic fiction—that we are creating dreams for our readers, dreams which must be rooted in real life if they are to be intensely powerful. The more closely a reader can identify with the book, the more she can respond to it and enjoy it. Women are both highly practical and deeply emotional, and what they want in their fiction is a mixture of warmly observed life and powerful emotion. All fiction is invented; the best fiction is close to reality yet with that added dimension of an escape into dreams.

*   *   *

Charlotte Lamb's series romances are characterized by energy and sensation despite their large number. For a considerable period of time, Lamb published one novel per month. Often identified by highly charged one-word titles (*Obsession, Frustration, Fever, Seduction*), her novels detail the romantic entanglements of characters with deep-seated problems, often related to sexuality.

Although Lamb's heroines are occasionally country girls, their most typical milieu is London. Some are secretaries to playboy businessmen; others are actresses, singers, or artists. They are usually young, occasionally naive, and always more inhibited than other women in the books. Her heroes are older, highly successful, and domineering without being excessively brutal. She knows how to suggest an appealing vulnerability in traditionally "macho" men.

Lamb often writes about heroines who have been victims of sexual trauma. In *Stranger in the Night* and *Seduction* her women are unwillingly seduced and are marked by the experience. She writes about troubled marriages in *Sensation* and *A Frozen Fire*. In *Dark Dominion* the hero is almost pathologically jealous. In *Frustration* the heroine is debilitated by the death of her husband. Most heroines need to be shown how to express sexuality; most heroes need to be taught fidelity. Although Lamb's topics are often more potentially sensational than those of other series writers, she handles the material with circumspection. Any author as prolific as Lamb will produce uneven work, but despite her productivity she is unusually inventive within the restricted range of series romance formulas.

—Kay Mussell

LAMONT, Marianne. *See* **RUNDLE, Anne**.

LANCASTER, Sheila. *See* **LAMB, Charlotte**.

LANCASTER, Vicky. *See* **ELSNA, Hebe**.

LANCE, Leslie. *See* **CHARLES, Theresa**.

LANE, Roumelia.   Address: c/o Mills and Boon Ltd., 15-16 Brooks Mews, London W1A 1DR, England.

ROMANCE AND GOTHIC PUBLICATIONS

Novels

Rose of the Desert.   London, Mills and Boon, 1967; Toronto, Harlequin, 1968.
Hideaway Heart.   London, Mills and Boon, 1967; Toronto, Harlequin, 1968.
House of the Winds.   London, Mills and Boon, and Toronto, Harlequin, 1968.
A Summer to Love.   London, Mills and Boon, 1968; Toronto, Harlequin, 1969.
Terminus Tehran.   London, Mills and Boon, 1969; Toronto, Harlequin, 1970.

Sea of Zanj.   London, Mills and Boon, and Toronto, Harlequin, 1969.
The Scented Hills.   London, Mills and Boon, 1970; Toronto, Harlequin, 1971.
Café Mimosa.   London, Mills and Boon, and Toronto, Harlequin, 1971.
In the Shade of the Palms.   London, Mills and Boon, 1972; Toronto, Harlequin, 1973.
Nurse at Noongwalla.   London, Mills and Boon, 1973; Toronto, Harlequin, 1974.
Across the Lagoon.   London, Mills and Boon, and Toronto, Harlequin, 1974.
Stormy Encounter.   London, Mills and Boon, 1974; Toronto, Harlequin, 1975.
Where the Moonflower Weaves.   London, Mills and Boon, 1974.
Harbour of Deceit.   London, Mills and Boon, and Toronto, Harlequin, 1975.
The Tenant of San Mateo.   London, Mills and Boon, and Toronto, Harlequin, 1976.
Himalayan Moonlight.   London, Mills and Boon, 1977.
Bamboo Wedding.   Toronto, Harlequin, 1977.
The Brightest Star.   London, Mills and Boon, 1978.
Hidden Rapture.   London, Mills and Boon, 1978; Toronto, Harlequin, 1979.
Second Spring.   London, Mills and Boon, 1980.

*   *   *

Roumelia Lane was first published in the Harlequin Romance series in 1968 and since then has easily established herself as one of the better romance writers. She has exceptional ability for combining exotic backgrounds with fresh, vivid characters that her readers thoroughly enjoy. The jungle forests of Ceylon, romantic, sunny Italy, and primitive Tanzania all become the stage for her novels, for she is one of the romance writers who deliberately draws her readers to far away places and unknown experiences.

Because of her penchant for unusual settings, Lane takes particular care in researching the material for her backgrounds. This is quite evident in novels such as *Where the Moonflower Weaves.* After her father's death, Jodi Lawrence tries to earn passage money back to England by caring for an older woman who is also returning to England. Blake Morrison is to take them by truck to the seaport to catch their ship, but during the trip a bridge collapses and they are left stranded deep in the Ceylon jungle. It takes them three weeks to reach civilization, and during this time they undergo terrifying experiences as they look for food, water, and shelter during their long march. The vivid detail and graphic descriptions of scenery and people make this novel one of her most fascinating.

Surprisingly, the background does not overpower the characters. Jodi Lawrence's quiet courage and sense of integrity help her withstand the animosity of Blake Morrison as he misunderstands her relationship with a neighboring planter just before they leave. The trek itself is a ruthless test of character and will which she stubbornly sets out to overcome. Blake Morrison exhibits the same sort of courage and resourcefulness in spite of overwhelming odds. Actually the entire story may be used as a classic example of plotting, for it shows man against man, man against self, and man against nature. The use of one such element makes a novel strong, but to combine all three elements of plotting successfully makes an exciting and unusually moving novel to read.

In *House of the Winds* Lane resorts to a similiar plotting technique, as Laurie Weldon sets out to convince Ryan Holt to take her on safari in Tanzania. She is determined to gain recognition as a photographer, and she feels that the photographs from the safari will achieve this purpose. The constant interplay of conflicting emotions against the dangerous background of wild animals and vast areas of wilderness offers Lane endless choice of motivation and plotting intricacies. Laurie is young, ambitious, and vulnerable, while Ryan is a hardened hunter and safari master.

A Summer to Love is an unexpected change of pace. Stacey Roberts takes a job as a tourist guide in Sorrento for the summer. It should have been fun, especially as she looked forward to working with Jeremy again, but she finds herself under the domination of the ruthless hotel manager, Mark Lawford, who sees to it she does a full day's job of keeping other people happy.

Nowhere is balance so evident as in the writing of Roumelia Lane. Her novels are exceptionally complicated in detail and characterization. Most of all, they are the sort of novels her readers avidly anticipate. Although she has evidently mastered the more gripping sort of novel, she yet manages to produce the occasional simple romance that her readers enjoy.

—Arlene Moore

LA TOURRETTE, Jacqueline. American. Born in Denver, Colorado, 5 May 1926. Educated at San Jose State University, California, 1948-51; trained as a nurse at St. Margaret's Hospital, Epping, Essex, 1958. Married David Gibeson in 1948 (divorced, 1970); three children. Teletype operator, Alaska Communications System, 1954-55; medical secretary, Massachusetts Institute of Technology, Cambridge, 1961-69. Since 1969, medical secretary, Kaiser-Permanente Medical Center, Santa Clara, California. Agent: Raines and Raines, 475 Fifth Avenue, New York, New York 10017, U.S.A.

ROMANCE AND GOTHIC PUBLICATIONS

Novels

   The Joseph Stone. New York, Nordon, 1971.
   A Matter of Sixpence. New York, Dell, 1972.
   The Madonna Creek Witch. New York, Dell, 1973.
   The Previous Lady. New York, Dell, 1974.
   The Pompeii Scroll. New York, Delacorte Press, 1975.
   Shadows in Umbria. New York, Putnam, 1979.
   The Wild Harp. New York, Fawcett, 1981.

*   *   *

Jacqueline La Tourrette's earlier novels are mostly horror stories in the style of Thomas Tryon. *The Madonna Creek Witch*, for example, is set in the Arizona Territory in the late 19th century, where a large, strange family is haunted by a witch. It was favorably received, some reviewers comparing it favorably with Tom Tryon's *The Other*.

The Previous Lady, also a horror novel involving little real action, concerns Amanda, a young woman who rents a secluded old English house from a lawyer. He is reluctant to let her have it, since the place has not been lived in since a former tenant went mad and died there. Amanda discovers a manuscript written by the insane tenant which tells about Christopher Lance who occupied the premises during the Victorian era. Naturally, Amanda becomes obsessed with the long-dead Lance and slowly begins losing her own sanity.

From these earlier novels, La Tourrette makes a sudden switch in style in *The Pompeii Scroll*, an adventurous and fun-filled story about collectors of illegal antiquities. The heroine, Joyce Lacey, digs up a smiling Etruscan statue in Greece which mysteriously disappears. She is framed for the theft and expelled from Greece in disgrace. Her pride in tatters, she retreats to Pompeii where she meets Antonio, a handsome Italian guide of archaeological sites. Together they begin a casual search for a legendary scroll stolen from Pompeii more than a century before, only to discover there is a connection between the missing scroll and the stolen statue. From this point the plot moves swiftly, providing sheer entertainment all the way. The dialogue is sophisticated and clever, and moves the plotline forward rather than just supplying filler. Inspector Vizzini is an excellently drawn character. Add to all this a love story with class, and you have a real treat.

Shadows in Umbria follows suit. This romantic suspense tale again takes place in Italy and involves a woman archaeologist, Christina Matthews, and a bullying Italian male archaeologist. They are digging up an Etruscan site on the land of an attractive Italian count whom the villagers consider in league with the devil. When the Count showers Christina with unwanted attention, she escapes him only to land herself in the arms of a grave robber. The story is rather implausible, and so many complications are often hard to make sense of. However, if the reader is willing to suspend disbelief, the novel is an interesting light read.

Embodying another change in style and content, *The Wild Harp* is a three-generational family saga about Irish immigrants who settle in Boston in the 1850's. The emphasis is on the women, who are the pillars of the family. The fate of the Noonans, after early years of squalor in Boston's Irish ghetto, takes a turn for the better when Mary is hired as a wet nurse by the wealthy Maddigan household. Mary's gifted daughter, Rosaleen, is allowed to attend tutored classes with the four Maddigan sons, one of whom she eventually marries. This is a well-told tale, well-paced and with fleshed-out characterizations.

All in all, Jacqueline La Tourrette is a talented author who seems to be trying out many different genres of fiction, achieving success in each of them. Any of her books can be recommended with confidence.

—Marilyn Lockhart

LEE, Elsie (née Williams).   Also writes as Elsie Cromwell; Norman Daniels; Jane Gordon; Lee Sheridan.   American.   Born in Brooklyn, New York, 24 January 1912. Attended Swarthmore College, Pennsylvania, 1929-32; Pratt Institute, New York, 1932-33. Married Marton Lee in 1941 (died). Librarian, Waterhouse and Company, New York, 1937-42; Office Manager, Reeves Laboratories, New York, 1942-45; Librarian, Gulf Oil Company, New York, 1947-51; Executive Secretary, Andrews Clark and Buckley, New York, 1951-53. Agent: Bill Berger Associates, 444 East 58th Street, New York, New York 10022.

ROMANCE AND GOTHIC PUBLICATIONS

Novels

The Blood Red Oscar. New York, Lancer, 1962.
Sam Benedict: Cast the First Stone (novelization of TV series; as Norman Daniels).   New York, Lancer, 1963.
A Comedy of Terrors (novelization of screenplay).   New York, Lancer, 1964.
The Masque of the Red Death (novelization of screenplay).   New York, Lancer, 1964.
Muscle Beach (novelization of screenplay).   New York, Lancer, 1964.
Season of Evil. New York, Lancer, 1965; as *Two Hearts Apart* (as Jane Gordon), London, Hale, 1973.
Dark Moon, Lost Lady. New York, Lancer, 1965; London, Hale, 1973.
Clouds over Vellanti. New York, Lancer, 1965; London, Hale, 1972.
The Curse of Carranca. New York, Lancer, 1966; as *The Second Romance*, London, Hale, 1974.
Mansion of the Golden Windows. New York, Lancer, 1966.
The Drifting Sands. New York, Lancer, 1966.

Sinister Abbey. New York, Lancer, 1967; as *Romance on the Rhine*, London, Hale, 1974.
The Spy at the Villa Miranda. New York, Lancer, 1967; as *The Unhappy Parting*, London, Hale, 1973.
Doctor's Office. New York, Lancer, 1968.
The Governess (as Elsie Cromwell). New York, Paperback Library, 1969; as *Guardian of Love*, London, Hale, 1972.
Satan's Coast. New York, Lancer, 1969; as *Mystery Castle*, London, Hale, 1973.
Fulfillment. New York, Lancer, 1969.
Barrow Sinister. New York, Dell, 1969; as *Romantic Assignment*, London, Hale, 1974.
Ivorstone Manor (as Elsie Cromwell). New York, Pocket Books, 1970; London, Hale, 1973.
Silence Is Golden. New York, Dell, 1971.
Wingarden. New York, Arbor House, 1971.
The Diplomatic Lover. New York, Dell, 1971.
Star of Danger. New York, Dell, 1971.
The Passions of Medora Graeme. New York, Arbor House, 1972.
A Prior Betrothal. New York, Arbor House, 1973; London, Hale, 1976.
The Wicked Guardian. New York, Dell, 1973; London, Sphere, 1979.
Second Season. New York, Dell, 1973.
An Eligible Connection. Bath, Chivers, 1974; New York, Dell, 1975.
Roomates. New York, Dell, 1976.
The Nabob's Widow. New York, Delacorte Press, 1976.
Mistress of Mount Fair. New York, Dell, 1977.

OTHER PUBLICATIONS

Other as Lee Sheridan (with Michael Sheridan)

How to Get the Most Out of Your Tape Recording. Flushing, New York, Robins, 1958.
More Fun with Your Tape Recorders and Stereo. Los Angeles, Trend, 1958.
The Bachelor's Cookbook. New York, Collier, 1962.

Other

The Exciting World of Rocks and Gems. Los Angeles, Trend, 1959.
Easy Gourmet Cooking. New York, Lancer, 1962.
At Home with Plants: A Guide to Successful Indoor Gardening. New York, Macmillan, and London, Collier Macmillan, 1966.
Second Easy Gourmet Cookbook. New York, Lancer, 1968.
Book of Simple Gourmet Cookery. New York, Arbor House, 1971.
Party Cookbook. New York, Arbor House, 1974.

*   *   *

Elsie Lee, who also writes as Elsie Cromwell and Jane Gordon, is a versatile author whose works include "modern gothics," Regency romances, and gourmet cookbooks. She began writing in the 1940's and sold her first stories to *Ladies Home Journal*. Those novels classified as modern gothics did not appear in print until the early 1960's. The period since then has been a prolific and successful one for Elsie Lee, resulting in the publication of more than 20 romantic novels.

Although others consider her a modern gothic writer, Elsie Lee says (in *The Writer*, May 1973), "...despite fifteen of my novels so advertised, I do not write gothics.... The novels I write are better described as fairy tales for grownups—primarily women...." She also points out how her novels differ from "true" gothics like *The Castle of Otranto*. Lee's novels are contemporary;

built around possible (although not probable) situations; contain little violence and terror; focus on characters who, although imaginary, are portrayed realistically—a young, usually American heroine who is intelligent, well-educated, and quick-witted plus a solid dependable, older hero who tends to underestimate the heroine at first and who always works at some career. Lee's novels also do not fit the gothic formula which requires, in addition to the hero and heroine, at least one minor male and female character. For Lee, there is the hero, heroine, and villain—and the secret or puzzle around which the plot revolves. Lee's novels are also more "spicy" than the gothics written by many others which typically gloss over the sexual aspects of the male-female relationship.

Two of Lee's most popular modern gothics—*The Passions of Medora Graeme* and *Wingarden*—illustrate the style and approach that form the core of her appeal to readers. *The Passions of Medora Graeme*, for example, has been called a "lovely little romance" but "spicier" than many others in that genre because of love affairs past and present and because of the "earthy" Greek setting. One reviewer (*Library Journal*, 15 October 1972) notes that the Greek island—where "Dolly-Medora-Medarling-Graeme" and Simeon Vladow meet—"...is a great healer, and their affair doesn't do them a bit of harm either." Dolly and Simeon, like most of Lee's leading characters, work in interesting fields. Dolly is a successful fabric and dress designer; Simeon is a promising London surgeon. What gets the plot going is their need for long vacations to recover from emotional upsets: Dolly's discovery that her business partner/lover wants to marry another woman and Simeon's loss of two patients, one of them his girlfriend. Lee also adds some social and economic reality to the story as Dolly and Simeon help the islanders to buy a new generator to power the looms critical to their economic livelihood.

In *Wingarden* Elsie Lee paints Chloe as an intelligent heroine who has very strong opinions and isn't afraid to voice them and who has a healthy streak of skepticism along with the requisite sense of responsibility to family and tradition. One critic commented about *Wingarden's* female lead, "For a gothic heroine, Chloe is unusually intelligent, forthright, and determined." The sole heir to the estate of a grandmother she never knew, Chloe successfully solves the "puzzle" by finding the missing letter of instruction her grandmother Amelia wrote before her death and by discovering what is really going at the supposedly "haunted" Wingarden. True to the contemporary setting and realistic characterization of her actors, Lee also does something that writers of modern gothics typically do not do. She incorporates into the plot an awareness of social issues (more fully realized than in *Medora Graeme* or other novels). *Wingarden* is set in Virginia, in a rigidly segregationist part of the South, and the interaction between Chloe's grandmother and her black servants reflects these long-standing patterns. On the surface, Amelia treated her black help no differently than the cultural definitions of the town prescribed. In actuality, however, she was concerned about their welfare and provided them with the opportunity to become self-sufficient through a bequest of property in her will. Lee thus portrays Amelia as a woman who is shrewd enough to avoid antagonizing the townspeople and unnecessarily risking outbreaks of racial violence.

Lee's ability to create realistic characters is evident in the portrait of Amelia that emerges via Chloe. Even though Amelia is dead as the novel begins, Elsie Lee makes her come alive through Chloe's insights into how her grandmother might have felt and acted towards the family and towards the blacks. There is almost a mystical sense of connection between Amelia and Chloe who never met but who look remarkably alike and have some of the same strong will and spirit.

Whether we describe her novels as "liberated modern gothics" or as "fairy tales for grown-ups," it is clear that Elsie Lee is a writer of skill and social awareness. Women readers in particular would find much to admire in her heroines. Previous research that we conducted on modern gothic novels suggested that the strong sex-role characterization of the heroines is a large part of the appeal of these novels. Most of the heroines in the gothics we analyzed were portrayed as toward the non-traditional end of the scale in terms of personality traits (i.e., not submissive or passive) and attitudes toward careers and marriage (i.e., likely to work and to have other goals besides finding a husband) (*Pacific Sociological Review*, April 1977). Clearly Elsie Lee's heroines would be of the same type and they are probably a major reason for the continuing appeal of her gothic romances.

—Josephine A. Ruggiero and Louise C. Weston

LEIGH, Roberta. *See* **LINDSAY, Rachel**.

LESLIE, Doris (née Oppenheim).   British.   Born in London, c. 1902. Educated privately in London, and in Brussels; studied art in Florence. Married 1) John Leslie (died); 2) Sir Walter Fergusson Hannay in 1936 (died, 1961). Served in Civil Defence, 1941-45. Address: The Grange, Felcourt, near East Grinstead, Sussex RH19 2LA, England. *Died 31 May 1982.*

ROMANCE AND GOTHIC PUBLICATIONS

Novels

The Starling. London, Hurst and Blackett, and New York, Century, 1927.
Fools in Mortar. London, Hurst and Blackett, and New York, Century, 1928.
The Echoing Green. London, Hurst and Blackett, 1929.
Terminus. London, Hurst and Blackett, 1931.
Puppets Parade. London, Lane, 1932.
Full Flavour. London, Lane, and New York, Macmillan, 1934.
Fair Company. London, Lane, and New York, Macmillan, 1936.
Concord in Jeopardy. London, Hutchinson, and New York, Macmillan, 1938.
Another Cynthia: The Adventures of Cynthia, Lady Ffulkes 1780-1850. London, Hutchinson, and New York, Macmillan, 1939.
Royal William: The Story of a Democrat. London, Hutchinson, 1940; New York, Macmillan, 1941.
House in the Dust. London, Hutchinson, and New York, Macmillan, 1942.
Polonaise. London, Hutchinson, 1943.
Folly's End. London, Hutchinson, 1944.
The Peverills. London, Hutchinson, 1946.
Wreath for Arabella. London, Hutchinson, 1948; New York, Popular Library, 1973.
That Enchantress. London, Hutchinson, 1950; New York, Popular Library, 1973.
A Toast to Lady Mary. London, Hutchinson, 1954; New York, Popular Library, 1973.
Peridot Flight. London, Hutchinson, 1956.
Tales of Grace and Favour (omnibus). London, Hutchinson, 1956.
As the Tree Falls. London, Hodder and Stoughton, 1958; as *The King's Traitor*, New York, Popular Library, 1973.
The Perfect Wife. London, Hodder and Stoughton, 1960; as *The Prime Minister's Wife*, New York, Doubleday, 1961.
I Return. London, Hodder and Stoughton, 1962; as *Vagabond's Way*, New York, Doubleday, 1962.
This for Caroline. London, Heinemann, 1964; New York, Popular Library, 1973.
Paragon Street. London, Heinemann, 1965.
The Sceptre and the Rose. London, Heinemann, 1967.
The Marriage of Martha Todd. London, Heinemann, 1968.
The Rebel Princess. London, Heinemann, 1970; New York, Popular Library, 1973.
A Young Wives' Tale. London, Heinemann, 1971.
The Desert Queen. London, Heinemann, 1972.
The Dragon's Head. London, Heinemann, 1973.
The Incredible Duchess. London, Heinemann, 1974.

Call Back Yesterday. London, Heinemann, 1975.
Notorious Lady. London, Heinemann, 1976.
The Warrior King. London, Heinemann, 1977.
Crown of Thorns. London, Heinemann, 1979.

OTHER PUBLICATIONS

Other

The Great Corinthian: A Portrait of the Prince Regent. London, Eyre and Spottiswoode, 1952; New York, Oxford University Press, 1953.

*   *   *

Doris Leslie has an impressive list of titles to her credit, both novels and "biographical
studies." Her period research is obviously intensive: seldom if ever can she be faulted in any
detail, and she projects a real sense of history vividly at work in her own mind's eye. She writes
of people important to her who, through her, become so to the reader. It is the day-to-dayness
of ordinary life that animates her novels, rather than engrossing plot or suspense. Events do
occur, but in an apparently formless, accidental way as in most lives, only forming recognizable
patterns in retrospect. Her characters, though convincing and well-rounded, seem all to speak
in the same voice, however their circumstances may differ; and while it is a voice worth hearing,
it provides little variety.

She is best known for her biographical studies, in part perhaps because she has ventured into
territories heretofore the province of the scholar only. Readers of the romantic-historic genre
have at their command literally dozens of titles based upon the familiar story of Elizabeth
Tudor, her tragic mother and monstrous golden father; similarly, there are scores of works
based on the lives of Queen Victoria, Empress Josephine, Louis XIV, and others of that
category of historical personage whose own vividly dramatic lives attract the romantic novelist
as a lightning rod draws the thunderbolt. But what other author has seen the possibilities
inherent in the relatively unfamiliar stories of Lady Blessington, bluff and foolish William IV,
or Queen Anne's beloved Lady Masham? Though Doris Leslie has traversed more popularly
familiar terrain with her stories of the Prince Regent, Caro Lamb, and Chopin, it is the lesser
historical personages in her pageant of fortune's fools and favourites that best hold the reader's
interest.

A failing in her work is the recurring tendency to suggest the workings of incomprehensible
providence at work in a tiresomely portentous manner; as in making reference, quite out of
context to the story in hand, to the fact that even as the action takes place, across the dark city,
that selfsame night, a young girl is untimely called from her bed in Kensington Palace...Vic-
toria! (She is also in the habit of referring to her own other novels in asterisked footnotes.)

In spite of a few such annoying mannerisms, as well as a propensity for documenting the facts
of a life in essay form, interpolating patches of very readable dialogue, and renaming it a study,
Doris Leslie has earned her popularity, if for no other reason than as the author of a painless
mini-course in history. She proves that history is peopled with characters any one of whom, if
singled out by a sympathetic, period-conscious writer, provides a fresh perspective on familiar,
often-worked literary and historical ground.

—Joan McGrath

LEWIS, Maynah.   British.   Born in Liverpool, Lancashire, 14 April 1919. Educated at schools in Scotland. Married Victor Lewis in 1936; one son. Professional musician and teacher; full-time writer from 1958. Recipient: Romantic Novelists Association Ayres Award, 1962, and Major Award, 1967, 1972. Agent: John Farquharson Ltd., 8 Bell Yard, London WC2A 2JU. Address: c/o Robert Hale Ltd., 45-47 Clerkenwell Green, London EC1R 0HT, England.

ROMANCE AND GOTHIC PUBLICATIONS

Novels

> *No Place for Love.*   London, Hurst and Blackett, 1963.
> *Give Me This Day.*   London, Hurst and Blackett, 1964.
> *See the Bright Morning.*   London, Hurst and Blackett, 1965.
> *Make Way for Tomorrow.*   London, Hurst and Blackett, 1966; New York, Beagle, 1973.
> *The Long, Hot Days.*   London, Hurst and Blackett, 1966.
> *The Future Is Forever.*   London, Hurst and Blackett, 1967.
> *Till Then, My Love.*   London, Hurst and Blackett, 1968.
> *Of No Fixed Abode.*   London, Hurst and Blackett, 1968.
> *Symphony for Two Players.*   London, Hurst and Blackett, 1969.
> *A Corner of Eden.*   London, Hurst and Blackett, 1970.
> *A Pride of Innocence.*   London, Hurst and Blackett, 1971; New York, Beagle, 1973.
> *Too Late for Tears.*   London, Hurst and Blackett, 1972.
> *The Town That Nearly Died.*   London, Collins, 1973.
> *The Miracle of Lac Blanche.*   London, Collins, 1973.
> *The Unforgiven.*   London, Collins, 1974; New York, Ace, 1976.
> *The Other Side of Paradise.*   London, Collins, 1975.
> *Yesterday Came Suddenly.*   London, Collins, 1975.
> *A Woman of Property.*   London, Collins, 1976.
> *These My Children.*   London, Collins, 1977.
> *Love Has Two Faces.*   London, Hale, 1981.
> *Barren Harvest.*   London, Hale, 1981.
> *Hour of the Siesta.*   London, Hale, 1982.

*   *   *

Maynah Lewis, a professional musician turned prolific novelist, has no doubt had little time to be idle, and this is reflected in the activity and diversity of her novels. Her heroes and heroines are all working (though not necessarily "working-class") people, deeply involved in their jobs or careers, be they in the legal or medical professions, or running a corner store. Each novel is set in different and definite surroundings: a Caribbean island, (*The Other Side of Paradise*), a small industrial Northern town (*A Woman of Property*), a home for handicapped children (*Love Has Two Faces*). The characters are not on the whole seekers of experience. Often they are settled, rather staid people forced into action by tangible problems: the loss of memory, the forces of big business, the difficulties of dealing with a delinquent child. Neither do they long for romance: love creeps up on them accidentally after an acquaintanceship, or reappears from a long-distant past.

Nowhere is this better illustrated than in *Yesterday Came Suddenly*, where the hero, Edward, a 38-year-old right-wing lawyer who has taken a public stand against declining moral standards, is approached out of the blue by the girlfriend of his university days, the mysterious, dark-eyed, apparently widowed Eleanor. Eleanor begs him to defend her delinquent son David, who, while driving a stolen car with a gang of friends, has run over and badly injured an elderly man. When Edward discovers that Eleanor has never been married and that David is indeed his own illegitimate son, he is thrown into confusion. Suddenly on the other side of the moral fence he flounders between his desire to protect his son, his renewed passion for Eleanor, and his unwillingness to be seen as a hypocrite in the eyes of his colleagues, his clinging mother, and his beautiful, clever, undemanding too-good-to-be-true doctor fiancée. But in typical Lewis style, his problems are sorted out as neatly as they happened: his colleagues rally round him, David is given a suspended sentence, his fiancée, retaining her pride, goes off to South Africa, sparing him even the ordeal of making a clean break with her, and Edward is reunited with his one real love, with the approval of her mother if not his own. Although Edward's dilemma is a real one, and well set up, he remains a dislikable character throughout the book, shirking responsibility wherever he can. One at times feels that this learned lawyer should, at his age, be a bit more grown-up.

Also guilty of shirking parental responsibility is Robert, the lawyer hero of *These My Children* who, until the death of his forceful wife prompts him into action, has taken no interest in the upbringing of his children. Now alone and lonely, Robert sets out to reestablish contact with his grown-up daughters and son. The theme of child/parent conflict re-emerges often in Lewis's books. More often than not the young are striking out by themselves in the face of parental opposition, either to pursue an "unsuitable" partner (Hilary and Carol in *These My Children*) or to take a stand against something they believe to be morally wrong (Veronica and Stuart in *A Woman of Property*). Any guilty feelings they may have about hurting or leaving an aged relative are, in the end, exonerated: Lewis's predilection for happy endings for all ensures a reunion in the end, by which time the parent is well on the way to forming a lasting relationship with someone of his or her own generation.

It is difficult to sum up work of such diversity as Maynah Lewis's. She is at her best in devising interesting plots and settings for her characters though one might wish, at times, that the tensions inherent in these situations could have been more fully explored. However, the richness of her novels has ensured her continuing popularity, and is the reason, no doubt, why she has twice been winner of the Romantic Novelists Association Major Award.

—Judith Summers

LEWTY, Marjorie (née Lobb). British. Born in Wallasey, Cheshire, 8 April 1906. Attended Queen Mary High School, Liverpool. Married Richard Arthur Lewty in 1933; one son and one daughter. Secretary, District Bank Ltd., Liverpool, 1923-33. Address: The Knapp, Studland, Swanage, Dorset BH19 3AE, England.

ROMANCE AND GOTHIC PUBLICATIONS

Novels

Never Call It Loving. London, Mills and Boon, 1958; Toronto, Harlequin, 1968.
The Million Stars. London, Mills and Boon, 1959.
The Imperfect Secretary. London, Mills and Boon, 1959; Toronto, Harlequin, 1967.
The Lucky One. London, Mills and Boon, 1961; Toronto, Harlequin, 1968.
This Must Be for Ever. London, Mills and Boon, 1962.
Alex Rayner, Dental Nurse. London, Mills and Boon, and Toronto, Harlequin, 1965.
Dental Nurse at Denley's. London, Mills and Boon, 1968; Toronto, Harlequin, 1969.
Town Nurse—Country Nurse. London, Mills and Boon, 1970; Toronto, Harlequin, 1971.
The Extraordinary Engagement. London, Mills and Boon, 1972; Toronto, Harlequin, 1973.
The Rest Is Magic. London, Mills and Boon, 1973; Toronto, Harlequin, 1974.

All Made of Wishes.   London, Mills and Boon, and Toronto, Harlequin, 1974.
Flowers in Stony Places.   London, Mills and Boon, and Toronto, Harlequin, 1975.
The Fire in the Diamond.   London, Mills and Boon, and Toronto, Harlequin, 1976.
To Catch a Butterfly.   London, Mills and Boon, and Toronto, Harlequin, 1977.
The Time and the Loving.   London, Mills and Boon, 1977; Toronto, Harlequin, 1978.
The Short Engagement.   London, Mills and Boon, and Toronto, Harlequin, 1978.
A Very Special Man.   London, Mills and Boon, 1979.
A Certain Smile.   London, Mills and Boon, 1979; Toronto, Harlequin, 1980.
Prisoner in Paradise.   London, Mills and Boon, 1980.
Love Is a Dangerous Game.   London, Mills and Boon, 1980.
Beyond the Lagoon.   London, Mills and Boon, 1981.

Marjorie Lewty comments:

All I can say about my work is that I write to please the reader, as well as myself. I believe the purpose of fiction is to tell a story, and that a story is what most people enjoy. I write romantic novels because I was born and brought up in a romantic age, the age of the 1920's, when there was still optimism in the world. I don't think romantic stories are necessarily "escapist," using the word in its pejorative sense, any more than a trip into the countryside is "escapist." I think the "romantic" formula corresponds to the basic myth of all time: the descent into despair, followed by the rise again to happiness—the happy ending. This myth is built into our culture, which would account for the popularity of the romantic novel through the ages.

*   *   *

Marjorie Lewty is a British writer who has developed her own individual style of writing romance novels. Usually her novels are written against a background to English towns and the countryside, so that much of the story development rests with the day in, day out activities of her characters as they meet and eventually fall in love. The strongest element in her writing is her characterization. Here she draws on her own interest in psychology to portray not only believable characters, but complex ones.

For instance, in *Flowers in Stony Places* she develops the character of Lisa, the sister of Samantha, her heroine in the novel. Lisa is a light, frivolous person who is shallow and self-centered to an unbelievable degree. She plays an indirect role in creating tension between the leading characters and appears at particularly crucial times in the story. Lewty's use of Lisa in the story to establish Samantha's character and to provide motivation for Adam Royle's attitude toward Samantha is particularly well done, and illustrates her ability to portray well-rounded characters. Besides Lisa and Samantha, Marjorie Lewty adds the character of Estelle Norton, the new matron for the school where Samantha and Adam Royle work. She is a cold, calculating person with little empathy for the boys in her care. Lewty's ability to balance the motivation of the three women in a single novel is quite remarkable and shows her command of characterization.

One of her most enjoyable novels is *The Imperfect Secretary*. In this story, Lewty develops the character of Carol Waring, described as an attractive girl who is warm-hearted, generous, and lively. But she is also young and impulsive, and frequently displays those qualities that are not considered "professional" in a good secretary. Her employer is determined to change her into his idea of a good secretary and much of the story revolves around his attempts to make her so. The hero, Clive Benedict, is the head of a large construction company and sees the task as a challenge. It is Carol's warm-heartedness that helps to solve a particularly nasty problem when a very old lady refuses to move from her cottage into a newer housing area. Officialdom sees her as cantankerous and obstinate, while Carol learns that she really fears losing touch with her grandson if he can not find her once she has left her old home. Carol constantly acts from instinctive qualities of goodness and kindness, rather than business-like efficiency. In the end, naturally, Clive Benedict finds that these qualities are far more important to him than an efficient secretary.

Carol Waring is typical of her heroines, and perhaps in a way Clive Benedict is just as typical of her heroes. They are often businessmen who have to make hard decisions and who have to maintain a wall of defense in order to be as successful as they are. It is not until the heroine learns more about him and is able to get beyond the outer wall that she realizes just what kind of difficulties the hero must constantly deal with. Frequently he is a sensitive person who is able to understand and empathize with the dreamers of the world.

Throughout her writing, Marjorie Lewty is able to maintain the suspense of the story and is able to inter-weave plot, motivation, and character in such a way that her readers are unaware of just how skillfully they are being led in a particular direction. There are no towering heights to be climbed, nor extraordinary depths to be plumbed; yet, her novels hold her readers and take them away from their own cares for a while, a fact that is extremely important to them and perhaps accounts for her popularity as a writer.

—Arlene Moore

LEY, Alice Chetwynd (née Humphrey). British. Born in Halifax, Yorkshire, 12 October 1913. Educated at King Edward VI Grammar School, Birmingham; London University, diploma in sociology 1962. Married Kenneth James Ley in 1945; two sons. Since 1963, Tutor in Creative Writing, Harrow College of Further Education, Middlesex. Past Chairman, Romantic Novelists Association. Agent: Curtis Brown Ltd., 1 Craven Hill, London W2 3EP. Address: 42 Cannonbury Avenue, Pinner, Middlesex HA5 1TS, England.

ROMANCE AND GOTHIC PUBLICATIONS

Novels

> *The Jewelled Snuff Box.* London, Hale, 1959; New York, Beagle, 1974.
> *The Georgian Rake.* London, Hale, 1960; New York, Beagle 1974.
> *The Guinea Stamp.* London, Hale, 1961; as *The Courting of Joanna*, New York, Ballantine, 1976.
> *Master of Liversedge.* London, Hale, 1966; as *The Master and the Maiden*, New York, Ballantine, 1977.
> *The Clandestine Betrothal.* London, Hale, 1967; New York, Ballantine, 1976.
> *The Toast of the Town.* London, Hale, 1969; New York, Ballantine, 1976.
> *Letters for a Spy.* London, Hale, 1970; as *The Sentimental Spy*, New York, Ballantine, 1977.
> *A Season at Brighton.* London, Hale, 1971; New York, Ballantine, 1976.
> *Tenant of Chesdene Manor.* London, Hale, 1974; as *Beloved Diana*, New York, Ballantine, 1977.
> *The Beau and the Bluestocking.* London, Hale, 1975; New York, Ballantine, 1977.
> *At Dark of the Moon.* London, Hale, 1977; New York, Ballantine, 1978.
> *An Advantageous Marriage.* London, Hale, 1977; New York, Ballantine, 1978.
> *A Regency Scandal.* New York, Ballantine, and London, Futura, 1979.
> *A Conformable Wife.* New York, Ballantine, 1981.

Alice Chetwynd Ley comments:

My novels are set in the late Georgian period, i.e., 1760-1816. Several are in the Regency period. I have made a study of the period when working on the Social History section of my Diploma course, and have always been a devotee of Jane Austen. This gives an authentic background to my work, but my novels are essentially romantic.

*   *   *

In a career spanning more than two decades, Alice Chetwynd Ley has proven herself to be one of the finest, most consistent authors of historical romances. In tone, style, and qualities her work is reminiscent of that of Georgette Heyer, yet she remains much less widely known.

Most of Ley's books are Regency romances, with a few taking place in the Georgian period. Like Heyer, she concentrates on developing her characters and giving them life. The care she takes in portraying even minor characters brings a depth to her stories not often found in formula romances, which frequently feature one- or two-dimensional figures.

Under Ley's pen, the aristocratic worlds of Georgian and Regency fashionable society comes to life. Enough movement to keep a story briskly paced is supplied, but the real focus is on the characters and their relationships. Feverish action is not necessary to interest the reader in the lovers of *The Clandestine Betrothal* or *The Beau and the Bluestocking*. Even in the more eventful novels, such as *Tenant of Chesdene Manor* or *The Jewelled Snuff Box*, the people are more important than specific events. The most action-filled of Ley's novels are those set against the background of the war with France. *The Guinea Stamp, At Dark of the Moon,* and *Letters for a Spy* all draw on the English fears of a French invasion and Napoleonic spies, yet most of the problems remain on a personal level for the protagonists. The heroes of these books are double agents or counter spies, and confusion of identities and mistaken motives lead to much of the action. Ley does manage to slip a few slightly unexpected twists into these plots when Elizabeth is the one suspected of being a spy in *Letter for a Spy* and the double agent, Captain Jackson, in *The Guinea Stamp* is revealed as also leading a double life in England.

The 1981 Ballantine edition of *A Conformable Wife* proclaims Alice Chetwynd Ley "the new queen of Regency romance." While in the main such a statement is accurate, it is somewhat misleading. It is true that she has authored many quality romances, yet her long career hardly qualifies her for a title as a *new* leader of the genre. Instead, real devotees of historical romances will recognize her as one of their best kept secrets.

—Barbara Kemp

LINDSAY, Rachel.   Also writes as Roberta Leigh; Janey Scott. Address: c/o Mills and Boon Ltd., 15-16 Brooks Mews, London W1A 1DR, England.

ROMANCE AND GOTHIC PUBLICATIONS

Novels

The Widening Stream. London, Hutchinson, 1952.
Alien Corn. London, Hutchinson, 1954; Toronto, Harlequin, 1973.
Healing Hands. London, Hutchinson, 1955.
Mask of Gold. London, Hutchinson, 1956; Toronto, Harlequin, 1974.
Castle in the Trees. London, Hurst and Blackett, 1958; Toronto, Harlequin, 1974.
House of Lorraine. London, Mills and Boon, 1959; Toronto, Harlequin, 1966.

The Taming of Laura.   London, Mills and Boon, 1959; Toronto, Harlequin, 1966.
Business Affair.   London, Mills and Boon, 1960; Toronto, Harlequin, 1974.
Heart of a Rose.   London, Mills and Boon, 1961; Toronto, Harlequin, 1965.
Song in My Heart.   London, Mills and Boon, 1961.
Lesley Forrest, M.D.   New York, Berkley, 1962.
Moonlight and Magic.   London, Mills and Boon, 1962; Toronto, Harlequin, 1972.
Design for Murder.   London, Mills and Boon, 1964.
No Business to Love.   London, Mills and Boon, 1966.
Love and Lucy Granger.   London, Mills and Boon, 1967; Toronto, Harlequin, 1972.
Price of Love.   London, Mills and Boon, 1967; Toronto, Harlequin, 1974.
Love and Dr. Forrest.   London, Mills and Boon, 1971; Toronto, Harlequin, 1978.
The Latitude of Love.   London, Mills and Boon, 1971.
A Question of Marriage.   London, Mills and Boon, 1972; Toronto, Harlequin, 1973.
Cage of Gold.   London, Mills and Boon, 1973; Toronto, Harlequin, 1974.
Chateau in Provence.   London, Mills and Boon, 1973.
Food for Love.   Toronto, Harlequin, 1974.
Affair in Venice.   London, Mills and Boon, and Toronto, Harlequin, 1975.
Love in Disguise.   London, Mills and Boon, and Toronto, Harlequin, 1975.
Innocent Deception.   London, Mills and Boon, and Toronto, Harlequin, 1975.
Prince for Sale.   London, Mills and Boon, and Toronto, Harlequin, 1975.
The Marquis Takes a Wife.   London, Mills and Boon, 1976; Toronto, Harlequin, 1977.
Roman Affair.   London, Mills and Boon, 1976; Toronto, Harlequin, 1977.
Secretary Wife.   London, Mills and Boon, and Toronto, Harlequin, 1976.
Tinsel Star.   London, Mills and Boon, 1976; Toronto, Harlequin, 1977.
A Man to Tame.   London, Mills and Boon, 1976; Toronto, Harlequin, 1977.
Forbidden Love.   Toronto, Harlequin, 1977.
Prescription for Love.   London, Mills and Boon, and Toronto, Harlequin, 1977.
Rough Diamond Lover.   Toronto, Harlequin, 1978.
An Affair to Forget.   Toronto, Harlequin, 1978.
Forgotten Marriage.   Toronto, Harlequin, 1978.
Brazilian Affair.   Toronto, Harlequin, 1978.
My Sister's Keeper.   London, Mills and Boon, 1979.
Man of Ice.   London, Mills and Boon, and Toronto, Harlequin, 1980.
Untouched Wife.   Toronto, Harlequin, 1981.

Novels as Roberta Leigh

In Name Only.   London, Falcon Press, 1951; Toronto, Harlequin, 1973.
Dark Inheritance.   London, Hutchinson, 1952; Toronto, Harlequin, 1968.
The Vengeful Heart.   London, Hutchinson, 1952; Toronto, Harlequin, 1970.
Beloved Ballerina.   London, Hutchinson, 1953; Toronto, Harlequin, 1974.
And Then Came Love.   London, Hutchinson, 1954; Toronto, Harlequin, 1974.
Pretence.   London, Hutchinson, 1956; Toronto, Harlequin, 1969.
Stacy.   London, Heinemann, 1958.
My Heart's a Dancer.   London, Mills and Boon, 1970; Toronto, Harlequin, 1973.
Cinderella in Mink.   London, Mills and Boon, 1973; Toronto, Harlequin, 1974.
If Dreams Came True.   London, Mills and Boon, 1974.
Shade of the Palms.   London, Mills and Boon, and Toronto, Harlequin, 1974.
Heart of the Lion.   Toronto, Harlequin, 1975.
Man in a Million.   London, Mills and Boon, 1975; Toronto, Harlequin, 1976.
Temporary Wife.   London, Mills and Boon, and Toronto, Harlequin, 1975.
Cupboard Love.   London, Mills and Boon, and Toronto, Harlequin, 1976.
To Buy a Bride.   London, Mills and Boon, and Toronto, Harlequin, 1976.
The Unwilling Bridegroom.   London, Mills and Boon, 1976; Toronto, Harlequin, 1977.
Man Without a Heart.   London, Mills and Boon, 1976; Toronto, Harlequin, 1977.
Girl for a Millionaire.   Toronto, Harlequin, 1977.
Too Young to Love.   Toronto, Harlequin, 1977.

Facts of Love.   London, Mills and Boon, 1978.
Night of Love.   London, Mills and Boon, 1978; New York, Fawcett, 1979.
The Savage Aristocrat.   London, Mills and Boon, 1978; New York, Fawcett, 1979.
Not a Marrying Man.   Toronto, Harlequin, 1978.
Love in Store.   New York, Fawcett, 1978.
Flower of the Desert.   New York, Fawcett, 1979.
Love and No Marriage.   London, Mills and Boon, 1980.
Rent a Wife.   London, Mills and Boon, 1980; as Rachel Lindsay, Toronto, Harlequin, 1980.
Wife for a Year.   London, Mills and Boon, 1980; as Rachel Lindsay, Toronto, Harlequin, 1981.
Love Match.   New York, Fawcett, 1980.
Confirmed Bachelor.   Toronto, Harlequin, 1981.

Novels as Janey Scott

Memory of Love.   London, Mills and Boon, 1959.
Melody of Love.   London, Mills and Boon, 1960.
A Time to Love.   London, Mills and Boon, 1960; revised edition, as *Unwanted Wife* (as Rachel Lindsay) Mills and Boon, 1976; Toronto, Harlequin, 1978.
Sara Gay—Model Girl [*in Mayfair, in New York, in Monte Carlo*].   London, World, 4 vols., 1961.

*   *   *

Rachel Lindsay's primary theme is how much easier it is to love than it is to trust. Her stories show passionate physical attraction between people from vastly different backgrounds, holding vastly different beliefs and values. Usually the girl is innocent and ordinary, while the man is rich, arrogant, and sexually experienced. Another standard motif is the patient Griselda story: an arrogant man assumes the innocent heroine to be devious and scheming and therefore treats her brutally and insultingly. She naturally falls in love with him and patiently puts up with his abuse until he realizes her innocence and abases himself before her. There is more sex in her novels then in most Harlequins, though heavy petting always stops short of consummation.

In *The Widening Stream* two people who love each other without knowing each other very well are pushed apart by the lies of a scheming woman. *The Taming of Laura* is a Cinderella story. Eric Berne suggested that after Cinderella married the prince she would still spend her time sweeping up the cinders. In this novel and in *Affair in Venice* and *Secretary Wife*, Lindsay's Cinderellas have this problem of adjusting to their new position and wealth. *Forgotten Marriage* is the patient Griselda story par excellence. The heroine has the double disadvantage of being accused of vile actions, and having amnesia and therefore being unable to disprove the accusations. While her falling in love with her accuser is incomprehensible, his subsequent groveling is satisfying to heroine and reader alike. In *Unwanted Wife* a refugee from an iron curtain country seeks her English husband only to find he is under the impression she has divorced him, and is planning to marry again. Since the heroine is blonde and beautiful, one can tell the difference between her and the doormat, though with some difficulty. Other patient Griselda stories include *Roman Affair* and *Man of Ice*. *An Affair to Forget* concerns a rock singer and a sweet country girl whose values are so different that only total surrender by one of them (guess who?) will make this relationship possible. *Song in My Heart* deals with a pop singer who falls in love with a married man. When his wife conveniently dies, the story becomes a murder mystery. *Prince of Love* reverses the normal situation; an arrogant woman doctor loves a man she regards as hopelessly frivolous and unreliable, and she is the one who has to change. *Design for Murder* is a murder mystery and love story set in the world of high fashion. In *A Man to Tame* a woman doctor overcomes sex discrimination, demonstrates her courage, and wins the heart of an arrogant man. In *Prescription for Love* neither hero nor heroine is sufficiently self-confident to admit their love. Were there no intermediary to resolve this romance, no doubt they would have pined genteely for each other for the rest of their lives. In *My Sister's Keeper* the heroine deeply distrusts the man she loves because of her preconceptions of his values. In *Love and No Marriage* a successful dress designer allows the hero to continue to believe she is a professional housekeeper, albeit 'a not very good one. *Wife for a Year* is another one of those books where only an intermediary can make the romance happen at all.

Bizarre and unlikely things happen in Lindsay's world: heroines rescue people from burning buildings and emerge with nary an unsightly scar; 22-year-old women own their own fabulously successful businesses; opera singers become rock singers; worst of all, her heroines live in a peculiarly friendless vacuum. Nevertheless, between her heroes and heroines, there is great emotional realism. Though some of her heroines do silly, irrational things, and several of her men are brutal and insensitive, most of her characters are reasonable people, trying to reconcile their differences and to develop trust and understanding as well as love.

—Marylaine Block

LOFTS, Norah (née Robinson). Also writes as Juliet Astley; Peter Curtis. British. Born in Shipdham, Norfolk, 27 August 1904. Educated at West Suffolk County School; Norwich Training College, teaching diploma 1925. Married 1) Geoffrey Lofts in 1931 (died, 1948), one son; 2) Robert Jorisch in 1949. Taught English and history at Guildhall Feoffment Girl's School, 1925-36. Recipient: Georgette Heyer Prize, for historical novel, 1978. Agent: Curtis Brown Ltd., 575 Madison Avenue, New York, New York 10022, U.S.A. Address: Northgate House, Bury St. Edmunds, Suffolk, England.

ROMANCE AND GOTHIC PUBLICATIONS

Novels

> *Here Was a Man: A Romantic History of Sir Walter Raleigh.*   London, Methuen, and New York, Knopf, 1936.
> *White Hell of Pity.*   London, Methuen, and New York, Knopf, 1937.
> *Requiem for Idols.*   London, Methuen, and New York, Knopf, 1938.
> *Out of This Nettle.*   London, Gollancz, 1938; as *Colin Lowrie*, New York, Knopf, 1939.
> *Blossom Like the Rose.*   London, Gollancz, and New York, Knopf, 1939.
> *Hester Roon.*   London, Davies, and New York, Knopf, 1940.
> *The Road to Revelation.*   London, Davies, 1941.
> *The Brittle Glass.*   London, Joseph, 1942; New York, Knopf, 1943.
> *Michael and All the Angels.*   London, Joseph, 1943; as *The Golden Fleece*, New York, Knopf, 1944.
> *Jassy.*   London, Joseph, and New York, Knopf, 1944.
> *To See a Fine Lady.*   London, Joseph, and New York, Knopf, 1946.
> *Silver Nutmeg.*   London, Joseph, and New York, Doubleday, 1947.
> *A Calf for Venus.*   London, Joseph, and New York, Doubleday, 1949; as *Letty*, New York, Pyramid, 1968.
> *Esther.*   New York, Macmillan, 1950; London, Joseph, 1951.
> *The Lute Player.*   London, Joseph, and New York, Doubleday, 1951.
> *Bless This House.*   London, Joseph, and New York, Doubleday, 1954.
> *Winter Harvest.*   New York, Doubleday, 1955.
> *Queen in Waiting.*   London, Joseph, 1955; as *Eleanor the Queen*, New York, Doubleday, 1955; as *Queen in Waiting*, Doubleday, 1958.

Afternoon of an Autocrat. London, Joseph, and New York, Doubleday, 1956; as *The Devil in Clevely*, Leeds, Morley Barker, 1968.
Scent of Cloves. New York, Doubleday, 1957; London, Hutchinson, 1958.
Suffolk Trilogy:
    The Town House. London, Hutchinson, and New York, Doubleday, 1959.
    The House at Old Vine. London, Hutchinson, and New York, Doubleday, 1961.
    The House at Sunset. New York, Doubleday, 1962; London, Hutchinson, 1963.
The Concubine: A Novel Based upon the Life of Anne Boleyn. New York, Doubleday, 1963; London, Hutchinson, 1964; as *Concubine*, London, Arrow, 1965.
How Far to Bethlehem? London, Hutchinson, and New York, Doubleday, 1965.
The Lost Ones. London, Hutchinson, 1969; as *The Lost Queen*, New York, Doubleday, 1969; London, Corgi, 1970.
Madselin. London, Corgi, 1969.
The King's Pleasure. New York, Doubleday, 1969; London, Hodder and Stoughton, 1970.
Lovers All Untrue. London, Hodder and Stoughton, and New York, Doubleday, 1970.
A Rose for Virtue. London, Hodder and Stoughton, and New York, Doubleday, 1971.
Charlotte. London, Hodder and Stoughton, 1972; as *Out of the Dark*, New York, Doubleday, 1972.
Nethergate. London, Hodder and Stoughton, and New York, Doubleday, 1973.
Crown of Aloes. London, Hodder and Stoughton, and New York, Doubleday, 1974.
Walk into My Parlour. London, Corgi, 1975.
Knight's Acre. London, Hodder and Stoughton, and New York, Doubleday, 1975.
The Homecoming. London, Hodder and Stoughton, 1975; New York, Doubleday, 1976.
Checkmate. London, Corgi, 1975; New York, Fawcett, 1978.
The Fall of Midas (as Juliet Astley). New York, Coward McCann, 1975; London, Joseph, 1976.
The Lonely Furrow. London, Hodder and Stoughton, 1976; New York, Doubleday, 1977.
Gad's Hall. London, Hodder and Stoughton, 1977; New York, Doubleday, 1978.
Copsi Castle (as Juliet Astley). London, Joseph, and New York, Coward McCann, 1978.
Haunted House. London, Hodder and Stoughton, 1978; as *The Haunting of Gad's Hall*, New York, Doubleday, 1979.
Day of the Butterfly. London, Bodley Head, 1979; New York, Doubleday, 1980.
A Wayside Tavern. London, Hodder and Stoughton, and New York, Doubleday, 1980.
The Old Priory. London, Bodley Head, 1981; New York, Doubleday, 1982.
The Claw. London, Hodder and Stoughton, 1981.

Novels as Peter Curtis

Dead March in Three Keys. London, Davies, 1940; as *No Question of Murder*, New York, Doubleday, 1959; as *The Bride of Moat House*, New York, Dell, 1969.
You're Best Alone. London, Macdonald, 1943.
Lady Living Alone. London, Macdonald, 1945.
The Devil's Own. London, Macdonald, and New York, Doubleday, 1960; as *The Witches*, London, Pan, 1966; as *The Little Wax Doll*, London, Hodder and Stoughton, and New York, Doubleday, 1970.

Short Stories

I Met a Gypsy. London, Methuen, and New York, Knopf, 1935.
Heaven in Your Hand and Other Stories. New York, Doubleday, 1958; London, Joseph, 1959.

Is Anybody There? London, Corgi, 1974; as *Hauntings: Is There Anybody There?*, New York, Doubleday, 1975.

Other

Women in the Old Testament: Twenty Psychological Portraits. London, Sampson Low, and New York, Macmillan, 1949.
Eternal France: A History of France 1789-1944, with Margery Weiner. New York, Doubleday, 1968; London, Hodder and Stoughton, 1969.
The Story of Maude Reed (juvenile). London, Transworld, 1971; as *The Maude Reed Tale*, New York, Nelson, 1972.
Rupert Hatton's Story (juvenile). London, Carousel Books, 1972.
Domestic Life in England. London, Weidenfeld and Nicolson, and New York, Doubleday, 1976.
Queens of Britain. London, Hodder and Stoughton, 1977; as *The Queens of England*, New York, Doubleday, 1977.
Emma Hamilton. London, Joseph, and New York, Coward McCann, 1978.
Anne Boleyn. New York, Coward McCann, and London, Orbis, 1979.

Norah Lofts comments:

Strictly speaking I don't think I belong in the romance or gothic class. I write books about ordinary people some of whom happen to live in the past. The love story is never dominant; most of my people are concerned with earning a living, achieving an ambition, holding their own in a harsh world. And gothic I never understood—I thought it was a form of architecture. I do tend to write about old houses because they fascinate me. Some of my houses are haunted—but never with spectres—mainly by emotions that have made impact on the atmosphere. Some of my houses are said to be cursed; but it is the people themselves who bring the bad luck into operation.

*   *   *

Norah Lofts has been writing historical romances for almost 50 years and has innumerable admirers. Above all, Lofts can tell a story: her inventive power, her very real gift of narrative, and her instinct for a story have been much praised. Her vigorous style of storytelling, whether in the first or the third person, carries the reader along as a multiplicity of events unfolds. Often in one historical romance the stories of several lives are told, sometimes down along the generations, and we see how these lives, socially or geographically remote from each other though they may be, touch and intertwine so as to affect each other irretrievably, for good or ill. Sometimes the stories span continents and oceans, as *Blossom Like the Rose* and *The Road to Revelation*, both set in England and the American colonies in the 17th century, and *Silver Nutmeg* and *Scent of Cloves*, both set in Europe and in the Dutch East Indies in the 17th century and involving "glove marriages" of girls sent out from Europe to marry unseen Dutch traders. Lofts's wide historical knowledge, which includes small social details as well as the details of great events, enables her to place her stories at home and abroad from the Anglo-Saxon period onwards. Her sense of history and her capacity to transmit the fascination of the past are remarkable, though it must be said that the first-person narrators in her historical romances have their narrative styles firmly rooted in the 20th century, regardless of the times in which they operate.

Lofts's first book was *I Met a Gypsy*, a collection of short stories which are linked by the gypsy blood which flows in the veins of a dominant character in each story. The stories range in time and location from the dissolution of the monasteries in England to a British mission in China in the 1930's. There is much in this book which is found again and again in Lofts's work:

the fascination with gypsies and their association with the supernatural; the dynastic or sequential ideas implicit in the arrangement of the stories which show a connection through history and through the generations; and the refusal to gloss over the brutality, nastiness, and squalor of previous ages. Sytlistically, the inter-linking of several first-person narratives into one book is a technique which Lofts uses very successfully in many novels.

Lofts has a strong sense of time and a strong sense of place. Many of her historical novels are set in Suffolk, and many of them are set around houses. Both landscape and houses have a permanency which their occupants lack, although the occupants may leave impressions. The "Suffolk Trilogy" (*The Town House, The House at Old Vine*, and *The House at Sunset*) spans six hundred years in the history of a house, from its beginnings as the home of a medieval wool-merchant to the present day, and *Bless This House* tells the story of the fortunes of a beautiful Elizabethan house in Suffolk in eight episodes, each narrated by a different character who plays a part in its history.

Lofts portrays with skill and sympathy the economic and social positions of women from highest to lowest. Indeed, her women characters are her most interesting. We see their reactions to chance and opportunities; we see what they make of their successes and failures, whether they make the best of their lot or become indifferent or embittered. There is an idea of "what you get and what you're prepared to pay for it" in the stories of many of Lofts's heroines, from Walter Raleigh's wife, Beth (in *Here Was a Man*), who has to share her husband with the ageing, coquettish Queen and with his own political and seafaring ambitions, to Hester (in *Hester Roon*) and the heroine of *Day of the Butterfly* who rise from the most abject and squalid poverty by their own efforts. Such women as these last two who are prepared to take their destinies into their own hands contrast sharply with, for instance, poor little Emmie in *White Hell of Pity*, who refuses the opportunity of further schooling out of an over-nice conscience and ends her days prematurely as an exhausted skivvy.

—Jean Buchanan

LOGAN, Mark. *See* **NICOLE, Christopher.**

LONDON, Laura. Pseudonym for Thomas Dale Curtis and Sharon Curtis. Americans. **CURTIS, Thomas Dale**: born in Antigo, Wisconsin, 11 November 1952. Attended University of Wisconsin, Madison. Married Sharon Curtis in 1970; two children. Has worked as a professional musician, newswriter, television reporter, actor, and truck driver. **CURTIS, Sharon**: born in Dahran, Saudi Arabia, 6 March 1951. Attended schools in Turkey, Pakistan, Iran; Marymount School for Girls, Kingston-on-Thames, Surrey; University of Wisconsin, Madison. Address: P.O. Box 175, Greendale, Wisconsin 53129, U.S.A.

ROMANCE AND GOTHIC PUBLICATIONS

Novels

A Heart Too Proud. New York, Dell, 1978.
The Bad Baron's Daughter. New York, Dell, 1978.
Moonlight Mist. New York, Dell, 1979.
Love's a Stage. New York, Dell, 1980.
The Gypsy Heiress. New York, Dell, 1981.

Laura London comments:

We've always wanted to be writers, and for us our career has been like a pleasant drift into a dream. Our finished works can be described as long conversations between the co-authors from which the interruptions have been edited. We believe in the romantic point of view and try to give our readers the quality craftsmanship they deserve.

We enjoy the research end of our work, and feel best when we can share some obscure fact with our readers in an original way. We read as many as 30 books to gain the background for one Regency romance.

*   *   *

A spunky, virginal heroine and a strong, handsome hero confront perilous situations in 19th-century England. This brief phrase sums up one of the most popular formulas for romantic fiction and all five of the novels by Laura London.

Why then would a reader select a London novel in such an overcrowded field? Certainly, historical details are not emphasized and the plots are not unusual. The answer lies in the dialogue between the hero and heroine and the occasional first-person narrative. There is a very modern quality that verges on the sarcastic when the verbal fencing begins. In the *Bad Baron's Daughter*, Katie (who had been found in a low tavern called "The Merry Maidenhead") rebels against Lord Linden's plans and tells him that she would rather "lose my maidenhead fifty times first." His calm response is to tell her that that is "an anatomical impossibility" and that her reputation cannot get any worse anyway. Frances, in *Love's a Stage*, protests David's lovemaking, "Because I intend to marry a virgin." David laughingly confesses that he, unfortunately, can no longer meet that requirement. This mocking style is found in all London's novels and is quite refreshing after a diet of saccharin prose. How else to explain an experienced nobleman (who also happens to be "The Bard of the Lakeland") who lets his bride bring her twin sister on their honeymoon (*Moonlight Mist*) or a mysterious highwayman whose claim to a title is supported by the strange physical characteristic of one blue eye and one brown (also in *Moonlight Mist*) or a villain who keeps a wolf on a leash and lets it loose to attack his enemies once every four years (*The Gypsy Heiress*)?

The copyright notice on each of the books credits Thomas Dale Curtis and Sharon Curtis. After reading one of the novels, one can easily picture a man and woman teaming up to write a spoof of romantic novels. All the appropriate conventions are observed, but the reader senses that the author's tongue is firmly planted in his/her cheek.

—Barbara Kemp

LORING, Emilie (née Baker). Also wrote as Josephine Story. American. Born in Boston, Massachusetts. Educated privately. Married Victor J. Loring; two sons. *Died 14 March 1951.*

ROMANCE AND GOTHIC PUBLICATIONS

Novels

The Trail of Conflict. Philadelphia, Penn, 1922; London, Unwin, 1923.
Here Comes the Sun! Philadelphia, Penn, 1924.
The Dragon-Slayer. London, Unwin, 1924.
A Certain Crossroad. Philadelphia, Penn, 1925.
The Solitary Horseman. Philadelphia, Penn, 1927.
Gay Courage. Philadelphia, Penn, 1928; London, Long, 1929.
Swift Water. Philadelphia, Penn, 1929.
Lighted Windows. Philadelphia, Penn, 1930; London, Hale, 1974.
Fair Tomorrow. Philadelphia, Penn, 1931; London, Stanley Paul, 1932.
Uncharted Seas. Philadelphia, Penn, 1932; London, Hale, 1975.
Hilltops Clear. Philadelphia, Penn, 1933; London, Stanley Paul, 1934.
Come On, Fortune! London, Stanley Paul, 1933.
We Ride the Gale! Philadelphia, Penn, 1934; London, Stanley Paul, 1935.
With Banners. Philadelphia, Penn, 1934; London, Stanley Paul, 1935.
It's a Great World! Philadelphia, Penn, 1935.
Give Me One Summer. Philadelphia, Penn, 1936.
As Long as I Live. Philadelphia, Penn, 1937; London, Hale, 1972.
Today Is Yours. Boston, Little Brown, 1938.
High of Heart. Boston, Little Brown, 1938.
Across the Years. Boston, Little Brown, 1939.
There Is Always Love. Boston, Little Brown, 1940; London, Foulsham, 1951.
Stars in Your Eyes. Boston, Little Brown, 1941; London, Nicholson and Watson, 1943.
Where Beauty Dwells. Boston, Little Brown, 1941.
Rainbow at Dusk. Boston, Little Brown, 1942; London, Hale, 1976.
When Hearts Are Light Again. Boston, Little Brown, 1943; London, Foulsham, 1953.
Keepers of the Faith. Boston, Little Brown, 1944; London, Hale, 1975.
Beyond the Sound of Guns. Boston, Little Brown, 1945.
Bright Skies. Boston, Little Brown, 1946.
Beckoning Trails. Boston, Little Brown, 1947; London, Foulsham, 1952.
I Hear Adventure Calling. Boston, Little Brown, 1948; London, Hale, 1976.
Love Came Laughing. Boston, Little Brown, 1949; London, Foulsham, 1951.
To Love and to Honor. Boston, Little Brown, 1950; London, Foulsham, 1951.
For All Your Life. Boston, Little Brown, 1952; London, Hale, 1970.
I Take This Man. Boston, Little Brown, 1954; London, Foulsham, 1955.
My Dearest Love. Boston, Little Brown, 1954; London, Hale, 1972; as *My Love*, London, Foulsham, 1955.
The Shadow of Suspicion. Boston, Little Brown, 1955; London, Hale, 1965.
What Then Is Love. Boston, Little Brown, 1956; London, Hale, 1965.
Look to the Stars. Boston, Little Brown, 1957; London, Hale, 1966; as *Scott Pelham's Princess*, London, Foulsham, 1958.
Behind the Cloud. Boston, Little Brown, 1958; London, Hale, 1967.
With This Ring. Boston, Little Brown, 1959; London, Hale, 1966.
How Can the Heart Forget. Boston, Little Brown, 1960; London, Hale, 1966.
Throw Wide the Door. Boston, Little Brown, 1962.
Follow Your Heart. Boston, Little Brown, 1963; London, Hale, 1964.
A Candle in Her Heart. Boston, Little Brown, 1964; London, Hale, 1969.
Forever and a Day. Boston, Little Brown, 1965.
Spring Always Comes. Boston, Little Brown, 1966; London, Hale, 1968.
A Key to Many Doors. Boston, Little Brown, 1967; London, Hale, 1969.

In Times Like These. Boston, Little Brown, 1968; London, Hale, 1976.
Love with Honor. Boston, Little Brown, 1969; London, Hale, 1970.
No Time for Love. Boston, Little Brown, 1970; London, Hale, 1971.
Forsaking All Others. Boston, Little Brown, 1971; London, Hale, 1973.
The Shining Years. Boston, Little Brown, 1972; London, Hale, 1974.

OTHER PUBLICATIONS

Play

Where's Peter? Philadelphia, Penn, 1928.

Other as Josephine Story

For the Comfort of the Family: A Vacation Experiment. New York, Doran, 1914.
The Mother in the House. Boston, Pilgrim Press, 1917.

*   *   *

Emilie Loring is an American writer of patriotic, moralistic romances that comment upon some of the major socio-political events occurring in the United States during the period in which they were published. Loring's version of the romance formula has had an enduring appeal, for, although her books were written in the first half of the century, their multiple printings up to the present day attest to their continued popularity.

Strong pro-Americanism is the most striking feature of Loring's fiction. Her books constitute a resounding defense of democratic capitalism. The heroines declare themselves to be fierce patriots ("my country, right or wrong"), and the heroes are either benevolent industrialists, war heroes, lawyers and politicians fighting for the "American Way," or "trouble-shooters for Uncle Sam." Whenever the American system of business or government is under attack, as is usually the case in Loring's plots, the main characters respond with impassioned speeches and may even burst into the Pledge of Allegiance to the Flag. Anyone who disagrees with this creed is considered to be a weak, inadequate person who blames society for his personal failures.

The moral tone of Loring's romances is consistent with her patriotic conservativeness. She bemoans the loosening of morals of the modern world, particularly the increase of divorce, and wishes for a return to stricter ethics. She continually attacks idleness, cheapness, spinelessness, selfishness, and pessimism, and admires integrity, modesty, graciousness, loyalty, sweetness, self-discipline, and a sense of humor.

Loring philosophizes most about marriage. Characters are apt to quote from the marriage service and discuss the components of a good marriage, as in *Swift Water*:

> ...marriage fundamentally is a matter of sympathetic companionship shot through and through with gleams of passion, love. It should be productive of fidelity, loyalty, responsibility, of the stamina to see a difficult situation through if necessary. It is not just the business of two persons. A marriage which breaks down threatens the institution.

When marriage breaks down, Loring adds elsewhere, society breaks down. Many romance writers portray love and courtship but stop short of portraying real marriages. Loring does not shirk this task. In fact, she frequently portrays even very unhappy marriages. These she uses to convey moral lessons. Loring advocates a "bite the bullet" approach to marriage. Once married, partners are irrevocably committed to each other, no matter what. Faithful spouses are always ultimately rewarded in Loring's novels. If one lives by a code of honor, "Things have a marvelous, unbelievable way of coming right." Thus, Loring's romances are optimistic and "up-lifting."

Loring differs from many writers of romances in another way as well. She describes and comments on crucial, contemporary social events such as World Wars I and II, the Korean conflict, Red scares, unionization, racketeer crime, wide-scale immigration, urbanization, and the Great Depression. Once again, her political conservatism is noticeably evident. For example, all union organizing is attributed to outside agitators, parasites, and ungrateful aliens. One hero (in *The Shadow of Suspicion*) tells a group of striking workers: "You've been getting a dose of propaganda. And do you know who paid for it? The Reds!" He proceeds to outline the evils of Russian communism. Loring's novels are full of traitors, spies, and subversives against whom one must be ever vigilant. Throughout her romances, Loring openly supports McCarthy-era tactics, the Cold War hostility, and the armaments race.

In addition to the romance and political intrigue, Loring's novels blend a number of stylistic and plot devices like humor, dialects, colloquialisms, and details of local color to make them distinctive. Every novel features amusing incidents which usually involve innocent but embarrassingly outspoken children or servants, or cute pets. Gay repartee also provides a sense of high spirits. Loring also has fun with characters' names which often reveal the nature of the character. Thus, a detective is called Tom Search; a formal butler is named Propper; a religious fanatic is Luther Calvin. These are rather heavy-handed and obvious, of course, but Loring apparently delights in them as they are a consistent pattern. Loring's minor characters (servants, farmers, and foreigners) speak in pronounced dialect with stereotypical mannerisms. For example, in *Across the Years* Loring describes a typical plump "Southern mammy" who talks like this: "Ah sure is glad to see yo', Mistuh Duke.... Let me tak' dat coat, honey-girl." While this technique adds "color" to Loring's writing style and is probably not intended to be racist, it is simplistic and condescending.

Loring has a fine eye for detail and she can skillfully create vivid scenes. However, she frequently relies too heavily on naming colors to evoke a mood. In addition, she sometimes gets trapped in a repetitive series of descriptive phrases that end up being irritating like in the following: "She darted in and out of a drove of bleating blackfaced sheep; did a running high jump over a squealing pig; ducked under the nose of a pawing colt; skirted a dog fight and shooed away a flock of cackling geese..." (*High of Heart*).

One final criticism of Loring's style stems from her moral lessons and patriotic lectures which result in some very stilted dialogue. One does not usually break into the Pledge of Allegiance in a casual, social conversation. Loring's flair for the dramatic leads her astray in these cases.

—Margaret Jensen

LORRIMER, Claire. Pseudonym for Patricia Denise Clark, née Robins; also wrote as Patricia Robins.   British.   Born in Hove, Sussex, 1 February 1921; daughter of Denise Robins, *q.v.* Educated at Parents' National Educational Union, Burgess Hill, Sussex, 1927-30; Effingham House, Bexhill-on-Sea, Sussex, 1930-35; Institut Prealpina, Switzerland, 1935-37; and in Munich, 1937-38. Served in the radar filter room, Women's Auxiliary Air Force, 1940-45: Flight Officer. Married D.C. Clark in 1948 (divorced); two sons and one daughter. Sub-Editor, *Woman's Illustrated*, London, 1938-40. Agent: Desmond Elliott, 3 Clifford Street, London, W.1. Address: Chiswell Barn, Marsh Green, Edenbridge, Kent TN8 5AP, England.

ROMANCE AND GOTHIC PUBLICATIONS

Novels

A Voice in the Dark. London, Souvenir Press, 1967; New York, Avon, 1968.
The Shadow Falls. New York, Avon, 1974.
Relentless Storm. New York, Avon, 1975; London, Arlington, 1979.
The Secret of Quarry House. New York, Avon, 1976.
Mavreen. London, Arlington, 1976; New York, Bantam, 1977.
Tamarisk. London, Arlington, 1978; New York, Bantam, 1979.
Chantal. London, Arlington, 1980; New York, Bantam, 1981.
The Chatelaine. London, Arlington, 1981.
The Wilderling. London, Arlington, 1982.

Novels as Patricia Robins

To the Stars. London, Hutchinson, 1944.
See No Evil. London, Hutchinson, 1945.
Statues of Snow. London, Hutchinson, 1947.
Three Loves. London, Hutchinson, 1949.
Awake My Heart. London, Hutchinson, 1950.
Beneath the Moon. London, Hutchinson, 1951.
Leave My Heart Alone. London, Hutchinson, 1951.
The Fair Deal. London, Hutchinson, 1952.
Heart's Desire. London, Hutchinson, 1953.
So This Is Love. London, Hutchinson, 1953.
Heaven in Our Hearts. London, Hutchinson, 1954.
One Who Cares. London, Hutchinson, 1954.
Love Cannot Die. London, Hutchinson, 1955.
The Foolish Heart. London, Hutchinson, 1956.
Give All to Love. London, Hutchinson, 1956.
Where Duty Lies. London, Hutchinson, 1957.
He Is Mine. London, Hurst and Blackett, 1957.
Love Must Wait. London, Hurst and Blackett, 1958.
Lonely Quest. London, Hurst and Blackett, 1959.
Lady Chatterley's Daughter. London, Consul, and New York, Ace, 1961.
The Last Chance. London, Hurst and Blackett, 1961.
The Long Wait. London, Hurst and Blackett, 1962.
The Runaways. London, Hurst and Blackett, 1962.
Seven Loves. London, Consul, 1962.
With All My Love. London, Hurst and Blackett, 1963.
The Constant Heart. London, Hurst and Blackett, 1964.
Second Love. London, Hurst and Blackett, 1964.
The Night Is Mine. London, Consul, 1964.
There Is But One. London, Hurst and Blackett, 1965.
No More Loving. London, Consul, 1965.
Topaze Island. London, Hurst and Blackett, 1965.
Love Me Tomorrow. London, Hurst and Blackett, 1966.
The Uncertain Joy. London, Hurst and Blackett, 1966.
Forbidden. London, Mayflower, 1967.
Sapphire in the Sand. London, Arrow, 1968.
Laugh on Friday. London, Hurst and Blackett, 1969.
No Stone Unturned. London, Hurst and Blackett, 1969.
Cinnabar House. London, Hurst and Blackett, 1970.
Under the Sky. London, Hurst and Blackett, 1970.
The Crimson Tapestry. London, Hurst and Blackett, 1972.

Play Fair with Love. London, Hurst and Blackett, 1972.
None But He. London, Hurst and Blackett, 1973.

OTHER PUBLICATIONS

Verse as Patricia Robins

Seven Days Leave. London, Hutchinson, 1943.

Other (juvenile) as Patricia Robins

The Adventures of the Three Baby Bunnies. London, Nicholson and Watson, 1934.
Tree Fairies. London, Hutchinson, 1945.
Sea Magic. London, Hutchinson, 1946.
The Heart of a Rose. London, Hutchinson, 1947.
The £100 Reward. Exeter, Wheaton, 1966.

Other

The Garden. London, Arlington, 1980.

Claire Lorrimer comments:

When I decided to become a free-lance writer after the war, it seemed natural to continue writing the kind of light romantic fiction I had been associated with as a junior sub editor on a magazine before the war. It did not occur to me to change to anything else until the 1970's when my agent, Desmond Elliott, suggested I could improve the standard of my work. I wrote *Mavreen* in 1975 and when it went immediately into the bestseller list in the USA, I decided to make a permanent change and virtually begin a new career. I like to think the standard of my work is improving with each book and the critical reviews I have been receiving suggest this is so. I prefer the relative realism of my Claire Lorrimers in which I try to make certain that no one says or does anything that in real life they might not have done or said, and although the stories are full of action and adventure I hope to convince my reader that these characters really could have existed and have led the lives I have given them. I often end up believing them real myself. Of all my reviews, I am most satisfied by George Thaw's (*Daily Mirror*) in which he concludes the *Chatelaine* review with the words: "A slice of life." I am never satisfied with the finished product. Of everything I have written in my life, my favourite is *The Garden.*

*   *   *

Claire Lorrimer's approach to her work is primarily instinctive. In her opinion, a story writes itself. The method has virtues, but the drawbacks are also evident at times. Many of her novels seem too long for the thematic material they support. There is a tendency towards verbosity, which often draws out the thread of a story to breaking point. This is particularly true of *Relentless Storm*, whose characters with their forbidden passions are the very stuff of gothic dream, but whose presentation fails to save a short story stretched to novel length. Characters lack depth, and the plot and its climaxes are predictable. It is melodramatic, but it fails to convince. *A Voice in the Dark* is more satisfying. The story is again conventional gothic romance, a young girl on holiday in Florence becoming involved with Italian aristocrats at their ancestral home. The long arm of coincidence is virtually dislocated in the opening pages, but the story moves more rapidly than *Relentless Storm*. The characters do not linger over their speeches, climaxes are reached without delay, and a happy ending secured at last. The least ambitious of her books, it is among the most successful.

It is the heroines of *Mavreen*, *Tamarisk*, and *Chantal* who have established their author's reputation. Mavreen sets the pace, and is the dominating presence of the trilogy. Natural daughter of an English nobleman, raised as a child by Sussex farmers, she enters into passionate love affairs with the French aristocrat Gerard de Valle and the titled highwayman Sir Perry Waite, taking part in the latter's robberies. She, together with Tamarisk and Chantal, tastes triumph and disaster in the aristocratic world of the Regency and enjoys the friendship of the great. The three heroines overshadow their men, although Gerard and Sir Perry are ably drawn. The novels are stories of individuals rather than a picture of the times—the Regency atmosphere is less strong than in the "Haggard" novels of Nicole—but this is unimportant. The characters compel and convince.

The Chatelaine is set in the early part of this century. Willow, daughter of an American millionaire, marries Rowell Rochford, not knowing the impoverished English nobleman is after her money. The Rochford mansion with its dominant matriarch, the dark secret of hereditary illness, and the imprisonment of Rowell's crippled sister all bring back gothic echoes of *A Voice in the Dark*. *The Chatelaine* is the most impressive of Lorrimer's novels to date, compact and well crafted. Willow, in her gradual assertion of independence from Rowell and his dragon of a mother, is at once interesting and credible. Her presence throws her male counterparts into the shade, but secondary characters are more fully realized in this work, and its appearance promises well for the Rochford books to come.

—Geoffrey Sadler

LOW, Dorothy Mackie.   Pseudonym for Lois Dorothea Low, née Pilkington; also writes as Zoe Cass; Lois Paxton.   British.   Born in Edinburgh, 15 July 1916. Attended Edinburgh Ladies' College (now Mary Erskine School). Married William Mackie Low in 1938; two sons. Has worked in insurance and as a literary agent. Chairman, Romantic Novelists Association, 1969-71. Address: High View, Shawcross Road, West Runton, Norfolk NR 27 9NA, England.

ROMANCE AND GOTHIC PUBLICATIONS

Novels

> *Isle for a Stranger*.   London, Hurst and Blackett, 1962; New York, Ace, 1968.
> *Dear Liar*.   London, Hurst and Blackett, 1963.
> *A Ripple on the Water*.   London, Hurst and Blackett, 1964.
> *The Intruder*.   London, Hurst and Blackett, 1965.
> *A House in the Country*.   London, Hurst and Blackett, 1968.
> *To Burgundy and Back*.   London, Hurst and Blackett, 1970; New York, Ace, 1973.

Novels as Lois Paxton

> *The Man Who Died Twice*.   London, Hurst and Blackett, 1968; New York, Ace, 1970.
> *The Quiet Sound of Fear*.   London, Hurst and Blackett, and New York, Hawthorn, 1971.
> *Who Goes There?*   London, Hurst and Blackett, 1972; New York, Ace, 1974.

Novels as Zoe Cass

Island of the Seven Hills. New York, Random House, 1974; London, Cassell, 1975.
The Silver Leopard. New York, Random House, 1976; London, Elek, 1978.
A Twist in the Silk. London, Elek, 1980.

*   *   *

Lois Dorothea Low writes under three pseudonyms. As Dorothy Mackie Low she writes romantic novels with authentic characters in believable situations. She does not over-glamourise lifestyles or write about impossibly idealistic love affairs. Realism is the key factor in these stories.

As Lois Paxton she writes tough suspense novels. In the Paxton books there is a love interest but the prime ingredient is suspense. The plot always revolves around a highly disturbing situation, yet one in which any girl might find herself. *The Quiet Sound of Fear* is probably the best of these.

In her Zoe Cass books she combines the two styles. They are long novels and best described as romantic suspense. The plots are strong and they carry a great deal of descriptive writing.

Low admits to finding the use of a pseudonym very challenging. She employs the same writing methods no matter which name she is using. She keeps a card index on characters, even minor ones, and so that no mistakes are made in location as the story proceeds, draws plans and maps. In the case of the Zoe Cass books, the story evolves around a craft or expertise which is always thoroughly researched. Although a voracious reader she reads very little romantic fiction and she doesn't feel that her work has been influenced by any other writer.

—Marion R. Harris

LOWNDES, Marie (Adelaide) Belloc. Also wrote as Philip Curtin. British. Born in 1868; sister of the writer Hilaire Belloc. Married the writer Frederic Sawrey Lowndes (died, 1940); one son and two daughters. *Died 14 November 1947.*

ROMANCE AND GOTHIC PUBLICATIONS

Novels (series: Duchess Laura)

The Heart of Penelope. London, Heinemann, 1904; New York, Dutton, 1915.
Barbara Rebell. London, Heinemann, 1905; New York, Dodge, 1907.
The Pulse of Life. London, Heinemann, 1908; New York, Dodd Mead, 1909.
The Uttermost Farthing. London, Heinemann, 1908; New York, Kennerley, 1909.
When No Man Pursueth. London, Heinemann, 1910; New York, Kennerley, 1911.
Jane Oglander. London, Heinemann, and New York, Scribner, 1911.
The Chink in the Armour. London, Methuen, and New York, Scribner, 1912; as *The House of Peril*, London, Readers Library, 1935.
Mary Pechell. London, Methuen, and New York, Scribner, 1912.

The Lodger. London, Methuen, and New York, Scribner, 1913.
The End of Her Honeymoon. New York, Scribner, 1913; London, Methuen, 1914.
Good Old Anna. London, Hutchinson, 1915; New York, Doran, 1916.
The Red Cross Barge. London, Smith Elder, 1916; New York, Doran, 1918.
Lilla: A Part of Her Life. London, Hutchinson, 1916; New York, Doran, 1917.
Love and Hatred. London, Chapman and Hall, and New York, Doran, 1917.
Out of the War? London, Chapman and Hall, 1918; as *Gentleman Anonymous*, London, Philip Allan, 1934.
From the Vasty Deep. London, Hutchinson, 1920; as *From Out the Vasty Deep*, New York, Doran, 1921.
The Lonely House. London, Hutchinson, and New York, Doran, 1920.
What Timmy Did. London, Hutchinson, 1921; New York, Doran, 1922.
The Terriford Mystery. London, Hutchinson, and New York, Doubleday, 1924.
What Really Happened. London, Hutchinson, and New York, Doubleday, 1926.
The Story of Ivy. London, Heinemann, 1927; New York, Doubleday, 1928.
Thou Shalt Not Kill. London, Hutchinson, 1927.
Cressida: No Mystery. London, Heinemann, 1928; New York, Knopf, 1930.
Duchess Laura: Certain Days of Her Life. London, Ward Lock, 1929; as *The Duchess Intervenes*, New York, Putnam, 1933.
Love's Revenge. London, Readers Library, 1929.
One of Those Ways. London, Heinemann, and New York, Knopf, 1929.
Letty Lynton. London, Heinemann, and New York, Cape and Smith, 1931.
Vanderlyn's Adventure. New York, Cape and Smith, 1931; as *The House by the Sea*, London, Heinemann, 1937.
Jenny Newstead. London, Heinemann, and New York, Putnam, 1932.
Love Is a Flame. London, Benn, 1932.
The Reason Why. London, Benn, 1932.
Duchess Laura: Further Days from Her Life. New York, Longman, 1933.
Another Man's Wife. London, Heinemann, and New York, Longman, 1934.
The Chianti Flask. New York, Longman, 1934; London, Heinemann, 1935.
Who Rides on a Tiger. New York, Longman, 1935; London, Heinemann, 1936.
And Call It Accident. New York, Longman, 1936; London, Hutchinson, 1939.
The Second Key. New York, Longman, 1936; as *The Injured Lover*, London, Hutchinson, 1939.
The Marriage-Broker. London, Heinemann, 1937; as *The Fortune of Bridget Malone*, New York, Longman, 1937.
Motive. London, Heinemann, 1938; as *Why It Happened*, New York, Longman, 1938.
Lizzie Borden: A Study in Conjecture. New York, Longman, 1939; London, Hutchinson, 1940.
Reckless Angel. New York, Longman, 1939.
The Christine Diamond. London, Hutchinson, and New York, Longman, 1940.
Before the Storm. New York, Longman, 1941.
She Dwelt with Beauty. London, Macmillan, 1949.

Short Stories

Studies in Wives. London, Heinemann, 1909; New York, Kennerley, 1910.
Studies in Love and Terror. London, Methuen, and New York, Scribner, 1913.
Why They Married. London, Heinemann, 1923.
Bread of Deceit. London, Hutchinson, 1925; as *Afterwards*, New York, Doubleday, 1925.
Some Men and Women. London, Hutchinson, 1925; New York, Doubleday, 1928.
What of the Night? New York, Dodd Mead, 1943.
A Labour of Hercules. London, Todd, 1943.

OTHER PUBLICATIONS

Plays

The Lonely House, with Charles Randolph, adaptation of the novel by Lowndes (pro-
duced Eastbourne, Sussex, 1924).
The Key: A Love Drama (as The Second Key, produced London, 1935).   London, Benn,
1930.
With All John's Love.   London, Benn, 1930.
Why Be Lonely?, with F.S.A. Lowndes.   London, Benn, 1931.
What Really Happened, adaptation of her own novel (produced London, 1936).   Lon-
don, Benn, 1932.
Her Last Adventure (produced London, 1936).
The Empress Eugenie.   New York, Longman, 1938.

Other

H.R.H. the Prince of Wales: An Account of His Career (published anonymously).
London, Richards, and New York, Appleton, 1898; revised edition, as His Most
Gracious Majesty King Edward VII, as Mrs. Belloc Lowndes, Richards, 1901.
The Philosophy of the Marquise (sketches and dialogues).   London, Richards, 1899.
T.R.H. the Prince and Princess of Wales (published anonymously).   London, Newnes,
1902.
Noted Murder Mysteries (as Philip Curtin).   London, Simpkin Marshall, 1914.
Told in Gallant Deeds: A Child's History of the War.   London, Nisbet, 1914.
"I, Too, Have Lived in Arcadia": A Record of Love and of Childhood.   London,
Macmillan, 1941; New York, Dodd Mead, 1942.
Where Love and Friendship Dwelt (autobiography).   London, Macmillan, and New
York, Dodd Mead, 1943.
The Merry Wives of Westminster (autobiography).   London, Macmillan, 1946.
A Passing World (autobiography).   London, Macmillan, 1948.
The Young Hilaire Belloc.   London, P.J. Kennedy, 1956.

Editor and Translator, with M. Shedlock, Edmund and Jules de Goncourt, with Letters
and Leaves from Their Journals.   London, Heinemann, and New York, Dodd Mead, 2
vols., 1895.

*   *   *

Marie Belloc Lowndes's romances capture changing moral values from Victorian elders to
Edwardian youth, from pre-war idealists to post-war cynics, the sense of propriety, respectability, and practicality in love of the one, the more liberal, convention-breaking affairs of the
other. Frequently her love stories involve elements of the supernatural, with seances, forewarn-
ings, and apparitions, or criminal activities that involve the reputations of young innocents
caught in a web of treachery. Staid and proper members of society find themselves unexpectedly seized by alien feelings of jealousy and shameless desire; young men and women sacrifice
their reputations and virtue for love or money, find themselves manipulated and abused, their
honesty questioned, their beloved driven into the arms of devious rivals. Occasionally the
situation is an adulterous one, pregnant with mixed feelings of love and remorse. Always
Lowndes portrays the joys and horrors of the everyday. Her forte is a compassionate understanding of the diversity and complexity of human motives, the shades of gray, the unspoken
and the hidden. Her novels are replete with sad adventuresses, rich but eccentric relatives,
gossipy neighbors, potential scandals, driving hatreds, and surprising human generosity. Her
historical romance She Dwelt with Beauty is typical of her domestic interests, focusing on the
courtship and marriage of Eugenie de Montijo and Louis Napoleon, not for the historical
repercussions, but for the human conflicts that grow out of the failure of the sexes to

understand their differing natures and needs: Napoleon's sexually rampant nature; Eugenie's naivety, her shock at his infidelities, her mixture of love and abhorrence.

Occasionally Lowndes's tales seem conventionally Victorian: a cold-hearted, rich, young man, rejected by a kind-hearted beauty, seeks revenge on his rival, a generous and much-admired new arrival with a dark past, only to find his own aunt aiding the young lovers' escape. Such novels usually feature a decaying manor, family scandal, and scheming relatives. But more frequently Lowndes depends on psychological portraits and ironic twists: an unexpected call announcing death traps a philanderer who has seduced his best friend's wife; another philanderer, dependent on the security of a bedridden wife to protect him from his various conquests' demands for marriage, finds one lover who takes his toying all too seriously, murders his wife, and leaves him to face the consequences; a betrayed wife realizes her own responsibility for her divorced husband's acts and, upon the death of his second wife, hesitantly returns to his arms; a wealthy widow, upon learning her ex-lover has seduced her daughter into a secret engagement, executes their mutual lover—for her daughter's sake; a greedy woman, obsessed by money, starves herself to death; thereafter, her bereaved husband squanders the hard-earned wealth on a poor, young, neighboring beauty (*Some Men and Women*). Often they verge on the gothic: a spoiled, self-righteous prude seeking revenge for her husband's infidelity in an illicit affair is warned from the act by the ghost of a woman whose illicit love she had once condemned; her insane husband having decapitated his rival in love, a terrified wife must return the head to the scene of horror to hide her shame and protect her family; a submarine captain and his mistress share a final farewell as the ship sinks, and the proud and loveless husband must use his wits to hide the scandal and preserve his honor (*Studies in Love and Terror*). The last focuses on the husband's guilt in the affair, and the cold self-possession that clearly alienated his gentle wife and allowed him to take the horror of her death so calmly. Always secret sins have public repercussions, and reputation is almost as important as survival.

Duchess Laura and *Duchess Laura, Further Days from Her Life*, sum up the contrast in generations, the first focusing on the very proper romance and marriage of a Victorian lady, the second, portraying episodically her forced readjustment to a changing world as she saves her son from a loveless marriage, helps an adventuress afford her true love, rescues a cynical young girl from the loathsome advances of a rich lecher, brings together an overprotected blind girl and a bitter, horribly scarred heir, prevents a repressed niece from poisoning her cantankerous old aunt, and faces the shock of her son wedding a poor, unattractive, roadhouse worker for her kindness and intelligence rather than family or beauty. Her difficulties in adjusting to the new morality and the breakdown of class differences among the younger generation are typical of the conflicts facing many of Lowndes's characters. *The Christine Diamond*, like many of her crime romances, deals with love beyond class bounds and the social patterns and taboos of upstairs/downstairs, as a rich young playboy takes pity on, then falls in love with, his aunt's secretary, to find he can win her love only by finding a stolen diamond and a clever thief. In *Reckless Angel* a spoiled debutante, moving in a rich, fast crowd, develops a reputation for carefree, thoughtless acts, yet becomes enamoured of a steady, puritanical naval officer whose only flaw is moral bondage to a grasping older woman; only involvement in murder and theft, and the near loss of love and reputation finally teach her to be more careful of her loyalties. In *Love Is a Flame*, an unusual mixture of the highly cynical and highly romantic, a hard-working young woman's honesty sends her lover into the arms of a spoiled and petulant acquaintance who marries him on a whim, then sends him to possible death; only after blackmail, murder, suicide, and a blinding, crippling war injury does true love win out.

Thus, Marie Belloc Lowndes portrays sympathetically domestic conflicts between generations, classes, and sexes; the misunderstandings and rationale of love; the attraction of opposites; the disillusionment of the naive; and the rewards of the faithful. With its commonplace horrors and its focus on the contradictory impulses of individuals, her canon reflects the war-induced breakdown of moral codes and the consequent confusion of decent characters caught in a morass of dimly understood shifting values. As a result, her work speaks to our time as well as her own.

—Gina Macdonald

LURGAN, Lester.   *See* **WYNNE, May**.

LUTYENS, Mary.   *See* **WYNDHAM, Esther**.

LYNN, Margaret.   Pseudonym for Gladys Starkey Battye.   Born in 1915. *Died*.

ROMANCE AND GOTHIC PUBLICATIONS

Novels

> *To See a Stranger*.   London, Hodder and Stoughton, 1961; New York, Doubleday, 1962.
> *Stranger by Night*.   London, Hodder and Stoughton, 1963; as *Mrs. Maitland's Affair*, New York, Doubleday, 1963.
> *Whisper of Darkness*.   London, Hodder and Stoughton, 1965; New York, Paperback Library, 1966.
> *A Light in the Window*.   London, Hodder and Stoughton, 1967; New York, Doubleday, 1968.
> *Sunday Evening*.   London, Hodder and Stoughton, 1969; New York, Doubleday, 1971.
> *Sweet Epitaph*.   London, Hodder and Stoughton, 1971; New York, Doubleday, 1972.

*   *   *

Margaret Lynn's novels of suspense appeal to all our latent paranoia. Her typical heroine is an isolated woman, surrounded by people she cannot trust, who suspect her of things she is certain she did not do, although the pressure of their suspicions sometimes forces her to question her own sanity. Lynn involves us totally with her heroine, and the reader believes in her despite her invidious position (for often enough we find the heroine is concealing something); because of this identification with the heroine, the level of suspense is high.

Her first novel, *To See a Stranger*, is her best. In it, a woman wakes up thinking she is a 20-year-old girl about to be married, and discovers she is instead a 40-year-old matron married to a man she dislikes; worse, she finds she does not like the person she apparently is. There is a claustrophobic feeling here, as we enter the mind of a woman convinced she must be going mad. In *Whisper of Darkness* a woman who all her life has been despised and bullied marries to achieve freedom and finds she is still tied by the terms of a will both to the house she hates and to her husband; to make things worse, everyone around her believes her responsible for a series of increasingly malicious tricks culminating in murder attempts on her husband. *A Light in the Window* deals with the wife of an Englishman accused of being a communist spy. Her life is threatened by a communist organization, while the police do not believe in her innocence. In

Sunday Evening a woman recovering from a nervous breakdown is suspected of the kidnap-murder of a child; her mind still clouded by her emotional breakdown, she not only cannot prove her innocence, but is not at all certain she *is* innocent. *Sweet Epitaph* is the least successful of her suspense novels, and much more akin to the conventional murder mystery. A woman is held captive for 42 days by unknown persons, apparently to keep her from seeing a dying relative who might alter his will in her favor. As in all Margaret Lynn's novels, truth is elusive and constantly shifting, and no one is to be trusted.

Few writers of Gothics have managed to create as much suspense and emotional involvement as Margaret Lynn has.

—Marylaine Block

MACARDLE, Dorothy (Margaret Callan).   Irish.   Born in 1899. Educated at University College, Dublin. Active in the Irish nationalist movement: jailed; taught at Alexandra College; became a journalist: correspondent at the League of Nations, Geneva; after World War II worked with displaced and refugee children. *Died 23 December 1958.*

ROMANCE AND GOTHIC PUBLICATIONS

Novels

>*Uneasy Freehold.*   London, Davies, 1941; as *The Uninvited*, New York, Doubleday, 1942.
>*The Seed Was Kind.*   London, Davies, 1944.
>*Fantastic Summer.*   London, Davies, 1946; as *The Unforeseen*, New York, Doubleday, 1946.
>*Dark Enchantment.*   London, Davies, and New York, Doubleday, 1953.

Short Stories

>*Earth-Bound: Nine Stories of Ireland.*   Worcester, Massachusetts, Harrigan Press, 1924.

Uncollected Short Story

>"Samhain," in *Best British Short Stories 1925*, edited by Edward J. O'Brien.   Boston, Houghton Mifflin, 1925.

OTHER PUBLICATIONS

Plays

>*Atonement* (produced Dublin, 1918).
>*Asthara* (produced Dublin, 1918).

Ann Kavanagh (produced Dublin, 1922).   New York, French, 1937.
The Old Man (produced Dublin, 1925).
Witch's Brew.   London, Deane, 1931.
The Children's Guest (juvenile).   London, Oxford University Press, 1940.
The Loving-Cup (juvenile).   London, Nelson, 1943.

Other

Tragedies of Kerry 1922-1923.   Dublin, Emton Press, 1924.
The Irish Republic: A Documented Chronicle of the Anglo-Irish Conflict and the Partitioning of Ireland, with a Detailed Account of the Period 1916-1923.   London, Gollancz, 1937; New York, Farrar Straus, 1965.
Without Fanfares: Some Reflections on the Republic of Eire.   Dublin, Gill, 1946.
Children of Europe: A Study of the Children of Liberated Countries....   London, Gollancz, 1949; Boston, Beacon Press, 1951.
Shakespeare, Man and Boy, edited by George Bott.   London, Faber, 1961.

*   *   *

Although Dorothy Macardle has written a long history of the Irish state and has been a performed playwright, she is best-remembered as the author of the supernatural romance *Uneasy Freehold* (American title, *The Uninvited*), which was made into a successful motion picture. Essentially a story of the persistence of emotions (expressed in fantastic terms), it describes the blighting effect of a haunting on what would otherwise have been a smooth, happy romance and marriage. For years Stella has been kept away from her dead father's closed house. When she enters, she awakens a haunting and her life is threatened. A mystery emerges, the solution to which is not likely to astonish the reader familiar with gothic devices. Instead, the reader is more likely to be impatient at the author's inability to characterize a male narrator. All in all, the motion picture *The Uninvited* (1944) is superior to the book.

A second supernatural novel, *Fantastic Summer* (American title, *The Unforeseen*), set in Ireland, is based on complications caused by the sudden emergence of the second sight. Virgilia Wilde is afflicted by premonitory visions that at first are only annoying, but become nightmarish when she foresees her daughter being strangled by her fianceP. (The situation is reminiscent of Hector Bolitho's "The House on Half-Moon Street.") The daughter's romance is interwoven with episodes of Virgilia's uncomfortable gift. Technically, the book is weaker than *Uneasy Freehold*, what with a feeble story line, flaccid characterizations, and excessive sentimentality. A foreword states that the story is based on fact, but it is not known whether this statement is meant seriously or is a literary device.

A third novel, *Dark Enchantment*, is set in the Maritime Alps of France. It has two themes, the maturation of a young Englishwoman tourist who stays in the area to become a helper in an inn, and the presence of ambivalent evil in the person of a gypsy witch. The witch's activities arouse the latent fears and brutalities of the natives. Treatment of both themes is superficial and confused, while the peasants are pallid if compared with similar types in the work of Ramuz.

—E.F. Bleiler

MACDONALD, Marcia.   *See* **HILL, Grace Livingston.**

MacGILL, Mrs. Patrick (Margaret MacGill, née Gibbons).

<small>ROMANCE AND GOTHIC PUBLICATIONS</small>

Novels

> *The Rose of Glenconnel.* London, Thomson, 1916.
> *An Anzac's Bride.* London, Jenkins, 1917.
> *Whom Love Hath Chosen.* London, Jenkins, 1919.
> *The Bartered Bride.* London, Jenkins, 1920.
> *Each Hour a Peril.* London, Thomson, 1921.
> *The Flame of Life.* London, Jenkins, 1921.
> *Hidden Fires.* London, Jenkins, 1921.
> *The Highest Bidder.* London, Thomson, 1921.
> *His Dupe.* London, Thomson, 1922.
> *Molly of the Lone Pine.* London, Thomson, 1922.
> *Shifting Sands.* London, Jenkins, 1922.
> *A Lover on Loan.* London, Jenkins, 1923.
> *Her Undying Past.* London, Jenkins, 1924.
> *Love—and Carol.* London, Jenkins, 1925.
> *Her Dancing Partner.* London, Jenkins, 1926.
> *Love's Defiance.* London, Thomson, 1926.
> *The Ukelele Girl.* London, Jenkins, 1927; as *His Ukelele Girl*, London, Thomson, 1927.
> *Dancers in the Dark.* London, Jenkins, 1929.
> *Painted Butterflies.* London, Jenkins, 1931.
> *Hollywood Madness.* London, Jenkins, 1936; as *Hollywood Star Dust*, New York,
>   Chelsea House, 1936.

<small>OTHER PUBLICATIONS</small>

Other

> *The "Good-Night" Stories* (juvenile; as Margaret Gibbons). London, Year Book Press,
>   1912.

*   *   *

Mrs. Patrick MacGill's first book, *The "Good-Night" Stories*, was a collection of stories for children. It has a stories-within-a-story framework, and is set in the Vane household whose numerous children are told bedtime stories by their mother before the Golden Dustman comes to throw magic dust on their eyes and send them to the enchanted realm of Slumberland. The stories are chiefly about fairies—"The bluebells tinkle merrily, and the fairies and elves form a ring round the Queen, who always sailed down in the moon to these gatherings (*sc.* on Hampstead Heath)."

Mrs. MacGill went from writing fairy stories for children to writing fairy stories for adults. Her romantic novels, which appeared between 1916 and 1936, are highly melodramatic, as their titles suggest. The plots are packed with incident—the result of genteel poverty, gambling fathers, spendthrift siblings, rascally employers, false accusations, bankruptcy, intrigue, treachery, deceit, gangsters—so that the hero and heroine are kept well apart until the final chapters.

The heroines of the earlier novels tend to be either unprotected orphan girls (such as the Rose of Glenconnel, born Rosalie Moran, who was brought up on a mining and lumber camp in the

Yukon and turns out to be the grand-daughter of a baronet) or young wives having trouble with their husbands (through shell-shock or a forced marriage). The heroines of the later novels (with an eye to changing social conditions) are in paid employment, doing jobs which are quite advanced for the time, glamorous, or even daring—"girl clerk," assistant in a Bond Street hat shop, society dress designer, Exhibition Dancer in a night club, film actress. Though the heroines do not vary much in type, their settings do, from the Canadian backwoods, to titled circles in London, to Hollywood. Mrs. Macgill seems to have been particularly smitten by "the Tinsel Kingdom, Filmdom's capital," and much of the action in her last two novels takes place in Hollywood, where (of course) two of her earlier works, *The Flame of Life* and *Hidden Fires*, are being turned into films. A *Times Literary Supplement* reviewer had already accused her of having an eye to "another mode of presentation than that of print" (1924 review of *Her Undying Past*).

Her literary style was as melodramatic as her plots, and did not change much over twenty novels: "She was shy now, this fragrant, beautiful little bride, and a burning, blushing face was pressed close to Ronald's breast. But the young trapper, with eyes and heart aflame, bent down and raised his wife's face to his own...(*The Rose of Glenconnel*, 1916); or " 'Let me look after you, sweetheart.' The low, deep voice was vibrant with passion, but very kindly and tender...as, stemming the tide of his own desire to press wild ecstatic kisses on the soft red mouth, he said, 'You are afraid of love, Peggy...' " (*Hollywood Madness*, 1936).

—Jean Buchanan

MACKINLAY, Leila (Antoinette Sterling). Also writes as Brenda Grey.   British.   Born in London, 5 September 1910. Attended Camden House School, London; trained as a singer and actress. Drama critic, *Dancing Times*, 1935-39, and since 1946 for *Amateur Stage*; publishers reader, and drama and verse adjudicator. Recipient: Romantic Novelists Association President's Prize, 1966. Address: 4P Portland Mansions, Chiltern Street, London W1M 1LF, England.

ROMANCE AND GOTHIC PUBLICATIONS

Novels

Little Mountebank.   London, Mills and Boon, 1930.
Fame's Fetters.   London, Mills and Boon, 1931.
Madame Juno.   London, Mills and Boon, 1931.
An Exotic Young Lady.   London, Mills and Boon, 1932.
Willed to Wed.   London, Mills and Boon, 1933.
The Pro's Daughter.   London, Ward Lock, 1934.
Shadow Lawn.   London, Ward Lock, 1934.
Love Goes South.   London, Ward Lock, 1935.
Into the Net.   London, Ward Lock, 1935.
Night Bell.   London, Ward Lock, 1936.
Young Man's Slave.   London, Ward Lock, 1936.
Doubting Heart.   London, Ward Lock, 1937.
Apron-Strings.   London, Ward Lock, 1937.
Caretaker Within.   London, Ward Lock, 1938.

Theme Song. London, Ward Lock, 1938.
Only Her Husband. London, Ward Lock, 1939.
The Reluctant Bride. London, Ward Lock, 1939.
Man Always Pays. London, Ward Lock, 1940.
Woman at the Wheel. London, Ward Lock, 1940.
Ridin' High. London, Ward Lock, 1941.
None Better Loved. London, Ward Lock, 1941.
Time on Her Hands. London, Ward Lock, 1942.
The Brave Live On. London, Ward Lock, 1942.
Green Limelight. London, Ward Lock, 1943.
Lady of the Torch. London, Ward Lock, 1944.
Two Walk Together. London, Ward Lock, 1945.
Piper's Pool. London, Ward Lock, 1946.
Piccadilly Inn. London, Ward Lock, 1946.
Blue Shutters. London, Ward Lock, 1947.
Echo of Applause. London, Ward Lock, 1948.
Peacock Hill. London, Ward Lock, 1948.
Restless Dream. London, Ward Lock, 1949.
Pilot's Point. London, Ward Lock, 1949.
Six Wax Candles. London, Ward Lock, 1950.
Spider Dance. London, Ward Lock, 1950.
Guilt's Pavilions. London, Ward Lock, 1951.
Five Houses. London, Ward Lock, 1952.
Unwise Wanderer. London, Ward Lock, 1952.
Cuckoo Cottage. London, Ward Lock, 1953.
She Married Another. London, Ward Lock, 1953.
Midnight Is Mine. London, Ward Lock, 1954.
Fiddler's Green. London, Ward Lock, 1954.
Vagabond Daughter. London, Ward Lock, 1955.
Riddle of a Lady. London, Ward Lock, 1955.
Man of the Moment. London, Ward Lock, 1956.
She Moved to Music. London, Ward Lock, 1956.
Divided Duty. London, Ward Lock, 1957.
Mantle of Innocence. London, Ward Lock, 1957.
Love on a Shoestring. London, Ward Lock, 1958.
The Secret in Her Life. London, Ward Lock, 1958.
Seven Red Roses. London, Ward Lock, 1959.
Uneasy Conquest. London, Ward Lock, 1959.
Food of Love. London, Ward Lock, 1960.
Spotlight on Susan. London, Ward Lock, 1960.
Beauty's Tears. London, Ward Lock, 1961.
Spring Rainbow. London, Ward Lock, 1961.
Vain Delights. London, Ward Lock, 1962.
Broken Armour. London, Ward Lock, 1963.
False Relations. London, Ward Lock, 1963.
Fool of Virtue. London, Ward Lock, 1964.
Practice for Sale. London, Ward Lock, 1964.
Ring of Hope. London, Ward Lock, 1965.
No Room for Loneliness. London, Ward Lock, 1965.
An Outside Chance. London, Ward Lock, 1966.
The Third Boat. London, Ward Lock, 1967.
Mists of the Moor. London, Ward Lock, 1967.
Frost at Dawn. London, Ward Lock, 1968.
Homesick for a Dream. London, Ward Lock, 1968.
Wanted—Girl Friday. London, Ward Lock, 1968.
Farewell to Sadness. London, Hale, 1970.
The Silken Purse. London, Hale, 1970.
Bridal Wreath. London, Hale, 1971.

Strange Involvement. London, Hale, 1972.
Birds of Silence. London, Hale, 1974.
Fortune's Slave. London, Hale, 1975.
Twilight Moment. London, Hale, 1976.
The Uphill Path. London, Hale, 1979.

Novels as Brenda Grey

Modern Micawbers. London, Eldon Press, 1933.
Stardust in Her Eyes. London, Gresham, 1964.
Girl of His Choice. London, Gresham, 1965.
How High the Moon. London, Gresham, 1966.
Throw Your Bouquet. London, Gresham, 1967.
A Very Special Person. London, Gresham, 1967.
Shadow of a Smile. London, Gresham, 1968.
Tread Softly on Dreams. London, Gresham, 1970.
Son of Summer. London, Gresham, 1970.
Mixed Singles. London, Gresham, 1971.
Husband in Name. London, Hale, 1972.

OTHER PUBLICATIONS

Other

Musical Productions. London, Jenkins, 1955.

*   *   *

Leila Mackinlay has had one of the longest careers of living romantic fiction writers. Her first novel, *Little Mountebank*, came out in 1930, and she has continued writing until the late 1970's. She has also written fiction under the name of Brenda Grey and drama criticism. She received the Romantic Novelists Association President's Prize in 1966.

Most of Mackinlay's novels concern the world of the theatre or singing, and her own training and involvement in the stage have served as a source of inspiration. Many of her books concern pupils or young entertainers. *An Exotic Young Lady*, for instance, is set in a popular environment of an Italian singing school in London and contains a very convincing description of this milieu.

The promotion of young and obscure theatrical talent has become a familiar theme, but there is a wide variety of plots, and love invariably is involved. In *Food of Love* the singer is a young miner and he has to be helped to overcome the disadvantages of his background and the jealous opposition of his small town fiancée. After the breaking off of the hero's engagement, a love triangle results between the hero's lady agent and her younger friend. The book is saved from being clichéd by a very sympathetic drawing of character, especially of the older woman whose attraction stirs in her long dormant feelings. A classic British theme of the time, the conflict between a rising hero and his working-class background is convincingly handled.

The world of the professional theatre can be inward looking but Mackinlay is able to give the reader a perspective on the life of a stage family in *An Outside Chance*. The position of second-team actors and actresses is convincingly summarised. The principal character, a young actress, is well drawn and shows us that she is quite normal and stable, somewhat against our expectations. True to a tradition in romance writing, glamour is pointed up by the grotesque: the heroine is the object of romantic advances from her fiancée's hideously crippled brother. The men are weak but the women are strong, and the heroine is able to cope with difficult situations and becomes the lynch pin of her own family.

True to the theatrical tradition, careers have their ups and downs. In *The Uphill Path* the

459

heroine is able to turn round her fortunes and rebuild her career; although painful memories are recalled, she rediscovers and renews her original love affair.

As well as a very accurate background setting of the theatre, Mackinlay gives a considerable credibility in her novels to her characters. Unexpected depths are found in people and she shows the hard work necessary for success. Ordinary people outside show business come across very well, too, and display a mature and steady attitude to emotional relationships despite being, in some cases, just out of their teens. Some minor characters, for instance in *Fool of Virtue*, are glaring exceptions to this rule.

Dialogue does not overburden her books and is neither trite nor silly. The plots are interesting and credible. The narrative is well written although occasionally slow.

The great achievement of Mackinlay is to be able to keep her books up to date for each decade. The heroine in *An Exotic Young Lady* of 1932 is an orthodox girl of the decade. *None Better Loved* of 1941 has an appropriate setting of air raid shelters. In *The Uphill Path* (1979) the modern post-1960's pop scene, its mores and attendant problems for a girl, is very well drawn as is the character of the girl herself.

As befits the tradition of romantic novels, Leila Mackinley's have a moral but it is palatable and does not spoil a good story.

—P.R. Meldrum

MacLEOD, Charlotte (Matilda).   Also writes as Alisa Craig; Matilda Hughes.   American. Born in Bath, New Brunswick, Canada, 12 November 1922. Educated at public schools in Weymouth, Massachusetts; Art Institute of Boston. Since 1952, member of the staff, currently Vice-President, N.H. Miller, advertising agency, Boston. Agent: Curtis Brown Ltd., 575 Madison Avenue, New York, New York 10022. Address: 177 Plympton Road, Sudbury, Massachusetts 01776, U.S.A.

ROMANCE AND GOTHIC PUBLICATIONS

Novels

> *Mystery of the White Knight*.   New York, Avalon, 1965.
> *The Food of Love* (as Matilda Hughes).   New York, Avalon, 1965.
> *Next Door to Danger*.   New York, Avalon, 1965.
> *Headlines for Caroline* (as Matilda Hughes).   New York, Avalon, 1967.
> *The Fat Lady's Ghost*.   New York, Weybright and Talley, 1968.
> *Ask Me No Questions*.   Philadelphia, Macrae Smith, 1971.
> *King Devil*.   New York, Atheneum, 1978.
> *Rest You Merry*.   New York, Doubleday, 1978; London, Collins, 1979.
> *The Family Vault*.   New York, Doubleday, 1979; London, Collins, 1980.
> *The Luck Runs Out*.   New York, Doubleday, 1979; London, Collins, 1981.
> *We Dare Not Go a-Hunting*.   New York, Atheneum, 1980.
> *The Withdrawing Room*.   New York, Doubleday, 1980.
> *The Palace Guard*.   New York, Doubleday, 1981.
> *Wrack and Rune*.   New York, Doubleday, 1982.

Novels as Alisa Craig (series: Madoc Rhys)

A Pint of Murder (Rhys).   New York, Doubleday, 1980.
The Grub-and-Stakers Move a Mountain.   New York, Doubleday, 1981.
Murder Goes Mumming (Rhys).   New York, Doubleday, 1981.

OTHER PUBLICATIONS

Other

Mouse's Vineyard (juvenile).   New York, Weybright and Talley, 1968.
Brass Pounder (juvenile).   Boston, Little Brown, 1971.
Astrology for Sceptics.   New York, Macmillan, 1972; London, Turnstone, 1973.

Manuscript Collection: Mugar Memorial Library, Boston University.

*   *   *

Charlotte MacLeod, who becomes Alisa Craig when she writes about her native Canada, is unfailingly entertaining in whatever genre she chooses to write. It is hard to say what one most appreciates in her books: her witty dialogue, her characters, or her cheerfully cynical view of the world.

That some of her novels are classed as young adult fiction has more to do with the publishers' marketing strategy than substance; they are perfectly satisfactory to adult readers of romantic suspense. The Fat Lady's Ghost is the least successful of these; in it, a snobbish and egotistical heroine turns into a likable human being, while solving a mystery involving a jewel thief and a haunted kitchen. King Devil is both a pleasing romance and a study in the banality of evil; characters who at first appear only to be foolish and mildly malicious turn out to be murderously egocentric. We Dare Not Go a-Hunting offers romance, kidnapping, and conflict between the full-time residents and rich summer visitors on an island community.

MacLeod has written three murder mysteries involving Peter Shandy, professor of agrology at Balaclava College. In the first, Rest You Merry, Shandy goes maliciously overboard with his house decorations for the campus Grand Illumination at Christmas. When he returns, he finds the campus busybody dead in his home, apparently fallen in the act of removing the offending decor. Peter correctly suspects murder and investigates. The plot is funny, the characters interesting, and the romance delightful. The Luck Runs Out is even better, involving a kidnapped sow, a murdered farrier, vigilant vegetarians, and three romances. Wrack and Rune is also very funny, though the romantic element is slim.

As Alisa Craig she has written three romantic mysteries. A Pint of Murder introduces Mountie Madoc Rhys, who looks like an unemployed plumber's assistant (they had expected a plainclothesman, but not that plain). He falls in love with one of the less likely suspects in two murders committed in a small town. Normal human absurdities are amusingly depicted. In The Grub-and-Stakers Move a Mountain a young woman discovers murder and civic corruption involving a plot to turn the "enchanted mountain," which is public property, into private property. While helping to solve the murder, she and her friends hastily put together a campaign to elect a candidate of their choice. Action is frenetic and funny, as the bad guys resort to skullduggery and the ladies retaliate. Madoc Rhys and his lady love return in Murder Goes Mumming to solve an Agatha Christie-style murder at a country estate during Christmas festivities. This is enjoyable, though her writing is less disciplined than usual, and Madoc tends to dote excessively.

MacLeod's more conventional murder mysteries, The Family Vault, The Withdrawing Room, and The Palace Guard, are equally witty, though more subdued, but as, after three novels, the leading characters have only now worked themselves up to a few discreet kisses, it will probably take a few more novels to get them to the point of being romantic enough to be discussed in this volume. Nevertheless they are recommended for all the usual virtues of

MacLeod's style: their strong sense of place and community, their wit, and their well-developed characters.

—Marylaine Block

MacLEOD, Jean S.   Also writes as Catherine Airlie.   British.   Bon in Glasgow, 20 January 1908. Educated at Bearsden Academy, near Glasgow; High School for Girls, Swansea, Wales. Married Lionel Walton in 1935; one son. Secretary, British Ministry of Labour, Newcastle-upon-Tyne, 1930-35. Recipient: Cartland Historical Novel Award, 1962. Agent: Mills and Boon Ltd., 15-16 Brooks Mews, London W1A 1DR, England. Address: Kilmelford, by Oban, Argyll, Scotland.

ROMANCE AND GOTHIC PUBLICATIONS

Novels

Life for Two.   London, Mills and Boon, 1936.
Human Symphony.   London, Mills and Boon, 1937.
Summer Rain.   London, Mills and Boon, 1938.
Sequel to Youth.   London, Mills and Boon, 1938.
Mist Across the Hills.   London, Mills and Boon, 1938; Toronto, Harlequin, 1967.
Dangerous Obsession.   London, Mills and Boon, 1938; Toronto, Harlequin, 1962.
Run Away from Love.   London, Mills and Boon, 1939; Toronto, Harlequin, 1961.
Return to Spring.   London, Mills and Boon, 1939; Toronto, Harlequin, 1971.
The Rainbow Isle.   London, Mills and Boon, 1939.
The Whim of Fate.   London, Mills and Boon, 1940.
Silent Bondage.   London, Mills and Boon, 1940; Toronto, Harlequin, 1961.
The Lonely Farrow.   London, Mills and Boon, 1940.
Heatherbloom.   London, Mills and Boon, 1940.
The Reckless Pilgrim.   London, Mills and Boon, 1941.
The Shadow of a Vow.   London, Mills and Boon, 1941.
One Way Out.   London, Mills and Boon, 1941.
Forbidden Rapture.   London, Mills and Boon, 1941.
Penalty for Living.   London, Mills and Boon, 1942.
Blind Journey.   London, Mills and Boon, 1942.
Bleak Heritage.   London, Mills and Boon, 1942; Toronto, Harlequin, 1970.
Reluctant Folly.   London, Mills and Boon, 1942.
Unseen To-morrow.   London, Mills and Boon, 1943.
The Rowan Tree.   London, Mills and Boon, 1943.
Flower o' the Broom.   London, Mills and Boon, 1943.
The Circle of Doubt.   London, Mills and Boon, 1943.
Lamont of Ardgoyne.   London, Mills and Boon, 1944.
Two Paths.   London, Mills and Boon, 1944; Toronto, Harlequin, 1966.
Brief Fulfillment.   London, Mills and Boon, 1945.
The Bridge of Years.   London, Mills and Boon, 1945.
This Much to Give.   London, Mills and Boon, 1945; Toronto, Harlequin, 1961.
One Love.   London, Mills and Boon, 1945; Toronto, Harlequin, 1970.

The Tranquil Haven. London, Mills and Boon, 1946.
Sown in the Wind. London, Mills and Boon, 1946; Toronto, Harlequin, 1970.
The House of Oliver. London, Mills and Boon, 1947; Toronto, Harlequin, 1968.
And We in Dreams. London, Mills and Boon, 1947.
The Chalet in the Sun. London, Mills and Boon, 1948.
Ravenscrag. London, Mills and Boon, 1948.
Above the Lattice. London, Mills and Boon, 1949.
To-morrow's Bargain. London, Mills and Boon, 1949.
Katherine. London, Mills and Boon, 1950.
The Valley of Palms. London, Mills and Boon, 1950; Toronto, Harlequin, 1963.
Roadway to the Past. London, Mills and Boon, 1951.
Once to Every Heart. London, Mills and Boon, 1951.
Cameron of Gare. London, Mills and Boon, 1952; Toronto, Harlequin, 1961.
Music at Midnight. London, Mills and Boon, 1952.
The Silent Valley. London, Mills and Boon, 1953; Toronto, Harlequin, 1958.
The Stranger in Their Midst. London, Mills and Boon, 1953; Toronto, Harlequin, 1961.
Dear Doctor Everett. London, Mills and Boon, 1954; Toronto, Harlequin, 1958.
The Man in Authority. London, Mills and Boon, 1954.
After Long Journeying. London, Mills and Boon, 1955.
Master of Glenkeith. London, Mills and Boon, 1955; Toronto, Harlequin, 1969.
The Way in the Dark. London, Mills and Boon, 1956; Toronto, Harlequin, 1960.
My Heart's in the Highlands. London, Mills and Boon, 1956; Toronto, Harlequin, 1963.
Journey in the Sun. London, Mills and Boon, 1957; Toronto, Harlequin, 1960.
The Prisoner of Love. London, Mills and Boon, 1958; Toronto, Harlequin, 1960.
The Gated Road. London, Mills and Boon, 1959; Toronto, Harlequin, 1960.
Air Ambulance. London, Mills and Boon, and Toronto, Harlequin, 1959.
The Little Doctor. London, Mills and Boon, and Toronto, Harlequin, 1960.
Nurse Lang. Toronto, Harlequin, 1960.
The White Cockade. London, Mills and Boon, 1960.
The Silver Dragon. London, Mills and Boon, 1961; Toronto, Harlequin, 1962.
Slave of the Wind. London, Mills and Boon, 1962; Toronto, Harlequin, 1969.
The Dark Fortune. London, Mills and Boon, 1962.
Mountain Clinic. Toronto, Harlequin, 1962.
Sugar Island. London, Mills and Boon, and Toronto, Harlequin, 1964.
The Black Cameron. London, Mills and Boon, and Toronto, Harlequin, 1964.
Crane Castle. London, Mills and Boon, and Toronto, Harlequin, 1965.
The Wolf of Heimra. London, Mills and Boon, 1965; Toronto, Harlequin, 1966.
Doctor's Daughter. Toronto, Harlequin, 1965.
The Tender Glory. London, Mills and Boon, 1965; Toronto, Harlequin, 1967.
The Drummer of Corrae. London, Mills and Boon, and Toronto, Harlequin, 1966.
Lament for a Lover. London, Mills and Boon, and Toronto, Harlequin, 1967.
The Master of Keills. London, Mills and Boon, 1967; Toronto, Harlequin, 1968.
The Bride of Mingalay. London, Mills and Boon, and Toronto, Harlequin, 1967.
The Moonflower. London, Mills and Boon, 1967; Toronto, Harlequin, 1968.
Summer Island. London, Mills and Boon, 1968; Toronto, Harlequin, 1969.
The Joshua Tree. London, Mills and Boon, 1970.
The Fortress. London, Mills and Boon, 1970.
The Way Through the Valley. London, Mills and Boon, and Toronto, Harlequin, 1971.
The Scent of Juniper. London, Mills and Boon, 1971.
Light in the Tower. Toronto, Harlequin, 1971.
Moment of Decision. Toronto, Harlequin, 1972.
Adam's Daughter. London, Mills and Boon, 1972; Toronto, Harlequin, 1973.
The Rainbow Days. London, Mills and Boon, and Toronto, Harlequin, 1973.
Over the Castle Wall. London, Mills and Boon, 1974.
Time Suspended. London, Mills and Boon, 1974; Toronto, Harlequin, 1975.
The Phantom Pipes. London, Mills and Boon, 1975.
Journey into Spring. Toronto, Harlequin, 1976.
Island Stranger. London, Mills and Boon, 1977; Toronto, Harlequin, 1978.

Viking Song. London, Mills and Boon, 1977.
The Ruaig Inheritance. London, Mills and Boon, 1978.
Search for Yesterday. London, Mills and Boon, and Toronto, Harlequin, 1978.
Meeting in Madrid. London, Mills and Boon, 1979.
Brief Enchantment. London, Mills and Boon, 1979.
Black Sand, White Sand. London, Mills and Boon, 1981.

Novels as Catherine Airlie

The Wild Macraes. London, Mills and Boon, 1948.
From Such a Seed. London, Mills and Boon, 1949.
The Restless Years. London, Mills and Boon, 1950.
Fabric of Dreams. London, Mills and Boon, 1951.
Strange Recompense. London, Mills and Boon, 1952; Toronto, Harlequin, 1960.
The Green Rushes. London, Mills and Boon, 1953; Toronto, Harlequin, 1968.
Hidden in the Wind. London, Mills and Boon, 1953.
A Wind Sighing. London, Mills and Boon, 1954; Toronto, Harlequin, 1969.
Nobody's Child. London, Mills and Boon, 1954; Toronto, Harlequin, 1968.
The Valley of Desire. London, Mills and Boon, 1955; Toronto, Harlequin, 1967.
The Ways of Love. London, Mills and Boon, 1955; Toronto, Harlequin, 1970.
The Mountain of Stars. London, Mills and Boon, 1956; Toronto, Harlequin, 1969.
The Unguarded Hour. London, Mills and Boon, 1956.
Land of Heart's Desire. London, Mills and Boon, 1957; Toronto, Harlequin, 1968.
Red Lotus. London, Mills and Boon, 1958; Toronto, Harlequin, 1968.
The Last of the Kintyres. London, Mills and Boon, 1959; Toronto, Harlequin, 1969.
Shadow on the Sun. London, Mills and Boon, 1960.
One Summer's Day. London, Mills and Boon, 1961; Toronto, Harlequin, 1966.
The Country of the Heart. London, Mills and Boon, 1961; Toronto, Harlequin, 1964.
The Unlived Year. London, Mills and Boon, 1962; Toronto, Harlequin, 1971.
Passing Strangers. London, Mills and Boon, 1963.
The Wheels of Chance. London, Mills and Boon, 1964.
The Sea Change. London, Mills and Boon, 1965.
Doctor Overboard. Toronto, Harlequin, 1966.
Nurse Jane in Teneriffe. Toronto, Harlequin, 1967.

Jean S. MacLeod comments:

After writing romantic and historical fiction for over 40 years I have come to the conclusion that I am happily employed in my chosen career which, even now, I would not like to be without. I have been most fortunate in my connection with Mills and Boon Ltd. and all the women's magazine editors with whom I have worked in that time.

*   *   *

Jean S. MacLeod is a writer who captivates the reader with unusual stories in exotic settings. It is obvious that she has thoroughly researched the background to her novels. Her characters seem to be equally at home in the mountains of Norway and the warmth of the Canary Islands as in her own native Scotland. More than mere settings, her milieux form an intrinsic part of the action, with unobtrusive descriptions of customs and natural phenomena providing an air of authenticity.

The majority of the novels are set in some part of Scotland: amid the cliffs and seas (*The Prisoner of Love*), in the Hebrides (*The Bride of Mingalay*), or in the Western Highlands (*Above the Lattice*). And in these books it is clear that the writer is in her element. However, there is an equal feeling of affinity in the novels which deal with less familiar places. The description of the Norwegian mountains in *The Mountain of Stars* (Catherine Airlie), for example, include many references to real places. The characters' observance of customs, such as that of the "bridal veil," whether real or not, also give an air of authenticity. This feeling of reality is also conveyed by the dialogues and interaction between the characters, such as that between Felicity and Philip in *Red Lotus*, whose relationship is moving and very plausible.

The force of the elements is strongly felt in all MacLeod's works, and one may even say that natural forces seem to influence events at times or at least to be in sympathy with them. In *Music at Midnight* Kay goes to Norway to take her dead sister's son to his grandparents. The writer manages to portray very convincingly the weighty fear of an avalanche, and in *Red Lotus* the volcanic eruption that traps Felicity and Philip on the mountain plays a frightening part in the action. *The Man in Authority* also contains a strong feeling of the power of places and the elements. Here, as in a number of these novels, the main character comes to possess a feeling of "belonging" to a location which was alien when the story began. Perhaps significantly, many of the novels (e.g., *After Long Journeying*) begin with someone standing on a quayside or waving from the deck of a ship at the commencement of a journey.

This travel element is often combined with a medical setting, a tried and tested favourite for romances of this kind. The formula is obviously well chosen in this case. The romances which MacLeod invents are often characterized by misunderstanding or lack of communication between the parties concerned. Margaret and Thor marry (in *The Mountain of Stars*) although each is under the illusion that the other does not love him. In *Time Suspended* Ruth at first thinks Logan could be either "a gentleman or a pirate," but they finally settle happily together in Antigua. So, too, in *The Bride of Maingalay* Rowena ends up marrying Andrew Fenwick despite her initial detestation.

In conclusion, it may be said that Jean MacLeod, whether writing under this name or her pseudonym of Catherine Airlie, has written carefully researched romances with some depth. The well-chosen settings combine effectively with the events of the plot to give an unusual and entertaining final product.

—Kim Paynter

* * *

MADDOCKS, Margaret (Kathleen Avern). British. Born in Caversham, Berkshire, 10 August 1906. Educated at St. Helen's School, Northwood, Middlesex, and in Dresden. Married Richard Maddocks in 1937 (died). Recipient: Romantic Novelists Association Major Award, 1962, 1965, 1970, 1976. Address: Asthall Cottage, Stogumber, Taunton, Somerset, England.

ROMANCE AND GOTHIC PUBLICATIONS

Novels

> *Come Lasses and Lads.* London, Hurst and Blackett, 1944.
> *The Quiet House.* London, Hurst and Blackett, 1947.
> *Remembered Spring.* London, Hurst and Blackett, 1949.
> *Fair Shines the Day.* London, Hurst and Blackett, 1952; as *The Open Door*, London, Hamlyn, 1980.
> *Piper's Tune.* London, Hurst and Blackett, 1954.
> *A Summer Gone.* London, Hurst and Blackett, 1957.
> *The Frozen Fountain.* London, Hurst and Blackett, 1959.
> *Larksbrook.* London, Hurst and Blackett, 1962.

The Green Grass. London, Hurst and Blackett, 1963.
November Tree. London, Hurst and Blackett, 1964.
The Silver Answer. London, Hurst and Blackett, 1965.
Dance Barefoot. London, Hurst and Blackett, 1966.
Fool's Enchantment. London, Hurst and Blackett, 1968.
Thea. London, Hurst and Blackett, 1969; New York, Ace, 1973.
The Weathercock. London, Hurst and Blackett, 1971; New York, Ace, 1973.
A View of the Sea. London, Hurst and Blackett, 1973.
The Moon Is Square. London, Hurst and Blackett, 1975.

Uncollected Short Stories

"The Third Tuesday," in *Good Housekeeping* (London), August 1955.
"Ginger for a Queen," in *Good Housekeeping* (London), 1956.

OTHER PUBLICATIONS

Other

An Unlessoned Girl (autobiography).   London, Hutchinson, 1977.

Margaret Maddocks comments:

Any writer must find it difficult to assess her own work honestly and objectively, so I can only say that I hope my books may be considered as well-written. They appear to be popular among all age groups in the nine countries where they have been published. This is probably because the reader can believe in the characters and the plot holds the interest to the end. They tend to cheer rather than depress. (Please note that they are NOT gothic.)

*   *   *

The heroines of Margaret Maddocks's novels are less concerned with finding true love than with finding themselves. The last thing on their minds is falling in love; rather they are concerned with rebuilding their lives after a time of great unhappiness, for example, the death of a spouse. Going it alone, after having depended on someone else to deal with the practicalities of life, may be tough, but Maddocks's heroines cope admirably. In fact they flourish, growing in spirit and personality as they meet and surmount the obstacles in their way. It is almost as if, in a brief but passionate marriage or a too-close relationship with a child, they have suppressed part of themselves. The constraints of adapting their temperaments to suit that of someone else are lifted, and the women are free to be, in fact they are forced to be, themselves. Such freedom brings its own difficulties, emotional and physical isolation being the most pressing. The characters yearn not for passion and romance, which they have experienced in the past, but for companionship and understanding, and someone to laugh with them at the problems that come their way. In short, the ability to make love seems a less important quality to look for in a lover than the ability to make a good joke.

Despite strong elements of realism in some novels, elements of clichéd romanticism are still to be found. Jane, the attractive young heroine of *The Silver Answer* (winner of the Romantic Novelists Association Major Award—one of four such awards that Maddocks has received), has been widowed after a brief passionate year of marriage. We meet her two years on, having recovered from the nervous breakdown and miscarriage that followed Alan's death, setting out over one summer to write a book about the mountaineering expedition in which he was tragically killed. Before long she has won the hearts of not one, not two, but three men! Two of these, the artistic, humorous Mike Harling and the sensible, understanding Lawrence Stafford, were friends of Alan's, and companions on the fatal expedition. The third is an untruthful actor, the hairy, "bear-like" egoistic Aubrey Charles. Though Jane declares that she could never fall in love again, and that she holds Mike and Lawrence responsible for Alan's death and thus "hates" them, her actual behaviour shows little evidence of this, and she spends the entire summer vacillating between the three men. After having a brief affair with the attractive/repulsive Aubrey, she ends up, rather predictably, with the man we knew she would end up with on page one. Still, elements of realism creep into the rather thin plot: the book that Jane writes over the summer turns out to be a rather self-indulgent failure, and is even rejected by her friends and former employers, who run a literary agency; and Jane's relationship with her aging, tight-lipped parents casts a gloomy shadow over the summer months.

The theme of child/parent relationships is one that obviously concerns Maddocks, and she deals with it admirably. The heroine of *Thea*, one of her most moving works, has recently been widowed after a long, superficially happy marriage to a man more than 20 years her senior. Not only must she now build a new life for herself but she must also cope with the problems of her two daughters, the rather remote and volatile Harriet whose stormy marriage is going through a crucial phase, and the endearing warm-hearted 18-year-old Lizzy, Thea's "other self." When Harriet walks out on her husband and arrives back on her mother's doorstep with her three-year-old son, and Lizzy falls in love with Jonah, a man Thea's age, Thea is forced to re-examine her marriage, which she finds to have had many faults, and is torn between concern for her children's futures and the need to explore and assert her own new-found independence. When she expresses her fears that Lizzy will, by marrying a man in a different generation, miss out on much of her youth, as she herself did, a rift forms for the first time between mother and daughter. Things are further complicated when Lizzy accuses Thea of wanting Jonah herself. *Thea* is a rich novel, realistic in plot and execution. The characters are all the more believable for having their imperfections (bad temper, insensitivity, Thea's obsession with feeding extra mouths), and the central portrait of a woman struggling for the first time in her life to put herself before her children is a convincing one.

The relationship between child and parent, or rather the lack of it, forms the basis of *The Moon Is Square*. In this case the "child" in question, teenage Stephen, far from needing his widowed mother Judith, disappears from home on the brink of the university career for which she has such high hopes. Left with no information of his whereabouts other than the fact that he is "walking to India," Judith, who had in the past turned down a proposal of marriage in order to devote herself to her son (or so she tells herself), is shocked, worried, and confused. Suddenly she realises that she had not really known Stephen as a person, so involved has she been in the world of romantic fiction, which she has been writing for financial reasons during her long widowhood. As in many of Margaret Maddocks's novels, the feeling of isolation predominates: the heroine has few friends, lives in an isolated country cottage, and has no one to turn to who understands her mixed reactions to Stephen's departure. The reappearance of her rejected suitor, Paul, and the rewarding if uneasy friendship she forms with one of Stephen's "drop-out" friends, Jan, through whom she begins to understand her son, lead her to reject the idea of forming a relationship with the attractive Paul, who treats her as "an unreasonable child," and towards a union of compassionate understanding with Jan's father, Ross.

Margaret Maddocks's novels are not so much about women falling in love as about women discovering themselves through adversity. Though, as in most romantic fiction, the hero and heroine get together in time for a happy, or at least hopeful, ending, what draws them together is companionship rather than passion, and far more important, and best explored, is what happens to them on the way.

—Judith Summers

MANLEY-TUCKER, Audrie.   Also writes as Linden Howard. Address: c/o Mills and Boon Ltd., 15-16 Brooks Mews, London W1A 1DR, England.

ROMANCE AND GOTHIC PUBLICATIONS

Novels

Leonie.   London, Mills and Boon, 1958.
Lost Melody.   London, Mills and Boon, 1959.
A Love Song in Springtime.   London, Mills and Boon, 1960.
Piper's Gate.   London, Mills and Boon, 1960.
Dark Bondage.   London, Mills and Boon, 1961.
A Memory of Summer.   London, Mills and Boon, 1961; New York, Paperback Library, 1966.
The Promise of Morning.   London, Mills and Boon, 1962.
Candlemas Street.   London, Mills and Boon, 1963.
The Loved and the Cherished.   London, Mills and Boon, 1964.
A Rainbow in My Hand.   London, Mills and Boon, 1965.
Shadow of Yesterday.   London, Mills and Boon, 1965.
Champagne Girl.   London, Mills and Boon, 1967.
Love, Spread Your Wings.   London, Mills and Boon, 1967; Toronto, Harlequin, 1973.
Door Without a Key.   London, Mills and Boon, 1967; Toronto, Harlequin, 1973.
Julie Barden, District Nurse.   London, Mills and Boon, 1968.
Return to Sender.   London, Mills and Boon, 1968.
Julie Barden, Doctor's Wife.   London, Mills and Boon, 1969.
A Room Without a Door.   London, Mills and Boon, 1970.
Assistance Unlimited.   London, Mills and Boon, 1971.
Every Goose a Swan.   London, Mills and Boon, 1972.
Shetland Summer.   London, Mills and Boon, 1973; New York, Pinnacle, 1980.
The Piper in the Hills.   London, Mills and Boon, 1974.
Life Begins Tomorrow.   London, Mills and Boon, 1975.
Two for Joy.   London, Mills and Boon, 1979.
Tamberlyn.   London, Mills and Boon, 1981.

Novels as Linden Howard

Foxglove Country.   New York, St. Martin's Press, 1977; London, Millington, 1978.
The Devil's Lady.   London, Millington, and New York, St. Martin's Press, 1980.

*   *   *

Audrie Manley-Tucker's romantic novels fulfil their function—to give enjoyment. It is one of her attributes that she makes really nice people interesting. The heroines are bright modern girls who tackle their problems with spirit and pluck. The reader identifies with them straightaway because they have to deal with difficulties that face every girl. Serena in *Shetland Summer*, for instance, is in love with a married man but is realistic enough to see there is no (happy) future in that. With characteristic courage she decides to make a clean break and goes off to Shetland.

Another bonus of Manley-Tucker's novels is her excellent description: "That hat in the milliner's window looked like an upturned rush basket spilling artificial daises and had two long streamers of pale green ribbon hanging down the back." An unusual little shop, a village garden, or the Scottish Highlands become vivid verbal paintings. The descriptions are so deftly inserted that they never hold up the narrative but enhance it.

As topical as today's news is the problem of the adopted child. Should she try to find her "real" mother and risk hurting her adoptive parents or stifle her curiosity and be content with her present environment? Sandy Drummond in *Every Goose a Swan* is determined to seek out her "mother," and she carries the reader along in her search.

With very few exceptions none of Audrie Manley-Tucker's heroines has glamorous jobs or goes to exotic places. They have ordinary jobs and mostly live at home with their parents. The same could be said of the men, the majority of whom are likable and worthy of the heroines. The few children appearing are life-like and not at all angelic.

Gothic novels by Audrie Manley-Tucker are written under the name of Linden Howard. These conform to the usual gothic tradition of a young girl facing a new life in an ancient mansion set in the country, and also facing, although she does not know it, hostility and danger. Manley-Tucker shows her adaptability in being able to tackle convincingly novels with so many restricted plot conventions. *Foxglove Country* and *The Devil's Lady* are excellent examples of this genre. The former novel has a powerful character (the grandfather) and a charming heroine in Sara Pryce. The background of the desolate Welsh Beacons adds to the tension and menace. There are accidents, death, and love stories woven into this fast-moving and convincing book. Manley-Tucker's descriptive gifts and perceptive insight into character makes this gothic compelling reading.

—Lucy Rogers and Peggy York

MANN, Deborah. *See* **BLOOM, Ursula.**

MANNERS, Alexandra. *See* **RUNDLE, Anne.**

MANNING, Marsha. *See* **GRIMSTEAD, Hettie.**

MARCHANT, Catherine. *See* **COOKSON, Catherine**.

MARSH, Jean. Pseudonym for Evelyn Marshall; also wrote as Lesley Bourne. British. Born in Pershore, Worcestershire, 2 December 1897. Educated at Bournville High School; Halesowen Grammar School; Oxford Senior Certificate for teaching. Married Gerald Eric Marshall in 1917; one son (dead) and one daughter. Teacher in Halesowen until 1919, then journalist for Thomson and Leng groups until late 1920's; contract writer for Amalgamated Press group until 1939; broadcaster during World War II; writer for *Children's Hour* until 1956. Agent: Shirley Russell, Rupert Crew Ltd., King's Mews, London WC1N 2JA. Address: The Spinney, Stourport Road, Bewdley, Worcestershire DY12 1BJ, England.

ROMANCE AND GOTHIC PUBLICATIONS

Novels

> *Sand Against the Wind*. London, Hale, 1973.
> *Loving Partnership*. London, Hale, 1978; Rolling Meadows, Illinois, Aston Hall, 1979.
> *The Family at Castle Trevissa*. London, Hale, 1979.
> *Sawdust and Dreams*. London, Hale, 1980.
> *Mistress of Tanglewood*. London, Hale, 1981.
> *Unbidden Dream*. London, Hale, 1981.
> *The Rekindled Flame*. London, Hale, 1982.
> *This Foolish Love*. London, Hale, 1982.

OTHER PUBLICATIONS

Novels

> *The Shore House Mystery*. London, Hamilton, 1931.
> *Murder Next Door*. London, Long, 1933.
> *Death Stalks the Bride*. London, Long, 1943.
> *Identity Unwanted*. London, Long, 1951.
> *Death Visits the Circus*. London, Long, 1953.
> *The Pattern Is Murder*. London, Long, 1954.
> *Death among the Stars*. London, Long, 1955.
> *Death at Peak Hour*. London, Long, 1957.

Plays

> Radio Serials: *Mystery of Castle Rock Zoo*, 1945; *On the Trail of the Albatross*, 1949; *Judith and the Dolls*, 1950; *Secret of the Pygmy Herd*, 1951; *Adventure with a Boffin*, 1952; *Death Visits the Circus*, 1952; *Ghost Ship*, 1952; *Helen Had a Daughter*, 1953; *Johnny Pilgrim Again*, 1953; *The Small Beginning*, 1954; *Valley of Silent Sound*, 1956; *The White Sapphire*, 1956; *Pocahontas*.

Other (juvenile)

On the Trail of the Albatross (adaptation of radio serial).   London, Burke, 1950.
Secret of the Pygmy Herd (adaptation of radio serial).   London, Burke, 1951.
Trouble for Tembo (as Lesley Bourne).   London, University of London Press, 1958.
Adventure with a Boffin (adaptation of radio serial).   London, University of London Press, 1962.
The Valley of Silent Sound (adaptation of radio serial).   London, University of London Press, 1962.

Other

Bewdley, XV Century Sanctuary Town.   Kinver, Halmar, 1979.
All Saints' Centenary.   Kinver, Halmar, 1980.

Jean Marsh comments:

I began my writing career at the end of World War I with the object, of necessity, of making a living at it. Being fortunate enough to have a contract with the multi-magazine publishers Amalgamated Press, this was possible. Short stories and serials were turned out as required by the group editor. With the advent of the 1939 war, most writings and broadcast talks were geared to the war effort both on home and overseas programmes. But at this time I discovered the delight of writing the kind of detective novels I had always wanted to write. These paved the way to writing adventure serials for BBC *Children's Hour* when the war ended. This was also the period when I wrote a number of adult radio plays and documentaries. After *Children's Hour* closed, I returned to the romantic novels written earlier as magazine serials. But now they have a country background, many of them featuring animals as well as human characters. These have proved popular first as series in *Woman's Story Magazine*, later in book form. I am still doing them. Fortunately even in one's eighties the creative urge is as strong as ever. It's the fingers that become a little stiff on the typewriter keys.

*   *   *

Jean Marsh's romantic novels are less about women falling in love than about women having to prove themselves as professionals in their work, and as valuable members of society. Her heroines live in small, inward-looking, closely-knit communities crowded with a multitude of characters whose lives and problems form the core of her plots. Such romance as there is is almost peripheral and is of a rather dated nature: girl meets boy, whom she secretly likes but who shows hostility or indifference towards her; drawn together by one, or many community dramas, they are united right at the end of the book when, after only one kiss, marriage is almost presumptuously assumed to be the natural outcome of their liking for one another. But, however slight the romantic involvement may be throughout the rest of the books, they all make for entertaining reading on one other count: as vivid portraits of small communities, struggling to create or to maintain a certain way of life.

Without exception Marsh picks rural settings for her romantic fiction. Her central characters are vets (*Loving Partnership*), managers of wild-life parks (*Unbidden Dream*), riding instructors (*Mistress of Tanglewood*), farming or circus people whose day-to-day lives bring them into close contact with a wide variety of animals. In *Sawdust and Dreams*, the story of Melissa, the teen-age daughter of a circus-owning family who is suddenly called upon to take over her sister-in-law's elephant act, we encounter the joys and difficulties of dealing with animals which are, though trained, still wild at heart. In *Unbidden Dream* the heroine, Sue, has taken over as vet in a newly established wild-life park, and has to cope with anything from a wounded lion to a baby giraffe. *The Family at Castle Trevissa* features, among other animals, a sick dolphin and a shoal of stranded seals. Though she tends at times towards a rather too sentimental attitude to her animals (piglets are being fattened up for market on the farm in *The Rekindled Flame* but there's not so much as a whisper of the word "abattoir"), Marsh deals

471

with the problems of looking after them with great compassion and authority, and this gives a great deal of authenticity to her work.

Animals are not the sole concern of the rural communities with which Marsh deals. Financial and personal problems loom large. In *The Rekindled Flame* the heroine, Betty, works as a free-lance farm accountant, and acts as unpaid confidante for all her clients. While she struggles to control her rekindled feelings for the business-minded Mark, an ex-boyfriend who has just returned from Canada to manage his uncle's farm, she acts as a good Samaritan, selflessly helping her neighbours to cope with their pressing problems. It is in the end her selfless devotion to the rather old-fashioned farming community which Mark, now used to the more go-ahead ways of Canadian agriculture, seems to despise, that draws him back to her: she has proved herself trustworthy both as a professional and a human being, and Mark, distrustful of women after a past experience, is free at last to express his love. Yet another man hostile to women is Steve, manager of a safari park and central male character of *Unbidden Dream*. Try as she might, the young heroine Sue, a veterinary surgeon, cannot get on friendly terms with him, though in her heart she harbours more than friendly feelings towards her new boss. Again, it is her courage and professional attitude which persuade Steve to trust her at last.

Trust is not an emotion that figures too highly in Marsh's closed communities. Secret vendettas against one or more characters provide added interest for her readers as well as the opportunity for her heroes and heroines to grow together over a little detective work (Melissa and Glen's search for the circus saboteur in *Sawdust and Dreams*). In *Unbidden Dream*, too, the future of a safari park is put in jeopardy after a series of mysterious "accidents." For many years a writer of mystery novels, it seems that Marsh is now unable to stop herself placing her characters under some kind of threat. The denouements of these small mysteries are, however, disappointingly handled, and might benefit from some further twist in the end.

Though not without their faults, the romantic novels of Jean Marsh are lively and interesting, certainly more so than the clichéd jacket covers imply.

—Judith Summers

MARSHALL, Edison (Tesla). Also wrote as Hall Hunter. American. Born in Rensselaer, Indiana, 28 August 1894. Educated at the University of Oregon, Eugene, 1913-16. Served in the United States Army Ordnance Field Services, 1918: Lieutenant; educational film writer for Department of Defense during World War II. Married Agnes Sharp Flythe in 1920; one son and one daughter. Hunter and explorer, then free-lance writer. Recipient: O. Henry Award, for short story, 1921. M.A.: University of Oregon, 1941. *Died 29 October 1967.*

ROMANCE AND GOTHIC PUBLICATIONS

Novels

> *Benjamin Blake.* New York, Farrar and Rinehart, 1941.
> *Great Smith.* New York, Farrar and Rinehart, 1943; London, Aldor, 1947.
> *The Upstart.* New York, Farrar Straus, 1945; London, World Distributors, 1959.
> *Yankee Pasha: The Adventures of Jason Starbuck.* New York, Farrar Straus, 1948; London, Redman, 1950.
> *Castle in the Swamp: A Tale of Old Carolina.* New York, Farrar Straus, 1948; London, Muller, 1949.
> *Gypsy Sixpence.* New York, Farrar Straus, 1949; London, Muller, 1950.
> *The Infinite Woman.* New York, Farrar Straus, 1950; London, Muller, 1951.

The Viking.   New York, Farrar Straus, 1951; London, Muller, 1952.
The Bengal Tiger: A Tale of India (as Hall Hunter).   New York, Doubleday, 1952; as *Rogue Gentleman*, as Edison Marshall, New York, Popular Library, 1963.
American Captain.   New York, Farrar Straus, 1954; as *Captain's Saga*, London, Muller, 1955.
Caravan to Xanadu: A Novel of Marco Polo.   New York, Farrar Straus, 1954; London, Muller, 1955.
The Gentleman.   New York, Farrar Straus, and London, Muller, 1956.
The Inevitable Hour: A Novel of Martinique.   New York, Putnam, 1957; London, Muller, 1958.
Princess Sophia.   New York, Doubleday, 1958; London, Muller, 1959.
The Pagan King.   New York, Doubleday, 1959; London, Muller, 1960.
Earth Giant.   New York, Doubleday, 1960; London, Muller, 1961.
West with the Vikings.   New York, Doubleday, 1961.
The Conqueror.   New York, Doubleday, 1962.
Cortez and Marina.   New York, Doubleday, 1963.
The Lost Colony.   New York, Doubleday, 1964.

Short Stories

The Heart of Little Shikara and Other Stories.   Boston, Little Brown, 1922; London, Hodder and Stoughton, 1924.
Love Stories of India.   New York, Farrar Straus, 1950.

OTHER PUBLICATIONS

Novels

The Voice of the Pack.   Boston, Little Brown, and London, Hodder and Stoughton, 1920.
The Strength of the Pines.   Boston, Little Brown, and London, Hodder and Stoughton, 1921.
The Snowshoe Trail.   Boston, Little Brown, and London, Hodder and Stoughton, 1921.
Shepherds of the Wild.   Boston, Little Brown, and London, Hodder and Stoughton, 1922.
The Sky Line of Spruce.   Boston, Little Brown, 1922; as *The Sky-Line*, London, Hodder and Stoughton, 1922.
The Land of Forgotten Men.   Boston, Little Brown, 1923; London, Hodder and Stoughton, 1924.
The Isle of Retribution.   Boston, Little Brown, and London, Hodder and Stoughton, 1923.
The Death Bell.   New York, Garden City Publishing Company, 1924.
Seward's Folly.   Boston, Little Brown, and London, Hodder and Stoughton, 1924.
The Sleeper of the Moonlit Ranges.   New York, Cosmopolitan, and London, Hodder and Stoughton, 1925.
Child of the Wild: A Story of Alaska.   New York, Cosmopolitan, and London, Hodder and Stoughton, 1926.
The Deadfall.   New York, Cosmopolitan, and London, Hodder and Stoughton, 1927.
The Far Call.   New York, Cosmopolitan, and London, Hodder and Stoughton, 1928.
The Fish Hawk.   New York, Cosmopolitan, and London, Hodder and Stoughton, 1929.
Singing Arrows.   London, Hodder and Stoughton, 1929.
The Missionary.   New York, Cosmopolitan, and London, Hodder and Stoughton, 1930.
The Doctor of Lonesome River.   New York, Cosmopolitan, and London, Hodder and Stoughton, 1931.

The Deputy at Snow Mountain. New York, Kinsey, and London, Hodder and Stoughton, 1932.
Forlorn Island. New York, Kinsey, and London, Hodder and Stoughton, 1932.
The Light in the Jungle. New York, Kinsey, 1933; as *Victory in the Jungle*, London, Hodder and Stoughton, 1933.
The Splendid Quest. New York, Kinsey, 1934.
Ogden's Strange Story. New York, Kinsey, 1934.
Dian of the Lost Land. New York, Kinsey, 1935; as *The Lost Land*, New York, Curtis, 1966.
Sam Campbell, Gentleman. New York, Kinsey, 1935; London, Hodder and Stoughton, 1936.
The Stolen God. New York, Kinsey, 1936; London, Hodder and Stoughton, 1937.
The White Brigand. New York, Kinsey, 1937; London, Hodder and Stoughton, 1938.
Darzee, Girl of India. New York, Kinsey, 1937; as *The Flower Dancer*, London, Hodder and Stoughton, 1937.
The Jewel of Malabar. New York, Kinsey, and London, Hodder and Stoughton, 1938.

Other

Ocean Gold (juvenile). New York, Harper, 1925.
Campfire Courage: The Woodsmoke Boys in the Canadian Rockies (juvenile). New York, Harper, 1926.
Shikar and Safari: Reminiscences of Jungle Hunting. New York, Farrar Straus, 1947; London, Museum Press, 1950.
The Heart of the Hunter (autobiography). New York, McGraw Hill, 1956; London, Muller, 1957.

*   *   *

Edison Marshall's long career was a sweeping curve upward to the position of the foremost historical novelist of the 1940's and 1950's, but since his death the reputation of his fiction has not so much declined as that fiction has simply been ignored. In spite of his success, including ten films based upon his works, he perhaps expected his fate when he said, "I am an anachronism, and my career is *contre tempes*."

His work falls neatly into two groups on the basis of both chronology and subject matter. Until the late 1930's, most of his writing consisted of short stories and magazine serials in the adventure-thriller genre. Many were based upon his own hunting expeditions around the world, especially in southern Asia and Alaska. "The Heart of Little Shikara," winner of the O. Henry prize in 1921, *The Light in the Jungle*, and *The Jewel of Malabar* are examples of the Asian stories. Even more prevalent are those set in Alaska or the American northwest; there are more than a dozen. Marshall stated that he was "Obsessed by nature to a degree of passion that would floor Freud," and these works are filled with close and accurate descriptions of nature, often to emphasize its redeeming power for various city types who find themselves suddenly amidst its wonders, as in *The Voice of the Pack, Shepherds of the Wild*, and *The Isle of Retribution*. Though the plots are often repetitive, these works can still have appeal for lovers of adventure and admirers of nature.

Even more successful with readers than these adventure stories were the historical novels beginning with *Benjamin Blake*. Ranging throughout history and varied in locale, they were novels of action and romance. Some centered on actual persons, as *Great Smith* (Captain John Smith) and *The Infinite Woman* (based on Lola Montez), while the central characters of others were imaginary: *Yankee Pasha* and *Gypsy Sixpence*. A major success was *The Viking*, with the legendary Ogier the Dane as its hero. Whether set in early America, India, the Caribbean, or Norseland, and whatever the time period, Marshall's novels were well-researched, fast-paced, and colorful in the presentation of customs and sights. The heroes and heroines were generally noble in deed, if not in title, and the sexual element was treated conservatively. With Marshall's many excellent qualities as a historical novelist, it may be that the lack of explicit sex is the reason for his being replaced by other novelists of lesser talent who provide titillation in historical guise for their readers. If so, that says more about the readers about than Marshall's ability as novelist.

—Earl F. Bargainnier

MARSHALL, Joanne. *See* **RUNDLE, Anne**.

MARSHALL, Rosamond (Van der Zee).   American.   Born in New York City, 17 October 1902. Educated at Miss Eaton's School, Pasadena, California; Lycée des Jeunes Filles, Dijon; Real Gymnasium, Vienna; University of Munich. Married Albert Earl Marshall (second marriage); one daughter. Amateur mountaineer. Recipient: New York *Herald Tribune* Festival award, for children's book, 1942. *Died 13 November 1957.*

ROMANCE AND GOTHIC PUBLICATIONS

Novels

    Kitty.   New York, Duell, 1943; London, Redman, 1956.
    Duchess Hotspur.   New York, Prentice Hall, 1946; London, Redman, 1958.
    Celeste.   New York, Prentice Hall, 1949.
    Laird's Choice.   New York, Prentice Hall, 1951; London, Redman, 1952.
    Bond of the Flesh.   New York, Doubleday, 1952; London, Redman, 1953.
    Jane Hadden.   New York, Prentice Hall, 1952; London, Redman, 1953.
    The Temptress.   New York, New American Library, 1952.
    The General's Wench.   New York, Prentice Hall, 1953; London, Redman, 1954.
    The Dollmaster.   New York, Prentice Hall, 1954; London, Redman, 1955; as *Mistress of Rogues*, New York, Popular Library, 1956.
    The Loving Meddler.   New York, Doubleday, 1954; London, Redman, 1955.
    Rogue Cavalier.   New York, Doubleday, 1955; London, Redman, 1956.
    The Rib of the Hawk.   New York, Appleton Century Crofts, 1956; London, Redman, 1957.
    Captain Ironhand.   New York, Appleton Century Crofts, and London, Redman, 1957.
    The Bixby Girls.   New York, Doubleday, 1957; London, Redman, 1958.

Other novels (in French): *L'Enfant du Cirque*, 1930; *La Main d'Acier*, 1931; *Plaisirs d'Amour*, 1932; *Le Vaisseau Fantôme*, 1933; *Vengeance du Sheik*, 1934; *Mystères de Chinatown*, 1934; *Mystères de Londres*, 1935.

Other (juvenile)

None But the Brave: A Story of Holland.   Boston, Houghton Mifflin, 1942; London, Hutchinson, 1946.
The Treasure of Shafto.   New York, Messner, 1946.

*   *   *

The traditional Horatio Alger "rags to riches" success story based upon hard work and righteous living has long been a favourite in the world of adult fairy tales, but Rosamond Marshall gave the old theme a surprising new twist with her best-selling period romance *Kitty*. This quite different success story tells of a nameless child of the 18th-century London gutters, her virginity sold for a few pence to a lecherous sexton when she was but eight years old by the heartless bawd who holds her bond. Kitty lives by petty theft and prostitution, until one day her gamin charm catches the eye of a great painter in want of a model. Thomas Gainsborough recognizes great beauty disguised by dirt, and the bath and arbitrary surname he provides for the lovely waif are her keys to a new life. Working her way up from man to man, finally attaining a peak of success as a duchess, Kitty has something the "Moll Flanders" version of fictional harlot lacked—a heart. She never forgets her own miserable beginnings, nor ceases to pity the plight of other child victims. At the height of her triumph, Kitty risks her own safety and happiness for the benefit of the wretched mill-children on her inherited estate.

As though to prove that a rake can progress in either direction, Rosamond Marshall followed the success of *Kitty* with another light-hearted romp, *Duchess Hotspur*, the tale of a high-born lady with an eclectic taste in lusty men, who falls in love at last with a penniless journalist. Duchess Percy thinks at first that it will be a simple matter to bring her scruffy lover up to a standard of appearances acceptable to her privileged circle by means of a few judicious gifts, but not so. He is a proud fellow, who regards such treatment as an insult to his manhood. A compromise must be reached between the wanton, lovely duchess and the stiff-necked quill-pusher, and it makes for a rousing tale.

Rosamond Marshall's books, considered daring in their day, are unlikely now to raise any eyebrows. Good humoured pre-Regency fun and games, they make cheerfully diverting bedtime stories.

—Joan McGrath

MARTIN, Rhona. Also writes as Rhona M. Neighbour.   British.   Born in London, 3 June 1922. Educated at various private schools; Redland High School, Bristol; West of England College of Art, 1937-39. Married 1) Peter Wilfrid Alcock in 1941 (divorced, 1957), two daughters; 2) Thomas Neighbour in 1959 (divorced). Fashion artist, Willsons Ltd., Bristol, 1940-41; clerk, Fire Guard Office, Weston-super-Mare, 1942-45; free-lance theatrical designer, 1946-48; catering manager, Club Labamba, Tunbridge Wells, 1963-68; Assistant Manager, Odeon, Sevenoaks, 1968-72; Accounts Secretary and Office Manager, Crown Chemical Company, Lamberhurst, Kent, 1972-79; then full-time writer. Recipient: Georgette Heyer Historical Novel Prize, 1978. Agent: John McLaughlin, Campbell Thomson and McLaughlin Ltd., 31 Newington Green, London N16 9PU. Address: 25 Henwood Crescent, Pembury, Kent TN2 4LJ, England.

Novels

Gallows Wedding.   London, Bodley Head, 1978; New York, Coward McCann, 1979.
Mango Walk.   London, Bodley Head, 1981; New York, Bantam, 1982.

Uncollected Short Stories as Rhona M. Neighbour

"Waiting for Mr. Right," in *Evening News* (London), September 1973.
"Nude with Knitting," in *Evening News* (London), July 1974.

Rhona Martin comments:

I am not sure that I would classify my writing as either romance or gothic—but then classification is in any case best left to the reader. With me, a novel comes from first one idea and then two, usually a character and a situation, which interact and grow in darkness until they are gnawing a hole in me and have to be got out of my system. I am blessed or cursed with a fertile imagination to which these tiny seeds of thought cling and germinate like mushroom spores, sometimes with little awareness on my part. Suddenly there they are, refusing to be suppressed or ignored, thrusting upwards towards the light and pushing up pavingstones if need be to get there. I prefer not to be tied to a category, modern, historical or whatever; it is people who interest me, their reactions to each other and to the situations in which they find themselves, and to explore these fascinating avenues one must be free. *Gallows Wedding* happened as a result of wondering how a girl would feel who is reduced to buying a stranger from the gallows for the sake of his protection...and how would the couple fare afterwards? As I could find no book to tell me, I had to write it myself in order to find out. *Mango Walk* sprang from a dream I was unable to shake off; the figures in it remained to haunt me until I gave in and put their story down on paper. From here my work could go in any direction. I have to write what fires me, and to quote from one of my own verses, "joy's a nymph, not captured one way twice."

*   *   *

In 1977 Rhona Martin won the first Historical Novel Prize awarded jointly by The Bodley Head and Corgi Paperbacks in memory of the late Georgette Heyer; but *Gallows Wedding* bears absolutely no resemblance to a Georgette Heyer Regency Romance. It is a love-story, but is tough (very) as well as tender.

Set in the reign of Henry VIII it is for once not about the Court, but about the lives of Henry's poorest subjects; and their lives were very poor indeed.

Rhona Martin pulls no punches. In places the story is horrific. But the horror arises naturally from the story and the violent period in which it is set. Henry's greed, egotism, and whimsical desire to marry his mistress led to religious and political upheavels on a vast scale, and the wanton destruction not only of much that was beautiful in England, but of people, too; and no one reading Rhona Martin's first book is left in any doubt about that.

It is *not* a "romantic" novel in the conventional sense, but it does throw light into dark corners of that particular period, and the love story of Hazel, the brave, loyal, doomed girl born with the Devil's mark on her body, and Black John, the outlaw she marries in a "Gallows Wedding" (a bastard in the ribald, not the literal, sense), is told with conviction.

The story is cleverly devised and the ending satisfying, though it leaves several questions hanging which the author promises to answer in a sequel.

Rhona Martin is not a fast or prolific writer. She researches deeply and writes meticulously and thoughtfully; and she is not one-track, or one-period, minded. So far she has published only two books, both highly original and quite different. The second, *Mango Walk*, published three years after the first, is set in the 1940's and 1950s, and is an even stranger and more unconventional love-story, in which two people widely separated by age and cultural background, attract hostility when they decide to share their lives.

Again, a courageous book, well-written and distinctive. Rhona Martin's development as a writer will be well worth watching. But don't, ever, expect from her books which soothe you to sleep, or touch merely the frivolous surface of life. She is a "romantic" writer in the strictly dictionary sense.

—Elizabeth Grey

MATHER, Anne. Also writes as Caroline Fleming. Address: c/o Mills and Boon Ltd., 15-16 Brooks Mews, London W1A 1DR, England.

ROMANCE AND GOTHIC PUBLICATIONS

Novels

> *Caroline.* London, Hale, 1965.
> *Beloved Stranger.* London, Hale, 1966.
> *Design for Loving.* London, Hale, 1966.
> *Masquerade.* London, Hale, 1966; Toronto, Harlequin, 1972.
> *The Arrogance of Love.* London, Hale, 1968; Toronto, Harlequin, 1976.
> *Dark Venetian* (as Caroline Fleming). London, Hale, 1969; as Anne Mather, Toronto, Harlequin, 1976.
> *The Enchanted Island.* London, Hale, 1969.
> *Dangerous Rhapsody.* London, Hale, 1969; Toronto, Harlequin, 1977.
> *Legend of Lexandros.* London, Mills and Boon, 1969; Toronto, Harlequin, 1973.
> *Dangerous Enchantment.* London, Mills and Boon, 1969; Toronto, Harlequin, 1974.
> *Tangled Tapestry.* London, Mills and Boon, 1969.
> *The Arrogant Duke.* London, Mills and Boon, and Toronto, Harlequin, 1970.
> *Charlotte's Hurricane.* London, Mills and Boon, 1970; Toronto, Harlequin, 1971.
> *Lord of Zaracus.* London, Mills and Boon, 1970; Toronto, Harlequin, 1972.
> *Sweet Revenge.* London, Mills and Boon, 1970; Toronto, Harlequin, 1973.
> *Who Rides the Tiger.* London, Mills and Boon, 1970; Toronto, Harlequin, 1973.
> *Moon Witch.* London, Mills and Boon, 1970; Toronto, Harlequin, 1974.
> *Master of Falcon's Head.* London, Mills and Boon, 1970; Toronto, Harlequin, 1974.
> *The Reluctant Governess.* London, Mills and Boon, 1971; Toronto, Harlequin, 1972.
> *The Pleasure and the Pain.* London, Mills and Boon, 1971; Toronto, Harlequin, 1973.
> *The Sanchez Tradition.* London, Mills and Boon, 1971; Toronto, Harlequin, 1973.
> *Storm in a Rain Barrel.* London, Mills and Boon, 1971; Toronto, Harlequin, 1973.
> *Dark Enemy.* London, Mills and Boon, 1971; Toronto, Harlequin, 1973.
> *All the Fire.* London, Mills and Boon, 1971; Toronto, Harlequin, 1976.
> *The High Valley.* London, Mills and Boon, 1971; Toronto, Harlequin, 1976.
> *The Autumn of the Witch.* London, Mills and Boon, 1972; Toronto, Harlequin, 1973.
> *Living with Adam.* London, Mills and Boon, 1972; Toronto, Harlequin, 1973.
> *A Distant Sound of Thunder.* London, Mills and Boon, 1972; Toronto, Harlequin, 1973.
> *Monkshood.* London, Mills and Boon, 1972; Toronto, Harlequin, 1973.

Prelude to Enchantment.   London, Mills and Boon, 1972; Toronto, Harlequin, 1974.
The Night of the Bulls.   London, Mills and Boon, 1972; Toronto, Harlequin, 1974.
Jake Howard's Wife.   London, Mills and Boon, 1973; Toronto, Harlequin, 1974.
A Savage Beauty.   London, Mills and Boon, 1973; Toronto, Harlequin, 1974.
Chase a Green Shadow.   London, Mills and Boon, 1973; Toronto, Harlequin, 1974.
White Rose of Winter.   London, Mills and Boon, 1973; Toronto, Harlequin, 1974.
Mask of Scars.   London, Mills and Boon, 1973; Toronto, Harlequin, 1975.
The Waterfalls of the Moon.   London, Mills and Boon, 1973; Toronto, Harlequin, 1975.
The Shrouded Web.   London, Mills and Boon, 1973; Toronto, Harlequin, 1976.
Seen by Candlelight.   Toronto, Harlequin, 1974.
Legacy of the Past.   Toronto, Harlequin, 1974.
Leopard in the Snow.   London, Mills and Boon, and Toronto, Harlequin, 1974.
The Japanese Screen.   London, Mills and Boon, 1974; Toronto, Harlequin, 1975.
Rachel Trevellyan.   London, Mills and Boon, 1974; Toronto, Harlequin, 1975.
Silver Fruit upon Silver Trees.   London, Mills and Boon, 1974; Toronto, Harlequin, 1975.
Dark Moonless Night.   London, Mills and Boon, 1974; Toronto, Harlequin, 1975.
Witchstone.   London, Mills and Boon, 1974; Toronto, Harlequin, 1975.
No Gentle Possession.   Toronto, Harlequin, 1975.
Pale Dawn, Dark Sunset.   London, Mills and Boon, and Toronto, Harlequin, 1975.
Take What You Want.   London, Mills and Boon, 1975; Toronto, Harlequin, 1976.
Come the Vintage.   London, Mills and Boon, 1975; Toronto, Harlequin, 1976.
Dark Castle.   London, Mills and Boon, 1975; Toronto, Harlequin, 1976.
Country of the Falcon.   London, Mills and Boon, 1975; Toronto, Harlequin, 1976.
For the Love of Sara.   London, Mills and Boon, 1975; Toronto, Harlequin, 1976.
Valley Deep, Mountain High.   London, Mills and Boon, 1976; Toronto, Harlequin, 1977.
The Smouldering Flame.   London, Mills and Boon, 1976; Toronto, Harlequin, 1977.
Wild Enchantress.   London, Mills and Boon, 1976; Toronto, Harlequin, 1977.
Beware the Beast.   London, Mills and Boon, 1976; Toronto, Harlequin, 1977.
Devil's Mount.   London, Mills and Boon, 1976; Toronto, Harlequin, 1977.
Forbidden.   London, Mills and Boon, 1976; Toronto, Harlequin, 1978.
Come Running.   London, Mills and Boon, 1976; Toronto, Harlequin, 1978.
Alien Wife.   Toronto, Harlequin, 1977.
The Medici Lover.   London, Mills and Boon, and Toronto, Harlequin, 1977.
Born Out of Love.   Toronto, Harlequin, 1977.
A Trial Marriage.   Toronto, Harlequin, 1977.
Devil in Velvet.   London, Mills and Boon, 1977; Toronto, Harlequin, 1978.
Loren's Baby.   London, Mills and Boon, and Toronto, Harlequin, 1978.
Rooted in Dishonour.   London, Mills and Boon, and Toronto, Harlequin, 1978.
Proud Harvest.   London, Mills and Boon, and Toronto, Harlequin, 1978.
Scorpions' Dance.   London, Mills and Boon, and Toronto, Harlequin, 1978.
Captive Destiny.   London, Mills and Boon, 1978; Toronto, Harlequin, 1981.
Fallen Angel.   London, Mills and Boon, 1978; Toronto, Harlequin, 1979.
Apollo's Seed.   London, Mills and Boon, 1979; Toronto, Harlequin, 1980.
Hell or High Water.   London, Mills and Boon, 1979.
The Judas Trap.   London, Mills and Boon, 1979.
Lure of Eagles.   London, Mills and Boon, and Toronto, Harlequin, 1979.
Melting Fire.   London, Mills and Boon, 1979.
Images of Love.   London, Mills and Boon, and Toronto, Harlequin, 1980.
Sandstorm.   London, Mills and Boon, and Toronto, Harlequin, 1980.
Spirit of Atlantis.   London, Mills and Boon, and Toronto, Harlequin, 1980.
Whisper of Darkness.   London, Mills and Boon, and Toronto, Harlequin, 1980.
Castles of Sand.   London, Mills and Boon, 1981.
Forbidden Flame.   London, Mills and Boon, and Toronto, Harlequin, 1981.
A Haunting Compulsion.   London, Mills and Boon, and Toronto, Harlequin, 1981.
Innocent Obsession.   London, Mills and Boon, and Toronto, Harlequin, 1981.
Edge of Temptation.   London, Mills and Boon, and Toronto, Harlequin, 1982.

Play

Screenplay: *Leopard in the Snow*, with Jill Hyem, 1973.

*   *   *

Among the most prolific of the series romance writers, Anne Mather often writes novels that are more complex than those of her contemporaries. Her books have more subplots and she employs more texture and mood in her stories. Occasionally, her books have subtle gothic overtones with brooding heroes who live in inaccessible and mysterious places with secret problems for the heroine to solve. In *Whisper of Darkness* the hero is maimed and convinced no one could love him. The heroine liberates him from his self-imposed exile and helps his troubled daughter, much as the heroines in "governess gothics" do although she has no mystery to solve. In *Edge of Temptation* and *Come Running* the hero is a married man whose wife must be disposed of before the characters can come together. Mather's heroines often seem less passive than those of other series romance writers. Although most of her novels are set in England, Mather also employs exotic locations abroad to provide romantic suspense. Because of her richer plots, her characters are occasionally kept apart by outside forces rather than by the internal conflicts and misunderstandings of most series romances.

By the end of the 1970's, Mather's annual production of novels had tapered off. She was one of the first series writers to use premarital sex in her novels and one of the few whose heroines fell in love with married men. But despite her innovations that move beyond the usual situations of series romances, Mather always handles potentially scandalous material with care and taste.

—Kay Mussell

MATTHEWS, Patricia (Anne, née Klein). Also writes as P.A. Brisco; Patty Brisco; Laura Wylie. American. Born in San Fernando, California, 1 July 1927. Educated at Pasadena Junior College, California; Mt. San Antonio Junior College, California; California State University, Los Angeles. Married 1) Marvin Brisco in 1946 (divorced, 1961), two sons; 2) Clayton Matthews in 1971. Secretary and administrator, California State University, 1959-77. Recipient: *West Coast Review of Books* award, 1979. Lives in Los Angeles. Address: c/o Bantam Books, 666 Fifth Avenue, New York, New York 10103, U.S.A.

Novels

Love's Avenging Heart.   New York, Pinnacle, and London, Corgi, 1977.
Love's Wildest Promise.   New York, Pinnacle, 1977; London, Corgi, 1978.
Love Forever More.   New York, Pinnacle, 1977; London, Corgi, 1978.
Love's Daring Dream.   New York, Pinnacle, 1978; London, Corgi, 1979.
Love's Pagan Heart.   New York, Pinnacle, 1978; London, Corgi, 1979.

Love's Magic Moment. New York, Pinnacle, and London, Corgi, 1979.
Love's Golden Destiny. New York, Pinnacle, 1979; London, Corgi, 1980.
The Night Visitor (as Laura Wylie). New York, Bantam, 1979.
Love's Raging Tide. New York, Pinnacle, and London, Corgi, 1980.
Love's Bold Journey. New York, Pinnacle, 1980.
Love's Sweet Agony. New York, Pinnacle, 1980; London, Corgi, 1981.
Tides of Love. New York, Bantam, and London, Corgi, 1981.
Midnight Whispers, with Clayton Matthews. New York, Bantam, 1981.
Embers of Dawn. New York, Bantam, 1982.

Novels as Patty Brisco, with Clayton Matthews

Horror at Gull House. New York, Belmont, 1970.
House of Candles. New York, Manor, 1973.
The Crystal Window. New York, Avon, 1973.
Mist of Evil. New York, Manor, 1976.

OTHER PUBLICATIONS

Novel as P.A. Brisco

The Other People. Reseda, California, Powell, 1979.

Verse

Love's Many Faces. New York, Bantam, 1979.

Other (juvenile) as Patty Brisco

Merry's Treasure. New York, Avalon, 1970.
The Carnival Mystery. New York, Scholastic, 1974.
The Campus Mystery. New York, Scholastic, 1977.
Raging Rapids. Minneapolis, Creative Education, 1979.
Too Much in Love. New York, Scholastic, 1979.

                        *   *   *

With a powerful blending of passion, violence, and intrigue Patricia Matthews has perfected her distinctive formula for the historical romance. Her heroines are sensual and wildly spirited, which is fortunate as they are usually subjected to a physical and psychological assault that would destroy less resilient characters. Unlike the leading ladies of traditional romantic novels, Matthews's heroines rarely retain their virginity beyond the opening chapters. There is none of the conventional slow build-up to physical contact, and the girls have to endure sadistic beatings and rapes, enforced prostitution and slavery.

Male characters from different backgrounds and occupations have astounding depths of brutality—even missionaries turn out to be lecherous! It is surprising, after suffering so much degradation at the hands of men, that Matthews's heroines are always able, eventually, to attain not only romantic but rapturous fulfilment. However, in spite of the hardships and humiliations that are heaped on them, they are not merely passive victims of circumstances. In *Love's Pagan Heart*, for example, a half-Hawaiian, half-English innocent has tremendous resilience; the teenage American heroine of *Love's Avenging Heart* is not only tough and voluptuous but calculating; and the leading character of *Love's Golden Destiny* is a late-Victorian New Yorker with intelligence and career ambitions.

Patricia Matthew's robustness of style triumphantly carries not only her heroines but her readers through her long and lusty books, which are modern romantic variants of the "colonial adventure." The author says that she is "a history buff" who refuses "to believe that love has gone out of style," and her novels certainly endorse her publisher's claim that historical backgrounds do not have to be textbookish! As Patty Brisco, she has written several successful and atmospheric Gothic stories.

—Mary Cadogan

MAXWELL, Vicky. *See* WORBOYS, Anne.

MAY, Wynne (Winifred Jean May). Lives in South Africa. Address: c/o Mills and Boon Ltd., 15-16 Brooks Mews, London W1A 1DR, England.

ROMANCE AND GOTHIC PUBLICATIONS

Novels

> *A Cluster of Palms.* London, Mills and Boon, 1967.
> *The Highest Peak.* London, Mills and Boon, 1967.
> *The Valley of Aloes.* London, Mills and Boon, and Toronto, Harlequin, 1967.
> *Tawny Are the Leaves.* London, Mills and Boon, 1968; Toronto, Harlequin, 1969.
> *Tamboti Moon.* London, Mills and Boon, and New York, Golden Press, 1969.
> *Where Breezes Falter.* London, Mills and Boon, 1970.
> *Sun, Sea and Sand.* London, Mills and Boon, 1970.
> *The Tide at Full.* London, Mills and Boon, 1971.
> *A Grain of Gold.* London, Mills and Boon, 1971.
> *A Slither of Silk.* London, Mills and Boon, 1972.
> *A Bowl of Stars.* London, Mills and Boon, and Toronto, Harlequin, 1973.
> *Pink Sands.* Toronto, Harlequin, 1974.
> *A Plume of Dust.* London, Mills and Boon, and Toronto, Harlequin, 1975.
> *A Plantation of Vines.* Toronto, Harlequin, 1977.
> *Island of Cyclones.* London, Mills and Boon, 1979.
> *A Scarf of Flame.* London, Mills and Boon, 1979.

*   *   *

Wynne May is one of the few romance writers who uses Africa and the Indian Ocean as backgrounds. With her, it is natural, however, for she has lived much of her life in South Africa. Her use of settings with which she is familiar makes her stories individual and instantly successful with her readers. In developing her backgrounds, she also tends to select the most fascinating elements to include in her stories.

Island of Cyclones describes the island of Mauritius in the Indian Ocean, with action set against the backgrounds of sugar cane plantations, expensive hotels, and an exclusive beauty clinic in one of these hotels. *A Plantation of Vines* uses the South African wine country as setting, while *A Scarf of Flame* tells about an African art gallery that is not far from a wild game reserve. Her unusual settings and the choice of detail she includes gives her readers a sense of modern South Africa. In fact, it plays a dominating role in her novels, but not to the point that her plots and characters are overshadowed.

Her heroes are often domineering men who are wealthy, successful, and extremely attractive. Philip de Berg in *A Plantation of Vines* owns a family home, one of the very old "Cape Houses" which he has turned into a hotel. He meets Nikki de Mist who returns to the country to take a job as a public relations specialist for the La Provence vineyard. Rey Stark in *A Scarf of Flame* combines a wild game reserve and a hotel that caters to very wealthy people. Although he has a constant attraction for women, Mistelle Hudson fights becoming just another woman to him as she helps her step-mother in her art gallery. Laurent Sevigny owns one of the fashionable hotels on Mauritius and it is here that Jade Lawford gets a job as a beauty consultant. She has arrived with the intention of marrying Marlow Lewis, a sugar cane planter.

While Wynne May uses considerable talent in depicting her characters and often creates sympathetic ones, her strongest creative ability centers on plot development. A wide range of secondary characters and conflicting needs frequently produces all sorts of plot complications. Usually the heroine and hero are, or seem to be, committed to other people and they seem on the verge of marriage to them. In *Island of Cyclones* Jade is planning to marry Marlow Lewis, but she falls in love with Laurent Sevigny. She believes him to be in love with Nicole de Speville or another woman. Actually Nicole and Marlow are in love and only the ending finds everyone sorted out with the right person. This somewhat complicated series of relationships naturally adds unusual and often conflicting clues to the plot line and offers a wide range of possible sub-plots and events.

Wynne May's readers have come to expect this kind of complexity and she does not disappoint them. Neither does she attempt to show her heroines as being too naive or dewy-eyed, although they are virtuous as all good heroines should be. In a way, they are feminine women who are on the edge of wanting and needing a permanent relationship which can only be marriage. There is an adult feeling about her heroines and less of the "girl" image to them. Overall, Wynne May offers well-balanced but complex novels that appeal to today's romance readers. Her unusual settings, sharply drawn characters, and intricate plots are just what they want.

—Arlene Moore

MAYBURY, Anne. Pseudonym for Anne Buxton, née Arundel; also writes as Katherine Troy. British. Married to Charles Burdon Buxton. Vice-President, Society of Women Journalists, and Romantic Novelists Association. Agent: A.M. Heath, 40-42 William IV Street, London WC2N 4DD, England.

Novels

The Best Love of All. London, Mills and Boon, 1932.
The Enchanted Kingdom. London, Mills and Boon, 1932.
The Love That Is Stronger Than Life. London, Mills and Boon, 1932.
Love Triumphant. London, Mills and Boon, 1932.
The Way of Compassion. London, Mills and Boon, 1933.
The Second Winning. London, Mills and Boon, 1933.
Farewell to Dreams. London, Mills and Boon, 1934.
Harness the Winds. London, Mills and Boon, 1934.
Catch at a Rainbow. London, Mills and Boon, 1935.
Come Autumn—Come Winter. London, Mills and Boon, 1935.
The Garden of Wishes. London, Mills and Boon, 1935.
The Starry Wood. London, Mills and Boon, 1935.
The Wondrous To-Morrow. London, Mills and Boon, 1936.
Give Me Back My Dreams. London, Mills and Boon, 1936.
Lovely Destiny. London, Mills and Boon, 1936.
The Stars Grow Pale. London, Mills and Boon, 1936.
This Errant Heart. London, Mills and Boon, 1937.
This Lovely Hour. London, Mills and Boon, 1937.
I Dare Not Dream. London, Mills and Boon, 1937.
Oh, Darling Joy! London, Mills and Boon, 1937.
Lady, It Is Spring! London, Mills and Boon, 1938.
The Shadow of My Loving. London, Mills and Boon, 1938.
They Dreamed Too Much. London, Mills and Boon, 1938.
Chained Eagle. London, Mills and Boon, 1939.
Gather Up the Years. London, Mills and Boon, 1939.
Return to Love. London, Mills and Boon, 1939.
The Barrier Between Us. London, Mills and Boon, 1940.
Dare to Marry. London, Mills and Boon, 1940.
I'll Walk with My Love. London, Mills and Boon, 1940.
Dangerous Living. London, Mills and Boon, 1941.
The Secret of the Rose. London, Collins, 1941.
All Enchantments Die. London, Collins, 1941.
To-Day We Live. London, Collins, 1942.
Arise, Oh Sun! London, Collins, 1942.
A Lady Fell in Love. London, Collins, 1943.
Journey into Morning. London, Collins, 1944; New York, Arcadia House, 1945.
Can I Forget You? London, Collins, 1944.
The Valley of Roses. London, Collins, 1945.
The Young Invader. London, Collins, 1947.
The Winds of Spring. London, Collins, 1948.
Storm Heaven. London, Collins, 1949.
The Sharon Women. London, Collins, 1950.
First, The Dream. London, Collins, 1951.
Goodbye, My Love. London, Collins, 1952.
The Music of Our House. London, Cherry Tree, 1952.
Her Name Was Eve. London, Collins, 1953.
The Heart Is Never Fair. London, Collins, 1954.
Prelude to Louise. London, Collins, 1954.
Follow Your Hearts. London, Collins, 1955.
The Other Juliet. London, Collins, 1955.
Forbidden. London, Collins, 1956.
Dear Lost Love. London, Collins, 1957.
Beloved Enemy. London, Collins, 1957.

The Stars Cannot Tell. London, Collins, 1958.
My Love Has a Secret. London, Collins, 1958.
The Gay of Heart. London, Collins, 1959.
The Rebel Heart. London, Collins, 1959.
Shadow of a Stranger. London, Collins, 1960; New York, Ace, 1966.
Bridge to the Moon. London, Collins, 1960.
Stay Until Tomorrow. London, Collins, 1961; New York, Ace, 1967.
The Night My Enemy. London, Collins, 1962; New York, Ace, 1967.
I Am Gabriella! London, Collins, 1962; New York, Ace, 1966; as *Gabriella*, London, Fontana, 1979.
Green Fire. London, Collins, 1963; New York, Ace, 1965.
My Dearest Elizabeth. London, Collins, 1964; as *The Brides of Bellenmore*, New York, Ace, 1964.
Pavilion at Monkshood. New York, Ace, 1965; London, Fontana, 1966.
Jessica. London, Collins, 1965.
The Moonlit Door. London, Hodder and Stoughton, and New York, Holt Rinehart, 1967.
The Minerva Stone. London, Hodder and Stoughton, and New York, Holt Rinehart, 1968.
Ride a White Dolphin. London, Hodder and Stoughton, and New York, Random House, 1971.
The Terracotta Palace. London, Hodder and Stoughton, and New York, Random House, 1971.
Walk in the Paradise Garden. New York, Random House, 1972; London, Collins, 1973.
The Midnight Dancers. New York, Random House, 1973; London, Collins, 1974.
Jessamy Court. New York, Random House, 1974; London, Collins, 1975.
The Jewelled Daughter. London, Collins, and New York, Random House, 1976.
Dark Star. New York, Random House, 1977; London, Collins, 1978.
Radiance. New York, Random House, 1979.

Novels as Katherine Troy

Someone Waiting. London, Collins, 1961; as Anne Maybury, New York, Ace, 1966.
Whisper in the Dark. London, Collins, 1961; as Anne Maybury, New York, Ace, 1966.
Enchanter's Nightshade. London, Collins, 1963; as *The Winds of Night* (as Anne Maybury), New York, Ace, 1967.
Falcon's Shadow. London, Collins, 1964; as Anne Maybury, New York, Ace, 1967.
The House of Fand. London, Collins, 1966; as Anne Maybury, New York, Ace, 1966.
The Night of the Enchantress. London, Hodder and Stoughton, 1967.
Farramonde. New York, McKay, 1968.
Storm over Roseheath. London, Hodder and Stoughton, 1969; as *Roseheath*, New York, McKay, 1969.

*   *   *

Anne Maybury has attracted a steady number of fans with her gothic novels, though she had earlier written many romances. Since about 1968 she has published approximately a book a year, and has never failed her audience in their expectations of a good gothic/romance, sensuously and delicately well-told. Maybury rises above the strait jacket of formula with well-conceived plots, sympathetic characters, and lushly described settings.

In Maybury's stories, the person under the most suspicion is the husband or the fiancé of the heroine, whom she both loves and suspects of foul deeds at the same time. The situation is complicated by the presence of a dependent, usually a child of nine or ten, or a friend for whom the heroine feels responsible. These relationships are complicated and tenuous, involving excruciating decisions for the heroine, often *for* the dependent and *against* the loved male. For example, Cathy Mountavon in *The Midnight Dancers* is responsible for Pippa, aged nine, her husband's child by his first wife. Pippa worships her father while innuendos abound that he is

485

responsible for her mother's death. These tangled relationships are always complicated by the heroine's doubt about her prospective/actual mate. The true male mate for the heroine usually emerges only at the conclusion as misunderstood and gallantly heroic, a Galahad who has been searching for the truth all along and trying to defend the heroine, all unknown to her or the reader. But these are not the males' stories; they belong to the woman as she independently explores both dangerous situations and her own emotions. The plots center on her ability not only to endure a threatening environment, but also to rise above situations bordering on the tragic.

Setting is always significant, varied, and expertly invoked. Maybury specializes in atmosphere, with the result that whether the setting is a castle in England or Rome, a pavilion in Hong Kong, or a house on a Greek island, the beauty of each serves as a contrast to the threatening atmosphere of the unknown—the unknown culture and the unfamiliar place. A fine balance is maintained between the heightened emotions of love and fear in a suffocating atmosphere of suspicion and the delicious beauty of each setting.

Maybury's heroines have come a long way from the fainting innocents of the first gothic fiction. Most are at the least able to support themselves; moreover, in *The Jeweled Daughter* Sarah Brendt is a trained gemologist and in *The Midnight Dancers* Cathy Mountavon is an artist trained in stained glass. That these heroines have professions introduces a new thread to the formulaic plot of new gothic, exploring the complications and rewards of further female independence. The villains are brilliant, but power mad. Insanity is the result of their being thwarted in whatever Machiavellian plans they have secretly laid throughout the novel. Of course, the twist is that they may be either male or female, the loved male or the female friend.

Maybury's stories represent the best and newest of the genre and can be counted on for vivid characters, basically sound plots, and carefully researched and lusciously described settings.

—Marilynn Motteler

McBAIN, Laurie (Lee).   American.   Born in Riverside, California, 15 October 1949. Educated at San Bernardino Valley College, California, and California State University, San Bernardino, 1967-72. Address: P.O. Box 24700, Route 3, Carmel, California, U.S.A.

ROMANCE AND GOTHIC PUBLICATIONS

Novels

Devil's Desire.   New York, Avon, 1975.
Moonstruck Madness.   New York, Avon, 1977; London, Futura, 1978.
Tears of Gold.   New York, Avon, and London, Futura, 1979.
Chance the Winds of Fortune.   New York, Avon, 1980.
Dark Before the Rising Sun.   New York, Avon, 1982.

*   *   *

With only four novels to her credit, Laurie McBain has already established herself as one of the most popular writers of sensual historical romances. Her style and the plots she creates put her in a class with Kathleen Woodiwiss as a leader in the genre.

Her stories are the type often described as "sweeping sagas," in which the heroine moves from adventure to adventure, usually in conflict with the hero. The action may take place in England, but often moves to other, more exotic locations. Mara O'Flynn (*Tears of Gold*) travels from England to California in Gold Rush days, and finally to Louisiana before embarking again for England. Rhea Dominick (*Chance the Winds of Fortune*) is sold as an indentured servant in the colonies and roams about the lush Caribbean before returning home. Sabrina Verrick (*Moonstruck Madness*) supports her family as a Robin Hood-style highwayman. Later Sabrina appears as Rhea's mother, a less-than-staid duchess, who agonizes about her daughter's adventures.

Descriptions of period dress and mannerisms fill the books, and much of the dialogue is laced with colloquialisms. This is obviously meant to help the reader "experience" the period, but at times the obsolete terms and phrases get in the way.

In spite of the locations and historical details, the main interest in McBain's novels remains the romance and its attendant problems. The course of true love is never allowed to run smoothly since there is always hostility between the hero and heroine. The hero is strong, older, usually cynical, and preferably titled. The heroine is young, relatively innocent, and something of a spitfire. The conflict between them allows for many twists and turns of a plot before she is tamed (at least a little) and he surrenders and confesses his love for her. Put this baldly, the characters and plots are pretty standard fare, but McBain succeeds in developing her characters within the limitations of the genre and inventing some interesting stories and subplots. Another plus for McBain is that she allows her heroines to mature. The original "spitfire" often seems to be little more than a spoiled brat rather than a woman fighting for independence, but McBain manages to alter the strident overtones as the romantic conflict is resolved.

—Barbara Kemp

McCORQUODALE, Barbara. *See* **CARTLAND, Barbara**.

McCUTCHEON, George Barr. Also wrote as Richard Greaves. American. Born near Lafayette, Indiana, 26 July 1866. Educated at Purdue University, Lafayette, two years. Married Marie Fay in 1904; one step-son. Reporter, *Journal*, 1889, columnist, *Sunday Journal*, 1890, and City Editor, 1893 and part-time staff member until 1905, *Courier*, all in Lafayette. President, Authors League, 1924-26. *Died 23 October 1928.*

ROMANCE AND GOTHIC PUBLICATIONS

Novels (series: Graustark)

Graustark: The Story of a Love Behind a Throne. Chicago, Stone, 1901; London, Richards, 1902.

Castle Craneycrow.   Chicago, Stone, 1902; London, Richards, 1903.
Brewster's Millions (as Richard Greaves).   Chicago, Stone, 1903; London, Collier, 1907.
The Sherrods.   New York, Dodd Mead, 1903; London, Ward Lock, 1905.
Beverly of Graustark.   New York, Dodd Mead, and London, Stevens and Brown, 1904.
The Day of the Dog.   New York, Dodd Mead, 1904; revised edition, 1916.
Nedra.   New York, Dodd Mead, and London, Stevens and Brown, 1905.
The Purple Parasol.   New York, Dodd Mead, 1905.
Cowardice Court.   New York, Dodd Mead, 1906.
Jane Cable.   New York, Dodd Mead, and London, Hodder and Stoughton, 1906.
The Flyers.   New York, Dodd Mead, and London, Stevens and Brown, 1907.
The Husbands of Edith.   New York, Dodd Mead, 1908; London, Holden and Har-
    dingham, 1912.
The Man from Brodney's.   New York, Dodd Mead, and London, Hodder and
    Stoughton, 1908.
The Alternative.   New York, Dodd Mead, 1909.
Truxton King: A Story of Graustark.   New York, Dodd Mead, and London, Stevens and
    Brown, 1909.
The Butterfly Man.   New York, Dodd Mead, 1910.
The Rose in the Ring.   New York, Dodd Mead, and London, Everett, 1910.
Mary Midthorne.   New York, Dodd Mead, and London, Stevens and Brown, 1911.
What's-His-Name.   New York, Dodd Mead, and London, Stevens and Brown, 1911.
The Hollow of Her Hand.   New York, Dodd Mead, and London, Stevens and Brown,
    1912.
A Fool and His Money.   New York, Dodd Mead, and London, Stevens and Brown,
    1913.
Black Is White.   New York, Dodd Mead, 1914; London, Everett, 1915.
The Prince of Graustark.   New York, Dodd Mead, and London, Stevens and Brown,
    1914.
Mr. Bingle.   New York, Dodd Mead, and London, Stevens and Brown, 1915.
From the Housetops.   New York, Dodd Mead, and London, Stevens and Brown, 1916.
The Light That Lies.   New York, Dodd Mead, 1916; London, Jenkins, 1917.
Green Fancy.   New York, Dodd Mead, 1917; London, Hodder and Stoughton, 1918.
The City of Masks.   New York, Dodd Mead, 1918; as *The Court of New York*, London,
    Melrose, 1919.
Shot with Crimson.   New York, Dodd Mead, 1918; London, Jenkins, 1920.
Sherry.   New York, Dodd Mead, 1919.
West Wind Drift.   New York, Dodd Mead, 1920; London, Nash, 1921.
Quill's Window.   New York, Dodd Mead, 1921; London, Nash, 1922.
Yollop.   New York, Dodd Mead, 1922.
Viola Gwyn.   New York, Dodd Mead, and London, Nash, 1922.
Oliver October.   New York, Dodd Mead, 1923; London, Harrap, 1924.
East of the Setting Sun: A Story of Graustark.   New York, Dodd Mead, 1924; London,
    Harrap, 1925.
Romeo in Moon Village.   New York, Dodd Mead, 1925; London, Nash, 1926.
The Inn of the Hawk and Raven: A Tale of Old Graustark.   New York, Dodd Mead,
    1926; London, Lane, 1927.
Kindling and Ashes; or, The Heart of Barbara Wayne.   New York, Dodd Mead, 1926;
    London, Lane, 1927.
Blades.   New York, Dodd Mead, and London, Lane, 1928.
The Merivales.   New York, Dodd Mead, 1929.

Short Stories

Her Weight in Gold.   Privately printed, 1911; revised edition, New York, Dodd Mead,
    1912.

OTHER PUBLICATIONS

Novel

The Daughter of Anderson Crow.   New York, Dodd Mead, and London, Hodder and
Stoughton, 1907.

Short Stories

Anderson Crow, Detective.   New York, Dodd Mead, 1920.
Anderson, The Joker, in Three Yarns, with Booth Tarkington and G.K. Chesterton.
Chicago, Blue Ribbon, 1924.

Plays

Brood House.   Privately printed, 1910.
One Score and Ten.   Privately printed, 1919.
Daddy Dumplings, with Earl Carroll (produced New York, 1920).

Other

Books Once Were Men: An Essay for Booklovers.   New York, Dodd Mead, 1931.
The Young Mathematician Series.   Skokie, Illinois, National Textbook, 6 vols., 1968-70.

*   *   *

George Barr McCutcheon wrote over 40 novels, a number of plays and novelettes, and
several essays, but he is best remembered for six popular romances, the Graustark stories.
    A product of the turn-of-the-century midwestern American imagination, McCutcheon
reflected both America's attraction to European culture and its self-conscious pride in her own
youth and independence during years when she was becoming a world power. McCutcheon's
work attempts to resolve this tension, yet gives America the edge in the argument. A faith in the
wholesomeness, ingenuity, and democracy of the optimistic American hero characterizes
McCutcheon's most important work.
    Related to adventure-romances like Anthony Hope's Prisoner of Zenda, and influenced by
his early reading in 19th-century dime novels, McCutcheon's Graustark books were predomi-
nantly departures from the domestic, female-protagonist romances of the 19th century and
excursions into a world of male action and resourcefulness. The Graustark novels are all set in a
mythical Balkan state and in and around Edelweiss, its central city. Most of the six novels are
male versions of the familiar Cinderella formula, but the commoner hero's reward for valor is
not money or Christian salvation, but acceptance by the aristocratic community. Sometimes
charmingly innocent before formal European ways, McCutcheon's heroes are over-simplified
Jamesian Americans abroad. Unlike Henry James's realistic characters, however, McCut-
cheons' heroes overcome countless obstacles and manage to save beautiful aristocratic women
from European villains and to bring them home to New York or Washington, D.C.
    The Graustark novels tend to begin slowly with background to the hero's search for love and
adventure, then pick up with his sudden, undermotivated attraction for a beautiful, mysterious
woman who leads him into a labyrinth of improbable intrigues and through a lengthy catalogue
of obstructions that increase in difficulty until the plot reaches a culminating action and the
hero's triumph. With his victory comes the defeat of evil forces and less worthy suitors for his
lover's hand, the stability of marriage, and the respect of the aristocrats who doubted his
abilities.
    In the best-selling Graustark, the first of the series, Count Halfont finds it difficult to accept
commoner hero Grenville Lorry's proposal of marriage to Graustark's Princess Yetive, even

though Halfont finds Lorry to be "the soul of honor, of courage, of manliness." Lorry's reply summarizes the democratic American bias throughout McCutcheon's books.

> ...every born American may become ruler of the greatest nation in the world—the United States. His home is his kingdom; his wife, his mother, his sisters are his queens and princesses; his fellow citizens are his admiring subjects if he is wise and good. In my land you will find the poor man climbing to the highest pinnacle side by side with the rich man....We recognize little as impossible. Until death destroys this power to love and to hope I must say to you that I shall not consider Princess Yetive beyond my reach.

Love triumphs: Lorry married the Princess, and with that marriage begins the saga that includes the continuing story of Yetive and Lorry in *Beverly of Graustark*, the tale of Prince Robin, the Lorrys' son and his protectors in *Truxton King*, Robin's courtship and marriage to an American woman in *The Prince of Graustark*, and the postwar adventures of an American writer in Graustark in *East of the Setting Sun*. The final Graustark novel, *The Inn of the Hawk and Raven*, returns to the years before Yetive's marriage to Lorry.

Although McCutcheon made his name on the Graustark books, he wrote 40 additional novels; many were similar formula romances with robust American heroes, but most were set in the United States. The best known of these, *Brewster's Millions*, published under the pseudonym Richard Greaves, became a popular film. In the American romances McCutcheon experimented more with realistic techniques, paying greater attention to local color settings, regional dialects, and humor.

McCutcheon's style and most of his characterizations are flat and pedestrian, his plot construction competent, but slow moving. His achievement comes in his clever conceptions for stories and most importantly in his creation of likeable, democratic American heroes of near-mythical proportions.

—Nancy Pogel

McELFRESH, (Elizabeth) Adeline. Also writes as John Cleveland; Jane Scott; Elizabeth Wesley. American. Born in Knox County, Indiana, 28 May 1918. Educated at a high school in Bruceville, Indiana. Proofreader, 1936-42, and feature editor, 1943-56, Vincennes *Sun-Commercial*, Indiana; reporter, Troy *Daily News*, Ohio, 1942-43. Since 1966, Director of Public Relations, Good Samaritan Hospital, Vincennes. Address: R.R.1, Vincennes, Indiana, U.S.A.

ROMANCE AND GOTHIC PUBLICATIONS

Novels

> *Charlotte Wade.* New York, Arcadia House, 1952.
> *Homecoming.* New York, Arcadia House, 1953.
> *The Old Baxter Place.* New York, Arcadia House, 1954.
> *Doctor Jane.* New York, Avalon, 1954; London, Corgi, 1958.
> *Ann and the Hoosier Doctor.* New York, Avalon, 1955; as *Hill Country Nurse*, New York, Bantam, 1959.

Young Doctor Randall. New York, Avalon, 1957.
Nurse Kathy. New York, Avalon, 1957.
Calling Doctor Jane. New York, Avalon, 1957; London, Corgi, 1959.
Dr. Jane's Mission. New York, Avalon, 1958.
Dr. Jane Comes Home. New York, Avalon, 1959; London, Corgi, 1961.
Kay Manion, M.D. New York, Dell, 1959; as *Kay Mannion, M.D.*, London, Corgi, 1960.
Team-Up for Ann. London, Ward Lock, 1959.
Wings for Nurse Bennett. New York, Dell, 1960.
Ann Kenyon, Surgeon. New York, Dell, 1960.
Dr. Jane's Choice. New York, Avalon, 1961.
To Each Her Dream. Indianapolis, Bobbs Merrill, 1961.
Night Call. New York, Dell, 1961.
Hospital Hill. New York, Dell, 1961.
Romantic Assignment. London, Ward Lock, 1961.
Jeff Benton, M.D. New York, Dell, 1962; London, Mayflower, 1964.
Jill Nolan, Surgical Nurse. New York, Dell, 1962.
Jill Nolan, R.N. New York, Dell, 1962.
Challenge for Dr. Jane. New York, Avalon, 1963.
Jill Nolan's Choice. New York, Dell, 1963.
The Magic Scalpel of Dr. Farrer. New York, Avalon, 1965.
Nurse Nolan's Private Duty. New York, Dell, 1966.
Dr. Jane, Interne. New York, Bantam, 1966.
Nurse for Mercy's Mission. New York, Belmont, 1976.

Novels as Elizabeth Wesley

Nora Meade, M.D. New York, Avalon, 1955; London, Corgi, 1958.
Ann Foster, Lab Technician. New York, Avalon, 1956.
Sharon James, Free-lance Photographer. New York, Avalon, 1956.
Polly's Summer Stock. New York, Avalon, 1957; as *Summer Stock Romance*, New York, Berkley, 1961.
Doctor Barbara. New York, Avalon, 1958.
Nurse Judy. New York, Avalon, 1958.
Jane Ryan, Dietician. New York, Avalon, 1959.
Doctor Dee. New York, Avalon, 1960.
Dr. Dee's Choice. New York, Avalon, 1962.
Dr. Dorothy's Choice. New York, Paperback Library, 1963.

Novels as Jane Scott

Barbara Owen, Girl Reporter. New York, Avalon, 1956.
Kay Rogers, Copy Writer. New York, Avalon, 1956.
A New Love for Cynthia. New York, Avalon, 1958.
Nurse Nancy. New York, Avalon, 1959.
A Nurse for Rebels' Run. New York, Avalon, 1960.

OTHER PUBLICATIONS

Novels

My Heart Went Dead. New York, Phoenix Press, 1949.
Murder with Roses. New York, Phoenix Press, 1950; London, Foulsham, 1953.
Keep Back the Dark. New York, Phoenix Press, 1951.

Minus One Corpse (as John Cleveland).   New York, Arcadia House, 1954.
Shattered Halo.   New York, Avalon, 1956; London, Ward Lock, 1960.

Other (juvenile)

Career for Jenny.   New York, Avalon, 1958.
Summer Change.   Indianapolis, Bobbs Merrill, 1960.

*   *   *

After writing a few early mystery novels, Adeline McElfresh found her niche in the medical-romance novel, and generally remained with it in the books published under her own name and under pseudonyms. Along with a number of individual novels, she wrote two longer series, the Dr. Jane stories and the Jill Nolan stories. However, similar situations, themes, and backgrounds run through both her series and separates, as she stays with her basic pattern. The novels are generally set in small towns in southern Indiana, with nurses and doctors at the local hospital as the chief characters. There are very detailed descriptions of operations and medical procedures; crises in the form of traffic accidents, fires, mine cave-ins, and natural disasters for the medics to cope with. The stories have a nice home-spun rural midwestern America feel to them. There is occasionally the more serious theme of the need for social reform, as in *Dr. Jane Comes Home*, in which a greedy industrialist provides sub-standard housing for his workers; and in *Jill Nolan, R.N.*, in which the nurse heroine leaves a doctor's wealthy society practice for a clinic in a small Kentucky town to work with poor coal-miners' families.

Romance plays a distinctly secondary role in these novels. While the heroines always have a romantic interest, usually a fellow medic, but often a local journalist, the love interest can shift from book to book in the series. The usual long descriptions of infatuations found in most romances take a back seat to long, and very good, descriptions of skull-fracture operations and deliveries of babies. In *Hospital Hill* the chief character, in a switch, is Chris Roman, a male doctor, in love with a woman journalist. But the themes remain the same. Chris must work to restore the hospital to the charitable clinic it had been in the past, before a new director put the emphasis on medicine for the well-to-do only. Another typical story, and one of the best, is *Kay Manion, M.D.* Kay, stranded in a flood in the small town of Woodbine, helps flood victims, stays on through a typhoid outbreak, and ultimately decides to leave her big-city hospital for life in Woodbine. While this is formula fiction, it is pleasantly written. The characters may be stock, and the plots may be predictable, but the feel for rural American life is good, and the medicine is above reproach.

—Necia A. Musser

McEVOY, Marjorie (née Harte).   Also writes as Marjorie Harte.   British.   Born in York. Educated at a private girls school. Married to William Noel McEvoy; one son and one daughter. Journalist; has also worked as a matron in a girls school and an auxiliary nurse. Agent: Jacintha Alexander, 47 Emperor's Gate, London S.W.7. Address: 54 Miriam Avenue, Chesterfield, Derbyshire S40 3NF, England.

Novels

No Castle of Dreams. London, Jenkins, 1960; New York, Lenox Hill Press, 1971.
A Red, Red Rose. London, Jenkins, 1960.
The Meaning of a Kiss. London, Jenkins, 1961.
Forever Faithful. London, Jenkins, 1962.
Softly Treads Danger. London, Jenkins, 1963; New York, Lenox Hill Press, 1967.
Calling Nurse Stewart. London, Jenkins, 1963.
Moon over the Danube. London, Jenkins, 1966.
Who Walks by Moonlight? London, Jenkins, 1966; New York, Lenox Hill Press, 1973.
Brazilian Stardust. New York, Arcadia House, 1967.
Dusky Cactus. London, Jenkins, 1968.
The Grenfell Legacy. London, Jenkins, 1968; New York, Pyramid, 1971.
The White Castello. London, Jenkins, 1969; as *Castle Doom*, New York, Lenox Hill
    Press, 1970.
The Hermitage Bell. New York, Lenox Hill Press, 1971.
My Love Johnny. London, Hale, 1971; as *Eaglescliffe*, New York, Lenox Hill Press,
    1971.
Peril at Polvellyn. New York, Beagle, 1973.
The Chinese Box. New York, Lenox Hill Press, 1973.
Ravensmount. New York, Beagle, 1974.
The Wych Stone. New York, Beagle, 1974.
The Queen of Spades. New York, Ballantine, 1975.
Echoes from the Past. New York, Doubleday, 1979.
Calabrian Summer. New York, Doubleday, 1980.

Novels as Marjorie Harte

A Call for the Doctor. London, Hale, 1961.
Goodbye, Doctor Garland. London, Hale, 1962.
Nurse in the Orient. London, Hale, 1962.
Doctors in Conflict. London, Hale, 1963.
Masquerade for a Nurse. London, Hale, 1964.
No Orchids for a Nurse. London, Hale, 1964; as *Strange Journey*, New York, Prestige,
    n.d.
Doctor Mysterious. London, Hale, 1965.
Cover Girl. London, Hale, 1968; as *The Closing Web*, New York, Lenox Hill Press,
    1973.
No Eden for a Nurse. London, Hale, 1971.

Marjorie McEvoy comments:

I am primarily an entertainer, but take care that details and locations are accurate. I travel abroad extensively to gain personal knowledge of my background, as well as researching. I have made two extended tours of India for my forthcoming novel of the Indian mutiny, *The Sleeping Tiger.*

*   *   *

Marjorie McEvoy writes gothic novels with all the proper accoutrements that are the substance of this genre. In a characteristic story a lovely heroine becomes innocently involved with a family possessed of an evil secret. All takes place in appropriately brooding, sinister environs dominated by an old, possibly haunted, mansion. The hero is quite handsome and the heroine is almost always attracted to him from the beginning, instinctively knowing that he is trustworthy. It is equally obvious of which person she must be wary, since from the moment of the first meeting, this odious character shows the darkness of his personality. In the background, ghostly cries or the ominous ringing of bells lend an aura of the supernatural although a more down-to-earth explanation usually occurs in the development. A typical example is *The Hermitage Bell*. The time is the mid-19th century and the setting a centuries old manor located in an isolated region of Wales. Desperately poor but ravishingly beautiful Victoria takes the position of companion to aged Lady Samantha, the strong-willed matriarch of the Tallyfont family. Very shortly Victoria realizes that this family's haunted past may spell danger for herself. The villain is David, Lady Samantha's adopted son, who wants the entire estate for himself. The hero is Huw, another adopted son with a brooding Celtic handsomeness that causes Victoria to fall in love immediately. Huw quite naturally reciprocates these feelings. David is responsible for some murder and mayhem but when he seeks to do away with Victoria, Huw is there to the rescue, proclaiming his everlasting love.

Under the pseudonym of Marjorie Harte, the author spins stories of romance, usually in a contemporary setting, and often involving a nurse as the heroine. Although an element of danger is frequently present, the main theme centers on how the heroine will overcome seemingly insurmountable obstacles to marry the man she loves. In *Strange Journey* nurse Sally Bloom takes a job in North Borneo to search for a husband missing for 6 years. She eventually finds him, only to discover that he suffers from amnesia and doesn't recognize her. Meanwhile she has fallen in love with the very married Dr. Dirk Greaves. When Dirk's wife leaves him for another man and Sally's husband conveniently dies of lung cancer the two protagonists are free to marry.

All of McEvoy/Harte's stories have standard plots with little intricacy; neither are the characters well developed. The narrative and dialogue of the romance stories are filled with colloquialisms that could annoy non-British readers, although this is not quite as obvious in the gothic novels because of the more formal language used. Some of the romance stories, moreover, tend to reflect a British colonialist attitude that more sensitive readers might find offensive. Still, this author's stories are fast-paced and there is enough action to keep the attention of avid gothic/romance readers.

—Patricia Altner

MELONEY, Franken. *See* **FRANKEN, Rose**.

MELVILLE, Anne. *See* **BETTERIDGE, Anne**.

MELVILLE, Jennie.   *See* **BUTLER, Gwendoline**.

MERLIN, Christina.   *See* **HEAVEN, Constance**.

MICHAELS, Barbara.   Pseudonym for Barbara (Louise) G(ross) Mertz; also writes as Elizabeth Peters.   American.   Born in Canton, Illinois, 29 September 1927. Educated at the University of Chicago Oriental Institute, Ph.D. 1952. Divorced; one daughter and one son. Address: c/o Dodd Mead, 79 Madison Avenue, New York, New York 10016, U.S.A.

ROMANCE AND GOTHIC PUBLICATIONS

Novels

   The Master of Blacktower.   New York, Appleton Century Crofts, 1966; London, Jenkins, 1967.
   Sons of the Wolf.   New York, Meredith, 1967; London, Jenkins, 1968.
   Ammie, Come Home.   New York, Meredith, 1968; London, Jenkins, 1969.
   Prince of Darkness.   New York, Meredith, 1969; London, Hodder and Stoughton, 1971.
   The Dark on the Other Side.   New York, Dodd Mead, 1970; London, Souvenir Press, 1973.
   Greygallows.   New York, Dodd Mead, 1972; London, Souvenir Press, 1974.
   The Crying Child.   New York, Dodd Mead, and London, Souvenir Press, 1973.
   Witch.   New York, Dodd Mead, 1973; London, Souvenir Press, 1975.
   House of Many Shadows.   New York, Dodd Mead, 1974; London, Souvenir Press, 1976.
   The Sea King's Daughter.   New York, Dodd Mead, 1975; London, Souvenir Press, 1977.
   Patriot's Dream.   New York, Dodd Mead, 1976; London, Souvenir Press, 1978.
   Wings of the Falcon.   New York, Dodd Mead, 1977.
   Wait for What Will Come.   New York, Dodd Mead, 1978.
   The Walker in Shadows.   New York, Dodd Mead, 1979.
   The Wizard's Daughter.   New York, Dodd Mead, 1980; London, Souvenir Press, 1982.
   Someone in the House.   New York, Dodd Mead, 1981.

Novels as Elizabeth Peters (series: Vicky Bliss; Jacqueline Kirby)

   The Jackal's Head.   New York, Meredith, 1968; London, Jenkins, 1969.
   The Camelot Caper.   New York, Meredith, 1969; London, Cassell, 1976.
   The Dead Sea Cipher.   New York, Dodd Mead, 1970; London, Cassell, 1975.

The Night of Four Hundred Rabbits. New York, Dodd Mead, 1971; as *Shadows in the Moonlight*, London, Hodder and Stoughton, 1975.

The Seventh Sinner (Kirby). New York, Dodd Mead, 1972; London, Hodder and Stoughton, 1975.

Borrower of the Night (Bliss). New York, Dodd Mead, 1973; London, Cassell, 1974.

The Murders of Richard III (Kirby). New York, Dodd Mead, 1974.

Crocodile on the Sandbank. New York, Dodd Mead, 1975; London, Cassell, 1976.

Legend in Green Velvet. New York, Dodd Mead, 1976; as *Ghost in Green Velvet*, London, Cassell, 1977.

Devil-May-Care. New York, Dodd Mead, 1977; London, Cassell, 1978.

Street of the Five Moons (Bliss). New York, Dodd Mead, 1978.

Summer of the Dragon. New York, Dodd Mead, 1979; London, Souvenir Press, 1980.

The Love Talker. New York, Dodd Mead, 1980; London, Souvenir Press, 1981.

The Curse of the Pharaohs. New York, Dodd Mead, 1981; London, Souvenir Press, 1982.

The Copenhagen Connection. New York, Congdon and Lattès, 1982.

OTHER PUBLICATIONS

Other as Barbara G. Mertz

Temples, Tombs, and Hieroglyphs: The Story of Egyptology. New York, Coward McCann, and London, Gollancz, 1964; revised edition, New York, Dodd Mead, 1978.

Red Land, Black Land: The World of the Ancient Egyptians. New York, Coward McCann, 1966; London, Hodder and Stoughton, 1967; revised edition, New York, Dodd Mead, 1978.

Two Thousand Years in Rome, with Richard Mertz. New York, Coward McCann, 1968; London, Dent, 1969.

Manuscript Collection: Mugar Memorial Library, Boston University.

*   *   *

Barbara Michaels is a pseudonym of Egyptologist Barbara G. Mertz, who also writes fiction under the name Elizabeth Peters. The Elizabeth Peters books are mystery/romances with strong detective elements; frequently, they have a background of archaelogical interest, and are either set in the modern period or comment upon an historical period from a modern perspective. Indeed, the best of these novels provide a kind of pastiche of the genre, with the heroine exhibiting more interest in her research than in snaring the hero. These books are lucidly written, and are infused with an irresistible combination of scholarly plausibility and good humour. The author's erudition is never conveyed as solemnity, and various academic details essential to the plots are presented with a notable lack of self-consciousness.

As Barbara Michaels, Mertz writes novels of historical romance, as well as books which explore facets of the supernatural. Imbued with the author's characteristic intelligence, these are, on the whole, rather less satisfying works, perhaps because the element of pastiche is missing. The best of the Michaels novels are those with a historical setting (*Wings of the Falcon*), or those in which a historical background figures prominently (*Wait for What Will Come*). Those which take place in the present, but in which supernatural events are rooted in history or legend (*Ammie, Come Home*), are more convincing than those in which the supernatural is a literal element in the plot (*The Dark on the Other Side*).

In fact, one has the sense that Mertz herself is uncomfortable with the supernatural as a theme, and her discomfort is revealed in occasional confusion of tone. Having saved the heroine from a husband who was a practicing warlock, the hero jokes about silver bullets; the psychiatrist who diagnosed a "delusion of lycanthropy" remarks: "You're her hero, aren't you? Fighting the powers of darkness for her soul....What are lions compared to that?" And the warlock must be destroyed not merely because he is deluded/evil, but because he is thinking of running for political office, and the (Jewish) analyst recognizes certain Hitlerian tendencies.

On the other hand, the historical romances contain writing which rivals the best of Elizabeth Peters, which is to say that, while not precisely tongue-in-cheek, they have a lightheartedness of tone which derives from the transparently contrived genre to which they belong. Accuracy of detail, combined with an intelligent presentation of female characters, sets these books apart from the mundane.

—Joanne Harack Hayne

MILES, Lady (Favell Mary Miles, née Hill).   British.   Born in Bath, Somerset. Married Sir Charles Miles in 1912 (died, 1966); two sons. *Died 3 January 1969.*

ROMANCE AND GOTHIC PUBLICATIONS

Novels

> *The Red Flame*.   London, Hutchinson, 1921.
> *Red, White, and Grey*.   London, Hutchinson, 1921.
> *Ralph Carey*.   London, Hutchinson, 1922.
> *Stony Ground*.   London, Hutchinson, 1923.
> *The Fanatic*.   London, Hutchinson, 1924.
> *Tread Softly*.   London, Hutchinson, 1926.
> *Love's Cousin*.   London, Hutchinson, 1927.
> *Dark Dream*.   London, Hutchinson, 1929.
> *Lorna Neale*.   London, Hutchinson, 1932.
> *This Flower*.   London, Hutchinson, 1933.
> *The Second Lesson*.   London, Hutchinson, 1936.

*   *   *

Lady Miles's first novel, *The Red Flame*, appeared in 1921. Her heroine is a red-haired *femme fatale* with a strange childhood in India behind her. She is "a lovely scrap of a disreputable thing, who'd look well à la mode on a tiger skin," and she goes through life (and her marriage) bringing unhappiness. The novel presents a picture of an unlovely character and her effect on others. The *Times Literary Supplement* reviewer pointed out that this novel "does not succeed in absorbing the attention of the reader," and this criticism continued to be made of subsequent novels, although reviewers acknowledged the care with which Lady Miles wrote.

The people in Lady Miles's novels tend to be unsympathetic characters and to live unhappy lives, frequently as the result of dismal and unloving childhoods. Consequently the stories of their lives abound in frustrated or misplaced affections, unfortunate marriages (of which they may or may not attempt to make the best), and cycles of failure in the capacity to love. Various ways of ensuring unhappiness are examined—obsession with religion (*The Fanatic*), obsession with spiritual forces communicating mysteriously à la Joan of Arc (*Dark Dream*), obsession with introspective questionings after an unhappy childhood (*Ralph Carey*), and vast oversensitiveness and over-imagination (*Lorna Neale*).

Emotions and motives are examined and analysed at considerable length both by the author (as narrator) and by the characters who think and talk a great deal about their relationships with one another ("What must Michael be thinking of her? Granted the courage of a mouse, she would not have deserted him, but she hadn't a mouse's courage. She always deserted those she loved...Glen? Glen had trusted her. She had led him to believe that she could save them both. The spirit is willing but the flesh is weak. The flesh is weak because the spirit is not willing enough; because, beneath a show of strength, the spirit is fatally weak, too. She had thrust Glen away...He, not Michael, needed her." *Lorna Neale*).

Plot, consequently, tends to arise from character, or to be a demonstration of character, and in some of the novels nothing much happens. The novels variously end unhappily, when the heroine falls down a quarry (*Dark Dream*) or walks into the sea in a religious ecstasy (*The Fanatic*), or with qualified happiness, when the hero and heroine decide to make the best of their lot or when (as the *TLS* said of *The Second Lesson*) disaster is averted but not very convincingly.

—Jean Buchanan

MILLAR, Margaret (Ellis, née Sturm). American. Born in Kitchener, Ontario, Canada, 5 February 1915. Educated at Kitchener Collegiate Institute, 1929-33; University of Toronto, 1933-36. Married the writer Kenneth Millar, i.e., Ross Macdonald, in 1938; one child (deceased). Screenwriter, Warner Brothers, Hollywood, 1945-46. President, Mystery Writers of America, 1957-58. Recipient: Mystery Writers of America Edgar Allan Poe Award, 1956; Los Angeles *Times* Woman of the Year Award, 1965. Agent: Harold Ober Associates Inc., 40 East 49th Street, New York, New York 10017. Address: 4420 Via Esperanza, Santa Barbara, California 93105, U.S.A.

ROMANCE AND GOTHIC PUBLICATIONS

Novels (series: Dr. Paul Prye; Inspector Sands)

> *The Invisible Worm* (Prye).   New York, Doubleday, 1941; London, Long, 1943.
> *The Weak-Eyed Bat* (Prye).   New York, Doubleday, 1942.
> *The Devil Loves Me* (Prye).   New York, Doubleday, 1942.
> *Wall of Eyes* (Sands).   New York, Random House, 1943; London, Lancer, 1966.
> *Fire Will Freeze.*   New York, Random House, 1944.
> *The Iron Gates* (Sands).   New York, Random House, 1945; as *Taste of Fears*, London, Hale, 1950.
> *Experiment in Springtime.*   New York, Random House, 1947.
> *It's All in the Family.*   New York, Random House, 1948.
> *The Cannibal Heart.*   New York, Random House, 1949; London, Hamish Hamilton, 1950.
> *Do Evil in Return.*   New York, Random House, 1950; London, Museum Press, 1952.
> *Vanish in an Instant.*   New York, Random House, 1952; London, Museum Press, 1953.
> *Rose's Last Summer.*   New York, Random House, 1952; London, Museum Press, 1954; as *The Lively Corpse*, New York, Dell, 1956.
> *Wives and Lovers.*   New York, Random House, 1954.
> *Beast in View.*   New York, Random House, and London, Gollancz, 1955.

An Air That Kills. New York, Random House, 1957; as The Soft Talkers, London,
   Gollancz, 1957.
The Listening Walls. New York, Random House, and London, Gollancz, 1959.
A Stranger in My Grave. New York, Random House, and London, Gollancz, 1960.
How Like an Angel. New York, Random House, and London, Gollancz, 1962.
The Fiend. New York, Random House, and London, Gollancz, 1964.
Beyond This Point Are Monsters. New York, Random House, 1970; London, Gollancz,
   1971.
Ask for Me Tomorrow. New York, Random House, 1976; London, Gollancz, 1977.
The Murder of Miranda. New York, Random House, 1979; London, Gollancz, 1980.
Mermaid. New York, Morrow, and London, Gollancz, 1982.

Uncollected Short Story

"Last Day in Lisbon," in Five Novels (New York), February 1943.

OTHER PUBLICATIONS

Other

The Birds and the Beasts Were There (autobiography). New York, Random House,
   1968.

*   *   *

The works of Margaret Millar have justly won recognition as mysteries. They develop tight
plots, parallel subplots, gripping suspense, and plausible characters. However, Millar's evocation of evil as psychologically motivated, resolved only psychologically, makes her works
interesting treatments of gothic as well as detective themes.
   A Stranger in My Grave, Millar's finest novel, illustrates the ways in which the author
combines mystery and gothic themes. Childless and overprotected housewife Daisy Harker is
haunted by nightmares of her own grave. To her horror, and that of her husband, she realizes
that she has in fact seen the grave; she determines to discover why she is dreaming about it. With
the help of Steve Pinata, a detective in search of his own identity, she discovers the truth; the
stranger in her grave is her real father, a Mexican-American whom her mother had denied and
whom her presumptive father had murdered in a jealous rage. Her identity discovered, her
nightmare purged, Daisy is able to leave her barren and dishonest marriage to begin a new and
healthy life with Pinata.
   While Steve Pinata acts as the detective of A Stranger in My Grave, he also acts as therapist,
helping Daisy to remember and accept people and events she has repressed. Moreover, Pinata's
motivation lies both in his sympathy for Daisy's search for identity and in his growing respect
and love for her. Daisy is both the victim and the pursuer of hidden evil, since the truth lies
hidden in her subconscious. Most important, the real resolution of A Stranger in My Grave is
the union between Daisy and Pinata, a marriage whose children will have the identity and
family love denied to their parents.
   Millar's mystery/gothics tend to deal with poor marital or sexual adjustment and to revolve
around women central characters. Do Evil in Return, Beast in View, and The Cannibal Heart
discuss the frightening consequences of repression that drives women to act out their fantasies
on the lives of others. Experiment in Springtime, Beyond This Point Are Monsters, and Ask for
Me Tomorrow demonstrate the unhealthy consequences of flawed marriage: jealousy, obsession, guilt, revenge. A last favorite Millar theme is sexual competition between women,
convincingly portrayed in Wall of Eyes, The Listening Walls, and The Murder of Miranda.
Millar's most gothic tale, The Fiend, parallels the struggle of a convicted child abuser to
overcome his attraction for a little girl to the little girl's own struggle to accept the flaws in her
parents' marriage and the sexual attractions between grownup men and women.

499

Millar's use of domestic themes and situations, her mastery of imagery, and her evocation of psychological horror question and analyse gothic evil as maladjustment in individuals and in the society that forms them. Her ability as a writer makes these analyses vivid and meaningful.

—Katherine Staples

MILLHISER, Marlys (Joy, née Enabnit).   American.   Born in Charles City, Iowa, 27 May 1938. Educated at the University of Iowa, Iowa City, 1956-60, B.A. in history, 1960; University of Colorado, Boulder, 1961-63, M.A. in history 1963. Married David Millhiser in 1960; one son and one daughter. History teacher, Boulder Valley schools, Lafayette, Colorado, 1963-65. Agent: Roberta Kent, Harry Ufland Agency, 190 North Canon Drive, Beverly Hills, California 90210. Address: 1743 Orchard Avenue, Boulder, Colorado 80302, U.S.A.

ROMANCE AND GOTHIC PUBLICATIONS

Novels

Michael's Wife.   New York, Putnam, 1972.
Nella Waits.   New York, Putnam, 1974.
Willing Hostage.   New York, Putnam, 1976.
The Mirror.   New York, Putnam, 1978.
Nightmare Country.   New York, Putnam, 1981.

Manuscript Collection: University of Wyoming, Laramie.

Marlys Millhiser comments:

I don't consider my work necessarily in a romance/gothic genre. I do not write to formula. But because I am female I tend to view life that way and I have no desire to imitate the other sex. So I do naturally include much of the human and especially female/male relationship in my stories. They've been billed as everything from romantic to supernatural to horror. My only hope is that they are not boring.

*   *   *

Marlys Millhiser can hardly be said to write escapist fiction. In fact, the settings, characters, and situations in her novels are often so grim that the reader must wonder why the *heroines* do not escape. Millhiser's command of descriptive language is excellent; so good, in fact, that it is difficult for a reader to become involved in her earliest works because of the unrelieved bleakness that she conveys. Her first novel, *Michael's Wife*, presents us with an amnesic young woman who returns to the husband that she abandoned and the child of whose existence she has been unaware. The husband seems to have murder in mind; his family makes no secret of their hatred for the prodigal wife. Even the secretary-babysitter seems determined to engineer Laurel's downfall or death. Further to complicate the situation all of these characters are isolated in a house in the desert. Laurel's stated reason for remaining in an environment so dangerous and unpleasant—that the child needs his mother—is unconvincing since the character of the boy remains two-dimensional and Laurel's relationship to him is somewhat undeveloped. The same sort of entrapment of the heroine occurs in each novel, yet only in *The Mirror* is one convinced that the young woman cannot free herself without physical or emotional trauma.

It is a measure of Millhiser's skill in plotting that her novels rise above such unpromising opening chapters to capture the reader's attention and interest. One can see an improvement in style from book to book, if not in the gloominess of setting and character. These novels are unusual for their genre in that, with the exception of *Willing Hostage*, they take place over very long spans of time. *The Mirror*, in fact, spans the lifetimes of a woman and her granddaughter. This time factor is one area in which Millhiser's increased skill is demonstrated in successive novels. *Michael's Wife* proceeds so slowly at times that the action seems almost to stop, while the later books are paced much more smoothly. It should also be noted that *Michael's Wife* with its detailed descriptions of hippies and their costumes is so typical that it now seems very dated. The later books have a more timeless, contemporary feeling about them.

The area in which this writer shines is in her handling of the supernatural. Both *Nella Waits* and *The Mirror* are supernatural tales. Both are exceptionally complex and yet vastly different from each other. The malevolent haunting and equivocal ending of *Nella Waits* is breathlessly believable. The transfer of souls in *The Mirror*, while not a new concept, is handled with a freshness and consistency that easily permit the reader's suspension of disbelief.

Millhiser's world is not easy to enter and not always entertaining in the lightest sense; but once the reader has entered, settings, characters, and style are secondary to the irresistible flow of these intricate plots.

—Susan Quinn Berneis

MITCHELL, Margaret (Munnerlyn). American. Born in Atlanta, Georgia, in 1900. Educated at the Washington Seminary, Atlanta, 1914-18; Smith College, Northampton, Massachusetts, 1918-19. Married John R. Marsh in 1925. Feature Writer and Reporter, *Atlanta Journal*, 1922-26. Recipient: Pulitzer Prize, 1937; Bohnenberger Memorial Award, 1938; New York Southern Society Gold Medal, 1938. M.A.: Smith College, 1939. *Died 16 August 1949.*

ROMANCE AND GOTHIC PUBLICATIONS

Novel

Gone with the Wind. New York and London, Macmillan, 1936.

OTHER PUBLICATIONS

Other

Margaret Mitchell's "Gone with the Wind" Letters 1936-1949, edited by Richard Harwell. New York, Macmillan, and London, Collier Macmillan, 1976.

*   *   *

In the 45 years since their first appearance, the characters in Margaret Mitchell's *Gone with the Wind* have stepped out of its pages and taken up permanent residence in our imaginations. They are a curious group, at once reductive romantic stereotypes, recognizably distinct individuals, and expansive mythic figures. Their author, for one, neither doubted nor denied that headstrong, thoughtless Scarlett O'Hara and cynical villainous Rhett Butler were stereotypes. But, she maintained, they were stock characters of a generation, not a genre. Rhett had to be a cynical rogue because the South of his day was populated by them, even as Scarlett was gritty and determined and mostly unscrupulous because that was the type of woman who survived and prospered in post-war Atlanta, of which she is a symbol. A histrionic plot was needed less to satisfy the demands of romance readers than to fulfill the exigencies of retelling events in Georgia during the 1860's. Yet these historical limitations work to Mitchell's advantage, for it is just this rootedness in time and place which allows her characters to become legendary. Scarlett, Rhett, Melanie, and Ashley can step out of Mitchell's pages and into myth because they have first been allowed to stand upon firm ground, in this case the red Georgia clay. For all their typicality, they are realistic, idiosyncratic characters whose choices are genuinely limited by their imagined existence in a real past.

The historically limited choices which Mitchell's characters make are well enough known: Scarlett's marriages, her killing of an intruding Yankee soldier, her manipulation of the postwar lumber business by hiring convicts, and, broadly, her decision to shoulder the responsiblity for the O'Hara household after its ruin; Melanie's constantly repeated decision to stand by Scarlett, and—if one can be said to choose a compulsion—her decision to remain ignorant of people's motives and acts; Ashley's decision to die spiritually with the old South (a culture into which, ironically, he hardly fits, as Gerald O'Hara testifies early in the novel), his willful indecision about his feelings for Scarlett; Rhett's scandalous profiteering, his belated decision to enlist in the South's lost cause, his will to protect his child from the shame of Scarlett's bad reputation, his final, irrevocable decision to leave. The pulling and pushing of emotions, which so many of these catalogued decisions achieve, is nothing new to romance fiction. What is different is that so many of these decisions are wrong, unwise, lead to unhappy outcomes for the principals, and do so permanently. Many a romance heroine has hastily married the wrong man like Scarlett, but few so knowingly. Many also have married the right man mistakenly, but few have finally declared their love only to have him leave permanently. Few romances, that is, take place in a world in which one can indeed be fatefully wrong.

Few, moreover, proceed at life's own pace, as does *Gone with the Wind*. The typically first-person narration of romance fiction is customarily urgent: whatever is going to happen is going to happen fast. Mitchell's novel, on the other hand, is leisurely. Although it builds to many climaxes, it does so always within the course of large events, sprawling beyond the confines of romance time (usually days or weeks) to cover ten years. Even the most conventionally romantic element of the book, the Rhett-Scarlett-Ashley triangle, upends expectation. Not only does it not turn out as we might have hoped, it doesn't even begin as it should. Scarlett's is a fatal, dogged desire for Ashley, but it does not start, as do most romances with an attraction/repulsion or as love-at-first-sight, but rather is an adolescent outgrowth in Scarlett of a long childhood friendship. Similarly, her belatedly recognized love for Rhett arises from their long living together in mutual dependence, not out of sudden, puzzling attraction. In *Gone with the Wind*, as in its readers' lives, people grow into affections, even as they sometimes outgrow them, and they do both within the context of larger, sometimes overwhelming, historical events.

Mitchell's pacing, her use of a solidly limiting past, and her characters' consequential choices set *Gone with the Wind* apart from other historical romances, making it more like *War and Peace* than like genre fiction. Is it excessive to compare a popular romance to a literary classic? Of course. Yet the extravagant comparison serves; for unlike other historical romances—and especially unlike most plantation novels—*Gone with the Wind* is set in the past not for its vagueness but for its specificity. If Mitchell's tortuous account of Scarlett and Ashley and Rhett is what keeps romance readers turning pages, what they are likely to find on the overleaf is not a passionate encounter, but instead an analysis of the role of profiteers in Georgia's wartime economy, or General Johnston's strategy in defending Atlanta, or the advantages of owning lumber in post-war, burnt-out Atlanta. Happily, Mitchell grinds her historical axes more quietly than her distant counterpart Tolstoy; economic and political details fit into the book as gracefully as Pittypat's swoons. What results is a neat dovetail joining of the historical and the individual, a book whose broad characters lead intensely personal lives and make consequential choices, the limits of which are determined far more by historical circumstances and inner compulsion than by the conventions of romance.

—Nancy Regan

MONTGOMERY, L(ucy) M(aud). Canadian. Born in Clifton, Prince Edward Island, 30 November 1874. Educated at schools in Cavendish, Prince Edward Island; Prince of Wales College, Charlottetown, Prince Edward Island, teacher's certificate, 1894, teacher's license 1895; Dalhousie College, Halifax, Nova Scotia, 1895-96. Married Ewan Macdonald in 1911; two sons. Schoolteacher, Bideford, 1894-95, 1896-97, and Lower Bedeque, 1897-98, both in Prince Edward Island; Assistant Postmistress, Cavendish, 1898-1911; Staff Member, Halifax *Echo*, 1901-02. Fellow, Royal Society of Arts, 1923. O.B.E. (Officer, Order of the British Empire), 1935. *Died 24 April 1942.*

ROMANCE AND GOTHIC PUBLICATIONS

Novels

Anne of Green Gables. Boston, Page, and London, Pitman, 1908.
Anne of Avonlea. Boston, Page, and London, Pitman, 1909.
Kilmeny of the Orchard. Boston, Page, and London, Pitman, 1910.
The Story Girl. Boston, Page, and London, Pitman, 1911.
The Golden Road. Boston, Page, 1913; London, Cassell, 1914.
Anne of the Island. Boston, Page, and London, Pitman, 1915.
Anne's House of Dreams. New York, Stokes, and London, Constable, 1917.
Rainbow Valley. Toronto, McClelland and Stewart, and New York, Stokes, 1919; London, Constable, 1920.
Rilla of Ingleside. Toronto, McClelland and Stewart, New York, Stokes, and London, Hodder and Stoughton, 1921.
Emily of New Moon. New York, Stokes, and London, Hodder and Stoughton, 1923.
Emily Climbs. New York, Stokes, and London, Hodder and Stoughton, 1925.
The Blue Castle. Toronto, McClelland and Stewart, New York, Stokes, and London, Hodder and Stoughton, 1926.
Emily's Quest. New York, Stokes, and London, Hodder and Stoughton, 1927.
Magic for Marigold. Toronto, McClelland and Stewart, New York, Stokes, and London, Hodder and Stoughton, 1929.
A Tangled Web. New York, Stokes, 1931; as *Aunt Becky Began It*, London, Hodder and Stoughton, 1931.
Pat of Silver Bush. New York, Stokes, and London, Hodder and Stoughton, 1933.
Mistress Pat: A Novel of Silver Bush. New York, Stokes, and London, Harrap, 1935.
Anne of Windy Poplars. New York, Stokes, 1936; as *Anne of Windy Willows*, London, Harrap, 1936.
Jane of Lantern Hill. Toronto, McClelland and Stewart, New York, Stokes, and London, Harrap, 1937.
Anne of Ingleside. New York, Stokes, and London, Harrap, 1939.

Short Stories

Chronicles of Avonlea.   Boston, Page, and London, Sampson Low, 1912.
Further Chronicles of Avonlea....   Boston, Page, 1920; London, Harrap, 1953.
The Road to Yesterday.   New York, McGraw Hill, 1974; London, Angus and Robertson, 1975.
The Doctor's Sweetheart and Other Stories.   New York, McGraw Hill, and London, Harrap, 1979.

OTHER PUBLICATIONS

Verse

The Watchman and Other Poems.   Toronto, McClelland and Stewart, 1916; New York, Stokes, 1917; London, Constable, 1920.

Other

Courageous Women, with Marian Keith and Mabel Burns McKinley.   Toronto, McClelland and Stewart, 1934.
The Green Gables Letters to Ephraim Weber, 1905-1909, edited by Wilfrid Eggleston. Toronto, Ryerson Press, 1960.
The Alpine Path: The Story of My Career.   Don Mills, Ontario, Fitzhenry and Whiteside, 1974.

Critical Studies: *The Years Before "Anne"* by Francis W.P. Bolger, n.p., Prince Edward Island Heritage Foundation, 1974; *The Wheel of Things: A Biography of L.M. Montgomery* by Mollie Gillen, Don Mills, Ontario, Fitzhenry and Whiteside, 1975, London, Harrap, 1976; *L.M. Montgomery: An Assessment* edited by John Robert Sorfleet, Guelph, Ontario, Canadian Children's Press, 1976.

*   *   *

L.M. Montgomery is of course rightly celebrated for novels like *Anne of Green Gables* and *Emily of New Moon* which have become classics of juvenile literature on both sides of the Atlantic. These are also, however, avidly read by grownups as well as children, and indeed their sequels, in which the young and rapturous heroines mature, have a distinctly adult appeal. The author's short stories (collected in *Chronicles of Avonlea, Further Chronicles of Avonlea, The Road to Yesterday*, and *The Doctor's Sweetheart*), though sometimes tenuously linked to the Green Gables characters, are set in a firmly adult world and contain little with which child readers would identify.

But to whatever age group her fiction is addressed, it always includes strong elements of romance. This is at one extreme cosily domestic and at the other ecstatically spiritual. Physical intensity plays little part in the books. It is significant that whenever a young man snatches his first kiss, the typical Montgomery heroine is likely to slap his face in fury. Despite the vividness of the girls' emotional response to life, they actually inhabit a well ordered housewifely world of newpin neatness where, one feels (to use one of Montgomery's own expressions) it must be a heinous sin to allow fluff-rolls to build up on one's linoleum. And so bodily sex, being a disorderly experience, is not allowed to disrupt the social tidiness of the stories. There is plenty of passion; it is sometimes folksy, sometimes fey—but never physical.

Anne, Emily, and other leading ladies have high flown flights of fantasy which spring from their passion for natural beauty. Emily, for example, has an extremely mobile soul which, we are told, slips easily away from mundane matters into "eternity" so that she can say with conviction: "I washed my soul free from dust in the aerial bath of a spring twilight." Similarly

Susette in *The Road to Yesterday* refreshes her inner being by "bathing her soul in dawn."

Montgomery's pattern of young love is predictable. After the heroine's initial and dramatic renunciation of romance ("I will not love—to love is to be a slave"), it creeps up from behind like a game of Grandma's Footsteps, catches her unawares, and explodes in a burst of ecstasy that is eventually consummated in happily married fecundity.

Fortunately, however, Anne, for example, never allows the claims of her many offspring and a very busy doctor-husband completely to eclipse her joy in her Lake of Shining Waters or the White Way of Delight. And Emily—who is on the threshold of marriage at the end of the trilogy that features her—will, one feels certain, not let domesticity radically dim her mystical "flashes," or her enjoyment of the sun-steeped ferns in her Land of Uprightness.

It must be said that Montgomery handles these tricky transitions from nature-waif to great-earth-mother far more skilfully than many authors who allow their juvenile heroines to mature in the course of a series. She is not only adept at tackling the theme of young love, but of middle-aged romance. (Significantly, perhaps, she did not marry until she was 36, as she devoted many years of her life to looking after an elderly relative, and the rival claims of love and duty are often featured in her books.) Later flowering love is a recurring theme in her story collections (particularly *The Road to Yesterday* and *The Doctor's Sweetheart*). These are full of misunderstandings, jiltings, estrangements, and nostalgia for what might have been; but also there are reconciliations and endeavours to resurrect romance in relationships that are—at least ostensibly—no longer touched by passion. There are also touches of ironic realism when, for example, Montgomery writes of fine but fading ladies who hold out against the attentions of male admirers for one or even two decades, until they find their own "air of distinction getting a little shopworn."

The complex processes of courtship and consummation in L.M. Montgomery's fiction are, as she says of the Canadian spring, "long and fickle and reluctant" but full of "unnameable" and haunting—"charm."

—Mary Cadogan

MOORE, Doris (Elizabeth) Langley. British. Educated in convent schools in South Africa and privately. Married Robin Sugden Moore in 1926 (divorced, 1942). Author and specialist in costume: Founder of the Museum of Costume, Bath, 1955, and designer of costumes for films. Recipient: British Academy Crawshay Prize, for non-fiction, 1975. Fellow, Royal Society of Literature. O.B.E. (Officer, Order of the British Empire), 1971. Address: 5 Prince Albert Road, London N.W. 1, England.

ROMANCE AND GOTHIC PUBLICATIONS

Novels

A Winter's Passion. London, Heinemann, 1932.
The Unknown Eros. London, Secker, 1935.
They Knew Her When: A Game of Snakes and Ladders. London, Rich and Cowan, 1938; as *A Game of Snakes and Ladders*, London, Cassell, 1955.
Not at Home. London, Cassell, 1948.
All Done by Kindness. London, Cassell, 1951; Philadelphia, Lippincott, 1952.
My Caravaggio Style. London, Cassell, and Philadelphia, Lippincott, 1959.

Other

> The Technique of the Love Affair (as A Gentlewoman).   London, Howe, and New York,
>   Simon and Schuster, 1928; revised edition, as Doris Langley Moore, London, Rich and
>   Cowan, 1936; New York, Knickerbocker, 1946.
> Pandora's Letter Box, Being a Discourse on Fashionable Life.   London, Howe, 1929.
> The Bride's Book; or, Young Housewife's Compendium (with June Moore, as Two Ladies
>   of England).   London, Howe, 1932; revised edition, as Our Loving Duty, as Doris
>   Langley Moore and June Moore, London, Rich and Cowan, 1936.
> The Pleasure of Your Company: A Text-Book of Hospitality, with June Moore.   Lon-
>   don, Howe, 1933; revised edition, London, Rich and Cowan, 1936.
> E. Nesbit: A Biography.   London, Benn, 1933; revised edition, Philadelphia, Chilton,
>   1966; Benn, 1967.
> The Vulgar Heart: An Enquiry into the Sentimental Tendencies of Public Opinion.
>   London, Cassell, 1945.
> Gallery of Fashion 1790-1822: From Plates by Heideloff and Ackermann.   London,
>   Batsford, 1949.
> The Woman in Fashion.   London, Batsford, 1949.
> Pleasure: A Discursive Guide Book.   London, Cassell, 1953.
> The Child in Fashion.   London, Batsford, 1953.
> The Great Byron Adventure.   Philadelphia, Lippincott, 1959.
> The Late Lord Byron: Posthumous Dramas.   London, Murray, and Philadelphia, Lip-
>   pincott, 1961.
> Marie and the Duke of H—: The Daydream Love Affair of Marie Bashkirtseff.   London,
>   Cassell, and Philadelphia, Lippincott, 1966.
> Fashion Through Fashion Plates 1771-1970.   London, Ward Lock, 1971; New York,
>   Potter, 1972.
> Lord Byron: Accounts Rendered.   London, Murray, and New York, Harper, 1974.
> Ada, Countess of Lovelace: Byron's Legitimate Daughter.   London, Murray, 1977.

> Editor, Good Fare: A Code of Cookery, by Édouard de Pomiane, translated by Blanche
>   Bowes.   London, Howe, 1932.

> Translator, Anacreon: 29 Odes.   London, Howe, 1926.
> Translator, Carlotta Grisi, by Serge Lifar.   London, Lehmann, 1947.

*   *   *

Doris Langley Moore's novels celebrate the pleasures of connoisseurship and the satisfac-
tions of art, the collector's world, "the little world where beauty was permanent and craftsmanship worth while" (They Knew Her When). Her novels, while not at all conventional romances,
are comedies which frequently end in marriage, and which seriously investigate the nature of
love, often from a contemporary woman's point of view. They complement her biographical
and critical works and are worthy and stylish artifacts from the author of Pleasure: A
Discursive Guide Book.

The Unknown Eros sets out most schematically Moore's concerns with the nature of
love—maternal, erotic, intellectual, religious, aesthetic—and gives primacy to the aesthetic.
Her heroine, because she is an honest artist, is granted a vision of Eros when the disparate faces
of love merge into one figure, that of a schoolboy singing at a speech day. The aesthetic impulse
also redeems the betrayals of the narrator of A Winter's Passion, for Caroline's lust for her
sister's lover is sparked by her unsatisfied artistic ambitions. These novels are more overtly
serious then the dazzlingly plotted comedies that follow.

In these, every turn of the plot, rooted in tics of character, is both surprising and inevitable.
All Done by Kindness is a merry chase after a recently discovered cache of Renaissance
masterpieces. The heroine's disinterested love, her honest connoisseurship, is the force which

leads to the defeat of the band of aesthetic pretenders, chief among them a dishonest art critic, and to her own marriage.

The narrator of *My Caravaggio Style* is brought to betray his aesthetic principles and his love for Byron by jealousy of his fiancée's attraction to the poet dead more than a hundred years. Quentin's preparations for his forgery of the lost Byron memoirs have the obsessive, hypnotic quality of preparations for a murder.

As *My Caravaggio Style* reprises the pattern and concerns of *All Done by Kindness*, so *Not at Home* repeats the romance pattern of *They Knew Her When*—the story of an actress stranded in Egypt after World War I who is reduced to the position of box office clerk in a cinema in Alexandria by the disastrous charity of a hypocritical friend. The comic resolution, Lucy's marriage to a duke, is deepened by the precise detailing of her slip from her class and the frightening despair engendered by poverty and exile. A similar confrontation between honesty and hypocrisy is repeated in *Not at Home*. This postwar novel recounts a domestic invasion in which the unlikely heroine, a middle-aged, botanical artist, Miss MacFarren, is rescued from a tendency toward spiritual smugness by her suffering at the hands of a slovenly and self-deluding tenant. Here is the most satisfying of Moore's investigations of beauty, friendship, and love, and the heroine's repossession of her solitary domain has overtones of a civilization restored.

—Karen Robertson

MORESBY, Louis.   *See* **BECK, L. Adams**.

MOSSOP, Irene.   *See* **CHARLES, Theresa**.

MOTLEY, Annette.   Address: c/o Hutchinson Publishing Group Ltd., 17-21 Conway Street, London W1P 5HL, England.

ROMANCE AND GOTHIC PUBLICATIONS

Novels

My Lady's Crusade.   London, Futura, 1977.
The Sins of the Lion.   London, Hutchinson, and New York, Stein and Day, 1979.

*   *   *

It is always a pleasure to find an author who can write intelligent historical fiction as well as tell a good love story. Annette Motley is such a writer. Here is an author who has thoroughly researched the periods covered in her two published novels, *Sins of the Lion* and *My Lady's Crusade*. Very cleverly Motley weaves historical background into natural conversations, unlike many writers who are given to allowing one character a long monolog. Instead she allows a flow of words and ideas with no artificiality as to why the characters should be discussing a certain event. As in so many tales of romance fiction, war, with all its passions and cruelities, serves as a background for handsome heroes and enticingly beautiful heroines. But in Motley's novels this background takes on an aspect of eerie reality. In each story the horrors of war and how it is experienced by the participants is described with stunning insight. To Richard the Lionheart *(My Lady's Crusade)* war becomes a way of life, a way to display his ruthless and bloodthirsty courage. For others, such as his more humanitarian lieutenant, Tristan de Jarnac, engagement in battle is necessary only when the cause is just. Killing to him then becomes an essential but unpleasant duty. In *Sins of the Lion* the Renaissance Prince Leone de Montevalenti desperately wishes to keep a hard-won peace for his city, but when war with his traitorous brother-in-law becomes inevitable, he reluctantly reverts to his warrior role. He leads his army to victory feeling like nothing less than a killing machine, completely devoid of fear for himself or compassion for his adversaries.

Although neither heroine participates in battle, each sees firsthand its brutality. In both novels it is their story which weaves all events together. The lovely Lady Eden of Hawkhurst *(My Lady's Crusade)* sets out to find her young husband Stephen who had left England years before to fight the Saracens in the Holy Land. Seen through her eyes the sights and sounds of the exotic and often barbarous Outremer pulsate with life. She suffers much privation in her lonely quest before aid and love come in the form of the chivalrous knight Tristan. *Sins of the Lion* is the story of Tulla, an exotically beautiful half-Greek, half-Turkish slave bought for the pleasure of Il Leone. As the aristocratic daughter of a Pasha, she possesses a pride which cannot allow her to become the willing mistress to the golden Prince, but eventually even this strong-minded lady falls under the spell of this complex man. In fact, it is her courage and loyalty which ultimately helps him defeat the enemy.

The characters in Motley's novels have flesh and blood reality. Eden's anguish is graphically described when she learns her husband has been seduced into a homosexual relationship with his Saracen captor. Along with this comes a touching portrait of Stephen's intense love for the Saracen and the misery felt for what he has become. Historical figures (Richard the Lionheart and Conrad de Montferrat in *My Lady's Crusade*, Sandro Bottecelli and Lorenzo de Medici in *Sins of the Lion*) are introduced naturally, and although not central characters, take on a life of their own. The reality of human suffering and joys coupled with a tale of romance characterize both novels.

—Patricia Altner

MURRAY, Frances. Pseudonym for Rosemary Booth, née Sutherland. British. Born in Glasgow, Lanark, 10 February 1928. Educated at the University of Glasgow, 1945-47; University of St. Andrews, Fife, M.A. 1965, diploma in education 1966. Married Robert Edward Booth in 1950; three daughters. History teacher, Perth Academy, Scotland, 1966-72. Since 1972, principal teacher of history, Linlathen High School, Dundee. School scriptwriter for BBC radio. Recipient: Romantic Novelists Association Major Award, 1974, and Elgin Prize, 1974. Address: c/o Hodder and Stoughton Ltd., Mill Road, Dunton Green, Sevenoaks, Kent TN13 2YA, England.

ROMANCE AND GOTHIC PUBLICATIONS

Novels

The Dear Colleague. London, Hodder and Stoughton, and New York, St. Martin's Press, 1972.
The Burning Lamp. London, Hodder and Stoughton, and New York, St. Martin's Press, 1973.
The Heroine's Sister. London, Hodder and Stoughton, and New York, St. Martin's Press, 1975.
Red Rowan Berry. London, Hodder and Stoughton, 1976; New York, St. Martin's Press, 1977.
Castaway. London, Hodder and Stoughton, 1978; New York, St. Martin's Press, 1979.

OTHER PUBLICATIONS

Other (juvenile)

Ponies on the Heather. London, Collins, 1966; revised edition, 1973.
Ponies and Parachutes. London, Hodder and Stoughton, 1975.
White Hope. London, Hodder and Stoughton, 1978.

*   *   *

If you like your history lessons presented in an easily comprehended manner aided by lots of romance and adventure, then Frances Murray is a safe bet. Her novels are always enjoyable, briskly paced, and set in unusual and interesting times and places. No matter where or when, her heroines are always spirited, liberated females who take command of their destinies with or without the hero's help.

Her first historical novel, *The Dear Colleague,* involved cloak and dagger politics in the British Foreign Office in Paris during Louis Napoleon's bid for emperor. The hero, Hector, and the heroine, Elizabeth, become husband and wife in an arranged marriage of convenience, naturally falling in love by the story's end. The grand finale includes a shoot-out at the Opera House in Paris where, thanks to Britain's intervention, Louis Napoleon escapes unharmed.

The Burning Lamp, almost more of a young adult title, again involves a liberated woman, Euphemia Witherspoon, who has trained as a nurse with Florence Nightingale and sets out for the Wild West to try to establish a hospital. In spite of Comanches, chauvinist townsmen, and incompetent doctors, Phemie still manages to get the hospital built and find herself a man.

The setting for *The Heroine's Sister,* a well-written romance adventure, is Venice in 1868, when it is still under Austrian rule. Again skullduggery and intrigue are the themes as the heroine, a wonderfully resourceful and courageous Victorian lady, foils the military and saves her tall dark Italian nobleman.

Red Rowan Berry is the least historical of her novels. Nineteenth-century Scotland provides the background for the romantic story of Janet Laidlaw and her quest through many trials and tribulations, including a bigamous marriage, to be reunited with her true love.

Another unusual setting occurs in *Castaway*, the tale of a young girl who is shipwrecked off the coast of Guernsey in 1804 at a time when Napoleon is readying troops to invade England. History takes precedence over romance as she finds it difficult to recognize friend from foe on an island filled with spies and smugglers. A lieutenant in Her Majesty's Royal Navy provides the brief love interest.

Frances Murray fills a much-needed niche in the historical-romance category. Being neither straight historical fiction nor a sweet-savage saga that uses historical settings to tell an erotic story of love, she falls comfortably in between granting readers the best of both worlds by giving them true historical romance.

—Marilyn Lockhart

MUSKETT, Netta (Rachel). British. Born in 1887. Former Vice-President, Romantic Novelists Association.

ROMANCE AND GOTHIC PUBLICATIONS

Novels

The Jade Spider. London, Hutchinson, 1927.
The Open Window. London, Hutchinson, 1930.
After Rain. London, Hutchinson, 1931.
The Flickering Lamp. London, Hutchinson, 1931.
A Mirror for Dreams. London, Hutchinson, 1931.
Nor Any Dawn. London, Hutchinson, 1932.
The Shallow Cup. London, Hutchinson, 1932.
Wings in the Dust. London, Hutchinson, 1933.
Plaster Cast. London, Hutchinson, 1933.
Painted Heaven. London, Hutchinson, 1934.
Silver-Gilt. London, Hutchinson, 1935; New York, Jove, 1978.
Tamarisk. London, Hutchinson, 1935.
Winter's Day. London, Hutchinson, 1936.
Misadventure. London, Hutchinson, 1936.
Alley-Cat. London, Hutchinson, 1937.
Middle Mist. London, Hutchinson, 1937.
Happy To-Morrow. London, Hutchinson, 1938.
The Shadow Market. London, Hutchinson, 1938.
Blue Haze. London, Hutchinson, 1939; New York, Jove, 1978.
To-Day Is Ours. London, Hutchinson, 1939.
Wide and Dark. London, Hutchinson, 1940.
Scarlet Heels. London, Hutchinson, 1940.
Twilight and Dawn. London, Hutchinson, 1941.
The Gilded Hoop. London, Hutchinson, 1941.
Love in Amber. London, Hutchinson, 1942.
Candle in the Sun. New York, Liveright, 1943; London, Hutchinson, 1960.
The Quiet Island. London, Hutchinson, 1943.
Time for Play. London, Hutchinson, 1943.

The Wire Blind. London, Hutchinson, 1944.
Golden Harvest. London, Hutchinson, 1944.
The Patchwork Quilt. London, Hutchinson, 1946.
Fire of Spring. London, Hutchinson, 1946.
The Clency Tradition. London, Hutchinson, 1947.
A Daughter for Julia. London, Hutchinson, 1948.
The Durrants. London, Hutchinson, 1948.
Living with Adam. London, Hutchinson, 1949.
Cast the Spear. London, Hutchinson, 1950; New York, Jove, 1978.
House of Many Windows. London, Hutchinson, 1950.
No May in October. London, Hutchinson, 1951.
The Long Road. London, Hale, 1951.
Rock Pine. London, Hale, 1952.
Safari for Seven. London, Hale, 1952.
Brocade. London, Hutchinson, 1953.
Red Dust. London, Hutchinson, 1954.
Philippa. London, Hutchinson, 1954.
Give Back Yesterday. London, Hutchinson, 1955.
Flowers from the Rock. London, Hutchinson, 1956.
Light from One Star. London, Hutchinson, 1956.
The Crown of Willow. London, Hutchinson, 1957.
The Fettered Past. London, Hutchinson, 1958.
Flame of the Forest. London, Hutchinson, 1958.
The High Fence. London, Hutchinson, 1959.
Through Many Waters. London, Hutchinson, 1961.
The Touchstone. London, Hutchinson, 1962.
The Weir House. London, Hutchinson, 1962.
Love and Deborah. London, Hutchinson, 1963.
Cloudbreak. London, Hutchinson, 1964.

*   *   *

Blue Haze, After Rain, Happy To-Morrow, Flame of the Forest, Through Many Waters, Painted Heaven—behind a succession of such pretty, light-hearted sounding titles lies the urgent attempt to deal conscientiously with serious human problems. After the 1914-18 war, a number of romantic novelists tackled those ethical problems which war had engendered. Netta Muskett looked, for instance, at the "surplus million" women, left on the shelf because of the huge numbers of young men killed in action. The heroine of *Painted Heaven* has the misfortune to lose fiancé, brothers, parents. The orphaned heroine, utterly alone in the world, is of course a much used device, since pathos can be added to her many other predicaments. Doomed to spinsterhood, with no chance of ever finding a husband, this heroine resolves to find "another kind of happiness" through an illegitimate child, only to discover that this offers false security, a false happiness which is no more than a "painted heaven."

By the mid 1950's, with changing social mores, and increasing sexual freedom, there were new problems to be solved. The dreaded peril of permissiveness was threatening to sweep away all that romantic novelists held to be most noble, dear, and beautiful. The reaction of some writers to the increased liberation going on in real life was to tighten up fictional virtue still more, to place their heroines on still higher pedestals. "The romantic novelist is almost alone in presenting a picture of true love, decent and honourable conduct, and the happiness which is the result of these 'old-fashioned things,' " explained a spokeswoman for the Romantic Novelists Association.

While some ignored the new problems, Netta Muskett seized upon them. Not for her the happy-ever-after ending with marriage at the last chapter. Marital unrest, failed marriage, middle-aged marriages, even unconsummated marriages, could provide daring food for thought, an opportunity for psychological insight into human difficulties. *Light from One Star* concerns the marital problems encountered by the older, thoughtful type of man if he mistaken-ly marries a younger woman. She is a glamorous, extroverted, television personality. This gives the clue to her flightly selfish behaviour as a bride. Career women, particularly in glamorous, self-advertising work, are not to be trusted. She accepts her husband's generous presents, and continental holidays, but refuses to sleep with him. Time and again, she "denies him his rights." And when, at long last, she finally resolves to give in/be a good wife/allow him to make love to her, which she does "with a pretty little lift of her head and an inviting look in her eyes," and the crude words, "Well—how, about it?," her husband has lost interest. He sadly, but wisely, tells her, "I'm not blaming you, my dear. I ought to have known. As a doctor, I ought to have realised *before it was too late*." Has the poor chap become impotent? Discretion prevents Netta Muskett delving any further into the problem.

Netta Muskett treats her problem novels to a special style of writing. Verbs are left out, random adverbs stuck in, commas here and there. This can be interpreted either, as one critic suggested, as "sloppy writing and false sentiment," or as a specially constructed, neo-realistic, semi-documentary prose appropriate to the important topic.

—Rachel Anderson

NEAL, Hilary. *See* **NORWAY, Kate**.

NEELS, Betty. Married; one daughter. Has worked as a nurse in the Netherlands and England. Address: c/o Mills and Boon Ltd., 15-16 Brooks Mews, London W1A 1DR, England.

ROMANCE AND GOTHIC PUBLICATIONS

Novels

   Amazon in an Apron. London, Mills and Boon, 1969.
   Blow Hot, Blow Cold. London, Mills and Boon, 1969; as *Surgeon from Holland*, Toronto, Harlequin, 1970.
   Sister Peters in Amsterdam. London, Mills and Boon, 1969; Toronto, Harlequin, 1970.
   Nurse in Holland. Toronto, Harlequin, 1970.
   Fate Is Remarkable. London, Mills and Boon, 1970; Toronto, Harlequin, 1971.
   Nurse Harriet Goes to Holland. Toronto, Harlequin, 1970.
   Damsel in Green. London, Mills and Boon, 1970; Toronto, Harlequin, 1971.
   The Fifth Day of Christmas. London, Mills and Boon, 1971; Toronto, Harlequin, 1972.
   Tangled Autumn. London, Mills and Boon, 1971; Toronto, Harlequin, 1972.
   Tulips for Augusta. London, Mills and Boon, and Toronto, Harlequin, 1971.
   Uncertain Summer. London, Mills and Boon, 1972; Toronto, Harlequin, 1974.
   Victory for Victoria. London, Mills and Boon, and Toronto, Harlequin, 1972.

Saturday's Child.   London, Mills and Boon, 1972; Toronto, Harlequin, 1973.
Tabitha in Moonlight.   London, Mills and Boon, 1972; Toronto, Harlequin, 1975.
Wish with the Candles.   London, Mills and Boon, and Toronto, Harlequin, 1972.
Three for a Wedding.   London, Mills and Boon, and Toronto, Harlequin, 1973.
Winter of Change.   London, Mills and Boon, and Toronto, Harlequin, 1973.
Enchanting Samantha.   London, Mills and Boon, 1973; Toronto, Harlequin, 1974.
Cassandra by Chance.   London, Mills and Boon, and Toronto, Harlequin, 1973.
Stars Through the Mist.   London, Mills and Boon, 1973; Toronto, Harlequin, 1974.
Cruise to a Wedding.   London, Mills and Boon, 1974; Toronto, Harlequin, 1975.
The End of the Rainbow.   London, Mills and Boon, 1974; Toronto, Harlequin, 1975.
The Gemel Ring.   London, Mills and Boon, and Toronto, Harlequin, 1974.
The Magic of Living.   London, Mills and Boon, 1974; Toronto, Harlequin, 1975.
Henrietta's Own Castle.   London, Mills and Boon, 1975; Toronto, Harlequin, 1976.
A Small Slice of Summer.   London, Mills and Boon, 1975; Toronto, Harlequin, 1977.
Heaven Is Gentle.   Toronto, Harlequin, 1975.
Tempestuous April.   London, Mills and Boon, 1975.
Cobweb Morning.   London, Mills and Boon, 1975; Toronto, Harlequin, 1976.
Roses for Christmas.   London, Mills and Boon, 1975; Toronto, Harlequin, 1976.
A Star Looks Down.   London, Mills and Boon, 1975; Toronto, Harlequin, 1976.
The Edge of Winter.   London, Mills and Boon, 1976; Toronto, Harlequin, 1977.
The Moon for Lavinia.   Toronto, Harlequin, 1976.
Gem of a Girl.   London, Mills and Boon, 1976; Toronto, Harlequin, 1977.
Esmeralda.   Toronto, Harlequin, 1976.
The Hasty Marriage.   Toronto, Harlequin, 1977.
A Matter of Chance.   Toronto, Harlequin, 1977.
Grasp a Nettle.   Toronto, Harlequin, 1977.
The Little Dragon.   London, Mills and Boon, 1977; Toronto, Harlequin, 1978.
Britannia All at Sea.   London, Mills and Boon, and Toronto, Harlequin, 1978.
Never While the Grass Grows.   London, Mills and Boon, 1978; Toronto, Harlequin, 1979.
Philomela's Miracle.   London, Mills and Boon, and Toronto, Harlequin, 1978.
Ring in a Teacup.   London, Mills and Boon, 1978.
Pineapple Girl.   Toronto, Harlequin, 1978.
Midnight Sun's Magic.   London, Mills and Boon, 1979; Toronto, Harlequin, n.d.
The Promise of Happiness.   London, Mills and Boon, 1979.
Sun and Candlelight.   London, Mills and Boon, 1979.
Winter Wedding.   Toronto, Harlequin, 1980.
Caroline's Waterloo.   London, Mills and Boon, 1980; Toronto, Harlequin, 1981.
Hannah.   London, Mills and Boon, 1980; Toronto, Harlequin, 1981.
Last April Fair.   London, Mills and Boon, 1980.
The Silver Thaw.   London, Mills and Boon, 1980; Toronto, Harlequin, 1981.
When May Follows.   London, Mills and Boon, 1980; Toronto, Harlequin, 1981.
Not Once but Twice.   Toronto, Harlequin, 1981.

*   *   *

There is a reassuring sameness in Betty Neels's novels that readers anticipate with pleasure. Her stories mirror her own life to a great extent for, although English, she married a Dutchman and lived and worked in Holland for a number of years before turning to writing. In fact, she could be one of her own heroines, for she was a registered nurse and worked in Dutch hospitals while living there.

It is impossible not to feel her deep affection for the Netherlands as she brings to life the placid, homely qualities of the people. At the same time, she uses skillful touches of description and scenery to entice her readers into an awareness of postage-stamp size gardens, flowering spring bulbs, and narrow, flowing canals that criss-cross the landscape. She carefully avoids the Dutch shoe and windmill clichés by concentrating on modern sights and events.

Her heroines are usually nurses in English hospitals. Often they are pleasing in appearance rather than beautiful; occasionally they are chubby or amazon-like instead of dainty, cute little things. But basically, all are sweet, loving girls who are dedicated to their profession; still, each hopes to meet and marry the right man for her.

Her heroes, however, are sleepy-eyed giants of lazy movement and calm unflappable manner. They are, in turn, highly respected and wealthy Dutch consultants who happen to be involved in a special medical situation that brings the heroine into a close relationship with them. Story development invariably moves from England to Holland and back again, and, for the most part, all of her novels have the same basic plot situation.

It is within this framework, however, that Betty Neels shows an unusual mastery of technique and emerges as a creative writer of romance fiction. From her earliest works, such as *Sister Peters in Amsterdam* or *Blow Hot, Blow Cold*, she constantly builds a careful picture of likeable characters, believable stories, and happy endings.

Frequently she varies her heroines' backgrounds, but usually they come from families who have reached professional levels either in medicine, the law, or the church. Occasionally, however, we find a drab little thing like Olympia Randle who is caught in a circle of enforced duty to an irascible, scheming aunt (*The End of the Rainbow*). Olympia finds that even duty eventually comes to an end, with the help of a willing outside force by the name of Waldo Van Der Graaf. For all that, however, Olympia yet has the innate manners and outlook of a lady so that she is able to fit into the doctor's home nicely. Often family responsibilities or difficulties may crop up for the heroine, but she is always able to balance these with a sensitive awareness of love or at least an understanding nature.

An added enjoyment in Betty Neels's novels is the frequent re-appearance of characters from earlier stories. Happy-ever-after is, indeed, a fact, as the reader is allowed to peek into the lives of people several years later as characters become part of a new story and are met again. Thus, Adelaide Peters meets and marries Coenraad Van Essen in *Sister Peters in Amsterdam*. In *Blow Hot, Blow Cold* Sophia Greenslade is introduced to her by Maximillian Van Oosterwelde. By then Adelaide and Coenraad have had a new little baby boy.

Overall, there is a placid, serene unfolding to Betty Neels's stories that gives the reader a sense of inevitableness. Things just could not end any other way. Perhaps this quality has much to do with her popularity. Certainly her novels are constantly being watched for by her readers, even though we already know it will be about an English nurse and a Dutch doctor.

—Arlene Moore

NEILAN, Sarah. British. Born in Newcastle-upon-Tyne. Educated at Oxford University, M.A. Married; four children. Book Editor for 12 years. Recipient: Mary Elgin Award, 1976. Agent: A.D. Peters, 10 Buckingham Street, London WC2N 6BU, England.

ROMANCE AND GOTHIC PUBLICATIONS

Novels

The Braganza Pursuit.   London, Hodder and Stoughton, and New York, Dutton, 1976.
An Air of Glory.   London, Hodder and Stoughton, and New York, Morrow, 1977.
Paradise.   London, Hodder and Stoughton, 1981; New York, St. Martin's Press, 1982.

Sarah Neilan comments:

I am primarily a storyteller, and try to produce a strong, exciting, fast-moving narrative, full of suspense (two of my three novels have been serialized), set against an authentic, unusual, and carefully researched historical background. My period is 1790-1840.

"A cheerful adventure gothic" was how one American reviewer described my first novel, *The Braganza Pursuit*, which was a governess story set in England and Brazil. My second novel, *An Air of Glory*, was about early immigrants to Nova Scotia; the book retraced a real journey (though with fictional characters). My current book, *Paradise*, is a remarkable family saga set among British frontier settlers in what is now southern Ontario, at the time of the war of 1812 between Canada and the U.S.A.

*   *   *

Sarah Neilan's progress as a novelist from fantasy with a base of history to fiction-based-on-fact has been an interesting one.

She claims to have dreamed the opening chapters of her first novel, *The Braganza Pursuit*, the historical details of which were completely unknown to her at the time; and those opening chapters do have the same highly coloured, highly charged, and crystalline quality of Coleridge's "Kubla Khan"—also the result of a dream.

The plot is fairly standard—the heroine being an early 19th-century penniless but gently born governess caught up in a sinister situation over which she has very little control—but the setting (the revolt in northern Brazil against the Braganzas) is dramatic, exotic, and unusual. The writing is equal to this bravely chosen background, being vigorous and vivid. The characters are convincing and the whole—often audacious—story roars along at a spanking rate.

In her second novel, *An Air of Glory*, Neilan has moved even nearer to history-as-it-happened. It is set, again, in the 19th century at a time when many Highlanders were being driven from their lands and forced, through sheer starvation, to cross the Atlantic to Canada in search of a new life. The description of the conditions in which these emigrants crossed the ocean is graphic, and in places horrific; but it is chiefly the characters in the story, their courage and resource, which capture the imagination and hold the attention. Neilan is married to a Canadian whose forebears actually did reach Canada in much the same way, and a good deal of her research has been done "on the ground," which explains the assurance with which she deals with the historical, and the personal, aspect of her work in this area. What she can do, and does with increasing skill, is graft on to actuality invention which irradiates the past.

Her third, and most ambitious, novel, *Paradise*, deals not with the journey to, and arrival in, Canada, but with life in the early years of settlement. In 1812, which is when the Clares and O'Maras set out to make a new life, the States had recently won their independence and there was still tension between the new Americans and the new Canadians. In addition to clearing forests and establishing farms the two families, whose new home was just north of the American border, must fight a war—and neither family is constitutionally fitted for either.

We all know in theory that life was precarious for such people. Sarah Neilan spells it out not only in dramatic, but in domestic, detail and by choosing Canada, rather than the over-exposed country to its south, she opens fresh doors on the experiences of our transatlantic cousins.

—Elizabeth Grey

NICHOLSON, Christina. *See* **NICOLE, Christopher**.

NICOLE, Christopher (Robin). Also writes as Leslie Arlen; Robin Cade; Peter Grange; Mark Logan; C.R. Nicholson; Christina Nicholson; Robin Nicholson; Alison York; Andrew York. British. Born in Georgetown, British Guiana, now Guyana, 7 December 1930. Educated at Harrison College, Barbados; Queen's College, Guyana. Married 1) Jean Barnett in 1951 (divorced), two sons and two daughters; 2) Diana de la Rue. Clerk, Royal Bank of Canada, in the West Indies, 1947-56. Lived in Guernsey for many years after 1957; now domiciled in the Bahamas. Agent: John Farquharson Ltd., 8 Bell Yard, London WC2A 2JU, England.

<small>ROMANCE AND GOTHIC PUBLICATIONS</small>

Novels (series: Amyot; Haggard; Hilton and Warner families)

Off White. London, Jarrolds, 1959.
Shadows in the Jungle. London, Jarrolds, 1961.
Ratoon. London, Jarrolds, and New York, St. Martin's Press, 1962.
Dark Noon. London, Jarrolds, 1963.
Amyot's Cay. London, Jarrolds, 1964.
Blood Amyot. London, Jarrolds, 1964.
The Amyot Crime. London, Jarrolds, 1965; New York, Bantam, 1974.
White Boy. London, Hutchinson, 1966.
The Self-Lovers. London, Hutchinson, 1968.
The Thunder and the Shouting. London, Hutchinson, and New York, Doubleday, 1969.
The Longest Pleasure. London, Hutchinson, 1970.
The Face of Evil. London, Hutchinson, 1971.
Lord of the Golden Fan. London, Cassell, 1973.
Heroes. London, Corgi, 1973.
Caribee (Hilton). London, Cassell, and New York, St. Martin's Press, 1974.
The Devil's Own (Hilton). London, Cassell, and New York, St. Martin's Press, 1975.
Mistress of Darkness (Hilton). London, Cassell, and New York, St. Martin's Press, 1976.
Black Dawn (Hilton). London, Cassell, and New York, St. Martin's Press, 1977.
Sunset (Hilton). London, Cassell, and New York, St. Martin's Press, 1978.
The Secret Memoirs of Lord Byron. Philadelphia, Lippincott, and London, Joseph, 1978; as *Lord of Sin*, London, Corgi, 1980.
The Fire and the Robe (as Alison York). London, W.H. Allen, and New York, Berkley, 1979.
The Scented Sword (as Alison York). London, W.H. Allen, 1980.
Haggard. London, Joseph, and New York, New American Library, 1980.
Haggard's Inheritance. London, Joseph, 1981; as *The Inheritors*, New York, New American Library, 1981.
The Friday Spy (as C.R. Nicholson). London, Corgi, 1981; as *A Passion for Treason* (as Robin Nicholson), New York, Jove, 1981.
The New Americans:
    Brothers and Enemies. New York, Jove, 1982.
    Lovers and Outlaws. New York, Jove, 1982.

Novels as Peter Grange

King Creole. London, Jarrolds, 1966.
The Devil's Emissary. London, Jarrolds, 1968.
The Tumult at the Gate. London, Jarrolds, 1970.
The Golden Goddess. London, Jarrolds, 1973.

Novels as Mark Logan

Tricolour. London, Macmillan, and New York, St. Martin's Press, 1976; as *The Captain's Woman*, New York, New American Library, 1977.
Guillotine. London, Macmillan, and New York, St. Martin's Press, 1976; as *French Kiss*, New York, New American Library, 1978.
Brumaire. London, Wingate, and New York, St. Martin's Press, 1978; as *December Passion*, New York, New American Library, 1979.

Novels as Christina Nicholson

The Power and the Passion. London, Corgi, and New York, Coward McCann, 1977.
The Savage Sands. London, Corgi, and New York, Coward McCann, 1978.
The Queen of Paris. London, Corgi, 1979.

Novels as Leslie Arlen

The Borodins:
  Love and Honour. New York, Jove, and London, Futura, 1980.
  War and Passion. New York, Jove, and London, Futura, 1981.
  Fate and Dreams. New York, Jove, and London, Futura, 1981.
  Destiny and Desire. New York, Jove, 1982.
  Rage and Desire. New York, Jove, 1982.

OTHER PUBLICATIONS

Novels as Andrew York

The Eliminator. London, Hutchinson, 1966; Philadelphia, Lippincott, 1967.
The Co-Ordinator. London, Hutchinson, and Philadelphia, Lippincott, 1967.
The Predator. London, Hutchinson, and Philadelphia, Lippincott, 1968.
The Deviator. London, Hutchinson, and Philadelphia, Lippincott, 1969.
The Dominator. London, Hutchinson, 1969; New York, Lancer, 1971.
The Infiltrator. London, Hutchinson, and New York, Doubleday, 1971.
The Expurgator. London, Hutchinson, 1972; New York, Doubleday, 1973.
The Captivator. London, Hutchinson, 1973; New York, Doubleday, 1974.
The Fear Dealers (as Robin Cade). London, Cassell, and New York, Simon and Schuster, 1974.
The Fascinator. London, Hutchinson, and New York, Doubleday, 1975.
Dark Passage. New York, Doubleday, 1975; London, Hutchinson, 1976.
Tallant for Trouble. London, Hutchinson, and New York, Doubleday, 1977.
Tallant for Disaster. London, Hutchinson, and New York, Doubleday, 1978.

Other (juvenile) as Andrew York

The Doom Fishermen. London, Hutchinson, 1969; as *Operation Destruct*, New York, Holt Rinehart, 1969.
Manhunt for a General. London, Hutchinson, 1970; as *Operation Manhunt*, New York, Holt Rinehart, 1970.
Where the Cavern Ends. London, Hutchinson, and New York, Holt Rinehart, 1971.
Appointment in Kiltone. London, Hutchinson, 1972; as *Operation Neptune*, New York, Holt Rinehart, 1972.

Other

> *West Indian Cricket.* London, Phoenix House, 1957.
> *The West Indies: Their People and History.* London, Hutchinson, 1965.
> *Introduction to Chess.* London, Corgi, 1973.

Christopher Nicole comments:

I am a romantic or a gothic writer simply because those are names currently in vogue for historical novels. I regard myself as an historical novelist. I also happen to be a romantic by nature and aim to retell history as entertainingly as possible.

*   *   *

Christopher Nicole denies the primacy of the intellect to stress the physical. Natural forces, the promptings of the senses, savage instincts in individuals and societies, are essentials of his work. His upbringing as a white man in the West Indies with their history of slavery, rebellion, and natural disaster is also evident.

Off White, his first novel, revolves around racial tensions and has an earthquake as its climax. *Ratoon* is, if anything, more accomplished. Based upon the Demerara slave insurrection of 1823, the book describes the relationship between a white woman planter and the black rebel who for a time holds her captive. The two share physical passion, and, though in the end they part, both are changed by the experience. The theme is skilfully handled by the author, who uses a pared understated style to bring out the nature of his characters. *Ratoon* has a pristine quality, and the strength of the writing is impressive.

Nicole's work under his own name is concerned mainly with the West Indian islands and their past. He has written a history of his own, but more memorable are his Amyot trilogy—*Amyot's Cay, Blood Amyot, The Amyot Crime*—a history of the Bahamas as seen by the Amyot family, and a longer five-volume saga depicting the fortunes of the Hiltons and Warners—*Caribee, The Devil's Own, Mistress of Darkness, Black Dawn*, and *Sunset*. Both sequences feature a succession of despots with undisputed power over the subjects of their plantation world, free to indulge their every desire. Often such power brings out their worst instincts, but some combine strong desires with equally strong ideals. Nicole has been claimed as showing the influence of Edgar Mittelholzer. Certainly some of the powerful matriarchs are reminiscent of the "Kaywana" novels, but the debt is overstressed. Nicole's work shows a greater warmth and humanity, and *Ratoon* is more impressive than anything the older man wrote.

Away from the Caribbean scene, Nicole has written effectively. *The Thunder and the Shouting*, the story of a Polish family during the last war, and the political thriller *The Longest Pleasure* are good examples. *The Face of Evil*, though less striking, is a capable story of witchcraft and ritual murder in modern Britain. He also has a variety of pseudonyms. As Andrew York he writes spy thrillers, and as Christina Nicholson produces tales of searing passion featuring tempestuous heroines. As C.R. Nicholson he follows the adventures of a beautiful double agent in *The Friday Spy*.

Lord of the Golden Fan describes the adventures of Will Adams, the first Englishman to set foot in Japan. Nicole outlines his rise as the friend of Prince Ieyeyasu, and his involvement in the struggle against the ruthless Princess Yodogimi. The story lacks nothing in excitement, with fearsome battle scenes and descriptions of Will's love for the half-caste Pinto Magdalena, consummated after an earthquake destroys Osaka. The differing lifestyles of puritan Europe and Japan are adroitly presented. *Lord of the Golden Fan* is a fine novel, its story compelling and its characters memorable. The vigour of the narrative cannot conceal its subtler insights.

Haggard and *Haggard's Inheritance* further explore the West Indian rulers, this time transplanted to England. Nicole follows two generations of Haggards from wealth in Barbados to the Derbyshire squirearchy, where their personalities bring them into conflict with the social order. The violence and brutality of the period are superbly portrayed as he traces the Haggard entanglements—sexual, political, and moral—through a network of bribery, rape, suicide, and incest, set against the background of the Napoleonic wars. The complex characters are revealed in a taut restrained style, the nature of Regency England brilliantly evoked.

Nicole's achievement tends to be overlooked. His portrayal of heroic man in the physical world—dominating his fellows, being dominated in turn by his own passions—is striking and individual. In the genre he has chosen, he cannot be bettered.

—Geoffrey Sadler

NORRIS, Kathleen (Thompson).   American.   Born in San Francisco, California, 16 July 1880. Educated at home; attended the University of California, Berkeley, 1905. Married the writer Charles Gilman Norris in 1909 (died, 1945); one son and two daughters. Worked as a bookkeeper, saleswoman, and teacher; society editor, *Evening Bulletin*, and reporter, *Call*, both San Francisco, 1907-09; free-lance writer from 1909. *Died 18 January 1966.*

ROMANCE AND GOTHIC PUBLICATIONS

Novels

   Mother.   New York, Macmillan, 1911.
   The Rich Mrs. Burgoyne.   New York, Macmillan, 1912.
   Saturday's Child.   New York, Macmillan, and London, Macmillan, 1914.
   The Treasure.   New York, Macmillan, 1914.
   The Story of Julia Page.   New York, Doubleday, and London, Murray, 1915.
   The Heart of Rachael.   New York, Doubleday, and London, Murray, 1916.
   Martie, The Unconquered.   New York, Doubleday, 1917; London, Murray, 1918.
   Undertow.   New York, Doubleday, and London, Curtis Brown, 1917.
   Josselyn's Wife.   New York, Doubleday, 1918; London, Murray, 1919.
   Sisters.   New York, Doubleday, and London, Murray, 1919.
   The Works.   New York, Doubleday, 11 vols., 1920.
   Harriet and the Piper.   New York, Doubleday, and London, Murray, 1920.
   The Beloved Woman.   New York, Doubleday, and London, Murray, 1921.
   Little Ships.   New York, Doubleday, 1921; London, Murray, 1925.
   Certain People of Importance.   New York, Doubleday, and London, Heinemann, 1922.
   Lucretia Lombard.   New York, Doubleday, and London, Curtis Brown, 1922.
   Butterfly.   New York, Doubleday, 1923; as *Poor Butterfly*, London, Heinemann, 1923.
   Uneducating Mary.   New York, Doubleday, 1923.
   Rose of the World.   New York, Doubleday, and London, Murray, 1924.
   The Callahans and the Murphys.   New York, Doubleday, and London, Heinemann, 1924.
   The Black Flemings.   New York, Doubleday, and London, Murray, 1926; as *Gabrielle*, New York, Paperback Library, 1965.
   Hildegarde.   New York, Doubleday, and London, Murray, 1926.
   Barberry Bush.   New York, Doubleday, 1927; London, Murray, 1929.
   My Best Girl.   New York, Burt, and London, Readers Library, 1927.
   The Sea Gull.   New York, Doubleday, 1927; London, Murray, 1938.
   Beauty and the Beast.   New York, Doubleday, 1928; as *Outlaw Love*, London, Murray, 1928.
   The Foolish Virgin.   New York, Doubleday, and London, Murray, 1928.
   Storm House.   New York, Doubleday, and London, Murray, 1929.

Red Silence. New York, Doubleday, and London, Murray, 1929.
The Lucky Lawrences. New York, Doubleday, and London, Murray, 1930.
Passion Flower. New York, Doubleday, and London, Murray, 1930.
Margaret Yorke. New York, Doubleday, 1930; London, Murray, 1931.
Belle-Mère. New York, Doubleday, 1931; London, Murray, 1932.
The Love of Julie Borel. New York, Doubleday, and London, Murray, 1931.
Treehaven. New York, Doubleday, and London, Murray, 1932.
Younger Sister. New York, Doubleday, 1932; as *Make Believe Wife*, London, Murray, 1947.
Second Hand Wife. New York, Doubleday, 1932; London, Murray, 1933.
Young Mother Hubbard. London, Benn, 1932.
Tangled Love. London, Murray, 1933.
The Angel in the House. New York, Doubleday, 1933.
Walls of Gold. New York, Doubleday, and London, Murray, 1933.
Wife for Sale. New York, Doubleday, 1933; London, Murray, 1934.
False Morning. London, Murray, 1934.
Maiden Voyage. New York, Doubleday, 1934.
Manhattan Love Song. New York, Doubleday, 1934.
Three Men and Diana. New York, Doubleday, and London, Murray, 1934.
Beauty's Daughter. New York, Doubleday, and London, Murray, 1935.
Shining Windows. New York, Doubleday, and London, Murray, 1935.
Woman in Love. New York, Doubleday, 1935; as *Tamara*, London, Murray, 1935.
The Mystery of Pine Point. London, Murray, 1936.
Secret Marriage. New York, Doubleday, and London, Murray, 1936.
The American Flaggs. New York, Doubleday, 1936; as *The Flagg Family*, London, Murray, 1936.
Bread into Roses. New York, Doubleday, and London, Murray, 1937.
You Can't Have Everything. New York, Doubleday, and London, Murray, 1937.
Heartbroken Melody. New York, Doubleday, and London, Murray, 1938.
Mystery House. New York, Doubleday, 1939.
Lost Sunrise. New York, Doubleday, and London, Murray, 1939.
The Runaway. New York, Doubleday, and London, Murray, 1939.
The Secret of the Marshbanks. New York, Doubleday, and London, Murray, 1940.
The World Is Like That. New York, Doubleday, and London, Murray, 1940.
April Escapade. London, Murray, 1941.
The Venables. New York, Doubleday, and London, Murray, 1941.
An Apple for Eve. New York, Doubleday, 1942; London, Murray, 1943.
Come Back to Me, Beloved. New York, Sun Dial Press, 1942; London, Murray, 1953; as *Motionless Shadows*, New York, Bart House, 1945.
Dina Cashman. New York, Doubleday, 1942; London, Murray, 1943.
Corner of Heaven. New York, Doubleday, 1943; London, Murray, 1944.
Love Calls the Tune. New York, Sun Dial Press, 1944; London, Murray, 1945.
Burned Fingers. New York, Doubleday, 1945; London, Murray, 1946.
Mink Coat. New York, Doubleday, and London, Murray, 1946.
The Secrets of Hillyard House. New York, Doubleday, 1947; as *Romance at Hillyard House*, London, Murray, 1948.
Christmas Eve. London, Murray, 1949.
High Holiday. New York, Doubleday, 1949.
Shadow Marriage. New York, Doubleday, and London, Murray, 1952.
Miss Harriet Townshend. New York, Doubleday, and London, Murray, 1955.
The Best of Kathleen Norris. Garden City, New York, Hanover House, 1955.
Through a Glass Darkly. New York, Doubleday, 1957; as *Cherry*, London, Murray, 1958.

Short Stories

Poor, Dear Margaret Kirby and Other Stories. New York, Macmillan, 1913.

Baker's Dozen. New York, Doubleday, 1938; as *Plain People*, London, Murray, 1938.
Star-Spangled Christmas. New York, Doubleday, 1942.
Over at the Crowleys'. New York, Doubleday, 1946.

Uncollected Short Story

"Security," in *Collier's* (Springfield, Ohio), 20 November 1948.

OTHER PUBLICATIONS

Plays

The Kelly Kid, with Dan Totheroh. Boston, Baker, 1926.
Victoria. New York, Doubleday, 1934.

Screenplay: *Lucretia Lombard* (*Flaming Passion*), with Bertram Millhauser and Sada Cowan, 1923.

Verse

One Nation Indivisible. New York, Doubleday, 1942.

Other

Noon: An Autobiographial Sketch. New York, Doubleday, 1925.
The Fun of Being a Mother. New York, Doubleday, and London, Heinemann, 1927.
Herbert Hoover as Seen by Kathleen Norris. Washington, D.C., Republican National
   Committee, 1928.
Home. New York, Dutton, 1928.
What Price Peace? A Handbook of Peace for American Women. New York, Double-
   day, 1928.
After the Honey Moon What? New York, Paulist Press, n.d.
Mother and Son. New York, Dutton, 1929.
Beauty in Letters. New York, Doubleday, 1930.
Hands Full of Living: Talks with American Women. New York, Doubleday, 1931.
My San Francisco. New York, Doubleday, 1932.
My California. New York, Doubleday, 1933.
Dedications. Privately printed, 1936.
*These I Like Best: The Favorite Novels and Stories of Kathleen Norris, Chosen by
   Herself.* New York, Doubleday, 1941.
Companionate Marriage. New York, Paulist Press, n.d.
Morning Light (juvenile). New York, Doubleday, 1950; as *Mary-Jo*, London, Dent,
   1952.
Family Gathering (memoirs). New York, Doubleday, and London, Murray, 1959.

*   *   *

Kathleen Norris has unfortunately been lumped together with the masses of popular magazine writers of the period from 1910 to 1950, and this, while appropriate for much of her work,
does a disservice to her best novels. Possibly a bit defensive about her work because of the more
"serious" (but utterly forgotten) work of her husband, Charles Norris (brother of Frank), she
saw herself as a professional writer, doing two or three serials a year for leading magazines, even
cutting back on her fiction when income tax made it appropriate to do so. But she said in her

autobiography: "Most of the critics did not take my work seriously, but then neither did I take the critics too seriously. My writing I took with deadly seriousness."

Certainly the critics were just to ignore much of her work. Norris's central mood hovers between the sentimental and the didactic; together they are a dangerous combination. It often leads to works which point a threadbare moral at the expense of much exploration of character. *The Treasure* (1914) is a "modern" story about social insecurity, "domestic science," and progress. The characters are used as counters in the thematic game—and the result is a "hard" story with little life to it. Usually Norris allows herself more space, but even so many of the novels center on obvious conflicts between ordinary folk and smart or rich people, usually with a romantic plot to keep the theme moving. *Rose of the World* contrasts a socially unacceptable girl with a rich snobbish family, but the girl is given the chance to have the last word, and marry the son of the family after all. *Mink Coat* contrasts a playboy New Yorker with an honest westerner by their effect on one woman. And other novels show rich or shiftless men damaging young susceptible girls. Perhaps a sacrifice has to be made to protect a relative or friend (*Lost Sunrise*)—but the long-term effect is usually a triumph for the heroine.

Norris emphasized her interest in "the fearful power of money upon human lives," and her stories are full of spendthrifts, unworkable household budgets, bank loans, wills, and middle-aged women who don't understand the principle of insurance. But another prime interest is the family itself, and her best novels are those which center on the family or clan as a preserver of traditional right action, even as an expression of the healthy melting pot of America itself.

Because Norris was from a prosperous Irish family from San Francisco, many of her works use this background. And she was not afraid to use simple or even slight themes: "I have no knowledge of those dark forces which fascinate modern writers. I write for people with simple needs and motives because I am like that myself." Her very first long story, *Mother*, brought her fame, and it initiates a constant Norris theme by having a strong sense of family—centered on the unassuming Mrs. Paget—act as a stabilizing force against the false values of a "smart" idle life: "the old beauty that had been hers was chiselled to a mere pure outline now, but there was a contagious serenity in Mrs. Paget's smile, a clear steadiness in her calm eyes, and her forehead, beneath an unfashionably plain sweep of hair, was untroubled and smooth." Other volumes also center on strong mothers (*Over at the Crowleys', The Callahans and the Murphys, Little Ships*), though sometimes the theme is reversed, so that a weak mother yields to a daughter who learns strength elsewhere (*The Venables*).

The two novels which most convincingly posit Norris's fictional values are *Certain People of Importance* and *The Flagg Family*, and the two books neatly represent two consecutive generations. The "certain people of importance" of the first novel are the members of the Crabtree family. The novel traces the Crabtrees in detail from their arrival in San Francisco in 1849 through the 40 or 50 years to the death of Reuben Crabtree. We see a family begun, a group of traditions started, rivalries and intimacies, financial and spiritual losses and gains— and life continues to surprise Reuben's daughters May and Fannie to the very end. The Flaggs represent the next generation, but their novel covers a shorter span of time (about 10 years) and has a firmer plot. The Flaggs are a large rich clan in northern California, the symbol of tradition and aristocracy to outsiders. Norris allows the clan to be penetrated by an outsider, not in order to debunk the Flaggs, but to show the value of the traditions the Flaggs have built up and learned to accept as part of their future, the richness of the strains that have fed them (English, Indian, Jewish, Italian, Dutch), the compromises that keep them afloat. Even the rather melodramatic plot superimposed on the more substantial edifice—should the newcomer Penelope divorce the spoiled Jeff Flagg to marry the more sedate cousin Tom Flagg?—is worked out in terms of the family theme.

Norris in these two books keeps her sentiments and nostalgia uncontaminated with didacticism, and the results are probing. She represents a second-generation American writer with second-generation American themes, and these are interesting yet today (vulgarized into sentimental myths as pervasive as Ozzie and Harriet or the Kennedys)—and presented with directness and precision.

—George Walsh

NORTON, Bess.   *See* **NORWAY, Kate**.

NORWAY, Kate.   Pseudonym for Olive Marion Norton, née Claydon; also writes as Hilary Neal; Bess Norton.   British.   Born 13 January 1913.   Educated at King Edward's School, Birmingham; Birmingham Children's Hospital; Manchester Royal Infirmary.   Married George Norton in 1938; one son and three daughters.   Nurse, 1930-36: in charge of first aid post during World War II; columnist, Birmingham *News*, 1954-59.   Counsellor, Citizens Advice Bureau. Agent: Laurence Pollinger Ltd., 18 Maddox Street, London W1R OEU.   Address: 1 Holly Lane, Four Oaks, Warwickshire, England.

ROMANCE AND GOTHIC PUBLICATIONS

Novels

   Sister Brookes of Bynd's.   London, Mills and Boon, 1957; as *Nurse Brookes*, Toronto, Harlequin, 1958.
   The Morning Star.   London, Mills and Boon, and Toronto, Harlequin, 1959.
   Junior Pro.   London, Mills and Boon, and Toronto, Harlequin, 1959.
   Nurse Elliot's Diary.   London, Mills and Boon, and Toronto, Harlequin, 1960.
   Waterfront Hospital.   London, Mills and Boon, 1961.
   The White Jacket.   London, Mills and Boon, 1961; Toronto, Harlequin, 1962.
   Goodbye, Johnny.   London, Mills and Boon, 1962.
   The Night People.   London, Mills and Boon, 1963.
   Nurse in Print.   London, Mills and Boon, 1963.
   The Seven Sleepers.   London, Mills and Boon, 1964.
   A Professional Secret.   London, Mills and Boon, 1964.
   The Lambs.   London, Mills and Boon, 1965.
   The Nightingale Touch.   London, Mills and Boon, 1966.
   Be My Guest.   London, Mills and Boon, 1966; as *Journey in the Dark*, London, Corgi, 1973.
   Merlin's Keep.   London, Mills and Boon, 1966.
   A Nourishing Life.   London, Mills and Boon, 1967.
   The Faithful Failure.   London, Mills and Boon, 1968.
   Dedication Jones.   London, Mills and Boon, 1969; Toronto, Harlequin, 1970.
   To Care Always.   London, Mills and Boon, 1970.
   Reluctant Nightingale.   London, Mills and Boon, 1970.
   Paper Halo.   London, Mills and Boon, 1970; Toronto, Harlequin, 1971.
   The Bedside Manner.   London, Mills and Boon, 1971.
   Casualty Speaking.   London, Mills and Boon, 1971.
   The Dutiful Tradition.   London, Mills and Boon, 1971.
   The Gingham Year.   London, Mills and Boon, 1973.
   Voices in the Night.   London, Mills and Boon, 1973.

Novels as Bess Norton

   The Quiet One.   London, Mills and Boon, 1959; Toronto, Harlequin, 1960.
   Night Duty at Duke's.   London, Mills and Boon, 1960.

The Red Chalet.   London, Mills and Boon, 1960.
The Summer Change.   London, Mills and Boon, 1961.
The Waiting Room.   London, Mills and Boon, 1961; Toronto, Harlequin, 1962.
A Nurse Is Born.   London, Mills and Boon, 1962; Toronto, Harlequin, 1963.
The Green Light.   London, Mills and Boon, 1963.
The Monday Man.   London, Mills and Boon, 1963.
St. Luke's Little Summer.   London, Mills and Boon, 1964.
A Miracle at Joe's.   London, Mills and Boon, 1965.
St. Julian's Day.   London, Mills and Boon, 1965.
What We're Here For.   London, Mills and Boon, 1966.
Night's Daughters.   London, Mills and Boon, 1966.
The Night Is Kind.   London, Mills and Boon, 1967.

Novels as Hilary Neal

Factory Nurse.   London, Mills and Boon, 1961; Toronto, Harlequin, 1964.
Tread Softly, Nurse.   London, Mills and Boon, and Toronto, Harlequin, 1962.
Star Patient.   London, Mills and Boon, 1963.
Love Letter.   London, Mills and Boon, 1963.
Houseman's Sister.   London, Mills and Boon, 1964.
Nurse Off Camera.   London, Mills and Boon, 1964.
Mr. Sister.   London, Mills and Boon, 1965.
The Team.   London, Mills and Boon, 1965.
Charge Nurse.   London, Mills and Boon, 1965.
A Simple Duty.   London, Mills and Boon, 1966.
Nurse Meg's Decision.   London, Mills and Boon, 1966.

OTHER PUBLICATIONS

Novels as Olive Norton

A School of Liars.   London, Cassell, 1966.
Now Lying Dead.   London, Cassell, 1967.
The Speight Street Angle.   London, Corgi, 1968.
Dead on Prediction.   London, Cassell, 1970.
The Corpse-Bird Cries.   London, Cassell, 1971.

Play

Radio Play: *Rose*, 1962.

Other as Olive Norton

Bob-a-Job Pony (juvenile).   London, Heinemann, 1961.

*   *   *

The hospital romance has become a popular and fertile branch of novel writing. It dates in Britain only from the start of the National Health Service in 1948, but Kate Norway has established herself as the most successful practitioner of this genre as well as being a crime writer.

Material for her many books is based on first-hand experience of hospital nursing in Britain, and on the whole the pictures she provides of hospitals are very truthful and realistic to the point of being workaday. There is, as a result, much technical medical detail, as well as clear examples of administrative systems, and much of the interest for many readers is contained in those two areas. The romance in many of her novels is intimately mixed with the work; it is even possible to see the romance aspect as subsidiary. Thus, a young reader contemplating a nursing career would read her novels for an inside picture of hospital life which will also be entertaining. *The Gingham Year*, in fact, deals with the transition of a girl from school to nursing. *The Lambs* concerns a group of student nurses.

Plots tend to follow a well-established pattern. They usually revolve around a young female nurse (occasionally doctor) who is dedicated, competent, and attractive. The nurse is attracted to several doctors and surgeons in the hospital, and can be warm and loving. Much of the interest in the plots is produced by a complicating of romantic situations involving the heroine. She is often disturbed in an initially inexplicable way by her attraction to a particular male. This attraction is often despite herself, and directed towards an unpromising suitor. At the same time she is involved with an ostensibly better candidate. Generally the least promising situation turns out to bring true love. Romantic plots are thus normally triangular: a little variety is added by including a subsidiary mystery involving crime. In *The White Jacket*, for instance, there is a masquerading murderer working in the hospital.

Another device used by Norway to add variety to plots is the accident which happens to nurse or doctor. In *Reluctant Nightingale* the nurse herself ends up needing nursing by those intruders, male nurses. Male nurses were once a controversial issue, and this remains true for the world in Norway's books, which is primarily a female one.

An interesting device occurs in *Voices in the Night* where the chapters form separate diaries written in a *sotto voce* style belonging to five characters. They are inter-related, and one sees hospital life from the view of the elderly spinster sister as well as the young nurse and young doctor. This device adds poignancy to the fact that one doctor is loved by two nurses.

Minor issues which appear in several books are motor car, and especially motor bike, accidents. Settings are commonly the English Midlands. The style of writing is simple with much lively dialogue but with a good deal of narrative in the first person; descriptive passages are not overlong. Character is not probed too deeply and judgments are often made in a snappy, personnel-management style.

—P.R. Meldrum

OGILVIE, Elisabeth (May).   American.   Born 20 May 1917. Educated at North Quincy High School, Massachusetts. Address: c/o McGraw-Hill Inc., 1221 Avenue of the Americas, New York, New York 10020, U.S.A.

ROMANCE AND GOTHIC PUBLICATIONS

Novels

    High Tide at Noon.   New York, Crowell, 1944; London, Harrap, 1945.
    Storm Tide.   New York, McGraw Hill, 1945; London, Harrap, 1947.
    Honeymoon (novelization of screenplay).   New York, Bartholomew House, 1947.
    The Ebbing Tide.   New York, Crowell, 1947; London, Harrap, 1948.
    Rowan Head.   New York, McGraw Hill, 1949; London, Harrap, 1950.
    The Dawning of the Day.   New York, McGraw Hill, 1954.

No Evil Angel.   New York, McGraw Hill, 1956; London, Harrap, 1957.
The Witch Door.   New York, McGraw Hill, 1959; London, W.H. Allen, 1961.
Call Home the Heart.   New York, McGraw Hill, 1962.
There May Be Heaven.   New York, McGraw Hill, 1966.
The Seasons Hereafter.   New York, McGraw Hill, 1966.
Waters on a Starry Night.   New York, McGraw Hill, 1968.
Bellwood.   New York, McGraw Hill, 1969.
The Face of Innocence.   New York, McGraw Hill, 1970.
A Theme for Reason.   New York, McGraw Hill, 1970.
Weep and Know Why.   New York, McGraw Hill, 1972.
Strawberries in the Sea.   New York, McGraw Hill, 1973.
Image of a Lover.   New York, McGraw Hill, 1974.
Where the Lost Aprils Are.   New York, McGraw Hill, 1975.
The Dreaming Swimmer.   New York, McGraw Hill, 1976.
An Answer in the Tide.   New York, McGraw Hill, 1978.
A Dancer in Yellow.   New York, McGraw Hill, 1979.
The Devil in Tartan.   New York, McGraw Hill, 1980.
The Silent Ones.   New York, McGraw Hill, 1981.

OTHER PUBLICATIONS

Other (juvenile)

My World Is an Island (for adults; reminiscences).   New York, McGraw Hill, 1950;
    London, Harrap, 1951.
Whistle for a Wind: Maine 1820.   New York, Scribner, 1954.
Blueberry Summer.   New York, McGraw Hill, 1956.
The Fabulous Year.   New York, McGraw Hill, 1958.
How Wide the Heart.   New York, McGraw Hill, 1959.
The Young Islanders.   New York, McGraw Hill, 1960.
Becky's Island.   New York, McGraw Hill, 1961.
Turn Around Twice.   New York, McGraw Hill, 1962; as *Mystery on Hopkins Island*,
    1966.
Ceiling of Amber.   New York, McGraw Hill, 1964.
Masquerade at Sea House.   New York, McGraw Hill, 1965.
The Pigeon Pair.   New York, McGraw Hill, 1967.
Come Aboard and Bring Your Dory.   New York, McGraw Hill, 1969; as *Nobody Knows
    about Tomorrow*, London, Heinemann, 1971.

*   *   *

Elisabeth Ogilvie is a writer in love with landscape. Her passion has been primarily directed toward the coastal islands of Maine, although she has extended it to Scotland in her most recent books. Her descriptions of the physical surroundings of her novels are so detailed and portrait-like that the setting almost becomes another character. By the final chapter of each of her books one is so minutely acquainted with every mood and view of the environment that one could be transported to that place and never feel lost. This sensitivity to scene gives these novels an immediacy and reality not often found in romantic novels today.

It is easy to call Ogilvie's works romantic novels; it is not easy to characterize them more specifically as each of her many books is different. Some, like *The Devil in Tartan*, could be classified as gothics while others, like *A Dancer in Yellow*, are nearly pure suspense. Many of her books are not classifiable beyond the feeling that a thread of romance binds the plot together. Her plots are rich and complex but at the same time easy for the reader to follow. The characters are as vivid as the settings. One feels that these people have lives apart from the span of time covered in the book, that the novel is merely a fascinating slice of a larger life. This feeling is reinforced by the author's ability to use the same characters in a second work as is the case with the cast of *Weep and Know Why*, most of whom appear again with equal success in *The Dreaming Swimmer*.

Even Ogilvie's use of the elements of romance cannot be described in general terms. Often her books conclude at a point that may be the germination of a romantic relationship rather than its culmination. She has also chosen, in *Weep and Know Why* and *The Dreaming Swimmer*, to follow a romance from earliest courtship through comfortable married life.

If there is an area of consistency in these novels it is in the characters of the heroes. Ogilvie seems to admire the taciturn, unemotional male who is deeply sensitive beneath a terse exterior. This is not to say that these men lack individuality or realism. Rather it seems that the writer began with a general type and fleshed him out to meet the demands of each story.

Perhaps the strongest appeal to the reader in Ogilvie's work is the ordinariness of her characters. Even the pseudo-Egyptian princess of *The Face of Innocence* is a normal girl grown into an unremarkable wife and mother. It is the sudden twistings and rearranging of the common events of life that gives rise to the plots. One can identify with these everyday people as they deal with upheavals that may be frightening but are also somehow familiar.

—Susan Quinn Berneis

O'GRADY, Rohan. Pseudonym for June O'Grady Skinner; also writes as A. Carleon. Canadian. Born in Vancouver, British Columbia, 23 July 1922. Married Frederick Snowden Skinner in 1948; three children. Newspaper librarian, then free-lance writer. Agent: Fox Chase Agency, 419 East 57th Street, New York, New York 10022, U.S.A. Address: 1243 River Drive, Port Coquitlam, British Columbia, V3E 1N7, Canada.

ROMANCE AND GOTHIC PUBLICATIONS

Novels

    O'Houlihan's Jest: A Lament for the Irish. New York, Macmillan, and London, Gollancz, 1961.
    Pippin's Journal; or, Rosemary Is for Remembrance. New York, Macmillan, 1962; London, Gollancz, 1963; as *Master of Montrolfe Hall*, New York, Ace, 1965.
    Let's Kill Uncle. New York, Macmillan, 1963; London, Longman, 1964.
    Bleak November. New York, Dial Press, 1970; London, Joseph, 1971.
    The May Spoon (as A. Carleon). New York, Beaufort, 1981.

Rohan O'Grady comments:

Each of my books is entirely different. I can not write to a formula. When an idea comes to me, I am caught up in its web, and am a captive of my characters until the last thread is unwound.

*   *   *

Rohan O'Grady is never predictable and is always intriguing. Each of her books is unique in its depiction of external horrors with internal manifestations.

Pippin's Journal spans several generations, with the sins of the fathers inflicted upon the sons in greater and greater degree. The modern Montrolfe, afflicted by club feet, a chiding Nanny, and a decaying ancestral manor, nearly dies from his encounter with a vengeful, ghostly enchantress. Once a young, beautiful, innocent girl, she tempts, beguiles, and destroys the descendants of the cynical, enigmatic Montrolfe who won her love and took her life. The main part of the book is the story of this strange relationship, her acquisition of the secret of the stolen fortune, her beguiling tricks to keep Montrolfe's favor, and the miscarriage of justice in punishing her supposed murderer. This book is the modern Montrolfe's atonement for his ancestor's crimes.

Let's Kill Uncle is an exciting story of two children who plot the murder of an ex-Commando "Uncle," a cold-blooded killer whose favorite author is the Marquis de Sade and whose past acts have been to eliminate the heirs to the family fortune—ten million dollars. Using hypnotic suggestion, the "uncle" has turned the young boy into a compulsive hooligan and liar to reduce his credibility and to make him more vulnerable to a future "accident." Nonetheless, friendly islanders, a tough but kindly Canadian Mountie, and an aging cougar the children befriend give them the courage to anticipate his acts of terror and death.

Bleak November seems to be the story of a splendid mansion, intentionally aged to hide its chilling past—the scene of multiple murders, a berserk father slaughtering his children. The house itself takes on an aura of horror, frightening and changing its tenants, who gradually glimpse its secrets and learn their previously unrealized ties to its past. There is a demon dog, a failed seance to exorcise ghost, and psychic manifestations of dead children who fill the days and afflict the nights. Finally reality becomes confused and, in an effective twist, the book becomes less a study of a haunted house than of a neurotic, possibly psychotic, narrator.

It is the close characterization and the unexpected final twists that make Rohan O'Grady's work memorable.

—Gina Macdonald

ONSTOTT, Kyle. *See* **HORNER, Lance**.

ORCZY, Baroness (Emma Magdalena Rosalia Maria Josefa Barbara Orczy).   British. Born in Tarna-Ors, Hungary, 23 September 1865. Educated in Brussels and Paris; West London School of Art; Heatherley School of Art, London. Married Montagu Barstow in 1894 (died, 1943); one son. Artist: exhibited work at the Royal Academy, London. *Died 12 November 1947.*

Novels (series: Sir Percy Blakeney, The Scarlet Pimpernel)

The Emperor's Candlesticks. London, Pearson, 1899; New York, Doscher, 1908.
The Scarlet Pimpernel. London, Greening, and New York, Putnam, 1905.
By the Gods Beloved. London, Greening, 1905; as *Beloved of the Gods*, New York,
   Knickerbocker Press, 1905; as *The Gates of Kamt*, New York, Dodd Mead, 1907.
A Son of the People. London, Greening, and New York, Putnam, 1906.
I Will Repay (Pimpernel). London, Greening, and Philadelphia, Lippincott, 1906.
In Mary's Reign. New York, Cupples and Leon, 1907.
The Tangled Skein. London, Greening, 1907.
Beau Brocade. Philadelphia, Lippincott, 1907; London, Greening, 1908.
The Elusive Pimpernel. London, Hutchinson, and New York, Dodd Mead, 1908.
The Nest of the Sparrowhawk. London, Greening, and New York, Stokes, 1909.
Petticoat Government. London, Hutchinson, 1910; as *Petticoat Rule*, New York,
   Doran, 1910.
A True Woman. London, Hutchinson, 1911; as *The Heart of a Woman*, New York,
   Doran, 1911.
Meadowsweet. London, Hutchinson, and New York, Doran, 1912.
Fire in the Stubble. London, Methuen, 1912; as *The Noble Rogue*, New York, Doran,
   1912.
Eldorado: A Story of the Scarlet Pimpernel. London, Hodder and Stoughton, and New
   York, Doran, 1913.
Unto Caesar. London, Hodder and Stoughton, and New York, Doran, 1914.
The Laughing Cavalier. London, Hodder and Stoughton, and New York, Doran, 1914.
A Bride of the Plains. London, Hutchinson, and New York, Doran, 1915.
The Bronze Eagle. London, Hodder and Stoughton, and New York, Doran, 1915.
Leatherface: A Tale of Old Flanders. London, Hodder and Stoughton, and New York,
   Doran, 1916.
A Sheaf of Bluebells. London, Hutchinson, and New York, Doran, 1917.
Lord Tony's Wife: An Adventure of the Scarlet Pimpernel. London, Hodder and
   Stoughton, and New York, Doran, 1917.
Flower o' the Lily. London, Hodder and Stoughton, 1918; New York, Doran, 1919.
The League of the Scarlet Pimpernel. London, Cassell, and New York, Doran, 1919.
His Majesty's Well-Beloved. London, Hodder and Stoughton, and New York, Doran,
   1919.
The First Sir Percy: An Adventure of the Laughing Cavalier. London, Hodder and
   Stoughton, 1920; New York, Doran, 1921.
Nicolette. London, Hodder and Stoughton, and New York, Doran, 1922.
The Triumph of the Scarlet Pimpernel. London, Hodder and Stoughton, and New
   York, Doran, 1922.
The Honourable Jim. London, Hodder and Stoughton, and New York, Doran, 1924.
Pimpernel and Rosemary. London, Cassell, 1924; New York, Doran, 1925.
The Celestial City. London, Hodder and Stoughton, and New York, Doran, 1926.
Sir Percy Hits Back: An Adventure of the Scarlet Pimpernel. London, Hodder and
   Stoughton, and New York, Doran, 1927.
Blue Eyes and Grey. London, Hodder and Stoughton, 1928; New York, Doubleday,
   1929.
Marivosa. London, Cassell, 1930; New York, Doubleday, 1931.
A Child of the Revolution. London, Cassell, and New York, Doubleday, 1932.
A Joyous Adventure. London, Hodder and Stoughton, and New York, Doubleday,
   1932.
The Way of the Scarlet Pimpernel. London, Hodder and Stoughton, 1933; New York,
   Putnam, 1934.
A Spy of Napoleon. London, Hodder and Stoughton, and New York, Putnam, 1934.
The Uncrowned King. London, Hodder and Stoughton, and New York, Putnam, 1935.

Sir Percy Leads the Band. London, Hodder and Stoughton, 1936.
The Divine Folly. London, Hodder and Stoughton, 1937.
No Greater Love. London, Hodder and Stoughton, 1938.
Mam'zelle Guillotine: An Adventure of the Scarlet Pimpernel. London, Hodder and Stoughton, 1940.
Pride of Race. London, Hodder and Stoughton, 1942.
Will-o'-the-Wisp. London, Hutchinson, 1947.

Short Stories

The Traitor. New York, Paget, 1912.
Two Good Patriots. New York, Paget, 1912.
The Old Scarecrow. New York, Paget, 1916.
A Question of Temptation. New York, Doran, 1925.
Adventures of the Scarlet Pimpernel. London, Hutchinson, and New York, Doubleday, 1929.
In the Rue Monge. New York, Doubleday, 1931.

OTHER PUBLICATIONS

Short Stories

The Case of Miss Elliott. London, Unwin, 1905.
The Old Man in the Corner. London, Greening, 1909; as *The Man in the Corner*, New York, Dodd Mead, 1909.
Lady Molly of Scotland Yard. London, Cassell, 1910; New York, Arno, 1976.
The Man in Grey, Being Episodes of the Chouan Conspiracies in Normandy During the First Empire. London, Cassell, and New York, Doran, 1918.
Castles in the Air. London, Cassell, 1921; New York, Doran, 1922.
The Old Man in the Corner Unravels the Mystery of the Khaki Tunic. New York, Doran, 1923.
The Old Man in the Corner Unravels the Mystery of the Pearl Necklace, and The Tragedy in Bishop's Road. New York, Doran, 1924.
The Old Man in the Corner Unravels the Mystery of the Russian Prince and of Dog's Tooth Cliff. New York, Doran, 1924.
The Old Man in the Corner Unravels the Mystery of the White Carnation, and The Montmartre Hat. New York, Doran, 1925.
The Old Man in the Corner Unravels the Mystery of the Fulton Gardens Mystery, and The Moorland Tragedy. New York, Doran, 1925.
The Miser of Maida Vale. New York, Doran, 1925.
Unravelled Knots. London, Hutchinson, 1925; New York, Doran, 1926.
Skin o' My Tooth. London, Hodder and Stoughton, and New York, Doubleday, 1928.

Plays

The Scarlet Pimpernel, with Montagu Barstow (produced Nottingham, 1903; London, 1905; New York, 1910).
The Sin of William Jackson, with Montagu Barstow (produced London, 1906).
Beau Brocade, with Montagu Barstow, adaptation of the novel by Orczy (produced Eastbourne, Sussex, and London, 1908).
The Duke's Wager (produced Manchester, 1911).
The Legion of Honour, adaptation of her novel *A Sheaf of Bluebells* (produced Bradford, 1918; London, 1921).

Leatherface, with Caryl Fiennes, adaptation of the novel by Orczy (produced Portsmouth and London, 1922).

Other

Les Beaux et les Dandys des Grands Siècles en Angleterre. Monaco, Société des Conférences, 1924.
The Scarlet Pimpernel Looks at the World (essays). London, John Heritage, 1933.
The Turbulent Duchess: H.R.H. Madame le Duchesse de Berri. London, Hodder and Stoughton, 1935; New York, Putnam, 1936.
Links in the Chain of Life (autobiography). London, Hutchinson, 1947.

Editor and Translator, with Montagu Barstow, *Old Hungarian Fairy Tales.* London, Dean, and Philadelphia, Wolf, 1895.
Editor and Translator, *The Enchanted Cat* (fairy tales). London, Dean, 1895.
Editor and Translator, *Fairyland's Beauty* (*The Suitors of Princess Fire-fly*). London, Dean, 1895.
Editor and Translator, *Uletka and the White Lizard* (fairy tales). London, Dean, 1895.

*   *   *

Romance in Baroness Orczy's stories is at more than one level, for she tackles with panache the romanticism of historical and improbably heroic adventures as well as sexual love. The shadow of the guillotine seems an unlikely breeding ground for the tender passion, but this is most potently conveyed in *The Scarlet Pimpernel* and its sequels which had as their background the French Revolution. Orczy's books are highly wrought and intensely atmospheric. There are vivid contrasts between the rabble-ridden, blood-running, and squalid streets of revolutionary Paris and the glittering splendorous of the court of King George III in England.

Sir Percy Blakeney seems to have been equally at home in both, ringing the changes from appearing at London balls and supper-parties as one of the Prince of Wales's favourite associates, to disguising himself as a "loathsome" looking old "jew trader," or some smelly market-hag or fisherman in order to whisk innocent potential victims away from the fury of the French mob, and the ever-devouring "Mam'zelle Guillotine." Those whom he rescued were more often than not aristocratic, and he drew his band of helpers—"The League of the Scarlet Pimpernel"—from the same class (Sir Andrew Ffoulkes, Lord Antony Dewhurst, Lord Hastings, etc.).

Generally speaking, artisans and even middle-class people did not show up too well in Baroness Orczy's stories. In spite of her attraction to strongly chivalric ideas, she writes about the "lower orders" with a distinct air of patronage and condescension, especially if they step out of line and fail to respect their "betters." (And, of course, nothing could be more disrespectful than putting the heads of these betters under the guillotine!)

Sir Percy, however, falls heavily in love with someone from a different class *and* a foreigner to boot—Marguerite St. Just, a French actress of considerable beauty and accomplishment who, until she recognizes the ruthless nature of the Revolution, is a republican. Naturally their married relationship is at first fraught with misunderstandings, and to conceal from Marguerite—as well as the rest of the world—that he is the Scarlet Pimpernel, Sir Percy assumes the role of inept but fashionable fop. Readers, of course, suspect his secret from the early stages of the first book, mainly because the foppish exterior never quite conceals his inner reserves of strength, humour, and compassion, or his romantic but slightly sardonic sense of chivalry: "The commands of a beautiful woman are binding on all mankind, even Cabinet Ministers...."

The action of the plot demands that the identity of the Scarlet Pimpernel, intrepid arch-enemy of the French Revolutionary government, *has* to be revealed to his friends and enemies at the end of the first book. Those that followed never quite achieved the same sense of drama or splendid style—but they were always rich in romantic interest. In different books from those in the Scarlet Pimpernel series, Barones Orczy created other gallant and upright English aristocrats but they lacked the charisma of Sir Percy and his associates.

Strangely enough, everything that worked so well in Orczy's creation of Sir Percy seems to have misfired when a little later on she produced a female righter-of-wrongs. In *Lady Molly of Scotland Yard*, the heroine from whom the book derives its name is, like Sir Percy, aristocratic, enigmatic, plucky, and adept at assuming disguises. But whereas Sir Percy remains a complex and endearing character, Lady Molly comes across as an arch and self-indulgent poseuse. However, although her place in literature is in the detective genre rather than the love-story, she is as much a romantic as Sir Percy. Unlike him, she never actually has to rescue her spouse from the threat of the guillotine—but she *does* vindicate his honour and secures his release from unjust imprisonment.

Baroness Orczy was adept not only in different literary genres but with different literary forms. *The Scarlet Pimpernel* was originally a successful play co-authored by Orczy and her husband Montagu Barstow. It was then re-written by the Baroness as a beautifully balanced and, of course, bestselling novel. All the other novels in the series are entertaining and dramatic, especially *The Elusive Pimpernel* and *I Will Repay*. In *Adventures of the Scarlet Pimpernel* she skilfully manipulates the romantic/suspense short story.

—Mary Cadogan

ØVSTEDAL, Barbara.   *See* **LAKER, Rosalind**.

PARGETER, Edith (Mary).   Also writes as Ellis Peters.   British.   Born in Horsehay, Shropshire, 28 September 1913. Educated at Dawley Church of England Elementary School, Shropshire; Coalbrookdale High School for Girls, Oxford School Certificate. Served in the Women's Royal Navy Service, 1940-45: British Empire Medal, 1944. Worked as a chemist's assistant, Dawley, 1933-40. Recipient: Mystery Writers of America Edgar Allan Poe Award, 1963; Czechoslovak Society for International Relations Gold Medal, 1968; Crime Writers Association Silver Dagger, 1981. Fellow, International Institute of Arts and Letters, 1961. Agent: Deborah Owen, 78 Narrow Street, London E14 8BP. Address: Parkville, Park Lane, Madeley, Telford, Shropshire TF7 5HE, England.

ROMANCE AND GOTHIC PUBLICATIONS

Novels (series: Brothers of Gwynedd)

> *Hortensius, Friend of Nero*.   London, Lovat Dickson, 1936; New York, Greystone Press, 1937.
> *Iron-Bound*.   London, Lovat Dickson, 1936.
> *The City Lies Foursquare*.   London, Heinemann, and New York, Reynal, 1939.

Ordinary People.   London, Heinemann, 1941; as *People of My Own*, New York, Reynal, 1942.
She Goes to War.   London, Heinemann, 1942.
The Eighth Champion of Christendom.   London, Heinemann, 1945.
Reluctant Odyssey.   London, Heinemann, 1946.
Warfare Accomplished.   London, Heinemann, 1947.
The Fair Young Phoenix.   London, Heinemann, 1948.
By Firelight.   London, Heinemann, 1948; as *By This Strange Fire*, New York, Reynal, 1948.
Lost Children.   London, Heinemann, 1951.
Holiday with Violence.   London, Heinemann, 1952.
This Rough Magic.   London, Heinemann, 1953.
Most Loving Mere Folly.   London, Heinemann, 1953.
The Soldier at the Door.   London, Heinemann, 1954.
A Means of Grace.   London, Heinemann, 1956.
The Heaven Tree.   London, Heinemann, and New York, Doubleday, 1960.
The Green Branch.   London, Heinemann, 1962.
The Scarlet Seed.   London, Heinemann, 1963.
A Bloody Field by Shrewsbury.   London, Macmillan, 1972; New York, Viking Press, 1973.
Sunrise in the West (Gwynedd).   London, Macmillan, 1974.
The Dragon at Noonday (Gwynedd).   London, Macmillan, 1975.
The Hounds of Sunset (Gwynedd).   London, Macmillan, 1976.
Afterglow and Nightfall (Gwynedd).   London, Macmillan, 1977.
The Marriage of Meggotta.   London, Macmillan, and New York, Viking Press, 1979.

Short Stories

The Lily Hand and Other Stories.   London, Macmillan, 1965.

OTHER PUBLICATIONS

Novels as Ellis Peters

Fallen into the Pit (as Edith Pargeter).   London, Heinemann, 1951.
Death Mask.   London, Collins, 1959; New York, Doubleday, 1960.
The Will and the Deed.   London, Collins, 1960; as *Where There's a Will*, New York, Doubleday, 1960; as *The Will and the Deed*, New York, Avon, 1966.
Death and the Joyful Woman.   London, Collins, 1961; New York, Doubleday, 1962.
Funeral of Figaro.   London, Collins, 1962; New York, Morrow, 1964.
Flight of a Witch.   London, Collins, 1964.
A Nice Derangement of Epitaphs.   London, Collins, 1965; as *Who Lies Here?*, New York, Morrow, 1965.
The Piper on the Mountain.   London, Collins, and New York, Morrow, 1966.
Black Is the Colour of My True-Love's Heart.   London, Collins, and New York, Doubleday, 1967.
The Grass-Widow's Tale.   London, Collins, and New York, Doubleday, 1968.
The House of Green Turf.   London, Collins, and New York, Morrow, 1969.
Mourning Raga.   London, Macmillan, 1969; New York, Morrow, 1970.
The Knocker on Death's Door.   London, Macmillan, 1970; New York, Morrow, 1971.
Death to the Landlords.   London, Macmillan, and New York, Morrow, 1972.
City of Gold and Shadows.   London, Macmillan, 1973; New York, Morrow, 1974.
The Horn of Roland.   London, Macmillan, and New York, Morrow, 1974.
Never Pick Up Hitch-Hikers!   London, Macmillan, and New York, Morrow, 1976.

A Morbid Taste for Bones: A Mediaeval Whodunnit. London, Macmillan, 1977; New York, Morrow, 1978.
Rainbow's End. London, Macmillan, 1978; New York, Morrow, 1979.
One Corpse Too Many. London, Macmillan, 1979; New York, Morrow, 1980.
Monk's-Hood. London, Macmillan, 1980; New York, Morrow, 1981.
Saint Peter's Fair. London, Macmillan, and New York, Morrow, 1981.
The Leper of Saint Giles. London, Macmillan, 1981; New York, Morrow, 1982.
The Virgin in the Ice. London, Macmillan, 1982.

Short Stories

The Assize of the Dying. London, Heinemann, and New York, Doubleday, 1958.

Plays

Radio Plays: *Mourning Raga* (as Ellis Peters), from her own novel, 1971; *The Heaven Tree*, 1975.

Other

The Coast of Bohemia. London, Heinemann, 1950.

Translator, *Tales of the Little Quarter: Stories*, by Jan Neruda. London, Heinemann, 1957; New York, Greenwood Press, 1976.
Translator, *The Sorrowful and Heroic Life of John Amos Comenius*, by Frantisek Kosík. Prague, State Educational Publishing House, 1958.
Translator, *A Handful of Linden Leaves: An Anthology of Czech Poetry*. Prague, Arta, 1958.
Translator, *Don Juan*, by Josef Toman. London, Heinemann, and New York, Knopf, 1958.
Translator, *The Abortionists*, by Valja Stýblová. London, Secker and Warburg, 1961.
Translator, *Granny*, by Bozena Nemcová. Prague, Artia, 1962; New York, Greenwood Press, 1976.
Translator, with others, *The Linden Tree* (anthology). Prague, Artia, 1962.
Translator, *The Terezín Requiem*, by Josef Bor. London, Heinemann, and New York, Knopf, 1963.
Translator, *Legends of Old Bohemia*, by Alois Jirásek. London, Hamlyn, 1963.
Translator, *May*, by Karel Hynek Mácha. Prague, Artia, 1965.
Translator, *The End of the Old Times*, by Vladislav Vancura. Prague, Artia, 1965.
Translator, *A Close Watch on the Trains*, by Bohumil Hrabal. London, Cape, 1968.
Translator, *Report on My Husband*, by Josefa Slánská. London, Macmillan, 1969.
Translator, *A Ship Named Hope*, by Ivan Klíma. London, Gollancz, 1970.
Translator, *Mozart in Prague*, by Jaroslav Seifert. Prague, Orbis, 1970.

*   *   *

A writer of many historical novels and mysteries, Edith Pargeter has special appeal for the romance/gothic reader through the medieval setting of so many of her works. Mystery fans have long been fascinated by her stories under the pseudonym Ellis Peters, which, along with many of her other novels, are often set in England's Middle Ages.

After publishing *The Marriage of Megotta*, Pargeter revealed that in writing historical novels she seems "to have retreated into the thirteenth century for keeps." This statement has a ring of truth since so many of her tales take place in that turbulent milieu. Her realistic depiction of daily hardships suffered by the common people, as well as of political intrigues among the nobility speaks clearly of thorough research. As examples, the wars and border skirmishes between England and Wales which dominated that era get close but fair scrutiny, and the often terrifying, quixotic behavior of the English monarchs is intelligently analyzed. She writes in the stylized prose generally associated with medieval historical fiction and carries it off well, managing to create in each character a distinct personality and a unique voice.

Her stories are not those of knights in shining armour riding out to rescue fair maidens but of real people caught in tragic events often not of their doing. In *The Heaven Tree* Harry Talvace discovers the cruelty of King John's character when the monarch orders the death of a young boy, Owen, foster son of the Welsh Prince Llewellyn. Harry's intense sense of justice will not allow him to stand by while this sentence is carried out. At the risk of his own life he engineers Owen's safe return to Wales. Later Llewellyn shows his gratitude by offering sanctuary to Harry's wife and infant son. *The Marriage of Megotta*, one of Pargeter's more recent novels, offers the poignant tale of two young people, Megotta and Richard, whose love has the purity and innocence reminiscent of Romeo and Juliet. But the scheming world of Henry III's court tears them apart and eventually causes the death of Megotta.

Pargeter's novels evoke the harsh realism of medieval life without dwelling on the brutality. This glossing over of unpleasantries sometimes leads to scenes and dialog that seem melodramatic, but the author's storytelling ability keeps the action moving and does not allow this to become a distraction.

—Patricia Altner

PARGETER, Margaret. British. Born in Northumberland. Widow; two sons. Address: c/o Mills and Boon Ltd., 15-16 Brooks Mews, London W1A 1DR, England.

ROMANCE AND GOTHIC PUBLICATIONS

Novels

Winds from the Sea. London, Mills and Boon, and Toronto, Harlequin, 1975.
The Kilted Stranger. London, Mills and Boon, 1975; Toronto, Harlequin, 1976.
Ride a Black Horse. London, Mills and Boon, 1975; Toronto, Harlequin, 1976.
Stormy Rapture. London, Mills and Boon, and Toronto, Harlequin, 1976.
Hold Me Captive. London, Mills and Boon, and Toronto, Harlequin, 1976.
Blue Skies, Dark Waters. London, Mills and Boon, 1976; Toronto, Harlequin, 1977.
Better to Forget. London, Mills and Boon, 1977; Toronto, Harlequin, 1978.
Never Go Back. Toronto, Harlequin, 1977.
The Jewelled Caftan. London, Mills and Boon, and Toronto, Harlequin, 1978.
Flamingo Moon. Toronto, Harlequin, 1978.
A Man Called Cameron. London, Mills and Boon, 1978.
Wild Inheritance. Toronto, Harlequin, 1978.
Marriage Impossible. London, Mills and Boon, 1978.
Midnight Magic. London, Mills and Boon, and Toronto, Harlequin, 1978.
The Wild Rowan. London, Mills and Boon, 1978; Toronto, Harlequin, 1979.
Autumn Song. London, Mills and Boon, 1979.
Boomerang Bride. London, Mills and Boon, 1979; Toronto, Harlequin, 1981.
The Devil's Bride. London, Mills and Boon, 1979.

Only You.   London, Mills and Boon, 1979.
Savage Possession.   London, Mills and Boon, 1979; Toronto, Harlequin, 1980.
Kiss of a Tyrant.   London, Mills and Boon, and Toronto, Harlequin, 1980.
Deception.   London, Mills and Boon, 1980; Toronto, Harlequin, 1981.
Dark Surrender.   London, Mills and Boon, 1980; Toronto, Harlequin, 1981.
The Dark Oasis.   London, Mills and Boon, 1980; Toronto, Harlequin, 1981.
The Loving Slave.   London, Mills and Boon, 1981.
Captivity.   London, Mills and Boon, and Toronto, Harlequin, 1981.

*   *   *

Margaret Pargeter is a relatively new British romance writer. She began being published in the mid-1970's and has continued since then to develop her own style of writing. It is a style that has instantly made her one of the more popular romance writers in years.

She is also one of the "new" romance writers who aims for realism by drawing on modern "literary" techniques of writing. Her plots are generally complicated as are her characters. Inner turmoil plays a constant counter-point as the heroine reacts to events in the novel and her own hopeless love for her hero. Tension, pathos, and despair provide constant reaction for her readers as she maintains near melodramatic levels of stress.

Her early novels do not have this heightened emotionalism, although they do have refreshing plots and well-balanced characters. *Better to Forget* and *Ride a Black Horse* are both in this traditional vein. Liza Dean in *Better to Forget* helps to prevent a fire in the large department store she works in. The shock of the accident and her own emotional problems cause Liza to lose her memory. She is taken care of by Grant Latham, the wealthy owner of the store. Jane Brown in *Ride a Black Horse* applies for a job in an exclusive stables and riding school at High Linton. She gets the job by falsifying her background. She eventually runs away after falling in love with the owner, Karl Grierson. Both of these novels depend on standard reactions and conflicts within the story.

Her recent novels have more complicated dimensions that quickly illustrate the complex development of character and Margaret Pargeter's development as a writer. In *The Devil's Bride* Sandra is forced by her cousin Alexandra into taking her place after her fiancé, Stein Freeman, is blinded in an accident. He is a well-known writer who spends much of his time in Greece. He discovers the deception and forces Sandra to marry him and return to Greece with him. His treatment of her is cruel and vindictive as he takes out his frustrations and anger on her. There is a constant pressure on Sandra as she grows to love him in spite of his action. Conflict is intense, and reader reaction is just as intense, for emotional buildup is continued and heightened until the very end of the novel.

Even more intense is *Boomerang Bride*. The character development is extremely complex and shows a wealth of complicated emotional reactions. In fact, it comes close to being a psychological study rather than a romance. The central thrust of the plot centers on the McLeods, an "Outback" station family. Only Wade McLeod and his grandfather are left, and their relationship is one of extreme dislike that borders on hate. The grandfather almost fanatically wants an heir for the station. In revenge, and hoping to prevent his grandfather's wishes from coming true, Wade marries Vicki. She is a temporary home-help and he considers her very ineligible. He presents his proposition as a business arrangement and Vicki agrees. He is determined not to have children! His passion and Vicki's unconscious provocation end that, however, and she becomes pregnant. Furious, Wade orders her to leave the station and she does—only to be brought back four years later with their son, Graham. The course of the story picks up their relationship and the final outcome centers on the people as they face the changes that have taken place over these years.

In assessing Margaret Pargeter as a writer, one must keep in mind the tremendous changes that have taken place in romance writing over the past few years. Many of these novels are filled with modern writing techniques and have a slightly different frame of reference than just romance. Stream of consciousness plays a much greater part in the novels, as does a more sophisticated outlook. Because of these elements, Margaret Pargeter probably appeals to a somewhat different audience from the traditional romance readers. She is also one of the

Harlequin Presents writers. These writers tend to show modern love against more complicated and emotional backgrounds.

—Arlene Moore

PAUL, Barbara.   *See* **LAKER, Rosalind.**

PAULEY, Barbara Anne (née Cotton).   American.   Born in Nashville, Tennessee, 12 January 1925. Attended Wellesley College, Cambridge, Massachusetts, 1942. Married Robert Reinhold Pauley in 1946; one daughter and three sons. Editorial assistant, Ideal Publishing Corporation, then free-lance writer. Agent: Blassingame McCauley and Wood, 60 East 42nd Street, Suite 924, New York, New York 10017. Address: 97 Larch Row, Wenham, Massachusetts 01984, U.S.A.

ROMANCE AND GOTHIC PUBLICATIONS

Novels

   Blood Kin. New York, Doubleday, 1972.
   Voices Long Hushed. New York, Doubleday, 1976.

*   *   *

To capture the passions, conflicts, and terrors of the Civil War, Barbara Anne Pauley focuses on a microcosm, an individual and familial situation, that reflects the broader problems of the times. *Blood Kin* focuses on a young Southern miss whose disillusionment and longing for lost relationships and the pleasures of a lost youth lead her to visit neighboring cousins, Union sympathizers firmly entrenched in a symbol of the dying South—a stately family plantation house. In *Voices Long Hushed* a young New England girl seeks her dubious heritage on a Southern plantation, ravaged by war, yet kept operative by poor, dependent Southern relations. In both, the conflicts, like those of the war itself, are family conflicts in which distant relatives conspire against the central characters—to acquire land or wealth or love, to hide sins, to work out personal hatreds.

In *Blood Kin* Leslie Hallam, deprived of family, land, and childhood by war, seeks to recreate her lost world of aristocratic and social comforts at Sycamore Knob, a magnificent Nashville plantation. She arrives amid stormy weather, only to find a more terrifying storm within, a frightening psychological turbulence beneath surface calm: a child terrorized by a nameless "bad thing" that haunts her nights and leaves her clothing bloodied; a fat, pasty-faced

537

woman, once beautiful, whose greed and passions make her strike out in jealousy; her arrogant brother, a model of decadent aristocratic weakness; a dashing, self-possessed confederate soldier, the family black sheep, seemingly crushed by his own spirited steed; a mysteriously wounded head of house whose wit, spirit, and sexuality capture the heart of a vulnerable cousin; a kindly Union officer who suspects but cannot prove fearful undercurrents and dangerous conspiracies. Nightmarish sequences follow: a deadly game of hide and seek, an attic excursion that nearly ends in death by fire, a mad dash in a swift carriage—fleeing madness only to find secret madness inescapable. Amid such gothic horrors, romance blossoms, first in the sudden, physical passion that draws together an experienced man-of-the-world and an inno-cent girl, and then a gentler, self-giving love that grows with time and proximity.

In *Voices Long Hushed* an uncle's will shatters a young orphan's tranquility. The loss of a lover and the discovery of a live mother, possibly a murderess and a madwoman, compel her to seek the truth of her inheritance at St. Cloud, her mother's plantation. There Stacy begins to untangle the web of deceit spun by an odd assortment of distant, conniving relatives. Her realization that her mother's innocence means another's guilt awakens the conflicts that produced the first murder 25 years before, and once again murder stalks the balconies and shadowy galleries of the old manor. A chain of gothic horrors ensues: an elevator shaft left open in the dark, a poisonous snake left in a bedroom, a slave dead in a trunk, a locked-room murder, a deadly drug that simulates insanity. As three men try to impose their will on pliable Stacy, relationships prove skewed; family hatreds and pre-war wounds are exposed. Destroying the evil depends on a cryptic journal hidden in a slave cabin and restoration of an amnesiac's memory by recreating childhood terror. Ultimately, the young Northern heiress finds her place in the South, and chooses a relationship tangled forever in the tight emotional knots of love and murder, of father killing father.

Together these novels seek to expose and exorcise the terrors and evils that separate brother from brother—the essence, for Pauley, of Civil War conflict—while suggesting the strength that allows one to build from ties on the shaky ground of old horrors, atrocities, and passions.

—Gina Macdonald

PEAKE, Lilian. British. Born in London. Married; has children. Has worked as secretary, typist, and journalist: reporter in High Wycombe, fashion writer in London, and writer for *Daily Herald* and *Woman* magazine. Address: c/o Mills and Boon Ltd., 15-16 Brooks Mews, London W1A 1DR, England.

ROMANCE AND GOTHIC PUBLICATIONS

Novels

Man of Granite.   London, Mills and Boon, 1971; Toronto, Harlequin, 1975.
This Moment in Time.   London, Mills and Boon, 1971; Toronto, Harlequin, 1972.
The Library Tree.   London, Mills and Boon, and Toronto, Harlequin, 1972.
Man Out of Reach.   London, Mills and Boon, 1972; Toronto, Harlequin, 1973.
The Real Thing.   London, Mills and Boon, 1972; Toronto, Harlequin, 1973.
A Girl Alone.   London, Mills and Boon, 1972; Toronto, Harlequin, 1978.
Mist Across the Moors.   London, Mills and Boon, and Toronto, Harlequin, 1972.
No Friend of Mine.   London, Mills and Boon, 1972; Toronto, Harlequin, 1977.

Gone Before Morning.   London, Mills and Boon, and Toronto, Harlequin, 1973.
Man in Charge.   London, Mills and Boon, and Toronto, Harlequin, 1973.
Familiar Stranger.   London, Mills and Boon, 1973; Toronto, Harlequin, 1976.
Till the End of Time.   London, Mills and Boon, 1973; Toronto, Harlequin, 1975.
The Dream on the Hill.   London, Mills and Boon, 1974; Toronto, Harlequin, 1975.
A Sense of Belonging.   London, Mills and Boon, and Toronto, Harlequin, 1974.
Master of the House.   London, Mills and Boon, and Toronto, Harlequin, 1974.
The Impossible Marriage.   Toronto, Harlequin, 1975.
Moonrise over the Mountains.   London, Mills and Boon, 1975; Toronto, Harlequin, 1976.
Heart in the Sunlight.   London, Mills and Boon, 1975; Toronto, Harlequin, 1976.
The Tender Night.   London, Mills and Boon, 1975; Toronto, Harlequin, 1976.
The Sun of Summer.   London, Mills and Boon, 1975; Toronto, Harlequin, 1976.
A Bitter Loving.   London, Mills and Boon, 1976; Toronto, Harlequin, 1977.
The Distant Dream.   London, Mills and Boon, and Toronto, Harlequin, 1976.
The Little Impostor.   London, Mills and Boon, 1976; Toronto, Harlequin, 1977.
Somewhere to Lay My Head.   London, Mills and Boon, and Toronto, Harlequin, 1977.
Passionate Involvement.   London, Mills and Boon, 1977; Toronto, Harlequin, 1978.
No Second Parting.   London, Mills and Boon, 1977.
This Man Her Enemy.   Toronto, Harlequin, 1977.
Day of Possession.   London, Mills and Boon, 1978.
Rebel in Love.   London, Mills and Boon, and Toronto, Harlequin, 1978.
Run for Your Love.   London, Mills and Boon, 1978; Toronto, Harlequin, 1980.
Dangerous Deception.   London, Mills and Boon, 1979; Toronto, Harlequin, 1980.
Enemy from the Past.   London, Mills and Boon, and Toronto, Harlequin, 1979.
Stranger on the Beach.   London, Mills and Boon, and Toronto, Harlequin, 1979.
Promise at Midnight.   London, Mills and Boon, 1980; Toronto, Harlequin, 1981.
A Ring for a Fortune.   London, Mills and Boon, and Toronto, Harlequin, 1980.
A Secret Affair.   London, Mills and Boon, 1980; Toronto, Harlequin, 1981.
Strangers into Lovers.   London, Mills and Boon, and Toronto, Harlequin, 1981.
Gregg Barratt's Woman.   London, Mills and Boon, and Toronto, Harlequin, 1981.
Across a Crowded Room.   Toronto, Harlequin, 1981.

*   *   *

Lilian Peake, a Mills and Boon/Harlequin Books author, has written several romances a year for over a decade without writing herself out, without overly-much repetition (except for the basic theme) from book to book, and without deterioration in quality. Her readability is high, and, surprisingly, the 21st book one reads is as entertaining as the first. She is a good, even superior, stylist, and her background enables her to give an accurate fine-tuned picture of contemporary English domestic and working life. Her limitation, if it is one in this genre, is that she writes the same story over each time, like variations on a musical theme. Her heroines are teachers, secretaries, department store buyers, laboratory assistants, or housekeepers. They are always in a subordinate position to some arrogant, overbearing, sardonic, but attractive man, with whom they have a running battle, interspersed with numerous romantic encounters, until the last pages of the story when the barriers are finally swept away. The novels are set in various parts of England, with the Yorkshire moors figuring several times (*Run for Your Love, The Tender Night*, and *Mist Across the Moors*). *The Sun of Summer* takes place on a Rhine cruise, and *Passionate Involvement* is set in Switzerland. The settings in the every-day English world serve to lend a patina of realism to balance the really heady romance in the novels. Events somehow always transpire to throw hero and heroine together in provocative situations. There are trips to conventions and scientific meetings, shared hotel rooms, school excursions and camping trips with shared sleeping bags. Sometimes there is a marriage of convenience, as in *Somewhere to Lay My Head* and *No Second Parting*, or a pretend engagement as in *Master of the House*. Whatever the circumstances the battle of the sexes goes on to the last. *Gone Before Morning* and *The Tender Night* are two of Peake's best stories. In the former a misogynist determined not to be trapped into marriage by his housekeeper finds himself succumbing, and in the latter a woman jilted by her fiancé is resolved not to fall in love again, but of course finds the one man who overcomes her resistance. Although Peake's novels are essentially backdrops in which she can place the many love scenes which are the purpose for the stories, it is remarkable how good style and well-fleshed-out plots, with lots of detail of every-day life, can produce such enjoyable results.

—Necia A. Musser

PEDLER, Margaret (Bass).   British.   Married.

ROMANCE AND GOTHIC PUBLICATIONS

Novels

This Splendid Folly.   London, Mills and Boon, 1918; New York, Doran, 1921.
The House of Dreams-Come-True.   London, Hodder and Stoughton, and New York, Doran, 1919.
The Hermit of Far End.   London, Hodder and Stoughton, 1919; New York, Doran, 1920.
The Lamp of Fate.   London, Hodder and Stoughton, 1920; New York, Doran, 1921.
The Moon Out of Reach.   London, Hodder and Stoughton, and New York, Doran, 1921.
The Vision of Desire.   London, Hodder and Stoughton, and New York, Doran, 1922.
The Barbarian Lover.   London, Hodder and Stoughton, and New York, Doran, 1923.
Red Ashes.   London, Hodder and Stoughton, 1924; New York, Doran, 1925.
The Better Love.   New York, Doran, 1924.
Her Brother's Keeper.   New York, Doran, 1924.
Mrs. Daventry's Reputation.   New York, Doran, 1924.
To-morrow's Tangle.   London, Hodder and Stoughton, 1925; New York, Doran, 1926.
Yesterday's Harvest.   London, Hodder and Stoughton, and New York, Doran, 1926.
Bitter Heritage.   London, Hodder and Stoughton, and New York, Doubleday, 1928.
The Guarded Halo.   London, Hodder and Stoughton, and New York, Doubleday, 1929.
Fire of Youth.   London, Hodder and Stoughton, and New York, Doubleday, 1930.
Many Ways.   London, Hodder and Stoughton, 1931.
Kindled Flame.   London, Hodder and Stoughton, and New York, Doubleday, 1931.
Desert Sand.   London, Hodder and Stoughton, and New York, Doubleday, 1932.
Pitiless Choice.   London, Hodder and Stoughton, 1933.
The Greater Courage.   New York, Doubleday, 1933.
Green Judgment.   London, Hodder and Stoughton, 1934; as *Distant Dawn*, New York, Doubleday, 1934.
The Shining Cloud.   London, Hodder and Stoughton, 1935; New York, Doubleday, 1936.
Flame in the Wind.   London, Hodder and Stoughton, and New York, Doubleday, 1937.
No Armour Against Fate.   London, Hodder and Stoughton, and New York, Doubleday, 1938.
Blind Loyalty.   London, Hodder and Stoughton, and New York, Doubleday, 1940.
Not Heaven Itself.   London, Hodder and Stoughton, 1940; New York, Doubleday, 1941.

Then Came the Test. London, Hodder and Stoughton, and New York, Doubleday, 1942.
No Gifts from Chance. London, Hodder and Stoughton, and New York, McBride, 1944.
Unless Two Be Agreed. London, Hodder and Stoughton, and New York, McBride, 1947.

Short Stories

Waves of Destiny. London, Hodder and Stoughton, and New York, Doran, 1924.
Checkered Paths. London, Hodder and Stoughton, 1935.

*   *   *

The stereotyped heroine of the 1930's was uncertain whether she wished to be liberated from man or dominated by him. It is indicative of this confusion (which was replacing the spiritual confusion on matters of the soul, of earlier heroines) that she often seeks out a lover who is paradoxically both fierce yet gentle, who can kiss with stormy, sudden passion, while simultaneously maintaining a "strange and lingering gentleness." This quality of kissing, difficult though it may be to achieve, is clearly seen as an attractive characteristic, for it has been adopted by a number of present-day heroes, who manage to kiss with "fierce yet tender passion."

Margaret Pedler went even further than just fierce tenderness, and invented in *The Barbarian Lover*, a strong, hard, arrogant man with sun-burned hatchet face, and obstinate straight-lipped mouth. He strides about the wide open spaces of the earth in travel-stained riding-kit, always on hand to rescue the heroine from whatever dangerous and unlikely situation she has got herself into. His first act of bravery and chivalry is to save her from a man-eating tiger seconds before it gobbles her up. Later, he rescues her when she is struck by lightning in a forest. He saves her from her bolting horse. He finally concludes that she is over-civilised and if only she would go camping with him, this would make a real woman of her.

"Or a savage," retorted Patricia.
"I suppose that's what you set me down for, isn't it?"
"I certainly think you're—primitive," she returned.
"So is God; so is nature. I don't want to be anything else. After all, it's the big primitive things that count."

The big primitive things in his life are birth, death, and the urgent desire to kiss her. Being a barbarian, he takes what he wants in every fibre of his being: "There was a fire in his eyes—a flaming light of passion barely held in leash that terrified her. He caught her roughly in his arms. His mouth sought hers, straining against it in fierce, possessive kisses. The love and passion which his iron will had thwarted and held back for months surged over her now in a resistless torrent. The gates had been opened. They could never again be closed."

Though to some extent afraid of this man's unleashed instincts, the girl ultimately gives in to her growing love for him, and learns to lie back and enjoy that fierce, barbarian, yet strangely gentle kissing, to yield tremulously to the imperious passion.

The Barbarian Lover was sold, in its first, 1923, version as one of "Hodders Ninepenny Series" in a jaunty jacket showing the barbarian lover himself, clutched at by the girl behind, both superimposed over a crossword puzzle. "First Read the Book," the jacket commands. "Then do the crossword." When re-issued in 1938; it was abridged.

Margaret Pedler's other 30-odd titles share similar tangled emotions, and unleashed passion.

—Rachel Anderson

PETER, Elizabeth O.

Novels

Confident Tomorrows. London, Hurst and Blackett, 1931.
The Third Miss Chance. London, Hurst and Blackett, 1933.
Familiar Treatment. London, Hurst and Blackett, 1940.
At Professor Chummy's. London, Sampson Low, 1946.
Compromise with Yesterday. London, Sampson Low, 1946.

* * *

Elizabeth O. Peter wrote only a few novels in the 1930's and early 1940's. There is, however, considerable development in style and mood between the first (*Confident Tomorrows*, 1931) and the last (*Compromise with Yesterday*, 1946). Both deal with the effects of war on romance. The melodrama and set-piece stiff-upper-lip situations of *Confident Tomorrows* fail to convince, but the unashamedly romantic plot of *Compromise with Yesterday* is skilfully and touchingly manipulated.

The first book was probably partly inspired by R.C. Sherriff's *Journey's End*. Jerry Mainwaring is, like Stanhope in Sherriff's play, only able to see the war through by taking to drink. He survives the first world war, but is by then an incurable alcoholic. Thelma ("Tim"), the wife who has adored him ever since they both were children, remains loyal—in spite of Jerry's drunkenness, debts, and degradation. But gradually she and Jerry's friend Michael fall in love, though they nobly damp down their feelings until almost the end of the book. Jerry's increasing depravity through drink, and his repeated reconciliations with Thelma lack conviction, mainly because the book's language is so often stilted: "Timmy...take me back. Let me be your husband again, and your lover, and your pal." But the romantic triangle is ultimately resolved successfully when, after Jerry strikes Thelma, Michael declares his love, and Jerry—as usual the worse for drink—gets killed in an accident.

By contrast, *Compromise with Yesterday* is vivid and compulsive from the beginning. David Allen, a first world war pilot who has become an Air Commodore in the RAF by the time of Hitler's war, represents not only the vulnerability of youthful romance but the potency of remembered love affairs. These are, of course, as Elizabeth O. Peter writes, "more powerful, more relentless than the living presence, which might disappoint or cease to enchant." The author uses the clichés of wartime romantic fiction with aplomb. Her descriptions of snatched meetings between lovers on leave and the fear of sudden death that formed the background of so many people's lives make haunting and memorable reading.

This novel gets as deeply under the emotional skin as, for example, Noël Coward's celebrated drama *Cavalcade*, which was also, like *Compromise with Yesterday*, a family saga of two wars and the years between. Elizabeth O. Peter uses the sweet-savage images of romance with such impact and intensity that it is surprising she did not follow up her last novel with further love stories.

—Mary Cadogan

PETERS, Maureen. Also writes as Veronica Black; Catherine Darby; Levanah Lloyd; Judith Rothman; Sharon Whitby. British. Born in Caernarvon, Wales, 3 March 1935. Educated at Caernarvon Grammar School, 1945-52; University College, Bangor, 1952-56, B.A. 1956, Dip.Ed. Married and divorced twice; two sons and two daughters. Address: Cae Ceridwen, Rhosbodrval, Caernarvon, Wales.

Novels

Elizabeth the Beloved.   London, Hale, 1965; New York, Beagle, 1972.
Katheryn, The Wanton Queen.   London, Hale, 1967; New York, Beagle, 1971.
Mary, The Infamous Queen.   London, Hale, 1968; New York, Beagle, 1971.
Bride for King James.   London, Hale, 1968.
Joan of the Lilies.   London, Hale, 1969.
The Rose of Hever.   London, Hale, 1969; as *Anne, The Rose of Hever*, New York,
     Beagle, 1971.
Flower of the Greys.   London, Hale, 1969.
Princess of Desire.   London, Hale, 1970; New York, Pinnacle, 1973.
Struggle for a Crown.   London, Hale, 1970.
Shadow of a Tudor.   London, Hale, 1971.
Seven for St. Crispin's Day.   London, Hale, 1971.
The Cloistered Flame.   London, Hale, 1971.
Jewel of the Greys.   London, Hale, 1972.
The Woodville Wench.   London, Hale, 1972.
Henry VIII and His Six Wives (novelization of screenplay).   London, Fontana, and New
     York, St. Martin's Press, 1972.
The Peacock Queen.   London, Hale, 1972.
The Virgin Queen.   New York, Pinnacle, 1972.
The Queen Who Never Was.   New York, Pinnacle, 1972.
Royal Escape.   Boston, Lincolnshire, Jones Blakey, 1972.
Destiny's Lady.   New York, Pinnacle, 1973.
The Gallows Herd.   London, Hale, 1973.
The Maid of Judah.   London, Hale, 1973.
Flawed Enchantress.   London, Hale, 1974.
So Fair and Foul a Queen.   London, Hale, 1974.
The Willow Maid.   London, Hale, 1974.
Curse of the Greys.   London, Hale, 1974.
With Murder in Mind (as Judith Rothman).   London, Hale, 1975.
The Queenmaker.   London, Hale, 1975.
Kate Alanna.   London, Hale, 1975.
A Child Called Freedom.   London, Hale, 1976.
Beggar Maid, Queen.   London, Hale, 1980.
I, The Maid.   London, Hale, 1980.
The Snow Blossom.   London, Hale, 1980.
Night of the Willow.   London, Hale, 1981.
Ravenscar.   London, Hale, 1981.

Novels as Veronica Black

Dangerous Inheritance.   London, Hale, 1969; New York, Paperback Library, 1970.
Portrait of Sarah.   London, Hale, 1969; New York, Berkley, 1973.
The Wayward Madonna.   London, Hale, and New York, Lenox Hill Press, 1970.
A Footfall in the Mist.   London, Hale, and New York, Lenox Hill Press, 1971.
Master of Malcarew.   London, Hale, and New York, Lenox Hill Press, 1971.
Enchanted Grotto.   London, Hale, 1972; New York, Lenox Hill Press, 1973.
Moonflete.   London, Hale, 1972; New York, Lenox Hill Press, 1973.
Fair Kilmeny.   London, Hale, and New York, Berkley, 1972.
Minstrel's Leap.   London, Hale, 1973.
Spin Me a Shadow.   London, Hale, 1974.
The House That Hated People.   London, Hale, 1974.
Tansy.   London, Hale, 1975.

Echo of Margaret. London, Hale, 1978.
Greengirl. London, Hale, 1979.
Pilgrim of Desire. London, Hale, 1979.
Flame in the Snow. London, Hale, 1980.
The Dragon and the Rose. London, Hale, 1982.

Novels as Sharon Whitby

The Last of the Greenwood. London, Hale, 1975; New York, Pyramid, 1976.
The Unforgotten Face. London, Hale, 1975.
Here Be Dragons. London, Hale, 1980.
The Silky. London, Hale, 1980.
The Houseless One. London, Hale, 1981.
No Song at Morningside. London, Hale, 1981.

Novels as Catherine Darby

Falcon Series:
1. *A Falcon for a Witch*. New York, Popular Library, and London, Hale, 1975.
2. *The King's Falcon*. New York, Popular Library, 1975; as *A Game of Falcons*, London, Hale, 1976.
3. *Fortune for a Falcon*. New York, Popular Library, 1975; London, Hale, 1976.
4. *Season of the Falcon*. New York, Popular Library, and London, Hale, 1976.
5. *Falcon Royal*. New York, Popular Library, 1976; as *A Pride of Falcons*, London, Hale, 1977.
6. *Falcon Tree*. New York, Popular Library, 1976; London, Hale, 1977.
7. *The Falcon and the Moon*. New York, Popular Library, 1976; London, Hale, 1978.
8. *Falcon Rising*. New York, Popular Library, 1976; London, Hale, 1978.
9. *Falcon Sunset*. New York, Popular Library, 1976; London, Hale, 1978.
10. *Seed of the Falcon*. New York, Popular Library, 1978; London, Hale, 1981.
11. *Falcon's Claw*. New York, Popular Library, 1978; London, Hale, 1982.
12. *Falcon to the Lure*. New York, Popular Library, 1978; London, Hale, 1982.
Moon Series:
1. *Whisper Down the Moon*. New York, Popular Library, 1977; London, Hale, 1978.
2. *Frost on the Moon*. New York, Popular Library, 1977; London, Hale, 1979.
3. *The Flaunting Moon*. New York, Popular Library, 1977; London, Hale, 1979.
4. *Sing Me a Moon*. New York, Popular Library, 1977; London, Hale, 1980.
5. *Cobweb Across the Moon*. New York, Popular Library, 1978; London, Hale, 1980.
6. *Moon in Pisces*. New York, Popular Library, 1978; London, Hale, 1981.
A Dream of Fair Serpents. London, Hale, and New York, Popular Library, 1979.

Novels as Belinda Grey

The Passionate Puritan. London, Mills and Boon, 1978; Toronto, Harlequin, 1979.
Loom of Love. London, Mills and Boon, 1979; Toronto, Harlequin, 1980.
Sweet Wind of Morning. London, Mills and Boon, 1979; Toronto, Harlequin, 1980.
Moon of Laughing Flame. London, Mills and Boon, and Toronto, Harlequin, 1980.
Daughter of Isis. London, Mills and Boon, and Toronto, Harlequin, 1981.
Glen of Frost. London, Mills and Boon, and Toronto, Harlequin, 1981.

Novels as Levanah Lloyd

A Maid Called Wanton. London, Futura, 1981.
Mail Order Bride. London, Futura, 1981.

Cauldron of Desire. London, Futura, 1981.
Dark Surrender. London, Futura, 1981.

OTHER PUBLICATIONS

Other

Jean Ingelow, Victorian Poetess. Ipswich, Boydell Press, and Totowa, New Jersey, Rowman and Littlefield, 1972.
An Enigma of Brontës. London, Hale, and New York, St. Martin's Press, 1974.

Maureen Peters comments:

A prolific writer. Writes easily, perhaps too easily, one idea succeeding another. Tries to keep up with but not give in to current trends and make each book the best of its kind. Enjoys using a variety of themes with a particular fondness for inducing a pleasurable terror in the reader. Enjoys Tudor and Plantagenet settings and the 19th century in the USA, also Red Indians and gypsies. Writes in longhand so greatest problem is keeping pace with flow of ideas.

*   *   *

Maureen Peters has written many excellent historical biographies beginning with those of royal personages, *Elizabeth the Beloved* blazing the trail. Following the undoubted success of this book, the author went on to write of Katheryn Howard, Mary, Lady Jane Grey and other Tudors, including the luckless Anne Boleyn in the moving *The Rose of Hever*. Obviously happy with the Tudors of whose period she exactly captured the romance, cruelty, and excitement, Peters continued her series with yet further stories of Henry VIII and his wives, seen through the eyes of the dying king—an unusual touch. This version of the great king's story is engrossing reading, and Peters was clever enough to convey the differences between the six queens, from the cloying Katherine of Aragon to the fascinating Anne Boleyn, the impish childishness of Katherine Howard to the final contentment he found with his last wife, who outlived him. Though stories of the Tudor period are legion, Peters's writing manages to instill a freshness and a reality of period that make one travel back in time.

So on through other novels still nudging history but with an occasional change of period, keeping the same ease of style and readability. *The Maid of Judah* provided a jump forward to Victorian days. This tale of a Jewish orphan's struggle against life in a brothel, with help from an old Jewish artist, and her love for a dancer, is dramatically set against an East End background. The heroine, Michal, is startlingly graphical, and the reader shares her loves and her miseries with pleasure. Peters has a simple style, but she manages to convey a word picture with consummate skill, choosing every one with care; even her choice of adjectives is just right for the mood of the time and place. The theme may seem sad but the telling of it skilfully removes any misery.

Tansy, *Kate Alanna*, and *A Child Called Freedom* constitute a family trilogy, each one complete in itself, yet making up a wonderful whole. The tale begins in Ireland with the young Tansy, whose dreams and passions puzzle her family. The sequel, *Kate Alanna*, reveals how she plans a new life in America with the dangers and excitement ahead, all faced with courage. The final book, *A Child Called Freedom*, is compelling reading, showing Tansy in America, and her love for Tom Wolf, a half Indian, which takes her to the Sacramento Trail. Here Peters has shown her versatility in writing authentically, with a caressing descriptive flair, of the tribal customs of the Indian and life in those pioneering days.

Maureen Peters is a young author already showing her real ability and versatility, and the promise of more such novels is rich indeed. Her first novels set a high standard which has been maintained, even surpassed, with each new book.

—Lornie Leete-Hodge

PETERS, Natasha. Address: c/o Fawcett, 1515 Broadway, New York, New York 10036, U.S.A.

ROMANCE AND GOTHIC PUBLICATIONS

Plays

    Savage Surrender. New York, Ace, 1977; London, Arrow, 1978.
    Dangerous Obsession. New York, Ace, 1978; London, Arrow, 1979.
    The Masquers. New York, Ace, 1979; London, Arrow, 1980.
    The Enticers. New York, Fawcett, 1981.

*   *   *

Historical settings vividly detailed, unbelievable characters in even less believable plots, rude talk and sexual encounters provocatively if not pornographically described—these form the basis of the historical romances of Natasha Peters.

Savage Surrender opens in a 19th-century French *château*, where the reader meets the novel's heroine, Elise Lesconflair, the spoiled and headstrong niece of Count Lesconflair and goddaughter of Napoleon. Elise grows up quickly, as she is, without her consent, betrothed to Baron Friederich Rolland von Meier, whom the willful Elise detests: "...so terribly dull...and so ugly.... Grotesquely ugly! That fat belly and those thin blond wisps of baby hair—yes, he looks just like a gigantic baby! And his breath stinks, too." In a fit of defiance, Elise runs out into the forest, sheds her clothing, and jumps into a swimming pond, where the "villainous" Garth McClelland stares at her boldly through "pale ice-blue eyes" and then proceeds to take advantage of the assumed invitation. Elise's indignant brothers force her to marry McClelland (posing as "Lord Armand Charles Alexandre Valadon, Marquis de Pellissier") despite her betrothal to the repugnant Baron. McClelland, alternately a "beast" and a gentle lover, takes his "hell-cat" Elise off to Nantes, where both board a slave ship headed for Africa and the West Indies. Elise is rescued from cruel Garth by pirate Jean Lafitte, who takes her to his home in Louisiana and installs her as his mistress. Amazingly, Elise and Garth McClelland find each other, villain and hell-cat are reunited, start a family, and eventually go "out of the gathering gloom of the forest into the brightness of the afternoon sun."

The Masquers is set in 18th-century Venice, "the beautiful, the sensual city of Venice," where "gondolas glide soundlessly through narrow canals, carrying masked lovers to secret trysts, while *cicisbei* (18th-century gallants, to the uninitiated) play court to bored noblewomen." Fosca Loredan is the beautiful and bored noblewoman heroine. Her husband is the aristocratic Alessandro; her lover, the bold revolutionary Rafaello Leopardi. The rest you know.

Pre-Communist Shanghai of the 1930's is the setting for *The Enticers*, a story of two sisters—Anne Fox, the "sensitive, passionate woman whose secret past bound her to this enigmatic land and stood between her and love forever," and Kit, Anne's gorgeous sister, "the queen of a razzle-dazzle social set, who ran from bed to bed savagely trying to fill an empty life"—and the two men they marry—Gilbert Lawrence, Anne's husband, "a doctor whose lust for his own wife's sister finally drove him to the sweet release of the East—opium," and James Innes, Kit's husband, a rich empire-builder "whose money bought his fashionable wife but could never pave his way into the high society he pretended to scorn."

Like the author's pseudonym, each "Natasha" novel dazzles with superficial exoticism, then "Peters" out in dull mundanity.

—Marcia G. Fuchs

PILCHER, Rosamunde (née Scott). Also wrote as Jane Fraser. British. Born in Lelant, Cornwall, 22 September 1924. Educated at St. Clares, Polwithen, Cornwall; Howell's School, Llandaff; Miss Kerr-Sanders Secretarial College. Served as a Wren, 1943-46. Married Graham Hope Pilcher in 1946; two daughters and two sons. Agent: Curtis Brown Ltd., 1 Craven Hill, London W2 3EP, England.

ROMANCE AND GOTHIC PUBLICATIONS

Novels

> *A Secret to Tell.* London, Collins, 1955.
> *April.* London, Collins, 1957.
> *On My Own.* London, Collins, 1965.
> *Sleeping Tiger.* London, Collins, 1967; New York, St. Martin's Press, 1974.
> *Another View.* London, Collins, 1969; New York, St. Martin's Press, 1974.
> *The End of the Summer.* London, Collins, 1971; New York, St. Martin's Press, 1975.
> *Snow in April.* London, Collins, 1972; New York, St. Martin's Press, 1975.
> *The Empty House.* London, Collins, 1973; New York, St. Martin's Press, 1975.
> *The Day of the Storm.* London, Collins, and New York, St. Martin's Press, 1975.
> *Under Gemini.* New York, St. Martin's Press, 1976; London, Collins, 1977.
> *Wild Mountain Thyme.* New York, St. Martin's Press, 1978; London, New English Library, 1980.

Novels as Jane Fraser

> *Half-way to the Moon.* London, Mills and Boon, 1949.
> *The Brown Fields.* London, Mills and Boon, 1951.
> *Dangerous Intruder.* London, Mills and Boon, 1951.
> *Young Bar.* London, Mills and Boon, 1952; Toronto, Harlequin, 1965.
> *A Day Like Spring.* London, Mills and Boon, 1953; Toronto, Harlequin, 1968.
> *Dear Tom.* London, Mills and Boon, 1954.
> *Bridge of Corvie.* London, Mills and Boon, 1956; New York, Fawcett, 1975.
> *A Family Affair.* London, Mills and Boon, 1958.
> *A Long Way from Home.* London, Mills and Boon, 1963; Toronto, Harlequin, 1964.
> *The Keeper's House.* London, Mills and Boon, 1963; Toronto, Harlequin, 1964.

Uncollected Short Stories

> "Touch of Magic," in *Good Housekeeping* (Des Moines, Iowa), May 1980.
> "Harbor of Love," in *Good Housekeeping* (Des Moines, Iowa), September 1980.

OTHER PUBLICATIONS

Plays

> *The Dashing White Sergeant*, with Charles C. Gairdner (produced London, 1955). London, Evans, 1955.
> *The Piper of Orde*, with Charles C. Gairdner. London, Evans, n.d.
> *The Tulip Major* (produced Dundee, 1957).

Rosamunde Pilcher comments:

I try in my work to strike a balance between the out-and-out romantic and the serious woman's writing of today. There is a huge market of intelligent women who sometimes wish to read a light novel without necessarily reading a load of out-dated rubbish. Over the 40 years I have been writing and selling, social conditions, behaviour, and expectations have changed drastically, and I have endeavoured always to keep a fresh and modern outlook, accepting the inevitable permissiveness, and incorporating it into my work, without necessarily condoning it nor encouraging the sort of loveless amorality which was prevalent in the 1960's. My short stories are not so much love stories, but more about human relations, i.e., the love which can exist, not simply between two young people, but also between mothers and children, brothers and sisters, old people and young people.

If the stories do not have a happy ending, then they always have a hopeful ending. Life is a succession of problems and decisions, and sometimes the best we can do is simply to come to terms with them.

* * *

American audiences have only recently discovered Rosamunde Pilcher, much to their delight. As the *New York Times Book Review* has stated, "I don't know where Rosamunde Pilcher has been all my life—but now that I've found her I'm not going to let her go!"

Pilcher got her earlier practice writing romance for the ever popular British publisher Mills and Boon. When her apprenticeship had been served, she emerged to write some of the best plotted, well-characterized enchanting romances to be found anywhere. There is a magical, timeless quality to her stories that charms even the most hard-hearted reader. Somehow they are always just perfect—in length, in dialogue, in everything that matters. Each one is a small gem and all are highly recommended to those who scoff at the genre. Pilcher provides a classy read that is positively addicting.

Sleeping Tiger is one of the best. Selina Bruce, a quiet sensible woman, is engaged to marry a quiet sensible man. Everything is quite proper—until one day she decides, on a sudden impulse, to take off for a Spanish island to search for her father and becomes entangled in a delightful love affair with a writer. The tone is wryly gentle with lots of sparkling dialogue that is a true pleasure to read.

Often the stories involve the replacing of a slightly tarnished old love with a new, forever-after love. This is the case in *The End of the Summer* where the heroine finally relinquishes her infatuation with her recklessly handsome cousin in exchange for the steady stable love of a lawyer from Scotland. In *The Empty House* the heroine, Virginia Keile, rediscovers an old flame who had broken her heart ten years ago and falls in love with him all over again, proving that he was worthy of her love in the first place. *Wild Mountain Thyme*'s plot revolves on the same basis, with Victoria Bradshaw renewing her broken affair with Oliver Dobbs only to realize, almost against her will, that she is in love with another, more worthy man.

Under Gemini concerns, naturally, a pair of identical twins. Flora, the good twin, is our heroine, and Rose is the bad one who wants Flora to impersonate her in the sticky situation into which she has landed herself. Lots of complications arise but all is settled quite to the reader's immense satisfaction.

With Rosamunde Pilcher's novels, the enjoyment is in the journey. Every step of the way is paved with all the hallmarks of quality one expects in a good writer, no matter what the scope of the work. Pilcher steadfastly provides it.

—Marilyn Lockhart

PLAGEMANN, Bentz.   American.   Born in Springfield, Ohio, 27 July 1913. Educated at Cathedral Latin High School, Cleveland. Served in the United States Navy, 1942-45. Married Catherine Witmer Emig in 1947 (died, 1976); one stepson. Worked in bookstores in Cleveland, Chicago, Detroit, and New York, 1932-42; Instructor in Journalism, New York University, 1946-47. Lives in Palisades, New York. Agent: Harold Matson Company, 22 East 40th Street, New York, New York 10016, U.S.A.

ROMANCE AND GOTHIC PUBLICATIONS

Novels

> *The Boxwood Maze.*   New York, Saturday Review Press, 1972.
> *Wolfe's Cloister.*   New York, Saturday Review Press, 1974.

OTHER PUBLICATIONS

Novels

> *William Walter.*   New York, Greystone Press, 1941.
> *All for the Best.*   New York, Simon and Schuster, 1946.
> *Into the Labyrinth.*   New York, Farrar Straus, 1948; London, Gollancz, 1949; as
>   *Downfall*, New York, Pyramid, 1952; as *The Sin Underneath*, Pyramid, 1956.
> *This Is Goggle; or, The Education of a Father.*   New York, McGraw Hill, 1955; as *My
>   Son Goggle*, London, Gollancz, 1955.
> *The Steel Cocoon.*   New York, Viking Press, 1958; London, Secker and Warburg, 1959.
> *Half the Fun.*   New York, Viking Press, and London, Cassell, 1961.
> *Father to the Man.*   New York, Morrow, 1964; London, Cassell, 1965.
> *The Best Is Yet to Be.*   New York, Morrow, 1966.
> *The Heart of Silence.*   New York, Morrow, 1967.
> *A World of Difference.*   New York, Morrow, 1969.

Other

> *My Place to Stand* (autobiography).   New York, Farrar Straus, 1949; London, Gollancz,
>   1950.
> *This Happy Place: Living the Good Life in America.*   New York, McCall, 1970.
> *How to Write a Story* (juvenile).   New York, Lothrop, 1971.

*   *   *

The author of many novels and an autobiography, Bentz Plagemann has made two forays into the world of gothic fiction, both competently written, enjoyable tales for fans of the genre.

In *The Boxwood Maze* a young girl goes to upstate New York to visit her somewhat dotty aunt who lives in a castle on the Hudson River. The obligatory cast of characters includes strange servants, a too-good-to-be-true long-lost cousin who is immediately recognizable as the bad guy, and the virile sinister good guy. Everything is here, from thumps in the night to the strange encounter in the graveyard. Although the result is a textbook gothic, this one is better written than many and with each new twist of the plot the reader is able to forget the formula and just enjoy.

Wolfe's Cloister is a Pennsylvania Dutch gothic that is just as spooky as anything set on the foggy moors of England. Amy Merriweather has been strictly raised by her grandmother who wants to prevent her from becoming like her much-married mother. When Amy sneaks off for a morning meeting with Munroe Patterson, Grandmother has a heart attack. Munroe sees her through the ensuing problems and sends her off to Pennsylvania, the home of her mother's first husband. It is here that the tricky story gets really underway with an ingenious plot that revolves on a clever handling of family lines. There is much symbolism for sophisticated readers to enjoy in this high quality gothic. Plagemann's performance in this second novel is more subtle and skilled than in *The Boxwood Maze*.

—Marilyn Lockhart

PLAIDY, Jean.   *See* **HOLT, Victoria.**

PLUMMER, Clare.   *See* **EMSLEY, Clare.**

PONSONBY, D(oris) A(lmon).   Also writes as Doris Rybot; Sarah Tempest.   British.   Born in Devonport, Devon, 23 March 1907. Educated at Shrewsbury High School for Girls; Villabelle, Neuchatel, Switzerland. Married John Rybot in 1933 (died). Journalist: sub-editor, Oxford *Times*, reporter, Aldershot *Gazette*, and free-lance writer for *South China Morning Post* and Hong Kong *Herald*, 1928-37. Agent: Curtis Brown Ltd., 1 Craven Hill, London W2 3EP, England.

ROMANCE AND GOTHIC PUBLICATIONS

Novels

> *The Gazebo.*   London, Hutchinson, 1945; as *If My Arms Could Hold* (as Doris Ponsonby), New York, Liveright, 1947.
> *Sophy Valentine.*   London, Hutchinson, 1946.
> *Merry Meeting.*   London, Hutchinson, 1948.
> *Strangers in My House.*   London, Hutchinson, 1948.
> *Bow Window in Green Street.*   London, Hutchinson, 1949.

Family of Jaspard. London, Hutchinson, 1950; as *The General* and *The Fortunate Adventure*, London, White Lion, 2 vols., 1971.
The Bristol Cousins. London, Hutchinson, 1951.
The Foolish Marriage. London, Hutchinson, 1952.
The Widow's Daughters. London, Hutchinson, 1953.
Royal Purple. London, Hutchinson, 1954.
Dogs in Clover. London, Hutchinson, 1954.
Conquesta's Caravan. London, Hutchinson, 1955.
Unhallowed House. London, Hutchinson, 1956.
So Bold a Choice. London, Hurst and Blackett, 1960.
Romany Sister (as Doris Rybot). London, Hale, 1960.
A Japanese Doll (as Doris Rybot). London, Hale, 1961.
A Living to Earn. London, Hurst and Blackett, 1961.
The Orphans. London, Hurst and Blackett, 1962.
Bells along the Neva. London, Hurst and Blackett, 1964.
The Jade Horse of Merle. London, Hurst and Blackett, 1966.
An Unusual Tudor. London, Hurst and Blackett, 1967.
A Winter of Fear (as Sarah Tempest). London, Hurst and Blackett, 1967; New York, Pyramid, 1968.
The Forgotten Heir. London, Hurst and Blackett, 1969.
The Heart in the Sand. London, Hurst and Blackett, 1970.
Mr. Florian's Fortune. London, Hurst and Blackett, 1971.
Flight from Hanover Square. London, Hurst and Blackett, 1972.
The Gamester's Daughter. London, Hurst and Blackett, 1974.
The Heir to Holtwood. London, Hurst and Blackett, 1975.
An Unnamed Gentlewoman. London, Hurst and Blackett, 1976.
Kaye's Walk. London, Hurst and Blackett, 1977.
Sir William. London, Hurst and Blackett, 1978.
Exhibition Summer. London, Hale, 1982.

OTHER PUBLICATIONS

Other

Call a Dog Hervey. London, Hutchinson, 1949.
The Lost Duchess: The Story of the Prince Consort's Mother. London, Chapman and Hall, 1958.
A Prisoner in Regent's Park. London, Chapman and Hall, 1961.

Other as Doris Rybot

The Popular Chow Chow, with Lydia Ingleton. London, Popular Dogs, 1954.
My Kingdom for a Donkey. London, Hutchinson, 1963.
A Donkey and a Dandelion. London, Hutchinson, 1966.
It Began Before Noah (on zoos). London, Joseph, 1972.

D.A. Ponsonby comments:

In all my historical stories and romances my main aim (apart from telling a good story) is to be as historically accurate as possible, not only in facts, but concerning manners, dress, social attitudes, and everything else.

*   *   *

It is over 30 years since D.A. Ponsonby's historical novels were first published, yet there is a freshness about them that makes them hold their attraction today.

Her sense of period is accurate and her shrewd knowledge of people splendidly evokes the time in which the tales are set. *The Gazebo*, her first novel, is a gripping family story revealing a young girl's awakening to love, her marriage and its problems. Much of her fiction is told by means of excellent descriptive passages with the conversations slipping into place effortlessly, avoiding the all-too-common failure of so many of today's writers of using mainly jerky conversations for narration.

The novel *Merry Meeting*, about the love of two orphans, begins in a foundling home in the cruel days of the 18th century. Their future lives are mingled, and the boy's eventual sacrifice fits exactly into the story. The author's ability to bring life to her characters ensures a convincing tale.

Bow Window in Green Street is set in 18th-century Bath, and all the hopes and excitement of Regency living are wonderfully captured. One feels one could again knock on the door of the very house in which they all lived. The Regency, in fact, was a favourite period for Ponsonby who vividly recreated its days in her novels. *The Widow's Daughters* is a more light-hearted story of a silly, scheming widow using her wiles to marry off her four daughters who had their own surprising ideas.

The well-worn themes of Regency novels take on a new meaning under this writer's narrative skill; the timelessness of her writing is its strong quality. Her sense of period and the fact that her stories can be read and re-read with ease makes them stand out in the morass of historical fiction. My regret is there are not more of them, though their exclusivity is another charm, making them novels to be treasured.

—Lornie Leete-Hodge

PORTER, Eleanor H(odgman). Also wrote as Eleanor Stuart. American. Born in Littleton, New Hampshire, 19 December 1868. Educated at the New England Conservatory of Music, Boston. Married John L. Porter in 1892. Choir and concert singer, then teacher; full-time writer from 1901. *Died 21 May 1920.*

Romance and Gothic Publications

Novels (series: Margaret; Miss Billy; Pollyanna)

Cross Currents: The Story of Margaret. Boston, Wilde, 1907; London, Harrap, 1928.
The Turn of the Tide: The Story of How Margaret Solved Her Problem. Chicago, Wilde, 1908; London, Harrap, 1928.
The Story of Marco. Cincinnati, Jennings and Graham, 1911; London, Stanley Paul, 1920.
Miss Billy. Boston, Page, 1911; London, Stanley Paul, 1914.
Miss Billy's Decision. Boston, Page, 1912; London, Stanley Paul, 1915.
Pollyanna. Boston, Page, and London, Pitman, 1913.
Miss Billy—Married. Boston, Page, 1914; London, Stanley Paul, 1915.
Pollyanna Grows Up. Boston, Page, and London, Pitman, 1915.
Just David. Boston, Houghton Mifflin, and London, Constable, 1916.
The Road to Understanding. Boston, Houghton Mifflin, and London, Constable, 1917.

Oh, Money! Money!   Boston, Houghton Mifflin, and London, Constable, 1918.
Dawn.   Boston, Houghton Mifflin, 1919; as *Keith's Dark Tower*, London, Constable, 1919.
Mary Marie.   Boston, Houghton Mifflin, and London, Constable, 1920.
Sister Sue.   Boston, Houghton Mifflin, and London, Constable, 1921.

Short Stories

The Tangled Threads.   Boston, Houghton Mifflin, 1919.
Across the Years.   Boston, Houghton Mifflin, 1919.
The Tie That Binds.   Boston, Houghton Mifflin, 1919.
Money, Love, and Kate, Together with The Story of a Nickel.   New York, Doran, 1923; London, Hodder and Stoughton, 1924.
Hustler Joe and Other Stories.   New York, Doran, 1924.
Little Pardner and Other Stories.   New York, Doran, 1926; London, Hodder and Stoughton, 1927.
Just Mother and Other Stories.   New York, Doran, 1927.
The Fortunate Mary.   New York, Doubleday, 1928.

OTHER PUBLICATIONS

Other (juvenile)

The Sunbridge Girls at Six Star Ranch (as Eleanor Stuart).   Boston, Page, 1913; as *Six Star Ranch*, Page, 1916; London, Harrap, 1928.

*   *   *

When Eleanor H. Porter died in her early fifties, having given up a singing career for writing only twenty years before, she left behind her over 20 volumes of fiction. From this prolific output, posterity has selected a single novel, *Pollyanna*, and given its name not to one who sees the best side of a bad situation, but to one who embraces a blind and foolish optimism. As with Harriet Beecher Stowe's Black Christ, so with Porter's little "glad" girl who brought happiness into lives as afflicted as her own—for who today would want to be called an Uncle Tom or a Pollyanna?

As a writer of children's stories—for and about children—Porter belongs in that very American line which runs from Mark Twain to Booth Tarkington. The boys are mischievous, the girls responsible; the boys disrupt the social order, though they (even Huck) ultimately conform to it, the girls work on it from within, and restore it with certain improvements. The boys foment misunderstandings between unconsenting adults, the girls resolve them. Tom Sawyer is constantly evading *his* Aunt Polly, Pollyanna nudges *hers* to the altar. Yet the status quo is not quite safe from either boys or girls: Porter's social blueprint, happily based upon feminine values, may be as subversive as Twain's "boy's" books, though repressed by the adult reader. For as a perceptive reviewer of 1913 noted, *Pollyanna* is "a book for grown-up people who will understand the criticism of convention; it would be a disaster if many little girls should undertake to imitate the heroine."

It is this "criticism of convention," however defused, which may give Porter some claim to our continuing attention. There is a genuine social conscience in her work which distinguished her from the Alice Hegan Rices and the Gene Stratton Porters, and brings her closer to the best of all these "cheerful" (if not always quite "glad") writers, Jean Webster. Porter's first novel, *Cross Currents*, sets the tone: a poor little rich girl is lost, and grows up in the slums, amid the sweatshops. The novel vigorously attacks the child labour of its day, and several of Porter's works at least touch upon social questions. *Pollyanna* certainly criticizes the same over-zealous social do-gooders who will be the villains of Griffith's film *Intolerance* three years later; *Mary*

Marie, in which the title character's odd name is a compromise agreed upon by warring parents, seriously discusses divorce; and *Pollyanna Grows Up* accuses the slum landlord.

Though the Six Star Ranch stories deal with a moderately mischievous group of six girls—"the happy hexagons"—Porter's typical heroine, as well as being a marital fixer, is, like Anne of Green Gables or Rebecca of Sunnybrook Farm, an orphan reaching for a family; and her arrangements are not always selfless, especially since she is so often poor. The formula works well enough with the girl at its centre, but two of Porter's more egregiously sentimental works fail by attempting to force the boy into this stereotyped role. *Dawn* finds a 15-year-old youth suddenly stricken with blindness; he turns away from human contact, but is won back by the love of the great eye surgeon's stepdaughter, who adopts a false identity to woo him (one wonders if Lloyd C. Douglas read this novel). And the hero of *Just David*, as *The Times* not unjustly remarked, "combines in his pathetic person the shortcomings of Lord Fauntleroy, Eric, and Humphrey in *Misunderstood*." Girls could still be prigs, but boys, after Tom, Huck, and Penrod, could not.

One (or three) of Porter's most effective works is the group of novels made up of *Miss Billy* (her first major success), *Miss Billy's Decision*, and *Miss Billy—Married*. Three settled bachelors receive a letter announcing the arrival of the forgotten godchild of the eldest. Because of her androgynous name, they assume that *she* is *he*, but their settled existence is in for a much greater discombobulation. Each falls in love with her, each proposes, and after several misunderstandings she marries the youngest. By June 1921, these three novels had sold 93, 78, and 86 thousand copies (*Pollyanna* at the same time had sold half a million, and, as James D. Hart has noted, Porter's publishers after her death commissioned five further writers of "their" Pollyanna series, which over 40 years sold two million copies).

Porter had a considerable talent for the short story—her novels tend to be episodic—and her best stories are collected in three volumes published the year before her death: *The Tangled Threads*, *The Tie That Binds*, and *Across the Years*, dealing with the three ages of love. The last collection especially shows her as a benign Mary Wilkins Freeman—the Yankee spareness and satiric bite of Freeman's famous "The Revolt of Mother" provides a point of comparison, one of many, with Porter's charming but sentimentally lenient "When Mother and Father Rebelled."

It is easy to sneer at Eleanor Porter. A reviewer of 1917, condemning one of her novels, predicts a large sale for it notwithstanding ("take it from a pessimist"). We do better to use as her epitaph the phrase of a reviewer of her second Pollyanna book: "after all, she has the right idea."

—Barrie Hayne

PORTER, Gene Stratton (Geneva Grace Stratton Porter). American. Born in Wabash County, Indiana, 17 August 1863. Attended public schools. Married Charles Darwin Porter in 1886; one daughter. Regular contributor, *McCall's Magazine*; Photographic Editor, *Recreation* magazine; member of the natural history department, *Outing* magazine; natural history photography specialist, *Photographic Times Annual Almanac*, four years. Founded Gene Stratton Porter Productions film company, 1922. *Died 6 December 1924.*

Novels

> *The Song of the Cardinal: A Love Story.*   Indianapolis, Bobbs Merrill, 1903; London, Hodder and Stoughton, 1913.
> *Freckles.*   New York, Doubleday, 1904; London, Murray, 1905.
> *At the Foot of the Rainbow.*   New York, Outing Publishing Company, 1907; London, Hodder and Stoughton, 1913.
> *A Girl of the Limberlost.*   New York, Doubleday, 1909; London, Hodder and Stoughton, 1911.
> *The Harvester.*   New York, Doubleday, and London, Hodder and Stoughton, 1911.
> *Laddie: A True-Blue Story.*   New York, Doubleday, and London, Murray, 1913.
> *Michael O'Halloran.*   New York, Doubleday, and London, Murray, 1915.
> *A Daughter of the Land.*   New York, Doubleday, and London, Murray, 1918.
> *Her Father's Daughter.*   New York, Doubleday, and London, Murray, 1921.
> *The White Flag.*   New York, Doubleday, and London, Murray, 1923.
> *The Keeper of the Bees.*   New York, Doubleday, and London, Hutchinson, 1925.
> *The Magic Garden.*   New York, Doubleday, and London, Hutchinson, 1927.

OTHER PUBLICATIONS

Play

> Screenplay: *A Girl of the Limberlost*, 1924.

Verse

> *Morning Face*, illustrated by the author.   New York, Doubleday, and London, Murray, 1916.
> *The Fire Bird.*   New York, Doubleday, and London, Murray, 1922.
> *Jesus of the Emerald.*   New York, Doubleday, and London, Murray, 1923.

Other

> *What I Have Done with Birds: Character Studies of Native American Birds.*   Indianapolis, Bobbs Merrill, 1907; revised edition, New York, Doubleday, 1917; as *Friends in Feathers*, London, Curtis Brown, 1917.
> *Birds of the Bible.*   Cincinnati, Jennings and Graham, 1909; London, Hodder and Stoughton, 1910.
> *Music of the Wild*, illustrated by the author.   Cincinnati, Jennings and Graham, and London, Hodder and Stoughton, 1910.
> *Moths of the Limberlost*, illustrated by the author.   New York, Doubleday, 1912; London, Hodder and Stoughton, 1913.
> *After the Flood.*   Indianapolis, Bobbs Merrill, 1912.
> *Birds of the Limberlost.*   New York, Doubleday, 1914.
> *Homing with the Birds.*   New York, Doubleday, and London, Murray, 1919.
> *Wings.*   New York, Doubleday, 1923.
> *Tales You Won't Believe* (natural history).   New York, Doubleday, and London, Heinemann, 1925.
> *Let Us Highly Resolve* (essays).   New York, Doubleday, and London, Heinemann, 1927.

Critical Studies: *The Lady of the Limberlost: The Life and Letters of Gene Stratton Porter* by Jeanette Porter Meehan, New York, Doubleday, 1928, as *Life and Letters of Gene Stratton Porter*, London, Hutchinson, 1928; *Gene Stratton Porter* by Bernard F. Richards, Boston, Twayne, 1980.

*   *   *

It seems incredible today that Gene Stratton Porter's books were once among the most popular all over the world, both in English and in translation; that they sold out edition after edition; and that several of them were the subjects of motion pictures. Surely never before or since did such cardboard creations capture and hold a more enthusiastic audience. A good many of her major characters were never even named; they were designated and remain The Swamp Angel, The Man of Affairs, The Bird Woman, and so on. Stereotypical characterization surely never has been carried to greater length. Her dialogue is a curious combination of simon-pure, frightfully long-winded passion and quirky lectures on diet and nature study, perpetrated by a writer totally deaf to the cadence of natural, colloquial speech; her code of values defies comprehension, muddling as it does fundamental issues of moral integrity and personal worth with trivial concerns of good form and etiquette relevant only to the turn of the century.

Still, when one has laughed at the quaint set speeches, purer-than-life heroes and positively incandescent heroines, and outmoded, bombastic philosophy, a glimmer of the charm that caught and held Gene Stratton Porter's millions of readers remains. She created a world of good, honest (if pompous) people who offered one another whole hearts and an enviable confidence in a wholesome, unspoiled world full of the bounty of nature that was to be theirs and their childrens'. "Homely" was to her a word of highest praise. A more cynical generation cannot share this perhaps blinkered simplicity—but it is surely to her credit that it is difficult to believe in the existence of a nuclear arms race while in imagination patrolling the Limberlost woodland trail with Freckles, or keeping bees in the beautiful blue garden with Jamie MacFarlane and his little Scout.

—Joan McGrath

PREEDY, George.   *See* **BOWEN, Marjorie.**

PRESTON, Ivy (Alice, née Kinross).   New Zealander.   Born in Timaru, 13 November 1913. Educated at Southburn Primary School, 1919-25; Timaru Technical College, 1925-26. Married Percival Edward James Preston in 1937 (died, 1956); two sons and two daughters. Address: 95 Church Street, Timaru, New Zealand.

ROMANCE AND GOTHIC PUBLICATIONS

Novels

Where Ratas Twine.   London, Wright and Brown, 1960.
None So Blind.   London, Wright and Brown, 1961.
Magic in Maoriland.   London, Wright and Brown, 1962.
Rosemary for Remembrance.   London, Hale, 1962.
Island of Enchantment.   London, Hale, 1963.
Tamarisk in Bloom.   London, Hale, 1963.
Hearts Do Not Break.   London, Hale, 1964.
The Blue Remembered Hills.   London, Hale, 1965.
Secret Love of Nurse Wilson.   London, Hale, 1966.
Enchanted Evening.   London, Hale, 1966.
Hospital on the Hill.   London, Hale, 1967.
Nicolette.   London, Hale, 1967.
Red Roses for a Nurse.   London, Hale, 1968.
Ticket of Destiny.   London, Hale, 1969.
April in Westland.   London, Hale, 1969.
A Fleeting Breath.   London, Hale, 1970; New York, Beagle, 1971.
Interrupted Journey.   London, Hale, 1970; New York, Beagle, 1971.
Portrait of Pierre.   London, Hale, 1971.
Petals in the Wind.   London, Hale, 1972.
Release the Past.   London, Hale, 1973.
Romance in Glenmore Street.   London, Hale, 1974; New York, Ace, 1978.
Voyage of Destiny.   London, Hale, 1974.
Moonlight on the Lake.   London, Hale, 1976.
The House above the Bay.   London, Hale, 1976.
Sunlit Seas.   London, Hale, 1977.
Where Stars May Lead.   London, Hale, 1978.
One Broken Dream.   London, Hale, 1979.
Mountain Magic.   London, Hale, 1979.
Summer at Willowbank.   London, Hale, 1980.
Interlude in Greece.   London, Hale, 1982.

OTHER PUBLICATIONS

Other

The Silver Stream (autobiography).   Christchurch, Pegasus Press, 1959.

Editor, with Margaret Smith, *Springbook: Seventy-Five Years of Progress* (on Springbook
   school).   Privately printed, 1970.

Ivy Preston comments:

   I had always intended to be a writer of romance novels for as long as I can remember but, in
the event, I began my writing career the wrong way round with an autobiography. Most people
wait until they are successful before venturing to write the story of their life. I wrote mine as an
ordinary housewife whom nobody except family, friends and neighbours had ever heard of.
Oddly enough it was reasonably successful. It was written as a tribute to my late husband who
had died suddenly in 1956 leaving me with four young children to bring up alone. Writing that
book helped rid me of the mental block I had suffered since his death and I was able to return to
the romance novels I had been trying unsuccessfully to write for several years, this time with

557

success. I now average one every nine months...like having a baby. Most have a New Zealand setting but now that my family have grown up I am able to travel to other countries and occasionally make use of these experiences for a change of background. I write romance stories because I enjoyed a very happy marriage relationship and believe strongly in love and romance.

*   *   *

Ivy Preston always writes under her own name and almost all of her 30 novels have a New Zealand setting. Although not formula stories, they are all written from the point of view of the heroine. Those not set in New Zealand have a New Zealand heroine and the story unfolds as seen through her eyes. Preston doesn't work from a synopsis but lets the characters develop the story. Although she selects backgrounds with care, these are of secondary importance: the characters are the reason for the book being written, since she strongly believes that it is the characters' actions and reactions that the reader is interested in. Because her books are romances she likes to choose romantic settings for the denouement, when all the ends are tidied up and the scene set for "happy ever after."

The "Anne" and "Emily" books by L.M. Montgomery, set in Canada, were a strong influence on Ivy during her childhood.

—Marion R. Harris

PRICE, Evadne. Pseudonym for Helen Zenna Smith. Born at sea, in 1896. Educated in West Maitland, New South Wales, and in Belgium. Worked for the Air Ministry during World War I. Married 1) C.A. Fletcher (died); 2) Kenneth A. Attiwell. Actress from 1906; then journalist.

ROMANCE AND GOTHIC PUBLICATIONS

Novels

    Diary of a Red-Haired Girl. London, Long, 1932.
    The Haunted Light. London, Long, 1933.
    Strip Girl. London, Hurst and Blackett, 1934.
    Probationer! London, Hurst and Blackett, 1934.
    Society Girl. London, Harrap, 1935.
    Red for Danger! London, Long, 1936.
    Glamour Girl. London, Harrap, 1937.
    The Dishonoured Wife. London, Jenkins, 1951.
    Escape to Marriage. London, Jenkins, 1952.
    My Pretty Sister. London, Jenkins, 1952.
    Her Stolen Life. London, Milestone, 1954.
    What the Heart Says. London, Hale, 1956.
    The Love Trap. London, Hale, 1958.
    Air Hostess in Love. London, Gresham, 1962.

Novels as Helen Zenna Smith

Not So Quiet...: Stepdaughters of War. London, Marriott, 1930; as *Stepdaughters of War*, New York, Dutton, 1930.
Women of the Aftermath. London, Long, 1931; as *One Woman's Freedom*, New York, Longman, 1932.
Shadow Women. London, Long, 1932.
They Lived with Me. London, Long, 1934.

OTHER PUBLICATIONS

Plays

The Phantom Light, with Joan Roy-Byford (as *The Haunted Light*, produced London, 1928; as *The Phantom Light*, produced London, 1937).   London, French, 1949.
Red for Danger (produced Richmond, Surrey, 1938).
Big Ben, with Ruby Miller (produced Malvern, Worcestershire, 1939).
Once a Crook, with Kenneth Attiwell (produced London, 1940).   London, French, 1943.
Who Killed My Sister?, with Kenneth Attiwell (produced London, 1942).
Three Wives Called Roland, with Kenneth Attiwell (produced London, 1943).
Through the Door (also director: produced London, 1946).
What Lies Beyond (also director: produced Margate, Kent, 1948).
Cabin for Three, with Kenneth Attiwell (produced Southsea, Hampshire, 1949).
Blonde for Danger (produced London, 1949).
Wanted on Voyage, with Kenneth Attiwell (produced Wimbledon, 1949).

Screenplays: *Wolf's Clothing*, with Brock Williams, 1936; *When the Poppies Bloom Again*, with Herbert Ayres, 1937; *Merry Comes to Town*, with Brock Williams, 1937; *Silver Top*, with Gerald Elliott and Dorothy Greenhill, 1938; *Lightning Conductor*, with J. Jefferson Farjeon and Ivor McLaren, 1938; *Not Wanted on Voyage*, with others, 1957.

Other (juvenile)

Just Jane.   London, John Hamilton, 1928.
Meet Jane.   London, Marriott, 1930.
Enter—Jane.   London, Newnes, 1932.
Jane the Fourth [*the Sleuth, the Unlucky, the Popular, the Patient, Gets Busy, at War*].   London, Hale, 7 vols., 1937-47.
She Stargazes (for adults; on astrology).   London, Ebury Press, 1965.

Theatrical Activities:

Director: **Plays** — *Through the Door*, London, 1946; *What Lies Beyond*, Margate, Kent, 1949.

Actress: **Plays** — in *Peter Pan* by J.M. Barrie, Sydney, 1906; Nang Ping in *Mr. Wu* by H.M. Vernon and Harold Owen, tour, 1914; toured in South Africa, and in *Oh, I Say* and *Within the Law*, 1915; Suzee in *Five Nights*, tour, 1919; Liliha in *The Bird of Paradise*, London, 1919, 1922; Sua-See in *The Dragon*, London, 1920; Tessie Kearns in *Merton of the Movies* by George S. Kaufman and Marc Connelly, London, 1923; Princess Angelica in *The Rose and the Ring*, London, 1923.

*   *   *

In Helen Zenna Smith's lighter books—which she wrote in the name of Evadne Price—there is often a distinctly drawing-room comedy flavour. (This applies also to her juvenile "Jane" books.) The heroines of her romantic novels often have theatrical careers or other glamorous jobs. These give Evadne Price ample opportunity to exploit her flair for lively, dramatic, or "bitchy" situations and relationships. The larger and more colourful than life quality of her love stories is enhanced by flashes of wit, and an overall feeling of exuberance.

Glamour Girl is one of her most incisive theatrical novels in which the temperamental "Glama Gaye"—"Britain's Premier Box-Office Attraction"—rides roughshod over everyone in her orbit—fellow performers, stage hands, dressers, and, most of all, her husband and secretary, who are eventually driven into each other's arms as a result of the star's ruthlessness. Theirs is, however, a triumph of true love—and Glama gets her just deserts in an uneasy relationship with a male "limelight idol" who is as fatally attractive and faithless as herself. The story has a slightly bizarre touch that is characteristic of Evadne Price's books; Glama, the striking beauty, and Elna, her rather drab secretary, are actually twin sisters, though the relationship is never publicly acknowledged. But Elna can overcome her mousiness sufficiently to disguise herself as Glama and "double" for her on assignments that Glama finds too dangerous—or too dull—to undertake.

Evadne Price uses this twin theme again with dramatic effect in *Air Hostess in Love*. Again, the quieter of the sisters, Judy, is a secretary, while the flashier one, Stella, has the glossy job of air hostess. And as in *Glamour Girl* the sedate young woman has sometimes to substitute for her sister in hazardous situations before her romantic difficulties with the man she loves can be resolved. Although Evadne Price skilfully enlists her readers' sympathies for conformist and "ordinary" heroines like these sisters of the high-powered actress or air hostess, she is at her best with more vivid characters, for example, the dancer Carole Iden in *The Love Trap*, who has "a flame of red hair" and "the permanent challenge" of "provocative green eyes." Carole in fact needs all the help that her startling good looks can bring her—because, at the beginning of the story, she has been made pregnant by a dashing test pilot who gets killed before he can marry her. She attracts an older and more stable man who offers her one of those marriages in-name-only that, in the romantic novel genre, always end happily with hero and heroine falling blissfully in love with each other. In some of her other books, Evadne Price persuasively exploits several inventive variations on the type of situation used in *The Love Trap*, *Glamour Girl*, and *Air Hostess in Love*.

—Mary Cadogan

PROLE, Lozania. *See* **BLOOM, Ursula.**

QUEST, Erica. *See* **BUCKINGHAM, Nancy.**

RAE, Hugh C.   *See* **STIRLING, Jessica.**

RADCLIFFE, Janette.   *See* **ROBERTS, Janet Louise.**

RANDALL, Florence Engel.   American.   Born in Brooklyn, New York, 18 October 1917. Attended Pratt Institute, New York, 1938; New York University, 1939. Married Murray C. Randall in 1939; three children. Agent: Raines and Raines, 475 Fifth Avenue, New York, New York 10017. Address: 88 Oxford Street, Great Neck, New York 11023, U.S.A.

ROMANCE AND GOTHIC PUBLICATIONS

Novels

   Hedgerow.   New York, Harcourt Brace, and London, Heinemann, 1967.
   The Place of Sapphires.   New York, Harcourt Brace, 1969; London, Millington, 1974.
   Haldane Station.   New York, Harcourt Brace, 1973; London, Millington, 1975.

Uncollected Short Stories

   "Thursday We Kiss," in *Seventeen* (Radnor, Pennsylvania), August 1962.
   "The Man Who Didn't Want to Go Home," in *Good Housekeeping* (Des Moines, Iowa), February 1963.
   "Heirloom," in *Redbook* (Dayton, Ohio), February 1963.
   "Close by My Side," in *Good Housekeeping* (Des Moines, Iowa), April 1963.
   "Meeting Place," in *Redbook* (Dayton, Ohio), May 1963.
   "Night Life," in *Redbook* (Dayton, Ohio), August 1963.
   "I Was Looking for You," in *Good Housekeeping* (Des Moines, Iowa), August 1963.
   "Heart of the House," in *Good Housekeeping* (Des Moines, Iowa), September 1963.
   "Newcomer," in *Redbook* (Dayton, Ohio), September 1963.
   "Please Call the Office," in *Redbook* (Dayton, Ohio), December 1963.
   "What Women Know Best," in *Good Housekeeping* (Des Moines, Iowa), February 1964.
   "No Beginning, No End," in *Redbook* (Dayton, Ohio), March 1964.
   "Friendship," in *Redbook* (Dayton, Ohio), September 1964.
   "So Near to Me," in *Good Housekeeping* (Des Moines, Iowa), January 1965.
   "No One Kicks Cans Any More," in *Redbook* (Dayton, Ohio), April 1965.
   "First Chill," in *Redbook* (Dayton, Ohio), October 1967.

"The Watchers," in *Impact*, edited by Donald L. Stansburg.   Englewood Cliffs, New Jersey, Prentice Hall, 1971.
"Night of Love," in *Good Housekeeping* (Des Moines, Iowa), October 1974.
"Me...and the Boy Next Door," in *Good Housekeeping* (Des Moines, Iowa), June 1978.

OTHER PUBLICATIONS

Other (juvenile)

The Almost Year.   New York, Atheneum, 1971.
A Watcher in the Woods.   New York, Atheneum, 1976; London, New English Library, n.d.

Manuscript Collection: Mugar Memorial Library, Boston University.

Florence Engel Randall comments:

Even though all of my adult novels could be classified as gothic since they contain the necessary ingredients of atmosphere, mystery, and romance, it seems to me they are gothic with a difference. These are modern novels, set in the present time and they vary, one from the other. *Hedgerow* takes place on a farm and is a straight mystery romance, but *The Place of Sapphires* is a romance set within the confines of a ghost story, and *Haldane Station*, since it deals with a form of time travel, could almost be called science fiction.

My "young adult" books are different as well. *The Almost Year* deals with a poltergeist and the race question. *A Watcher in the Woods* is science fiction that has its focus not only in the imagination but reality as well. It has been made into a movie by Walt Disney Productions.

                         *   *   *

While she was writing romantic short stories in the early 1960's, Florence Engel Randall dreamed of producing a novel. She writes each chapter as she would a short story, yet leaves each incomplete in itself, linked to the others. She allows her characters and her unconscious mind to determine the flow of the story rather than planning the plot in advance.

The heroine of *Hedgerow* is a young ballet student who takes a summer babysitting job as a change from her grueling practice schedule after an illness forces her to rest. She becomes curious about the strange suicide of a member of the Hedge family and is determined to discover its cause. She pries into the family secrets until she deserves the results of the fury she induces. But love conquers all and this novel has more pure romance than the ones that follow.

The Place of Sapphires deals with a ghost and possession. After an accident in which their parents are killed, two sisters take a house which is reputed to be haunted. The injured girl occupies the room of Alarice, the deceased younger sister of the owner, and begins to reflect the behavior of the dead woman. The story is told from the points of view of the two sisters and the ghost in separate sections which relate the same events from three different perspectives. The contrast is striking and well done.

The Almost Year derived from research undertaken for the previous work. The idea of a poltergeist developed into a 15-year-old black girl sent from the ghetto to live with a middle-class white family for nine months. Resentment, anger, and suspicion spark the poltergeist which symbolizes the girl's misery and frustration. An American Library Association Notable Book, this novel for young adults handles the racial problem with skill, but the poltergeist received mixed reviews.

Haldane Station reveals the author's fascination with time. She uses time measured inwardly or subjectively in a series of flash-forwards as Rachel "remembers" things that have not happened yet and then finds herself in the future remembering much of the past. But the future is not as she recalls it. The complex plot is intriguing, but not every reader will enjoy it.

A Watcher in the Woods also has a time theme. Jan begins to feel the emotions of a girl who seems to be trying to lead her to the resolution of the unsolved disappearance of a child almost 50 years before. When other members of the family are also contacted by the watcher, the child's mother is invited to visit in an attempt to reunite them. The first-person narrative is filled with a 15-year-old's preoccupations, but curiosity is very strong, both in the characters and in the reader.

Randall has developed from a writer of sweet romance short stories into the successful author of occult-like novels and has carved a small niche for herself in the annals of gothic romance literature.

—Andrea Lee Shuey

RANDALL, Rona. British. Born in Birkenhead, Cheshire. Educated at Birkenhead High School; Pitman's College, London. Married Frederick Walter Shamrock; one son. Worked in theatre repertory companies, three years, then a journalist: Chairman, Women's Press Club of London, 1962-63. Recipient: Romantic Novelists Association Major Award, 1969. Address: Conifers, Pembury Road, Tunbridge Wells, Kent TN2 4ND, England.

ROMANCE AND GOTHIC PUBLICATIONS

Novels

The Moon Returns. London, Collins, 1942.
Doctor Havelock's Wife. London, Collins, 1943.
Rebel Wife. London, Collins, 1944.
The Late Mrs. Lane. London, Collins, 1945; New York, Arcadia House, 1946.
The Howards of Saxondale. London, Collins, 1946.
That Girl, Jennifer! New York, Arcadia House, 1946.
The Fleeting Hour. London, Collins, 1947.
I Married a Doctor. London, Collins, 1947; as *The Doctor Takes a Wife*, New York, Arcadia House, 1947.
The Street of the Singing Fountain. London, Collins, 1948.
Shadows on the Sand. London, Collins, 1949; New York, Ace, 1973.
Delayed Harvest. London, Collins, 1950.
Young Doctor Kenway. London, Collins, 1950.
The Island Doctor. London, Collins, 1951.
Bright Morning. London, Collins, 1952.
Girls in White. London, Collins, and New York, Arcadia House, 1952.
Young Sir Galahad. London, Collins, 1953.
Journey to Love. London, Collins, 1953; New York, Ace, 1972.
Faith, Hope, and Charity. London, Collins, 1954.
The Merry Andrews. London, Collins, 1954.
Desert Flower. London, Collins, 1955.
Journey to Arcady. New York, Arcadia House, 1955.
Leap in the Dark. London, Collins, 1956; New York, Ace, 1967.
A Girl Called Ann. London, Collins, 1956; New York, Ace, 1973.
Runaway from Love. London, Collins, 1956.

The Cedar Tree. London, Collins, 1957.
The Doctor Falls in Love. London, Collins, 1958.
Nurse Stacey Comes Aboard. London, Collins, 1958; New York, Ace, 1968.
Love and Dr. Maynard. London, Collins, 1959.
Enchanted Eden. London, Collins, 1960.
Sister at Sea. London, Collins, 1960.
Hotel De Luxe. London, Collins, 1961; New York, Ace, 1967.
Girl in Love. London, Collins, 1961.
House Surgeon at Luke's. London, Collins, 1962.
Walk into My Parlour. London, Collins, 1962; New York, Ace, 1967; revised edition, as
    Lyonhurst, London, Fontana, and New York, Ballantine, 1977.
Lab Nurse. New York, Berkley, 1962.
The Silver Cord. London, Collins, 1963; New York, Ace, 1968.
The Willow Herb. London, Collins, 1965; New York, Ace, 1967.
Seven Days from Midnight. London, Collins, 1965; New York, Ace, 1967.
Arrogant Duke. London, Collins, 1966; New York, Ace, 1972.
Knight's Keep. London, Collins, and New York, Ace, 1967.
Broken Tapestry. London, Hurst and Blackett, 1969; New York, Ace, 1973.
The Witching Hour. London, Hurst and Blackett, and New York, Ace, 1970.
Silent Thunder. London, Hurst and Blackett, 1971.
Mountain of Fear. New York, Ace, 1972.
Time Remembered, Time Lost. New York, Ace, 1973.
Glenrannoch. London, Collins, 1973; as *The Midnight Walker*, New York, Ace, 1973.
Dragonmede. London, Collins, and New York, Simon and Schuster, 1974.
Watchman's Stone. London, Collins, and New York, Simon and Schuster, 1975.
The Eagle at the Gate. New York, Coward McCann, 1977; London, Hamish Hamilton,
    1978.
Gods of Mars. New York, Ballantine, 1977.
The Mating Dance. London, Hamish Hamilton, and New York, Coward McCann,
    1979.
The Ladies of Hanover Square. London, Hamish Hamilton, and New York, Coward
    McCann, 1981.

OTHER PUBLICATIONS

Other

Jordan and the Holy Land. London, Muller, 1968.

*   *   *

A common theme found in Rona Randall's stories concerns a young woman who becomes involved with a handsome man unworthy of her love. Often the heroine actually marries this man and shares with him a passionate relationship, all the time believing that they will live happily ever after. At first all goes well, but slowly sinister aspects of his personality emerge. Fortunately there is always another man around willing to offer the kind of love she deserves. Though not necessarily handsome, he is a robust individual who impresses the heroine with a powerful masculine presence. In what has become standard romantic form, the hero and heroine are initially incompatible, often because of his overbearing personality or sarcastic wit. Typically, he is a medical doctor and through the tender care of his patients Randall shows the reader and the heroine his intrinsic goodness.

This format is ideal for the gothic novel of which Randall has written several. Probably one of her best known is *Dragonmede*. In this Victorian tale Eustacia Rochdale falls in love with the aristocratic Julian Kershaw. Although Eustacia is well educated, her family background (a mother who runs an illegal gambling establishment) leaves much to be desired. However, the young man seems genuinely to love her and eventually proposes marriage. She is ecstatic until her first glimpse of the ancestral home, Dragonmede, whereupon a feeling of foreboding engulfs her. Her fears are not unfounded for, although Julian proves to be a passionate husband, he has a brooding, sadistic side that eventually destroys Eustacia's love for him. Other sinister characters abound, and with Julian's murder she finds herself in mortal danger. In the end it is the love of a virile young doctor that saves her life and gives her the happy marriage she has always wanted.

An earlier work with a similar plot but fewer of the gothic trappings is *Shadows on the Sand*. Sorrel Dean, a young architect, journeys to Beirut in order to join her fiancé Richard Baily, an archeologist working at a desert site. Soon she finds that he is involved in the theft of valuable relics uncovered by the expedition. Although Sorrel is never directly in danger, her innocent association with this dark character causes her a great deal of emotional stress. Again it is a taciturn but basically compassionate medical doctor who proves to be her true love.

Variations on the eternal triangle theme also run through many of Randall's stories. Often the heroine discovers that the man she first loved is not all he seems as when his involvement with another woman can no longer be ignored. In *Dragonmede* Julian, although married to Eustacia, still keeps the wickedly beautiful Victoria on the side. In *Watchman's Stone* the lovely Elizabeth marries Calum only to discover his affair with her younger sister. In *The Mating Dance* pretty blonde Lucinda finds her worthless husband in bed with her older sister Clementine, an irrepressible lady whose obvious enjoyment of sex is in sharp contrast to Lucy's more conventional attitude.

Randall's fiction contains elements of drama, action, and excitement. Her excellent portrayal of the various characters, especially the heroines, makes the reader care what happens to them. With a fluid writing style this author weaves engaging tales of women in love.

—Patricia Altner

RAYNER, Claire (Berenice). Also writes as Sheila Brandon; Ann Lynton; Ruth Martin. British. Born 22 January 1931. Married Desmond Rayner in 1957; one daughter and two sons. Nurse in the pediatric department, Whittington Hospital, London, until 1960; television presenter, Pebble Mill program; Columnist, as Ruth Martin for nine years, and since 1975 as Claire Rayner, *Woman's Own*, London. Agent: Michael Horniman, A.P. Watt Ltd., 26-28 Bedford Row, London WC1R 4HL. Address: Holly Wood House, Harrow-on-the-Hill, Middlesex HA1 3BU, England.

ROMANCE AND GOTHIC PUBLICATIONS

Novels

The Performers:
   Gower Street. London, Cassell, and New York, Simon and Schuster, 1973.
   The Haymarket. London, Cassell, and New York, Simon and Schuster, 1974.
   Paddington Green. London, Cassell, and New York, Simon and Schuster, 1975.
   Soho Square. London, Cassell, and New York, Putnam, 1976.
   Bedford Row. London, Cassell, and New York, Putnam, 1977.
   Long Acre. London, Cassell, 1978; as *Covent Garden*, New York, Putnam, 1978.
   Charing Cross. London, Cassell, and New York, Putnam, 1979.
   The Strand. London, Cassell, and New York, Putnam, 1980.

Chelsea Reach. London, Weidenfeld and Nicolson, 1982.

Novels as Sheila Brandon

The Final Year. London, Corgi, 1962.
Cottage Hospital. London, Corgi, 1963.
Children's Ward. London, Corgi, 1964.
The Lonely One. London, Corgi, 1965.
The Doctors of Downlands. London, Corgi, 1968.
The Private Wing. London, Corgi, 1971.
Nurse in the Sun. London, Corgi, 1972.

OTHER PUBLICATIONS

Novels

Shilling a Pound Pears. London, Hart Davis, 1964.
The House on the Fen. London, Corgi, and New York, Bantam, 1967.
Starch of Aprons. London, Hale, 1967; as *The Hive*, London, Corgi, 1968.
Lady Mislaid. London, Corgi, 1968.
Death on the Table. London, Corgi, 1969.
The Meddlers. London, Cassell, and New York, Simon and Schuster, 1970.
A Time to Heal. London, Cassell, and New York, Simon and Schuster, 1972.
The Burning Summer. London, Allison and Busby, 1972.
Sisters. London, Hutchinson, 1978.
Reprise. London, Hutchinson, 1980.
The Running Years. London, Hutchinson, 1981.

Other

Mothers and Midwives. London, Allen and Unwin, 1962.
What Happens in the Hospital. London, Hart Davis, 1963.
The Calendar of Childhood: A Guide for All Mothers. London, Ebury Press, 1964.
Your Baby. London, Hamlyn, 1965.
Careers with Children. London, Hale, 1966.
Housework—The Easy Way. London, Corgi, 1967.
Mothercraft (as Ann Lynton). London, Corgi, 1967.
Shall I Be a Nurse? Exeter, Wheaton, 1967.
Home Nursing and Family Health. London, Transworld, 1967.
101 Facts an Expectant Mother Should Know. London, Dickens Press, 1967.
For Children: Equipping a Home for a Growing Family. London, Macdonald, 1967.
Essentials of Out-patient Nursing. London, Arlington, 1967.
101 Key Facts of Practical Baby Care. London, Dickens Press, 1967.
A Parent's Guide to Sex Education. London, Corgi, 1968; Garden City, New York,
   Dolphin, 1969.
People in Love: A Modern Guide to Sex in Marriage. London, Hamlyn, 1968; revised
   edition, as *About Sex*, London, Fontana, 1972.
Woman's Medical Dictionary. London, Corgi, 1971.
When to Call the Doctor—What to Do Whilst Waiting. London, Corgi, 1972.
The Shy Person's Book. London, Wolfe, 1973; New York, McKay, 1974.
Childcare Made Simple. London, W.H. Allen, 1973.
Where Do I Come From? Answers to a Child's Questions about Sex. London, Arling-
   ton, 1974.
You Know More Than You Think You Do. London, MIND Council, 1975.

Kitchen Garden, with Keith Fordyce.   London, Independent Television Publications, 1976.
More Kitchen Garden, with Keith Fordyce.   London, Independent Television Publications, 1977.
Family Feelings: Understanding Your Child from 0 to Five.   London, Arrow, 1977.
Claire Rayner Answers Your 100 Questions on Pregnancy.   London, BBC Publications, 1977.
The Body Book (juvenile).   London, G. Whizzard, 1978; Woodbury, New York, Barron's, 1980.
Related to Sex.   New York and London, Paddington Press, 1979.
Everything Your Doctor Would Tell You If He Had the Time.   London, Cassell, and New York, Putnam, 1980.
Claire Rayner's Lifeguide: A Commonsense Approach to Modern Living.   London, New English Library, 1980.
Baby and Young Child Care: A Practical Guide for Parents of Children Aged 0-5 Years.   Maidenhead, Berkshire, Purnell, 1981.

Editor (as Ruth Martin), *Before the Baby—and After*.   London, Hurst and Blackett, 1958.
Editor, *The Mitchell Beazley Atlas of the Body and Mind*.   London, Mitchell Beazley, 1976; as *Rand McNally Atlas of the Body and Mind*, Chicago, Rand McNally, 1976.

*   *   *

Claire Rayner is a professional writer in the best sense. She works very hard, to a tight schedule. She writes with authority and her research is impeccable, whether she be writing factually or fictionally. Talking of her historical fiction she once said: "If I say it was hot and muggy one August day in 1825 there's no need to check the meteorological records. I've done it already." This sums up her almost pernickety attitude to accuracy.

She is known widely for her journalism, largely based on her medical training. She has been an "Agony Auntie" for many years, writing Problem Pages in magazines and newspapers and appearing on television in the same role, as well as on more general programmes, such as (on radio) *The News Quiz* and *Any Questions*. In short, she has become a personality, and, in addition, a respected writer of non-fiction books on psychological and sexual problems, family health, and child care.

The fund of knowledge gained in these fields stands behind her work as a novelist. She has written many novels. In the 1960's, as Sheila Brandon, she wrote romantic hospital fiction and two gothics. But nearly 10 years ago she began to write a series with perhaps the greatest appeal for romantic fiction readers, again using her medical knowledge, but adding another facet of her interests and experience, the theatre. And she set the scene back in time.

The Performers series begins in the early 1800's. Claire Rayner plans that it should run to at least a dozen volumes. Each has, as its title, the name of a London street appropriate to the plot. The first volume, *Gower Street*, begins the dual stories of Abel Lackland and Lilith Lucas, two guttersnipes with intelligence, ambition, ruthlessness—and luck. The violence of their mutual attraction is mixed with antagonism and resentment, and it is this clash of emotions which pervades the whole series as their proliferating progeny become, in various ways, its victims.

Apart from being a good, practical, professional writer Claire Rayner is a born storyteller. She handles the increasingly complex strands of her story and growing list of characters adroitly. And her stories are full of "character" as well as characters. Each is permeated with interesting information about medical practice and the London theatre in the Victorian era—though the author is clever enough not to let her in-depth research intrude.

She is also adept at the art of "letting go" the initial characters, allowing later generations to take centre stage. By the time we reach Book 3 (*Paddington Green*) Abel and Lilith are middle-aged and at the height of their professions, Abel an eminent surgeon, Lilith an equally famous actress. Their characters have hardened, and it is the intertwining stories of their children which engage our interest—especially that of Abel's daughter Abby, whose romance with a handsome Jew introduces virtually insurmountable new difficulties.

But although the story is beginning to "spread out," the two families remain locked in their love-hate relationship. In Book 6 (*Long Acre*), which brings the story up to the 1860's, two of Lilith's grandchildren return to England from America to take the London theatre by storm. Inevitably their paths cross those of Abel's grandchildren, and the sparks begin to fly all over again.

This book marks the end of an era, but on the final page the beginning of a new episode promises to carry the story on for at least a further generation. By this time the reader is hooked anyway—lured on partly by the fascinating detail of the settings, period, and plot, partly by the sharpness and variety of the characters, and their interdependence.

At the time of writing eight volumes of the saga have been published. Claire Rayner shows no sign of flagging. She has, however, continued to vary her style outside the series, producing two modern novels *Sisters* and *Reprise*, which cannot by any means be described as romantic, and a long (200,000 word) novel on the twin themes of survival and money—its diverse effects on people in general and, specifically, down the ages on one migrant Jewish clan—*The Running Years*.

Claire Rayner has a passionate interest in what makes people tick, what makes relationships work, or go wrong. This is obviously why her medical/psychological non-fiction is so successful and popular. It is also why she writes good novels. Her people are real, vulnerable, fallible and it is from the clash of their strengths and weaknesses that the stories grow.

—Elizabeth Grey

REID, Henrietta.   Address: c/o Mills and Boon Ltd., 15-16 Brooks Mews, London W1A 1DR, England.

ROMANCE AND GOTHIC PUBLICATIONS

Novels

Island of Secrets.   London, Mills and Boon, 1965.
Return to Candelriggs.   London, Mills and Boon, 1966.
Daughter of Lir.   London, Mills and Boon, 1966.
Man of the Islands.   London, Mills and Boon, 1966; Toronto, Harlequin, 1967.
My Dark Rapparee.   London, Mills and Boon, 1966; Toronto, Harlequin, 1967.
Substitute for Love.   London, Mills and Boon, 1967; Toronto, Harlequin, 1968.
Bridal Tapestry.   London, Mills and Boon, 1967.
Falcon's Keep.   London, Mills and Boon, 1968; Toronto, Harlequin, 1969.
Beloved Sparrow.   London, Mills and Boon, 1968; Toronto, Harlequin, 1969.
Laird of Storr.   London, Mills and Boon, and Toronto, Harlequin, 1968.
Reluctant Masquerade.   London, Mills and Boon, 1969; Toronto, Harlequin, 1970.
The Thorn Tree.   London, Mills and Boon, 1969.
The Black Delaney.   London, Mills and Boon, 1970; Toronto, Harlequin, 1971.
Hunter's Moon.   London, Mills and Boon, and Toronto, Harlequin, 1970.
Rival Sisters.   London, Mills and Boon, 1970; Toronto, Harlequin, 1971.
The Made Marriage.   London, Mills and Boon, and Toronto, Harlequin, 1971.
Sister of the Bride.   London, Mills and Boon, 1971; Toronto, Harlequin, 1972.
Garth of Tregillis.   London, Mills and Boon, and Toronto, Harlequin, 1972.
The Torrent.   London, Mills and Boon, 1972.

Bride of Ravenscourt. London, Mills and Boon, 1972.
Dark Usurper. London, Mills and Boon, 1972.
Bird of Prey. London, Mills and Boon, 1973; Toronto, Harlequin, 1974.
Intruder at Windgates. London, Mills and Boon, and Toronto, Harlequin, 1973.
Dragon Island. London, Mills and Boon, 1974; Toronto, Harlequin, 1975.
The Man at the Helm. London, Mills and Boon, and Toronto, Harlequin, 1975.
The Tartan Ribbon. London, Mills and Boon, 1976; Toronto, Harlequin, 1977.
Love's Puppet. Toronto, Harlequin, 1976.
Greek Bridal. Toronto, Harlequin, 1976.
Push the Past Behind. Toronto, Harlequin, 1977.
Tomorrow Brings Enchantment. London, Mills and Boon, 1978.
Paradise Plantation. London, Mills and Boon, and Toronto, Harlequin, 1979.
Lord of the Isles. Toronto, Harlequin, 1981.

*   *   *

Henrietta Reid's novels may read like modern versions of Cinderella, but in reality they are delightful examples of "happy ever after" love stories. She is another writer who finds young innocence full of enchanting possibilities as she sets the stage for her heroines.

Although she does vary the approaches in her novels, she has, perhaps, unconsciously developed a certain kind of pattern that lets her make the fullest use of her gift in creating heartwarming stories. In at least three novels, she portrays a sensitive girl/child heroine who has suddenly been pushed out of her secure nest into the world of strangers. In *Hunter's Moon* Gillian Blake's Aunt Fisher has had to sell her home and move in with a friend her own age. To make it possible for her to do so, Gillian sets out to find a job on her own, by hitch-hiking. Although she has never held a job, she is sure she can get one because she is "good with her hands."

Just as precipitous is Nicola Fletcher in *The Black Delaney* as she is suddenly pitch-forked into the household of Rowan Delaney. Her Aunt Doris decides she has no further need of her now that her own daughter is marrying. Finally, Mandy in *Laird of Storr* is suddenly offered a home by an unknown aunt after spending her life in an orphanage. Mandy, of course, is not aware that her aunt really wants an unpaid servant for the moment.

This tendency to throw her heroine into the deep end naturally gives Reid a wide range of plot complications and offers numerous chances for character development. Her heroines are ingenuous and they are guileless. It makes a touching story for her readers as she is able to show them winning the hero's love without losing that inner radiance of goodness that characterizes them. This is not to imply that they do not grow and mature. Experience must add to a person's knowledge, but their experiences merely re-inforce their own standards of behavior and beliefs. In this sense, their innocence is their protection and one of the strongest impulses of attraction for the heroes.

Reid is able to maintain a strong balance in developing the characters of her heroes. While successful, forceful, and confident, they are yet gentlemen in the true sense of the word. Steven Charlton in *Hunter's Moon* is a business man who maintains a home in the country. His mother and the daughter of an old family friend live there also. He is somewhat cynical, an eligible bachelor, and at heart a "softy." Alisdair Storr in *Laird of Storr* is quite similar in character and outlook. He is just as forceful and holds a place of respect in the community because of his position but also because of his own personality. Rowan Delaney's careless acceptance of Nicola in *The Black Delaney* is typical of a strong man who might befriend a stray kitten, and this is his attitude towards her. He is careless and absent-minded, if impatient, as he tries to fit her into his life and home.

For the most part, Reid's backgrounds are sketched with a minimum of detail and only as it helps to move the story along. She does use the natural world, however, to help establish the heroine's sensitivity and gentleness as she frequently reacts to the beauty around her. Neither does she restrict herself to English scenes, for several of her novels are placed in other parts of the world.

In summarizing Henrietta Reid as a romance writer, one must acknowledge her talent for portraying her heroines so charmingly. What makes them so nice is the fact that she makes them believable, in spite of modern standards and ideas. In a way, her readers may see her heroines as personifications of modern girls in spite of changing mores. They seem to enjoy the idealistic outlook for it offers endless possibilities for freshness and hope to them.

—Arlene Moore

RENIER, Elizabeth.   Pseudonym for Betty Doreen Baker, née Flook.   British.   Born in Bristol, 22 November 1916. Educated at the Collegiate School, and Merchant Venturers College, both Bristol. Served in the Voluntary Aid Detachment, attached to the Royal Army Medical Corps, 1940-42. Married Frank Edward Baker (died). Has worked as a doctor's secretary; volunteer, Family Planning Association, 1958-62. Recipient: Romantic Novelists Association Warwick Award, 1962. Address: Inchcoulter Cottage, 15 Douglas Avenue, Exmouth, Devon, England.

ROMANCE AND GOTHIC PUBLICATIONS

Novels

> *The Generous Vine*.   London, Hurst and Blackett, 1962; New York, Ace, 1972.
> *The House of Water*.   London, Hurst and Blackett, 1963; New York, Ace, 1972.
> *Blade of Justice*.   London, Hurst and Blackett, 1965; New York, Ace, 1972.
> *If This Be Treason*.   London, Hurst and Blackett, 1965; as *If This Be Love*, New York, Ace, 1971.
> *Valley of Nightingales*.   London, Hurst and Blackett, 1966.
> *A Singing in the Woods*.   London, Hurst and Blackett, 1966; New York, Ace, 1972.
> *Prelude to Freedom*.   London, Hurst and Blackett, 1967; as *Prelude to Love*, New York, Ace, 1972.
> *The House of Granite*.   London, Hurst and Blackett, 1968; New York, Ace, 1971.
> *By Sun and Candlelight*.   London, Hurst and Blackett, 1968; New York, Ace, 1973.
> *Tomorrow Comes the Sun*.   London, Hurst and Blackett, 1969; New York, Ace, 1971.
> *The Spanish Doll*.   London, Hurst and Blackett, 1970; New York, Ace, 1972.
> *Valley of Secrets*.   London, Hurst and Blackett, 1970; New York, Ace, 1972.
> *Woman from the Sea*.   London, Hurst and Blackett, 1971; New York, Ace, n.d.
> *The Renshawe Inheritance*.   London, Hurst and Blackett, 1972; New York, Ace, 1973.
> *A Time for Rejoicing*.   London, Hurst and Blackett, and New York, Ace, 1973.
> *Ravenstor*.   London, Hurst and Blackett, 1974.
> *Yesterday's Mischief*.   London, Hurst and Blackett, 1975.
> *The Moving Dream*.   London, Hurst and Blackett, 1977; New York, Fawcett, 1978.
> *Landscape of the Heart*.   London, Hurst and Blackett, 1978; New York, Fawcett, 1979.

OTHER PUBLICATIONS

Other (juvenile)

> *The Lightkeepers*.   London, Hamish Hamilton, 1977.
> *The Stone People*.   London, Hamish Hamilton, 1978.

The Dangerous Journey. London, Hamish Hamilton, 1979.
The Post-rider. London, Hamish Hamilton, 1980.

*   *   *

"Do not hit those children like that as if you were herding cattle." "Cattle'd fetch a better price, m'lady." These lines from Elizabeth Renier's *A Singing in the Woods* typify a dominant theme in her works, that of the wealthy heroine dedicating herself to improving conditions among the less fortunate. This egalitarian theme echoes her own avocational interest in working with deprived children. What is particularly impressive about Renier's novels, however, is a second theme, that of a young heiress pitted against the male dominance which surrounds her in the Devonshire area during the Georgian period. She masterfully creates the spirited innocence of the wealthy heroine of the time, allowing her lady to become a formidable challenge for the male counterpart. She effortlessly depicts the prosaic figure of a lovely woman amidst the splendor of her affluence but at the same time provides her with more than a superficial personality. Renier's heroine is eager to know about the world which surrounds her; she is an amalgam of fiestiness, tenaciousness, and strength. Renier captures the rebellious nature of a woman with power during this period without losing the harmony of the poignantly described period setting. The lady always possesses a strong feeling for the grandeur of her homeland, whether it be Stant Lydeard of *A Singing in the Woods*, Merriott of *The Renshawe Inheritance*, or similar settings. The reader can trust the character to be true to her ideals throughout the novel.

Renier's writing is refreshingly free from affectation, simply paced. The plot usually presents an energetic promenade of adventures which entangle the heroine and the hero (frequently land disputes create the dilemmas); but the potentially intolerable wooing scenes are pruned to crisp-in-form but tender-in-content meetings, punctuated with convincing descriptions of historical and graphical details. The heroes range from engaging swashbucklers to the more diffident gentlemen whose psychological strength outperforms their physical strength. Even Renier's minor characters are effective and memorable sketches.

Renier is an equal master in creating the ambiance of the period, providing the reader with an almost illustrated tour, a topo-cosmography of the Devonshire area with detailed descriptions that almost allow the reader to scent the aroma of the salt air.

Using these themes and style, Renier consistently writes well. With efficacy she creates a stimulating romance novel.

—W.M. von Zharen

RIEFE, Barbara. Pseudonym for Alan Riefe. American. Born in Waterbury, Connecticut, 18 May 1925. Educated at Colby College, Waterville, Maine, B.A. 1950. Served in the United States Army during World War II. Married 1) Martha Daggett in 1948 (died, 1949); 2) Barbara Dube in 1955; four children. Free-lance writer. Agent: Knox Burger Associates, 39½ Washington Square South, New York, New York 10012, U.S.A.

ROMANCE AND GOTHIC PUBLICATIONS

Novels

> *Barringer House*. New York, Popular Library, 1976.
> *Rowleston*. New York, Popular Library, 1976.
> *Auldearn House*. New York, Popular Library, 1976.
> *This Ravaged Heart*. Chicago, Playboy Press, 1977; London, Sphere, 1979.
> *Far Beyond Desire*. Chicago, Playboy Press, 1978; London, Sphere, 1980.
> *Fire and Flesh*. Chicago, Playboy Press, 1978.
> *Tempt Not This Flesh*. Chicago, Playboy Press, 1979.
> *Blackfire*. Chicago, Playboy Press, 1980.
> *So Wicked the Heart*. Chicago, Playboy Press, 1980.
> *Olivia*. Chicago, Playboy Press, 1981.
> *Wild Fire*. Chicago, Playboy Press, 1981.

OTHER PUBLICATIONS as Alan Riefe

Novels

> *The Lady Killers*. New York, Popular Library, 1975; London, New English Library,
> 1976.
> *The Conspirators*. New York, Popular Library, 1975; London, New English Library,
> 1977.
> *The Black Widower*. New York, Popular Library, 1975.
> *The Silver Puma*. New York, Popular Library, 1975.
> *The Bullet-Proof Man*. New York, Popular Library, 1975.
> *The Killer with the Golden Touch*. New York, Popular Library, 1975.
> *Tyger at Bay*. New York, Popular Library, 1976.
> *Tyger by the Tail*. New York, Popular Library, 1976.
> *The Smile on the Face of the Tyger*. New York, Popular Library, 1976.
> *Tyger and the Lady*. New York, Popular Library, 1976.
> *Hold That Tyger*. New York, Popular Library, 1976.
> *Tyger, Tyger, Burning Out*. New York, Popular Library, 1976.

Short Stories

> *Tales of Horror*. New York, Pocket Books, 1965.

Plays

> Television Writing: *Masquerade Party*, 8 years; *Keep Talking*, 2 years; and plays for
> *Pulitzer Prize Playhouse* and *Studio One* series.

Other

> *Vip's Illustrated Woman Driver's Manual*. New York, Fawcett, 1966.
> *Am I Your President?*, with others. New York, Curtis, 1972.

> Editor, with Dick Harrington, *Sanford and Son*. New York, Curtis, 1973.

*   *   *

Since 1976, Alan Riefe, writing under the pseudonym of Barbara Riefe, has turned his writing skills to the genre of historical romance with varying success. Riefe has a solid understanding of those elements which are of interest to the romance reader—true love, adventure in foreign lands, fast-paced action, and a sprinkling of spicy sex, all set in a time period gone by, and eventually leading to the beloved "happy ending."

Riefe's plots are often based on the separation of loved ones by unfortunate circumstances and the ensuing struggle by the loved ones against nearly impossible odds to become reunited. Riefe is at his best when he sends his characters on adventures, most often by sea. His sense of geographical detail—ranging from the United States to Capri to Tasmania to the Far East—and his knowledge of the sea and seafaring vessels add much in the way of credibility to his stories. In addition, fast-paced action, detailed description, and crisp dialogue serve to keep the reader actively interested in what is going to happen next. It is, after all, a good story that the reader of popular fiction is looking for; the main failure of books in the genre of popular fiction comes from the reader's fading desire to want to know what happens next, for there is generally insufficient character development, or logical cause and effect plot—which causes character development and growth—on which to rely in the event of lapses in the story.

When Riefe finds himself in danger of being uninteresting because the reader has become confident of the story's outcome, he uses coincidences and surprises—i.e., information which is known only to him—to cause a reversal or modification in the situation which heightens the reader's interest. Riefe also uses several subplots which are related to, and ultimately merge with, the main plot. These subplots are usually the various adventures of the separated loved ones. Rapid alternations between one plot and another (usually occurring in different geographical locations) serve to maintain and rekindle the reader's interest. (In one instance—in *This Ravaged Heart*—because of the use of witchcraft, the separation is made not only geographical but also temporal.) Should either of these methods fail, there are often graphic sexual interludes to add excitement.

Characterization and character development in these novels are often weak, as is generally the case in popular fiction, and many of the characters remain flat and undeveloped since they are, after all, merely vehicles for the action. Understandably, the character of the heroine is most clearly defined (although it doesn't often develop further in the course of the novel). The heroine exhibits "true, undying love" and the expected moral character necessary to being a good wife. In addition to female beauty and alluring female charms, the traits of solid judgement, intelligence, great mental and emotional strength, and superhuman stamina reveal themselves when she is separated from her husband and allow her to outwit her adversaries and overcome apparently insurmountable situations, ultimately resulting in the rescue of the loved one. These heroines do not bear up under close scrutiny, for they are almost superhuman figures, the good aspects of several men and women rolled into one, but their dialogue when well contrived convinces the reader—momentarily, at least—that it is otherwise. The reader is quite willing to overlook the flaw in the interest of entertainment. Riefe departs from the typical damsel-in-distress romance heroine, and makes his heroines much more products of this century, than of the previous century where he places them in time.

All in all, when Riefe balances the elements which he uses in his novels, he is capable of producing a well-wrought, gripping bit of entertainment that rivals that of many of his competitors. This is especially evident in the first volume of the Dandridge trilogy, *This Ravaged Heart*, perhaps the best of his romance novels. The second book, *Far Beyond Desire*, is also quite solid entertainment, although there is a prevalence of sexual interludes. The last book, *Fire and Flesh*, becomes a bit tedious because the reader must wade through a great deal of predictable exposition before arriving at the expected ending.

—Michael Held

RINEHART, Mary Roberts. American. Born in Pittsburgh, Pennsylvania, in 1876. Educated in elementary and high schools in Pittsburgh; Pittsburgh Training School for nurses, graduated 1896. Married Dr. Stanley Marshall Rinehart in 1896 (died, 1932); three sons. Full-time writer from 1903. Correspondent for *Saturday Evening Post* in World War I; reported Presidential nominating conventions. Lived in Pittsburgh until 1920, in Washington, D.C., 1920-32, and in New York City from 1932. Recipient: Mystery Writers of America Special Award, 1953. Litt.D.: George Washington University, Washington, D.C., 1923. *Died 22 September 1958.*

ROMANCE AND GOTHIC PUBLICATIONS

Novels (series: Nurse Hilda Adams, "Miss Pinkerton")

The Circular Staircase. Indianapolis, Bobbs Merrill, 1908; London, Cassell, 1909.
When a Man Marries. Indianapolis, Bobbs Merrill, 1909; London, Hodder and Stoughton, 1920.
The Man in Lower Ten. Indianapolis, Bobbs Merrill, and London, Cassell, 1909.
The Window at the White Cat. Indianapolis, Bobbs Merrill, 1910; London, Nash, 1911.
Where There's a Will. Indianapolis, Bobbs Merrill, 1912.
The Case of Jennie Brice. Indianapolis, Bobbs Merrill, 1913; London, Hodder and Stoughton, 1919.
The After House. Boston, Houghton Mifflin, 1914; London, Simpkin Marshall, 1915.
The Street of Seven Stars. Boston, Houghton Mifflin, 1914; London, Cassell, 1915.
K. Boston, Houghton Mifflin, and London, Smith Elder, 1915.
Bab, A Sub-Deb. New York, Doran, 1917; London, Hodder and Stoughton, 1920.
Long Live the King! Boston, Houghton Mifflin, and London, Murray, 1917.
Twenty-Three and a Half Hours' Leave. New York, Doran, 1918.
The Amazing Interlude. New York, Doran, and London, Murray, 1918.
Dangerous Days. New York, Doran, and London, Hodder and Stoughton, 1919.
The Truce of God. New York, Doran, 1920.
A Poor Wise Man. New York, Doran, and London, Hodder and Stoughton, 1920.
Sight Unseen, and The Confession. New York, Doran, and London, Hodder and Stoughton, 1921.
The Breaking Point. New York, Doran, and London, Hodder and Stoughton, 1922.
The Out Trail. New York, Doran, 1923.
The Red Lamp. New York, Doran, 1925; as *The Mystery Lamp*, London, Hodder and Stoughton, 1925.
The Bat (novelization of play), with Avery Hopwood. New York, Doran, and London, Cassell, 1926.
Lost Ecstasy. New York, Doran, and London, Hodder and Stoughton, 1927; as *I Take This Woman*, New York, Grosset and Dunlap, 1927.
Two Flights Up. New York, Doubleday, and London, Hodder and Stoughton, 1928.
This Strange Adventure. New York, Doubleday, and London, Hodder and Stoughton, 1929.
The Door. New York, Farrar and Rinehart, and London, Hodder and Stoughton, 1930.
Miss Pinkerton. New York, Farrar and Rinehart, 1932; as *The Double Alibi*, London, Cassell, 1932.
Mary Roberts Rinehart's Crime Book (Adams; novelets). New York, Farrar and Rinehart, 1933; London, Cassell, 1958.
The Album. New York, Farrar and Rinehart, and London, Cassell, 1933.
The State Versus Elinor Norton. New York, Farrar and Rinehart, 1934; as *The Case of Elinor Norton*, London, Cassell, 1934.
Mr. Cohen Takes a Walk. New York, Farrar and Rinehart, 1934.
The Doctor. New York, Farrar and Rinehart, and London, Cassell, 1936.
The Wall. New York, Farrar and Rinehart, and London, Cassell, 1938.
The Great Mistake. New York, Farrar and Rinehart, 1940; London, Cassell, 1941.

Haunted Lady (Adams).   New York, Farrar and Rinehart, and London, Cassell, 1942.
The Yellow Room.   New York, Farrar and Rinehart, 1945; London, Cassell, 1949.
The Curve of the Catenary.   New York, Royce, 1945.
A Light in the Window.   New York, Rinehart, and London, Cassell, 1948.
Episode of the Wandering Knife: Three Mystery Tales.   New York, Rinehart, 1950; as
   The Wandering Knife, London, Cassell, 1952.
The Swimming Pool.   New York, Rinehart, 1952; as *The Pool*, London, Cassell, 1952.

Short Stories (series: Letitia "Tish" Carberry)

The Amazing Adventures of Letitia Carberry.   Indianapolis, Bobbs Merrill, 1911; Lon-
   don, Hodder and Stoughton, 1919.
Tish.   Boston, Houghton Mifflin, 1916; London, Hodder and Stoughton, 1917.
Love Stories.   New York, Doran, 1920.
Affinities and Other Stories.   New York, Doran, and London, Hodder and Stoughton,
   1920.
More Tish.   New York, Doran, and London, Hodder and Stoughton, 1921.
Temperamental People.   New York, Doran, and London, Hodder and Stoughton, 1924.
Tish Plays the Game.   New York, Doran, 1926; London, Hodder and Stoughton, 1927.
Nomad's Land.   New York, Doran, 1926.
The Romantics.   New York, Farrar and Rinehart, 1929; London, Hodder and Stoughton,
   1930.
Married People.   New York, Farrar and Rinehart, and London, Cassell, 1937.
Tish Marches On.   New York, Farrar and Rinehart, 1937; London, Cassell, 1938.
Familiar Faces: Stories of People You Know.   New York, Farrar and Rinehart, 1941;
   London, Cassell, 1943.
Alibi for Isabel and Other Stories.   New York, Farrar and Rinehart, 1944; London,
   Cassell, 1946.
The Frightened Wife and Other Murder Stories.   New York, Rinehart, 1953; London,
   Cassell, 1954.
The Best of Tish.   New York, Rinehart, 1955; London, Cassell, 1956.

OTHER PUBLICATIONS

Plays

Seven Days, with Avery Hopwood (produced Trenton and New York, 1909; Harrogate,
   1913; London, 1915).   New York, French, 1931.
Cheer Up (produced New York, 1912).
Spanish Love, with Avery Hopwood (produced New York, 1920).
The Bat, with Avery Hopwood, adaptation of the novel *The Circular Staircase* by
   Rinehart (produced New York, 1920; London, 1921).   New York, French, 1931.
The Breaking Point (produced New York, 1923).

Screenplay: *Aflame in the Sky*, with Ewart Anderson, 1927.

Other

Kings, Queens, and Pawns: An American Woman at the Front.   New York, Doran,
   1915.
Through Glacier Park: Seeing America First with Howard Eaton.   Boston, Houghton
   Mifflin, 1916.
The Altar of Freedom.   Boston, Houghton Mifflin, 1917.

Tenting Tonight: A Chronicle of Sport and Adventure in Glacier Park and the Cascade Mountains. Boston, Houghton Mifflin, 1918.
Isn't That Just Like a Man! New York, Doran, 1920.
My Story (autobiography). New York, Farrar and Rinehart, 1931; London, Cassell, 1932; revised edition, New York, Rinehart, 1948.
Writing Is Work. Boston, The Writer, 1939.

Manuscript Collection: University of Pittsburgh Library.

Critical Study: *Improbable Fiction: The Life of Mary Roberts Rinehart* by Jan Cohn, Pittsburgh, University of Pittsburgh Press, 1980.

*   *   *

When Mary Roberts Rinehart turned her pen from mystery with romance to romance by itself, her "world" was still dominated by large houses with servants. This versatile craftsman produced novels and stories of sentiment, humor, and happy endings. Taken together, they offer a limited social history of the U.S.A. from the late 19th century to the late 1940's.

Early romances foreshadow. *When a Man Marries* is farce; its complications include a two-hour substitute "wife" for the visit of an aunt who doles an allowance, an ex-wife, and a butler with small pox. Vienna is the setting for *The Street of Seven Stars*, the romance of young Americans, the girl studying music, the man, medicine. They take care of a dying young boy. In *K*, "K", a surgeon, is a steadying influence on an idealist nurse.

World War I is a backdrop for several works. *The Amazing Interlude* concerns an American girl who dispensed soup, cigarettes, and pure love to wounded soldiers behind the front lines and returned to wait for Henri, her Belgian true-love. *Dangerous Days* centers on a wealthy and patriotic munitions manufacturer, his plant, and his stale marriage. Only the Armistice finally offers a bright future. Hilarity in *Twenty-Three and a Half Hours' Leave* results from a quartermaster's attempt to deal with the problem of no uniforms for a troop about to sail. *Bab, A Sub-Deb* is also very amusing as 17-year-old Barbara Putnam Thatcher records her Experiences, some "sickning." "For is not Romanse itself but breif, the thing of an hour, at least to the Other Sex?" During World War I, she helps to capture a spy.

The war is part of the ambitious scope of *This Strange Adventure* (life), a narrative of the Colfax family, mainly of the enduring Missy, from the 1880's to the war, and of *The Doctor* which chronicles the overlapping professional and love lives of Dr. Arden from 1910 to 1927. In *A Light in the Window* the light is placed by the mother of Ricky for a son off to World War I and by Ricky herself for her son and daughter off to World War II. Lives and loves of two generations of a family unfold.

Other romances vary. *Long Live the King!* has a charming ten-year-old hero, European Prince Otto. *A Poor Wise Man* is an ill-advised attempt to delve into labor problems after WW I, and *The Truce of God* documents a change of heart on Christmas day in medieval times. Through the marriage of a cowboy and an Eastern girl, *Lost Ecstasy* contrasts the hardships of life in the West and the easy, sometimes superficial, life in the affluent East. Slight is the parable of *Mr. Cohen Takes a Walk*; wealthy and elderly, he returns refreshed by good deeds.

Titles of the collections of short stories, except those of Tish, reveal diversified love stories. For 30 years, Tish (Letitia Carberry) led Lizzie, the narrator, and Aggie, the long-suffering, into the wild and woolly adventures of the M.A.T. (Middle-Aged Trio). Laugh provoking, the stories are full of spirit, including that of Charlie Sand, nephew, and of the medicinal blackberry cordial.

In a long career, Rinehart proved an able storyteller, her plots more complex than can be noted here. For readers of the 1980's, a weakness is the assumption that the best place for women, in spite of talent or intelligence, is in the home. Her humor cannot be faulted.

—Jane Gottschalk

RITCHIE, Claire. Also writes as Sharon Heath. Address: c/o Robert Hale Ltd., 45-47 Clerkenwell Green, London EC1R OHT, England.

Romance and Gothic Publications

Novels

The Sheltered Flame. London, Hodder and Stoughton, 1949.
Love Builds a House. London, Hodder and Stoughton, 1950.
Bright Meadows. London, Hodder and Stoughton, 1951.
Durable Fire. London, Hodder and Stoughton, 1951.
Lighted Windows. London, Hodder and Stoughton, 1952.
The Green Bough. London, Hodder and Stoughton, 1953.
The Heart Turns Homeward. London, Hodder and Stoughton, 1953.
The Gentle Wind. London, Hodder and Stoughton, 1954.
Sun on the Sea. London, Hodder and Stoughton, 1954.
Gift of the Heart. London, Hale, 1955.
Mending Flower. London, Hale, 1955.
The White Violet. London, Hale, 1956.
Dreaming River. London, Hale, 1957.
Love Will Lend Wings. London, Hale, 1957.
Date with an Angel. London, Hale, 1958.
The Sunflower's Look. London, Hale, 1958.
The Tempest and the Song. London, Hale, 1959.
Vagrant Dream. London, Hale, 1959.
Hatful of Cowslips. London, Hale, 1960.
Shadowed Paradise. London, Hale, 1960.
Sweet Bloom. London, Hale, 1961.
The Fair Adventure. London, Hale, 1961.
Doctor's Joy. London, Hale, 1962.
Heartsease Grows Here. London, Hale, 1962.
Summer at Silverwood. London, Hale, 1962.
You'll Love Me Yet. London, Hale, 1963.
Circle of Gold. London, Hale, 1964.
Ride on Singing. London, Hale, 1964.
For a Dream's Sake. London, Hale, 1965.
The Love That Follows. London, Hale, 1966.
To Greet the Morning. London, Hale, 1966.
Hope Is My Pillow. London, Hale, 1967.
As Waits the Sky. London, Hale, 1969.
This Summer's Rose. London, Hale, 1970.
Give All to Love. London, Hale, 1971.
Dream in the Heart. London, Hale, 1972.
Rainbow Romance. London, Hale, 1974.
Castle Perilous. London, Hale, 1979.
Season for Singing. London, Hale, 1979.
Lodestone for Luck. London, Hale, 1980.

Novels as Sharon Heath

A Vacation for Nurse Dean. New York, Ace, 1966.
Nurse at Moorcroft Manor. New York, Ace, 1967.
Nurse on Castle Island. New York, Ace, 1968; as *Master of Trelona* (as Claire Ritchie), London, Hale, 1977.
Nurse at Shadow Manor. New York, Ace, 1973.

Nurse Elaine and the Sapphire Star.   New York, Ace, 1973; as *Starshine for Sweethearts* (as Claire Ritchie), London, Hale, 1976.

OTHER PUBLICATIONS

Verse

The White Garden and Other Poems.   Crayke, Yorkshire, Guild Press, 1957.
The Mirror and Other Poems.   Walton on Thames, Surrey, Outposts, 1970.

Other

Writing the Romantic Novel.   London, Bond Street, 1962.

*   *   *

Claire Ritchie writes romantic novels in the modern idiom: novels which are light and readable by young but mature adults.

The heroines in Ritchie's novels are the up-to-date young ladies of their respective generations, as in *Bright Meadows* (1951) or *Castle Perilous* (1979). The girls are not beautiful but pretty and attractive. They are generally rather ordinary, and, though somewhat experienced in love, still at a formative age. The experiences in the novels help them to mature, to develop a competence in life through a testing experience. Ritchie sets her later novels in holiday or seaside locations with some added glamour; the plots become more complex and action-filled, with an element of mystery and skulduggery which sometimes appears contrived and unrealistic, as in *Castle Perilous.*

There are moral lessons, but Ritchie has learned to put them across in a more subtle way than the "Loyalty is a rare quality nowadays" type of remark in *Bright Meadows.* The experiences of the main characters instill in them a wisdom.

The incidental detail such as descriptions of women and the men who love them and the minor aspects of relationships are well handled. The novels are easy to read, having comparatively little dialogue and simple sentences. The main criticism that can be made is that the books are too chaste by modern standards. There is little passion in, for instance, *This Summer Rose* (1970) where the hero makes do with confessing to himself that he is in love. The romantic climax of this novel is, in fact, an offer to share the middle years.

—P.R. Meldrum

ROBERTS, Irene (née Williamson).   Also writes as Roberta Carr; Elizabeth Harle; I.M. Roberts; Ivor Roberts; Iris Rowland; Irene Shaw.   British.   Born in London, 27 September 1925. Left school at age 13. Served in the Women's Land Army during World War II. Married Terence Granville Leonard Roberts in 1947; two sons and one daughter. Worked as shop assistant, typist, and saleswoman, then journalist and writer: woman's page editor, *South Hams Review,* 1977-79, and weekly book reviewer in provincial newspapers. Since 1978, Tutor in Creative Writing, Kingsbridge Community College. Agent: John F. Gibson, 70 Windsor

Road, Bexhill-on-Sea, Sussex. Address: Alpha House, Higher Town, Marlborough, Kingsbridge, South Devon TQ7 3RL, England.

ROMANCE AND GOTHIC PUBLICATIONS

Novels

    Love Song of the Sea.   London, Fleetway, 1960.
    Squirrel Walk.   London, Gresham, 1961.
    Only to Part.   London, Fleetway, 1961.
    Wind of Fate.   London, Gresham, 1961.
    Beloved Rascals.   London, Gresham, 1962.
    The Shrine of Marigolds.   London, Gresham, 1962.
    Come Back Beloved.   London, Gresham, 1962.
    The Dark Night.   London, Fleetway, 1962.
    Sweet Sorrel.   London, Gresham, 1963.
    Tangle of Gold Lace .   London, Gresham, 1963.
    Cry of the Gulls.   London, Fleetway, 1963.
    The Whisper of Sea-Bells.   London, Hale, 1964.
    Echo of Flutes.   London, Hale, 1965.
    The Mountain Sang.   London, Hale, 1965.
    Where Flamingoes Fly.   London, Hale, 1966.
    A Handful of Stars.   London, Hale, 1967.
    Shadows on the Moon.   London, Hale, 1968.
    Jungle Nurse.   London, Hale, 1968.
    Love Comes to Larkswood.   London, Hale, 1968.
    Alpine Nurse.   London, Hale, 1968.
    Nurse in the Hills.   London, Hale, 1969.
    The Lion and the Sun.   London, Hale, 1969.
    Thunder Heights.   London, Hale, 1969.
    Surgeon in Tibet.   London, Hale, 1970.
    Birds Without Bars.   London, Hale, 1970.
    The Shrine of Fire.   London, Hale, 1970.
    Gull Haven.   London, Hale, 1971.
    Sister at Sea.   London, Hale, 1971.
    Moon over the Temple.   London, Hale, 1972.
    The Golden Pagoda.   London, Hale, 1972.
    Desert Nurse.   London, Hale, 1976.
    Nurse in Nepal.   London, Hale, 1976.
    Stars above Raffael.   London, Hale, 1977.
    Hawks Barton.   London, Hale, 1979.
    Symphony of Bells.   London, Hale, 1980.
    Nurse Moonlight.   London, Hale, 1980.
    Weave Me a Moonbeam.   London, Hale, 1982.
    Jasmine for a Nurse.   London, Hale, 1982.
    Sister on Leave.   London, Hale, 1982.

Novels as Iris Rowland

    The Tangled Web.   London, Gresham, 1962.
    Island in the Mist.   London, Gresham, 1962.
    The Morning Star.   London, Gresham, 1963.
    With Fire and Flowers.   London, Gresham, 1963.
    Golden Flower.   London, Gresham, 1964.
    A Fountain of Roses.   London, Gresham, 1966.

Valley of Bells. London, Gresham, 1967.
Blue Feathers. London, Gresham, 1967.
A Veil of Rushes. London, Gresham, 1967.
To Be Beloved. London, Gresham, 1968.
Rose Island. London, Gresham, 1969.
Cherries and Candlelight. London, Gresham, 1969.
Nurse at Kama Hall. London, Gresham, 1969.
Moon over Moncrieff. London, Gresham, 1969; New York, Lenox Hill Press, 1974.
The Knave of Hearts. London, Hale, 1970.
Star-Drift. London, Gresham, 1970.
Rainbow River. London, Gresham, 1970.
The Wild Summer. London, Gresham, 1970.
Orange Blossom for Tara. London, Gresham, 1971.
Blossoms in the Snow. London, Gresham, 1971.
Sister Julia. London, Hale, 1972.
To Lisa with Love. London, Hale, 1975.
Golden Bubbles. London, Hale, 1976.
Hunter's Dawn. London, Hale, 1977.
Forgotten Dreams. London, Hale, 1978.
Golden Triangle. London, Hale, 1978.
Dance Ballerina Dance. London, Hale, 1980.

Novels as Roberta Carr

Red Runs the Sunset. London, Gresham, 1963.
Sea Maiden. London, Gresham, 1965.
Fire Dragon. London, Gresham, 1967.
Golden Interlude. London, Gresham, 1970.

Novels as Elizabeth Harle

Golden Rain. London, Gresham, 1964; as Irene Roberts, New York, Belmont, 1966.
Gay Rowan. London, Gresham, 1965.
Sandy. London, Gresham, 1967.
Spray of Red Roses. London, Gresham, 1971.
The Silver Summer. London, Hale, 1971.
Buy Me a Dream. London, Hale, 1972.
The Burning Flame. London, Hale, 1979.

Novels as Irene Shaw

The House of Lydia. London, Wright and Brown, 1967.
Moonstone Manor. London, Wright and Brown, 1968; as *Murder's Mansion*, New York, Doubleday, 1976.
The Olive Branch. London, Wright and Brown, 1968.

OTHER PUBLICATIONS

Novels as Ivor Roberts

Jump into Hell! London, Brown Watson, 1960.
Trial by Water. London, Micron, 1961.
Green Hell. London, Micron, 1961.

The Throne of Pharaohs (as I.M. Roberts). London, Hale, 1974.
Hatshepsut, Queen of the Nile (as I.M. Roberts). London, Hale, 1976.

Other (juvenile)

Laughing Is for Fun. London, Micron, 1963.
Holidays for Hanbury. London, Micron, 1964.

Irene Roberts comments:

To me writing is as natural as breathing. It is something that I had to do. To this end it was necessary to educate myself and to learn to type and spell. Writing is, I find, as exciting as the first real Spring day after a bad Winter. I choose my characters and their situations from a great imaginary mixing-bowl of words that I keep in my head. I knead and shape these words into colourful beads that I love to string together in an interesting, meaningful way. While I am writing I am at one with my characters. I laugh with them and I feel their pain—that is why nine times out of ten I give them happy endings.

*   *   *

Irene Roberts is currently working on her 95th book. As Ivor Roberts she writes War novels. As Irene Roberts she turns out both doctor/nurse romances and contemporary Gothics. Elizabeth Harle is the name she uses for what she describes as sweet romances, the sort of sweet innocent romances that can be read and enjoyed by women from 12 to 90 plus, stories that quicken the heart without bringing a blush to the cheeks. As Iris Rowland she writes mystery or straight romance novels; as Roberta Carr again the genre is straight romance. Many of her contemporary gothic novels appear under the name Irene Shaw. Historical novels based on fact appear under her I.M. Roberts by-line. Covering such a wide span it is not surprising that she has been influenced by such widely differing authors as Rider Haggard, Edgar Rice Burroughs, and Arnold Bennett's mystical work *The Glimpse*. This latter, she claims, had a great effect on her. Jean Plaidy's historical works and the Victoria Holt romances have also played some part in shaping her writings.

—Marion R. Harris

ROBERTS, Janet Louise. Also writes as Louisa Bronte; Rebecca Danton; Janette Radcliffe. American. Born in New Britain, Connecticut, 20 January 1925. Educated at Fairview High School, Dayton, Ohio; Otterbein College, Westerville, Ohio, B.A. 1946; Columbia University School of Library Science, New York, M.S. 1966. Clerk typist; reference librarian, Dayton and Montgomery County Public Library, Dayton, 1966-78; then full-time writer. Recipient: Porgie Award (*West Coast Review of Books*), 1980. H.H.D.: Otterbein College, 1979. Agent: Jay Garon, Garon-Brooke Associates, 415 Central Park West, New York, New York 10025. Address: 100 North Jefferson Street, Apartment 702, Dayton, Ohio 45402, U.S.A.

ROMANCE AND GOTHIC PUBLICATIONS

Novels

    Jewels of Terror. New York, Lancer, 1970.
    Love Song. New York, Pinnacle, 1970.
    The Weeping Lady. New York, Lancer, 1971.
    Ravenswood. New York, Avon, 1971.
    Dark Rose. New York, Lancer, 1971.
    The Devil's Own. New York, Avon, 1972.
    The Curse of Kenton. New York, Avon, 1972.
    A Marriage of Inconvenience. New York, Dell, 1972.
    Rivertown. New York, Avon, 1972.
    My Lady Mischief. New York, Dell, 1973.
    The Dancing Doll. New York, Dell, 1973.
    The Dornstein Icon. New York, Avon, 1973.
    The Golden Thistle. New York, Dell, 1973.
    Isle of the Dolphins. New York, Dell, 1973.
    La Casa Dorada. New York, Dell, 1973.
    The Cardross Luck. New York, Dell, 1974.
    The First Waltz. New York, Dell, 1974.
    Castlereagh. New York, Pocket Books, 1975.
    Jade Vendetta. New York, Pocket Books, 1976.
    Wilderness Inn. New York, Pocket Books, 1976.
    Island of Desire. New York, Ballantine, and London, Sphere, 1977.
    Black Pearls. New York, Ballantine, 1979; London, Sphere, 1980.
    Golden Lotus. New York, Warner, 1979.
    Silver Jasmine. New York, Warner, 1980.
    Flamenco Rose. New York, Warner, 1981.
    Forget Me Not. New York, Warner, 1982.

Novels as Rebecca Danton

    Sign of the Golden Goose. New York, Popular Library, 1972.
    Black Horse Tavern. New York, Popular Library, 1972.
    Amethyst Love. New York, Fawcett, 1977.
    Fire Opals. New York, Fawcett, 1977.
    Ship of Hate. New York, Dell, 1977.
    Star Sapphire. New York, Fawcett, 1979.
    The Highland Brooch. New York, Fawcett, 1980.
    Ruby Heart. New York, Fawcett, 1980.

Novels as Louisa Bronte (series: Greystone)

    Lord Satan. New York, Avon, 1972.
    Her Demon Lover. New York, Avon, 1973.
    Greystone Tavern. New York, Ballantine, 1975.
    Gathering at Greystone. New York, Ballantine, 1976.
    Greystone Heritage. New York, Ballantine, 1976.
    Casino at Greystone. New York, Ballantine, 1976.
    Moonlight at Greystone. New York, Ballantine, 1976.
    The Vallette Heritage. New York, Jove, 1978; London, Fontana, 1979.
    The Van Rhyne Heritage. New York, Jove, 1979; London, Fontana, 1980.

Novels as Janette Radcliffe

The Blue-Eyed Gypsy. New York, Dell, 1974.
The Moonlight Gondola. New York, Dell, 1975.
The Gentleman Pirate. New York, Dell, 1975.
White Jasmine. New York, Dell, 1976.
Lord Stephen's Lady. New York, Dell, 1976.
The Azure Castle. New York, Dell, 1976.
The Topaz Charm. New York, Dell, 1976.
A Gift of Violets. New York, Dell, 1977.
The Heart Awakens. New York, Dell, 1977.
Scarlet Secrets. New York, Dell, 1977.
Stormy Surrender. New York, Dell, 1978; London, Sphere, 1979.
Hidden Fires. New York, Dell, 1978.
American Baroness. New York, Dell, 1980.
The Court of the Flowering Peach. New York, Dell, 1981.

Janet Louise Roberts comments:

I have always loved to write, since childhood. There is a deep pleasure in working with words, and making them say just what I feel. I find the world unsatisfactory, and in my fiction I try to make things come out the way I want them to, and I love happy endings. My writing is romantic, not realistic. Writing is a profession requiring long study and much dedicated work. There is a tremendous satisfaction in conquering the difficulties. It is no fun to do something simple, anybody can. I like to do the hard problems, because when one gets to the top of the mountain one feels tremendous pride and joy in the conquering of the struggle to get there.

*   *   *

Writing under her own name and three pseudonyms (Janette Radcliffe, Rebecca Danton and Louisa Bronte), Janet Louise Roberts is one of the most prolific of today's romance novelists. She writes modern, gothic, and historical romances and has even produced a few "occult romances," in which the devil or a demon takes the place of the traditional hero (*The Devil's Own, Isle of the Dolphins, Lord Satan, Her Demon Lover*).

Although Roberts's books show some variety in plot, setting, and time period, they remain basically the same. Her work is one of the easiest to spot regardless of the pseudonym used. One of the most constant aspects to be found in her stories is her treatment of women. Even in a genre under fire for being sexist, Roberts's heroines have much to endure. Whether the hero is an arrogant aristocrat (*The Dornstein Icon, A Marriage of Inconvenience, Star Sapphire*) or a captain of industry (*Golden Lotus, Flamenco Rose*), he is rough and overbearing. The woman may put up some token resistance, but she remains totally ineffectual in the face of male domination. It is not uncommon for the heroine to be raped by the hero at least once in the story. Sexual details are not very explicit, but the lack of tenderness and the idea of sex as punishment are apparent. Often the woman is held captive (*The Dornstein Icon, The Court of the Flowering Peach*) until she learns to love her captor. This may or may not be within the marriage bond, and the captivity may be emotional or financial rather than strictly physical, but it is clear that the woman is unable to act in her own interests or do anything but submit to the all-conquering male.

Roberts's books are frequently marred by idiosyncracies. One is her seeming obsession with food. A review of one of her novels once said that reading a Janet Louise Roberts book is like reading a cookbook, and that is not far from the truth. Elaborate descriptions of food and its preparation abound, usually with little or no relation to the story. Another fetish is what only can be termed a "wonder salve." No matter the injury—gunshot wound, concussion, sprain—it can be cured by applying a salve. One cannot help but think that a description of a realistic treatment would not be difficult to write. Roberts also leaps into ridiculous, if not insulting, attempts at conveying ethnic accents. In *Wilderness Inn* two Indians sum up their rescue of the heroine from an unknown attacker by saying, "He grab you, try to carry you away. We watch, we see. We run like hell!" In *Casino Greystone* Fran's Italian accent is implied by dialogue like this: "Won't-a never find Enid there...She'll-a be swept out-a to sea."

Such patently silly descriptions and dialogue make her stories less believable, but Roberts's fans are forgiving. In spite of her failings, she remains one of the most popular of the romance novelists. Her view of women as pretty dolls to be used and manipulated by men certainly must cause feminists to gnash their teeth, but she obviously strikes a responsive chord among her readers.

—Barbara Kemp

ROBERTS, Willo Davis. American. Born in Grand Rapids, Michigan, 29 May 1928. Educated at a high school in Pontiac, Michigan, graduated 1946. Married David W. Roberts in 1949; two daughters and two sons. Has worked in hospitals and doctors offices; currently conducts a writers workshop in Granite Falls, Washington. Agent: Curtis Brown Ltd., 575 Madison Avenue, New York, New York 10022. Address: 12020 Engebretson Road, Granite Falls, Washington 98252, U.S.A.

Romance and Gothic Publications

Novels

Murder at Grand Bay. New York, Arcadia House, 1955.
The Girl Who Wasn't There. New York, Arcadia House, 1957.
Murder Is So Easy. Fresno, California, Vega, 1961.
The Suspected Four. Fresno, California, Vega, 1962.
Nurse Kay's Conquest. New York, Ace, 1966.
Once a Nurse. New York, Ace, 1966.
Nurse at Mystery Villa. New York, Ace, 1967.
Return to Darkness. New York, Lancer, 1969.
Shroud of Fog. New York, Ace, 1970.
Devil Boy. New York, New American Library, 1970; London, New English Library, 1971.
The Waiting Darkness. New York, Lancer, 1970.
Shadow of a Past Love. New York, Lancer, 1970.
The House at Fern Canyon. New York, Lancer, 1970.
The Tarot Spell. New York, Lancer, 1970.
Invitation to Evil. New York, Lancer, 1970.
The Terror Trap. New York, Lancer, 1971.
King's Pawn. New York, Lancer, 1971.
The Gates of Montrain. New York, Lancer, 1971.
The Watchers. New York, Lancer, 1971.
The Ghosts of Harrel. New York, Lancer, 1971.
Inherit the Darkness. New York, Lancer, 1972.
Nurse in Danger. New York, Ace, 1972.
Becca's Child. New York, Lancer, 1972.
Sing a Dark Song. New York, Lancer, 1972.

The Nurses. New York, Ace, 1972; as *The Secret Lives of the Nurses*, London, Pan, 1975.
The Face of Danger. New York, Lancer, 1972.
Dangerous Legacy. New York, Lancer, 1972.
Sinister Gardens. New York, Lancer, 1972.
The M.D. New York, Lancer, 1972.
The Evil Children. New York, Lancer, 1973.
The Gods in Green. New York, Lancer, 1973.
Nurse Robin. New York, Lenox Hill Press, 1973.
Didn't Anybody Know My Wife? New York, Putnam, 1974; London, Hale, 1978.
White Jade. New York, Doubleday, 1975.
Key Witness. New York, Putnam, 1975; London, Hale, 1978.
Expendable. New York, Doubleday, 1976; London, Hale, 1979.
The Jaubert Ring. New York, Doubleday, 1976.
The House of Imposters. New York, Popular Library, 1977.
Cape of Black Sands. New York, Popular Library, 1977.
Act of Fear. New York, Doubleday, 1977; London, Hale, 1978.
The Black Pearl series:
   Dark Dowry. New York, Popular Library, 1978.
   The Cade Curse. New York, Popular Library, 1978.
   The Stuart Stain. New York, Popular Library, 1978.
   The Devil's Double. New York, Popular Library, 1978.
   The Radkin Revenge. New York, Popular Library, 1979.
   The Hellfire Heritage. New York, Popular Library, 1979.
   The Macomber Menace. New York, Popular Library, 1979.
   The Gresham Ghost. New York, Popular Library, 1980.
The Search for Willie. New York, Popular Library, 1980.
Destiny's Women. New York, Popular Library, 1980.
The Face at the Window. Toronto, Harlequin, 1981.
A Long Time to Hate. New York, Avon, 1982.

OTHER PUBLICATIONS

Other (juvenile)

The View from the Cherry Tree. New York, Atheneum, 1975.
Don't Hurt Laurie! New York, Atheneum, 1977.
The Minden Curse. New York, Atheneum, 1978.
More Minden Curses. New York, Atheneum, 1980.
The Girl with the Silver Eyes. New York, Atheneum, 1980.

*   *   *

The first quality which one recognizes in Willo Davis Roberts's work is her inclusion and perceptive descriptions of accident "victims" and/or health problems. The penchant and thoroughness of her depiction may be the result of her medical training. In any event this accuracy lends credibility to her facile, trim plots. The majority of her novels emphasize mystery-romance more than gothic. *Invitation to Evil, King's Pawn*, and *Shroud of Fog*, all deal with deadly danger, catenulate episodes leading up to the answer to "who did it." Many of her novels have New England settings, and Roberts appears well-versed in this topography, placing the novels in remote areas. The elements of mystery are straightforward and unruffled: a concubitant heroine meets a hero with more than an abundance of panache, usually a man of almost superhuman indestructibility. Physical suffering in proportions excelling what mere mortals could endure occurs during the plot development. Events that at first seem tangentially related become part of the not-too-complicated interplay.

The heroine in *King's Pawn* continually and desperately needs to be reassured, assuming a volitionless capacity and eagerness to believe in the hero after the crises she endures: kidnapping, a fall from the tower into the ocean, etc. This is a plausible response, therefore, and she never becomes the awe-inspiring blank found in the heroines of many other romance novelists' pages. Indeed, the pain which the heroine suffers is vividly described, forcing the reader to explore and experience the discomfort with the victim. The graphic detail enables the reader to excuse the air of the miraculous which surrounds her survival.

A problem encountered frequently in her novels is her too hastily drawn conclusions in which all the sources of tension are conveniently reconciled. The abrupt endings are particularly disturbing in light of the otherwise well-constructed exposition.

Although her conclusions are often a disappointment, the reader can nonetheless be caught up in Willo Davis Roberts's love of the mystery.

—W.M. von Zharen

ROBINS, Denise (Naomi, née Klein).   Also writes as Denise Chesterton; Ashley French; Harriet Gray; Hervey Hamilton; Julia Kane; Francesca Wright.   British.   Born in London, 1 February 1897. Educated at schools in Staten Island, New York, and San Diego, and at The Convent, Upper Norwood, London. Married 1) Arthur Robins in 1918 (divorced, 1938), three daughters, including Claire Lorrimer, *q.v.*; 2) O'Neill Pearson in 1939. Journalist, Dundee *Courier*, Scotland, 1914-15, then free-lance writer, broadcaster, and journalist. Since 1954, editor of the advice column, *She*, magazine, London. Founding Member, 1960, and President, 1960-66, Romantic Novelists Association. Address: 15 Oathall Road, Haywards Heath, Sussex RH16 3EG, England.

ROMANCE AND GOTHIC PUBLICATIONS

Novels

> *The Marriage Bond.*   London, Hodder and Stoughton, 1924.
> *Sealed Lips.*   London, Hodder and Stoughton, 1924.
> *The Forbidden Bride.*   London, Newnes, 1926.
> *The Man Between.*   London Newnes, 1926.
> *The Passionate Awakening.*   London, Newnes, 1926.
> *Forbidden Love.*   London, Newnes, 1927.
> *The Inevitable End.*   London, Mills and Boon, 1927.
> *Jonquil.*   London, Mills and Boon, 1927.
> *The Triumph of the Rat.*   London, Philip Allan, 1927.
> *Desire Is Blind.*   London, Mills and Boon, 1928.
> *The Passionate Flame.*   London, Mills and Boon, 1928.
> *White Jade.*   London, Mills and Boon, 1928.
> *Women Who Seek.*   London, Mills and Boon, 1928.
> *The Dark Death.*   London, Mills and Boon, 1929.
> *The Enduring Flame.*   London, Mills and Boon, 1929; New York, Ballantine, 1975.
> *Heavy Clay.*   London, Mills and Boon, 1929.
> *Love Was a Jest.*   London, Mills and Boon, 1929.
> *And All Because....*   London, Mills and Boon, 1930; as *Love's Victory*, New York, Watt, 1933.

It Wasn't Love. London, Mills and Boon, 1930.

Swing of Youth. London, Mills and Boon, 1930.

Heat Wave: The Story of the Play by Roland Pertwee. London, Mills and Boon, 1930.

Crowns, Pounds, and Guineas. London, Mills and Boon, 1931; as *The Wild Bird*, New York, Watt, 1932.

Fever of Love. London, Mills and Boon, 1931.

Lovers of Janine. London, Mills and Boon, 1931.

Second Best. London, Mills and Boon, 1931; New York, Watt, 1933.

Blaze of Love. London, Mills and Boon, 1932.

The Boundary Line. London, Mills and Boon, and New York, Watt, 1932.

The Secret Hour. London, Mills and Boon, 1932.

There Are Limits. London, Mills and Boon, 1932; as *No Sacrifice*, New York, Watt, 1934.

Gay Defeat. London, Mills and Boon, 1933.

Life's a Game. London, Mills and Boon, 1933.

Men Are Only Human. London, Mills and Boon, and New York, Macaulay, 1933.

Shatter the Sky. London, Mills and Boon, 1933.

Strange Rapture. London, Mills and Boon, 1933.

Brief Ecstasy. London, Mills and Boon, 1934; New York, Ballantine, 1976.

Never Give All. London, Mills and Boon, and New York, Macaulay, 1934.

Slave-Woman. London, Mills and Boon, 1934; New York, Macaulay, 1935.

Sweet Love. London, Mills and Boon, 1934.

All This for Love. London, Mills and Boon, 1935.

Climb to the Stars. London, Nicholson and Watson, 1935.

How Great the Price. London, Mills and Boon, 1935.

Life and Love. London, Nicholson and Watson, 1935; New York, Avon, 1978.

Murder in Mayfair (novelization of play). London, Mills and Boon, 1935.

Love Game. London, Nicholson and Watson, 1936.

Those Who Love. London, Nicholson and Watson, 1936.

Were I Thy Bride. London, Nicholson and Watson, 1936; New York, Pyramid, 1966; as *Betrayal*, London, Hodder and Stoughton, 1976.

Kiss of Youth. London, Nicholson and Watson, 1937; New York, Avon, 1975.

Set Me Free. London, Nicholson and Watson, 1937.

The Tiger in Men. London, Nicholson and Watson, 1937; New York, Avon, 1979.

The Woman's Side of It. London, Nicholson and Watson, 1937.

Family Holiday (as Hervey Hamilton). London, Nicholson and Watson, 1937.

Restless Heart. London, Nicholson and Watson, 1938; New York, Arcadia House, 1940.

Since We Love. London, Nicholson and Watson, 1938; New York, Arcadia House, 1941.

You Have Chosen. London, Nicholson and Watson, 1938; New York, Ballantine, 1975.

Dear Loyalty. London, Nicholson and Watson, 1939.

Gypsy Lover. London, Nicholson and Watson, 1939.

I, Too, Have Loved. London, Nicholson and Watson, 1939; New York, Avon, 1979.

Officer's Wife. London, Nicholson and Watson, 1939.

Island of Flowers. London, Nicholson and Watson, 1940; New York, Avon, 1977.

Little We Know. London, Hutchinson, 1940.

Sweet Sorrow. London, Nicholson and Watson, 1940; as *Forget That I Remember*, New York, Arcadia House, 1940.

To Love Is to Live. London, Hutchinson, 1940.

If This Be Destiny. London, Hutchinson, 1941.

Set the Stars Alight. London, Hutchinson, 1941; New York, Avon, 1979.

Winged Love. London, Hutchinson, 1941; New York, Avon, 1978.

Love Is Enough. London, Hutchinson, 1941; New York, Avon, 1975.

This One Night. London, Hutchinson, 1942; New York, Avon, 1975.

War Marriage. London, Hutchinson, 1942; as *Let Me Love*, London, Hodder and Stoughton, 1979.

What Matters Most. London, Hutchinson, 1942.

The Changing Years. London, Hutchinson, 1943; New York, Beagle, 1974.

Daughter Knows Best. London, Hutchinson, 1943.

Dust of Dreams. London, Hutchinson, 1943; New York, Avon, 1976.

Escape to Love. London, Hutchinson, 1943; New York, Avon, 1976.

This Spring of Love. London, Hutchinson, 1943.

War Changes Everything. London, Todd, 1943.

Give Me Back My Heart. London, Hutchinson, 1944; New York, Avon, 1976.

How to Forget. London, Hutchinson, 1944.

Never Look Back. London, Hutchinson, 1944.

Desert Rapture. London, Hutchinson, 1945; New York, Avon, 1979.

Love So Young. London, Hutchinson, 1945.

All for You. London, Hutchinson, 1946; New York, Ballantine, 1975.

Heart's Desire. London, Foster, 1946.

Greater Than All. London, Hutchinson, 1946.

Separation. London, Foster, 1946.

The Story of Veronica. London, Hutchinson, 1946.

Figs in Frost (as Hervey Hamilton). London, Macdonald, 1946.

Forgive Me, My Love. Hanley, Staffordshire, Docker, 1947.

More Than Love. London, Hutchinson, 1947.

Could I Forget. London, Hutchinson, 1948; New York, Avon, 1976.

Khamsin. London, Hutchinson, 1948; New York, Avon, 1978.

Love Me No More! London, Hutchinson, 1948.

The Hard Way. London, Hutchinson, 1949.

To Love Again. London, Hutchinson, 1949; Toronto, Harlequin, 1961.

The Uncertain Heart. London, Hutchinson, 1949; New York, Avon, 1977.

The Feast Is Finished. London, Hutchinson, 1950; New York, Avon, 1979.

Love Hath an Island. London, Hutchinson, 1950.

Heart of Paris. London, Hutchinson, 1951.

Infatuation. London, Hutchinson, 1951.

Only My Dreams. London, Hutchinson, 1951; New York, Avon, 1976.

Second Marriage. London, Hutchinson, 1951; New York, Avon, 1979.

Something to Love. London, Hutchinson, 1951.

The Other Love. London, Hutchinson, 1952.

Strange Meeting. London, Hutchinson, 1952.

The First Long Kiss. London, Hutchinson, 1953; New York, Avon, 1976.

My True Love. London, Hutchinson, 1953; New York, Avon, 1977.

The Loves of Lucrezia (as Francesca Wright). London, Rich and Cowan, 1953; New York, Popular Library, 1954.

The Long Shadow. London, Hutchinson, 1954; New York, Avon, 1979.

Venetian Rhapsody. London, Hutchinson, 1954; New York, Avon, 1979.

Bitter-Sweet. London, Hutchinson, 1955.

The Unshaken Loyalty. London, Hutchinson, 1955.

All That Matters. London, Hutchinson, 1956.

The Enchanted Island. London, Hutchinson, 1956; New York, Avon, 1974.

The Seagull's Cry. London, Hutchinson, 1957; New York, Avon, 1979.

The Noble One. London, Hodder and Stoughton, 1957.

Chateau of Flowers. London, Hodder and Stoughton, 1958.

The Untrodden Snow. London, Hodder and Stoughton, 1958.

Do Not Go, My Love. London, Hodder and Stoughton, 1959; New York, Ballantine, 1974.

We Two Together. London, Hodder and Stoughton, 1959.

The Unlit Fire. London, Hodder and Stoughton, 1960.

Arrow in the Heart. London, Hodder and Stoughton, 1960.

I Should Have Known. London, Hodder and Stoughton, 1961.

A Promise for Ever. London, Hodder and Stoughton, 1961.

Put Back the Clock. London, Hodder and Stoughton, 1962; New York, Pyramid, 1967.

Mad Is the Heart. London, Hodder and Stoughton, 1963.

Nightingale's Song. London, Hodder and Stoughton, 1963; New York, Pyramid, 1966.

Reputation. London, Hodder and Stoughton, 1963.
Meet Me in Monte Carlo. London, Arrow, 1964; New York, Avon, 1979.
Moment of Love. London, Hodder and Stoughton, 1964; New York, Pyramid, 1966.
Loving and Giving. London, Hodder and Stoughton, 1965; New York, Ballantine, 1975.
The Strong Heart. London, Hodder and Stoughton, 1965.
O Love! O Fire! London, Panther, 1966.
Lightning Strikes Twice. London, Hodder and Stoughton, 1966.
The Crash. London, Hodder and Stoughton, 1966.
Wait for Tomorrow. London, Hodder and Stoughton, 1967.
House of the Seventh Cross. London, Hodder and Stoughton, 1967; as *House by the Watch Tower*, New York, Arcadia House, 1968.
Laurence, My Love. London, Hodder and Stoughton, 1968.
Love and Desire and Hate. London, Hodder and Stoughton, 1969.
A Love Like Ours. London, Hodder and Stoughton, 1969; New York, Ballantine, 1976.
She-Devil: The Story of Jezebel (as Francesca Wright). London, Corgi, 1970; revised edition, as *Jezebel* (as Denise Robins), London, Hodder and Stoughton, 1977.
Sweet Cassandra. London, Hodder and Stoughton, 1970.
Forbidden. London, Hodder and Stoughton, 1971.
The Snow Must Return. London, Hodder and Stoughton, 1971.
The Other Side of Love. London, Hodder and Stoughton, 1973; New York, Ballantine, 1975.
Twice Have I Loved. London, Hodder and Stoughton, 1973; New York, Ballantine, 1975.
Dark Corridor. London, Hodder and Stoughton, 1974.
Two Loves. New York, Bantam, 1975.
Come Back Yesterday. London, Hodder and Stoughton, 1976.
Fauna (omnibus). New York, Avon, 1978.

Novels as Ashley French

Once Is Enough. London, Hutchinson, 1953.
The Bitter Core. London, Hutchinson, 1954.
Breaking Point. London, Hutchinson, 1956; as Denise Robins, New York, Bantam, 1975.

Novels as Harriet Gray

Gold for the Gay Masters. London, Rich and Cowan, 1954; New York, Avon, 1956.
Bride of Doom. London, Rich and Cowan, 1956; as *Bride of Violence*, New York, Avon, 1957.
The Flame and the Frost. London, Rich and Cowan, 1957; in *Fauna* (as Denise Robins), 1978.
Dance in the Dust. London, Hale, 1959; as Denise Robins, New York, Avon, 1978.
My Lady Destiny. London, Hale, 1961; as Denise Robins, New York, Avon, 1978.

Novels as Denise Chesterton

Two Loves. London, Merit, 1955.
The Price of Folly. London, Merit, 1955.
When a Woman Loves. London, Merit, 1955.

Novels as Julia Kane

Dark Secret Love. London, Hodder and Stoughton, 1962.

The Sin Was Mine.   London, Hodder and Stoughton, 1964.
Time Runs Out.   London, Hodder and Stoughton, 1965.

Short Stories

One Night in Ceylon and Others.   London, Mills and Boon, 1931.
Light the Candles.   London, Hurst and Blackett, 1959.

OTHER PUBLICATIONS

Play

Light the Candles, with Michael Pertwee, adaptation of the story by Robins.   London, English Theatre Guild, 1957.

Verse

Love Poems and Others.   London, Mills and Boon, 1930.

Other

Stranger Than Fiction: Denise Robins Tells Her Life Story.   London, Hodder and Stoughton, 1965.

Editor, *The World of Romance* (anthology).   London, New English Library, 1964.

*   *   *

Denise Robins is worth noting not just for her prolificity in writing around 170 novels in over 50 years, but for the variety of subject and character treatment she has produced within this genre. Most of her books concentrate on the contemporary love story, and she has exploited nearly every conceivable situation both inside and outside marriage. Even in her early works, the often taboo subjects of divorce and extra-marital relationships are handled with care and sensitivity, as in the poignant *More Than Love*, in which a young girl tells of her affair with a married man, and all the problems such a relationship incurs. Both *Put Back the Clock* and *The Crash* concern marriage on the rebound; *The Bitter Core* deals with the marriage of a woman in her forties to a much younger man; *Give Me Back My Heart* is about an arranged marriage and the girl's struggle to marry the man of her choice; while *O Love! O Fire!* introduces the moral dilemma facing Candy, who, after much heart-searching, sleeps with her boyfriend, only to become pregnant and bear his child while realizing gradually that her love was mere infatuation. Another controversial topic, even today, that of a mother leaving her children with their father, is the theme of both *Figs in Frost* and *Once Is Enough*. The latter tells of a mother's attempts to see her daughter against her estranged husband's will; her mental anguish, the child's bewilderment at being the centre of the struggle, and the subsequent, inevitable tragedy are all movingly described. Occasionally the fast-moving plots sport equal measures of suspense and romance, as in the strong and passionate drama *Heat Wave*, set in Malaya.

The characters and settings are equally as varied as the themes. The central protagonists range in age from 18 to the mid-forties, and vary considerably in temperament and social background: they are treated in reasonable depth, changed for good or bad by the physical and emotional experiences they undergo. The settings of the novels embrace the streets of London, fashionable Paris, the Swiss mountains, and more exotic places such as Egypt, Ceylon, and Morocco, described with just enough authenticity to imbue the story with their particular flavour; sometimes a place is set more firmly in the memory, like the Chateau de Lurmines in

The Snow Must Return. The character of each decade of the 20th century can also be seen over the range of her novels, especially in fashion details, the intrusion of the Second World War, the slowly changing attitudes towards divorce and infidelity, and the freedom of women in particular regarding careers and financial and moral independence, and the author keeps up-to-date with both social and political scenes in order to give each novel a realistic touch.

Denise Robins has also produced five historical romances under the pseudonym Harriet Gray. *Gold for the Gay Master, Bride of Doom*, and *The Flame and the Frost* make up a trilogy set in the late Georgian and early Victorian periods, tracing the history of a beautiful quadroon slave and her descendants. The stories are well punctuated with dramatic climaxes, moving fast and furiously against a rich backcloth of elaborately painted characters and settings. The two fictional biographies about Lucrezia Borgia and Jezebel, written under the name Francesca Wright, are highly embellished accounts, but equally well filled with drama, romance, and excitement. Of her two collections of short stories, *One Night in Celyon and Others* is by far the stronger work, with each tale a swift, vigorous slice of life, often with a neat, unexpected twist at the end, as in "Perfectly Acted," "This Is Marriage," and the title story.

Although with such a vast output, some of her work is bound to be slighter in form, lacking pace, less well-worked-out, and with weaker characterization, Denise Robins writes with a smooth, firm confidence gained from years of consistent popularity; plot and sub-plot move rapidly in a polished flow across the page, the various entanglements neatly resolving to a happy climax, with the passions of both young and old relayed with a sympathy born of experience and observation.

—Tessa Rose Chester

ROBINS, Patricia. *See* **LORRIMER, Claire**.

ROBY, Mary Linn. Also writes as Pamela D'Arcy; Georgina Grey; Elizabeth Welles; Mary Wilson. American. Born in Bangor, Maine, 31 March 1930. Educated at the University of Maine, Orono, B.A. 1951 (Phi Beta Kappa). Married Kinley E. Roby in 1951; two children. History teacher at State College High School, Pennsylvania, and Orono High School. Since 1972, English teacher, Concord/Carlisle High School, Massachusetts. Agent: Lenniger Literary Agency, 104 East 40th Street, New York, New York 10016, U.S.A.

ROMANCE AND GOTHIC PUBLICATIONS

Novels

Still as the Grave. New York, Dodd Mead, 1964; London, Collins, 1965.
Afraid of the Dark. New York, Dodd Mead, 1965.

Before I Die. London, Hale, 1966.
Cat and Mouse. London, Hale, 1967.
In the Dead of the Night. New York, New American Library, 1969.
Pennies on Her Eyes. New York, New American Library, 1969.
All Your Lovely Words Are Spoken. New York, Ace, 1970.
Some Die in Their Beds. New York, New American Library, 1970.
If She Should Die. New York, New American Library, 1970.
Lie Quiet in Your Grave. New York, New American Library, 1970.
That Fatal Touch. New York, New American Library, 1970.
Dig a Narrow Grave. New York, New American Library, 1971.
This Land Turns Evil Slowly. New York, New American Library, 1971.
Reap the Whirlwind. New York, New American Library, 1972.
And Die Remembering. New York, New American Library, 1972.
When the Witch Is Dead. New York, New American Library, 1972.
The White Peacock. New York, Hawthorn, 1972; as *The Cry of the Peacock*, Aylesbury,
    Buckinghamshire, Milton House, 1974.
Shadow over Grove House. New York, New American Library, 1973.
Speak No Evil of the Dead. New York, New American Library, 1973.
The House at Kilgallen. New York, New American Library, 1973.
The Broken Key. New York, Hawthorn, 1973; Aylesbury, Buckinghamshire, Milton
    House, 1974.
Marsh House. New York, Hawthorn, 1974; London, Milton House, 1975.
The Tower Room. New York, Hawthorn, 1974; London, Milton House, 1975.
The Silent Walls. New York, New American Library, 1974.
The Changeling (as Mary Wilson). New York, Dell, 1975.
Wind of Death (as Mary Wilson). New York, Dell, 1976.
Christobel. New York, Berkley, 1976.
The Treasure Chest. New York, Berkley, 1976.
Seagull Crag (as Elizabeth Welles). New York, Pocket Books, 1977.
The Hidden Book. New York, Berkley, 1977.
Trapped. New York, Dell, 1977.
A Heritage of Strangers. New York, Berkley, 1978.
Fortune's Smile. New York, Warner, 1979.
My Lady's Mask. New York, Warner, 1979.
Passing Fancy. New York, Dell, 1980.
Love's Wilful Call. New York, Warner, 1981.

Novels as Georgina Grey

The Hesitant Heir. New York, Fawcett, 1978.
Turn of the Cards. New York, Fawcett, 1979.
Both Sides of the Coin. New York, Fawcett, 1980.
Fashion's Frown. New York, Fawcett, 1980.
Franklin's Folly. New York, Fawcett, 1980.
The Last Cotillion. New York, Fawcett, 1980.
The Bartered Bridegroom. New York, Fawcett, 1981.
The Queen's Quadrille. New York, Fawcett, 1981.
The Reluctant Rivals. New York, Fawcett, 1981.

Novels as Pamela D'Arcy

Angel in the House. New York, Jove, 1980.
Heritage of the Heart. New York, Jove, 1980.
Magic Moment. New York, Jove, 1980.

*   *   *

Whether she is writing a contemporary gothic or a historical romance, Mary Linn Roby manages to produce a competent, if not exceptional, novel.

Her gothics have all the required ingredients: brooding manors, danger and murder, complicated personal relationships (at least one of which will obviously lead to love), and last minute denouements. *The Tower Room* is a good example of Roby's gothic formula. Family and acquaintances gather in an isolated cliffside castle. An autocratic old woman manipulates those around her, reviving old memories and reopening old wounds. Several murders take place and the young heroine finds herself in danger. Everyone is under suspicion, although the reader obviously knows that the hero and heroine are innocent. The tangled plot is gradually unraveled, the true villain revealed, and justice quickly and efficiently served.

Like her gothics, Roby's Regency romances can be viewed as good representatives of the prevailing formula for the genre. Bright, independent heroines and steadfast heroes overcome numerous obstacles to find true love and happiness. Roby does show one common theme or motif in these romances: the stage or the roles and impersonations carried out by the characters. A major stumbling block to Jennifer's happiness in *Passing Fancy* is the deception practiced by the Earl of Watching when he poses as the less important Sir John Evans. In *Love's Wilful Call* Hannah struggles to follow her father's footsteps in the theatre, yet when she reaches her goal she realizes that she really yearns more for the love of Lord Derwent. Roby brings both themes together in *My Lady's Mask*. Caroline plays the role of a great society lady and becomes involved with several theatre people, most notably the playwright, Lord Troyan, to whom she loses her heart. In spite of many difficulties encountered by the characters, Roby manages to end all of these novels in a happy spate of engagements and weddings. In the category of happy endings, however, few novels can beat *Fortune's Smile*, in which Roby provides at least four engagements and hints at two more to come, all in the final two chapters. Everyone is provided with a satisfactory partner.

As an author of both gothic novels and historical romances, Roby knows the conventions. She includes all the right elements, and the results are enjoyable but lack that extra spark that puts an author's work in the first rank.

—Barbara Kemp

ROGERS, Rosemary (née Jansze).   American.   Born in Panadura, Ceylon, 7 December 1932. Educated at the University of Ceylon, Colombo, B.A. Married 1) Summa Navaratnam (divorced), two daughters; 2) Leroy Rogers (divorced), two sons. Feature writer and information officer, Associated Newspapers of Ceylon, Colombo, 1959-62; secretary, Travis Air Force Base, California, 1964-69, and Solano County Parks Department, Fairfield, California, 1969-74. Formerly, reporter, Fairfield *Daily Republic*. Address: c/o Avon, 959 Eighth Avenue, New York, New York 10019, U.S.A.

ROMANCE AND GOTHIC PUBLICATIONS

Novels

   Sweet Savage Love.   New York, Avon, 1974; London, Futura, 1977.
   The Wildest Heart.   New York, Avon, 1974; London, Futura, 1978.
   Dark Fires.   New York, Avon, 1975; London, Futura, 1977.
   Wicked Loving Lies.   New York, Avon, 1976; London, Futura, 1977.

The Crowd Pleasers.   New York, Avon, 1978; revised edition, 1980.
The Insiders.   New York, Avon, and London, Futura, 1979.
Lost Love, Last Love.   New York, Avon, 1980.
Love Play.   New York, Avon, 1981; London, Sphere, 1982.

*   *   *

In 1974 Avon published Rosemary Rogers's first swashbuckling tale of passion, *Sweet Savage Love*, a historical novel whose title gave a name to an entire genre. In this story and those that follow the respective heroines suffer ravishment by an assortment of men, slavery, torture (but nothing, of course, that mars their breathtaking beauty), plus a host of other horrors that would certainly devastate the normal human female. However, these ladies emerge triumphant with the man they have loved and hated for approximately 600 pages. The Rosemary Rogers heroine is always lovely and ardently desired by every man who meets her. She inevitably thinks of herself as willful and independent but somehow develops a spine of jelly when forced into the arms of the hero.

The male protagonist in hot pursuit of the maiden (which she usually is for the first few pages) must be virile, handsome, well educated or at least highly intelligent, but most of all must have a savagery in his lovemaking. Rogers has stated that all her male leads are modeled on the macho cowboy image of Clint Eastwood. Inevitably the heroine's innocence is taken from her by this male animal, who releases in her body an unimaginable passion. Heights of fulfillment the average person may never experience are reached over and over whenever the sweet/savage lovers copulate. The passages depicting this sexual ecstasy leave little to the imagination, but the language, however explicit, is rarely coarse.

Rogers's early novels, such as *Sweet Savage Love, The Wildest Heart*, and *Wicked Loving Lies*, are typical of the novels known in the publishing trade as "bodice busters." Set in the 19th century the hero and heroine fight and bed their way across Europe and the American West. From the descriptions of the countryside and the inhabitants, it is apparent that Rogers knows this era of European and American history well. All this is convincing background to what one book jacket described as "a tale of unquenched desire...united in a blaze of undying passion and infinite love." This quite accurately captures the essence of a Rosemary Rogers novel.

In *Sweet Savage Love* Ginny Brandon and Steve Morgan, travelling through Texas and Mexico, leave a fiery trail of passion, hate, lust, and ultimately love. But this is only the beginning of their story for there are two more episodes of this burning saga. In each Ginny and Steve separate (because of some absurd misunderstanding) and go again and again through the hate, lust, love routine. Meanwhile each has tried to find consolation in the arms of others, but their desire for one another cannot be quenched.

The author's more recent novels have contemporary settings, although the basic sweet/savage theme remains. In *The Crowd Pleasers* a young and aristocratic actress/model becomes reluctantly involved with Webb Carnahan, an earthy, dominant male with a hint of cruelty. *Love Play* has the virginal and very uptight British Sara agreeing to impersonate her younger, outrageously liberated American half-sister Delight. This would permit young sis to elope with her rich boyfriend and to escape the evil clutches of his older brother, Marco. Sara and Marco quickly become antagonists although their mutual lust gets in the way of their interminable arguing.

Although these novels follow a predictable pattern, the plots are often intricate and imaginative, and are built on a foundation of vivid, realistic, often witty dialog. Intrigue of some sort often surrounds the protagonists, throwing them together, then flinging them apart. But always incredible good fortune brings the lovers together for a passionate and searing conclusion. Love stories with a sadomasochistic touch have made Rosemary Rogers one of today's more popular writers.

—Patricia Altner

ROME, Margaret.   British.   Married; one son. Address: c/o Mills and Boon Ltd., 15-16 Brooks Mews, London W1A 1DR, England.

ROMANCE AND GOTHIC PUBLICATIONS

Novels

The Lottery for Matthew Devlin.   London, Mills and Boon, 1968.
The Marriage of Caroline Lindsay.   London, Mills and Boon, 1968; Toronto, Harlequin, 1974.
A Chance to Win.   Toronto, Harlequin, 1969.
Flower of the Marsh.   London, Mills and Boon, 1969.
Man of Fire.   London, Mills and Boon, 1970; Toronto, Harlequin, 1974.
Bird of Paradise.   London, Mills and Boon, 1970; Toronto, Harlequin, 1973.
Chateau of Flowers.   London, Mills and Boon, 1971; Toronto, Harlequin, 1972.
The Girl at Eagles' Mount.   London, Mills and Boon, 1971; Toronto, Harlequin, 1973.
Bride of the Rif.   London, Mills and Boon, and Toronto, Harlequin, 1972.
Island of Pearls.   London, Mills and Boon, 1973; Toronto, Harlequin, 1974.
The Bartered Bride.   London, Mills and Boon, 1973; Toronto, Harlequin, 1975.
Palace of the Hawk.   London, Mills and Boon, 1974; Toronto, Harlequin, 1975.
Valley of Paradise.   Toronto, Harlequin, 1975.
Cove of Promises.   London, Mills and Boon, 1975; Toronto, Harlequin, 1976.
The Girl at Dane's Dyke.   London, Mills and Boon, and Toronto, Harlequin, 1975.
Adam's Rib.   London, Mills and Boon, and Toronto, Harlequin, 1976.
Bride of Zarco.   London, Mills and Boon, 1976; Toronto, Harlequin, 1977.
Lion of Venice.   London, Mills and Boon, 1977; Toronto, Harlequin, 1978.
The Thistle and the Rose.   Toronto, Harlequin, 1977.
Son of Adam.   London, Mills and Boon, 1978.
Castle of the Fountains.   London, Mills and Boon, 1979.
Champagne Spring.   London, Mills and Boon, 1979; Toronto, Harlequin, 1980.
Isle of Calypso.   London, Mills and Boon, 1979.
Marriage by Capture.   London, Mills and Boon, 1980.
Miss High and Mighty.   London, Mills and Boon, 1980; Toronto, Harlequin, 1981.
The Wild Man.   London, Mills and Boon, 1980; Toronto, Harlequin, 1981.
Second-Best Bride.   Toronto, Harlequin, 1981.

*   *   *

Margaret Rome is an English writer of romance fiction who has been widely published for a number of years. Apparently her own restlessness and curiosity led her in search of change and new experience. She often held jobs such as waitress, theatre usher, office and shop assistant, but all became such humdrum day-in-and-day-out events that eventually she turned to writing to express herself fully. Whatever the cause, however, Rome has her own way of creating enjoyable stories. She is able to develop well-rounded, believable characters that go beyond the stereotype "romance" image. Her female characters reflect their background, and they grow from their past and their own inner beliefs.

Fleur, in Chateau of Flowers, is the only child of an elderly couple, her father being a minister. She is a gentle, giving child who marries a blind man because he needs her, aware even as she does so that he does not love her. She travels to his home in the south of France where perfume is made and faces constant inner turmoil because of Alain's inability to accept his blindness.

Tina Donnelly (Man of Fire) joins a botanical expedition into the unexplored parts of the Amazon basin in search of rare plant specimens. She does this in spite of the fact that she is deathly afraid of the jungle; to make the situation worse, she must substitute for her aunt who has injured herself.

Finally, there is Sara Battle (Bride of the Rif) who swears revenge against Señor Felipe de

Panza who has accused her grandfather of cheating at cards. She pretends to be in love with his nephew, Alvarso de Leon, and is presented to the family as his "close friend." In order to prevent any closer ties between the nephew and Sara, Felipe kidnaps Sara, takes her to the area of Morocco where the Rifs live, and goes through a marriage ceremony with her.

Dominating characteristics of sensitivity, courage and, most of all, true femininity are illustrated in all of her female characters. She portrays her heroines especially well in situations where modern concepts of morals or social standards are being advocated or substituted for older ideals, so that the heroine faces more than the usual obstacles before she discovers her heart. Often she is placed in a position of accepting, or seeming to accept, the current "social standard"; yet, she herself clings to a firm belief in older, virtuous ideals. Frequently she is misunderstood by the man she falls in love with because of her seemingly modern outlook and not until nearly the end of the story does it become evident that, for all of her surface sophistication, she is still a naive and virtuous girl. In fact, her sometimes prickly attitudes and flippant manners are her form of self-protection in a world she can't feel comfortable in, but must deal with.

Rome's male characters stand out equally well as they display masculine qualities that balance and temper those of her heroines. All are just enough older to insure a greater degree of sophistication. Their experience helps in letting them understand the real persons the heroines try to hide, and makes it possible for them to see beneath the surface. While most are wealthy, they yet are people of authority who work. Arrogant maleness is tempered with flashes of gentleness and tenderness that show a balanced, assured man of the world. They usually possess all the traits that women instinctively seek—that is, strength, decisiveness, and, most of all, a belief in their own abilities to guide their own lives and those of their loved ones.

If Rome's characters are well presented, her plots and settings are equally interesting, since she lets her stories unfold against the background of the Amazon jungle, the exotic islands of Tahiti, or the canals of Venice. Detail of locale is skillfully woven throughout the stories and lend an added touch of realism. In fact, it is this variation of background that permits some of her plots to work. In both *Man of Fire* and *Bride of the Rif* the heroines must fight against physical difficulties as well as mental ones. Physical danger alone forces the heroine to cope with new emotions and experiences at a time when she has little reserves to call upon. Yet in each of her stories the heroine displays unexpected qualities of courage and determination to achieve her happiness.

Basically, Margaret Rome is a storyteller. She combines intriguing characters with very strong plots that keep her readers involved. She draws heavily on male/female encounters in such a way that conflict is immediate and sustaining. Finally, she brings those same qualities of curiosity and love of new experiences and adventures to her novels as she has to her own life.

—Arlene Moore

ROSS, Catherine. *See* **BEATY, Betty.**

ROWLAND, Iris. *See* **ROBERTS, Irene**.

ROWLANDS, Effie. *See* **ALBANESI, Madame**.

RUCK, Berta (Amy Roberta Ruck).   British.   Born in Murree, India, 2 August 1878. Educated at St. Winifred's School, Bangor, Wales; Lambeth School of Art, and Slade School of Art, both London; Calorossi's, Paris. Married the writer Oliver Onions in 1909 (died, 1961); two sons. *Died 11 August 1978.*

ROMANCE AND GOTHIC PUBLICATIONS

Novels

> *His Official Fiancée*.   London, Hutchinson, and New York, Dodd Mead, 1914.
> *The Courtship of Rosamond Fayre*.   London, Hutchinson, 1915; as *The Wooing of Rosamond Fayre*, New York, Dodd Mead, 1915.
> *The Lad with Wings*.   London, Hutchinson, 1915; as *The Boy with Wings*, New York, Dodd Mead, 1915.
> *Miss Million's Maid*.   New York, Dodd Mead, 1915; London, Hutchinson, 1916.
> *The Girls at His Billet*.   London, Hutchinson, and New York, Dodd Mead, 1916.
> *In Another Girl's Shoes*.   New York, Dodd Mead, 1916; London, Hodder and Stoughton, 1917.
> *The Bridge of Kisses*.   London, Hutchinson, 1917; New York, Dodd Mead, 1920.
> *Three of Hearts*.   New York, Dodd Mead, 1917; London, Hodder and Stoughton, 1918.
> *The Girl Who Proposed!*   London, Hodder and Stoughton, 1918.
> *The Years for Rachel*.   London, Hodder and Stoughton, and New York, Dodd Mead, 1918.
> *Arabella the Awful*.   London, Hodder and Stoughton, 1918.
> *The Disturbing Charm*.   London, Hodder and Stoughton, and New York, Dodd Mead, 1919.
> *The Land-Girl's Love Story*.   London, Hodder and Stoughton, and New York, Dodd Mead, 1919
> *The Wrong Mr. Right*.   London, Hodder and Stoughton, 1919; New York, Dodd Mead, 1922.
> *Sweethearts Unmet*.   New York, Dodd Mead, 1919; London, Hodder and Stoughton, 1922.

Sweet Stranger. London, Hodder and Stoughton, and New York, Dodd Mead, 1921.

The Arrant Rover. London, Hodder and Stoughton, and New York, Dodd Mead, 1921.

Under False Pretences. London, Hodder and Stoughton, 1922.

The Subconscious Courtship. London, Hodder and Stoughton, and New York, Dodd Mead, 1922.

The Bride Who Ran Away—Nurse Henderson. London, Hodder and Stoughton, 1922.

The Elopement of Eve and Prince Playfellow. London, Hodder and Stoughton, 1922.

Sir or Madam? London, Hutchinson, and New York, Dodd Mead, 1923.

The Dancing Star. London, Hodder and Stoughton, and New York, Dodd Mead, 1923.

The Clouded Pearl. London, Hodder and Stoughton, and New York, Dodd Mead, 1924.

The Leap Year Girl. New York, Dodd Mead, 1924.

Lucky in Love. London, Hodder and Stoughton, and New York, Dodd Mead, 1924.

Kneel to the Prettiest. London, Hodder and Stoughton, and New York, Dodd Mead, 1925.

The Immortal Girl. London, Hodder and Stoughton, and New York, Dodd Mead, 1925.

Her Pirate Partner. London, Hodder and Stoughton, 1926; New York, Dodd Mead, 1927.

The Pearl Thief. London, Hodder and Stoughton, and New York, Dodd Mead, 1926.

The Mind of a Minx. London, Hodder and Stoughton, and New York, Dodd Mead, 1927.

Money for One. London, Hodder and Stoughton, 1927; New York, Dodd Mead, 1928.

One of the Chorus. London, Hodder and Stoughton, 1928; as *Joy-Ride*, New York, Dodd Mead, 1929.

The Youngest Venus; or, The Love Story of a Plain Girl. London, Hodder and Stoughton, and New York, Dodd Mead, 1928.

The Unkissed Bride. London, Hodder and Stoughton, and New York, Dodd Mead, 1929.

To-day's Daughter. London, Hodder and Stoughton, 1929; New York, Dodd Mead, 1930.

Post-War Girl. London, Hutchinson, 1930.

Missing Girl. London, Cassell, 1930; as *The Love-Hater*, New York, Dodd Mead, 1930.

Offer of Marriage. London, Cassell, 1930; New York, Dodd Mead, 1931.

Forced Landing. London, Cassell, 1931.

Dance Partner. New York, Dodd Mead, 1931.

The Lap of Luxury. London, Cassell, 1931; New York, Dodd Mead, 1932.

This Year, Next Year, Sometime—. London, Cassell, and New York, Dodd Mead, 1932.

Sudden Sweetheart. London, Cassell, 1932; New York, Dodd Mead, 1933.

Understudy. London, Hodder and Stoughton, and New York, Dodd Mead, 1933.

Eleventh Hour Lover. London, Hutchinson, 1933.

Change Here for Happiness, Written Especially for Those Who Want Some Happy Hours—and a Change! London, Hodder and Stoughton, and New York, Dodd Mead, 1933.

The Best Time Ever. London, Hodder and Stoughton, and New York, Dodd Mead, 1934.

Sunburst. London, Hodder and Stoughton, and New York, Dodd Mead, 1934.

Sunshine-Stealer: The Story of a Cruise. London, Hodder and Stoughton, and New York, Dodd Mead, 1935.

A Star in Love. London, Hodder and Stoughton, and New York, Dodd Mead, 1935.

Spring Comes to Miss Lonely Heart. London, Hodder and Stoughton, 1936; as *Spring Comes*, New York, Dodd Mead, 1936.

Half-Past Kissing Time. London, Hodder and Stoughton, 1936; as *Sleeping Beauty*, New York, Dodd Mead, 1936.

Love on Second Thoughts. London, Hodder and Stoughton, 1936; New York, Dodd Mead, 1937.

Romance Royal. London, Hodder and Stoughton, and New York, Dodd Mead, 1937.

Love Comes Again Later. London, Hodder and Stoughton, and New York, Dodd Mead, 1938.

Handmaid to Fame. London, Hodder and Stoughton, 1938; New York, Dodd Mead, 1939.

Wedding March. London, Hodder and Stoughton, and New York, Dodd Mead, 1938.

Mock-Honeymoon. London, Mills and Boon, and New York, Dodd Mead, 1939.

Arabella Arrives. New York, Dodd Mead, 1939.

Out to Marry Money. London, Mills and Boon, 1940; as *It Was Left to Peter*, New York, Dodd Mead, 1940.

He Learnt about Women. London, Mills and Boon, 1940; as *He Learned about Women*, New York, Dodd Mead, 1940.

Pennies from Heaven. London, Mills and Boon, 1940; as *Money Isn't Everything*, New York, Dodd Mead, 1940; revised edition, as *Third Love Lucky*, London, Hurst and Blackett, 1958; as *Third Time Lucky*, Dodd Mead, 1958.

Fiancées Count as Relatives. London, Mills and Boon, 1941; as *Fiancées Are Relatives*, New York, Dodd Mead, 1941.

Jade Earrings. New York, Dodd Mead, 1941.

Waltz-Contest. London, Mills and Boon, and New York, Dodd Mead, 1941.

Spinster's Progress. London, Mills and Boon, and New York, Dodd Mead, 1942.

Quarrel and Kiss. London, Mills and Boon, 1942.

Footlight Fever. New York, Dodd Mead, 1942.

Bread-and-Grease-Paint. London, Hutchinson, 1943.

Shining Chance. London, Hutchinson, and New York, Dodd Mead, 1944.

Intruder Marriage. New York, Dodd Mead, 1944; London, Hutchinson, 1945.

You Are the One. New York, Dodd Mead, 1945; London, Hutchinson, 1946.

Surprise Engagement. New York, Dodd Mead, 1946; London, Hutchinson, 1947.

Throw Away Yesterday. London, Hutchinson, and New York, Dodd Mead, 1946.

Tomboy in Lace. London, Hutchinson, and New York, Dodd Mead, 1947.

She Danced in the Ballet. New York, Dodd Mead, 1948; London, Hutchinson, 1949.

Love and Apron-Strings. London, Hutchinson, 1949; as *Gentle Tyrant*, New York, Dodd Mead, 1949.

Hopeful Journey. London, Hutchinson, 1950; as *Joyful Journey*, New York, Dodd Mead, 1950.

Love at a Festival. London, Hutchinson, and New York, Dodd Mead, 1951.

Song of the Lark. London, Hutchinson, 1951; as *The Rising of the Lark*, New York, Dodd Mead, 1951.

Spice of Life. London, Hutchinson, and New York, Dodd Mead, 1952.

Fantastic Holiday. London, Hutchinson, and New York, Dodd Mead, 1953.

Marriage Is a Blind Date. London, Hutchinson, 1953; as *Blind Date*, New York, Dodd Mead, 1953.

The Men in Her Life. London, Hutchinson, and New York, Dodd Mead, 1954.

We All Have Our Secrets. London, Hutchinson, and New York, Dodd Mead, 1955.

Romance in Two Keys. New York, Dodd Mead, 1955; as *Romance of a Film Star*, London, Hutchinson, 1956.

A Wish a Day. London, Hutchinson, and New York, Dodd Mead, 1956.

Admirer Unknown. New York, Dodd Mead, 1957.

Leap Year Love. London, Hurst and Blackett, 1957; as *Leap Year Romance*, New York, Dodd Mead, 1957.

Mystery Boy-Friend. London, Hutchinson, 1957.

Romantic Afterthought. London, Hurst and Blackett, and New York, Dodd Mead, 1959.

Love and a Rich Girl. London, Hurst and Blackett, and New York, Dodd Mead, 1960.

Sherry and the Ghosts. London, Hurst and Blackett, 1961; New York, Dodd Mead, 1962.

Diamond Engagement Ring. London, Hurst and Blackett, 1962.

Runaway Lovers. London, Hurst and Blackett, 1963.

Rendezvous in Zagarella. London, Hurst and Blackett, 1964.

Shopping for a Husband. London, Hurst and Blackett, 1967.

Short Stories

Khaki and Kisses. London, Hutchinson, 1915.
The Great Unmet. New York, Harper's Bazaar, 1918.
Rufus on the Rebound. New York, Harper's Bazaar, 1918.
The Dream Domesticated. New York, Harper's Bazaar, 1918.
The Girl Who Was Too Good-Looking. London, Hodder and Stoughton, 1920.
The Post-War Girl and Other Stories. London, Hutchinson, 1922.
Wanted on the Voyage. London, Cassell, 1930.

OTHER PUBLICATIONS

Other

American Snap-Shots. New York, Dodd Mead, 1920.
The Berta Ruck Birthday Book, with Quotations. London, Hodder and Stoughton, and
   New York, Dodd Mead, 1920.
A Story-Teller Tells the Truth: Reminiscences and Notes. London, Hutchinson, 1935.
A Smile for the Past (autobiography). London, Hutchinson, 1959.
A Trickle of Welsh Blood. London, Hutchinson, 1967.
An Asset to Wales. London, Hutchinson, 1970.
Ancestral Voices. London, Hutchinson, 1972.

*   *   *

The Edwardian era is seen by many as a Golden Age of Romance, a time of gaiety, extravagance, luxury, and flamboyant wealth. Berta Ruck, who published the first of her many novels in 1914, used this background for a number of her stories. "The Edwardian dinner parties," she said recalling that time in a radio interview: "I've been to those...when I was very young and I don't think such things again exist...those long tables full of guests, and being 'taken in' to dinner. And the long skirts—skirt after skirt after skirt with perhaps a champagne cork caught in the flounce, you'd occasionally see. Masses of flowers—an absolute jungle of pink sweet peas and white gypsophila."

Ruck proved to be an adaptable writer, changing her background, and style according to the times in which she lived. *Arabella the Awful* (1918) is a simple, cheery little tale with some light-hearted satire on the aristocracy thrown in, and jokey references to the German's silliness, and the Englishman's bravery, and was clearly intended as a morale-raiser in time of war. In 1922 appeared a story with a nursing background, *The Bride Who Ran Away*. And, like so many romantic novelists, she too was lured by the desert: "That was, of course, one of those never-to-be-forgotten nights. The moon, instead of being silver, made everything amber and gold—the sands of the desert, I suppose—and the camels. Everything was so ageless. "In the 1960's, she was up with the times as is shown by *Shopping for a Husband*, a novel dedicated to Heather Jenner, a principal and founder of one of the country's largest marriage bureaux, and written about the seemingly unromantic topic of marriage bureau matches. Kate, on the shelf in her late twenties, and desperate for a marriage, is finally driven, as the title suggests, to go shopping for a husband. After working through numerous men on the bureau's books, she falls for a staggeringly rich north-country steel magnate, and proves that the services of a bureau can be as legitimate and wonderful a way of discovering true love as any more chancey, flash-in-the-pan meeting. As Heather Jenner, the bureau principal, explained in a book about modern marriage: "The whole social concept of marriage has changed, but a man still seeks a wife who fits in with his background and who comes of wholesome stock."

After 50 years of writing, the rather cloying, sickly-sweet, flavour of the earliest stories had given way to a quasi-stream of consciousness style, jerky and chatty, which leaves out finite verbs, definite articles and pronouns, while making the fullest possible use of upper case letters, unorthodox punctuation, and italics, sometimes entire paragraphs being italicised.

Her attitude to her work was optimistic. When accused of leaving out the "unpleasant realities" of life, she justified it like this:

I belong to the School of Thought (the Non-Thinking School, if you like) that considers "compensating dream fiction," not as opiate, but as tonic, and prefers to leave the tale on a note definitely gay and hopeful. People condemn the story-teller's cheerfully tidied-up last chapter as the flight from reality. Personally I regard it as the entrance into the original real world.

To the people who ask me why I can't face facts, I would suggest that it takes all kind of facts to make a world; why should I not describe those I prefer? Why, people ask, do I falsify Life? Why, I ask, do they? I think it is very wrong to give Youth the impression that it is unalterably doomed to disappointment. *"C'est en croyant aux roses,"* says a French proverb, *"qu'on les fait éçlore."* It is by believing in roses that one brings them into bloom...

It is my creed that the world was created to go merry as a marriage-bell and for the whole human race to be healthy, wealthy and wise enough to be happy on all cylinders.

—Rachel Anderson

RUNDLE, Anne (née Lamb).   Also writes as Georgianna Bell; Marianne Lamont; Alexandra Manners; Joanne Marshall; Jeanne Sanders.   British.   Born in Berwick-on-Tweed, Northumberland. Attended army schools, and Berwick High School for Girls. Married Edwin Charles Rundle in 1949; one daughter and two sons. Civil servant, Berwick, Newcastle-upon-Tyne, and London, to 1951. Recipient: Romantic Novelists Association Netta Muskett Award, 1967, and Major Award, 1970, 1971. Agent: John McLaughlin, Campbell Thomson and McLaughlin, 31 Newington Green, London N16 9PU, England. Address: Cloy Cottage, Knowe Road, Brodick, Arran KA27 8BY, Scotland.

ROMANCE AND GOTHIC PUBLICATIONS

Novels

The Moon Marriage. London, Hurst and Blackett, 1967.
Swordlight. London, Hurst and Blackett, 1968.
Forest of Fear. London, Hurst and Blackett, 1969.
Passionate Jade (as Georgianna Bell). London, Fontana, 1969; New York, Pocket Books, 1981.
Rakehell. London, Hurst and Blackett, 1970.
Lost Lotus. London, Hale, 1972.
Amberwood. London, Hale, 1972; New York, Bantam, 1974.
Spindrift (as Jeanne Sanders). London, Hale, 1974.
Heronbrook. New York, Bantam, 1974; London, Hale, 1975.
Judith Lammeter. London, Hale, 1976.
Grey Ghyll. London, Hale, 1978; New York, St. Martin's Press, 1979.

Novels as Joanne Marshall

Cuckoo at Candlemas.   London, Jenkins, 1968.
Cat on a Broomstick.   London, Jenkins, 1969.
The Dreaming Tower.   London, Jenkins, 1969.
Flower of Silence.   London, Mills and Boon, 1970; New York, Avon, 1974.
Babylon Was Dust.   London, Mills and Boon, 1971.
Wild Boar Wood.   London, Mills and Boon, 1972; New York, Avon, 1973.
The Trellised Walk.   London, Mills and Boon, 1973.
Sea-Song.   London, Mills and Boon, 1973.
Follow a Shadow.   London, Collins, and New York, Putnam, 1974.
Valley of Tall Chimneys.   London, Collins, 1975.
Last Act.   London, Collins, and New York, Putnam, 1976.
The Peacock Bed.   London, Collins, and New York, St. Martin's Press, 1978.

Novels as Marianne Lamont

Dark Changeling.   London, Hurst and Blackett, 1970; New York, Avon, 1973.
Green Glass Moon.   London, Hurst and Blackett, 1970.
Bitter Bride-Bed.   London, Hurst and Blackett, 1971.
Nine Moons Wasted.   London, Constable, and New York, Putnam, 1977.
Horns of the Moon.   London, Constable, 1979.

Novels as Alexandra Manners

The Stone Maiden.   New York, Putnam, 1973; London, Millington, 1974.
Candles in the Wood.   New York, Putnam, 1974; London, Millington, 1975.
The Singing Swans.   New York, Putnam, 1975; London, Millington, 1976.
Sable Hunter.   New York, Putnam, 1977; London, Collins, 1978; as *Cardigan Square*,
    New York, Berkley, 1977.
Wildford's Daughter.   New York, Putnam, 1978; as *The White Moths*, London, Collins,
    1979.
Echoing Yesterday.   London, Corgi, 1981.
Karran Kinrade.   London, Corgi, 1982.

OTHER PUBLICATIONS

Other (juvenile)

Dragonscale.   London, Hutchinson, 1969.
Tamlane.   London, Hutchinson, 1970.

*   *   *

Anne Rundle began her writing career by winning the Romantic Novelists Association Netta Muskett Award with her historical novel *The Moon Marriage*, based on the Jacobite Rebellion. Rundle spent her childhood with grandparents in Berwick: the loneliness of her formative years, coupled with growing up in a town so rich in history, was a main step to her becoming a writer.

Rundle is a self-taught writer, and her work has been influenced by numerous writers, in particular Daphne du Maurier, but also Winston Graham, R.L. Delderfield, Dorothy Eden, Catherine Gaskin, and Mary Stewart. In more recent years the works of Diane Pearson, Elizabeth Byrd, and P.D. James, who write books that have a harder core, have inspired her writings. Just as her work has been influenced by a variety of different writers, so her books have appeared under a variety of pseudonyms. Her earliest works appeared under her own name, but she has used the name Marianne Lamont for historical romance, Alexandra Manners for longer gothic novels, and Joanne Marshall for straight romance.

Rundle attributes her success in so many facets of romance writing to her being a Gemini and having the ability readily to take on the mantle of four different people when changing her writing style. This, coupled with a fertile imagination, self-discipline, and determination have combined to produce over 25 titles. Her lifelong interest in amateur dramatics has also obviously reinforced her ability to visualise action as in stage setting, a strong point of many of the dramatic scenes in her work.

—Marion R. Harris

SABATINI, Rafael. British. Born in Jesi, Italy, 29 April 1875. Educated at Ecole Cantonale, Zoug, Switzerland, and in Oporto, Portugal. Served in the War Office Intelligence Department during World War I. Married 1) Ruth Goad Dixon in 1905 (divorced); 2) Mrs. Christine Dixon in 1935. Lived in Clifford, Herefordshire. *Died 13 February 1950.*

ROMANCE AND GOTHIC PUBLICATIONS

Novels (series: Captain Blood)

The Lovers of Yvonne. London, Pearson, 1902; as *The Suitors of Yvonne*, New York, Putnam, 1902.
The Tavern Knight. London, Richards, 1904; Boston, Houghton Mifflin, 1927.
Bardelys the Magnificent. London, Nash, 1906; Boston, Houghton Mifflin, 1923.
The Trampling of the Lilies. London, Hutchinson, 1906; Boston, Houghton Mifflin, 1924.
Love-at-Arms. London, Hutchinson, 1907; Boston, Houghton Mifflin, 1924.
The Shame of Molly. London, Hutchinson, 1908; Boston, Houghton Mifflin, 1924.
St. Martin's Summer. London, Hutchinson, 1909; Boston, Houghton Mifflin, 1924.
Anthony Wilding. London, Hutchinson, 1910; as *Arms and the Maid; or, Anthony Wilding*, New York, Putnam, 1910.
The Lion's Skin. London, Stanley Paul, and Boston, Houghton Mifflin, 1911.
The Justice of the Duke. London, Stanley Paul, 1912.
The Strolling Saint. London, Stanley Paul, 1913; Boston, Houghton Mifflin, 1924.
The Gates of Doom. London, Stanley Paul, 1914; Boston, Houghton Mifflin, 1926.
The Sea-Hawk. London, Secker, and Philadelphia, Lippincott, 1915.
The Banner of the Bull: Three Episodes in the Career of Cesare Borgia. London, Secker, and Philadelphia, Lippincott, 1915; first episode published as *The Urbinian*, Boston, Houghton Mifflin, 1924.
The Snare. London, Secker, and Philadelphia, Lippincott, 1915.
Scaramouche: A Romance of the French Revolution. London, Hutchinson, and Boston, Houghton Mifflin, 1921.
Captain Blood, His Odyssey. London, Hutchinson, and Boston, Houghton Mifflin, 1922.
Fortune's Fool. London, Hutchinson, and Boston, Houghton Mifflin, 1923.
Mistress Wilding. Boston, Houghton Mifflin, 1924.

The Carolinian. London, Hutchinson, and Boston, Houghton Mifflin, 1925.
Bellarion the Fortunate. London, Hutchinson, and Boston, Houghton Mifflin, 1926.
The Nuptials of Corbal. London, Hutchinson, and Boston, Houghton Mifflin, 1927.
The Hounds of God. London, Hutchinson, and Boston, Houghton Mifflin, 1928.
The Romantic Prince. London, Hutchinson, and Boston, Houghton Mifflin, 1929.
The Reaping. London, Readers Library, 1929.
The Minion. London, Hutchinson, 1930; as *The King's Minion*, Boston, Houghton Mifflin, 1930.
Captain Blood Returns. Boston, Houghton Mifflin, 1931; as *The Chronicles of Captain Blood*, London, Hutchinson, 1932.
The Black Swan. London, Hutchinson, and Boston, Houghton Mifflin, 1932.
The Stalking Horse. London, Hutchinson, and Boston, Houghton Mifflin, 1933.
Venetian Masque. London, Hutchinson, and Boston, Houghton Mifflin, 1934.
Chivalry. London, Hutchinson, and Boston, Houghton Mifflin, 1935.
The Fortunes of Captain Blood. London, Hutchinson, and Boston, Houghton Mifflin, 1936.
The Lost King. London, Hutchinson, and Boston, Houghton Mifflin, 1937.
The Sword of Islam. London, Hutchinson, and Boston, Houghton Mifflin, 1939.
The Marquis of Carabas. London, Hutchinson, 1940; as *Master-at-Arms*, Boston, Houghton Mifflin, 1940.
Columbus. London, Hutchinson, and Boston, Houghton Mifflin, 1942.
King in Prussia. London, Hutchinson, 1944; as *The Birth of Mischief*, Boston, Houghton Mifflin, 1945.
The Gamester. London, Hutchinson, and Boston, Houghton Mifflin, 1949.
Saga of the Sea (omnibus). London, Hutchinson, 1953.
Sinner, Saint, and Jester (omnibus). London, Hutchinson, 1954.
In the Shadow of the Guillotine. (omnibus). London, Hutchinson, 1955; Boston, Houghton Mifflin, 1956.

Short Stories

The Historical Nights' Entertainment, 1st-3rd series. Boston, Houghton Mifflin, 3 vols., 1917-38; London, Secker, 1 vol., 1918; London, Hutchinson, 2 vols., 1919-37.
Stories of Love, Intrigue, and Battle, Being Selected Works of Rafael Sabatini. Boston, Houghton Mifflin, 1931.
Turbulent Tales. London, Hutchinson, 1946.

OTHER PUBLICATIONS

Plays

Kuomi, The Jester, with Stephanie Baring (produced Luton, Bedfordshire, 1903).
Bardelys the Magnificent, with Henry Hamilton, adaptation of the novel by Sabatini (produced Birmingham, 1910; London, 1911).
Fugitives (produced London, 1911).
The Rattlesnake, with J.E. Harold Terry (produced New York, 1921; London, 1922).
Scaramouche, adaptation of his own novel (produced New York, 1923; Glasgow and London, 1927).
In the Snare, with Leon M. Lion, adaptation of the novel *The Snare* by Sabatini (produced London, 1924).
The Carolinian, with J.E. Harold Terry (produced Detroit and New York, 1925).
The Tyrant: An Episode in the Life of Cesare Borgia (produced Birmingham and London, 1925; New York, 1930). London, Hutchinson, 1925.

Screenplays: *Bluff*, 1921; *The Recoil*, 1922; *The Scourge* (*Fortune's Fool*), 1922.

Other

The Life of Cesare Borgia of Grance.   London, Stanley Paul, 1911; New York, Bren-
    tano's, 1912.
Torquemada and the Spanish Inquisition.   London, Stanley Paul, and New York,
    Brentano's, 1913; revised edition, Stanley Paul, and Boston, Houghton Mifflin, 1924.
Heroic Lives.   London, Hutchinson, and Boston, Houghton Mifflin, 1934.

Editor, A Century of Sea Stories.   London, Hutchinson, 1934.
Editor, A Century of Historical Stories.   London, Hutchinson, 1936.
Editor, The Book of the Sea Trout, by Hamish Stuart.   London, Cape, 1952.

*   *   *

Rafael Sabatini was called the "new Dumas" by his admirers and a sleight-of-hand artist with
a "bag of tricks" by skeptics, but his narratives are well crafted and often sparkle with crisp
dialogue and rousing adventure. The settings of what he called his period novels ranged over
several centuries in England, France, Italy, and in the Caribbean during the heyday of piracy,
with a few more scattered around America, Spain, Venice, and elsewhere. In addition to his
romantic novels Sabatini wrote fiction and accounts of historical incidents for his three
volumes of Historical Nights' Entertainment, recreated episodes from the Spanish Inquisition,
and wrote novelizations and sketches of the lives of such cultural heroes as Columbus, Saint
Francis of Assisi, Joan of Arc, Lord Nelson, and Florence Nightingale. He seems to have read
history with great voracity, but he had no more respect for historians than many of them had
for his own versions of past events.
    Sabatini had been writing historical fiction, biography, and romance for over 30 years when
he summarized his views on the writer's responsibilities to his art. Historians, Sabatini argued,
are not necessarily more faithful to their material than are period novelists, and they seldom
write as well. Citing the accounts of William Tell, the Man in the Iron Mask, and incestual
relations among the Borgias as legends which had crept into histories of Europe, Sabatini finds
that historical "facts" are all too often based on repeated errors, sensationalism, and the biased
reports of dubious witnesses. He says of one of his characters in Captain Blood who has just
carried off a successful lie that "there was a great historian lost in Wolverstone. He had the right
imagination that knows just how far to colour it so as to change its shape for his own purposes."
Good period fiction, on the other hand, requires equally serious research, a faithfulness to
historical personages and events, and shrewd analysis of the available evidence. According to
Sabatini there are basically three kinds of period novels: those which are concerned entirely
with historical characters and happenings, those involving imaginary characters set "against a
real background to which story and characters must bear some real and true relationship," and
those which blend "events that are reasonably and logically imagined, and characters that lived
with characters that the author has invented."
    Sabatini's The Minion (U.S. title: The King's Minion) for which he "scarcely invented even a
minor character," is an example of the first type. The novel is concerned with intrigues leading
to the murder of Sir Thomas Overbury in the court of James I, and Sabatini finds "as a result of
close study and close reasoning" that there were initially two conspiracies which later became
entangled. Scaramouche, which is subtitled "A Romance," is the second type: the title character
is imaginary, but the setting is faithful to the milieu of revolutionary France. The hero is "the
natural offspring of the circumstances and habits of mind of the time," which molded his
character and shaped his fortunes. Scaramouche is aptly titled a romance. After being banished
from the estate of his foster father, André-Louis Moreau takes the name Scaramouche and
joins a traveling band of players. The death of a friend at the hands of a vicious aristocrat leads
Scaramouche to seek revenge, and in turn become a notorious polemicist, a fencing master, and
a Revolutionary hero. In seeking revenge, André clashes with the aristocrat over an actress he
thinks he loves and the lady he has always loved. At the culmination of the Revolution André
learns that the aristocrat is his father. This psychological drama is woven interestingly into the
players' story where the troup moves from hard times under feudal leadership to great success
through André's skills as an early capitalist; he collects personnel, organizes bookings, writes
advertising, composes plays based on the classics, and stars in performances.

Sabatini's third kind of novel, a combination of the period novel and the historical romance, is found in *Captain Blood*. Peter Blood is based on Henry Pitman, an English surgeon who was sold into slavery at Barbados after being sentenced to death by Jeffreys at the Bloody Assize for ministering to wounded rebels during Monmouth's Rebellion. Sabatini follows Pitman's biography up to the point of his escape, then follows John [or A. O.] Exquemelin's *History of the Bucaniers of America* and other accounts, including that of Henry Morgan, for models of buccaneer adventures and characters. The success of *Captain Blood* led to *The Chronicles of Captain Blood* (U.S. title: *Captain Blood Returns*) in 1931 and *The Fortunes of Captain Blood* in 1936. The sea is an ideal setting and piracy a useful mode for portraying the struggle for reasonable loyalties inc a world of shifting alliances. Like those in *The Sea-Hawk* and *The Black Swan*, Captain Blood's adventures allows Sabatini to play on those gray areas surrounding allegiance to particular nations, religions, and ideals of personal integrity.

In *The Sea-Hawk* Sir Oliver Tressilan loses his estate and is enslaved by Moslems after his brother accuses him of a murder he himself had committed, but Tressilan makes himself invaluable to his master and becomes Sakr-el-Bahr the pirate. *The Black Swan* finds French ex-buccaneer Charles de Bernis drawn into alliance with the last of the renegade pirates, Tom Leach, in order to save his own life.

Sabatini's fiction is effective to the extent that he creates an opposition between the picaresque milieu in which the action takes place and the chivalric idealism of the protagonists. In a world of court intrigues, war, and such outlawry as piracy the hero's position is associated with or appears to be compromised by shadowy motives and actions. Despite his protestations, in the lady's eyes the gentleman is compromised, because his chivalrous manner is at odds with what she sees of his actions in the world. Since the hero's immersion in the picaresque life has usually resulted from a betrayal of some sort, he must extract himself by avenging wrongs while he attempts to gain or regain his fortune. While he is away the lady should have the "womanliness to be guided by natural instincts in the selection of her mate," but an admirable woman is courted by many men and since she distrusts him she might, "for position, riches, and a great title barter herself in marriage," or be less cautious with another suitor. The reader identifies the love match early and much of the tension of the novels results from suspension of the courtship during periods of vigorous action. Because the potential lovers are ignorant or distrustful of one another's feelings yet drawn together by an instinctively powerful attraction, meetings between them crackle with misunderstandings and disdainful wit.

Sabatini's period novels and romances have not lost their charm over time for those readers willing to suspend disbelief in their romantic premises. His most popular works inspired motion pictures and he turned some of them into successful stage productions. His popularity weathered the abuse of critics who would have had more realism and historians who demanded more footnotes. His bag of tricks, which included stock characters, a liberal use of "Chance," predictably honorable heroes and heroines, unlikely misunderstandings and so on, seldom intrude into the magical moments of high action and grand verbal exchanges. Readers who made *Scaramouche*, *The Sea-Hawk*, *Mistress Wilding*, *The Carolinian*, and *Captain Blood* best sellers were responding not merely to the lure of romantic fiction, but to energy and courage inspired by one of its most capable spokesmen.

—Larry N. Landrum

ST. JOHN, Mabel.   Pseudonym for Henry St. John Cooper.

Novels

    Most Cruelly Wronged.   London, Amalgamated Press, 1907.
    Only a Singing Girl.   London, Amalgamated Press, 1907.
    Rival Beauties.   London, Amalgamated Press, 1907.
    Under a Ban.   London, Amalgamated Press, 1907.
    Her Father's Sin.   London, Amalgamated Press, 1908.
    Polly Green: A School Story [*and Coosha, at Cambridge, —Engaged, in Society, at Twenty-One*].   London, Amalgamated Press, 6 vols., 1909-11.
    Romany Ruth: A Gipsy Love Story.   London, Amalgamated Press, 1909.
    Just a Barmaid.   London, Amalgamated Press, 1909.
    A Daughter Scorned.   London, Amalgamated Press, 1911.
    Jane Em'ly.   London, Amalgamated Press, 1911.
    The Twins of Twineham.   London, Amalgamated Press, 1911.
    The Dear Old Home.   London, Amalgamated Press, 1912.
    The Best Woman in the World.   London, Fleetway House, 1913.
    Nell of the Camp; or, The Pride of the Prairie.   London, Fleetway House, 1913.
    The Outcasts of Crowthorpe College.   London, Fleetway House, 1913.
    The Schoolgirl Bride.   London, Fleetway House, 1913.
    Faults on Both Sides.   London, Fleetway House, 1914.
    Fine Feathers! or, The Wife Who Would Be Smart.   London, Fleetway House, 1914.
    From Mill to Mansion.   London, Fleetway House, 1914.
    Kiddy, The Coffee-Stall Girl.   London, Fleetway House, 1914.
    Little Miss Millions.   London, Fleetway House, 1914.
    Married to Her Master.   London, Fleetway House, 1914.
    My Lancashire Queen.   London, Fleetway House, 1914.
    Sally in Our Alley.   London, Fleetway House, 1914.
    The Ticket-of-Leave Girl.   London, Fleetway House, 1914.
    When a Girl's Pretty.   London, Fleetway House, 1914.
    John Jordan, Slave-Driver.   London, Fleetway House, 1915.
    Just Jane Ann.   London, Fleetway House, 1915.
    The Lass That Loved a Sailor.   London, Fleetway House, 1915.
    Maggie Darling.   London, Fleetway House, 1915.
    My Girl, Regan.   London, Fleetway House, 1915.
    The Post Office Girl.   London, Fleetway House, 1915.
    Shielded from the World.   London, Fleetway House, 1915.
    Too Wilful for Words!   London, Fleetway House, 1915.
    The Worst Wife in the World.   London, Fleetway House, 1915.
    Born in Prison: The Story of a Mill-Girl's Sacrifice.   London, Fleetway House, 1916.
    Cook at School.   London, Fleetway House, 1916.
    How the Money Goes!   London, Fleetway House, 1916.
    In Mother's Place.   London, Fleetway House, 1916.
    The Mistress of the Fifth Standard.   London, Fleetway House, 1916.
    The Soul of the Mill.   London, Fleetway House, 1916.
    The Best Girls Are Here.   London, Fleetway House, 1917.
    Daisy Earns Her Living.   London, Fleetway House, 1917.
    Daisy Peach Abroad.   London, Fleetway House, 1917.
    Liz o' Loomland.   London, Fleetway House, 1917.
    Married at School.   London, Fleetway House, 1917.
    Our Nell.   London, Fleetway House, 1917.
    The "Sixpenny Ha'penny" Duchess.   London, Fleetway House, 1917.
    What a Woman Can Do!   London, Fleetway House, 1917.

The Autograph Hunters. London, Fleetway House, 1918.
Dolly Daydreams! London, Fleetway House, 1918.
For Her Lover's Sake. London, Fleetway House, 1918.
His Sealed Lips! or, The Tale He Would Not Tell! London, Fleetway House, 1918.
Little and Good. London, Fleetway House, 1918.
Little Miss Innocence. London, Fleetway House, 1918.
Millgirl and Dreamer. London, Fleetway House, 1918.
Old Smith's Nurse. London, Fleetway House, 1918.
Pearl of the West. London, Fleetway House, 1918.
Her Stolen Baby. London, Fleetway House, 1919.
Apronstrings. London, Amalgamated Press, 1919.
Ashamed of the Shop; or, Miss High-and-Mighty. London, Amalgamated Press, 1919.
The Belle of the Works. London, Amalgamated Press, 1919.
The Favourite Wins! or, The Bookmaker's Bride. London, Amalgamated Press, 1919.
Good Gracious, Marian! London, Amalgamated Press, 1919.
The Little "Gutter Girl." London, Amalgamated Press, 1919.
Betty on the Stage. London, Amalgamated Press, 1920.
The Wife Who Dragged Him Down! London, Amalgamated Press, 1920.
A Boxer's Sweetheart. London, Amalgamated Press, 1920.
The Wife Who Would Be "Master"! London, Amalgamated Press, 1920.
The Cinderella Girl. London, Amalgamated Press, 1920.
In the Shadows! London, Amalgamated Press, 1920.
Mary Ellen—Mill-Lass. London, Amalgamated Press, 1920.
Mill-Lass o' Mine! London, Amalgamated Press, 1920.
Wedded But Not Wooed; or, Marry Me—Or Go to Prison! London, Amalgamated Press, 1920.
From Pillar to Post; or, No Home of Her Own. London, Amalgamated Press, 1921.
Wife—or Housekeeper? London, Amalgamated Press, 1921.
A House, But Not a Home. London, Amalgamated Press, 1921.
The Husband, The Wife, and the Friend. London, Amalgamated Press, 1921.
A Jealous Wife's Revenge! London, Amalgamated Press, 1921.
Just Jane Em'ly. London, Amalgamated Press, 1921.
Little Miss Lancashire; or, Moll o' the Mill. London, Amalgamated Press, 1921.
Lonely Little Lucy. London, Amalgamated Press, 1921.
Mad for Dress! London, Amalgamated Press, 1921.
Sally All-Smiles. London, Amalgamated Press, 1921.
The School Against Her! London, Amalgamated Press, 1921.
Scorned by "His" Mother. London, Amalgamated Press, 1921.
Ann All-Alone: The Story of a Girl's Great Self-Sacrifice. London, Amalgamated Press, 1922.
Wife or Maid? or, Scorned by Her Workmates. London, Amalgamated Press, 1922.
The Brute! London, Amalgamated Press, 1922.
We Want Our Mummy! London, Amalgamated Press, 1922.
Gipsy Born! London, Amalgamated Press, 1922.
Tattling Tongues. London, Amalgamated Press, 1922.
The Gipsy Schoolgirl. London, Amalgamated Press, 1922.
Girl of the Prairie. London, Amalgamated Press, 1922.
The Home Without a Father! London, Amalgamated Press, 1922.
Mother Knows Best! or, Uttered in Anger! London, Amalgamated Press, 1922.
Mr. Leslie's School for Girls. London, Amalgamated Press, 1922.
Nobody's Girl. London, Amalgamated Press, 1922.
Rich Girl—Charity Girl! London, Amalgamated Press, 1922.
Blood Money! London, Amalgamated Press, 1923.
The Disappearance of Barbara. London, Amalgamated Press, 1923.
Such a Fine Fellow! London, Amalgamated Press, 1923.
The Gipsy Actress. London, Amalgamated Press, 1923.
The Girl Who Married the Wrong Man! London, Amalgamated Press, 1923.
He Couldn't Take Money! or, The "Old Fool" of the Family! London, Amalgamated

Press, 1923.
His Wife—or His Mother? or, No Home of Her Own. London, Amalgamated Press, 1923.
I'm Not a Common Girl! London, Amalgamated Press, 1923.
Jenny Luck of Brendon's Mills. London, Amalgamated Press, 1923.
The New Girl at Bellforth. London, Amalgamated Press, 1923.
The Second Husband. London, Amalgamated Press, 1923.
Secrets of the Shop! London, Amalgamated Press, 1923.
Too Old for Her Husband! London, Amalgamated Press, 1924.
Bringing Up Becky! London, Amalgamated Press, 1924.
She Was an Actress. London, Amalgamated Press, 1924.
Go Borrowing—Go Sorrowing. London, Amalgamated Press, 1924.
A Son to Be Proud Of! London, Amalgamated Press, 1924.
He Married a Mill-Lass. London, Amalgamated Press, 1924.
The Island Girl. London, Amalgamated Press, 1924.
Married to His Wife's Family. London, Amalgamated Press, 1924.
She Wrecked Their Home! or, A Son's a Son till He Takes Him a Wife. London, Amalgamated Press, 1924.
Midsummer Madness! London, Amalgamated Press, 1924.
The Mill-Girl's Bargain! London, Amalgamated Press, 1924.
My Man of the Mill! London, Amalgamated Press, 1924.
Poisoned Lives! London, Amalgamated Press, 1924.
The "Sports" of Lyndale. London, Amalgamated Press, 1925.
As the World Judged. London, Amalgamated Press, 1925.
When There's Love at Home. London, Amalgamated Press, 1925.
A Girl's Good Name. London, Amalgamated Press, 1925.
Where Is My Child To-night? London, Amalgamated Press, 1925.
Just 'Liz-beth Ann. London, Amalgamated Press, 1925.
Longing for Love. London, Amalgamated Press, 1925.
Pride Parted Them! London, Amalgamated Press, 1925.
Shamed by Her Husband! London, Amalgamated Press, 1925.
She Posed as Their Friend! London, Amalgamated Press, 1925.
She Shall Never Call You Mother! London, Amalgamated Press, 1925.
And Still She Loved Him. London, Amalgamated Press, 1926.
The Daughter He Didn't Want! London, Amalgamated Press, 1926.
Some Mother's Child! London, Amalgamated Press, 1926.
It Is My Duty! London, Amalgamated Press, 1926.
The Life He Led Her! London, Amalgamated Press, 1926.
Love Needs Telling. London, Amalgamated Press, 1926.
Maggie of Marley's Mill. London, Amalgamated Press, 1926.
The Man Who Married Again. London, Amalgamated Press, 1926.
Rivals at School—Rivals Through Life! London, Amalgamated Press, 1926.
She Sold Her Child! London, Amalgamated Press, 1927.
He'll Never Marry You! London, Amalgamated Press, 1927.
Thou Shalt Love Thy Neighbour—. London, Amalgamated Press, 1927.
Lizbeth Rose. London, Amalgamated Press, 1927.
Tied to Her Apron Strings! London, Amalgamated Press, 1927.
The Long, Long Wooing. London, Amalgamated Press, 1927.
Loved for Her Money. London, Amalgamated Press, 1927.
The New Girl. London, Amalgamated Press, 1927.
She'll Never Marry My Son! London, Amalgamated Press, 1927.
Some Mother's Son! London, Amalgamated Press, 1928.
A Beggar at Her Husband's Door! London, Amalgamated Press, 1928.
Utterly Alone! London, Amalgamated Press, 1928.
His Wife or His Work? London, Amalgamated Press, 1928.
His Wife's Secret! London, Amalgamated Press, 1928.
Nobody Wants You! London, Amalgamated Press, 1928.
He Shall Not Marry a Mill-Lass! London, Amalgamated Press, 1929.

The Husband She Wanted. London, Amalgamated Press, 1930.
Jess o' Jordan's. London, Amalgamated Press, 1930.
Wedded—But Alone! London, Amalgamated Press, 1930.
Another Girl Won Him. London, Amalgamated Press, 1935.

Novels as Henry St. John Cooper

The Master of the Mill. London, Amalgamated Press, 1910.
A Shop-Girl's Revenge. London, Fleetway House, 1914.
The Cotton King. London, Fleetway House, 1915.
The Lass He Left Behind Him! London, Fleetway House, 1915.
The Black Sheep; or, Who Is My Brother? London, Fleetway House, 1916.
Ready—Aye Ready! A Story of the Bull-Dogs of the Ocean. London, Fleetway House, 1916.
The Man with the Money. London, Fleetway House, 1917.
Hero or Scamp? London, Fleetway House, 1918.
Miss Bolo; or, A Spy in the Home. London, Fleetway House, 1918.
The Man of Her Dreams. London, Amalgamated Press, 1919.
The Mill Queen. London, Fleetway House, 1919.
Sunny Ducrow. London, Sampson Low, 1919.
There's Just One Girl. London, Amalgamated Press, 1919.
Vagabond Jess. London, Amalgamated Press, 1919.
"Wild-Fire" Nan. London, Amalgamated Press, 1919.
Fair and False; or, A Whited Sepulchre. London, Amalgamated Press, 1920.
Her Mother-in-Law. London, Amalgamated Press, 1920.
James Bevanwood, Baronet. London, Sampson Low, 1920.
Just a Cottage Maid. London, Amalgamated Press, 1920.
A Lodger in His Own Home. London, Amalgamated Press, 1920.
Married to a Miser. London, Amalgamated Press, 1920.
Men Were Deceivers Ever. London, Amalgamated Press, 1920.
Mountain Lovers. London, Amalgamated Press, 1920.
Two Men and a Maid. London, Amalgamated Press, 1920.
Elizabeth in Dreamland. London, Amalgamated Press, 1921.
The Garden of Memories. London, Sampson Low, 1921.
The Island of Eve. London, Amalgamated Press, 1921.
Love's Waif. London, Amalgamated Press, 1921.
Mabel St. John's Schooldays. London, Amalgamated Press, 1921.
Madge o' the Mill. London, Amalgamated Press, 1921.
Prison-Stained! London, Amalgamated Press, 1921.
We're Not Wanted Now! London, Amalgamated Press, 1921.
Carniss and Company. London, Sampson Low, 1922.
Above Her Station. London, Amalgamated Press, 1922.
A Daughter of the Loom; or, Go and Marry Your Mill-Girl! London, Amalgamated Press, 1922.
Fairweather Friends! or, Fleeced by His Family! London, Amalgamated Press, 1922.
The Imaginary Marriage. London, Sampson Low, 1922.
Poverty's Daughter. London, Amalgamated Press, 1922.
A Snake in the Grass. London, Amalgamated Press, 1922.
The Vagabond's Daughter. London, Amalgamated Press, 1922.
Could She Forgive? London, Amalgamated Press, 1923.
Gipsy Love. London, Amalgamated Press, 1923.
The "Head" of the Family; or, Despised by Them All! London, Amalgamated Press, 1923.
Hidden Hearts. London, Amalgamated Press, 1923.
Kidnapped. London, Amalgamated Press, 1923.
Mary Faithful. London, Amalgamated Press, 1923.
Son o' Mine! London, Amalgamated Press, 1923.

Too Common for Him! London, Amalgamated Press, 1923.
Two's Company...; or, Young Folks Are Best Alone. London, Amalgamated Press, 1923.
Yield Not to Temptation! London, Amalgamated Press, 1923.
The Broken Barrier. London, Amalgamated Press, 1924.
His Wife from the Kitchen! London, Amalgamated Press, 1924.
Just Plain Jim! or, One of the Rank and File. London, Amalgamated Press, 1924.
A Lover in Rags. London, Amalgamated Press, 1924.
Redway Street. London, Amalgamated Press, 1924.
The Unwanted Heiress. London, Amalgamated Press, 1924.
The Fortunes of Sally Luck. London, Sampson Low, 1925.
Lose Money—Lose Friends! London, Amalgamated Press, 1925.
Nan of No Man's Land. London, Amalgamated Press, 1925.
The Cottar's Daughter. London, Amalgamated Press, 1926.
The Gallant Lover: A Queen Anne Story. London, Sampson Low, 1926.
The Golconda Necklace. London, Sampson Low, 1926.
Whoso Diggeth a Pit—. London, Amalgamated Press, 1926.
The Woman Who Parted Them! London, Amalgamated Press, 1926.
The Amazing Tramp. London, Amalgamated Press, 1927.
Morning Glory. London, Sampson Low, 1927.
Golden Bait. London, Sampson Low, 1928.
The Red Veil. London, Sampson Low, 1928.
As Fate Decrees. London, Sampson Low, 1929.
Compromise. London, Sampson Low, 1929.
Retribution. London, Sampson Low, 1930.
The Millionaire Tramp. London, Sampson Low, 1930.
When a Man Loves. London, Sampson Low, 1931.
The Forbidden Road. London, Sampson Low, 1931.
Love That Divided. London, Sampson Low, 1932.
The Splendid Love. London, Sampson Low, 1932.
When Love Compels. London, Sampson Low, 1933.
Dangerous Paths. London, Sampson Low, 1933.
As a Woman Wills. London, Sampson Low, 1934.
The Hush Marriage. London, Sampson Low, 1934.
Toils of Silence. London, Sampson Low, 1935.
A Woman's Way. London, Sampson Low, 1935.
At Grips with Fate. London, Sampson Low, 1936.
The Call of Love. London, Sampson Low, 1936.

OTHER PUBLICATIONS

Other

Bull-Dogs and Bull-Dog Breeding. London, Jarrolds, 1905.
Bulldogs and Bulldog Men. London, Jarrolds, 1908.
Bulldogs and All about Them. London, Jarrolds, 1914.

*   *   *

Henry St. John Cooper was a prolific and wide-ranging author. He not only churned out thousands of words of women's fiction every week, but regularly wrote stories of tough, Borstal-like boarding-schools for several boys' papers.

As Mabel St. John he was one of the most popular writers of Lord Northcliffe's *Girls' Friend, Girls' Reader,* and *Girls' Home.* Before the first world war, these periodicals catered for hard-working and frequently exploited working-girl readers, whose education had begun and ended at elementary schools. St. John's championship of the underdog and the sheer gusto of the stories combined to create an instant recipe for success. (A large number of these magazine serial romances were subsequently reissued in the form of inexpensive paperback books.) Millgirl and maid-of-all-work readers could easily identify with St. John's heroines, who often occupied similar positions to their own (*Just a Barmaid, Liz o' Loomland*, etc.). The fictional "slaveys" and factory workers, however, had the advantage of stumbling more easily on redemptive romance with the bosses' sons than their real-life counterparts were likely to do in the rigid class divisions of Edwardian society.

Henry St. John, who was half-brother to Gladys Cooper, the celebrated actress, used theatrical settings for many of his stories. *Sunny Ducrow* is an attractive account of stage ambitions in a working-class girl. However, his theatre novels owed more to the rumbustious good humour of the music-hall than to the serious drama at which his sister excelled. Until "Mr. Right" came along to provide a permanent escape from their poorly paid drudgery, several St. John heroines abandoned "skivvying" for a career "on the halls," where they would achieve success through unusual enterprise and endeavour. (Em Hammond, for example, despite her much vaunted "yellow hair," manages convincingly to play the part of an Arab girl and also—no mean achievement this—to whistle "The Man Who Broke the Bank at Monte Carlo" through her yashmak!)

The apotheosis of romantic madcap appeal was achieved in Polly Green, whom St. John starred in six of his books. Rather surprisingly, Polly is not a working-class girl but a college student at Cambridge, where she inspires wholesale adulation from male undergraduates. Later she has London society at her feet, and enters into a forced engagement with a horribly ruthless member of the ruling class, whom she sensibly throws over as soon as circumstances permit. Happily he then not only commits suicide but obligingly leaves Polly his fortune, thus smoothing her way to marriage with her besotted but impecunious true love (Mabel St. John championing the underdog again!). A notable feature of the Polly Green stories is that Polly had a very long-standing friendship, on equal terms, with Coocha, an outspoken and extremely lively natured black girl. This was for its time a progressive step, but one that seemed immensely popular with Edwardian readers.

With their melodramatic plots and flashes of iconoclastic humour, the St. John romantic novels are certainly not in the classic mould. Their earthy acuteness, however, makes them more memorable than many mainstream love stories.

—Mary Cadogan

ST. JOHN, Nicole. Pseudonym for Norma Johnston. American. Born in Ridgewood, New Jersey. Educated at Ramsey public schools, New Jersey; Montclair State College, New Jersey, B.A.; studied acting at American Theatre Wing, New York. Has worked as actress, editor, teacher, and businesswoman. Agent: McIntosh and Otis Inc., 475 Fifth Avenue, New York, New York 10017, U.S.A.; or, A.M. Heath, 40-42 William IV Street, London WC2N 4DD, England.

ROMANCE AND GOTHIC PUBLICATIONS

Novels

The Medici Ring.   New York, Random House, 1975; London, Collins, 1976.
Wychwood.   New York, Random House, 1976; London, Heinemann, 1978.

Guinever's Gift.   New York, Random House, 1977; London, Heinemann, 1979.

OTHER PUBLICATIONS

Novels (juvenile) as Norma Johnston

The Wishing Star.   New York, Funk and Wagnalls, 1963.
The Wider Heart.   New York, Funk and Wagnalls, 1964.
Ready or Not.   New York, Funk and Wagnalls, 1965.
The Bridge Between.   New York, Funk and Wagnalls, 1966.
The Keeping Days.   New York, Atheneum, 1973.
Glory in the Flower.   New York, Atheneum, 1974.
Of Time and of Seasons.   New York, Atheneum, 1975.
Strangers Dark and Gold.   New York, Atheneum, 1975.
A Striving after Wind.   New York, Atheneum, 1976.
The Sanctuary Tree.   New York, Atheneum, 1977.
A Mustard Seed of Magic.   New York, Atheneum, 1977.
If You Love Me, Let Me Go.   New York, Atheneum, 1978.
The Swallow's Song.   New York, Atheneum, 1978.
Both Sides Now.   New York, Atheneum, 1978.
The Crucible Year.   New York, Atheneum, 1979.
Pride of Lions.   New York, Atheneum, 1979.
A Nice Girl Like You.   New York, Atheneum, 1980.
Myself and I.   New York, Atheneum, 1981.

Manuscript Collection: Rutgers University Library, New Brunswick, New Jersey.

*   *   *

"I draw my strength from England," says the American novelist Nicole St. John. Indeed, English history is the underlying theme—the *bas-relief*, if you will—of two of St. John's novels. Hidden within *Wychwood* is the story of Catherine Parr, widow of Henry VIII, and her lover Thomas Seymour, as well as ancient Anglo-Saxon occult rituals. *Guinever's Gift* is a re-enactment of the Arthurian legend, as the central characters investigate its historical validity. *The Medici Ring*, the author's first novel, reveals her appreciation of fine art and antiques. Further, St. John's love of English literature is reflected in her frequent references to Sir Thomas Malory, Shakespeare, Tennyson.

These are novels in the classic gothic tradition. Heroines (who tell their own stories) are always young and pretty, bright, curious, spunky, and alone in the world (typically, Lavinia Stanton, of *The Medici Ring*, is a "young, impecunious, overeducated orphan"). All heroes in St. John's novels are older and wiser, dark and mysterious, with flashing eyes (in short, *Jane Eyre*'s Rochester). The standard settings are: a mansion—the Culhaine mansion, on Marlborough Street in Boston, in *The Medici Ring*; Avalon, an Arthurian-type country house, in *Guinever's Gift*; an English cottage (Wychwood); each with many rooms, staircases, and hallways, some of them, of course, secret. The time: the Victorian Age. The plots that unfold are captivating and suspenseful.

Impelled by instinct, interest, and her newly orphaned status, the heroine is directed to the mansion (or country home or cottage), and there meets the dark stranger who, when his veil of mystery drops, will be revealed as her hero. In *The Medici Ring* the orphan Lavinia Stanton suffers another loss when her guardian, "Uncle" Eustace Robinson, dies, leaving her with only a 15th-century ruby ring and a knowledge of art and antiques. Lavinia is invited by Damaris Culhaine, an old school friend, to help catalogue the family's collection of Renaissance art. The Culhaine mansion contains not only paintings and sculpture and jewels, but many mysteries: the possible poisoning of Damaris; the Marchesa Marina Orsini, Damaris's aunt; the theft and forgery of some of the Culhaine's valuable art works; the untimely death (some years before) of

Damaris's mother, Isabel; and Damaris's father, the "emerald-eyed" Ross Culhaine. The figures in a hidden Renaissance tapestry unravel these mysteries for Lavinia.

Wychwood, named for the English country cottage to which the orphan sisters Camilla and Nell Jardin move when Nell is paralyzed by an accident at boarding school, likewise abounds in mysteries and apparitions, particularly the "ghost of the Copper Maid." Camilla risks her life and sanity to discover the riddle of her inheritance and the secrets behind the frightening events that occur at Wychwood. Aided by a mysterious neighbor, Jeremy Bushell, she uncovers the secret story of Catherine Parr and Thomas Seymour, and gains her own rightful inheritance.

In *Guinever's Gift* Lydian Wentworth, after the death of her father, travels to Avalon at the invitation of Lord Charles Ransome, a scholar of the Arthurian legend. Although paralyzed, Charles further invites Lydian to marry him. She accepts. Lydian, Charles, and Lawrence Stearns, Charles's young research assistant, seem fated to re-enact the lives of Guinever, Arthur, and Lancelot, until Lydian's courage, determination, and her own knowledge of Arthurian lore save them from the tragic triangle.

Nicole St. John writes with an easy elegance and literary *connaissance* that make her a worthy successor to the Brontës.

—Marcia G. Fuchs

SALISBURY, Carola. Pseudonym for Michael Butterworth; also writes as Sarah Kemp. British. Born 10 January 1924. Served in the Royal Naval Volunteer Reserve: Lieutenant. Married Jenny Spalding in 1957; one son and four daughters, and one daughter by previous marriage. Tutor in drawing, Nottingham College of Art, 1950-51; Editor, Art Director, and Managing Editor, Fleetway Publications, London, 1952-63. Agent: Georges Borchardt, 136 East 57th Street, New York, New York 10022, U.S.A. Address: 13 Lansdown Crescent, Bath, Avon, England.

ROMANCE AND GOTHIC PUBLICATIONS

Novels

Mallion's Pride. London, Collins, 1975; as *The Pride of the Trevallions*, New York, Doubleday, 1975.
Dark Inheritance. New York, Doubleday, 1975; London, Collins, 1976.
The "Dolphin" Summer. New York, Doubleday, 1976; London, Collins, 1977.
The Winter Bride. London, Collins, and New York, Doubleday, 1978.
The Shadowed Spring. London, Collins, and New York, Doubleday, 1980.
Count Vronsky's Daughter. London, Collins, and New York, Doubleday, 1981.

OTHER PUBLICATIONS

Novels as Michael Butterworth

The Soundless Scream. London, Long, and New York, Doubleday, 1967.
Walk Softly, In Fear. London, Long, 1968.

Vanishing Act.   London, Collins, 1970; as *The Uneasy Sun*, New York, Doubleday, 1970.
Flowers for a Dead Witch.   London, Collins, and New York, Doubleday, 1971.
The Black Look.   London, Collins, and New York, Doubleday, 1972.
Villa on the Shore.   London, Collins, 1973; New York, Doubleday, 1974.
The Man in the Sopwith Camel.   London, Collins, 1974; New York, Doubleday, 1975.
Remains to Be Seen.   London, Collins, and New York, Doubleday, 1976.
Festival! London, Collins, 1976.
X Marks the Spot.   London, Collins, and New York, Doubleday, 1978.
Over the Edge (as Sarah Kemp).   New York, Doubleday, 1979.

*   *   *

Michael Butterworth, under the name of Carola Salisbury, is one of the best of the current crop of gothic novelists. His experience as a mystery writer clearly shows as he develops the tension of the story, releasing it in exciting, unexpected endings. The sudden realization that Piers Trevallion is still alive (*Mallion's Pride*), the discovery that Melloney has faked her invalid state (*The "Dolphin" Summer*), and the final revelation that an entire diplomatic mission has been a red herring to protect the real emissary (*The Shadowed Spring*) all show Butterworth's ability to develop and sustain a feeling of true suspense.

Equal attention is paid to the solid development of the characters. Especially noteworthy is the first-person narrative of the heroines. Feminine thoughts and feelings are expressed so naturally that no thought is given to the fact that the author is in reality a man. Seen through a woman's eyes, the action is described with just the right mixture of curiosity and fear, without lapsing into the hysteria which sometimes passes for sensitivity when depicting a gently bred woman confronted by the violence and terror in a gothic novel.

The theme of the past affecting the present and the future is prevalent in the Salisbury novels. Previous events and actions taken by others weave a web which draws the current characters into a situation that explodes into a resolution of the mystery. Often the secret lies buried in a great family's history, as described in *Mallion's Pride* and *Dark Inheritance*. Old crimes are resurrected to haunt the present in *The "Dolphin" Summer* and *The Winter Bride*. Even the classics serve to provide a past for *Count Vronsky's Daughter*, in which Anna Karenina's daughter is the heroine.

The Salisbury novels are carefully plotted to provide about average suspense and intrigue, with many twists to the plots which keep the reader guessing to the very end. Insanity, or at the least instability, lurks in the minds of the least likely characters. The stories are peopled by colorful, complex characters who engage a reader's imagination and interest. Distinguished by action, adventure, and excitement, these novels must rank high on any list of period gothics.

—Barbara Kemp

SANDERS, Dorothy Lucie.   *See* **WALKER, Lucy**.

SAWLEY, Petra.   Address: c/o Robert Hale Ltd., 45-47 Clerkenwell Green, London EC1R 0HT, England.

ROMANCE AND GOTHIC PUBLICATIONS

Novels

No Time for Love.   London, Gresham, 1967.
No Place for Love.   London, Gresham, 1967.
Love on Ice.   London, Gresham, 1967.
Their Mysterious Patient.   London, Gresham, 1970.
Love's Dark Shadow.   London, Gresham, 1970.
That Strange Holiday.   London, Hale, 1972.
Doctor with a Past.   London, Hale, 1973.
Dream of Past Loves.   London, Hale, 1975.

*   *   *

Petra Sawley writes rather light romances for young girls in suitable settings such as the ice-skating world, nursing, and veterinary surgery.

In *Love on Ice* there is much background detail about ice skating as well as romance. The heroine has three men in her life and looks forward to a happy future with the most wealthy and cosmopolitan of them. In *No Place for Love* there is excitement when the secretary heroine is kidnapped, but there is a happy ending when she resolves her doubts about her real love. There are several exciting unexpected events in *No Time for Love*, where the career-minded veterinary surgeon works in a mysterious dockland part of London and is involved in a river chase down the Thames. Her chosen love is a traditional mainstay of the romantic novel—a good-looking doctor—and she cries in the last line because she is very happy.

A doctor is also the male counterpart to the nurse in *Their Mysterious Patient* but, rather against the conventions of fictional doctors, he turns out to be a psychiatrist. He is not, however, inordinately passionate, but the girl is aware of the subtleties of body language when she realises that the sensation of feeling Mike's arm against her means that she is something special. A rather exciting background of a castle in Spain plus mystery adds to the appeal of this book as do the light mysteries in *That Strange Holiday* and *Doctor with a Past*.

The plots of Sawley's novels basically concern a heroine and two male suitors, and most of the interest revolves around the development of romance with the girls coming to a decision as to which of them she really loves. The men in the heroine's life are generally wealthy but are surrounded by a certain amount of controlled tragedy and have had experience of life and women. Some novels concern the employer-employee situation.

Characters are not very complex, but girls tend to explore their feelings a good deal, see marriage as their goal, and cry during final love scenes. There is much circumstantial glamour in the books derived from settings involving Wales, Scotland, foreign travel, castles, and large houses. The novels are chaste, and dialogue between sweethearts is very trite.

—P.R. Meldrum

SCOTT, Jane. *See* **McELFRESH, Adeline**.

SCOTT, Janey. *See* **LINDSAY, Rachel**.

SEALE, Sara. Pseudonym for A.D.L. MacPherson.

ROMANCE AND GOTHIC PUBLICATIONS

Novels

Beggars May Sing. London, Mills and Boon, 1932; Toronto, Harlequin, 1968.
Chase the Moon. London, Mills and Boon, 1933.
Summer Spell. London, Mills and Boon, 1937.
Grace Before Meat. London, Mills and Boon, 1938.
This Merry Bond. London, Mills and Boon, 1938; Toronto, Harlequin, 1961.
Spread Your Wings. London, Mills and Boon, 1939.
Green Grass Growing. London, Mills and Boon, 1940.
Stormy Petrel. London, Mills and Boon, 1941.
Barn Dance. London, Mills and Boon, 1941.
The Silver Sty. London, Mills and Boon, 1941; Toronto, Harlequin, 1976.
House of Glass. London, Mills and Boon, 1944; as *Maggy*, Toronto, Harlequin, 1959.
Folly to Be Wise. London, Mills and Boon, 1946; Toronto, Harlequin, 1966.
The Reluctant Orphan. London, Mills and Boon, 1947; as *Orphan Bride*, Toronto, Harlequin, 1962.
The English Tutor. London, Mills and Boon, 1948; Toronto, Harlequin, 1968.
The Gentle Prisoner. London, Mills and Boon, 1949; Toronto, Harlequin, 1962.
These Delights. London, Mills and Boon, 1949; Toronto, Harlequin, 1965.
Then She Fled Me. London, Mills and Boon, 1950; Toronto, Harlequin, 1963.
The Young Amanda. London, Mills and Boon, 1950; Toronto, Harlequin, 1966.
The Dark Stranger. London, Mills and Boon, 1951; Toronto, Harlequin, 1964.
Wintersbride. London, Mills and Boon, 1951; Toronto, Harlequin, 1960.
The Lordly One. London, Mills and Boon, 1952; Toronto, Harlequin, 1968.
The Forbidden Island. London, Mills and Boon, 1953; Toronto, Harlequin, 1963.
Turn to the West. London, Mills and Boon, 1953.
The Truant Spirit. London, Mills and Boon, 1954; Toronto, Harlequin, 1969.
Time of Grace. London, Mills and Boon, 1955; Toronto, Harlequin, 1965.
Child Friday. London, Mills and Boon, 1956; Toronto, Harlequin, 1965.
Sister to Cinderella. London, Mills and Boon, 1956.

I Know My Love. London, Mills and Boon, 1957; Toronto, Harlequin, 1969.
Trevallion. London, Mills and Boon, 1957; Toronto, Harlequin, 1967.
Lucy Lamb. London, Mills and Boon, 1958; Toronto, Harlequin, 1963.
Charity Child. London, Mills and Boon, 1959; Toronto, Harlequin, 1966.
Dear Dragon. London, Mills and Boon, 1959; Toronto, Harlequin, 1964.
Cloud Castle. London, Mills and Boon, 1960; Toronto, Harlequin, 1967.
The Only Charity. London, Mills and Boon, 1961; Toronto, Harlequin, 1962.
Valentine's Day. London, Mills and Boon, 1962.
The Reluctant Landlord. London, Mills and Boon, 1962.
Doctor's Ward. London, Mills and Boon, and Toronto, Harlequin, 1962.
By Candlelight. London, Mills and Boon, 1963.
The Youngest Bridesmaid. London, Mills and Boon, 1963; Toronto, Harlequin, 1964.
The Third Uncle. London, Mills and Boon, 1964; Toronto, Harlequin, 1965.
To Catch a Unicorn. London, Mills and Boon, 1964; Toronto, Harlequin, 1975.
Green Girl. London, Mills and Boon, 1965; Toronto, Harlequin, 1966.
The Truant Bride. London, Mills and Boon, 1966; Toronto, Harlequin, 1967.
Penny Plain. London, Mills and Boon, 1967; Toronto, Harlequin, 1968.
That Young Person. London, Mills and Boon, 1969; Toronto, Harlequin, 1970.
The Queen of Hearts. Toronto, Harlequin, 1969.
Dear Professor. London, Mills and Boon, 1970; Toronto, Harlequin, 1971.
Mr. Brown. London, Mills and Boon, 1971; as *The Unknown Mr. Brown*, Toronto, Harlequin, 1972.
My Heart's Desire. Toronto, Harlequin, 1976.

*   *   *

Sara Seale is the pen name of Mrs. A.D.L. MacPherson, a romance writer who wrote from the 1930's to the 1960's. Her first book, *Beggars May Sing* (1932), was the first of almost 50 romances. She often used Irish backgrounds in her novels as well as settings in England and Cornwall.

Her romances have an unusual simplicity and innocence in them that make them strongly evocative and almost timeless in their enjoyment. They are deceptively simple, however, in the sense that Seale brings a highly developed writing skill to them so that their simplicity actually hides a subtle sense of sophistication and complexity.

Her heroines are typically sweet and awakened, often lacking in the usual standards of beauty and attractiveness. They are child-like, fey little creatures who drift somewhere between earth and heaven in a hazy cocoon of rose-tinted dreams, except when age-old wisdom of woman-kind unexpectedly emerges to confound the hero's more earthy beliefs and attitudes about women and love. Their fragile sweetness and charm prevent their naive provocations from becoming blatant efforts to captivate. The fact that these qualities are, in fact, captivating is usually accidental and quite beyond the heroines' intent.

Worldly-wise and world-weary heroes offer instant resistance to the heroines. Experience, knowledge, and often their own unhappiness prove too strong and effective a teacher to let them believe their instinctive reactions. Only gradually do they acknowledge the fact that the heroine holds the key to their ultimate happiness.

In a sense, Seale's novels have an individuality about them that make them remembered and enjoyed over and over again. Her heroines are not goody-goody, trite little charmers who will quickly take on the tired sophistication of older women. Their beliefs and goodness come from within and show Seale's creative ability to an outstanding degree. Goodness, naturalness, and true sensitivity combine in the heroines to make them feminine and womanly in the best sense of the words. They find happiness in little things; they give happiness by practicing constant instinctive virtues that are neatly balanced by quick repartee, occasional glimpses of temper, and natural sweetness of thought.

In at least three of her novels Sara Seale uses the same type of opening and it proves to be very effective. Basically the story begins with the arrival of the heroine in a strange and usually unwelcoming household. In *Dear Dragon*, a novel set in Cornwall, Alice Brown is thrust rather crudely into the Pendragon house to take care of a child. Bride Aherne in *That Young Person* arrives at Queen's Acre from Ireland to visit her intended's family. She is also to win approval for their marriage from Simon Spender, the estate's trustee. Finally, *My Heart's Desire* moves Gael Cassella from the rural beauty of Ireland's Galway to the fascinating delights and difficulties of "swinging" London.

In each novel the arrival of the heroine acts as a catalyst as she unconsciously draws attention to attitudes and actions of the people living there. False ideals, sophisticated deception, and weakness of character suddenly stand out for what they really are as the heroine reacts to them. In *That Young Person* Simon Spender sheds his cold, monkish outlook and succumbs to warm childish pleasures such as a snow-ball fight with Bride. Alice's rather naive and child-like habit of truthfulness forces the members of the Pendragon family to take stock of themselves. She does it, however, in a way that helps each to discover his own hopes and wishes in life. Gael's fey-like characteristic of seeing good in everyone at first repels the sophisticated members of Richard Saracen's family. His aunt and his cousin as well as their friends find her odd ways embarrassing and often dreadful. At the end, however, they all discover that her qualities and outlook on life are all that really matter, regardless of financial position.

Perhaps the best illustration of Sara Seale's heroines is in the following: "He looked into her strange eyes and saw there something infinitely older, infinitely wiser than himself. 'You are my conscience, my friend, and my true love,' he said simply."

Somehow Sara Seale's readers understood the difference between her heroines and those of other writers. Naivety and the lack of sophistication are usual traits of heroines, but hers are drawn with an inner strength of knowledge and an ability to hold with solid truths of principle. In her novels, light romance takes on an added dimension. They offer pictures of the best qualities in life that women and girls hope to find in their own lives.

—Arlene Moore

SEIFERT, Elizabeth. Also wrote as Ellen Ashley. American. Born in Washington, Missouri, 19 June 1897. Educated at Washington University, St. Louis, A.B. 1918. Married John J. Gasparotti in 1920 (died); three sons and one daughter. Recipient: *Redbook*-Dodd Mead Award, 1938. Agent: Lurton Blassingame, 60 East 42nd Street, New York, New York 10017. Address: 511 Fort Street, Moberly, Missouri 65270, U.S.A.

ROMANCE AND GOTHIC PUBLICATIONS

Novels

> *Young Doctor Galahad*. New York, Dodd Mead, 1938; as *Young Doctor*, London, Collins, 1939.
> *A Great Day*. New York, Dodd Mead, 1939; London, Collins, 1940.
> *Thus Doctor Mallory*. New York, Dodd Mead, 1940; as *Doctor Mallory*, London, Collins, 1941.
> *Hillbilly Doctor*. New York, Dodd Mead, 1940; as *Doctor Bill*, London, Collins, 1941.
> *Bright Scalpel*. New York, Dodd Mead, 1941; as *Healing Hands*, London, Collins, 1942.
> *Army Doctor*. New York, Dodd Mead, 1942; London, Collins, 1943.
> *Surgeon in Charge*. New York, Dodd Mead, 1942; London, Collins, 1945.
> *A Certain Doctor French*. New York, Dodd Mead, 1943; London, Collins, 1944.
> *Bright Banners*. New York, Dodd Mead, 1943.

Girl in Overalls: A Novel of Women in Defense Today (as Ellen Ashley).   New York,
   Dodd Mead, 1943.
Girl Intern.   New York, Dodd Mead, 1944; as *Doctor Chris*, London, Collins, 1946.
Dr. Ellison's Decision.   New York, Dodd Mead, 1944.
Dr. Woodward's Ambition.   New York, Dodd Mead, 1945; London, Collins, 1946.
Orchard Hill.   New York, Dodd Mead, 1945; London, Collins, 1947.
Old Doc.   New York, Dodd Mead, 1946; London, Collins, 1948.
Dusty Spring.   New York, Dodd Mead, 1946.
Take Three Doctors.   New York, Dodd Mead, 1947; London, Collins, 1949.
So Young, So Fair.   New York, Dodd Mead, 1947; London, Collins, 1948.
The Glass and the Trumpet.   New York, Dodd Mead, 1948.
Hospital Zone.   New York, Dodd Mead, 1948.
The Bright Coin.   New York, Dodd Mead, 1949; as *The Doctor Dares*, London, Collins,
   1950.
Homecoming.   New York, Dodd Mead, 1950.
Pride of the South.   London, Collins, 1950.
The Story of Andrea Fields.   New York, Dodd Mead, 1950.
Miss Doctor.   New York, Dodd Mead, 1951; as *Woman Doctor*, London, Collins, 1951.
Doctor of Mercy.   New York, Dodd Mead, 1951; London, Collins, 1953.
The Strange Loyalty of Dr. Carlisle.   New York, Dodd Mead, 1952; as *The Case of Dr.
   Carlisle*, London, Collins, 1953.
The Doctor Takes a Wife.   New York, Dodd Mead, 1952; London, Collins, 1954.
Doctor Mollie.   London, Collins, 1952.
The Doctor Disagrees.   New York, Dodd Mead, 1953; London, Collins, 1954.
Lucinda Marries the Doctor.   New York, Dodd Mead, 1953; London, Collins, 1955.
Doctor at the Crossroads.   New York, Dodd Mead, 1954; London, Collins, 1955.
Marriage for Three.   New York, Dodd Mead, 1954; London, Collins, 1956.
A Doctor in the Family.   New York, Dodd Mead, 1955; London, Collins, 1956.
Challenge for Doctor Mays.   New York, Dodd Mead, 1955; as *Doctor Mays*, London,
   Collins, 1957.
A Doctor for Blue Jay Cove.   New York, Dodd Mead, 1956; as *Doctor's Orders*,
   London, Collins, 1958.
A Call for Doctor Barton.   New York, Dodd Mead; 1956; London, Collins, 1957.
Substitute Doctor.   New York, Dodd Mead, 1957; London, Collins, 1958.
The Doctor's Husband.   New York, Dodd Mead, 1957; London, Collins, 1959.
The New Doctor.   New York, Dodd Mead, 1958; as *Doctor Jamie*, London,   Collins,
   1959.
Love Calls the Doctor.   New York, Dodd Mead, 1958; London, Collins, 1960.
Home-Town Doctor.   New York, Dodd Mead, 1959; London, Collins, 1960.
Doctor on Trial.   London, Dodd Mead, 1959; London, Collins, 1961.
When Doctors Marry.   New York, Dodd Mead, 1960; London, Collins, 1961.
Doctors on Parade (omnibus).   New York, Dodd Mead, 1960.
The Doctor's Bride.   New York, Dodd Mead, 1960; London, Collins, 1962.
The Doctor Makes a Choice.   New York, Dodd Mead, 1961; London, Collins, 1962.
Dr. Jeremy's Wife.   New York, Dodd Mead, 1961; London, Collins, 1963.
The Honor of Dr. Shelton.   New York, Dodd Mead, 1962; London, Collins, 1963.
The Doctor's Strange Secret.   New York, Dodd Mead, 1962; London, Collins, 1964.
Dr. Scott, Surgeon on Call.   New York, Dodd Mead, 1963; as *Surgeon on Call*, London,
   Collins, 1965.
Legacy for a Doctor.   New York, Dodd Mead, 1963; London, Collins, 1964.
Katie's Young Doctor.   New York, Dodd Mead, 1964; London, Collins, 1965.
A Doctor Comes to Bayard.   New York, Dodd Mead, 1964; London, Collins, 1966.
Doctor Samaritan.   New York, Dodd Mead, 1965; London, Collins, 1966.
Ordeal of Three Doctors.   New York, Dodd Mead, 1965; London, Collins, 1967.
Hegerty, M.D.   New York, Dodd Mead, 1966; London, Collins, 1967.
Pay the Doctor.   New York, Dodd Mead, 1966; London, Collins, 1968.
Doctor with a Mission.   New York, Dodd Mead, 1967; London, Collins, 1969.
The Rival Doctors.   New York, Dodd Mead, 1967; London, Collins, 1969.

The Doctor's Confession.   New York, Dodd Mead, 1968; London, Collins, 1971.
To Wed a Doctor.   New York, Dodd Mead, 1968; London, Collins, 1970.
Bachelor Doctor.   New York, Dodd Mead, 1969; London, Collins, 1971.
For Love of a Doctor.   New York, Dodd Mead, 1969; London, Collins, 1970.
Doctor's Kingdom.   New York, Dodd Mead, 1970.
The Doctor's Two Lives.   New York, Dodd Mead, 1970; London, Collins, 1972.
Doctor in Judgment.   New York, Dodd Mead, 1971; London, Collins, 1972.
The Doctor's Second Love.   New York, Dodd Mead, 1971; London, Collins, 1973.
Doctor's Destiny.   New York, Dodd Mead, and London, Collins, 1972.
The Doctor's Reputation.   New York, Dodd Mead, 1972; London, Collins, 1974.
The Doctor's Private Life.   New York, Dodd Mead, and London, Collins, 1973.
The Two Faces of Dr. Collier.   New York, Dodd Mead, 1973; London, Collins, 1974.
The Doctor and Mathilda.   New York, Dodd Mead, 1974; London, Collins, 1976.
Doctor in Love.   New York, Dodd Mead, 1974; London, Collins, 1976.
The Doctor's Daughter.   New York, Dodd Mead, 1974; London, Collins, 1975.
Four Doctors, Four Wives.   New York, Dodd Mead, 1975; London, Collins, 1976.
The Doctor's Affair.   New York, Dodd Mead, 1975; London, Collins, 1977.
Two Doctors and a Girl.   New York, Dodd Mead, 1976; London, Collins, 1978.
The Doctor's Desperate Hour.   New York, Dodd Mead, 1976; London, Collins, 1977.
Doctor Tuck.   New York, Dodd Mead, 1977; London, Collins, 1979.
The Doctors of Eden Place.   New York, Dodd Mead, 1977; London, Collins, 1978.
The Doctors Were Brothers.   New York, Dodd Mead, 1978; London, Collins, 1980.
Rebel Doctor.   New York, Dodd Mead, 1978; London, Collins, 1980.
The Doctor's Promise.   New York, Dodd Mead, 1979; London, Collins, 1981.
The Problems of Doctor A.   New York, Dodd Mead, 1979; London, Collins, 1981.

Manuscript Collection: Boston University.

Elizabeth Seifert comments:

I have written novels of current life, often in small towns of America, and with only a few exceptions the subject matter has been medical.

*   *   *

One is not likely to find Elizabeth Seifert citations on academic reading lists, nor mention of her in college library catalogs or critical reference works; but go to almost any public library in the country and you will find book after book, or you would if so many weren't in circulation, of this prolific writer—who has produced one or two novels a year since 1938. Her popularity has surely stood the test of time, for it was less than ten years ago that most of her early work was reprinted. Nearly all Seifert's books have also been published in England, and many have been published in 14 other countries as well. How can this phenomenon be explained? Is the general reading public so intrigued by the mystique of the medical profession that any title with "doctor" in it, as nearly all Seifert's titles have, will be avidly sought after? There's much more to it than this.

Though Elizabeth Seifert's books have medical backgrounds and center primarily on the professional, social, and ethical problems of doctors and their families, usually in an American midwestern setting, they cannot be defined as medical fiction. Her stories are about people who happen to be doctors. Her books are easy to read and consist almost entirely of brief descriptions and dialogue. The reader is not subjected to long paragraphs of exposition. We learn about the characters by how they look, what they wear, what they say, and the plots unfold through their words and actions. We know what their homes look like, how they are furnished, how they are landscaped. And we know these people—for they exist in every neighborhood in the Western world. Though her characters belong to a glamorous profession, they do the same things readers do—bake pies, tell each other how to raise their children, help each other look for lost dogs, plan programs for cub scouts, grapple with problems of middle age. Seifert's male characters are apt to be heroic and larger than life, but she is right on target with women, their strengths and weaknesses, their hopes and fears. She generally closes with happy endings; but often they are bittersweet, as with her first book, the $10,000 prize novel— *Young Doctor Galahad*, whose protagonist won a professional battle but slid gallantly into marriage with a woman he didn't love.

Though her first novel dealt well with a post-depression town and proselytized in favor of clinics and socialized medicine, much to the chagrin of many doctors then as now—indeed, though the theme of public health is prevalent in many of her novels—her stories do not reflect the changing influences and current events of half a century, nor do they keep up with the many technological advances. But human nature does not change with the times, so her early novels are as valid in their characterizations as the later ones. Many of them form the Bayard Books, named for a Missouri town, featuring the same characters, one time in major roles, and the next only incidentally. The Bayard Folk become our own families, and it's no wonder that we eagerly wish to learn what happens to them. Elizabeth Seifert is successful because she is plain, direct, and recognizable; and because she likes people.

—Marion Hanscom

SETON, Anya.   British.   Born in New York City; daughter of the writer Ernest Thompson Seton. Educated privately in England; attended Oxford University. Married twice; three children. Former Member of the Editorial Board, *Writers Magazine*. Address: Binney Lane, Old Greenwich, Connecticut 06870, U.S.A.

ROMANCE AND GOTHIC PUBLICATIONS

Novels

My Theodosia. Boston, Houghton Mifflin, 1941; London, Hodder and Stoughton, 1945.
Dragonwyck. Boston, Houghton Mifflin, 1944; London, Hodder and Stoughton, 1945.
The Turquoise. Boston, Houghton Mifflin, and London, Hodder and Stoughton, 1946.
The Hearth and the Eagle. Boston, Houghton Mifflin, and London, Hodder and Stoughton, 1948.
Foxfire. Boston, Houghton Mifflin, and London, Hodder and Stoughton, 1951.
Katherine. Boston, Houghton Mifflin, and London, Hodder and Stoughton, 1954.
The Winthrop Woman. Boston, Houghton Mifflin, and London, Hodder and Stoughton, 1958.
Devil Water. Boston, Houghton Mifflin, and London, Hodder and Stoughton, 1962.
Avalon. Boston, Houghton Mifflin, 1965; London, Hodder and Stoughton, 1966.
Green Darkness. Boston, Houghton Mifflin, and London, Hodder and Stoughton, 1972.

Uncollected Short Stories

"Fun Tomorrow," in *Ladies Home Journal* (Philadelphia), November 1942.
"We'll Come Back," in *American Magazine* (Springfield, Ohio), May 1943.
"Back Track to Love," in *Ladies Home Journal* (Philadelphia), May 1946.

OTHER PUBLICATIONS

Other (juvenile)

The Mistletoe and Sword: A Story of Roman Britain. New York, Doubleday, 1955;
Leicester, Brockhampton Press, 1956.
Washington Irving. Boston, Houghton Mifflin, 1960.
Smouldering Fires. New York, Doubleday, 1975; London, Hodder and Stoughton,
1976.

*   *   *

As a writer of long, meticulously researched historical romances, Anya Seton may be the best
of her generation. Her output is relatively small for a romance writer, but the quality is
uniformly high. Unlike some of her contemporaries who choose a historical period and stay
with it for book after book, Seton selects a different time and place for each novel. She often
uses actual men and women in history as the basis for her plots, and she makes their stories both
interesting and compelling.

Seton's early novel *Dragonwyck* is a straight gothic romance set along the Hudson River
among the descendants of Dutch settlers. *The Hearth and Eagle* is a romance set in Marble-
head, Massachusetts. Both these novels had interest, but it was in *My Theodosia* that Seton
displayed what would become the hallmark of her work: fictional recreations of the lives of
actual historical women. *My Theodosia* is the story of Theodosia Burr, the daughter of the
American scapegrace politician Aaron Burr. Seton considered historical controversies about
the Burrs as well as the legends that grew up around the romantic Theodosia, including stories
about her early romance with Meriwether Lewis and about her mysterious death.

Seton's classic novel is probably *Katherine*, a fictional treatment of the life of Katherine
Swynford, mistress and later wife of John of Gaunt, Duke of Lancaster, in the 14th century.
Katherine is significant to history because of a fluke—her descendants (born bastards but
legitimized by Parliament) won the War of the Roses, making her a direct ancestress of the
British Royal Family. Seton's research for *Katherine* was extensive and meticulous. She used
original documents in Middle French and Middle English to supplement her Latin, and she
addressed historical controversies about the character of John of Gaunt, a difficult task
considering the nature of the sources for the period. She also created an engaging fictional
portrait of Katherine's brother-in-law, Geoffrey Chaucer. The "Author's Note" delineates her
research methods and the way she approached her subjects before she began to write.

In *Katherine* and later novels—*Devil Water, Avalon, The Winthrop Woman*—Seton blends
historical accuracy (insofar as she can) with legend to produce love stories appealing to modern
sensibilities. She portrays women who rise above historical limitations and who exemplify
contemporary values about love, marriage, and family. Although Katherine Swynford lived in
an age that valued women for their family connections more than personal qualities and in
which marriage was often more political alliance than love match, Seton's Katherine is a
woman who transcends her time. She is portrayed as an excellent wife and mother, even in an
early marriage of convenience. After her long illicit liaison with John of Gaunt she deserves her
elevation to Duchess of Lancaster because she remained faithful to him and genuinely repented
for her sins against morality. The political realities of 14th-century England may have denied
her a place as his wife until late in their lives, but because her situation was not "her fault," she
could be redeemed from disgrace.

The Winthrop Woman, one of the all-time American bestsellers, is about Elizabeth Winthrop, the scandalous niece of John Winthrop who was the first governor of the Massachusetts
Bay Colony. Again, Seton plays out the love story against a background of historical limits on
women's lives. Elizabeth's desire for true love was thwarted by a repressive Puritan society.
Devil Water, set in 18th-century England and America, is about the life of a woman who may
exist only in a family legend. Most of the minor characters, however, are real; and Seton mixes
fact and legend convincingly. *Avalon*, set in 10th-century England, Cornwall, and Iceland,
takes her even farther away from the known and factual as she delineates the Age of Faith
against a background of vicious Viking raids. *Green Darkness* is about the Protestant Refor-

mation, although in this book Seton dabbles in reincarnation and sets short sections in the modern world. Other books, including *The Turquoise* and *Foxfire*, are not based on fact.

In many of her books, Seton uses an author's note to inform readers of both her research methods and her formulations about historical truth. She acknowledges that the lives of women in history were of only passing interest to the historical record and that it is extraordinarily difficult to recreate personal lives and motivations after many centuries. She describes how she determines the most likely version of the truth. In her books, fact and fiction often work together effectively to produce lengthy and fascinating portraits of her characters. Unlike some other authors in her subfield of romance, she does not take shortcuts or distort the historical record; instead, she spins her tale within the limits of the known.

Seton has the ability to use history as the vehicle for a compelling love story. Her books move quickly, building a record of historical detail without letting research dominate her characters. Her descriptions of places are both evocative and accurate, so that even today many of the locations about which she writes can be found without recourse to a map.

Seton's historical romances have remained in print over many years; it is her ability to make history accessible to modern readers that makes her stand out among her competitors.

—Kay Mussell

SHAW, Irene. *See* **ROBERTS, Irene.**

SHEARING, Joseph. *See* **BOWEN, Marjorie.**

SHELLABARGER, Samuel. Also wrote as John Esteven; Peter Loring. American. Born in Washington, D.C., 18 May 1888. Educated at private schools; Princeton University, New Jersey, 1905-09, A.B. 1909; studied in Munich, 1910-11; Harvard University, Cambridge, Massachusetts, 1911-14, Ph.D. 1917. Served in Ordnance and Military Intelligence, and as Assistant Military Attaché, U.S. Legation, Stockholm, 1918-19: Captain. Married Vivan Borg in 1915; two sons and two daughters. Instructor, 1914-16, and Assistant Professor of English, 1919-23, Princeton University; lived in Europe, 1923-31; Headmaster, Columbus School for Girls, Ohio, 1938-46; then full-time writer. *Died 20 March 1954.*

Novels

The Black Gale.   New York, Century, 1929.
Grief Before Night (as Peter Loring).   Philadelphia, Macrae Smith, 1938; London,
    Hodder and Stoughton, 1939.
Miss Rolling Stone (as Peter Loring).   Philadelphia, Macrae Smith, 1939; as *He Travels
    Alone*, London, Hodder and Stoughton, 1939.
Captain from Castile.   Boston, Little Brown, 1945; London, Macmillan, 1947.
Prince of Foxes.   Boston, Little Brown, 1947; London, Hamish Hamilton, 1948.
The King's Cavalier.   Boston, Little Brown, 1950; as *Blaise of France*, London, Hamish
    Hamilton, 1950.
Lord Vanity.   Boston, Little Brown, 1953; London, Collins, 1954.
Tolbecken.   Boston, Little Brown, 1956; London, Bles, 1957.

Novels as John Esteven

The Door of Death.   New York, Century, 1928; London, Methuen, 1929.
Voodoo.   New York, Doubleday, and London, Hutchinson, 1930.
By Night at Dinsmore.   New York, Doubleday, and London, Harrap, 1935.
While Murder Waits.   London, Harrap, 1936; New York, Doubleday, 1937.
Graveyard Watch.   New York, Modern Age, 1938.
Blind Man's Night.   London, Hodder and Stoughton, 1938.
Assurance Double Sure.   London, Hodder and Stoughton, 1939.

Other

The Chevalier Bayard: A Study in Fading Chivalry.   New York, Century, 1928.
Lord Chesterfield.   New York and London, Macmillan, 1935.
Lord Chesterfield and Manners (lecture).   Claremont, California, Pomona College,
    1938.
Lord Chesterfield and His World.   Boston, Little Brown, 1951.
The Token (juvenile).   Boston, Little Brown, 1955.

*   *   *

Samuel Shellabarger is one of those rare authors who made a financially successful transition from academic life to fiction. Though his most famous novels are rousing adventures, he will be best remembered for his meticulous attention to historical detail, particularly of 16th century Spain, Italy, and France. In his major novels, *Captain from Castile, Prince of Foxes, The King's Cavalier*, and *Lord Vanity*, his mastery of genealogy, battles, customs, manners, and folklore is impressive. His backgrounds create an authentic surface realism that survives the sometimes overly melodramatic plots and superficial characterization often found in the historical romance. It is tempting to dismiss the literary aspects of Shellabarger's fiction, which critics who have underestimated the difficulty of the genre have sometimes done, yet moments of art are found throughout his work.

Shellabarger's early Rae Norse mysteries carried the pen name John Esteven. As Peter Loring he wrote *Miss Rolling Stone*, a romance set in Baghdad, and *Grief Before Night*, a light novel of tangled love which drew its background from Shellabarger's residence in Sweden prior to and during World War I. It was not until the publication of *Captain from Castile* in 1945, however, that Shellabarger achieved widespread popular success. After the publication of this book several of his novels would be adapted to the motion pictures and for more than a decade he could be assured of a receptive audience.

Since *Captain from Castile* represents the pinnacle of Shellabarger's success, it is useful to delineate several of its major themes. The story follows the youthful son of a Spanish Don, Pedro de Vargas, from his infatuation with the aristocrat Duena Luisa through his adventures with Cortes in Mexico and back to Spain. Woven into the plot is the conflict in Pedro's mind between the traditional match with Luisa, representing the now decadent chivalric ideal, and Pedro's "natural" attraction to the tavern dancer, Catana, who follows him from Spain to Mexico and back. The episodic adventures of the novel are provided by the conquest of Mexico and the machinations of the arch villain de Silva, who betrays the innocent de Vargas family to the Inquisition, casually marries Luisa in Pedro's absence, allows Pedro and several comrades to be captured for humiliation and sacrifice by the Aztecs, and tries to have Pedro executed for betraying the king. Shellabarger neatly parallels the Spanish Inquisition with Aztec sacrificial rites and has a corrupt Inquisitor burned by the Aztecs. Underlying the surface of the novel are characteristic American ambivalences of the time toward success and race. In order to avoid having Pedro directly profit from the slaughter of the Aztecs, Shellabarger has Pedro's own treasure given to him by an Indian whom he had helped escape from brutal servitude in Spain. The Aztecs and Indians are nevertheless inferior; Montezuma's "stone-age self could not cope with the thrust of Cortes's personality," and though the Indians side with the Spanish against the Aztecs, "it was the white force that counted."

Pedro is not the clever hero of picaresque Romance, he is more akin to those of Horatio Alger, and the Aztecs might as well have been lifted from a western. Pedro does change from a spirited youth dominated by his father to a man tempered by his experiences, but as a character he remains undistinguished. Shellabarger further mined the 16th-century in *Prince of Foxes*, set in the court of the Borgias in Italy, and in *The King's Cavalier*, set in France during the reign of Francis I, while he moved the action of *Lord Vanity* to 18th-century England, Italy, and France. In these novels Shellabarger continued his struggle to create believable characters and eliminate cumbersome plots while developing competent and sometimes brilliant settings and backgrounds.

—Larry N. Landrum

SINCLAIR, Olga (Ellen). Also writes as Ellen Clare.   British.   Born in Watton, Norfolk, 23 January 1923. Educated at Convent of the Sacred Heart, Swaffham, Norfolk. Married Stanley G. Sinclair in 1945; three sons. Since 1966, Justice of the Peace for Norfolk. Recipient: Society of Authors Margaret Rhondda Award, 1972. Address: Dove House Farm, Potter Heigham, Norfolk NR29 5LJ, England.

ROMANCE AND GOTHIC PUBLICATIONS

Novels

The Man at the Manor.   London, Gresham, 1967; New York, Dell, 1972.
Man of the River.   London, Hale, 1968.
Hearts by the Tower.   London, Hale, 1968; as *Night of the Black Tower*, New York, Lancer, 1968.

Bitter Sweet Summer. London, Hale, 1970; New York, Simon and Schuster, 1972.
Wild Dream. London, Hale, 1973.
Tenant of Binningham Hall. London, Woman's Weekly Library, 1975.
Where the Cigale Sings. London, Woman's Weekly Library, 1976.
My Dear Fugitive. London, Hale, 1976.
Never Fall in Love. London, Hale, 1977.
Master of Melthorpe. London, Hale, 1979.
Gypsy Julie. London, Woman's Weekly Library, 1979.
Ripening Vine (as Ellen Clare). London, Mills and Boon, 1981.

OTHER PUBLICATIONS

Other (juvenile)

Gypsies. Oxford, Blackwell, 1967.
Dancing in Britain. Oxford, Blackwell, 1970.
Children's Games. Oxford, Blackwell, 1972.
Toys and Toymaking. Oxford, Blackwell, 1975.
Gypsy Girl. London, Collins, 1981.

Olga Sinclair comments:

A great deal of my work has a rural background, often set in my beloved home county of Norfolk, with its long stretch of coastline, slow-flowing rivers, broad lakes, and country traditions. Other books have been based on foreign travel—notably *Bitter Sweet Summer* which was written after a fateful family holiday to Czechoslovakia the year the Russians invaded to cut short the "Prague Spring."

Some of my children's books reflect a fascination for gypsies. This came about because we renovated a derelict horse-drawn "vardo," travelled with it, and met many of those strange, unorthodox and sometimes romantic people.

*   *   *

Olga Sinclair has written romantic and historical fiction with fairly plain plots and characters. Her romantic fiction normally has a Norfolk setting and she writes with familiarity of the attractive English countryside. She has, however, used other settings such as a seaside town in *Hearts by the Tower* or Czechoslovakia, Austria, and Germany in *Bitter Sweet Summer*. The background adds a lot to Sinclair's novels, the Czechoslovakia of 1968 adding topical excitement to the rather pedestrian story line and a contrast to the tranquility of the Austrian countryside.

Sinclair is, however, at home setting her books in Norfolk. The loneliness of the Norfolk broads in winter features in *Wild Dream*, and the broads also feature in *Master of Melthorpe* and *Man of the River*. Sinclair's world is the world of village life rather than town life, although her heroines have often lived some time in London.

The novels revolve around young women as heroines, and generally concern triangles of attraction towards two lovers, one of whom is much less charming and worthy of her love than the other. Her first feelings towards a fiancé she comes to question, as in *Man of the River*, and is gradually attracted towards another suitor. In *Master of Melthorpe* the heroine at first finds the Lord of the Manor too dominating and arrogant, but ends up realizing his real nature and consenting to marry him.

Suspense features strongly, and the heroine is often surprised by the sudden unravelling of an enigmatic young man (*Bitter Sweet Summer*). Other novels employ strange plots with interesting twists. The heroine in *Wild Dream* is in peril in a black magic context; her father has a mystery past and she an unknown half-sister in *Man of the River*. Mysterious circumstances surround the heroine's predecessor, as wife in *Hearts by the Tower*, or as fiancée in *Master of*

Melthorpe. Plots can be rather contrived and depend heavily on the "mystery" as a central feature.

Characters are sometimes rather shallow, as the father in *Never Fall in Love*, although the women are developed a good deal more particularly as regards their romantic feelings. Love is, however, very chaste, and a kiss or an offer of marriage can be the climax of a book.

—P.R. Meldrum

SLAUGHTER, Frank G(ill). Also wrote as G. Arnold Haygood; C.V. Terry. American. Born in Washington, D.C., 25 February 1908. Educated at Oxford High School, North Carolina; Duke University, Durham, North Carolina, A.B. (magna cum laude) 1926; Johns Hopkins Medical School, Baltimore, M.D. 1930. Served in the United States Army Medical Corps, 1942-46: Lieutenant Colonel. Married Jane Mundy in 1933; two sons. Intern and resident surgeon, Jefferson Hospital, Roanoke, Virginia, 1930-34; resident in thoracic surgery, Herman Kiefer Hospital, Detroit, 1934; staff surgeon, Riverside Hospital, Jacksonville, Florida, 1934-42; then full-time writer. Fellow, American College of Surgeons. D.H.L.: Jacksonville University, Florida. Agent: Brandt and Brandt, 1501 Broadway, New York, New York 10036. Address: Box 14, Ortega Station, Jacksonville, Florida 32210, U.S.A.

ROMANCE AND GOTHIC PUBLICATIONS

Novels

> *That None Should Die.* New York, Doubleday, 1941; London, Jarrolds, 1942.
> *Spencer Brade, M.D.* New York, Doubleday, 1942; London, Jarrolds, 1943.
> *Air Surgeon.* New York, Doubleday, 1943; London, Jarrolds, 1944.
> *Battle Surgeon.* New York, Doubleday, 1944.
> *A Touch of Glory.* New York, Doubleday, 1945; London, Jarrolds, 1946.
> *In a Dark Garden.* New York, Doubleday, 1946; London, Jarrolds, 1952.
> *The Golden Isle.* New York, Doubleday, 1947; London, Jarrolds, 1950.
> *Sangaree.* New York, Doubleday, 1948; London, Jarrolds, 1950.
> *Divine Mistress.* New York, Doubleday, 1949; London, Jarrolds, 1951.
> *The Stubborn Heart.* New York, Doubleday, 1950; London, Jarrolds, 1953.
> *Fort Everglades.* New York, Doubleday, and London, Jarrolds, 1951.
> *The Road to Bithynia: A Novel of Luke, The Beloved Physician.* New York, Doubleday, 1951; London, Jarrolds, 1952.
> *East Side General.* New York, Doubleday, 1952; London, Jarrolds, 1953.
> *Storm Haven.* New York, Doubleday, 1953; London, Jarrolds, 1954.
> *The Galileans: A Novel of Mary Magdalene.* New York, Doubleday, 1953; London, Jarrolds, 1954.
> *The Song of Ruth.* New York, Doubleday, 1954; London, Jarrolds, 1955.
> *The Healer.* New York, Doubleday, and London, Jarrolds, 1955.
> *Flight from Natchez.* New York, Doubleday, 1955; London, Jarrolds, 1956.
> *The Scarlet Cord: A Novel of the Woman of Jericho.* New York, Doubleday, and London, Jarrolds, 1956.

The Warrior. New York, Doubleday, 1956; as *The Flaming Frontier*, London, Jarrolds, 1957.
The Mapmaker: A Novel of the Days of Prince Henry, The Navigator. New York, Doubleday, 1957; London, Jarrolds, 1958.
Sword and Scalpel. New York, Doubleday, and London, Jarrolds, 1957.
Daybreak. New York, Doubleday, and London, Jarrolds, 1958.
Deep Is the Shadow (as G. Arnold Haygood). New York, Doubleday, 1959; London, Hutchinson, 1975; as *Shadow of Evil* (as Frank G. Slaughter), New York, Pocket Books, 1975.
The Crown and the Cross: The Life of Christ. Cleveland, World, and London, Jarrolds, 1959.
The Thorn of Arimathea. New York, Doubleday, and London, Jarrolds, 1959.
Lorena. New York, Doubleday, 1959; London, Hutchinson, 1960.
Pilgrims in Paradise. New York, Doubleday, 1960; as *Puritans in Paradise*, London, Hutchinson, 1960.
Epidemic! New York, Doubleday, and London, Hutchinson, 1961.
The Curse of Jezebel: A Novel of the Biblical Queen of Evil. New York, Doubleday, 1961; as *Queen of Evil*, London, Hutchinson, 1962.
Tomorrow's Miracle. New York, Doubleday, and London, Hutchinson, 1962.
Devil's Harvest. New York, Doubleday, and London, Hutchinson, 1963.
Upon This Rock: A Novel of Simon Peter, Prince of the Apostles. New York, Coward McCann, 1963; London, Hutchinson, 1964.
A Savage Place. New York, Doubleday, and London, Hutchinson, 1964.
Constantine: The Miracle of the Flaming Cross. New York, Doubleday, 1965; London, Hutchinson, 1966.
The Purple Quest: A Novel of Seafaring Adventure in the Ancient World. New York, Doubleday, and London, Hutchinson, 1965.
Surgeon, U.S.A. New York, Doubleday, 1966; as *War Surgeon*, London, Hutchinson, 1967.
Doctors' Wives. New York, Doubleday, 1967; London, Hutchinson, 1971.
God's Warrior. New York, Doubleday, and London, Hutchinson, 1967.
The Sins of Herod: A Novel of Rome and the Early Church. New York, Doubleday, 1968; London, Hutchinson, 1969.
Surgeon's Choice: A Novel of Medicine Tomorrow. New York, Doubleday, and London, Hutchinson, 1969.
Countdown. New York, Doubleday, and London, Hutchinson, 1970.
Code Five. New York, Doubleday, 1971; London, Hutchinson, 1972.
Convention, M.D.: A Novel of Medical In-Fighting. New York, Doubleday, 1972; London, Hutchinson, 1973.
Women in White. New York, Doubleday, 1974; as *Lifeblood*, London, Hutchinson, 1974.
Stonewall Brigade. New York, Doubleday, 1975; London, Hutchinson, 1976.
Plague Ship. New York, Doubleday, 1976; London, Hutchinson, 1977.
Devil's Gamble. New York, Doubleday, 1977; London, Hutchinson, 1978.
The Passionate Rebel. New York, Doubleday, and London, Hutchinson, 1979.
Gospel Fever: A Novel about America's Most Beloved TV Evangelist. New York, Doubleday, 1980.
Doctor's Daughters. New York, Doubleday, 1981; London, Hutchinson, 1982.

Novels as C.V. Terry

Buccaneer Surgeon. New York, Hanover House, 1954; as *Buccaneer Doctor*, London, Jarrolds, 1955.
Darien Venture. New York, Hanover House, and London, Jarrolds, 1955.
The Golden Ones. New York, Hanover House, 1955; London, Jarrolds, 1958.
The Deadly Lady of Madagascar. New York, Doubleday, and London, Jarrolds, 1959.

OTHER PUBLICATIONS

Play

Screenplay: *Naked in the Sun*, with John Hugh, 1957.

Other

The New Science of Surgery. New York, Messner, 1946; London, Low, 1948; revised
edition, as *Science and Surgery*, New York, Permabooks, 1956.
Medicine for Moderns: The New Science of Psychosomatic Medicine. New York,
Messner, 1947; London, Jarrolds, 1953; as *The New Way to Mental and Physical
Health*, New York, Grosset and Dunlap, 1949; as *Your Body and Your Mind*, New
York, New American Library, 1953.
Immortal Magyar: Semmelweis, Conqueror of Childbed Fever. New York, Schuman,
1950; as *Semmelweis, Conqueror of Childbed Fever*, New York, Collier, 1961.
Apalachee Gold: The Fabulous Adventures of Cabeza de Vaca (juvenile). New York,
Doubleday, 1954; London, Hutchinson, 1955.
The Land and the Promise: The Greatest Stories from the Bible. Cleveland, World,
1960; London, Hutchinson, 1961.
David, Warrior and King: A Biblical Biography. Cleveland, World, 1962; London,
Hutchinson, 1963.

Manuscript Collections: Mugar Memorial Library, Boston University; Duke University,
Durham, North Carolina.

Frank G. Slaughter comments:

I am primarily a storyteller who writes to entertain and also inform. As such, I am
meticulous in my research and polish my writings through an average of ten revisions. Critics
have dubbed me "the undisputed master of medical fiction," an accolade I prize very much.

*   *   *

Though Frank G. Slaughter has been turning out novels at the rate of about one every ten
months for the last 40 years, he received very little critical comment in the 1970's. He doesn't
need it. His books will sell anyway. He is still a master craftsman, a professional who is expert
at moving a story along from one climax to the next. Novice writers need only study a few of
Slaughter's novels to learn about structure and style. Slaughter must be a happy millionaire by
now. Over sixty million copies of his books have been sold, in 21 countries.

Though his talent is clearly evident in his depiction of action, background, color, and plot,
Slaughter lacks the touch of genius that would make him a great writer. His characterizations
fall short. His people are just not believable. They talk in long, long sentences, especially in the
medical novels which comprise the largest segment of his work. On the positive side, the
medical novels surely do keep up with the time as far as medical technology and current events
are concerned—from exposing to the public eye the none too admirable practices of many
physicians in *That None Should Die*, to big city summer gang wars and public housing
development problems in *Epidemic!*, to the energy shortage, Haitian refugees, and Florida
condominiums in his latest novel *Doctor's Daughters*; from his physician protagonists in all
kinds of situation and through all the wars this nation has suffered to the very recent
controversy surrounding the inordinate number of coronary by-pass operations being done
that might better be treated medically. His empathy with people, however, fails to keep pace,
especially his women who do not even begin to reflect the very real changes that women have
undergone in the last half of the 20th century. In my review of *Women in White* (1974), I wrote,

"Lest anyone think this new medical novel promotes the women's cause, forget it. The nurses are fine women; the female doctors have reached their high standing through judicious use of their lovely bodies, not their intellect." In *Doctor's Daughters* (1981) he made a stab at rectifying this by featuring three sisters, all of them successful doctors in their own right who earned their caducei by study and hard work. But the denouement of the tale is the finding of a true love for each one, all in one short week. Slaughter's women are glossy counterfeits. A pattern has emerged in most of his novels, even some of the biblical ones. There is usually a crusading hero, most often a physician with a cause, and two women, one of them naughty; the other, good, wholesome, and eminently marriageable. When the subject of demonic possession was in vogue, Slaughter brought these two women together in one body in *Devil's Gamble*—a neat trick.

Slaughter's novels are of three types: historical, biblical, and medical, or frequently a combination of these. His historical novels are least pedantic. They neither preach nor present long treatises on surgical procedures. When he writes under the name of C.V. Terry he seems to have more fun. His language is expansive and adventuresome. He tends more to the ribald and is freer in his portrayals of sexual encounters. In all his work, the historical research is accurate if lacking depth. His descriptions of places and events are marvelous—there is an especially graphic scene of a sea battle in *The Purple Quest*—but the significance of the events is not his primary concern. In both the historical and biblical novels, Slaughter has commandeered excessive dramatic licence when dealing with those famed personages who actually walked this earth by putting his words into their mouths and by ascribing his feelings to their hearts and minds.

Readers of gothic and romance literature have much to thank Frank Slaughter for. He has lifted them out of their armchairs to many lands in many times, and perhaps sent some scurrying to their encyclopedias to learn more about the Phoenicians, the Spanish Inquisition, the Civil War. Many have turned to their bibles to read what the scriptures have to say about Ruth, Jezebel, and Christ. What's more, his fascinating descriptions of dazzling new medical equipment and sophisticated technology have reassured his fans that they can enjoy long and healthy lives. With all this magic, who really cares that his characters lack vitality!

—Marion Hanscom

SMITH, Doris E(dna Elliott). Irish. Born in Dublin, 12 August 1919. Educated at Alexandra College, Dublin. Since 1938, has worked for an insurance group, Dublin. Recipient: Romantic Novelists Association Major Award, 1969. Lives in Dublin. Address: c/o Robert Hale Ltd., 45-47 Clerkenwell Green, London EC1R 0HT, England.

ROMANCE AND GOTHIC PUBLICATIONS

Novels

Star to My Barque. London, Ward Lock, 1964.
The Thornwood. London, Ward Lock, 1966.
Song from a Lemon Tree. London, Ward Lock, 1966.
The Deep Are Dumb. London, Ward Lock, 1967.
Comfort and Keep. London, Ward Lock, 1968.
Fire is for Sharing. London, Mills and Boon, 1968; Toronto, Harlequin, 1969.

To Sing Me Home. London, Mills and Boon, 1969; Toronto, Harlequin, 1970.
Seven of Magpies. London, Mills and Boon, and Toronto, Harlequin, 1970.
Cup of Kindness. London, Mills and Boon, 1971.
The Young Green Corn. London, Mills and Boon, 1971.
Dear Deceiver. London, Mills and Boon, and Toronto, Harlequin, 1972.
The One and Only. London, Mills and Boon, and Toronto, Harlequin, 1973.
The Marrying Kind. London, Mills and Boon, 1974.
Green Apple Love. London, Mills and Boon, 1974.
Haste to the Wedding. London, Mills and Boon, 1974.
Cotswold Honey. Toronto, Harlequin, 1975.
Smuggled Love. Toronto, Harlequin, 1976.
Wild Heart. Toronto, Harlequin, 1977.
My Love Came Back. London, Mills and Boon, 1978.
Mix Me a Man. London, Mills and Boon, 1978.
Noah's Daughter. London, Hale, 1982.

*   *   *

Doris E. Smith was born in Ireland and grew up near Dublin. Her childhood years were spent there just before the Second World War and were quite happy ones. They opened her mind and imagination to all sorts of influences which later emerged in her writing. Her natural facility with words edged her towards writing, but she was over 40 before she was published. Although not a prolific writer, she is yet a good one. Recognition for her ability came in 1969 when the Romantic Novelists Association awarded her their prize for the best romance of that year.

Her novels combine a very slight hint of Irish charm, and an obvious love of words and descriptions. She is, in fact, one of the "happy" writers who loves a good romance and who can't refrain from producing one every so often.

Predictably she uses an Irish background in some of her novels, *Smuggled Love*, for instance, or *Dear Deceiver*. In the latter, she uses that part of Ireland she is most familiar with, the Wicklow area near Dublin. She has not limited herself to this background, however, for several of her novels take place against the physical beauty of the Cotswolds and the low rolling hills of the border country between Scotland and England. Smith has a slow, yet captivating way of letting her stories unfold, for she blends dialogue, description, and action in just the right amount to entice her readers on.

One of her more recent novels, *Wild Heart*, is perhaps one of the best examples of her work and illustrates the care and planning that goes into her work. Victoria Elliott inherits a cottage in the Selkirk area of Scotland from her Great-Aunt Elizabeth and she goes there planning to sell it. Her sister, Lorraine, also goes with her. She has just experienced a shock as her fiancé has had second thoughts about marriage just days before their wedding. During the novel, Lorraine grows up and realizes that she herself contributed to this decision by her weaknesses and immaturity. Victoria, on the other hand, is one of the "fighters" of the world who tries to stand on her own feet just as her Great-Aunt had. The owner of the near-by castle is Dugald Douglas and, from their first meeting, Victoria is intrigued by him. Her efforts to redevelop her aunt's animal shelter and later to deny her growing love for Dugald are the major focus points in the novel. The counterpoint of Lorraine's problems plays a motivating force in the plot. Smith has her character's personality well in hand during the novel. She is able to show the underlying facets of their personality in such a way that one is instantly sympathetic towards them. For all of Victoria's considerable success in her own field, she is still the sensitive child that her Great-Aunt had befriended with the words "welcome to my world"—a world of stray dogs and abandoned kittens.

Smith's obvious love of animals emerges frequently as she uses settings that incorporate them. Charlotte Lavender in *Cotswold Honey* is a veterinary nurse who leaves a practice to go into a rural one. Dugald Douglas in *Wild Heart* has a famous kennel and raises and trains hunting dogs.

Doris Smith's novels are quiet ones in a way; emotional yes, even unhappy at times, but the reader is allowed to peek behind the scenes and understands that everything will right itself before the ending. Misunderstandings and mis-read hints or words are clarified so that the reader leaves her novels with a sense of happy completion.

—Arlene Moore

SMITH, Lady Eleanor (Furneaux). British. Born in Birkenhead, Cheshire, in 1902. Educated at Miss Douglas's School, London, and at a boarding school. Journalist: gossip columnist and film critic for London *Dispatch*, *Sphere*, and *Bystander*. *Died 20 October 1945*.

<small>ROMANCE AND GOTHIC PUBLICATIONS</small>

Novels

> *Red Wagon: A Study of the Tober*. London, Gollancz, and Indianapolis, Bobbs Merrill, 1930.
> *Flamenco*. London, Gollancz, and Indianapolis, Bobbs Merrill, 1931.
> *Ballerina*. London, Gollancz, and Indianapolis, Bobbs Merrill, 1932.
> *Tzigane*. London, Hutchinson, 1935; as *Romany*, Indianapolis, Bobbs Merrill, 1935.
> *Portrait of a Lady*. London, Hutchinson, 1936; New York, Doubleday, 1937.
> *The Spanish House*. London, Hutchinson, and New York, Doubleday, 1938.
> *Lovers' Meeting*. London, Hutchinson, and New York, Doubleday, 1940.
> *The Man in Grey: A Regency Romance*. London, Hutchinson, 1941; New York, Doubleday, 1942.
> *A Dark and Splendid Passion*. New York, Ace, 1941.
> *Caravan*. London, Hutchinson, and New York, Doubleday, 1943.
> *Magic Lantern*. London, Hutchinson, 1944; New York, Doubleday, 1945.

Short Stories

> *Satan's Circus and Other Stories*. London, Gollancz, 1932; Indianapolis, Bobbs Merrill, 1934.
> *Christmas Tree*. London, Gollancz, and Indianapolis, Bobbs Merrill, 1933; as *Seven Trees*, Bobbs Merrill, 1935 (?).

<small>OTHER PUBLICATIONS</small>

Other

> *Life's a Circus* (autobiography). London, Longman, 1939; New York, Doubleday, 1940.
> *British Circus Life*, edited by W.J. Turner. London, Harrap, 1948.
> *The Etiquette of Letter Writing*. Hemel Hempstead, Hertfordshire, John Dickinson, 1950 (?).

Critical Study: *Lady Eleanor Smith: A Memoir* by Lord Birkenhead, London, Hutchinson, 1953.

*   *   *

Lady Eleanor Smith claimed that she was partly of gypsy ancestry. It is not known whether this is true, but gypsies certainly play a large part in her fiction, both realistically and symbolically. In one aspect the gypsy displays a mode of life around carnivals or on the drom (road); in the other, the gypsy is a dark, brooding lover, a symbol of a highly felt sexuality that is both free and tragic.

Smith's first novel, *Red Wagon*, was based on her travels, in 1920's, as a sort of publicity agent with a circus. Set in the 19th century, it describes the life history of Joe Prince, one-time roustabout, who marries a gypsy and eventually acquires his own circus. It is noteworthy for a wealth of realistic detail about circus life. Similarly pseudo-biographical is *Ballerina*, the tragic story of a Victorian dancing girl who becomes a prima ballerina, but suffers a sad decline and death.

Gypsies are central to six of Smith's novels. *Flamenco* and *The Spanish House* echo *Wuthering Heights*, with gypsies as sex symbols and with alienation plots. *Flamenco* describes the life of a gypsy dancing girl closely, while *The Spanish House* has excellent pictures of carnival life, together with episodes set in Hollywood that are almost prophetic of the career of Marilyn Monroe. In *Romany* (British title *Tzigane*) a gypsy dancing girl, madly in love with Brazil, a gypsy animal trainer, marries a gorgio (non-gypsy) when she thinks Brazil is dead. Years later, happily married, she must decide what to do when Brazil turns up. *Portrait of a Lady*, Victorian in setting, depicts a married woman who has the strength of character to resist the remarkable charms of a young gypsy. *Magic Lantern* describes the marriage of a Devon squire to a gypsy girl, and the life of their son. *Caravan*, however, is concerned more with adventure and political intrigue than with heightened emotional situations, and is perhaps ultimately grounded upon George Borrow's adventures among the gypsies of Spain.

In addition to her gypsy gothic fiction, Miss Smith wrote a historical romance, *The Man in Grey*, which is similar to *Vanity Fair* in basic situation, and several supernatural stories. *Lovers' Meeting*, which invokes love, magic, and time travel to the past, is well done, and is unusual (for this type of story) in not having a happy ending. *Satan's Circus and Other Stories* contains several supernatural stories that used to be anthologized frequently in the 1930's and 1940's.

Lady Eleanor Smith's fiction usually displays an odd contrast between, on the one hand, highly romantic themes, florid sexuality, and exaggerated emotion, and, on the other hand, many realistic characterizations and detailed, almost ethnographic accounts of subculture life. Her work is primarily fiction of event, told in a clear, detached manner, without analysis, but nicely paced and often fascinating in its detail.

—E.F. Bleiler

———————————————

SMITH, Helen Zenna.   *See* **PRICE, Evadne.**

———————————————

SMITH, Joan. American. Born in 1938. Address: c/o Fawcett, 1515 Broadway, New York, New York 10036, U.S.A.

ROMANCE AND GOTHIC PUBLICATIONS

Novels

>   *An Affair of the Heart*. New York, Fawcett, 1977.
>   *Escapade*. New York, Fawcett, 1977.
>   *La Comtesse*. New York, Fawcett, 1978.
>   *Imprudent Lady*. New York, Walker, 1978.
>   *Dame Durden's Daughter*. New York, Walker, 1978.
>   *Aunt Sophie's Diamonds*. New York, Fawcett, 1979.
>   *Flowers of Eden*. New York, Fawcett, 1979.
>   *Sweet and Twenty*. New York, Fawcett, 1979.
>   *Talk of the Town*. New York, Walker, 1979.
>   *Aurora*. New York, Walker, 1980.
>   *Babe*. New York, Fawcett, 1980.
>   *Endure My Heart*. New York, Fawcett, 1980.
>   *Lace for Milady*. New York, Walker, 1980.
>   *Delsie*. New York, Fawcett, 1981.
>   *Lover's Vows*. New York, Fawcett, 1981.
>   *Love's Way*. New York, Walker, 1982.

*   *   *

Of all the Georgette Heyer imitators, Joan Smith has been the most successful in duplicating Heyer's wit. Her heroines and heroes are always intelligent, and their conversations always amusing. She also has Heyer's gift for depicting various kinds of entertaining fools and dolts as minor characters. As comedies of character, these romances have much more substance than most in the genre. Unfortunately, her best books are her earliest, and her more recent works are in some cases somewhat dull.

An Affair of the Heart is her first book, and one of her wittiest. A girl who lacks beauty, in a family of beauties, wins the heart of a lord, but can't believe it, especially when this lord's foolish best friend keeps telling her about her predecessor, complicating both the relationship and the plot. In *Escapade* (modeled on Heyer's *Sylvester*?) a young woman who writes a gossip column falls in love with the chief target of her column. Among the minor characters, the three young ladies competing for the attentions of the hero are outstandingly absurd and amusing. In *Aunt Sophie's Diamonds*, the diamonds, which are supposed to be buried with her, touch off an inspired comedy, resembling Heyer's *The Talisman Ring* (in situation, rather than plot). The heroine is a 24-year-old woman, deprived all her life of adventure, romance, and even friendship, who enters wholeheartedly into the young people's plans to dig up the corpse; the happy result for her is adventure, friendship, and romance. *La Comtesse* is a conventional good-bad girl story, in which Lord Dashford investigates the possibility that "la Comtesse" is a Napoleonic spy, and falls in love with her despite himself. The story is not up to Smith's usual standard. *Imprudent Lady* is akin to Heyer's *Venetia* and *Black Sheep* in that an unworldly maiden lady receives the confidences of a confirmed rake, who falls in love with her. As the hero and heroine are writers, we are given a glimpse of the Regency's literary figures as well. The hero and heroine are among Smith's wittiest, and the heroine's uncle is a memorable ass. *Aurora* is about a missing heir, an heiress who wants him to stay that way, and a girl who falls in love with the soi-disant heir. This is unusual among Smith's works in the presence of downright villainy. *Endure My Heart* and *Lace for Milady* are both about smuggling. The heroine of *Endure My Heart* falls into the leadership of a band of smugglers, but falls in love with the man assigned to catch them. Smith actually makes this sound plausible, and it is one of her entertaining books. *Lace for Milady* doesn't work anywhere near so well. *Delsie*, one of Smith's most recent works, is poor. It resembles *The Reluctant Widow* in every way except that it is not interesting. *Lover's Vows* again deals with a woman in her mid-twenties, surrounded by fools, and unappreciated except by the hero. It is not prime Smith, but even at that, it is well-written.

Despite the derivative nature of her work, Smith is capable of considerable originality and imagination. Her attention to period detail is excellent, though she occasionally jars the reader with a glaring anachronism. Even though her more recent works are not up to the standard she herself set, there is always a good chance that her books will provide entertainment and pleasure.

—Marylaine Block

SNOW, Lyndon. *See* **ELSNA, Hebe**.

SOMERS, Suzanne. *See* **DANIELS, Dorothy**.

STEEL, Danielle. American. Born in New York City. Educated at schools in Europe; New York University and Parsons School of Design. Married; has children. Helped start a public relations firm in New York; writer since 1973. Agent: Phyllis Westberg, Harold Ober Associates, 40 East 49th Street, New York, New York 10017, U.S.A.

<small>ROMANCE AND GOTHIC PUBLICATIONS</small>

Novels

> *Going Home.* New York, Pocket Books, 1973; London, Sphere, 1980.
> *Passion's Promise.* New York, Dell, 1977; as *Golden Moments*, London, Sphere, 1980.
> *Now and Forever.* New York, Dell, 1978; London, Sphere, 1979.
> *The Promise* (novelization of screenplay). New York, Dell, and London, Sphere, 1978.
> *Season of Passion.* New York, Dell, and London, Sphere, 1979.
> *The Ring.* New York, Delacorte Press, 1980; London, Sphere, 1982.

Loving. New York, Dell, 1980; Loughton, Essex, Piatkus, 1981.
To Love Again. New York, Dell, 1980.
Remembrance. New York, Delacorte Press, 1981; London, Hodder and Stoughton, 1982.
Palomino. New York, Dell, 1981; Loughton, Essex, Piatkus, 1982.
Summer's End. New York, Dell, 1981.
A Perfect Stranger. New York, Dell, and Loughton, Essex, Piatkus, 1982.
Once in a Lifetime. New York, Dell, 1982.

OTHER PUBLICATIONS

Verse

Love: Poems. New York, Dell, 1981.

*   *   *

Danielle Steel writes about the women who inhabit the upper echelon of society. She presents no serious psychological portraits of these characters, but the trappings of the good life—the best and most expensive restaurants, the designer dresses, Gucci shoes and bags, posh parties—are described in loving detail by a lady who knows whereof she speaks. She has mastered the art of creating sumptuous scenes of life at the top. The heroines all have good breeding and class. It's obvious by the way they walk, talk, or toss an always luxurious mane of hair. These women have the kind of looks and style that make others envious, yet each one suffers some terrible romantic tragedy that in the end makes her a stronger, freer person. Still, there is always a man close by just in case she needs to lean on someone.

These modern day heroines brim with talent—usually writing or painting—but must seek fulfillment in a society that often admires them only for their beauty. Some find a way to accomplish this through love, such as Kezia Saint Martin (*Passion's Promise*) whose lover convinces her she can break out of her gilded cage to become a serious writer. Another example is Deanna Durcas (*Summer's End*) whose affair with a handsome art dealer allows her to defy a husband who had consistently ridiculed her efforts at painting and go on to establish herself as an artist. Nothing comes easily to these women, even while living in the luxurious surroundings of New York, San Francisco, or some exotic European locale. They must truly suffer. The aforementioned Kezia shares an all consuming love with Lucas only to lose him first to prison and then death. In *Now and Forever* Jessica Clarke lives through the nightmare of her husband's trial for rape and his year-long imprisonment. And in *The Ring* Kassandra von Gotthard and her daughter Ariana both love and lose their men in the horror that engulfed Nazi Germany.

There is an element of melodrama inherent in all of Steel's tales, and her characters, despite their physical and social similarities, are distinctive and have a certain appeal. Her ear for dialog is excellent which helps make an occasional far-fetched situation seem believable. Bittersweet love and smoldering passion, not explicit sex, are the hallmarks of this author's novels.

—Patricia Altner

STEEN, Marguerite. Also wrote as Lennox Dryden; Jane Nicholson. British. Born Marguerite Elena May Benson in Liverpool, Lancashire, 12 May 1894; took surname of foster parents. Educated privately, and at Moorhurst School, Lancashire, 5 years; Kendal High School; Froebel School, Sheffield, 3 years. Kindergarten teacher in Hertfordshire, 1914-18; taught dance and eurythmics, Halifax, 1919-22; toured with the Fred Terry-Julia Neilson theatrical company, 1923-26; teacher and writer after 1926; columnist, *Sunday Graphic*, London, in 1940's. Fellow, Royal Society of Literature. *Died 4 August 1975.*

ROMANCE AND GOTHIC PUBLICATIONS

Novels

The Gilt Cage. London, Bles, 1926; New York, Doran, 1927.
Duel in the Dark. London, Bles, 1928; as *Dark Duel*, New York, Stokes, 1929.
The Reluctant Madonna. London, Cassell, 1929; New York, Stokes, 1930.
They That Go Down. London, Cassell, 1930; as *They That Go Down in Ships*, New York, Cosmopolitan, 1931.
Ancestors (as Lennox Dryden). London, Cassell, 1930.
When the Wind Blows. London, Cassell, 1931.
Unicorn. London, Gollancz, 1931; New York, Century, 1932.
The Wise and the Foolish Virgins. London, Gollancz, and Boston, Little Brown, 1932.
Spider. London, Gollancz, and Boston, Little Brown, 1933.
Stallion. London, Gollancz, and Boston, Little Brown, 1933.
Matador. London, Gollancz, and Boston, Little Brown, 1934.
The One-Eyed Moon. London, Gollancz, and Boston, Little Brown, 1935.
The Tavern. London, Gollancz, 1935; Indianapolis, Bobbs Merrill, 1936.
Return of a Heroine. London, Gollancz, and Indianapolis, Bobbs Merrill, 1936.
Who Would Have Daughters? London, Collins, 1937.
The Marriage Will Not Take Place. London, Collins, 1938.
Family Ties. London, Collins, 1939.
The Flood trilogy:
    The Sun Is My Undoing. London, Collins, and New York, Viking Press, 1941.
    Twilight on the Floods. London, Collins, and New York, Doubleday, 1949.
    Phoenix Rising. London, Collins, 1952; as *Jehovah Blues*, New York, Doubleday, 1952.
Shelter (as Jane Nicholson). London, Harrap, and New York, Viking Press, 1941.
Rose Timson. London, Collins, 1946; as *Bell Timson*, New York, Doubleday, 1946.
Granada Window. London, Falcon Press, 1949.
The Swan. London, Hart Davis, 1951; Boston, Houghton Mifflin, 1953.
Anna Fitzalan. London, Collins, and New York, Doubleday, 1953.
Bulls of Parral. London, Collins, and New York, Doubleday, 1954.
The Unquiet Spirit. London, Collins, 1955; New York, Doubleday, 1956.
The Tower. London, Collins, 1959; New York, Doubleday, 1960.
The Woman in the Back Seat. London, Collins, and New York, Doubleday, 1959.
A Candle in the Sun. London, Longman, and New York, Doubleday, 1964.

Short Stories

A Kind of Insolence and Other Stories. London, Collins, 1940.

Plays

Oakfields Plays, Including the Inglemere Christmas Play (juvenile).   London, Nicholson and Watson, 1932.
Peepshow (juvenile).   London, Nicholson and Watson, 1933.
Matador, with Matheson Lang, adaptation of the novel by Steen (produced Edinburgh, 1937).
French for Love, with Derek Patmore (produced London, 1939).   London, Collins, 1940.
The Grand Manner (produced Manchester, 1942).

Screenplays: *The Man from Morocco*, with others, 1945; *Beware of Pity*, with W.P. Lipscomb and Elizabeth Baron, 1946.

Other

Hugh Walpole: A Study.   London, Nicholson and Watson, and New York, Doubleday, 1933.
The Lost One: A Biography of Mary—Perdita—Robinson.   London, Methuen, 1933.
William Nicholson.   London, Collins, 1943.
Little White King (on cats).   London, Joseph, and Cleveland, World, 1956.
A Pride of Terrys: A Family Saga.   London, Longman, 1962; Westport, Connecticut, Greenwood Press, 1978.
Looking Glass: An Autobiography.   London, Longman, 1966.
Pier Glass: More Autobiography.   London, Longman, 1968.

*   *   *

Born in Liverpool in 1894, Marguerite Steen was persuaded to take up writing by her friends, among them the author Hugh Walpole and the famous actress Ellen Terry. Her novels reflect her extensive travelling, with Bristol, Spain, and the American Deep South providing a focus for some of her finest work. Bristol is the setting of her first significant book, *They That Go Down*, which describes the adventures of the lively Jane Carradus and her press-ganged lover during the period of Trafalgar. The style is strong—if elaborate in description—and characters and period strikingly portrayed. Steen's early work tends to the gothic, fixing on fierce extremes of human nature in remote situations. The headstrong Sanchia Mullyon of *When the Wind Blows* is a typical example. So too is Jim Devoke, the womanising "hero" of *Stallion*, a more impressive novel where a sensual violence pervades the pages. Jim's infidelities—a parallel to the stud services of the prize shire stallion he leads from one farm to the next—lead him to the satanic Tamar, whose love takes a savage toll when he rejects her at last. The quiet rural setting and stable family background serve to throw the characters into sharper relief.

Steen's mature fiction shows a change of emphasis, as well as a heightening of perception. The style is more direct and forceful, shorn of the earlier description. There is too a greater reliance on contemporary themes. Without a doubt her most important work is to be found in the "Spanish" novels and the trilogy based on the fortunes of the Flood family of Bristol. In the former, her knowledge of Spain and identification with its tradition—embodied in the ritual of the bull-fight—are used to great effect. *Matador*, with its story of the retired torero living vicariously through his sons, is memorable as a study of the Spanish character in action. The theme of the bull-fight was subsequently pursued, with success, in *Bulls of Parral*. The Flood trilogy follows the family of Bristol slavers to success and opulence as legitimate traders and squires, and examines the conflict of ideals raised by their inextricable involvement with Africa and the blacks. *The Sun Is My Undoing*, a bestseller and Book Society Choice, remains the best known, but its sequel, *Twilight on the Floods*, is equally good, switching adroitly from Victorian Bristol to West Africa at the time of the Ashantie war. *Phoenix Rising*, the final volume of the trilogy, is less satisfying, perhaps due to its being heavily cut prior to publication. Nevertheless, the trilogy as a whole deserves to be ranked with Steen's finest achievements.

Though less significant than the Spanish and Flood trilogies, a number of the contemporary novels are well worth consideration. *Family Ties* is an excellent study of personal lives in crisis in the publishing world, and both *Anna Fitzalan* and *Rose Timson*—the latter of a story of a mother's obsessive love for her daughters—are outstanding analyses of female character. Though not highly regarded by the author, her last novel, *A Candle in the Sun*, is a clear and effective presentation of marital breakdown and its effects on a growing child.

—Geoffrey Sadler

STEVENSON, Anne.   Address: c/o William Morrow Inc., 105 Madison Avenue, New York, New York 10016, U.S.A.

ROMANCE AND GOTHIC PUBLICATIONS

Novels

Ralph Dacre.   New York, Walker, and London, Collins, 1967.
Flash of Splendour.   London, Collins, 1968.
A Relative Stranger.   New York, Putnam, and London, Collins, 1970.
A Game of Statues.   New York, Putnam, and London, Collins, 1972.
The French Inheritance.   New York, Putnam, and London, Collins, 1974.
Coil of Serpents.   New York, Putnam, and London, Collins, 1977.
Mask of Treason.   New York, Putnam, 1979; Loughton, Essex, Piatkus, 1981.
Turkish Rondo.   New York, Morrow, and Loughton, Essex, Piatkus, 1981.

*   *   *

Anne Stevenson's special gift as a writer of romantic suspense is her ability to place ordinary people in extraordinary, even improbable situations and yet to retain a strong sense of reality. The heroines of her novels are neither so glamorous and sophisticated nor so young and beautiful that the average reader cannot sympathize or identify with them. At the same time these women, from shop assistant to operatic costume designer, are not insipid marionettes wandering heedlessly into dangerous situations. Instead each deals competently with the challenges that she faces without relinquishing control of her life to the men who appear to offer protection and love. In fact, the crises weathered by these women serve to strengthen them.

It is notable that one of Stevenson's novels, *The French Inheritance*, features a hero rather than a heroine, with two female characters competing for his affections. This is a very neat reversal of the usual gothic pattern. The hero is as believable and as deftly drawn as all of Stevenson's creations. If a weakness can be found in any of these works it might be the occasionally jarring note in characterization. As an example, Ben, the child in *A Game of Statues*, seems at times both younger and older than his stated age of eight. Some of the other less-central characters, like Mr. Rizzio in *Coil of Serpents*, lean close to caricature. These faintly false notes are only jarring in retrospect, however, since all the characters in the novels are woven so firmly into compelling plots that the reader is carried along.

Stevenson has a brisk and straightforward prose style which avoids the florid descriptive passages that often mark this genre. She also has a remarkably accurate ear for dialogue that renders such description unnecessary.

The plots of these relatively long novels are reminiscent of the work of both Mary Stewart and Helen MacInnes, although they are in no way derivative. The resolutions of the plots are neither obvious nor entirely unexpected, although several of the books feature a clever last-minute twist at the moment that a less confident writer might conclude the tale. No loose end ever remains dangling; often a minor character or scene from an early chapter is pivotal.

The romance element is invariably handled with delicacy and restraint. Romance is, of course, integral to novels of this kind, but these stories stand on their own as adventures. As well-crafted contemporary works of suspense these books are likely to appeal to readers of gothics and to those ordinarily put off by the gothic approach.

—Susan Quinn Berneis

STEVENSON, D(orothy) E(mily).   British.   Born in Edinburgh, in 1892. Educated privately in England and France. Married James Reid Peploe in 1916; two sons and one daughter. *Died 30 December 1973.*

Romance and Gothic Publications

Novels (series: Mrs. Tim; Miss Buncle)

Peter West.   London, Chambers, 1923.
Mrs. Tim of the Regiment (published anonymously).   London, Cape, 1932; as *Mrs. Tim Christie*, New York, Holt Rinehart, 1973.
Miss Buncle's Book.   London, Jenkins, 1934; New York, Farrar and Rinehart, 1937.
Golden Days.   London, Jenkins, 1934.
Divorced from Reality.   London, Jenkins, 1935; as *Miss Dean's Dilemma*, New York, Farrar and Rinehart, 1938; as *The Young Clementina*, London, Collins, and New York, Holt Rinehart, 1970.
Miss Buncle, Married.   London, Jenkins, 1936; New York, Farrar and Rinehart, 1937.
Smouldering Fire.   London, Jenkins, 1936; New York, Farrar and Rinehart, 1938.
The Empty World: A Romance of the Future.   London, Jenkins, 1936; as *A World in Spell*, New York, Farrar and Rinehart, 1939.
The Story of Rosabelle Shaw.   London, Chambers, 1937; New York, Farrar and Rinehart, 1939; as *Rosabelle Shaw*, London, Collins, 1967.
Miss Bun, The Baker's Daughter.   London, Collins, 1938; as *The Baker's Daughter*, New York, Farrar and Rinehart, 1938.
Green Money.   London, Collins, and New York, Farrar and Rinehart, 1939.
The English Air.   London, Collins, and New York, Farrar and Rinehart, 1940.
Rochester's Wife.   London, Collins, and New York, Farrar and Rinehart, 1940.
Spring Magic.   New York, Farrar and Rinehart, 1941; London, Collins, 1942.
Mrs. Tim Carries On.   London, Collins, and New York, Farrar and Rinehart, 1941.
Mrs. Tim (omnibus).   London, Collins, 1941.
Crooked Adam.   New York, Farrar and Rinehart, 1942; London, Collins, 1969.
Celia's House.   London, Collins, and New York, Farrar and Rinehart, 1943.

The Two Mrs. Abbotts.   London, Collins, and New York, Farrar and Rinehart, 1943.
Listening Valley.   London, Collins, and New York, Farrar and Rinehart, 1944.
The Four Graces.   London, Collins, and New York, Rinehart, 1946.
Kate Hardy.   London, Collins, and New York, Rinehart, 1947.
Mrs. Tim Gets a Job.   London, Collins, and New York, Rinehart, 1947.
Young Mrs. Savage.   London, Collins, 1948; New York, Rinehart, 1949.
Trilogy:
  Vittoria Cottage.   London, Collins, and New York, Rinehart, 1949.
  Music in the Hills.   London, Collins, and New York, Rinehart, 1950.
  Winter and Rough Weather.   London, Collins, 1951; as *Shoulder the Sky*, New York,
    Rinehart, 1951.
Mrs. Tim Flies Home.   London, Collins, and New York, Rinehart, 1952.
Five Windows.   London, Collins, and New York, Rinehart, 1953.
Charlotte Fairlie.   London, Collins, 1954; as *Blow the Wind Southerly*, New York,
    Rinehart, 1954.
Amberwell.   London, Collins, and New York, Rinehart, 1955.
Summerhills.   London, Collins, and New York, Rinehart, 1956.
The Tall Stranger.   London, Collins, and New York, Rinehart, 1957.
Anna and Her Daughters.   London, Collins, and New York, Rinehart, 1958.
Still Glides the Stream.   London, Collins, and New York, Rinehart, 1959.
The Musgraves.   London, Collins, and New York, Holt Rinehart, 1960.
Bel Lamington.   London, Collins, and New York, Holt Rinehart, 1961.
Fletchers End.   London, Collins, and New York, Holt Rinehart, 1962.
The Blue Sapphire.   London, Collins, and New York, Holt Rinehart, 1963.
Miss Buncle (omnibus).   New York, Holt Rinehart, 1964.
Katherine Wentworth.   London, Collins, and New York, Holt Rinehart, 1964.
Katherine's Marriage.   London, Collins, 1965; as *The Marriage of Katherine*, New
    York, Holt Rinehart, 1965.
The House on the Cliff.   London, Collins, and New York, Holt Rinehart, 1966.
Sarah Morris Remembers.   London, Collins, and New York, Holt Rinehart, 1967.
Sarah's Cottage.   London, Collins, and New York, Holt Rinehart, 1968.
Gerald and Elizabeth.   London, Collins, and New York, Holt Rinehart, 1969.
The House of the Deer.   London, Collins, 1970; New York, Holt Rinehart, 1971.

OTHER PUBLICATIONS

Verse

Meadow-Flowers.   London, Macdonald, 1915.
The Starry Mantle: Poems.   London, Stockwell, 1926.

Other (juvenile)

Alister and Co.: Poems.   New York, Farrar and Rinehart, 1940.
It's Nice to Be Me (verse).   London, Methuen, 1943.

*   *   *

The author of innumerable romances and family chronicles, as well as the popular "Mrs. Tim" books, D.E. Stevenson is an excellent example of a romance writer who expands the possibilities of the genre while recognizing its limitations.

Her novels might best be classified as novels of manners, in the same way as Dorothy L. Sayers's works are so described in the detective genre. The interest lies always in the development and exploration of character, in both the individual and collective sense. Thus, the Mrs. Tim novels, written in the epistolary mode, reveal not only Mrs. Tim's own psychological development, but also the changing nature of English wartime society. Her other novels, while they can be read on their own, often allude to characters and locations in previous works. What emerges is a kind of *roman fleuve* of English life and culture of a particular kind, at a particular time. This effect strikes one as being essentially unselfconscious, though it is obviously the result of considerable skill.

There is very little element of the gothic in Stevenson's work; what there is exists mainly in an atmosphere which is always essential to plot or theme: Celia's ghost in *Celia's House* is not so much an agent of the supernatural as of the house itself (the real "hero" of the novel). The house, Dunnian, goes through various changes during the novel, over the period of the two world wars, and thus is both a device for revealing social change and a symbol of continuity.

While primarily novels of character, Stevenson's works are noteworthy also for their effective realization of locale. The Scottish setting of *Sarah's Cottage* is vividly described, as are the English locations in the same book. Setting is effectively related to character, and vice-versa; indeed, the interconnection of character and setting might be said to be a recurring theme in the novels, particularly in those with an Anglo-Germanic interest (*Sarah's Cottage, The English Air*).

Though skillfully plotted, the novels lack a major element of mystery or suspense of a conventional kind. Even when a mystery precipitates the plot, as in *Green Money*, it is ultimately a mystery of character, a why-dunnit rather than a who-dunnit. In *The English Air* the wartime exploits of the hero, Franz, are presented not as elements of an espionage thriller, but in relation to the character and his romance with his English cousin. Nevertheless, the novels are utterly engrossing, and probably represent the pure English modern romance at its very best.

—Joanne Harack Hayne

STEVENSON, Florence.   Also writes as Zandra Colt; Lucia Curzon; Zabrina Faire.   American.   Born in Los Angeles, California. Educated at Yale University, New Haven, Connecticut; University of Southern California, Los Angeles, B.A., M.A. Drama columnist, Los Angeles *Mirror*, 1949-50; editorial assistant, *Mademoiselle*, New York, 1956-57; press assistant, James D. Proctor, 1957-58; Assistant Editor, 1959-60, and Contributing Editor, 1960-70, *Opera News*, New York; columnist ("Opera Boutique"), *Metropolitan Opera Program*, New York, for ten years; columnist ("Things of Beauty"), *Lincoln Center Program*, New York, for ten years; Associate Editor, *FM Guide*, New York, 1964-65; Contributing Editor, *Weight Watchers*, 1968-75, and *New Ingenue*, 1974-75, both New York. Agent: Phyllis Westberg, Harold Ober Associates, 40 East 49th Street, New York, New York 10017. Address: 227 East 57th Street, New York, New York 10022, U.S.A.

ROMANCE AND GOTHIC PUBLICATIONS

Novels (series: Kitty Telefair)

Ophelia.   New York, New American Library, 1968.
Feast of Eggshells.   New York, New American Library, 1970.
The Curse of the Concullens.   New York, World, 1970.
The Witching Hour (Telefair).   New York, Award, 1971.
Where Satan Dwells (Telefair).   New York, Award, 1971.
Bianca, with Patricia Hagan Murray.   New York, New American Library, 1973.

Kilmeny in the Dark Wood.   New York, New American Library, 1973.
Altar of Evil (Telefair).   New York, Award, 1973.
The Mistress of Devil's Manor (Telefair).   New York, Award, 1973.
The Sorcerer of the Castle (Telefair).   New York, Award, 1974.
Dark Odyssey.   New York, New American Library, 1974.
The Ides of November.   New York, New American Library, 1975.
A Shadow on the House.   New York, New American Library, 1975.
Witch's Crossing.   New York, New American Library, 1975.
The Silent Watcher (Telefair).   New York, Award, 1975.
A Darkness on the Stairs.   New York, New American Library, 1976.
The House at Luxor.   New York, New American Library, 1976.
Dark Encounter.   New York, New American Library, 1977.
The Horror from the Tombs.   New York, Award, 1977.
Julie.   New York, New American Library, 1978.
The Golden Galatea.   New York, Jove, 1979.
The Moonlight Variations.   New York, Jove, 1981.
The Cactus Rose (as Zandra Colt).   New York, Jove, 1982.

Novels as Zabrina Faire

Lady Blue.   New York, Warner, 1979.
The Midnight Match.   New York, Warner, 1979.
The Romany Rebel.   New York, Warner, 1979.
Enchanting Jenny.   New York, Warner, 1979.
Wicked Cousin.   New York, Warner, 1980.
Athena's Airs.   New York, Warner, 1980.
Bold Pursuit.   New York, Warner, 1980.
Pretender to Love.   New York, Warner, 1981.
Pretty Kitty.   New York, Warner, 1981.
Tiffany's True Love.   New York, Warner, 1981.

Novels as Lucia Curzon

The Chadbourne Luck.   New York, Jove, 1981.
Adverse Alliance.   New York, Jove, 1981.
The Mourning Bride.   New York, Jove, 1982.

OTHER PUBLICATIONS

Other

The Story of Aida, Based on the Opera by Giuseppe Verdi (juvenile).   New York, Putnam, 1965.
Call Me Counselor, with Sara Halbert.   Philadelphia, Lippincott, 1977.

*   *   *

It is hard not to like an author who can inject as much humor in her books as can Florence Stevenson. Lucinda Ayers, a governess in *The Curse of the Concullens*, must be one of the most indomitable gothic heroines ever created. A mere slip of a girl, she encounters and copes with just about every occult manifestation possible. She befriends both the local banshee and the family vampire and deals calmly with the fact that her two young charges are werewolves. Even an encounter with the Devil himself does not shake her. Dimitri O'Hagan is an appropriately mysterious and brooding hero, given to clandestine activities. In fact he is an Irish patriot working against the hated British. The intrepid Lucy solves all the mysteries and manages to bring a degree of happiness to a remarkably unfortunate family, at the same time finding true love for herself.

Stevenson's selection of a pseudonym for most of her Regency novels, Zabrina Faire, again reflects a sense of humor and mischief. *Lady Blue*, one of Zabrina Faire's early novels, has a predictably happy ending after a somewhat rocky romance, but Stevenson develops the plot along some rather unusual lines. Meriel, also a governess, is the victim of a malicious prank played by her young charge. He spills ink on her hair, turning it blue. Dismissed for slapping him, Meriel is hired by Lord Farr to impersonate a ghostly blue lady. Later she is kidnapped and forced to perform in a circus sideshow as a blue mermaid. Lord Farr, who luckily is a proficient magician, uses his skills to rescue her and foil the villains.

Unfortunately for those who appreciate such humor, Stevenson's later Regencies, both by Faire and her later pseudonym, Lucia Curzon, are standard formula novels. All the conventions are followed quite competently. The results are enjoyable to read but not readily distinguishable from most similar books. It is Stevenson's occasional humorous novel, gently spoofing the genre, which sets her apart, adding real sparkle to her work and keeping readers hoping for more.

—Barbara Kemp

STEWART, Mary (Florence Elinor, née Rainbow). British. Born in Sunderland, County Durham, 17 September 1916. Educated at Eden Hall, Penrith, Cumberland; Skellfield School, Ripon, Yorkshire; St. Hild's College, University of Durham, B.A. (honours) 1938, M.A. 1941. Served in the Royal Observer Corps during World War II. Married Sir Frederick Henry Stewart in 1945. Lecturer in English, Durham University, 1941-45; Part-time Lecturer in English, St. Hild's Training College, Durham, and Durham University, 1948-56. Recipient: Crime Writers Association Silver Dagger, 1961; Frederick Niven Award, 1971; Scottish Arts Council Award, 1975. Fellow, Royal Society of Arts, 1968. Lives in Edinburgh. Address: c/o Hodder and Stoughton Ltd., Mill Road, Dunton Green, Sevenoaks, Kent TN13 2YA, England.

ROMANCE AND GOTHIC PUBLICATIONS

Novels

Madam, Will You Talk? London, Hodder and Stoughton, 1955; New York, Mill, 1956.
Wildfire at Midnight. London, Hodder and Stoughton, and New York, Appleton Century Crofts, 1956.
Thunder on the Right. London, Hodder and Stoughton, 1957; New York, Mill, 1958.
Nine Coaches Waiting. London, Hodder and Stoughton, 1958; New York, Mill, 1959.
My Brother Michael. London, Hodder and Stoughton, and New York, Mill, 1960.
The Ivy Tree. London, Hodder and Stoughton, 1961; New York, Mill, 1962.
The Moon-Spinners. London, Hodder and Stoughton, 1962; New York, Mill, 1963.
This Rough Magic. London, Hodder and Stoughton, and New York, Mill, 1964.
Airs above the Ground. London, Hodder and Stoughton, and New York, Mill, 1965.
The Gabriel Hounds. London, Hodder and Stoughton, and New York, Mill, 1967.

The Wind off the Small Isles. London, Hodder and Stoughton, 1968.
The Crystal Cave. London, Hodder and Stoughton, and New York, Morrow, 1970.
The Hollow Hills. London, Hodder and Stoughton, and New York, Morrow, 1973.
Touch Not the Cat. London, Hodder and Stoughton, and New York, Morrow, 1976.
The Last Enchantment. London, Hodder and Stoughton, and New York, Morrow, 1979.

OTHER PUBLICATIONS

Plays

Radio Plays: *Lift from a Stranger*, *Call Me at Ten-Thirty*, *The Crime of Mr. Merry*, and *The Lord of Langdale*, 1957-58.

Other (juvenile)

The Little Broomstick. Leicester, Brockhampton Press, 1971; New York, Morrow, 1972.
Ludo and the Star Horse. Leicester, Brockhampton Press, 1974; New York, Morrow, 1975.
A Walk in Wolf Wood. London, Hodder and Stoughton, and New York, Morrow, 1980.

*   *   *

Although Mary Stewart's novels are usually categorized as contemporary or gothic romances because of their subject matter and plot lines, it may be unfair to label her a genre writer. From 1955 through 1967, Stewart wrote a highly popular set of novels of romantic suspense that, for convenience, were often reviewed as gothics. But, although her novels had similarities to those of Victoria Holt and Phyllis Whitney (her two most popular contemporaries), Stewart transcended their work and the formula romance of which these were the three most significant writers. After *The Gabriel Hounds* Stewart turned to historical romance, writing a trilogy (*The Crystal Cave*, *The Hollow Hills*, and *The Last Enchantment*) about Merlin and Arthur, a series that differed from her other books. In the mid-1970's she published *Touch Not the Cat*, a return to her earlier work but with a plot that depended upon telepathy, a new ingredient for her fiction. She has also written fantasies for children.

Of her romance writings, Stewart's most important work came during her earlier period, although the Merlin trilogy may be her most enduring literary contribution. From *Madam, Will You Talk?* to *The Gabriel Hounds*, her books were excellent and original romances that relied heavily upon her ability to evoke a place, to create complex characters, and to weave sophisticated and compelling stories.

Her two best contemporary romances are *Nine Coaches Waiting* and *My Brother Michael*, set respectively in France and Greece. *Nine Coaches Waiting* is her only "governess gothic," a novel about an orphaned heroine who is employed to teach the heir to a vast French estate. When she discovers the child's life is in danger, the heroine protects him and earns the love of the boy's older cousin, who has not been—despite appearances—a part of the conspiracy. Stewart's academic background in literature informs this novel as it does each of her others. The heroine consciously recalls her literary predecessors (especially Cinderella and Jane Eyre) as Stewart plays off the resonance of the literary history of romance against the modern heroine's sensibility and experience.

My Brother Michael employs a background of ancient and recent Greek history, myth, and legend with thematic elements from John Donne. The heroine joins the hero's search for the truth about the fate of his brother, who died during World War II near Delphi. In addition to learning what had happened, the characters also find a buried ancient Greek statue.

Wildfire at Midnight, set on the Isle of Skye, works against a background of ancient Celtic myth. *This Rough Magic*, on Corfu, finds it inspiration in Shakespeare's *The Tempest*. *The Gabriel Hounds* derives from the story of Lady Hester Stanhope. Other novels are set in the south of France, in Northumbria, and in Austria. In each, Stewart evokes the place in a rich and compelling manner.

The originality of her literary sensibility is most fully realized in the nature of her characters. Stewart's heroes and heroines are people of commitment, not just to each other as in many other romances but especially to others and to abstract concepts of truth and justice. Their values may seem archaic in the modern world, but Stewart portrays them so sensitively that they remain believable. Without preaching or moralizing, she places her characters in situations of extreme danger where it would be acceptable for them to walk away from someone else's trouble. They do not, and her delineation of their motivation and personal growth is always crucial to understanding their stories.

Although each of Stewart's contemporary romances contains a love story as an integral part of the plot, she does not allow the vicissitudes of the lovers to dominate. Her characters are selfless, sometimes (as the heroine of *Nine Coaches Waiting*) making decisions that require the apparent sacrifice of the love affair in the cause of justice. But despite their "stiff upper lip" morality, the heroines are attractive, lively, and admirable without being either stuffy or priggish. She portrays the success of the love relationship as a product of the heroine's maturity rather than as an end in itself.

In addition, Stewart is a fine stylist. Reviewers consistently praise the quality of her prose, especially her descriptions of food and place as well as the charm and good humor with which her heroines tell their tales. Without padding her stories with extraneous details, she describes her scenes vividly, offering not a travelogue but a concrete sense of what it must be like to experience an exotic place fraught with dramatic and emotional events. Mary Stewart defies categorization because, although her books may resemble those of other writers, she remains, even in her weaker books, a writer of uncommon originality and grace. She may work within a formula, but her scene is the larger setting of romance through centuries of literature, making her novels both rewarding and inimitable.

—Kay Mussell

STIRLING, Jessica.   Pseudonym for Peggie Coghlan and Hugh C. Rae.   British.   **COGH-LAN, Peggie**: born in Glasgow, 26 January 1920. Educated at Notre Dame High School. Married Eugene O. Coghlan; two daughters. Address: 109 Mugdock Road, Milngavie, Dunbartonshire, Scotland.   **RAE, Hugh C(rauford)**: also writes as Robert Crawford; Stuart Stern. Born in Glasgow, Scotland, 22 November 1935. Attended secondary school in Glasgow. Served in the Royal Air Force, 1954-56. Married Elizabeth Dunn in 1960; one daughter. Assistant to antiquarian bookseller, 1952-65, then full-time writer. Address: Drumore Farm Cottage, Balfron Station, Stirlingshire, Scotland. Agent: Fraser and Dunlop Scripts Ltd., 91 Regent Street, London W1R 8RU, England.

ROMANCE AND GOTHIC PUBLICATIONS

Novels

The Spoiled Earth.   London, Hodder and Stoughton, 1974; as *Strathmore*, New York, Delacorte Press, 1975.

The Hiring Fair. London, Hodder and Stoughton, 1976; as *Call Home the Heart*, New York, St. Martin's Press, 1977.

The Dresden Finch. New York, Delacorte Press, 1976; as *Beloved Sinner*, London, Pan, 1976.

The Dark Pasture. London, Hodder and Stoughton, 1977; New York, St. Martin's Press, 1978.

The Deep Well at Noon. London, Hodder and Stoughton, 1979; New York, St. Martin's Press, 1980.

The Blue Evening Gone. London, Hodder and Stoughton, and New York, St. Martin's Press, 1981.

The Gates of Midnight. London, Hodder and Stoughton, 1982.

OTHER PUBLICATIONS by Hugh C. Rae

Novels

Skinner. London, Blond, and New York, Viking Press, 1965.

Night Pillow. London, Blond, and New York, Viking Press, 1967.

A Few Small Bones. London, Blond, 1968; as *The House at Balnesmoor*, New York, Coward McCann, 1969.

The Interview. London, Blond, and New York, Coward McCann, 1969.

The Saturday Epic. London, Blond, and New York, Coward McCann, 1970.

The Marksman. London, Constable, and New York, Coward McCann, 1971.

The Shooting Gallery. London, Constable, and New York, Coward McCann, 1972.

The Rock Harvest. London, Constable, 1973.

The Rookery. London, Constable, and New York, St. Martin's Press, 1974.

Harkfast. London, Constable, and New York, St. Martin's Press, 1976.

The Minotaur Factor (as Stuart Stern). Chicago, Playboy Press, 1977.

Sullivan. London, Constable, 1978.

The Haunting of Waverley Falls. London, Constable, 1980.

Novels as Robert Crawford

The Shroud Society. London, Constable, and New York, Putnam, 1969.

Cockleburr. London, Constable, 1969; as Hugh C. Rae, New York, Putnam, 1970; as *Pay as You Die*, New York, Berkley, 1971.

Kiss the Boss Goodbye. London, Constable, 1970; New York, Putnam, 1971.

The Badger's Daughter. London, Constable, 1971.

Whip Hand. London, Constable, 1972.

Peggie Coghlan comments:

For many years my writing was slanted exclusively in the direction of the magazine field. It was my friend and mentor Hugh C. Rae who suggested that I change direction and write a novel. The help and guidance I received from Mr. Rae cannot be estimated, and it is no exaggeration to say that without him the books would not have been written.

Contemplating the first book, and being a member of a fairly large family, I suppose it was natural that I should decide to write a family story. For me, the work of a book is divided into two parts. First, the research, which I enjoy very much and tend to spin out far beyond what is required, and the actual writing which is hard and demanding work but is at the same time deeply satisfying when what appears on the printed page nearly approximated what, at the beginning, I planned in my head and felt in my heart.

A picture, it is said, is worth more than a thousand words, so equally, too, will not a thousand words evoke a memorable picture? That, to me, is what novel writing is all about.

*   *   *

The strong female protagonists of Jessica Stirling's novels are believable, attractive, and beleaguered by difficulties. They "carry on" and show their mettle while remaining stable and appealingly feminine. Careful character development and settings which powerfully complement and justify these characters are distinctive features of Stirling's fiction.

The search for dignity, independence, and love by Mirrin Stalker of the Strathmore trilogy is played out against the background of a coal-mining village in the last century in Scotland. The feudal system in which she and her family seem trapped begins to show some cracks, and Mirrin is among the first to realize that coalmaster Houston Lamont is as human and touchable as she, and therefore as vulnerable. Mirrin and her proud family get caught up in the changes taking place. The proprieties and bleakness of this narrow society are intricately presented with the powerful characters gaining advantages only to lose them again.

Holly Beckman, in *The Deep Well at Noon* and *The Blue Evening Gone*, must also contend with disadvantage while trying to find her place in the world. Her disreputable father and evil brother pose continuous threats to the position she works so hard to maintain. In the first novel Holly finds her niche in the antiques trade in London just after World War I. Her employer, a kindly mentor, provides her with a share of the business after his death, giving her the chance to make something of herself. The antiques business adds interest and validity to both novels and allows Holly to obtain respectability and eventual affluence. Her personal life is often in turmoil, however. In *The Blue Evening Gone* Holly's mid-thirties "crisis" is portrayed beautifully in counterpoint to the turmoil in Europe in the years prior to World War II. Her intelligence and integrity, which serve her well in business, see her through these and other difficult times.

Stirling has also created intriguing male characters. One doesn't easily forget the brilliant and haughty Drew Stalker who, in *The Dark Pasture*, mellows only enough to seem human at last. Nor does one pass lightly over the men in Holly Beckman's life, from the caddish David Aspinall, her first lover, to highly sensitive Christopher Deems, the husband who perishes; as well as steadfast Kennedy King, her second husband and business partner, and attractive, but callow Peter Freeman, the American dancer who almost spoils it all.

Stirling's stories are well crafted, believably plotted, with intriguing characters seemingly constructed around the belief that Drew Stalker expressed in an off-guard moment, "You are, you can be, what you choose to be."

—Allayne C. Heyduk

STRATTON, Rebecca. Also writes as Lucy Gillen.   British.   Served in the Women's Auxiliary Air Force and the Fire Service during World War II. Worked at many jobs before becoming a civil servant for the Coventry County Court, 1957-67; then a full-time writer. Address: c/o Mills and Boon Ltd., 15-16 Brooks Mews, London W1A 1DR, England.

ROMANCE AND GOTHIC PUBLICATIONS

Novels

The Golden Madonna.   London, Mills and Boon, 1973; Toronto, Harlequin, 1974.
The Bride of Romano.   London, Mills and Boon, 1973; Toronto, Harlequin, 1974.

Castles in Spain. Toronto, Harlequin, 1974.
The Yellow Moon. London, Mills and Boon, 1974; Toronto, Harlequin, 1975.
Island of Darkness. London, Mills and Boon, 1974; Toronto, Harlequin, 1975.
Autumn Concerto. London, Mills and Boon, 1974; Toronto, Harlequin, 1975.
The Flight of the Hawk. London, Mills and Boon, 1974; Toronto, Harlequin, 1975.
Run from the Wind. London, Mills and Boon, and Toronto, Harlequin, 1974.
Fairwinds. London, Mills and Boon, and Toronto, Harlequin, 1974.
The Warm Wind of Farik. London, Mills and Boon, and Toronto, Harlequin, 1975.
Firebird. London, Mills and Boon, and Toronto, Harlequin, 1975.
The Fire and the Fury. London, Mills and Boon, 1975; Toronto, Harlequin, 1976.
The Goddess of Mavisu. London, Mills and Boon, 1975; Toronto, Harlequin, 1976.
Isle of the Golden Drum. London, Mills and Boon, 1975; Toronto, Harlequin, 1976.
Moon Tide. London, Mills and Boon, 1975; Toronto, Harlequin, 1976.
The White Dolphin. London, Mills and Boon, 1976.
Proud Stranger. Toronto, Harlequin, 1976.
The Road to Gafsa. London, Mills and Boon, 1976; Toronto, Harlequin, 1977.
Gemini Child. London, Mills and Boon, 1976; Toronto, Harlequin, 1977.
Chateau d'Armor. London, Mills and Boon, and Toronto, Harlequin, 1976.
Dream of Winter. London, Mills and Boon, 1977; Toronto, Harlequin, 1978.
Girl in a White Hat. London, Mills and Boon, and Toronto, Harlequin, 1977.
More Than a Dream. Toronto, Harlequin, 1977.
Spindrift. London, Mills and Boon, 1977; Toronto, Harlequin, 1978.
Lost Heritage. London, Mills and Boon, 1978.
Image of Love. London, Mills and Boon, and Toronto, Harlequin, 1978.
Bargain for Paradise. London, Mills and Boon, and Toronto, Harlequin, 1978.
The Corsican Bandit. London, Mills and Boon, and Toronto, Harlequin, 1978.
The Eagle of the Vincella. London, Mills and Boon, 1978.
Inherit the Sun. Toronto, Harlequin, 1978.
The Sign of the Ram. Toronto, Harlequin, 1978.
The Velvet Glove. Toronto, Harlequin, 1978.
Close to the Heart. London, Mills and Boon, and Toronto, Harlequin, 1979.
Lark in an Alien Sky. London, Mills and Boon, and Toronto, Harlequin, 1979.
The Tears of Venus. London, Mills and Boon, 1979; Toronto, Harlequin, 1980.
Trader's Cay. London, Mills and Boon, 1980.
The Leo Man. London, Mills and Boon, 1980.
The Inherited Bride. London, Mills and Boon, 1980.
Apollo's Daughter. London, Mills and Boon, 1980.
The Black Invader. London, Mills and Boon, 1981.
Black Enigma. London, Mills and Boon, 1981.
The Silken Cage. London, Mills and Boon, 1981.

Novels as Lucy Gillen

The Ross Inheritance. London, Mills and Boon, 1969.
Good Morning, Doctor Houston. London, Mills and Boon, 1969; Toronto, Harlequin, 1970.
The Silver Fishes. London, Mills and Boon, 1969; Toronto, Harlequin, 1970.
A Wife for Andrew. London, Mills and Boon, 1969; Toronto, Harlequin, 1970.
Heir to Glen Ghyll. London, Mills and Boon, and Toronto, Harlequin, 1970.
Nurse Helen. London, Mills and Boon, 1970; Toronto, Harlequin, 1971.
Doctor Toby. London, Mills and Boon, 1970; Toronto, Harlequin, 1972.
The Girl at Smuggler's Rest. London, Mills and Boon, 1970; Toronto, Harlequin, 1971.
My Beautiful Heathen. London, Mills and Boon, 1970; Toronto, Harlequin, 1972.
The Whispering Sea. London, Mills and Boon, 1971.
Winter at Cray. London, Mills and Boon, 1971; Toronto, Harlequin, 1972.
Dance of Fire. London, Mills and Boon, 1971.
Marriage by Request. London, Mills and Boon, and Toronto, Harlequin, 1971.

Summer Season. London, Mills and Boon, 1971; Toronto, Harlequin, 1973.
The Enchanted Ring. London, Mills and Boon, 1971; Toronto, Harlequin, 1973.
Sweet Kate. London, Mills and Boon, 1971; Toronto, Harlequin, 1973.
That Man Next Door. London, Mills and Boon, 1971; Toronto, Harlequin, 1972.
A Time Remembered. London, Mills and Boon, 1971; Toronto, Harlequin, 1973.
The Pretty Witch. London, Mills and Boon, 1971; Toronto, Harlequin, 1974.
Dangerous Stranger. London, Mills and Boon, 1972; Toronto, Harlequin, 1973.
Glen of Sighs. London, Mills and Boon, 1972; Toronto, Harlequin, 1975.
Means to an End. London, Mills and Boon, 1972; Toronto, Harlequin, 1975.
The Changing Years. London, Mills and Boon, 1972; Toronto, Harlequin, 1975.
Painted Wings. London, Mills and Boon, 1972; Toronto, Harlequin, 1974.
The Pengelly Jade. London, Mills and Boon, 1972; Toronto, Harlequin, 1974.
The Runaway Bride. London, Mills and Boon, 1972; Toronto, Harlequin, 1974.
An Echo of Spring. London, Mills and Boon, 1973.
Moment of Truth. London, Mills and Boon, 1973.
A Touch of Honey. London, Mills and Boon, 1973; Toronto, Harlequin, 1975.
Gentle Tyrant. London, Mills and Boon, 1973; Toronto, Harlequin, 1975.
A Handful of Stars. London, Mills and Boon, 1973; Toronto, Harlequin, 1976.
The Stairway to Enchantment. London, Mills and Boon, 1973; Toronto, Harlequin, 1975.
Come, Walk with Me. London, Mills and Boon, 1974.
Web of Silver. London, Mills and Boon, 1974; Toronto, Harlequin, 1975.
All the Summer Long. London, Mills and Boon, 1975; Toronto, Harlequin, 1976.
Return to Deepwater. London, Mills and Boon, 1975; Toronto, Harlequin, 1976.
The Hungry Tide. Toronto, Harlequin, 1976.
The House of Kingdom. London, Mills and Boon, and Toronto, Harlequin, 1976.
Master of Ben Ross. Toronto, Harlequin, 1977.
Back of Beyond. Toronto, Harlequin, 1978.
Heron's Point. Toronto, Harlequin, 1978.
Hepburn's Quay. London, Mills and Boon, 1979.
The Storm Eagle. London, Mills and Boon, 1980.

*   *   *

Rebecca Stratton is an unexpected mixture of late blooming talent, a checkered working career, and an unusual ability to write romances. In all, she has produced over 80 novels since 1969, with roughly half of them published under her pseudonym, Lucy Gillen. There is a progressive development evident in her work as she moves from sweet simplicity to the more sophisticated involvement that modern readers are looking for. In fact, two of her more recent novels appeared in the Harlequin Presents series. Because of this development, her readers sometimes find it difficult to decide which type of romance they prefer.

Writing as Lucy Gillen, her novels are more traditional with the plot kept fairly simple. Conflict actually depends on the heroine's gradual awakening love, but in a slow, puzzled way that finds her wondering what is happening even as the hero declares himself. That is the situation that Kim Anders is in the novel *That Man Next Door*. Kim has come to stay with an aunt and uncle and hopes to get a job as a secretary to a writer that lives near them. She also meets James Fleming and the three small relatives whom he is temporarily caring for. Since he lives right next door, their continued meeting can't be avoided, much as she would like to, considering his dislike of and cruelty to the children. Because of his attitude, Kim finds herself becoming more and more involved with them and in spite of childish remarks soon learns that the children have exaggerated his attitude. Her job as secretary, the return of James's former girl friend, and constant upsets with the children offer numerous chances for misunderstandings and reactions. Through the whole story, Kim's emotional reactions swing constantly from gradual liking to renewed dislike. Finally, when she hears that he is going to marry, she forces herself to accept the fact that she had mistaken her feelings and his seeming encouragement. "You *will* marry me, won't you?" forces her to revise her thoughts as the final misunderstanding is reconciled. Generally, the tone is light, although Kim is aware of unfamiliar emotional turmoil. The sub-plots and minor incidents offer humor and at times satisfaction as Kim feels that she has managed to score a point against James's rather autocratic disregard of the children.

Lost Heritage (Rebecca Stratton) offers a different kind of romance, for ultimate happiness seems very dim to Charlotte Kennedy as she encounters Raoul Menais. Suspense is much more heightened, character conflict more frequent and more damaging as Charlotte takes a job as a secretary/companion to Lizette Menais. Charlotte learns that she was adopted as a baby and was given a bracelet with the name "Menais" on it. With her adoptive parents dead, Charlotte sets out to learn about her real parents. As she travels to France to live with the family, she gradually learns the hidden secrets of the Menais family. Confrontation with Raoul Menais occurs as he becomes suspicious of her when she is slowly drawn into the family conflicts. Tension is high as twenty-year-old events surface and Charlotte learns the truth about her family. Charlotte's constant need to remain in the background, yet her equally compelling need to protect her employer, Lizette, forces her to face repeated difficulties with Raoul and others in the family. The fact that she falls in love with Raoul is an added burden to her heart for she feels that nothing can ever come of it, especially if her birth is questionable. The end, of course, gives her her answers and her heart's desire.

Readers instantly react to the different styles that Rebecca Stratton uses in her novels, and certainly there are many readers who prefer her Lucy Gillen stories. However, since 1974 she has gradually chosen to write under her own name and in the more sophisticated style that is becoming more acceptable to modern readers. Perhaps young love and tender naivety are becoming less realistic, even unbelievable, in today's world. Certainly Rebecca Stratton's novels tend to be more complex with hidden psychological situations and sharper character delineations.

—Arlene Moore

STUBBS, Jean.   British.   Born in Denton, Lancashire, 23 October 1926. Educated at Manchester High School for Girls, 1938-44; Manchester School of Art, 1944-47. Married; one daughter and one son. Since 1966, regular reviewer, *Books and Bookmen*, London. Recipient: Tom-Gallon Trust Award, for short story, 1965. Agent: Teresa Sacco, Macmillan London Ltd., Little Essex Street, London WC2R 3LF. Address: Trewin, Nancegollan, near Helston, Cornwall TR13 0AJ, England.

ROMANCE AND GOTHIC PUBLICATIONS

Novels (series: Howarth Chronicles)

The Rose-Grower.   London, Macmillan, 1962; New York, St. Martin's Press, 1963.
The Travellers.   London, Macmillan, and New York, St. Martin's Press, 1963.
Hanrahan's Colony.   London, Macmillan, 1964.
The Straw Crown.   London, Macmillan, 1966.
The Passing Star.   London, Macmillan, 1970; as *Eleanora Duse*, New York, Stein and Day, 1970.
An Unknown Welshman.   London, Macmillan, and New York, Stein and Day, 1972.
A Timeless Place.   London, Macmillan, 1978.
Kit's Hill (Howarth).   London, Macmillan, 1978; as *By Our Beginnings*, New York, St. Martin's Press, 1979.

The Ironmaster (Howarth). London, Macmillan, 1981; as *An Imperfect Joy*, New York, St. Martin's Press, 1981.
The Vivian Inheritance (Howarth). London, Macmillan, 1982.

OTHER PUBLICATIONS

Novels

My Grand Enemy. London, Macmillan, 1967; New York, Stein and Day, 1968.
The Case of Kitty Ogilvie. London, Macmillan, 1970; New York, Walker, 1971.
Dear Laura. London, Macmillan, and New York, Stein and Day, 1973.
The Painted Face. London, Macmillan, and New York, Stein and Day, 1974.
The Golden Crucible. New York, Stein and Day, 1976; London, Macmillan, 1977.

Play

Television Play: *Family Christmas*, 1965.

*   *   *

The author of many novels, short stories, and a television play, Jean Stubbs is a writer whose works defy easy classification. She has described her crime novels as "why-done-its and not who-done-its"; yet this distinction fails to capture the unique qualities of meticulous historical detail and compelling characterization which the works embody. An intriguing paradox is that, while two of these novels are re-constructions of actual crimes (*My Grand Enemy, The Case of Kitty Ogilvie*), they are presented in a thoroughly imaginative way; conversely, the Inspector Lintott novels (*Dear Laura, The Painted Face, The Golden Crucible*), which are wholly fictional, give the impression of being part fact. These novels are mysteries in the most general sense, presenting a series of contrasts between fact and fantasy, reality and dream—between, in short, life and art.

Such dichotomies appear as recurring motifs in the other novels as well. In *The Rose-Grower*, for example, we are presented with the history of a man's life from his own point of view, from the point of view of other characters, and from an objective narrative viewpoint; these views ebb and flow, advance and recede as the man himself grapples with a personification of death. The degree to which this "history" is a creation of the rose-grower as thwarted artist, or is merely the reconstruction of a sick man, is never absolutely clear. Hence, if the plot takes an occasionally fanciful turn, this seems appropriate to the dream logic of the narrative, with its blending of past and present.

Characterization is clearly more important to Stubbs than plot. On the other hand, her use of historical setting is never as a mere backdrop for the characters. Rather, characters are shown in the act of defining themselves, and this can only be accomplished in a social context. In *The Straw Crown* Stubbs presents a mythical island colony, steeped in archaic and exclusive tradition, faced with the necessity of disbanding because their island is to be used for nuclear tests. The confrontation between the old and the new values, occasionally comic and invariably touching, is embodied in the character of a female archaeologist who comes to study the tribe. Indubitably a woman of the present, she is also compellingly linked to the past. Her struggles to save the island, and to sort out her own relationships and values, are presented with sympathy. What might be regarded as fantastic plots become, in the author's intelligent hands, means of examining, through the eyes of her characters, our own assumptions about the nature of reality.

—Joanne Harack Hayne

SUMMERS, Essie (Ethel Snelson Summers).   New Zealander.   Born in Christchurch, 24 July 1912. Educated at North Linwood Primary School; Christchurch Technical College. Married to William Flett; one son and one daughter. Prior to World War II, worked for Londontown Drapers, Christchurch, for seven years, and as a costing clerk for four years. Columnist ("Parish Meditations," as Tamsin), Timaru *Herald*, for six years; also wrote a column for the Christchurch *Star*, and a marriage guidance column. Address: c/o Mills and Boon Ltd., 15-16 Brooks Mews, London W1A 1DR, England.

Romance and Gothic Publications

Novels

New Zealand Inheritance.   London, Mills and Boon, 1957; as *Heatherleigh*, Toronto, Harlequin, 1963.
The Time and the Place.   London, Mills and Boon, 1958; Toronto, Harlequin, 1964.
Bachelors Galore.   London, Mills and Boon, 1958; Toronto, Harlequin, 1965.
The Lark in the Meadow.   London, Mills and Boon, 1959.
The Master of Tawhai.   London, Mills and Boon, 1959; Toronto, Harlequin, 1965.
Moon over the Alps.   London, Mills and Boon, 1960; Toronto, Harlequin, 1964.
Come Blossom-Time, My Love.   London, Mills and Boon, 1961; Toronto, Harlequin, 1963.
Nurse Abroad.   Toronto, Harlequin, 1961; London, Mills and Boon, 1967.
No Roses in June.   London, Mills and Boon, 1961; Toronto, Harlequin, 1962.
The House of the Shining Tide.   London, Mills and Boon, 1962; Toronto, Harlequin, 1963.
South to Forget.   London, Mills and Boon, 1963; Toronto, Harlequin, 1964.
Where No Roads Go.   London, Mills and Boon, and Toronto, Harlequin, 1963.
Bride in Flight.   London, Mills and Boon, 1964; Toronto, Harlequin, 1965.
The Smoke and the Fire.   London, Mills and Boon, and Toronto, Harlequin, 1964.
No Legacy for Lindsay.   London, Mills and Boon, and Toronto, Harlequin, 1965.
No Orchids by Request.   London, Mills and Boon, 1965; Toronto, Harlequin, 1966.
Sweet Are the Ways.   London, Mills and Boon, 1965; Toronto, Harlequin, 1966.
Heir to Windrush Hill.   London, Mills and Boon, and Toronto, Harlequin, 1966.
His Serene Miss Smith.   London, Mills and Boon, 1966; Toronto, Harlequin, 1967.
Postscript to Yesterday.   London, Mills and Boon, 1966; Toronto, Harlequin, 1967.
A Place Called Paradise.   London, Mills and Boon, and Toronto, Harlequin, 1967.
Rosalind Comes Home.   London, Mills and Boon, 1968; Toronto, Harlequin, 1969.
Meet on My Ground.   London, Mills and Boon, 1968; Toronto, Harlequin, 1969.
The Kindled Fire.   London, Mills and Boon, 1969; Toronto, Harlequin, 1970.
Revolt—and Virginia.   London, Mills and Boon, and Toronto, Harlequin, 1969.
The Bay of the Nightingales.   London, Mills and Boon, and Toronto, Harlequin, 1970.
Summer in December.   London, Mills and Boon, and Toronto, Harlequin, 1970.
Return to Dragonshill.   London, Mills and Boon, and Toronto, Harlequin, 1971.
The House on Gregor's Brae.   London, Mills and Boon, and Toronto, Harlequin, 1971.
South Island Stowaway.   London, Mills and Boon, 1971; Toronto, Harlequin, 1972.
The Forbidden Valley.   Toronto, Harlequin, 1973.
A Touch of Magic.   London, Mills and Boon, and Toronto, Harlequin, 1973.
Through All the Years.   London, Mills and Boon, 1974; Toronto, Harlequin, 1975.
The Gold of Noon.   London, Mills and Boon, 1974; Toronto, Harlequin, 1975.
Anne of Strathallan.   London, Mills and Boon, and Toronto, Harlequin, 1975.
Beyond the Foothills.   London, Mills and Boon, and Toronto, Harlequin, 1976.
Not by Appointment.   London, Mills and Boon, and Toronto, Harlequin, 1976.
Adair of Starlight Peaks.   London, Mills and Boon, 1977; Toronto, Harlequin, 1978.
Goblin Hill.   Toronto, Harlequin, 1977.
The Lake of the Kingfisher.   London, Mills and Boon, 1978.
Spring in September.   London, Mills and Boon, and Toronto, Harlequin, 1978.

My Lady of the Fuchsias. London, Mills and Boon, and Toronto, Harlequin, 1979.
One More River to Cross. London, Mills and Boon, 1979.
Autumn in April. London, Mills and Boon, 1981.
Daughters of the Misty Gorges. London, Mills and Boon, 1981.

OTHER PUBLICATIONS

Other

The Essie Summers Story. London, Mills and Boon, 1974.

*   *   *

Essie Summers, a New Zealand writer with a strong English background, grew up with traditions that honor the poet and storyteller. Perhaps this background accounts for her unique qualities as a writer of romance fiction. One does not sit down to read a novel by her with the intent of passing a brief hour or so. Her books have to be approached with plenty of time on one's hands and they have to be saved for that special time when one needs a real sense of re-creation. For that is what Essie Summers does: she re-creates whole families, generations even, that fill her novels with deep vibrant love, both for each other and for their country, New Zealand.

Pace in her novels lends a slow unfolding of the story and characters so that one is able to grasp the subtle elements of conflict and tension between the main characters of the story. While most of her novels show initial antagonism between the lead characters, Summers will occasionally have a situation where another character deliberately causes trouble for those in love. For the most part, however, Summers depends on her characters to move the story along and to show the developing plot to her readers.

Usually her novels take place in remote farming areas of the country, and this in itself gives an added dimension to her works, for action, motivation, and resolution take place against an almost panoramic background of harsh, rugged country and hard-working people. It is impossible not to gain an understanding of the earlier settlers of the country and those who still hold the land as she incorporates these struggles in her stories.

For instance, in *Return to Dragonshill*, the heroine, Henrietta, agrees to return to the high-country sheep ranch to act as governess to the children there. She also meets the man she had loved (and she thought lost) several years ago for he has returned as well. His reason for returning is to build a bridge over an impassable river, an undertaking that is going to open that part of the country up to all-weather travel for the first time. Within her cast of characters, Essie Summers takes special pains to create the character of Madame. She is one hundred years old; she and her husband were the very first settlers in that part of the country. Reminiscences of early tragedies, of stark, primitive living conditions, are woven into the narrative in such a way that one feels and sees the hardships of these early settlers.

Touches of homey, sentimental events instill a mood of serenity as Madame brings out scrap books of those early days containing touches of poetry, mention of short stories and essays, as well as newspaper clippings that tell of those early years. There is a sense of timelessness and security that touches the lives of the characters in the stories, but also the lives of her readers, for much of the faith and belief that shines through these little scraps reach out to them as well.

Over and over again Summers draws vivid pictures of their way of life. Her ability to re-create the mood and life of her country and to people it with strong, sensitive characters shows remarkable creativity. The slow unfolding of her stories draws her readers toward the characters and makes them want to know that they do find a much deserved happiness. In a way, her readers feel that they have sat down with a long cozy letter from home that tells the joys and sorrows of well-loved friends and relatives. Of all modern romance writers, Essie Summers has taken this unique way of telling her stories and has made it her own.

—Arlene Moore

SWAN, Annie S. Also wrote as David Lyall. British. Born in Mountskip, Gorebridge, Scotland. Educated at the Queen Street Ladies' College, Edinburgh; and privately. Married James Burnett Smith in 1883 (died, 1927); one daughter and one son. Writer and journalist from the 1870's: Editor, *The Woman at Home* magazine, London, 1893-1917, the Annie S. Swan Penny Stories, later Penny Weekly, 1898-99, and the *Annie S. Swan Annual* from 1924. *Died 17 June 1943.*

ROMANCE AND GOTHIC PUBLICATIONS

Novels

>   *Ups and Downs: A Family Chronicle.* London, Charing Cross, 1878.
>   *Shadowed Lives.* Glasgow, Marr, 1880.
>   *Bess: The Story of a Waif.* Glasgow, Marr, 1880.
>   *Grandmother's Child.* London, Partridge, 1882; as *Grannie's Little Girl*, 1925.
>   *Inside the Haven.* London, Blackie, 1882.
>   *Aldersyde: A Border Tale of Seventy Years Ago.* Edinburgh, Oliphant, and New York, Carter, 1883.
>   *The Better Part.* London, Partridge, 1884.
>   *Carlowrie; or, Among Lothian Folks.* Edinburgh, Oliphant, 1884; Cincinnati, Jennings and Pye, n.d.
>   *Dorothea Kirke; or, Free to Serve.* Edinburgh, Oliphant, and Cincinnati, Cranston and Stowe, 1884.
>   *Mark Desborough's Vow.* London, Partridge, 1884.
>   *Ursula Vivian, The Sister-Mother.* Edinburgh, Oliphant, 1884; Cincinnati, Cranston and Stowe, 1890.
>   *Warner's Chase; or, The Gentle Heart.* London, Blackie, 1884.
>   *Adam Hepburn's Vow: A Tale of Kirk and Covenant.* London, Cassell, 1885; New York, Cassell, 1888.
>   *A Divided House: A Study from Life.* Edinburgh, Oliphant, 1885.
>   *Thankful Rest.* London, Nelson, 1885.
>   *Freedom's Sword: A Tale of the Days of Wallace and Bruce.* London, Cassell, 1886.
>   *The Gates of Eden: A Story of Endeavour.* Edinburgh, Oliphant, 1886; Cincinnati, Cranston and Stowe, 1890.
>   *Robert Martin's Lesson.* Edinburgh, Oliphant, 1886; Cincinnati, Cranston and Stowe, 1890.
>   *Sundered Hearts.* Edinburgh, Oliphant, 1886.
>   *Thomas Dryburgh's Dream: A Story of the Sick Children's Hospital.* Edinburgh, Oliphant, 1886.
>   *Briar and Palm: A Study of Circumstance and Influence.* Edinburgh, Oliphant, 1887; Cincinnati, Cranston and Stowe, 1890.
>   *Jack's Year of Trial.* London, Nelson, 1887.
>   *The Strait Gate.* London, Partridge, 1887.
>   *Doris Cheyne: The Study of a Noble Life.* Edinburgh, Oliphant, 1888; Cincinnati, Cranston and Stowe, 1890.
>   *Hazell & Sons, Brewers.* Edinburgh, Oliphant, 1888; Cincinnati, Cranston and Stowe, 1891.
>   *The Secret Panel.* Edinburgh, Oliphant, 1888.
>   *St. Veda's; or, The Pearl of Orr's Haven.* Edinburgh, Oliphant, 1889; Cincinnati, Cranston and Stowe, n.d.
>   *Sheila.* Edinburgh, Anderson and Ferrier, 1890; Cincinnati, Cranston and Stowe, 1891.
>   *Across Her Path.* Cincinnati, Cranston and Stowe, 1890; London, Leng, 1925.
>   *Maitland of Laurieston: A Family History.* Edinburgh, Oliphant, 1890; Cincinnati, Jennings and Pye, n.d.
>   *A Vexed Inheritance.* Edinburgh, Oliphant, 1890; Cincinnati, Cranston and Stowe, 1893.

The Ayres of Studleigh. Edinburgh, Oliphant, and New York, Hunt and Eaton, 1891.
Who Shall Serve? A Story for the Times. Edinburgh, Oliphant, 1891.
The Guinea Stamp: A Story of Modern Glasgow. Edinburgh, Oliphant, and Cincinnati, Cranston and Stowe, 1892.
A Bitter Debt: A Tale of the Black Country. London, Hutchinson, 1893.
Homespun: A Study of Simple Folk. London, Hutchinson, 1893; New York, Dutton, n.d.
The Answer to a Christmas Prayer. New York, Collier, 1894.
A Foolish Marriage: An Edinburgh Story of Student Life. London, Hutchinson, 1894.
A Lost Ideal. Edinburgh, Oliphant, 1894.
A Victory Won. London, Hutchinson, 1895.
Fettered Yet Free: A Study in Heredity. New York, Dodd Mead, 1895.
Elizabeth Glen, M.B.: The Experience of a Lady Doctor. London, Hutchinson, 1895.
Kinsfolk. London, Hutchinson, 1896.
A Stormy Voyager. London, Hutchinson, 1896.
The Curse of Cowden. London, Hutchinson, 1897.
Mrs. Keith Hamilton, M.B.: More Experiences of Elizabeth Glen. London, Hutchinson, 1897.
The Ne'er-Do-Weel. London, Hutchinson, 1897.
Conscience Money (as David Lyall). London, Hodder and Stoughton, 1898.
Greater Love (as David Lyall). London, Hodder and Stoughton, 1898.
Not Yet: A Page from a Noble Life. London, Hutchinson, 1898.
Wyndham's Daughter: A Story of To-day. London, Hutchinson, 1898.
A Son of Erin. London, Hutchinson, 1899.
Twice Tried. Cincinnati, Cranston and Stowe, n.d.; London, Leng, 1928.
An American Wife. London, Hutchinson, 1900; as *An American Woman*, New York, Dutton, n.d.
The Burden-Bearers. London, Hutchinson, 1900.
Love Grown Cold. London, Methuen, 1902.
Mary Garth: A Clydeside Romance. London, Hodder and Stoughton, 1904.
Christian's Cross; or, Tested and True. London, Hodder and Stoughton, 1905.
Love, The Master Key. London, Hodder and Stoughton, 1905.
A Mask of Gold: The Mystery of the Meadows. London, Hodder and Stoughton, 1906.
Nancy Nicholson; or, Who Shall Be Heir? London, Hodder and Stoughton, 1906.
Love Unlocks the Door. London, Hodder and Stoughton, 1907.
Anne Hyde, Travelling Companion. London, Hodder and Stoughton, 1908.
The Broad Road. London, Hurst and Blackett, 1908.
Hester Lane. London, Hodder and Stoughton, 1908.
The Inheritance. London, Hodder and Stoughton, 1909.
The Old Moorings: A Story of Modern Life. London, Hodder and Stoughton, 1909.
Love's Barrier. London, Cassell, 1910.
Love's Miracle. London, Hodder and Stoughton, 1910.
Margaret Holroyd; or, The Pioneers. London, Hodder and Stoughton, 1910.
The Mystery of Barry Ingram. London, Cassell, 1910.
Rhona Keith. London, Hodder and Stoughton, 1910.
What Shall It Profit? or, Roden's Choice. London, Partridge, 1910.
The Last of Their Race. London, Hodder and Stoughton, 1911.
To Follow the Lead. London, Kelly, 1911.
The Bondage of Riches. London, Partridge, 1912.
A Favourite of Fortune. London, Cassell, 1912.
Woven of the Wind. London, Hodder and Stoughton, 1912.
The Bridge Builders. London, Hodder and Stoughton, 1913.
The Farrants: A Story of Struggle and Victory. London, Kelly, 1913.
The Fairweathers: A Story of the Old World and the New. London, Hodder and Stoughton, 1913.
Prairie Fires. London, Cassell, 1913.
Corroding Gold. London, Cassell, 1914.
Meg Hamilton: An Ayrshire Romance. London, Hodder and Stoughton, 1914.

Love Gives Itself: The Story of a Blood Feud.   London, Hodder and Stoughton, 1915.
The Step-Mother.   London, Hodder and Stoughton, 1915.
The Woman's Part.   London, Hodder and Stoughton, 1916.
Young Blood.   London, Hodder and Stoughton, 1917.
Hands Across the Sea.   London, Oliphant, 1919.
The Ruling Passion.   London, Leng, 1920.
The Ivory God.   London, Hodder and Stoughton, 1923.
Macleod's Wife: A Highland Romance.   London, Hodder and Stoughton, 1924.
A Maid of the Isles: A Romance of Skye.   London, Hodder and Stoughton, 1924.
Wrongs Righted.   London, Leng, 1924.
Elsie Thorburn.   London, Leng, 1926; as *The World Well Lost*, 1935.
Closed Doors.   London, Leng, 1926.
The Pendulum.   London, Hodder and Stoughton, 1926; New York, Doran, 1927.
For Love of Betty.   London, Leng, 1928.
Love the Prodigal.   London, Leng, 1929.
Fiona Macrae.   London, Leng, 1929; as *The Pride of Fiona Macrae*, 1934.
A Wild Harvest.   London, Leng, 1929.
The Forerunners.   London, Hodder and Stoughton, 1930.
The House on the Rock.   London, Leng, 1930.
The Marching Feet.   London, Hodder and Stoughton, 1931.
The Luck of the Livingstones.   London, Leng, 1932.
The Maclure Mystery.   London, Leng, 1932.
The Shore Beyond.   London, Hodder and Stoughton, 1932.
Christine Against the World.   London, Leng, 1933.
The Last of the Laidlaws: A Romance of the Border.   London, Leng, 1933.
The Little Stranger.   London, Leng, 1933.
A Winsome Witch.   London, Leng, 1933.
The Purchase Price.   London, Leng, 1934.
Between the Tides.   London, Hodder and Stoughton, 1935.
A Homing Bird.   London, Leng, 1935.
The Way of Escape.   London, Leng, 1935.
A Breaker of Hearts.   London, Leng, 1937.
A Portrait of Destiny.   London, Leng, 1937.
The Road to Damascus.   London, Hodder and Stoughton, 1937.
The Family Secret.   London, Leng, 1938.
The Greater Freedom.   London, Leng, 1938.
The Head of the House.   London, Leng, 1938.
The White House of Marisaig; or, The Interloper.   London, Leng, 1938.
The Witch in Pink.   London, Leng, 1938.
Double Lives.   London, Leng, 1939.
These Are Our Masters.   London, Hodder and Stoughton, 1939.
A Trust Betrayed.   London, Leng, 1939.
The Uninvited Guest.   London, Leng, 1939.
Peggy Fordyce.   London, Leng, 1940.
Proud Patricia.   London, Leng, 1940.
Rebel Hearts.   London, Leng, 1940.
The Secret of Skye.   London, Leng, 1940.
The Third Generation.   London, Leng, 1940.
Dreams Come True.   London, Leng, 1941.
The Mischief-Makers.   London, Leng, 1941.
The Younger Brother.   London, Leng, 1941.
The Dark House.   London, Leng, 1941.
The Family Name.   London, Leng, 1942.
Who Are the Heathen? London, Hodder and Stoughton, 1942.

Short Stories

Climbing the Hill.   London, Blackie, 1883.

For Lucy's Sake: A Homely Story. London, Partridge, 1883.
Katie's Christmas Lesson. Edinburgh, Oliphant, 1883.
Marion Forsyth; or, Unspotted from the World. Edinburgh, Oliphant, 1883; with *Mistaken*, Cincinnati, Cranston and Stowe, 1892.
Mistaken. Edinburgh, Oliphant, 1883; with *Marion Forsyth*, Cincinnati, Cranston and Stowe, 1892.
Tony's Memorable Christmas. Edinburgh, Oliphant, 1883.
A Year at Coverley. London, Blackie, 1883.
The Bonnie Jean. Glasgow, Scottish Temperance Society, 1884.
Holidays at Sunnycroft. London, Blackie, 1885.
Wilful Winnie. London, Nelson, 1886.
Miss Baxter's Bequest. Edinburgh, Oliphant, 1888.
Climbing the Hill and Other Stories. London, Blackie, 1891.
A Bachelor in Search of a Wife, and Roger Marcham's Ward. Edinburgh, Oliphant, 1892.
The Bonnie Jean and Other Stories. Edinburgh, Oliphant, 1895.
The Secret of Dunston Mere. London, Hodder and Stoughton, 1898.
For the Sake of the Family. London, Hodder and Stoughton, 1898.
An Elder Brother. London, Hodder and Stoughton, 1898.
A Runaway Daughter. London, Hodder and Stoughton, 1898.
The Lady Housekeeper. London, Hodder and Stoughton, 1898.
A Blessing in Disguise. London, Hodder and Stoughton, 1898.
Alone in Paris. London, Hodder and Stoughton, 1898.
The Wedding of Kitty Barton. London, Hodder and Stoughton, 1898.
In Haste to Be Rich. London, Hodder and Stoughton, 1898.
The Dream of Mary Muldoon. London, Hodder and Stoughton, 1898.
Jasper Dennison's Christmas. London, Hodder and Stoughton, 1898.
Seth Newcome's Wife. London, Hodder and Stoughton, 1898.
The False and the True. London, Hodder and Stoughton, 1898.
Stephen Glyn. London, Hodder and Stoughton, 1898.
Married in Haste. London, Hodder and Stoughton, 1898.
What She Could. London, Hodder and Stoughton, 1898.
Sir Roderick's Will: A Love Story. London, Hodder and Stoughton, 1898.
Two Friends. London, Hodder and Stoughton, 1898.
A Married Man. London, Hodder and Stoughton, 1898.
An Only Son. London, Hodder and Stoughton, 1898.
A New Woman. London, Hodder and Stoughton, 1898.
Aunt Anne's Money. London, Hodder and Stoughton, 1898.
After Many Years. London, Hodder and Stoughton, 1899.
A Truant Wife. London, Hodder and Stoughton, 1899.
Good Out of Evil. London, Hodder and Stoughton, 1899.
Gable Farm. London, Hodder and Stoughton, 1899.
A Blessing in Disguise and Other Stories. London, Hodder and Stoughton, 1902.
The False and the True and Other Stories. London, Hodder and Stoughton, 1902.
Good Out of Evil and Other Stories. London, Hodder and Stoughton, 1902.
An Only Son and Other Stories. London, Hodder and Stoughton, 1902.
The Secret of Dunston Mere and Other Stories. London, Hodder and Stoughton, 1902.
Stephen Glyn and Other Stories. London, Hodder and Stoughton, 1902.
The Homecoming of the Boys. Edinburgh, Clark, 1916.
For Lucy's Sake and Other Stories. London, Wright and Brown, 1935.
The Collected Stories of Annie S. Swan. London, Clarke, 1942.

OTHER PUBLICATIONS

Verse

Songs of Memory and Hope. Edinburgh, Nimmo, and New York, Caldwell, 1911; as *Love's Crown*, Nimmo, 1913.

Other

> *Courtship and Marriage, and the Gentle Art of Home-Making.* London, Hutchinson, 1893.
> *Memories of Margaret Grainger, Schoolmistress.* London, Hutchinson, 1896.
> *From a Turret Window.* London, Hodder and Stoughton, 1902.
> *The Outsiders, Being a Sketch of the Social Work of the Salvation Army.* London, Salvation Army, 1905.
> *Letters to a War Bride.* London, Hodder and Stoughton, 1915.
> *An Englishwoman's Home.* New York, Doran, 1918.
> *As Others See Her.* Boston, Houghton Mifflin, 1919; as *America at Home: Impressions of a Visit in War Time*, London, Oliphant, 1920.
> *My Life: An Autobiography.* London, Nicholson and Watson, 1934.
> *We Travel Alone.* London, Nicholson and Watson, 1935.
> *The Land I Love.* London, Nicholson and Watson, 1936.
> *Seed Time and Harvest: The Story of the Hundred Years' Work of the Women's Foreign Mission of the Church of Scotland.* London, Nelson, 1937.
> *The Enchanted Door: A Fireside Philosophy.* London, Nicholson and Watson, 1938.
> *The Letters of Annie S. Swan*, edited by Mildred Robertson Nicoll. London, Hodder and Stoughton, 1945.

*   *   *

Annie Swan was, in her day, in the league of superwriters of romantic fiction, and is said to have written over 250 novels and stories. Her advice was even marketed in non-fiction form. Her works were reprinted as late as the 1950's but today are largely of antiquarian interest, being unreadable by modern standards.

Settings of some of her novels are firmly of their period, such as the family-run department store in *Love, The Master Key* (1905) or the suffragette movement in *Margaret Holroyd* (1910). Some of the backgrounds are historical settings: *A Mask of Gold* (1906), *The Forerunners* (1930), and *Woven of the Wind* (1912) all have early 19th-century Scottish settings. It is not the historical novels which appear so dated, however, but the turn-of-the-century life which is often effectively portrayed, such as the hard-heartedness of City of London financiers in *What Shall It Profit?* (1910), or the penny trams so many of her heroines take and the toques that so many of them wear.

The world that Annie Swan sees is essentially the world seen through women's eyes. This world is often hard ("It's a hard thing to be a woman") on the unemancipated women who live and sometimes work in it. Downtrodden shop assistants and servants get much less out of life than the upper-class ladies who also populate this world, and live by a hard, but also a Christian, fatalism. Pride is fierce and reputation important, even among those who suffer a genteel poverty, as in *Love Unlocks the Door* (1907); this novel also stresses the tight bonds of 19th-century social order. There is much thwarted ambition, thwarted nature, and stifled love in Swan's novels.

Some of the webs of relationships rival in complexity those of the novels of George Eliot but do not contain her intellectual depth. Many of the plots are very contrived in appearance, containing secret marriages and runaway sons and daughters. There are sometimes, as in *Love Unlocks the Door* and *For Lucy's Sake* (1883), violent confrontations between two principal male characters over the love of a girl. As well as some melodrama, there is also plenty of maudlin sentimentality, as in the death of Lucy, the climax of *For Lucy's Sake*, and the use of her gravestone inscription as the last few lines of the story.

The location of many of her books is Scotland and northeast England sometimes serves to add an element of caricature to character portrayal of oppressed women. The picture of Edinburgh in which she portrays the carefully graded strata of Scottish society is particularly authentic. But the use of the dialect "Scotch" language by many characters (sometimes only at unguarded moments) lessens their credibility and also makes the books difficult for the modern reader; the Geordie dialect transliteration is almost incomprehensible. In her later novels, Swan uses less dialogue (*The Pendulum*, 1926), but uses a rather more exaggerated style of description.

Annie Swan had a keen ear for the social groundswell of the period she lived in, and keeps this sense of period updated in her later novels. The characters in the later books tend to be better dressed, higher in the social scale, and English. Swan's characterisation is much improved in her later novels, but this is offset by open invocation of the Christian religion and almost mystical tendencies. Her love scenes are always very chaste.

—P.R. Meldrum

TATE, Ellalice. *See* **HOLT, Victoria**.

TATTERSALL, (Honor) Jill (née Blunt). British. Born in Tintagel, Cornwall, 18 December 1931. Educated privately in England and Switzerland. Married Robin Erskine Tattersall in 1953; four sons. Has worked as gift wrapper, typist, model, actress, receptionist, horse trainer, and nursery school teacher. Agent: Michael Horniman, A.P. Watt Ltd., 26-28 Bedford Row, London WC1R 4HL. Address: 26 East Street, Alresford, Hampshire, England.

ROMANCE AND GOTHIC PUBLICATIONS

Novels

A Summer's Cloud. London, Collins, 1965.
Enchanter's Castle. London, Collins, 1966.
The Midnight Oak. London, Collins, 1967.
Lyonesse Abbey. London, Collins, and New York, Morrow, 1968.
A Time at Tarragon. London, Collins, 1969.
Lady Ingram's Retreat. London, Collins, 1970; as *Lady Ingram's Room*, New York, Morrow, 1981.
Midsummer Masque. London, Collins, and New York, Morrow, 1972.
The Wild Hunt. London, Hodder and Stoughton, and New York, Morrow, 1974.
The Witches of All Saints. London, Hodder and Stoughton, and New York, Morrow, 1975.
The Shadows of Castle Fosse. New York, Morrow, and London, Hodder and Stoughton, 1976.
Chanters Chase. New York, Morrow, and London, Hodder and Stoughton, 1978.
Dark at Noon. New York, Morrow, and London, Hodder and Stoughton, 1979.
Damnation Reef. New York, Morrow, 1979; London, Hodder and Stoughton, 1980.

Jill Tattersall comments:

Mystery and romance in period settings, with detailed backgrounds.

*   *   *

Jill Tattersall's novels present the reader with a complete catalog of the most tried and true gothic literary devices. She skillfully manipulates forbidding castles, malevolent happenings, plucky heroines, and tormented heroes. With these familiar strands she weaves complicated stories, building and sustaining suspense until the very end.

Not unexpectedly, the heroines are beautiful, virtuous young women, who are appealingly feisty. Orphaned or lacking adequate familial protection, they must make their ways in an indifferent or hostile world. Each has a combination of curiosity and courage which enables her to solve the mystery facing her and, in the process, intrigue and attract the brooding, enigmatic hero. It is through the efforts of these inquisitive females that strong men, who are otherwise quite capable, are saved from sinister, ensnaring pasts and bleak futures. In *Lyonesse Abbey* it is Tessa who not only uncovers the secret of Damon's brother, but probes until she learns the truth of his brother's madness. Knowing that it is the result of an accident rather than an inherited flaw frees Damon to lead a normal life as husband and father. Perdita, in *Enchanter's Castle*, is used as the key to unlock the puzzles of the disappearance of Sir Owen and the death of his son, Sir Irwyn. Again, the truth frees her love, Sir Gareth, by cleaning the stains of patricide and suicide from the family honor.

Madness, witchcraft, the supernatural, and legends all play large parts in creating the suspense in Tattersall's books. Sometimes, as in *Chanters Chase*, it is all taken quite seriously, with no "logical" explanations given to dilute the tale involving witchcraft and a sibyl with her crystal ball. In other cases, rational causes for seemingly unexplainable happenings are offered. *Enchanter's Castle* is full of the presence of Arthur, Merlin, and other characters of Welsh legend. While it is the pervasive sense of these mythical and supernatural personages that ultimately is the source of the family tragedy, the actual deaths are the result of direct human action. On occasion, however, Tattersall seems almost to parody these suspenseful devices. The ghoulish band of body snatchers in *The Midnight Oak* becomes much less sinister when revealed to be a group of common smugglers, and Damon's unusual father (*Lyonesse Abbey*) seems to mock the idea of madness when he arrives in full regalia as a Muslim.

Like most authors of gothic tales, Tattersall varies little from the approved formula in terms of actual plots. The similarity in story lines can usually be discerned, but it is very apparent in *A Summer's Cloud* and *The Midnight Oak*. Only the hero and heroine are different in each, and even their problems are basically the same. In *A Summer's Cloud* Henrietta is torn between her love for Lord St. Ives and her patriotic duty to stop his nefarious, possibly traitorous activities. Her cousin, Sophia, faces the same dilemma in *The Midnight Oak* when she falls in love with Guy Carleton whom she believes to be the leader of the resurrectionists. Most of the other characters, all residents of West Mead, Essex, appear in both books, although their roles vary in importance. Perhaps the most surprising thing is that Tattersall chose Sophia as the heroine of the second novel after portraying her as such a spoiled, petulant child in the first.

Jill Tattersall's work must be classified with the gothic genre, but within this formula she has developed a distinct style. While her stories are not strikingly original, they are suspenseful, well-written, and highly entertaining. The willing suspension of disbelief, necessary in reading a gothic novel, is easy to achieve when reading a Tattersall book.

—Barbara Kemp

TEMPEST, Jan. *See* **CHARLES, Theresa**.

TERRY, C.V. *See* **SLAUGHTER, Frank G.**

THANE, Elswyth. American. Born in Burlington, Iowa, 16 May 1900. Married the naturalist William Beebe in 1927 (died, 1962). Journalist and film writer. Agent: Jo Stewart, 201 East 66th Street, New York, New York 10021. Address: Wilmington, Vermont 05363, U.S.A.

ROMANCE AND GOTHIC PUBLICATIONS

Novels (series: Williamsburg)

    Riders of the Wind. New York, Stokes, 1926; London, Murray, 1928.
    Echo Answers. New York, Stokes, and London, Murray, 1927.
    His Elizabeth. New York, Stokes, and London, Murray, 1928.
    Cloth of Gold. New York, Stokes, and London, Murray, 1929.
    Bound to Happen. New York and London, Putnam, 1930.
    Queen's Folly. New York, Harcourt Brace, and London, Constable, 1937.
    Tryst. New York, Harcourt Brace, and London, Constable, 1939.
    Remember Today: Leaves from a Guardian Angel's Notebook. New York, Duell, 1941;
        London, Hale, 1948.
    From This Day Forward. New York, Duell, 1941; London, Hale, 1947.
    Williamsburg series:
        Dawn's Early Light. New York, Duell, 1943; London, Hale, 1945.
        Yankee Stranger. New York, Duell, 1944; London, Hale, 1947.
        Ever After. New York, Duell, 1945; London, Hale, 1948.
        The Light Heart. New York, Duell, 1947; London, Hale, 1950.
        Kissing Kin. New York, Duell, 1948; London, Hale, 1951.
        This Was Tomorrow. New York, Duell, 1951; London, Hale, 1952.
        Homing. New York, Duell, 1957; London, Hale, 1958.
    Melody. New York, Duell, 1950; London, Hale, 1952.
    The Lost General. New York, Duell, 1953; London, Hale, 1954.
    Letter to a Stranger. New York, Duell, 1954; London, Hale, 1955.

Uncollected Short Stories

"Martha," in *Ladies Home Journal* (Philadelphia), February 1954.
"The Bride," in *Ladies Home Journal* (Philadelphia), February 1959.

OTHER PUBLICATIONS

Plays

The Tudor Wench (produced London, 1933). London, French, 1933.
Young Mr. Disraeli (produced London, 1934; New York, 1937). London, French, 1935.
Bound to Happen (produced New York, 1939).

Other

The Tudor Wench. New York, Brewer Warren and Putnam, 1932; London, Hurst and Blackett, 1933.
Young Mr. Disraeli. New York, Harcourt Brace, and London, Constable, 1936.
England Was an Island Once. New York, Harcourt Brace, 1940; London, Constable, 1941.
The Bird Who Made Good. New York, Duell, 1947.
Reluctant Farmer. New York, Duell, 1950; as *The Strength of the Hills*, New York, Christian Herald House, 1976.
The Family Quarrel: A Journey Through the Years of the Revolution. New York, Duell, 1959; London, Hale, 1960.
Washington's Lady. New York, Duell, 1960.
Potomac Squire. New York, Duell, 1963.
Mount Vernon Is Ours: The Story of its Preservation. New York, Duell, 1966.
Mount Vernon: The Legacy: The Story of Its Preservation and Care since 1885. Philadelphia, Lippincott, 1967.
Mount Vernon Family (juvenile). New York, Macmillan, 1968.
The Virginia Colony (juvenile). New York, Macmillan, 1969.
Dolley Madison: Her Life and Times. New York, Macmillan, 1970.
The Fighting Quaker: Nathanael Greene. New York, Hawthorn, 1972.

*   *   *

Elswyth Thane is a prolific writer notable for the variety of her work. While she has written a number of contemporary romantic novels in addition to her well-known biographies, she has achieved greatest success with her historical romances, especially the popular Williamsburg novels. Her early works, all set in England, are improbably romantic adventures, in which briefly sketched characters move through confusing plots. *Queen's Folly* was the first work to break out of this mold with some success, and also introduced a supernatural theme which was to recur in Thane's later work. The characters in *Queen's Folly* are rather less fanciful than their predecessors, but Thane's major breakthrough is in her use of historical settings. Her most successful and most popular works combine her love of England and her ability convincingly to depict the past in love stores which still charm modern readers.

The Williamsburg novels follow the fortunes of the intertwined Day-Sprague-Campion families from just before the American Revolution to the London blitz in the Second World War. Her characters experience the Revolutionary War (*Dawn's Early Light*), the Civil War (*Yankee Stranger*), the Spanish-American War (*Ever After*), World War I (*The Light Heart*), the rise of the Nazis (*Kissing Kin* and *This Was Tomorrow*), and the early stages of World War II (*Homing*). The plots are organized around historical events which Thane takes pains to describe accurately. Her descriptions of Williamsburg, New York in the 1890's, and the Cotswolds are quite detailed, and provide depth to the novels. While there are no real villains

(Prince Conrad in the *The Light Heart* and his son, Victor, in *This Was Tomorrow* come close, but are tragically flawed rather than utterly wicked), war and totalitarianism are the serious threats to her lovers' happiness. The Williamsburg novels should be read as part of a series, although the first three can stand on their own.

For all Thane's characters, family is tremendously important, and her few orphans (Julian in *Dawn's Early Light*, Gwen and Dinah in *Ever After*) find not just mates, but roots and well-branched family trees. The men are brave in battle and crisis, and they are portrayed as level-headed fellows used to taking charge and coping with major and minor tragedies. Many are journalists (Julian Day is a writer, Cabot and Bracken Murray and Jeff Day are newsmen), a device which allows them to observe and comment on the historical events of their periods. Thane's women are occasionally independent (Phoebe Sprague in *The Light Heart* is a writer) but are happy to settle down in blissful domesticity after their romantic adventures. From that secure position they can occasionally aid the next generation in its respective romantic involvements. Thane's heroines are frequently in need of rescue—from a drunken father, Yankee soldiers, the wreck of the Lusitania, even the snares of a Nazi spy—by her capable and experienced heroes. The lovers feel passion, but consummate their love discreetly within marriage—these novels are not "bodice-rippers." In *Homing* the hero and heroine are reincarnations of Julian and Tibby, the main characters of the first Williamsburg novel (*Dawn's Early Light*), and the rescue is mutual. Mab/Tibby saves Jeff/Julian from his depression while he in turn rescues her from her own fears.

Elswyth Thane used her own experiences and her careful historical research to enrich her work, so that her historical novels are somewhat denser and more compelling than others of the genre. Her attractive and likeable characters are easy to care for, and Thane's readers are carried into a happy world where men are true and women are gentle, and where true love triumphs, despite the adversities of war and revolution. The modern reader may be occasionally jarred to encounter stereotypes like the happy loyal slaves of the Williamsburg novels, but Thane's intent is to entertain, not to expose the less attractive aspects of the past.

—Mary C. Lynn

THORNE, Nicola. *See* **ELLERBECK, Rosemary**.

THORPE, Kay. Address: c/o Mills and Boon Ltd., 15-16 Brooks Mews, London W1A 1DR, England.

Novels

Devon Interlude. London, Mills and Boon, 1968; Toronto, Harlequin, 1969.
The Last of the Mallorys. London, Mills and Boon, and Toronto, Harlequin, 1968.
Opportune Marriage. London, Mills and Boon, 1968; Toronto, Harlequin, 1975.
Rising Star. London, Mills and Boon, and Toronto, Harlequin, 1969.
Curtain Call. London, Mills and Boon, and Toronto, Harlequin, 1971.
Not Wanted on Voyage. London, Mills and Boon, and Toronto, Harlequin, 1972.
Olive Island. London, Mills and Boon, 1972; Toronto, Harlequin, 1973.
Sawdust Season. London, Mills and Boon, and Toronto, Harlequin, 1972.
Man in a Box. London, Mills and Boon, 1972.
An Apple in Eden. London, Mills and Boon, 1973; Toronto, Harlequin, 1974.
The Man at Kambala. London, Mills and Boon, 1973; Toronto, Harlequin, 1974.
Remember This Stranger. London, Mills and Boon, 1974.
The Iron Man. London, Mills and Boon, 1974; Toronto, Harlequin, 1975.
The Shifting Sands. London, Mills and Boon, and Toronto, Harlequin, 1975.
Sugar Cane Harvest. London, Mills and Boon, 1975; Toronto, Harlequin, 1976.
The Royal Affair. Toronto, Harlequin, 1976.
Safari South. London, Mills and Boon, 1976; Toronto, Harlequin, 1977.
The River Lord. Toronto, Harlequin, 1977.
Storm Passage. Toronto, Harlequin, 1977.
Lord of La Pampa. London, Mills and Boon, 1977; Toronto, Harlequin, 1978.
Bitter Alliance. London, Mills and Boon, 1978.
Full Circle. London, Mills and Boon, 1978.
Timber Boss. London, Mills and Boon, and Toronto, Harlequin, 1978.
The Wilderness Trail. London, Mills and Boon, 1978; Toronto, Harlequin, 1979.
Caribbean Encounter. Toronto, Harlequin, 1978.
The Dividing Line. London, Mills and Boon, 1979; Toronto, Harlequin, 1980.
The Man from Tripoli. London, Mills and Boon, and Toronto, Harlequin, 1979.
This Side of Paradise. London, Mills and Boon, 1979; Toronto, Harlequin, 1980.
Chance Meeting. London, Mills and Boon, and Toronto, Harlequin, 1980.
No Passing Fancy. London, Mills and Boon, 1980.
Copper Lake. London, Mills and Boon, and Toronto, Harlequin, 1981.
Floodtide. Toronto, Harlequin, 1981.

* * *

Kay Thorpe's slow but steady output of series romances since 1968 includes a number of carefully crafted formula stories. She is particularly adept at portraying heroines in interesting professions and at writing novels that hinge upon successive misunderstandings and misinterpretations between potential lovers. Her books move swiftly and maintain their suspense.

In some books, her heroines are "spoiled brats," too immature to sustain adult relationships. Inevitably, they behave badly and alienate their lovers or husbands. In others, she portrays women who are misinterpreted as "gold diggers," who must somehow convince the heroes to trust them. She sets her novels in exciting and interesting places: the theatre, the circus, a cruise ship, a department store, or a newspaper office. Her women are usually competent in their fields, even though they must be instructed in love by the heroes.

An unusual feature of Thorpe's romances is that she sometimes leaves the relationship with room to grow at the end of the book. Most other series romance writers describe a complete reconciliation by the final page, but Thorpe does not always wrap up the ends so neatly. In *Bitter Alliance* and *Floodtide* her heroes at the end have not learned the difference between "wanting" and "loving," a critical issue in most series romances, for without an acknowledgement of that distinction, no self-respecting heroine can submit sexually to the hero. Thorpe's heroines remain confident that the hero will change in time and so they agree to be patient.

Because Thorpe is less prolific than many of her colleagues, her novels are sometimes more complex than theirs. She has been prominent as a series writer because of the care with which she constructs her plots.

—Kay Mussell

THORPE, Sylvia. Pseudonym for June Sylvia Thimblethorpe. Born in London, in 1926. Educated at a school in Brondesbury, Kilburn High School for Girls, Slade School of Fine Arts, and University College, all London. Secretary, 1949-52; school teacher, 1952-53. Recipient: Romantic Novelists Association Historical Award, 1971. Address: c/o Hutchinson Publishing Group Ltd., 17-21 Conway Street, London W1P 5HL, England.

ROMANCE AND GOTHIC PUBLICATIONS

Novels

The Scandalous Lady Robin. London, Hutchinson, 1950; New York, Fawcett, 1975.
The Sword and the Shadow. London, Hutchinson, 1951; New York, Fawcett, 1976.
Beggar on Horseback. London, Hutchinson, 1953; New York, Fawcett, 1977.
Smugglers' Moon. London, Rich and Cowan, 1955; as *Strangers on the Moor*, New York, Pyramid, 1966.
The Golden Panther. London, Rich and Cowan, 1956; New York, Fawcett, 1976.
Sword of Vengeance. London, Rich and Cowan, 1957; New York, Fawcett, 1977.
Rogues' Covenant. London, Hurst and Blackett, 1957; New York, Fawcett, 1976.
Captain Gallant. London, Hurst and Blackett, 1958; New York, Fawcett, 1978.
Beloved Rebel. London, Hurst and Blackett, 1959; New York, Fawcett, 1978.
Romantic Lady. London, Hurst and Blackett, 1960; New York, Fawcett, 1976.
The Devil's Bondsman. London, Hurst and Blackett, 1961; New York, Fawcett, 1980.
The Highwayman. London, Hurst and Blackett, 1962; New York, Fawcett, 1979.
The House at Bell Orchard. London, Hurst and Blackett, 1962; New York, Fawcett, 1979.
The Reluctant Adventuress. London, Hurst and Blackett, 1963; New York, Fawcett, 1974.
Fair Shine the Day. London, Hurst and Blackett, 1964; New York, Fawcett, 1977.
Spring Will Come Again. London, Hurst and Blackett, 1965; New York, Fawcett, 1974.
The Changing Tide. London, Hurst and Blackett, 1967; New York, Fawcett, 1978.
Dark Heritage. London, Hurst and Blackett, 1968; as *Tarrington Chase*, London, Corgi, 1977.
No More A-Roving. London, Hurst and Blackett, 1970; New York, Fawcett, 1979.
The Scarlet Domino. London, Hurst and Blackett, 1970; New York, Fawcett, 1975.
The Scapegrace. London, Hurst and Blackett, 1971; New York, Fawcett, 1978.
Dark Enchantress. London, Hurst and Blackett, 1973; New York, Fawcett, 1980.
The Silver Nightingale. London, Hurst and Blackett, and New York, Fawcett, 1974.
The Witches of Conyngton. London, Hurst and Blackett, 1976.
A Flash of Scarlet. New York, Fawcett, 1978.
The Varleigh Medallion. London, Hurst and Blackett, and New York, Fawcett, 1979.
The Avenhurst Inheritance. London, Hutchinson, 1981.

*   *   *

June Sylvia Thimblethorpe, better known as Sylvia Thorpe, is a very prolific historical novelist. Her stories are marked by careful attention to historical detail and extremely well-drawn characters.

Her Regency romances are among the best written. Combining romance with adventure and intrigue, they are filled with believable, sympathetic people. *The Silver Nightingale* is both a mystery and a love story in which snowbound travelers are threatened by a killer. Justin, Lord Chayle, must flush out the murderer in order to protect his fiancée, Sarah. In *Romantic Lady* Caroline's impetuousness leads her into danger and involves Guy Ravenshaw in several rescues in spite of himself. Thorpe's ladies are spirited and courageous, and are suitable mates for their dashing partners.

Similar in nature to the Regencies are Thorpe's Georgian romances. The same mixture of romance and adventure is present, with slightly more emphasis on forceful action as befits an earlier age. The heroes tend to be more roguish in these novels. The hero of *Captain Gallant* is a daring highwayman. Geraint St. Arvan (*The Scarlet Domino*) is taken from the Common Debtors' Ward in Newgate to marry Antonia. Philip Digby in *Rogues' Covenant* has a mysterious past that leads to violence. In spite of these flaws (which really make the characters more interesting), these men are reformed, or at least captured, by the love of their heroines.

Many of Thorpe's historical romances are set in even earlier times. The Commonwealth under Cromwell is not one of the most popular eras for historical novelists to use, but it provides extremely fertile ground for Thorpe's imagination. The exiles and wanderers created by the English Civil War provide excellent material for action-packed tales of rogues and pirates. Set against the lush tropical background of the Caribbean, bold love stories come alive in the true swashbuckling tradition. Using a place and time of violent men, Thorpe wisely puts more focus on the men in these stories, but does so without slighting the women or diluting the romance. Thorpe's talent can be seen in the fact that women can read these novels for the romance, while men can enjoy an escape to high adventure. *The Golden Panther, No More A-Roving, The Devil's Bondsman*, and *The Sword and the Shadow* are all examples of Thorpe's ability to portray some rousing action.

In sum, Sylvia Thorpe is a consummate storyteller. Her craftsmanship is evident in each of her novels, raising them above standard formula stories. Many authors could learn a great deal about writing historical romances by reading her books.

—Barbara Kemp

TRANTER, Nigel (Godwin). Also writes as Nye Tredgold. British. Born in Glasgow, Scotland, 23 November 1909. Educated at St. James's Episcopal School, Edinburgh, 3 years; George Heriot's School, Edinburgh, 9 years. Served in the Royal Artillery during World War II: Lieutenant. Married May Jean Campbell Grieve in 1933; one daughter, and one son (dead). Accountant and inspector in family insurance company, Edinburgh, 1929-39. Since 1946, full-time writer, broadcaster, and lecturer. Chairman, Scottish Convention, Edinburgh, 1948-51; Scottish President, P.E.N., 1962-66; Scottish Chairman, Society of Authors, 1966-74, and National Book League, 1973-78. M.A.: Edinburgh University, 1971. Knight Commander, Order of St. Lazarus of Jerusalem, 1961. Address: Quarry House, Aberlady, East Lothian EH32 0QB, Scotland.

Novels

Trespass. Edinburgh, Moray Press, 1937.
Mammon's Daughter. London, Ward Lock, 1939.
Harsh Heritage. London, Ward Lock, 1939.
Eagles Feathers. London, Ward Lock, 1941.
Watershed. London, Ward Lock, 1941.
The Gilded Fleece. London, Ward Lock, 1942.
Delayed Action. London, Ward Lock, 1944.
Tinker's Pride. London, Ward Lock, 1945.
Man's Estate. London, Ward Lock, 1946.
Flight of Dutchmen. London, Ward Lock, 1947.
Island Twilight. London, Ward Lock, 1947.
Root and Branch. London, Ward Lock, 1948.
Colours Flying. London, Ward Lock, 1948.
The Chosen Course. London, Ward Lock, 1949.
Fair Game. London, Ward Lock, 1950.
High Spirits. London, Collins, 1950.
The Freebooters. London, Ward Lock, 1950.
Tidewrack. London, Ward Lock, 1951.
Fast and Loose. London, Ward Lock, 1951.
Bridal Path. London, Ward Lock, 1952.
Cheviot Chase. London, Ward Lock, 1952.
Ducks and Drakes. London, Ward Lock, 1953.
The Queen's Grace. London, Ward Lock, 1953.
Rum Week. London, Ward Lock, 1954.
The Night Riders. London, Ward Lock, 1954.
There Are Worse Jungles. London, Ward Lock, 1955.
Rio d'Oro. London, Ward Lock, 1955.
The Long Coffin. London, Ward Lock, 1956.
MacGregor's Gathering. London, Hodder and Stoughton, 1957.
The Enduring Flame. London, Hodder and Stoughton, 1957.
Balefire. London, Hodder and Stoughton, 1958.
The Stone. London, Hodder and Stoughton, 1958; New York, Putnam, 1959.
The Man Behind the Curtain. London, Hodder and Stoughton, 1959.
The Clansman. London, Hodder and Stoughton, 1959.
Spanish Galleon. London, Hodder and Stoughton, 1960.
The Flockmasters. London, Hodder and Stoughton, 1960.
Kettle of Fish. London, Hodder and Stoughton, 1961.
The Master of Gray. London, Hodder and Stoughton, 1961.
Drug on the Market. London, Hodder and Stoughton, 1962.
Gold for Prince Charlie. London, Hodder and Stoughton, 1962.
The Courtesan. London, Hodder and Stoughton, 1963.
Chain of Destiny. London, Hodder and Stoughton, 1964.
Past Master. London, Hodder and Stoughton, 1965.
A Stake in the Kingdom. London, Hodder and Stoughton, 1966.
Lion Let Loose. London, Hodder and Stoughton, 1967.
Cable from Kabul. London, Hodder and Stoughton, 1968.
Black Douglas. London, Hodder and Stoughton, 1968.
Robert the Bruce:
    The Steps to the Empty Throne. London, Hodder and Stoughton, 1969; New York, St. Martin's Press, 1971.
    The Path of the Hero King. London, Hodder and Stoughton, 1970; New York, St. Martin's Press, 1973.
    The Price of the King's Peace. London, Hodder and Stoughton, 1971; New York, St. Martin's Press, 1973.

The Young Montrose. London, Hodder and Stoughton, 1972.
Montrose, The Captain-General. London, Hodder and Stoughton, 1973.
The Wisest Fool. London, Hodder and Stoughton, 1974.
The Wallace. London, Hodder and Stoughton, 1975.
Stuart Trilogy:
  Lords of Misrule. London, Hodder and Stoughton, 1976.
  A Folly of Princes. London, Hodder and Stoughton, 1977.
  The Captive King. London, Hodder and Stoughton, 1977.
Macbeth the King. London, Hodder and Stoughton, 1978.
Margaret the Queen. London, Hodder and Stoughton, 1979.
David the Prince. London, Hodder and Stoughton, 1980.
True Thomas. London, Hodder and Stoughton, 1981.
The Patriot. London, Hodder and Stoughton, 1982.

OTHER PUBLICATIONS

Novels as Nye Tredgold

Thirsty Range. London, Ward Lock, 1949.
Heartbreak Valley. London, Ward Lock, 1950.
The Big Corral. London, Ward Lock, 1952.
Trail Herd. London, Ward Lock, 1952.
Desert Doublecross. London, Ward Lock, 1953.
Cloven Hooves. London, Ward Lock, 1954.
Dynamite Trail. London, Ward Lock, 1955.
Rancher Renegade. London, Ward Lock, 1956.
Trailing Trouble. London, Ward Lock, 1957.
Dead Reckoning. London, Ward Lock, 1957.
Bloodstone Trail. London, Ward Lock, 1958.

Other (juvenile)

Spaniards' Isle. Leicester, Brockhampton Press, 1958.
Border Rising. Leicester, Brockhampton Press, 1959.
Nestor the Monster. Leicester, Brockhampton Press, 1960.
Birds of a Feather. Leicester, Brockhampton Press, 1961.
The Deer Poachers. London, Blackie, 1961.
Something Very Fishy. London, Collins, 1962.
Give a Dog a Bad Name. London, Collins, 1963; New York, Platt and Munk, 1964.
Silver Island. London, Nelson, 1964.
Smoke Across the Highlands. New York, Platt and Munk, 1964.
Pursuit. London, Collins, 1965.
Fire and High Water. London, Collins, 1967.
Tinker Tess. London, Dobson, 1967.
To the Rescue. London, Dobson, 1968.

Other

The Fortalices and Early Mansions of Southern Scotland 1400-1650. Edinburgh, Moray Press, 1935.
The Fortified House in Scotland. Edinburgh, Oliver and Boyd, 4 vols., 1962-66; London, Chambers, 1 vol., 1970.
The Pegasus Book of Scotland. London, Dobson, 1964.
Outlaw of The highlands: Rob Roy. London, Dobson, 1965.

Land of the Scots. London, Hodder and Stoughton, and New York, Weybright and
   Talley, 1968.
The Queen's Scotland. London, Hodder and Stoughton, 4 vols., 1971-77.
Portrait of the Border Country. London, Hale, 1972.
Portrait of the Lothians. London, Hale, 1979.
Nigel Tranter's Scotland: A Very Personal View. Glasgow, Drew, 1981.

Editor, *No Tigers in the Hindu Kush*, by Philip Tranter. London, Hodder and
   Stoughton, 1968.

Manuscript Collection: National Library of Scotland, Edinburgh.

Nigel Tranter comments:

Wrote ordinary novels of adventure and romance, usually set in Scotland, from 1938
onwards, including four written in army during active service. In 1961 wrote *The Master of
Gray*, first of long and carefully researched historical novels, since when have concentrated on
these, in an attempt to cover most of the spectrum of Scotland's colourful and dramatic story,
in a way which would make it palatable for the ordinary reader who would seldom open a
"straight" history book. Have endeavoured to stick closely to fact as far as possible with the
very minimum of invented characters.

*   *   *

Nigel Tranter is a prolific writer of historical novels dealing with almost every aspect and
every period of Scottish history—indeed to read his books is to take a painless course in that
subject. He is obviously a scrupulous and indefatigable researcher, setting great store by
accuracy, and he turns history into novels by adding romantic fiction to historical fact. For
instance, in *Gold for Prince Charlie* the historical fact that the French gold which was sent to
Scotland in 1745 arrived too late to be of use in the Jacobite rebellion is used to make an
exciting adventure for Duncan McGregor and Caroline Cameron. In *MacGregor's Gathering*
he uses the facts that Rob Roy strove to get the proscription of the clan lifted and that he was
against the Act of Union, but adds to that the love story of Rob Roy's nephew. *The Clansman*
is Tranter's interpretation of Rob Roy's behaviour at Sherrifmuir when he did not fight but
held the MacGregors immobile in the midst of battle.

But Tranter's real forte is the fictional biography. He has covered practically the whole
conspectus of Scottish history in a series of biographical novels, beginning in the Celtic twilight
with *Macbeth the King*, in which he gives us something different from the dramatic but
inaccurate picture drawn by Shakespeare and puts Macbeth where he belongs in Scottish
history. In *Margaret the Queen* he draws a portrait of the Saxon princess who married
Malcolm Canmore and civilised the Scottish court. Margaret was made a saint but she emerges
from the book as a warm human being. *David the Prince* tells of Scotland in the 12th century,
and the 13th century is covered by *True Thomas*, a book which puts at the centre the legendary
Thomas the Rhymer, poet and prophet, rather than Alexander III, although we learn his story
too. *The Wallace* continues the account of that bleak, cruel era when England and Scotland
were perpetually at war. Wallace is, of course, one of Scotland's great heroes and is so
portrayed by Tranter, and Edward I (known to English history as Longshanks and Lawgiver
and above all Hammer of the Scots) emerges as a double-dyed villain. All these books lead up
to Robert the Bruce, the most famous Scottish king who is known even to English children
because of the spider—Tranter takes three books to tell his story, *The Steps to the Empty
Throne*, *The Path of the Hero King*, and *The Price of the King's Peace*.

There are many more historical novels: the rise of the house of Stuart is covered in *Lords of
Misrule*, *A Folly of Princes*, and *The Captive Crown*, and so it goes on through the years. *Lion
Let Loose* tells of James I, *Chain of Destiny* James IV, and his series featuring the Master of
Grey contrasts the Tudor court of Elizabeth with the Scottish court. All these books are
craftsmanlike works with accurate history, but alas with no great sense of period. You do not

get the feeling which some novelists convey that through the eyes of the main character you are looking at a very different scene, living at a different period, assessing things differently because the values of that character are different from your own. You never seem to get inside the skins of the people of earlier times. The dialogue is stilted and often very strangely punctuated. Although I admire his industry and his accuracy, Nigel Tranter's books do not come alive for me.

—Pamela Cleaver

TROLLOPE, Joanna. Pseudonym for Joanna Potter; also writes as Caroline Harvey. British. Born in England, 9 December 1943. Educated at St. Hugh's College, Oxford (Gamble Scholar), 1962-65, M.A. Married David Potter in 1966; two daughters. Since 1968, teacher in preparatory schools and adult and foreign student classes. Agent: A.D. Peters, 10 Buckingham Street, London WC2N 6BU. Address: 16 William Mews, Lowndes Square, London S.W.1, England.

ROMANCE AND GOTHIC PUBLICATIONS

Novels

Eliza Stanhope. London, Hutchinson, 1978; New York, Dutton, 1979.
Parson Harding's Daughter. London, Hutchinson, 1979; as *Mistaken Virtues*, New York, Dutton, 1980.
Leaves from the Valley. London, Hutchinson, 1980.
Charlotte, Alexandra (as Caroline Harvey). London, Octopus, 1980.
The City of Gems. London, Hutchinson, 1981.

Joanna Trollope comments:

There are, certainly, love stories in my books, but they are only a part of the whole. The whole is my desire to bring history to life, not just to superimpose a 20th-century story on to a historical background. I want to give a sense of life as it was lived in the past, and to that end I do more than twice as much research as I need for each book so that I am, myself, thoroughly familiar with each period.

*   *   *

Joanna Trollope writes good historical novels, with a foundation of solid research which never obtrudes.

Her first, *Eliza Stanhope*, is loosely based on the experiences of the wife of one of Wellington's ADCs, who married for love—a comparatively unusual event in those days. In Trollope's story, after a brief period of marital bliss Captain Francis Beaumont, recalled to the colours when Napoleon escapes from Elba, takes his wife with him to Brussels. Trollope writes dazzlingly about the gay life of the city as the Battle of Waterloo draws near, about the famous Ball held on the actual eve of fighting, and also about the battle itself—for Eliza, disguised as an ensign, follows her beloved Francis to the field of Waterloo, where, her thin disguise soon penetrated, she is recruited to help one of the surgeons in his awful task of salvaging what lives he can.

Trollope writes equally well about love and battles—an unusual combination of talents. *Eliza Stanhope* is a highly accomplished novel, written with sensitivity, charm, and a real feeling for the period. The characters live, and have individuality. As a first novel it was astonishing; but it was followed by three more, each in its turn an advance on the previous books. All are quite different.

Parson Harding's Daughter, which won the Romantic Novelists Association Major Award, is set largely in the India of Warren Hastings; *Leaves from the Valley* adheres closely to the events of the Crimean War. *The City of Gems*, her most ambitious novel, is set against the unusual background of Mandalay in the 1880's, when the rule of King Thibaw and Queen Supayalat of the Kingdom of Ava in Upper Burma is nearing its imperious end. Meanwhile the couple dominate the squalid, exotic city and enthral beautiful, arrogant Maria Beresford, English daughter of a failed tea-planter—one of Trollope's most inspired—and exasperating— heroines, whose expectation of admiration and submission is absolute, but who seems incapable of accepting or giving affection. Likewise the hero, Archie Tennant, is one of the most fully realised and likeable of the author's characters. And the feeling of mounting tension as the social order disintegrates is handled with firm assurance.

As Caroline Harvey, Joanna Trollope writes stories in a lighter vein, with nice touches of humour. So far only two have been published, jointly in one paperback volume. *Charlotte* has the background of Victorian Afghanistan—a lovely, rip-roaring yarn told with gusto and obvious enjoyment, about the sort of intrepid English woman of that period who threw convention to the winds and as a result had a gloriously colourful, adventurous and rewarding life. *Alexandra* is about her Edwardian grand-daughter who, inheriting a residual lawlessness, takes off from her home in a Scottish castle for Cornwall, where she resolutely does her own thing—her "thing" being quite different from her Grannie's. Although written more lightly, these two stories are just as successful as those by Joanna Trollope, and written with just as much care.

—Elizabeth Grey

TORDAY, Ursula. *See* **BLACKSTOCK, Charity.**

TROY, Katherine. *See* **MAYBURY, Anne.**

VAIZEY, Mrs. George de Horne (Jessie Bell Vaizey, née Mansergh).   British.   Born in 1857.

ROMANCE AND GOTHIC PUBLICATIONS

Novels

> *A Rose-Coloured Thread.*   London, Bowden, 1898.
> *About Peggy Saville.*   London, Religious Tract Society, 1900; New York, Putnam, 1917.
> *Sisters Three.*   London and New York, Cassell, 1900.
> *Tom and Some Other Girls: A Public School Story.*   London and New York, Cassell, 1901.
> *More about Peggy.*   London, Religious Tract Society, 1901.
> *A Houseful of Girls.*   London, Religious Tract Society, 1902.
> *Pixie O'Shaughnessy.*   London, Religious Tract Society, 1903; Philadelphia, Jacobs, 1907.
> *More about Pixie.*   London, Religious Tract Society, 1903.
> *The Daughters of a Genius: Story of a Brave Endeavour.*   London, Chambers, and Philadelphia, Lippincott, 1903.
> *How Like the King.*   London, Bousfield, 1905.
> *The Heart of Una Sackville.*   London, Partridge, 1907.
> *The Fortunes of the Farrells.*   London, Religious Tract Society, 1907; Philadelphia, Jacobs, 1908.
> *Betty Trevor.*   London, Religious Tract Society, 1907; New York, Putnam, 1917.
> *Big Game: A Story for Girls.*   London, Religious Tract Society, 1908.
> *Flaming June.*   London, Cassell, 1908.
> *The Conquest of Chrystabel.*   London, Cassell, 1909.
> *A Question of Marriage.*   London, Hodder and Stoughton, 1910; New York, Putnam, 1911.
> *Etheldreda the Ready: A School Story.*   London and New York, Cassell, 1910.
> *Cynthia Charrington.*   London and New York, Cassell, 1911.
> *A Honeymoon in Hiding.*   London and New York, Cassell, 1911.
> *The Adventures of Billie Belshaw.*   London, Mills and Boon, 1912.
> *A College Girl.*   London, Religious Tract Society, 1913; New York, Putnam, 1916.
> *An Unknown Lover.*   London, Mills and Boon, and New York, Putnam, 1913.
> *Grizel Married.*   London, Mills and Boon, 1914; as *Lady Cassandra*, New York, Putnam, 1914.
> *The Love Affairs of Pixie.*   London, Religious Tract Society, 1914.
> *Salt of Life.*   London, Mills and Boon, 1915.
> *The Independence of Claire.*   London, Religious Tract Society, 1915.
> *The Lady of the Basement Flat.*   London, Religious Tract Society, 1917.
> *Harriet Mannering's Paying Guests.*   London, Mills and Boon, 1917.

Short Stories

> *Old Friends and New.*   London, Hodder and Stoughton, 1909.
> *What a Man Wills.*   London, Cassell, and New York, Putnam, 1915.
> *The Right Arm and Other Stories.*   London, Mills and Boon, 1918.

*   *   *

Most of Mrs. de Horne Vaizey's novels dealt with "the essence of femininity in the springtide of life," and several were originally serialised in the *Girl's Own Paper*. They cannot, however, be classified as juvenile fiction but are essentially light Edwardian romances designed to appeal both to teenage girls and adult women.

For their time, the stories were refreshingly vigorous. Mrs. Vaizey sent a string of heroines to college or to embark upon careers, although she actually disapproved of women's suffrage, and considered that men should manage the country and the business world. Even the most lively of her girls would eventually be forced into the realization that a woman's place was firmly in "the shelter of her lover's arms" and subsequently, of course, in acquiescent domesticity.

Her most perceptive and rewarding book is *The Independence of Claire*, which vividly highlights a 19-year-old high-school teacher's struggles against poverty and prejudice, from which romance happily provides the ultimate escape. However, her most loved character is without doubt Pixie O'Shaughnessy, "the wild Irish tornado." Pixie must have been one of the first of the irrepressible Irish heroines who were eventually to become stock figures in the English light fiction genre. She progresses from exuberant schoolgirl—"the joy and terror of the school," in fact—to elegant adult in the course of the three books that describe her exploits.

These and the Peggy Saville stories were the most popular of Mrs. Vaizey's works, but the author preferred *Salt of Life*, which was based on the experiences of her own family and friends. This is a perceptive and witty story about two families of girls on the threshold of adult life and romance. The romantic threads in her family sagas are low key rather than lush, but nevertheless effective. And at least the male characters for whom her heroines abdicate all their career ambitions are three-dimensional people, and not simply the cyphers of simplistic (and boring) masculinity that are featured in more run-of-the-mill romantic novels.

—Mary Cadogan

VAN SLYKE, Helen (Lenore, née Vogt). Also wrote as Sharon Ashton. American. Born in Washington, D.C., 9 July 1919. Married William Woodward Van Slyke in 1946 (divorced, 1952). Fashion Editor, Washington *Evening Star*, 1938-43; Beauty Editor, 1945-55, and Promotion Director, 1955-60, *Glamour* magazine, New York; Promotion and Advertising Director, Henri Bendel, New York, 1960-61; Vice-President and Creative Director, Norman Craig and Kummel, advertising agency, New York, 1961-63; President, House of Fragrance (Genesco), New York, 1963-68; Vice-President for Creative Activities, Helena Rubinstein, New York, 1968-72; then full-time writer and lecturer. *Died in 1979.*

ROMANCE AND GOTHIC PUBLICATIONS

Novels

The Rich and the Righteous. New York, Doubleday, 1971; London, Cassell, 1972.
All Visitors Must Be Announced. New York, Doubleday, 1972; London, Cassell, 1973; as *The Best People*, New York, Popular Library, 1976.
The Heart Listens. New York, Doubleday, 1973; London, New English Library, 1974.
The Santa Ana Wind (as Sharon Ashton). New York, Doubleday, 1974; London, New English Library, 1975.
The Mixed Blessing. New York, Doubleday, 1975; London, New English Library, 1976.
The Best Place to Be. New York, Doubleday, and London, New English Library, 1976.
Always Is Not Forever. New York, Doubleday, 1977; London, New English Library, 1978.
Sisters and Strangers. New York, Doubleday, 1978; London, Heinemann, 1979.
A Necessary Woman. New York, Doubleday, and London, Heinemann, 1979.

No Love Lost. Philadelphia, Lippincott, and London, Heinemann, 1980.
Public Smiles, Private Tears, completed by James Elward. New York, Harper, 1982.

*   *   *

Helen Van Slyke viewed her books pragmatically: "perhaps what I write is romantic, sentimental nonsense, but if two million or more people want to read it, that's important. If you're in a business, you should act as if you're in a business, with something to sell, and every now and then you must forget about artistic merit. I know I don't write literature, for heaven's sake...."

What she did write and promote are phenomenally successful "women's novels," which she referred to as "soap operas between covers." Only the first book has a man as its central character. In the rest, the main characters are women who are usually affluent and often middle-aged. They confront problems familiar to the contemporary reader. Sheila Callahan in *The Best Place to Be* faces widowhood. Alice Winters (*Sister and Strangers*) is married to a wife beater. Charlene Jenkins (*The Heart Listens*) is married to a black man, and her daughter Toni (*The Mixed Blessing*) must resolve identity problems resulting from her inter-racial heritage. Mary Morgan (*A Necessary Woman*) has to deal with her successful career and a weak husband.

Like Mary, Van Slyke's women are generally stronger than their male counterparts. Some of them use their strength to help others. Elizabeth Quigly (*The Heart Listens* and *The Mixed Blessing*) works indefatigably for her family and friends. Others use their power to destroy people's lives. Mary Morgan's sister Pat seduces Mary's husband to hurt her sister.

Although Van Slyke's women enjoy sex, they are more likely to remain faithful to their marriage commitments than are their husbands, many of whom assume that extramarital liaisons are a male prerogative. In *No Love Lost* that attitude eventually drives Pauline Thresher to leave her husband—with her mother-in-law's support.

Van Slyke's women need and like men, but they also have strong relationships with other women. A letter from her daughter helps Sheila Callahan resolve a long-standing conflict with her own mother. Relationships between sisters are explored in *A Necessary Woman* and *Sisters and Strangers*. The importance of friendship between women is evident in *Always Is Not Forever*. Susan Langdon's former boss is honest enough to help Susan confront her drinking problem, marital difficulties, and need for an identity apart from her husband.

But the exploration of character never dominates Van Slyke's action-filled stories. Like the soap operas to which she compared her books, her plots include one crisis after another. Van Slyke believed in "the power of storytelling" to reach her readers with a tale "that is comprehensible within the realm of their own experience." The popularity of her books bears witness to her success in meeting her goal.

—Kathy Piehl

VERYAN, Patricia. Pseudonym for Patricia V. Bannister. British/American (dual citizenship). Born in London, England, 21 November 1923. Educated at Mitcham Central Girls School, Surrey, 1934-37; Miss Lodge Secretarial School, London, 1937-38. Married Allan Louis Berg in 1946 (died, 1980); one daughter and one son. Secretary, Navy, Army, and Air Force Institutes, London, 1938-40, Columbia Pictures, London, 1940-42, United States Army, London, Paris, and Frankfurt, 1942-46, Pacific Telephone, Sacramento, California, 1949, National Cash Register Company, Los Angeles, 1950, Southern Counties Gas Company, Los Angeles, 1951-52, and Humble Oil and Refining Company, Los Angeles, 1952-55. Since 1971,

Secretary for Graduate Affairs, University of California, Riverside. Agent: Richard Curtis, Richard Curtis Associates, 156 East 52nd Street, New York, New York 10022. Address: 6111 Del Ray Court, Riverside, California 92506, U.S.A.

ROMANCE AND GOTHIC PUBLICATIONS

Novels

> *The Lord and the Gypsy.* New York, Walker, 1978; as *Debt of Honour*, London, Souvenir Press, 1980.
> *Love's Duet.* New York, Walker, 1979; as *A Perfect Match*, London, Souvenir Press, 1981.
> *Mistress of Willowvale.* New York, Walker, 1980.
> *Nanette.* New York, Walker, 1981.
> *Feather Castles.* New York, St. Martin's Press, 1982.

Patricia Veryan comments:

Almost every period of history has its highlights, its subtle nuances of life at every level that would warrant much happy digging and delving into, so as to gain a fairly well-rounded picture of the time. Of them all, however, I am most fascinated by Britain's crowded past: the perilous days of the Stuarts, the Jacobite uprisings, and the Regency (1811-20). This latter time I find especially intriguing, for it was surely, as Sir Arthur Bryant dubbed it, "The Age of Elegance." Were one to cover the era fully, and from every side, there must be some very dark pages, of course; and some, perhaps darkest of all, shadowed by the shape of things to come. I am not a historian, however, although I attempt to hold true to historical detail. I do not write to moralise, or educate, but to entertain, and if I may thereby leave my reader with a little deeper appreciation of the period, why, so much the better.

And what a period it was! The Napoleonic Wars, and the incredible heroism of the men who fought them on land and sea, whether French, English, or their Allies. The many-faceted Regent himself, later to become George IV, who, despite his numerous failings, encouraged a deeper interest in art, music, and architecture, and left us so rich a heritage of beauty. The preoccupation with manners, the niceties of fashion, and that rare and wonderful intangible, the Code of Honour. Regency gentlemen lived, and sometimes died, by this same Code that valued honour above all things, and next to honour, courage, loyalty, and gentleness. By its unwritten yet inviolate precepts, parents must be respected and obeyed; women revered; children, the weak, and the helpless protected. A man's character was judged by his adherence to his given word, and the crime unforgivable was cowardice. A religion rather? Perhaps. A religion seldom spoken of, but quietly lived. It was a time of contrasts we now find astounding; of sordid poverty and squalor, and great wealth; medical horrors, and the emergence of self-cleanliness; exquisitely gowned ladies instructed from the cradle in the graces and attributes necessary to becoming a good wife, gallant gentlemen, and the savageries of child labour; oppression and tyranny, and yet withal a prosperity unrivalled in the Europe of that day, and a nationwide and innate courtesy and chivalry.

Against this rich canvas, my books are set. They may differ slightly from others of the genre, in that I perhaps insert a trifle more of action and adventure than is the usual fashion, for it was so much a period of action.

If I have, to any extent, achieved success, much of the credit must go to my superb teachers. These have been many, for from every author one gleans something. In my own field however, two were outstanding: the first of these was Jeffery Farnol, who wrote with such gentleness, warmth, and charm, in the early years of this century; the second, Georgette Heyer, whose wit, masterful style, rich humour, and knowledge of her period, were so incomparable. Without these two great friends, whom I dearly loved, and from whom I learned so much, countless happy hours would have been lost to me. For this, besides what they taught me, I do most humbly, if posthumously, thank them.

To others I leave the task of painting the harsh realities of life; the bewilderments of today's world; the savageries of drugs and the pity of lost morality. Life is difficult enough to live, I do not choose to carry such harshness into my writing. I fashion my tales lightly, in the hope that my readers—especially those who may be wearied of the daily grind, or ill, or discouraged, or lonely (surely the cruellest of sorrows)—may perhaps find a smile, or a tug at the heartstrings, or a tingle of excitement within the pages of my books, and thus escape to the thunderous elegance that was, not so long ago—the Regency.

*   *   *

Although Patricia Veryan's body of work is still relatively small, she has already proven herself adept at creating some of the most interesting characters and intriguing stories to be found in historical romances. She has researched the period (usually 19th-century England) well and writes convincingly of the manners of the time.

A basic theme in her work is the preservation of honor and integrity in the face of betrayal and suffering. Both men and women must bear the burden, sometimes with great loneliness. In *Mistress of Willowvale* Leonie braves public disgrace and the contempt of the man she loves to protect her nephew and the memory of her sister. The Marquis of Damon, hero of *Love's Duet*, endures his father's scorn and the shame of a dishonorable reputation in order to bring the true villains to justice. In other cases, such as that of Lucian St. Clair in *The Lord and the Gypsy*, the suffering endured is a means to ultimate reparation for past wrongs committed.

Veryan's books are distinguished by well-developed central characters and many interesting minor personages. There is great romantic involvement, but no explicit sexual details. In fact, Veryan reserves some of her longest, most detailed passages for carefully orchestrated mayhem, which 'forms an integral part of the suffering to be borne by the hero. Lucian St. Clair participates in, and almost loses, a brutal sword duel; Harry Redmond (*Nanette*) becomes a fugitive hunted throughout England and eventually is thrown into Newgate; and Christopher Thorndyke (*Mistress of Willowvale*) is branded a traitor and narrowly avoids death in an all-out battle which takes place in a kitchen. Detailed as the descriptions of the action become, there is no gratuitous violence. Veryan tempers all the serious themes and actions with a very satisfying love story.

An unusual aspect of her work has been the gradual forging of a complete social world for her characters. Where other authors often rely on real historical figures, such as the Prince Regent, to create the sense of aristocratic society in which their characters move, Veryan introduces her readers to new members of that society in each book and mentions others who have already made an appearance. There is a real sense of continuity when the same people appear or are referred to in book after book. These appearances never seem contrived but are worked into the narrative quite naturally. After a while, it is like receiving news of an old friend.

—Barbara Kemp

WADE, Jennifer. Pseudonym for Joy DeWeese-Wehen. Anglo-American. Born in Penang, Malaysia, 31 October 1936. Educated at St. Christopher's School, Victoria, British Columbia; Norfolk House, Victoria; The Banff School, Alberta; Mayfield School, Pasadena, California; St. Margaret's School, Waterbury, Connecticut; Marylhurst College, Oregon; Queen's College, London. Editorial Assistant, *The Diplomat* magazine, 1960's. Since 1976, West Coast Editor, *Antique Monthly, Horizon*, and *The Gray Letter*. Address: 1931 Funston Avenue, San Francisco, California 94116, U.S.A.

ROMANCE AND GOTHIC PUBLICATIONS

Novel

The Singing Wind.   New York, Coward McCann, 1977.

OTHER PUBLICATIONS

Other (juvenile) as Joy DeWeese-Wehen

Stairway to a Secret.   New York, Dutton, 1953.
The Tower in the Sky.   New York, Dutton, 1955.
Stranger at Golden Hill.   New York, Duell, 1961; as *The Golden Hill Mystery*, New
   York, Berkley, 1964.
The Silver Cricket.   New York, Duell, 1966.
So Far from Malabar.   New York, Hawthorn, 1970.

Manuscript Collection (juvenile works): University of Southern Mississippi, Hattiesburg.

Jennifer Wade comments:

In my adult novels, I would like to entertain the reader with a suspenseful yet heart-warming story, while introducing them to another country and another era—in the case of *The Singing Wind* it was 19th-century Dorset. To this end I do a great deal of research, so that all details of architecture, furniture, food, costume, daily life, etc., are authentic and informative. I also like to include one unusual element to give the book a little more lasting value than entertainment alone. *The Singing Wind* featured, woven into the plot and setting, a great deal of history and background of bee-lore, apiculture, and the legends, folk-lore, and details of bee-keeping in 19th-century England. My next novel will spotlight the story of English 18th-century silver, and so on.

*   *   *

For those who like their gothics with a bit of fun, Jennifer Wade's only published novel, *The Singing Wind*, has a lot to offer. The protagonist, Deborah Bond, is a best-selling fiction writer in Victorian England when she learns that she has inherited her uncle's estate, Secretts. Poor Uncle Josiah had died mysteriously—the supposed victim of a bee's sting. Deborah must learn the daily running of the estate and try to discover the truth about her uncle's death. Neighbors and friends fall increasingly under suspicion as they begin to reveal their true characters. Her best friend, Lavinia, a bluestocking, discloses the fact that she was engaged to the dead Josiah. Her neighbor, Sir Launceston Powers, her most ardent suitor, seems eager all of a sudden to be rid of her, and Antony Strang announces that he has been hired, unbeknownst to anyone, as Secrett's beemaster.

The title of the novel refers to the hum of contented bees in their hive and Mr. Stang, a skilled beemaster, evokes the "singing wind" from his beehives. Intertwined smoothly throughout the story are interesting facts about the bees who actually manage to save the heroine in an exciting finale. Before the story's close, Deborah has helped to uncover a criminal operation while exposing the surprising villain (it's a woman).

Wade writes enthusiastically, often ending chapters on a cliffhanging note and she offers a multitude of references on antique furniture, fabrics, painters, and food. Her style is at once sincere and mildly satirical—she never takes herself too seriously, thereby allowing the reader

to have a good time throughout. On the basis of this unusual well-written novel, we can hope to
see more of Jennifer Wade.

—Marilyn Lockhart

WALKER, Lucy. Pseudonym for Dorothy Lucy Sanders, née McClemans; also writes as
Shelley Dean. Australian. Born in Boulder Gold Fields, Western Australia, 4 May 1907.
Educated at Perth College, Western Australia, 10 years; University of Western Australia,
Nedlands, part-time study, 4 years; Claremont Teachers College, teachers certificate 1938.
Married Colsell S. Sanders in 1936; two sons and one daughter. Teacher in Western Australia,
1928-36, and in London, 1936-38. Former Member of the State Advisory Board to the
Australian Broadcasting Commission, and Member of the State Library Board, Western
Australia. Address: 20 Jukes Way, Wembley Gardens, Western Australia 6016, Australia.

ROMANCE AND GOTHIC PUBLICATIONS

Novels

The One Who Kisses. London, Collins, 1954.
Sweet and Faraway. London, Collins, 1955; New York, Arcadia House, 1957.
Come Home, Dear! London, Collins, 1956; New York, Ballantine, 1975.
Heaven Is Here. London, Collins, and New York, Arcadia House, 1957.
Master of Ransome. London, Collins, and New York, Arcadia House, 1958.
Orchard Hill. New York, Arcadia House, 1958.
The Stranger from the North. London, Collins, 1959; New York, Ballantine, 1976.
Kingdom of the Heart. London, Collins, 1959; New York, Ballantine, 1971.
Love in a Cloud. London, Collins, 1960.
The Loving Heart. London, Collins, 1960.
The Moonshiner. London, Collins, 1961; as *Cupboard Love*, New York, Arcadia
    House, 1963.
Wife to Order. London, Collins, 1961; New York, Arcadia House, 1962.
The Distant Hills. London, Collins, 1962.
Down in the Forest. London, Collins, 1962.
The Call of the Pines. London, Collins, 1963; New York, Arcadia House, 1966.
Follow Your Star. London, Collins, 1963; New York, Ballantine, 1976.
The Man from Outback. London, Collins, 1964; New York, Ballantine, 1974.
A Man Called Masters. London, Collins, 1965; New York, Ballantine, 1976.
The Other Girl. London, Collins, 1965; New York, Arcadia House, 1967.
Reaching for the Stars. London, Collins, 1966; New York, Ballantine, 1976.
The Ranger in the Hills. London, Collins, 1966.
South Sea Island (as Shelley Dean). London, Mills and Boon, 1966.
Island in the South (as Shelley Dean). London, Mills and Boon, 1967.
The River Is Down. London, Collins, 1967; New York, Ballantine, 1972.
Home at Sundown. London, Collins, 1968; New York, Ballantine, 1976.
The Gone-Away Man. London, Collins, 1969; New York, Ballantine, 1974.
Joyday for Jodi. London, Collins, 1971; New York, Ballantine, 1976.
The Mountain That Went to the Sea. London, Collins, 1971; New York, Beagle, 1973.

Girl Alone. London, Collins, 1973; New York, Ballantine, 1976.
The Runaway Girl. London, Collins, and New York, Ballantine, 1975.
Gamma's Girl. London, Collins, 1977.
So Much Love. New York, Ballantine, 1977.

Novels as Dorothy Lucie Sanders

Fairies on the Doorstep. Sydney, Australasian, 1948; as *Pool of Dreams* (as Lucy
    Walker), New York, Ballantine, 1973.
The Randy. Sydney, Australasian, 1948.
Pepper Tree series:
    Six for Heaven. London, Hodder and Stoughton, 1952.
    Shining River. London, Hodder and Stoughton, 1954.
    Waterfall. London, Hodder and Stoughton, 1956; as *The Bell Branch* (as Lucy
        Walker), London, Collins, 1971; New York, Ballantine, 1972.
    Ribbons in Her Hair. London, Hodder and Stoughton, 1957.
    Pepper Tree Bay. London, Hodder and Stoughton, 1959.
    Monday in Summer. London, Hodder and Stoughton, 1961.

*   *   *

Within recent years, Australia has produced several outstanding romance writers. Few,
however, achieve quite the same originality as Lucy Walker for she does more than use
Australia as a background for her books.

Woven intricately through her novels and adding in some cases a tremendous emotional
quality are the nearly mystical elements of aboriginal beliefs and customs. These touches lend
support to the romantic involvement and seem to heighten the sense of inevitability as two
people find each other. Not only does she use these native elements in her writing, but she also
uses situations and events that may be unique to Australia, given their land tenure and mining
policies. Thus we find Katie James in *The Ranger in the Hills* involved with mining surveys and
the race to see that a mining right is recognized first.

In *So Much Love* Nairee has such close empathy with the aboriginal people that she
unconsciously carries out a simple, primitive ritual of creating her own "spirit land" by making
a circle of pretty stones and dotting larger ones in its middle. Symbolically the circle is the home
of a person's spirit. Nairee is a young girl, brought up in the outback by an old woman. She is an
orphan who yet has people interested in her future. Her return to The Patch in the Outback is
the beginning of the story as she finally learns who she is and to whom she really belongs.

Lucy Walker's heroines are typically nice girls, a little strong minded, often naive and
groping into adulthood. They are not aggressively women's lib candidates; however, they don't
mind trying something new and illustrate a determined sense of independence in their actions
and outlook. *Kingdom of the Heart*, for instance, is about a girl who inherits half a cattle farm
in the Australian outback and proceeds to go to live there. Kimberly Wentworth in *Home at
Sundown* joins a botanical expedition into the outback to find samples of rare plants for
medical studies.

Typically Lucy Walker's heroes are older, more experienced men. Often they are wealthy
"station" owners who have developed a sixth sense in avoiding the matrimonial trap. They flirt,
and they draw women to them unwittingly and unintentionally at times by their masculinity
and their habit of superiority. Frequently they personify their surroundings as they take on the
bleak harshness of their land.

Lucy Walker balances the force of her characters against the force of the physical background where the story takes place. Constantly the tremendous isolation of the people living in
the outback shapes and moves her characters. This isolation of station life in turn brings out
qualities in character that she skillfully exploits to the fullest. In *Down in the Forest* Kim Baxter
is more than a station manager; he is also appointed to turn his part of the country, the Darjalup
district, into an international show case for foreign visitors. A bush fire neatly sets him back to
the beginning and the story progresses from the arrival of Jill Dawson to become his right-hand
man in this gigantic undertaking.

In *The Call of the Pines* a plane crash leaves four people stranded in the dense outback jungle. Cherry Landin is a young girl hired to help with the children of the station and she is one of those in the plane. Stephen Denton, the owner of the station, has to call on all his ability to lead them out of the jungle and along a cattle trail until they are rescued, all the while watching out for poisonous plants, dangerous animals, and still finding them food and water for the journey.

In all, Lucy Walker gives her readers an unusual glimpse into another world entirely. Given the nature of her country, she could not create her novels without building on its uniqueness, and over and over again this special feeling for Australia comes through. In a sense, one could not justifiably say she uses Australia as a background; it is too much a part of the story, too much of a character within it, to be merely considered background.

—Arlene Moore

WALSH, Sheila. Also writes as Sophie Leyton. British. Born in Birmingham, 10 October 1928. Educated at Notre Dame Convent, Birkdale, Southport. Married Desmond Walsh in 1950; two daughters. Secretary, Romantic Novelists Association. Recipient: Romantic Novelists Association Netta Muskett Award, 1973. Address: 35 Coudray Road, Southport, Merseyside PR9 9NL, England.

ROMANCE AND GOTHIC PUBLICATIONS

Novels

> *The Golden Songbird*. London, Hurst and Blackett, and New York, New American Library, 1975.
> *Madalena*. London, Hurst and Blackett, 1976; New York, New American Library, 1977.
> *The Sergeant Major's Daughter*. London, Hurst and Blackett, 1977; New York, New American Library, 1978.
> *A Fine Silk Purse*. London, Hurst and Blackett, 1978; as *Lord Gilmore's Bride*, New York, New American Library, 1979.
> *The Incomparable Miss Brady*. London, Hutchinson, and New York, New American Library, 1980.
> *Lady Cecily's Dilemma* (as Sophie Leyton). London, Octopus, 1980.
> *The Rose Domino*. New York, New American Library, 1981; London, Hutchinson, 1982.

Sheila Walsh comments:

All my books to date have been set in or around the Regency period, and are essentially light-hearted amusing stories in the Georgette Heyer tradition—an entertaining "read," I hope, for anyone wanting to forget their problems for a little while.

*   *   *

Sheila Walsh is one of the best of the current Regency novelists. Her novels are marked by well-developed, sympathetic characters and intriguing, if predictable, plots. She is skillful in following the conventions of the genre, combining dangerous situations for her heroines with appealing love stories.

The focal point of Walsh's stories is obviously the heroine. Each of these women is proud, fiercely independent, and seeks her own solutions to her problems. Felicity (*The Sergeant Major's Daughter*) is severely beaten by the villain but continues to operate a village school, even at the risk of her own life. Clementina (*The Incomparable Miss Brady*) is abducted by an unprincipled rake, but succeeds in defending herself. The hero arrives to save her, only to find her tending her wounded abductor. Pilar (*Lord Gilmore's Bride*) saves her husband and father by killing her wicked uncle. Although their efforts may be thwarted by superior strength or numbers, these heroines think and act courageously.

Walsh is also successful in creating some interesting perils, which allow a great deal of action to develop. Incarceration in a brothel (*The Golden Songbird*), blackmail (*The Rose Domino*), and fire (*The Sergeant Major's Daughter*) are only a few of the dangers which threaten the lives and honor of the heroines.

The male counterparts to these resourceful women are cast in the common mold of the handsome, somewhat dictatorial rake. It is obvious from the start of each novel that the two temperaments will lead to a clash of wills. That, after all, is a major source of interest in the Regency novel. Walsh, however, manages to keep the antagonistic aspects of such relationships within bounds and develop her characters so that the reader can believe in the development of mutual respect and affection and the inevitable happy ending.

—Barbara Kemp

WARREN, Mary Douglas. *See* **GREIG, Maysie**.

WATSON, Julia. *See* **FITZGERALD, Julia**.

WAY, Margaret. Address: c/o Mills and Boon Ltd., 15-16 Brooks Mews, London W1A 1DR, England.

Novels

Blaze of Silk. London, Mills and Boon, 1970; Toronto, Harlequin, 1971.
King Country. London, Mills and Boon, 1970; Toronto, Harlequin, 1971.
The Time of the Jacaranda. London, Mills and Boon, and Toronto, Harlequin, 1970.
Return to Belle Amber. London, Mills and Boon, 1971; Toronto, Harlequin, 1974.
Summer Magic. London, Mills and Boon, 1971; Toronto, Harlequin, 1972.
Bauhinia Junction. London, Mills and Boon, 1971; Toronto, Harlequin, 1975.
The Man from Bahl Bahla. London, Mills and Boon, and Toronto, Harlequin, 1971.
Noonfire. London, Mills and Boon, 1972; Toronto, Harlequin, 1973.
Ring of Jade. London, Mills and Boon, and Toronto, Harlequin, 1972.
A Man Like Daintree. London, Mills and Boon, 1972; Toronto, Harlequin, 1975.
Copper Moon. London, Mills and Boon, 1972; Toronto, Harlequin, 1975.
The Rainbow Bird. London, Mills and Boon, 1972; Toronto, Harlequin, 1975.
Storm over Mandargi. London, Mills and Boon, 1973; Toronto, Harlequin, 1974.
Sweet Sundown. London, Mills and Boon, 1974; Toronto, Harlequin, 1975.
The Love Theme. London, Mills and Boon, and Toronto, Harlequin, 1974.
McCabe's Kingdom. London, Mills and Boon, 1974; Toronto, Harlequin, 1975.
Wind River. Toronto, Harlequin, 1974.
Reeds of Honey. London, Mills and Boon, and Toronto, Harlequin, 1975.
Storm Flower. London, Mills and Boon, 1975; Toronto, Harlequin, 1976.
A Lesson in Loving. London, Mills and Boon, 1975; Toronto, Harlequin, 1976.
Flight into Yesterday. London, Mills and Boon, and Toronto, Harlequin, 1976.
The Man on Half-Moon. London, Mills and Boon, 1976; Toronto, Harlequin, 1977.
Red Cliffs of Malpara. London, Mills and Boon, and Toronto, Harlequin, 1976.
Swans' Reach. Toronto, Harlequin, 1977.
One Way Ticket. Toronto, Harlequin, 1977.
The Awakening Flame. London, Mills and Boon, and Toronto, Harlequin, 1978.
Wake the Sleeping Tiger. London, Mills and Boon, 1978.
The Wild Swan. London, Mills and Boon, and Toronto, Harlequin, 1978.
Ring of Fire. London, Mills and Boon, 1978; Toronto, Harlequin, 1979.
Portrait of Jaime. Toronto, Harlequin, 1978.
Mutiny in Paradise. Toronto, Harlequin, 1978.
Black Ingo. Toronto, Harlequin, 1978.
Blue Lotus. London, Mills and Boon, 1979; Toronto, Harlequin, 1980.
The Butterfly and the Baron. London, Mills and Boon, 1979; Toronto, Harlequin, 1980.
Valley of the Moon. London, Mills and Boon, 1979.
White Magnolia. London, Mills and Boon, 1979.
The Winds of Heaven. London, Mills and Boon, 1979.
The Golden Puma. London, Mills and Boon, 1980.
Flamingo Park. London, Mills and Boon, 1980; Toronto, Harlequin, 1981.
Lord of the High Valley. London, Mills and Boon, 1980; Toronto, Harlequin, 1981.
Temple of Fire. London, Mills and Boon, 1980; Toronto, Harlequin, 1981.
Shadow Dance. Toronto, Harlequin, 1981.
A Season for Change. Toronto, Harlequin, 1981.

*   *   *

Margaret Way began writing for Mills and Boon and Harlequin in 1970. Since then, she has had over 40 novels published. The backgrounds that she uses in her novels indicate that she is an Australian romance writer who is especially familar with that country. Queensland and the "Outback" figure frequently as physical locations where her characters meet and fall in love. While she does make use of the physical background, and her descriptions are both enjoyable and informative, this is not the element that stands out in her writing. Rather, Margaret Way has a unique and highly creative method of developing elliptical dialogue that moves her novels along as she shows her characters meeting and instinctively fighting one another. This ability to develop tense, lightning-struck scenes between her heroines and heroes is uniquely her own.

Her heroines are generally young, innocent things who often have known the hero as a child. Genny in *Black Ingo* is typical of the sort of female lead characters that she develops. Earlier events cause antagonism as she goes to visit her cousin, Ingo Faulkner, on the outback station of Tandarro. The reader has an immediate awareness of the instant male/female confrontation that occurs when they meet again after several years.

Both Genny and Ingo have had traumatic childhoods that have left marks on their characters. Genny's mother is a child-like scatty female who indulges in numerous love affairs which usually end in marriage. The effect of her mother's affairs, however, influences Genny and her ideals of love and marriage. Her exposure to this sort of background through her formative teen-age years makes it especially hard for her to see that love and marriage can be the natural outcome of a relationship. Ingo has had a similar background, for his mother deserted him and left him with his father and a straitlaced aunt with little feminine gentleness. Their childhood influences naturally make both extremely suspicious of the opposite sex and far harder to understand in their reactions.

The principal characters in *Return to Belle Amber* have similar kinds of problems to overcome. Karen Hartmann has been taught by her mother from her early teen years to hate her father's family and all members of it. Her mother's death leaves her to bring up her ten-year-old brother. The death, however, brings Guy Amber back into the life as he persuades her to make Belle Amber her home again. Karen must fight to overcome her mother's spiteful reactions to the Amber family and she must learn to tolerate and later love Guy Amber, first as the head of the family and then as the man who breached her defenses and won her heart.

It is not until well into the novels that the subtle shift of emphasis takes place and the girl is able to realize that her apparent antagonism really is a dawning physical awareness of the hero as a man. The earlier overtones of hostility may have started from her misunderstanding of a situation, but slowly the heroine realizes that her reaction is all wrong and for all the wrong reasons. Generally, the hero is aware of her reactions and feelings and is aware of the actual causes, so that his cryptic retorts and subtle hints seem to be more than merely taunting insults at times. It is as if he promises and warns her all at the same time. Few writers have her talent for saying so little and hinting at so much.

Margaret Way's skill in creating fascinating characters is reinforced by her ability to develop tight emotional scenes between her leading characters. Her readers are kept constantly involved with the movement of the story and the slow unfolding of the contest between the girl and the man. Margaret Way has a truly individualized style of writing that her readers look forward to with each new novel. They know that they will be entertained by fast-paced, elusive dialogue, and characters that are enjoyable to know.

—Arlene Moore

WEBB, Jean Francis.   Also writes as Ethel Hamill; Roberta Morrison; Lee Davis Willoughby.   American.   Born in White Plains, New York, 1 October 1910. Educated at Amherst College, Massachusetts, 1927-31, B.A. 1931. Married Nancy Bukeley in 1936; four sons. Actor in repertory, 1932-33; worked at Bergdorf-Goodman, New York, 1933; then full-time writer. Taught writing courses at the University of Hawaii, Honolulu, 1958. Member of the Board of Directors, Mystery Writers of America, 1975-79, and since 1981. Agent: McIntosh and Otis, 475 Fifth Avenue, New York, New York 10017; or, Barbara Lowenstein Associates, 250 West 57th Street, New York, New York 10019. Address: 242 East 72nd Street, New York, New York 10021, U.S.A.

Novels

> *Love They Must.* New York, Washburn, 1933.
> *Tree of Evil* (as Roberta Morrison). New York, Paperback Library, 1966.
> *The Craigshaw Curse.* New York, Meredith Press, 1968.
> *Carnavaron's Castle.* New York, Meredith Press, 1969.
> *Roses from a Haunted Garden.* New York, McKay, 1971.
> *Somewhere Within This House.* New York, McKay, 1973.
> *The Bride of Cairngore.* New York, McKay, 1974.

Novels as Ethel Hamill

> *Reveille for Romance.* New York, Arcadia House, 1946.
> *Challenge to Love.* New York, Arcadia House, 1946.
> *Honeymoon in Honolulu.* New York, Avalon, 1950; London, Foulsham, 1952.
> *Tower in the Forest.* New York, Avalon, 1951; as *Tower of Dreams*, London, Ward Lock, 1961.
> *Nurse on Horseback.* New York, Avalon, 1952; London, Ward Lock, 1960.
> *The Dancing Mermaid.* New York, Avalon, 1952; as *All for Love*, New York, Paperback Library, 1965.
> *Bluegrass Doctor.* New York, Avalon, 1953.
> *The Minister's Daughter.* New York, Avalon, 1953.
> *Gloria and the Bullfighter.* New York, Avalon, 1954.
> *A Nurse Comes Home.* New York, Avalon, 1954; as *Nurse Elizabeth Comes Home*, London, Foulsham, 1955.
> *Runaway Nurse.* New York, Avalon, 1955; London, Ward Lock, 1959.
> *A Nurse for Galleon Key.* New York, Avalon, 1957.
> *The Golden Image.* New York, Avalon, 1959.
> *Aloha Nurse.* New York, Avalon, 1961.
> *Sudden Love.* New York, Avalon, 1962.
> *The Nurse from Hawaii.* New York, Avalon, 1964.

Short Stories

> *Forty Brothers.* Menasha, Wisconsin, Collegiate Press, 1934.

Novels

> *No Match for Murder.* New York, Macmillan, 1942.
> *Little Women* (novelization of screenplay). New York, Dell, 1949.
> *Anna Lucasta* (novelization of screenplay). New York, Dell, 1949.
> *King Solomon's Mines* (novelization of screenplay). New York, Dell, 1950.
> *Is This Coffin Taken?* New York, Zebra, 1978.
> *The Cajuns* (as Lee Davis Willoughby). New York, Dell, 1981.

Plays

> *Cabaña* (produced White Plains, New York, 1933).

The Fate That Is Worse Than Death (produced White Plains, New York, 1933).

Radio Plays: *Chick Carter, Boy Detective* series, 1943-45.

Other

Golden Feathers (juvenile), with Nancy Webb.   New York, Avalon, 1954.
The Hawaiian Islands from Monarchy to Democracy, with Nancy Webb.   New York,
   Viking Press, 1956; revised edition, 1963.
Kaiulani, Crown Princess of Hawaii, with Nancy Webb.   New York, Viking Press, 1962.
Will Shakespeare and His America, with Nancy Webb.   New York, Viking Press, 1964.
The Dark House (juvenile).   New York, Scholastic, 1982.

Jean Francis Webb comments:

My writing over the years has been so diverse that any description of it would be difficult.
During the 1930's, 1940's, and 1950's, when magazine fiction was still in demand, my work
encompassed romance, western, detective, and adventure stories for a wide variety of slick and
pulp publications. As Ethel Hamill (my mother's name) I have since done many career-girl
novels, and under my own name a string of gothics and mysteries. In recent years, believing
soft-cover novels to be the probable future of popular fiction, I have been turning more and
more in that direction. I have few illusions as to the rare literary quality of my work; but I try to
write each "entertainment" to the best of my ability.

*   *   *

Jean Francis Webb has been writing professionally since 1931. He has written a great deal of
formula fiction in which the "new" girl falls in love. But the course of true love is not always
smooth and misunderstandings occur before romance wins out. This is the theme of his many
novels written under the pseudonym Ethel Hamill. They are light and typical of the paperback
romance variety.

Webb's last five novels are of the gothic genre. The first of these, *The Craigshaw Curse*, has
been compared to Hawthorne's *The House of the Seven Gables*. Beautiful Constance Craigshaw is called home suddenly to contend with a ghost walking the family mansion in swampy
Florida. Her timorous secretary accompanies her and does some investigating on her own. Jill's
life is endangered after she is shadowed by a newspaperman and a stranger. The description of
the estate is detailed and fascinating, and the characters are well drawn.

The building in *Carnavaron's Castle* would make a fabulous movie set. A modern castle of
medieval design complete with ruins is the home of the widow of the romantic actor, Charles
Carnavaron. Jennifer is the first to visit the remote island off the coast of Maine. She revels in
the famous man's relics but finds much more than a museum. She is attacked by a ghost and
haunted by a younger copy of the actor. Webb weaves a complicated plot into a thrilling maze
of history and romance.

The last three novels are set in Hawaii and give a good picture of the island's history. Legend
and description combined with interesting stories make all three worth reading. In *Roses from
a Haunted Garden* Bethany is terrified that her husband intends to kill her. Not enough clues
are given for the villain's actions, and the reader is left with the feeling that something has been
omitted. Although Bethany is incredibly naive, her terror is realistic and the reader is compelled
to keep turning pages all the way to the end. In *Somewhere Within This House* Ellen arrives in
Hawaii in 1886 to find the true cause of her fiancé's death and is caught up in the missionary
versus royalist struggle of pre-annexation. She is employed to care for the blind daughter of a
dead Hawaiian princess, and finds the answers to several mysteries. Here, too, is painful yet
glorious love in an exciting gothic. Jessica (*The Bride of Cairngore*) is hired to convert a
long-deserted mansion into a small hotel. Her client is the duplicate of his great-grandfather
who supposedly murdered his wife, the reputed ghost of this house. Jessica is drawn to three
men and finds she does not trust any of them when she is stranded after dark and chased

through the deserted unlighted building by a tangible human being. This is a real "haunting," all tightly told and neatly explained.

Webb is a careful writer with well-thought-out plots, believable characters, and superb descriptive ability. He offers his readers many hours of enjoyment.

—Andrea Lee Shuey

WEBSTER, Jean (Alice Jane Chandler Webster). American. Born in Fredonia, New York, 24 July 1876; grandniece of the writer Mark Twain. Educated at schools in Fredonia; Lady Jane Grey School, Binghamton, New York, graduated 1896; Vassar College, Poughkeepsie, New York, B.A. in English and economics 1901. Married Glenn Ford McKinney in 1915; one daughter. *Died 11 June 1916.*

ROMANCE AND GOTHIC PUBLICATIONS

Novels (series: Patty)

> *The Wheat Princess.* New York, Century, 1905; London, Hodder and Stoughton, 1916.
> *Jerry, Junior.* New York, Century, 1907; as *Jerry*, London, Hodder and Stoughton, 1916.
> *The Four-Pools Mystery* (published anonymously). New York, Century, 1908; as Jean Webster, London, Hodder and Stoughton, 1916.
> *Much Ado about Peter.* New York, Doubleday, 1909; London, Hodder and Stoughton, 1917.
> *Daddy-Long-Legs.* New York, Century, 1912; London, Hodder and Stoughton, 1913.
> *Dear Enemy.* New York, Century, and London, Hodder and Stoughton, 1915.

Short Stories

> *When Patty Went to College.* New York, Century, 1903; as *Patty and Priscilla*, London, Hodder and Stoughton, 1915.
> *Just Patty.* New York, Century, 1911; London, Hodder and Stoughton, 1915.

OTHER PUBLICATIONS

Play

> *Daddy Long-Legs*, adaptation of her own novel (produced New York, 1914). New York, French, 1922; London, French, 1927.

Verse

> *Vitriol and Lilacs.* Cleveland, Press of Flozari, 1943.

*   *   *

Mark Twain was Jean Webster's "Uncle Sam": her maternal grandmother was Jane Clemens, Twain's elder sister, and her father was Charles Webster, Twain's publisher and partner, whose imprint appears on both *Huckleberry Finn* and General Grant's memoirs. After the failure of Twain's finances with the Paige typesetter in the late 1890's, Twain used Charley Webster as his scapegoat ("not a man, but a hog," as he wrote to W.D. Howells). That Jean Webster at Vassar did not admit to the relationship with Twain may partly be traced to family animosities; her brother, 50 years later in *Mark Twain, Businessman*, noted that their great-uncle "never forgave anyone he had injured," and that though "a joy to live with," he was "a devil to do business with." But Twain privately praised Jean Webster's first book (the only one he lived to read): "it is limpid, bright, sometimes brilliant; it is easy, flowing, effortless, & brimming with girlish spirits.... Its humor is genuine, & not often overstrained."

With her Southern mother and Northern father, there is in Jean Webster something of the same division that one sees in her great-uncle. She wrote one mystery novel, *The Four-Pools Mystery*, the only work she published anonymously, in which a postwar plantation system is seen approvingly, and comic darkies abound, but in which the lordly temper of the master is seen as more responsible for his murder than the black who actually kills him—whom he has beaten, and who is allowed to escape the penalty of the law.

Of all her sentimental contemporaries—Mrs. Rice, Mrs. Wiggin, Mrs. Montgomery, the two Mrs. Porters—she comes closest to combining romance effectively with realism—surely Twain's great strength, though with her the realism most often takes the form of social concern. Implicitly, her most famous work, *Daddy-Long-Legs*, is a criticism of the contemporary treatment of the orphan; it is no fortuity that it produced, at Vassar and elsewhere, a system of sponsorship of parentless children by wealthy undergraduates. Her own favorite of her novels, *The Wheat Princess*, has elements of a Jamesian international novel—set in Italy and peopled largely by Americans—but it is more informed by a sense of the wrong done by the heroine's father, a tycoon who has cornered the wheat market. His action produces a famine amongst the Italian peasantry, who in revenge besiege the villa occupied by his brother, a philanthropist; and the heroine too is endangered. "Some day," the hero says at the end of the book, "I will tell you that I'm proud to be an American. Don't ask me just yet." Which sounds more like Pudd'nhead Wilson than Pollyanna.

It is this "combination of serious social modernity with the other modernity of gayety and humor" (as the *New York Times* saw it in 1915) which marks Webster's best work, *Daddy-Long-Legs* and its sequel *Dear Enemy*. The heroines of both novels, especially Judy of the first, are resourceful, much less accepting of their lots than Rebecca, Anne, or even (a special case) Pollyanna. Judy has been played by Ruth Chatterton in Webster's own stage adaptation, and by Mary Pickford on the screen; and these are happier visual equivalents than her later impersonators. Judy fits Pickford's image of contemporary American girlhood better than the more conventionally girlish Rebecca or Pollyanna do—Shirley Temple, who repeated these last two roles, would be impossible as Judy. Even Janet Gaynor and Leslie Caron, however, are sentimentalized versions of the original—further stages in the normal evolution of a bestselling character, blurring and domesticating what may be threatening or anti-social.

Judy is generally thought to be based on Webster's college mate and fellow writer Adelaide Crapsey; so too is her next most attractive character, the Patty of her first book, as well as of *Just Patty*. The stories in *When Patty Went to College*, published in the Vassar newspaper, find the enterprising girl in a variety of scrapes, from which she almost always emerges triumphant—whether applying her Social Studies to her Latin class and leading a "Virgil strike," or enrolling a fictitious student in the German club; her specialty is "local color" ("Baron Münchhausen himself would have blushed at her creations"). Patty is a more elegant Judy, equipped with wealthy parents; and in her private schools she is free of the restrictions of the orphanage.

But all of these "juvenile" works create enclosed women's worlds into which men intrude as schoolmasters, janitors, brothers, fathers, occasionally suitors. That in her most popular work the suitor is also the father, the "daddy" long legs, may say something about Webster's own urge to tame and even rival the highly undomesticated, dominating father of the Clemens family (Charley Webster had died when Jean was 15). But it no doubt says a great deal more about the continued appeal of her books to adolescent girls—if there are still such—who want the marital palm without the dust.

—Barrie Hayne

WESLEY, Elizabeth.   *See* **McELFRESH, Adeline.**

WESTMACOTT, Mary. Pseudonym for Agatha Mary Clarissa Christie, née Miller.   British. Born in Torquay, Devon, 15 September 1890. Educated privately at home; studied singing and piano in Paris. Married 1) Colonel Archibald Christie in 1914 (divorced, 1928), one daughter; 2) the archaeologist Max Mallowan in 1930. Served as a Voluntary Aid Detachment nurse in a Red Cross Hospital in Torquay during World War I, and worked in the dispensary of University College Hospital, London, during World War II; also assisted her husband on excavations in Iraq and Syria and on the Assyrian cities. President, Detection Club. Recipient: Mystery Writers of America Grand Master Award, 1954; New York Drama Critics Circle Award, 1955. D.Litt.: University of Exeter, 1961. Fellow, Royal Society of Literature, 1950. C.B.E. (Commander, Order of the British Empire), 1956; D.B.E. (Dame Commander, Order of the British Empire), 1971. *Died 12 January 1976.*

ROMANCE AND GOTHIC PUBLICATIONS

Novels

> *Giants' Bread.*   London, Collins, and New York, Doubleday, 1930.
> *Unfinished Portrait.*   London, Collins, and New York, Doubleday, 1934.
> *Absent in the Spring.*   London, Collins, and New York, Farrar and Rinehart, 1944.
> *The Rose and the Yew Tree.*   London, Heinemann, and New York, Rinehart, 1948.
> *A Daughter's a Daughter.*   London, Heinemann, 1952; New York, Dell, 1963.
> *The Burden.*   London, Heinemann, 1956; New York, Dell, 1963.

OTHER PUBLICATIONS as Agatha Christie

Novels

> *The Mysterious Affair at Styles.*   London, Lane, 1920; New York, Dodd Mead, 1927.
> *The Secret Adversary.*   London, Lane, and New York, Dodd Mead, 1922.

The Murder on the Links. London, Lane, and New York, Dodd Mead, 1923.
The Man in the Brown Suit. London, Lane, and New York, Dodd Mead, 1924.
The Secret of Chimneys. London, Lane, and New York, Dodd Mead, 1925.
The Murder of Roger Ackroyd. London, Collins, and New York, Dodd Mead, 1926.
The Big Four. London, Collins, and New York, Dodd Mead, 1927.
The Mystery of the Blue Train. London, Collins, and New York, Dodd Mead, 1928.
The Seven Dials Mystery. London, Collins, and New York, Dodd Mead, 1929.
The Murder at the Vicarage. London, Collins, and New York, Dodd Mead, 1930.
The Floating Admiral, with others. London, Hodder and Stoughton, 1931; New York, Doubleday, 1932.
The Sittaford Mystery. London, Collins, 1931; as *The Murder at Hazelmoor*, New York, Dodd Mead, 1931.
Peril at End House. London, Collins, and New York, Dodd Mead, 1932.
Lord Edgware Dies. London, Collins, 1933; as *Thirteen at Dinner*, New York, Dodd Mead, 1933.
Why Didn't They Ask Evans? London, Collins, 1934; as *The Boomerang Clue*, New York, Dodd Mead, 1935.
Murder on the Orient Express. London, Collins, 1934; as *Murder in the Calais Coach*, New York, Dodd Mead, 1934.
Murder in Three Acts. New York, Dodd Mead, 1934; as *Three Act Tragedy*, London, Collins, 1935.
Death in the Clouds. London, Collins, 1935; as *Death in the Air*, New York, Dodd Mead, 1935.
The A.B.C. Murders. London, Collins, and New York, Dodd Mead, 1936; as *The Alphabet Murders*, New York, Pocket Books, 1966.
Cards on the Table. London, Collins, 1936; New York, Dodd Mead, 1937.
Murder in Mesopotamia. London, Collins, and New York, Dodd Mead, 1936.
Death on the Nile. London, Collins, 1937; New York, Dodd Mead, 1938.
Dumb Witness. London, Collins, 1937; as *Poirot Loses a Client*, New York, Dodd Mead, 1937.
Appointment with Death. London, Collins, and New York, Dodd Mead, 1938.
Hercule Poirot's Christmas. London, Collins, 1938; as *Murder for Christmas*, New York, Dodd Mead, 1939; as *A Holiday for Murder*, New York, Avon, 1947.
Murder Is Easy. London, Collins, 1939; as *Easy to Kill*, New York, Dodd Mead, 1939.
Ten Little Niggers. London, Collins, 1939; as *And Then There Were None*, New York, Dodd Mead, 1940; as *Ten Little Indians*, New York, Pocket Books, 1965.
One, Two, Buckle My Shoe. London, Collins, 1940; as *The Patriotic Murders*, New York, Dodd Mead, 1941; as *An Overdose of Death*, New York, Dell, 1953.
Sad Cypress. London, Collins, and New York, Dodd Mead, 1940.
Evil under the Sun. London, Collins, and New York, Dodd Mead, 1941.
N or M? London, Collins, and New York, Dodd Mead, 1941.
The Body in the Library. London, Collins, and New York, Dodd Mead, 1942.
The Moving Finger. New York, Dodd Mead, 1942; London, Collins, 1943.
Five Little Pigs. Lodnon, Collins, 1942; as *Murder in Retrospect*, New York, Dodd Mead, 1942.
Death Comes as the End. New York, Dodd Mead, 1944; London, Collins, 1945.
Towards Zero. London, Collins, and New York, Dodd Mead, 1944.
Sparkling Cyanide. London, Collins, 1945; as *Remembered Death*, New York, Dodd Mead, 1945.
The Hollow. London, Collins, and New York, Dodd Mead, 1946; as *Murder after Hours*, New York, Dell, 1954.
Taken at the Flood. London, Collins, 1948; as *There Is a Tide...*, New York, Dodd Mead, 1948.
Crooked House. Lodnon, Collins, and New York, Dodd Mead, 1949.
A Murder Is Announced. London, Collins, and New York, Dodd Mead, 1950.
They Came to Baghdad. London, Collins, and New York, Dodd Mead, 1951.
They Do It with Mirrors. London, Collins, 1952; as *Murder with Mirrors*, New York, Dodd Mead, 1952.

Mrs. McGinty's Dead.   London, Collins, and New York, Dodd Mead, 1952; as *Blood Will Tell*, New York, Detective Book Club, 1952.

After the Funeral.   London, Collins, 1953; as *Funerals Are Fatal*, New York, Dodd Mead, 1953; as *Murder at the Gallop*, London, Fontana, 1963.

A Pocket Full of Rye.   London, Collins, 1953; New York, Dodd Mead, 1954.

Destination Unknown.   London, Collins, 1954; as *So Many Steps to Death*, New York, Dodd Mead, 1955.

Hickory, Dickory, Dock.   London, Collins, 1955; as *Hickory, Dickory, Death*, New York, Dodd Mead, 1955.

Dead Man's Folly.   London, Collins, and New York, Dodd Mead, 1956.

4:50 from Paddington.   London, Collins, 1957; as *What Mrs. McGillicuddy Saw!*, New York, Dodd Mead, 1957; as *Murder She Said*, New York, Pocket Books, 1961.

Ordeal by Innocence.   London, Collins, 1958; New York, Dodd Mead, 1959.

Cat among the Pigeons.   London, Collins, 1959; New York, Dodd Mead, 1960.

The Pale Horse.   London, Collins, 1961; New York, Dodd Mead, 1962.

The Mirror Crack'd from Side to Side.   London, Collins, 1962; as *The Mirror Crack'd*, New York, Dodd Mead, 1963.

The Clocks.   London, Collins, 1963; New York, Dodd Mead, 1964.

A Caribbean Mystery.   London, Collins, 1964; New York, Dodd Mead, 1965.

At Bertram's Hotel.   London, Collins, 1965; New York, Dodd Mead, 1966.

Third Girl.   London, Collins, 1966; New York, Dodd Mead, 1967.

Endless Night.   London, Collins, 1967; New York, Dodd Mead, 1968.

By the Pricking of My Thumbs.   London, Collins, and New York, Dodd Mead, 1968.

Hallowe'en Party.   London, Collins, and New York, Dodd Mead, 1969.

Passenger to Frankfurt.   London, Collins, and New York, Dodd Mead, 1970.

Nemesis.   London, Collins, and New York, Dodd Mead, 1971.

Elephants Can Remember.   London Collins, and New York, Dodd Mead, 1972.

Postern of Fate.   London, Collins, and New York, Dodd Mead, 1973.

Curtain: Hercule Poirot's Last Case.   London, Collins, and New York, Dodd Mead, 1975.

Sleeping Murder.   London, Collins, and New York, Dodd Mead, 1976.

Short Stories

Poirot Investigates.   London, Lane, 1924; New York, Dodd Mead, 1925.

Partners in Crime.   London, Collins, and New York, Dodd Mead, 1929; reprinted in part as *The Sunningdale Mystery*, Collins, 1933.

The Under Dog.   London, Readers Library, 1929.

The Mysterious Mr. Quin.   London, Collins, and New York, Dodd Mead, 1930.

The Thirteen Problems.   London, Collins, 1932; as *The Tuesday Club Murders*, New York, Dodd Mead, 1933; selection, as *The Mystery of the Blue Geranium and Other Tuesday Club Murders*, New York, Bantam, 1940.

The Hound of Death and Other Stories.   London, Collins, 1933.

Parker Pyne Investigates.   London, Collins, 1934; as *Mr. Parker Pyne, Detective*, New York, Dodd Mead, 1934.

The Listerdale Mystery and Other Stories.   London, Collins, 1934.

Murder in the Mews and Three Other Poirot Cases.   London, Collins, 1937; as *Dead Man's Mirror and Other Stories*, New York, Dodd Mead, 1937.

The Regatta Mystery and Other Stories.   New York, Dodd Mead, 1939.

The Mystery of the Baghdad Chest.   Los Angeles, Bantam, 1943.

The Mystery of the Crime in Cabin 66.   Los Angeles, Bantam, 1943.

Poirot and the Regatta Mystery.   Los Angeles, Bantam, 1943.

Poirot on Holiday.   London, Todd, 1943.

Problem at Pollensa Bay, and Christmas Adventure.   London, Todd, 1943.

The Veiled Lady, and The Mystery of the Baghdad Chest.   London, Todd, 1944.

Poirot Knows the Murderer.   London, Todd, 1946.

Poirot Lends a Hand.   London, Todd, 1946.

The Labours of Hercules. London, Collins, and New York, Dodd Mead, 1947.
The Witness for the Prosecution and Other Stories. New York, Dodd Mead, 1948.
The Mousetrap and Other Stories. New York, Dell, 1949; as *Three Blind Mice and Other Stories*, New York, Dodd Mead, 1950.
The Under Dog and Other Stories. New York, Dodd Mead, 1951.
The Adventure of the Christmas Pudding, and Selection of Entrées. London, Collins, 1960.
Double Sin and Other Stories. New York, Dodd Mead, 1961.
13 for Luck! A Selection of Mystery Stories for Young Readers. New York, Dodd Mead, 1961; London, Collins, 1966.
Surprise! Surprise! A Collection of Mystery Stories with Unexpected Endings, edited by Raymond T. Bond. New York, Dodd Mead, 1965.
Star over Bethlehem and Other Stories (as Agatha Christie Mallowan). London, Collins, and New York, Dodd Mead, 1965.
13 Clues for Miss Marple. New York, Dodd Mead, 1966.
The Golden Ball and Other Stories. New York, Dodd Mead, 1971.
Poirot's Early Cases. London, Collins, 1974; as *Hercule Poirot's Early Cases*, New York, Dodd Mead, 1974.
Miss Marple's Final Cases and Two Other Stories. London, Collins, 1979.

Plays

Black Coffee (produced London, 1930). London, Ashley, and Boston, Baker, 1934.
Ten Little Niggers, adaptation of her own novel (produced Wimbledon and London, 1943). London, French, 1944; as *Ten Little Indians* (produced New York, 1944), New York, French, 1946.
Appointment with Death, adaptation of her own novel (produced Glasgow and London, 1945). London, French, 1956; in *The Mousetrap and Other Plays*, 1978.
Murder on the Nile, adaptation of her novel *Death on the Nile* (as *Little Horizon*, produced Wimbledon, 1945; as *Murder on the Nile* produced London and New York, 1946). London and New York, French, 1948.
The Hollow, adaptation of her own novel (produced Cambridge and London, 1951; Princeton, New Jersey, 1952; New York, 1978). London and New York, French, 1952.
The Mousetrap, adaptation of her story "Three Blind Mice" (broadcast, 1952; produced Nottingham and London, 1952; New York, 1960). London and New York, French, 1954.
Witness for the Prosecution, adaptation of her own story (produced Nottingham and London, 1953; New York, 1954). London and New York, French, 1954.
Spider's Web (produced Nottingham and London, 1954; New York, 1974). London and New York, French, 1957.
Towards Zero, with Gerald Verner, adaptation of the novel by Christie (produced Nottingham and London, 1956). New York, Dramatists Play Service, 1957; London, French, 1958.
Verdict (produced Wolverhampton and London, 1958). London, French, 1958; in *The Mousetrap and Other Plays*, 1978.
The Unexpected Guest (produced Bristol and London, 1958). London, French, 1958; in *The Mouse Trap and Other Plays*, 1978.
Go Back for Murder, adaptation of her novel *Five Little Pigs* (produced Edinburgh and London, 1960). London, French, 1960; in *The Mousetrap and Other Plays*, 1978.
Rule of Three: Afternoon at the Seaside, The Patient, The Rats (produced Aberdeen and London, 1962; *The Rats* produced New York, 1974; *The Patient* produced New York, 1978). London, French, 3 vols., 1963.
Fiddlers Three (produced Southsea, 1971; London, 1972).
Akhnaton (as *Akhnaton and Nefertiti*, produced New York, 1979; as *Akhnaton*, produced London, 1980). London, Collins, and New York, Dodd Mead, 1973.
The Mousetrap and Other Plays (includes *Witness for the Prosecution, Ten Little*

Indians, Appointment with Death, The Hollow, Towards Zero, Verdict, Go Back for Murder). New York, Dodd Mead, 1978.

Radio Plays: *The Mousetrap*, 1952; *Personal Call*, 1960.

Verse

The Road of Dreams. London, Bles, 1925.
Poems. London, Collins, and New York, Dodd Mead, 1973.

Other

Come, Tell Me How You Live (travel). London, Collins, and New York, Dodd Mead, 1946; revised edition, 1976.
An Autobiography. London, Collins, and New York, Dodd Mead, 1977.

Bibliography: by Louise Barnard, in *A Talent to Deceive: An Appreciation of Agatha Christie* by Robert Barnard, London, Collins, and New York, Dodd Mead, 1980.

Critical Study: *The Life and Crimes of Agatha Christie* by Charles Osborne, London, Collins, 1982.

*   *   *

Agatha Christie was a product of the English upper middle class. That society with which she was so familiar became the setting for her plots during the more than 56 years of her writing life. Her dozens of mystery novels are known to readers around the world. Since her death in 1976, many writers of the genre have been billed as Christie's successors. And Christie fans are frustrated that the annual Christie mystery is no longer the event they eagerly awaited each year.

There was another side to Christie the writer. Even staunch Christie fans may be unaware that she wrote six romances under a pseudonym. Writing as Mary Westmacott was Agatha Christie's alternative to plotting mysteries as well as her escape from being First Lady or Queen of Mysteries. While she was a best seller in the mystery field, her six "straight" novels never enjoyed the same success.

Christie was ingenious in outlining mysteries, and when she wrote her romance novels she put them together like detective novels with an element of mystery introduced into each. The Westmacott mystery factor, however, revolved around people's character or relationships among individuals. Christie was better able to introduce psychological elements into her Westmacott books than in her mysteries. Some read like psychological studies of the characters.

However, Dame Agatha Christie was never able to become a great success as a romance or gothic writer. Indeed, if she had not also been Agatha Christie, Mary Westmacott might have disappeared from the literary world forever.

The Westmacott novels are simple in style. The plots are uncomplicated. They are all about women and their problems or their life style. If one reads any of the Christie biographies or even her autobiography, another common trait becomes apparent: much that transpires in the novels resembles events in Christie's life.

In *Giants' Bread*, the first of the Westmacott romances, Christie utilized her love for music in the plot and emphasized making choices based on personal preference as well as society's expectations. This book appeared about the time of her remarriage, two years after her divorce from Archibald Christie. There is a typical Christie country house setting. Tragic deaths in the Boer War and World War I create twists in the plots and force the characters into unfamiliar life styles. It was while her first husband was serving in World War I that Christie began writing; her first mystery was finally accepted for publication in 1920. After her husband's return from the war, the marriage began to founder. Thus, while planning and writing *Giants' Bread*, Christie herself was undergoing drastic changes in her life.

Christie's own childhood had been fairly quiet. She had been tutored by her mother and then had studied music in Paris. In both *Giants' Bread* and *Unfinished Portrait* the nursery motif, complete with mauve iris wallpaper, is repeated. In both these novels there is a tragedy leading to reduced family circumstances. Divorce from a husband depicted as a philanderer is another parallel to Christie's own life. Some biographers have felt Miriam in *Unfinished Business* is based on Christie's mother.

It was ten years before *Absent in the Spring* was published. The chief character, a woman en route back to England after visiting one daughter, spends several days in an isolated desert region, and begins thinking how she has controlled her husband's life to meet her desires in life rather than his, and how she has stage managed both daughters' lives. The isolation of the area and the lack of companionship force her into long periods of reflection. She must face the knowledge that she hasn't been the perfect wife and mother. Whether this is a parallel to Christie's life we don't know, but she incorporated her Middle East experiences with her second husband in to the plot. Christie, writing from first hand experience, effectively depicts the isolation of the desert.

One of the talents of Christie the mystery writer was her use of narrators to tell the story. In *The Rose and the Yew Tree* an invalid becomes the very observant narrator of village life. Making unpopular life choices is the theme; characters with questionable backgrounds are the participants.

The last two Westmacott novels were written in the 1950's. *A Daughter's a Daughter* reverses the theme of *Absent in the Spring* with the daughter trying to manage her mother's romantic life. The two women almost reach the destructive point in their relationship before they realize what is happening. In *The Burden* a sister is guilt ridden by her brother's death and her wish for her sister's death. She seeks refuge in working for good causes.

Characteristic of the Westmacott books are several factors: deaths, usually in a war, causing reduced financial circumstances; choices made that are based on what society expects; the difficulty of making decisions that will change one's life; punishment of self for misdeeds imagined or real. Several settings or parts of stories are carried from book to book.

Because of her use of events from her own life, the reader may wonder if the plotting and writing of these romance novels was a form of catharsis for her. Was Mary Westmacott the depicter of what Christie envisioned happening or wanted to happen? The Westmacott novels often end unresolved or with endings unsatisfactory to the characters. Is this how Christie expected life to be? These novels lack the spark and plotting of the Christie mysteries, but offer a glimpse into how Agatha Christie viewed life.

—Jennifer Cargill

WESTWOOD, Gwen (née Knox). British. Born in Warrington, Lancashire, 27 June 1915. Educated at the University of Birmingham, B.A. 1936. Married Gladwin Westwood in 1938; two children. Former teacher. Address: 422 Blackburn Road, Durban, Natal, South Africa.

ROMANCE AND GOTHIC PUBLICATIONS

Novels

Keeper of the Heart. London, Mills and Boon, and Toronto, Harlequin, 1969.
Bright Wilderness. London, Mills and Boon, 1969; Toronto, Harlequin, 1970.
The Emerald Cuckoo. London, Mills and Boon, 1970; Toronto, Harlequin, 1971.
Castle of the Unicorn. London, Mills and Boon, and Toronto, Harlequin, 1971.
Pirate of the Sun. London, Mills and Boon, and Toronto, Harlequin, 1972.
Citadel of Swallows. London, Mills and Boon, and Toronto, Harlequin, 1973.
Sweet Roots and Honey. London, Mills and Boon, 1974; Toronto, Harlequin, 1975.
Ross of Silver Ridge. London, Mills and Boon, 1975; Toronto, Harlequin, 1976.
Blossoming Gold. London, Mills and Boon, and Toronto, Harlequin, 1976.
Bride of Bonamour. London, Mills and Boon, and Toronto, Harlequin, 1977.
A Place for Lovers. London, Mills and Boon, 1978.
Forgotten Bride. London, Mills and Boon, 1980.
Zulu Moon. London, Mills and Boon, 1980; Toronto, Harlequin, 1981.

OTHER PUBLICATIONS

Other (juvenile)

Monkey Business. London, Hamish Hamilton, 1965.
The Gentle Dolphin. London, Hamish Hamilton, 1965.
The Red Elephant Blanket. London, Hamish Hamilton, 1966.
The Pumpkin Year. London, Hamish Hamilton, 1966.
Narni of the Desert. London, Hamish Hamilton, 1967; Chicago, Rand McNally, 1968.
A Home for Digby. London, Hamish Hamilton, 1968.

*   *   *

Gwen Westwood's love affair with South Africa began the day she left England to join her future husband in South Africa. There her husband's career took them to various parts of that country and they lived in several places before settling in Durban. Two factors have made her a talented romance writer; the first is, of course, her wide knowledge of South Africa and her obvious love of the country with all of its colorful history. The second factor is her own life, for she seems to draw upon her own years of love and happiness as she writes her romances. Although she favors her own country in many of her novels, she does write of other countries.

Citadel of Swallows takes place in Greece. In this novel Stacey Grant and a friend, Lauren, go to the Greek islands, Lauren for a modeling assignment and Stacey merely to see Lauren's brother again. It is Stacey's belief that she and Lauren's brother have an "understanding." In fact, she had given him most of her savings so he would have time to write an anticipated best seller. Her encounter with Stavros Demetrios, however, changes everything as she falls in love with him. In this novel, Stacey is the traditional romance heroine as she makes bumbling mistakes and says things that instantly tell of her naivety. Stavros is also a traditional romance character and has all the sophisticated élan that any good hero should have.

In *Ross of Silver Ridge* Taryn Bartlett is hired to accompany three children from London to South Africa and to stay with them as their housekeeper. Taryn is twenty, an orphan now that her grandparents have died, and is totally unsuited for most kinds of work since she has had no formal training. She finds her own age and inexperience a definite problem as Ross Trent, the children's uncle, finds her far too young for the job. Her efforts to control the children and to fit into his home prove unusually difficult for her, and additionally she quickly succumbs to Ross's undeniable attraction. The fact that another woman, Coral Swann, is the most likely woman to be his wife complicates Taryn's emotions, and much of the story centers on her efforts to deny or suppress her love for Ross. After all, he is wealthy, important, and extremely eligible, what could she offer him that he would want!

In another novel, we find Perry Vaughan returning to South Africa to see Tarquin Winslow, her husband. The title, of course, gives the clue—*Forgotten Bride*. She returns after five years to find that an accident the day after their secret marriage has caused him to lose any memory of her. The illness of her aunt, the death of her grandparents, and the spite of a jealous woman all brought about the circumstances that Perry faces as she first tries to deny her love, and then slowly gives in to it, only to have him reject her completely until surgery restores his memory and his love.

These three novels illustrate the transitional stages of Gwen Westwood as a writer. Her heroines begin in the traditional manner, but slowly she emphasizes more complexity of character, more inner strength and sureness in her heroines. The innocence of Stacey gives way to the gradual maturing of Taryn and then to the more adult character of Perry as she faces the crumbling of carefully built defenses after long lonely years. Her gradual shift from young, unawakened love to rejected love is more than simple plot complication, for it shows a more experienced hand at developing her female characters.

—Arlene Moore

WHITBY, Sharon. *See* **PETERS, Maureen.**

WHITNEY, Phyllis A(yame). American. Born in Yokohama, Japan, 9 September 1903. Educated at schools in Japan, China, the Philippines, Berkeley, California, San Antonio, Texas; graduated from high school in Chicago, 1924. Married 1) George Garner in 1925 (divorced, 1945), one daughter, 2) Lovell Jahnke in 1950 (died, 1973). Children's Book Editor, Chicago *Sun*, 1942-46, and Philadelphia *Inquirer*, 1946-48; Instructor in Juvenile Fiction Writing, Northwestern University, Evanston, Illinois, 1945-46, and New York University, 1947-58. Past President, Mystery Writers of America. Recipient: Youth Today Award, 1947; Mystery Writers of America Edgar Allan Poe Award, for juvenile, 1961, 1964. Agent: McIntosh and Otis Inc., 475 Fifth Avenue, New York, New York 10017, U.S.A.

ROMANCE AND GOTHIC PUBLICATIONS

Novels

> *Red Is for Murder.* Chicago, Ziff Davis, 1943; as *The Red Carnelian*, New York, Paperback Library, 1968; London, Coronet, 1976.
> *The Quicksilver Pool.* New York, Appleton Century Crofts, 1955; London, Coronet, 1973.

The Trembling Hills. New York, Appleton Century Crofts, 1956; London, Coronet, 1974.

Skye Cameron. New York, Appleton Century Crofts, 1957; London, Hurst and Blackett, 1959.

The Moonflower. New York, Appleton Century Crofts, 1958; as *The Mask and the Moonflower,* London, Hurst and Blackett, 1960.

Thunder Heights. New York, Appleton Century Crofts, 1960; London, Coronet, 1973.

Blue Fire. New York, Appleton Century Crofts, 1961; London, Hodder and Stoughton, 1962.

Window on the Square. New York, Appleton Century Crofts, 1962; London, Coronet, 1969.

Seven Tears for Apollo. New York, Appleton Century Crofts, 1963; London, Coronet, 1969.

Black Amber. New York, Appleton Century Crofts, 1964; London, Hale, 1965.

Sea Jade. New York, Appleton Century Crofts, 1964; London, Hale, 1966.

Columbella. New York, Doubleday, 1966; London, Hale, 1967.

Silverhill. New York, Doubleday, 1967; London, Heinemann, 1968.

Hunter's Green. New York, Doubleday, 1968; London, Heinemann, 1969.

The Winter People. New York, Doubleday, 1969; London, Heinemann, 1970.

Lost Island. New York, Doubleday, 1970; London, Heinemann, 1971.

Listen for the Whisperer. New York, Doubleday, and London, Heinemann, 1972.

Snowfire. New York, Doubleday, and London, Heinemann, 1973.

The Turquoise Mask. New York, Doubleday, 1974; London, Heinemann, 1975.

Spindrift. New York, Doubleday, and London, Heinemann, 1975.

The Golden Unicorn. New York, Doubleday, 1976; London, Heinemann, 1977.

The Stone Bull. New York, Doubleday, and London, Heinemann, 1977.

The Glass Flame. New York, Doubleday, 1978; London, Heinemann, 1979.

Domino. New York, Doubleday, 1979; London, Heinemann, 1980.

Poinciana. New York, Doubleday, and London, Heinemann, 1980.

Vermilion. New York, Doubleday, 1981; London, Heinemann, 1982.

Uncollected Short Stories

"Gallant Rogue," in *All-Story* (New York), 1 March 1933.

"Clinging Vine—1935," in *All-Story* (New York), 12 January 1935.

"How Do You Get That Way?," in *All-Story* (New York), 1 June 1935.

"Love among the Goldfish," in *All-Story* (New York), 28 August 1937.

"Miss Gayheart," in *All-Story* (New York), 16 October 1937.

"Ice Cream Man," in *All-Story* (New York), 18 December 1937.

"The Bug Lady," in *All-Story* (New York), 19 February 1938.

"The Man Who Loved a Dummy," in *All-Story* (New York), 16 April 1938.

"Five Dogs and a Man," in *All-Story* (New York), 25 June 1938.

"Don't Send Me Valentines," in *All-Story* (New York), 18 February and 25 February 1939.

"The Perfumed Cat," in *All-Story* (New York), 15 April 1939.

"Love of Tomorrow," in *All-Story* (New York), 15 July 1939.

OTHER PUBLICATIONS

Novels (juvenile)

A Place for Ann. Boston, Houghton Mifflin, 1941.

A Star for Ginny. Boston, Houghton Mifflin, 1942.

A Window for Julie. Boston, Houghton Mifflin, 1943.

The Silver Inkwell. Boston, Houghton Mifflin, 1945.

Willow Hill.   New York, Reynal, 1947.
Ever After.   Boston, Houghton Mifflin, 1948.
Mystery of the Gulls.   Philadelphia, Westminster Press, 1949.
Linda's Homecoming.   Philadelphia, McKay, 1950.
The Island of Dark Woods.   Philadelphia, Westminster Press, 1951; as *Mystery of the Strange Traveler*, 1967.
Love Me, Love Me Not.   Boston, Houghton Mifflin, 1952.
Mystery of the Black Diamonds.   Philadelphia, Westminster Press, 1954; as *Black Diamonds*, Leicester, Brockhampton Press, 1957.
Step to the Music.   New York, Crowell, 1953.
A Long Time Coming.   Philadelphia, McKay, 1954.
Mystery on the Isle of Skye.   Philadelphia, Westminster Press, 1955.
The Fire and the Gold.   New York, Crowell, 1956.
The Highest Dream.   Philadelphia, McKay, 1956.
Mystery of the Green Cat.   Philadelphia, Westminster Press, 1957.
Secret of the Samurai Sword.   Philadelphia, Westminster Press, 1958.
Creole Holiday.   Philadelphia, Westminster Press, 1959.
Mystery of the Haunted Pool.   Philadelphia, Westminster Press, 1960.
Secret of the Tiger's Eye.   Philadelphia, Westminster Press, 1961.
Mystery of the Golden Horn.   Philadelphia, Westminster Press, 1962.
Mystery of the Hidden Hand.   Philadelphia, Westminster Press, 1963.
Secret of the Emerald Star.   Philadelphia, Westminster Press, 1964.
Mystery of the Angry Idol.   Philadelphia, Westminster Press, 1965.
Secret of the Spotted Shell.   Philadelphia, Westminster Press, 1967.
Secret of Goblin Glen.   Philadelphia, Westminster Press, 1968.
The Mystery of the Crimson Ghost.   Philadelphia, Westminster Press, 1969.
Secret of the Missing Footprint.   Philadelphia, Westminster Press, 1969.
The Vanishing Scarecrow.   Philadelphia, Westminster Press, 1971.
Nobody Likes Trina.   Philadelphia, Westminster Press, 1972.
Mystery of the Scowling Boy.   Philadelphia, Westminster Press, 1973.
Secret of Haunted Mesa.   Philadelphia, Westminster Press, 1975.
Secret of the Stone Face.   Philadelphia, Westminster Press, 1977.

Other

Writing Juvenile Fiction.   Boston, The Writer, 1947; revised edition, 1960.
Writing Juvenile Stories and Novels.   Boston, The Writer, 1976.
"Gothic Mysteries," in *The Mystery Story*, edited by John Ball.   San Diego, University of California Extension, 1976.
Guide to Fiction Writing.   Boston, The Writer, 1982.

Manuscript Collection: Mugar Memorial Library, Boston University.

Phyllis A. Whitney comments:

Since I have lived in many different places, I have no "roots." Thus I must look for a fresh setting for each suspense novel I write. Once I have chosen my setting, I visit it to collect impressions and information firsthand. Then I do a great deal of research at home. Eventually, I develop a young woman character with a serious problem facing her, and in my imagination I set her down in the background I mean to use. Around her I place other characters who will bring conflict and further problems into her life. As these characters grow, both in my mind and on paper, my story begins to emerge a bit at a time, until the whole thing is clear before I write. The setting itself often becomes an important character in my novels.

*   *   *

When I was growing up, my mother and those friends of hers who were avid readers were discriminating in their addictions: not just any romance would do. It ought to be historical, spirited, suspenseful, and if it had a bit of literary merit that didn't hurt at all. Any new Victoria Holt sufficed, as did the latest by Mary Stewart or Daphne du Maurier. What these writers offered my mother and her friends was not simply romantic intrigue, but rather romance with a decidedly British accent. All the more surprising then that in the mid-1960's those ladies added to their brief, cherished list of favorites the books of Phyllis A. Whitney—an American, and one, moreover, who set her romances mainly in America and almost exclusively in modern dress. Place and time, those two staples of Gothic fiction, had been transformed, at least for my mother's circle, from "an old house in England a long time ago" to "here and now."

Not exactly down the street, of course. Whitney chooses her settings for their romantic possibilities. Yet she avoids the predictably romantic American locations, those places which resonate loudest in the American psyche: the South, Los Angeles, New York. The latter she uses only historically (*Window on the Square*), or as a point of departure from which the heroines of *Vermilion*, *The Winter People*, *Sea Jade*, *Domino* and several other books flee, seeking sanctuary or confronting the past in ancestral homes elsewhere. Remarkable in Whitney is where "elsewhere" is. She has a proclivity for sustaining romantic suspense in what could easily be prosaic locations—the Poconos and Catskills, the Hamptons, New Hampshire, even northern New Jersey, all resort areas for the middle class. Whitney achieves this transformation of these otherwise hum-drum locales by means of some standard gothic devices: the heroine's seeming isolation amid a hostile household whose shifting moods she only dimly understands; the gothic house itself, be it old hotel or mansion; the careful removal of dailiness. In a Whitney novel, as in other gothics, characters gather for meals less to eat than to confront each other, dress not to keep warm but to show off the latest fashions, and go to bed mostly to be disturbed by ominous noises, bad dreams, and an occasional murderer. Furthermore, while virtually all of Whitney's heroines are "career-girls," hardly a one continues to work during the course of the novel, except at a new job, often of near-servant status: a governess, companion, or hostess.

This displacement from accustomed work, and usually from what had been home, is all the more appropriate since Whitney has created a species of romance fiction which might be called Tourist Gothic. She writes well and lovingly of the various places in which her books are set, but always with the enthusiasm of a visitor, not with an inhabitant's long knowledge of place. Thus Whitney provides her readers with a kind of exciting vacation, replete with interesting locations, confusing romances, and outright danger. Book after book is set in or near a resort: in the Tennessee or New Hampshire mountains, at a reconstructed Colorado mining town, near Santa Fe or Tlaquepaque, in a Newport mansion or a palatial hotel in the shadowy Catskills. What reader wouldn't love to spend a week in one of these places, under the spell of an older man by whom she will feel, as does Megan Kincaid of *Window on the Square*, "unaccountably drawn and yet a little repelled?"

If these resort locations are chosen for romance and heightened by contrived isolation, they also serve for Whitney an educative function. As others have noted, Americans like a little learning with their light reading; in so pragmatic a culture nothing should be just for pleasure and even on vacation one should learn. A Whitney heroine learns about her own resourcefulness and the true feelings of those around her, especially those of that attractive but disconcerting older man. But she, and consequently the reader, learns more as well. Each of Whitney's romances instructs us in some facet of local color or history: Caribbean seashells and hurricanes in *Columbella*, Turkish mosaics in *Black Amber*, Japanese netsuke in *Poinciana*, herbalism in *Thunder Heights*, Hopi Indian culture in *Vermilion*, topiary in *Hunter's Green*, South African diamonds and apartheid in *Blue Fire*. The list is as long as Whitney's publication history, for each novel supplies a new location and with it a new factual knowledge.

Constant in Whitney's work, however, is her preoccupation with art and her passion for environmentally sound architecture and land developement. That art would figure prominently is not surprising, the unstable artist being a common enough romantic device. And Whitney does use artists conventionally, creating in *The Winter People*, *The Golden Unicorn*, *Thunder Heights*, and *Window on the Square* tortured, often deranged, painters and sculptors. Occasionally she goes against type, presenting in *The Stone Bull* a sculptor whose work is expressive of the dark side of his nature but whose actions are good, and in *Vermilion*, the Indian paintings of Alice Spencer whose art is angry but whose personality is deeply calm. The artistic process itself holds a fascination for Whitney beyond romantic convention; her characters seem constantly perplexed by its moral and emotional valence, as if the author herself were ambivalent about the worth of an art deeper than that which she practices.

The value of an architecture mindful of its surroundings Whitney easily recognizes, however. Her passion for beautiful building and sound development drives the plots of several novels. In *Thunder Heights*, set in the 19th-century Hudson Valley, the engineer hero dreams of bridging the river in a careful, environmentally sound manner; in *The Trembling Hills*, which takes place in San Francisco during the year of the great earthquake, a young architect enthuses about the new Chicago School which has been "preaching that form should follow function" and predicts great things from "a young fellow named Wright...." The contemporary issue of land use comes up in *The Glass Flame* where the love interest is an architect and planner who is building a lake community in the Tennessee hills, even as in the earlier book, *The Winter People*, the main conflict centers on the pontential development of a wilderness area. Whitney's devotion to this topic is peculiar to her romances, even as her knowledge of architecture extends beyond the traditional Gothic devices of towers and secret passageways. From the Norwegian kirks in *Listen for the Whisperer* to the reconstructed mining town in *Domino*, Whitney uses architecture for its tangible as well as symbolic value.

A tourist's enthusiasm, some local learning, a passion for good houses on well-used land: these hardly seem the stuff of which romantic dreams are woven. But such is Whitney's gift that she can make the prosaic mysterious and transform business and environmental issues into the source of romantic conflicts. This is her distinct contribution, I think, for in other ways her novels are unfailingly conventional. I can pick any book at random from my stack of Whitney novels and know as well before as after I open it that her heroine will be alone, will have recently lost one or both parents, will have been devoted to her father and at odds with her mother, and—most importantly—will be about to investigate the past, usually her own familial past, to confront some long repressed, traumatic event. Romance readers want certain constants, of course, what Whitney herself has referred to as "the dear familiar landscape" of romance: the lone woman, the toubling man, the mysterious danger. She provides all these, but happily is an inventive enough writer to twist her own devices when they become tired, as in the recent *Vermilion* where the familiar Whitney convention of giving her heroine a vague, partial, terrifying memory of a violent or criminal act witnessed in childhood is transformed into the haunting of the narrator's adult self by a spirited imaginary playmate, a doppelganger who expresses the heroine's more violent emotions. If Whitney's psychology is not deep here, it is convincing, for as she has done now in nearly 30 romance novels she assures her readers that even a young woman haunted by a repressed memory of violence or by an imaginary friend unwilling to be banished may be resourceful enough to undo wrongs, save herself from danger, and win the love of a strong, mysterious man. It's not so unlikely, really. Not when we have been made to believe that gothic romance may exist in prosaic north Jersey and that anything at all may happen on the resort vacations that are Phyllis Whitney's books.

—Nancy Regan

WILLIAMS, Claudette. Address: c/o Fawcett, 1515 Broadway, New York, New York 10036, U.S.A.

ROMANCE AND GOTHIC PUBLICATIONS

Novels

Spring Gambit. New York, Fawcett, 1976.
Sassy. New York, Fawcett, 1977.
Sunday's Child. New York, Fawcett, 1977.
After the Storm. New York, Fawcett, 1977.
Blades of Passion. New York, Fawcett, 1978; London, Arrow, 1979.
Cotillion for Mandy. New York, Fawcett, 1978.
Myriah. New York, Fawcett, 1978.
Cassandra. New York, Fawcett, and London, Arrow, 1979.
Jewelene. New York, Fawcett, 1979.
Lacey. New York, Fawcett, 1979.
Mary, Sweet Mary. New York, Fawcett, 1980.
Naughty Lady Ness. New York, Fawcett, 1980.
Passion's Pride. New York, Fawcett, 1980.
Desert Rose, English Moon. New York, Fawcett, 1981.

*   *   *

Claudette Williams seems to be an author with a split personality. Where most writers of historical romances stick with one style or formula, at least for each pseudonym, Williams produces two distinct types of books under one name.

Her largest output has been in the familiar Regency formula novel. *Spring Gambit*, *Sassy*, *Jewelene*, *Lacey* are only some examples of her work in this genre. Her virginal heroines and handsome, rakish heroes fit the common mold but are elevated by some engaging dialogue. The earlier novels in this vein (*After the Storm*, *Sassy*, *Sunday's Child*) allowed for more development of character and plot, but the more recent titles seem to be hurried and place greater reliance on the formula: a little bit of danger to the heroine, but rescue always in time. Rarely is there a hint of more than a kiss or, perhaps, a discreetly passionate embrace.

Readers accustomed to this fare were in for a shock when *Blades of Passion* appeared. Suddenly Williams joined the ranks of those authors producing steamy, explicit sex scenes. The rules of the game change in this formula. Here the heroine loses her virginity before marriage but remains true to the hero throughout. Rape becomes seduction as lust turns into tenderness. The books are longer and so there are more dangerous situations to encounter, but most of the plot revolves around the antagonism which exists between hero and heroine, and how long it will take them to recognize it as love. *Passion's Pride* and, to a lesser extent, *Cassandra*, follow this formula too. *Passion's Pride* is less successful than *Blades of Passion* because of an awkward attempt to develop two parallel stories which only occasionally touch on one another. *Desert Rose, English Moon* is Williams's only novel in a modern setting, but all the elements of *Blades of Passion* are present.

Claudette Williams is a good romantic novelist. She has the ability to create likeable characters, and while her stories may stretch the reader's credulity, they are no more far-fetched than most other historical romances.

—Barbara Kemp

WILLIAMSON, C.N. and A.M. Also wrote as Charles de Crespigny; M.P. Revere; Dona Teresa de Savallo; Alice Stuyvesant; Mrs. Harcourt Williamson. **WILLIAMSON, C(harles) N(orris):** British. Born in Exeter, in 1859. Educated at University College, London. Married Alice Livingston in 1895. Journalist: staff member, *Graphic*, 1882-90; Founding Editor, *Black and White* magazine, 1891. *Died 3 October 1920.* **WILLIAMSON, A(lice) M(uriel, née Livingston):** born near Poughkeepsie, New York, in 1869. Educated privately. Lived in England after 1893. *Died 24 September 1933.*

<small>ROMANCE AND GOTHIC PUBLICATIONS</small>

Novels

The Lightning Conductor: The Strange Adventures of a Motor-Car. London, Methuen, 1902; New York, Holt, 1903.

The Princess Passes: A Romance of a Motor Car. London, Methuen, 1904; New York, Holt, 1905.

My Friend the Chauffeur. London, Methuen, and New York, McClure, 1905.

The Car of Destiny and Its Errand to Spain. London, Methuen, 1906; as The Car of Destiny, New York, McClure, 1906.

Lady Betty Across the Water. London, Methuen, and New York, McClure, 1906.

Rosemary in Search of a Father. London, Hodder and Stoughton, and New York, McClure, 1906; as Rosemary: A Christmas Story, New York, Burt, 1909.

The Botor Chaperon. London, Methuen, 1907; as The Chauffeur and the Chaperon, New York, McClure, 1908; as The Chaperon, New York, Burt, 1912.

The Powers and Maxine. New York, Empire, 1907.

The Marquis of Loveland. New York, McClure, 1908.

Love and the Spy. London, Leng, 1908.

The Motor Maid. London, Hodder and Stoughton, 1909; New York, Doubleday, 1910.

Set in Silver. London, Methuen, and New York, Doubleday, 1909.

The Golden Silence. London, Methuen, and New York, Doubleday, 1910.

Lord Loveland Discovers America. London, Methuen, and New York, Doubleday, 1910.

The Demon. London, Methuen, 1912.

The Heather Moon. London, Methuen, and New York, Doubleday, 1912.

The Guests of Hercules. London, Methuen, and New York, Doubleday, 1912; as Mary at Monte Carlo, Methuen, 1920.

Champion: The Story of a Motor Car. London, Cassell, 1913.

The Love Pirate. London, Methuen, 1913; as The Port of Adventure, New York, Doubleday, 1913.

The Wedding Day. London, Methuen, 1914.

A Soldier of the Legion. London, Methuen, and New York, Doubleday, 1914.

It Happened in Egypt. London, Methuen, and New York, Doubleday, 1914.

Secret History. London, Methuen, 1915; as Secret History Revealed by Lady Peggy O'Malley, New York, Doubleday, 1915.

The Shop-Girl. London, Methuen, and New York, Grosset and Dunlap, 1916; as Winnie Childs, The Shop Girl, Grosset and Dunlap, 1926.

The War Wedding. London, Methuen, 1916; as Where the Path Breaks (as Captain Charles de Crespigny), New York, Century, 1916.

The Lightning Conductress. London, Methuen, 1916; as The Lightning Conductress Discovers America, New York, Doubleday, 1916.

Angel Unawares: A Story of Christmas Eve. New York, Harper, 1916.

This Woman to This Man. London, Methuen, 1917.

The Cowboy Countess. London, Methuen, 1917.

Tiger Lily. London, Mills and Boon, 1917.

Lord John in New York. London, Methuen, 1918.

Crucifix Corner: A Story of Everyman's Land.   London, Methuen, 1918; as *Everyman's Land*, New York, Doubleday, 1918.
Briar Rose.   London, Odhams, 1919.
The Lion's Mouse.   London, Methuen, and New York, Doubleday, 1919.
The Second Latchkey.   New York, Doubleday, 1920.
The Dummy Hand.   London, Hutchinson, 1920.
Alias Richard Power.   London, Hodder and Stoughton, 1921.
The Great Pearl Secret.   London, Methuen, and New York, Doubleday, 1921.
The House of Silence.   London, Hodder and Stoughton, 1921.
The Night of the Wedding.   London, Hodder and Stoughton, 1921; New York, Doran, 1923.
Vision House.   New York, Doubleday, 1921.
The Brightener.   New York, Doubleday, 1921; London, Hutchinson, 1922.
The Lady from the Air.   London, Hodder and Stoughton, 1922; New York, Doubleday, 1923.

Novels by A.M. Williamson

The Barn Stormers, Being the Tragical Side of a Comedy.   London, Hutchinson, 1897; as Mrs. Harcourt Williamson, New York, Stokes, 1897.
Fortune's Sport.   London, Pearson, 1898.
A Woman in Grey.   London and New York, Routledge, 1898.
Lady Mary of the Dark House.   London, Bowden, 1898.
The House by the Lock.   London, Bowden, 1899; New York, Dodge, 1906.
The Newspaper Girl.   London, Pearson, 1899.
My Lady Cinderella.   London, Routledge, 1900; New York, Dodge, 1906.
Ordered South.   London, Routledge, 1900.
The Adventure of Princess Sylvie.   London, Methuen, 1900; as *The Princess Virginia*, New York, McClure, 1909.
Queen Sweetheart.   London, White, 1901.
A Bid for a Coronet.   London, Routledge, 1901.
'Twixt Devil and Deep Sea.   London, Pearson, 1901.
Papa.   London, Methuen, 1902.
The Silent Battle.   London, Hurst and Blackett, 1902; New York, Doubleday, 1909.
The Woman Who Dared.   London, Methuen, 1903.
The Little White Nun.   London, White, 1903.
The Sea Could Tell.   London, Methuen, 1904.
The Turnstile of Night.   London, Hurst and Blackett, 1904.
The Castle of Shadows.   London, Methuen, 1905; New York, Hudson Press, 1909.
The Girl Who Had Nothing.   London, Ward Lock, 1905.
The House of the Lost Court (as Dona Teresa de Savallo).   New York, McClure, 1908.
The Underground Syndicate.   London, Hodder and Stoughton, 1910.
The Vanity Box (as Alice Stuyvesant).   New York, Doubleday, 1911; as A.M. Williamson, London, Hodder and Stoughton, 1913.
The Flower Forbidden.   London, Hodder and Stoughton, 1911.
The Girl of the Passion Play.   London, Hodder and Stoughton, 1911.
The Bride's Hero (as M.P. Revere).   New York, Stokes, 1912.
To M.L.G.; or, He Who Passes.   New York, Stokes, 1912.
The Life Mask.   New York, Stokes, 1913.
What I Found Out in the House of a German Prince, by an English Governess.   London, Chapman and Hall, and New York, Stokes, 1915.
Name the Woman.   London, Methuen, 1924.
The Million Dollar Doll.   New York, Doran, 1924.
The Man Himself.   London, Philpot, 1925.
Secret Gold.   London, Methuen, and New York, Doubleday, 1925.
Publicity for Anne.   London, Mills and Boon, 1926.
Cancelled Love.   London, Methuen, 1926; as *Golden Butterfly*, New York, Doran, 1926.

Sheikh Bill. London, Mills and Boon, 1927; as *Bill—The Sheik*, New York, Doran, 1927.
Hollywood Love. London, Chapman and Hall, 1928.
Black Sleeves: It Happened in Hollywood. London, Chapman and Hall, 1928.
Children of the Zodiac. London, Chapman and Hall, 1929.
Frozen Slippers. London, Chapman and Hall, 1930.
The Golden Carpet. London, Chapman and Hall, 1931.
Honeymoon Hate. London, Chapman and Hall, 1931.
Bewitched. London, Chapman and Hall, and New York, Kinsey, 1932.
Last Year's Wife. London, Benn, 1932.
Keep This Door Shut. London, Benn, 1933.
The Lightning Conductor Comes Back. London, Chapman and Hall, 1933.
The Girl in the Secret. London, Wright and Brown, 1934.

Short Stories

Scarlet Runner. London, Methuen, 1908.
The Minx Goes to the Front. London, Mills and Boon, 1919.
Berry Goes to Monte Carlo. London, Mills and Boon, 1921.
The Fortune Hunters and Others. London, Mills and Boon, 1923.
The Indian Princess (by A.M. Williamson). London, Mills and Boon, 1924.
Told at Monte Carlo (by A.M. Williamson). London, Mills and Boon, 1926; as *Black Incense: Tales of Monte Carlo*, New York, Doran, 1926.

OTHER PUBLICATIONS by A.M. Williamson

Other

Memoirs of the Life and Writings of Thomas Carlyle, by C.N. Williamson and Richard Herne Shepherd. London, W.H. Allen, 1881.
Queen Alexandra, The Nation's Pride. London, Partridge, 1902.
Princess Mary's Locked Book (published anonymously). London, Cassell, 1912; New York, Cassell, 1913.
The Bride's Breviary (published anonymously). London, Hodder and Stoughton, 1912.
The Lure of Monte Carlo. London, Mills and Boon, 1924; New York, Doubleday, 1926.
Alice in Movieland. London, Philpot, 1927; New York, Appleton, 1928.
The Inky Way (autobiography). London, Chapman and Hall, and New York, Putnam, 1931.

*   *   *

Charles Norris Williamson of Exeter, England, had co-authored a book on Thomas Carlyle before he met Miss Alice Muriel Livingston of Poughkeepsie, New York, and after their marriage (in 1895) they combined their literary talents to write books of a very different nature. These were mostly romantic novels with motoring and travel backgrounds. Charles's informed interest in science and engineering gave the stories a sense of technical modernity, while Alice seems to have injected them with robust romanticism.

There is an Edwardian charm even in the novels that appeared during the 1920's, and much of the Williamsons' best work was published between 1900 and 1910. The couple made their home at Cap Martin and gave many of their books a continental setting, though the main characters, expectedly, were often British or American. *The Lightning Conductor, The Princess Passes, The Car of Destiny,* and *My Friend the Chauffeur* are notable examples of the Williamsons' roaming-European-romances, which convey motoring and sight-seeing adventures with wit and whimsy. The stories are, for their time, fast moving, and only romantic clinches are allowed sometimes to slow down the crackling pace.

In *The Botor Chaperon* three pairs of lovers—assortedly Dutch, English, and American—take to the canals and waterways of Holland. Anglo-American themes are expectedly prominent in the novels. The hero is frequently an impeccable English milord whose opinions (at first) seem to the more questioning American heroine to have survived "crusted and spider-webbed from the cellars of the Stone Age" (*Lord John in New York* and *Lord Loveland Discovers America*). Nevertheless the Williamsons appear to have a very soft spot for upper-crust Englishmen (though less for their female counterparts). Their aristocratic male arrogance could of course eventually be loosened by American honesty and liveliness, as embodied by a string of attractive heroines.

Many of these leading girl characters pursue careers, though romance generally marks the end of job ambitions. *The Newspaper Girl*, which Mrs. Williamson wrote on her own, is a briskly perceptive account of an American incognito-heiress trying to scrape a living in London as a "penny-a-liner journalist," but ending up, with relief, as an English Lady-by-marriage. The Williamsons apparently relished the creation of witty vignettes of exotic continental or American women trying to make advances to restrained Englishmen, and nobody does this better in their novels than Maxine de Renzie, the Polish actress/spy operating in Paris in *Love and the Spy*. She is beautiful, cultivated, quick-witted, and far-seeing in the plots and counterplots of espionage—and, of course, of romance.

—Mary Cadogan

WINSOR, Kathleen. American. Born in Olivia, Minnesota, 16 October 1919. Educated at the University of California, Berkleley, A.B. 1938. Married 1) Robert Herwig in 1936 (divorced, 1946); 2) the musician Artie Shaw in 1946; 3) Paul A. Porter in 1956 (died, 1975); 4) Arnold Robert Krakower. Reporter and receptionist, Oakland *Tribune*, California, 1937-38; story consultant for *Dreams in the Dust* television series, 1971. Address: c/o Doubleday and Company, 245 Park Avenue, New York, New York 10017, U.S.A.

ROMANCE AND GOTHIC PUBLICATIONS

Novels

   Forever Amber. New York, Macmillan, 1944; London, Macdonald, 1945.
   Star Money. New York, Appleton Century Crofts, and London, Macdonald, 1950.
   The Lovers. New York, Appleton Century Crofts, and London, Macdonald, 1952.
   America, With Love. New York, Putnam, 1957; London, Davies, 1958.
   Wanderers Eastward, Wanderers West. New York, Random House, and London, Davies, 1965.
   Calais. New York, Doubleday, 1979; London, Sidgwick and Jackson, 1980.

*   *   *

Kathleen Winsor writes serious novels. To say this is at once to acknowledge Winsor's ambitions and to lament her humorlessness. Romance fiction is not known for its wittiness, to be sure, but it is light reading. Winsor has something else in mind than providing escapist fantasies for her audience; in fact, for all the love affairs in her books, she does not really write romances. Rather, she writes leisurely, languid, temporizing stories of driven, obsessive women. If Winsor books are a species of romance then it is the romance of ambition she details. Her women are in love neither with love itself nor with a strong, rescuing man, but instead with their own achievements, having wrested from life what they most needed.

Baldly stated, what Winsor's women need from life is success: to be a star, to beloved, to have money. Not the swooning passive ladies of light romance, Winsor's heroines typically achieve fame, adoration, and wealth through their own dogged efforts. "I've worked hard for what I have," choruses Shireen Delaney throughout *Star Money*, reminding the reader again and again of the four and a half years she spent writing the bestseller which has made her rich and famous. Such effort apparently excuses all manner of unscrupulous behavior, both in Shireen and in Winsor's other heroines. Ambitious and sensual, greedy, uncaring and often fickle, Amber St. Clare sets the pattern for these heroines, for she is above all determined. At first Amber seems determined to find love with Bruce Carlton, to take life on his terms. But as the novel unfolds at its languid pace it becomes clear that so romantic a goal is unfit for a Winsor heroine. Like her later incarnations, Shireen and Lily Malone, Amber is an opportunist; her unscrupulous will to prosper lifts her from the placid village of Marygreen to the London stage and ultimately to Charles II's court and bedroom. That she steals and whores and murders along the way is inconsequential to heroine and author alike. Arguably, the scandalous Amber is bested—if not punished—at the end of the novel, chasing off to America after Bruce because she has been deceived. Yet because so many previous times in *Forever Amber* events that have looked bad for her have turned out well, it is hard to believe she won't land on her feet. This lack of punishment is a refreshing change from romance fictions generic insistence on the goodliness of its heroines. Amber is a rogue, even as Shireen Delaney in *Star Money* is a feckless ravener and Lily Malone of *Calais* is a vengeful tyrant. Moreover, all these women are sensualists, women who, unlike the typical romance heriones, do not deny or misidentify their sexual longings. Again, this is a refreshing change from the enforced and often hypocritical chastity present in most romances.

Given these driven, sensual, unscrupulous central characters, it is surprising that Winsor's books are strangely uncompelling. With the partial exception of *Calais*, none builds to a climax; most end arbitrarily. Amber could as easily continue her adventures in Virginia; Shireen might as well have another affair, since having seen her devour most of the men in *Star Money* without so much as a hiccough, we've no reason to suppose that the wreck of her marriage is going to give her dyspepsia. Winsor's novels don't end so much as they stop, and prior to stopping they have wandered (as in the aptly named *Wanderers Eastward, Wanderers West*) and gone on nearly "forever." The dilatory pace of her narratives is all the more surprising considering Winsor's obvious love of drama. Her major heroines are all connected with the theater; in fact, Winsor's most convincing and memorable character is Lily Malone/ Arlette Morgan of *Calais*, her most rounded novel. Unlike Winsor's earlier works, *Calais* moves toward a necessary, not arbitrary resolution. When Lily Malone drops into the sea, she has been doomed by—though not punished for—her intractable remembrance of things, sadness, and loss—her tenacious vengeance on the past.

"Everything seems pretty grim with you," Shireen Delaney's secretary tells her toward the end of *Star Money* (a title expressive of Winsor's preoccupations), and to an entent this judgment applies to Winsor's works as a whole. Was there ever a bawdy romp less joyful that *Forever Amber* or a success story more cheerless than *Star Money*? Like her heroines, Winsor commands our respect with her thoroughness, her concentration, her diligent effort, but her novels, which mix strangely langorous prose with obsessive subjects, fail finally to engage our full attention and sympathy.

—Nancy Regan

WINSPEAR, Violet. British. Born in London. Address: c/o Mills and Boon Ltd., 15-16 Brooks Mews, London W1A 1DR, England.

ROMANCE AND GOTHIC PUBLICATIONS

Novels

Lucifer's Angel. London, Mills and Boon, and Toronto, Harlequin, 1961.
Wife Without Kisses. London, Mills and Boon, 1961; Toronto, Harlequin, 1973.
The Strange Waif. London, Mills and Boon, 1962; Toronto, Harlequin, 1974.
House of Strangers. London, Mills and Boon, 1963; Toronto, Harlequin, 1973.
Beloved Tyrant. London, Mills and Boon, 1964; Toronto, Harlequin, 1966.
Cap Flamingo. London, Mills and Boon, 1964; as *Nurse at Cap Flamingo*, Toronto, Harlequin, 1965.
Love's Prisoner. London, Mills and Boon, 1964; Toronto, Harlequin, 1974.
Bride's Dilemma. London, Mills and Boon, 1965; Toronto, Harlequin, 1966.
Desert Doctor. London, Mills and Boon, and Toronto, Harlequin, 1965.
The Tower of the Captive. London, Mills and Boon, 1966; Toronto, Harlequin, 1967.
The Viking Stranger. London, Mills and Boon, 1966; Toronto, Harlequin, 1967.
Tender Is the Tyrant. London, Mills and Boon, 1967; Toronto, Harlequin, 1968.
The Honey Is Bitter. London, Mills and Boon, 1967; Toronto, Harlequin, 1973.
Beloved Castaway. London, Mills and Boon, 1968; Toronto, Harlequin, 1971.
Court of the Veils. London, Mills and Boon, 1968; Toronto, Harlequin, 1969.
The Dangerous Delight. London, Mills and Boon, 1968; Toronto, Harlequin, 1969.
Pilgrim's Castle. London, Mills and Boon, 1969; Toronto, Harlequin, 1973.
The Unwilling Bride. London, Mills and Boon, 1969; Toronto, Harlequin, 1973.
Blue Jasmine. London, Mills and Boon, 1969; Toronto, Harlequin, 1970.
Dragon Bay. London, Mills and Boon, 1969; Toronto, Harlequin, 1973.
Palace of the Peacocks. London, Mills and Boon, and Toronto, Harlequin, 1969.
The Chateau of St. Avrell. London, Mills and Boon, 1970; Toronto, Harlequin, 1974.
The Cazalet Bride. London, Mills and Boon, and Toronto, Harlequin, 1970.
Tawny Sands. London, Mills and Boon, 1970; Toronto, Harlequin, 1974.
Black Douglas. London, Mills and Boon, 1971; Toronto, Harlequin, 1972.
Dear Puritan. London, Mills and Boon, 1971; Toronto, Harlequin, 1973.
Bride to Lucifer. London, Mills and Boon, 1971; Toronto, Harlequin, 1973.
The Castle of the Seven Lilacs. London, Mills and Boon, and Toronto, Harlequin, 1971.
Raintree Valley. London, Mills and Boon, 1971; Toronto, Harlequin, 1972.
The Little Nobody. London, Mills and Boon, 1972; Toronto, Harlequin, 1973.
The Pagan Island. London, Mills and Boon, and Toronto, Harlequin, 1972.
Rapture of the Desert. London, Mills and Boon, 1972; Toronto, Harlequin, 1973.
The Silver Slave. London, Mills and Boon, and Toronto, Harlequin, 1972.
The Glass Castle. London, Mills and Boon, 1973; Toronto, Harlequin, 1974.
Devil in a Silver Room. London, Mills and Boon, and Toronto, Harlequin, 1973.
Forbidden Rapture. London, Mills and Boon, 1973; Toronto, Harlequin, 1974.
The Kisses and the Wine. London, Mills and Boon, and Toronto, Harlequin, 1973.
Palace of the Pomegranate. London, Mills and Boon, 1974; Toronto, Harlequin, 1975.
The Girl at Golden Hawk. London, Mills and Boon, 1974; Toronto, Harlequin, 1975.
The Noble Savage. London, Mills and Boon, 1974; Toronto, Harlequin, 1975.
Satan Took a Bride. London, Mills and Boon, 1975; Toronto, Harlequin, 1976.
Dearest Demon. London, Mills and Boon, 1975; Toronto, Harlequin, 1976.
The Devil's Darling. London, Mills and Boon, and Toronto, Harlequin, 1975.
Darling Infidel. London, Mills and Boon, and Toronto, Harlequin, 1976.
The Burning Sands. London, Mills and Boon, 1976; Toronto, Harlequin, 1977.
The Child of Judas. London, Mills and Boon, and Toronto, Harlequin, 1976.
The Sun Tower. London, Mills and Boon, 1976; Toronto, Harlequin, 1977.

The Sin of Cynara. London, Mills and Boon, and Toronto, Harlequin, 1976.
The Loved and the Feared. London, Mills and Boon, 1977; Toronto, Harlequin, 1978.
Love Battle. London, Mills and Boon, 1977; Toronto, Harlequin, 1978.
Love in a Stranger's Arms. London, Mills and Boon, and Toronto, Harlequin, 1977.
Passionate Sinner. London, Mills and Boon, 1977; Toronto, Harlequin, 1978.
Time of the Temptress. London, Mills and Boon, 1977; Toronto, Harlequin, 1978.
The Valdez Marriage. London, Mills and Boon, 1978; Toronto, Harlequin, 1979.
The Awakening of Alice. London, Mills and Boon, and Toronto, Harlequin, 1978.
Desire Has No Mercy. London, Mills and Boon, 1979.
The Sheik's Captive. London, Mills and Boon, 1979.
Love Is the Honey. London, Mills and Boon, and Toronto, Harlequin, 1980.
A Girl Possessed. London, Mills and Boon, 1980; Toronto, Harlequin, 1981.
Love's Agony. London, Mills and Boon, and Toronto, Harlequin, 1981.

*   *   *

Violet Winspear has said: "I am a true spinster of romances, for in the old days the word spinster meant a woman who spun, and in the writing of a story one spins and weaves and forms a pattern that is hoped will prove pleasant and satisfactory" (*Thirty Years of Harlequin*, 1979). In fact, a distinctive pattern has been woven into Winspear's storytelling, a pattern that has fulfilled the hopes of readers for over 20 years. Realizing people's need for escape, Winspear creates fast-paced, dramatic romances set in exotic lands inhabited by strange and wonderful peoples.

Winspear's romances feature immediate, intense conflict between the hero and the heroine which gives way to passionate unification by the end of the novel. As early as page ten, the hero and heroine are engaged in open warfare. Often their first words to each other are hostile; their first encounter may lead to physical violence between them. They are attracted to each other, but are initially repulsed by the strength of their feelings. Winspear uses extreme contrasts and emphasizes the attraction of opposites to build the tension between the hero and heroine: heaven and hell, pleasure and pain, devil and angel, love and hate, saint and sinner, fire and ice, hard and soft, dark and fair.

The hero in Winspear's novels is an impossibly strong, dominant man who is smoothly cultured but who, at the slightest provocation from the heroine, reverts to the type of his primitive ancestors. Be he Danish, Greek, Spanish, or Arabic, the hero is a pagan and a pirate. Book titles like *Bride to Lucifer*, *Dearest Demon*, and *Satan Took a Bride* make reference to the demonic qualities of the hero. The hero is the most compelling character in a Winspear romance because he is a man with a secret. Neither the heroine nor the reader initially knows why the hero is attractively scarred, why he is so bitter about women, why he is temporarily estranged from his family, or why he is evasive about his past. Gradually, the hero's misleading devilish reputation is stripped away to reveal the saint within. He is a man who puts others before himself and his business, who is capable of making noble sacrifices without any acknowledgement, and who is capable of controlling his powerful sexuality even when incredibly aroused.

The typical Winspear heroine undergoes the reverse process. In the beginning, she is the ice-cool angel with the modesty of a Madonna. She is like an "ice bombe, bursting with chilled cream and the tang of bitter cherry." However, contact with the hero melts that icy exterior and reveals the temperamental sensualist within. Thus, the conflict and its resolution not only lead to a marriage of opposites, but also allow both characters to express previously hidden aspects of their selves. The reader is willing to allow Winspear her excesses and exaggerations of character traits because this is such a satisfying conclusion.

Winspear's flamboyancy is also apparent in her writing style. She has a stock of romantic words which inevitably surface in her descriptions of characters, objects, or scenery. These are words like tawny, creamy, smoky, silken, taut, honey, and savage, the latter because "...there is generally a touch of savagery in anything truly romantic, as if it has to be tested by steel or fire." Winspear is willing to invent new forms of words if they are evocative, for example, "...he brought her tigerishly close to him...." She frequently hyphenates words for romantic effect as well (the hero's "iron-hard jaw" or "sun-dark skin," the "honey-warm air").

Another characteristic of Winspear's writing is that she liberally sprinkles foreign names and expressions, particularly endearments, throughout the novel. She does not concentrate on any one country or locale. Rather she varies her settings by writing about the Caribbean, South America, the Middle East, Europe, and the United States. Interestingly, in a genre that has usually been purged of any overt political references, Winspear does mention the political turmoil found in some of the countries she writes about, and she occasionally uses it as part of the plot, although such references are generally kept vague. Winspear's heroes are always citizens of these exciting lands but the heroines are invariably English.

The sense of worldly sophistication created in the novels by the multi-lingualism is further heightened by Winspear's literary references to Dante, Byron, Chekov, Balzac, Browning, etc. The hero and heroine are likely to recite bits of poetry and prose during the course of the story. Winspear also likes to use mythology as a motif in her romances. Thus the hero and heroine will be compared to mythological characters such as Apollo and Daphne or Proserpina and Aidoneus, or "romantic" historical figures like the Sabine women and their captors. Winspear also borrows from other popular fiction. For instance, *Blue Jasmine* is very closely modeled after E.M. Hull's *The Sheik*.

When asked why she does not write about an ordinary Englishman, a "Herbert Smith," or her childhood home in London's East End, Winspear replied: "Quite frankly I do often write about Herbert Smith but I give him a more romantic name and disguise him in a tailored suit." She added: "I often write about the East End, for my Eastern bazaars are straight out of Petticoat Lane. My Greeks and Italians reside there, the aroma of exotic food has been breathed there... I have often plucked strands for my stories from that rich tapestry." The results show that Winspear has the ability to transform her observations of everyday people, places, and events into glamorous romances.

—Margaret Jensen

WINSTON, Daoma. American. Born in Washington, D.C., 3 November 1922. Educated at George Washington University, Washington, D.C., A.B. 1946 (Phi Beta Kappa). Married Murray Strasberg in 1944. Lives in Washington, D.C. Agent: Jay Garon-Brooke Associates, 415 Central Park West, New York, New York 10025.

ROMANCE AND GOTHIC PUBLICATIONS

Novels (series: Bracken's World)

> *Tormented Lovers.* Derby, Connecticut, Monarch, 1962.
> *Love Her, She's Yours.* Derby, Connecticut, Monarch, 1963.
> *The Secrets of Cromwell Crossing.* New York, Lancer, 1965.
> *Sinister Stone.* New York, Paperback Library, 1966.
> *The Wakefield Witches.* New York, Award, 1966.
> *The Mansion of Smiling Masks.* New York, New American Library, 1967.
> *Shadow of an Unknown Woman.* New York, Lancer, 1967; Loughton, Essex, Piatkus, 1979.
> *The Castle of Closing Doors.* New York, Belmont, 1967.
> *The Carnaby Curse.* New York, Belmont, 1967.
> *Shadow on Mercer Mountain.* New York, Lancer, 1967.
> *Pity My Love.* New York, Belmont, 1967.

The Trificante Treasure. New York, Lancer, 1968.
Moderns. New York, Pyramid, 1968.
The Long and Living Shadow. New York, Belmont, 1968.
Bracken's World. New York, Paperback Library, 1969.
Mrs. Berrigan's Dirty Book. New York, Lancer, 1970.
Beach Generation. New York, Lancer, 1970.
Wild Country (Bracken's World). New York, Paperback Library, 1970.
Dennison Hill. New York, Paperback Library, 1970.
House of Mirror Images. New York, Lancer, 1970.
Sound Stage (Bracken's World). New York, Paperback Library, 1970.
The Love of Lucifer. New York, Lancer, 1970.
The Vampire Curse. New York, Paperback Library, 1971.
Flight of a Fallen Angel. New York, Lancer, 1971.
The Devil's Daughter. New York, Lancer, 1971.
The Devil's Princess. New York, Lancer, 1971; Loughton, Essex, Piatkus, 1980.
Seminar in Evil. New York, Lancer, 1972.
The Victim. New York, Popular Library, 1972.
The Return. New York, Avon, 1972.
The Inheritance. New York, Avon, 1972.
Kingdom's Castle. New York, Berkley, 1972; Loughton, Essex, Piatkus, 1981.
Skeleton Key. New York, Avon, 1972; Loughton, Essex, Piatkus, 1980; as *The May-eroni Myth*, New York, Lancer, 1972.
Moorhaven. New York, Avon, 1973; London, Futura, 1976.
The Trap. New York, Popular Library, 1973.
The Unforgotten. New York, Berkley, 1973.
The Haversham Legacy. New York, Simon and Schuster, 1974; London, Futura, 1977.
Mills of the Gods. New York, Avon, 1974; London, Macdonald and Jane's, 1980.
Emerald Station. New York, Avon, 1974; London, Futura, 1977.
The Golden Valley. New York, Simon and Schuster, 1975; London, Futura, 1978.
Death Watch. New York, Ace, 1975.
A Visit after Dark. New York, Ace, 1975.
Walk Around the Square. New York, Ace, 1975.
Gallows Way. New York, Simon and Schuster, 1976; London, Macdonald and Jane's, 1978.
The Dream Killers. New York, Ace, 1976.
The Adventuress. New York, Simon and Schuster, 1978; London, Macdonald and Jane's, 1979.
The Lotteries. New York, Morrow, and London, Macdonald, 1980.
A Sweet Familiarity. New York, Arbor House, 1981.
Mira. New York, Arbor House, 1982.

*   *   *

The novels of Daoma Winston contain much romance but also complex stories and psychology. They centre around women rather than men and involve a fairly deep level of characterisation. They seem to be divisible into two types: long historical novels and shorter works that, but for the added romantic element, could fall into the category of mystery novels. These latter are very exciting and contain a well-developed crescendo of suspense, to which the romantic element is subordinate.

The heroines are strong, complex, and exceedingly logical, and have to deal with serious family problems as well as very masculine but wayward men. Usually one or more of the minor characters poses a mortal threat to the heroine, either because of greed, jealousy, envy, or desire for revenge. In fact, apart from a difference in setting and background detail, her shorter novels are really explorations of one theme: strong emotions becoming twisted and serving as motives for destruction. The heroines find themselves in ever-increasing danger as a series of mysterious deaths occur, each death coming closer to the heroine herself. It is the heroine who ultimately uncovers the killer and his motive; the heroine to whom the killer reveals all in an exciting but contrived denouement.

The bizarre features prominently, as in, for example, the spiritualist cult in *The Devil's Princess* or the curse of the Mayeroni in *Skeleton Key*. Except in her historical novels, the plots and backgrounds appear contrived and far-fetched.

Winston's historical novels such as *Moorhaven*, *The Golden Valley* and *Gallows Way* are more powerful and substantial and have met with greater popularity in Britain than her other works. Unfortunately she does not exploit her skill in recreating historical events, instead using the setting primarily as a vehicle for her exploration of the emotions and motive already mentioned. This leads to a weakening of the romantic thriller element, since romance is often delayed until the very end of the novel when the heroine is finally moved by the hero's love for her. The historical element is often overpowered by a strong, all-pervading sense of doom. The action is sometimes spread over several generations, as in *Moorhaven*, and this compounds the doom which afflicts the inhabitants of the Golden Valley and the family mansion Moorhaven.

An interesting feature of character drawing is the way that twins are used as main characters (*House of Mirror Images*, *Skeleton Key*, *Kingdom's Castle*, *The Golden Valley*): considerable attention is devoted to their psychological (and sometimes pathological) interdependence. Winston likes to explore situations in which grown-up children are brought to a state where they cause violence because of their parents keeping them as children beyond childhood. Their settings are, however, stylised and they often appear mannequin-like.

Winston has latterly developed a sure touch and mastered the craft of romantic novel writing. In her latest novels, her work has matured, and she now develops stronger plots and story lines as well as a faster pace of action. In *Mills of the Gods* these features are combined with an accurate and minutely researched historical setting at the turn of the century. The vivid descriptions of clothes and facial appearances provide a comprehensive catalogue of the minutiae of romantic attraction. Personal attracton grows and wanes against a strong background of family and social disturbance, but people are perhaps more forward sexually than might be expected for the time. In *The Lotteries* the setting again includes New England but is largely a rather grimy and greasy contemporary America. A favourite theme of fortune and its twists reappears, as does the theme of the disadvantages of wealth. The emotions and behaviour shown are, however, very up-to-date as are the sexual mores of the characters.

Daoma Winston provides, in addition to romantic escape, useful insights into some bogeys of the American psyche.

—P.R. Meldrum

WOODIWISS, Kathleen E. American. Born in Alexandria, Louisiana. Educated at schools in Alexandria. Married to Ross Woodiwiss; three sons. Address: c/o Avon Books, 959 Eighth Avenue, New York, New York 10019, U.S.A.

ROMANCE AND GOTHIC PUBLICATIONS

Novels

The Flame and the Flower.   New York, Avon, 1972; London, Futura, 1975.
The Wolf and the Dove.   New York, Avon, 1974.
Shanna.   New York, Avon, and London, Futura, 1977.
Ashes in the Wind.   New York, Avon, 1979.

*   *   *

Although Kathleen E. Woodiwiss has published only four romances to date, her impact on the genre, especially as it is produced in the United States, has been substantial, if not revolutionary. When *The Flame and the Flower*, her first novel, arrived at Avon Books in 1972, the field of romance publishing was still dominated by the contemporary "gothics" of writers such as Mary Stewart, Victoria Holt, and Phyllis Whitney. A good three hundred pages longer than the gothics, *The Flame and the Flower* differed from them further in that it contained long, erotic passages describing the sexual encounters of heroine and hero in surprising detail. When Woodiwiss's novel met with immediate success, her publishers followed it with Rosemary Rogers's similar *Sweet Savage Love* and then created a new romantic sub-genre that has since been dubbed "the erotic historical" or, less reverently, "the bodice-ripper."

Woodiwiss's novels, which include, in addition to *The Flame and the Flower*, *The Wolf and the Dove*, *Shanna*, and *Ashes in the Wind*, do not deserve the latter epithet, as do those of some of her imitators. Although her heroines encounter male violence as Heather does in *The Flame and the Flower* when she is raped by her future husband because he thinks her a prostitute, Woodiwiss never multiplies such scenes or dwells on their brutal details simply to titillate her readers. Not only are such events rare in her books but they are also carefully integrated into complex plots which all focus on the *gradual* development of love between the two principal characters. Unlike many of the writers of this subgenre who keep the heroine and hero apart until the final pages of the novel, Woodiwiss brings them into contact early in the tale. Having established their initial attraction for each other, she then shows how love develops between two extraordinary individuals, emphasizes that the relationship must be cultivated carefully, and demonstrates that compromise, tenderness, and generosity are necessary to maintain it. The erotic scenes in all of Woodiwiss's novels are presented as integral parts of this deepening relationship and, as a consequence, she places most of her emphasis on the increasing tenderness with which the hero treats the heroine.

Woodiwiss's stories are further distinguished from those of her imitators by the fact that her characters exhibit somewhat more androgynous personalities than do those that typically populate the genre. Although all her heroines are unusually beautiful, sensitive, and particularly adept at nursing or caring for others, they are also asserted to be willful, forceful, intelligent, and capable of initiating action on their own. Interestingly enough, each Woodiwiss heroine is more independent and active than was her prececessor. Aislinn (*The Wolf and the Dove*) and Shanna (*Shanna*) both challenge their heroes in ways Heather (*The Flame and the Flower*) does not, just as they are portrayed as the intellectual equals of their men. This apparent emphasis on equality is carried even further in *Ashes in the Wind* when Alaina masquerades as a boy throughout the entire first half of the novel, saves the hero's life, and generally proves herself capable of fending for herself. The heroes, on the other hand, though typically Byronic, commanding, and spectacularly male, are also capable of reflection, sympathy, and tenderness. By the end of her novels, each Woodiwiss hero, like Brandon in *The Flame and the Flower*, confesses openly his dependence on the heroine and his love for her special qualities. It seems possible, then, that although she does not challenge the validity of the romance's essential message that female happiness can be secured most successfuly in the arms of a protective male, Kathleen Woodiwiss has been influenced by the feminism of the 1970's to the extent that she unfailingly asserts verbally that her heroines are not mere children whose every whim and desire must be gratified by a man. Rather, she insists, they are independent women who desire a loving relationship that is also an equal partnership. Her extraordinary and sudden popularity may well have been a function of this ability to embody some of the ideas of the feminist movement in changed character types without also upsetting the traditional structural relationship between the sexes.

—Janice Radway

WORBOYS, Anne (Annette Isobel Worboys, née Eyre).   Also writes as Annette Eyre; Vicky Maxwell; Anne Eyre Worboys.   British.   Born in Auckland, New Zealand. Served in the Royal New Zealand Air Force, 1942-45. Married Walter Worboys in 1946; two daughters. Recipient: Mary Elgin Award, 1975; Romantic Novelists Association Major Award, 1977. Agent: David Higham Associates Ltd., 5-8 Lower John Street, London W1R 4HA. Address: The White House, Leigh, near Tonbridge, Kent, England.

ROMANCE AND GOTHIC PUBLICATIONS

Novels

> *The Lion of Delos*.   New York, Delacorte Press, 1974; London, Hodder and Stoughton, 1975.
> *Every Man a King*.   London, Hodder and Stoughton, 1975; New York, Scribner, 1976; as *Rendezvous with Fear*, New York, Ace, 1977.
> *The Barrancourt Destiny*.   London, Hodder and Stoughton, 1977; New York, Scribner, 1978.
> *The Bhunda Jewels*.   London, Severn House, 1980; New York, Ace, 1981.
> *Run, Sara, Run*.   New York, Scribner, 1981; London, Severn House, 1982.

Novels as Anne Eyre Worboys

> *Dream of Petals Whim*.   London, Ward Lock, 1961.
> *Palm Rock and Paradise*.   London, Ward Lock, 1961.
> *Call for a Stranger*.   London, Ward Lock, 1962.

Novels as Annette Eyre

> *Three Strings to a Fortune*.   London, Hurst and Blackett, 1962.
> *Visit to Rata Creek*.   London, Hurst and Blackett, 1964.
> *The Valley of Yesterday*.   London, Hurst and Blackett, 1965.
> *A Net to Catch the Wind*.   London, Hurst and Blackett, 1966.
> *Return to Bellbird Country*.   London, Hurst and Blackett, 1966.
> *The House of Five Pines*.   London, Hurst and Blackett, 1967.
> *The River and Wilderness*.   London, Hurst and Blackett, 1967; as *Give Me Your Love*, New York, New American Library, 1975.
> *A Wind from the Hill*.   London, Hurst and Blackett, 1968.
> *Thorn-Apple*.   London, Hurst and Blackett, 1968.
> *Tread Softly in the Sun*.   London, Hurst and Blackett, 1969.
> *The Little Millstones*.   London, Hurst and Blackett, 1970.
> *Dolphin Bay*.   London, Hurst and Blackett, 1970.
> *Rainbow Child*.   London, Hurst and Blackett, 1971.
> *The Magnolia Room*.   London, Hurst and Blackett, 1972; New York, New American Library, 1975.
> *Venetian Inheritance*.   London, Hurst and Blackett, 1973; New York, New American Library, 1975.

Novels as Vicky Maxwell

> *Chosen Child*.   London, Collins, 1973; New York, Ace, 1980.
> *Flight to the Villa Mistra*.   London, Collins, 1973; New York, Ace, 1981.
> *The Way of the Tamarisk*.   London, Collins, 1974; as Anne Worboys, New York, Delacorte Press, 1975.

High Hostage.   London, Collins, 1976.
The Other Side of Summer.   London, Collins, 1977; New York, Ace, 1979.

*   *   *

Anne Worboys is a prolific writer of romance and romantic suspense novels who always turns out a readable, well-paced story. As Annette Eyre, she writes romance novels in the standard format. Under the pseudonym Vicky Maxwell, she writes novels of suspense. Similar in construction and content to the Vicky Maxwell titles are the novels issued under the name Anne Worboys. With one exception, these are the most well-written and interesting fiction of this enjoyable author.

The Lion of Delos, her first, combines a setting on the sunny Greek island of Mykonos with the slightly confusing plot of a missing twin sister. Well-wrought dialog and flashes of real excellence in the storyline provide a preview of her later works.

Every Man a King proves to be one of her best books, an intriguing story set in Spain with its roots in the Spanish Civil War over 30 years ago. Suzanne Cole comes to discover the mystery surrounding her stepmother's involvement with the wealthy de Merito family. The scenery is spectacular and a ride on horses through the Sierra Nevadas provides a thrilling finale.

The Barrancourt Destiny is a fitting followup to *Every Man a King*. Again family problems and mysteries dominate as Victoria Brown comes to England to solve the riddle of her family background and her possible connection to the Barrancourts of Alconleigh. She is lucky enough to find a job there, meeting first the heir (who is having an affair with his father's young wife) and then cousin Louis, enigmatic and handsome, who takes care of the riding stables. The mystery aspect is quite well-handled, and the romance is a charmer complete with a tension-filled midnight tour by candlelight of the estate.

Unfortunately, Worboys's latest novel, *Run, Sara, Run*, more of a mystery than her usual romantic suspense, is an annoying, unsatisfying tale of an actress, Sara Tindale, who along with her baby is being stalked by a vengeful killer. Part of the disappointment derives from the fact that the reader expects another *Barrancourt Destiny*.

—Marilyn Lockhart

WREN, P(ercival) C(hristopher).   British.   Born in Devonshire, in 1885.   Educated at Oxford University, M.A. Married; one son. Worked as schoolmaster, journalist, farm hand, explorer, hunter, soldier: trooper in a British cavalry regiment, and served in the French Foreign Legion; lived in India: Assistant Director of Education, Bombay, 10 years, and Justice of the Peace; Major in the Indian Forces in East Africa during World War I: invalided home. *Died 22 November 1941.*

ROMANCE AND GOTHIC PUBLICATIONS

Novels

   Father Gregory; or, Lures and Failures: A Tale of Hindostan.   London, Longman, 1913;
      New York, Stokes, 1926.
   Snake and Sword.   London, Longman, 1914; as *The Snake and the Sword*, New York,
      Stokes, 1923.

The Wages of Virtue. London, Murray, 1916; New York, Stokes, 1917.
Driftwood Spars. London, Longman, 1916; New York, Stokes, 1927.
Cupid in Africa; or, The Baking of Bertram in Love and War—A Character Study.
   London, Cranton, 1920.
Beau Geste. London, Murray, 1924; New York, Stokes, 1925.
Beau Sabreur. London, Murray, and New York, Stokes, 1926.
Beau Ideal. London, Murray, and New York, Stokes, 1928.
Soldiers of Misfortune: The Story of Otho Belleme. London, Murray, and New York,
   Stokes, 1929.
Mysterious Waye: The Story of "The Unsetting Sun." London, Murray, and New
   York, Stokes, 1930.
The Mammon of Righteousness: The Story of Coxe and the Box. London, Murray,
   1930; as *Mammon*, New York, Stokes, 1930.
Sowing Glory: The Memoirs of "Mary Ambree," The English Woman—Legionary.
   London, Murray, and New York, Stokes, 1931.
Valiant Dust. London, Murray, and New York, Stokes, 1932.
Action and Passion. London, Murray, and New York, Stokes, 1933.
Beggars' Horses. London, Murray, 1934; as *The Dark Woman*, Philadelphia, Macrae
   Smith, 1943.
Sinbad the Soldier. London, Murray, and Boston, Houghton Mifflin, 1935.
Explosion. London, Murray, 1935.
Spanish Maine. London, Murray, 1935; as *The Desert Heritage*, Boston, Houghton
   Mifflin, 1935.
Fort in the Jungle: The Extraordinary Adventures of Sinbad Dysart in Tonkin. Lon-
   don, Murray, and Boston, Houghton Mifflin, 1936.
Bubble Reputation. London, Murray, 1936; as *The Courtenay Treasure*, Boston,
   Houghton Mifflin, 1936.
The Man of a Ghost. London, Murray, 1937; as *The Spur of Pride*, Boston, Houghton
   Mifflin, 1937.
Worth Wile. London, Murray, 1937; as *To the Hilt*, Boston, Houghton Mifflin, 1937.
Cardboard Castle. London, Murray, and Boston, Houghton Mifflin, 1938.
Paper Prison. London, Murray, 1939; as *The Man the Devil Didn't Want*, Philadel-
   phia, Macrae Smith, 1940.
The Disappearance of General Jason. London, Murray, 1940.
Two Feet from Heaven. London, Murray, 1940; Philadelphia, Macrae Smith, 1941.
Stories of the Foreign Legion (omnibus). London, Murray, 1947.

Short Stories

Dew and Mildew: Semi-Detached Stories from Karabad, India. London, Longman,
   1912; as *Dew and Mildew: A Loose-Knit Tale of Hindustan*, New York, Stokes, 1927.
Stepsons of France. London, Murray, and New York, Stokes, 1917.
*The Young Stagers, Being Further Faites and Gestes of the Junior Curlton Club of
   Karabad, India....* London, Longman, 1917; New York, Stokes, 1926.
*Good Gestes: Stories of Beau Geste, His Brothers, and Certain of Their Comrades in the
   French Foreign Legion.* London, Murray, and New York, Stokes, 1929.
Flawed Blades: Tales from the Foreign Legion. London, Murray, and New York,
   Stokes, 1933.
Port o' Missing Men: Strange Tale of the Stranger Regiment. London, Murray, 1934;
   Philadelphia, Macrae Smith, 1943.
Rough Shooting: True Tales and Strange Stories. London, Murray, 1938; Philadel-
   phia, Macrae Smith, 1944.
Odd—But Even So: Stories Stranger Than Fiction. London, Murray, 1941; Philadel-
   phia, Macrae Smith, 1942.
The Hunting of Henri. London, Vallancey Press, 1944.
Dead Men's Boot and Other Tales from the Foreign Legion. London, Gryphon, 1949.

OTHER PUBLICATIONS

Other

The Indian Teacher's Guide to the Theory and Practice of Mental, Moral, and Physical
    Education. Bombay, Longman, 1910.
Indian School Organization, Management, Discipline, Tone, and Equipment, Being the
    Indian Headmaster's Guide. Bombay, Longman, 1911.
The "Direct" Teaching of English in Indian Schools. Bombay, Longman, 1911.
Chemistry and First Aid for Standard VII, with H.E.H. Pratt. Bombay, Longman,
    1913.
Physics and Mechanics, with N.B. Macmillan. Bombay, Longman, 1914.
With the Prince Through Canada, New Zealand, and Australia. Bombay, Athenaeum
    Press, 1922.
Work, Wealth, and Wages (juvenile), revision of a work by Ernest F. Row. Bombay,
    Cooper, 1950.
First Lessons in English Grammar. Bombay, Cooper, 1961.

Editor, The World and India, Adapted for Use in Indian Schools. Calcutta, Oxford
    University Press, 1905.
Editor, Ivanhoe (simplified), by Scott. London, Frowde, 1912.
Editor, Longmans' Science Series for Indian High Schools. Bombay, Longman, 11
    vols., 1913-14.
Editor, Gulliver's Travels (simplified), by Swift. Calcutta, Oxford University Press,
    1963.

*   *   *

P.C. Wren's works range from potboilers indistinguishable from the fulminations of pulp
writers to novels that presented an integrated world-view and fully developed characters; these
latter efforts were recognizable bids for recognition as a serious artist—a recognition that his
popularity seemed to preclude. Wren mixed melodrama with the lightest comic banter, exotic
settings with the most brutal realism, and romantic idealism with an almost overwhelmingly
cynical fatalism.

The melodrama in Wren most often grows out of basic conflicts; circumstances demand the
characters choose a course of action that frustrates personal needs but satisfies the character's
sense of honor. Wren was also not afraid of employing outdated superstitions—e.g., prenatal
conditioning (Snake and Sword) or yogic telepathy (Beggars' Horses)—in order to underscore
his basic interest in fiction: men in a state of struggle, in which the external conflict only works
as a metaphor for the internal conflict. Wren's melodramatic (Dickensian?) use of coincidence
also serves a purpose apparently unnoticed by his contemporaries: it represents an attachment
to Oriental fatalism that is deeply rooted in his own Anglo-Saxon origins—the warrior in
conflict with Wyrd, with only individual courage and the aid of kinsmen to stave off an
inevitable death.

Beneath the melodrama is the humorous banter of English boys that changes little as the
public-school heroes grow into men. In Wren, the inevitable and thankless manifest destiny of
the British Empire to shape the remote corners of the world is often set forth in schoolboy
exchanges that counterpoint a complex emotional and psychological framework reminiscent
of Conrad, though without his allusive obscurity. His characters are usually joined in a
metaphorical or actual fraternity, most commonly in a military unit in which family relationships are disguised (Beau Geste) or unknown (Wages of Virtue). This ironic, half-humorous
approach shows events in multiple focus: the stiff-upper-lip narration often reveals, beneath
the total belief in Great Britain, a tottering personal emotional security pivoting on a conflict of
honor against survival. Though the values of British upbringing appear never to be questioned,
circumstances ironically point to an emotionally empty or fateful universe that overwhelms the
values of the individual. The bland assurances of organized religion ring hollow for Wren's

characters. Only in death does the sense of purpose or significance of individual life seem vindicated.

The most successful of Wren's books was *Beau Geste*, which incorporates the most characteristic themes and values of Wren's world-view. This story of three brothers who join the Foreign Legion in order to preserve the family honor and fulfill their own boyhood military fantasies becomes an elaborately realized celebration of the theme of human brotherhood. The Gestes (the Anglo-French pun, as always in Wren, is intended) are orphans whose real family is unknown to us. Their rootlessness is paralleled by the international and anonymous make-up of the French Foreign Legion whose brotherhood the Gestes soon join. The existential overtones of the defense of Fort Zinderneuf are obvious today through hindsight, but it may be doubted that many of Wren's original readers caught the philosophical significance of the repeated ascents of the watchtower by men marked for death or the dead soldiers standing watch at the machicolations while Digby prepares Beau's "Viking's funeral." Death with honor is the ultimate seal of human commitments. These themes of the commitment to brotherhood and of disguised relationships recur in the two sequels to *Beau Geste*: *Beau Sabreur* and *Beau Ideal*. (*Good Gestes*, Wren's farewell to the characters that made him famous, is a set of excellent stories that add nothing to our knowledge of the Gestes and could have been about anybody. And an indirectly connected work, *Spanish Maine*, appeared in 1935.)

Other series characters appear in later works, though none so fully or satisfactorily drawn as the Gestes. Sinclair Noel Brody Dysart ("Sinbad") appears in *Action and Passion*, *Sinbad the Soldier*, and *The Fort in the Jungle*. Several figures involved in British intelligence in India recur in novels the most interesting of which is *Beggars' Horses*, an ironic *tour de force*. This novel examines the disastrous effects on a handful of skeptical inquirers into the alleged prophecies of a famous yogi when the angry yogi *grants* each of them their dearest wish. Another outstanding departure is the neglected masterpiece of psychological disintegation and sexual captivity, *Mammon of Righteousness*, in which Wren's insights into the effects of repression result in one of his most agonizing and involving stories.

In the face of all this sardonic irony, with characters moving under the shadow of immanent death, there is still in Wren's best work the clear affirmation that life has meaning, despite the efforts of a universe apparently anitpathetic to human hopes and wishes. That meaning lies in commitment to our essential brotherhood and to the values and traditions of the British Empire.

—Thomas R. Tietze

WYNDHAM, Esther.   Pseudonym for Mary Lutyens.   British.   Born in London, 31 July 1908; daughter of the architect Edwin Lutyens. Educated at home; Queen's College, London, 1919-23. Married 1) Anthony Sewell in 1930, one daughter; 2) Joseph G. Links in 1945. Writer from 1930: Columnist ("Mrs. Marriott"), *Woman's Weekly*, for a few months during World War II. Fellow, Royal Society of Literature, 1976. Agent: Curtis Brown Ltd., 1 Craven Hill, London W2 3EP. Address: 2 Hyde Park Street, London W2 2JN, England.

ROMANCE AND GOTHIC PUBLICATIONS

Novels

   Come Back, Elizabeth.   London, Nimmo Hay and Mitchell, 1948.

Black Charles.   London, Mills and Boon, 1952; Toronto, Harlequin, 1962.
Man of Steel.   London, Mills and Boon, 1952.
Mistress of Merryweather.   London, Mills and Boon, 1953.
Master of the Manor.   London, Mills and Boon, 1953.
Above the Clouds.   London, Mills and Boon, 1954; Toronto, Harlequin, 1964.
Tiger Hall.   London, Mills and Boon, 1954; Toronto, Harlequin, 1965.
Once You Have Found Him.   London, Mills and Boon, 1954; Toronto, Harlequin, 1964.
The House of Discontent.   London, Mills and Boon, 1955; Toronto, Harlequin, 1966.
The Blue Rose.   London, Mills and Boon, 1957; Toronto, Harlequin, 1967.

OTHER PUBLICATIONS as Mary Lutyens

Novels

Perchance to Dream.   London, Murray, 1935.
Rose and Thorn.   London, Murray, 1936.
Spider's Silk.   London, Joseph, 1939.
Family Colouring.   London, Joseph, 1940.
A Path of Gold.   London, Joseph, 1941.
Together and Alone.   London, Joseph, 1942.
So Near to Heaven.   London, Joseph, 1943.
And Now There Is You.   London, Hale, 1953.
Week-End at Hurtmore.   London, Hutchinson, 1954.
The Lucian Legend.   London, Hutchinson, 1955.
Meeting in Venice.   London, Hutchinson, 1956.
Cleo.   London, Joseph, 1973; New York, Stein and Day, 1974.

Short Stories

Forthcoming Marriages.   London, Murray, and New York, Dutton, 1933.

Other

Julie and the Narrow Valley (juvenile).   London, Guildford Press, 1947.
To Be Young: Some Chapters of Autobiography.   London, Hart Davis, 1959.
The Ruskins and the Grays.   London, Murray, 1972.
Krishnamurti: The Years of Awakening.   London, Murray, and New York, Farrar Straus, 1975.
The Lyttons in India: An Account of Lord Lytton's Viceroyalty 1876-1880.   London, Murray, 1979.
Edwin Lutyens.   London, Murray, 1980.

Editor, *Lady Lytton's Court Diary.*   London, Hart Davis, 1960.
Editor, *Effie in Venice.*   London, Murray, 1965; as *Young Mrs. Ruskin in Venice: Her Picture of Society and Life with John Ruskin 1849-1852*, New York, Vanguard Press, 1966.
Editor, *Millais and the Ruskins.*   London, Murray, 1967; New York, Vanguard Press, 1968.
Editor, *Freedom from the Known*, by Krishnamurti.   London, Gollancz, 1968; New York, Harper, 1969.
Editor, *The Only Revolution*, by Krishnamurti.   London, Gollancz, and New York, Harper, 1970.

Editor, *The Penguin Krishnamurti Reader* [and second reader].   London, Penguin, 2 vols., 1970-73.
Editor, *The Urgency of Change*, by Krishnamurti.   London, Gollancz, 1971.
Editor, *Krishnamurti's Notebook*.   London, Gollancz, and New York, Harper, 1976.

Esther Wyndham comments:

I first started writing romantic serials in the late 1930's under the pseudonym of Esther Wyndham to supplement the inadequate income I was making from the novels I *wanted* to write. Since the fees were high and the stories were afterwards published as books, this work was very rewarding financially. The ten serials I wrote came out either in *Woman's Weekly* or *Woman and Home*. I had a wonderful editor at the Amalgamated Press, Winifred Johnson, who had first approached me and who taught me this difficult craft which should never be underrated. For ten instalments the hero and heroine had to meet constantly, yet could not be brought together until the last instalment, and each instalment had to end with an emotional cliff-hanger.

The hero and heroine had to conform to Miss Johnson's romantic formula. Lady Diana Spencer would never have qualified as a Johnson heroine, except that she was a virgin and loved children, for she was far too beautiful, too rich, and had had too easy a life. The Prince of Wales might just have squeezed through as a Johnson hero, for in spite of being a prince he worked hard, had had rumoured involvements with other girls, and had not declared himself until the last instalment; however, there was a quality of mystery lacking in him.

One never penetrated the hero's mind until the end of the story, whereas every nuance of the heroine's feelings was revealed. In some stories she started by hating the hero because of his supposed arrogance until about instalment three when she began to feel drawn to him in spite of her better judgement. His behaviour was always a mystery to her. Disappointment and chagrin quickly followed those rare occasions when she felt he *cared*. There must invariably be another girl or older woman to make mischief out of jealousy, for it was only through misunderstandings on both sides that the couple could be kept apart for 70,000 words. A foreign setting was always a help.

The hero had to be brave, strong, rich, and frantically busy. It was best if he was self-made; if an aristocrat with inherited wealth he must be a model landlord who laboured to improve his estate for the sake of his tenants. The spirited heroine must not only have a wonderful way with children and old people but some previous tragedy or hardship in her life. And, of course, she had to work hard for her living. It was her character rather than her looks that attracted; she became beautiful only at rare moments, preferably when the hero was looking at her without her knowing it. Naturally, she became permanently beautiful at the end when irradiated with requited love.

Miss Johnson would give me guide-lines: "We want a heroine this time of about 28 who feels that life has passed her by," or, "Let's have a young girl in your next who has never been in love before." When writing in the war years it was easier to have a hero in a reserved occupation, hence Miss Johnson's plea to her authors after the war, "*Please*, no more farmers or doctors." When once the characters and story-line were more or less settled one wrote from the heart. To write down would have been fatal and I never felt any temptation to do so.

Miss J. only started publishing a serial when she had the complete story. This had not been the rule when she first entered the office as a junior. The great Ethel M. Dell had then been writing serials for the Amalgamated Press, and in a late instalment of one story it transpired to the horror of the editor that the unwed heroine was going to have a baby. She searched frantically through previous instalments to see when this could have happened and found that the heroine had come back one day from a walk with the hero with harebells in her hair. Thereafter the injunction ran through the office, "No more harebells."

I would write an instalment in three or four days and post it to Miss J. Next day her assistant would ring up either to say, "Go ahead," or "Miss Johnson would like to see you." Dread words, for I knew that somehow I had gone off the rails and would have to re-write the instalment. There was no arguing with Miss J. because she was quite deaf. Since her magazines sold widely in Ireland there must not be the slightest hint of impropriety, let alone "harebells." In one story when my hero was in Washington with the heroine, his secretary, and I had allowed her to sleep in the sitting-room of his hotel suite because all the hotels were full (a situation helpful to romance), Miss J. sent me a telegram, for I had gone abroad between instalments: "Please make another effort to find Elizabeth a room of her own." And when I was writing my first story, almost every instalment of which had to be re-written, and I had made the hero say that he was feeling ill in order to get away from a party, she wrote indignantly, "Who can have respect for a man who feels ill at a party?" A great editor, but one who could hardly have functioned successfully today.

*   *   *

It was one of Mary Lutyens's stories in *Forthcoming Marriages* that led to her being invited by Winifred Johnson to contribute romantic serials to the Amalgamated Press's women's papers. The first half of this story ("Mr. Raymond Skedley and Miss Katherine N. Robinson") conveyed the current of the heroine's thoughts on her wedding morning; the second half was concerned with emotional incidents leading up to and surrounding the ceremony later that day. Without perhaps realizing it, Mary Lutyens had already arrived at a satisfying and atmospheric balance of inner and outer mood that was exactly appropriate to the romantic story, and, as "Esther Wyndham," in her subsequent serial/novels she explored and exploited this to the full.

In the tradition of the genre, her heroines suffer the usual tremulous feelings of inadequacy that are sparked off by the challenge of relating to handsome but arrogant and enigmatic heroes. Esther Wyndham's leading ladies, however, are spirited, capable of decisive action, and, occasionally, of going against the tide of public opinion. (Generally they are working girls who take their careers quite seriously—an advanced shorthand-typist in *Come Back, Elizabeth*, a dedicated bookseller's assistant in *Above the Clouds*, an antique dealer in *Black Charles*.)

Even when overwhelmed by masculine magnetism and the intensity of their own sexual/romantic feelings, these heroines resolutely cling to a few robust strands of inner resource and intellectual independence. Their honest and slightly rueful self-awareness makes them interesting and extremely sympathetic to read about, and marks them as forerunners of the intelligent and highly individualised heroines who were two or three decades later to be at the centre of thriller romances by Mary Stewart in England, and Barbara Michaels in the USA.

The stories are tightly structured, and punctuated with humorous incident to counterbalance strong suspense. There is plenty of the latter, because the novels were originally written as serials with cliff hanger endings to each episode.

The author's vivid feeling for place gives the books a special intensity, but, though adept at evoking exotic foreign and romantic settings (Venice, for example, in *Above the Clouds*), Esther Wyndham is at her best with the traditional English country house background (as in *Black Charles*). This is, expectedly, not gruesomely Gothic but graciously Lutyens-esque!

—Mary Cadogan

WYNNE, May. Pseudonym for Mabel Winifred Knowles; also wrote as Lester Lurgan. British. Born in Streatham, London, in January 1875. Educated at home. Worked in an East End Church of England mission.

ROMANCE AND GOTHIC PUBLICATIONS

Novels

In the Shadows; or, Thoughts for Mourners. London, Marshall, 1900.
Sympathy. London, Skeffington, 1901.
Mollie's Adventures. London, Russell, 1903.
For Faith and Navarre. London, Long, 1904.
Ronald Lindsay. London, Long, 1905.
A King's Tragedy. London, Digby Long, 1905.
The Temptation of Philip Carr. London, Sonnenschein, 1905.
Theodore. London, Rivers, 1906.
Maid of Brittany. London, Greening, 1906.
The Goal. London, Digby Long, 1907.
When Terror Ruled. London, Greening, 1907.
Henry of Navarre: A Romance of August, 1572 (as Mabel W. Knowles). New York,
     Putnam, 1908; as May Wynne, London, Greening, 1909.
Let Erin Remember. London, Greening, 1908.
The Tailor of Vitré. London, Gay and Hancock, 1908.
For Church and Chieftain. London, Mills and Boon, 1909.
For Charles the Rover. London, Greening, 1909; New York, Fenno, 1911.
The Gipsy Count. New York, McBride, 1909.
A Blot on the Escutcheon. New York, Fenno, n.d., London, Mills and Boon, 1910.
A King's Masquerade. London, Greening, 1910.
Mistress Cynthia. London, Greening, 1910.
The Gallant Graham. London, Greening, 1911.
Honour's Fetters. London, Stanley Paul, 1911.
The Claim That Won. London, Everett, 1912.
Hey for Cavaliers! London, Greening, 1912.
The Red Fleur-de-Lys. London, Stanley Paul, 1912.
The Brave Brigands. London, Stanley Paul, 1913.
The Destiny of Claude. London, Stanley Paul, 1913.
The Secret of the Zenana. London, Greening, 1913.
Goring's Girl. London, Mascot, 1914.
The Hero of Urbino. London, Stanley Paul, 1914.
Murray Finds a Chum. London, Stanley Paul, 1914.
The Silent Captain. London, Stanley Paul, 1914.
The Regent's Gift. London, Chapman and Hall, 1915.
Foes of Freedom. London, Chapman and Hall, 1916.
An English Girl in Serbia. London, Collins, 1916.
The Gipsy King. London, Chapman and Hall, 1917.
The Lyons Mail. London, Jarrolds, 1917.
Marcel of the "Zephyrs." London, Jarrolds, 1917.
The Master Wit: A Story of Boccaccio. London, Greening, 1917.
Penance. London, Mascot, 1917.
A Spy for Napoleon. London, Jarrolds, 1917.
The Taint of Tragedy. London, Mascot, 1917.
Three's Company. London, Blackie, 1917.
The "Veiled Lady," with Draycot M. Dell. London, Jarrolds, 1918.
The King of a Day. London, Jarrolds, 1918.
Queen Jennie. London, Chapman and Hall, 1918.
Stranded in Belgium. London, Blackie, 1918.
The Red Whirlpool, with Draycott M. Dell. London, Jarrolds, 1919.
The Curse of Gold. London, Aldine, 1919.
Dick. London, Religious Tract Society, 1919.
Phyllis in France. London, Blackie, 1919.
Robin the Prodigal. London, Jarrolds, 1919.

A Run for His Money. London, Aldine, 1919.
The Adventures of Dolly Dingle. London, Jarrolds, 1920.
A Prince of Intrigue: A Romance of Mazeppa. London, Jarrolds, 1920.
Adventures of Two. London, Blackie, 1920.
A Gallant of Spain. London, Stanley Paul, 1920.
Janie's Great Mistake. London, Odhams Press, 1920.
Mervyn, Jock, or Joe. London, Blackie, 1921.
Mog Megone. London, Jarrolds, 1921.
My Lady's Honour. London, Lloyds, 1921.
The Spendthrift Duke. London, Holden and Hardingham, 1921.
The Red Rose of Lancaster. London, Holden and Hardingham, 1922.
A Trap for Navarre. London, Holden, 1922.
A King in the Lists. London, Stanley Paul, 1922.
The Girls of the Veldt Farm. London, Pearson, 1922.
The Ambitions of Jill. London, Long, 1923.
The Witch-Finder. London, Jarrolds, 1923.
Blundering Bettina. London, Religious Tract Society, 1924.
Jill the Hostage. London, Pearson, 1925.
Hootie Toots of Hollow Tree. Philadelphia, Altemus, 1925.
Rachel Lee. London, Leng, 1925.
Hazel Asks Why. London, Ward Lock, 1926.
Gwennola. London, Rivers, 1926.
The Fires of Youth. London, Rivers, 1927.
Plotted in Darkness. London, Stanley Paul, 1927.
King Mandarin's Challenge. London, Stanley Paul, 1927.
A Royal Traitor. London, Stanley Paul, 1927.
Love's Penalty. London, Stanley Paul, 1927.
Terry the Black Sheep. London, Pearson, 1928.
The Girls of Mackland Court. London, Ward Lock, 1928.
The Terror of the Moor. London, Rivers, 1928.
Gipsy-Spelled. London, Rivers, 1929.
The House of Whispers. London, Ward Lock, 1929.
Red Fruit. London, Ward Lock, 1929.
Hamlet: A Romance from Shakespeare's Play. London, Rivers, 1930.
Juliet of the Mill. London, Ward Lock, 1931.
The Girl Upstairs. London, Thomson, 1932.
The Unseen Witness. London, Leng, 1932.
Stella Maris. London, Leng, 1932.
Who Was Wendy? London, Newnes, 1932.
The Heart of Glenayrt. London, Nelson, 1932.
Pixie's Mysterious Mission. London, Newnes, 1933.
Enter Jenny Wren. London, Ward Lock, 1933.
Malys Rockell. London, Ward Lock, 1934.
The Smugglers of Penreen. London, Religious Tract Society, 1934.
Up to Val. London, Newnes, 1935.
Tangled Fates. London, Mellifont Press, 1935.
Flower o' the Moor. London, Houghton and Scott-Snell, 1935.
The Choice of Mavis. London, Mellifont Press, 1935.
Bunny the Aunt. London, Religious Tract Society, 1936.
The Haunted Ranch. London, Dean, 1936.
Thirteen for Luck. London, Ward Lock, 1936.
Vivette on Trial. London, Queensway Press, 1936.
The Secret of Brick House. London, Ward Lock, 1937.
Temptation. London, Mellifont Press, 1937.
Two Maids of Rosemarkie. London, Epworth Press, 1937.
The Luck of Penrayne. London, Religious Tract Society, 1937.
Audrey on Approval. London, Ward Lock, 1937.
The Girl Sandy. London, Ward Lock, 1938.

Whither? London, Cranston, 1938.
The Unexpected Adventure. London, Ward Lock, 1939.
The Coming of Verity. London, Ward Lock, 1940.
Love Dismayed. London, Mellifont Press, 1942.
Echoed from the Past. London, Mellifont Press, 1944.
The Pursuing Shadow. London, Mellifont Press, 1944.
The Unsuspected Witness. London, Mellifont Press, 1945.
The Secret of the Caves. London, Mellifont Press, 1945.
Ginger Ellen. London, Nelson, 1947.
The Great Adventure. London, Ward Lock, 1948.
Secrets of the Rockies. London, Ward Lock, 1954.

Novels as Lester Lurgan

Bohemian Blood. London, Greening, 1910.
The Mill-Owner. London, Greening, 1910.
The League of the Triangle. London, Greening, 1911.
A Message from Mars. London, Greening, 1912.
The Ban. London, Stanley Paul, 1912.
The Wrestler on the Shore. London, Everett, 1912.

OTHER PUBLICATIONS

Other (juvenile)

Love's Objects; or, Some Thoughts for Young Girls. London, Nisbet, 1899.
Jimmie: The Tales of a Little Black Bear. London, Partridge, 1910.
Phil's Cousin: A Holiday Tale. London, Blackie, 1912.
The Story of Heather. London, Nelson, 1912.
Crackers: The Tale of a Mischievous Monkey. London, Partridge, 1912.
The Life and Reign of Victoria the Good. London, Stanley Paul, 1913.
Tony's Chums. London, Blackie, 1915.
When Auntie Lil Took Charge. London, Blackie, 1915.
A Cousin from Canada. London, Blackie, 1918.
The Honour of the School. London, Nisbet, 1918.
The Heroine of Chelton School. London, Stanley Paul, 1919.
The Little Girl Beautiful. London, Religious Tract Society, 1919.
Nan and Ken. London, Nelson, 1919.
Nipper and Co. London, Stanley Paul, 1919.
Scouts for Serbia. London, Nelson, 1919.
Comrades from Canada. London, Blackie, 1919.
The Seven Champions of Christendom. London, Jarrolds, 1919.
The Girls of Beechcroft School. London, Religious Tract Society, 1920.
Roseleen at School. London, Cassell, 1920.
Three Bears and Gwen. London, Blackie, 1920.
Little Ladyship. London, Religious Tract Society, 1921.
Lost in the Jungle. London, Stanley Paul, 1921.
Peggy's First Term. London, Ward Lock, 1922.
Angela Goes to School. London, Jarrolds, 1922; Cleveland, World, 1929.
Christmas at Holford. London, Blackie, 1922.
Two Girls in the Wild. London, Blackie, 1923.
The Best of Chums. London, Ward Lock, 1923.
A Heather Holiday. London, Blackie, 1923; as *Wendy's Adventure in Scotland*, 1933;
  as *An Adventurous Holiday* (reader), 1933.
The Girl Who Played the Game. London, Ward Lock, 1924.

Bertie, Bobby, and Belle. London, Blackie, 1924.
The Girls of Clanways Farm. London, Cassell, 1924.
Kits at Clynton Court School. London, Warne, 1924.
The Sunshine Children. London, Nelson, 1924.
Three and One Over. London, Cassell, 1924.
Two and a Chum. London, Pearson, 1924.
The Girls of Old Grange School. London, Ward Lock, 1925.
Over the Hills and Far Away. London, Children's Companion, 1925.
Dare-All Jack and the Cousins. London, Children's Companion, 1925.
Carol of Hollydene School. London, Sampson Low, 1926.
The Secret of Carrock School. London, Jarrolds, 1926.
Diccon the Impossible. London, Children's Companion, 1926.
The Girl over the Wall. London, Girl's Own Paper, 1926.
Jean Plays Her Part. London, Girl's Own Paper, 1926.
Dinah's Secret. London, Children's Companion, 1927.
Jean of the Lumber Camp. London, Ward Lock, 1927.
Robin Hood to the Rescue. Exeter, Wheaton, 1927.
Little Sally Mandy's Christmas Present. Philadelphia, Altemus, 1929.
The Guide's Honour. London, Warne, 1929.
A Term to Remember. London, Aldine, 1930.
Two Girls in the Hawk's Den. London, Pearson, 1930.
Bobbety the Brownie. London, Warne, 1930.
The Masked Rider. Chicago, Laidlaw, 1931.
Patient Pat Joins the Circus. Philadelphia, Altemus, 1931.
Peter Rabbit and the Big Black Crows. Philadelphia, Altemus, 1931.
The Peter Rabbit Playtime Story Book. Philadelphia, Altemus, 1931.
Girls of the Pansy Patrol. London, Aldine, 1931.
Patsy from the Wilds. London, Warne, 1931.
The Old Brigade. London, Girl's Own Paper, 1932.
The Secret of Marigold Marnell. London, Girl's Own Paper, 1932.
The School Mystery. London, Readers Library, 1933.
Comrades to Robin Hood. London, Religious Tract Society, 1934.
The Mysterious Island. London, Mellifont Press, 1935.
Their Girl Chum. London, Religious Tract Society, 1935.
Under Cap'n Drake. London, Boy's Own Paper, 1935.
"Peter," The New Girl. London, Queensway Press, 1936.
The Daring of Star. London, Girl's Own Paper, 1936.
The Lend-a-Hand Holiday. London, Epworth Press, 1938.
Heather the Second. London, Nelson, 1938.
The Term of Many Adventures. London, Nelson, 1939.
Little Brown Tala. London, Mellifont Press, 1944.
Brown Tala Finds Little Tulsi. London, Mellifont Press, 1945.
Little Brown Tala Stories. London, Harrap, 1947.
Patch the Piebald. Croydon, Surrey, Blue Book, 1947.
Playing the Game. Croydon, Surrey, Blue Book, 1947.
Snow Fairies. London, Mellifont Press, 1947.
Sally Comes to School. London, Ward Lock, 1949.
The Furry Fairies. London, Mellifont Press, 1949.
Merion Plays the Game. London, Readers Library, 1950.

*   *   *

May Wynne infused romantic elements into the juvenile stories at which she excelled in the form of exotic locations and charismatic personalities. Her love stories for adults also exploit glamorously foreign settings and colourful people like gipsies or intrepid adventurer-explorers. *The Gipsy King* (1917) includes characters of both these types. Bampfylde Carew, who starts off as something of a wastrel, leaves his vicarage home, attracted by "the merry fiddling of the gipsies...and the crackling of their wood fires," sounds that, apparently, "echo

louder, more enticing, more alluring than the sonorous music of his father's preaching...."
Wynne thus sets the scene for a much-used theme in her romances: the conflict between duty,
which she sees as synonymous with the acceptance of orthodox Christianity, and the attractions of the "free" and socially untrammelled life. Generally she includes the finding of true
love and its attendant pattern of committal to married domesticity as part and parcel of the
hero or heroine's redemptive adoption of a religious faith. However, Bampfylde Carew has a
long way to go (roaming with the gipsies, having lusty adventures on the high seas and in the
Indian territories of America) before he is eventually brought back to the path of Christian
virtue by loyal and loving Letty Gray, from his own village.

The Fires of Youth (1927) is concerned with similar issues, and particularly with the return
to rustic roots (also equatable in Wynne's stories with the romantic and religious experience).
For Tom Tarrock, illusions of freedom take the shape of making money in a big way—but like
Bampfylde in The Gipsy King, and many other of this author's heroes, he has an innocent
village girl (in this case Jessamy Windell, who becomes a Church Army Sister), waiting
patiently to feel—eventually—his passionate but purified kiss on her "firm, sweet lips."

With her insistent linking of romantic and domestic love to Christian conversion, May
Wynne is harking back to the mood of many Victorian "tales of home life." Her love stories,
however, have less of the retributive tone of their 19th-century forerunners, though they never
achieve the liveliness of her juvenile stories.

—Mary Cadogan

YARBRO, Chelsea Quinn. American. Born in Berkeley, California, 15 September 1942.
Attended San Francisco State College, 1960-63. Married Donald P. Simpson in 1969
(divorced, 1982). Theatre manager and playwright, Mirthmakers Children's Theatre, San
Francisco, 1961-64; children's counsellor, 1963; cartographer, C.E. Erickson and Associates,
Oakland, California, 1963-70; composer; card and palm reader, 1974-78. Secretary, Science
Fiction Writers of America, 1970-72. Agent: Kirby McCauley, 425 Park Avenue South, New
York, New York 10016. Address: 1921 El Dorado Avenue, Berkeley, California 94707, U.S.A.

ROMANCE AND GOTHIC PUBLICATIONS

Novels (series: Count Saint Germain)

Ogilvie, Tallant, and Moon. New York, Putnam, 1976.
Hotel Transylvania: A Novel of Forbidden Love (Saint Germain). New York, St.
    Martin's Press, 1978; London, New English Library, 1981.
Music When Sweet Voices Die. New York, Putnam, 1979.
The Palace (Saint Germain). New York, St. Martin's Press, 1979; London, New English
    Library, 1981.
Blood Games (Saint Germain). New York, St. Martin's Press, 1980.
Sins of Omission. New York, New American Library, 1980.
Ariosto. New York, Pocket Books, 1980.
Dead and Buried. New York, Warner, 1980.
Path of the Eclipse (Saint Germain). New York, St. Martin's Press, 1981.
Tempting Fate (Saint Germain). New York, St. Martin's Press, 1982.
A Taste of Wine (as Vanessa Pryor). New York, Pocket Books, 1982.

OTHER PUBLICATIONS

Novels

Time of the Fourth Horseman.   New York, Doubleday, 1976; London, Sidgwick and
   Jackson, 1980.
False Dawn.   New York, Doubleday, 1978; London, Sidgwick and Jackson, 1979.

Short Stories

Cautionary Tales.   New York, Doubleday, 1978; expanded edition, New York, Warner,
   and London, Sidgwick and Jackson, 1980.

Play

The Little-Girl Dragon of Alabaster-on-Fenwick (produced San Francisco, 1973).

Other

Messages from Michael.   Chicago, Playboy Press, 1979.

Editor, with Thomas N. Scortia, *Two Views of Wonder*.   New York, Ballantine, 1973.

*   *   *

Known to science-fiction and mystery readers, Chelsea Quinn Yarbro attracted a new
audience with the 1978 publication of *Hotel Transylvania*. Here she introduced to gothic and
historical romance readers the lustful vampire Count Saint Germain. His sustenance came
from blood, but never did he wish to terrify or harm his victims. He searched instead for love
and understanding. Whenever passion was present the energy he received became greatly
increased while his partner experienced raptures no human male could possible induce.
Through the four books in the Saint Germain series, the reader begins to understand the nature
of the vampire as it exists in the mind of the author. Evil is not an intrinsic vampire trait,
something Saint Germain proves over and over again in his championship of good causes. In
addition, this vampire has achieved a sort of immortality, never aging or changing physically.
Death can only come through fire, decapitation or severing of the spinal column, or long
exposure to sunlight or water without the protection of native soil worn in specially constructed shoes. Native soil also lines his bed and the foundation of his house. In its presence, he
absorbs the soil's life sustaining radiation. Coming originally from Eastern Europe he travels
throughout the world seeking true love and an end to intense loneliness.
   The Saint Germain stories, all set in various historical periods, dwell on episodes of fear and
violence. The setting for *Hotel Transylvania* is mid-18th-century Paris, where the exquisite
Madelaine De Montalia becomes the victim of a satanic cult. In *The Palace* the incredibly
beautiful Demitrice, former mistress of Lorenzo the Magnificent, is arrested and tortured by
the followers of Savonarola. Olivia, a character whose letters of love and friendship appear in
The Palace and *Path of the Eclipse*, is the heroine of *Blood Games*, a tale of debauchery set in
the Rome of Nero. The most recent novel, *Path of the Eclipse*, finds Saint Germain fleeing the
Mongol invasion of China and entering the exotic world of India. Here he must battle the cruel
priestess of the evil goddess Kali in order to save the life of his current love, Padmiri.
   Violence is graphically described in Yarbro's novels, while scenes of love have a more
elusive, highly erotic quality, as when Saint Germain, who as a vampire cannot make love as
most men do, skillfully uses his hands and mouth. A practiced writer, Yarbro immerses her
readers in historical time displaying a rhythmic, flowing style to conjure up the mood of the

period. Although often classified as gothic, the Saint Germain series will appeal to general readers as well as romance fans.

—Patricia Altner

YATES, Dornford. Pseudonym for Cecil William Mercer. British. Born in Upper Walmer, Kent, 7 August 1885. Educated at St. Clare, Walmer, 1894-99; Harrow School, 1899-1904; University College, Oxford (President, Dramatic Society, 1907), B.A. in jurisprudence 1907; Inner Temple, London: called to the Bar 1909. Served in the 3rd County of London Yeomanry in Egypt and Salonika during World War I: Captain; with the East Africa Command, 1942-43, then in Southern Rhodesia forces: Major. Married 1) Bettine Stokes Edwards in 1919 (marriage dissolved, 1933), one son; 2) Elizabeth Lucy Bowie in 1934. Practicing solicitor from 1909: worked on the Crippen case, 1910; lived in France after World War I, and in Southern Rhodesia after World War II. *Died 5 March 1960.*

ROMANCE AND GOTHIC PUBLICATIONS

Novels

> *Anthony Lyveden*. London, Ward Lock, 1921.
> *Valerie French*. London, Ward Lock, 1923.
> *The Stolen March*. London, Ward Lock, 1926; New York, Minton Balch, 1933.
> *Blind Corner*. London, Hodder and Stoughton, and New York, Minton Balch, 1927.
> *Perishable Goods*. London, Hodder and Stoughton, and New York, Minton Balch, 1928.
> *Blood Royal*. London, Hodder and Stoughton, 1929; New York, Minton Balch, 1930.
> *Summer Fruit*. New York, Minton Balch, 1929.
> *Fire Below*. London, Hodder and Stoughton, 1930; as *By Royal Command*, New York, Minton Balch, 1931.
> *Adele & Co.* New York, Minton Balch, 1931; London, Hodder and Stoughton, 1932.
> *Safe Custody*. London, Hodder and Stoughton, and New York, Minton Balch, 1932.
> *Storm Music*. London, Hodder and Stoughton, and New York, Minton Balch, 1934.
> *She Fell among Thieves*. London, Hodder and Stoughton, and New York, Minton Balch, 1935.
> *She Painted Her Face*. London, Ward Lock, and New York, Putnam, 1937.
> *This Publican*. London, Ward Lock, 1938; as *The Devil in Satin*, New York, Doubleday, 1938.
> *Gale Warning*. London, Ward Lock, 1939; New York, Putnam 1940.
> *Shoal Water*. London, Ward Lock, 1940; New York, Putnam 1941.
> *An Eye for a Tooth*. London, Ward Lock, 1943; New York, Putnam 1944.
> *The House That Berry Built*. London, Ward Lock, and New York, Putnam 1945.
> *Red in the Morning*. London, Ward Lock, 1946; as *Were Death Denied*, New York, Putnam 1946.
> *Cost Price*. London, Ward Lock, 1949; as *The Laughing Bacchante*, New York, Putnam 1949.
> *Lower Than Vermin*. London, Ward Lock, 1950.
> *Ne'er-Do-Well*. London, Ward Lock, 1954.

Wife Apparent.   London, Ward Lock, 1956.

Short Stories

The Brother of Daphne.   London, Ward Lock, 1914.
The Courts of Idleness.   London, Ward Lock, 1920.
Berry and Co.   London, Ward Lock, 1921; New York, Minton Balch, 1928.
Jonah and Co.   London, Ward Lock, 1922; New York, Minton Balch, 1927.
And Five Were Foolish.   London, Ward Lock, 1924.
As Other Men Are.   London, Ward Lock, 1925.
Maiden Stakes.   London, Ward Lock, 1929.
And Berry Came Too.   London, Ward Lock, and New York, Minton Balch, 1936.
Period Stuff.   London, Ward Lock, 1942.
The Berry Scene.   London, Ward Lock, and New York, Minton Balch, 1947.

Uncollected Short Stories

"Valerie," in *Windsor Magazine* (London), 1919.
"Court Cards," in *Windsor Magazine* (London), 1927.
"The Real Thing," in *Windsor Magazine* (London), 1937.

OTHER PUBLICATIONS

Play

Eastward Ho!, with Oscar Asche, music by Grace Torrens and John Ansell (produced London, 1919).

Other

As Berry and I Were Saying.   London, Ward Lock, 1952.
B-Berry and I Look Back.   London, Ward Lock, 1958.

Critical Study: *Dornford Yates: A Biography* by A. J. Smithers, London, Hodder and Stoughton, 1982.

*   *   *

Dornford Yates reflected the modes and manners of certain sections of English society with an accuracy derived from personal acquaintance. With little fear of contradiction, one may describe him as a romantic. His books can certainly be placed in that category, but it is necessary to use the dictionary definition of the term. With Yates a love affair is not the be-all and end-all of romance, and his books encompass chivalry, imagination, fantasy, and passion in its widest sense. He is in the romantic tradition of John Buchan, Anthony Hope, Conan Doyle and "Sapper."

Yates is a good example of a writer whose books mirror his own experience and social scene, if only as a starting point from which he develops plots and characters somewhat larger than life. His education at Harrow and Oxford, his profession as a barrister, his war service as an officer, his extensive travelling and love of elegant cars, his residence in the South of France and the colonies are all reflected in the sort of fiction he wrote and the characters he created. His books were once described by *The Times* as affording the maximum of entertainment with the minimum of likelihood, and they found in their heyday countless readers who were clearly eager to lose themselves in his world, perhaps attracted by the snob appeal of the Yates milieu and certainly enthralled by what Milton Crane called "the verve and excitement by which the puppets are manipulated."

His early stories, collected in such volumes as *The Brother of Daphne, The Courts of Idleness*, and *Berry and Co.*, secured for Yates a reputation as an accomplished spinner of light-hearted yarns. His fictional family, the Pleydells and the Mansels, became over many years a very real institution to the reading public. Although their social position and their houses, White Ladies and Gracedieu, were beyond the personal experience of the average reader, even in those more affluent years of the British Empire, they must have held for many the fascination and curiosity value of their present-day equivalents in mass-media soap opera. Yates gave his faithful readers what they clearly enjoyed; not always to be taken too seriously, he projected in his stories a certain boyishness and irresponsibility together with an element of Victorian romance. Although he wrote exclusively of the leisured classes, he did so with authority; the world of White Ladies had social stability as its essence, of which Yates heartily approved and of which he was part. Indeed, the stories were an expression of Yates himself in the person of the witty and amorous Boy Pleydell.

Such social stability can be threatened, however, and this is where Yates can be related to such writers as Buchan and "Sapper," and contributed his influence to a whole school of gentlemen-adventurers which endured well into the second half of the twentieth century. Leslie Charteris owes something to Yates, and it would not be fanciful to suggest that even the more explicit and brutal Ian Fleming carried on the Yates tradition. The basic thesis, as seen in Yates and his contemporaries and developed by later writers, is that any threat to the British way of life (and particularly to the security of the upper classes) must be resisted with vigour until the status quo is restored. Where other writers tended to see violence as the only way to meet villainy and aggression, Yates had the more British approach and depicted violence less gratuitously.

From the cloistered atmosphere of the gentlemen's clubs, Yates heroes set forth to engage the enemy. A spin-off from the Berry Pleydell books, cousin Jonah Mansel is the principal heroic figure in such works as *Blind Corner, She Fell among Thieves, An Eye for a Tooth*, and *Cost Price*. A much-travelled bachelor, with distinguished service in the Great War (including counter-espionage), Jonah spends the inter-war years as a free-lance crime-fighter and returns to the Secret Service in 1939. His partner in adventure, William Chandos, is also the narrator of their exploits in what are called the "Chandos Books" in Yates's bibliography, which distinguishes them, from the family-related but lighter Berry books. Jonah and Chandos complement each other, with qualities and abilities that make for a first-class team equipped for adventure and romance. Well-heeled Jonah, with combat skills and friends in high places, is the manly hero with the stiff upper lip, whereas Chandos is equally tough in a tight corner but supplies most of the romantic interest with the devastatingly beautiful women who populate their escapades. They take readers into a world of unreality, where the economic need to earn one's daily bread is absent and there is unlimited time to indulge in the pursuit of those described by someone (was it Charteris?) as the un-Godly.

Yates was, above all, a highly competent storyteller. In spite of his often quaint use of language, the readability of his books is not in question. His motivation has sometimes been criticised—was he Fascist in his depiction of the lower orders, and in his use and treatment of obviously Jewish villains, or was he merely in keeping with the popular literature of his time? He was, of course, a great lover of England and a protector of the traditions of his class, and in many respects his books are a yearning for the England of yesteryear. Although time has not stood still, his books can be read and enjoyed today because they can be placed in the context of their time and Yates's own world. His snob appeal has disintegrated, but perhaps we still need a dream world, especially when presented to us with what Cyril Connolly described in 1935 as "a wit that is ageless united to a courtesy that is extinct."

—Melvyn Barnes

YERBY, Frank (Garvin). American. Born in Augusta, Georgia, 5 September 1916. Educated at Paine College, Augusta, A.B. 1937; Fisk University, Nashville, Tennessee, M.A. 1938; University of Chicago, 1939. Married 1) Flora Helen Claire Williams in 1941 (divorced), two sons and two daughters; 2) Blanca Calle Pérez in 1956. Instructor, Florida Agricultural and Mechanical College, Tallahassee, 1938-39, and Southern University and A. and M. College, Baton Rouge, Louisiana, 1939-41; Laboratory Technician, Ford Motor Company, Dearborn, Michigan, 1941-44; Magnaflux Inspector, Ranger (Fairchild) Aircraft, Jamaica, New York, 1944-45; full-time writer from 1945; settled in Madrid, 1954. Recipient: O. Henry Award, 1944. Agent: Owen Laster, William Morris Agency, 1350 Avenue of the Americas, New York, New York 10019, U.S.A. Address: Edificio Torres Blancas, Apartamento 710, Avenida de America 37, Madrid 2, Spain.

ROMANCE AND GOTHIC PUBLICATIONS

Novels

The Foxes of Harrow. New York, Dial Press, 1946; London, Heinemann, 1947.
The Vixens. New York, Dial Press, 1947; London, Heinemann, 1948.
The Golden Hawk. New York, Dial Press, 1948; London, Heinemann, 1949.
Pride's Castle. New York, Dial Press, 1949; London, Heinemann, 1950.
Floodtide. New York, Dial Press, 1950; London, Heinemann, 1951.
A Woman Called Fancy. New York, Dial Press, 1951; London, Heinemann, 1952.
The Saracen Blade. New York, Dial Press, 1952; London, Heinemann, 1953.
The Devil's Laughter. New York, Dial Press, 1953; London, Heinemann, 1954.
Benton's Row. New York, Dial Press, 1954; London, Heinemann, 1955.
Bride of Liberty. New York, Dial Press, 1954; London, Heinemann, 1955.
The Treasure of Pleasant Valley. New York, Dial Press, 1955; London, Heinemann, 1956.
Captain Rebel. New York, Dial Press, 1956; London, Heinemann, 1957.
Fairoaks. New York, Dial Press, 1957; London, Heinemann, 1958.
The Serpent and the Staff. New York, Dial Press, 1958; London, Heinemann, 1959.
Jarrett's Jade. New York, Dial Press, 1959; London, Heinemann, 1960.
Gillian. New York, Dial Press, 1960; London, Heinemann, 1961.
The Garfield Honor. New York, Dial Press, 1961; London, Heinemann, 1962.
Griffin's Way. New York, Dial Press, 1962; London, Heinemann, 1963.
The Old Gods Laugh: A Modern Romance. New York, Dial Press, and London, Heinemann, 1964.
An Odor of Sanctity. New York, Dial Press, 1965; London, Heinemann, 1966.
Goat Song: A Novel of Ancient Greece. New York, Dial Press, 1967; London, Heinemann, 1968.
Judas, My Brother: The Story of the Thirteenth Disciple. New York, Dial Press, and London, Heinemann, 1969.
Speak Now. New York, Dial Press, 1969; London, Heinemann, 1970.
The Dahomean. New York, Dial Press, 1971; as The Man from Dahomey, London, Heinemann, 1971.
The Girl from Storyville: A Victorian Novel. New York, Dial Press, and London, Heinemann, 1972.
The Voyage Unplanned. New York, Dial Press, and London, Heinemann, 1974.
Tobias and the Angel. New York, Dial Press, and London, Heinemann, 1975.
A Rose for Ana María. New York, Dial Press, and London, Heinemann, 1976.
Hail the Conquering Hero. New York, Dial Press, 1977; London, Heinemann, 1978.
A Darkness at Ingraham's Crest. New York, Dial Press, 1979.
Western: A Saga of the Great Plains. New York, Dial Press, 1982.

Manuscript Collection: Mugar Memorial Library, Boston University.

Critical Studies: *Behind the Magnolia Mask: Frank Yerby as Critic of the South* by William Werdna Hill, Jr., unpublished thesis, Auburn University, Alabama, 1968; *The Unembarrassed Muse* by Russel B. Nye, New York, Dial Press, 1970; *Anti-Heroic Perspectives in the Life and Works of Frank Yerby* by James Lee Hill, unpublished thesis, University of Iowa, 1976.

*   *   *

In writing nearly 30 novels, most of which are historical, Frank Yerby has become the most popularly successful black novelist yet to appear in the United States. His novels have made him rich but have brought him little critical acclaim; rather, his works sell in the millions while being dismissed by most critics as melodramatic potboilers aimed solely at the cash register. He has also been consistently attacked for betraying his race by not continuing to write the social protest fiction, such as the often anthologized "Health Card," with which he began his career. Over the years, in facing this charge, Yerby has repeatedly used some variation of a single defence: "The novelist hasn't any right to inflict on the public his private ideas on politics, religion or race." This attitude is directly related to his view of the novel itself: "a novel is not life, but a deliberate distortion of it, solely designed to give pleasure to a reader"; that is, Yerby considers his fiction romance and its purpose "entertainment," his own word. Nevertheless, in such late works as *Speak Now*, a modern novel of inter-racial love, and *The Dahomean*, as much treatise on African culture as novel, Yerby has written seriously, if not always with full control, on racial injustice and the black heritage.

His longest statement on his fiction appears in "How and Why I Write the Costume Novel" (*Harper's Magazine*, October 1959). Though he states that he does extensive research, the notes always bulking larger than the finished novel, and though there are often notes and references (*The Saracen Blade* has 17 pages of notes as an appendix), as well as historical digressions, even lectures, Yerby prefers "costume novel" to historical novel, for he says that his publishers rightly remove "ninety-nine and ninety-nine one-hundredths" of the history so that the novels will entertain. Aside from the history, his principal elements are a picaresque protagonist, who must be a dominant male, emotionally immature, which Yerby defines as "romantic," in his relationships with women; an even more emotionally immature beautiful heroine; understated sex; "a strong, exteriorized conflict, personified in a continuing, antago-nist or antagonists," and presented dramatically; and as a theme, "something ennobling to life." He states that he has been most successful with the theme of "the eternal warfare of the sexes," but the true underlying theme of most of his fiction, and frequently expressed by his protagonists, is one that he says he has held since the late 1930's: "many, if not most, of life's problems cannot be solved at all."

Yerby's usually long novels have complex, if episodic, plot lines, providing for the introduc-tion (and then elimination) of numerous minor characters, as well as historical color, whether sordid, exotic, or idyllic. In some ways Yerby is a direct descendant of Sir Walter Scott: in his use of a clash of cultures—masters and slaves, aristocrats and plebeians, Saracens or Moors and Christians, Guelfs and Ghibellines, etc.—as a plot-unifying principle, and in the young hero, always more modern in thought and feeling than his adversaries, thrown into a world different from what he has previously known to make his way amidst brutality and treachery. In a sense, though the romance plot (most often of lovers separated by social circumstances) plays a much larger part in Yerby's novels than in Scott's, it still serves as a thread upon which to hang the historical events and local color and to demonstrate that clash of cultures.

Except for the few early short stories and the two novels *The Old Gods Laugh* and *Speak Now*, Yerby's work ranges widely in history. His first novel, *The Foxes of Harrow*, which is set in Louisiana, was a gigantic success, and it has been followed by a number of antebellum, Civil War, and Reconstruction novels, including, among others, *The Vixens*, *Floodtide*, *A Woman Called Fancy*, *Benton's Row*, *Griffin's Way*, and *A Darkness at Ingraham's Crest*. As a result, Yerby is associated in most readers' minds with the romance of the Old South, but it is hardly a "moonlight and magnolias" South, though all of the paraphernalia of that tradition is present—white-columned mansions on huge plantations, crinolined ladies, extensive descrip-tion of food, manners, etc. Instead, it is a world of parvenues, greedy entrepreneurs, racists, and blind chauvinists, where wealth and position are more important than humanity. When not writing about his native South, Yerby has moved back in time from the French and American Revolutions (*The Devil's Laughter* and *Bride of Liberty*), through the 17th century

(*The Golden Hawk*), the Middle Ages (*An Odor of Sanctity* and *The Saracen Blade*), the time of Christ (*Judas, My Brother*) to ancient Greece (*Goat Song*). Such works are written to the same formulas as those of the Old South, being, however, usually more episodic and covering more territory through the hero's travels. Their antagonists are similar, if more powerful, and identical motives—greed, lust for power, rivalry in love—generate the conflict.

To explain the enormous popularity of Yerby's novels is ultimately impossible, for other writers have used the same plot formulas, the same perfervid prose, the same aura of eroticism, and the same strongly typed and contrasted characters, without coming near his sales or public fame. Perhaps the principal reason, despite his critical reputation, is that readers can sense an ethical underpinning to the exciting action and sexy romance. His heroes are nearly always idealists or sceptics, and often the idealists become sceptics, if not stoics, thus fulfilling the theme that most of man's problems have no solutions. This existential view, however bleak, pervades the novels and accounts for the frequent less-than-happy endings. Yerby has yet to be taken as seriously as he deserves by either literary or sociological critics, the fate of most extremely popular writers. Yet his historical fiction is firmly based upon mid-20th-century *angst*, and in the interplay between historical action and contemporary sensibility lies the nexus of his achievement.

—Earl F. Bargainnier

YORKE, Katherine. *See* **ELLERBECK, Rosemary.**

TITLE
INDEX

The following list of titles includes all novels and short story collections listed in the romance and gothic publications sections of the entries in the book. The name(s) in parenthesis after the title is meant to direct the reader to the appropriate entry where full publication information is given. The date given is that of first publication; alternative and revised titles are listed with their appropriate dates.

Abbeygate (Cecily Crowe), 1977
Abbot's House, The (Hebe Elsna), 1969
Abduction (Charlotte Lamb), 1981
Abiding City, The (Ursula Bloom), 1958
Abode of Love, The (Marjorie Bowen, as Joseph Shearing), 1945
About Mrs. Leslie (Viña Delmar), 1950
Above All Things (Madame Albanesi, as Effie Rowlands), 1915
Above Her Station (Mabel St. John, as Henry St. John Cooper), 1922
Above Rubies (Anne Hampson), 1978
Above the Clouds (Esther Wyndham), 1954
Above the Lattice (Jean S. MacLeod), 1949
Abraham, Prince of Ur (W.G. Hardy), 1935
Absent in the Spring (Mary Westmacott), 1944
Accident Call (Elizabeth Harrison), 1971
Accidental Bride (Susan Barrie), 1967
Accompanied by His Wife (Mary Burchell), 1941
Ace of Cads, The (Michael Arlen), 1927
Acquittal (Hebe Elsna, as Laura Conway), 1973
Across a Crowded Room (Lilian Peake), 1981
Across Her Path (Annie S. Swan), 1890
Across the Counter (Mary Burchell), 1960
Across the Lagoon (Roumelia Lane), 1974
Across the Years (Emilie Loring), 1939
Across the Years (Eleanor H. Porter), 1919
Act of Darkness, An (Phyllis Hastings), 1969
Act of Fear (Willo Davis Roberts), 1977
Act of God (Margaret Kennedy), 1955
Acting Sister (Ursula Bloom, as Sheila Burns), 1968
Action and Passion (P.C. Wren), 1933
Action at Aquila (Hervey Allen), 1938
Activities of Lavie Jutt, The (Countess Barcynska, as Marguerite Barclay), 1911
Adair of Starlight Peaks (Essie Summers), 1977
Adam and Evelina (Charity Blackstock, as Paula Allardyce), 1956
Adam Hepburn's Vow (Annie S. Swan), 1885
Adam Penfeather, Buccaneer (Jeffery Farnol), 1940
Adam's Daughters (Jean S. MacLeod), 1972
Adam's Daughters (Ursula Bloom), 1947

Adam's Eden (Faith Baldwin), 1977
Adam's Rib (Charity Blackstock, as Paula Allardyce), 1963
Adam's Rib (Margaret Rome), 1976
Adele & Co. (Dornford Yates), 1931
Admiral of the Ocean-Sea (Mary Johnston), 1923
Admiral's House, The (Nan Asquith), 1969
Admiral's Lady, The (Mary Ann Gibbs), 1975
Admirer Unknown (Berta Ruck), 1957
Adorable Doctor, The (Ursula Bloom, as Mary Essex), 1968
Adrien Leroy (Charles Garvice), 1912
Adultress, The (Victoria Holt, as Philippa Carr), 1982
Advantageous Marriage, An (Alice Chetwynd Ley), 1977
Adventure in Romance (Ursula Bloom, as Sheila Burns), 1955
Adventure of Princess Sylvie, The (A.M. Williamson), 1900
Adventurer, The (Barbara Cartland), 1977
Adventurers, The (Jane Aiken Hodge), 1965
Adventures of Billie Belshaw, The (Mrs. George de Horne Vaizey), 1912
Adventures of Dolly Dingle, The (May Wynne), 1920
Adventures of Napoleon Prince, The (May Edginton), 1912
Adventures of Two (May Wynne), 1920
Adventuress, The (Daoma Winston), 1978
Adventurous Heart (Ursula Bloom, as Sheila Burns), 1940
Adversaries, The (Pamela Bennetts), 1969
Adverse Alliance (Florence Stevenson, as Lucia Curzon), 1981
Aegean Quest (Elizabeth Ashton), 1977
Affair at Alkali, The (Virginia Coffman), 1960
Affair at Marrakesh (Dorothy Daniels), 1968
Affair in Hong Kong (Dorothy Daniels), 1969
Affair in Tangier, The (Kathryn Blair), 1962
Affair in Venice (Rachel Lindsay), 1975
Affair of the Heart, An (Joan Smith), 1977
Affair to Forget, An (Rachel Lindsay), 1978
Affairs of Love (Glenna Finley), 1980
Affairs of Men (Marjorie Bowen), 1922
Affinities (Mary Roberts Rinehart), 1920

Afraid (Barbara Cartland), 1981

Afraid of the Dark (Mary Linn Roby), 1965

African Dream (Elizabeth Hoy), 1971

African Mountain, The (Isobel Chace), 1960

After All (Hebe Elsna, as Lyndon Snow), 1961

After House, The (Mary Roberts Rinehart), 1914

After Long Journeying (Jean S. MacLeod), 1955

After Many Days (Madame Albanesi, as Effie Rowlands), 1910

After Many Years (Annie S. Swan), 1899

After Office Hours (Mary Burchell), 1939

After Rain (Netta Muskett), 1931

After Sundown (Anne Hampson), 1974

After the Lady (Charity Blackstock, as Paula Allardyce), 1954

After the Night (Barbara Cartland), 1944

After the Storm (Janet Dailey), 1975

After the Storm (Claudette Williams), 1977

After the Verdict (Robert Hichens), 1924

After Tomorrow (Maysie Greig, as Jennifer Ames), 1951

After Tomorrow (Robert Hichens), 1895

After-Glow (Ruby M. Ayres), 1936

Afterglow, The (Rose Burghley), 1966

Afterglow, The (Robert Hichens), 1935

Afterglow and Nightfall (Edith Pargeter), 1977

Afternoon for Lizards (Dorothy Eden), 1962

Afternoon of an Autocrat (Norah Lofts), 1956

Afternoon Walk (Dorothy Eden), 1971

Afterwards (Marie Belloc Lowndes), 1925

Against the Stream (Barbara Cartland), 1946

Against the World (Madame Albanesi, as Effie Rowlands), 1923

Against This Rapture (Barbara Cartland), 1947

Age Cannot Wither (Ursula Bloom), 1942

Air Ambulance (Jean S. MacLeod), 1959

Air Hostess in Love (Evadne Price), 1962

Air Liner (Ursula Bloom, as Sheila Burns), 1948

Air Ministry, Room 28 (Gilbert Frankau), 1942

Air of Glory, An (Sarah Neilan), 1977

Air Surgeon (Frank G. Slaughter), 1943

Air That Kills, An (Margaret Millar), 1957

Air Ticket (Susan Barrie), 1957

Airing in a Closed Carriage (Marjorie Bowen, as Joseph Shearing), 1943

Airs above the Ground (Mary Stewart), 1965

Albatross, The (Charlotte Armstrong), 1957

Albert the Beloved (Ursula Bloom, as Lozania Prole), 1974

Album, The (Mary Roberts Rinehart), 1933

Album Leaf (Marjorie Bowen, as Joseph Shearing), 1933

Aldersyde (Annie S. Swan), 1882

Alex and the Raynhams (Iris Bromige), 1961

Alex Rayner, Dental Nurse (Marjorie Lewty), 1965

Alexa (Anne Betteridge, as Anne Melville), 1979

Alexa (Victoria Holt, as Eleanor Burford), 1948

Alexandra (Joanna Trollope, as Caroline Harvey), 1980

Alexandrovitch Is Missing! (Anne Edwards), 1970

Alias Richard Power (C.N. and A.M. Williamson), 1921

Alibi for Isabel (Mary Roberts Rinehart), 1944

Alibi for Murder (Charlotte Armstrong), 1956

Alice, Where Art Thou? (Elizabeth Cadell), 1959

Alice, Where Are You? (Theresa Charles, as Leslie Lance), 1940

Alien Corn (Ursula Bloom), 1947

Alien Corn (Rachel Lindsay), 1954

Alien Wife (Anne Mather), 1977

Alimony (Faith Baldwin), 1929

Alinor (Roberta Gellis), 1978

All Done by Kindness (Doris Langley Moore), 1951

All Earth to Love (Phyllis Hastings), 1968

All Else Is Folly (Catherine Gaskin), 1951

All Enchantment Die (Anne Maybury), 1941

All for Love (Patricia Gallagher), 1981

All for Love (Jean Francis Webb, as Ethel Hamill), 1965

All for You (Denise Robins), 1946

All I Ask (Theresa Charles, as Fay Chandos), 1939

All in the Day's Work (Hebe Elsna, as Lyndon Snow), 1950

All Is Not Fair in Love (Charles Garvice), 1913

All Made of Wishes (Marjorie Lewty), 1974

All Men Are Murderers (Charity Blackstock), 1958

All My Enemies (Rosemary Harris), 1967

All Our Tomorrows (Hebe Elsna, as Vicky Lancaster), 1958

All Over Again (Ruby M. Ayres), 1934

All over the Town (R.F. Delderfield), 1947

All Past Years (Hebe Elsna, as Vicky Lancaster), 1949

All Swans (Hebe Elsna), 1932

All That Glitters (Frances Parkinson Keyes), 1941

All That Matters (Denise Robins), 1956

All the Days of Summer (Joyce Dingwell), 1978

All the Fire (Anne Mather), 1971

All the Queen's Men (Evelyn Anthony), 1960

All the Summer Long (Rebecca Stratton, as Lucy Gillen), 1975

All the Trumpets Sounded (W.G. Hardy), 1942

All Things Come Round (G.B. Burgin), 1929

All This and Heaven Too (Rachel Field), 1938

All This for Love (Denise Robins), 1935

All This I Gave (Theresa Charles, as Jan Tempest), 1937

All Through the Night (Grace Livingston Hill), 1945

All Visitors Ashore (Hebe Elsna), 1938

All Visitors Must Be Announced (Helen Van Slyke), 1972

All Your Lovely Word Are Spoken (Mary Linn Roby), 1970

Allan Quartermain series (H. Rider Haggard)

Allandale's Daughters (G.B. Burgin), 1928

Allegra (Clare Darcy), 1975

Alley-Cat (Netta Muskett), 1937

All's Well with the World (Madame Albanesi), 1932

All-the-Way Man, The (Joyce Dingwell), 1980

Almond, Wild Almond (D.K. Broster), 1933

Aloha Means Goodbye (Naomi A. Hintze), 1972

Aloha Nurse (Jean Francis Webb, as Ethel Hamill), 1961

Alone in Paris (Barbara Cartland), 1978

Alone in Paris (Annie S. Swan), 1898

Alone with Me (Hebe Elsna, as Lyndon Snow), 1955

Along a Dark Path (Velda Johnston), 1967

Alpine Coach, The (Virginia Coffman), 1976

Alpine Doctor (Rose Burghley), 1970

Alpine Nurse (Irene Roberts), 1968

Alpine Rhapsody (Elizabeth Ashton), 1973

Also the Hills (Frances Parkinson Keyes), 1943

Altar of Evil (Florence Stevenson), 1973

Altar of Honour, The (Ethel M. Dell), 1929

Alternative, The (George Barr McCutcheon), 1909

Always a Rainbow (Gloria Bevan), 1975

Always Another Man (Theresa Charles, as Jan Tempest), 1941

Always Is Not Forever (Helen Van Slyke), 1977

Always Remember (Hebe Elsna, as Lyndon Snow), 1954

Always Tomorrow (Ruby M. Ayres), 1933

Always Yours (Mary Burchell), 1941

Alyx (Lolah Burford), 1977

Amateur Gentleman, The (Jeffery Farnol), 1913

Amateur Governess, The (Mary Ann Gibbs), 1964

Amaranth Flower, The (Eleanor Farnes), 1979

Amazing Interlude, The (Mary Roberts Rinehart), 1918

Amazing Marriage, The (Hebe Elsna, as Vicky Lancaster), 1958

Amazing Tramp, The (Mabel St. John, as Henry St. John Cooper), 1927

Amazon in an Apron (Betty Neels), 1969

Ambassadress, The (Frances Parkinson Keyes), 1938

Amber Cat, The (Mary Ann Gibbs, as Elizabeth Ford), 1976

Amber Five (Betty Beaty), 1958

Amberstone (Pamela Bennetts), 1980

Amberwell (D.E. Stevenson), 1955

Amberwood (Anne Rundle), 1972

Ambitions of Jill, The (May Wynne), 1923

Ambulance Call (Elizabeth Harrison), 1972

America, with Love (Kathleen Winsor), 1957

American Baroness (Janet Louise Roberts, as Janette Radcliffe), 1980

American Beauty (Edna Ferber), 1931

American Bred (Rose Franken, as Franken Meloney), 1941

American Captain (Edison Marshall), 1954

American Family (Faith Baldwin), 1935

American Flaggs (Kathleen Norris), 1936

American Heiress, The (Dorothy Eden), 1980

American Wife, An (Annie S. Swan), 1900

American Woman, An (Annie S. Swan)

Amethyst Love (Janet Louise Roberts, as Rebecca Danton), 1977

Amethyst Meadows, The (Iris Danbury), 1974

Ammie, Come Home (Barbara Michaels), 1968

Among the Wolves and Other Tales (David Case), 1982

Among Those Present (Edna Ferber), 1923

Amorelle (Grace Livingston Hill), 1934

Amorous Bicycle, The (Ursula Bloom, as Mary Essex), 1944

Amyot series (Christopher Nicole)

And All Because... (Denise Robins), 1930

And Be Thy Love (Rose Burghley), 1958

And Berry Came Too (Dornford Yates), 1936

And Call It Accident (Marie Belloc Lowndes), 1936

And Die Remembering (Mary Linn Roby), 1972

And Falsely Pledge My Love (Mary Burchell), 1957

And Five Were Foolish (Dornford Yates), 1924

And New Stars Burn (Faith Baldwin), 1941

And No Regrets (Kathryn Blair, as Rosalind Brett), 1948

And Now the Screaming Starts (David Case), 1973

And Now Tomorrow (Rachel Field), 1942

And Sometimes Death (Charlotte Armstrong, as Jo Valentine), 1954

And Still She Loved Him (Mabel St. John), 1926

And Still They Dream (Ruby M. Ayres), 1938

And Then Came Love (Rachel Lindsay, as Roberta Leigh), 1954

And Then Face to Face (Susan Ertz), 1927

And Then There Was Georgia (Jane Blackmore), 1975

And Then You Came (Ann Bridge), 1948

And We in Dreams (Jean S. MacLeod), 1947

Ancestors (Marguerite Steen, as Lennox Dryden), 1930

Ancient Sin, The (Michael Arlen), 1930

Andrew Leicester's Wife (Madame Albanesi, as Effie Rowlands)

Angel in Hell, An (Barbara Cartland), 1976

Angel in the House, The (Kathleen Norris), 1933

Angel in the House (Mary Linn Roby, as Pamela D'Arcy), 1980

Angel of Evil (Madame Albanesi, as Effie Rowlands), 1905

Angel of His Presence, The (Grace Livingston Hill), 1902

Angel Unawares (C.N. and A.M. Williamson), 1916

Angel Who Couldn't Sing, The (Sophia Cleugh), 1935

Angela's Lover (Charles Garvice, as Caroline Hart)

Angel's Eyes (Countess Barcynska), 1957

Angel's Kiss (Countess Barcynska, as Oliver Sandys), 1937

Angel's Tear (Jane Blackmore), 1974

Anger in the Sky (Susan Ertz), 1943

Angevin King, The (Pamela Bennetts), 1972

Angry Man, The (Joyce Dingwell), 1979

Anitra's Dance (Fannie Hurst), 1934

Ann All-Alone (Mabel St. John), 1921

Ann and the Hoosier Doctor (Adeline McElfresh), 1955

Ann Foster, Lab Technician (Adeline McElfresh, as Elizabeth Wesley), 1956

Ann Kenyon, Surgeon (Adeline McElfresh), 1960

Ann, The Gentle (Katheryn Kimbrough), 1978

Anna and Her Daughters (D.E. Stevenson), 1958

Anna Fitzalan (Marguerite Steen), 1953

Anna Heritage (Mary Howard), 1944

Anne Boleyn (Evelyn Anthony), 1957

Anne Boleyn (L. Adams Beck, as E. Barrington), 1932

Anne Hyde, Travelling Companion (Annie S. Swan), 1908

Anne Marguerite (Sophia Cleugh), 1932

Anne of Austria (Evelyn Anthony), 1968

Anne of Cleves (Julia Fitzgerald, as Julia Hamilton), 1972

Anne of Green Gables series (L.M. Montgomery)

Anne of Strathallan (Essie Summers), 1975

Anne, The Rose of Hever (Maureen Peters), 1971

Another Cynthia (Doris Leslie), 1939

Another Girl Won Him (Mabel St. John), 1935

Another Man's Murder (Mignon Eberhart), 1957

Another Man's Wife (Marie Belloc Lowndes), 1934

Another View (Rosamunde Pilcher), 1969

Another Time, Another Place (Katrina Britt), 1981

Another Woman's House (Mignon Eberhart), 1947

Another Woman's Shoes (Theresa Charles, as Fay Chandos), 1939

Answer as a Man (Taylor Caldwell), 1981

Answer in the Tide, An (Elisabeth Ogilvie), 1978

Answer to a Christmas Prayer, The (Annie S. Swan), 1894

Answer to Heaven (Patricia Gallagher), 1964

Anthony Adverse (Hervey Allen), 1933

Anthony Lyveden (Dornford Yates), 1921

Anthony Wilding (Rafael Sabatini), 1910

Antic Years, The (Rose Franken), 1958

Antonia (Naomi Jacob), 1954

Any Two Can Play (Elizabeth Cadell), 1981

Any Village (Faith Baldwin), 1971

Anything But Love (Maysie Greig, as Jennifer Ames), 1933

Anything Can Happen (Hebe Elsna, as Lyndon Snow), 1962

Anywoman (Fannie Hurst), 1950

Anzac's Bride, An (Mrs. Patrick MacGill), 1917

Apollo Fountain, The (Dorothy Daniels), 1974

Apollo's Daughter (Rebecca Stratton), 1980

Apollo's Seed (Anne Mather), 1979

Apothecary's Daughter, The (Mary Ann Gibbs), 1962

Appassionata (Fannie Hurst), 1926

Apple for Eve, An (Kathleen Norris), 1943

Apple in Eden, An (Kay Thorpe), 1973

Apples of Gold (Warwick Deeping), 1923

Apple Tree, The (Daphne du Maurier), 1952

April (Rosamunde Pilcher), 1957

April After, An (Ursula Bloom), 1928

April Escapade (Kathleen Norris), 1941

Apple for the Doctor, An (Ursula Bloom, as Mary Essex), 1950

April Girl, An (Iris Bromige), 1967

April Gold (Grace Livingston Hill), 1936

April in Westland (Ivy Preston), 1969

April Lady (Georgette Heyer), 1957

April Wooing (Iris Bromige), 1951

April's Day (Ruby M. Ayres), 1945

April's Grave (Susan Howatch), 1969

Apron-Strings (Leila Mackinlay), 1937

Apronstrings (Mabel St. John), 1919

Arabella (Georgette Heyer), 1949

Arabella Arrives (Berta Ruck), 1939

Arabella the Awful (Berta Ruck), 1918

Araby (Baroness von Hutten), 1904

Ardath (Marie Corelli), 1889

Ariel Custer (Grace Livingston Hill), 1925

Ariosto (Chelsea Quinn Yarbro), 1980

Arise, Oh Sun! (Anne Maybury), 1942

Arizona Star (Faith Baldwin), 1945

Arkady (Anne Duffield), 1948

Arm and the Darkness, The (Taylor Caldwell), 1943

Armour Against Love (Barbara Cartland), 1945

Arms and the Maid (Rafael Sabatini), 1910

Army Doctor (Elizabeth Seifert), 1942

Around the Rugged Rock (Elizabeth Cadell), 1954

Arranged Marriage, The (Flora Kidd), 1980

Arrant Rover, An (Berta Ruck), 1921

Arrogance of Love, The (Anne Mather), 1968

Arrogant Duke, The (Anne Mather), 1970

Arrogant Duke (Rona Randall), 1966

Arrow in My Heart, An (Hebe Elsna, as Lyndon Snow), 1972

Arrow in the Heart (Denise Robins), 1960

Arrow of Love, An (Barbara Cartland), 1975

As a Man Loves (Madame Albanesi), 1936

As a Woman Wills (Mabel St. John, as Henry St. John Cooper), 1934

As Bends the Bough (Ursula Bloom), 1952

As Eagles Fly (Barbara Cartland), 1975

As Fate Decreases (Mabel St. John, as Henry St. John Cooper), 1929

As Long as I Live (Emilie Loring), 1937

As Long as You Live (Phyllis Hastings), 1951

As Other Men Are (Dornford Yates), 1925

As the Tree Falls (Doris Leslie), 1958

As the World Judged (Mabel St. John), 1925

As Waits the Sky (Claire Ritchie), 1969

Ashamed of the Shop (Mabel St. John), 1919

Ashes in the Wind (Kathleen E. Woodiwiss), 1979

Ashes of Falconwyck (Dorothy Daniels, as Angela Gray), 1973

Ashes of Love (Charles Garvice), 1910

Ask for Me Tomorrow (Margaret Millar), 1976

Ask Me Again (Theresa Charles, as Jan Tempest), 1955

Ask Only Love (Elizabeth Hoy), 1943

Ask the Parlourmaid (Maysie Greig), 1939

Assassin, The (Evelyn Anthony), 1970

Assignment to Love (Maysie Greig, as Jennifer Ames), 1953

Assistance Unlimited (Audrie Manley-Tucker), 1971

Assistant Matron (Ursula Bloom, as Mary Essex), 1967

Assurance Double Sure (Samuel Shellabarger, as John Esteven), 1939

Astra (Grace Livingston Hill), 1941

Astrologer (Countess Barcynska), 1944

Astrov Inheritance, The (Constance Heaven), 1973

Astrov Legacy, The (Constance Heaven), 1973

At a Touch I Yield (Theresa Charles), 1952

At Dark of the Moon (Alice Chetwynd Ley), 1977

At First Sight (Mary Burchell), 1950

At Great Cost (Madame Albanesi, as Effie Rowlands), 1895

At Grips with Fate (Mabel St. John, as Henry

St. John Cooper), 1936

At Her Mercy (Madame Albanesi, as Effie Rowlands), 1914

At Love's Call (Charles Garvice), 1909

At Professor Chummy's (Elizabeth O. Peter), 1946

At the Foot of the Rainbow (Gene Stratton Porter), 1907

At the Same Time Tomorrow (Maysie Greig, as Jennifer Ames), 1944

At the Villa Massina (Kathryn Blair, as Celine Conway), 1958

At Tuxter's (G.B. Burgin), 1895

Athena's Airs (Florence Stevenson, as Zabrina Faire), 1980

Atkinson Heritage, The (Mollie Hardwick), 1978

Atlantic Sky, The (Betty Beaty), 1967

Attic Rope, The (Dorothy Daniels), 1970

Audacious Adventuress, The (Barbara Cartland), 1971

Audrey (Mary Johnston), 1902

Audrey on Approval (May Wynne), 1937

Augusta, The First (Katheryn Kimbrough), 1975

Augusta, The Second (Katheryn Kimbrough), 1979

Auldearn House (Barbara Riefe), 1976

Aunt Anne's Money (Annie S. Swan), 1898

Aunt Beardie (Marjorie Bowen, as Joseph Shearing), 1940

Aunt Becky Began It (L.M. Montgomery), 1931

Aunt Crete's Emancipation (Grace Livingston Hill), 1911

Aunt Sophie's Diamond (Joan Smith), 1979

Aurora (Joan Smith), 1980

Australian Hospital (Joyce Dingwell), 1955

Autobiography of Cornelius Blake, The (Marjorie Bowen, as George Preedy), 1934

Autocrat of Melhurst, The (Anne Hampson), 1969

Autograph Hunters, The (Mabel St. John), 1918

Autumn Concerto (Rebecca Stratton), 1974

Autumn Conquest (Charlotte Lamb), 1978

Autumn Fires (Ruby M. Ayres), 1951

Autumn in April (Essie Summers), 1981

Autumn of the Witch, The (Anne Mather), 1972

Autumn Song (Margaret Pargeter), 1979

Autumn Twilight (Anne Hampson), 1975

Autumn Wedding (Susan Barrie, as Anita Charles), 1963

Avalon (Anya Seton), 1965

Avenhurst Inheritance, The (Sylvia Thorpe), 1981

Avenue Goes to War, The (R.F. Delderfield), 1958

Avenue of the Dead, The (Evelyn Anthony), 1981

Avenue Story, The (R.F. Delderfield), 1964

Awake and Rehearse (Louis Bromfield), 1929

Awake My Heart (Claire Lorrime, as Patricia Robins), 1950

Awake, My Love! (Theresa Charles, as Fay Chandos), 1942

Awakening (Maud Diver), 1911

Awakening Flame, The (Margaret Way), 1978

Awakening of Alice, The (Violet Winspear), 1978

Away from Each Other (Theresa Charles, as Fay Chandos), 1944

Away Went Love (Mary Burchell), 1945

Axwater (Gwendoline Butler, as Jennie Melville), 1978

Ayesha (H. Rider Haggard), 1905

Ayres of Studleigh, The (Annie S. Swan), 1891

Azure Castle, The (Janet Louise Roberts, as Janette Radcliffe), 1976

Bab (Mary Roberts Rinehart), 1917

Babe (Joan Smith), 1980

Babes in the Wood (Michael Arlen), 1929

Babylon Was Dust (Anne Rundle, as Joanne Marshall), 1971

Bacchante, The (Robert Hichens), 1927

Bacchante and the Nun, The (Robert Hichens), 1927

Bachelor Doctor (Elizabeth Seifert), 1969

Bachelor Girls, The (Mary Howard), 1968

Bachelor Heaven (Mollie Chappell), 1958

Bachelor Husband, A (Ruby M. Ayres), 1920

Bachelor in Search of a Wife, A (Annie S. Swan), 1892

Bachelor Territory (Gloria Bevan), 1977

Bachelor's Bride (Theresa Charles, as Jan Tempest), 1946

Bachelors Galore (Essie Summers), 1958

Bachelor's Tonic (Countess Barcynska, as Oliver Sandys), 1951

Back of Beyond (Rebecca Stratton, as Lucy Gillen), 1978

Back Street (Fannie Hurst), 1931

Back to the Honey-Pot (Countess Barcynska), 1925

Background to Hyacinthe (Elizabeth Hoy), 1949

Bad Baron's Daughter, The (Laura London)

Bad Girl (Viña Delmar), 1928

Bad Girl Leaves Town, A (Maysie Greig), 1933

Bad Lad (Countess Barcynska, as Oliver Sandys), 1930

Bag of Saffron, The (Baroness von Hutten), 1917

Bagatelle (Marjorie Bowen, as George Preedy), 1930

Baker's Daughter, The (D.E. Stevenson), 1938

Baker's Dozen (Kathleen Norris), 1938

Balance Wheel, The (Taylor Caldwell), 1951

Balcony, The (Frances Cowen), 1962

Balefire (Nigel Tranter), 1958

Ballad-Maker of Paris, The (Charity Blackstock, as Ursula Torday), 1935

Ballerina (Lady Eleanor Smith), 1932

Balloon Man, The (Charlotte Armstrong), 1968

Bamboo Wedding (Roumelia Lane), 1977

Ban, The (May Wynne, as Lester Lurgan), 1912

Bandit and the Priest, The (Audrey Erskine-Lindop), 1953

Banner of the Bull, The (Rafael Sabatini), 1915

Banshee Tide, The (Alice Dwyer-Joyce), 1977

Barabbas (Marie Corelli), 1893

Barbara Owen, Grip Reporter (Adeline McElfresh, as Jane Scott), 1956

Barbara Rebell (Marie Belloc Lowndes), 1905

Barbara, The Valiant (Katheryn Kimbrough), 1977

Barbara's Love Story (Madame Albanesi, as Effie Rowlands), 1911

Barbarian Lover, The (Margaret Pedler), 1924

Barbary Moon (Kathryn Blair), 1954

Barbary Sheep (Robert Hichens), 1907

Barberry Bush (Kathleen Norris), 1927

Bardelys the Magnificent (Rafael Sabatini), 1906

Bargain Bride, The (Flora Kidd), 1976

Bargain for Paradise (Rebecca Stratton), 1978

Bargain in Love (Hebe Elsna, as Laura Conway), 1960

Barn Dance (Sara Seale), 1941

Barn Stormers, The (A.M. Williamson), 1897

Barons of Runnymede, The (Pamela Bennetts), 1974

Barrancourt Destiny, The (Anne Worboys), 1977

Barren Corn (Georgette Heyer), 1930

Barren Harvest (Maynah Lewis), 1981

Barren Metal (Naomi Jacob), 1936

Barrier Between Us, The (Anne Maybury), 1940

Barriers Between (Charles Garvice), 1910

Barringer House (Barbara Riefe), 1976

Barrow Sinister (Elsie Lee), 1969

Bars of Iron, The (Ethel M. Dell), 1915

Bartered Bride, The (Mrs. Patrick MacGill), 1920

Bartered Bride, The (Margaret Rome), 1973

Bartered Bridegroom, The (Mary Linn Roby, as Georgina Grey), 1981

Bartholomew Fair (Phyllis Hastings), 1974

Base Metal (Ursula Bloom), 1928

Bastard King, The (Victoria Holt, as Jean Plaidy), 1974

Bat, The (Mary Roberts Rinehart), 1926

Bath Tangle (Georgette Heyer), 1955

Battle Dress (Betty Beaty, as Catherine Ross), 1979

Battle of Love (Kathryn Blair), 1961

Battle of the Queens, The (Victoria Holt, as Jean Plaidy), 1978

Battle of the Villa Fiorita, The (Rumer Godden), 1963

Battle Surgeon (Frank G. Slaughter), 1944

Bauhinia Junction (Margaret Way), 1971

Bay of Moonlight, The (Rose Burghley), 1968

Bay of the Nightingales, The (Essie Summers), 1970

Bayou Road, The (Mignon Eberhart), 1979

Bazalgettes, The (E.M. Delafield), 1935

Be All and End All (Evelyn Berckman), 1976

Be More Than Dreams (Elizabeth Hoy), 1968

Be My Guest (Elizabeth Cadell), 1964

Be My Guest (Kate Norway), 1966

Be Still, My Heart (Theresa Charles, as Jan Tempest), 1936

Be True to Me (Hebe Elsna, as Laura Conway), 1957

Beach Generation (Daoma Winston), 1970

Beach House, The (Virginia Coffman), 1970

Beads of Nemesis, The (Isobel Chace, as Elizabeth Hunter), 1974

Beast in View (Margaret Millar), 1955

Beatrice (H. Rider Haggard), 1890

Beau and the Bluestocking, The (Alice Chetwynd Ley), 1975

Beau Brocade (Baroness Orczy), 1907

Beau Barron's Lady (Pamela Bennetts), 1981

Beau Geste (P.C. Wren), 1924

Beau Ideal (P.C. Wren), 1928

Beau Sabreur (P.C. Wren), 1926

Beau Wyndham (Georgette Heyer), 1941

Beaumaroy Home from the Wars (Anthony Hope), 1919

Beaumont Tradition, The (Dorothy Daniels), 1971

Beautiful Is Vanished, The (Taylor Caldwell), 1951

Beauty (Faith Baldwin), 1933

Beauty and the Beast (Kathleen Norris), 1928

Beauty for Ashes (Grace Livingston Hill), 1935

Beauty of the Season, The (Charles Garvice), 1910

Beauty Surgeon, The (Ursula Bloom, as Sheila Burns), 1967

Beauty's Daughter (Mollie Hardwick), 1976

Beauty's Daughter (Kathleen Norris), 1935

Beauty's Tears (Leila Mackinlay), 1961

Beauvallet (Georgette Heyer), 1929

Because I Love You (Susan Inglis), 1940

Because I Wear Your Ring (Theresa Charles, as Fay Chandos), 1947

Because My Love Is Come (Theresa Charles, as Jan Tempest), 1938

Because My Love Is Coming (Theresa Charles, as Jan Tempest), 1958

Because of Doctor Danville (Elizabeth Hoy), 1956

Because of Stephen (Grace Livingston Hill), 1904

Because of These Things... (Marjorie Bowen), 1915

Because There Is Hope (Theresa Charles, as Jan Tempest), 1958

Because You're Mine (Hettie Grimstead, as Marsha Manning), 1960

Becca's Child (Willo Davis Roberts), 1972

Beckoning, The (Virginia Coffman), 1965

Beckoning Dream, The (Evelyn Berckman), 1955

Beckoning from Moura, The (Virginia Coffman), 1977

Beckoning Trails (Emilie Loring), 1947

Bed Disturbed, The (Victoria Holt, as Elbur Ford), 1952

Bed of Grass (Janet Dailey), 1979

Bedford Row (Claire Rayner), 1977

Bedford Village (Hervey Allen), 1944

Bedside Manner, The (Kate Norway), 1971

Beechy (Baroness von Hutten), 1909

Before I Die (Mary Linn Roby), 1966

Before I Kissed (Mary Howard), 1955

Before I Make You Mine (Theresa Charles, as Fay Chandos), 1938

Before the Storm (Marie Belloc Lowndes), 1941

Beggar at Her Husband's Door, A (Mabel St. John), 1928

Beggar Girl's Gift (Hebe Elsna, as Vicky Lancaster), 1943

Beggar Maid, Queen (Maureen Peters), 1980

Beggar Man, The (Ruby M. Ayres), 1920

Beggar on Horseback (Sylvia Thorpe), 1953

Beggar Wished..., A (Barbara Cartland), 1934

Beggarman (Grace Livingston Hill), 1932

Beggars' Horses (P.C. Wren), 1934

Beggars May Sing (Sara Seale), 1932

Begin to Live (Victoria Holt, as Eleanor Burford), 1956

Behind the Cloud (Emilie Loring), 1958

Behold, Here's Poison! (Georgette Heyer), 1936

Believe in To-morrow (Nan Asquith), 1955

Believe Me, Beloved— (Theresa Charles, as Jan Tempest), 1936

Believe the Heart (Victoria Holt, as Eleanor Burford), 1950

Believers, The (Janice Holt Giles), 1957

Bel Lamington (D.E. Stevenson), 1961

Bell, The (Dorothy Daniels), 1971

Bell Branch, The (Lucy Walker), 1971

Bell Timson (Marguerite Steen), 1946

Bella (Jilly Cooper), 1976

Bella (Dorothy Eden), 1964

Bella Donna (Robert Hichens), 1909

Bellarion the Fortunate (Rafael Sabatini), 1926

Belle of Santiago, The (G.B. Burgin), 1911

Belle of the Works, The (Mabel St. John), 1919

Belles of Vaudroy, The (G.B. Burgin), 1906

Belle-Mère (Kathleen Norris), 1931

Bellerose Bargain, The (Robyn Carr), 1982

Bells along the Neva (D.A. Ponsonby), 1964

Bells of Bruges, The (Elizabeth Ashton), 1973

Bells of St. Martin, The (Betty Beaty, as Karen Campbell), 1979

Bells of the City, The (Charlotte Lamb, as Sheila Coates), 1975

Bells Still Ring, The (Ursula Bloom, as Sheila Burns), 1976

Bellwood (Elisabeth Ogilvie), 1969

Beloved (Viña Delmar), 1956

Beloved and Unforgettable (Ursula Bloom, as Sheila Burns), 1953

Beloved Ballerina (Rachel Lindsay, as Roberta Leigh), 1953

Beloved Burden (Countess Barcynska), 1954

Beloved Castaway (Violet Winspear), 1968

Beloved Creditor (Ursula Bloom), 1939

Beloved Diana (Alice Chetwynd Ley), 1977

Beloved Enemies (Susan Barrie, as Pamela Kent), 1967

Beloved Enemy, The (Madame Albanesi), 1913

Beloved Enemy (Anne Duffield), 1950

Beloved Enemy (Anne Maybury), 1957

Beloved Knight (Maysie Greig, as Jennifer Ames), 1959

Beloved Man, The (Ursula Bloom, as Sheila Burns), 1957

Beloved of the Gods (Baroness Orczy), 1905

Beloved Physician, The (Naomi Jacob), 1930

Beloved Rake (Anne Hampson), 1972

Beloved Rascals (Irene Roberts), 1962

Beloved Rebel (Sylvia Thorpe), 1959

Beloved Sinner (Jessica Stirling), 1976

Beloved Sparrow (Henrietta Reid), 1968

Beloved Stranger (Jane Blackmore), 1953

Beloved Stranger (Anne Mather), 1966

Beloved Stranger, The (Grace Livingston Hill), 1933

Beloved Tyrant (Violet Winspear), 1964

Beloved Vagabond (Anne Hampson), 1981

Beloved Woman, The (Kathleen Norris), 1921

Below the Salt (Thomas B. Costain), 1957

Belshazzar (H. Rider Haggard), 1930

Beltane the Smith (Jeffery Farnol), 1915

Belvedere, The (Mary Ann Gibbs, as Elizabeth Ford), 1973

Bend in the River, The (Iris Bromige), 1975

Bend Sinister (Juliet Dymoke), 1962

Beneath a Spell (Madame Albanesi, as Effie Rowlands), 1900

Beneath the Magic (Robert Hichens), 1950

Beneath the Moon (Claire Lorrimer, as Patricia Robins), 1951

Beneath the Passion Flower (Marjorie Bowen, as George Preedy), 1932

Benefactress, The (Elizabeth), 1901

Benevolent Despot, The (Elizabeth Ashton), 1970

Bengal Tiger, The (Edison Marshall, as Hall Hunter), 1962

Benita (H. Rider Haggard), 1906

Benjamin Blake (Edison Marshall), 1941

Benton's Row (Frank Yerby), 1954

Berry and Co. (Dornford Yates), 1921

Berry Goes to Monte Carlo (C.N. and A.M. Williamson), 1921

Berry Scene, The (Dornford Yates), 1947

Bertrand of Brittany (Warwick Deeping), 1908

Beside a Norman Tower (Mazo de la Roche), 1934

Bess (Annie S. Swan), 1880

Bess of the Woods (Warwick Deeping), 1906

Best Girls Are Here, The (Mabel St. John), 1917

Best Love of All, The (Anne Maybury), 1932

Best Loved Person (Hebe Elsna, as Lyndon Snow), 1976

Best Man, The (Grace Livingston Hill), 1914

Best People, The (Helen Van Slyke), 1976

Best Place to Be, The (Helen Van Slyke), 1976

Best Time Ever, The (Berta Ruck), 1934

Best Wishes (May Edginton), 1942

Best Woman in the World, The (Mabel St. John), 1913

Beth Mason (Madame Albanesi, as Effie Rowlands), 1913

Betrayal (Denise Robins), 1976

Better Love, The (Margaret Pedler), 1924

Better Part, The (Annie S. Swan), 1884

Better Than Life (Charles Garvice), 1910

Better to Eat You, The (Charlotte Armstrong), 1954

Better to Forget (Margaret Pargeter), 1977

Better to Marry (Ursula Bloom), 1933

Betty (Faith Baldwin), 1928

Betty on the Stage (Mabel St. John), 1920

Betty Trevor (Mrs. George de Horne Vaizey), 1907

Between the Rides (Annie S. Swan), 1935

Between You and Me (Ruby M. Ayres), 1935

Bevy of Maids, A (Anne Duffield), 1941

Beware My Heart (Glenna Finley), 1978

Beware of the Banquet (Joan Aiken), 1966

Beware of the Stranger (Janet Dailey), 1978

Beware the Heart (Anne Mather), 1976

Beware the Night (Jane Blackmore), 1958

Bewildered Heart (Kathryn Blair), 1950

Bewitched (Barbara Cartland), 1975

Bewitched (A.M. Williamson), 1932

Beyond Control (Flora Kidd), 1981

Beyond Reasonable Doubt (Hebe Elsna), 1962

Beyond the Blue Mountains (Victoria Holt, as Jean Plaidy), 1947

Beyond the Foothills (Essie Summers), 1976

Beyond the Lagoon (Marjorie Lewty), 1981

Beyond the Mountain (Nan Asquith), 1970

Beyond the Ranges (Gloria Bevan), 1970

Beyond the Rocks (Elinor Glyn), 1906

Beyond the Sound of Guns (Emilie Loring), 1945

Beyond the Sunset (Flora Kidd), 1973

Beyond the Sweet Waters (Anne Hampson), 1970

Beyond This Point Are Monsters (Margaret

Millar), 1970

Bhunda Jewels, The (Anne Worboys), 1980

Bianca (Florence Stevenson), 1973

Bid for a Coronet, A (A.M. Williamson), 1901

Bid Me Love (Mollie Chappell), 1967

Bid Time Return (Hebe Elsna), 1979

Big Ben (Ruby M. Ayres), 1939

Big Blue Soldier, The (Grace Livingston Hill), 1923

Big Family, The (Viña Delmar), 1961

Big Fellah, The (Ruby M. Ayres), 1931

Big Frogs and Little Frogs (Susan Ertz), 1938

Big Game (Mrs. George de Horne Vaizey), 1908

Big Man, The (Mary Howard), 1965

Big Sky Country (Janet Dailey), 1978

Bill—The Sheik (A.M. Williamson), 1927

Bird in a Storm, A (Madame Albanesi), 1924

Bird in the Chimney, The (Dorothy Eden), 1963

Bird of Paradise (Margaret Rome), 1970

Bird of Prey (Henrietta Reid), 1973

Birds, The (Daphne du Maurier), 1968

Birds' Fountain (Baroness von Hutten), 1915

Birds in the Tree, The (Elizabeth Goudge), 1940

Bird's Nest, The (Shirley Jackson), 1955

Birds of Mingalay, The (Jean S. MacLeod), 1967

Birds of Silence (Leila Mackinlay), 1974

Birds Without Bars (Irene Roberts), 1970

Birdwatcher, The (Ethel Edison Gordon), 1974

Birth of Mischief, The (Rafael Sabatini), 1945

Bishop of Hell, The (Marjorie Bowen), 1949

Bit of a Bounder, A (Mary Ann Gibbs), 1952

Bitter Alliance (Kay Thorpe), 1978

Bitter Conquest, The (Charity Blackstock), 1959

Bitter Core, The (Denise Robins, as Ashley French), 1954

Bitter Debt, A (Annie S. Swan), 1893

Bitter Heritage (Margaret Pedler), 1928

Bitter Honey (Jane Blackmore), 1960

Bitter Lotus (Louis Bromfield), 1944

Bitter Loving, A (Lilian Peake), 1976

Bitter Love (Jane Blackmore), 1956

Bitter Rapture (Anne Duffield), 1937

Bitter Reason, The (Frances Cowen), 1966

Bitter Sweet (Madame Albanesi, as Effie Rowlands), 1910

Bitter Sweet Summer (Olga Sinclair), 1970

Bitter Winds (Barbara Cartland), 1938

Bitter Winds of Love, The (Barbara Cartland), 1976

Bittersweet (Ursula Bloom), 1978

Bitter-Sweet (Denise Robins), 1955

Bixby Girls, The (Rosamond Marshall), 1957

Black Amber (Phyllis A. Whitney), 1964

Black Bartlemy's Treasure (Jeffery Farnol), 1920

Black Benedicts, The (Susan Barrie, as Anita Charles), 1956

Black Cameron, The (Jean S. MacLeod), 1964

Black Charles (Esther Wyndham), 1952

Black Dawn (Christopher Nicole), 1977

Black Delaney, The (Henrietta Reid), 1970

Black Douglas (Nigel Tranter), 1968

Black Douglas (Violet Winspear), 1971

"Black Duchess," The (Alanna Knight), 1980

Black Eagle, The (Anne Hampson), 1973

Black Enigma (Rebecca Stratton), 1981

Black Flemings, The (Kathleen Norris), 1926

Black Gale, The (Samuel Shellabarger), 1929

Black Harvest (Countess Barcynska), 1960

Black Heart and White Heart (H. Rider Haggard), 1900

Black Heather (Virginia Coffman), 1966

Black Horse Tavern (Janet Louise Roberts, as Rebecca Danton), 1972

Black Incense (A.M. Williamson), 1926

Black Ingo (Margaret Way), 1978

Black Invaders, The (Rebecca Stratton), 1981

Black Is White (George Barr McCutcheon), 1915

Black Knight, The (Ethel M. Dell), 1926

Black Knight, The (Flora Kidd), 1976

Black Magic (Marjorie Bowen), 1909

Black Man—White Maiden (Marjorie Bowen, as George Preedy), 1941

Black Milestone, The (Catherine Gavin), 1941

Black Moth, The (Georgette Heyer), 1921

Black Narcissus (Rumer Godden), 1939

Black Panther, The (Barbara Cartland), 1939

Black Pearl series (Willo Davis Roberts)

Black Pearls (Janet Louise Roberts), 1979

Black Plantagenet, The (Pamela Bennetts), 1969

Black Rose, The (Thomas B. Costain), 1945

Black Sand, White Sand (Jean S. MacLeod), 1981

Black Sheep, The (Ruby M. Ayres), 1917

Black Sheep (Georgette Heyer), 1966

Black Sheep, The (Mabel St. John, as Henry St. John Cooper), 1916

Black Sheep, White Lamb (Dorothy Salisbury Davis), 1965

Black Sleeves (A.M. Williamson), 1928

Black Spaniel, The (Robert Hichens), 1905
Black Sun, The (Lance Horner), 1967
Black Swan, The (Rafael Sabatini), 1932
Black Virgin of the Gold Mountain, The (Phyllis Hastings), 1956
Black-Eyed Stranger, The (Charlotte Armstrong), 1951
Blackfire (Barbara Riefe), 1980
Black-Out Symphony (Countess Barcynska), 1942
Blackthorn (Dorothy Daniels), 1975
Blackwell's Ghost (Dorothy Daniels, as Angela Gray), 1972
Blade of Justice (Elizabeth Renier), 1965
Blades (George Barr McCutcheon), 1928
Blades of Passion (Claudette Williams), 1978
Bladon's Rock (Susan Barrie, as Pamela Kent), 1963
Blaise of France (Samuel Shellabarger), 1950
Blaize (Anne Betteridge, as Anne Melville), 1981
Blake's Reach (Catherine Gaskin), 1958
Blanche Fury (Marjorie Bowen, as Joseph Shearing), 1939
Blaze of Love (Denise Robins), 1932
Blaze of Noon (Victoria Holt, as Eleanor Burford), 1958
Blaze of Silk (Margaret Way), 1970
Blaze of Sunlight (Faith Baldwin), 1959
Blazon of Passion (Stephanie Blake), 1978
Bleak Heritage (Jean S. MacLeod), 1942
Bleak November (Rohan O'Grady), 1970
Bledding Sorrow (Marilyn Harris), 1976
Bless This House (Norah Lofts), 1954
Blessed Plot, The (Evelyn Berckman), 1976
Blessing in Disguise, The (Eleanor Farnes), 1958
Blessing in Disguise, A (Annie S. Swan), 1898
Blind Corner (Dornford Yates), 1927
Blind Date (Berta Ruck), 1953
Blind Journey (Jean S. MacLeod), 1942
Blind Loyalty (Margaret Pedler), 1940
Blind Man's Night (Samuel Shellabarger, as John Esteven), 1939
Blind Man's Year (Warwick Deeping), 1937
Blind Miller, The (Catherine Cookson), 1963
Blind Villain, The (Evelyn Berckman), 1957
Blind-Girl's-Buff (Evelyn Berckman), 1962
Blinkeyes (Countess Barcynska, as Oliver Sandys), 1925
Blood Games (Chelsea Quinn Yarbro), 1980
Blood Kin (Barbara Anne Pauley), 1972
Blood Money! (Mabel St. John), 1923
Blood Red Oscar, The (Elsie Lee), 1962
Blood Royal (Dornford Yates), 1929

Blood Sport (Virginia Coffman, as Victor Cross), 1966
Bloodied Toga, The (W.G. Hardy), 1979
Bloodstock (Margaret Irwin), 1953
Bloody Field by Shrewsbury, A (Edith Pargeter), 1972
Bloom on the Gorse (Eleanor Farnes), 1941
Blossom Like the Rose (Norah Lofts), 1939
Blossoming Gold (Gwen Westwood), 1976
Blossoms in the Snow (Irene Roberts, as Iris Rowland), 1971
Blot on the Escutcheon, A (May Wynne)
Blow Hot, Blow Cold (Betty Neels), 1969
Blow the Wind Southerly (D.E. Stevenson), 1954
Blue Camellia (Frances Parkinson Keyes), 1957
Blue Caribbean, The (Kathryn Blair, as Celine Conway), 1954
Blue Castle, The (L.M. Montgomery), 1926
Blue Cockade, The (Mary Ann Gibbs, as Elizabeth Ford), 1943
Blue Devil Suite (Dorothy Daniels), 1968
Blue Evening Gone, The (Jessica Stirling), 1981
Blue Eyes and Grey (Baroness Orczy), 1928
Blue Falcon, The (Robyn Carr), 1981
Blue Feathers (Irene Roberts, as Iris Rowland), 1967
Blue Fire (Phyllis A. Whitney), 1961
Blue Haze (Netta Muskett), 1939
Blue Heather (Barbara Cartland, as Barbara McCorquodale), 1953
Blue Hills of Sintra (Anne Hampson), 1973
Blue Horizons (Faith Baldwin), 1942
Blue Jacaranda, The (Elizabeth Hoy), 1975
Blue Jasmine (Violet Winspear), 1969
Blue Lenses, The (Daphne du Maurier), 1970
Blue Lotus (Margaret Way), 1979
Blue Remembered Hills, The (Ivy Preston), 1965
Blue Rose, The (Esther Wyndham), 1957
Blue Ruin (Grace Livingston Hill), 1928
Blue Sapphire, The (D.E. Stevenson), 1963
Blue Shutters (Leila Mackinlay), 1947
Blue Skies, Dark Waters (Margaret Pargeter), 1976
Blue Sky of Spring, The (Elizabeth Cadell), 1956
Blue-Eyed Gypsy, The (Janet Louise Roberts, as Janette Radcliffe), 1974
Blue-Eyed Witch, The (Barbara Cartland), 1976
Bluegrass Doctor (Jean Francis Webb, as Ethel Hamill), 1953

Bluegrass King (Janet Dailey), 1977
Bluewater (Warwick Deeping), 1939
Blunder of an Innocent, The (Madame Albanesi), 1899
Blundering Bettina (May Wynne), 1924
Blunt Instrument, A (Georgette Heyer), 1938
Bohemian Blood (May Wynne, as Lester Lurgan), 1910
Bolambo Affair, The (Kathryn Blair, as Rosalind Brett), 1961
Bold Pursuit (Florence Stevenson, as Zabrina Faire), 1980
Bond of Blood (Roberta Gellis), 1965
Bond of the Flesh (Rosamond Marshall), 1952
Bondage of Riches, The (Annie S. Swan), 1912
Bondman, The (Hall Caine), 1889
Bonds of Matrimony, The (Isobel Chace, as Elizabeth Hunter), 1975
Bonfire in the Dusk (Iris Danbury), 1965
Bonnie Jean, The (Annie S. Swan), 1884
Boomerang Bride (Margaret Pargeter), 1979
Boomerang Girl, The (Joyce Dingwell), 1962
Bored Bridegroom, The (Barbara Cartland), 1974
Borgia Bull, The (Pamela Bennetts), 1968
Borgia Prince, The (Pamela Bennetts), 1975
Born for Love (Ursula Bloom), 1978
Born for Victory (Juliet Dymoke), 1960
Born in Prison (Mabel St. John), 1916
Born Out of Love (Anne Mather), 1977
Born to be King (Constance Gluyas), 1974
Borodins series (Christopher Nicole, as Leslie Arlen)
Borrowed Plumes (Elizabeth Ashton), 1980
Borrower of the Night (Barbara Michaels, as Elizabeth Peters), 1973
Boss Man from Ogallala (Janet Dailey), 1975
Boss of Bali Creek (Anne Hampson), 1973
Boss's Daughter, The (Joyce Dingwell), 1978
Both Sides of the Coin (Mary Linn Roby, as Georgina Grey), 1980
Botor Chaperon, The (C.N. and A.M. Williamson), 1907
Bound to Happen (Elswyth Thane), 1930
Boundary Line, The (Denise Robins), 1932
Boundless Water (Marjorie Bowen), 1926
Boutique of the Singing Clocks, The (Ursula Bloom, as Lozania Prole), 1969
Bow to the Storm (Mary Howard), 1950
Bow Window in Green Street (D.A. Ponsonby), 1949
Bowl of Stars, A (Wynne May), 1973
Boxer's Sweetheart, A (Mabel St. John), 1920

Boxwood Maze, The (Bentz Plagemann), 1972
Boy (Marie Corelli), 1900
Boy in the House, A (Mazo de la Roche), 1952
Boy with Wings, The (Berta Ruck), 1915
Bracelet, The (Robert Hichens), 1930
Bracken's World (Daoma Winston), 1969
Braganza Pursuit, The (Sarah Neilan), 1976
Brass (May Edginton), 1910
Brass Islands, The (Alice Dwyer-Joyce), 1974
Brave Barbara (Madame Albanesi), 1901
Brave Brigands, The (May Wynne), 1913
Brave Employments (Marjorie Bowen), 1931
Brave Heart (Madame Albanesi, as Effie Rowlands), 1911
Brave in Heart, The (Mary Burchell), 1948
Brave Live On, The (Leila Mackinlay), 1942
Brave Love (Madame Albanesi, as Effie Rowlands), 1926
Brazilian Affair (Rachel Lindsay), 1978
Brazilian Stardust (Marjorie McEvoy), 1967
Bread into Roses (Kathleen Norris), 1937
Bread of Deceit (Marie Belloc Lowndes), 1925
Bread of Tears, The (G.B. Burgin), 1899
Bread-and-Grease-Paint (Berta Ruck), 1943
Breadwinners (Ursula Bloom), 1932
Breaker of Hearts, A (Annie S. Swan), 1937
Breakfast with the Nikolides (Rumer Godden), 1942
Breaking Point (Daphne du Maurier), 1959
Breaking Point, The (Mary Roberts Rinehart), 1922
Breaking Point (Denise Robins, as Ashley French), 1956
Breath of Air, A (Rumer Godden), 1950
Breath of Life (Faith Baldwin), 1942
Brentwood (Grace Livingston Hill), 1937
Breeze from Camelot, The (Viña Delmar), 1959
Breeze from the Bosphorus (Elizabeth Ashton), 1978
Breta's Double (Charles Garvice), 1911
Brethren, The (H. Rider Haggard), 1904
Brewster's Millions (George Barr McCutcheon, as Richard Greaves), 1903
Briar and Palm (Annie S. Swan), 1887
Briar Patch, The (Charity Blackstock), 1960
Briar Rose (C.N. and A.M. Williamson), 1919
Bridal Affair (Glenna Finley), 1972
Bridal Array (Elizabeth Cadell), 1957
Bridal Black (Dorothy Daniels), 1980
Bridal Lamp, The (Patricia Ainsworth), 1975

Bridal Path (Nigel Tranter), 1952

Bridal Sweet (Ursula Bloom, as Sheila Burns), 1942

Bridal Tapestry (Henrietta Reid), 1967

Bridal Wreath (Leila Mackinlay), 1971

Bride Alone (Ursula Bloom, as Sheila Burns), 1943

Bride by Arrangement (Rose Burghley), 1960

Bride by Candlelight (Dorothy Eden), 1954

Bride for a Night (Anne Hampson), 1979

Bride for King James (Maureen Peters), 1968

Bride in Flight (Essie Summers), 1964

Bride in the Sun (Isobel Chace, as Elizabeth Hunter), 1980

Bride in Waiting (Susan Barrie), 1961

Bride—Maybe (Ursula Bloom, as Sheila Burns), 1946

Bride of Alaine (Rose Burghley), 1966

Bride of Bonamour (Gwen Westwood), 1977

Bride of Caringore, The (Jean Francis Webb), 1974

Bride of Doom (Denise Robins, as Harriet Gray), 1956

Bride of Emersham (Theresa Charles, as Leslie Lance), 1967

Bride of Kylsaig (Iris Danbury), 1963

Bride of Lenore (Dorothy Denise, as Cynthia Kavanaugh), 1966

Bride of Liberty (Frank Yerby), 1954

Bride of Moat House, The (Norah Lofts, as Peter Curtis), 1969

Bride of Pendorric (Victoria Holt), 1963

Bride of Ravenscourt (Henrietta Reid), 1972

Bride of Romano, The (Rebecca Stratton), 1973

Bride of the Delta Queen, The (Janet Dailey), 1978

Bride of the Plains, A (Baroness Orczy), 1915

Bride of the Rif (Margaret Rome), 1972

Bride of Violence (Denise Robins, as Harriet Gray), 1975

Bride of Zarco (Margaret Rome), 1976

Bride Price, The (Isobel Chace, as Elizabeth Hunter), 1974

Bride to Lucifer (Violet Winspear), 1971

Bride to the King (Barbara Cartland), 1980

Bride Who Ran Away—Nurse Henderson, The (Berta Ruck), 1922

Bride's Dilemma (Violet Winspear), 1965

Bride's Hero, The (A.M. Williamson, as M.P. Revere), 1912

Brides of Bellenmore, The (Anne Maybury), 1964

Brides of Friedberg, The (Gwendoline Butler), 1977

Bridge Builders, The (Annie S. Swan), 1913

Bridge of Corvie (Rosamunde Pilcher, as Jane Fraser), 1956

Bridge of Desire (Warwick Deeping), 1916

Bridge of Fear, The (Dorothy Eden), 1966

Bridge of Kisses, The (Berta Ruck), 1917

Bridge of Strange Music, The (Jane Blackmore), 1952

Bridge of Years, The (Jean S. MacLeod), 1945

Bridge to the Moon (Anne Maybury), 1960

Bridge to Yesterday, The (Constance Gluyas), 1981

Bridie Climbing (Rosemary Ellerbeck, as Nicola Thorne), 1969

Brief Ecstasy (Denise Robins), 1934

Brief Enchantment (Jean S. MacLeod), 1979

Brief Excursion (Eleanor Farnes), 1944

Brief Fulfillment (Jean S. MacLeod), 1945

Brief Heroine (Hebe Elsna), 1937

Brief Is the Glory (Constance Gluyas), 1975

Brief Rapture (Anne Duffield), 1938

Brief Return (Mignon Eberhart), 1939

Brief Springtime (Ursula Bloom), 1957

Bright Arrows (Grace Livingston Hill), 1946

Bright Banners (Elizabeth Seifert), 1943

Bright Coin, The (Elizabeth Seifert), 1949

Bright Destiny (Ruby M. Ayres), 1952

Bright Face of Honour (Hebe Elsna, as Lyndon Snow), 1965

Bright Flows the River (Taylor Caldwell), 1978

Bright Meadows (Claire Ritchie), 1951

Bright Morning (Rona Randall), 1952

Bright Promise (Mollie Chappell), 1960

Bright Scalpel (Elizabeth Seifert), 1941

Bright Skies (Emilie Loring), 1946

Bright Son of York (Pamela Bennetts), 1971

Bright Tomorrow (Victoria Holt, as Eleanor Burford), 1952

Bright Wilderness (Gwen Westwood), 1969

Bright Winter (Theresa Charles, as Leslie Lance), 1965

Brightener, The (C.N. and A.M. Williamson), 1921

Brightest Star, The (Roumelia Lane), 1978

Brimming Cup, The (Hebe Elsna), 1965

Brimstone in the Garden (Elizabeth Cadell), 1950

Bringing Up Becky! (Mabel St. John), 1924

Bristol Cousins, The (D.A. Ponsonby), 1951

Britannia All at Sea (Betty Neels), 1978

Brittany Blue (Isobel Chace), 1967

Brittle Bondage (Kathryn Blair, as Rosalind Brett), 1951

Brittle Glass, The (Norah Lofts), 1942

Brittle Shadow, The (Ursula Bloom), 1938

Broad Highway, The (Jeffery Farnol), 1910

Broad Road, The (Annie S. Swan), 1908

Broadway Interlude (Faith Baldwin), 1929

Brocade (Netta Muskett), 1953

Broken Armour (Leila Mackinlay), 1963

Broken Barrier, The (Mabel St. John, as Henry St. John Cooper), 1924

Broken Barriers (Barbara Cartland), 1938

Broken Bough, The (Iris Bromige), 1973

Broken Gate, The (Theresa Charles, as Jan Tempest), 1940

Broken Halo, The (Florence L. Barclay), 1913

Broken Key, The (Mary Linn Roby), 1973

Broken Sphinx, The (Katheryn Kimbrough), 1972

Broken Tapestry (Rona Randall), 1967

Broken Wing, The (Mary Burchell), 1966

Bronze Eagle, The (Baroness Orczy), 1915

Brooding Lake, The (Dorothy Eden), 1966

Broomsticks in the Hall (Jane Blackmore), 1970

Brother of Daphne, The (Dornford Yates), 1914

Brother Sinister (Katheryn Kimbrough, as Charlotte Bramwell), 1973

Brothers and Enemies (Christopher Nicole), 1982

Brown Eyes of Mary, The (Madame Albanesi), 1905

Brown Fields, The (Rosamunde Pilcher, as Jane Fraser), 1951

Brown Sugar (Ruby M. Ayres), 1921

Brumaire (Christopher Nicole, as Mark Logan), 1978

Brute!, The (Mabel St. John), 1922

Bubble over Thorn (Countess Barcynska), 1951

Bubble Reputation (P.C. Wren), 1936

Bubbling Springs (Anne Duffield), 1940

Buccaneer Doctor (Frank G. Slaughter, as C.V. Terry), 1955

Buccaneer Surgeon (Frank G. Slaughter, as C.V. Terry), 1954

Bulls of Parral (Marguerite Steen), 1954

Bunch of Blue Ribbons, A (Madame Albanesi, as Effie Rowlands), 1926

Bunny the Aunt (May Wynne), 1936

Burden, The (Mary Westmacott), 1956

Burden-Bearers, The (Annie S. Swan), 1900

Burned Fingers (Kathleen Norris), 1945

Burning Beacon, The (Theresa Charles), 1956

Burning Flame, The (Hettie Grimstead), 1956

Burning Flame, The (Irene Roberts, as Elizabeth Harle), 1979

Burning Glass, The (Marjorie Bowen), 1918

Burning Is a Substitute for Loving (Gwendoline Butler, as Jennie Melville), 1963

Burning Lamp, The (Frances Murray), 1973

Burning Memories (Charlotte Lamb, as Laura Hardy), 1981

Burning Sands, The (Violet Winspear), 1976

Bury the Past (Maysie Greig, as Jennifer Ames), 1938

Business Affair (Rachel Lindsay), 1960

But Joy Kissed Me (Hebe Elsna, as Lyndon Snow), 1942

But Never Free (Barbara Cartland), 1937

But Not for Me (Mary Burchell), 1938

But Yesterday— (Maud Diver), 1927

Butter Market House (Mary Ann Gibbs, as Elizabeth Ford), 1958

Buttercup Joe (Phyllis Hastings), 1980

Buttered Side Down (Edna Ferber), 1912

Butterflies (Countess Barcynska, as Oliver Sandys), 1932

Butterflies in the Rain (Countess Barcynska, as Oliver Sandys), 1958

Butterfly (Kathleen Norris), 1923

Butterfly and the Baron, The (Margaret Way), 1979

Butterfly Man, The (George Barr McCutcheon), 1910

Butterfly Picnic, The (Joan Aiken), 1972

Butterfly's Hour, A (Hebe Elsna, as Laura Conway), 1964

Butternut Tree, The (Betty Beaty), 1958

Buy Me a Dream (Irene Roberts, as Elizabeth Harle), 1972

By Candlelight (Sara Seale), 1963

By Dangerous Ways (Charles Garvice), 1909

By Firelight (Edith Pargeter), 1948

By Fountains Wild (Anne Hampson), 1970

By Love Transformed (Hebe Elsna, as Laura Conway), 1959

By Night at Dinsmore (Samuel Shellabarger, as John Esteven), 1935

By Order of the Company (Mary Johnston), 1900

By Our Beginnings (Jean Stubbs), 1979

By Request (Ethel M. Dell), 1927

By Royal Command (Dornford Yates), 1931

By Sun and Candlelight (Elizabeth Renier), 1968

By the Gate of Pity (Ruby M. Ayres), 1927

By the Gods Beloved (Baroness Orczy), 1905

By the World Forgot (Ruby M. Ayres), 1932

By This Strange Fire (Edith Pargeter), 1948

By Way of the Silverthorns (Grace Livingston Hill), 1941

By Yet Another Door (Jane Arbor), 1950

Byeways (Robert Hichens), 1897

Cable from Kabul (Nigel Tranter), 1968

Cactus and the Crown, The (Catherine Gavin), 1962

Cactus Has Courage, The (Ursula Bloom), 1961

Cactus Rose, The (Florence Stevenson, as Zandra Colt), 1982

Cade Curse, The (Willo Davis Roberts), 1978

Cadence of Portugal (Isobel Chace), 1972

Caduceus Tree, The (Dorothy Daniels, as Suzanne Somers), 1961

Café Mimosa (Roumelia Lane), 1971

Cafeteria (Hebe Elsna), 1946

Cage of Gold (Rachel Lindsay), 1973

Cake Without Icing (Maysie Greig), 1932

Calabrian Summer (Marjorie McEvoy), 1980

Calais (Kathleen Winsor), 1979

Calder series (Janet Dailey)

Caldwell Shadow, The (Dorothy Daniels), 1973

Calf for Venus, A (Norah Lofts), 1949

Call—And I'll Come (Mary Burchell), 1937

Call after Midnight (Mignon Eberhart), 1964

Call Back Love (Rose Franken, as Margaret Grant), 1937

Call Back Yesterday (Charlotte Lamb), 1978

Call Back Yesterday (Doris Leslie), 1975

Call for a Stranger (Anne Worboys, as Anne Eyre Worboys), 1962

Call for Doctor Barton, A (Elizabeth Seifert), 1956

Call for the Doctor, A (Marjorie McEvoy, as Marjorie Harte), 1961

Call Her Fannie (May Edginton), 1930

Call Home the Heart (Elisabeth Ogilvie), 1962

Call Home the Heart (Jessica Stirling), 1977

Call in the Night (Susan Howatch), 1967

Call of Glengarron (Nancy Buckingham), 1968

Call of Love, The (Mabel St. John, as Henry St. John Cooper), 1936

Call of the Blood, The (Robert Hichens), 1906

Call of the Blood (Victoria Holt, as Kathleen Kellow), 1956

Call of the Flesh (Virginia Coffman), 1968

Call of the Heart (Barbara Cartland), 1975

Call of the Heart, The (Charles Garvice), 1914

Call of the Heathen (Anne Hampson), 1980

Call of the Outback (Anne Hampson), 1976

Call of the Pines, The (Lucy Walker), 1963

Call of the Veld (Anne Hampson), 1977

Callahans and the Murphys, The (Kathleen Norris), 1924

Calling Dr. Savage (Marion Collin), 1970

Calling Nurse Stewart (Marjorie McEvoy), 1963

Calm Waters (Countess Barcynska, as Oliver Sandys), 1940

Came a Cavalier (Frances Parkinson Keyes), 1947

Came a Stranger (Kathryn Blair, as Celine Conway), 1960

Camelot Caper, The (Barbara Michaels, as Elizabeth Peters), 1969

Cameos (Marie Corelli), 1896

Cameron of Gare (Jean S. MacLeod), 1952

Can I Forget You? (Anne Maybury), 1944

Canadian Affair (Flora Kidd), 1979

Canary Yellow (Elizabeth Cadell), 1965

Cancelled Love (A.M. Williamson), 1926

Candidate for Love (Maysie Greig), 1947

Candidate's Wife, The (Virginia Coffman), 1968

Candle for the Dragon, A (Mary Francis Craig), 1973

Candle for St. Jude, A (Rumer Godden), 1948

Candle in Her Heart, A (Emilie Loring), 1964

Candle in the Sun (Dorothy Daniels), 1968

Candle in the Sun (Netta Muskett), 1943

Candle in the Sun, A (Marguerite Steen), 1964

Candle Light (Ruby M. Ayres), 1924

Candle Rekindled, The (Patricia Ainsworth), 1969

Candlemas Street (Audrie Manley-Tucker), 1963

Candles for Love (Hettie Grimstead), 1954

Candles in the Wind (Maud Diver), 1909

Candles in the Wood (Anne Rundle, as Alexandra Manners), 1974

Candles of the Night, The (Phyllis Hastings), 1977

Candleshades (Ursula Bloom), 1927

Candy (Baroness von Hutten), 1925

Candytuft—I Mean Veronica (Mabel Barnes Grundy), 1914

Cane Music (Joyce Dingwell), 1975

Cannibal Heart, The (Margaret Millar), 1949

Canopy of Rose Leaves, A (Isobel Chace), 1976

Cap Flamingo (Violet Winspear), 1964

Cap of Youth, The (Madame Albanesi), 1914

1963

Case of Jennie Brice, The (Mary Roberts Rinehart), 1913

Case of Susan Dare, The (Mignon Eberhart), 1934

Case of the Weird Sisters, The (Charlotte Armstrong), 1932

Cashelmara (Susan Howatch), 1974

Cassandra (Claudette Williams), 1979

Cassandra by Chance (Betty Neels), 1973

Cast a Long Shadow (Hebe Elsna), 1976

Cast the Spear (Netta Muskett), 1950

Castaway (Frances Murray), 1978

Castle at Witches' Coven (Virginia Coffman), 1966

Castle Barebane (Joan Aiken), 1976

Castle Barra (Virginia Coffman), 1966

Castle Clodha (Alanna Knight), 1972

Castle Craneycrow (George Barr McCutcheon), 1902

Castle Doom (Marjorie McEvoy), 1970

Castle Dor (Daphne du Maurier), 1962

Castle in Spain (Anne Duffield), 1958

Castle in Spain, A (Eleanor Farnes), 1971

Castle in the Air (Maysie Greig), 1947

Castle in the Swamp (Edison Marshall), 1948

Castle in the Trees (Rachel Lindsay), 1958

Castle Kelpiesloch (Theresa Charles), 1973

Castle Man, The (G.B. Burgin), 1898

Castle Morvant (Dorothy Daniels), 1972

Castle of Closing Doors, The (Daoma Winston), 1967

Castle of Eagles (Constance Heaven), 1974

Castle of Fear, The (Barbara Cartland), 1974

Castle of Foxes (Alanna Knight), 1981

Castle of Shadows, The (A.M. Williamson), 1905

Castle of Temptation (Flora Kidd), 1978

Castle of the Fountains (Margaret Rome), 1979

Castle of the Seven Lilacs, The (Violet Winspear), 1971

Castle of the Unicorn (Gwen Westwood), 1971

Castle on the Hill, The (Elizabeth Goudge), 1941

Castle Perilous (Velda Johnston), 1971

Castle Perilous (Claire Ritchie), 1979

Castle Raven (Laura Black), 1978

Castle Thunderbird (Susan Barrie), 1965

Castlereagh (Janet Louise Roberts), 1975

Castles in Spain (Victoria Holt, as Eleanor Burford), 1954

Castles in Spain (Rebecca Stratton), 1974

Castles in the Air (Patricia Gallagher), 1976

Castles of Sand (Anne Mather), 1981

Castile for Isabella (Victoria Holt, as Jean Plaidy), 1960

Casualty Speaking (Kate Norway), 1971

Casualty Ward (Ursula Bloom, as Sheila Burns), 1968

Cat and Mouse (Mary Linn Roby), 1967

Cat on a Broomstick (Anne Rundle, as Joanne Marshall), 1969

Catch at a Rainbow (Anne Maybury), 1935

Catch-as-Catch-Can (Charlotte Armstrong), 1952

Catch Up to Love (Maysie Greig), 1960

Catherine de' Medici (Victoria Holt, as Jean Plaidy), 1969

Cat's Prey (Dorothy Eden), 1952

Cattleman, The (Joyce Dingwell), 1974

Cauldron of Desire (Maureen Peters, as Levanah Lloyd), 1981

Cave of the White Rose, The (Flora Kidd), 1972

Cazalet Bride, The (Violet Winspear), 1970

Cease Firing (Mary Johnston), 1912

Cecily (Clare Darcy), 1972

Cedar Tree, The (Rona Randall), 1957

Celeste (Rosamond Marshall), 1949

Celestial City, The (Baroness Orczy), 1926

Celia's House (D.E. Stevenson), 1943

Cell, The (David Case), 1969

Ceremony of the Innocent (Taylor Caldwell), 1976

Certain Crossroad, A (Emilie Loring), 1925

Certain Doctor French, A (Elizabeth Seifert), 1943

Certain People of Importance (Kathleen Norris), 1922

Certain Smile, A (Marjorie Lewty), 1979

Certain Spring, The (Nan Asquith), 1956

Certified Bride, A (Countess Barcynska), 1928

Chadbourne Luck, The (Florence Stevenson, as Lucia Curzon), 1981

Chain of Destiny (Nigel Tranter), 1964

Chained Eagle (Anne Maybury), 1939

Chains of Love, The (Anne Betteridge), 1965

Chalet Diabolique (Virginia Coffman), 1971

Chalet in the Sun, The (Jean S. MacLeod), 1948

Challenge for Doctor Mays (Elizabeth Seifert), 1955

Challenge of Love, The (Warwick Deeping), 1932

Challenge of Spring, The (Iris Bromige), 1965

Challenge to Clarissa (E.M. Delafield), 1931

Challenge to Happiness (Maysie Greig), 1936

Challenge to Love (Jean Francis Webb, as Ethel Hamill), 1946

Challengers, The (Grace Livingston Hill), 1932

Champagne Girl (Audrie Manley-Tucker), 1967

Champagne Kiss, The (Countess Barcynska, as Oliver Sandys), 1929

Champagne Spring (Margaret Rome), 1979

Champion (C.N. and A.M. Williamson), 1913

Chance Encounter (Hettie Grimstead, as Marsha Manning), 1975

Chance for Love, A (Iris Bromige), 1975

Chance Meeting (Kay Thorpe), 1980

Chance of a Lifetime, The (Grace Livingston Hill), 1931

Chance Romance, The (Ursula Bloom, as Sheila Burns), 1948

Chance the Winds of Fortune (Lauria McBain), 1980

Chance to Win, A (Margaret Rome), 1969

Change Here for Happiness (Berta Ruck), 1933

Change of Air, A (Anthony Hope), 1893

Change of Heart (Madame Albanesi, as Effie Rowlands)

Change of Heart (Faith Baldwin), 1944

Change of Heart, A (Ursula Bloom), 1979

Change of Heart, A (Eleanor Farnes), 1963

Changeling, The (Mary Linn Roby, as Mary Wilson), 1975

Changeling Queen, The (Julia Fitzgerald, as Julia Hamilton), 1977

Changing Pilots (Ruby M. Ayres), 1932

Changing Tide, The (Sylvia Thorpe), 1967

Changing Years, The (Denise Robins), 1943

Changing Years (Rebecca Stratton, as Lucy Gillen), 1972

Chantal (Claire Lorrimer), 1980

Chantemerle (D.K. Broster), 1911

Chanters Chase (Jill Tattersall), 1978

Chaperon, The (C.N. and A.M. Williamson), 1912

Chaperone, The (Ethel Edison Gordon), 1973

Chappy—That's All (Countess Barcynska, as Oliver Sandys), 1922

Charge Nurse (Kate Norway, as Hilary Neal), 1965

Charing Cross (Claire Rayner), 1979

Charity Child (Sara Seale), 1959

Charity Girl, A (Madame Albanesi, as Effie Rowlands), 1900

Charity Girl (Georgette Heyer), 1970

Charity's Chosen (Ruby M. Ayres), 1926

Charles Rex (Ethel M. Dell), 1922

Charles II (Victoria Holt, as Jean Plaidy), 1972

Charles the King (Evelyn Anthony), 1961

Charlie Come Home (R.F. Delderfield), 1976

Charlie Is My Darling (Mollie Hardwick), 1977

Charlotte (Norah Lofts), 1972

Charlotte (Joanna Trollope, as Caroline Harvey), 1980

Charlotte Fairlie (D.E. Stevenson), 1954

Charlotte Wade (Adeline McElfresh), 1952

Charlotte's Hurricane (Anne Mather), 1970

Charmed Circle (Susan Ertz), 1956

Charmian, Lady Vibart (Jeffery Farnol), 1932

Charming Couple, A (Mary Ann Gibbs, as Elizabeth Ford), 1975

Chase a Green Shadow (Anne Mather), 1973

Chase a Rainbow (Hettie Grimstead), 1968

Chase the Moon (Sara Seale), 1933

Chaste Diana, The (L. Adams Beck, as E. Barrington), 1923

Chautauqua Idyl, A (Grace Livingston Hill), 1887

Chateau d'Armor (Rebecca Stratton), 1976

Chateau in Provence (Rachel Lindsay), 1973

Chateau in the Palms (Anne Hampson), 1979

Chateau of Fire, The (Susan Barrie, as Pamela Kent), 1961

Chateau of Flowers (Denise Robins), 1958

Chateau of Flowers (Margaret Rome), 1971

Chateau of Pines (Iris Danbury), 1969

Chateau of St. Avrell, The (Violet Winspear), 1970

Chatelaine, The (Claire Lorrimer), 1981

Chauffeur and the Chaperon, The (C.N. and A.M. Williamson), 1908

Cheap Day Return (R.F. Delderfield), 1967

Cheats, The (Marjorie Bowen), 1920

Checkered Paths (Margaret Pedler), 1935

Checkmate (Dorothy Dunnett), 1975

Checkmate (Norah Lofts), 1975

Checquered Pattern (Iris Bromige), 1947

Cheerful, By Request (Edna Ferber), 1918

Chelsea Reach (Claire Rayner), 1982

Chelynne (Robyn Carr), 1980

Cherished One, The (Hebe Elsna), 1974

Cherries and Candlelight (Irene Roberts, as Iris Rowland), 1969

Cherry (Countess Barcynska, as Oliver Sandys), 1929

Cherry (Kathleen Norris), 1958

Cherry Blossom Love (Maysie Greig), 1961

Cherry Hat, The (Ursula Bloom), 1904

Cherry-Blossom Clinic (Isobel Chace, as Elizabeth Hunter), 1961

Cherrystones (Countess Barcynska, as Oliver Sandys), 1959

Chess Players, The (Frances Parkinson Keyes), 1960

Cheval Glass, The (Ursula Bloom), 1973

Cheviot Chase (Nigel Tranter), 1952

Chianti Flask, The (Marie Belloc Lowndes), 1934

Chicagoans, The (Mary Francis Craig, as M.S. Craig), 1981

Chicane (Countess Barcynska, as Oliver Sandys), 1912

Chieftain, The (Alice Dwyer-Joyce), 1980

Chieftain Without a Heart, The (Barbara Cartland), 1978

Chiffon Scarf, The (Mignon Eberhart), 1939

Child Called Freedom, A (Maureen Peters), 1976

Child Friday (Sara Seale), 1956

Child from the Sea, The (Elizabeth Goudge), 1970

Child in Their Midst, The (May Edginton), 1937

Child of Darkness (Dorothy Daniels), 1974

Child of Judas, The (Violet Winspear), 1976

Child of Music (Mary Burchell), 1970

Child of Night (Anne Edwards), 1975

Child of Passion (Hebe Elsna), 1928

Child of Storm (H. Rider Haggard), 1913

Child of the Revolution, A (Baroness Orczy), 1932

Child of the Sun (Lance Horner), 1966

Child Royal (D.K. Broster), 1937

Children of Houndstooth, The (Katheryn Kimbrough), 1972

Children of the Zodiac (A.M. Williamson), 1929

Children's Nurse (Kathryn Blair), 1961

Children's Ward (Claire Rayner, as Sheila Brandon), 1964

China Court (Rumer Godden), 1961

China Princess, The (Hebe Elsna), 1965

Chinese Box, The (Marjorie McEvoy), 1973

Chinese Door, The (Virginia Coffman), 1967

Chinese Puzzle (Rumer Godden), 1936

Chink in the Armour, The (Marie Belloc Lowndes), 1912

Chip and the Block, The (E.M. Delafield), 1925

Chivalry (Rafael Sabatini), 1935

Chocolate Cobweb, The (Charlotte Armstrong), 1948

Choice of Mavis, The (May Wynne), 1935

Choose the One You'll Marry (Mary Burchell), 1960

Choose Which You Will (Mary Burchell), 1949

Chosen Child (Anne Worboys, as Vicky Maxwell), 1973

Chosen Course, The (Nigel Tranter), 1949

Christening Party (Hebe Elsna, as Lyndon Snow), 1945

Christian, The (Hall Caine), 1897

Christian Marlowe's Daughter (Frances Parkinson Keyes), 1934

Christian's Cross (Annie S. Swan), 1905

Christina (Anne Eliot, as Caroline Arnett), 1980

Christine (Elizabeth, as Alice Cholmondeley), 1917

Christine Against the World (Annie S. Swan), 1933

Christine Diamond, The (Marie Belloc Lowndes), 1940

Christmas Bride, The (Grace Livingston Hill), 1934

Christmas Eve (Kathleen Norris), 1949

Christmas in London (Rachel Field), 1946

Christmas Tree (Lady Eleanor Smith), 1933

Christobel (Mary Linn Roby), 1976

Christopher and Columbus (Elizabeth), 1919

Christopher Strong (Gilbert Frankau), 1932

Chronicles of Avonlea (L.M. Montgomery), 1912

Chronicles of Count Antonio, The (Anthony Hope), 1895

Chronicles of the Imp, The (Jeffery Farnol), 1915

Cimarron (Edna Ferber), 1930

Cinder Path, The (Catherine Cookson), 1978

Cinderella after Midnight (Mary Burchell), 1945

Cinderella Girl, The (Mabel St. John), 1920

Cinderella Had Two Sisters (Theresa Charles, as Jan Tempest), 1948

Cinderella in Mink (Rachel Lindsay, as Roberta Leigh), 1973

Cinnabar House (Claire Lorrimer, as Patricia Robins), 1970

Circle in the Water, The (Marjorie Bowen), 1939

Circle of Doubt, The (Jean S. MacLeod), 1943

Circle of Dreams (Hettie Grimstead, as Marsha Manning), 1962

Circle of Evil (Velda Johnston), 1972

Circle of Gold (Claire Ritchie), 1964

Circle of Guilt (Dorothy Daniels), 1976

Circular Staircase, The (Mary Roberts Rinehart), 1908

Cissy (Madame Albanesi), 1913

Citadel of Swallows (Gwen Westwood), 1973

City in the Dawn, The (Hervey Allen), 1950

City Lies Foursquare, The (Edith Pargeter), 1939

City Nurse (Jane Arbor), 1956

City of Bells, The (Elizabeth Goudge), 1936

City of Dreams (Elizabeth Hoy), 1959

City of Fire, The (Grace Livingston Hill), 1922

City of Gems, The (Joanna Trollope), 1981

City of Libertines, The (W.G. Hardy), 1957

City of Masks, The (George Barr McCutcheon), 1918

City of Palms (Susan Barrie, as Pamela Kent), 1957

Civil Contract, A (Georgette Heyer), 1961

Claim That Won, The (May Wynne), 1912

Claire (Charles Garvice), 1899

Claire and Circumstances (Madame Albanesi), 1928

Clandara (Evelyn Anthony), 1963

Clandestine Betrothal, The (Alice Chetwynd Ley), 1967

Clansman, The (Nigel Tranter), 1959

Clarissa (Anne Eliot, as Caroline Arnett), 1976

Claudia (Anne Eliot, as Caroline Arnett), 1978

Claudia series (Rose Franken)

Claudine's Daughter (Rosalind Laker), 1979

Claw, The (Norah Lofts), 1981

Clay Hand, The (Dorothy Salisbury Davis), 1950

Clear Stream, The (Madame Albanesi), 1930

Clemency Page (Hebe Elsna), 1947

Clency Tradition, The (Netta Muskett), 1947

Cleopatra (L. Adams Beck, as E. Barrington), 1934

Cleopatra (H. Rider Haggard), 1889

Cleric's Secret, The (Warwick Deeping), 1944

Cliffs of Dread, The (Virginia Coffman), 1972

Cliffside Castle (Dorothy Daniels), 1965

Climb to the Stars (Denise Robins), 1935

Climbing the Hill (Annie S.Swan) , 1883

Cloak and Dagger Lover (Maysie Greig), 1955

Cloistered Flame, The (Maureen Peters), 1971

Cloisterman, The (Juliet Dymoke), 1969

Close to the Heart (Rebecca Stratton), 1979

Close Your Eyes (Theresa Charles, as Jan Tempest), 1947

Closed Doors (Annie S. Swan), 1926

Closing Door, The (Jane Blackmore), 1955

Closing Web, The (Marjorie McEvoy, as Marjorie Harte), 1973

Cloth of Gold (Elswyth Thane), 1929

Cloud Castle (Sara Seale), 1960

Cloud over Malverton (Nancy Buckingham), 1967

Cloudbreak (Netta Muskett), 1964

Clouded Moon, The (Mary Howard), 1948

Clouded Pearl, The (Berta Ruck), 1924

Clouded Veil, The (Isobel Chace), 1976

Clouds over Vellanti (Elsie Lee), 1965

Cloudy Jewel (Grace Livingston Hill), 1920

Clove Orange (Joyce Dingwell), 1967

Cluster of Palms, A (Wynne May), 1967

Cluster of Separate Sparks, A (Joan Aiken), 1972

Clyde Valley (Catherine Gavin), 1938

Cobweb Mist, The (Hebe Elsna, as Vicky Lancaster), 1961

Cobweb Morning (Betty Neels), 1975

Code Five (Frank G. Slaughter), 1971

Coffee at Dobree's (Elizabeth Harrison), 1965

"Coffin" series (Gwendoline Butler)

Coil of Serpents (Anne Stevenson), 1977

Coin of Love, The (Barbara Cartland), 1956

Colin Lowrie (Norah Lofts), 1939

Colla's Children (Alanna Knight), 1982

College Girl, A (Mrs. George de Horne Vaizey), 1913

Colonel Quaritch, V.C. (H. Rider Haggard), 1888

Colorado (Louis Bromfield), 1947

Colour Blind (Catherine Cookson), 1953

Coloured Lights (Madame Albanesi), 1931

Colours Flying (Nigel Tranter), 1948

Colours of the Night, The (Betty Beaty, as Catherine Ross), 1962

Columbella (Phyllis A. Whitney), 1966

Columbus (Rafael Sabatini), 1942

Come and Get It (Edna Ferber), 1935

Come Autumn—Come Winter (Anne Maybury), 1935

Come Back Beloved (Irene Roberts), 1962

Come Back, Elizabeth (Esther Wyndham), 1948

Come Back, Miranda (Anne Duffield), 1955

Come Back My Dream (Elizabeth Hoy), 1942

Come Back to Love (Joyce Dingwell), 1980

Come Back to Me, Beloved (Kathleen Norris), 1942

Come Back Yesterday (Denise Robins), 1976

Come Be My Guest (Elizabeth Cadell), 1964

Come Blossom-Time, My Love (Essie Summers), 1961

Come by Chance (Mollie Chappell), 1963

Come Home and Be Killed (Gwendoline Butler, as Jennie Melville) , 1962

Come Home Charlie and Face Them (R.F. Delderfield), 1969

Come Home, Dear! (Lucy Walker), 1956

Come Lasses and Lads (Margaret Maddocks), 1944

Come Love, Come Hope (Iris Bromige), 1962

Come On, Fortune! (Emilie Loring), 1933

Come Out to Play (Margaret Irwin), 1914

Come Pour the Wine (Cynthia Freeman), 1981

Come Running (Anne Mather), 1976

Come the Vintage (Anne Mather), 1975

Come to My Wedding (Ruby M. Ayres), 1933

Come to My Wedding (Hebe Elsna, as Lyndon Snow), 1949

Come, Walk with Me (Rebecca Stratton, as Lucy Gillen), 1974

Come Wind, Come Weather (Daphne du Maurier), 1940

Comedies of Courtship (Anthony Hope), 1896

Comedy of Terrors, A (Elsie Lee), 1964

Comfort and Keep (Doris E. Smith), 1968

Coming of Verity, The (May Wynne), 1940

Coming Through the Rye (Grace Livingston Hill), 1926

Common Cheat, A (Sophia Cleugh), 1928

Complacent Wife, The (Barbara Cartland), 1972

Compromise (Ruby M. Ayres), 1935

Compromise (Mabel St. John, as Henry St. John Cooper), 1929

Compromise with Yesterday (Elizabeth O. Peter), 1946

Compulsion (Charlotte Lamb), 1980

Comtesse, La (Joan Smith), 1978

Concerning Peter Jackson (Gilbert Frankau), 1931

Concession (Katheryn Kimbrough, as Ann Ashton), 1981

Concord in Jeopardy (Doris Leslie), 1938

Concubine, The (Norah Lofts), 1963

Confident Tomorrows (Elizabeth O. Peter), 1931

Confirmed Bachelor (Rachel Lindsay, as Roberta Leigh), 1981

Conflict (Faith Baldwin), 1935

Conformable Wife, A (Alice Chetwynd Ley), 1981

Conjurer's Daughter, The (Hebe Elsna, as Lyndon Snow), 1979

Conjuror (Countess Barcynska), 1950

Connelly's Castle (Gloria Bevan), 1974.

Conover's Folly (Dorothy Daniels), 1972

Conway Touch, The (Iris Bromige), 1958

Conquered by Love (Barbara Cartland), 1977

Conqueror, The (Georgette Heyer), 1931

Conqueror, The (Edison Marshall), 1962

Conquest of Chrystabel, The (Mrs. George de Horne Vaizey), 1909

Conquesta's Caravan (D.A. Ponsonby), 1955

Conscience Money (Annie S. Swan, as David Lyall), 1898

Consequences (E.M. Delafield), 1919

Conservatory, The (Phyllis Hastings), 1973

Consider the Lilies (Elizabeth Cadell, as Harriet Ainsworth), 1956

Consider the Lilies (Daphne du Maurier), 1944

Consider These Women (Hebe Elsna), 1954

Consort to the Queen (Ursula Bloom, as Lozania Prole), 1959

Constant Heart, The (Ruby M. Ayres), 1941

Constant Heart, The (Eleanor Farnes), 1956

Constant Heart, The (Claire Lorrimer, as Patricia Robins), 1964

Constant Image, The (Marcia Davenport), 1960

Constant Nymph, The (Margaret Kennedy), 1924

Constant Rabbit, The (Countess Barcynska, as Oliver Sandys), 1949

Constantine (Frank G. Slaughter), 1965

Consulting Surgeon (Jane Arbor), 1959

Contract, The (Elinor Glyn), 1913

Contrary Mary (Madame Albanesi, as Effie Rowlands), 1910

Convention, M.D. (Frank G. Slaughter), 1972

Convenient Marriage, The (Georgette Heyer), 1934

Convert, The (Hebe Elsna), 1952

Cook at School (Mabel St. John), 1916

Coolibah Creek (Anne Hampson), 1979

Coombe St. Mary's (Maud Diver), 1925

Copenhagen Connection, The (Barbara Michaels, as Elizabeth Peters), 1982

Copper Lake (Kay Thorpe), 1981

Copper Moon (Margaret Way), 1972

Copsi Castle (Norah Lofts, as Juliet Astley), 1978

Coral Tree, The (Joyce Dingwell), 1958

Corinthian, The (Georgette Heyer), 1940

Cormac Legend, The (Dorothy Daniels), 1979

Corn in Egypt (Warwick Deeping), 1941

Cornelian Strand, The (Alice Dwyer-Joyce), 1982

Corner House (Mary Burchell), 1959

Corner of Eden, A (Maynah Lewis), 1970

Corner of Heaven (Kathleen Norris), 1944

Corner Shop, The (Elizabeth Cadell), 1966

Cornish Hearth, The (Isobel Chace), 1975

Cornish Heiress, The (Roberta Gellis), 1981

Cornish Rhapsody (Ursula Bloom, as Sheila Burns), 1972

Coronet of Shame, A (Charles Garvice), 1900

Corporation Boss (Joyce Dingwell), 1975

Corporation Wife (Catherine Gaskin), 1960

Corroding Gold (Annie S. Swan), 1914

Corsican Bandit, The (Rebecca Stratton), 1978

Cortez and Marina (Edison Marshall), 1963

Cost Price (Dornford Yates), 1949

Cotillion (Georgette Heyer), 1953

Cotillion for Mandy (Claudette Williams), 1978

Cotswold Honey (Doris E. Smith), 1975

Cottage at Drimble, The (Mary Ann Gibbs, as Elizabeth Ford), 1958

Cottage Hospital (Claire Rayner, as Sheila Brandon), 1963

Cottage in Spain, A (Kathryn Blair, as Rosalind Brett), 1955

Cottager's Daughter, The (Mary Howard), 1972

Cottar's Daughter, The (Mabel St. John, as Henry St. John Cooper), 1926

Cotton King, The (Mabel St. John, as Henry St., John Cooper), 1915

Couching at the Door (D.K. Broster), 1942

Could I Forget (Denise Robins), 1948

Could She Forgive? (Mabel St. John, as Henry St. John Cooper), 1923

Coulton's Wife (Madame Albanesi, as Effie Rowlands), 1930

Count the Stars (Barbara Cartland), 1981

Count Vronsky's Daughter (Carola Salisbury), 1981

Countdown (Frank G. Slaughter), 1970

Counterpoint (Isabelle Holland), 1980

Countess (Mary Howard, as Josephine Edgar), 1978

Countess Fanny, The (Marjorie Bowen), 1928

Countess Glika (Warwick Deeping), 1919

Country Air (Mollie Chappell), 1977

Country Holiday, A (Mary Ann Gibbs, as Elizabeth Ford), 1966

Country Love (Charles Garvice), 1912

Country Nurse (Dorothy Daniels), 1963

Country of the Falcon (Anne Mather), 1975

Country of the Heart, The (Jean S. MacLeod, as Catherine Airlie), 1961

Courage of Love, The (Madame Albanesi), 1930

Court of New York, The (George Barr McCutcheon), 1919

Court of the Flowering Peach, The (Janet Louise Roberts, as Janette Radcliffe), 1981

Court of the Veils (Violet Winspear), 1968

Courtenay Treasure, The (P.C. Wren), 1936

Courtesan, The (Nigel Tranter), 1963

Courting of Joanna, The (Alice Chetwynd Ley), 1976

Courts of Idleness, The (Dornford Yates), 1920

Courtship of Rosamond Fayre, The (Berta Ruck), 1915

Cousin Kate (Georgette Heyer), 1968

Cousin Mark (Elizabeth Ashton), 1971

Cousin to Terror (Katheryn Kimbrough, as Charlotte Bramwell), 1972

Cousins by Courtesy (Theresa Charles, as Leslie Lance, 1977

Cousins May Kiss (Theresa Charles, as Fay Chandos), 1948

Cove of Promises (Margaret Rome), 1975

Cover Girl (Marjorie McEvoy, as Marjorie Harte), 1968

Cove's End (Susan Hufford), 1977

Cowardice Court (George Barr McCutcheon), 1906

Cowardly Custard (Baroness von Hutten), 1936

Cowboy Countess, The (C.N. and A.M. Williamson), 1917

Craddock's Kingdom (Theresa Charles, as Jan Tempest), 1957

Craigshaw Curse, The (Jean Francis Webb), 1968

Crane Castle (Jean S. MacLeod), 1965

Cranes of Inycus, The (Mary Francis Craig), 1974

Crash, The (Denise Robins), 1966

Crazy Quilt (Ursula Bloom), 1933

Creature of the Twilight, A (Russell Kirk), 1966

Creatures of Destiny (Charles Garvice)

Crescendo (Charlotte Lamb), 1980

Crescent Carnival (Frances Parkinson Keyes), 1942

Crescent Moon, The (Isobel Chace, as Elizabeth Hunter), 1973

Cresselly Inheritance, The (Jane Blackmore), 1973

Cressida (Clare Darcy), 1977

Cressida (Marie Belloc Lowndes), 1928

Cressy (Mollie Chappell), 1973

Crime at Honotassa, The (Mignon Eberhart),

1962

Crime of Laura Sarelle, The (Marjorie Bowen, as Joseph Shearing), 1941

Crimes of Old London (Marjorie Bowen), 1919

Crimson Mountain (Grace Livingston Hill), 1942

Crimson Paw (Mignon Eberhart), 1959

Crimson Ramblers, The (Countess Barcynska, as Oliver Sandys), 1927

Crimson Roses (Grace Livingston Hill), 1928

Crimson Tapestry, The (Claire Lorrimer, as Patricia Robins), 1972

Crinklenose (Countes Barcynska, as Oliver Sandys), 1938

Crisis at St. Chad's (Theresa Charles), 1977

Crista Moon (Hebe Elsna), 1936

Croatan (Mary Johnston), 1923

Crocodile on the Sandbank (Barbara Michaels, as Elizabeth Peters), 1975

Crooked Adam (D.E. Stevenson), 1942

Crooked Coronet, The (Michael Arlen), 1937

Crooked Furrow, The (Jeffery Farnol), 1937

Cross Currents (Eleanor H. Porter), 1907

Crow Hollow (Dorothy Eden), 1950

Crowd Pleasers, The (Rosemary Rogers), 1978

Crown and the Cross, The (Frank G. Slaughter), 1959

Crown and the Shadow, The (Pamela Hill), 1955

Crown Estate, The (Evelyn Berckman), 1976

Crown for a Lady (Elizabeth Hoy), 1937

Crown for Normandy, A (Pamela Bennetts), 1971

Crown of Aloes (Norah Lofts), 1974

Crown of Flowers (Joyce Dingwell), 1969

Crown of Thorns (Doris Leslie), 1979

Crown of Willow (Elizabeth Ashton), 1975

Crown of Willow, The (Netta Muskett), 1957

Crown Usurped, A (Charlotte Lamb, as Sheila Coates), 1972

Crowned Lovers, The (L. Adams Beck, as E. Barrington), 1935

Crowning Glory (Phyllis Hastings), 1952

Crowns, Pounds, and Guineas (Denise Robins), 1931

Crucifix Corner (C.N. and A.M. Williamson), 1918

Cruel Count, The (Barbara Cartland), 1974

Cruel Flame, The (Charlotte Lamb), 1978

Cruise (Maysie Grieg, as Jennifer Ames), 1934

Cruise Ship Nurse (Dorothy Daniels), 1963

Cruise to a Wedding (Betty Neels), 1974

Cruiser in the Bay, The (Katrina Britt), 1975

Cry of the Gulls (Irene Roberts), 1963

Cry of the Peacock, The (Mary Linn Roby), 1974

Cry the Soft Rain (Alice Dwyer-Joyce), 1972

Cry Witch (Naomi A. Hintze), 1975

Crying Child, The (Barbara Michaels), 1973

Crystal Cave, The (Mary Stewart), 1970

Crystal Clear (Elizabeth Cadell), 1953

Crystal Crow, The (Joan Aiken), 1968

Crystal Gull, The (Lucilla Andrews), 1978

Crystal Spring, The (Eleanor Farnes), 1940

Crystal Villa, The (Mary Howard), 1970

Crystal Window, The (Patricia Matthews, as Patty Brisco), 1973

Cuckoo at Candlemas (Anne Rundle, as Joanne Marshall), 1968

Cuckoo Cottage (Leila Mackinlay), 1953

Cuckoo in Spring, The (Elizabeth Cadell), 1954

Cuckoo in the Night (Susan Barrie, as Pamela Kent), 1966

Cuckoo Never Weds, The (Ursula Bloom, as Sheila Burns), 1950

Cup of Kindness (Doris E. Smith), 1971

Cup, The Blade, or the Gun, The (Mignon Eberhart), 1961

Cupid in Africa (P.C. Wren), 1920

Cupid Rides Pillion (Barbara Cartland), 1952

Cupboard Love (Rachel Lindsay, as Roberta Leigh), 1976

Cupboard Love (Lucy Walker), 1963

Curate's Egg, The (Baroness von Hutten), 1930

Curious Happenings (Marjorie Bowen), 1917

Curled Hands, The (Countess Barcynska, as Oliver Sandys), 1926

Curse Not the King (Evelyn Anthony), 1954

Curse of Carranca, The (Elsie Lee), 1966

Curse of Cowden, The (Annie S. Swan), 1897

Curse of Gold, The (May Wynne), 1919

Curse of Halewood, The (Rosalind Laker, as Barbara Paul), 1976

Curse of Jezebel, The (Frank G. Slaughter), 1961

Curse of Kenton, The (Janet Louise Roberts), 1972

Curse of Mallory Hall, The (Dorothy Daniels), 1970

Curse of the Clan, The (Barbara Cartland), 1977

Curse of the Clodaghs, The (Frances Cowen), 1974

Curse of the Concullens, The (Florence Stev-

1964

Dangerous Legacy (Willo Davis Roberts), 1972

Dangerous Living (Anne Maybury), 1941

Dangerous Love (Jane Blackmore), 1958

Dangerous Loving (Mary Burchell), 1963

Dangerous Masquerade (Janet Dailey), 1976

Dangerous Obsession (Jean S. MacLeod), 1938

Dangerous Obsession (Natasha Peters), 1978

Dangerous Paths (Mabel St. John, as Henry St. John Cooper), 1933

Danerous Pretence (Flora Kidd), 1977

Dangerous Rhapsody (Anne Mather), 1969

Dangerous Stranger (Rebecca Stratton, as Lucy Gillen), 1972

Dangerous to Know (Elizabeth Ashton), 1974

Dangerous Waters (Kathryn Blair, as Rosalind Brett), 1960

Dangerous Winter, The (Suzanne Ebel), 1965

Dangerous Woman, A (Madame Albanesi, as Effie Rowlands), 1910

Dangerous Years, The (Gilbert Frankau), 1937

Dangerous Yesterday (Nan Asquith), 1967

Daniel Airlie (Robert Hichens), 1937

Danielle, My Darling (Ursula Bloom, as Mary Essex), 1954

Danny Boy (Alice Dwyer-Joyce), 1979

Danse Macabre (Victoria Holt, as Kathleen Kellow), 1952

Daphne Deane (Grace Livingston Hill), 1937

Darcourt (Isabelle Holland), 1976

Dare and Do (Madame Albanesi, as Effie Rowlands), 1911

Dare I Be Happy? (Mary Burchell), 1943

Dare to Love (Glenna Finley), 1977

Dare to Marry (Anne Maybury), 1940

Dare-Devil Doctor (Ursula Bloom, as Mary Essex), 1965

Darien Venture (Frank G. Slaughter, as C.V. Terry), 1955

Daring Deception, The (Barbara Cartland), 1973

Daring Deception, The (Eleanor Farnes), 1965

Dark and Splendid Passion, A (Lady Eleanor Smith), 1941

Dark Angel (Elizabeth Ashton), 1974

Dark Ann (Marjorie Bowen), 1927

Dark at Noon (Jill Tattersall), 1979

Dark Avenger (Anne Hampson), 1972

Dark Before the Rising Sun (Laurie McBain), 1982

Dark Beneath the Pines, The (Anne Eliot),

1974

Dark Between the Stars, The (Jane Blackmore), 1961

Dark Beyond Moura, The (Virginia Coffman), 1977

Dark Bondage (Audrie Manley-Tucker), 1961

Dark Carnival (Maysie Greig), 1950

Dark Castle (Anne Mather), 1975

Dark Changeling (Anne Rundle, as Marianne Lamont), 1970

Dark Corridor (Denise Robins), 1974

Dark Death, The (Denise Robins), 1929

Dark Dominion (Charlotte Lamb), 1979

Dark Dowry (Willo Davis Roberts), 1978

Dark Dream (Hebe Elsna, as Laura Conway), 1976

Dark Dream (Lady Miles), 1929

Dark Duel (Marguerite Steen), 1929

Dark Eden (Barbara Kevern), 1973

Dark Enchantment (Dorothy Macardle), 1953

Dark Enchantress (Sylvia Thorpe), 1973

Dark Enemy (Anne Mather), 1971

Dark Farm, The (Ursula Bloom, as Mary Essex), 1974

Dark Fires (Rosemary Rogers), 1975

Dark Fortune, The (Jean S. MacLeod), 1962

Dark Garden The (Mignon Eberhart), 1933

Dark Gentleman (Ruby M. Ayres), 1953

Dark Gentleman, Fair Lady (Ursula Bloom, as Mary Essex), 1951

Dark Heritage (Dorothy Daniels), 1976

Dark Heritage (Sylvia Thorpe), 1968

Dark Hills Shine (Anne Hampson), 1971

Dark Horse, The (Rumer Godden), 1981

Dark Horse, Dark Rider (Elizabeth Hoy), 1960

Dark House, The (Warwick Deeping), 1942

Dark House, The (Annie S. Swan), 1941

Dark Inheritance (Rachel Lindsay, as Roberta Leigh), 1952

Dark Inheritance (Carola Salisbury), 1975

Dark Interval (Joan Aiken), 1967

Dark Island (Dorothy Daniels), 1972

Dark Legacy (Theresa Charles), 1968

Dark Loch, The (Elizabeth Hoy), 1948

Dark Master (Charlotte Lamb), 1979

Dark Mile, The (D.K. Broster), 1929

Dark Moment, The (Ann Bridge), 1951

Dark Moon, Lost Lady (Elsie Lee), 1965

Dark Moonless Night (Anne Mather), 1974

Dark Morality (Mary Howard), 1932

Dark Night, The (Irene Roberts), 1962

Dark Noon (Christopher Nicole), 1963

Dark Oasis, The (Margaret Pargeter), 1980

Dark Odyssey (Florence Stevenson), 1974

Dark on the Other Side, The (Barbara Michaels), 1970

Dark Palazzo, The (Virginia Coffman), 1973

Dark Pasture, The (Jessica Stirling), 1977

Dark Priestess (Juanita Coulson), 1979

Dark Rider, The (Dorothy Daniels, as Geraldine Thayer), 1961

Dark Rosaleen (Marjorie Bowen), 1932

Dark Rose (Janet Louise Roberts), 1971

Dark Secret Love (Denise Robins, as Julia Kane), 1962

Dark Shore, The (Susan Howatch), 1965

Dark Stage, The (Dorothy Daniels), 1970

Dark Star (Anne Maybury), 1977

Dark Stranger, The (Theresa Charles, as Leslie Lance), 1946

Dark Stranger, The (Sara Seale), 1951

Dark Stream, The (Barbara Cartland), 1944

Dark Summer, The (Nancy Buckingham), 1968

Dark Sunlight (Maysie Greig, as Jennifer Ames), 1943

Dark Surrender (Margaret Pargeter), 1980

Dark Surrender (Maureen Peters, as Levanah Lloyd), 1981

Dark Sweet Wanton (Charlotte Lamb, as Sheila Lancaster), 1979

Dark Symmetry (Hebe Elsna, as Laura Conway), 1973

Dark Tower, The (Ursula Bloom, as Mary Essex), 1957

Dark Tower, The (Mary Howard, as Josephine Edgar), 1965

Dark Usurper (Henrietta Reid), 1972

Dark Venetian (Anne Mather, as Caroline Fleming), 1969

Dark Villa (Dorothy Daniels), 1966

Dark Waters (Marian Cockrell), 1944

Dark Woman, The (P.C.Wren), 1943

Dark-Eyed Queen, The (Ursula Bloom, as Lozania Prole), 1967

Dark-eyed Sister, The (Ursula Bloom, as Sheila Burns), 1968

Darkhaven (Dorothy Daniels), 1965

Darkness and the Dawn, The (Thomas B. Costain), 1959

Darkness at Ingraham's Crest, A (Frank Yerby), 1979

Darkness Falling (Barbara Kevern), 1974

Darkness on the Stairs, A (Florence Stevenson), 1976

Darkwater (Dorothy Eden), 1964

Darling Clementine (Dorothy Eden), 1955

Darling Clementine (Maysie Greig), 1946

Darling District Nurse (Ursula Bloom, as Rachel Harvey), 1970

Darling Infidel (Violet Winspear), 1976

Darling Jenny (Janet Dailey), 1978

Date with a Doctor (Ursula Bloom, as Mary Essex), 1962

Date with an Angel (Claire Ritchie), 1958

Date with Danger (Maysie Greig), 1952

Daughter, The (Charity Blackstock), 1970

Daughter at Home (Hebe Elsna, as Vicky Lancaster), 1939

Daughter for Julia, A (Netta Muskett), 1948

Daughter He Didn't Want! The (Mabel St. John), 1926

Daughter Knows Best (Denise Robins), 1943

Daughter of Anna (Victoria Holt, as Eleanor Burford), 1941

Daughter of Destiny (Stephanie Blake), 1977

Daughter of Isis (Maureen Peters, as Belinda Grey), 1981

Daughter of Lir (Henrietta Reid), 1966

Daughter of Midnight (Pamela Hill), 1979

Daughter of Satan (Victoria Holt, as Jean Plaidy), 1952

Daughter of the Devil (Ursula Bloom, as Lozania Prole), 1963

Daughter of the House (Catherine Gaskin), 1952

Daughter of the the Land, A (Gene Stratton Porter), 1918

Daughter of the Loom, A (Mabel St. John, as Henry St. John Cooper), 1922

Daughter Scorned, A (Mabel St. John), 1911

Daughter's a Daughter, A (Mary Westmacott), 1952

Daughters of a Genius, The (Mrs. George de Horne Vaizey), 1903

Daughters of Ardmore Hall, The (Dorothy Eden), 1968

Daughters of Babylon, The (Robert Hichens), 1899

Daughters of Spain (Victoria Holt, as Jean Plaidy), 1961

Daughters of the House, The (Rosemary Ellerbeck as Nicola Thorne), 1981

Daughters of the Misty Gorges (Essie Summers), 1981

Daughters of the Rectory (Ursula Bloom), 1955

David the Prince (Nigel Tranter), 1980

Dawn (H. Rider Haggard), 1884

Dawn (Eleanor H. Porter), 1919

Dawn Chorus, The (Victoria Holt, as Eleanor Burford), 1959

Dawn of Love, The (Barbara Cartland), 1980

Dawn O'Hara, The Girl Who Laughed (Edna

Ferber), 1911

Dawn on the High Mountain (Susan Barrie, as Pamela Kent), 1961

Dawn of the Morning (Grace Livingston Hill), 1911

Dawn Steals Softly, The (Anne Hampson), 1980

Dawn Through the Shutters (Hebe Elsna, as Vicky Lancaster), 1937

Dawning of the Day, The (Elisabeth Ogilvie), 1954

Dawning Splendour, The (Susan Barrie, as Pamela Kent), 1963

Dawn's Early Light (Elswyth Thane), 1943

Day Comes Round, The (Ruby M. Ayres), 1949

Day Like Spring, A (Rosamunde Pilcher, as Jane Fraser), 1953

Day of Grace, A (Hebe Elsna), 1952

Day of Possession (Lilian Peake), 1978

Day of Roses (Hettie Grimstead, as Marsha Manning), 1976

Day of the Butterfly (Norah Lofts), 1979

Day of the Dancing Sun (Phyllis Hastings), 1971

Day of the Dog, The (George Barr McCutcheon), 1904

Day of the Storm, The (Mary Ann Gibbs, as Elizabeth Ford), 1971

Day of the Storm, The (Rosamunde Pilcher), 1975

Day That the Rain Came Down, The (Isobel Chace), 1970

Daybreak (Frank G. Slaughter), 1958

Daylight Fear, The (Frances Cowen), 1969

Days of Winter, The (Cynthia Freeman), 1978

Dazzle on the Sea, The (Flora Kidd), 1971

Dead and Buried (Chelsea Quinn Yarbro), 1980

Dead in a Row (Gwendoline Butler), 1957

Dead March in Three Keys (Norah Lofts, as Peter Curtis), 1940

Dead Men's Boot (P.C. Wren), 1949

Dead Men's Plans (Mignon Eberhart), 1952

Dead Sea Cipher, The (Barbara Michaels, as Elizabeth Peters), 1970

Deadly Is the Diamond (Mignon Eberhart), 1942

Deadly Lady of Madagascar, The (Frank G. Slaughter, as C.V. Terry), 1959

Deadly Travellers, The (Dorothy Eden), 1959

Dean's Watch, The (Elizabeth Goudge), 1960

Dear Adversary (Kathryn Blair), 1953

Dear and Glorious Physician (Taylor Caldwell), 1959

Dear Benefactor (Anne Hampson), 1976

Dear Chance (Victoria Hlt, as Eleanor Burford), 1947

Dear Colleague, My (Frances Murray), 1972

Dear Deceiver (Doris E. Smith), 1972

Dear Delusion (Victoria Holt, as Eleanor Burford), 1952

Dear Doctor Everett (Jean S. MacLeod), 1954

Dear Dragon (Sara Seale), 1959

Dear Enemy (Jean Webster), 1915

Dear Fugitive (Elizabeth Hoy), 1960

Dear Intruder (Jane Arbor), 1955

Dear Kate (Suzanne Ebel), 1972

Dear Liar (Dorothy Mackie Low), 1963

Dear Lost Love (Anne Maybury), 1957

Dear Loyalty (Denise Robins), 1939

Dear Mr. Dean (Countess Barcynska, as Oliver Sandys), 1957

Dear Old Home, The (Mabel St. John), 1912

Dear Plutocrat (Anne Hampson), 1973

Dear Professor (Sara Seale), 1970

Dear Puritan (Violet Winspear), 1971

Dear Sir (Mary Burchell), 1958

Dear Stranger (Anne Hampson), 1973

Dear Stranger (Elizabeth Hoy), 1946

Dear Tiberius (Susan Barrie), 1956

Dear Tom (Rosamunde Pilcher, as Jane Fraser), 1954

Dear Trustee (Mary Burchell), 1958

Dear Yesterday (Hebe Elsna, as Lyndon Snow), 1946

Dearest Demon (Violet Winspear), 1975

Dearest Doctor (Ursula Bloom, as Rachel Harvey), 1968

Dearest Enemy (Hebe Elsna, as Lyndon Snow), 1953

Dearest Enemy (Kathryn Blair), 1951

Dearest Mamma (Hebe Elsna, as Laura Conway), 1969

Dearest Neighbour (Mollie Chapell), 1981

Dearly Beloved (Mary Burchell), 1944

Death among Friends (Elizabeth Cadell, as Harriet Ainsworth), 1964

Death Descending (Betty Beaty, as Karen Campbell), 1976

Death Filled the Glass (Charlotte Armstrong), 1945

Death in the Fog (Mignon Eberhart), 1934

Death in the Life, A (Dorothy Salisbury Davis), 1976

Death in the Stocks (Georgette Heyer), 1935

Death Is a Red Rose (Dorothy Eden), 1956

Death Lives Next Door (Gwendoline Butler),

1960

Death My Lover (Charity Blackstock, as Paula Allardyce), 1959

Death of an Old Sinner (Dorothy Salisbury Davis), 1957

Death of the Red King (Pamela Bennetts), 1976

Death Strikes Out (Glenna Finley), 1957

Death Watch (Daoma Winston), 1975

Death-Scented Flower, The (Phyllis Hastings), 1977

Deb and Destiny (Susan Inglis), 1950

Debt of Honor (Barbara Cartland), 1970

Debt of Honour (Patricia Veryan), 1980

Debutante in Uniform (Maysie Greig), 1938

Decameron Cocktails (Countess Barcynska), 1926

December Love (Robert Hichens), 1922

December Passion (Christopher Nicole, as Mark Logan), 1979

Deception, The (Dorothy Daniels, as Cynthia Kavanaugh), 1966

Deception (Margaret Pargeter), 1980

Deck with Flowers (Elizabeth Cadell), 1973

Dedication Jones (Kate Norway), 1969

Deed of Innocence (Jane Blackmore), 1969

Deemster, The (Hall Caine), 1887

Deep Are Dumb, The (Doris E. Smith), 1967

Deep in the Forest (Joyce Dingwell), 1976

Deep Is the Shadow (Frank G. Slaughter, as G. Arnold Haygood), 1959

Deep Pool, The (Jane Blackmore), 1972

Deep Well at Noon, The (Jessica Stirling), 1979

Deep, Wide River, The (Eleanor Farnes), 1947

Defector, The (Evelyn Anthony), 1980

Defender of the Faith (Marjorie Bowen), 1911

Defenders of the Faith (Victoria Holt, as Ellalice Tate), 1956

Definite Object (Jeffery Farnol), 1917

Delayed Action (Nigel Tranter), 1944

Delayed Harvest (Rona Randall), 1950

Delicate Deceit, A (Susan Hufford), 1976

Delight (Mazo de la Roche), 1926

Delsie (Joan Smith), 1981

Delta Blood (Barbara Ferry Johnson), 1977

deMaury Papers, The (Isabelle Holland), 1977

Demi-Semi Nurse (Joyce Dingwell), 1969

Demon, The (C.N. and A.M. Williamson), 1912

Demon Tower, The (Virginia Coffman), 1966

de Montfort Legacy, The (Pamela Bennetts),

1973

Dennison Hill (Daoma Winston), 1970

Dental Nurse at Denley's (Marjorie Lewty), 1968

Depart in Peace (Dorothy Eden), 1979

Departing Wings (Faith Baldwin), 1927

Deputy Pet (Countess Barcynska, as Oliver Sandys), 1945

Desert Barbarian (Charlotte Lamb), 1978

Desert Castle, The (Isobel Chace), 1976

Desert Doctor (Violet Winspear), 1965

Desert Doorway (Susan Barrie, as Pamela Kent), 1956

Desert Flower (Rona Randall), 1955

Desert Gold (Susan Barrie, as Pamela Kent), 1968

Desert Healer, The (E.M. Hull), 1923

Desert Heritage, The (P.C. Wren), 1935

Desert Moon (Anne Duffield), 1939

Desert Nurse (Jane Arbor), 1963

Desert Nurse (Irene Roberts), 1976

Desert Queen, The (Doris Leslie), 1972

Desert Rapture (Denise Robins), 1945

Desert Rose, English Moon (Claudette Williams), 1981

Desert Sand (Margaret Pedler), 1932

Design for Loving (Mary Burchell), 1972

Design for Loving (Anne Mather), 1966

Design for Murder (Nancy Buckingham, as Erica Quest), 1981

Design for Murder (Rachel Lindsay), 1964

Desire (Charlotte Lamb), 1981

Desire Has No Mercy (Violet Winspear), 1979

Desire Is Blind (Denise Robins), 1928

Desire Is Not Dead (Ursula Bloom, as Sheila Burns), 1947

Desire of His Life, The (Ethel M. Dell), 1914

Desire of the Heart (Barbara Cartland), 1954

Desmond's Daughter (Maud Diver), 1916

Desperate Defiance (Barbara Cartland), 1936

Desperate Holiday, The (Frances Cowen), 1962

Destiny and Desire (Christopher Nicole, as Leslie Arlen), 1982

Destiny of Claude, The (May Wynne), 1913

Destiny's Lady (Maureen Peters), 1973

Destiny's Women (Willo Davis Roberts), 1980

Details of Jeremy (Audrey Erskine-Lindop), 1955

Detection Unlimited (Georgette Heyer), 1953

Detour (Faith Baldwin), 1942

Deveron Hall (Velda Johnston), 1976

Devices and Desires (Susan Ertz), 1972

Devil and Mary Ann, The (Catherine Cookson), 1958

Devil and Miss Hay, The (Charlotte Lamb, as Sheila Holland), 1977

Devil Boy (Willo Davis Roberts), 1970

Devil Drives, The (Jane Arbor), 1979

Devil in a Silver Room (Violet Winspear), 1973

Devil in Clevely, The (Norah Lofts), 1968

Devil in Harbour, The (Catherine Gavin), 1968

Devil in Love, The (Barbara Cartland), 1975

Devil in My Heart (Mary Howard), 1941

Devil in Satin, The (Dornford Yates), 1938

Devil in Tartan, The (Elisabeth Ogilvie), 1980

Devil in Velvet (Anne Mather), 1978

Devil Loves Me, The (Margaret Millar), 1942

Devil of Aske, The (Pamela Hill), 1972

Devil on Horseback, The (Victoria Holt), 1977

Devil on Lammas Night, The (Susan Howatch), 1970

Devil Snar'd, The (Marjorie Bowen, as George Preedy), 1932

Devil Vicar, The (Virginia Coffman), 1966

Devil Water (Anya Seton), 1962

Devil-May-Care (Barbara Michaels, as Elizabeth Peters), 1977

Devil's Advocate, The (Taylor Caldwell), 1952

Devil's Arms, The (Charlotte Lamb), 1978

Devil's Bondsman, The (Sylvia Thorpe), 1961

Devil's Bride, The (Margaret Pargeter), 1979

Devil's Cub (Georgette Heyer), 1934

Devil's Darling, The (Violet Winspear), 1975

Devil's Daughter, The (Daoma Winston), 1971

Devil's Desire (Laurie McBain), 1975

Devil's Double, The (Willo Davis Roberts), 1978

Devil's Due, The (G.B. Burgin), 1905

Devil's Emissary, The (Christopher Nicole, as Peter Grange), 1968

Devil's Fire, Love's Revenge (Rosalind Laker, as Barbara Paul), 1976

Devil's Gamble (Frank G. Slaughter), 1977

Devil's Harvest (Frank G. Slaughter), 1963

Devil's Hole, The (Patricia Ainsworth), 1971

Devil's Innocent, The (Mary Howard, as Josephine Edgar), 1972

Devil's Jig, The (Marjorie Bowen, as Robert Paye), 1930

Devil's Laughter, The (Frank Yerby), 1953

Devil's Mistress, The (Virginia Coffman), 1969

Devil's Motor, The (Marie Corelli), 1910

Devil's Mount (Anne Mather), 1976

Devil's Own, The (Norah Lofts, as Peter Curtis), 1960

Devil's Own, The (Christopher Nicole), 1975

Devil's Own, The (Janet Louise Roberts), 1972

Devil's Princess, The (Daoma Winston), 1971

Devil's Sonata, The (Susan Hufford), 1976

Devil's Vineyard, The (Barbara Kevern), 1975

Devil's Virgin, The (Virginia Coffman), 1970

Devon Interlude (Kay Thorpe), 1968

Dew and Mildew (P.C. Wren), 1912

Dewdrops (Margaret Kennedy), 1928

Dewey Death (Charity Blackstock), 1956

Diablo Manor (Dorothy Daniels), 1971

Diamond Cage, The (Alice Dwyer-Joyce), 1976

Diamond Engagement Ring (Berta Ruck), 1962

Diana (R.F. Delderfield), 1960

Diana and Destiny (Charles Garvice), 1906

Diana Comes Home (Iris Bromige), 1955

Diana Falls in Love (Madame Albanesi), 1919

Diana Goes to Tokyo (Maysie Greig, as Jennifer Ames), 1961

Diana of Dreams (G.B. Burgin), 1910

Diana's Destiny (Charles Garvice)

Diary of a Provincial Lady (E.M. Delafield), 1930

Diary of a Red-Haired Girl (Evadne Price), 1932

Dick (May Wynne), 1919

Dick Heriot's Wife (Susan Inglis), 1947

Dickie Dilver (G.B. Burgin), 1912

Dickon (Marjorie Bowen), 1929

Did She? (Elinor Glyn), 1934

Didn't Anybody Know My Wife? (Willo Davis Roberts), 1974

Die She Must (Baroness von Hutten), 1934

Died on a Rainy Sunday (Joan Aiken), 1972

Different Kind of Summer, A (Gwendoline Butler, as Jennie Melville), 1967

Difficult Decision (Janet Dailey), 1980

Difficult to Love (Hebe Elsna, as Lyndon Snow), 1963

Dig a Narrow Grave (Mary Linn Roby), 1971

Dimbie and I—and Amelia (Mabel Barnes Grundy), 1907

Dina Cashman (Kathleen Norris), 1942

Dinah (Mary Ann Gibbs), 1981

Dinah Faire (Virginia Coffman), 1979

Dinah's Husband (Ursula Bloom), 1941

Dine and Be Dead (Gwendoline Butler), 1960

Leslie Lance), 1980

Dr. Irresistible, M.D. (Ursula Bloom, as Sheila Burns), 1962

Doctor Is a Lady, The (Maysie Greig), 1962

Doctor Is Engaged, The (Nan Asquith), 1962

Doctor Jamie (Elizabeth Seifert), 1959

Doctor Jane series (Adeline McElfresh)

Dr. Jeremy's Wife (Elizabeth Seifert), 1961

Doctor Makes a Choice, The (Elizabeth Seifert), 1961

Doctor Mallory (Elizabeth Seifert), 1941

Doctor Max (Eleanor Farnes), 1963

Doctor Mays (Elizabeth Seifert), 1957

Doctor Mollie (Elizabeth Seifert), 1952

Doctor Mysterious (Marjorie McEvoy, as Marjorie Harte), 1965

Doctor of Mercy (Elizabeth Seifert), 1951

Doctor on Call (Ursula Bloom, as Mary Essex), 1961

Doctor on Duty Bound (Ursula Bloom, as Mary Essex), 1969

Doctor on Trial (Elizabeth Seifert), 1959

Doctor on Wings (Maysie Greig), 1966

Doctor Overboard (Jean S. MacLeod, as Catherine Airlie), 1966

Doctor Robert Comes Around (Nan Asquith), 1965

Dr. Ross series (Alice Dwyer-Joyce)

Doctor Samaritan (Elizabeth Seifert), 1965

Dr. Scott, Surgeon on Call (Elizabeth Seifert), 1963

Doctor Takes a Holiday, The (Maysie Greig, as Jennifer Ames), 1969

Doctor Takes a Wife, The (Rona Randall), 1947

Doctor Takes a Wife, The (Elizabeth Seifert), 1952

Doctor Ted's Clinic (Maysie Greig, as Jennifer Ames), 1967

Doctor Therne (H. Rider Haggard), 1898

Doctor to the Rescue (Ursula Bloom, as Sheila Burns), 1961

Doctor Toby (Rebecca Stratton, as Lucy Gillen), 1970

Doctor Tuck (Elizabeth Seifert), 1977

Doctor Westland (Kathryn Blair), 1965

Doctor Who Fell in Love, The (Ursula Bloom, as Rachel Harvey), 1974

Doctor with a Mission (Elizabeth Seifert), 1967

Doctor with a Past (Petra Sawley), 1973

Dr. Wodward's Ambition (Elizabeth Seifert), 1945

Doctor's Affair, The (Elizabeth Seifert), 1975

Doctors Are Different (Theresa Charles, as Fay Chandos), 1954

Doctor's Assistant (Kathryn Blair, as Celine Conway), 1964

Doctor's Bride, The (Elizabeth Seifert), 1960

Doctor's Circle, The (Eleanor Farnes), 1970

Doctor's Confession, The (Elizabeth Seifert), 1968

Doctor's Daughter, The (Charity Blackstock, as Paula Allardyce), 1955

Doctor's Daughter (Jean S. MacLeod), 1965

Doctor's Daughter, The (Elizabeth Seifert), 1974

Doctor's Daughters (Frank G. Slaughter), 1981

Doctor's Delusion, The (Marion Collin), 1967

Doctor's Desperate Hour, The (Elizabeth Seifert), 1976

Doctor's Destiny (Elizabeth Seifert), 1972

Doctor's Distress (Ursula Bloom, as Sheila Burns), 1964

Doctor's Husband, The (Elizabeth Seifert), 1957

Doctors in Conflict (Marjorie McEvoy, as Marjorie Harte), 1963

Doctor's Joy (Claire Ritchie), 1962

Doctor's Kingdom (Elizabeth Seifert), 1970

Doctor's Love, A (Ursula Bloom, as Mary Essex), 1974

Doctor's Nurse (Maysie Greig, as Jennifer Ames), 1959

Doctors of Downlands, The (Claire Rayner, as Sheila Brandon), 1968

Doctors of Eden Place, The (Elizabeth Seifert), 1977

Doctor's Office (Elsie Lee), 1968

Doctors on Parade (Elizabeth Seifert), 1960

Doctor's Orders (Eleanor Farnes), 1963

Doctor's Orders (Elizabeth Seifert), 1958

Doctor's Private Life, The (Elizabeth Seifert), 1973

Doctor's Promise, The (Elizabeth Seifert), 1979

Doctor's Reputation, The (Elizabeth Seifert), 1972

Doctor's Second Love, The (Elizabeth Seifert), 1971

Doctor's Strange Secret, The (Elizabeth Seifert), 1962

Doctor's Sweetheart, The (L.M. Montgomery), 1979

Doctors Three (Marion Collin), 1964

Doctor's Two Lives, The (Elizabeth Seifert), 1970

Doctor's Ward (Sara Seale), 1962

Doctors Were Brothers, The (Elizabeth

Dream of Winter (Rebecca Stratton), 1977

Dream on the Hill, The (Lilian Peake), 1974

Dream Prevails, The (Maud Diver), 1938

Dream Street (Hettie Grimstead), 1959

Dream Tea (L. Adams Beck), 1934

Dream That Happened, The (May Edginton), 1926

Dream Towers (Charity Blackstock), 1981

Dream Walker, The (Charlotte Armstrong), 1955

Dream Within, The (Barbara Cartland), 1947

Dreamer Wakes, The (Ruby M. Ayres), 1945

Dreaming River (Claire Ritchie), 1957

Dreaming Suburb, The (R.F. Delderfield), 1958

Dreaming Swimmer, The (Elisabeth Ogilvie), 1976

Dreaming Tower, The (Anne Rundle, as Joanne Marshall), 1969

Dreams and Delights (L. Adams Beck), 1926

Dreams Come True (Annie S. Swan), 1941

Dreams Do Come True (Barbara Cartland), 1981

Dreams Get You Nowhere (Maysie Greig), 1937

Dreams in the Sun (Hettie Grimstead, as Marsha Manning), 1967

Dresden Finch, The (Jessica Stirling), 1976

Drift of Jasmine, A (Joyce Dingwell), 1977

Drifting Sands, The (Elsie Lee), 1966

Driftwood Spars (P.C. Wren), 1916

Drink (Hall Caine), 1906

Drink for the Bridge, A (Alanna Knight), 1976

Driving of Desire, The (Ursula Bloom), 1925

Drop of the Dice, The (Victoria Holt, as Philippa Carr), 1981

Drug on the Market (Nigel Tranter), 1962

Drum (Lance Horner), 1962

Drummer and the Song, The (Joyce Dingwell), 1969

Drummer of Corrae, The (Jean S. MacLeod), 1966

Drums of Love, The (Barbara Cartland), 1979

Drury Randall (Mary Johnston), 1934

Drusilla's Point of View (Madame Albanesi), 1908

Duchess (Mary Howard, as Josephine Edgar), 1976

Duchess Disappeared, The (Barbara Cartland), 1979

Duchess Hotspur (Rosamond Marshall), 1946

Duchess in Disguise (Caroline Courtney), 1979

Duchess Intervenes, The (Marie Belloc Lowndes), 1933

Duchess Laura (Marie Belloc Lowndes), 1929

Duchess of Duke Street, The (Mollie Hardwick), 1976

Ducks and Drakes (Nigel Tranter), 1953

Duel in the Dark (Marguerite Steen), 1928

Duel of Desire (Charlotte Lamb), 1978

Duel of Hearts, A (Barbara Cartland), 1949

Duel of Queens, The (L. Adams Beck, as E. Barrington), 1930

Duel with Destiny, A (Barbara Cartland), 1977

Dueling Oaks (Dorothy Daniels, as Danielle Dorsett), 1972

Duet (Dorothy Daniels), 1968

Duke and the Preacher's Daughter, The (Barbara Cartland), 1979

Duke's Strategem, The (G.B. Burgin), 1931

Duke's Twins, The (G.B. Burgin) , 1914

Dulcie (Charles Garvice), 1910

Dull Dead, The (Gwendoline Butler), 1958

Dummy Hand, The (C.N. and A.M. Williamson), 1920

Duncan Dynasty, The (Dorothy Daniels), 1973

Duplicate Death (Georgette Heyer), 1951

Durable Fire (Claire Ritchie), 1951

Durrants, The (Netta Muskett), 1948

Duskin (Grace Livingston Hill), 1929

Dust in the Sunlight (Catherine Gaskin), 1950

Dust Is My Pillow (Phyllis Hastings), 1955

Dust of Dreams (Denise Robins), 1943

Dusky Cactus (Marjorie McEvoy), 1968

Dusty Dawn (Anne Duffield), 1949

Dusty Spring (Elizabeth Seifert), 1946

Dutiful Tradition, The (Kate Norway), 1971

Dweller on the Threshold, The (Robert Hichens), 1911

Dwelling (Grace Livingston Hill), 1938

Dwelling Place, The (Catherine Cookson), 1971

Dynasty of Death (Taylor Caldwell), 1938

Each Hour a Peril (Mrs. Patrick MacGill), 1921

Each Song Twice Over (Jane Arbor), 1948

Eager Search, The (Ruby M. Ayres), 1923

Eagle at the Gate, The (Rona Randall), 1977

Eagle of Degarra, The (Iris Danbury), 1966

Eagle of the Vincella, The (Rebecca Stratton), 1978

Eagle Swooped, An (Anne Hampson), 1970

Eagle's Feathers (Nigel Tranter), 1941

Eagles Gather, The (Taylor Caldwell), 1940
Eagle's Nest, The (Dorothy Daniels), 1967
Eaglescliffe (Marjorie McEvoy), 1971
Earl's Daughter, The (Charles Garvice), 1910
Earl's Heir, The (Charles Garvice)
Early Autumn (Louis Bromfield), 1926
Early Blossom (Hebe Elsna, as Lyndon Snow), 1946
Earth Giant (Edison Marshall), 1960
Earth-Bound (Dorothy Macardle), 1924
East of the Setting Sun (George Barr McCutcheon), 1924
East Side General (Frank G. Slaughter), 1952
East Side, West Side (Marcia Davenport), 1947
Ebbing Tide, The (Elisabeth Ogilvie), 1947
Echo Answers (Elswyth Thane), 1927
Echo from Afar (Hebe Elsna), 1945
Echo of Applause (Leila Mackinlay), 1948
Echo of Flutes (Irene Roberts), 1965
Echo of Margaret (Maureen Peters, as Veronica Black), 1978
Echo of Spring, An (Rebecca Stratton, as Lucy Gillen), 1973
Echoed from the Past (May Wynne), 1944
Echoes from the Macabre (Daphne du Maurier), 1976
Echoes from the Past (Marjorie McEvoy), 1979
Echoes of Another Spring (Faith Baldwin), 1965
Echoes of Love (Elisabeth Beresford), 1979
Echoing Green, The (Doris Leslie), 1929
Echoing Yesterday (Anne Rundle, as Alexandra Manners), 1981
Eddy and Edouard (Baroness von Hutten), 1928
Eden Passion, The (Marilyn Harris), 1979
Eden Rising (Marilyn Harris), 1982
Edge of Beyond, The (Isobel Chace), 1973
Edge of Glass (Catherine Gaskin), 1967
Edge of Temptation (Anne Mather), 1982
Edge of Terror (Frances Cowen), 1970
Edge of Winter, The (Betty Neels), 1976
Edinburgh Excursion (Lucilla Andrews), 1970
Edna's Secret Marriage (Charles Garvice), 1905
Edward, Edward (Lolah Burford), 1973
Edward Longshanks (Victoria Holt, as Jean Plaidy), 1979
Edwardian Day-Dream (Ursula Bloom), 1972
Eighth Champion of Christendom, The (Edith Pargeter), 1945
Elaine (Charles Garvice), 1911
Elder Brother, An (Annie S. Swan), 1898

Elder Sister (Maysie Greig, as Jennifer Ames), 1938
Eldest Daughter, The (Hebe Elsna), 1974
Eldorado (Baroness Orczy), 1913
Eleanor Jowitt, Antiques (Ursula Bloom), 1950
Eleanor of Aquitaine (Charlotte Lamb, as Sheila Holland), 1978
Eleanor the Queen (Norah Lofts), 1955
Eleanora Duse (Jean Stubbs), 1970
Electric Torch, The (Ethel M. Dell), 1934
Eleventh Hour Lover (Berta Ruck), 1933
Elgin Marble, The (Baroness von Hutten), 1937
Eligible Connection, An (Elsie Lee), 1974
Elissa (H. Rider Haggard), 1900
Eliza (Charity Blackstock, as Paula Allardyce), 1975
Eliza Stanhope (Joanna Trollope), 1978
Elizabeth (Evelyn Anthony), 1960
Elizabeth and the Prince of Spain (Margaret Irwin), 1953
Elizabeth Browne, Children's Nurse (Kathryn Blair, as Rosalind Brett), 1965
Elizabeth, Captive Princess (Margaret Irwin), 1948
Elizabeth Glen, M.B. (Annie S. Swan), 1895
Elizabeth in Dreamland (Mabel St. John, as Henry St. John Cooper), 1921
Elizabeth the Beloved (Maureen Peters), 1965
Elizabeth Visits America (Elinor Glyn), 1909
Elizabethan Lover (Barbara Cartland), 1953
Elopement of Eve and Prince Playfellow, The (Berta Ruck), 1922
Elsie Brant's Romance (Madame Albanesi, as Effie Rowlands), 1913
Elsie Thorburn (Annie S. Swan), 1926
Elusive Crown, The (Hebe Elsna), 1973
Elusive Earl, The (Barbara Cartland), 1976
Elusive Harmony (Mary Burchell), 1976
Elusive Lover, The (Frances Cowen), 1981
Elusive Quest, The (Frances Cowen), 1965
Elyza (Clare Darcy), 1976
Embers of Dawn (Patricia Matthews), 1982
Embroidered Sunset, The (Joan Aiken), 1970
Emerald (Suzanne Ebel, as Suzanne Goodwin), 1980
Emerald Cuckoo, The (Gwen Westwood), 1970
Emerald Garden,The (Katrina Britt), 1976
Emerald Hill (Dorothy Daniels), 1970
Emerald Station (Daoma Winston), 1974
Emergency Call (Elizabeth Harrison), 1970
Emergency in the Pyrenees (Ann Bridge), 1965

Emergency Wife (May Edginton), 1937

Emily (Charity Blackstock, as Paula Allardyce), 1976

Emily (Jilly Cooper), 1975

Emily series (L.M. Montgomery)

Emma Hart (Ursula Bloom, as Lozania Prole), 1951

Emma McChesney & Co. (Edna Ferber), 1915

Emperor's Candlesticks, The (Baroness Orczy), 1899

Emperor's Daughter, The (Julia Fitzgerald, as Julia Hamilton), 1978

Empress of Hearts, The (L. Adams Beck, as E. Barrington), 1928

Empty Heart, The (Mary Ann Gibbs, as Elizabeth Ford), 1957

Empty House, The (Rosamunde Pilcher), 1973

Empty World, The (D.E. Stevenson), 1936

Enchanted, The (Viña Delmar), 1965

Enchanted, The (Elizabeth Hoy), 1952

Enchanted April, The (Elizabeth), 1922

Enchanted August (Hettie Grimstead), 1955

Enchanted Barn, The (Grace Livingston Hill), 1918

Enchanted Cup, The (Patricia Ainsworth), 1980

Enchanted Dawn (Anne Hampson), 1972

Enchanted Eden (Rona Randall), 1960

Enchanted Evening (Ivy Preston), 1966

Enchanted Garden, The (Iris Bromige), 1956

Enchanted Grotto, (Maureen Peters, as Veronica Black), 1972

Enchanted Island, The (Eleanor Farnes), 1970

Enchanted Island, The (Anne Mather), 1969

Enchanted Island, The (Denise Robins), 1956

Enchanted Journey (Ursula Bloom), 1933

Enchanted Kingdom, The (Anne Maybury), 1932

Enchanted Moment, The (Barbara Cartland), 1949

Enchanted Oasis (Faith Baldwin), 1938

Enchanted Ring, The (Rebecca Stratton, as Lucy Gillen), 1971

Enchanted Valley (Theresa Charles, as Jan Tempest), 1954

Enchanted Waltz, The (Barbara Cartland), 1955

Enchanted Wilderness (Elizabeth Hoy), 1940

Enchanted Wood, The (Elizabeth Ashton), 1971

Enchanted Woods, The (Katrina Britt), 1978

Enchanter's Castle (Jill Tattersall), 1966

Enchanter's Nightshade (Ann Bridge), 1937

Enchanter's Nightshade (Anne Maybury, as Katherine Troy), 1963

Enchanting Clementina (Sophia Cleugh), 1930

Enchanting Courtesan, The (Ursula Bloom, as Lozania Prole), 1955

Enchanting Evil, The (Barbara Cartland), 1968

Enchanting Island, The (Kathryn Blair), 1952

Enchanting Jenny (Florence Stevenson, as Zabrina Faire), 1979

Enchanting Princess, The (Ursula Bloom, as Lozania Prole), 1970

Enchanting Samantha (Betty Neels), 1973

Enchantment (Anne Duffield), 1937

Enchantment (Hebe Elsna, as Laura Conway), 1956

Enchantment (Mary Ann Gibbs), 1952

Enchantment in Blue (Flora Kidd), 1975

Enchantress, The (Rosemary Ellerbeck, as Katherine Yorke), 1979

Encounter, The (Charity Blackstock), 1971

Encounter at Alpenrose (Iris Bromige), 1970

End Crowns All, The (Madame Albanesi, as Effie Rowlands), 1906

End of Her Honeymoon, The (Marie Belloc Lowndes), 1913

End of the Rainbow, The (Betty Neels), 1974

End of the Summer, The (Rosamunde Pilcher), 1971

End of the World, The (Viña Delmar), 1934

Endearing Young Charms (Mollie Chappell), 1957

Endure My Heart (Joan Smith), 1980

Enduring Flame, The (Denise Robins), 1929

Enduring Flame, The (Nigel Tranter), 1957

Enduring Hills, The (Janice Holt Giles), 1950

Enemy and Brother (Dorothy Salisbury Davis), 1966

Enemy from the Past (Lilian Peake), 1979

Enemy in Camp (Janet Dailey), 1980

Enemy in the House (Mignon Eberhart), 1962

Enemy Lover (Susan Barrie, as Pamela Kent), 1964

Enemy of Love (Virginia Coffman), 1977

English Air, The (D.E. Stevenson), 1940

English Boss, The (Joyce Dingwell), 1964

English Daughter, The (Isobel Chace), 1972

English Girl in Serbia, An (May Wynne), 1916

English Heiress, The (Roberta Gellis), 1980

English Paragon, The (Marjorie Bowen), 1930

English Rose (Mary Ann Gibbs, as Elizabeth Ford), 1953

English Tutor, The (Sara Seale), 1948

English Wife, The (Charity Blackstock), 1964

Entanglement (Catherine Fellows), 1979

Enter Jenny Wren (May Wynne), 1933

Enter Mrs. Belchamber (Elizabeth Cadell), 1951

Entertainment, The (E.M. Delafield), 1927

Enticers, The (Natasha Peters), 1981

Envious Casca (Georgette Heyer), 1941

Envious Eliza (Madame Albanesi), 1909

Envoy from Elizabeth (Pamela Bennett), 1970

Epidemic! (Frank G. Slaughter), 1961

Episode at Toledo, The (Ann Bridge), 1966

Episode of Sparrows, An (Rumer Godden), 1955

Episode of the Wandering Knife (Mary Roberts Rinehart), 1950

Epitaph for Three Women (Victoria Holt, as Jean Plaidy), 1981

Eric Brighteyes (H. Rider Haggard), 1891

Ernestine Sophie (Sophia Cleugh), 1925

Errant Bride (Elizabeth Ashton), 1973

Escapade (Joan Smith), 1977

Escape from Passion (Barbara Cartland), 1945

Escape the Night (Mignon Eberhart), 1944

Escape to Happiness (Elisabeth Beresford), 1964

Escape to Love (Denise Robins), 1943

Escape to Marriage (Evadne Price), 1952

Escape to Paradise (Hettie Grimstead), 1956

Escape to Yesterday (Gilbert Frankau), 1942

Escort (Daphne du Maurier), 1943

Esmeralda (Betty Neels), 1976

Esther (Norah Lofts), 1950

Eternal Circle (Jane Arbor), 1952

Eternal City, The (Hall Caine), 1901

Eternal Justice (G.B. Burgin), 1932

Eternal Summer (Anne Hampson), 1969

Eternal Tomorrow, The (Ursula Bloom), 1929

Etheldreda the Ready (Mrs. George de Horne Vaizey), 1910

Etruscan Smile, The (Velda Johnston), 1977

Eugenia (Clare Darcy), 1977

Eugénie (Marjorie Bowen), 1971

Eugenie (Hester W. Chapman), 1961

Eve and I (Theresa Charles, as Fay Chandos), 1943

Eve Didn't Care (Ursula Bloom, as Mary Essex), 1941

Eve Originals (Dorothy Daniels), 1962

Evelyn, The Ambitious (Katheryn Kimbrough), 1978

Evening Star (Faith Baldwin), 1966

Ever After (Elswyth Thane), 1945

Ever Thine (Hester W. Chapman), 1951

Evergreen Gallant (Victoria Holt, as Jean Plaidy), 1965

Every Goose a Swan (Audrie Manley-Tucker), 1972

Every Man a King (Anne Worboys), 1975

Every Other Gift (Naomi Jacob), 1950

Every Soul Hath Its Song (Fannie Hurst), 1914

Every Woman's Doctor (Maysie Greig), 1964

Every Woman's Man (Maysie Greig), 1961

Everyman's Land (C.N. and A.M. Williamson), 1918

Everyone Loves Lorraine (Hebe Elsna), 1941

Everywoman (Gilbert Frankau), 1933

Evil at Queens Priory, The (Virginia Coffman), 1973

Evil at Roger's Cross (Catherine Cookson, as Catherine Marchant), 1966

Evil Children, The (Willo Davis Roberts), 1973

Evil in the House (Victoria Holt, as Elbur Ford), 1954

Evil of Time, The (Evelyn Berckman), 1954

Except My Love (Mary Burchell), 1937

Exchange of Hearts (Betty Beaty), 1980

Exchange Royal (Marjorie Bowen), 1940

Exhibition Summer (D.A. Ponsonby), 1982

Exile (Warwick Deeping), 1930

Exile, The (Mary Johnston), 1927

Exiles (Warwick Deeping), 1930

Exit Betty (Grace Livingston Hill), 1920

Exit Renee (Countess Barcynska), 1934

Exorcism, The (Charity Blackstock), 1961

Exorcism of Jenny Slade, The (Dorothy Daniels), 1974

Exotic Young Lady, An (Leila Mackinlay), 1932

Expendable (Willo Davis Roberts), 1976

Expensive (May Edginton), 1947

Expensive Lady (May Edginton), 1934

Experiment in Love (May Edginton), 1939

Experiment in Springtime (Margaret Millar), 1947

Experiments in Crime (Gilbert Frankau), 1937

Expiation (Elizabeth), 1929

Explorer, The (Frances Parkinson Keyes), 1964

Explorers of the Dawn (Mazo de la Roche), 1922

Explosion (P.C. Wren), 1935

Explosion of Love, The (Barbara Cartland), 1980

Exquisite Perdita, The (L. Adams Beck, as E. Barrington), 1926

Extraordinary Engagement, The (Marjorie Lewty), 1972

Eye for a Tooth, An (Dornford Yates), 1943

Eyes of Doctor Karl, The (Ursula Bloom, as Sheila Burns), 1962

Eyes of Love, The (Warwick Deeping), 1933

Eyes of Love (Charles Garvice)

Fabric of Dreams (Jean S. MacLeod, as Catherine Airlie), 1951

Fabulous Island, The (Katrina Britt), 1970

Fabulous Marriage, The (Hebe Elsna, as Lyndon Snow), 1961

Fabulous Nell Gwynne, The (Ursula Bloom, as Lozania Prole), 1954

Facade (Ursula Bloom), 1948

Face at the Window, The (Willo Davis Roberts), 1981

Face in the Shadows, The (Velda Johnston), 1971

Face of an Angel (Dorothy Eden, as Mary Paradise), 1961

Face of Danger, The (Willo Davis Roberts), 1972

Face of Evil, The (Christopher Nicole), 1971

Face of Innocence, The (Elisabeth Ogilvie), 1970

Face the Music—for Love (Theresa Charles, as Jan Tempest), 1938

Factor's Wife, The (Charity Blackstock), 1964

Factory Nurse (Kate Norway, as Hilary Neal), 1961

Facts of Love (Rachel Lindsay, as Roberta Leigh), 1978

Fade Out (Naomi Jacob), 1937

Faint Heart, The (Ruby M. Ayres), 1926

Faint Heart, Fair Lady (Maysie Greig), 1932

Faint with Pursuit (Ursula Bloom, as Sheila Burns), 1949

Fair Adventure, The (Claire Ritchie), 1961

Fair and False (Mable St. John, as Henry St. John Cooper), 1920

Fair Company (Doris Leslie), 1936

Fair Deal, The (Claire Lorrimer, as Patricia Robins), 1952

Fair Game (Nigel Tranter), 1950

Fair Horizon (Kathryn Blair, as Rosalind Brett), 1952

Fair Imposter, A (Charles Garvice), 1909

Fair Invader, The (Kathryn Blair), 1952

Fair Island, The (Anne Hampson), 1972

Fair Kilmeny (Maureen Peters, as Veronica Black), 1972

Fair Lady (May Edginton), 1929

Fair Margaret (H. Rider Haggard), 1907

Fair Prisoner (Iris Bromige), 1960

Fair Shine the Day (Sylvia Thorpe), 1964

Fair Shines the Day (Margaret Maddocks), 1952

Fair Tomorrow (Emilie Loring), 1931

Fair Warning (Mignon Eberhart), 1936

Fair Wind of Love (Rosalind Laker), 1974

Fair Young Phoenix, The (Edith Pargeter), 1948

Fair Young Widow, The (Marjorie Bowen, as George Preedy), 1939

Fairer Than She (Theresa Charles), 1953

Fairies' Baby, The (Elizabeth Goudge), 1919

Fairies on the Doorstep (Lucy Walker, as Dorothy Lucie Sanders), 1948

Fairoaks (Frank Yerby), 1957

Fairweather Friends! (Mabel St. John, as Henry St. John Cooper), 1922

Fairwinds (Rebecca Stratton), 1974

Fairweathers, The (Annie S. Swan), 1913

Fairytales (Cynthia Freeman), 1977

Faith, Hope, and Charity (Rona Randall), 1954

Faithful Failure, The (Kate Norway), 1968

Faithful Fool, The (G.B. Burgin), 1921

Faithful Heart, The (Katrina Brett), 1977

Faithful Traitor, A (Madame Albanesi, as Effie Rowlands), 1896

Faithless Dove, The (Ursula Bloom), 1945

Faithless Friend, The (Eleanor Farnes), 1949

Faithless One, The (Elizabeth Hoy), 1966

Falcon series (Maureen Peters, as Catherine Darby)

Falcon for a Queen, A (Catherine Gaskin), 1972

Falcon Gold (Rosemary Ellerbeck, as Katherine Yorke), 1980

Falcon on the Hill (Charlotte Lamb, as Sheila Holland), 1974

Falconhurst series (Horner, Lance)

Falcon's Keep (Henrietta Reid), 1968

Falcon's Shadow (Anne Maybury, as Katherine Troy), 1966

Fall of Midas, The (Norah Lofts, as Juliet Astley), 1975

Fallen Angel (Anne Mather), 1978

Fallen Woman (Julia Fitzgerald), 1981

Falling Stream (Hester W. Chapman), 1954

False and the True, The (Annie S. Swan), 1898

False and True (Madame Albanesi, as Effie Rowlands)

False Colours (Georgette Heyer), 1963

False Faith (Madame Albanesi, as Effie

Rowlands), 1911

False Morning (Kathleen Norris), 1934

False Relations (Leila Mackinlay), 1963

False Star (Anne Duffield), 1939

Fame's Fetters (Leila Mackinlay), 1931

Familiar Faces (Mary Roberts Rinehart), 1941

Familiar Stranger (Lilian Peake), 1973

Familiar Treatment (Elizabeth O. Peter), 1940

Families Are Such Fun (Theresa Charles, as Fay Chandos), 1952

Family, The (Ruby M. Ayres), 1928

Family (Elinor Glyn), 1919

Family! (Fannie Hurst), 1960

Family Affair (Mignon Eberhart), 1981

Family Affair, A (Charlotte Lamb), 1974

Family Affair, A (Rosamunde Pilcher, as Jane Fraser), 1958

Family Affairs (Catherine Gaskin), 1980

Family at Castle Trevissa, The (Jean Marsh), 1979

Family at the Farm, The (Theresa Charles, as Leslie Lance), 1978

Family Fortune (Mignon Eberhart), 1976

Family Feeling, The (Suzanne Ebel), 1973

Family Gathering (Elizabeth Cadell), 1979

Family Holiday (Denise Robins, as Hervey Hamilton), 1937

Family Likeness, A (Anna Gilbert), 1977

Family Name, The (Annie S. Swan), 1942

Family of Jaspard (D.A. Ponsonby), 1950

Family Orchestra (Mary Howard), 1945

Family Portraits (Mollie Chappell), 1973

Family Secret, The (Annie S. Swan), 1938

Family Ties (Marguerite Steen), 1939

Family Web, The (Iris Bromige), 1963

Famous Island (Katrina Britt), 1973

Fanatic, The (Lady Miles), 1924

Fanfare for Lovers (Elizabeth Hoy), 1953

Fannie's Fortune (May Edginton), 1932

Fanny Herself (Edna Ferber), 1917

Fanny McBride (Catherine Cookson), 1959

Fantasia (Warwick Deeping), 1939

Fantastic Holiday (Berta Ruck), 1953

Fantastic Summer (Dorothy Macardle), 1946

Fantoccini (Countess Barcynska), 1930

Fanuela (G.B. Burgin), 1907

Far Beyond Desire (Barbara Riefe), 1978

Far Blue Horizons (Mary Howard), 1940

Far Flies the Eagle (Evelyn Anthony), 1955

Far from Jupiter (Phyllis Hastings), 1952

Far Sanctuary (Jane Arbor), 1958

Far Seeks the Heart (Rosalind Laker), 1970

Far to Seek (Maud Diver), 1921

Farewell Romance (Gilbert Frankau), 1936

Farewell the Tranquil Mind (R.F. Delderfield), 1950

Farewell to Dreams (Anne Maybury), 1934

Farewell to Sadness (Leila Mackinlay), 1970

Farewell to Veronica (Hebe Elsna, as Vicky Lancaster), 1940

Farm, The (Louis Bromfield), 1933

Farm by the Sea (Theresa Charles, as Fay Chandos), 1967

Farmer Holy's Daughter (Charles Garvice), 1908

Faro's Daughter (Georgette Heyer), 1941

Farramonde (Anne Maybury, as Katherine Troy), 1968

Farrants, The (Annie S. Swan), 1913

Fascinating Doctor, The (Ursula Bloom, as Mary Essex), 1972

Fashion's Frown (Mary Linn Roby, as Georgina Grey), 1980

Fast and Loose (Nigel Tranter), 1951

Faster! Faster! (E.M. Delafield), 1936

Fatal Ruby, The (Charles Garvice), 1909

Fate (Charles Garvice), 1912

Fate and Dreams (Christopher Nicole, as Leslie Arlen), 1981

Fate Is Remarkable (Betty Neels), 1970

Fateful Fraud, A (G.B. Burgin), 1934

Fateful Promise (Madame Albanesi, as Effie Rowlands)

Fateful Summer, The (Velda Johnston), 1981

Father (Elizabeth), 1931

Father Abraham (W.G. Hardy), 1935

Father Gregory (P.C. Wren), 1913

Father Stafford (Anthony Hope), 1891

Fault of One, The (Madame Albanesi, as Effie Rowlands), 1897

Faults on Both Sides (Mabel St. John), 1914

Fauna (Denise Robins), 1978

Favourite of Fortune, A (Annie S. Swan), 1912

Favourite Wife (May Edginton), 1936

Favourite Wins!, The (Mabel St. Johns), 1919

Fear Kissed My Lips (Maysie Greig, as Jennifer Ames), 1947

Fear No More (Hester W. Chapman), 1968

Fear of Heights, A (Virginia Coffman), 1973

Fear Stalks the Bayou (Juanita Coulson), 1976

Fearful Paradise, The (Maysie Greig, as Jennifer Ames), 1953

Feast, The (Margaret Kennedy), 1950

Feast Is Finished, The (Denise Robins), 1950

Feast of Eggshells (Florence Stevenson), 1970

Feast of the Candles (Iris Danbury), 1968

Feast of the Peacock, The (Phyllis Hastings), 1978

Feather (Ruby M. Ayres), 1935

Feather Castles (Patricia Veryan), 1982

Feather in the Wind (Iris Danbury), 1959

Feathered Shaft, The (Jane Arbor), 1970

Feathers in the Fire (Catherine Cookson), 1971

Feel of Silk, The (Joyce Dingwell), 1967

Felix (Robert Hichens), 1904

Female Editor (Charles Garvice), 1908

Fen Tiger, The (Catherine Cookson, as Catherine Marchant), 1963

Fengriffen (David Case), 1970

Fenwick Houses (Catherine Cookson), 1960

Festival (May Edginton), 1931

Festival Summer (Charlotte Lamb), 1977

Fetch, The (Marjorie Bowen, as Joseph Shearing), 1942

Fettered Past, The (Netta Muskett), 1958

Fettered Yet Free (Annie S. Swan), 1895

Fetters of Hate (Anne Hampson), 1974

Fever (Charlotte Lamb), 1979

Fever of Love (Denise Robins), 1931

Few Days in Endel, A (Lucilla Andrews, as Diana Gordon), 1968

Few Fiends to Tea, A (Virginia Coffman), 1967

Fiametta (Anne Duffield), 1956

Fiancees Are Relatives (Berta Ruck), 1941

Fiancées Count as Relatives (Berta Ruck), 1941

Fickle Fortune (Charles Garvice), 1912

Fiddler's Green (Leila Mackinlay), 1954

Field of Roses, The (Phyllis Hastings), 1955

Field of the Forty Footsteps (Phyllis Hastings), 1978

Fielding's Folly (Frances Parkinson Keyes), 1940

Fiend, The (Margaret Millar), 1964

Fiesta San Antonio (Janet Dailey), 1977

Fifteen Streets, The (Catherine Cookson), 1952

Fifth Day of Christmas, The (Betty Neels), 1971

Fighting Spirit, The (Madame Albanesi, as Effie Rowlands), 1930

Figs in Frost (Denise Robins, as Hervey Hamilton), 1946

File on Devlin, The (Catherine Gaskin), 1965

Final Hour, The (Taylor Caldwell), 1944

Final Test, The (G.B. Burgin), 1928

Final Year, The (Claire Rayner, as Sheila Brandon), 1962

Finch's Fortune (Mazo de la Roche), 1931

Find Another Eden (Theresa Charles, as Fay Chandos), 1953

Find Me a River (Janice Holt Giles), 1964

Find Out the Way (Mary Burchell), 1946

Findernes' Flowers (Marjorie Bowen, as George Preedy), 1941

Finding of Jasper Holt, The (Grace Livingston Hill), 1916

Fine Feathers (Madame Albanesi, as Effie Rowlands), 1928

Fine Feathers! (Mabel St. John), 1914

Fine Romance, A (Katrina Britt), 1969

Fine Silk Purse, A (Sheila Walsh), 1978

Finger to Her Lips, A (Evelyn Berckman), 1971

Finished (H. Rider Haggard), 1917

Fiona (Catherine Gaskin), 1970

Fiona Macrae (Annie S. Swan), 1929

Fire and Flesh (Barbara Riefe), 1978

Fire and Ice (Janet Dailey), 1975

Fire and the Robe, The (Christopher Nicole, as Alison York), 1979

Fire and the Fury, The (Rebecca Stratton), 1975

Fire and the Rose, The (Ursula Bloom), 1977

Fire Below (Dornford Yates), 1930

Fire Dawn (Virginia Coffman), 1978

Fire Down Below (Margaret Irwin), 1928

Fire Dragon (Irene Roberts, as Roberta Carr), 1967

Fire in the Diamond, The (Marjorie Lewty), 1976

Fire Is for Sharing (Doris E. Smith), 1968

Fire Meets Fire (Anne Hampson), 1976

Fire of Driftwood, A (D.K. Broster), 1932

Fire of Love, The (Barbara Cartland), 1964

Fire of Spring (Netta Muskett), 1946

Fire of the Andes (Juanita Coulson), 1979

Fire of Youth (Margaret Pedler), 1930

Fire on the Snow (Barbara Cartland), 1975

Fire Opal (Pamela Hill), 1980

Fire Opals (Janet Louise Roberts, as Rebecca Danton), 1977

Fire Will Freeze (Margaret Millar), 1944

Firebird (Rebecca Stratton), 1975

Fires of Brimstone, The (Patricia Gallagher), 1966

Fires of Glenlochy, The (Constance Heaven), 1976

Fires of Spring (Hettie Grimstead), 1973

Fires of Torretta, The (Iris Danbury), 1974

Fires of Youth, The (May Wynne), 1927

First and Favourite Wife (Theresa Charles, as Fay Chandos), 1952

First and Last (Charles Garvice), 1908

First Class, Lady? (Barbara Cartland), 1935

First Elizabeth, The (Ursula Bloom), 1953

First I Must Forget (Theresa Charles, as Virginia Storm), 1951

First Lady Brendon, The (Robert Hichens), 1931

First Long Kiss, The (Denise Robins), 1953

First Love (E.M. Delafield), 1929

First Love—Last Love (Mary Burchell), 1946

First, The Dream (Anne Maybury), 1951

First Waltz, The (Janet Louise Roberts), 1974

First Week in September, The (Hebe Elsna), 1940

First Year, The (Lucilla Andrews), 1957

First-Time of Asking (Theresa Charles, as Jan Tempest), 1954

Fishy, Said the Admiral (Elizabeth Cadell), 1948

Five and Ten (Fannie Hurst), 1929

Five Farthings (Mollie Chappell), 1974

Five for Sorrow, Ten for Joy (Rumer Godden), 1979

Five Houses (Leila Mackinlay), 1952

Five Mrs. Lorrimers (Hebe Elsna, as Laura Conway), 1966

Five Passengers from Lisbon (Mignon Eberhart), 1946

Five People (Marjorie Bowen), 1925

Five Windows (D.E. Stevenson), 1953

Five Winds (Marjorie Bowen), 1927

Five Women (Faith Baldwin), 1942

Five-Hooded Cobra, The (Countess Barcynska, as Oliver Sandys), 1932

Five-Minute Marriage, The (Joan Aiken), 1977

Fixed as the Stars (Hebe Elsna, as Vicky Lancaster), 1946

Flagg Family, The (Kathleen Norris), 1936

Flamboyant Tree, The (Isobel Chace), 1972

Flame and the Flower, The (Kathleen E. Woodiwiss), 1972

Flame and the Frost, The (Denise Robins, as Harriet Gray), 1957

Flame in Fiji (Gloria Bevan), 1973

Flame in the Snow (Maureen Peters, as Veronica Black), 1980

Flame Is Love, The (Barbara Cartland), 1975

Flame of Fate (Anne Hampson), 1975

Flame of Life (Mrs. Patrick MacGill), 1921

Flame of Love, The (Madame Albanesi, as Effie Rowlands), 1923

Flame of the Forest (Netta Muskett), 1958

Flame of the South (Constance Gluyas), 1979

Flamenco (Lady Eleanor Smith), 1931

Flamenco Rose (Janet Louise Roberts), 1981

Flames (Robert Hichens), 1897

Flames in the Wind (Margaret Pedler), 1937

Flaming Felicia (Anne Duffield), 1934

Flaming Frontier, The (Frank G. Slaughter), 1957

Flaming Janet (Pamela Hill), 1954

Flaming June (Mrs. George de Horne Vaizey), 1908

Flamingo Flying South (Joyce Dingwell), 1974

Flamingo Moon (Margaret Pargeter), 1978

Flamingo Park (Margaret Way), 1980

Flamingoes on the Lake (Isobel Chace), 1961

Flash of Emerald (Jane Arbor), 1977

Flash of Scarlet, A (Sylvia Thorpe), 1978

Flash of Splendour (Anne Stevenson), 1968

Flaunting Extravagant Queen (Victoria Holt, as Jean Plaidy), 1957

Flavia (Naomi Jacob), 1965

Flawed Blades (P.C. Wren), 1933

Flawed Enchantress (Maureen Peters), 1974

Fledgling, The (Elizabeth Cadell), 1975

Fleeing Shadows (Anne Duffield), 1934

Fleeting Breath, A (Ivy Preston), 1970

Fleeting Hour, The (Rona Randall), 1947

Flesh and the Devil (Victoria Holt, as Elbur Ford), 1950

Fletchers End (D.E. Stevenson), 1962

Fleurette of Four Corners (G.B. Burgin), 1925

Flickering Candle, The (Patricia Ainsworth), 1968

Flickering Lamp, The (Netta Muskett), 1931

Flies (Baroness von Hutten), 1927

Flight from Hanover Square (D.A. Ponsonby), 1972

Flight from Natchez (Frank G. Slaughter), 1955

Flight into Fear (Maysie Greig, as Jennifer Ames), 1954

Flight into Love (Jane Blackmore), 1964

Flight into Yesterday (Margaret Way), 1976

Flight of a Fallen Angel (Daoma Winston), 1971

Flight of Dutchmen (Nigel Tranter), 1947

Flight of the Falcon, The (Ursula Bloom), 1969

Flight of the Falcon, The (Daphne du Maurier), 1965

Flight of the Hawk, The (Rebecca Stratton), 1974

Flight of the Heron, The (D.K. Broster), 1925

Flight of the Swan, The (Eleanor Farnes), 1959

Flight of the Swan, The (Charlotte Lamb, as Sheila Coates), 1973

Flight to Happiness (Maysie Greig, as Jennifer Ames), 1950

Flight to the Stars (Susan Barrie, as Pamela Kent), 1959

Flight to the Villa Mistra (Anne Worboys, as Vicky Maxwell), 1973

Flirt and the Flapper, The (Elinor Glyn), 1930

Flockmasters, The (Nigel Tranter), 1960

Flood of Passion (Ursula Bloom), 1932

Floodtide (Kay Thorpe), 1981

Floodtide (Frank Yerby), 1950

Florentine Spring (Charlotte Lamb), 1977 ´

Floris (Charles Garvice), 1910

Flower and the Fruit, The (Theresa Charles, as Jan Tempest), 1964

Flower and the Nettle, The (Theresa Charles), 1975

Flower Forbidden, The (A.M. Williamson), 1911

Flower of Ethiopia (Isobel Chace), 1969

Flower of Silence (Anne Rundle, as Joanne Marshall), 1970

Flower o' the Broom (Jean S. MacLeod), 1943

Flower of the Desert (Rachel Lindsay, as Roberta Leigh), 1979

Flower of the Greys (Maureen Peters), 1969

Flower of the Heart (Hettie Grimstead, as Marsha Manning), 1963

Flower o' the Lily (Baroness Orczy), 1918

Flower o' the Moor (May Wynne), 1935

Flower of the Morning (Kathryn Blair, as Celine Conway), 1960

Flower of the Nettle (Jane Arbor), 1953

Flower on the Rock, The (Jane Arbor), 1972

Flowering Cactus, The (Isobel Chace), 1970

Flowering Desert (Elizabeth Hoy), 1965

Flowering Wilderness (Kathryn Blair), 1951

Flowering Year, The (Iris Bromige), 1959

Flowers for Lilian (Anna Gilbert), 1980

Flowers for My Love (Katrina Britt), 1979

Flowers for the Doctor (Lucilla Andrews), 1963

Flowers for the God of Love (Barbara Cartland), 1978

Flowers from the Rock (Netta Muskett), 1956

Flowers in Stony Places (Marjorie Lewty), 1975

Flowers in the Wind (Kathryn Blair, as Celine Conway), 1954

Flowers of Eden (Joan Smith), 1979

Flowers of Fire (Stephanie Blake), 1977

Flowers of Fire (G.B. Burgin), 1908

Flowers of the Marsh (Margaret Rome), 1969

Flutter of White Wings (Elizabeth Ashton), 1972

Fly Away, Love (Betty Beaty), 1975

Fly Banners of Silk (Rosalind Laker), 1981

Fly Beyond the Sunset (Anne Hampson), 1978

Flyers, The (George Barr McCutcheon), 1907

Flying Dutchman (Michael Arlen), 1939

Flying Nurse, The (Ursula Bloom, as Sheila Burns), 1967

Flying Swans, The (Ursula Bloom), 1940

Foes (Mary Johnston), 1918

Foes of Freedom (May Wynne), 1916

Fog (Mary Ann Gibbs, as Elizabeth Ford), 1933

Foggy, Foggy Dew, The (Charity Blackstock), 1958

Follies of the King, The (Victoria Holt, as Jean Plaidy), 1980

Follow a Shadow (Anne Hampson), 1971

Follow a Shadow (Anne Rundle, as Joanne Marshall), 1974

Follow a Stranger (Charlotte Lamb), 1973

Follow the Shadow (Ruby M. Ayres), 1936

Follow Your Dream (Maysie Greig, as Jennifer Ames), 1957

Follow Your Heart (Emilie Loring), 1963

Follow Your Hearts (Anne Maybury), 1955

Follow Your Love (Maysie Greig), 1959

Follow Your Star (Hebe Elsna, as Lyndon Snow), 1941

Follow Your Star (Lucy Walker), 1963

Following of the Star, The (Florence L. Barclay), 1911

Folly by Candlelight (Charlotte Lamb, as Sheila Holland), 1978

Folly Island (Warwick Deeping), 1939

Folly of Eustace, The (Robert Hichens), 1896

Folly of Princes, A (Nigel Tranter), 1977

Folly of the Heart (Jane Arbor), 1955

Folly of the Heart (Rose Burghley), 1967

Folly to Be Wise (Sara Seale), 1946

Folly's End (Doris Leslie), 1944

Fond Fancy (Marjorie Bowen), 1932

Food for Love (Barbara Cartland), 1975

Food for Love (Rachel Lindsay), 1974

Food of Love (Leila Mackinlay), 1960

Fool and His Money, A (George Barr McCutcheon), 1913

Fool, Be Still (Fannie Hurst), 1964

Fool Beloved, The (Jeffery Farnol), 1949

Fool of the Family, The (Margaret Kennedy), 1930

Fool of Virtue (Leila Mackinlay), 1964

Foolish Heart, The (Claire Lorrimer, as Patricia Robins), 1956

Foolish Marriage, The (D.A. Ponsonby), 1952

Foolish Marriage, A (Annie S. Swan), 1894

Foolish Virgin, The (Kathleen Norris), 1929

Fool's Enchantment (Margaret Maddocks), 1969

Fool's Haven (Mary Howard), 1954

Fools in Mortar (Doris Leslie), 1928

Footfall in the Mist, A (Maureen Peters, as Veronica Black), 1971

Footlight Fever (Berta Ruck), 1942

Footsteps in the Dark (Georgette Heyer), 1932

Footsteps in the Fog (Pamela Bennetts), 1979

For a Dream's Sake (Theresa Charles, as Fay Chandos), 1949

For a Dream's Sake (Hebe Elsna, as Laura Conway), 1967

For a Dream's Sake (Claire Ritchie), 1965

For All Eternity (Barbara Cartland), 1981

For All Your Life (Emilie Loring), 1952

For an Earldom (Charles Garvice)

For Bitter or Worse (Janet Dailey), 1978

For Charles the Rover (May Wynne), 1909

For Church and Chieftan (May Wynne), 1909

For Ever and a Day (Madame Albanesi, as Effie Rowlands), 1911

For Ever and Ever (Mary Burchell), 1956

For Ever True (Madame Albanesi, as Effie Rowlands), 1904

For Faith and Navarre (May Wynne), 1904

For Her Lover's Sake (Mabel St. John), 1918

For Her Only (Charles Garvice), 1902

For Her to See (Marjorie Bowen, as Joseph Shearing), 1947

For I Have Lived Today (Alice Dwyer-Joyce), 1971

For Love (Ruby M. Ayres), 1918

For Love Alone (Hebe Elsna, as Lyndon Snow), 1957

For Love and Honor (Madame Albanesi, as Effie Rowlands)

For Love of a Doctor (Elizabeth Seifert), 1969

For Love of a Pagan (Anne Hampson), 1978

For Love of Anne Lambert (Madame Albanesi), 1910

For Love of Betty (Annie S. Swan), 1928

For Love of Sigrid (Madame Albanesi, as Effie Rowlands), 1906

For Love of Speranza (Madame Albanesi, as Effie Rowlands), 1910

For Love of the King (Ursula Bloom, as Lozania Prole), 1960

For Love or Honor (Charles Garvice, as Caroline Hart)

For Love's Sake Only (Elizabeth Hoy), 1951

For Lucy's Sake (Annie S. Swan), 1883

For Mike's Sake (Janet Dailey), 1979

For My Great Folly (Thomas B. Costain), 1942

For My Sins (Kathryn Blair, as Rosalind Brett), 1966

For the Love of God (Janet Dailey), 1981

For the Love of Sara (Anne Mather), 1975

For the Sake of the Family (Annie S. Swan), 1898

For Those in Love (Theresa Charles, as Jan Tempest), 1956

For What? (Barbara Cartland), 1930

Forbidden (Claire Lorrimer, as Patricia Robins), 1967

Forbidden (Anne Mather), 1976

Forbidden (Anne Maybury), 1956

Forbidden (Denise Robins), 1971

Forbidden Bride, The (Denise Robins), 1926

Forbidden Fiancé (Ursula Bloom, as Mary Essex), 1957

Forbidden Fire (Charlotte Lamb), 1979

Forbidden Flame (Anne Mather), 1981

Forbidden Island, The (Sara Seale), 1953

Forbidden Love (Caroline Courtney), 1980

Forbidden Love (Rachel Lindsay), 1977

Forbidden Love (Denise Robins), 1927

Forbidden Rapture (Jean S. MacLeod), 1941

Forbidden Rapture (Violet Winspear), 1973

Forbidden Road, The (Madame Albanesi), 1908

Forbidden Road, The (Mabel St. John, as Henry St. John Cooper), 1931

Forbidden Valley, The (Essie Summers), 1973

Forever Amber (Kathleen Winsor), 1944

Forever and a Day (Emilie Loring), 1965

Forever Autumn (Ursula Bloom), 1979

Forever Faithful (Marjorie McEvoy), 1962

Forever To-morrow (Anne Duffield), 1946

Forced Landing (Berta Ruck), 1931

Foreign Girl, The (Anne Betteridge), 1960

Forerunners, The (Annie S. Swan), 1930

Forest and the Fort, The (Hervey Allen), 1943

Forest Lure, The (G.B. Burgin), 1926

Forest of Fear (Anne Rundle), 1969

Forest of Stone, The (Phyllis Hastings, as Julia Mayfield), 1957

Forest of Terrible Things, The (E.M. Hull), 1939

Forget Me Not (Janet Louise Roberts), 1982

Forget Not Ariadne (Pamela Hill), 1965

Forget That I Remember (Denise Robins), 1940

Forget-Me-Not (Marjorie Bowen, as Joseph Shearing), 1932

Forgive Me, My Love (Denise Robins), 1947

Forgotten Bride (Gwen Westwood), 1980

Forgotten City, The (Barbara Cartland), 1936

Forgotten Dreams (Irene Roberts, as Iris Rowland), 1978

Forgotten Heir, The (D.A. Ponsonby), 1969

Forgotten Marriage (Rachel Lindsay), 1978

Forgotten Smile, The (Margaret Kennedy), 1961

Forsaking All Others (Emilie Loring), 1971

Fort Everglades (Frank G. Slaughter), 1951

Fort in the Jungle (P.C. Wren), 1936

Fortress, The (Catherine Gavin), 1964

Fortress, The (Jean S. MacLeod), 1970

Fortunate, The (D.A. Ponsonby), 1971

Fortunate Mary, The (Eleanor H. Porter), 1928

Fortune Hunter, The (Ruby M. Ayres), 1921

Fortune Hunters, The (Joan Aiken), 1965

Fortune Hunters, The (C.N. and A.M. Williamson), 1923

Fortune in Romance, A (Maysie Greig), 1940

Fortune My Foe (Audrey Erskine-Lindop), 1947

Fortune's Fool (Rafael Sabatini), 1923

Fortune's Footballs (G.B. Burgin), 1897

Fortunes of Bridget Malone, The (Marie Belloc Lowndes), 1937

Fortunes of Garin, The (Mary Johnston), 1915

Fortunes of Love, The (Caroline Courtney), 1980

Fortunes of Sally Luck, The (Mabel St. John, as Henry St. John Cooper), 1925

Fortunes of Springfield, The (Eleanor Farnes), 1955

Fortunes of the Farrells, The (Mrs. George de Horne Vaizey), 1907

Fortune's Slave (Leila Mackinlay), 1975

Fortune's Smile (Mary Linn Roby), 1979

Fortune's Sport (A.M. Williamson), 1898

Four-Pools Mystery, The (Jean Webster), 1908

40 Acres and No Mule (Janice Holt Giles), 1952

Forty Brothers (Jean Francis Webb), 1934

Forty Is Beginning (Ursula Bloom, as Mary Essex), 1952

Found Treasure (Grace Livingston Hill, as Marcia Macdonald), 1928

Founder of the House, The (Naomi Jacob), 1935

Foundling, The (Georgette Heyer), 1948

Fountain of Roses, A (Irene Roberts, as Iris Rowland), 1966

Fountain of Youth, The (Phyllis Hastings), 1959

Four Days in June (Mary Ann Gibbs, as Elizabeth Ford), 1951

Four Doctors, Four Wives (Elizabeth Seifert), 1975

Four Generations (Naomi Jacob), 1934

Four Graces, The (D.E. Stevenson), 1946

Four of Hearts (Hettie Grimstead, as Marsha Manning), 1967

Four Roads to Windrush (Susan Barrie), 1957

Four-Part Setting (Ann Bridge), 1939

1492 (Mary Johnston), 1922

Fourth Cedar, The (Ursula Bloom), 1944

Fourth Chamber, The (Marjorie Bowen, as George Preedy), 1944

Fourth Man on the Rope, The (Evelyn Berckman), 1972

Fox from His Lair, The (Elizabeth Cadell), 1965

Fox Farm (Warwick Deeping), 1911

Foxes of Harrow, The (Frank Yerby), 1946

Foxfire (Anya Seton), 1951

Fractured Silence, The (Frances Cowen), 1969

Fragile Years, The (Rose Franken), 1952

Fragrant Flower (Barbara Cartland), 1976

Frame of Dreams, A (Barbara Cartland), 1975

Frances Fights for Herself (Madame Albanesi, as Effie Rowlands), 1934

Francesca (Hebe Elsna, as Lyndon Snow), 1970

Franklin's Folly (Mary Linn Roby, as Georgina Grey), 1980

Fräulein Schmidt and Mr. Anstruther (Elizabeth), 1907

Freckles (Gene Stratton Porter), 1904

Freddy for Fun (Ursula Bloom, as Mary Essex), 1943

Frederica (Georgette Heyer), 1965

Free from Fear (Barbara Cartland), 1980

Freebody Heiress, The (Ethel Edison Gordon), 1974

Freebooters, The (Nigel Tranter), 1950

Freedom's Sword (Annie S. Swan), 1886

Freer's Cove (Ethel Edison Gordon), 1972

Freeways, The (Viña Delmar), 1971

French Bride, The (Evelyn Anthony), 1964

French Girl in Love (Maysie Greig), 1963

French Husband, The (Ethel Edison Gordon), 1977

French Inheritance, The (Anne Stevenson), 1974

French Kiss (Christopher Nicole, as Mark Logan), 1978

Frenchman, The (Velda Johnston), 1976

Frenchman and the Lady, The (Elizabeth Cadell), 1952

Frenchman's Creek (Daphne du Maurier), 1941

Frenchwoman, The (Rosalind Laker, as Barbara Paul), 1977

Friday Spy, The (Christopher Nicole, as C.R. Nicholson), 1981

Friday's Child (Georgette Heyer), 1944

Friday's Laughter (Joyce Dingwell), 1972

Friend of the Bride (Hettie Grimstead, as Marsha Manning), 1968

Friendly Air, The (Elizabeth Cadell), 1970

Frightened Bride, The (Barbara Cartland), 1975

Frightened Heart, The (Maysie Greig, as Jennifer Ames), 1952

Frightened Wife, The (Mary Roberts Rinehart), 1953

Fringe of Heaven (Gloria Bevan), 1978

Frivolous Cupid (Anthony Hope), 1895

From Fairest Flower (Theresa Charles), 1969

From Hell to Heaven (Barbara Cartland), 1981

From Mill to Mansion (Mabel St. John), 1914

From Out the Vasty Deep (Marie Belloc Lowndes), 1921

From Pillar to Post (Mabel St. John), 1921

From Satan, With Love (Virginia Coffman), 1972

From Such a Seed (Jean S. MacLeod, as Catherine Airlie), 1949

From the Housetops (George Barr McCutcheon), 1916

From the Vasty Deep (Marie Belloc Lowndes), 1920

From This Dark Stairway (Mignon Eberhart), 1931

From This Day Forward (Ruby M. Ayres), 1934

From This Day Forward (Betty Beaty, as Catherine Ross), 1959

From This Day Forward (Elswyth Thane), 1941

From Want to Wealth (Charles Garvice, as Caroline Hart)

From Worse Than Death (Charles Garvice, as Caroline Hart)

Frontier Passage (Ann Bridge), 1942

Frost and the Fire, The (Gloria Bevan), 1973

Frost at Dawn (Leila Mackinlay), 1968

Frozen Fire, A (Charlotte Lamb), 1980

Frozen Fountain, The (Margaret Maddocks), 1959

Frozen Slippers (A.M. Williamson), 1930

Fruit of the Tree (May Edginton), 1947

Fruit on the Bough (Ursula Bloom), 1931

Fruitful Vine, The (Robert Hichens), 1911

Fruits of the Year (Eleanor Farnes), 1942

Frustration (Charlotte Lamb), 1979

Fugitive from Love, A (Barbara Cartland), 1978

Fugitive from Love (Theresa Charles, as Fay Chandos), 1950

Fugitive Romantic, The (Ursula Bloom, as Mary Essex), 1960

Fugue in Time, A (Rumer Godden), 1945

Fulfillment (Elsie Lee), 1969

Full Circle (Kay Thorpe), 1978

Full Flavour (Doris Leslie), 1934

Full Fruit Flavour (Ursula Bloom, as Mary Essex), 1949

Full Meridian (Naomi Jacob), 1939

Full Summer's Kiss (Hettie Grimstead, as Marsha Manning), 1966

Full Tide (Kathryn Blair, as Celine Conway), 1954

Future Is Forever, The (Maynah Lewis), 1967

Gable Farm (Annie S. Swan), 1899

Gabriel Hounds, The (Mary Stewart), 1967

Gabriella (Anne Maybury), 1979

Gabrielle (Kathleen Norris), 1965

Gad's Hall (Norah Lofts), 1977

Gail Talbot (Hebe Elsna), 1953

Galahad's Garden (G.B. Burgin), 1908

Galaxy, The (Susan Ertz), 1929

Gale Warning (Dornford Yates), 1939

Galileans, The (Frank G. Slaughter), 1953

Gallant, The (Charity Blackstock), 1962

Gallant Graham, The (May Wynne), 1911

Gallant Lover, The (Mabel St. John, as Henry St. John Cooper), 1926

Gallant of Spain, A (May Wynne), 1920

Gallants, The (L. Adams Beck, as E. Barrington), 1924

Gallant's Fancy (Flora Kidd), 1974

Gallows Herd, The (Maureen Peters), 1973

Gallows Way (Daoma Winston), 1976

Gallows Wedding (Rhona Martin), 1978

Gamble with Hearts, A (Barbara Cartland),

1975

Gamble with Love, A (Ruby M. Ayres), 1922

Gambling Man, The (Catherine Cookson), 1975

Game and the Candle, The (Margaret Kennedy), 1928

Game in Diamonds (Elizabeth Cadell), 1976

Game of Hazard, A (Charity Blackstock, as Paula Allardyce), 1955

Game of Hearts, A (G.B. Burgin), 1915

Game of Kings, The (Dorothy Dunnett), 1961

Game of Life, The (Madame Albanesi, as Effie Rowlands), 1910

Game of Love (Charles Garvice, as Caroline Hart)

Game of Statues, A (Anne Stevenson), 1972

Gamester, The (Rafael Sabatini), 1949

Gamester's Daughter, The (D.A. Ponsonby), 1974

Gamma's Girl (Lucy Walker), 1977

Garden for My Child, A (Ursula Bloom), 1946

Garden Oats (Faith Baldwin), 1929

Garden of Allah, The (Robert Hichens), 1904

Garden of Don José, The (Rose Burghley), 1964

Garden of Memories, The (Mabel St. John, as Henry St. John Cooper), 1921

Garden of Persephone, The (Nan Asquith), 1967

Garden of Shadows (Virginia Coffman), 1973

Garden of the Gods, The (Elizabeth Ashton), 1978

Garden of Vision, The (L. Adams Beck), 1929

Garden of Wishes, The (Anne Maybury), 1935

Garden Room, The (Mollie Chappell), 1964

Gardenia, The (Robert Hichens), 1934

Gardenia Tree, The (Susan Barrie, as Pamela Kent), 1965

Garfield Honor, The (Frank Yerby), 1961

Garland of Marigolds, A (Isobel Chace), 1967

Garland of Youth, The (Madame Albanesi, as Effie Rowlands), 1923

Garment, The (Catherine Cookson), 1962

Garment of Gold, The (Countess Barcynska, as Oliver Sandys), 1921

Garth of Tregillis (Henrietta Reid), 1972

Gascoigne's Ghost (G.B. Burgin), 1896

Gaslight Sonatas (Fannie Hurst), 1918

Gate Leads Nowhere, The (Mary Howard), 1953

Gate Marked "Private," The (Ethel M. Dell), 1928

Gates of Happiness, The (Madame Albanesi,

as Effie Rowlands), 1927

Gated Road, The (Ursula Bloom), 1963

Gated Road, The (Jean S. MacLeod), 1959

Gates of Dawn, The (Susan Barrie), 1954

Gates of Doom, The (Rafael Sabatini), 1914

Gates of Eden, The (Annie S. Swan), 1886

Gates of Kami, The (Baroness Orczy), 1907

Gates of Midnight, The (Jessica Stirling), 1982

Gates of Montrain, The (Willo Davis Roberts), 1971

Gates of Morning, The (Phyllis Hastings), 1973

Gates of Paradise, The (Robert Hichens), 1930

Gates of Steel (Anne Hampson), 1970

Gateway to Nowhere (Frances Cowen), 1978

Gather Up the Years (Anne Maybury), 1939

Gay Courage (Emilie Loring), 1928

Gay Defeat (Denise Robins), 1933

Gay Fiesta (Anne Duffield), 1938

Gay Galliard, The (Margaret Irwin), 1941

Gay Intruder (Iris Bromige), 1954

Gay Is Life (Mary Howard), 1943

Gay Knight I Love (Theresa Charles, as Fay Chandos), 1938

Gay Life (E.M. Delafield), 1933

Gay Lord Robert (Victoria Holt, as Jean Plaidy), 1955

Gay of Heart, The (Anne Maybury), 1959

Gay Pursuit (Elizabeth Cadell), 1948

Gay Rowan (Irene Roberts, as Elizabeth Harle), 1965

Gay Unfortunate, The (Hebe Elsna), 1958

Gaynor Women, The (Virginia Coffman), 1978

Gazebo, The (D.A. Ponsonby), 1945

Geisha in the House (Maysie Greig, as Jennifer Ames), 1963

Gem of a Girl (Betty Neels), 1976

Gemel Ring, The (Betty Neels), 1974

Gemini Child (Rebecca Stratton), 1976

Gene (Rumer Godden), 1968

General, The (D.A. Ponsonby), 1971

General Crack (Marjorie Bowen, as George Preedy), 1928

General's Wench, The (Rosamond Marshall), 1954

Generous Vine, The (Elizabeth Renier), 1962

Gentian Hill (Elizabeth Goudge), 1949

Gentle Despot, A (G.B. Burgin), 1919

Gentle Flame, The (Katrina Britt), 1971

Gentle Highwayman, The (Charity Blackstock, as Paula Allardyce), 1961

Gentle Invader, The (Iris Danbury), 1957

Gentle Murderer, A (Dorothy Salisbury Davis), 1951

Gentle Obsession, The (Frances Cowen), 1968

Gentle Prisoner, The (Sara Seale), 1949

Gentle Sex, The (Charity Blackstock, as Paula Allardyce), 1974

Gentle Tyrant (Berta Ruck), 1949

Gentle Tyrant (Rebecca Stratton, as Lucy Gillen), 1973

Gentle Wind, The (Claire Ritchie), 1954

Gentleman, The (Edison Marshall), 1956

Gentleman Anonymous (Marie Belloc Lowndes), 1934

Gentleman Called, A (Dorothy Salisbury Davis), 1958

Gentleman Called James, A (Ursula Bloom, as Mary Essex), 1951

Gentleman in Love, A (Barbara Cartland), 1980

Gentleman Pirate, The (Janet Louise Roberts, as Janette Radcliffe), 1975

Gentleman Rogue (Charity Blackstock, as Paula Allardyce), 1975

Gentlemen Go By, The (Elizabeth Cadell), 1954

Gentlemen's Agreement (Baroness von Hutten), 1936

Georgian Rake, The (Alice Chetwynd Ley), 1960

Georgina (Clare Darcy), 1971

Gerald and Elizabeth (D.E. Stevenson), 1969

Gerald Cranston's Lady (Gilbert Frankau), 1924

Geste of Duke Jocelyn, The (Jeffery Farnol), 1919

Ghost Dancers, The (Dorothy Daniels, as Angela Gray), 1971

Ghost in Green Velvet (Barbara Michaels), 1977

Ghost in Monte Carlo, A (Barbara Cartland), 1951

Ghost Kings, The (H. Rider Haggard), 1908

Ghost of Archie Gilroy, The (Charity Blackstock, as Paula Allardyce), 1970

Ghost of Fiddler's Hill, The (Ursula Bloom, as Mary Essex), 1968

Ghost of June (Theresa Charles, as Jan Tempest), 1942

Ghost Song (Dorothy Daniels), 1974

Ghost Stories (Michael Arlen), 1927

Ghost That Haunted a King, The (Ursula Bloom, as Lozania Prole), 1963

Ghost Town (Charity Blackstock), 1976

Ghost Who Fell in Love, The (Barbara Cartland), 1978

Ghosts of Fontenoy, The (Charity Blackstock, as Charlotte Keppel), 1981

Ghosts of Harrel, The (Willo Davis Roberts), 1971

Giant (Edna Ferber), 1952

Giant in Chains, A (Marjorie Bowen), 1938

Giant of Medabi (Janet Dailey), 1978

Giants' Bread (Mary Westmacott), 1930

Gideon Faber's Choice (Susan Barrie, as Pamela Kent), 1965

Gift of My Heart, The (Hebe Elsna, as Lyndon Snow), 1949

Gift of the Heart (Claire Ritchie), 1955

Gift of Violets, A (Janet Louise Roberts, as Janette Radcliffe), 1977

Gift Shop, The (Charlotte Armstrong), 1967

Gifted Friend (Hebe Elsna, as Laura Conway), 1965

Gigolo (Edna Ferber), 1920

Gilded Fleece, The (Nigel Tranter), 1942

Gilded Hoop, The (Netta Muskett), 1941

Gilded Ladder, The (Hebe Elsna), 1945

Gilded Splendour (Rosalind Laker), 1982

Gillian (Frank Yerby), 1960

Gilliane (Roberta Gellis), 1979

Gilt Cage, The (Marguerite Steen), 1926

Ginger Ellen (May Wynne), 1947

Ginger Griffin, The (Ann Bridge), 1934

Gingerbread House, The (Alice Dwyer-Joyce), 1977

Ginger-Jar, The (Countess Barcynska, as Oliver Sandys), 1926

Gingham Year, The (Kate Norway), 1973

Gipsy Actress, The (Mabel St. John), 1923

Gipsy Born! (Mabel St. John), 1922

Gipsy Count, The (May Wynne), 1909

Gipsy Flower (Ursula Bloom), 1949

Gipsy King, The (May Wynne), 1917

Gipsy Love (Mabel St. John, as Henry St. John Cooper), 1923

Gipsy Lover, The (Ursula Bloom, as Rachel Harvey), 1973

Gipsy Schoolgirl, The (Mabel St. John), 1922

Gipsy Vans Come Through, The (Ursula Bloom), 1936

Gipsy-Spelled (May Wynne), 1929

Girl, The (Catherine Cookson), 1977

Girl Alone (Jane Blackmore), 1964

Girl Alone, A (Lilian Peake), 1972

Girl Alone (Lucy Walker), 1973

Girl and Her Money, A (Maysie Greig), 1971

Girl at Dane's Dyke, The (Margaret Rome), 1975

Girl at Eagles' Mount, The (Margaret Rome), 1971

Girl at Golden Hawk, The (Violet Winspear), 1974

Girl at Smuggler's Rest, The (Rebecca Stratton, as Lucy Gillen), 1970

Girl at Snowy River, The (Joyce Dingwell), 1959

Girl at White Draft, The (Kathryn Blair, as Rosalind Brett), 1962

Girl by the Sea (Suzanne Ebel), 1974

Girl Called Ann, A (Rona Randall), 1956

Girl Called Evelyn, A (Theresa Charles), 1959

Girl Called Tegi, A (Katrina Britt), 1980

Girl Disappears, A (Hebe Elsna), 1953

Girl for a Millionaire (Rachel Lindsay, as Roberta Leigh), 1977

Girl for Sale, A (Mabel Barnes Grundy), 1920

Girl from Montana, The (Grace Livingston Hill), 1908

Girl from Nowhere, The (Maysie Greig), 1936

Girl from Paris, The (Joan Aiken), 1982

Girl from Rome, The (Nan Asquith), 1973

Girl from Storyville, The (Frank Yerby), 1972

Girl from the South, A (Charles Garvice), 1910

Girl in Blue (Katrina Britt), 1976

Girl in a White Hat (Rebecca Stratton), 1977

Girl in Jeopardy (Maysie Greig), 1967

Girl in Love, The (Charles Garvice), 1919

Girl in Love (Rona Randall), 1961

Girl in Overalls (Elizabeth Seifert, as Ellen Ashley), 1943

Girl in the 'bacca Shop, The (Charles Garvice), 1920

Girl in the Blue Dress, The (Mary Burchell), 1958

Girl in the Green Valley, The (Elizabeth Hoy), 1973

Girl in the Mauve Mini, The (Theresa Charles, as Leslie Lance), 1979

Girl in the Secret, The (A.M. Williamson), 1934

Girl Intern (Elizabeth Seifert), 1944

Girl Men Talked About, The (Maysie Greig), 1938

Girl Must Marry, A (Maysie Greig), 1931

Girl Named Smith, A (Jane Arbor), 1960

Girl Next Door, The (Ruby M. Ayres), 1919

Girl of His Choice (Leila Mackinlay, as Brenda Grey), 1965

Girl of Spirit, A (Charles Garvice), 1906

Girl of the Limberlost, A (Gene Stratton Porter), 1909

Girl of the Prairie (Mabel St. John), 1922

Girl of the Woods, The (Grace Livingston Hill), 1942

Girl of the Passion Play, The (A.M. Williamson), 1911

Girl on His Hands (Maysie Greig), 1939

Girl on the Make (Faith Baldwin), 1932

Girl Outside, The (Anne Betteridge), 1971

Girl Possessed, A (Violet Winspear), 1980

Girl Sandy, The (May Wynne), 1938

Girl to Come Home To, A (Grace Livingston Hill), 1945

Girl Upstairs, The (May Wynne), 1932

Girl Who Got Out, The (G.B. Burgin), 1916

Girl Who Had Nothing, The (A.M. Williamson), 1905

Girl Who Loved Crippen, The (Ursula Bloom), 1955

Girl Who Married the Wrong Man!, The (Mabel S. John), 1923

Girl Who Proposed!, The (Berta Ruck), 1918

Girl Who Was Brave, The (Madame Albanesi, as Effie Rowlands), 1916

Girl Who Was Too Good-Looking, The (Berta Ruck), 1920

Girl Who Wasn't There, The (Willo Davis Roberts), 1957

Girl Who Wasn't Welcome, The (Maysie Greig), 1969

Girl with a Challenge (Mary Burchell), 1965

Girl with a Heart, A (Madame Albanesi, as Effie Rowlands), 1911

Girl with a Million (Maysie Greig), 1945

Girl with a Secret, The (Charlotte Armstrong), 1959

Girl Without a Heart, The (Charles Garvice), 1912

Girl Without Credit (Maysie Greig), 1941

Girl Without Money (Maysie Greig), 1957

Girlie (Ursula Bloom), 1904

Girls, The (Rosemary Ellerbeck, as Nicola Thorne), 1967

Girls, The (Edna Ferber), 1921

Girls at His Billet, The (Berta Ruck), 1916

Girl's Good Name, A (Mabel St. John), 1925

Girls in White (Rona Randall), 1952

Girl's Kingdom, The (Madame Albanesi, as Effie Rowlands)

Girls of Mackland Court, The (May Wynne), 1928

Girls of the Veldt Farm, The (May Wynne), 1922

Give All to Love (Claire Lorrimer, as Patricia Robins), 1956

Give All to Love (Claire Ritchie), 1971

Give Back Yesterday (Netta Muskett), 1955

Give Her Gardenias (Theresa Charles, as Jan Tempest), 1953

Give Love the Air (Faith Baldwin), 1947

Give Me Back My Dreams (Anne Maybury), 1936

Give Me Back My Heart (Denise Robins), 1944

Give Me New Wings (Elizabeth Hoy), 1944

Give Me One Summer (Emilie Loring), 1936

Give Me This Day (Maynha Lewis), 1964

Give Me the Daggers (Catherine Gavin), 1972

Give Me Your Love (Anne Worboys, as Annette Eyre), 1975

Give Us This Day (R.F. Delderfield), 1973

Giving Him Up (Ruby M. Ayres), 1930

Glad Heart, The (Madame Albanesi), 1910

Glad Summer, The (Jeffery Farnol), 1951

Glamour Girl (Evadne Price), 1937

Glass and the Trumpet, The (Elizabeth Seifert), 1948

Glass Castle, The (Violet Winspear), 1973

Glass Flame, The (Phyllis A. Whitney), 1978

Glass Heiress, The (Alice Dwyer-Joyce), 1981

Glass Palace, The (Mary Ann Gibbs), 1973

Glass Slipper, The (Mignon Eberhart), 1938

Glass Virgin, The (Catherine Cookson), 1969

Glass-Blowers, The (Daphne du Maurier), 1963

Gleam in the North, The (D.K. Broster), 1927

Glen of Frost (Maureen Peters, as Belinda Grey), 1981

Glen of Sighs (Rebeca Stratton, as Lucy Gillen), 1972

Glen o' Weeping, The (Marjorie Bowen), 1907

Glendraco (Laura Black), 1977

Glenrannoch (Rona Randall), 1973

Glittering Heights (Anne Duffield), 1936

Glittering Lights, The (Barbara Cartland), 1974

Glitter-Dust, The (Alice Dwyer-Joyce), 1978

Gloria and the Bullfighter (Jean Francis Webb, as Ethel Hammill), 1954

Glorious Apollo (L. Adams Beck, as E. Barrington), 1925

Glorious Flames (Elinor Glyn), 1932

Glory and the Lightning (Taylor Caldwell), 1974

Glory of Egypt, The (L. Adams Beck, as Louis Moresby), 1926

Go Borrowing—Go Sorrowing! (Mabel St. John), 1924

Goal, The (May Wynne), 1907

Goat Song (Frank Yerby), 1967

Goblin Hill (Essie Summers), 1977

God and Mr. Aaronson (Countess Barcynska), 1937

God and the King (Marjorie Bowen), 1911

God and the Wedding Dress (Marjorie Bowen), 1938

God in the Car, The (Anthony Hope), 1894

God Is an Englishman (R.F. Delderfield), 1970

God Must Be Sad (Fannie Hurst), 1961

God Speed the Night (Dorothy Salisbury Davis), 1968

God Within Him, The (Robert Hichens), 1926

Goddess and the Gaiety Girl, The (Barbara Cartland), 1980

Goddess of Gray's Inn, A (G.B. Burgin), 1901

Goddess of Mavisu, The (Rebecca Stratton), 1975

Goddess of the Green Room (Victoria Holt, as Jean Plaidy), 1971

Gods Forget, The (Barbara Cartland), 1939

God's Good Man (Marie Corelli), 1904

Gods in Green, The (Willo Davis Roberts), 1973

Gods of Mars (Rona Randall), 1977

God's Playthings (Marjorie Bowen), 1912

God's Warrior (Frank G. Slaughter), 1967

Going All the Way (Susan Hufford), 1980

Going Home (Danielle Steel), 1973

Golconda Necklace, The (Mabel St. John, as Henry St. John Cooper), 1926

Gold for Gay Masters (Denise Robins, as Harriet Gray), 1954

Gold for My Girl (Jane Blackmore), 1967

Gold for Prince Charlie (Nigel Tranter), 1962

Gold in the Dust (Madame Albanesi), 1929

Gold in the Gutter, The (Charles Garvice), 1907

Gold Is the Sunrise (Anne Hampson), 1971

Gold of Apollo, The (Charlotte Lamb, as Sheila Holland), 1976

Gold of Noon, The (Essie Summers), 1974

Gold Pennies (Rose Franken), 1938

Gold Shoe, The (Grace Livingston Hill), 1930

Gold Slippers, The (Frances Parkinson Keyes), 1958

Golden Apollo (Phyllis Hastings), 1958

Golden Apple Island (Jane Arbor), 1967

Golden Bait (Mabel St. John, as Henry St. John Cooper), 1928

Golden Bubbles (Irene Roberts, as Iris Rowland), 1976

Golden Butterfly (A.M. Williamson), 1926

Golden Cage, The (Iris Bromige), 1950

Golden Carpet, The (A.M. Williamson), 1931

Golden Collar, The (Elizabeth Cadell), 1969

Golden Cord, The (Warwick Deeping), 1935

Golden Dawn, A (Madame Albanesi, as Effie Rowlands), 1912

Golden Days (D.E. Stevenson), 1934

Golden Flame, The (Ursula Bloom), 1941

Golden Fleece, The (Norah Lofts), 1944

Golden Flower (Irene Roberts, as Iris Rowland), 1964

Golden Future (Hebe Elsna, as Lyndon Snow), 1950

Golden Galatea, The (Florence Stevenson), 1979

Golden Garden, The (Maysie Greig), 1968

Golden Girl, The (Elizabeth Ashton), 1978

Golden Goddess, The (Christopher Nicole, as Peter Grange), 1973

Golden Gondola, The (Barbara Cartland), 1958

Golden Harvest (Netta Muskett), 1944

Golden Hawk, The (Frank Yerby), 1948

Golden Horizons (Anne Duffield), 1935

Golden Illusion, The (Barbara Cartland), 1976

Golden Image, The (Jean Francis Webb, as Ethel Hamill), 1959

Golden Interlude (Irene Roberts, as Roberta Carr), 1970

Golden Isle, The (Frank G. Slaughter), 1947

Golden Lotus (Janet Louise Roberts), 1979

Golden Madonna, The (Rebecca Stratton), 1973

Golden Marguerite, The (Virginia Coffman, as Anne Stanfield), 1981

Golden Moment, The (Hettie Grimstead), 1962

Golden Moments (Danielle Steel), 1980

Golden Ones, The (Frank G. Slaughter, as C.V. Terry), 1958

Golden Packet, The (Dorothy Daniels, as Angela Gray), 1971

Golden Pagoda, The (Irene Roberts), 1972

Golden Panther, The (Sylvia Thorpe), 1956

Golden Peaks, The (Eleanor Farnes), 1951

Golden Penny, The (G.B. Burgin), 1937

Golden Puma, The (Margaret Way), 1980

Golden Rain (Irene Roberts as Elizabeth Harle), 1964

Golden Road, The (L.M. Montgomery), 1913

Golden Roof, The (Marjorie Bowen), 1928

Golden Rose, The (Kathryn Blair), 1959

Golden Silence, The (C.N. and A.M. Williamson), 1910

Golden Shoestring, The (Faith Baldwin), 1949

Golden Snail, The (Countess Barcynska), 1927

Golden Songbird, The (Sheila Walsh), 1975

Golden Stud (Lance Horner), 1975

Golden Summer (Iris Bromige), 1972

Golden Summer, The (Anne Duffield), 1954

Golden Thistle, The (Janet Louise Roberts), 1973

Golden Triangle (Irene Roberts, as Iris Rowland), 1978

Golden Unicorn, The (Phyllis A. Whitney), 1976

Golden Valley, The (Daoma Winston), 1975

Golden Venture, The (Ursula Bloom), 1938

Golden Violet, The (Marjorie Bowen as Joseph Shearing), 1936

Goldsmith's Wife, The (Victoria Holt, as Jean Plaidy), 1950

Gollantz Saga (Naomi Jacob)

Gone Before Morning (Lilian Peake), 1973

Gone with the Wind (Margaret Mitchell), 1936

Gone-Away Man, The (Lucy Walker), 1969

God Gestes (P.C. Wren), 1929

Good Gracious, Marian! (Mabel St. John), 1919

Good Man's Love, A (E.M. Delafield), 1932

Good Morning, Doctor Houston (Rebecca Stratton, as Lucy Gillen), 1969

Good Old Anna (Marie Belloc Lowndes), 1915

Good Out of Evil (Annie S. Swan), 1899

Good Sport (Maysie Greig), 1934

Good Woman, A (Louis Bromfield), 1927

Goodbye, Doctor Galahad (Marjorie McEvoy, as Marjorie Harte), 1962

Goodbye, Johnny (Kate Norway), 1962

Good-bye, Julie Scott (Alice Abbott), 1975

Goodbye, My Love (Anne Maybury), 1952

Gorgeous Brute (Countess Barcynska), 1949

Gorgeous Lover, The (Marjorie Bowen), 1929

Goring's Girl (May Wynne), 1914

Gospel Fever (Frank G. Slaughter), 1980

Gossamer Dream, The (Ursula Bloom), 1931

Gossip (Anne Duffield), 1938

Governess, The (Elsie Lee, as Elsie Cromwell), 1969

Governor of England, The (Marjorie Bowen), 1913

Gower Street (Claire Rayner), 1973

Grace Before Meat (Sara Seale), 1938

Grace Latouche and the Warringtons (Marjorie Bowen), 1931

Graces, The (L. Adams Beck, as E. Barrington), 1934

Gracious Lady, The (Ursula Bloom), 1955

Grafton Girls, The (Mary Howard), 1956

Grain of Gold, A (Wynne May), 1971

Granada Window (Marguerite Steen), 1949

Grand Duchess, The (Anne Duffield), 1954

Grand Man, A (Catherine Cookson), 1954

Grand Relations (Maysie Greig), 1940

Grand Sophy, The (Georgette Heyer), 1950

Grandmère (Viña Delmar), 1967

Grandmother and the Priests (Taylor Caldwell), 1963

Grandmother's Child (Annie S. Swan), 1882

Grasp a Nettle (Betty Neels), 1977

Graustark series (George Barr McCutcheon)

Grave of Truth, The (Evelyn Anthony), 1979

Graveyard Watch (Samuel Shellabarger, as John Estevan), 1938

Great Adventure, The (Janice Holt Giles), 1966

Great Adventure, The (May Wynne), 1948

Great Amulet, The (Maud Diver), 1908

Great Beginning, The (Ursula Bloom), 1924

Great Black Oxen (Naomi Jacob), 1962

Great Day, A (Elizabeth Seifert), 1939

Great Husband Hunt, The (Mabel Barnes Grundy), 1922

Great Laughter (Fannie Hurst), 1936

Great Lion of God (Taylor Caldwell), 1970

Great Miss Driver, The (Anthony Hope), 1908

Great Mistake, The (Mary Roberts Rinehart), 1940

Great Moment, The (Elinor Glyn), 1923

Great Pearl Secret, The (C.N. and A.M. Williamson), 1921

Great Romantic, The (L. Adams Beck, as E. Barrington), 1933

Great Roxhythe, The (Georgette Heyer), 1922

Great Smith (Edison Marshall), 1943

Great Son (Edna Ferber), 1945

Great Tradition, The (Frances Parkinson Keyes), 1939

Great Unmet, The (Berta Ruck), 1918

Great Valley, The (Mary Johnston), 1926

Greater Courage, The (Margaret Pedler), 1933

Greater Freedom, The (Annie S. Swan), 1938

Greater Gain, The (G.B. Burgin), 1917

Greater Happiness, The (Katrina Britt), 1974

Greater Love (Annie S. Swan, as David Lyall), 1898

Greater Than All (Denise Robins), 1946

Greatest Nurse of Them All, The (Ursula Bloom, as Lozania Prole), 1968

Greatheart (Ethel M. Dell), 1918

Grecian Rhapsody (Anne Duffield), 1938

Greek Bridal (Henrietta Reid) , 1976

Greek Wedding (Jane Aiken Hodge), 1970

Green Apple Love (Doris E. Smith), 1974

Green Bay Tree, The (Louis Bromfield), 1924

Green Beetle, The (Mary Ann Gibbs, as Elizabeth Ford), 1972

Green Bough, The (Claire Ritchie), 1953

Green Branch, The (Edith Pargeter), 1962

Green Caravan, The (Countess Barcynska, as Oliver Sandys), 1922

Green Carnation, The (Robert Hichens), 1894

Green Country, The (Madame Albanesi), 1927

Green Darkness (Anya Seton), 1972

Green Dolphin Country (Elizabeth Goudge), 1944

Green Dolphin Street (Elizabeth Goudge), 1944

Green Empress, The (Elizabeth Cadell), 1958

Green Fancy (George Barr McCutcheon), 1917

Green Fire (Anne Maybury), 1963

Green Gauntlet, The (R.F. Delderfield), 1968

Green Girl (Sara Seale), 1965

Green Glass Moon (Anne Rundle, as Marianne Lamont), 1970

Green Grass, The (Margaret Maddocks), 1963

Green Grass Growing (Sara Seale), 1940

Green Harvest (Elizabeth Ashton), 1977

Green Hat, The (Michael Arlen), 1924

Green Judgment (Margaret Pedler), 1934

Green Lacquer Pavillon, The (Helen Beauclerk), 1926

Green Leaves (Kathryn Blair, as Rosalind Brett), 1947

Green Light, The (Kate Norway, as Bess Norton), 1963

Green Limelight (Leila Mackinlay), 1943

Green Money (D.E. Stevenson), 1939

Green Mountain Man (Janet Dailey), 1978

Green Patch, The (Baroness von Hutten), 1910

Green Rushes, The (Jean S. MacLeod, as Catherine Airlie), 1953

Green Salamander, The (Pamela Hill), 1977

Green Valleys (Madame Albanesi, as Effie Rowlands), 1932

Greenfingers Farm (Joyce Dingwell), 1955

Greengage Summer, The (Rumer Godden), 1958

Greengirl (Maureen Peters, as Veronica Black), 1979

Greenwood Shady, The (Elizabeth Cadell), 1951

Gregg Barratt's Woman (Lilian Peake), 1981

Grenelle (Isabelle Holland), 1976

Grenfell Legacy, The (Marjorie McEvoy), 1968

Gresham Ghost, The (Willo Davis Roberts), 1980

Grey Ghyll (Anne Rundle), 1978

Greygallows (Barbara Michaels), 1972

Greystone series (Janet Louis Roberts, as Louisa Bronte)

Grief Before Night (Samuel Shellabarger, as Peter Loring), 1938

Griffin's Way (Frank Yerby), 1962

Grizel Married (Mrs. George de Horne Vaizey), 1914

Groping (Naomi Jacob), 1933

Grove of Olives, A (Suzanne Ebel), 1976

Grow Up, Little Lady! (Theresa Charles, as Jan Tempest), 1937

Growing Moon, A (Jane Arbor), 1977

Growing Season, The (Charlotte Lamb, as Sheila Holland), 1975

Growth of a Man (Mazo de la Roche), 1938

Guarded Gates, The (Katrina Britt), 1973

Guarded Halo, The (Margaret Pedler), 1929

Guardian, The (Mary Ann Gibbs), 1958

Guardian Nurse (Joyce Dingwell), 1970

Guardian of Love (Elsie Lee, as Elsie Cromwell), 1972

Guardian of the Heart (Carolina Courtney), 1979

Guardian of Willow House, The (Dorothy Daniels), 1975

Guests of Hercules, The (C.N. and A.M. Williamson), 1912

Guillotine (Christopher Nicole, as Mark Logan), 1976

Guilt's Pavillions (Leila Mackinlay), 1951

Guinea Stamp, The (Alice Chetwyne Ley), 1961

Guinea Stamp, The (Annie S. Swan), 1892

Guinevere's Lover (Elinor Glyn), 1913

Guinever's Gift (Nicole St. John), 1977

Gull Haven (Irene Roberts), 1971

Guy Mervyn (Florence L. Barclay, as Brandon Roy), 1891

Guyfford of Weare (Jeffery Farnol), 1928

Gwenda (Mabel Barnes Grundy), 1910

Gwendolen (Clare Darcy), 1978

Gwennola (May Wynne), 1926

Gyfford of Weare (Jeffery Farnol), 1928

Gypsy Flame (Ursula Bloom), 1979

Gypsy, Gypsy (Rumer Godden), 1940

Gypsy Heiress, The (Laura London), 1981

Gypsy Julie (Olga Sinclair), 1979

Gypsy Lover (Denise Robins), 1939

Gypsy Sixpence (Edison Marshall), 1949

Gypsy Virtue (Hebe Elsna, as Vicky Lancaster), 1936

Habit of Love, The (Joyce Dingwell), 1974

Habsburg series (Julia Fitzgerald, as Julia Hamilton)

Hagar (Mary Johnston), 1913

Haggard series (Christopher Nicole)

Hail the Conquering Hero (Frank Yerby), 1977

Haircut for Samson (Ursula Bloom, as Mary Essex), 1940

Halcyone (Elinor Glyn), 1912

Haldane Station (Florence Engel Randall), 1973

Half a Hero (Anthony Hope), 1893

Half a World Away (Gloria Bevan), 1980

Half Open Door, The (Madame Albenesi), 1934

Half Portions (Edna Ferber), 1920

Half Sisters (Hebe Elsna), 1934

Half-Enchanted, The (Suzanne Ebel), 1964

Half-Past Kissing Time (Berta Ruck), 1936

Half-Way to the Moon (Rosamunde Pilcher, as Jane Fraser), 1949

Hallelujah (Fannie Hurst), 1944

Halo, The (Baroness von Hutten), 1907

Halo for the Dead, A (Barbara Cartland), 1972

Hamlet (May Wynne), 1930

Hammer of the Scots (Victoria Holt, as Jean Plaidy), 1981

Hammersleigh (Rosemary Ellerbeck), 1976

Hand in Glove (Mignon Eberhart), 1937

Hand of Fate, The (Madame Albensi, as Effie Rowlands), 1914

Hand Painted (Countess Barcynska), 1925

Handful of Silver, A (Isobel Chace), 1968

Handful of Stars, A (Irene Roberts), 1967

Handful of Stars, A (Rebecca Stratton, as Lucy Gillen), 1973

Handmaid to Fame (Berta Ruck), 1938

Hands Across the Sea (Annie S. Swan), 1919

Hands of Veronica, The (Fannie Hurst), 1947

Hangman's Whip, The (Mignon Eberhart), 1940

Hangsaman (Shirley Jackson), 1951

Hannah (Betty Neels), 1980

Hannah Fowler (Janice Holt Giles), 1956

Hannah Massey (Catherine Cookson), 1965

Hanrahan's Colony (Jean Stubbs), 1964

Happiest Year, The (Hebe Elsna), 1944

Happiness Can't Wait (Susan Inglis), 1950

Happiness Hill (Grace Livingston Hill), 1932

Happiness Stone, The (Countess Barcynska, as Oliver Sandys), 1956

Happy Birthday to You (Hebe Elsna), 1951

Happy Christmas (Daphne du Maurier), 1940

Happy Cinderella, The (Hebe Elsna, as Vicky Lancaster), 1943

Happy Day (Countess Barcynska, as Oliver Sandys), 1934

Happy Endings (Ruby M. Ayres), 1935

Happy Enterprise, The (Eleanor Farnes), 1958

Happy Event (Hebe Elsna, as Lyndon Snow), 1960

Happy Fortress, The (Iris Bromige), 1978

Happy Harvest, The (Jeffery Farnol), 1939

Happy Hearts, The (Countess Barcynska, as Oliver Sandys), 1962

Happy House (Baroness von Hutten), 1919

Happy Is the Wooing (Theresa Charles, as Jan Tempest), 1952

Happy Island (Maysie Greig, as Jennifer Ames), 1964

Happy Man, The (Phyllis Hastings), 1957

Happy Mummers, The (Countess Barcynska, as Oliver Sandys), 1937

Happy Now I Go (Theresa Charles), 1947

Happy To-Morrow (Netta Muskett), 1938

Happy with Either (Theresa Charles, as Jan Tempest), 1946

Harbin's Ridge (Janice Holt Giles), 1951

Harbour Lights (Anne Duffield), 1953

Harbour of Deceit (Roumelia Lane), 1975

Harbour of Love (Anne Hampson), 1977

Hard to Win (Hebe Elsna, as Laura Conway), 1956

Hard-Hearted Doctor, The (Ursula Bloom, as Mary Essex), 1964

Hard Way, The (Denise Robins), 1949

Harlot's Daughter, The (Phyllis Hastings), 1967

Harness the Winds (Anne Maybury), 1934

Harps in the Wind (Robert Hichens), 1945

Harriet (Jilly Cooper), 1976

Harriet and the Piper (Kathleen Norris), 1920

Harriet Mannering's Paying Guests (Mrs. George de Horne Vaizey), 1917

Harriet, The Haunted (Katheryn Kimbrough), 1976

Harry's Last Love (Ursula Bloom, as Lozania Prole), 1958

Harsh Heritage (Nigel Tranter), 1939

Harvest is Mine, The (May Edginton), 1944

Harvest of a House (Ursula Bloom), 1935

Harvest of Hope (Faith Baldwin), 1962

Harvester, The (Gene Stratton Porter), 1911

Harvest-Home Come Sunday (Ursula Bloom), 1962

Haste to the Wedding (Doris E. Smith), 1974

Hasting Day, The (Mollie Chappell), 1970

Hasty Marriage, The (Betty Neels), 1977

Hasty Wedding (Mignon Eberhart), 1938

Hate Begins at Home (Joan Aiken), 1967

Hate That Lasts, The (G.B. Burgin), 1925

Hatful of Cowslips (Claire Ritchie), 1960

Haunted Castle (Norah Lofts), 1978

Haunted Headsman, The (Ursula Bloom, as Lozania Prole), 1965

Haunted Lady (Mary Roberts Rinehart), 1942

Haunted Landscape, A (Iris Bromige), 1976

Haunted Life (Charles Garvice, as Caroline Hart)

Haunted Light, The (Evadne Price), 1933

Haunted Place, A (Virginia Coffman), 1966

Haunted Portrait, The (Katheryn Kimbrough, as Ann Ashton), 1976

Haunted Ranch, The (May Wynne), 1936

Haunted Sisters, The (Victoria Holt, as Jean Plaidy), 1966

Haunted Summer (Anne Edwards), 1972

Haunted Vintage, The (Marjorie Bowen), 1921

Haunting Compulsion, A (Anne Mather), 1981

Haunting Me (Charity Blackstock, as Paula Allardyce), 1978

Haunting of Gas's Hall, The (Norah Lofts), 1979

Haunting of Helen Farley, The (Frances Cowen), 1976

Haunting of Hill House, The (Shirley Jackson), 1959

Haunting of Sara Lessingham, The (Pamela Bennetts, as Margaret James), 1978

Hauntings (Norah Lofts), 1975

Have Courage, My Heart (Mary Howard), 1943

Haversham Legacy, The (Daoma Winston), 1974

Hawaii for Danger (Naomi A. Hintze), 1973

Hawk and the Dove, The (Anne Hampson), 1970

Hawk in a Blue Sky (Charlotte Lamb), 1977

Hawkridge (Jane Blackmore), 1976

Hawks Barton (Irene Roberts), 1979

Hawk's Head (Theresa Charles, as Leslie Lance), 1981

Haymaker, The (Elizabeth Cadell), 1972

Haymarket, The (Claire Rayner), 1974

Hazard of Hearts, A (Barbara Cartland), 1949

Hazards of Belinda, The (Sophia Cleugh), 1933

Hazel Asks Why (May Wynne), 1926

Hazel of Heatherland (Mabel Barnes Grundy), 1906

Hazell & Sons, Brewers (Annie S. Swan), 1888

He and Hecuba (Baroness von Hutton), 1905

He Couldn't Take Money! (Mabel St. John), 1923

He Is Mine (Claire Lorrimer, as Patricia Robins), 1957

He Learnt about Women (Berta Ruck), 1940

He Loves Me, He Loves Me Not (Charles Garvice), 1911

He Married a Doctor (Faith Baldwin), 1944

He Married a Mill-Lass (Mabel St. John), 1924

He Married His Parlourmaid (Countess Barcynska), 1929

He Shall Not Marry a Mill-Lass! (Mabel St. John), 1929

He Travels Alone (Samuel Shellabarger, as Peter Loring), 1939

Head of Chancery (Betty Beaty), 1972

"Head" of the Family, The (Mabel St. John, as Henry St. John Cooper), 1923

Head of the House, The (Hebe Elsna, as Lyndon Snow), 1967

Head of the House (Grace Livingston Hill), 1940

Head of the House, The (Annie S. Swan), 1938

Healer, The (Frank G. Slaughter), 1955

Healer of Hearts (Katrina Britt), 1969

Healing Hands (Rachel Lindsay), 1955

Healing Hands (Elizabeth Seifert), 1942

Healing Time, The (Lucilla Andrews), 1969

Health unto His Majesty, A (Victoria Holt, as Jean Plaidy), 1956

Heart Alone, The (Hettie Grimstead, as Marsha Manning), 1959

Heart Appeal (Maysie Greig), 1934

Heart Awakens, The (Janet Louise Roberts, as Janette Radcliffe), 1977

Heart Cannot Forget, The (Mary Burchell), 1953

Heart Expects Adventure, The (Jane Arbor), 1951

Heart for Sale, A (Madame Albanesi), 1929

Heart for Heart (Charles Garvice)

Heart Has Wings, The (Faith Baldwin), 1937

Heart, Have You No Wisdom? (Elizabeth Hoy), 1962

Heart in Darkness (Maysie Greig, as Jennifer Ames), 1947

Heart in the Sand, The (D.A. Ponsonby), 1970

Heart in the Sunlight (Lilian Peake), 1975

Heart Is Broken, A (Barbara Cartland), 1972

Heart Is Never Fair, The (Anne Maybury), 1954

Heart Is Stolen, A (Barbara Cartland), 1980

Heart Line, The (Madame Albanesi, as Effie Rowlands), 1936

Heart Listens, The (Helen Van Slyke), 1973

Heart Must Choose, The (Mary Burchell), 1953

Heart of a Maid, The (Charles Garvice), 1910

Heart of a Rose (Rachel Lindsay), 1961

Heart of a Woman, The (Madame Albanesi, as Effie Rowlands), 1913

Heart of a Woman, The (Baroness Orczy), 1911

Heart of Angela Brent, The (Madame Albanesi, as Effie Rowlands), 1917

Heart of Glenayrt, The (May Wynne), 1932

Heart of Hetta, The (Madame Albanesi, as Effie Rowlands), 1900

Heart of Honour (Caroline Courtney), 1982

Heart of Marble (Nancy Buckingham), 1967

Heart of His Heart (Madame Albanesi), 1911

Heart of Little Shikara, The (Edison (Marshall), 1922

Heart of Paris (Denise Robins), 1951

Heart of Penelope, The (Marie Belloc Lowndes), 1904

Heart of Princess Osra, The (Anthony Hope), 1896

Heart of Rachael, The (Kathleen Norris), 1916

Heart of Stone (Janet Dailey), 1980

Heart of the Family, The (Elizabeth Goudge), 1953

Heart of the House, The (Naomi Jacob), 1951

Heart of the Lion, The (Victoria Holt, as Jean Plaidy), 1977

Heart of the Lion (Rachel Lindsay, as Roberta Leigh), 1975

Heart of the World (H. Rider Haggard), 1895

Heart of Una Sackville, The (Mrs. George de Horne Vaizey), 1907

Heart Remembers, The (Faith Baldwin), 1941

Heart Remembers, The (Elizabeth Hoy), 1946

Heart Specialist (Susan Barrie), 1958

Heart Surgeon (Ursula Bloom, as Mary Essex), 1971

Heart, Take Care! (Elizabeth Hoy), 1940

Heart to Be Won, A (Hebe Elsna, as Lyndon Snow), 1958

Heart Too Proud, A (Laura London), 1978

Heart Triumphant, The (Barbara Cartland), 1976

Heart Turns Homeward, The (Claire Ritchie), 1953

Heartbreak for Two (Maysie Greig), 1942

Heartbreak Marriage, The (Ruby M. Ayres), 1929

Heartbreak Surgeon (Ursula Bloom, as Sheila Burns), 1963

Heartbreaker (Hebe Elsna, as Vicky Lancaster), 1938

Heartbreaker (Charlotte Lamb), 1981

Heartbroken Melody (Kathleen Norris), 1938

Hearth and the Eagle, The (Anya Seton), 1948

Heart's Afire (Victoria Holt, as Eleanor Burford), 1954

Hearts and Sweethearts (Madame Albanesi), 1916

Hearts at Random (Elizabeth Hoy), 1942

Hearts at War (Madame Albanesi, as Effie Rowlands), 1913

Hearts by the Tower (Olga Sinclair), 1968

Heart's Desire (Claire Lorrimer, as Patricia Robins), 1953

Heart's Desire (Denise Robins), 1946

Hearts Do Not Break (Ivy Preston), 1964

Hearts for Gold (Countess Barcynska), 1938

Heart's Haven (Elizabeth Hoy), 1945

Hearts of Fire (Charles Garvice, as Caroline Hart)

Heart's Triumph, A (Madame Albanesi, as Effie Rowlands), 1912

Heartsease Grows Here (Claire Ritchie), 1962

Heat Wave (Denise Robins), 1930

Heather Moon, The (C.N. and A.M. Williamson), 1912

Heatherbloom (Jean S. MacLeod), 1940

Heathercleigh (Essie Summers), 1963

Heaven in Our Hearts (Claire Lorrimer, as Patricia Robins), 1954

Heaven in Your Hand (Norah Lofts), 1958

Heaven Is Gentle (Betty Neels), 1975

Heaven Is Here (Lucy Walker), 1957

Heaven Is High (Anne Hampson), 1970

Heaven Isn't Here (Maysie Greig), 1941

Heaven Lies Ahead (Ursula Bloom, as Sara Sloane), 1951

Heaven Tree, The (Edith Pargeter), 1960

Heavy Clay (Denise Robins), 1929

Hedgerow (Florence Engel Randall), 1967

He'll Never Marry You! (Mabel St. John), 1927

Heel of Achilles, The (E.M. Delafield), 1921

Hegerty, M.D. (Elizabeth Seifert), 1966

Heir of Garlands, The (Hebe Elsna), 1968

Heir of Starvelings, The (Evelyn Berckman), 1967

Heir of Vering (Charles Garvice), 1902

Heir to Glen Ghyll (Rebecca Stratton, as Lucy Gillen), 1970

Heir to Holtwood, The (D.A. Ponsonby), 1975

Heir to Kuragin (Constance Heaven), 1978

Heir to Windrush Hill (Essie Summers), 1966

Heiress, The (Evelyn Anthony), 1964

Heiress Apparent (Hebe Elsna, as Laura Conway), 1966

Heiress of Frascati, The (Marjorie Bowen, as Joseph Shearing), 1966

Heiress Presumptive (Hebe Elsna), 1981

Heiress to Wolfskill (Katheryn Kimbrough), 1973

Heirs of Love, The (Barbara Ferry Johnson), 1980

Helen (Georgette Heyer), 1928

Helena's Path (Anthony Hope), 1907

Hell of High Water (Anne Mather), 1979

Hell! Said the Duchess (Michael Arlen), 1934

Hell-Cat and the King, The (Barbara Cartland), 1977

Hellfire Heritage, The (Willo Davis Roberts), 1979

Helping Hersey (Baroness von Hutten), 1914

Henrietta's Own Castle (Betty Neels), 1975

Henry VIII and His Six Wives (Maureen Peters), 1972

Henry of Navarre (May Wynne, as Mabel W. Knowles), 1908

Henry of the High Rock (Juliet Dymoke), 1971

Henry's Golden Queen (Ursula Bloom, as Lozania Prole), 1964

Hepburn's Quay (Rebecca Stratton, as Lucy Gillen), 1979

Her Brother's Keeper (Margaret Pedler), 1924

Her Dancing Partner (Mrs. Patrick MacGill), 1926

Her Demon Lover (Janet Louise Roberts, as Louisa Bronte), 1973

Her Father's Daughter (Gene Stratton Porter), 1921

Her Father's Sin (Mabel St. John), 1908

Her Father's Wish (Madame Albanesi, as Effie Rowlands), 1937

Her French Husband (Phyllis Hastings), 1956

Her Golden Secret (Madame Albanesi, as Effie Rowlands)

Her Heart's Desire (Charles Garvice), 1900

Her Heart's Desire (Maysie Greig, as Jennifer Ames), 1961

Her Heart's Longing (Madame Albanesi, as Effie Rowlands), 1910.

Her Humble Lover (Charles Garvice), 1904.

Her Husband (Madame Albanesi, as Effie Rowlands), 1914

Her Husband and Her Love (Madame Albanesi, as Effie Rowlands), 1905

Her Kingdom (Madame Albanesi, as Effie Rowlands), 1910

Her Love So True (Charles Garvice)

Her Mad Month (Mabel Barnes Grundy), 1917

Her Mistake (Madame Albanesi, as Effie Rowlands), 1911

Her Mother-in-Law (Mabel St. John, as Henry St. John Cooper), 1920

Her Name Was Eve (Anne Maybury), 1953

Her Pirate Partner (Berta Ruck), 1926

Her Punishment (Madame Albanesi, as Effie Rowlands), 1910

Her Ransom (Charles Garvice), 1903

Her Right to Love (Charles Garvice, as Caroline Hart)

Her Sister's Children (Mary Burchell), 1965

Her Stolen Baby (Mabel St. John), 1919

Her Stolen Life (Evadne Price), 1954

Her Undying Past (Mrs. Patrick MacGill), 1924

Her Way and His (Ruby M. Ayres), 1921

Her Wedding Garment (Grace Livingston Hill), 1932

Her Weight in Gold (George Barr McCutcheon), 1911

Her Wild Voice Singing (Elizabeth Hoy), 1963

Her World of Men (Maysie Greig, as Jennifer Ames), 1937

Herb of Grace, The (Elizabeth Goudge), 1948

Herb of Healing, The (G.B. Burgin), 1915

Here Be Dragons (Maureen Peters, as Sharon Whitby), 1980

Here Comes a Candle (Jane Aiken Hodge), 1967

Here Comes the Sun! (Emilie Loring), 1924

Here I Belong (Mary Burchell), 1951

Here Lies Margot (Pamela Hill), 1957

Here Lies Our Soveriegn Lord (Victoria Holt, as Jean Plaidy), 1957

Here Today and Gone Tomorrow (Louis Bromfield), 1934

Here Was a Man (Norah Lofts), 1936

Heritage, The (Frances Parkinson Keyes), 1968

Heritage of Folly (Catherine Cookson, as Catherine Merchant), 1962

Heritage of Hate, A (Charles Garvice), 1909

Heritage of Strangers, A (Mary Linn Roby), 1978

Heritage of the House (Mary Linn Roby, as Pamela D'Arcy), 1980

Heritage Perilous (Jeffery Farnol), 1946

Hermit of Bonneville, The (G.B. Burgin), 1904

Hermit of Far End, The (Margaret Pedler), 1919

Hermitage Bell, The (Marjorie McEvoy), 1971

Hermitage Hill (Dorothy Daniels), 1978

Hermits of Gray's Inn, The (G.B. Burgin), 1899

Hero for Love's Sake (Madame Albanesi, as Effie Rowlands)

Hero of Herat, The (Maud Diver), 1912

Hero of Urbino, The (May Wynne), 1914

Hero or Scamp? (Mabel St. John, as Henry St. John Cooper), 1918

Heroes (Christopher Nicole), 1973

Heroes of Clone, The (Margaret Kennedy), 1957

Heroine's Sister, The (Frances Murray), 1975

Heron's Nest (Mary Ann Gibbs, as Elizabeth Ford), 1960

Heron's Point (Rebecca Stratton, as Lucy Gillen), 1978

Herring's Nest, The (Ursula Bloom, as Mary Essex), 1949

Hesitant Heart, The (Anne Edwards), 1974

Hesitant Heir, The (Mary Linn Roby, as Georgina Grey), 1978

Hesitation Waltz (Eleanor Farnes), 1939

Hester (Brian Cleeve), 1979

Hester Lane (Annie S. Swan), 1908

Hester Roon (Norah Lofts), 1940

Hester Trefusis (Madame Albanesi, as Effie Rowlands), 1912

Heu-Heu (H. Rider Haggard), 1924

Hey for Cavaliers! (May Wynne), 1912

Heywood Inheritance, The (Catherine Fellows), 1975

Hibiscus House (Theresa Charles, as Fay Chandos), 1955

Hidden Book, The (Mary Linn Roby), 1977

Hidden Evil, The (Barbara Cartland), 1963

Hidden Fires (Mrs. Patrick McGill), 1921

Hidden Fires (Janet Louise Roberts, as Janette

Radcliffe), 1978

Hidden Gift, The (Madame Albanesi), 1936

Hidden Heart, The (Barbara Cartland), 1946

Hidden Hearts (Mabel St. John, as Henry St. John Cooper), 1923

Hidden in the Wind (Jean S. MacLeod, as Catherine Airlie), 1953

Hidden Rapture (Roumelia Lane), 1978

Hidden Terror, A (Charles Garvice, as Caroline Hart), 1910

Hideaway Heart (Roumelia Lane), 1967

High Adventure, The (Jeffery Farnol), 1926

High Fence, The (Netta Muskett), 1959

High Heaven (Anne Duffield), 1939

High Holiday (Kathleen Norris), 1949

High Hostage (Anne Worboys, as Vicky Maxwell), 1976

High Master of Clere (Jane Arbor), 1966

High of Heart (Emilie Loring), 1938

High Noon (Ruby M. Ayres), 1936

High Road, The (Faith Baldwin), 1939

High Road (Maysie Greig, as Mary Douglas Warren), 1954

High Spirits (Nigel Tranter), 1950

High Terrace, The (Virginia Coffman), 1966

High Tide at Noon (Elisabeth Ogilvie), 1944

High Towers (Thomas B. Costain), 1949

High Valley, The (Anne Mather), 1971

High-Country Wife (Gloria Bevan), 1974

Highest Bidder, The (Ruby M. Ayres), 1921

Highest Bidder, The (Mrs. Patrick MacGill), 1921

Highest Peak, The (Wynne May), 1967

Highland Brooch, The (Janet Louise Roberts, as Rebecca Danton), 1980

Highland Holiday (Susan Inglis), 1952

Highland Interlude (Lucilla Andrews), 1968

Highland Masquerade (Mary Elgin), 1966

Highland Mist (Rose Burghley), 1962

Highwayman, The (Sylvia Thorpe), 1962

Hilary in His Heart (Theresa Charles, as Jan Tempest), 1938

Hilary on Her Own (Mabel Barnes Grundy), 1908

Hildegarde (Kathleen Norris), 1927

Hill Country Nurse (Adeline McElfresh), 1959

Hillbilly Doctor (Elizabeth Seifert), 1940

Hills Beyond, The (Katrina Britt), 1978

Hills of Fire (Dorothy Daniels), 1973

Hills of Kalamata (Anne Hampson), 1976

Hills of Maketu, The (Gloria Bevan), 1969

Hilltops Clear (Emilie Loring), 1933

Himalayan Moonlight (Roumelia Lane), 1977

Hindu, The (Robert Hichens), 1917

Hired Baby, The (Marie Corelli), 1891

Hiring Fair, The (Jessica Stirling), 1976

His Dupe (Mrs. Patrick MacGill), 1922

His Elizabeth (Elswyth Thane), 1928

His Guardian Angel (Charles Garvice), 1911

His Hour (Elinor Glyn), 1910

His Lordship (G.B. Burgin), 1893

His Love So True (Charles Garvice), 1896

His Majesty's Well-Beloved (Baroness Orczy), 1919

His Official Fiancee (Berta Ruck), 1914

His One Love (Madame Albanesi, as Effie Rowlands), 1912

His Perfect Trust (Charles Garvice)

His Sealed Lips! (Mabel St. John), 1918

His Serene Miss Smith (Essie Summers), 1966

His Shadow on the Wall (Hebe Elsna, as Lyndon Snow), 1965

His Ukelele Girl (Mrs. Patrick MacGill), 1927

His Wife—or His Mother? (Mabel St. John), 1923

His Wife or His Work? (Mabel St. John), 1928

His Wife's Secret (Mabel St. John), 1928

His Word of Honour (Ruby M. Ayres), 1921

Historical Nights' Entertainment, The (Rafael Sabatini)

Hold Back the Heart (Ursula Bloom, as Sheila Burns), 1951

Hold Hard, My Heart (Ursula Bloom, as Sheila Burns), 1946

Hold Me Captive (Margaret Pargeter), 1976

Hold On to Your Heart (Faith Baldwin), 1976

Holiday (May Edginton), 1933

Holiday Affair (Hettie Grimstead, as Marsha Manning), 1969

Holiday Engagement, A (Mary Ann Gibbs, as Elizabeth Ford), 1963

Holiday for Love (Glenna Finley), 1976

Holiday with Violence (Edith Pargeter), 1953

Holidays at Sunnycroft (Annie S. Swan), 1885

Hollow Hills, The (Mary Stewart), 1973

Hollow of Her Hand, The (George Barr McCutcheon), 1912

Hollywood Honeymoon (Countess Barcynska, as Oliver Sandys), 1939

Hollywood Love (A.M. Williamson), 1928

Hollywood Madness (Mrs. Patrick MacGill), 1936

Hollywood Star Dust (Mrs. Patrick MacGill), 1936

Holy Flower, The (H. Rider Haggard), 1915

Holy Orders (Marie Corelli), 1910

Homage to a Rose (Pamela Hill), 1979
Home at Sundown (Lucy Walker), 1968
Home for Jocelyn, A (Eleanor Farnes), 1953
Home for Joy, A (Mary Burchell), 1968
Home for the Wedding (Elizabeth Cadell), 1971
Home from the Sky (Iris Danbury), 1964
Home Is Goodbye (Isobel Chace), 1971
Home Is the Hero (Theresa Charles, as Fay Chandos), 1946
Home to My Country (Mary Howard), 1971
Home Without a Father, The (Mabel St. John), 1922
Homecoming (Hebe Elsna, as Vicky Lancaster), 1951
Homecoming, The (Norah Lofts), 1975
Homecoming (Adeline McElfresh), 1953
Homecoming (Elizabeth Seifert), 1950
Homecoming of the Boys, The (Annie S. Swan), 1916
Homeplace, The (Janet Dailey), 1976
Homesick for a Dream (Leila Mackinlay), 1968
Homespun (Annie S. Swan), 1893
Home-Town Doctor (Elizabeth Seifert), 1959
Homeward Bound (Eleanor Farnes), 1975
Homeward the Heart (Elizabeth Hoy), 1964
Homeward Winds the River (Barbara Ferry Johnson), 1979
Homing (Grace Livingston Hill), 1938
Homing (Elswyth Thane), 1957
Homing Bird, A (Annie S. Swan), 1935
Honey (Mary Burchell), 1959
Honey for Tea (Elizabeth Cadell), 1961
Honey Is Bitter, The (Violet Winspear), 1967
Honey Island (Nan Asquith), 1957
Honey Pot, The (Countess Barcynska), 1916
Honeyball Farm (Ethel M. Dell), 1937
Honeymoon (Elisabeth Ogilvie), 1947
Honeymoon Alone (Maysie Greig, as Jennifer Ames), 1940
Honeymoon for One (Maysie Greig), 1971
Honeymoon Hate (A.M. Williamson), 1931
Honeymoon in Hiding, A (Mrs. George de Horne Vaizey), 1911
Honeymoon Honolulu (Jean Francis Webb, as Ethel Hamill), 1950
Honeymoon in Manila (Maysie Greig, as Jennifer Ames), 1962
Honeymoon Island (Ursula Bloom), 1938
Honeymoon Holiday (Elizabeth Hoy), 1967
Honeymoons Arranged (Maysie Greig), 1938
Honor Bound (Faith Baldwin), 1934
Honor Bright (Frances Parkinson Keyes), 1936

Honor Girl, The (Grace Livingston Hill, as Marcia Macdonald), 1927
Honor of Dr. Shelton, The (Elizabeth Seifert), 1962
Honor's Price (Ursula Bloom), 1979
Honour Comes Back— (Naomi Jacob), 1935
Honour of Four Corners, The (G.B. Burgin), 1934
Honourable Jim, The (Baroness Orczy), 1924
Honourable Mr. Twanish, The (Jeffery Farnol), 1913
Honoured Guest (Hebe Elsna, as Lyndon Snow), 1952
Honour's a Mistress (Naomi Jacob), 1947
Honour's Fetters (May Wynne), 1911
Hootie Toots of Hollow Tree (May Wynne), 1925
Hope Is My Pillow (Claire Ritchie), 1967
Hopeful Journey (Berta Ruck), 1950
Horatia (Mary Ann Gibbs), 1961
Horns of the Moon (Anne Rundle, as Marianne Lamont), 1979
Horror at Gull House (Patricia Matthews, as Patty Brisco), 1970
Horror from the Tomb, The (Florence Stevenson), 1977
Horseman Riding By, A (R.F. Delderfield), 1966
Hortensius, Friend of Nero (Edith Pargeter), 1936
Hospital Call (Elizabeth Harrison), 1975
Hospital Circles (Lucilla Andrews), 1967
Hospital Corridors (Mary Burchell), 1955
Hospital Hill (Adeline McElfresh), 1961
Hospital of Fatima, The (Isobel Chace), 1963
Hospital of the Heart (Ursula Bloom, as Mary Essex), 1966
Hospital on the Hill (Ivy Preston), 1967
Hospital Summer, A (Lucilla Andrews), 1958
Hospital Zone (Elizabeth Seifert), 1948
Hostage Bride, The (Janet Dailey), 1981
Hostage Most Royal (Alanna Knight, as Margaret Hope), 1979
Hostile Shore, The (Catherine Gavin), 1940
Hot Day in High Summer (Phyllis Hastings), 1962
Hotel at Treloan (Susan Barrie), 1964
Hotel Belvedere (Iris Danbury), 1961
Hotel by the Loch (Iris Danbury), 1968
Hotel De Luxe (Rona Randall), 1961
Hotel Hostess (Faith Baldwin), 1938
Hotel Jacarandas (Katrina Britt), 1980
Hotel Mirador (Kathryn Blair, as Rosalind Brett), 1959
Hotel Southerly (Joyce Dingwell), 1968

Shaw), 1967

House of Many Doors, The (Dorothy Daniels), 1971

House of Many Shadows (Barbara Michaels), 1974

House of Many Windows (Netta Muskett), 1950

House of Men (Catherine Cookson, as Catherine Marchant), 1963

House of Mirror Images (Daoma Winston), 1970

House of Oliver, The (Jean S. MacLeod), 1947

House of Peril, The (Marie Belloc Lowndes), 1912

House of Pines (Theresa Charles, as Jan Tempest), 1975

House of Ravensbourne, The (Mary Ann Gibbs), 1965

House of Scissors, The (Isobel Chace), 1972

House of Seven Courts (Dorothy Daniels), 1967

House of Silence (Dorothy Daniels), 1980

House of Silence, The (C.N. and A.M. Williamson), 1921

House of Spies, The (Warwick Deeping), 1913

House of Stolen Memories (Dorothy Daniels), 1967

House of Storm (Mignon Eberhart), 1949

House of Strangers (Violet Winspear), 1963

House of Sunshine, The (Madame Albanesi, as Effie Rowlands), 1912

House of Terror (Evelyn Berckman), 1960

House of the Deer, The (D.E. Stevenson), 1970

House of the Eagles, The (Elizabeth Ashton), 1974

House of the Laird, The (Susan Barrie), 1956

House of the Lost Court, The (A.M. Williamson, as Dona Teresa de Savallo), 1908

House of the Pines (Theresa Charles, as Jan Tempest), 1946

House of the Seventh Cross (Denise Robins), 1967

House of the Shining Tide, The (Essie Summers), 1962

House of the Twelve Caesars (Phyllis Hastings), 1975

House of the Winds (Roumelia Lane), 1968

House of War, The (Catherine Gavin), 1970

House of Water, The (Elizabeth Renier), 1963

House of Whispers, The (May Wynne), 1929

House on Brinden Water, The (Nan Asquith), 1958

House on Circus Hill, The (Dorothy Daniels), 1972

House on Gregor's Brae, The (Essie Summers), 1971

House on Hay Hill, The (Dorothy Eden), 1976

House on Malador Street, The (Phyllis Hastings), 1970

House on the Cliff, The (D.E. Stevenson), 1966

House on the Fens, The (Catherine Cookson, as Catherine Marchant), 1965

House on the Hill, The (Ursula Bloom), 1977

House on the Left Bank, The (Velda Johnston), 1975

House on the Moat, The (Virginia Coffman), 1972

House on the Nile, The (Anne Duffield), 1937

House on the Rock, The (Annie S. Swan), 1930

House on the Rocks (Theresa Charles), 1962

House on the Roof, The (Mignon Eberhart), 1935

House on the Strand, The (Daphne du Maurier), 1969

House on Thunder Hill, The (Dorothy Daniels, as Suzanne Somers), 1973

House on Twyford Street, The (Constance Gluyas), 1976

House on Windswept Ridge, The (Katheryn Kimbrough), 1971

House Party (E.M. Delafield), 1931

House Possessed, A (Charity Blackstock), 1962

House Surgeon at Luke's (Rona Randall), 1962

House That Berry Built, The (Dornford Yates), 1945

House That Died Alone, The (Ursula Bloom), 1964

House That Hated People, The (Maureen Peters, as Veronica Black), 1974

House That Jane Built, The (Madame Albanesi), 1921

House with the Myrtle, The (Mary Ann Gibbs, as Elizabeth Ford), 1942

House with the Watching, The (Naomi A. Hintze), 1970

House Without a Heart, The (Frances Cowen), 1978

House Without Love, A (Iris Bromige), 1964

Houseful of Girls, A (Mrs. George de Horne Vaizey), 1902

Houseless One, The (Maureen Peters, as Sharon Whitby), 1981

Houseman's Sister (Kate Norway, as Hilary Neal), 1964

Hovering Darkness, The (Evelyn Berckman), 1957

How Can I Forget? (Theresa Charles, as Jan Tempest), 1948

How Dark, My Lady! (Ursula Bloom), 1951

How Dear Is My Delight! (Ursula Bloom, as Sheila Burns), 1955

How Far to Bethlehem? (Norah Lofts), 1965

How Great the Price (Denise Robins), 1935

How High the Moon (Leila Mackinlay, as Brenda Grey), 1966

How Like an Angel (Margaret Millar), 1962

How Like the King (Mrs. George de Horne Vaizey), 1905

How Many Miles to Babylon? (Margaret Irwin), 1913

How Much You Mean to Me (Theresa Charles), 1966

How Rich Is Love? (Ursula Bloom, as Sheila Burns), 1957

How Sleep the Brave (Catherine Gavin), 1980

How the Money Goes! (Mabel St. John), 1916

How to Forget (Denise Robins), 1944

Howards of Saxondale, The (Rona Randall), 1946

Howling in the Woods, A (Velda Johnston), 1968

Human Symphony (Jean S. MacLeod), 1937

Humbug (E.M. Delafield), 1922

Humoresque (Fannie Hurst), 1919

Hundredth Chance, The (Ethel M. Dell), 1917

Hundredth Man, The (G.B. Burgin), 1927

Hungry for Love (Barbara Cartland), 1976

Hungry Hill (Daphne du Maurier), 1943

Hungry Tide, The (Rebecca Stratton, as Lucy Gillen), 1976

Hunt with the Hounds (Mignon Eberhart), 1950

Hunter in the Shadows, The (Gwendoline Butler, as Jennie Melville), 1969

Hunter of the East (Anne Hampson), 1973

Hunter's Dawn (Irene Roberts, as Iris Rowland), 1977

Hunter's Green (Phyllis A. Whitney), 1968

Hunter's Mate (Jane Blackmore), 1971

Hunter's Moon, The (Ursula Bloom), 1969

Hunter's Moon (Henrietta Reid), 1970

Hunting of Henri, The (P.C. Wren), 1944

Hunting Shirt (Mary Johnston), 1931

Husband, The (Catherine Cookson), 1976

Husband and Foe (Madame Albanesi, as Effie Rowlands), 1900

Husband for Hire (Theresa Charles, as Fay Chandos), 1940

Husband Hunters, The (Barbara Cartland), 1976

Husband in Name (Leila Mackinlay, as Brenda Grey), 1972

Husband She Wanted, The (Mabel St. John), 1930

Husband, The Wife, and the Friend, The (Mabel St. John), 1921

Husbands at Home (Theresa Charles, as Fay Chandos), 1955

Husbands of Edith, The (George Barr McCutcheon), 1908

Hush Marriage, The (Mabel St. John, as Henry St. John Cooper), 1934

Hustler Joe (Eleanor H. Porter), 1924

Hut by the River, The (G.B. Burgin), 1916

Hyde Place (Virginia Coffman), 1974

I Am Gabriella! (Anne Maybury), 1962

I and My Heart (Joyce Dingwell), 1967

I Bequeath (Hebe Elsna), 1955

I Came to the Castle (Velda Johnston), 1969

I Came to the Highlands (Velda Johnston), 1975

I Could Be Good to You (Charity Blackstock, as Charlotte Keppel), 1980

I Dare Not Dream (Anne Maybury), 1937

I Dwelt in High Places (Marjorie Bowen), 1933

I Have Lived Today (Hebe Elsna), 1944

I Hear Adventure Calling (Emilie Loring), 1948

I, Judas (Taylor Caldwell), 1977

I Know a Maiden (Madame Albanesi), 1906

I Know My Life (Catherine Gaskin), 1962

I Know My Love (Sara Seale), 1957

I Know Not Whither (Hebe Elsna, as Laura Conway), 1979

I Like You So Much (May Edginton), 1933

I Live Again (Warwick Deeping), 1942

I Lost My Heart (Maysie Greig), 1935

I Love a Lass (Elizabeth Cadell), 1956

I Loved a Fairy (Countess Barcynska), 1933

I Loved Her Yesterday (Maysie Greig), 1945

I Married a Doctor (Rona Randall), 1947

I Married Mr. Richardson (Maysie Greig, as Jennifer Ames), 1945

I Met a Gypsy (Norah Lofts), 1935

I Met Him Again (Maysie Greig), 1948

I Met Murder on the Way (Charity Blackstock), 1977

ing), 1946

In a Dark Garden (Frank G. Slaughter), 1946

In a Glass Darkly (Janet Caird), 1966

In Another Girl's Shoes (Berta Ruck), 1916

In Cupid's Chains (Charles Garvice), 1902

In Daffodil Time (Madame Albanesi, as Effie Rowlands), 1913

In Exchange for Love (Charles Garvice), 1914

In Fine Feathers (Charles Garvice), 1912

In Haste to Be Rich (Annie S. Swan), 1898

In Love (Rosemary Ellerbeck, as Nicola Thorne), 1974

In Love with Claire (Madame Albanesi), 1932

In Love's Land (Madame Albanesi, as Effie Rowlands), 1912

In Mary's Reign (Baroness Orczy), 1907

In Me My Enemy (Audrey Erskine-Lindop), 1948

In Mother's Place (Mabel St. John), 1916

In Name Only (Rachel Lindsay, as Roberta Leigh), 1951

In Search of Love (Hebe Elsna, as Vicky Lancaster), 1955

In Search of Mr. Rochester (Mollie Chappell), 1976

In Storm and in Calm (Lucilla Andrews), 1975

In the Arms of Love (Barbara Cartland), 1981

In the Cool of the Day (Susan Ertz), 1961

In the Day's March (Ruby M. Ayres), 1930

In the Dead of the Night (Mary Linn Roby), 1969

In the Matter of a Letter (Charles Garvice), 1908

In the Mountains (Elizabeth), 1920

In the Portico (Baroness von Hutten), 1931

In the Rue Monge (Baroness Orczy), 1931

In the Shade of the Palms (Roumelia Lane), 1972

In the Shadow of the Guillotine (Rafael Sabatini), 1956

In the Shadows (Dorothy Daniels), 1978

In the Shadows (Mabel St. John), 1920

In the Shadows (May Wynne), 1900

In the Way (Grace Livingston Hill), 1897

In the Wilderness (Robert Hichens), 1917

In This House of Brede (Rumer Godden), 1969

In Times Like These (Emilie Loring), 1968

In Tune with Wedding Bells (Grace Livingston Hill), 1941

In Wolf's Clothing (Charles Garvice), 1908

Incident at a Corner (Charlotte Armstrong), 1959

Incident at Villa Rahmana (Anne Eliot), 1972

Inclination to Murder (Rosemary Ellerbeck), 1965

Incognito (Robert Hichens), 1947

Incomparable Miss Brady, The (Sheila Walsh), 1980

Incredible Duchess, The (Doris Leslie), 1974

Incredible Honeymoon, The (Barbara Cartland), 1976

Incredible Year, The (Faith Baldwin), 1929

Incumbent, The (Pamela Hill), 1974

Indecent Exposure (Evelyn Berckman), 1975

Independence of Claire, The (Mrs. George de Horne Vaizey), 1915

Indian Princess, The (A.M. Williamson), 1924

Indiscretion of the Duchess, The (Anthony Hope), 1894

Indiscretions of the Queen (Victoria Holt, as Jean Plaidy), 1970

Indy Man, The (Janet Dailey), 1978

Inevitable End, The (Denise Robins), 1927

Inevitable Hour, The (Edison Marshall), 1957

Infamous Army, An (Georgette Heyer), 1937

Infatuation (Denise Robins), 1951

Infinite Woman, The (Edison Marshall), 1950

Inherit My Heart (Mary Burchell), 1962

Inherit the Darkness (Willo Davis Roberts), 1972

Inherit the Sun (Rebecca Stratton), 1978

Inheritance, The (Annie S. Swan), 1909

Inheritance, The (Daoma Winston), 1972

Inherited Bride, The (Rebecca Stratton), 1980

Injured Lover, The (Marie Belloc Lowndes), 1939

Inland Paradise (Joyce Dingwell), 1976

Inn of the Hawk and Raven, The (George Barr McCutcheon), 1926

Innocent (Marie Corelli), 1914

Innocent and the Wicked, The (Phyllis Hastings), 1956

Innocent Bystander (Faith Baldwin), 1934

Innocent Deception (Rachel Lindsay), 1975

Innocent Enchantress (Hebe Elsna, as Laura Conway), 1953

Innocent Flower, The (Charlotte Armstrong), 1945

Innocent Girl, An (Charles Garvice), 1898

Innocent Heiress (Barbara Cartland), 1970

Innocent in Paris (Barbara Cartland), 1971

Innocent Obsession (Anne Mather), 1981

Inscrutable Nymph, The (Anne Duffield), 1942

Inside the Haven (Annie S. Swan), 1882

Insiders, The (Rosemary Rogers), 1979

Instead of the Thorn (Georgette Heyer), 1923

Interloper (Madame Albanesi, as Effie Rowlands)

Interloper, The (Gwendoline Butler), 1959

Interloper, The (Mary Howard), 1967

Interlude for Love (Susan Barrie, as Anita Charles), 1958

Interlude in Greece (Ivy Preston), 1982

Interrupted Journey (Ivy Preston), 1970

Intimate Story (Rose Franken), 1955

Into a Golden Land (Elizabeth Hoy), 1971

Into the Net (Leila Mackinlay), 1935

Introduction to Sally (Elizabeth), 1926

Intruder, The (Mary Howard), 1959

Intruder, The (Dorothy Mackie Low), 1965

Intruder at Windgates (Henrietta Reid), 1973

Intruder Marriage (Berta Ruck), 1944

Intrusions of Peggy, The (Anthony Hope), 1902

Invalided Out (Ruby M. Ayres), 1918

Invincible Amelia, The (Madame Albanesi), 1909

Invisible Cord, The (Catherine Cookson), 1975

Invisible Worm, The (Margaret Millar), 1941

Invitation, The (Catherine Cookson), 1970

Invitation to Evil (Willo Davis Roberts), 1970

Invitation to Folly (Susan Ertz), 1953

Invitation to Love (May Edginton), 1944

Iris (Charles Garvice), 1914

Iris in Winter (Elizabeth Cadell), 1949

Irish Beauties, The (L. Adams Beck, as E. Barrington), 1931

Irish Boy, The (Naomi Jacob), 1955

Irish Lover, An (Madame Albanesi, as Effie Rowlands), 1914

Iron Facade, The (Catherine Cookson, as Catherine Marchant), 1976

Iron Gates, The (Margaret Millar), 1945

Iron Man, The (Kay Thorpe), 1974

Iron-Bound (Edith Pargeter), 1936

Ironmaster, The (Jean Stubbs), 1981

Ironwood (Gwendoline Butler, as Jennie Melville), 1972

Irresistible Buck, The (Barbara Cartland), 1972

Irresistible Force, The (Barbara Cartland), 1978

Irresponsibles, The (Mary Ann Gibbs, as Elizabeth Ford), 1946

Is Anybody There? (Norah Lofts), 1974

Isabella and Fredinand (Victoria Holt, as Jean Plaidy), 1970

Isabelle, The Frantic (Katheryn Kimbrough), 1978

Island Affair (Hettie Grimstead), 1971

Island Doctor, The (Rona Randall), 1951

Island for Dreams (Katrina Britt), 1980

Island Girl, The (Mabel St. John), 1924

Island House (Theresa Charles, as Leslie Lance), 1976

Island in the Mist (Irene Roberts, as Iris Rowland), 1962

Island in the South (Lucy Walker, as Shelley Dean), 1967

Island Magic (Elizabeth Goudge), 1934

Island Nurse (Dorothy Daniels), 1964

Island of Bitter Memories (Dorothy Daniels), 1974

Island of Cyclones (Wynne May), 1979

Island of Darkness (Rebecca Stratton), 1974

Island of Desire (Janet Louise Roberts), 1977

Island of Enchantment (Ivy Preston), 1963

Island of Eve, The (Mabel St. John, as Henry St. John Cooper), 1921

Island of Evil (Dorothy Daniels), 1970

Island of Flowers (Denise Robins), 1940

Island of Mermaids (Iris Danbury), 1970

Island of Pearls (Margaret Rome), 1973

Island of Secrets (Henrietta Reid), 1965

Island of Shadows (Elisabeth Beresford), 1966

Island of the Seven Hills (Dorothy Mackie Low, as Zoe Cass), 1974

Island Stranger (Jean S. MacLeod), 1977

Island Twilight (Nigel Tranter), 1947

Isle at the Rainbow's End (Anne Hampson), 1976

Isle for a Stranger (Dorothy Mackie Low), 1962

Isle of Calypso (Margaret Rome), 1979

Isle of Desire (Anne Hampson), 1978

Isle of Pomegranates (Iris Danbury), 1969

Isle of the Dolphins (Janet Louise Roberts), 1973

Isle of the Golden Drum (Rebecca Stratton), 1975

Isle of the Rainbow (Anne Hampson), 1970

Isle of the Undead (Virginia Coffman), 1969

It (Elinor Glyn), 1927

It Began in Te Rangi (Gloria Bevan), 1971

It Began in Vauxhall Gardens (Victoria Holt, as Kathleen Kellow), 1955

It Couldn't Happen to Me (Jane Blackmore), 1962

It Had to Be You (Elizabeth Hoy), 1940

It Had to Happen (Louis Bromfield), 1936

It Happened in Egypt (C.N. and A.M. Williamson), 1914

It Happened in Paris (Elizabeth Hoy), 1970

It Happened One Flight (Maysie Greig), 1951

It Is My Duty! (Mabel St. John), 1926

It Started in Hongkong (Maysie Greig, as Jennifer Ames), 1961

It Takes All Kinds (Louis Bromfield), 1939

It Was Left to Peter (Berta Ruck), 1940

It Was Like This (Hervey Allen), 1940

It Was Romance (Mary Howard), 1939

It Wasn't Love (Denise Robins), 1930

Italian Woman, The (Victoria Holt, as Jean Plaidy), 1952

It's a Great World (Emilie Loring), 1935

It's All in the Family (Margaret Millar), 1948

It's Lonely Without You (Hebe Elsna, as Laura Conway), 1962

It's Rumoured in the Village (Mary Burchell), 1946

It's Spring, My Heart! (Ursula Bloom, as Mary Essex), 1958

It's Wise to Forget (Elizabeth Hoy), 1945

I've Always Loved You (Maysie Greig), 1943

Ivorstone Manor (Elsie Lee, as Elsie Cromwell), 1970

Ivory Cane, The (Janet Dailey), 1977

Ivory Child, The (H. Rider Haggard), 1916

Ivory God, The (Annie S. Swan), 1920

Ivy Tree, The (Mary Stewart), 1961

Jacaranda Island (Iris Danbury), 1972

Jack Be Nimble (Countess Barcynska, as Oliver Sandys), 1941

Jackal's Head, The (Barbara Michaels, as Elizabeth Peters), 1968

Jackie (Countess Barcynska), 1921

Jackpot, The (Countess Barcynska), 1957

Jack's Year of Trial (Annie S. Swan), 1887

Jacob Ussher (Naomi Jacob), 1925

Jade Dragon, The (Nancy Buckingham), 1974

Jade Earrings (Berta Ruck), 1941

Jade Green (Dorothy Daniels), 1973

Jade Horse of Merle, The (D.A. Ponsonby), 1966

Jade of Destiny, The (Jeffery Farnol), 1931

Jade Spider, The (Netta Muskett), 1927

Jade Vendetta (Janet Louise Roberts), 1976

Jake Howard's Wife (Anne Mather), 1973

Jalna series (Mazo de la Roche)

Jamaica Inn (Daphne du Maurier), 1936

James Bevanwood, Baronet (Mabel St. John, as Henry St. John Cooper), 1920

Jane (Marie Corelli), 1897

Jane Cable (George Barr McCutcheon), 1906

Jane Em'ly (Mabel St. John), 1911

Jane Hadden (Rosamond Marshall), 1952

Jane of Lantern Hill (L.M. Montgomery), 1937

Jane Oglander (Marie Belloc Lowndes), 1911

Jane Ryan, Dietician (Adeline McElfresh, as Elizabeth Wesley), 1959

Jane, The Courageous (Katheryn Kimbrough), 1975

Janice (Maysie Greig), 1947

Janie's Great Mistake (May Wynne), 1920

Janus Imperative, The (Evelyn Anthony), 1980

Japanese Doll, A (D.A. Ponsonby, as Doris Rybot), 1961

Japanese Lantern, The (Isobel Chace), 1960

Japanese Screen, The (Anne Mather), 1974

Jarrett's Jade (Frank Yerby), 1959

Jasmine Farm (Elizabeth), 1934

Jasmine for a Nurse (Irene Roberts), 1982

Jasmine Harvest (Jane Arbor), 1963

Jasmine—Take Care! (Maysie Greig), 1930

Jasper Dennison's Christmas (Annie S. Swan), 1898

Jassy (Norah Lofts), 1944

Jaubert Ring, The (Willo Davis Roberts), 1976

Jealous Wife's Revenge!, A (Mabel St. John), 1921

Jeanne (Charles Garvice), 1902

Jeanne Margot (Sophia Cleugh), 1927

Jeff Benton, M.D. (Adeline McElfresh), 1962

Jehovah Blues (Marguerite Steen), 1952

Jennifer James, R.N. (Dorothy Daniels), 1962

Jenny Luck of Brendon's Mills (Mabel St. John), 1923

Jenny Newstead (Marie Belloc Lowndes), 1932

Jenny W.R.E.N. (Ursula Bloom, as Sheila Burns), 1945

Jerry (Jean Webster), 1916

Jerry, Junior (Jean Webster), 1907

Jess (H. Rider Haggard), 1887

Jess Mawney, Queen's Nurse (Jane Arbor), 1954

Jess o' Jordan's (Mabel St. John), 1930

Jessamy Court (Anne Maybury), 1974

Jessica (Anne Maybury), 1965

Jest, The (Marjorie Bowen), 1922

Jest of Fate, A (Charles Garvice), 1904

Jewel of Death (Evelyn Berckman), 1968

Jewel of the Greys (Maureen Peters), 1972

Jewelene (Claudette Williams), 1979

Jewelled Caftan, The (Margaret Pargeter), 1978

Jewelled Daughter, The (Anne Maybury), 1976

Jewelled Snuff Box, The (Alice Chetwynd Ley), 1959

Jewels of Terror (Janet Louise Roberts), 1970

Jezebel (Denise Robins), 1977

Jig-Saw (Barbara Cartland), 1925

Jill (E.M. Delafield), 1926

Jill Nolan series (Adeline McElfresh)

Jill Takes a Chance (Susan Inglis), 1949

Jill the Hostage (May Wynne), 1925

Jinks (Countess Barcynska, as Oliver Sandys), 1930

Joan Haste (H. Rider Haggard), 1895

Joan of the Lilies (Maureen Peters), 1969

Joan of the Tower (Warwick Deeping), 1911

Joanna (Jane Blackmore), 1963

Joanna (Roberta Gellis), 1978

Joanna at the Grange (Mary Burchell), 1957

Joanne, The Unpredictable (Katheryn Kimbrough), 1976

Job for Jenny, A (Faith Baldwin), 1945

Job's Niece (Grace Livingston Hill), 1927

John Galbraith's Wife (Madame Albanesi, as Effie Rowlands), 1910

John Helsby's Wife (Madame Albanesi, as Effie Rowlands), 1920

John Jordan, Slave-Driver (Mabel St. John), 1915

John o' the Green (Jeffery Farnol), 1935

Johnny Danger (Charity Blackstock, as Paula Allardyce), 1960

Johnny Osage (Janice Holt Giles), 1960

Jonah and Co. (Dornford Yates), 1922

Jonquil (Denise Robins), 1927

Joshua Tree, The (Jean S. MacLeod), 1970

Jonty in Love (Anne Hampson), 1975

Joseph Stone, The (Jacqueline La Tourrette), 1971

Josselyn's Wife (Kathleen Norris), 1918

Journey for Two Travellers (Eleanor Farnes), 1946

Journey from a Foreign Land (Anne Betteridge), 1972

Journey from Yesterday (Suzanne Ebel), 1963

Journey Home (Hebe Elsna, as Laura Conway), 1978

Journey Home, The (Hettie Grimstead), 1950

Journey in the Dark (Susan Barrie, as Pamela Kent), 1962

Journey in the Dark (Maysie Greig, as Jennifer Ames), 1945

Journey in the Dark (Kate Norway), 1973

Journey in the Sun (Jean S. MacLeod), 1957

Journey into Morning (Anne Maybury), 1944

Journey into Spring (Jean S. MacLeod), 1976

Journey into Stone (Audrey Erskine-Lindop), 1972

Journey into Terror (Dorothy Daniels), 1971

Journey to Arcady (Rona Randall), 1955

Journey to Love (Glenna Finley), 1970

Journey to Love (Rona Randall), 1953

Journey to Paradise (Barbara Cartland), 1974

Journey Up, The (Robert Hichens), 1938

Journey's End (Evelyn Berckman), 1977

Journey's Eve (Elizabeth Cadell), 1953

Joy Comes After (Countess Barcynska), 1943

Joy Girl, The (May Edginton), 1927

Joy of Life, The (Madame Albanesi, as Effie Rowlands), 1913

Joy Shop, The (Countess Barcynska), 1931

Joy Street (Frances Parkinson Keyes), 1950

Joyce, The Beloved (Katheryn Kimbrough), 1979

Joyday for Jodi (Lucy Walker), 1971

Joyful Journey (Berta Ruck), 1950

Joyous Adventure, The (Elizabeth Ashton), 1979

Joyous Adventure, A (Countess Barcynska), 1932

Joyous Story of Astrid, The (L. Adams Beck), 1931

Joy-Ride (Berta Ruck), 1929

Jubilee Hospital (Theresa Charles, as Jan Tempest), 1966

Judas Cat, The (Dorothy Salisbury Davis), 1949

Judas Figure, The (Audrey Erskine-Lindop), 1956

Judas Flowering (Jane Aiken Hodge), 1976

Judas Iscariot—Traitor! (Ursula Bloom, as Lozania Prole), 1971

Judas Kiss, The (Victoria Holt), 1981

Judas, My Brother (Frank Yerby), 1969

Judas Trap, The (Anne Mather), 1979

Judge of Jerusalem, The (Ursula Bloom), 1926

Judge of the Four Corners, The (G.B. Burgin), 1896

Judgement of the Sword, The (Maud Diver), 1913

Judged by Fate (Madame Albanesi, as Effie Rowlands), 1913

Judgement of Love, The (Barbara Cartland), 1978

Judith (Brian Cleeve), 1978

Judith Lammeter (Anne Rundle), 1976

Juice of the Pomegranate, The (Ethel M. Dell), 1938

Julia Ballantyne (Marjorie Bowen, as George Preedy), 1952

Julia in Ireland (Ann Bridge), 1973

Julia Involved (Ann Bridge), 1962

Julia Roseingrave (Marjorie Bowen, as Robert

Paye), 1933

Julia's Sister (Suzanne Ebel), 1982

Julia (Pamela Hill), 1967

Julia (Baroness von Hutten), 1924

Julian Probert (Susan Ertz), 1931

Julie (Florence Stevenson), 1978

Julie Barden series (Audrie Manley-Tucker)

Juliet of the Mill (May Wynne), 1931

June for Enchantment (Elizabeth Hoy), 1949

June in Her Eyes (Theresa Charles, as Fay Chandos), 1949

Jungle, The (Charity Blackstock), 1972

Jungle Captive (E.M. Hull), 1939

Jungle Nurse (Irene Roberts), 1968

Jungle of Desire (Flora Kidd), 1977

Junior Pro (Kate Norway), 1959

Juniper Tree, The (Faith Baldwin), 1952

Juniper Hill (Dorothy Daniels), 1976

Jury of One (Mignon Eberhart), 1961

Just a Barmaid (Mabel St. John), 1909

Just a Cottage Maid (Mabel St. John, as Henry St. John Cooper), 1920

Just a Girl (Charles Garvice), 1898

Just a Little Longer (Theresa Charles, as Fay Chandos), 1944

Just a Nice Girl (Mary Burchell), 1941

Just Around the Corner (Fannie Hurst), 1914

Just Around the Corner (Mary Ann Gibbs, as Elizabeth Ford), 1952

Just Before the Wedding (Theresa Charles, as Fay Chandos), 1954

Just David (Eleanor H. Porter), 1916

Just for One Weekend (Theresa Charles), 1978

Just Jane Ann (Mabel St. John), 1915

Just Jane Em'ly (Mabel St. John), 1921

Just Lil (Countess Barcynska, as Oliver Sandys), 1933

Just 'Liz-beth Ann (Mabel St. John), 1925

Just Mother (Eleanor H. Porter), 1927

Just Off Piccadilly (Barbara Cartland), 1933

Just Plain Jim! (Mabel St. John, as Henry St. John Cooper), 1924

Just You Wait (Evelyn Berckman), 1973

Justice by Midnight (Jeffery Farnol), 1956

Justice of the Duke, The (Rafael Sabatini), 1912

K (Mary Roberts Rinehart), 1915

Karen's Memory (Anne Duffield), 1939

Karma of Love, The (Barbara Cartland), 1974

Karran Kinrade (Anne Rundle, as Alexandra Manners), 1982

Kate (Brian Cleeve), 1977

Kata Alanna (Maureen Peters), 1975

Kate Hardy (D.E. Stevenson), 1947

Kate Hannigan (Catherine Cookson), 1950

Kate, The Curious (Katheryn Kimbrough), 1976

Katharine of Aragon (Victoria Holt, as Jean Plaidy), 1968

Katharine, The Virgin Widow (Victoria Holt, as Jean Plaidy), 1961

Katharine's Yesterday (Grace Livingston Hill), 1895

Katherine (Jean S. MacLeod), 1950

Katherine (Anya Seton), 1954

Katherine of Aragon (Julia Fitzgerald, as Julia Hamilton), 1972

Katherine, The Returned (Katheryn Kimbrough), 1980

Katherine the Tragic Tudor (Julia Fitzgerald, as Julia Hamilton), 1974

Katherine Wentworth (D.E. Stevenson), 1964

Katherine's Marriage (D.E. Stevenson), 1965

Katheryn, The Wanton Queen (Maureen Peters), 1967

Katie Mulholland (Catherine Cookson), 1967

Katie's Christmas Lesson (Annie S. Swan), 1883

Katie's Young Doctor (Elizabeth Seifert), 1964

Kay Manion, M.D. (Adeline McElfresh), 1959

Kay Rogers, Copy Writer (Adeline McElfresh, as Jane Scott), 1956

Kaye's Walk (D.A. Ponsonby), 1977

Keep Cheery (Countess Barcynska), 1937

Keep This Door Shut (A.M. Williamson), 1933

Keeper of the Bees, The (Gene Stratton Porter), 1925

Keeper of the Door, The (Ethel M. Dell), 1915

Keeper of the Heart (Gwen Westwood), 1969

Keeper's House, The (Rosamunde Pilcher, as Jane Fraser), 1963

Keepers of the Faith (Emilie Loring), 1944

Keith's Dark Tower (Eleanor H. Porter), 1919

Kenny (Louis Bromfield), 1947

Kentuckians, The (Janice Holt Giles), 1953

Kept Woman (Viña Delmar), 1929

Kerry (Grace Livingston Hill), 1931

Kettle of Fish (Nigel Tranter), 1961

Key, The (Barbara Kevern), 1974

Key Diablo (Dorothy Daniels), 1971

Key of Dreams, The (L. Adams Beck), 1922

Key to Many Doors, A (Emilie Loring), 1967

Key Witness (Willo Davis Roberts), 1975

Keys from a Window (Evelyn Berckman), 1965

Khaki and Kisses (Berta Ruck), 1915

Khamsin (Denise Robins), 1948

Kiddy, The Coffee-Stall Girl (Mabel St. John), 1914

Kidnapped (Mabel St. John, as Henry St. John Cooper), 1923

Kilgaren (Isabelle Holland), 1974

Kilmeny in the Dark Wood (Florence Stevenson), 1973

Kilmeny of the Orchard (L.M. Montgomery), 1910

Kilted Stranger, The (Margaret Pargeter), 1975

Kind of Insolence, A (Marguerite Steen), 1940

Kind of War, A (Pamela Haines), 1976

Kind of Warfare, A (Juliet Dymoke), 1981

Kinder Love, The (Theresa Charles), 1955

Kindled Fire, The (Essie Summers), 1969

Kindled Flame (Margaret Pedler), 1931

Kindling and Ashes (George Barr McCutcheon), 1926

Kindly Giant, The (Joyce Dingwell), 1964

King and a Coward, A (Madame Albanesi, as Effie Rowlands), 1899

King Behind the King, The (Warwick Deeping), 1914

King Country (Margaret Way), 1970

King Creole (Christopher Nicole, as Peter Grange), 1966

King Henry's Sweetheart (Ursula Bloom, as Lozania Prole), 1967

King Hereafter (Dorothy Dunnett), 1982

King in Prussia (Rafael Sabatini), 1944

King in the Lists, A (May Wynne), 1922

King Liveth, The (Jeffery Farnol), 1943

King Mandarin's Challenge (May Wynne), 1927

King of a Day, The (May Wynne), 1918

King of Four Corners, The (G.B. Burgin), 1910

King of Spades, The (Katrina Britt), 1974

King of the Castle, The (Susan Barrie, as Anita Charles), 1963

King of the Castle, The (Victoria Holt), 1967

King Solomon's Mines (H. Rider Haggard), 1885

Kingdom of a Heart, The (Madame Albanesi, as Effie Rowlands), 1899

Kingdom of the Heart (Lucy Walker), 1959

Kingdom's Castle (Daoma Winston), 1972

Kingfisher Morning (Charlotte Lamb), 1977

Kingfisher Tide (Jane Arbor), 1965

Kingfishers Catch Fire (Rumer Godden), 1953

King's Bastard, The (Hebe Elsna), 1971

King's Brat (Constance Gluyas), 1972

King's Cavalier, The (Samuel Shellabarger), 1950

King's Daughter, The (Ursula Bloom, as Lozania Prole), 1975

King's Favourite, The (Marjorie Bowen), 1971

King's General, The (Daphne du Maurier), 1946

King's Legacy (Constance Heaven, as Constance Fecher), 1967

King's Masquerade, A (May Wynne), 1910

King's Minion, The (Rafael Sabatini), 1930

King's Mirror, The (Anthony Hope), 1899

King's Mistress, The (Julia Fitzgerald, as Julia Watson), 1970

King's Mistress, The (Victoria Holt, as Jean Plaidy), 1952

King's Pawn (Willo Davis Roberts), 1971

King's Plaything, A (Ursula Bloom, as Lozania Prole), 1962

King's Pleasure, The (Ursula Bloom, as Lozania Prole), 1954

King's Pleasure, The (Victoria Holt, as Jean Plaidy), 1949

King's Pleasure, The (Norah Lofts), 1969

King's Rhapsody (Hester W. Chapman), 1950

King's Secret Matter, The (Victoria Holt, as Jean Plaidy), 1962

King's Tragedy, A (May Wynne), 1905

King's Traitor, The (Doris Leslie), 1973

King's Vixen, The (Pamela Hill), 1954

King's Wife, The (Ursula Bloom), 1950

Kings-at-Arms (Marjorie Bowen), 1918

Kingsmead (Baroness von Hutten), 1909

Kinsfolk (Annie S. Swan), 1896

Kinsman's Sin (Madame Albanesi, as Effie Rowlands)

Kirkby's Changeling (Madeleine Brent), 1975

Kirkland Revels (Victoria Holt), 1962

Kiss, The (G.B. Burgin), 1924

Kiss a Stranger (Glenna Finley), 1972

Kiss—and Forget (Theresa Charles, as Jan Tempest), 1936

Kiss for the King, A (Barbara Cartland), 1975

Kiss from Satan, A (Anne Hampson), 1973

Kiss in a Gondola, A (Katrina Britt), 1968

Kiss in Sunlight (Maysie Greig), 1956

Kiss in the Sun, A (Hettie Grimstead), 1959

Kiss Me Again, Stranger (Daphne du Maurier), 1953

Kiss of a Tyrant (Margaret Pargeter), 1980

Kiss of Hot Sun (Nancy Buckingham), 1969

Kiss of Life, The (Barbara Cartland), 1981

Kiss of Paris, The (Barbara Cartland, as Barbara McCorquodale), 1956

Kiss of Promise (Maysie Greig), 1960

Kiss of Silk, A (Barbara Cartland, as Barbara McCorquodale), 1959

Kiss of Youth (Denise Robins), 1937

Kiss of the Devil, The (Barbara Cartland), 1955

Kiss the Moon (Countess Barcynska, as Oliver Sandys), 1951

Kiss the Moonlight (Barbara Cartland), 1977

Kisses and the Wine, The (Violet Winspear), 1973

Kisses for Three (Hettie Grimstead, as Marsha Manning), 1958

Kissing Gate, The (Joyce Dingwell), 1975

Kissing Gate, The (Pamela Haines), 1981

Kissing Kin (Elswyth Thane), 1948

Kit's Hill (Jean Stubbs), 1978

Kitty (Warwick Deeping), 1927

Kitty (Rosamond Marshall), 1943

Knave of Diamonds, The (Ethel M. Dell), 1913

Knave of Hearts, The (Barbara Cartland), 1950

Knave of Hearts, The (Irene Roberts, as Iris Rowland), 1970

Kneel to the Prettiest (Berta Ruck), 1925

Knight in Red Armor (Dorothy Daniels), 1966

Knight of Spain, A (Marjorie Bowen), 1913

Knight's Acre (Norah Lofts), 1975

Knight's Honor (Roberta Gellis), 1964

Knight's Keep (Rona Randall), 1967

Knock at Midnight, The (Charity Blackstock), 1966

Knock Four Times (Margaret Irwin), 1927

Knock on the Door, The (Robert Hichens), 1909

Knot Garden, The (Marjorie Bowen, as George Preedy), 1933

Kona Winds (Janet Dailey), 1979

Kowhai Country (Gloria Bevan), 1979

Kyra's Fate (Charles Garvice), 1908

Lab Nurse (Rona Randall), 1962

Labour of Hercules, A (Marie Belloc Lowndes), 1943

Lace for Milady (Joan Smith), 1980

Lacey (Claudette Williams), 1979

Lachlan's Woman (Alice Dwyer-Joyce), 1979

Lacquer Couch, The (Anne Duffield), 1928

Lad with Wings, The (Berta Ruck), 1915

Ladder of Understanding (Jane Arbor), 1949

Laddie (Gene Stratton Porter), 1913

Ladies, The (L. Adams Beck, as E. Barrington), 1922

Ladies of Hanover Square, The (Rona Randall), 1981

Ladies of Lark, The (Mollier Chappell), 1965

Ladies of Lyndon, The (Margaret Kennedy), 1923

Ladies of the Manor, The (G.B. Burgin), 1903

Ladies Only (May Edginton), 1922

Ladies' Pleasaunce (May Edginton), 1951

Lady and the Pirate, The (Charity Blackstock, as Paula Allardyce), 1957

Lady and the Unicorn, The (Rumer Godden), 1937

Lady Betty Across the Water (C.N. and A.M. Williamson), 1906

Lady Blanche Farm (Frances Parkinson Keyes), 1931

Lady Blue (Florence Stevenson, as Zabrina Faire), 1979

Lady Cassandra (Mrs. George de Horne Vaizey), 1914

Lady Cecily's Dilemma (Sheila Walsh, as Sophie Leyton), 1980

Lady Chatterly's Daughter (Claire Lorrimer, as Patricia Robins), 1961

Lady Fell in Love, A (Mary Howard), 1956

Lady Fell in Love, A (Anne Maybury), 1943

Lady Feo's Daughter (Madame Albanesi, as Effie Rowlands), 1926

Lady from London, The (Ruby M. Ayres), 1944

Lady from the Air, The (C.N. and A.M. Williamson), 1922

Lady Housekeeper, The (Annie S. Swan), 1898

Lady in a Veil (Marjorie Bowen, as George Preedy), 1943

Lady in Berkshire, A (Mary Ann Gibbs), 1970

Lady in the Limelight (Elizabeth Ashton), 1976

Lady in the Mist (Theresa Charles), 1966

Lady Ingram's Retreat (Jill Tattersall), 1970

Lady Ingram's Room (Jill Tattersall), 1981

Lady, It Is Spring! (Anne Maybury), 1938

Lady Living Alone (Norah Lofts, as Peter Curtis), 1945

Lady—Look Ahead (Hebe Elsna, as Vicky Lancaster), 1944

Lady Mary of the Dark House (A.M. Williamson), 1898

Lady Mary's Money (G.B. Burgin), 1918

Lady Misjudged (Hebe Elsna), 1941

Lady of Blossholme, The (H. Rider Haggard), 1909

Lady of Darracourt, The (Charles Garvice), 1902

Lady of Mallow (Dorothy Eden), 1962

Lady of Quality (Georgette Heyer), 1972

Lady of Spain, A (G.B. Burgin), 1911

Lady of the Basement Flat, The (Mrs. George de Horne Vaizey), 1917

Lady on the Coin (Hebe Elsna), 1963

Lady of the Garter (Juliet Dymoke), 1979

Lady of the Heavens, The (H. Rider Haggard), 1908

Lady of the Lakes (Rosemary Ellerbeck, as Katherine Yorke), 1981

Lady of the Pool, The (Anthony Hope), 1894

Lady of the Shadows (Dorothy Daniels), 1968

Lady of the Torch (Leila Mackinlay), 1944

Lady of Wildersley, The (Mary Howard, as Josephine Edgar), 1975

Lady Pamela (Clare Darcy), 1975

Lady Patricia's Faith (Madame Albanesi, as Effie Rowlands), 1913

Lady Serena, The (Virginia Coffman, as Jeanne Duval), 1979

Lady! This Is Love! (Ursula Bloom, as Sheila Burns), 1938

Ladybird (Grace Livingston Hill), 1930

Laird of Glenfernie, The (Mary Johnston), 1919

Laird of Locharrun, The (Anne Hampson), 1980

Laird of Storr (Henrietta Reid), 1968

Laird's Choice (Rosamond Marshall), 1951

Lake of Darkness, The (Frances Cowen), 1971

Lake of Shadows (Jane Arbor), 1964

Lake of the Kingfisher, The (Essie Summers), 1978

Lamb to the Slaughter (Dorothy Eden), 1953

Lambs, The (Kate Norway), 1965

Lame Daddy (Countess Barcynska, as Oliver Sandys), 1942

Lame Englishman, The (Warwick Deeping), 1910

Lament for a Lost Lover (Victoria Holt, as Philippa Carr), 1977

Lament for a Lover (Jean S. MacLeod), 1967

Lament for Four Brides (Evelyn Berckman), 1959

Lament for Lost Lovers (Alanna Knight), 1972

Lamont of Ardgoyne (Jean S. MacLeod), 1944

Lamp in the Desert, The (Ethel M. Dell), 1919

Lamp of Fate, The (Margaret Pedler), 1920

Lamp of Friendship, The (Madame Albanesi, as Effie Rowlands), 1936

Lamplight (May Edginton), 1930

Lancaster Men (Janet Dailey), 1981

Land Beyond the Mountains, The (Janice Holt Giles), 1958

Land Called Deseret, A (Janet Dailey), 1979

Land of Enchantment (Janet Dailey), 1975

Land of Heart's Desire (Jean S. MacLeod, as Catherine Airlie), 1957

Land of Silence, The (G.B. Burgin), 1904

Land of the Far Island (Victoria Holt), 1975

Land of the Lotus-Eaters, The (Isobel Chace), 1966

Land-Girl's Love Story, The (Berta Ruck), 1919

Landscape of the Heart (Elizabeth Renier), 1978

Language of the Heart (Elizabeth Cadell), 1962

Lanier Riddle, The (Dorothy Daniels), 1972

Lantern in the Night, A (Charlotte Lamb, as Sheila Holland), 1973

Lantern Lane (Warwick Deeping), 1921

Lantern-Light (Anne Duffield), 1933

Lap of Luxury, The (Berta Ruck), 1931

Lark Ascending (Mazo de la Roche), 1932

Lark in an Alien Sky (Rebecca Stratton), 1979

Lark in the Meadow, The (Essie Summers), 1959

Lark Shall Sing, The (Elizabeth Cadell), 1955

Larksbrook (Margaret Maddocks), 1962

Larrabee Heiress, The (Dorothy Daniels), 1972

Larry Vincent (Frances Parkinson Keyes), 1953

Lass a King Loved, The (Ursula Bloom, as Lozania Prole), 1975

Lass He Left Behind Him!, The (Mabel St. John, as Henry St. John Cooper), 1915

Lass That Loved a Sailor, The (Mabel St. John), 1915

Last Act (Jane Aiken Hodge), 1979

Last Act (Anne Rundle, as Joanne Marshall), 1976

Last April Fair (Betty Neels), 1980

Last Bouquet, The (Marjorie Bowen), 1932

Last Chance, The (Claire Lorrimer, as Patricia Robins), 1961

Last Confession, The (Hall Caine), 1892

Last Cotillion, The (Mary Linn Roby, as Georgina Grey), 1981

Last Enchantment, The (Mary Stewart), 1979

Last Love, The (Thomas B. Costain), 1963

Last Love of a King, The (Ursula Bloom, as Lozania Prole), 1974

Last Movement (Joan Aiken), 1977

Last of the Greenwood, The (Maureen Peters, as Sharon Whitby), 1975

Last of the Kintyres, The (Jean S. MacLeod, as Catherine Airlie), 1959

Last of the Laidlaws, The (Annie S. Swan), 1933

Last of the Mallorys, The (Kay Thorpe), 1968

Last of the Mansions, The (Dorothy Daniels), 1966

Last of the Stuarts, The (Victoria Holt, as Jean Plaidy), 1977

Last of the Tudors, The (Julia Fitzgerald, as Julia Hamilton), 1971

Last of Their Race, The (Annie S. Swan), 1911

Last Straw for Harriet (Elizabeth Cadell), 1947

Last Time, The (Robert Hichens), 1923

Last Tsarina, The (Ursula Bloom, as Lozania Prole), 1970

Last Year's Roses (Theresa Charles, as Fay Chandos), 1945

Last Year's Wife (A.M. Williamson), 1932

Lasting Lover, The (Ursula Bloom, as Sheila Burns), 1960

Latchkeys (Hebe Elsna, as Lyndon Snow), 1978

Late and Soon (E.M. Delafield), 1943

Late Clare Beame, The (Taylor Caldwell), 1963

Late Lark Singing, A (Naomi Jacob), 1952

Late Mrs. Fonsell, The (Velda Johnston), 1972

Late Mrs. Lane, The (Rona Randall), 1945

Late Rapture (Jane Arbor), 1978

Lattimer Legend, The (Dorothy Daniels), 1971

Lattimore Arch, The (Dorothy Daniels, as Angela Gray), 1971

Lattitude of Love, The (Rachel Lindsay), 1971

Laugh on Friday (Claire Lorrimer, as Patricia Robins), 1969

Laughing Bacchante, The (Dornford Yates), 1949

Laughing Cavalier (Maysie Greig), 1932

Laughing Cavalier, The (Baroness Orczy), 1914

Laughing Ghost, The (Dorothy Eden), 1943

Laughing House (Warwick Deeping), 1946

Laughing Lady, The (Ursula Bloom), 1936

Laughing Queen, The (L. Adams Beck, as E. Barrington), 1929

Laughing Stranger, The (Viña Delmar), 1953

Laughter and Love Remain (Countess Barcynska, as Oliver Sandys), 1962

Laughter in Cheyne Walk (Ursula Bloom), 1936

Laughter of Life, The (Madame Albanesi), 1908

Laura Sarelle (Marjorie Bowen, as Joseph Shearing), 1940

Laurel of Stonystream (Faith Baldwin), 1923

Laurell'd Captains (Marjorie Bowen, as George Preedy), 1935

Laurence, My Love (Denise Robins), 1968

Laurian Vale (Iris Bromige), 1952

Lavender's Love Story (Madame Albanesi, as Effie Rowlands), 1912

Lay On, Mac Duff (Charlotte Armstrong), 1942

Leading Lady (Daphne du Maurier), 1945

Leaf in the Storm (Anne Hampson), 1978

Leaf Turned Down, A (Madame Albanesi), 1936

League of the Triangle, The (May Wynne, as Lester Lurgan), 1911

Leap in the Dark (Rona Randall), 1956

Leap Year Girl, The (Berta Ruck), 1924

Leap Year Romance (Berta Ruck), 1957

Leap Year Love (Berta Ruck), 1957

Leaping Flame, The (Barbara Cartland), 1942

Learn to Laugh Again (Countess Barcynska, as Oliver Sandys), 1947

Leatherface (Baroness Orczy), 1916

Leave It to Nancy (Theresa Charles, as Fay Chandos), 1953

Leave Love to Itself (Charles Garvice), 1908

Leave Me My Love (Victoria Holt, as Eleanor Burford), 1953

Leave My Heart Alone (Claire Lorrimer, as Patricia Robins), 1951

Leaves Before the Storm (Ursula Bloom), 1937

Leaves from the Valley (Joanna Trollope), 1980

Leavetaking, The (Anna Gilbert), 1979

Led by Love (Charles Garvice), 1903

Legacy for a Doctor (Elizabeth Seifert), 1963

Legacy of Fear (Virginia Coffman), 1979

Legacy of Pride (Charity Blackstock, as Paula Allardyce), 1975

Legacy of the Past (Anne Mather), 1974

Legend, The (Evelyn Anthony), 1969

Legend in Green Velvet (Barbara Michaels, as Elizabeth Peters), 1976

Legend of Baverstock Manor, The (Nancy Buckingham), 1968

Legend of Death (Dorothy Daniels), 1980

Legend of Katmandu, The (Isobel Chace), 1969

Legend of Lexandros (Anne Mather), 1969

Legend of Roscano, The (Iris Danbury), 1971

Legend of the Loch (Alanna Knight), 1969

Legend of the Seventh Virgin, The (Victoria Holt), 1965

Legend of the Swans, The (Flora Kidd), 1974

Leila Vane's Burden (Madame Albanesi, as Effie Rowlands), 1911

Leland Legacy, The (Dorothy Daniels), 1965

Lemmings, The (Charity Blackstock), 1969

Lemon in the Backet (Charlotte Armstrong), 1967

Lenient God, The (Naomi Jacob), 1937

Leo Man, The (Rebecca Stratton), 1980

Leola Dale's Fortune (Charles Garvice), 1901

Leonie (Audrie Manley-Tucker), 1958

Leonora (Catherine Fellows), 1972

Leopard and the Lily, The (Marjorie Bowen), 1909

Leopard in the Snow (Anne Mather), 1974

Leopards and Spots (Naomi Jacob), 1942

Lesley Forrest, M.D. (Rachel Lindsay), 1962

Leslie's Loyalty (Charles Garvice), 1911

Lesson in Loving, A (Mollie Chappell), 1961

Lesson in Loving, A (Margaret Way), 1975

Lessons in Love (Barbara Cartland), 1974

Let Erin Remember (May Wynne), 1908

Let Love Come Last (Taylor Caldwell), 1948

Let Me Love (Denise Robins), 1979

Let the Storm Burst (Countess Barcynska), 1941

Let's All Be Happy (Countess Barcynska, as Oliver Sandys), 1952

Let's Do the Town (Faith Baldwin), 1942

Let's Kill Uncle (Rohan O'Grady), 1963

Letter from Don, A (Mary Burchell), 1950

Letter from Lydia, A (Mollie Chappell), 1974

Letter from Spain, A (Frances Parkinson Keyes), 1959

Letter to a Stranger (Elswyth Thane), 1954

Letter to My Love (Elizabeth Cadell), 1963

Letter to My Love, A (Theresa Charles, as Fay Chandos), 1942

Letters for a Spy (Alice Chetwynd Ley), 1970

Letters from Fleet Street (Countess Barcynska, as Marguerite Barclay), 1912

Letty (Clare Darcy), 1980

Letty (Norah Lofts), 1968

Letty and the Law (Faith Baldwin), 1940

Letty Lynton (Marie Belloc Lowndes), 1931

Lewis Rand (Mary Johnston), 1908

Libertine in Love (Caroline Courtney), 1982

Library Tree, The (Lilian Peake), 1972

Lie Quiet in Your Grave (Mary Linn Roby), 1970

Life—and Erica (Gilbert Frankau), 1924

Life and Love (Denise Robins), 1935

Life and Mary Ann (Catherine Cookson), 1962

Life Begins Tomorrow (Audrie Manley-Tucker), 1975

Life Everlasting, The (Marie Corelli), 1911

Life for Two (Jean S. MacLeod), 1936

Life He Led Her!, The (Mabel St. John), 1926

Life Isn't So Bad (May Edginton), 1929

Life Line, The (Madame Albanesi, as Effie Rowlands), 1924

Life Mask, The (A.M. Williamson), 1913

Life Steps In (Ruby M. Ayres), 1928

Lifeblood (Frank G. Slaughter), 1974

Life's a Game (Denise Robins), 1933

Life's Love, A (Madame Albanesi, as Effie Rowlands), 1911

Light from One Star (Netta Muskett), 1956

Light Heart, The (Elswyth Thane), 1947

Light in the Swamp, The (Velda Johnston), 1970

Light in the Tower (Jean S. MacLeod), 1971

Light in the Ward, The (Lucilla Andrews), 1965

Light in the Window, A (Margaret Lynn), 1967

Light in the Window, A (Mary Roberts Rinehart), 1948

Light of the Moon (Barbara Cartland), 1979

Light on Lucrezia (Victoria Holt, as Jean Plaidy), 1959

Light That Lies, The (George Barr McCutcheon), 1916

Light the Candles (Denise Robins), 1959

Light to the Heart, A (Barbara Cartland, as Barbara McCorquodale), 1962

Lighted Windows (Emilie Loring), 1930

Lighted Windows (Claire Ritchie), 1952

Lighthearted Quest, The (Ann Bridge), 1956

Lightning Conductor series (C.N. and A.M. Williamson)

Lightning Strikes Twice (Denise Robins), 1966

Lightning Tree, The (Joan Aiken), 1980

Lights and Shadows (Madame Albanesi, as Effie Rowlands), 1929

Lights of Love (Barbara Cartland, as Barbara McCorquodale), 1958

Like Summer Brave (Hebe Elsna), 1938

Lil, The Dancing Girl (Charles Garvice, as Caroline Hart)

Lilac Is for Sharing, The (Jane Blackmore), 1969

Lilamani (Maud Diver), 1911

Lilith (Victoria Holt, as Kathleen Kellow), 1954

Lilla (Marie Belloc Lowndes), 1916

Lillian Harley (Marian Cockrell), 1943

Lillian's Vow (Charles Garvice, as Caroline Hart)

Lily Christine (Michael Alren), 1928

Lily Hand, The (Edith Pargeter), 1965

Lily Pond, The (Dorothy Daniels), 1965

Lily-of-the-Valley (Ursula Bloom), 1938

Limelight for Jane (Mary Ann Gibbs, as Elizabeth Ford), 1970

Limmerston Hall (Hester W. Chapman), 1972

Linden Leaf, The (Jane Arbor), 1971

Lindy Lou (Sophia Cleugh), 1934

Link in the Chain, A (Hebe Elsna), 1975

Linked by Fate (Charles Garvice), 1905

Linnet Singing, A (Dorothy Eden), 1972

Linnie (Charles Garvice), 1908

Lion and the Sun, The (Irene Roberts), 1960

Lion Let Loose (Nigel Tranter), 1967

Lion of Delos, The (Anne Worboys), 1974

Lion of Justice, The (Victoria Holt, as Jean Plaidy), 1975

Lion of Mortimer, The (Juliet Dymoke), 1979

Lion of Trevarrock (Constance Heaven, as Constance Fecher), 1969

Lion of Venice (Margaret Rome), 1977

Lion Triumphant, The (Victoria Holt, as Philippa Carr), 1974

Lionors (Barbara Ferry Johnson), 1975

Lion's Legacy, The (Juliet Dymole), 1974

Lion's Mouse, The (C.N. and A.M. Williamson), 1919

Lion's Shadow, The (Isobel Chace, as Elizabeth Hunter), 1980

Lion's Skin, The (Rafael Sabatini), 1911

Lion-Tamer, The (E.M. Hull), 1928

Lips for a Stranger (Maysie Greig, as Jennifer Ames), 1949

Listen for the Whisperer (Phyllis A. Whitney), 1970

Listen, Please Listen (Naomi A. Hintze), 1972

Listen to Danger (Dorothy Eden), 1959

Listener, The (Taylor Caldwell), 1960

Listening Valley (D.E. Stevenson), 1944

Listening Walls, The (Margaret Millar), 1959

Little Adventure, The (Barbara Cartland), 1973

Little and Good (Ruby M. Ayres), 1940

Little and Good (Mabel St. John), 1918

Little Bit of Luck, A (Anne Betteridge), 1967

Little Brothers, The (Dorothy Salisbury Davis), 1973

Little Brown Girl (Theresa Charles, as Jan Tempest), 1940

Little Brown Mouse, A (Madame Albanesi), 1906

Little Doctor, The (Jean S. MacLeod), 1960

Little Dragon, The (Betty Neels), 1977

Little Goddess, The (Hebe Elsna), 1961

Little "Gutter Girl," The (Mabel St. John), 1919

Little Heiress, The (Frances Cowen), 1961

Little Imposter, The (Lilian Peake), 1976

Little Kit (Madame Albanesi, as Effie Rowlands), 1895

Little Lady, The (Madame Albanesi), 1937

Little Lady Charles (Madame Albanesi, as Effie Rowlands), 1899

Little Lady in Lodgings, The (Ruby M. Ayres), 1922

Little Less Than Kind, A (Charlotte Armstrong), 1963

Little Man, The (Ruby M. Ayres), 1931

Little Matron of the Cottage Hospital, The (Ursula Bloom, as Rachel Harvey), 1969

Little Millstones, The (Anne Worboys, as Annette Eyre), 1970

Little Miss Innocence (Mabel St. John), 1918

Little Miss Lancashire (Mabel St. John), 1921

Little Miss Millions (Mabel St. John), 1914

Little Mountebank (Leila Mackinlay), 1930

Little Nobody, The (Violet Winspear), 1972

Little Nurse, The (Ursula Bloom, as Mary Essex), 1967

Little Pardner (Eleanor H. Porter), 1926

Little Pretender, The (Barbara Cartland), 1951

Little Princess (Charles Garvice, as Caroline Hart)

Little Ships (Kathleen Norris), 1921

Little Sinner, The (Ruby M. Ayres), 1940

Little Sister (Mary Burchell), 1939

Little Sisters Don't Count (Maysie Greig), 1932

Little Stranger, The (Annie S. Swan), 1933

Little Tiger (Anthony Hope), 1925

Little Victoria, The (Ursula Bloom, as Lozania Prole), 1957

Little Wax Doll, The (Norah Lofts, as Peter

Curtis), 1970

Little We Know (Denise Robins), 1940

Little White Doves of Love (Barbara Cartland), 1980

Little White Nun, The (A.M. Williamson), 1903

Little Wig-Maker of Bread Street, The (Ursula Bloom, as Lozania Prole), 1959

Littl'st Lover, The (Ruby M. Ayres), 1917

Live Bait, The (Ethel M. Dell), 1932

Live Happily—Love Song (Ursula Bloom, as Sheila Burns), 1952

Lively Corpse, The (Margaret Millar), 1956

Lives of a Woman (Baroness von Hutten), 1935

Living Apart (Ruby M. Ayres), 1937

Living to Earn, A (D.A. Ponsonby), 1961

Living with Adam (Anne Mather), 1972

Living with Adam (Netta Muskett), 1949

Living with Paula (Hebe Elsna, as Laura Conway), 1972

Liz o' Loomland (Mabel St. John), 1917

Lizbeth Rose (Mabel St. John), 1927

Lizzie (Shirley Jackson), 1957

Lizzie Borden (Marie Belloc Lowndes), 1939

Lo, Michael! (Grace Livingston Hill), 1913

Loaded Stick, The (Naomi Jacob), 1934

Loch, The (Janet Caird), 1968

Lodestone for Luck (Claire Ritchie), 1980

Lodger, The (Marie Belloc Lowndes), 1913

Lodger in His Own Home, A (Mabel St. John, as Henry St. John Cooper), 1920

Log of a Naval Officer's Wife, The (Ursula Bloom), 1932

Lombard Cavalcade, The (Virginia Coffman), 1982

London and Paris (Daphne du Maurier), 1945

London, Here I Come (Maysie Greig), 1951

London Venture, The (Michael Arlen), 1920

Londoners, The (Robert Hichens), 1898

Lone Point (Grace Livingston Hill), 1898

Lonely Bride, The (Anne Duffield), 1947

Lonely Doctor, The (Faith Baldwin), 1964

Lonely Dreamer, The (Hebe Elsna), 1961

Lonely Farrow, The (Jean S. MacLeod), 1940

Lonely Furrow (Maud Diver), 1923

Lonely Furrow, The (Norah Lofts), 1976

Lonely House, The (Jane Blackmore), 1957

Lonely House, The (Marie Belloc Lowndes), 1920

Lonely Little Lucy (Mabel St. John), 1921

Lonely Man, The (Faith Baldwin), 1964

Lonely Man, The (Gilbert Frankau), 1932

Lonely Night (Jane Blackmore), 1969

Lonely One, The (Claire Rayner, as Sheila Brandon), 1965

Lonely Parade (Fannie Hurst), 1942

Lonely Place, The (Dorothy Daniels), 1978

Lonely Quest (Claire Lorrimer, as Patricia Robins), 1959

Lonely Road, The (Jeffery Farnol), 1938

Lonely Shadow (Ursula Bloom), 1942

Lonely Strangers, The (Charity Blackstock), 1972

Lonesome Road, The (Theresa Charles, as Jan Tempest), 1966

Long Acre (Claire Rayner), 1978

Long and Living Shadow, The (Daoma Winston), 1968

Long Arm of the Prince, The (Evelyn Berckman), 1968

Long Barnaby (Phyllis Hastings), 1961

Long Coffin, The (Nigel Tranter), 1956

Long Corridor, The (Catherine Cookson), 1965

Long Dance of Love, The (Anne Betteridge), 1963

Long Division (Hester W. Chapman), 1943

Long, Hot Days, The (Maynah Lewis), 1966

Long Lane to Happiness, The (Ruby M. Ayres), 1915

Long Live the King! (Mary Roberts Rinehart), 1918

Long, Long Wooing, The (Mabel St. John), 1927

Long Masquerade, The (Madeleine Brent), 1981

Long Road, The (Netta Muskett), 1951

Long Roll, The (Mary Johnston), 1911

Long Shadow, The (Denise Robins), 1954

Long Shadows (Naomi Jacob), 1964

Long Summer Days (R.F. Delderfield), 1974

Long Surrender, The (Charlotte Lamb), 1978

Long Time Ago, A (Margaret Kennedy), 1932

Long Time to Hate, A (Willo Davis Roberts), 1982

Long Wait, The (Claire Lorrimer, as Patricia Robins), 1962

Long Way from Home, A (Rosamunde Pilcher, as Jane Fraser), 1963

Long Way Home, The (Theresa Charles, as Jan Tempest), 1943

Long Week-End, A (Margaret Kennedy), 1927

Longest Pleasure, The (Christopher Nicole), 1970

Longing for Love (Mabel St. John), 1925

Look, Listen, and Love (Barbara Cartland),

1977
Look of Innocence, The (Anna Gilbert), 1975
Look Out for Liza (Faith Baldwin), 1950
Look to the Spring (Ruby M. Ayres), 1932
Look to the Stars (Emilie Loring), 1957
Looking-Glass (Virginia Coffman), 1979
Loom of Fate, The (Charles Garvice), 1913
Loom of Love (Maureen Peters, as Belinda Grey), 1979
Loose Ladies (Viña Delmar), 1929
Lorena (Frank G. Slaughter), 1959
Lord and Mary Ann, The (Catherine Cookson), 1956
Lord and the Gypsy, The (Patricia Veryan), 1978
Lord Gilmore's Bride (Sheila Walsh), 1979
Lord John in New York (C.N. and A.M. Williamson), 1918
Lord Loveland Discovers America (C.N. and A.M. Williamson), 1910
Lord of Greenwich, The (Juliet Dymoke), 1980
Lord of Himself (Charles Garvice), 1911
Lord of La Pampa (Kay Thorpe), 1977
Lord of Little Langton, The (G.B. Burgin), 1924
Lord of Ravensley (Constance Heaven), 1978
Lord of Sin (Christopher Nicole), 1980
Lord of the Golden Fan (Christopher Nicole), 1973
Lord of the High Lonesome (Janet Dailey), 1980
Lord of the High Valley (Margaret Way), 1980
Lord of the Hollow Dark (Russell Kirk), 1979
Lord of the Isles (Henrietta Reid), 1981
Lord of the Manor (Jane Blackmore), 1975
Lord of Zaracus (Anne Mather), 1970
Lord Ravenscar's Revenge (Barbara Cartland), 1978
Lord Satan (Janet Louise Roberts, as Louisa Bronte), 1972
Lord Sin (Constance Gluyas), 1980
Lord Stephen's Lady (Janet Louise Roberts, as Janette Radcliffe), 1976
Lord Tony's Wife (Baroness Orczy), 1917
Lord Vanity (Samuel Shellabarger), 1953
Lordly One, The (Sara Seale), 1952
Lords of Lancaster, The (Pamela Bennetts), 1973
Lords of Misrule (Nigel Tranter), 1976
Lordship of Love, The (Baroness von Hutten), 1909
Loren's Baby (Anne Mather), 1978
Lorimer series (Anne Betteridge, as Anne

Melville)
Loring Mystery, The (Jeffery Farnol), 1925
Lorna Neale (Lady Miles), 1932
Lorrie (Charles Garvice), 1899
Lose Money—Lose Friends! (Mabel St. John, as Henry St. John Cooper), 1925
Lost Children (Edith Pargeter), 1951
Lost Colony, The (Edison Marshall), 1964
Lost Ecstasy (Mary Roberts Rinehart), 1927
Lost Enchantment (Barbara Cartland), 1972
Lost Garden The (Jane Aiken Hodge), 1982
Lost General, The (Elswyth Thane), 1953
Lost Heritage (Rebecca Stratton), 1978
Lost Ideal, A (Annie S. Swan), 1894
Lost Island (Phyllis A. Whitney), 1970
Lost King, The (Rafael Sabatini), 1937
Lost Lake (Russell Kirk), 1966
Lost Laughter (Barbara Cartland), 1980
Lost Lotus (Anne Rundle), 1972
Lost Love (Barbara Cartland), 1970
Lost Love, Last Love (Rosemary Rogers), 1980
Lost Madonna, The (Isabelle Holland), 1981
Lost Melody (Audrie Manley-Tucker), 1959
Lost Message, The (Grace Livingston Hill), 1938
Lost One, The (Frances Cowen), 1977
Lost Ones, The (Norah Lofts), 1969
Lost Property (Ruby M. Ayres), 1943
Lost Queen, the (Norah Lofts), 1969
Lost Summer (Theresa Charles, as Fay Chandos), 1948
Lost Sunrise (Kathleen Norris), 1939
Lotteries, The (Daoma Winston), 1980
Lottery, The (Shirley Jackson), 1949
Lottery for Matthew Devlin, The (Margaret Rome), 1968
Louis, The Well-Beloved (Victoria Holt, as Jean Plaidy), 1959
Louise, The Restless (Katheryn Kimbrough), 1978
Lovable Stranger (Anne Duffield), 1949
Love (Elizabeth), 1925
Love Almost Lost, A (Madame Albanesi, as Effie Rowlands), 1905
Love Alters Not (Flora Kidd), 1967
Love among the Ruins (Warwick Deeping), 1904
Love and a Lie (Ruby M. Ayres), 1923
Love and a Lie (Charles Garvice)
Love and a Rich Girl (Berta Ruck), 1960
Love and Apron-Strings (Berta Ruck), 1949
Love—and Carol (Mrs. Patrick MacGill), 1925
Love and Deborah (Netta Muskett), 1963

Love and Desire and Hate (Denise Robins), 1969

Love and Doctor Benedict (Joyce Dingwell), 1978

Love and Dr. Forrest (Rachel Lindsay), 1971

Love and Dr. Maynard (Rona Randall), 1959

Love and Hatred (Marie Belloc Lowndes), 1917

Love and Honour (Christopher Nicole, as Leslie Arlen), 1980

Love and Let Me Go (Maysie Greig), 1935

Love and Linda (Barbara Cartland), 1976

Love and Louisa (Madame Albanesi), 1902

Love and Lucy Brown (Joyce Dingwell), 1975

Love and Lucy Granger (Rachel Lindsay), 1967

Love and Mary Ann (Catherine Cookson), 1962

Love and No Marriage (Rachel Lindsay, as Roberta Leigh), 1980

Love and the Kentish Maid (Betty Beaty), 1971

Love and the Loathsome Leopard (Barbara Cartland), 1977

Love and the Locusts (G.B. Burgin), 1922

Love—and the Philosopher (Marie Corelli), 1923

Love and the S.S. Beatrice (Elisabeth Beresford), 1972

Love and the Spy (C.N. and A.M. Williamson), 1908

Love at a Festival (Berta Ruck), 1951

Love at Forty (Barbara Cartland), 1977

Love Battle (Violet Winspear), 1977

Love Builds a House (Claire Ritchie), 1950

Love Calls Me Home (Hebe Elsna, as Laura Conway), 1952

Love Calls the Doctor (Elizabeth Seifert), 1958

Love Calls the Tune (Kathleen Norris), 1944

Love Came Laughing (Emilie Loring), 1949

Love Campaign, The (Suzanne Ebel), 1965

Love Cannot Die (Claire Lorrimer, as Patricia Robins), 1955

Love Child, The (Victoria Holt, as Eleanor Burford), 1950

Love Climbs In (Barbara Cartland), 1979

Love Comedy, A (Charles Garvice), 1908

Love Comes Again Later (Berta Ruck), 1938

Love Comes to Larkswood (Irene Roberts), 1968

Love Comes to Mary (Ruby M. Ayres), 1932

Love Comes Unseen (Ruby M. Ayres), 1943

Love Decided (Charles Garvice), 1904

Love Deferred (Anne Duffield), 1951

Love Dismayed (May Wynne), 1942

Love Eternal (H. Rider Haggard), 1918

Love for a Rogue (Glenna Finley), 1976

Love for Love (Madame Albanesi, as Effie Rowlands), 1910

Love for Sale (Barbara Cartland), 1980

Love Forbidden, A (Jane Blackmore), 1974

Love Forbidden (Barbara Cartland, as Barbara McCorquodale), 1957

Love Game (Denise Robins), 1936

Love Gives Itself (Annie S. Swan), 1915

Love Goes South (Leila Mackinlay), 1935

Love Grown Cold (Annie S. Swan), 1902

Love Has His Way (Barbara Cartland), 1980

Love Has No Resurrection (E.M. Delafield), 1939

Love Has No Secrets (Ursula Bloom, as Rachel Harvey), 1972

Love Has Two Faces (Hettie Grimstead), 1962

Love Has Two Faces (Maynah Lewis), 1981

Love Hath an Island (Anne Hampson), 1970

Love Hath an Island (Denise Robins), 1950

Love Her, She's Yours (Daoma Winston), 1963

Love Him or Leave Him (Mary Burchell), 1950

Love Holds the Cards (Barbara Cartland), 1965

Love, Honour, and Obey (Maysie Greig), 1933

Love in a Cloud (Lucy Walker), 1960

Love in a Far Country (Maysie Greig, as Jennifer Ames), 1960

Love in a Mist (Charlotte Lamb, as Sheila Holland), 1971

Love in a Rainy Country (Anne Betteridge), 1969

Love in a Snare (Charles Garvice), 1912

Love in a Stranger's Arms (Violet Winspear), 1977

Love in Amber (Netta Muskett), 1942

Love in Apron Strings (Elizabeth Hoy), 1933

Love in Danger (Glenna Finley), 1973

Love in Disguise (Rachel Lindsay), 1975

Love in Hiding (Barbara Cartland), 1959

Love in Pity (Barbara Cartland), 1977

Love in Store (Rachel Lindsay, as Roberta Leigh), 1978

Love in the Afternoon (Rose Burghley), 1959

Love in the Clouds (Barbara Cartland), 1979

Love in the Dark (Barbara Cartland), 1979

Love in the East (Maysie Greig, as Jennifer Ames), 1960

Love in the Moon (Barbara Cartland), 1980

Love Is a Dangerous Game (Marjorie Lewty), 1980

Love Is a Flame (Marie Belloc Lowndes), 1932

Love Is a Flower (Countess Barcynska, as Oliver Sandys), 1938

Love Is a Frenzy (Charlotte Lamb), 1979

Love Is a Gamble (Maysie Greig, as Jennifer Ames), 1954

Love Is a Gambler (Maysie Greig), 1958

Love Is a Lady (Countess Barcynska), 1945

Love Is a Thief (Maysie Greig), 1959

Love Is an Eagle (Barbara Cartland), 1951

Love Is Contraband (Barbara Cartland), 1968

Love Is Dangerous (Barbara Cartland, as Barbara McCorquodale), 1963

Love Is Enough (Denise Robins), 1941

Love Is Everything (Ursula Bloom), 1933

Love Is Fire (Flora Kidd), 1971

Love Is Innocent (Barbara Cartland), 1975

Love Is Mine (Barbara Cartland, as Barbara McCorquodale), 1952

Love Is My Reason (Mary Burchell), 1957

Love Is My Reason (Suzanne Ebel, as Suzanne Goodwin), 1982

Love Is So Blind (Ruby M. Ayres), 1933

Love Is the Enemy (Barbara Cartland), 1952

Love Is the Honey (Violet Winspear), 1980

Love Itself (Elinor Elyn), 1924

Love Leaves at Midnight (Barbara Cartland), 1978

Love Letter (Kate Norway, as Hilary Neal), 1963

Love Lies North (Glenna Finley), 1972

Love Like Ours, A (Denise Robins), 1969

Love Locked In (Barbara Cartland), 1977

Love, Lords, and Lady-Birds (Barbara Cartland), 1978

Love Made the Choice (Mary Burchell), 1942

Love Maggy (Countess Barcynska), 1918

Love Match, A (Madame Albanesi, as Effie Rowlands), 1912

Love Match, The (Hebe Elsna), 1956

Love Match, The (Catherine Fellows), 1977

Love Match (Rachel Lindsay, as Roberta Leigh), 1980

Love Me (Maysie Greig), 1971

Love Me for Ever (Barbara Cartland), 1953

Love Me for Ever (Hebe Elsna, as Lyndon Snow), 1955

Love Me Forever (Patricia Matthews), 1977

Love Me No More! (Denise Robins), 1948

Love Me To-morrow (Ursula Bloom, as Sheila Burns), 1952

Love Me Tomorrow (Claire Lorrimer, as Patricia Robins), 1966

Love Must Wait (Claire Lorrimer, as Patricia Robins), 1958

Love Needs Telling (Mabel St. John), 1926

Love Never Dies (Countess Barcynska), 1943

Love of a Life Time (Charles Garvice)

Love of His Life, The (Madame Albanesi, as Effie Rowlands), 1912

Love of Julie Borel, The (Kathleen Norris), 1931

Love of Long Ago, The (Marie Corelli), 1920

Love of Lucifer, The (Daoma Winston), 1970

Love of Robert Dennison, The (Ruby M. Ayres), 1921

Love of the Foolish Angel, The (Helen Beauclerk), 1929

Love of the Lion, The (Dorothy Daniels, as Angela Gray), 1980

Love, Old and New (Ursula Bloom), 1933

Love on a Shoestring (Leila Mackinlay), 1958

Love on Dark Wings (Maysie Greig, as Jennifer Ames), 1957

Love on Ice (Petra Sawley), 1967

Love on Second Thoughts (Berta Ruck), 1936

Love on the Run (Barbara Cartland, as Barbara McCorquodale), 1965

Love Pirate, The (Barbara Cartland), 1977

Love Pirate, The (C.N. and A.M. Williamson), 1913

Love Play (Rosemary Rogers), 1981

Love Remembered (Elisabeth Beresford), 1970

Love So Young (Denise Robins), 1945

Love Song (Julia Fitzgerald, as Julia Watson), 1981

Love Song (Janet Louise Roberts), 1970

Love Song in Springtime, A (Audrie Manley-Tucker), 1960

Love Song of the Sea (Irene Roberts), 1960

Love, Spread Your Wings (Audrie Manley-Tucker), 1967

Love Stories of India (Edison Marshall), 1950

Love Story of Dr. Duke, The (Ursula Bloom, as Mary Essex), 1960

Love Story of Nurse Julie, The (Ursula Bloom, as Rachel Harvey), 1975

Love Talker, The (Barbara Michaels, as Elizabeth Peters), 1980

Love That Divided (Mabel St. John, as Henry St. John Cooper), 1932

Love That Follows, The (Claire Ritchie), 1966

Love That Is Stronger Than Life, The (Anne Maybury), 1932

Love That Lasts, The (G.B. Burgin), 1913

Love That Lasts, The (Theresa Charles, as

Leslie Lance), 1974

Love That Lives, The (Madame Albanesi), 1937

Love, The Adventurous (Charles Garvice), 1917

Love, The Magician (Suzanne Ebel), 1956

Love, The Master Key (Annie S. Swan), 1905

Love the Prodigal (Annie S. Swan), 1929

Love, The Tyrant (Charles Garvice), 1905

Love Theme, The (Margaret Way), 1974

Love They Must (Jean Francis Webb), 1933

Love This Enemy (Kathryn Blair), 1958

Love This Stranger (Kathryn Blair, as Rosalind Brett), 1951

Love to the Rescue (Barbara Cartland), 1967

Love Token (Roberta Gellis, as Priscilla Hamilton), 1979

Love Trap, The (Viña Delmar), 1949

Love Trap, The (Evadne Price), 1958

Love Triumphant (Caroline Courtney), 1980

Love Triumphant (Anne Maybury), 1932

Love under Fire (Barbara Cartland), 1960

Love Unlocks the Door (Annie S. Swan), 1907

Love Unmasked (Caroline Courtney), 1979

Love Was a Jest (Denise Robins), 1929

Love While You Wait (Theresa Charles, as Jan Tempest), 1944

Love Will Lend Wings (Claire Ritchie), 1957

Love Will Win (Maysie Greig), 1969

Love Wins (Madame Albanesi, as Effie Rowlands), 1912

Love with Honor (Emilie Loring), 1969

Love Without Wings (Ruby M. Ayres), 1953

Love-at-Arms (Rafael Sabatini), 1907

Lovechild, The (Julia Fitzgerald, as Julia Watson), 1967

Love-Child, The (Victoria Holt, as Philippa Carr), 1978

Loved and the Cherished, The (Audrie Manley-Tucker), 1964

Loved and the Feared, The (Violet Winspear), 1977

Loved for Her Money (Mabel St. John), 1927

Love-Girl (May Edginton), 1931

Love-Hater, The (Berta Ruck), 1930

Love-in-a-Mist (Madame Albanesi), 1907

Loveless Marriage, A (Ruby M. Ayres), 1921

Lovely Clay (Maysie Greig), 1930

Lovely Day, The (Hettie Grimstead), 1970

Lovely Destiny (Anne Maybury), 1936

Lovely, Though Late (Theresa Charles, as Jan Tempest), 1946

Lovely Wanton, The (Constance Heaven, as Constance Fecher), 1977

Lover, The (Daphne du Maurier), 1961

Lover Come Lonely (Hettie Grimstead, as Marsha Manning), 1965

Lover on Loan, A (Mrs. Patrick MacGill), 1923

Lover in Rags, A (Mabel St. John, as Henry St. John Cooper), 1924

Lover Who Died, The (Ruby M. Ayres), 1922

Lovers (Ruby M. Ayres) , 1929

Lovers, The (Kathleen Winsor), 1952

Lovers All Untrue (Norah Lofts), 1970

Lovers and Outlaws (Christopher Nicole), 1982

Lover's Fate (Anthony Hope), 1894

Lovers in Darkness (Hebe Elsna, as Vicky Lancaster), 1955

Lovers in Paradise (Barbara Cartland), 1978

Lovers in the Dark (Maysie Greig, as Jennifer Ames), 1946

Lovers in Waiting (Hebe Elsna, as Laura Conway), 1962

Lovers' Knots (Marjorie Bowen), 1912

Lovers' Meeting (Eleanor Farnes), 1962

Lovers Meeting (Mollie Hardwick), 1979

Lovers' Meeting (Lady Eleanor Smith), 1940

Lovers of Janine (Denise Robins), 1931

Lovers of Yvonne, The (Rafael Sabatini), 1902

Lover's Staff (Hebe Elsna, as Vicky Lancaster), 1954

Lovers under the Sun (Maysie Greig), 1954

Lover's Vows (Joan Smith), 1981

Love's a Puzzle (Faith Baldwin), 1933

Love's a Stage (Laura London), 1981

Love's Agony (Violet Winspear), 1981

Love's Avenging Heart (Patricia Matthews), 1977

Love's Barrier (Annie S. Swan), 1910

Love's Blindness (Elinor Glyn), 1926

Love's Bold Journey (Patricia Matthews), 1980

Love's Bright Flame (Charlotte Lamb, as Sheila Holland), 1978

Love's Cousin (Lady Miles), 1927

Love's Cruel Whim (Madame Albanesi, as Effie Rowlands)

Love's Daring Dream (Patricia Matthews), 1978

Love's Dark Shadow (Petra Sawley), 1970

Love's Defiance (Mrs. Patrick MacGill), 1926

Love's Dilemma (Charles Garvice), 1902

Love's Duet (Patricia Veryan), 1979

Love's Fire (Madame Albanesi, as Effie Rowlands), 1911

Love's Golden Destiny (Patricia Matthews),

1979

Love's Greatest Gift (Madame Albanesi, as Effie Rowlands), 1906

Love's Harvest (Madame Albanesi, as Effie Rowlands), 1911

Love's Hidden Fire (Glenna Finley), 1971

Love's Hour (Elinor Glyn), 1932

Love's Last Reward (Countess Barcynska), 1920

Love's Logic (Anthony Hope), 1908

Love's Magic Moment (Patricia Matthews), 1979

Love's Magic Spell (Glenna Finley), 1974

Love's Mask (Madame Albanesi, as Effie Rowlands), 1913

Love's Masquerade (Caroline Courtney), 1981

Love's Memory (Anne Duffield), 1936

Love's Miracle (Annie S. Swan), 1910

Loves of a Virgin Princess, The (Ursula Bloom, as Lozania Prole), 1968

Loves of an Actress, The (Baroness von Hutten), 1929

Loves of Lucrezia, The (Denise Robins, as Francesca Wright), 1953

Love's Pagan Heart (Patricia Matthews), 1978

Love's Penalty (May Wynne), 1927

Love's Playthings (Ursula Bloom), 1932

Love's Prisoner (Hebe Elsna, as Laura Conway), 1954

Love's Prisoner (Violet Winspear), 1964

Love's Puppet (Henrietta Reid), 1976

Love's Raging Tide (Patricia Matthews), 1980

Love's Revenge (Marie Belloc Lowndes), 1929

Love's Rugged Path (Charles Garvice, as Caroline Hart)

Love's Second Chance (Hebe Elsna, as Vicky Lancaster), 1962

Love's Sweet Agony (Patricia Matthews), 1980

Love's Temptation (Glenna Finley), 1979

Love's Victory (Denise Robins), 1933

Love's Waif (Mabel St. John, as Henry St. John Cooper), 1921

Love's Way (Joan Smith), 1982

Love's Wildest Promise (Patricia Matthews), 1977

Love's Wilful Call (Mary Linn Roby), 1981

Love's Young Dream (Madame Albanesi, as Effie Rowlands), 1914

Love-Story of Aliette Brunton, The (Gilbert Frankau), 1922

Loving (Danielle Steel), 1980

Loving and Giving (Eleanor Farnes), 1968

Loving and Giving (Denise Robins), 1965

Loving Heart, The (Mollie Chappell), 1977

Loving Heart, The (Susan Inglis), 1954

Loving Heart, The (Lucy Walker), 1960

Loving Is Different (Hebe Elsna, as Laura Conway), 1964

Loving Is Giving (Mary Burchell), 1956

Loving Meddler, The (Rosamond Marshall), 1954

Loving Partnership (Jean Marsh), 1978

Loving Sands, Deadly Sands (Charity Blackstock, as Charlotte Keppel), 1975

Loving Slave, The (Margaret Pargeter), 1981

Loving Spirit, The (Daphne du Maurier), 1931

Loving You Always (Hebe Elsna, as Laura Conway), 1953

Low Country Liar (Janet Dailey), 1979

Lower Than Vermin (Dornford Yates), 1950

Loyal Defence, A (Madame Albanesi, as Effie Rowlands), 1932

Loyal in All (Mary Burchell), 1957

Loyal Lady (Sophia Cleugh), 1932

Loyal Man's Love, A (Madame Albanesi, as Effie Rowlands), 1910

Loyalty (Madame Albanesi), 1930

Lucifer and the Angel (Barbara Cartland), 1980

Lucifer Cove series (Virginia Coffman)

Lucifer's Angel (Violet Winspear), 1961

Lucile Cléry (Marjorie Bowen, as Joseph Shearing), 1932

Lucille (Charles Garvice)

Lucinda (Anthony Hope), 1920

Lucinda Marries the Doctor (Elizabeth Seifert), 1953

Luck of Penrayne, The (May Wynne), 1937

Luck of the Livingstones, The (Annie S. Swan), 1932

Luckiest Lady, The (Ruby M. Ayres), 1927

Lucky in Love (Berta Ruck), 1924

Lucky Lawrences, The (Kathleen Norris), 1930

Lucky Number, The (Ethel M. Dell), 1920

Lucky One, The (Marjorie Lewty), 1961

Lucretia Lombard (Kathleen Norris), 1922

Lucrezia Borgia (Victoria Holt, as Jean Plaidy), 1976

Lucy (Hester W. Chapman), 1965

Lucy Carmichael (Margaret Kennedy), 1951

Lucy in London (Hettie Grimstead, as Marsha Manning), 1964

Lucy Lamb (Sara Seale), 1958

Lucy's Cottage (Pamela Bennetts), 1981

Lummox (Fannie Hurst), 1923

Lure of Eagles (Anne Mather), 1979
Lute Player, The (Norah Lofts), 1951
Luxury Husband, The (Maysie Greig), 1928
Lydia (Clare Darcy), 1973
Lydian Inheritance, The (Iris Bromige), 1966
Lyndley Waters (Marjorie Bowen, as George Preedy), 1942
Lynmara Legacy, The (Catherine Gaskin), 1975
Lyonesse Abbey (Jill Tattersall), 1968
Lyonhurst (Rona Randall), 1977
Lyons Mail, The (May Wynne), 1917
Lyon's Share, A (Janet Dailey), 1977
Lyra, My Love (Theresa Charles, as Jan Tempest), 1969
Lysbeth (H. Rider Haggard), 1901

M.D., The (Willo Davis Roberts), 1972
Mabel St. John's Schooldays (Mabel St. John, as Henry St. John Cooper), 1921
Macbeth the King (Nigel Tranter), 1978
MacGregor's Gathering (Nigel Tranter), 1957
Macleod's Wife (Annie S. Swan), 1924
Maclure Mystery, The (Annie S. Swan), 1932
MacLyon (Lolah Burford), 1974
Macomber Menace, The (Willo Davis Roberts), 1979
Mad Barbara (Warwick Deeping), 1908
Mad for Dress! (Mabel St. John), 1921
Mad Is the Heart (Denise Robins), 1963
Madalena (Sheila Walsh), 1976
Madam, Will You Talk? (Mary Stewart), 1955
Madam, You Must Die (Charity Blackstock, as Charlotte Keppel), 1974
Madame Adastra (Countess Barcynska, as Oliver Sandys), 1964
Madame Castel's Lodger (Frances Parkinson Keyes), 1962
Madame Claire (Susan Ertz), 1923
Madame du Barry (Victoria Holt, as Ellalice Tate), 1959
Madame Fears the Dark (Margaret Irwin), 1935
Madame Juno (Leila Mackinlay), 1931
Madame Tudor (Constance Gluyas), 1979
Madame Serpent (Victoria Holt, as Jean Plaidy), 1951
Maddalena (Pamela Hill), 1963
Madderleys Married, The (Theresa Charles, as Jan Tempest), 1963
Made in Heaven (Hebe Elsna, as Lyndon Snow), 1952

Made Marriage, The (Henrietta Reid), 1971
Made to Marry (Theresa Charles, as Fay Chandos), 1944
Madeleine (Catherine Gavin), 1957
Madge o' the Mill (Mabel St. John, as Henry St. John Cooper), 1921
Madness of Love, The (Madame Albanesi, as Effie Rowlands), 1911
Madness of Love (Charles Garvice, as Caroline Hart)
Madonna Creek Witch, The (Jacqueline La Tourrette), 1973
Madonna of the Seven Hills (Victoria Holt, as Jean Plaidy), 1958
Madselin (Norah Lofts), 1969
Mag Pye (Baroness von Hutten) , 1917
Magie Darling (Mabel St. John), 1915
Maggie, Her Marriage (Taylor Caldwell), 1953
Maggie of Marley's Mill (Mabel St. John), 1926
Maggie Rowan (Catherine Cookson), 1954
Maggy (Sara Seale), 1959
Magic and Mary Rose (Faith Baldwin), 1924
Magic City, The (Hettie Grimstead, as Marsha Mannning), 1973
Magic for Marigold (L.M. Montgomery), 1929
Magic Garden, The (Gene Stratton Porter), 1927
Magic in Maoriland (Ivy Preston), 1962
Magic Lantern (Lady Eleanor Smith), 1944
Magic Moment (Mary Linn Roby, as Pamela D' Arcy), 1980
Magic of Living, The (Betty Neels), 1974
Magic of Love, The (Barbara Cartland), 1977
Magic of the Moon (Hettie Grimstead, as Marsha Manning), 1961
Magic or Mirage (Barbara Cartland), 1978
Magic Place, A (Iris Bromige), 1971
Magic Ring, The (Dorothy Daniels), 1978
Magic Scalpel of Dr. Farrer, The (Adeline McElfresh), 1965
Magic Symphony (Eleanor Farnes), 1952
Magnificent Courtesan, The (Ursula Bloom, as Lozania Prole), 1950
Magnificent Marriage, The (Barbara Cartland), 1974
Magnolia Room, The (Anne Worboys, as Annette Eyre), 1972
Mahatma and the Hare, The (H. Rider Haggard), 1911
Mahdi, The (Hall Caine), 1894
Mahound, The (Lance Horner), 1969
Maid Called Wanton, A (Maureen Peters, as

Levanah Lloyd), 1981

Maid of Brittany (May Wynne), 1906

Maid of Judah, The (Maureen Peters), 1973

Maid of Stonystream, The (Faith Baldwin), 1924

Maid of the Isles, A (Annie S. Swan), 1924

Maida (Charles Garvice), 1901

Maiden Castle (Charlotte Lamb, as Sheila Holland), 1978

Maiden Flight (Betty Beaty), 1956

Maiden Stakes (Dornford Yates), 1929

Maiden Voyage (Kathleen Norris), 1934

Mail Order Bride (Maureen Peters, as Levanah Lloyd), 1981

Maisie's Romance (Madame Albanesi), 1910

Maitland of Laurieston (Annie S. Swan), 1890

Maiwa's Revenge (H. Rider Haggard), 1888

Make Believe Wife (Kathleen Norris), 1947

Make Me a Murderer (Gwendoline Butler), 1961

Make the Man Notice You (Maysie Greig, as Jennifer Ames), 1940

Make Way for Tomorrow (Gloria Bevan), 1971

Make Way for Tomorrow (Maynah Lewis), 1966

Make-Believe (Faith Baldwin), 1930

Making of a Lover, The (Ruby M. Ayres), 1921

Making of a Man, The (Ruby M. Ayres), 1915

Malady in Madeira, The (Ann Bridge), 1969

Malaspiga Exit, The (Evelyn Anthony), 1974

Malice of Men, The (Warwick Deeping), 1939

Mallen series (Catherine Cookson)

Mallion's Pride (Carola Salisbury) , 1975

Malvie Inheritance, The (Pamela Hill), 1973

Malys Rockell (May Wynne), 1934

Mammon (P.C. Wren) , 1930

Mammon of Righteousness, The (P.C. Wren), 1930

Mammon's Daughter (Nigel Tranter), 1939

Mam'zelle Guillotine (Baroness Orczy), 1940

Man Always Pays (Leila Mackinlay), 1940

Man and His Model, A (Anthony Hope)

Man and Maid (Elinor Glyn), 1922

Man and the Moment, The (Elinor Glyn), 1914

Man—and Waif (Theresa Charles, as Jan Tempest), 1938

Man at Kambala, The (Kay Thorpe), 1973

Man at Key West (Katrina Britt), 1982

Man at Mulera, The (Kathryn Blair), 1959

Man at the Gate, The (Madame Albanesi, as Effie Rowlands), 1911

Man at the Helm, The (Henrietta Reid), 1975

Man at the Manor, The (Olga Sinclair), 1967

Man Behind, The (G.B. Burgin), 1923

Man Behind the Curtain, The (Nigel Tranter), 1959

Man Between, The (Denise Robins), 1926

Man Called Cameron, A (Margaret Pargeter), 1978

Man Called Masters, A (Lucy Walker), 1965

Man for Always, A (Nancy Bucking, as Nancy John), 1981

Man for Margaret, A (Theresa Charles, as Fay Chandos), 1945

Man for Me, The (Theresa Charles), 1965

Man Friday (Ruby M. Ayres), 1943

Man from Bahl Bahla, The (Margaret Way), 1971

Man from Brodney's, The (George Barr McCutcheon), 1908

Man from Ceylon, The (Ruby M. Ayres), 1950

Man from Dahomey, The (Frank Yerby), 1971

Man from Outback, The (Lucy Walker), 1964

Man from Singapore, The (Mary Howard), 1946

Man from the Mists, A (Mary Elgin), 1965

Man from the Sea (Susan Barrie, as Pamela Kent), 1968

Man from the Valley, The (Joyce Dingwell), 1966

Man from the West, A (Madame Albanesi, as Effie Rowlands), 1927

Man from Tripoli, The (Kay Thorpe), 1979

Man from Turkey, The (G.B. Burgin), 1921

Man from Yesterday, The (Dorothy Daniels), 1970

Man Himself, The (A.M. Williamson), 1925

Man in a Box (Kay Thorpe), 1972

Man in a Million (Rachel Lindsay, as Roberta Leigh), 1975

Man in Authority, The (Jean S. MacLeod), 1954

Man in Chains (Warwick Deeping), 1953

Man in Charge (Lilian Peake), 1973

Man in Grey, The (Lady Eleanor Smith), 1941

Man in Her Life, The (Ruby M. Ayres), 1935

Man in Lower Ten, The (Mary Roberts Rinehart), 1909

Man in the Corner, The (G.B. Burgin), 1939

Man in the Mirror, The (Robert Hichens),

1950

Man Is Always Right, The (Maysie Greig), 1940

Man Like Daintree, A (Margaret Way), 1972

Man Missing (Mignon Eberhart), 1954

Man Next Door, The (Mignon Eberhart), 1943

Man of a Ghost, The (P.C. Wren), 1937

Man of Destiny (Rose Burghley), 1965

Man of Fire (Margaret Rome), 1970

Man of Granite (Lilian Peake), 1971

Man of Her Dreams, The (Mabel St. John, as Henry St. John Cooper), 1919

Man of His Word, A (Ruby M. Ayres), 1916

Man of Ice (Rachel Lindsay), 1980

Man of Kent, A (Isobel Chace), 1973

Man of Mark, A (Anthony Hope), 1890

Man of My Dreams (Theresa Charles, as Fay Chandos), 1937

Man of Power (Jan Blackmore), 1966

Man of Steel (Esther Wyndham), 1952

Man of Stone (Mary Howard), 1958

Man of the Desert, The (Grace Livingston Hill) , 1914

Man of the Family (Theresa Charles, as Leslie Lance), 1952

Man of the Islands (Henrietta Reid), 1966

Man of the Moment (Leila Mackinlay), 1956

Man of the Outback (Anne Hampson), 1980

Man of the River (Olga Sinclair), 1968

Man of Wrath, The (Charity Blackstock, as Paula Allardyce), 1956

Man on Half-Moon, The (Margaret Way), 1976

Man on the Island, The (Marion Collin), 1968

Man on the Peak, The (Katrina Britt), 1979

Man on the White Horse, The (Warwick Deeping), 1934

Man She Bought, The (Maysie Greig), 1930

Man She Loved,The (Madame Albanesi, as Effie Rowlands), 1900

Man She Married, The (Madame Albanesi, as Effie Rowlands), 1910

Man the Devil Didn't Want, The (P.C. Wren), 1940

Man the Women Loved, The (Ruby M. Ayres), 1925

Man to Be Feared, A (Anne Hampson), 1976

Man to Follow, A (Theresa Charles, as Fay Chandos), 1943

Man to Protect You, A (Maysie Greig), 1939

Man to Tame, A (Rachel Lindsay), 1976

Man under Authority, A (Ethel M. Dell), 1925

Man Who Broke the Rule, The (May Edgin-

ton), 1919

Man Who Came Back, The (Susan Barrie, as Pamela Kent), 1967

Man Who Cried, The (Catherine Cookson), 1979

Man Who Dared, The (May Edginton), 1923

Man Who Died, The (G.B. Burgin), 1903

Man Who Died Twice, The (Dorothy Mackie Low, as Lois Paxton), 1968

Man Who Found Himself, The (Naomi Jacob), 1929

Man Who Had Everything, The (Louis Brom-field), 1935

Man Who Listens, The (Taylor Caldwell), 1961

Man Who Lived Alone, The (Ruby M. Ayres), 1950

Man Who Married Again, The (Mabel St. John), 1926

Man Who Wasn't Mac, The (Theresa Charles, as Fay Chandos), 1939

Man Who Went Back, The (Warwick Deep-ing), 1940

Man with One Hand, The (Fannie Hurst), 1953

Man with the Broken Nose, The (Michael Arlen), 1927

Man with the Money, The (Mabel St. John, as Henry St. John Cooper), 1917

Man with the Scales, The (Marjorie Bowen), 1954

Man Without a Heart (Anne Hampson), 1981

Man Without a Heart (Rachel Lindsay, as Roberta Leigh), 1976

Man Without a Heart, The (Ruby M. Ayres), 1923

Mandingo (Lance Horner), 1957

Mandolins of Mantori (Iris Danbury), 1973

Manetta's Marriage (G.B. Burgin), 1922

Mango Walk (Rhona Martin), 1981

Manhattan Love Song (Kathleen Norris), 1934

Manhattan Nights (Faith Baldwin), 1937

Man-Made Miracle (Theresa Charles), 1948

Mannequin (Fannie Hurst), 1928

Manor Farm, The (Maysie Greig, as Mary Douglas Warren), 1951

Man's Estate (Nigel Tranter), 1946

Man's Way, The (Ruby M. Ayres), 1921

Man's World (Charlotte Lamb), 1980

Mansion of Lost Memories (Dorothy Daniels), 1969

Mansion of Smiling Masks, The (Daoma Winston), 1967

Mansion of the Golden Windows (Elsie Lee),

1966

Mantle of Innocence (Leila Mackinlay), 1957

Manxman, The (Hall Caine), 1894

Many a Human Heart (Hebe Elsna, as Vicky Lancaster), 1954

Many Ways (Margaret Pedler), 1931

Mapmaker, The (Frank G. Slaughter), 1957

Marble Angel, The (Dorothy Daniels), 1970

Marble City, The (G.B Burgin), 1905

Marble Hills (Dorothy Daniels), 1975

Marble Leaf (Dorothy Daniels), 1966

Marble Mountain (Iris Danbury), 1964

Marcaboth Women, The (Viña Delmar), 1951

Marcel of the "Zephyrs" (May Wynne), 1917

Marchwood (Iris Bromige), 1949

Marching Feet, The (Annie S. Swan), 1931

Marchington Inheritance, The (Isabelle Holland), 1979

Marcia (Grace Livingston Hill), 1921

Marcia Drayton (Charles Garvice), 1908

Marcia Schuyler (Grace Livingston Hill), 1908

Marcia, The Innocent (Katheryn Kimbrough), 1976

Margaret (H. Rider Haggard), 1907

Margaret Dent (Madame Albanesi, as Effie Rowlands), 1913

Margaret, The Faithful (Katheryn Kimbrough), 1975

Margaret the Queen (Nigel Tranter), 1979

Margaret Yorke (Kathleen Norris), 1930

Margery Daw (Madame Albanesi), 1886

Marguerite's Wonderful Year (Mabel Barnes Grundy), 1906

Maria (Baroness von Hutten), 1914

Marian Sax (Madame Albanesi), 1905

Marianna (Nancy Buckingham), 1981

Marie (H. Rider Haggard), 1912

Mariette's Lovers (G.B. Burgin), 1925

Marigold (Grace Livingston Hill), 1938

Marionette (Pamela Bennetts), 1979

Marion Forsyth (Annie S. Swan), 1883

Maris (Grace Livingston Hill), 1938

Marivosa (Baroness Orczy), 1930

Marjorie of Scotland (Pamela Hill), 1956

Mark Desborough's Vow (Annie S. Swan), 1884

Mark of the Hand, The (Charlotte Armstrong), 1963

Marks upon the Snow (Hebe Elsna), 1960

Marlborough's Unfair Lady (Ursula Bloom, as Lozania Prole), 1965

Marquess, The (Mary Ann Gibbs), 1982

Marquis, The (Charles Garvice), 1896

Marquis and Miss Jones, The (Pamela Ben-

netts), 1981

Marquis of Carabas, The (Rafael Sabatini), 1940

Marquis of Loveland, The (C.N. and A.M. Williamson), 1908

Marquis Takes a Wife, The (Rachel Lindsay), 1976

Marquis Who Hated Women, The (Barbara Cartland), 1977

Marr'd in Making (Baroness von Hutten), 1901

Marriage and Mary Ann (Catherine Cookson), 1964

Marriage Bond, The (Denise Robins), 1924

Marriage-Broker, The (Marie Belloc Lowndes), 1937

Marriage by Capture (Margaret Rome), 1980

Marriage by Conquest (Warwick Deeping), 1915

Marriage by Request (Rebecca Stratton, as Lucy Gillen), 1971

Marriage Chest, The (Dorothy Eden), 1965

Marriage for Three (Elizabeth Seifert), 1954

Marriage Handicap, The (Ruby M. Ayres), 1925

Marriage Has Been Arranged, A (Charity Blackstock, as Paula Allardyce), 1959

Marriage Impossible (Margaret Pargeter), 1978

Marriage in Heaven (Ursula Bloom), 1943

Marriage in Mexico (Flora Kidd), 1978

Marriage Is a Blind Date (Berta Ruck), 1953

Marriage Masque, The (Catherine Fellows), 1974

Marriage Merger, The (Glenna Finley), 1978

Marriage of Barry Wicklow, The (Ruby M. Ayres), 1920

Marriage of Caroline Lindsay, The (Margaret Rome), 1968

Marriage of Inconvenience, A (Janet Louise Roberts), 1972

Marriage of Katherine, The (D.E. Stevenson), 1965

Marriage of Leonora (Ursula Bloom), 1953

Marriage of Margaret, The (Madame Albanesi), 1909

Marriage of Martha Todd, The (Doris Leslie), 1968

Marriage of Mary Chard, The (Susan Inglis), 1935

Marriage of Meggotta, The (Edith Pargeter), 1979

Marriage of Pierrot (Ursula Bloom), 1936

Marriage Racket, The (Viña Delmar), 1933

Marriage Wheel, The (Susan Barrie), 1968

Marriage Will Not Take Place, The (Marguerite Steen), 1938

Marriage Without a Ring (Maysie Greig), 1972

Married at School (Mabel St. John), 1917

Married at Sight (Charles Garvice), 1894

Married in Haste (Victoria Holt, as Eleanor Burford), 1956

Married in Haste (Annie S. Swan), 1898

Married Life (May Edginton), 1917

Married Lover, The (Victoria Holt, as Eleanor Burford), 1942

Married Man, A (Annie S. Swan), 1898

Married Man's Girl (Susan Inglis), 1934

Married or Unmarried (Robert Hichens), 1941

Married People (Mary Roberts Rinehart), 1937

Married Quarters (Maysie Greig), 1964

Married to a Miser (Mabel St. John, as Henry St. John Cooper), 1920

Married to Her Master (Mabel St. John), 1914

Married to His Wife's Family (Mabel St. John), 1924

Marriott Hall (Dorothy Daniels), 1965

Marry a Stranger (Susan Barrie), 1954

Marry for Money (Faith Baldwin), 1948

Marry in Haste (Maysie Greig), 1935

Marry in Haste (Jane Aiken Hodge), 1969

Marry to Taste (Ursula Bloom, as Mary Essex), 1942

Marrying Kind, The (Elizabeth Cadell), 1980

Marrying Kind, The (Hebe Elsna), 1957

Marrying Kind, The (Doris E. Smith), 1974

Marsanne (Virginia Coffman), 1976

Marsh Blood (Lucilla Andrews, as Joanna Marcus), 1980

Marsh House (Mary Linn Roby), 1974

Marshall Family, The (Mary Burchell), 1967

Martie, The Unconquered (Kathleen Norris), 1917

Martin Conisby's Vengeance (Jeffery Farnol), 1921

Martin Make-Believe (Gilbert Frankau), 1930

Martin Valliant (Warwick Deeping), 1917

Martyrdom (Warwick Deeping), 1929

Martyred Love (Charles Garvice), 1902

Mary Ann and Bill (Catherine Cookson), 1967

Mary Ann and Jane (Mabel Barnes Grundy), 1944

Mary Anne (Daphne du Maurier), 1954

Mary Ann's Angels (Catherine Cookson), 1965

Mary Arden (Grace Livingston Hill), 1948

Mary at Monte Carlo (C.N. and A.M. Williamson), 1920

Mary Dunbar's Love (Madame Albanesi, as Effie Rowlands), 1921

Mary Ellen—Mill-Lass (Mabel St. John), 1920

Mary Faithful (Mabel St. John, as Henry St. John Cooper), 1923

Mary Garth (Annie S. Swan), 1904

Mary Hallam (Susan Ertz), 1947

Mary Marie (Eleanor H. Porter), 1920

Mary Midthorne (George Barr McCutcheon), 1911

Mary of Delight (Naomi Jacob), 1949

Mary of Marion Isle (H. Rider Haggard), 1929

Mary Olivane (Hebe Elsna), 1973

Mary Pechell (Marie Belloc Lowndes), 1912

Mary, Queen of France (Victoria Holt, as Jean Plaidy), 1964

Mary, Sweet Mary (Claudette Williams), 1980

Mary, The Infamous Queen (Maureen Peters), 1968

Mary Wakefield (Mazo de la Roche), 1949

Masculine Touch, The (Katrina Britt), 1970

Mask, The (Robert Hichens), 1951

Mask and the Moonflower, The (Phyllis A. Whitney), 1960

Mask of Comedy, The (Hebe Elsna), 1970

Mask of Evil (Charlotte Armstrong), 1958

Mask of Gold (Rachel Lindsay), 1956

Mask of Gold, A (Annie S. Swan), 1906

Mask of Love, The (Barbara Cartland), 1975

Mask of Scars (Anne Mather), 1973

Mask of the Enchantress, The (Victoria Holt), 1980

Mask of Treason (Anne Stevenson), 1979

Masque, The (Charlotte Lamb, as Sheila Holland), 1979

Masque by Gaslight (Virginia Coffman), 1970

Masque of Satan (Virginia Coffman), 1971

Masque of the Red Death, The (Elsie Lee), 1964

Masquerade (Anne Mather), 1966

Masquerade for a Nurse (Marjorie McEvoy, as Marjorie Harte), 1964

Masquerade for Love (Hebe Elsna, as Vicky Lancaster), 1938

Masquerade in Venice (Velda Johnston), 1973

Masqueraders, The (Georgette Heyer), 1928

Masquers, The (Natasha Peters), 1979

Master and the Maiden, The (Alice Chetwynd Ley), 1977

Master at Arms (Betty Beaty), 1973

Master Fiddler, The (Janet Dailey), 1977

Master Man, The (Ruby M. Ayres), 1920

Master of Ben Ross (Rebecca Stratton, as Lucy Gillen), 1977

Master of Blacktower, The (Barbara Michaels), 1966

Master of Blue Mire, The (Virginia Coffman), 1971

Master of Comus (Charlotte Lamb), 1977

Master of Falcon's Head (Anne Mather), 1970

Master of Forrestmead (Anne Hampson), 1978

Master of Glenkeith (Jean S. MacLeod), 1955

Master of Gray, The (Nigel Tranter), 1961

Master of Heronsbridge, The (Iris Bromige), 1969

Master of Jethart, The (Alice Dwyer-Joyce), 1976

Master of Keills, The (Jean S. MacLeod), 1967

Master of Liversedge (Alice Chetwynd Ley), 1966

Master of Love (Glenna Finley), 1978

Master of Lynch Towers, The (Madame Albanesi, as Effie Rowlands), 1910

Master of Mahia (Gloria Bevan), 1981

Master of Malcarew (Maureen Peters, as Veronica Black), 1971

Master of Man, The (Hall Caine), 1921

Master of Melincourt (Susan Barrie), 1966

Master of Melthorpe (Olga Sinclair), 1979

Master of Montrolfe Hall (Rohan O'Grady), 1965

Master of Moonrock (Anne Hampson), 1973

Master of Penrose, The (Jane Aiken Hodge), 1968

Master of Ransome (Lucy Walker), 1958

Master of Stair, The (Marjorie Bowen), 1907

Master of the House (Lilian Peake), 1974

Master of the Manor (Esther Wyndham), 1953

Master of the Mill, The (Mabel St. John, as Henry St. John Cooper), 1910

Master of the Tawhai, The (Essie Summers), 1959

Master of Trelona (Claire Ritchie), 1977

Master Wit, The (May Wynne), 1917

Master-at-Arms (Rafael Sabatini), 1940

Master-Christian, The (Marie Corelli), 1902

Masterson (Gilbert Frankau), 1926

Matador (Marguerite Steen), 1934

Match Is Made, A (Theresa Charles, as Jan Tempest), 1950

Matched Pearls (Grace Livingston Hill), 1933

Matchmakers, The (Janet Dailey), 1978

Matherson Marriage, The (Ruby M. Ayres), 1922

Matilda, Governess of the English (Sophia Cleugh), 1924

Mating Dance, The (Rona Randall), 1979

Mating of Marcus, The (Mabel Barnes Grundy), 1923

Mating Season, The (Janet Dailey), 1980

Matter of Business, A (Jeffery Farnol), 1940

Matter of Chance, A (Betty Neels), 1977

Matter of Sixpence, A (Jacqueline La Tourrette), 1972

Matthew, Mark, Luke, and John (Ursula Bloom), 1954

Maulever Hall (Jane Aiken Hodge), 1964

Maurice Durant (Charles Garvice), 1875

Maverton Heiress, The (Theresa Charles, as Leslie Lance), 1975

Mavis of Green Hill (Faith Baldwin), 1921

Mavreen (Claire Lorrimer), 1976

May Fair (Michael Arlen), 1925

May Spoon, The (Rohan O'Grady, as A. Carleon), 1981

Maya Temple (Dorothy Daniels), 1972

Mayenga Farm (Kathryn Blair), 1951

Mayeroni Myth, The (Daoma Winston), 1972

McCabe's Kingdom (Margaret Way), 1974

McKeever (Viña Delmar), 1976

McLeod's Folly (Louis Bromfield), 1948

Meadowsweet (Countess Barcynska, as Oliver Sandys), 1942

Meadowsweet (Baroness Orczy), 1912

Meaning of a Kiss, The (Marjorie McEvoy), 1961

Means of Grace, A (Edith Pargeter), 1956

Means to an End (Rebecca Stratton, as Lucy Gillen), 1972

Meant for Each Other (Mary Burchell), 1945

Meant to Meet (Theresa Charles, as Jan Tempest), 1967

Measure of Love, The (Mollie Chappell), 1961

Medical Center (Faith Baldwin), 1940

Medici Lover, The (Anne Mather), 1977

Medici Mistress (Julia Fitzgerald, as Julia Watson), 1968

Medici Ring, The (Nicole St. John), 1975

Mediterranean Madness (Ursula Bloom), 1934

Medusa Connection, The (Frances Cowen), 1976

Meet Love on Holiday (Ursula Bloom, as Sheila Burns), 1940

Meet Me Again (Mary Burchell), 1954

Meet Me by Moonlight (Theresa Charles, as Jan Tempest), 1953

Meet Me in Istanbul (Susan Barrie, as Pamela Kent), 1958

Meet Me in Monte Carlo (Denise Robins), 1964

Meet on My Ground (Essie Summers), 1968

Meet the Sun Halfway (Jane Arbor), 1974

Meeting in Madrid (Jean S. MacLeod), 1979

Meeting in the Spring (Mary Ann Gibbs, as Elizabeth Ford), 1954

Meg (Dorothy Daniels), 1979

Meg Hamilton (Annie S. Swan), 1914

Melbury Square (Dorothy Eden), 1970

Melinda (Anne Eliot, as Caroline Arnett), 1975

Melissa (Taylor Caldwell), 1948

Melody (Elswyth Thane), 1950

Melody of Love (Rachel Lindsay, as Janey Scott), 1960

Melody of Malice (Susan Hufford), 1979

Melon in the Cornfield, The (Charity Blackstock), 1969

Melora (Mignon Eberhart), 1959

Melting Fire (Anne Mather), 1979

Mem, The (Baroness von Hutten), 1934

Memory of Love (Rachel Lindsay, as Janey Scott), 1959

Memory of Summer, A (Audrie Manley-Tucker), 1961

Memory Serves My Love (Jane Arbor), 1952

Men Act That Way (Maysie Greig), 1933

Men and Angels (Elizabeth Cadell), 1952

Men Are Only Human (Denise Robins), 1933

Men Are So Strange (Hebe Elsna, as Vicky Lancaster), 1937

Men Are Such Fools! (Faith Baldwin), 1936

Men as Her Stepping Stones (Maysie Greig, as Ann Barclay), 1937

Men Dislike Women (Michael Arlen), 1931

Men in Her Life, The (Berta Ruck), 1954

Men Made the Town (Ruby M. Ayres), 1931

Men, Maids, and Mustard-Pot (Gilbert Frankau), 1924

Men of the Frontier Force, The (Maud Diver), 1930

Men on White Horses (Pamela Haines), 1978

Men Out of Reach (Lilian Peake), 1972

Men Were Deceivers Ever (Mabel St. John, as Henry St. John Cooper), 1920

Menagerie, The (Catherine Cookson), 1958

Mending Flower (Claire Ritchie), 1955

Menfreya (Victoria Holt), 1966

Menfreya in the Morning (Victoria Holt), 1966

Merchant's Daughter, The (Charlotte Lamb, as Sheila Holland), 1980

Merely Murder (Georgette Heyer), 1935

Merivales, The (George Barr McCutcheon), 1929

Merlin's Keep (Madeleine Brent), 1977

Merlin's Keep (Kate Norway), 1966

Mermaid (Margaret Millar), 1982

Merrily All the Way (Countess Barcynska, as Oliver Sandys), 1943

Merry Andrews, The (Rona Randall), 1954

Merry Goes the Time (Eleanor Farnes), 1935

Merry Meeting (D.A. Ponsonby), 1948

Mervyn, Jock, or Joe (May Wynne), 1921

Message from Hong Kong (Mignon Eberhart), 1969

Message from Mars, A (May Wynne, as Lester Lurgan), 1912

Messalina of the Suburbs (E.M. Delafield), 1924

Messenger of Love (Barbara Cartland), 1961

Mice for Amusement (Baroness von Hutten), 1933

Michael and All the Angels (Norah Lofts), 1943

Michael Forth (Mary Johnston), 1919

Michael O'Halloran (Gene Stratton Porter), 1915

Michael's Wife (Gilbert Frankau), 1948

Michael's Wife (Marlys Millhiser), 1972

Michaelmas Tree, The (Pamela Bennetts), 1982

Midas Touch, The (Margaret Kennedy), 1938

Midday Moon (Dorothy Daniels), 1966

Middle Mist (Netta Muskett), 1937

Middle Window, The (Elizabeth Goudge), 1935

Midnight Dancers, The (Anne Maybury), 1973

Midnight Encounter (Glenna Finley), 1981

Midnight Is Mine (Leila Mackinlay), 1954

Midnight Match, The (Florence Stevenson, as Zabrina Faire), 1979

Midnight Matinée (Hebe Elsna), 1949

Midnight Music (Margaret Pargeter), 1978

Midnight Oak, The (Jill Tattersall), 1967

Midnight Sailing (Susan Hufford), 1975

Midnight Sun, The (Katrina Britt), 1979

Midnight Sun's Magic (Betty Neels), 1979

Midnight Walker, The (Rona Randall), 1973

Midnight Whispers (Patricia Matthews), 1981

Midsummer Madness! (Mabel St. John), 1924

Midsummer Masque (Jill Tattersall), 1972

Mighty Atom, The (Marie Corelli), 1896

Mignonette (Marjorie Bowen, as Joseph Shearing), 1948

Miklos Alexandrovitch Is Missing (Anne Edwards), 1970

Milady Charlotte (Victoria Holt, as Kathleen Kellow), 1959

Mill Queen, The (Mabel St. John, as Henry St. John Cooper), 1919

Millgirl and Dreamer (Mabel St. John), 1918

Mill-Girl's Bargain!, The (Mabel St. John), 1924

Millijoy, The Determined (Katheryn Kimbrough), 1977

Milliner's Shop, The (Mary Ann Gibbs), 1981

Million, The (Robert Hichens), 1940

Million Dollar Doll, The (A.M. Williamson), 1924

Million Stars, The (Marjorie Lewty), 1959

Millionaire Tramp, The (Mabel St. John, as Henry St. John Cooper), 1930

Millionaire's Daughter, The (Dorothy Eden), 1973

Mill-Lass o' Mine! (Mabel St. John), 1920

Mill-Owner, The (May Wynne, as Lester Lurgan), 1910

Mills of the Gods (Daoma Winston), 1974

Milly Comes to Town (Countess Barcynska), 1928

Mind of a Minx, The (Berta Ruck), 1927

Mine for a Day (Mary Burchell), 1951

Minerva Stone, The (Anne Maybury), 1968

Minion, The (Rafael Sabatini), 1930

Ministering Angel, A (Madame Albanesi, as Effie Rowlands), 1933

Minister's Daughter, The (Jean Francis Webb, as Ethel Hamilton), 1953

Minister's Son, The (Grace Livingston Hill), 1938

Mink Coat (Kathleen Norris), 1946

Minstrel's Court (Hebe Elsna), 1963

Minstrel's Leap (Maureen Peters, as Veronica Black), 1973

Mint Walk (Countess Barcynska), 1927

Minx Goes to the Front, The (C.N. and A.M. Williamson), 1919

Mira (Daoma Winston), 1982

Miracle at Joe's, A (Kate Norway, as Bess Norton), 1965

Miracle at St. Burno's, The (Victoria Holt, as Philippa Carr), 1972

Miracle of Lac Blanche, The (Maynah Lewis), 1973

Miracle Stone of Wales, The (Countess Barcynska, as Marguerite Barclay), 1957

Mirage for Love (Elizabeth Hoy), 1939

Mirage of Love (Ursula Bloom), 1978

Mirage on the Horizon (Ursula Bloom), 1974

Miranda (Jane Blackmore), 1966

Miranda (Grace Livingston Hill), 1914

Mirror, The (Marlys Millhiser), 1978

Mirror for Dreams, A (Netta Muskett), 1931

Mirror of the Sun, The (Charity Blackstock, as Ursula Torday), 1938

Misadventure (Netta Muskett), 1936

Misadventures of Bethany Price, The (Marian Cockrell), 1979

Mischief (Charlotte Armstrong), 1950

Mischief-Makers, The (Annie S. Swan), 1941

Miss Baxter's Bequest (Annie S. Swan), 1888

Miss Bede Is Staying (Anna Gilbert), 1982

Miss Billy series (Eleanor J. Porter)

Miss Bolo (Mabel St. John, as Henry St. John Cooper), 1918

Miss Bun, The Baxter's Daughter (D.E. Stevenson), 1938

Miss Buncle series (D.E. Stevenson)

Miss Charley (Charity Blackstock), 1979

Miss Charlotte's Fancy (Charlotte Lamb, as Sheila Holland), 1980

Miss Carmichael's Conscience (Baroness von Hutten), 1900

Miss Dean's Dilemma (D.E. Stevenson), 1938

Miss Delicia Allen (Mary Johnston), 1933

Miss Doctor (Elizabeth Seifert), 1951

Miss Estcourt (Charles Garvice), 1911

Miss Fenny (Charity Blackstock), 1957

Miss Harriet Townshend (Kathleen Norris), 1955

Miss High and Mighty (Margaret Rome), 1980

Miss Jonas's Boy (Charity Blackstock, as Paula Allardyce), 1972

Miss Lavinia's Call (Grace Livingston Hill), 1949

Miss Martha Mary Crawford (Catherine Cookson, as Catherine Marchant), 1975

Miss Mayhew and Ming Yun (Anne Duffield), 1928

Miss Miranda's Walk (Betty Beaty), 1967

Miss Mission's Maid (Berta Ruck), 1915

Miss Nobody from Nowhere (Elizabeth Ashton), 1975

Miss Paraffin (Countess Barcynska, as Oliver Sandys), 1944

Miss Philadelphia Smith (Charity Blackstock, as Paula Allardyce), 1977

Miss Pinkerton (Mary Roberts Rinehart), 1932

Miss Rolling Stone (Samuel Shellabarger, as Peter Loring), 1939

Mists of Memory, The (Catherine Cookson, as Catherine Marchant), 1965

Mists of Mourning, The (Dorothy Daniels, as Suzanne Somers), 1966

Mists of the Moor (Leila Mackinlay), 1967

Misty Angel (Countess Barcynska, as Oliver Sandys), 1931

Mixed Blessing, The (Helen Van Slyke), 1975

Mixed Blessings (Marian Cockrell), 1978

Mixed Company (Marian Cockrell), 1979

Mixed Marriage (Elizabeth Cadell), 1963

Mix Me a Man (Doris E. Smith), 1978

Mixed Singles (Leila Mackinlay, as Brenda Grey), 1971

Mock-Honeymoon (Berta Ruck), 1939

Model Girl's Farm (Theresa Charles, as Fay Chandos), 1958

Modern Eve, A (May Edginton), 1913

Modern Hero, A (Louis Bromfield), 1932

Modern Juliet (Charles Garvice), 1900

Modern Micawbers (Leila Mackinlay, as Brenda Grey), 1933

Modern Witch, A (Madame Albanesi, as Effie Rowlands), 1912

Moderns (Daoma Winston), 1968

Mog Megone (May Wynne), 1921

Mollie's Adventures (May Wynne), 1903

Molly of the Lone Pine (Mrs. Patrick Mac-Gill), 1922

Moment I Saw You, The (Theresa Charles, as Jan Tempest), 1941

Moment in Paris, A (Rose Burghley), 1961

Moment of Decision (Jean S. MacLeod), 1972

Moment of Love (Denise Robins), 1964

Moment of Truth (Hebe Elsna, as Lyndon Snow), 1968

Moment of Truth (Rebecca Stratton, as Lucy Gillen), 1973

Moncrieff (Isabelle Holland), 1975

Monday in Summer (Lucy Walker, as Dorothy Lucie Sanders), 1961

Monday Man, The (Kate Norway, as Bess Norton), 1963

Monday's Child (Mollie Hardwick), 1981

Money for One (Berta Ruck), 1927

Money Isn't Everything (Berta Ruck), 1940

Money, Love, and Kate (Eleanor H. Porter), 1923

Money, Magic, and Marriage (Barbara Cartland), 1980

Money! Money! Money! (May Edginton), 1931

Money Moon, The (Jeffery Farnol), 1911

Money or Wife? (Madame Albanesi, as Effie Rowlands), 1914

Moneyman, The (Thomas B. Costain), 1947

Monkey on a Chain (Charity Blackstock), 1965

Monkey Tree in a Flower Pot (Ursula Bloom), 1958

Monkey-Puzzle (Baroness von Hutten), 1932

Monkshood (Anne Mather), 1972

Monte Carlo (Dorothy Daniels), 1981

Montezuma's Daughter (H. Rider Haggard), 1893

Montrose, The Captain-General (Nigel Tranter), 1973

Mooltiki (Rumer Godden), 1957

Moon series (Maureen Peters, as Catherine Darby)

Moon and Bride's Hill, The (Susan Barrie, as Anita Charles), 1958

Moon at the Full (Susan Barrie), 1961

Moon Dragon (Anne Hampson), 1978

Moon for Lavinia, The (Betty Neels), 1976

Moon in a Bucket, The (Mary Ann Gibbs), 1972

Moon in the Water, The (Ruby M. Ayres), 1939

Moon into Blood, The (Catherine Gavin), 1966

Moon Is Square, The (Margaret Maddocks), 1975

Moon Marriage, The (Anne Rundle), 1967

Moon of Israel (H. Rider Haggard), 1918

Moon of Laughing Flame (Maureen Peters, as Belinda Grey), 1980

Moon of Romance, The (Madame Albanesi), 1932

Moon Out of Reach, The (Margaret Pedler), 1921

Moon over Africa (Susan Barrie, as Pamela Kent), 1955

Moon over Eden (Barbara Cartland), 1976

Moon over Moncrieff (Irene Roberts, as Iris Rowland), 1969

Moon over Stamboul (Anne Duffield), 1936

Moon over the Alps (Essie Summers), 1960

Moon over the Danube (Marjorie McEvoy), 1966

Moon over the Temple (Irene Roberts), 1972

Moon over the Water (Maysie Greig, as Mary Douglas Warren), 1956

Moon Returns, The (Rona Randall), 1942

Moon Shadow, The (Katheryn Kimbrough, as Kym Allyson), 1976

Moon Song (Ursula Bloom), 1953

Moon Through Glass, The (Madame Albanesi), 1928

Moon Tide (Rebecca Stratton), 1975

Moon Witch (Anne Mather), 1970

Moon Without Stars (Anne Hampson), 1974

Moonflete (Maureen Peters, as Veronica Black), 1972

Moonflower, The (Jean S. MacLeod), 1967

Moonflower, The (Phyllis A. Whitney), 1958

Moonlight and Magic (Rachel Lindsay), 1962

Moonlight Gondola, The (Janet Louise Roberts, as Janette Radcliffe), 1975

Moonlight Mist (Laura London), 1979

Moonlight on the Lake (Ivy Preston), 1976

Moonlight on the Nile (Elizabeth Ashton), 1979

Moonlight Variations, The (Florence Stevenson), 1981

Moonlight Witchery (Hebe Elsna, as Lyndon Snow), 1959

Moonlighters, The (Charity Blackstock, as Paula Allardyce), 1966

Moonlit Door, The (Anne Maybury), 1967

Moonlit Way, The (Alice Dwyer-Joyce), 1974

Moonraker's Bride (Madeleine Brent), 1973

Moonrise over the Mountains (Lilian Peake), 1975

Moon's Our Home, The (Faith Baldwin), 1936

Moonshiner, The (Lucy Walker), 1961

Moon-Spinners, The (Mary Stewart), 1962

Moonstone Manor (Irene Roberts, as Irene Shaw), 1968

Moonstruck Madness (Laurie McBain), 1977

Moorhaven (Daoma Winston), 1973

Moorland Magic (Elizabeth Ashton), 1973

Mops (Countess Barcynska, as Oliver Sandys), 1928

More Than Conqueror (Grace Livingston Hill), 1944

More Than a Dream (Rebecca Stratton), 1977

More Than Friendship (Mary Howard), 1960

More Than Love (Denise Robins), 1947

Morning Glory (Mabel St. John, as Henry St. John Cooper), 1927

Morning Star (H. Rider Haggard), 1910

Morning Star, The (Kate Norway), 1959

Morning Star, The (Irene Roberts, as Iris Rowland), 1963

Morning Will Come, The (Naomi Jacob), 1953

Mortimer Brice (Robert Hichens), 1932

Moss Rose (Marjorie Bowen, as Joseph Shearing), 1934

Most Auspicious Star, A (Suzanne Ebel), 1968

Most Cruelly Wronged (Mabel St. John), 1907

Most Loving Mere Folly (Edith Pargeter), 1953

Most Romantic City, A (Mary Ann Gibbs), 1976

Most Sacred of All (Jeffery Farnol), 1948

Mostly by Moonlight (Dorothy Daniels), 1968

Mother (Kathleen Norris), 1911

Mother Knows Best (Edna Ferber), 1927

Mother Knows Best! (Mabel St. John), 1922

Mother-in-Law (Baroness von Hutten), 1922

Motionless Shadows (Kathleen Norris), 1945

Motive (Marie Belloc Lowndes), 1938

Motor Maid, The (C.N. and A.M. Williamson), 1909

Mountain and the Tree, The (Helen Beauclerk), 1935

Mountain Clinic (Jean S. MacLeod), 1962

Mountain Heritage (Elizabeth Ashton), 1976

Mountain Lovers (Mabel St. John, aa Henry St. John Cooper), 1920

Mountain Magic (Susan Barrie), 1964

Mountain Magic (Ivy Preston), 1979

Mountain of Fear (Rona Randall), 1972

Mountain of Light, The (Catherine Gavin), 1944

Mountain of Stars, The (Jean S. MacLeod, as Catherine Airlie), 1956

Mountain Sang, The (Irene Roberts), 1965

Mountain That Went to the Sea, The (Lucy Walker), 1971

Mountford Show (Mary Ann Gibbs, as Elizabeth Ford), 1948

Moura (Virginia Coffman), 1959

Mourning Bride, The (Florence Stevenson, as Lucia Curzon), 1982

Mourning Trees, The (Velda Johnston), 1972

Mouth of Truth, The (Isobel Chace), 1977

Moving Dream, The (Elizabeth Renier), 1977

Much Ado about Peter (Jean Webster), 1909

Much-Loved (Ruby M. Ayres), 1934

Mud on My Stockings (Countess Barcynska, as Oliver Sandys), 1938

Murder at Grand Bay (Willo Davis Roberts), 1955

Murder by an Aristocrat (Mignon Eberhart), 1932

Murder by Nail (Jeffery Farnol), 1942

Murder Has a Pretty Face (Gwendoline Butler, as Jennie Melville), 1981

Murder in Mayfair (Denise Robins), 1935

Murder in the Tower, The (Victoria Holt, as Jean Plaidy), 1964

Murder in Waiting (Mignon Eberhart), 1973

Murder Is So Easy (Willo Davis Roberts), 1961

Murder Most Royal (Victoria Holt, as Jean Plaidy), 1949

Murder of Delicia, The (Marie Corelli), 1896

Murder of Miranda, The (Margaret Millar), 1979

Murder of My Patient (Mignon Eberhart), 1934

Murder Reflected (Janet Caird), 1965

Murder Remote (Janet Caird), 1973

Murder Scholastic (Janet Caird), 1967

Murderers' Houses (Gwendoline Butler, as Jennie Melville), 1964

Murdering Kind, The (Gwendoline Butler), 1958

Murder's Mansion (Irene Roberts, as Irene Shaw), 1976

Murder's Nest (Charlotte Armstrong), 1954

Murders of Richard III, The (Barbara Michaels, as Elizabeth Peters), 1974

Murray Finds a Chum (May Wynne), 1914

Muscle Beach (Elsie Lee), 1964

Musgraves, The (D.E. Stevenson), 1960

Music at Midnight (Jean S. MacLeod), 1952

Music I Heard with You (Elizabeth Hoy), 1969

Music in the Hills (D.E. Stevenson), 1950

Music in Winter (Suzanne Ebel), 1975

Music of Our House, The (Anne Maybury), 1952

Music of the Heart (Mary Burchell), 1972

Music When Sweet Voices Die (Chelsea Quinn Yarbro), 1979

Must the Dream End (Hebe Elsna, as Vicky Lancaster), 1941

Mustee, The (Lance Horner), 1967

Mutiny in Paradise (Margaret Way), 1978

Mutual Look, The (Joyce Dingwell), 1973

My Beautiful Heathen (Rebecca Stratton, as Lucy Gillen), 1970

My Best Girl (Kathleen Norris), 1927

My Brother Michael (Mary Stewart), 1960

My Brother's Keeper (Marcia Davenport), 1954

My Brother's Wife (Hebe Elsna, as Lyndon Snow), 1964

My Caravaggio Style (Doris Langley Moore), 1959

My Cousin Lola (Hebe Elsna, as Lyndon Snow), 1966

My Cousin Rachel (Daphne du Maurier), 1951

My Dark Rapparee (Henrietta Reid), 1966

My Dear (May Edginton), 1929

My Dear Aunt Flora (Elizabeth Cadell), 1946

My Dear Cousin (Kathryn Blair, as Celine Conway), 1959

My Dear Fugitive (Olga Sinclair), 1976

My Dear Lady (Hebe Elsna), 1957

My Dear Lover England (Pamela Bennetts), 1975

My Dear Miss Emma (Charity Blackstock, as Paula Allardyce), 1958

My Dearest Elizabeth (Anne Maybury), 1964

My Dearest Love (Emilie Loring), 1954

My Desert Friend (Robert Hichens), 1931

My Dream Fulfilled (Hebe Elsna, as Lyndon Snow), 1962

My Dream Is Yours (Nan Asquith), 1954

My Enemy and I (Theresa Charles), 1941

My Enemy the Queen (Victoria Holt), 1978

My Fellow Laborer (H. Rider Haggard), 1888

My Friend the Chauffeur (C.N. and A.M. Williamson), 1905

My Friend the Professor (Lucilla Andrews), 1960

My Girl, Regan (Mabel St. John), 1915

My Heart a Traitor (Iris Danbury), 1958

My Heart at Your Feet (Susan Barrie, as Anita Charles), 1957

My Heart Has Wings (Elizabeth Hoy), 1957

My Heart Remembers (Flora Kidd), 1971

My Heart's a Dancer (Rachel Lindsay, as Roberta Leigh), 1970

My Heart's Desire (Sara Seale), 1976

My Heart's Down Under (Maysie Greig), 1951

My Heart's in the Highlands (Jean S. MacLeod), 1956

My Heart's Right There (Florence L. Barclay), 1914

My Lady Benbrook (Constance Gluyas), 1975

My Lady Caprice (Jeffery Farnol), 1907

My Lady Cinderella (A.M. Williamson), 1900

My Lady Destiny (Denise Robins, as Harriet Gray), 1961

My Lady Disdain (Elizabeth Ashton), 1976

My Lady Mischief (Janet Louise Roberts), 1973

My Lady of Dreadwood (Madame Albanesi, as Effie Rowlands), 1906

My Lady of Snow (Charles Garvice), 1908

My Lady of the Fuchsias (Essie Summers), 1979

My Lady Pride (Charles Garvice), 1902

My Lady's Crusade (Annette Motley), 1977

My Lady's Honour (May Wynne), 1921

My Lady's Mask (Mary Linn Roby), 1979
My Lancashire Queen (Mabel St. John), 1914
My "Little Bit" (Marie Corelli), 1919
My Lord Foxe (Constance Gluyas), 1976
My Lord John (Georgette Heyer), 1975
My Lord of Wrybourne (Jeffery Farnol), 1948
My Love (Emilie Loring), 1955
My Love Came Back (Doris E. Smith), 1978
My Love Has a Secret (Anne Maybury), 1958
My Love Johnny (Marjorie McEvoy), 1971
My Love Kitty (Charles Garvice), 1911
My Man of the Mill! (Mabel St. John), 1924
My! My Little Queen! (Ursula Bloom, as Lozania Prole), 1961
My Name Is Clary Brown (Charity Blackstock, as Charlotte Keppel), 1976
My Old Love Came (Ruby M. Ayres), 1930
My Old Love Came (Mary Burchell), 1943
My Only Love (Theresa Charles, as Jan Tempest), 1939
My Pretty Sister (Evadne Price), 1954
My Secret Love (Elizabeth Hoy), 1967
My Sister Celia (Mary Burchell), 1961
My Sister Erica (Jane Blackmore), 1973
My Sister Sophie (Mary Howard, as Josephine Edgar), 1964
My Sister's Keeper (Rachel Lindsay), 1979
My Surgeon Neighbour (Jane Arbor)
My Tattered Loving (Marjorie Bowen, as George Preedy), 1937
My Theodosia (Anya Seton), 1941
My True Love (Theresa Charles), 1971
My True Love (Denise Robins), 1953
My Wanton Tudor Rose (Ursula Bloom, as Lozania Prole), 1956
My Wonderful Wife (Marie Corelli), 1889
Myriah (Claudette Williams), 1978
Mysterious Maid-Servant, The (Barbara Cartland), 1977
Mysterious Waye (P.C. Wren), 1930
Mystery at Little Heaven (Viña Delmar), 1933
Mystery Boy-Friend (Berta Ruck), 1957
Mystery Castle (Elsie Lee), 1973
Mystery Flowers (Grace Livingston Hill), 1936
Mystery House (Kathleen Norris), 1939
Mystery Lamp, The (Mary Roberts Rinehart), 1925
Mystery of Barry Ingram, The (Annie S. Swan), 1910
Mystery of Hunting's End, The (Mignon Eberhart), 1930
Mystery of Mary, The (Grace Livingston Hill), 1912
Mystery of Pine Point, The (Kathleen Norris), 1936
Mystic Manor (Dorothy Daniels, as Helen Gray Weston), 1966
Mystic Rose (Patricia Gallagher), 1977

Nabob's Widow, The (Elsie Lee), 1976
Nada the Lily (H. Rider Haggard), 1892
Naked Battle, The (Barbara Cartland), 1977
Name in Lights, A (Suzanne Ebel), 1968
Name Is Mary, The (Fannie Hurst), 1951
Name the Woman (A.M. Williamson), 1924
Nameless Bess (Charles Garvice, as Caroline Hart)
Nameless Coffin, A (Gwendoline Butler), 1966
Nan—and the New Owner (Theresa Charles, as Fay Chandos), 1959
Nan of No Man's Land (Mabel St. John, as Henry St. John Cooper), 1925
Nance (Charles Garvice), 1900
Nancy Nicholson (Annie S. Swan), 1906
Nancy, The Daring (Katheryn Kimbrough), 1976
Nanette (Patricia Beryan), 1981
Naughty Lady Ness (Claudette Williams), 1980
Navy Blue Lady (Hettie Grimstead), 1951
Necessary Woman, A (Helen Van Slyke), 1979
Nedra (George Barr McCutcheon), 1905
Ne'er-Do-Well, The (Annie S. Swan), 1897
Nell Alone (Gwendoline Butler, as Jennie Melville), 1966
Nell Gwyn (Marjorie Bowen), 1926
Nell of Shorne Mills (Charles Garvice), 1900
Nell of the Camp (Mabel St. John), 1913
Nellie (Charles Garvice), 1913
Nellie, The Obvious (Katheryn Kimbrough), 1978
Nelson's Love (Ursula Bloom, as Lozania Prole), 1966
Nest of the Sparrowhawk, The (Baroness Orczy), 1909
Nesting Cats (Ursula Bloom, as Mary Essex), 1941
Net to Catch the Wind, A (Anne Worboys, as Annette Eyre), 1966
Nethergate (Norah Lofts), 1973
Nevada Gunslinger (Virginia Coffman), 1962
"Never Again!" Said Nicola (Theresa Charles, as Jan Tempest), 1944
Never Another Love (Theresa Charles, as Jan

Tempest), 1949

Never Call It Loving (Dorothy Eden), 1966

Never Call It Loving (Marjorie Lewty), 1958

Never Fall in Love (Olga Sinclair), 1977

Never Give All (Denise Robins), 1934

Never Go Back (Margaret Pargeter), 1977

Never Laugh at Love (Barbara Cartland), 1976

Never Look Back (Mignon Eberhart), 1951

Never Look Back (Denise Robins), 1944

Never the Same (Maysie Greig), 1970

Never Victorious, Never Defeated (Taylor Caldwell), 1954

Never While the Grass Grows (Betty Neels), 1978

Ne'er-Do-Well (Dornford Yates), 1954

New Americans series (Christopher Nicole)

New Broom, The (Joyce Dingwell), 1974

New Day, A (Countess Barcynska, as Oliver Sandys), 1957

New Doctor, The (Elizabeth Seifert), 1958

New Girl, The (Mabel St. John), 1927

New Girl at Bellforth, The (Mabel St. John), 1923

New Girl in Town (Faith Baldwin), 1975

New Kind of Killer, An Old Kind of Death, A (Gwendoline Butler, as Jennie Melville), 1970

New Life for Joanna, A (Iris Bromige), 1958

New Lord Whinbridge, The (Theresa Charles, as Leslie Lance), 1973

New Love, The (Robert Hichens), 1895

New Love for Cynthia, A (Adeline McElfresh, as Jane Scott), 1958

New Moon Through a Window (Maysie Greig), 1937

New Name, A (Grace Livingston Hill), 1926

New Orleans Lady (Viña Delmar), 1949

New Owner, The (Iris Bromige), 1956

New Sister Theater, The (Lucilla Andrews), 1964

New Way of Life, A (Robert Hichens), 1942

New Woman, A (Annie S. Swan), 1898

New Zealand Inheritance (Essie Summers), 1957

New Zealander, The (Joyce Dingwell), 1963

Newspaper Girl, The (A.M. Williamson), 1899

Next of Kin (Mignon Eberhart), 1982

Next Tuesday (Ursula Bloom), 1949

Nice Bloke, The (Catherine Cookson), 1969

Nice Girl Comes to Town, A (Maysie Greig), 1930

Nice Girl's Story, The (Rosemary Harris), 1968

Nickel Nurse (Joyce Dingwell), 1970

Nicola (Dorothy Daniels), 1980

Nicola (Audrey Erskine-Lindop), 1959

Nicolette (Baroness Orczy), 1922

Nicolette (Ivy Preston), 1967

Night at Sea Abbey (Virginia Coffman), 1972

Night Bell (Leila Mackinlay), 1936

Night Call (Adeline McElfresh), 1961

Night Duty at Duke's (Kate Norway, as Bess Norton), 1960

Night in Bombay (Louis Bromfield), 1940

Night in Cold Harbour, A (Margaret Kennedy), 1960

Night Is Kind, The (Kate Norway, as Bess Norton), 1967

Night Is Mine, The (Claire Lorrimer, as Patricia Robins), 1964

Night Music (Charlotte Lamb), 1980

Night My Enemy, The (Anne Maybury), 1962

Night of Carnival (Maysie Greig, as Jennifer Ames), 1956

Night of Stars (Victoria Holt, as Eleanor Burford), 1960

Night of Tears (Katheryn Kimbrough, as John M. Kimbro), 1976

Night of the Black Tower (Olga Sinclair), 1968

Night of the Bonfire (Jane Blackmore), 1974

Night of the Bulls, The (Anne Mather), 1972

Night of the Cotillion, The (Janet Dailey), 1976

Night of the Enchantress, The (Anne Maybury, as Katherine Troy), 1967

Night of Four Hundred Rabbits, The (Barbara Michaels, as Elizabeth Peters), 1971

Night of Love (Rachel Lindsay, as Roberta Leigh), 1978

Night of the Letter, The (Dorothy Eden), 1967

Night of the Party, The (Iris Bromige), 1974

Night of the Party, The (Hebe Elsna, as Laura Conway), 1969

Night of the Singing Birds (Susan Barrie), 1970

Night of the Stranger, The (Jane Blackmore), 1961

Night of the Wedding, The (C.N. and A.M. Williamson), 1921

Night of the Willow (Maureen Peters), 1981

Night of the Wolf, The (Constance Heaven, as Constance Fecher), 1972

Night of the Yellow Moon (Flora Kidd), 1977

Night on the Mountain (Flora Kidd), 1973

Night People, The (Kate Norway), 1963

Night Riders, The (Nigel Tranter), 1954

Night Shade (Dorothy Daniels), 1976

Night the Roof Blew Off, The (Phyllis Hastings), 1962

Night Visitor, The (Patricia Matthews, as Laura Wylie), 1979

Night Way (Janet Dailey), 1981

Nightbound (Robert Hichens), 1951

Nightcap and Plume (Marjorie Bowen, as George Preedy), 1945

Nightfall (Dorothy Daniels), 1977

Nightingale Once Sang, A (Ursula Bloom, as Mary Essex), 1958

Nightingale Sang, A (Barbara Cartland), 1979

Nightingale Touch, The (Kate Norway), 1966

Nightingales (Mary Burchell), 1980

Nightingale's Song (Denise Robins), 1963

Nightmare at Riverview (Dorothy Daniels, as Angela Gray), 1973

Nightmare Chase, The (Evelyn Berckman), 1975

Nightmare Country (Marlys Millhiser), 1981

Nightmare Ends, The (Frances Cowen), 1970

Night's Dark Secret (Marjorie Bowen, as Margaret Campbell), 1975

Night's Daughters (Kate Norway, as Bess Norton), 1966

Nightshade at Morning (Ursula Bloom), 1944

Nile Dusk (Susan Barrie, as Pamela Kent), 1972

Nina (Susan Ertz), 1924

Nine Coaches Waiting (Mary Stewart), 1958

Nine Lives (Ursula Bloom), 1951

Nine Moons Wasted (Anne Rundle, as Marianne Lamont), 1977

Nine O'Clock Tide (Mignon Eberhart), 1978

Ninth Earl, The (Jeffery Farnol), 1950

Ninth Vibration, The (L. Adams Beck), 1922

Nitana (G.B. Burgin), 1928

No Armour Against Fate (Margaret Pedler), 1938

No Bed of Roses (Faith Baldwin), 1973

No Business to Love (Rachel Lindsay), 1966

No Castle of Dreams (Marjorie McEvoy), 1960

No Darkness for Love (Barbara Cartland), 1974

No Dowry for Jennifer (Maysie Greig), 1957

No Easy Way (Naomi Jacob), 1938

No Eden for a Nurse (Marjorie McEvoy, as Marjorie Harte), 1971

No Escape from Love (Barbara Cartland), 1977

No Escape from Love (Theresa Charles, as Fay Chandos), 1937

No Evil Angel (Elisabeth Ogilvie), 1956

No Faint Heart (Countess Barcynska, as Oliver Sandys), 1943

No Females Wanted (Joyce Dingwell), 1970

No Fields of Amaranth (Hebe Elsna), 1943

No Friend of Mine (Lilian Peake), 1972

No Gentle Possession (Anne Mather), 1975

No Gifts from Chance (Margaret Pedler), 1944

No Good as a Nurse (Hebe Elsna, as Vicky Lancaster), 1962

No Greater Love (Patricia Gallagher), 1979

No Greater Love (Baroness Orczy), 1938

No Heart Is Free (Barbara Cartland), 1948

No Hearts to Break (Susan Ertz), 1937

No Hero—This (Warwick Deeping), 1936

No Just Cause (Susan Barrie), 1965

No Known Grave (Evelyn Berckman), 1958

No Lady Buys a Cot (Ursula Bloom), 1943

No Lady in Bed (Ursula Bloom), 1944

No Lady in the Cart (Ursula Bloom), 1949

No Lady with a Pen (Ursula Bloom), 1947

No Laggard in Love (Theresa Charles, as Leslie Lance), 1971

No Lease for Love (Jane Arbor), 1950

No Legacy for Lindsay (Essie Summers), 1965

No Limit to Love (Theresa Charles, as Fay Chandos), 1937

No Love Lost (Helen Van Slyke), 1980

No May in October (Netta Muskett), 1951

No More A-Roving (Sylvia Thorpe), 1970

No More Loving (Claire Lorrimer, as Patricia Robins), 1965

No One Hears But Him (Taylor Caldwell), 1966

No One Now Will Know (E.M. Delafield), 1941

No Orchids by Request (Essie Summers), 1965

No Orchids for a Nurse (Marjorie McEvoy, as Marjorie Harte), 1964

No Other Haven (Kathryn Blair), 1950

No Other Man— (Theresa Charles, as Jan Tempest), 1937

No Passing Fancy (Kay Thorpe), 1980

No Peace for the Wicked (Charity Blackstock, as Ursula Torday), 1937

No Place for Love (Maynah Lewis), 1963

No Place for Love (Petra Sawley), 1967

No Private Heaven (Faith Baldwin), 1946

No Quarter Asked (Janet Dailey), 1974

No Question of Murder (Norah Lofts, as Peter Curtis), 1959

No Real Relation (Mary Burchell), 1953

No Retreat from Love (Maysie Greig), 1942

No Regrets (Hebe Elsna, as Laura Conway), 1958

No Room at the Inn (Edna Ferber), 1941

No Room for Joanna (Mary Ann Gibbs, as Elizabeth Ford), 1964

No Room for Loneliness (Leila Mackinlay), 1965

No Roses in June (Essie Summers), 1961

No Sacrifice (Denise Robins), 1934

No Second Parting (Lilian Peake), 1977

No Shallow Stream (Hebe Elsna), 1950

No Silver Spoon (Jane Arbor), 1959

No Song at Morningside (Maureen Peters, as Sharon Whitby), 1981

No Sooner Met (Isobel Chace, as Elizabeth Hunter), 1965

No Stone Unturned (Claire Lorrimer, as Patricia Robins), 1969

No Summer Beauty (Theresa Charles, as Leslie Lance), 1967

No Tears Tomorrow (Dorothy Daniels, as Helaine Ross), 1962

No Through Road (Theresa Charles), 1960

No Time for a Man (Theresa Charles, as Jan Tempest), 1942

No Time for Love (Barbara Cartland), 1976

No Time for Love (Emilie Loring), 1970

No Time for Love (Petra Sawley), 1967

No Time for Tears (Cynthia Freeman), 1981

No Trespassers in Love (Ursula Bloom, as Sheila Burns), 1949

No Way Home (Marjorie Bowen, as George Preedy), 1947

No Wind of Blame (Georgette Heyer), 1939

Noah's Daughter (Doris E. Smith), 1982

Noble One, The (Denise Robins), 1957

Noble Rogue, The (Baroness Orczy), 1912

Noble Savage, The (Violet Winspear), 1974

Nobody Asked Me (Mary Burchell), 1937

Nobody Else—Ever (Theresa Charles, as Jan Tempest), 1950

Nobody Wants You! (Mabel St. John), 1928

Nobody's Child (Jean S. MacLeod, as Catherine Airlie), 1954

Nobody's Girl (Mabel St. John), 1922

Nobody's in Town (Edna Ferber), 1938

Nobody's Lovers (Ruby M. Ayres), 1921

Nobody's Wife (Charles Garvice, as Caroline Hart)

Nomad's Land (Mary Roberts Rinehart), 1926

None Better Loved (Leila Mackinlay), 1941

None But He (Claire Lorrimer, as Patricia Robins), 1973

None Dare Call It Treason (Catherine Gavin), 1978

None So Blind (Ivy Preston), 1961

None So Pretty (Margaret Irwin), 1930

Nonesuch, The (Georgette Heyer), 1962

Noonfire (Margaret Way), 1972

Nor Any Dawn (Netta Muskett), 1932

Nor Evil Dreams (Rosemary Harris), 1974

Nora Meade, M.D. (Adeline McElfresh, as Elizabeth Wesley), 1955

Norah (Pamela Hill), 1976

Norah Stroyan (Pamela Hill), 1976

Northern Magic (Janet Dailey), 1982

Northwater (Cecily Crowe), 1968

Not a Marrying Man (Rachel Lindsay, as Roberta Leigh), 1978

Not after Midnight (Daphne du Maurier), 1971

Not at Home (Doris Langley Moore), 1948

Not by Appointment (Essie Summers), 1976

Not Far from Heaven (Anne Hampson), 1974

Not for This Alone (Theresa Charles, as Jan Tempest), 1945

Not Free to Love (Ursula Bloom, as Sheila Burns), 1950

Not Heaven Itself (Margaret Pedler), 1940

Not in Our Stars (Victoria Holt, as Eleanor Burford), 1945

Not in the Calendar (Margaret Kennedy), 1964

Not Love Alone (Barbara Cartland), 1933

Not Once but Twice (Betty Neels), 1981

Not One of Us (Maysie Greig, as Jennifer Ames), 1939

Not So Quiet (Evadne Price, as Helen Zenna Smith), 1930

Not under the Law (Grace Livingston Hill), 1925

Not Wanted on Voyage (Kay Thorpe), 1972

Not Without You (Mary Burchell), 1947

Not Yet (Annie S. Swan), 1898

Notable Princess, A (Florence L. Barclay), 1905

Nothing Hurts for Long (Daphne du Maurier), 1943

Nothing Is Safe (E.M. Delafield), 1937

Nothing Lovelier (Ruby M. Ayres), 1942

Notorious Gentleman, The (Charlotte Lamb, as Sheila Holland), 1980

Notorious Lady (Doris Leslie), 1976

Notorious Mrs. Gatacre, The (Baroness von Hutten), 1933

Nourishing Life, A (Kate Norway), 1967

November Tree (Margaret Maddocks), 1964

Now and Always (Theresa Charles, as Jan Tempest), 1950

Now and Forever (Danielle Steel), 1978
Now Barrabas Was a Robber (Ursula Bloom, as Deborah Mann), 1968
Now East, Now West (Susan Ertz), 1927
Now I Can Forget (Theresa Charles, as Leslie Lance), 1973
Now Rough—Now Smooth (Barbara Cartland), 1941
Now That April's Gone (Victoria Holt, as Eleanor Burford), 1961
Now We Set Out (Susan Ertz), 1934
Numbered Account, The (Ann Bridge), 1960
Nun's Castle (Gwendoline Butler, as Jennie Melville), 1973
Nuptials of Corbal, The (Rafael Sabatini), 1927
Nurse Abroad (Essie Summers), 1961
Nurse Alice in Love (Theresa Charles), 1964
Nurse Alison's Trust (Mary Burchell), 1964
Nurse at Barbazon, A (Kathryn Blair), 1964
Nurse at Cap Flamingo (Violet Winspear), 1965
Nurse at Danger Mansion (Dorothy Daniels), 1966
Nurse at Kama Hall (Irene Roberts, as Iris Rowland), 1969
Nurse at Mystery Villa (Willo Davis Roberts), 1967
Nurse at Noongwalla (Roumelia Lane), 1973
Nurse at Rowanbank (Flora Kidd), 1966
Nurse at St. Catherine's (Maysie Greig), 1963
Nurse at Moorcroft Manor (Claire Ritchie, as Sharon Heath), 1967
Nurse at Shadow Manor (Claire Ritchie, as Sharon Heath), 1973
Nurse at the Top (Marion Collin), 1964
Nurse Atholl Returns (Jane Arbor)
Nurse Brookes (Kate Norway), 1958
Nurse by Accident (Theresa Charles), 1974
Nurse Called Liza, A (Ursula Bloom, as Mary Essex), 1973
Nurse Comes Home, A (Jean Francis Webb, as Ethel Hamill), 1954
Nurse Elaine and the Sapphire Star (Claire Ritchie, as Sharon Heath), 1973
Nurse Elizabeth Comes Home (Jean Francis Webb, as Ethel Hamill), 1955
Nurse Elliot's Diary (Kate Norway), 1960
Nurse Errant (Lucilla Andrews), 1961
Nurse for Doctor Keith, A (Dorothy Daniels), 1962
Nurse for Galleon Key, A (Jean Francis Webb, as Ethel Hamill), 1957
Nurse for Mercy's Mission (Adeline McElfresh), 1976

Nurse for Rebels' Run, A (Adeline McElfresh, as Jane Scott), 1960
Nurse from Hawaii, The (Jean Francis Webb, as Ethel Hamill), 1964
Nurse from Killarney (Ursula Bloom, as Mary Essex), 1963
Nurse Greve (Jane Arbor)
Nurse Harriet Goes to Holland (Betty Neels), 1970
Nurse Helen (Rebecca Stratton, as Lucy Gillen), 1970
Nurse in Danger (Maysie Greig), 1964
Nurse in Danger (Willo Davis Roberts), 1972
Nurse in Holland (Betty Neels), 1970
Nurse in Nepal (Irene Roberts), 1976
Nurse in Print (Kate Norway), 1963
Nurse in the Dark (Marion Collin), 1965
Nurse in the Hills (Irene Roberts), 1969
Nurse in the Orient (Marjorie McEvoy, as Marjorie Harte), 1962
Nurse in the Sun (Claire Rayner, as Sheila Brandon), 1972
Nurse in the Woods (Theresa Charles, as Leslie Lance), 1969
Nurse in Waiting (Jane Arbor), 1962
Nurse Is Born, A (Kate Norway, as Bess Norton), 1962
Nurse Jane in Teneriffe (Jean S. MacLeod, as Catherine Airlie), 1967
Nurse Jess (Joyce Dingwell), 1959
Nurse Judy (Adeline McElfresh, as Elizabeth Wesley), 1958
Nurse Kathy (Adeline McElfresh), 1957
Nurse Kay's Conquest (Willo Davis Roberts), 1966
Nurse Lang (Jean S. MacLeod), 1960
Nurse Laurie (Kathryn Blair), 1962
Nurse Maria (Marion Collin), 1963
Nurse Marika (Mary Burchell), 1963
Nurse Marlowe (Jane Arbor), 1959
Nurse Meg's Decision (Kate Norway, as Hilary Neal), 1966
Nurse Moonlight (Irene Roberts), 1980
Nurse Nancy (Adeline McElfresh, as Jane Scott), 1959
Nurse Nolan (Susan Barrie), 1961
Nurse of All Work (Jane Arbor), 1962
Nurse Off Camera (Kate Norway, as Hilary Neal), 1964
Nurse on an Island (Marion Collin), 1970
Nurse on Bodmin Moor (Ursula Bloom, as Rachel Harvey), 1970
Nurse on Castle Island (Claire Ritchie, as Sharon Heath), 1968
Nurse on Holiday (Kathryn Blair, as Rosa-

lind Brett), 1963

Nurse on Horseback (Jean Francis Webb, as Ethel Hamill), 1952

Nurse Pro Tem (Glenna Finley), 1967

Nurse Robin (Willo Davis Roberts), 1973

Nurse Smith, Cook (Joyce Dingwell), 1968

Nurse Stacey Comes Abroad (Rona Randall), 1958

Nurse Trent's Children (Joyce Dingwell), 1961

Nurse Verena in Weirwater (Theresa Charles, as Leslie Lance), 1970

Nurse Who Fell in Love, The (Ursula Bloom, as Mary Essex), 1972

Nurse Who Shocked the Matron, The (Ursula Bloom, as Sheila Burns), 1970

Nurse Willow's Ward (Theresa Charles, as Jan Tempest), 1965

Nursery Maid, The (Mary Ann Gibbs), 1975

Nurses, The (Willo Davis Roberts), 1972

Nurse's Holiday (Maysie Greig, as Jennifer Ames), 1965

Nurse's Story (Maysie Greig, as Jennifer Ames), 1965

O Love! O Fire! (Denise Robins), 1966

Obsession (Charlotte Lamb), 1980

Obsession of Victoria Gracen, The (Grace Livingston Hill), 1915

Obstacle Race, The (Ethel M. Dell), 1921

Occupying Power, The (Evelyn Anthony), 1973

Octavia (Charity Blackstock, as Paula Allardyce), 1965

Octavia (Jilly Cooper), 1977

October Cabaret, The (Nancy Buckingham, as Erica Quest), 1979

October Witch, The (Alanna Knight), 1971

Odd—But Even So (P.C. Wren), 1941

Odds, The (Ethel M. Dell), 1925

Odds on Love (Maysie Greig), 1936

Odious Duke, The (Barbara Cartland), 1973

Odor of Sanctity, An (Frank Yerby), 1965

Of Great Riches (Rose Franken), 1937

Of Lena Geyer (Marcia Davenport), 1936

Of Love and Intrigue (Virginia Coffman), 1969

Of No Fixed Abode (Maynah Lewis), 1968

Of the Ring of Earls (Juliet Dymoke), 1970

Of Time and the Seasons (Nicole St. John), 1975

Of Wind and Fire (Jane Blackmore), 1980

Off White (Christopher Nicole), 1959

Offer of Marriage (Berta Ruck), 1930

Office Wife, The (Faith Baldwin), 1930

Officer's Wife (Denise Robins), 1939

Ogilvie, Tallant, and Moon (Chelsea Quinn Yarbro), 1976

Oh, Darling Joy! (Anne Maybury), 1937

Oh! James! (May Edginton), 1914

Oh, Money! Money! (Eleanor H. Porter), 1918

O'Houlihan's Jest (Rohan O'Grady), 1961

Ola and the Sea Wolf (Barbara Cartland), 1980

Old Adam, The (Ursula Bloom), 1967

Old Baxter Place, The (Adeline McElfresh), 1954

Old Doc (Elizabeth Seifert), 1946

Old Dominion, The (Mary Johnston), 1899

Old Elm Tree, The (Ursula Bloom), 1974

Old Friends and New (Mrs. George de Horne Vaizey), 1909

Old Glory (Anne Duffield), 1942

Old Gods Laugh, The (Frank Yerby), 1964

Old Gray Homestead, The (Frances Parkinson Keyes), 1919

Old Hat (Countess Barcynska, as Oliver Sandys), 1939

Old House of Fear (Russell Kirk), 1961

Old Hunting Lodge, The (Susan Inglis), 1961

"Old Man's" Marriage (G.B. Burgin), 1897

Old Mischief (Warwick Deeping), 1950

Old Moorings, The (Annie S. Swan), 1909

Old Patch's Medley (Marjorie Bowen), 1930

Old Priory, The (Norah Lofts), 1981

Old Pybus (Warwick Deeping), 1928

Old Rectory, The (Ursula Bloom), 1973

Old Roses (Countess Barcynska, as Oliver Sandys), 1923

Old Scarecrow, The (Baroness Orczy), 1916

Old Sinners Never Die (Dorothy Salisbury Davis), 1959

Old Smith's Nurse (Mabel St. John), 1918

Old Wine and New (Warwick Deeping), 1932

Old World Dies, The (Warwick Deeping), 1954

Old-Fashioned Heart (Ruby M. Ayres), 1953

Olive Branch, The (Irene Roberts, as Irene Shaw), 1968

Olive Island (Kay Thorpe), 1973

Oliver October (George Barr McCutcheon), 1923

Oliver Trenton, K.C. (Gilbert Frankau), 1951

Olivia (Charles Garvice), 1902

Olivia (Barbara Riefe), 1981

Olivia and Others (Charles Garvice), 1908

Olivia Mary (Madame Albanesi), 1912

Olivia, The Tormented (Katheryn Kimbrough),

1976

On Call (Elizabeth Harrison), 1974

On Love's Altar (Charles Garvice), 1892

On My Own (Rosamunde Pilcher), 1965

On the Air (Mary Burchell), 1956

On the High Road (Madame Albanesi, as Effie Rowlands), 1914

On the Night of the Seventh Moon (Victoria Holt), 1972

On the Screen (Robert Hichens), 1929

On the Wings of Love (Madame Albanesi, as Effie Rowlands)

Once a Nurse (Willo Davis Roberts), 1966

Once He Was Mine (May Edginton), 1940

Once in a Life (Charles Garvice), 1910

Once in a Lifetime (Danielle Steel), 1982

Once Is Enough (Denise Robins, as Ashley French), 1953

Once to Every Heart (Jean S. MacLeod), 1951

Once upon a Kiss (Hettie Grimstead), 1965

Once You Have Found Him (Esther Wyndham), 1954

One and Only, The (Doris E. Smith), 1973

One Basket (Edna Ferber), 1947

One Between, The (Frances Cowen), 1967

One Brief Sweet Hour (Jane Arbor), 1980

One Broken Dream (Ivy Preston), 1979

One Coin in the Fountain (Susan Barrie, as Anita Charles), 1957

One Dark Night (Pamela Bennetts), 1978

One Day, My Love (Iris Bromige), 1980

One Enchanted Summer (Iris Danbury), 1958

One Fight More (Susan Ertz), 1939

One Fine Day (Mary Ann Gibbs, as Elizabeth Ford), 1954

One Girl in the World, The (Charles Garvice), 1915

One Little Room (Mollie Chappell), 1960

One Love (Jean S. MacLeod), 1945

One Man Too Many (Virginia Coffman), 1968

One Man's Evil (Madame Albanesi, as Effie Rowlands), 1900

One Man's Heart (Mary Burchell), 1940

One Month at Sea (Ruby M. Ayres), 1929

One More River to Cross (Essie Summers), 1979

One More Time (Faith Baldwin), 1972

One Night in Ceylon (Denise Robins), 1931

One Night in London (Lucilla Andrews), 1979

One of the Boys (Janet Dailey), 1980

One of the Chorus (Berta Ruck), 1928

One of the Crowd (Madame Albanesi), 1913

One of the Family (Mary Burchell), 1939

One of Those Ways (Marie Belloc Lowndes), 1929

One Room for His Highness (Maysie Greig), 1944

One Sees Stars (Ruby M. Ayres), 1952

One Step from Heaven (Elizabeth Hoy), 1943

One String for Her Bow (Joyce Dingwell), 1970

One String for Nurse Bow (Joyce Dingwell), 1969

One Summer (Ruby M. Ayres), 1930

One Summer's Day (Jean S. MacLeod, as Catherine Airlie), 1961

One Thing I Wanted, The (Theresa Charles, as Jan Tempest), 1944

One to Live With (Ruby M. Ayres), 1938

One Traveller Returns (G.B. Burgin), 1931

One Unwanted, The (Ruby M. Ayres), 1921

One Way Out, The (Baroness von Hutten), 1906

One Way Out (Jean S. MacLeod), 1941

One Way Ticket (Margaret Way), 1977

One Way to Venice (Jane Aiken Hodge), 1974

One Who Cares (Claire Lorrimer, as Patricia Robins), 1954

One Who Counted, The (Madame Albanesi), 1937

One Who Forgot, The (Ruby M. Ayres), 1919

One Who Kisses, The (Lucy Walker), 1954

One Who Looked On, The (Hebe Elsna, as Lyndon Snow), 1965

One Who Paid, The (Madame Albanesi, as Effie Rowlands), 1935

One Who Remembers (Theresa Charles), 1976

One Who Stood By, The (Ruby M. Ayres), 1923

One Woman, The (Madame Albanesi, as Effie Rowlands), 1911

One Woman Too Many (Ruby M. Ayres), 1952

One Woman's Freedom (Evadne Price, as Helen Zenna Smith), 1932

One-Eyed Moon, The (Marguerite Steen), 1935

One-Faced Girl, The (Charlotte Armstrong), 1963

One-Man Girl (Maysie Greig), 1931

Only a Girl's Love (Charles Garvice), 1901

Only a Singing Girl (Mabel St. John), 1907

Only a Touch (Theresa Charles, as Fay Chandos), 1941

Only Charity, The (Sara Seale), 1961

Only Her Husband (Leila Mackinlay), 1939

Only Love (Barbara Cartland), 1980

Only My Dreams (Denise Robins), 1951

Only My Heart to Give (Nan Asquith), 1955

Only One Love (Charles Garvice), 1910

Only Our Love (Iris Bromige), 1968

Only Son, An (Annie S. Swan), 1898

Only to Part (Irene Roberts), 1961

Only World, The (G.B. Burgin), 1906

Only You (Margaret Pargeter), 1979

Open Day at the Manor (Mary Ann Gibbs, as Elizabeth Ford), 1977

Open Door, The (Margaret Maddocks), 1980

Open Not the Door (Katrina Britt), 1978

Open the Door to Love (Theresa Charles, as Jan Tempest), 1952

Open Window, The (Netta Muskett), 1930

Open Wings (Barbara Cartland), 1942

Openers of the Gate, The (L. Adams Beck), 1930

Opening Flower, The (Eleanor Farnes), 1948

Open Ophelia (Florence Stevenson), 1968

Ophelia, The Anxious (Katheryn Kimbrough), 1977

Opportune Marriage (Kay Thorpe), 1968

Optimist, The (E.M. Delafield), 1922

Oracles, The (Margaret Kennedy), 1955

Orange Blossom for Sandra (Ursula Bloom), 1951

Orange Blossom for Tara (Irene Roberts, as Iris Rowland), 1971

Orange Blossom Shop, The (Theresa Charles, as Jan Tempest), 1946

Orange Blossoms (Marjorie Bowen, as Joseph Shearing), 1938

Orange Sash, The (Juliet Dymoke), 1958

Oranges and Lemons (Isobel Chace), 1967

Orchard Hill (Elizabeth Seifert), 1945

Orchard Hill (Lucy Waker), 1958

Orchards (Warwick Deeping), 1922

Orchid Girl (Theresa Charles, as Leslie Lance), 1978

Orchids for the Bride (Hettie Grimstead), 1967

Ordeal of Elizabeth, The (Elizabeth), 1901

Ordeal of Three Doctors (Elizabeth Seifert), 1965

Ordered South (A.M. Williamson), 1900

Ordinary People (Edith Pargeter), 1941

Orphan Bride (Sara Seale), 1962

Orphans, The (D.A. Ponsonby), 1962

Other Cathy, The (Nancy Buckingham), 1978

Other Girl, The (Charles Garvice), 1911

Other Juliet, The (Anne Maybury), 1955

Other Linding Girl, The (Mary Burchell), 1966

Other Lips Have Loved You (Mary Burchell), 1938

Other Love, The (Denise Robins), 1952

Other Men's Arms (Maysie Greig, as Ann Barclay), 1936

Other Miss Donne, The (Jane Arbor), 1971

Other One, The (Theresa Charles, as Fay Chandos), 1953

Other People's Fires (Hebe Elsna), 1931

Other Room, The (Jane Blackmore), 1968

Other Side of Love, The (Denise Robins), 1973

Other Side of Paradise, The (Maynah Lewis), 1975

Other Side of Summer, The (Anne Worboys, as Vicky Maxwell), 1977

Other Side of the Street, The (Shirley Jackson), 1956

Other Woman, The (Viña Delmar), 1930

Other Woman, The (Charles Garvice), 1905

Other Women's Beauty (Maysie Greig), 1938

Oubliette, The (Jeffery Farnol), 1912

Our Admirable Betty (Jeffery Farnol), 1918

Our Avenue (Ruby M. Ayres), 1922

Our Dearest Emma (Ursula Bloom, as Lozania Prole), 1949

Our Lady of Marble (Ursula Bloom), 1926

Our Lady of the Beeches (Baroness von Hutten), 1902

Our Little Life (Hebe Elsna), 1942

Our Miss Penny (Hettie Grimstead, as Marsha Manning), 1964

Our Nell (Mabel St. John), 1917

Out of a Clear Sky (Madame Albanesi, as Effie Rowlands), 1925

Out of Reach (Barbara Cartland), 1945

Out of the Dark (Nan Asquith), 1972

Out of the Dark (Norah Lofts), 1972

Out of the House (Margaret Irwin), 1916

Out of the Past (Charles Garvice)

Out of the Shadows (Anne Duffield), 1944

Out of the Storm (Grace Livingston Hill, as Marcia Macdonald), 1929

Out of the Swim (G.B. Burgin), 1930

Out of the War? (Marie Belloc Lowndes), 1918

Out of the Whirlwind (Audrey Erskine-Lindop), 1951

Out of This Nettle (Norah Lofts), 1938

Out to Marry Money (Berta Ruck), 1940

Out Trail, The (Mary Roberts Rinehart), 1923

Outcast of the Family, An (Charles Garvice), 1900

Outcasts of Crowthorpe College, The (Mabel

St. John), 1913

Outer Ring, The (Audrey Erskine-Lindop), 1955

Outlaw Love (Kathleen Norris), 1928

Outrageous Fortune (Mary Ann Gibbs, as Elizabeth Ford), 1955

Outrageous Lady, The (Barbara Cartland), 1977

Outside Chance, An (Leila Mackinlay), 1966

Over at the Crowleys' (Kathleen Norris), 1946

Over the Blue Mountains (Mary Burchell), 1952

Over the Castle Wall (Jean S. MacLeod), 1974

Over the Hills (Jeffery Farnol), 1930

Overheard (Ruby M. Ayres), 1925

Overlooker, The (Phyllis Hastings), 1982

Overseas Nurse (Maysie Greig, as Jennifer Ames), 1961

Owner Gone Abroad (Ruby M. Ayres), 1937

Pacific Cavalcade (Virginia Coffman), 1980

Pack Mule (Ursula Bloom), 1931

Pact Without Desire (Jane Arbor), 1979

Paddington Green (Claire Rayner), 1975

Pagan Encounter (Charlotte Lamb), 1978

Pagan Interlude (Kathryn Blair, as Rosalind Brett), 1947

Pagan Island, The (Violet Winspear), 1972

Pagan King, The (Edison Marshall), 1959

Pagan Lover (Anne Hampson), 1980

Pageant of Victory, A (Jeffery Farnol), 1936

Pagoda, The (Marjorie Bowen), 1927

Paid For! (Charles Garvice), 1892

Painted Angel (Marjorie Bowen, as George Preedy), 1938

Painted Butterflies (Mrs. Patrick MacGill), 1931

Painted Ceiling, The (Eleanor Farnes), 1961

Painted Heaven (Netta Muskett), 1934

Painted Lady, The (Ursula Bloom), 1945

Painted Palace, The (Iris Danbury), 1977

Painted Virgin (Hettie Grimstead), 1931

Painted Wings (Rebecca Stratton, as Lucy Gillen), 1972

Palace, The (Chelsea Quinn Yarbro), 1979

Palace of the Hawk (Margaret Rome), 1974

Palace of the Peacocks (Violet Winspear), 1969

Palace of the Pomegranate (Violet Winspear), 1974

Pale Betrayer, The (Dorothy Salisbury Davis), 1966

Pale Dawn, Dark Sunset (Anne Mather), 1975

Palm Rock and Paradise (Anne Worboys, as Anne Eyre Worboys), 1961

Palomino (Danielle Steel), 1981

Pam series (Baroness von Hutten)

Pandora (Elisabeth Beresford), 1974

Pandora Lifts the Veil (Maysie Greig, as Jennifer Ames), 1932

Papa (A.M. Williamson), 1902

Paper Halo (Kate Norway), 1970

Paper Marriage, The (Flora Kidd), 1974

Paper Prison (P.C. Wren), 1939

Paper Roses (Ruby M. Ayres), 1916

Parade of Peacocks, A (Elizabeth Ashton), 1972

Paradine Case, The (Robert Hichens), 1933

Paradise (Anne Duffield), 1936

Paradise (Sarah Neilan), 1981

Paradise Island (Elisabeth Beresford), 1963

Paradise Place (Warwick Deeping), 1949

Paradise Plantation (Henrietta Reid), 1979

Paradise Row (Charity Blackstock, as Paula Allardyce), 1976

Paragon Street (Doris Leslie), 1963

Parasites, The (Daphne du Maurier), 1949

Parcel of Land, A (Mary Ann Gibbs), 1969

Parents Are a Problem (Maysie Greig), 1933

Paris—And My Love (Mary Burchell), 1960

Parisian Adventure (Elizabeth Ashton), 1970

Parkerstown Delegate, The (Grace Livingston Hill), 1892

Parson Harding's Daughter (Joanna Trollope), 1979

Parson's House (Elizabeth Cadell), 1977

Partners (Grace Livingston Hill), 1940

Partners Are a Problem (Theresa Charles, as Fay Chandos), 1957

Partners for Playtime (Mary Howard), 1938

Parts Unknown (Frances Parkinson Keyes), 1938

Party in Dolly Creek (Charity Blackstock), 1967

Passage Perilous, A (Naomi Jacob), 1948

Passage to Pontefract (Victoria Holt, as Jean Plaidy), 1981

Passerby, The (Ethel M. Dell), 1925

Passing Fancy (Mary Linn Roby), 1980

Passing Star, The (Jean Stubbs), 1970

Passing Strangers (Jean S. MacLeod, as Catherine Airlie), 1963

Passing Sweet (Hebe Elsna, as Vicky Lancaster), 1953

Passion and the Flower, The (Barbara Cartland), 1978

Passion Flower (Marjorie Bowen), 1932

Passion Flower, A (Charles Garvice), 1910

Passion Flower (Kathleen Norris), 1930

Passion for Treason, A (Christopher Nicole, as Robin Nicholson), 1981

Passionate Adventure, The (Ursula Bloom, as Sheila Burns), 1936

Passionate Attachment (Barbara Cartland), 1935

Passionate Awakening, The (Denise Robins), 1926

Passionate Encounter (Flora Kidd), 1979

Passionate Enemies, The (Victoria Holt, as Jean Plaidy), 1976

Passionate Flame, The (Denise Robins), 1928

Passionate Heart, The (Ursula Bloom), 1930

Passionate Interlude (Anne Duffield), 1931

Passionate Involvement (Lilian Peake), 1977

Passionate Jade (Anne Rundle, as Georgianna Bell), 1969

Passionate Kindness, The (Alanna Knight), 1974

Passionate Pilgrim, The (Barbara Cartland, as Barbara McCorquodale), 1952

Passionate Puritan, The (Maureen Peters, as Belinda Grey), 1978

Passionate Rebel, The (Frank G. Slaughter), 1979

Passionate Rivals, The (Hettie Grimstead, as Marsha Manning), 1978

Passionate Savage, The (Constance Gluyas), 1980

Passionate Sinner (Violet Winspear), 1977

Passionate Springtime, The (Ursula Bloom, as Mary Essex), 1956

Passionate Stranger (Flora Kidd), 1981

Passionate Summer, The (Hettie Grimstead), 1953

Passionate Witness (Victoria Holt, as Eleanor Burford), 1941

Passions in the Sand (Barbara Cartland), 1976

Passions of Medora Graeme, The (Elsie Lee), 1972

Passion's Pride (Claudette Williams), 1980

Passion's Promie (Danielle Steel), 1977

Passion's Slave (Mary Francis Craig, as Alexis Hill), 1979

Passport to Happiness (Maysie Greig), 1955

Passport to Love (Hettie Grimstead, as Marsha Manning), 1958

Past Master (Nigel Tranter), 1965

Past Must Die, The (Hebe Elsna, as Vicky Lancaster), 1959

Past Tense of Love, The (Elizabeth Cadell), 1970

Pastel (Georgette Heyer), 1929

Pastoral (Ursula Bloom), 1934

Pastor's Wife, The (Elizabeth), 1914

Pat of Silver Bush (L.M. Montgomery), 1935

Patch of Blue, The (Grace Livingston Hill), 1932

Patchwork Quilt, The (Netta Muskett), 1946

Path of the Eclipse (Chelsea Quinn Yarbro), 1981

Path of the Hero King, The (Nigel Tranter), 1970

Path of the Moonfish, The (Betty Beaty), 1964

Path to Love, The (Hettie Grimstead), 1960

Paths of Summer, The (Iris Bromige), 1979

Pathway to Paradise (Maysie Greig), 1942

Patient in Love (Theresa Charles), 1963

Patient in Room 18, The (Mignon Eberhart), 1929

Patricia (Grace Livingston Hill), 1939

Patricia and Life (Madame Albanesi), 1920

Patricia Plays a Part (Mabel Barnes Grundy), 1913

Patricia, The Beautiful (Katheryn Kimbrough), 1975

Patriot, The (Nigel Tranter), 1982

Patriot's Dream (Barbara Michaels), 1976

Pattern, The (Mignon Eberhart), 1937

Pattern (Rose Franken), 1925

Pattern of Murder (Mignon Eberhart), 1948

Patty series (Jean Webster)

Paul in Possession (Ruby M. Ayres), 1924

Pavement of Pearl, A (Iris Danbury), 1975

Pavilion (Ursula Bloom), 1951

Pavilion at Monkswood (Anne Maybury), 1965

Pavilion of Honour, The (Marjorie Bowen, as George Preedy), 1932

Pawn in Frankincense (Dorothy Dunnett), 1969

Pay Me Tomorrow (Mary Burchell), 1940

Pay the Doctor (Elizabeth Seifert), 1966

Paying Pests (Mabel Barnes Grundy), 1941

Payment in Full (Anne Hampson), 1980

Peach's Progress, The (May Edginton), 1927

Peacock Bed, The (Anne Rundle, as Joanne Marshall), 1978

Peacock Hill (Leila Mackinlay), 1948

Peacock Queen, The (Maureen Peters), 1972

Peacock Spring, The (Rumer Godden), 1975

Pearl of the Habsburgs, The (Julia Fitzgerald, as Julia Hamilton), 1978

Pearl of the West (Mabel St. John), 1918

Pearl Thief, The (Berta Ruck), 1926

Pearl-Maiden (H. Rider Haggard), 1903

Peggy series (Mrs. George de Horne Vaizey)

Peggy by Request (Ethel M. Dell), 1928

Peggy Fordyce (Annie S. Swan), 1940

Peggy of Beacon Hill (Maysie Greig), 1924

Peggy, The Concerned (Katheryn Kimbrough), 1981

Peggy the Pilgrim (G.B. Burgin), 1907

Peking Picnic (Ann Bridge), 1932

Pelicans, The (E.M. Delafield), 1918

Penalty for Living (Jean S. MacLeod), 1942

Penance (May Wynne), 1917

Pendulum, The (Annie S. Swan), 1926

Pengelly Jade, The (Rebecca Stratton, as Lucy Gillen), 1972

Penhallow (Georgette Heyer), 1942

Penmarris (Susan Howatch), 1971

Pennies from Heaven (Berta Ruck), 1940

Pennies on Her Eyes (Mary Linn Roby), 1969

Penniless Heir, The (Barbara Cartland), 1974

Penniless Heiress, The (Mary Ann Gibbs), 1975

Penny Box, The (Alice Dwyer-Joyce), 1981

Penny Plain (Sara Seale), 1967

People Are So Respectable (Hebe Elsna), 1937

People from the Sea, The (Velda Johnston), 1979

People in Glass House (Charity Blackstock), 1975

People of My Own (Edith Pargeter), 1942

People of the Mist, The (H. Rider Haggard), 1894

People on the Hill, The (Velda Johnston), 1971

Pepper Tree Bay (Lucy Walker, as Dorothy Lucie Sanders), 1959

Perchance to Dream (Ursula Bloom), 1971

Perchance to Marry (Kathryn Blair, as Celine Conway), 1961

Perdita's Prince (Victoria Holt, as Jean Plaidy), 1969

Peregrine's Progress (Jeffery Farnol), 1922

Perfect Marriage (Hebe Elsna, as Vicky Lancaster), 1949

Perfect Match, A (Patricia Veryan), 1981

Perfect Stranger, A (Suzanne Ebel), 1966

Perfect Stranger, A (Danielle Steel), 1982

Perfect Wife, The (Doris Leslie), 1960

Perfect Wife and Mother, The (Rosemary Ellerbeck, as Nicola Thorne), 1980

Perfection of Love, The (Barbara Cartland), 1980

Perfume of the Rainbow, The (L. Adams Beck), 1923

Peridot Flight (Doris Leslie), 1956

Peril at Polvellyn (Marjorie McEvoy), 1973

Perilous Quest (Maysie Greig, as Jennifer Ames), 1960

Perilous Waters (Jane Blackmore), 1954

Period Stuff (Dornford Yates), 1942

Perishable Goods (Dornford Yates), 1928

Perrine (Dorothy Daniels), 1978

Persian Price, The (Evelyn Anthony), 1975

Persian Ransom, The (Evelyn Anthony), 1975

Persistent Lover, The (Eleanor Farnes), 1958

Person in the House, The (G.B. Burgin), 1900

Personal Affair (Flora Kidd), 1981

Personality Plus (Edna Ferber), 1914

Perturbing Spirit (Janet Caird), 1966

Petals Drifting (Anne Hampson), 1971

Petals in the Wind (Ivy Preston), 1972

Peter, A Parasite (Madame Albanesi), 1901

Peter Day-by-Day (Countess Barcynska, as Marguerite Barclay), 1916

Peter Jackson, Cigar Merchant (Gilbert Frankau), 1920

Peter Jameson (Gilbert Frankau), 1920

Peter West (D.E. Stevenson), 1923

Petticoat Government (Baroness Orczy), 1910

Petticoat Rule (Baroness Orczy), 1910

Peverills, The (Doris Leslie), 1946

Phantasy (Anne Duffield), 1932

Phantom Cottage, The (Velda Johnston), 1970

Phantom Flame of Wind House, The (Katheryn Kimbrough), 1973

Phantom Lover, The (Ruby M. Ayres), 1919

Phantom Pipes, The (Jean S. MacLeod), 1975

Phantom Reflection, The (Katheryn Kimbrough, as Ann Ashton), 1978

Phenwick Women series (Katheryn Kimbrough)

Philippa (Netta Muskett), 1954

Phillippa (Charles Garvice)

Philomela's Miracle (Betty Neels), 1978

Philosopher's Daughter, The (Susan Ertz), 1976

Phoebe Dean (Grace Livingston Hill), 1909

Phoenix Rising (Marguerite Steen), 1952

Phroso (Anthony Hope), 1897

Phyllis in France (May Wynne), 1919

Physicians, The (Elizabeth Harrison), 1966

Piccadilly Inn (Leila Mackinlay), 1946

Pick Up and Smile (Countess Barcynska), 1936

Pied Tulip, The (Elizabeth Ashton), 1969

Pierrepont's Daughters (G.B. Burgin), 1935

Pilate's Wife (Ursula Bloom, as Deborah Mann), 1976

Pilgrim of Desire (Maureen Peters, as Veronica Black), 1979

Pilgrim Soul, The (Ursula Bloom), 1932

Pilgrim's Castle (Violet Winspear), 1969

Pilgrims in Paradise (Frank G. Slaughter), 1960

Pilgrim's Inn (Elizabeth Goudge), 1948

Pilgrims of Circumstance (G.B. Burgin), 1920

Pillar of Iron, A (Taylor Caldwell), 1965

Pilot's Point (Leila Mackinlay), 1949

Pineapple Girl (Betty Neels), 1978

Pink Sands (Wynne May), 1974

Pious Fraud, A (G.B. Burgin), 1938

Pious Pilgrimage, The (Elizabeth), 1901

Piper in the Hills, The (Audrie Manley-Tucker), 1974

Piper's Gate (Audrie Manley-Tucker), 1960

Piper's Pool (Leila Mackinlay), 1946

Piper's Tune (Margaret Maddocks), 1954

"Piping Times," The (Jeffery Farnol), 1945

Pippa (Mabel Barnes Grundy), 1932

Pippin's Journal (Rohan O'Grady), 1962

Piracy (Michael Arlen), 1922

Pirate of the Sun (Gwen Westwood), 1972

Pistols for Two (Georgette Heyer), 1960

Pitiless Choice (Margaret Pedler), 1933

Pity My Love (Daoma Winston), 1967

Pixie series (Mrs. George de Horne Vaizey)

Pixie's Mysterious Mission (May Wynne), 1933

Place Called Paradise, A (Essie Summers), 1967

Place for Everyone, A (Anne Betteridge), 1977

Place for Lovers, A (Gwen Westwood), 1978

Place of Ravens, A (Pamela Hill), 1980

Place of Sapphires, The (Florence Engel Randall), 1969

Place of Stones, The (Constance Heaven), 1975

Place to Stand, A (Ann Bridge), 1953

Plague Ship (Frank G. Slaughter), 1976

Plain People (Kathleen Norris), 1938

Plantagenet Prelude, The (Victoria Holt, as Jean Plaidy), 1977

Plantation Boss, The (Anne Hampson), 1972

Plantation Doctor (Kathryn Blair), 1962

Plantation Moon (Gloria Bevan), 1978

Plantation of Vines, A (Wynne May), 1977

Planter and the Tree, The (Ruby M. Ayres), 1926

Plaster Cast (Netta Muskett), 1933

Play Fair with Love (Claire Lorrimer, as Patricia Robins), 1972

Playboy, The (Warwick Deeping), 1948

Player King, The (Elizabeth Ashton), 1975

Player Queen (Constance Heaven, as Constance Fecher), 1968

Playing with Fire (Charlotte Lamb, as Laura Hardy), 1981

Pleasant Husband, The (Marjorie Bowen), 1921

Please Burn after Reading (Ursula Bloom, as Sheila Burns), 1954

Pleasure and the Pain, The (Anne Mather), 1971

Pleasure Garden, The (Countess Barcynska, as Oliver Sandys), 1923

Pleasure Seekers, The (Mary Howard), 1970

Plotted in Darkness (May Wynne), 1927

Plough, The (Naomi Jacob), 1928

Plum Thicket, The (Janice Holt Giles), 1954

Plume of Dust, A (Wynne May), 1975

Poellenberg Inheritance, The (Evelyn Anthony), 1972

Poinciana (Phyllis A. Whitney), 1980

Poison Flower (Dorothy Daniels), 1977

Poison in Pimlico (Victoria Holt, as Elbur Ford), 1950

Poisoned Lives! (Mabel St. John), 1924

Poisoners, The (Marjorie Bowen, as George Preedy), 1936

Point of View, The (Elinor Glyn), 1913

Polly Kettle (Mary Ann Gibbs), 1963

Polly, The Worried (Katheryn Kimbrough), 1978

Pollyanna series (Eleanor H. Porter)

Polly's Summer Stock (Adeline McElfresh, as Elizabeth Wesley), 1957

Polonaise (Doris Leslie), 1943

Pompeii Scroll, The (Jacqueline La Tourrette), 1975

Pool, The (Mary Roberts Rinehart), 1952

Pool of Dreams (Lucy Walker), 1971

Pool of Pink Lilies (Joyce Dingwell), 1970

Poor Butterfly (Hebe Elsna, as Lyndon Snow), 1951

Poor, Dear Margaret Kirby (Kathleen Norris), 1913

Poor Millionaire, A (G.B. Burgin), 1933

Poor Relation (Hebe Elsna, as Lyndon Snow), 1968

Poor Straws! (Naomi Jacob), 1933

Poor Wise Man, A (Mary Roberts Rinehart), 1920

Poor Young People! (May Edginton), 1939

Poppet & Co. (Countess Barcynska, as Oliver Sandys), 1944

Poppies in the Corn (Madame Albanesi), 1911

Poppy and the Rose, The (Countess Barcynska, as Oliver Sandys), 1962

Port of Adventure, The (C.N. and A.M. Williamson), 1913

Port o' Missing Men (P.C. Wren), 1934

Portrait in Gold (Patricia Ainsworth), 1971

Portrait of a Gentleman in Colours, A (Jeffery Farnol), 1935

Portrait of a Lady (Lady Eleanor Smith), 1936

Portrait of a Playboy (Warwick Deeping), 1947

Portrait of a Witch (Dorothy Daniels), 1976

Portrait of Destiny, A (Annie S. Swan), 1937

Portrait of Jaime (Margaret Way), 1978

Portrait of Jill (Suzanne Ebel), 1972

Portrait of Lorraine (Hebe Elsna, as Laura Conway), 1971

Portrait of Paula (Hettie Grimstead), 1968

Portrait of Pierre (Ivy Preston), 1971

Portrait of Sarah (Maureen Peters, as Veronica Black), 1969

Portrait of Susan (Kathryn Blair, as Rosalind Brett), 1956

Portraits (Cynthia Freeman), 1979

Portugese Affair, A (Anne Betteridge), 1966

Portugese Escape, The (Ann Bridge), 1958

Possessed, The (Dorothy Daniels), 1975

Possession (Louis Bromfield), 1925

Possession (Mazo de la Roche), 1923

Possession (Charlotte Lamb), 1979

Possession of Tracy Corbin, The (Dorothy Daniels), 1973

Post of Honor (R.F. Delderfield), 1974

Post Office Girl, The (Mabel St. John), 1915

Postmark Murder (Mignon Eberhart), 1956

Postscript to Yesterday (Essie Summers), 1966

Post-War Girl (Berta Ruck), 1930

Poverty's Daughter (Mabel St. John, as Henry St. John Cooper), 1922

Powder and Patch (Georgette Heyer), 1930

Power (Naomi Jacob), 1927

Power and the Passion, The (Christopher Nicole, as Christina Nicholson), 1977

Power and the Prince, The (Barbara Cartland), 1980

Power of Love, The (Madame Albanesi, as Effie Rowlands), 1911

Power to Kill, The (Robert Hichens), 1934

Powers and Maxine, The (C.N. and A.M. Williamson), 1907

Practice for Sale (Leila Mackinlay), 1964

Prairie Fires (Annie S. Swan), 1913

Precious Waif (Anne Hampson), 1969

Predestined (Anne Duffield), 1929

Prelude for Two Queens (Hebe Elsna), 1972

Prelude to Enchantment (Anne Mather), 1972

Prelude to Freedom (Elizabeath Renier), 1967

Prelude to Louise (Anne Maybury), 1954

Prelude to Love (Elizabeth Renier), 1972

Prelude to Yesterday (Ursula Bloom), 1961

Prescription for Love (Rachel Lindsay), 1977

Prescription for Melissa (Alice Dwyer-Joyce), 1974

Presence and the Power, The (Marjorie Bowen), 1924

Presence in an Empty Room, A (Velda Johnston), 1980

President Is Born, A (Fannie Hurst), 1928

Pretence (Rachel Lindsay, as Roberta Leigh), 1956

Pretender to Love (Florence Stevenson, as Zabrina Faire), 1981

Pretenders, The (Mary Howard), 1962

Prettiest Girl, The (Mary Burchell), 1955

Pretty Dear (Countess Barcynska), 1920

Pretty Horse-Breakers, The (Barbara Cartland), 1971

Pretty Kitty (Florence Stevenson, as Zabrina Faire), 1981

Pretty One, The (Maysie Greig), 1937

Pretty Ones, The (Dorothy Eden), 1957

Pretty Penelope (Madame Albanesi, as Effie Rowlands), 1907

Pretty Polly Pennington (Madame Albanesi), 1908

Pretty Witch, The (Rebecca Stratton, as Lucy Gillen), 1971

Pretty, Witty Nell! (Ursula Bloom, as Lozania Prole), 1953

Previous Lady, The (Jacqueline Tourrette), 1974

Price Is Love, The (Barbara Cartland, as Barbara McCorquodale), 1960

Price of Folly, The (Denise Robins, as Denise Chesterton), 1955

Price of Honor (Charles Garvice)

Price of Honour, The (Charles Garvice, as Charles Gibson)

Price of Inheritance (Alice Dwyer-Joyce), 1963

Price of Love (Rachel Lindsay), 1967

Price of Pleasure, The (Hebe Elsna), 1937

Price of the King's Peace, The (Nigel Tranter), 1971

Price of Things, The (Elinor Glyn), 1919

Price Paid, The (Madame Albanesi, as Effie Rowlands), 1914

Pride and Power (Anne Hampson), 1974

Pride and the Poor Princess (Barbara Cartland), 1980

Pride of Eve, The (Warwick Deeping), 1914

Pride of Fiona Macrae, The (Annie S. Swan), 1934

Pride of Her Life (Charles Garvice)

Pride of Innocence, A (Maynah Lewis), 1971

Pride of Lions, A (Isobel Chace), 1972

Pride of Lions, A (Juliet Dymoke), 1978

Pride of Madeira (Isobel Chace, as Elizabeth Hunter), 1977

Pride of Race (Baroness Orczy), 1942

Pride of the Morning (Victoria Holt, as Eleanor Burford), 1958

Pride of the Peacock, The (Victoria Holt), 1976

Pride of the South (Elizabeth Seifert), 1950

Pride of the Trevallions, The (Carola Salisbury), 1975

Pride Parted Them! (Mabel St. John), 1925

Pride's Castle (Frank Yerby), 1949

Priestess of the Damned (Virginia Coffman), 1970

Prima Donna (Hebe Elsna, as Lyndon Snow), 1963

Prime Minister's Wife, The (Doris Leslie), 1961

Primrose Bride, The (Kathryn Blair), 1961

Primula (Majorie Bowen, as George Preedy), 1941

Primula and Hyacinth (Ursula Bloom, as Sheila Burns), 1950

Prince and Heretic (Marjorie Bowen), 1914

Prince and the Pekingese, The (Barbara Cartland), 1979

Prince and the Quakeress, The (Victoria Holt, as Jean Plaidy), 1968

Prince Charming (Countess Barcynska, as Oliver Sandys), 1937

Prince for Portia, A (Theresa Charles, as Jan Tempest), 1943

Prince for Sale (Rachel Lindsay), 1975

Prince of Darkness, The (Victoria Holt, as Jean Plaidy), 1978

Prince of Darkness (Barbara Michaels), 1969

Prince of Eden, The (Marilyn Harris), 1978

Prince of Foxes (Samuel Shellabarger), 1947

Prince of Intrigue, A (May Wynne), 1920

Prince Philanderer (Ursula Bloom, as Lozania Prole), 1968

Prince's Darling, The (Marjorie Bowen, as George Preedy), 1930

Prince's Story (Countess Barcynska), 1959

Princess and the Pagan, The (Julia Fitzgerald), 1982

Princess Charming (Madame Albanesi, as Effie Rowlands), 1931

Princess in Distress, A (Barbara Cartland), 1978

Princess in Love (Hebe Elsna, as Vicky Lancaster), 1957

Princess of All Linds, The (Russell Kirk), 1979

Princess of Celle, The (Victoria Holt, as Jean Plaidy), 1967

Princess Passes, The (Ruby M. Ayres), 1931

Princess Passes, The (Frances Cowen, as Eleanor Hyde), 1979

Princess Passes, The (C.N. and A.M. Williamson), 1904

Princess Priscilla's Fortnight, The (Elizabeth), 1905

Princess Sophia (Edison Marshall), 1958

Princess Virginia, The (A.M. Williamson), 1909

Princess's Game, The (Ethel M. Dell), 1920

Print Petticoat, The (Lucilla Andrews), 1954

Prior Betrothal, A (Elsie Lee), 1973

Prison Wall, The (Ethel M. Dell), 1932

Prisoner in Paradise (Marjorie Lewty), 1980

Prisoner of Love, The (Barbara Cartland), 1979

Prisoner of Love, The (Jean S. MacLeod), 1958

Prisoner of Malville Hall, The (Dorothy Daniels), 1973

Prisoner of Passion (Nancy Buckingham, as Nancy John), 1981

Prisoner of the Heart (Charlotte Lamb, as Sheila Holland), 1972

Prisoner of Zenda, The (Anthony Hope), 1894

Prisoners of Hope, The (Mary Johnston), 1898

Prisoner-Stained! (Mabel St. John, as Henry St. John Cooper), 1921

Private Duty (Faith Baldwin), 1936

Private Hotel—Anywhere (Mabel Barnes Grundy), 1937

Private Wing, The (Claire Rayner, as Sheila Brandon), 1971

Probationer (Evadne Price), 1934

Problems of Doctor A, The (Elizabeth Seifert), 1979

Problems of Love, The (Barbara Cartland), 1978

Procession (Fannie Hurst), 1929

Prodigal Girl, The (Grace Livingston Hill), 1929

Prodigal Heart, The (Susan Ertz), 1950

Prodigal Son, The (Hall Caine), 1904

Professional Hero (Maysie Greig), 1943

Professional Lover (Maysie Greig), 1933

Professional Secret, A (Kate Norway), 1964

Progress of Julius, The (Daphne du Maurier), 1933

Prologue to Love, A (Taylor Caldwell), 1961

Promise, The (Danielle Steel), 1978

Promise at Midnight (Lilian Peake), 1980

Promise for Ever, A (Denise Robins), 1961

Promise of Delight (Mary Howard), 1952

Promise of Happiness, The (Betty Neels), 1979

Promise of Morning, The (Audrie Manley-Tucker), 1962

Promise of Murder, The (Mignon Eberhart), 1961

Promise of Paradise (Theresa Charles, as Jan Tempest), 1949

Promises (Catherine Gaskin), 1982

Promising Affair, A (Glenna Finley), 1974

Property of a Gentleman, The (Catherine Gaskin), 1974

Prophet of Berkeley Square, The (Robert Hichens), 1901

Prophetic Marriage, The (Warwick Deeping), 1920

Props (Naomi Jacob), 1932

Pro's Daughter, The (Leila Mackinlay), 1934

Proselyte, The (Susan Ertz), 1933

Protégé, The (Charlotte Armstrong), 1970

Proud Citadel (Theresa Charles), 1967

Proud Citadel (Elizabeth Hoy), 1942

Proud Harvest (Anne Mather), 1978

Proud Lover, The (Hettie Grimstead, as Marsha Manning), 1966

Proud Patricia (Annie S. Swan), 1940

Proud Princess, The (Barbara Cartland), 1976

Proud Servant, The (Margaret Irwin), 1934

Proud Stranger (Rebecca Stratton), 1976

Provincial Lady series (E.M. Delafield)

Prude and the Prodigal, The (Barbara Cartland), 1980

Prudence (Jilly Cooper), 1978

Prudence Langford's Ordeal (Madame Albanesi, as Effie Rowlands), 1914

Psychiatrist's Wife, The (Roberta Gellis, as Leah Jacobs), 1966

Public Smiles, Private Tears (Helen Van Slyke), 1982

Publicity Baby (Countess Barcynska), 1935

Publicity for Anne (A.M. Williamson), 1926

Puller of Strings, The (G.B. Burgin), 1917

Pullman (Ethel M. Dell), 1930

Pulse of Life, The (Marie Belloc Lowndes), 1908

Punch and Judy (Madame Albanesi), 1919

Punished with Love (Barbara Cartland), 1980

Punishment of a Vixen (Barbara Cartland), 1977

Puppets Parade (Doris Leslie), 1932

Purchase Price, The (Annie S. Swan), 1934

Pure and Untouched (Barbara Cartland), 1981

Pure as the Lily (Catherine Cookson), 1972

Puritan Strain, The (Faith Baldwin), 1935

Puritans in Paradise (Frank G. Slaughter), 1960

Purple and the Gold, The (Dorothy Daniels), 1980

Purple Parasol, The (George Barr McCutcheon), 1905

Purple Quest, The (Frank G. Slaughter), 1965

Pursuing Shadow, The (May Wynne), 1944

Pursuit and the Capture, The (Eleanor Farnes), 1966

Pursuit of Pleasure, The (Hebe Elsna), 1969

Push the Past Behind (Henrietta Reid), 1977

Put Back the Clock (Denise Robins), 1962

Put Love Aside (Susan Inglis), 1939

Pyramid, The (Robert Hichens), 1936

Quaint Place (Countess Barcynska, as Oliver Sandys), 1952

Quality of Music, A (Rose Burghley), 1966

Quarrel and Kiss (Berta Ruck), 1942

Queen and Lord M, The (Victoria Holt, as Jean Plaidy), 1973

Queen and the Gypsy, The (Constance Heaven), 1977

Queen Anne's Lace (Frances Parkinson Keyes), 1930

Queen for England, A (Ursula Bloom, as Lozania Prole), 1957

Queen for the Regent, A (Ursula Bloom, as Lozania Prole), 1971

Queen from Provence, The (Victoria Holt, as Jean Plaidy), 1979

Queen Guillotine (Ursula Bloom, as Lozania Prole), 1962

Queen in Waiting (Victoria Holt, as Jean Plaidy), 1967

Queen in Waiting (Norah Lofts), 1955

Queen Jennie (May Wynne), 1918

Queen Jezebel (Victoria Holt, as Jean Plaidy), 1953

Queen Kate (Charles Garvice), 1909

Queen of Diamonds, The (Victoria Holt, as Ellalice Tate), 1958

Queen of Evil (Frank G. Slaughter), 1962

Queen of Hearts, The (Sara Seale), 1969

Queen of Paris, The (Christopher Nicole, as Christina Nicholson), 1979

Queen of Spades, The (Marjorie McEvoy), 1975

Queen of the Dawn (H. Rider Haggard), 1925

Queen Sheba's Ring (H. Rider Haggard), 1910

Queen Sweetheart (A.M. Williamson) , 1901

Queen Who Never Was, The (Maureen Peters), 1972

Queen Who Was a Nun, The (Ursula Bloom, as Lozania Prole), 1967

Queenmaker, The (Maureen Peters), 1975

Queen's Affair, The (Ursula Bloom), 1979

Queen's Caprice (Marjorie Bowen, as George Preedy), 1934

Queen's Captain, The (Alanna Knight, as Margaret Hope), 1978

Queen's Confession, The (Victoria Holt), 1968

Queen's Daughters, The (Ursula Bloom, as Lozania Prole), 1973

Queen's Delight (Constance Heaven, as Constance Fecher), 1966

Queen's Favorite (Constance Heaven, as Constance Fecher), 1974

Queen's Favourites, The (Victoria Holt, as Jean Plaidy), 1966

Queen's Folly (Elswyth Thane), 1937

Queen's Grace, The (Nigel Tranter), 1953

Queen's Harbour (Mary Ann Gibbs, as Elizabeth Ford), 1944

Queen's Husband, The (Victoria Holt, as Jean Plaidy), 1973

Queen's Letter, The (Charlotte Lamb, as Sheila Coates), 1973

Queen's Messenger, The (Barbara Cartland), 1971

Queen's Midwife, The (Ursula Bloom, as Lozania Prole), 1961

Queen's Nurse (Jane Arbor), 1960

Queen's Play (Dorothy Dunnett), 1964

Queen's Quadrille, The (Mary Linn Roby, as Georgina Grey), 1981

Queen's Ward, The (Hebe Elsna), 1966

Quest, The (Nan Asquith), 1964

Quest for Alexis (Nancy Buckingham), 1973

Quest of Glory, The (Marjorie Bowen), 1912

Quest of Youth, The (Jeffery Farnol), 1927

Questing Heart, The (Elizabeth Ashton), 1978

Questing Trout, The (Ursula Bloom), 1934

Question of Marriage, A (Rachel Lindsay), 1972

Question of Marriage, A (Mrs. George de Horne Vaizey), 1910

Question of Quality, A (Madame Albanesi), 1909

Question of Temptation, A (Baroness Orczy), 1925

Quick and the Dead, The (Pamela Bennetts), 1980

Quicksilver Pool, The (Phyllis A. Whitney), 1955

Quiet Gentleman, The (Georgette Heyer), 1951

Quiet Heart, The (Susan Barrie), 1966

Quiet Heart (Rose Franken), 1954

Quiet Hills, The (Iris Bromige), 1967

Quiet Holiday (Kathryn Blair, as Rosalind Brett), 1957

Quiet House, The (Margaret Maddocks), 1947

Quiet Island, The (Netta Muskett), 1943

Quiet One, The (Kate Norway, as Bess Norton), 1959

Quiet Sound of Fear, The (Dorothy Mackie Low, as Lois Paxton), 1971

Quiet Valley, The (Eleanor Farnes), 1944

Quiet Village, The (Ursula Bloom), 1965

Quiet Wards, The (Lucilla Andrews), 1956

Quill's Window (George Barr McCutcheon), 1921

Quisanté (Anthony Hope), 1900

R.S.V.P. Murder (Mignon Eberhart), 1965

Race for Love, The (Barbara Cartland), 1978

Rachel, The Possessed (Katheryn Kimbrough), 1975

Rachel Lee (May Wynne), 1925

Rachel Trevellyan (Anne Mather), 1974

Radiance (Anne Maybury), 1979

Radkin Revenge, The (Willo Davis Roberts), 1979

Ragamuffin (Maysie Greig), 1929

Rage and Desire (Christopher Nicole, as Leslie Arlen), 1982

Raging Waters, The (Dorothy Daniels), 1970

Rainbow after Rain (Theresa Charles), 1977

Rainbow at Dusk (Emilie Loring), 1942

Rainbow Bird, The (Margaret Way), 1972

Rainbow Child (Anne Worboys, as Annette Eyre), 1971

Rainbow Cottage (Grace Livingston Hill), 1934

Rainbow Days, The (Jean S. MacLeod), 1973

Rainbow Glass, The (Alice Dwyer-Joyce),

1973

Rainbow in My Hand, A (Audrie Manley-Tucker), 1965

Rainbow Isle, The (Jean S. MacLeod), 1939

Rainbow River (Irene Roberts, as Iris Rowland), 1970

Rainbow Romance (Claire Ritchie), 1974

Rainbow Shell, The (Iris Danbury), 1960

Rainbow to Heaven, A (Barbara Cartland), 1976

Rainbow Valley (L.M. Montgomery), 1919

Rains Came, The (Louis Bromfield), 1937

Raintree Valley (Violet Winspear), 1971

Rakehell (Anne Rundle), 1970

Rake's Progress, The (Marjorie Bowen), 1912

Ralph Carey (Lady Miles), 1922

Ralph Dacre (Anne Stevenson), 1967

Rancher Needs a Wife, The (Kathryn Blair, as Celine Conway), 1962

Rancho Rio, El (Mignon Eberhart), 1970

Randy, The (Lucy Walker, as Dorothy Lucie Sanders), 1948

Ranger in the Hills, A (Lucy Walker), 1966

Ransom, The (Grace Livingston Hill), 1933

Rapture (Phyllis Hastings), 1966

Rapture in My Rags (Phyllis Hastings), 1954

Rapture of the Desert (Violet Winspear), 1972

Ratoon (Christopher Nicole), 1962

Ravelston Affair, The (Elizabeth Harrison), 1967

Raven Wings (Anne Edwards), 1977

Ravenburn (Laura Black), 1978

Ravenden (Jane Blackmore), 1976

Ravenscar (Maureen Peters), 1981

Ravenscrag (Jean S. MacLeod), 1948

Ravenscroft (Dorothy Eden), 1965

Raven's Forge (Gwendoline Butler, as Jennie Melville), 1975

Ravensley Touch, The (Constance Heaven), 1982

Ravensmount (Marjorie McEvoy), 1974

Ravenstor (Elizabeth Renier), 1974

Ravenswood, (Janet Louise Roberts), 1971

Ravenswood Hall (Dorothy Daniels, as Angela Gray), 1973

Ravishers, The (Virginia Coffman, as Jeanne Duval), 1980

Raw Summer (Jane Blackmore), 1967

Raxl, Voodoo Princess (Dorothy Daniels), 1970

Reach for the Shadows (Alice Dwyer-Joyce), 1972

Reaching for the Stars (Lucy Walker), 1966

Ready—Aye Ready! (Mabel St. John, as Henry St. John Cooper), 1916

Real Gold (Madame Albanesi, as Effie Rowlands), 1924

Real Thing, The (Lilian Peake), 1972

Realms of Gold, The (Isobel Chace, as Elizabeth Hunter), 1976

Reap the Whirlwind (Anne Hampson), 1975

Reap the Whirlwind (Mary Linn Roby), 1972

Reaping, The (Rafael Sabatini), 1929

Reason Why, The (Elinor Glyn), 1911

Reason Why, The (Marie Belloc Lowndes), 1932

Rebecca (Daphne du Maurier), 1938

Rebecca, The Mysterious (Katheryn Kimbrough), 1975

Rebel Against Love (Elizabeth Ashton), 1981

Rebel Bride, The (Anne Hampson), 1971

Rebel Doctor (Elizabeth Seifert), 1978

Rebel Heart, The (Anne Maybury), 1959

Rebel Hearts (Annie S. Swan), 1940

Rebel Heiress (Jane Aiken Hodge), 1975

Rebel in Love (Lilian Peake), 1978

Rebel Lover, The (Charity Blackstock, as Paula Allardyce), 1979

Rebel Princess (Evelyn Anthony), 1953

Rebel Princess, The (Doris Leslie), 1970

Rebel Wife (Rona Randall), 1944

Receipt for Hardness (Hebe Elsna), 1935

Receipt for Murder (Gwendoline Butler), 1956

Reckless (May Edginton), 1932

Reckless Adventure (Eleanor Farnes), 1942

Reckless Angel (Marie Belloc Lowndes), 1939

Reckless Pilgrim, The (Jean S. MacLeod), 1941

Re-Creations (Grace Livingston Hill), 1924

Red Ashes (Margaret Pedler), 1924

Red Carnelian, The (Phyllis A. Whitney), 1968

Red Chalet, The (Kate Norway, as Bess Norton), 1960

Red Cherry Summer (Rosalind Laker, as Barbara Øvstedal), 1973

Red Cliffs, The (Eleanor Farnes), 1961

Red Cliffs of Malpara (Margaret Way), 1976

Red Cross Barge, The (Marie Belloc Lowndes), 1916

Red Dust (Netta Muskett), 1954

Red Eve (H. Rider Haggard), 1912

Red Flame, The (Lady Miles), 1921

Red Fleur-de-Lys, The (May Wynne), 1912

Red for Danger! (Evadne Price), 1936

Red Fruit (May Wynne), 1929

Red Ginger Blossom (Joyce Dingwell), 1972

Red Hair (Elinor Glyn)

Red in the Morning (Dornford Yates), 1946

Red Is for Murder (Phyllis A. Whitney), 1943

Red Lamp, The (Mary Roberts Rinehart), 1925

Red Lotus (Jean S. MacLeod, as Catherine Airlie), 1958

Red, Red Rose, A (Marjorie McEvoy), 1960

Red Rose of Anjou (Victoria Holt, as Jean Plaidy), 1982

Red Rose of Lancaster, The (May Wynne), 1922

Red Roses for a Nurse (Ivy Preston), 1968

Red Rowan Berrry (Frances Murray), 1976

Red Runs the Sunset (Irene Roberts, as Roberta Carr), 1963

Red Saint, The (Warwick Deeping), 1909

Red Signal, The (Grace Livingston Hill), 1919

Red Silence (Kathleen Norris), 1929

Red Sky at Morning (Margaret Kennedy), 1927

Red Sky at Night (Victoria Holt, as Eleanor Burford), 1959

Red Sky at Night: Lovers' Delight? (Jane Aiken Hodge), 1977

Red Staircase, The (Gwendoline Butler), 1979

Red Veil, The (Mabel St. John, as Henry St. John Cooper), 1928

Red Wagon (Lady Eleanor Smith), 1930

Red Whirlpool, The (May Wynne), 1919

Red, White, and Grey (Lady Miles), 1921

Redeemed by Love (Charles Garvice, as Caroline Hart)

Red-Headed Bastard (Hebe Elsna), 1981

Redway Street (Mabel St. John, as Henry St. John Cooper), 1924

Reeds of Honey (Margaret Way), 1975

Reef of Dreams (Mary Howard), 1942

Reflection (Katheryn Kimbrough, as Ann Ashton), 1979

Reflections of Ambrosine, The (Elinor Glyn), 1902

Regency Buck (Georgette Heyer), 1935

Regency Rogue (Pamela Bennetts), 1981

Regency Scandal, A (Alice Chetwynd Ley), 1979

Regent's Daughter, The (Victoria Holt, as Jean Plaidy), 1971

Regent's Gift, The (May Wynne), 1915

Regina (Clare Darcy), 1976

Rehearsal for Love (Faith Baldwin), 1940

Reilly's Woman (Janet Dailey), 1978

Rekindled Flame, The (Elizabeth Ashton), 1980

Rekindled Flame, The (Jean Marsh), 1982

Relative Stranger, A (Anne Stevenson), 1970

Release the Past (Ivy Preston), 1973

Relenting Fate, A (Charles Garvice), 1912

Relentless Storm (Claire Lorrimer), 1975

Reluctant Adventuress, The (Sylvia Thorpe), 1963

Reluctant Bride, The (Barbara Cartland), 1970

Reluctant Bride, The (Hettie Grimstead), 1957

Reluctant Bride, The (Leila Mackinlay), 1939

Reluctant Cinderella, The (Maysie Greig, as Jennifer Ames), 1952

Reluctant Folly (Jean S. MacLeod), 1942

Reluctant Governess, The (Anne Mather), 1971

Reluctant Guest, The (Kathryn Blair, as Rosalind Brett), 1959

Reluctant Landlord, The (Sara Seale), 1962

Reluctant Madonna, The (Marguerite Steen), 1929

Reluctant Maiden, The (Glenna Finley), 1975

Reluctant Masquerade (Henrietta Reid), 1969

Reluctant Millionaire (Maysie Greig), 1944

Reluctant Nightingale (Kate Norway), 1970

Reluctant Odyssey (Edith Pargeter), 1947

Reluctant Orphan, The (Sara Seale), 1947

Reluctant Partnership (Elizabeth Ashton), 1979

Reluctant Relation (Mary Burchell), 1961

Reluctant Rivals, The (Mary Linn Roby, as Georgina Grey), 1981

Reluctant Voyager (Katrina Britt), 1973

Reluctant Widow, The (Georgette Heyer), 1946

Remedy for Love (Flora Kidd), 1972

Remember September (Joyce Dingwell), 1978

Remember This Stranger (Kay Thorpe), 1974

Remember Today (Elswyth Thane), 1941

Remembered Kiss, The (Ruby M. Ayres), 1918

Remembered Serenade (Mary Burchell), 1975

Remembered Spring (Margaret Maddocks), 1949

Remembering Louise (Anna Gilbert), 1978

Remembrance (Danielle Steel), 1981

Rendezvous, The (Evelyn Anthony), 1967

Rendezvous, The (Daphne du Maurier), 1980

Rendezvous (Rose Franken), 1954

Rendezvous in Lisbon (Iris Danbury), 1967

Rendezvous in Venice (Elizabeth Ashton), 1978

Rendezvous in Zagarella (Berta Ruck), 1964

Rendezvous with Fear (Anne Worboys), 1977

Renegade Girl (Mary Ann Gibbs), 1981

Renny's Daughter (Mazo de la Roche), 1951

Renshawe Inheritance, The (Elizabeth Renier), 1972

Rent a Wife (Rachel Lindsay, as Roberta Leigh), 1980

Repeating Pattern, The (Mary Howard), 1968

Repent at Leisure (Anne Duffield), 1945

Reprieve (Warwick Deeping), 1945

Reputation (Denise Robins), 1963

Requiem for Idols (Norah Lofts), 1938

Respectable Miss Parkington-Smith, The (Charity Blackstock, as Paula Allardyce), 1964

Rest Is Magic, The (Marjorie Lewty), 1973

Rest Is Silence, The (Virginia Coffman), 1967

Rest of My Life with You, The (Faith Baldwin), 1942

Restless Beauty (Maysie Greig, as Jennifer Ames), 1944

Restless Dream (Leila Mackinlay), 1949

Restless Heart, The (Elisabeth Beresford), 1982

Restless Heart (Denise Robins), 1938

Restless Lady, The (Frances Parkinson Keyes), 1963

Restless Passion, The (Viña Delmar), 1947

Restless Years, The (Jean S. MacLeod, as Catherine Airlie), 1950

Retreat from Love (Maysie Greig), 1937

Retribution (Charlotte Lamb), 1981

Retribution (Mabel St. John, as Henry St. John Cooper), 1930

Return, The (Evelyn Anthony), 1978

Return, The (Daoma Winston), 1972

Return Engagement (Glenna Finley), 1981

Return I Dare Not (Margaret Kennedy), 1931

Return Journey (Ruby M. Ayres), 1938

Return Journey (R.F. Delderfield), 1974

Return Journey (May Edginton), 1935

Return Match (Elizabeth Cadell), 1979

Return of a Heroine (Marguerite Steen), 1936

Return of Simon (Kathryn Blair, as Celine Conway), 1953

Return of the Cuckoo, The (Theresa Charles, as Leslie Lance), 1976

Return of the Petticoat, The (Warwick Deeping), 1909

Return to Aylforth (Anne Eliot), 1967

Return to Bellbird Country (Anne Worboys, as Annette Eyre), 1966

Return to Belle Amber (Margaret Way), 1971

Return to Candelriggs (Henrietta Reid), 1966

Return to Darkness (Willo Davis Roberts), 1969

Return to Deepwater (Rebecca Stratton, as Lucy Gillen), 1975

Return to Delphi (Anne Betteridge), 1964

Return to Dragonshill (Essie Summers), 1971

Return to Glenshael (Mary Elgin), 1965

Return to King's Mere (Theresa Charles, as Leslie Lance), 1967

Return to Love (Jane Blackmore), 1964

Return to Love (Mary Howard), 1946

Return to Love (Anne Maybury), 1939

Return to Sender (Audrey Manley-Tucker), 1968

Return to Silbersee (Jane Arbor), 1978

Return to Spring (Jean S. MacLeod), 1939

Return to Terror (Theresa Charles), 1966

Return to Tremarth (Susan Barrie), 1969

Return to Tremarth (Rose Burghley), 1969

Return to Vienna (Nancy Buckingham), 1971

Return to Wuthering Heights (Rosemary Ellerbeck, as Anna L'Estrange), 1977

Returned Empty (Florence L. Barclay), 1920

Reuben (Charles Garvice), 1912

Reunion in Reno (Maysie Greig, as Mary Douglas Warren), 1941

Reveille for Romance (Jean Francis Webb, as Ethel Hamill), 1946

Reversion to Type, A (E.M. Delafield), 1923

Revolt—and Virginia (Essie Summers), 1969

Revolt of Sarah Perkins, The (Marian Cockrell), 1965

Revolt of the Eaglets, The (Victoria Holt, as Jean Plaidy), 1977

Rhapsody of Love, A (Barbara Cartland), 1977

Rhiannon (Roberta Gellis), 1982

Rhona Keith (Annie S. Swan), 1910

Rhythm of Flamenco, The (Isobel Chace), 1966

Rib of the Hawk, The (Rosamond Marshall), 1956

Ribbons and Laces (Ruby M. Ayres), 1924

Ribbons in Her Hair (Lucy Walker, as Dorothy Lucie Sanders), 1957

Ribs of Death, The (Joan Aiken), 1967

Rich and the Righteous, The (Helen Van Slyke), 1971

Rich Are Different, The (Susan Howatch), 1977

Rich Are Not Proud, The (Maysie Greig, as Mary Douglas Warren), 1942

Rich Girl—Charity Girl (Mabel St. John), 1922

Rich Girl, Poor Girl (Faith Baldwin), 1938

Rich Man, Poor Girl (Maysie Greig), 1935

Rich Mrs. Burgoyne, The (Kathleen Norris),

1912

Rich Twin, Poor Twin (Maysie Greig), 1940

Richard and the Knights of God (Pamela Bennetts), 1970

Richard Chatterton, V.C. (Ruby M. Ayres), 1915

Richest Girl in the World (Virginia Coffman), 1967

Richest Man, The (May Edginton), 1952

Riddle of a Lady (Leila Mackinlay), 1955

Ride a Black Horse (Margaret Pargeter), 1975

Ride a White Dolphin (Anne Maybury), 1971

Ride on Singing (Claire Ritchie), 1964

Ride the Blue Riband (Rosalind Laker), 1977

Ride the Thunder (Janet Dailey), 1981

Ride with Me (Thomas B. Costain), 1944

Riders of the Wind (Elswyth Thane), 1926

Ridin' High (Leila Mackinlay), 1941

Right Arm, The (Mrs. George de Horne Vaizey), 1918

Right Grand Girl, A (Mary Howard), 1972

Rilla of Ingleside (L.M. Montgomery), 1921

Rio d'Oro (Nigel Tranter), 1955

Ring, The (Danielle Steel), 1980

Ring for a Fortune, A (Lilian Peake), 1980

Ring for Nurse Raine (Theresa Charles), 1962

Ring in a Teacup (Betty Neels), 1978

Ring o' Roses (Lucilla Andrews), 1972

Ring of Fire (Margaret Way), 1978

Ring of Hope (Leila Mackinlay), 1965

Ring of Jade (Margaret Way), 1972

Ring on Her Finger, A (Mary Burchell), 1953

Ring the Bell Softly (Pamela Bennetts), 1978

Ring Tree, The (Ursula Bloom), 1964

Ring Without Romance (Maysie Greig, as Jennifer Ames), 1940

Ringed Castle, The (Dorothy Dunnett), 1971

Ripening Vine (Olga Sinclair, as Ellen Clare), 1982

Ripple on the Water, A (Dorothy Mackie Low), 1964

Rising of the Lark, The (Berta Ruck), 1951

Rising Star (Kay Thorpe), 1969

Rival Beauties (Mabel St. John), 1907

Rival Doctors, The (Elizabeth Seifert), 1967

Rival Heiresses (Charles Garvice, as Caroline Hart)

Rival Sisters (Henrietta Reid), 1970

Rivals at School—Rivals Through Life! (Mabel St. John), 1926

River, The (Rumer Godden), 1946

River and Wilderness, The (Anne Worboys, as Annette Eyre), 1967

River Is Down, The (Lucy Walker), 1967

River Lodge (Elizabeth Cadell), 1949

River Lord, The (Kay Thorpe), 1977

River Nurse (Joyce Dingwell), 1962

River Road, The (Frances Parkinson Keyes), 1945

River Voices (Suzanne Ebel), 1976

Rivertown (Janet Louise Roberts), 1972

Road, The (Warwick Deeping), 1931

Road Boss, The (Joyce Dingwell), 1976

Road That Bends, The (Ruby M. Ayres), 1916

Road Through the Wall, The (Shirley Jackson), 1948

Road to Bithynia, The (Frank G. Slaughter), 1951

Road to Damascus, The (Annie S. Swan), 1937

Road to Gafsa, The (Rebecca Stratton), 1976

Road to Revelation, The (Norah Lofts), 1941

Road to the Border, The (Elizabeth Ashton), 1974

Road to Understanding, The (Eleanor H. Porter), 1917

Road to Yesterday, The (L.M. Montgomery), 1974

Roadway to the Past (Jean S. MacLeod), 1951

Roast Beef, Medium (Edna Ferber), 1913

Robert Martin's Lesson (Annie S. Swan), 1886

Robert the Bruce series (Nigel Tranter)

Robin in a Cage, A (Ursula Bloom), 1943

Robin the Prodigal (May Wynne), 1919

Rochester, The Mad Earl (Victoria Holt, as Kathleen Kellow), 1957

Rochester's Wife (D.E. Stevenson), 1940

Rock and Sand (Naomi Jacob), 1926

Rock Pine (Netta Muskett), 1952

Rocklitz, The (Marjorie Bowen, as George Preedy), 1930

Rocks of Arachenza, The (Elizabeth Ashton), 1973

Rocks of Valpré, The (Ethel M. Dell), 1913

Rococo (Marjorie Bowen), 1921

Rogue, The (Janet Dailey), 1980

Rogue Cavalier (Rosamond Marshall), 1955

Rogue Gentleman (Edison Marshall), 1963

Rogue Roman (Lance Horner), 1965

Rogues' Covenant (Sylvia Thorpe), 1957

Rogue's Lady, The (Charity Blackstock, as Paula Allardyce), 1979

Rogue's Mistress (Constance Gluyas), 1977

Rolande (Clare Darcy), 1978

Roman Affair (Rachel Lindsay), 1976

Roman Summer (Jane Arbor), 1973

Romance and Nurse Margaret (Ursula Bloom, as Sheila Burns), 1972

Romance at Hillyard House (Kathleen Norris), 1948

Romance at Wrecker's End (Theresa Charles, as Leslie Lance), 1976

Romance for Rose (Theresa Charles, as Jan Tempest), 1959

Romance for Sale (Maysie Greig, as Jennifer Ames), 1934

Romance in Glenmore Street (Ivy Preston), 1974

Romance in Two Keys (Berta Ruck), 1955

Romance Is Always Young (Hebe Elsna, as Lyndon Snow), 1957

Romance Is Mine (Ursula Bloom, as Sheila Burns), 1941

Romance of a Film Star (Berta Ruck), 1956

Romance of a Rogue, The (Ruby M. Ayres), 1923

Romance of Atlantic, The (Taylor Caldwell), 1976

Romance of Charles Dickens, The (Ursula Bloom), 1960

Romance of Dr. Dinah, The (Ursula Bloom, as Mary Essex), 1967

Romance of Jenny W.R.E.N. (Ursula Bloom, as Sheila Burns), 1944

Romance of Summer (Ursula Bloom, as Mary Essex), 1959

Romance of Two Worlds, A (Marie Corelli), 1886

Romance on a Cruise (Maysie Greig), 1935

Romance on Ice (Theresa Charles, as Jan Tempest), 1942

Romance on the Rhine (Elsie Lee), 1974

Romance Royal (Berta Ruck), 1937

Romantic Afterthought (Berta Ruck), 1959

Romantic Assignment (Elsie Lee), 1974

Romantic Assignment (Adeline McElfresh), 1961

Romantic Cottage Hospital (Ursula Bloom, as Sheila Burns), 1967

Romantic Frenchman, The (Mary Ann Gibbs), 1967

Romantic Fugitive (Ursula Bloom, as Sheila Burns), 1943

Romantic Intruder (Ursula Bloom, as Sheila Burns), 1952

Romantic Journey (Nancy Buddingham), 1968

Romantic Lady, The (Michael Arlen), 1921

Romantic Lady (Sylvia Thorpe), 1960

Romantic Melody (Eleanor Farnes), 1938

Romantic Prince, The (Rafael Sabatini), 1929

Romantic Rivals, The (Carolina Courtney), 1980

Romantic Spirit, The (Glenna Finley), 1973

Romantic Summer Sea (Ursula Bloom, as Sheila Burns), 1956

Romantic Theatre Sister (Ursula Bloom, as Mary Essex), 1965

Romantic Touch, The (Theresa Charles, as Fay Chandos), 1957

Romantic Widow, The (Mollie Chappell), 1978

Romantics, The (Mary Roberts Rinehart), 1929

Romany (Lady Eleanor Smoth), 1935

Romany Curse, The (Dorothy Daniels, as Suzanne Somers), 1971

Romany Rebel, The (Florence Stevenson, as Zabrina Faire), 1979

Romany Sister (D.A. Ponsonby, as Doris Rybot), 1960

Romeo in Moon Village (George Barr McCutcheon), 1925

Ronald Lindsay (May Wynne), 1905

Room in the Tower, The (Jane Blackmore), 1972

Room with Dark Mirrors, A (Velda Johnston), 1975

Room Without a Door, A (Audrie Manley-Tucker), 1970

Roomates (Elsie Lee), 1976

Rooms at Mrs. Oliver's (Victoria Holt, as Kathleen Kellow), 1953

Rooney (Catherine Cookson), 1957

Root and Branch (Nigel Tranter), 1948

Rooted in Dishonour (Anne Mather), 1978

Roots (Naomi Jacob), 1931

Roper's Row (Warwick Deeping), 1929

Rosa Mundi (Ethel M. Dell), 1921

Rosabelle Shaw (D.E. Stevenson), 1967

Rosalie's Career (Faith Baldwin), 1928

Rosalind Comes Home (Essie Summers), 1968

Rosary, The (Florence L. Barclay), 1909

Rose and the Thorn, The (Eleanor Farnes), 1968

Rose and the Yew Tree, The (Mary Westmacott), 1948

Rose Domino, The (Sheila Walsh), 1981

Rose for Ana María, A (Frank Yerby), 1976

Rose for Virtue, A (Norah Lofts), 1971

Rose from Lucifer, A (Anne Hampson), 1979

Rose Galbraith (Grace Livingston Hill), 1940

Rose in Heather, A (Suzanne Ebel), 1978

Rose in the Bud (Susan Barrie), 1966

Rose in the Rind, The (George Barr McCutcheon), 1910

Rose Island (Irene Roberts, as Iris Rowland), 1969

Rose o' the Sea (Countess Barcynska), 1920

Rose of the Dawn, The (Ethel M. Dell), 1917

Rose of Glenconnel, The (Mrs. Patrick Mac-Gill), 1916

Rose of Hever, The (Maureen Peters), 1969

Home of Life, The (Madame Albanesi, as Effie Rowlands), 1912

Rose of the Desert (Roumelia Lane), 1967

Rose of the World (Kathleen Norris), 1924

Rose of Yesterday, The (Madame Albanesi), 1908

Rose Princess, The (Theresa Charles, as Leslie Lance), 1979

Rose, Rose, Where Are You? (Rosemary Ellerbeck), 1978

Rose Sweetman (Ursula Bloom), 1933

Rose Timson (Marguerite Steen), 1946

Roseanne (Madame Albanesi), 1922

Rosebud and Stardust (Ursula Bloom, as Sheila Burns), 1951

Rose-Coloured Thread, A (Mrs. George de Horne Vaizey), 1898

Rose-Grower, The (Jean Stubbs), 1962

Roseheath (Anne Maybury, as Katherine Troy), 1969

Roselynde Chronicles, The (Roberta Gellis)

Rosemary (C.N. and A.M. Williamson), 1909

Rosemary—For Forgetting (Ruby M. Ayres), 1941

Rosemary for Remembrance (Ivy Preston), 1962

Rosemary in Search of a Father (C.N. and A.M. Williamson), 1906

Rosemary Tree, The (Elizabeth Goudge), 1956

Roses for Breakfast (Hettie Grimstead), 1970

Roses for Christmas (Betty Neels), 1975

Roses for the Bride (Hettie Grimstead, as Marsha Manning), 1962

Roses from a Haunted Garden (Jean Francis Webb), 1971

Roses in the Snow (Elizabeth Hoy), 1936

Rose's Last Summer (Margaret Millar), 1952

Roses round the Door (Elisabeth Beresford), 1965

Rosevean (Iris Bromige), 1962

Rose-Walled Castle, The (Iris Danbury), 1959

Rosewood Box, The (Mary Burchell), 1970

Ross Inheritance, The (Rebecca Stratton, as Lucy Gillen), 1969

Ross of Silver Ridge (Gwen Westwood), 1975

Rough Diamond Lover (Rachel Lindsay), 1978

Rough Seas to Sunrise (Maysie Greig, as Jennifer Ames), 1956

Rough Shooting (P.C. Wren), 1938

Rough Weather (Iris Bromige) , 1972

Round Dozen (Elizabeth Cadell), 1978

Round Tower, The (Catherine Cookson), 1968

Rowan Head (Elisabeth Ogilvie), 1949

Rowan Tree, The (Jean S. MacLeod), 1943

Rowleston (Barbara Riefe), 1976

Royal Affair, The (Kay Thorpe), 1976

Royal Box, the (Frances Parkinson Keyes), 1954

Royal Deputy (Hebe Elsna, as Vicky Lancaster), 1957

Royal Escape (Georgette Heyer), 1938

Royal Escape (Maureen Peters), 1972

Royal Flush (Margaret Irwin), 1932

Royal Griffin, The (Juliet Dymoke), 1978

Royal Intrigue (Evelyn Anthony), 1954

Royal Pledge, The (Barbara Cartland), 1970

Royal Purple (Susan Barrie), 1962

Royal Purple (D.A. Ponsonby), 1954

Royal Regiment (Gilbert Frankau), 1938

Royal Road to Fotheringay (Victoria Holt, as Jean Plaidy), 1955

Royal Signet (Charles Garvice)

Royal Slave (Julia Fitzgerald), 1978

Royal Summons (Elizabeth Cadell), 1973

Royal Swords at Agincourt (Pamela Bennetts), 1971

Royal Traitor, A (May Wynne), 1927

Royal William (Doris Leslie), 1940

Ruaig Inheritance, The (Jean S. MacLeod), 1978

Rubber Princess, A (G.B. Burgin), 1919

Rubies (L. Adams Beck, as Louis Moresby), 1927

Rubies for My Love (Eleanor Farnes), 1969

Ruby (Viña Delmar), 1956

Ruby Heart (Janet Louise Roberts, as Rebecca Danton), 1980

Rufus on the Rebound (Berta Ruck), 1918

Rugged Path, The (Charles Garvice), 1908

Rule Britannia (Daphne du Maurier), 1972

Ruling Passion, The (Annie S. Swan), 1920

Rum Week (Nigel Tranter), 1954

Run Away from Love (Jean S. MacLeod), 1939

Run for His Money, A (May Wynne), 1919

Run for Your Love (Lilian Peake), 1978

Run from the Wind (Rebecca Stratton), 1974

Run, Sara, Run (Anne Worboys), 1981
Run Scared (Mignon Eberhart), 1963
Runaway, The (Kathleen Norris), 1939
Runaway Bride (Jane Aiken Hodge), 1975
Runaway Bride (Elizabeth Hoy), 1939
Runaway Bride, The (Rebecca Stratton, as Lucy Gillen), 1972
Runaway Daughter, A (Annie S. Swan), 1898
Runaway from Love (Rona Randall), 1956
Runaway Girl, The (Lucy Walker), 1975
Runaway Heart, The (Barbara Cartland, as Barbara McCorquodale), 1961
Runaway Lovers (Berta Ruck), 1963
Runaway Nurse (Jean Francis Webb, as Ethel Hamill), 1955
Runaway Star, A (Barbara Cartland), 1978
Runaway Visitors, The (Eleanor Farnes), 1973
Runaways, The (Claire Lorrimer, as Patricia Robins), 1962
Running Free (Countess Barcynska), 1929
Running Thursday (Phyllis Hastings), 1980
Rupert of Hentzau (Anthony Hope), 1898
Russet Jacket, The (Countess Barcynska), 1924
Rust of Rome, The (Warwick Deeping), 1910
Rustle of Bamboo, The (Kathryn Blair, as Celine Conway), 1957
Ruth, The Unsuspecting (Kathryn Kimbrough), 1977
Ruthless Rake, The (Barbara Cartland), 1974
Ruth's Romance (Madame Albanesi, as Effie Rowlands), 1913

S.O.S. Queenie (Countess Barcynska, as Oliver Sandys), 1928
Sable Hunter (Anne Rundle, as Alexandra Manners), 1977
Sackcloth into Silk (Warwick Deeping), 1935
Sacked City, The (Marjorie Bowen, as George Preedy), 1949
Sacred Bullock, The (Mazo de la Roche), 1939
Sacrifice, The (Anne Betteridge), 1973
Sacrifice to Art (Charles Garvice), 1908
Safari for Seven (Netta Muskett), 1952
Safari South (Kay Thorpe), 1976
Safe Bridge, The (Frances Parkinson Keyes), 1934
Safe Custody (Dornford Yates), 1932
Safety for My Love (Hebe Elsna, as Laura Conway), 1963
Safety-Curtain, The (Ethel M. Dell), 1917
Saffron (Julia Fitzgerald, as Julia Watson), 1972

Saffron Sky, The (Isobel Chace), 1968
Saffroned Bridesails (Naomi Jacob, as Ellington Hray), 1928
Saga at Forty (Barbara Cartland), 1937
Saga of the Sea (Rafael Sabatini), 1953
Sail a Jeweled Ship (Rosalind Laker), 1971
Sailor's Love (Ursula Bloom, as Mary Essex), 1961
Saint and the Sinner, The (Barbara Cartland), 1977
St. Julian's Day (Kate Norway, as Bess Norton), 1965
St. Luke's Little Summer (Kate Norway, as Bess Norton), 1964
St. Martin's Summer (Rafael Sabatini), 1909
Saint or Sinner? (Victoria Holt, as Eleanor Burford), 1951
Saint or Satyr? (Elinor Glyn), 1933
St. Thomas's Eve (Victoria Holt, as Jean Plaidy), 1954
St. Veda's (Annie S. Swan), 1889
Salamanca Drum, The (Dorothy Eden), 1977
Salamander (Julia Fitzgerald), 1981
Sally All-Smiles (Mabel St. John), 1921
Sally Gets Married (Madame Albanesi), 1927
Sally in a Service Flat (Mabel Barnes Grundy), 1934
Sally in Her Alley (Madame Albanesi), 1925
Sally in Our Alley (Mabel St. John), 1914
Sally in the Sunshine (Elizabeth Hoy), 1937
Sally of Sloper's (Countess Barcynska, as Oliver Sandys), 1930
Sally Scarth (Naomi Jacob), 1940
Sally Serene (Countess Barcynska, as Oliver Sandys), 1924
Sally's Sweetheart (G.B. Burgin), 1923
Salt Harbor (Maysie Greig, as Mary Douglas Warren), 1953
Salt of Life (Mrs. George de Horne Vaizey), 1915
Salt of the Earth (Ruby M. Ayres), 1946
Salute Me Darling (Maysie Greig), 1942
Sam Benedict (Elsie Lee), 1963
Samantha (Dorothy Eden), 1960
Sample of Prejudice (Charles Garvice), 1908
Sanchez Tradition, The (Anne Mather), 1971
Sanctuary in the Desert (Elizabeth Ashton), 1976
Sand Against the Wind (Jean Marsh), 1973
Sandals for My Feet (Phyllis Hastings), 1960
Sandflower (Jane Arbor), 1959
Sandstorm (Anne Mather), 1980
Sandy (Irene Roberts, as Elizabeth Harle), 1967

Sangaree (Frank G. Slaughter), 1948

Sangor Hospital Story, The (Ursula Bloom, as Mary Essex), 1963

Sanity Jane (Countess Barcynska), 1919

Santa Ana Wind, The (Helen Van Slyke, as Sharon Ashton), 1974

Santiago Road (Lance Horner), 1967

Sapphire in the Sand (Claire Lorrimer, as Patricia Robins), 1968

Sara (Brian Cleeve), 1976

Sara Dane (Catherine Gaskin), 1954

Sara Gay series (Rachel Lindsay, as Janey Scott)

Sara Steps In (Susan Inglis), 1947

Saracen Blade, The (Frank Yerby), 1952

Saraband for Two Sisters (Victoria Holt, as Philippa Carr), 1976

Sarah Morris Remembers (D.E. Stevenson), 1967

Sarah's Cottage (D.E. Stevenson), 1968

Sarah's Story (Mollie Hardwick), 1973

Saratoga (Dorothy Daniels), 1981

Saratoga Trunk (Edna Ferber), 1941

Sassy (Claudette Williams), 1977

Satan and the Nymph (Anne Hampson), 1976

Satan Took a Bride (Violet Winspear), 1975

Satan's Circus (Lady Eleanor Smith), 1932

Satan's Coast (Elsie Lee), 1969

Satan's Sunset (Susan Hufford), 1977

Satin Straps (Maysie Greig), 1929

Saturday's Child (Elisabeth Beresford), 1968

Saturday's Child (Betty Neels), 1972

Saturday's Child (Kathleen Norris), 1914

Savage Aristocrat, The (Rachel Lindsay, as Roberta Leigh), 1978

Savage Beauty, A (Anne Mather), 1973

Savage Eden (Constance Gluyas), 1976

Savage Land (Janet Dailey), 1974

Savage Place, A (Frank G. Slaughter), 1964

Savage Possession (Margaret Pargeter), 1979

Savage Sands, The (Christopher Nicole, as Christina Nicholson), 1978

Savage Surrender (Charlotte Lamb), 1980

Savage Surrender (Natasha Peters), 1977

Savanna (Janice Holt Giles), 1961

Savannah Purchase (Jane Aiken Hodge), 1971

Sawdust (Barbara Cartland), 1926

Sawdust and Dreams (Jean Marsh), 1980

Sawdust and Spangles (Marion Collin), 1972

Sawdust Season (Kay Thorpe), 1972

Saxon's Folly (Hebe Elsna), 1966

Say Yes, Samantha (Barbara Cartland), 1975

Say You're Sorry (Theresa Charles, as Jan Tempest), 1939

Scandalous Lady Robin, The (Sylvia Thorpe), 1950

Scales of Love (Hettie Grimstead), 1957

Scapegoat, The (Hall Caine), 1891

Scapegoat, The (Daphne du Maurier), 1957

Scapegrace, The (Sylvia Thorpe), 1971

Scar, The (Ruby M. Ayres), 1920

Scaramouche (Rafael Sabatini), 1921

Scarecrow Lover (Phyllis Hastings), 1960

Scarf of Flame, A (Wynne May), 1979

Scarlet Cloak, The (Victoria Holt, as Ellalice Tate), 1957

Scarlet Cord, The (Frank G. Slaughter), 1956

Scarlet Domino, The (Sylvia Thorpe), 1970

Scarlet Heels (Netta Muskett), 1940

Scarlet Kisses (Stephanie Blake), 1981

Scarlet Mantle, The (W.G. Hardy), 1978

Scarlet Night (Dorothy Salisbury Davis), 1980

Scarlet Pimpernel series (Baroness Orczy)

Scarlet Runner (C.N. and A.M. Williamson), 1908

Scarlet Secrets (Janet Louise Roberts, as Janette Radcliffe), 1977

Scarlet Seed, The (Edith Pargeter), 1963

Scarlet Woman (Julia Fitzgerald), 1979

Scarlet Women, The (Julia Fitzgerald, as Jane de Vere), 1969

Scent of Cloves (Norah Lofts), 1957

Scent of Juniper, The (Jean S. MacLeod), 1971

Scent of Sandalwood, The (Elizabeth Ashton), 1974

Scent of Water, The (Elizabeth Goudge), 1963

Scented Danger (Frances Cowen), 1966

Scented Hills, The (Roumelia Lane), 1970

Scented Island, The (Iris Danbury), 1976

Scented Sword, The (Christopher Nicole, as Alison York), 1980

Sceptre and the Rose, The (Doris Leslie), 1967

School Against Her!, The (Mabel St. John), 1921

School for Hearts, A (Madame Albanesi, as Effie Rowlands), 1934

Schoolgirl Bride, The (Mabel St. John), 1913

Schoolmaster's Daughters, The (Dorothy Eden), 1948

Scorched Wings (Elizabeth Ashton), 1972

Scorned by "His" Mother (Mabel St. John), 1921

Scorpion's Dance (Anne Mather), 1978

Scott Pelham's Princess (Emilie Loring), 1958

Screen Lover (Maysie Greig), 1969

Screen Test for Laurel (Dorothy Daniels), 1967

Scribblers' Club, The (Charles Garvice), 1909

Sculptor's Wooing (Charles Garvice)

Sea Change, The (Jean S. MacLeod, as Catherine Airlie), 1965

Sea Could Tell, The (A.M. Williamson), 1904

Sea Fret (Ursula Bloom), 1953

Sea Gull, The (Kathleen Norris), 1927

Sea Jade (Phyllis A. Whitney), 1964

Sea King's Daughter, The (Barbara Michaels), 1975

Sea Maiden (Irene Roberts, as Roberta Carr), 1965

Sea of Zanj (Roumelia Lane), 1969

Sea Urchins, The (Mary Ann Gibbs), 1968

Sea Without a Haven, The (D.K. Broster), 1941

Seacage (Lolah Burford), 1979

Seagull Crag (Mary Linn Roby, as Elizabeth Welles), 1977

Seagull's Cry, The (Denise Robins), 1957

Sea-Hawk, The (Rafael Sabatini), 1915

Sealed Lips (Denise Robins), 1924

Search, The (Grace Livingston Hill), 1919

Search for a Background (Naomi Jacob), 1960

Search for Love (Barbara Cartland), 1937

Search for Willie, The (Willo Davis Roberts), 1980

Search for Yesterday (Jean S. MacLeod), 1978

Search at Brighton, A (Alice Chetwynd Ley), 1971

Season for Change, A (Margaret Way), 1981

Season for Singing (Claire Ritchie), 1979

Season of Enchantment, A (Eleanor Farnes), 1956

Season of Evil (Elsie Lee), 1965

Season of Passion (Danielle Steel), 1979

Sea-Song (Anne Rundle, as Joanne Marshall), 1973

Season's Greetings, The (Hebe Elsna), 1954

Seasons Hereafter, The (Elisabeth Ogilvie), 1966

Second Best (Denise Robins), 1931

Second Best Wife (Isobel Chace), 1978

Second Chance (Joyce Dingwell), 1956

Second Hand Wife (Kathleen Norris), 1932

Second Harvest (Naomi Jacob), 1954

Second Honeymoon, The (Ruby M. Ayres), 1918

Second Honeymoon (Theresa Charles), 1970

Second Husband, The (Mabel St. John), 1923

Second Key, The (Marie Belloc Lowndes), 1936

Second Latchkey, The (C.N. and A.M. Williamson), 1920

Second Lesson, The (Lady Miles), 1936

Second Love (Claire Lorrimer, as Patricia Robins), 1964

Second Marriage (Mary Burchell), 1971

Second Marriage (Denise Robins), 1951

Second Mrs. Rivers, The (Iris Bromige), 1960

Second Romance, The (Elsie Lee), 1974

Second Season (Elsie Lee), 1973

"Second Sighter's" Daughter, The (G.B. Burgin), 1913

Second Spring (Roumelia Lane), 1980

Second String (Anthony Hope), 1910

Second Thoughts (Hebe Elsna, as Lyndon Snow), 1941

Second Tomorrow (Anne Hampson), 1980

Second Winning, The (Anne Maybury), 1933

Second Youth (Warwick Deeping), 1919

Second-Best Bride (Margaret Rome), 1981

Secret Affair, A (Lilian Peake), 1980

Secret Armour, The (Lucilla Andrews), 1955

Secret Fear, The (Barbara Cartland), 1970

Secret Gold (A.M. Williamson), 1925

Secret Heart, The (Barbara Cartland), 1970

Secret Heart, The (Susan Inglis), 1959

Secret Heiress (Eleanor Farnes), 1956

Secret History (C.N. and A.M. Williamson), 1915

Secret Hour, The (Denise Robins), 1932

Secret in Her Life, The (Leila Mackinlay), 1958

Secret Information (Robert Hichens), 1938

Secret Lives (Hebe Elsna, as Vicky Lancaster), 1960

Secret Lives of the Nurses, The (Willo Davis Roberts), 1975

Secret Love of Nurse Wilson (Ivy Preston), 1966

Secret Lover, The (Ursula Bloom), 1930

Secret Marriage (Kathryn Blair, as Rosalind Brett), 1947

Secret Marriage, The (Isobel Chace), 1966

Secret Marriage (Kathleen Norris), 1936

Secret Memoirs of Lord Byron, The (Christopher Nicole), 1978

Secret of Brick House, The (May Wynne), 1937

Secret of Dunston Mere, The (Annie S. Swan), 1898

Secret of Quarry House, The (Claire Lorrimer), 1976

Secret of Seven Oaks, The (Juanita Coulson), 1972

Secret of Shower Tree, The (Virginia Coffman), 1966

Secret of Skye, The (Annie S. Swan), 1940

Secret of the Caves, The (May Wynne), 1945

Secret of the Ghostly Shroud, The (Nancy Buckingham), 1969

Secret of the Glen, The (Barbara Cartland), 1976

Secret of the Rose, The (Anne Maybury), 1941

Secret of the Tower, The (Anthony Hope), 1919

Secret of the Zenana, The (May Wynne), 1913

Secret of Weir House, The (Frances Cowen), 1975

Secret Panel, The (Annie S. Swan), 1888

Secret Power, The (Marie Corelli), 1921

Secret Sanctuary, The (Warwick Deeping), 1923

Secret Services (Gilbert Frankau), 1934

Secret Sins (Stephanie Blake), 1980

Secret to Tell, A (Rosamunde Pilcher), 1955

Secret Woman, The (Victoria Holt), 1970

Secretary Wife (Rachel Lindsay), 1976

Secrets of Cromwell Crossing, The (Daoma Winston), 1965

Secrets of Hillyard House, The (Kathleen Norris), 1947

Secrets of the Marshbanks, The (Kathleen Norris), 1940

Secrets of the Rockies (May Wynne), 1954

Secrets of the Shop! (Mabel St. John), 1923

Secrets to Keep (Charlotte Lamb, as Sheila Holland), 1980

Seduction (Charlotte Lamb), 1980

See My Shining Palace (Hebe Elsna), 1942

See No Evil (Clair Lorrimer, as Patricia Robins), 1945

See the Bright Morning (Maynah Lewis), 1965

Seed Was Kind, The (Dorothy Macardle), 1944

Seeds of Enchantment, The (Gilbert Frankau), 1921

Seeing Life! (Marjorie Bowen), 1923

Seen by Candlelight (Anne Mather), 1974

Seen Unknown... (Naomi Jacob), 1931

Self-Appointed Saint, The (Audrey Erskine-Lindop), 1975

Self-Lovers, The (Christopher Nicole), 1968

Self-Made Woman (Faith Baldwin), 1932

Selina's Love Story (Madame Albanesi, as Effie Rowlands)

Seminar in Evil (Daoma Winston), 1972

Senator Marlowe's Daughter (Frances Parkinson Keyes), 1933

Send for Miss Marshall (Maysie Greig), 1959

Sensation (Charlotte Lamb), 1979

Sense of Belonging, A (Lilian Peake), 1974

Sentimental Family, The (Ursula Bloom), 1951

Sentimental Journey (Janet Dailey), 1979

Sentimental Spy, The (Alice Chetwynd Ley), 1977

Separation (Denise Robins), 1946

September Street (Joyce Dingwell), 1969

September's Girl (Hettie Grimstead), 1969

Sequel to Youth (Jean S. MacLeod), 1938

Sequence 1905-1912, The (Elinor Glyn), 1913

Serena (Mollie Chappell), 1980

Serenade of Santa Rose (Iris Danbury), 1970

Sergeant Major's Daughter, The (Sheila Walsh), 1977

Serpent and the Staff, The (Frank Yerby), 1958

Serpent in Eden (Juliet Dymoke), 1973

Serpent in Eden, A (Eleanor Farnes), 1971

Serpent in the Garden, The (Ethel M. Dell), 1938

Serpent of Satan, A (Barbara Cartland), 1979

Serpent's Tooth, The (Warwick Deeping), 1956

Servant of the Public, A (Anthony Hope), 1905

Set in Silver (C.N. and A.M. Williamson), 1909

Set Me Free (Denise Robins), 1937

Set the Stars Alight (Denise Robins), 1941

Set with Green Herbs (Marjorie Bowen), 1933

Seth Newcome's Wife (Annie S. Swan), 1898

Seton's Wife (Mollie Chappell), 1975

Settled Out of Court (G.B. Burgin), 1898

Seven Days from Midnight (Rona Randall), 1965

Seven Deadly Sins, The (Marjorie Bowen), 1926

Seven for St. Crispin's Day (Maureen Peters), 1971

Seven Loves (Claire Lorrimer, as Patricia Robins), 1962

Seven Men Came Back (Warwick Deeping), 1934

Seven Men of Gascony (R.F. Delderfield), 1949

Seven of Magpies (Doris E. Smith), 1970

Seven Red Roses (Leila Mackinlay), 1959

Seven Seats to the Moon (Charlotte Armstrong), 1969

Seven Sleepers, The (Kate Norway), 1964

Seven Streams, The (Warwick Deeping), 1905

Seven Tears for Apollo (Phyllis A. Whitney), 1963

Seven Trees (Lady Eleanor Smith)

Seventeen Widows of Sans Souce, The (Charlotte Armstrong), 1959

Seventeenth Stair, The (Rosalind Laker, as Barbara Paul), 1975

Seventh Commandment, The (Elinor Glyn)

Seventh Hour, The (Grace Livingston Hill), 1939

Seventh Sinner, The (Barbara Michaels, as Elizabeth Peters), 1972

Sevier Secret, The (Dorothy Daniels), 1967

Sew a Fine Seam (Mary Howard), 1954

Shabby Summer (Warwick Deeping), 1939

Shade of Darkness, A (Hebe Elsna), 1954

Shade of the Palms (Rachel Lindsay, as Roberta Leigh), 1974

Shadow, The (Jeffery Farnol), 1929

Shadow Across My Heart (Maysie Greig, as Jennifer Ames), 1948

Shadow Between, The (Anne Hampson), 1977

Shadow Box, The (Virginia Coffman), 1966

Shadow Dance (Margaret Way), 1981

Shadow Falls, The (Claire Lorrimer), 1974

Shadow Glen (Dorothy Daniels), 1965

Shadow Lawn (Leila Mackinlay), 1934

Shadow Man, The (Ruby M. Ayres), 1919

Shadow Market, The (Netta Muskett), 1938

Shadow Marriage (Hebe Elsna, as Laura Conway), 1961

Shadow Marriage (Kathleen Norris), 1952

Shadow of a Crime, The (Hall Caine), 1885

Shadow of a Lady (Jane Aiken Hodge), 1973

Shadow of a Lion (Anne Edwards), 1972

Shadow of a Man (Dorothy Daniels), 1975

Shadow of a Past Love (Willo Davis Roberts), 1970

Shadow of a Smile (Leila Mackinlay, as Brenda Grey), 1968

Shadow of a Stranger (Anne Maybury), 1960

Shadow of a Tudor (Maureen Peters), 1971

Shadow of a Vow, The (Jean S. MacLeod), 1941

Shadow of a Witch (Dorothy Eden, as Mary Paradise), 1962

Shadow of an Unknown Woman (Daoma Winston), 1967

Shadow of Apollo (Anne Hampson), 1981

Shadow of Evil (Frank G. Slaughter), 1975

Shadow of Her Life (Charles Garvice)

Shadow of Murder, The (Charity Blackstock), 1959

Shadow of My Loving, The (Anne Maybury), 1938

Shadow of Palaces (Pamela Hill), 1955

Shadow of Polperro, The (Frances Cowen), 1969

Shadow of Sin (Barbara Cartland), 1975

Shadow of Suspicion, The (Eleanor Farnes), 1972

Shadow of Suspicion, The (Emilie Loring), 1955

Shadow of the Court, The (Marion Collin), 1967

Shadow of the East, The (E.M. Hull), 1921

Shadow of the Hills (Elizabeth Hoy), 1938

Shadow of the Lynx, The (Victoria Holt), 1971

Shadow of the Pines, The (Anne Duffield), 1940

Shadow of the Pomegranate, The (Victoria Holt, as Jean Plaidy), 1962

Shadow of Theale (Frances Cowen), 1974

Shadow of Yesterday (Audrie Manley-Tucker), 1965

Shadow on Mercer Mountain (Daoma Winston), 1967

Shadow on Mockways, The (Marjorie Bowen), 1932

Shadow on the House, A (Florence Stevenson), 1975

Shadow on the Sun (Jean S. MacLeod, as Catherine Airlie), 1960

Shadow over Grove House (Mary Linn Roby), 1973

Shadow over Pheasant Heath, The (Katheryn Kimbrough), 1974

Shadow over the Island (Maysie Greig, as Mary Douglas Warren), 1955

Shadow Queen, The (Alanna Knight, as Margaret Hope), 1979

Shadow Wife, The (Madame Albanesi), 1925

Shadow Wife, The (Dorothy Eden), 1968

Shadow Woman (Evadne Price, as Helen Zenna Smith), 1932

Shadowed Happiness, A (Madame Albanesi, as Effie Rowlands), 1906

Shadowed Lives (Annie S. Swan), 1880

Shadowed Lover (Charity Blackstock, as Paula Allardyce), 1977

Shadowed Paradise (Claire Ritchie), 1960

Shadowed Spring, The (Carola Salisbury), 1980

Shadows Across the Sun (Maysie Greig, as Jennifer Ames), 1955

Shadows at Dawn (Charlotte Lamb, as Sheila

Holland), 1975

Shadows from the Past (Dorothy Daniels), 1972

Shadows in the Jungle (Christopher Nicole), 1961

Shadows in the Moonlight (Barbara Michaels, as Elizabeth Peters), 1975

Shadows in the Sun (Mary Howard), 1957

Shadows in Umbria (Jacqueline La Tourrette), 1979

Shadows of Castle Fosse, The (Jill Tattersall), 1976

Shadows of Passion (Patricia Gallagher), 1971

Shadows of the Past (Mary Francis Craig), 1976

Shadows of Tomorrow (Dorothy Daniels), 1971

Shadows of Yesterday (Marjorie Bowen), 1916

Shadows on a Throne (Juliet Dymoke), 1976

Shadows on a Wall (Helen Beauclerk), 1941

Shadows on the Moon (Irene Roberts), 1968

Shadows on the Sand (Elizabeth Hoy), 1974

Shadows on the Sand (Rona Randall), 1949

Shadows on the Water (Elizabeth Cadell, as Harriet Ainsworth), 1958

Shadows Waiting (Anne Eliot), 1969

Shadowy Third, The (Theresa Charles), 1968

Shady Grove (Janice Holt Giles), 1968

Shake Down the Moon (Hettie Grimstead), 1966

Shall Love Be Lost? (Iris Bromige), 1974

Shallow Cup, The (Netta Muskett), 1932

Shame of Molly, The (Rafael Sabatini), 1908

Shamed by Her Husband (Mabel St. John), 1925

Shanna (Kathleen E. Woodiwiss), 1977

Shannon (Patricia Gallagher), 1967

Sharon James, Free-Lance Photographer (Adeline McElfresh, as Elizabeth Wesley), 1956

Sharon Women, The (Anne Maybury), 1950

Sharrow (Baroness von Hutten), 1910

Shatter the Rainbow (Elizabeth Hoy), 1946

Shatter the Sky (Denise Robins), 1933

She (H. Rider Haggard), 1886

She and Allan (H. Rider Haggard), 1921

She Acted on Impulse (Susan Inglis), 1936

She Asked for It (Evelyn Berckman), 1969

She Danced in the Ballet (Berta Ruck), 1948

She Dwelt with Beauty (Marie Belloc Lowndes), 1949

She Fell among Thieves (Dornford Yates), 1935

She Goes to War (Edith Pargeter), 1942

She Had What It Takes (Ursula Bloom, as Mary Essex), 1952

She Loved Him (Charles Garvice), 1899

She Loved Not Wisely (Charles Garvice, as Caroline Hart)

She Married Another (Leila Mackinlay), 1953

She Moved to Music (Leila Mackinlay), 1956

She Painted Her Face (Dornford Yates), 1937

She Posed as Their Friend (Mabel St. John), 1925

She Saw Them Go By (Hester W. Chapman), 1933

She Shall Never Call You Mother! (Mabel St. John), 1925

She Sold Her Child! (Mabel St. John), 1927

She Walked into His Parlour (Maysie Greig), 1934

She Was an Actress (Mabel St. John), 1924

She Wrecked Their Home! (Mabel St. John), 1924

Sheaf of Bluebells, A (Baroness Orczy), 1917

She-Devil (Denise Robins, as Francesca Wright), 1970

Sheep's-Head and Babylon (Marjorie Bowen), 1929

Sheik, The (E.M. Hull), 1919

Sheikh Bill (A.M. Williamson), 1927

Sheik's Captive, The (Violet Winspear), 1979

Sheila (Annie S. Swan), 1890

She'll Never Marry My Son! (Mabel St. John), 1927

She'll Take the High Road (Maysie Greig, as Jennifer Ames), 1948

Shelter (Marguerite Steen, as Jane Nicholson), 1941

Sheltered Flame, The (Claire Ritchie), 1949

Sheltering Tree, A (Iris Bromige), 1970

Sherrods, The (George Barr McCutcheon), 1903

Sherry (George Barr McCutcheon), 1919

Sherry and the Ghosts (Berta Ruck), 1961

She's All the World to Me (Hall Caine), 1885

Shetland Summer (Audrie Manley-Tucker), 1973

She-Wolf, The (Pamela Bennetts), 1975

Shield of Love, The (Warwick Deeping), 1940

Shielded from the World (Mabel St. John), 1915

Shifting Sands (Mrs. Patrick MacGill), 1922

Shifting Sands, The (Kay Thorpe), 1975

Shine My Wings (Countess Barcynska, as Oliver Sandys), 1954

Shining Chance (Berta Ruck), 1944

Shining Cloud, The (Margaret Pedler), 1935

Shining Failure (Countess Barcynska, as Oliver Sandys), 1950

Shining River (Lucy Walker, as Dorothy Lucie Sanders), 1954

Shining Windows (Kathleen Norris), 1935

Shining Years, The (Emilie Loring), 1972

Ship in a Bottle (Ursula Bloom), 1962

Ship of Hate (Janet Louise Roberts, as Rebecca Danton), 1977

Ships Come Home (Countess Barcynska), 1922

Ship's Doctor (Maysie Greig), 1966

Ships in the Bay! (D.K. Broster), 1931

Ships of Youth (Maud Diver), 1931

Ship's Surgeon (Kathryn Blair, as Celine Conway), 1962

Shirt Front, The (Charity Blackstock), 1977

Shivering Sands, The (Victoria Holt), 1969

Shoal Water (Dornford Yates), 1940

Shock Wave (Dorothy Salisbury Davis), 1972

Shooting Star (Anne Betteridge), 1968

Shop on Threnody Street, The (Mary Francis Craig, as Mary Francis Shura), 1972

Shop-Girl, The (C.N. and A.M. Williamson), 1916

Shop-Girl's Revenge, A (Mabel St. John, as Henry St. John Cooper), 1914

Shopping for a Husband (Berta Ruck), 1967

Shore Beyond, The (Annie S. Swan), 1932

Short Engagement, The (Marjorie Lewty), 1978

Short Lease (Hebe Elsna, as Vicky Lancaster), 1950

Short-Cut to the Stars (Theresa Charles, as Jan Tempest), 1949

Shot with Crimson (George Barr McCutcheon), 1918

Shoulder the Sky (D.E. Stevenson), 1951

Show Boat (Edna Ferber), 1926

Show Me (Janet Dailey), 1976

Show Must Go On, The (Countess Barcynska, as Oliver Sandys), 1936

Shriek in the Midnight Tower, A (Katheryn Kimbrough), 1975

Shrine of Fire, The (Irene Roberts), 1970

Shrine of Marigolds, The (Irene Roberts), 1962

Shripney Lady, The (Rosalind Laker), 1972

Shroud of Fog (Willo Davis Roberts), 1970

Shroud of Silence (Nancy Buckingham), 1970

Shrouded Tower, The (Theresa Charles), 1966

Shrouded Walls, The (Susan Howatch), 1968

Shrouded Way, The (Janet Caird), 1973

Shrouded Web, The (Anne Mather), 1973

Sicilian Summer (Elizabeth Ashton), 1980

Siege in the Sun (Dorothy Eden), 1967

Siege Perilous (Maud Diver), 1924

Sigh No More (Elizabeth Ashton), 1973

Sight Unseen (Audrey Erskine-Lindop), 1969

Sight Unseen (Mary Roberts Rinehart), 1921

Sign of Love, The (Barbara Cartland), 1977

Sign of the Golden Goose (Janet Louise Roberts, as Rebecca Danton), 1972

Sign of the Ram, The (Rebecca Stratton), 1978

Signa's Sweetheart (Charles Garvice), 1910

Signpost Has Four Arms, The (Phyllis Hastings), 1957

Signpost to Love (Barbara Cartland), 1980

Silence Is Golden (Hebe Elsna, as Lyndon Snow), 1958

Silence Is Golden (Elsie Lee), 1971

Silence of Herondale, The (Joan Aiken), 1964

Silent Battle, The (A.M. Williamson), 1902

Silent Bondage (Jean S. MacLeod), 1940

Silent Captain, The (May Wynne), 1914

Silent Halls of Ashenden, The (Dorothy Daniels), 1973

Silent Lady, The (Alice Dwyer-Joyce), 1964

Silent Nightingale, The (Iris Danbury), 1961

Silent Ones, The (Elisabeth Ogilvie), 1981

Silent Pool, The (Frances Cowen), 1977

Silent Song (Lucilla Andrews), 1973

Silent Thunder (Rona Randall), 1971

Silent Valley, The (Jean S. MacLeod), 1953

Silent Walls, The (Mary Linn Roby), 1974

Silent Watcher, The (Florence Stevenson), 1975

Silken Bond, The (Flora Kidd), 1980

Silken Cage, The (Rebecca Stratton), 1981

Silken Purse, The (Leila Mackinlay), 1970

Silken Trap, The (Charlotte Lamb), 1979

Silky, The (Maureen Peters, as Sharon Whitby), 1980

Silver Answer, The (Margaret Maddocks), 1965

Silver Arrow (Elizabeth Ashton), 1980

Silver Boy, The (Hebe Elsna), 1936

Silver Bride, The (Ethel M. Dell), 1932

Silver Castle, The (Nancy Buckingham, as Erica Quest), 1978

Silver Chain, The (Elisabeth Beresford), 1980

Silver Chalice, The (Thomas B. Costain), 1952

Silver Cord, The (Rona Randall), 1963

Silver Cross (Mary Johnston), 1922

Silver Dolphin, The (Velda Johnston), 1979

Silver Dragon, The (Jean S. MacLeod), 1961

Silver Falcon, The (Evelyn Anthony), 1977

Silver Fishes, The (Rebecca Stratton, as Lucy Gillen), 1969

Silver Fruit upon Silver Trees (Anne Mather), 1974

Silver Jasmine (Janet Louise Roberts), 1980

Silver Leopard, The (Dorothy Mackie Low, as Zoe Cass), 1976

Silver Maiden (Elizabeth Hoy), 1951

Silver Nightingale, The (Sylvia Thorpe), 1974

Silver Nutmeg (Norah Lofts), 1947

Silver Orchids (Ursula Bloom), 1941

Silver Peaks (Anne Duffield), 1935

Silver Ring, The (Ursula Bloom), 1955

Silver Slave, The (Violet Winspear), 1972

Silver Summer, The (Irene Roberts, as Elizabeth Harle), 1971

Silver Stallion, The (Iris Danbury), 1973

Silver Sty, The (Sara Seale), 1941

Silver Thaw, The (Betty Neels), 1980

Silver Tree, The (Katrina Britt), 1977

Silver Unicorn (Jane Blackmore), 1977

Silver Wedding (Ruby M. Ayres), 1937

Silver Wedding, The (Ethel M. Dell), 1932

Silver Wings (Grace Livingston Hill), 1931

Silver-Gilt (Netta Muskett), 1935

Silverhill (Phyllis A. Whitney), 1967

Simon Dale (Anthony Hope), 1898

Simon the Coldheart (Georgette Heyer), 1925

Simple Case of Ill-Will, A (Evelyn Berckman), 1964

Simple Duty, A (Kate Norway, as Hilary Neal), 1966

Simple Savage, A (G.B. Burgin), 1909

Simple Simon (Madame Albanesi), 1907

Sin of Cynara, The (Violet Winspear), 1976

Sin of Eve, The (May Edginton), 1913

Sin Was Mine, The (Denise Roberts, as Julia Kane), 1964

Sinbad the Soldier (P.C. Wren), 1935

Since First We Met (Theresa Charles, as Fay Chandos), 1948

Since Summer (Mollie Chappell), 1967

Since We Love (Denise Robins), 1938

Sincerity (Warwick Deeping), 1912

Sing a Dark Song (Willo Davis Roberts), 1972

Sing for Your Supper (Hebe Elsna), 1970

Sing Witch, Sing Death (Roberta Gellis), 1975

Singer Not the Song, The (Audrey Erskine-Lindop), 1953

Singer Passes, The (Maud Diver), 1934

Singing Heart, The (Elizabeth Cadell), 1959

Singing in the Wilderness (Isobel Chace), 1976

Singing in the Woods, A (Elizabeth Renier), 1966

Singing Shadows (Dorothy Eden), 1940

Singing Swans, The (Anne Rundle, as Alexandra Manners), 1975

Singing Uphill (Countess Barcynska, as Oliver Sandys), 1940

Singing Waters (Ann Bridge), 1946

Singing Wind, The (Jennifer Wade), 1977

Single to New York (Anne Betteridge), 1965

Sinister Abbey (Elsie Lee), 1967

Sinister Gardens (Willo Davis Roberts), 1972

Sinister Island, The (Maysie Greig, as Jennifer Ames), 1968

Sinister Melody (Frances Cowen), 1976

Sinister Stone (Daoma Winston), 1966

Sinner, Saint, and Jester (Rafael Sabatini), 1954

Sinners in Paradise (Maysie Greig, as Jennifer Ames), 1963

Sins of Herod, The (Frank G. Slaughter), 1968

Sins of Omission (Chelsea Quinn Yarbro), 1980

Sins of the Fathers (Susan Howatch), 1980

Sins of the Lion, The (Anne Motley), 1979

Sir Boxer (Countess Barcynska, as Oliver Sandys), 1934

Sir Isumbras at the Ford (D.K. Broster), 1918

Sir John Dering (Jeffery Farnol), 1923

Sir Mortimer (Mary Johnston), 1904

Sir or Madam? (Berta Ruck), 1923

Sir Percy series (Baroness Orczy)

Sir Roderick's Will (Annie S. Swan), 1898

Sir William (D.A. Ponsonby), 1978

Siren Song (Roberta Gellis), 1981

Siren's Heart (Madame Albanesi, as Effie Rowlands)

Sirocco (Anne Betteridge), 1970

Sister Anne (Madame Albanesi), 1908

Sister at Sea (Rona Randall), 1960

Sister at Sea (Irene Roberts), 1971

Sister Brookes of Bynd's (Kate Norway), 1957

Sister Christine (Susan Inglis), 1953

Sister Julia (Irene Roberts, as Iris Rowland), 1972

Sister Loving Heart (Ursula Bloom, as Sheila Burns), 1971

Sister Marion's Summer (Hettie Grimstead, as Marsha Manning), 1965

Sister of the Bride (Henrietta Reid), 1971

Sister of the Housemaster (Eleanor Farnes), 1954

Sister on Leave (Irene Roberts), 1982

Sister Peters in Amsterdam (Betty Neels), 1969

Sister Pussycat (Joyce Dingwell), 1971

Sister Rose's Holiday (Hettie Grimstead), 1975

Sister Sue (Eleanor H. Porter), 1921

Sister Sylvan (Theresa Charles, as Fay Chandos), 1962

Sister to a Stranger (Ursula Bloom, as Rachel Harvey), 1971

Sister to Cinderella (Sara Seale), 1956

Sisters, The (Hebe Elsna, as Laura Conway), 1971

Sisters (Kathleen Norris), 1919

Sisters and Strangers (Helen Van Slyke), 1978

Sisters in Love (Theresa Charles, as Leslie Lance), 1960

Sisters in Love (Mollie Hardwick), 1979

Sisters of Valcour (Dorothy Daniels), 1981

Sisters Three (Mrs. George de Horn Vaizey), 1900

Six Days (Elinor Glyn), 1924

Six Fools and a Fairy (Ursula Bloom, as Mary Essex), 1948

Six for Heaven (Lucy Walker, as Dorothy Lucie Sanders), 1952

Six Impossible Things (Elizabeth Cadell), 1961

Six Passengers for the "Sweet Bird" (Charity Blackstock, as Paula Allardyce), 1967

Six Wax Candles (Leila Mackinlay), 1950

Six White Horses (Janet Dailey), 1977

Six-Fingered Stud (Lance Horner), 1975

Six-Horse Hitch (Janice Holt Giles), 1969

Sixpence in Her Shoe (Mary Howard), 1950

"Sixpenny Ha' penny" Duchess, The (Mabel St. John), 1917

Sixth of October, The (Robert Hichens), 1936

Sixth Wife, The (Victoria Holt, as Jean Plaidy), 1953

Skeleton Key (Daoma Winston), 1972

Skin Deep (Susan Hufford), 1978

Skye Cameron (Phyllis A. Whitney), 1957

Skyscraper (Faith Baldwin), 1931

Skyscraper Hotel (Hettie Grimstead, as Marsha Manning), 1959

Skyscraper Souls (Faith Baldwin), 1931

Slade (Warwick Deeping), 1943

Slanderers, The (Warwick Deeping), 1905

Slave, The (Robert Hichens), 1899

Slave Lady (Julia Fitzgerald), 1980

Slave of the Lake (Charles Garvice), 1908

Slave of the Wind (Jean S. MacLeod), 1962

Slave Ship, The (Mary Johnston), 1924

Slaves of Allah, The (G.B. Burgin), 1909

Slaves of Love, The (Barbara Cartland), 1976

Slaves of the Ring (G.B. Burgin), 1936

Slave-Woman (Denise Robins), 1934

Sleep in the Woods (Dorothy Eden), 1960

Sleeping Beauty (Faith Baldwin), 1947

Sleeping Beauty (Berta Ruck), 1936

Sleeping Bride, The (Dorothy Eden), 1959

Sleeping Dogs (Mabel Barnes Grundy), 1924

Sleeping Tiger (Rosamunde Pilcher), 1967

Sleeping Swords (Barbara Cartland, as Barbara McCorquodale), 1942

Slinky Jane (Catherine Cookson), 1959

Slither of Silk, A (Wynne May), 1972

Slow Awakening, The (Catherine Cookson, as Catherine Marchant), 1976

Small Slice of Summer, A (Betty Neels), 1975

Small Tawny Cat, The (Virginia Coffman), 1967

Smile in the Mirror (Countess Barcynska), 1963

Smile of the Stranger, The (Joan Aiken), 1978

Smith (Warwick Deeping), 1932

Smith and the Pharaohs (H. Rider Haggard), 1920

Smoke and the Fire, The (Essie Summers), 1964

Smoke into Flame (Jane Arbor), 1976

Smouldering Fire (D.E. Stevenson), 1936

Smouldering Flame, The (Anne Mather), 1976

Smuggled Heart, The (Barbara Cartland), 1959

Smuggled Love (Doris E. Smith), 1976

Smuggler's Bride, The (Rosalind Laker), 1975

Smugglers' Moon (Sylvia Thorpe), 1955

Smugglers of Penreen, The (May Wynne), 1934

Snake and Sword (P.C. Wren), 1914

Snake and the Sword, The (P.C. Wren), 1923

Snake in the Grass (Hebe Elsna, as Vicky Lancaster), 1961

Snake in the Grass, A (Mabel St. John, as Henry St. John Cooper), 1922

Snake-Bite (Robert Hichens), 1919

Snare, The (Rafael Sabatini), 1915

Snare the Wild Heart (Elizabeth Hoy), 1955

Snow Blossom, The (Maureen Peters), 1980

Snow in April (Rosamunde Pilcher), 1972

Snow in Summer (Madame Albanesi), 1932

Snow Mountain, The (Catherine Gavin), 1973

Snow Must Return, The (Denise Robins), 1971

Snow Queen, The (Julia Fitzgerald, as Julia Hamilton), 1978

Snowfire (Phyllis A. Whitney), 1973

So Big (Edna Ferber), 1924

So Bold a Choice (D.A. Ponsonby), 1960

So Dear to My Heart (Susan Barrie), 1956

So Deep Suspicion (Mary Ann Gibbs, as Elizabeth Ford), 1950

So Evil My Love (Marjorie Bowen, as Joseph Shearing), 1947

So Fair and Foul a Queen (Maureen Peters), 1974

So Fair My Love (Hebe Elsna, as Lyndon Snow), 1956

So Fair, So False (Charles Garvice), 1902

So Frail a Thing (Helen Beauclerk), 1940

So Like a Man (Madame Albanesi, as Effie Rowlands), 1905

So Loved and So Far (Elizabeth Hoy), 1954

So Many Miles (Ruby M. Ayres), 1932

So Many Tomorrows (Nancy Buckingham, as Nancy John), 1982

So Many Worlds (Hebe Elsna, as Vicky Lancaster), 1948

So Much Good (Gilbert Frankau), 1928

So Much Love (Lucy Walker), 1977

So Nearly Lost (Charles Garvice), 1902

So Nearly Married (Theresa Charles, as Fay Chandos), 1956

So New to Love (Hebe Elsna, as Laura Conway), 1955

So the Dreams Depart (Victoria Holt, as Eleanor Burford), 1944

So This Is Love (Claire Lorrimer, as Patricia Robins), 1954

So Wicked My Desire (Stephanie Blake), 1979

So Wicked the Heart (Barbara Riefe), 1980

So Wild a Heart (Velda Johnston, as Veronica Jason), 1981

So Young, So Fair (Elizabeth Seifert), 1947

Society Girl (Evadne Price), 1935

Soft Talkers, The (Margaret Millar), 1957

Softly Treads Danger (Marjorie McEvoy), 1963

Soho Square (Claire Rayner), 1976

Soldier and the Ladies, The (May Edginton), 1947

Soldier from Virginia, The (Marjorie Bowen), 1912

Soldier of the Legion, A (C.N. and A.M. Williamson), 1914

Soldier at the Door, The (Edith Pargeter), 1954

Soldiers and Lovers (Mary Howard), 1973

Soldiers' Daughters Never Cry (Audrey Erskine-Lindop), 1948

Soldiers of Misfortune (P.C. Wren), 1929

Solitary Horseman, The (Emilie Loring), 1927

Some Day (Ruby M. Ayres), 1935

Some Day My Love (Hettie Grimstead, as Marsha Manning), 1968

Some Day You'll Love Me (Hebe Elsna, as Lyndon Snow), 1960

Some Die in Their Beds (Mary Linn Roby), 1970

Some Men and Women (Marie Belloc Lowndes), 1925

Some Mother's Child (Mabel St. John), 1926

Some Mother's Son! (Mabel St. John), 1928

Somebody Else (Ruby M. Ayres), 1936

Someone in the House (Barbara Michaels), 1981

Someone New to Love (Theresa Charles, as Jan Tempest), 1936

Someone Waiting (Anne Maybury, as Katherine Troy), 1961

Someone Who Cares (Theresa Charles, as Leslie Lance), 1982

Somersault (Suzanne Ebel), 1971

Something Between (Marian Cockrell), 1946

Something Blue (Charlotte Armstrong), 1962

Something Extra (Janet Dailey), 1975

Something Special (Faith Baldwin), 1940

Something to Love (Denise Robins), 1951

Sometimes Spring Is Late (Ruby M. Ayres), 1941

Sometimes Spring Returns (Hebe Elsna, as Vicky Lancaster), 1940

Somewhere to Lay My Head (Lilian Peake), 1977

Somewhere Within This House (Jean Francis Webb), 1973

Son of a Hundred Kings (Thomas B. Costain), 1950

Son of Adam (Margaret Rome), 1978

Son of Erin, A (Annie S. Swan), 1899

Son of Hagar, A (Hall Caine), 1887

Son of Mammon, A (G.B. Burgin), 1901

Son o' Mine! (Mabel St. John, as Henry St. John Cooper), 1923

Son of Summer (Leila Mackinlay, as Brenda Grey), 1970

Son of the Morning (Gilbert Frankau), 1949

Son of the People, A (Baroness Orczy), 1906

Son of York (Julia Fitzgerald, as Julia Hamilton), 1973

Son to Be Proud Of!, A (Mabel St. John), 1924

Song and the Sea, The (Isobel Chace), 1962

Song Begins, A (Mary Burchell), 1965

Song Bird (Sophia Cleugh), 1930

Song Cycle (Mary Burchell), 1974

Song from a Lemon Tree (Doris E. Smith), 1966

Song in My Heart (Rachel Lindsay), 1961

Song in the House, The (Ann Bridge), 1936

Song of Life (Fannie Hurst), 1927

Song of Love, A (Barbara Cartland), 1980

Song of Miriam, The (Marie Corelli), 1898

Song of Philomel, The (Ursula Bloom), 1950

Song of Ruth, The (Frank G. Slaughter), 1954

Song of Salome, The (Ursula Bloom, as Deborah Mann), 1969

Song of Summer (Eleanor Farnes), 1954

Song of Surrender (Hettie Grimstead), 1953

Song of the Cardinal, The (Gene Stratton Porter), 1903

Song of the Lark (Berta Ruck), 1951

Song of the Mockingbird (Anne Duffield), 1946

Song of the Siren, The (Victoria Holt, as Philippa Carr), 1980

Song of the Waves (Anne Hampson), 1976

Songless Wood, The (Hebe Elsna, as Lyndon Snow), 1979

Sonora Sundown (Janet Dailey), 1978

Sons and the Daughters, The (Patricia Gallagher), 1961

Sons of the Sheik, The (E.M. Hull), 1925

Sons of the Wolf (Barbara Michaels), 1967

Sooner or Later (Elinor Glyn), 1933

Sophia (Charlotte Lamb, as Sheila Holland), 1979

Sophy of Kravonia (Anthony Hope), 1906

Sophy Valentine (D.A. Ponsonby), 1946

Sorcerer of the Castle, The (Florence Stevenson), 1974

Sorcerers, The (Countess Barcynska, as Oliver Sandys), 1927

Sorrell and Son (Warwick Deeping), 1925

Sorrows of Satan, The (Marie Corelli), 1895

Soul of Lilith, The (Marie Corelli), 1892

Soul of Mary Olivane, The (Hebe Elsna), 1949

Soul of the Mill, The (Mabel St. John), 1916

Sound of the Trumpet, The (Grace Livingston Hill), 1943

Sound of Thunder, The (Taylor Caldwell), 1957

Sound Stage (Daoma Winston), 1970

South Island Stowaway (Essie Summers), 1971

South of Capricorn (Anne Hampson), 1975

South of Mandraki (Anne Hampson), 1971

South of the Moon (Anne Hampson), 1979

South Sea Island (Lucy Walker, as Shelley Dean), 1966

South to Forget (Essie Summers), 1963

South to the Sun (Betty Beaty), 1956

Southarn Folly (Charity Blackstock, as Paula Allardyce), 1958

Southern Nights (Janey Dailey), 1980

Southern Star (Maysie Greig, as Mary Douglas Warren), 1950

Souvenir from Sweden (Rosalind Laker, as Barbara Øvstedal), 1974

Sovereign's Key (Rosalind Laker), 1969

Sowing Glory (P.C. Wren), 1931

Sown among Thorns (Ethel M. Dell), 1939

Sown in the Wind (Jean S. MacLeod), 1946

Spain for the Sovereigns (Victoria Holt, as Jean Plaidy), 1960

Spangles (Countess Barcynska, as Oliver Sandys), 1934

Spanish Bride, The (Georgette Heyer), 1940

Spanish Bridegroom, The (Victoria Holt, as Jean Plaidy), 1954

Spanish Chapel, The (Dorothy Daniels), 1972

Spanish Doll, The (Elizabeth Renier), 1970

Spanish Galleon (Nigel Tranter), 1960

Spanish Grandee, The (Katrina Britt), 1975

Spanish House, The (Nancy Buckingham, as Nancy John), 1981

Spanish House, The (Lady Eleanor Smith), 1938

Spanish Inheritance, The (Isobel Chace, as Elizabeth Hunter), 1975

Spanish Lace (Joyce Dingwell), 1969

Spanish Maine (P.C. Wren), 1935

Spanish Summer, The (Mary Howard), 1977

Speak No Evil (Mignon Eberhart), 1941

Speak No Evil of the Dead (Mary Linn Roby), 1973

Speak Now (Frank Yerby), 1969

Speak to Me of Love (Dorothy Eden), 1972

Special Breed (Janice Holt Giles), 1966

Specter of Dolphin Cove, The (Katheryn Kimbrough), 1973

Spectral Bride, The (Marjorie Bowen, as Joseph Shearing), 1942

Spell of Ursula, The (Madame Albanesi, as Effie Rowlands), 1894

Spencer Brade, M.D. (Frank G. Slaughter), 1942

Spending of the Pile, The (G.B. Burgin), 1924

Spendthrift Duke, The (May Wynne), 1921

Spice Box (Grace Livingston Hill), 1943

Spice of Life (Berta Ruck), 1952

Spiced with Cloves (Isobel Chace, as Elizabeth Hunter), 1962

Spider (Marguerite Steen), 1933

Spider and the Fly, The (Charles Garvice)

Spider Dance (Leila Mackinlay), 1950

Spider in the Cup, The (Marjorie Bowen, as Joseph Shearing), 1934

Spider's Web, The (Isobel Chace), 1966

Spilled Salt (Ursula Bloom), 1927

Spin Me a Shadow (Maureen Peters, as Veronica Black), 1974

Spindrift (Anne Rundle, as Jeanne Sanders), 1974

Spindrift (Rebecca Stratton), 1977

Spindrift (Phyllis A. Whitney), 1975

Spinster of This Parish (Hebe Elsna, as Lyndon Snow), 1966

Spinster's Progress (Berta Ruck), 1942

Spirit in Prison, A (Robert Hichens), 1908

Spirit of Atlantis (Anne Mather), 1980

Spirit of Bambatse, The (H. Rider Haggard), 1906

Spirit of the Time, The (Robert Hichens), 1921

Splendid Destiny, A (Madame Albanesi, as Effie Rowlands), 1910

Splendid Friend, The (Madame Albanesi, as Effie Rowlands), 1917

Splendid Legacy, The (Eleanor Farnes), 1973

Splendid Love (Madame Albanesi, as Effie Rowlands), 1911

Splendid Love, The (Mabel St. John, as Henry St. John Cooper), 1932

Splendid Man, The (Madame Albanesi, as Effie Rowlands), 1905

Spoiled Earth, The (Jessica Stirling), 1974

Spoilt Music (Ruby M. Ayres), 1926

Sport Royal (Anthony Hope), 1893

"Sports" of Lyndale, The (Mabel St. John), 1925

Spotlight on Susan (Leila Mackinlay), 1960

Spray of Edelweiss, A (Katrina Britt), 1972

Spray of Red Roses (Irene Roberts, as Elizabeth Harle), 1971

Spread Wings (Ursula Bloom), 1933

Spread Your Wings (Sara Seale), 1939

Spreading Sails (Theresa Charles, as Leslie Lance), 1963

Sprig Muslin (Georgette Heyer), 1956

Spring (Sophia Cleugh), 1929

Spring Always Comes (Emilie Loring), 1966

Spring at the Villa (Kathryn Blair, as Rosalind Brett), 1961

Spring Comes (Berta Ruck), 1936

Spring Comes to Miss Lonely Heart (Berta Ruck), 1936

Spring Comes to the Crescent (Mary Ann Gibbs, as Elizabeth Ford), 1949

Spring Gambit (Claudette Williams), 1976

Spring Green (Elizabeth Cadell), 1953

Spring in Morocco (Anne Betteridge), 1962

Spring in September (Ursula Bloom), 1941

Spring in September (Essie Summers), 1978

Spring in the Heart (Madame Albanesi, as Effie Rowlands), 1929

Spring Madness of Mr. Sermon, The (R.F. Delderfield), 1963

Spring Magic (D.E. Stevenson), 1941

Spring of a Lion, The (H. Rider Haggard), 1899

Spring of the Tiger, The (Victoria Holt), 1979

Spring Picture (Daphne du Maurier), 1945

Spring Rainbow (Leila Mackinlay), 1961

Spring Will Come Again (Sylvia Thorpe), 1965

Springtime for Sally (Theresa Charles, as Leslie Lance), 1962

Spring-Time of Love, The (Charles Garvice), 1910

Spun by the Moon (Theresa Charles, as Leslie Lance), 1960

Spur of Pride, The (P.C. Wren), 1937

Spurned Proposal (Madame Albanesi, as Effie Rowlands)

Spy at the Villa Miranda, The (Elsie Lee), 1967

Spy Concerto, The (Constance Heaven, as Christina Merlin), 1980

Spy for Napoleon, A (May Wynne), 1917

Spy of Napoleon, A (Baroness Orczy), 1934

Squire (Countess Barcynska, as Oliver Sandys), 1932

Squirrel Walk (Irene Roberts), 1961

Stacy (Rachel Lindsay, as Roberta Leigh), 1958

Stage of Love (Suzanne Ebel, as Cecily Shelbourne), 1978

Stairway to Enchantment, The (Rebecca Stratton, as Lucy Gillen), 1973

Stake in the Game, The (Evelyn Berckman), 1971

Stake in the Kingdom, A (Nigel Tranter), 1966

Stalemate (Evelyn Berckman), 1966

Stalking Horse, The (Rafael Sabatini), 1933

Stalking Terror, The (Virginia Coffman), 1977

Stallion (Marguerite Steen), 1933

Stamboul Love (Anne Duffield), 1934

Standish Place, The (Isabelle Holland), 1976

Star Creek (Susan Barrie, as Pamela Kent),

1965

Star in Love, A (Berta Ruck), 1935

Star in the Dark, A (Madame Albanesi), 1933

Star Looks Down, A (Betty Neels), 1975

Star Money (Kathleen Winsor), 1950

Star of Danger (Elsie Lee), 1971

Star of Desire (Hettie Grimstead, as Marsha Manning), 1961

Star of Lancaster, The (Victoria Holt, as Jean Plaidy), 1981

Star on Her Shoulder (Faith Baldwin), 1942

Star Patient (Kate Norway, as Hilary Neal), 1963

Star Quality (Mary Burchell), 1959

Star Sapphire (Janet Louise Roberts, as Rebecca Danton), 1979

Star to My Barque (Doris E. Smith), 1964

Star-Crossed (Mary Howard), 1949

Star-Crossed (Charlotte Lamb), 1976

Star-Drift (Irene Roberts, as Iris Rowland), 1970

Star-Dust (Fannie Hurst), 1921

Stardust in Her Eyes (Leila Mackinlay, as Brenda Grey), 1964

Starless Night (Ruby M. Ayres), 1943

Starling, The (Doris Leslie), 1927

Starry Wood, The (Anne Maybury), 1935

Stars above Raffael (Irene Roberts), 1977

Stars Are My Children, The (Phyllis Hastings), 1970

Stars Cannot Tell, The (Anne Maybury), 1958

Stars Grow Pale, The (Anne Maybury), 1936

Stars in Her Eyes (Barbara Cartland), 1971

Stars in My Heart (Barbara Cartland), 1957

Stars in Your Eyes (Emilie Loring), 1941

Stars of San Cecilio, The (Susan Barrie), 1958

Stars of Spring (Anne Hampson), 1971

Stars over Egypt (Elizabeth Hoy), 1938

Stars over Sarawak (Anne Hampson), 1974

Stars Through the Mist (Betty Neels), 1973

Starshine for Sweethearts (Claire Ritchie), 1976

Star-Spangled Christmas (Kathleen Norris), 1942

State Versus Elinor Norton, The (Mary Roberts Rinehart), 1934

Stateroom for Two (Glenna Finley), 1980

Station Wagon in Spain (Frances Parkinson Keyes), 1959

Station Wagon Set (Faith Baldwin), 1939

Statues of Snow (Claire Lorrimer, as Patricia Robins), 1947

Staunch as a Woman (Charles Garvice), 1903

Staunch of the Heart (Charles Garvice), 1903

Stay But till Tomorrow (Iris Bromige), 1946

Stay Through the Night (Flora Kidd), 1979

Stay Until Tomorrow (Anne Maybury), 1961

Steadfast Lover, The (Elisabeth Beresford), 1980

Steady Burns the Candle (Patricia Ainsworth), 1970

Stealer of Hearts (Hebe Elsna, as Lyndon Snow), 1959

Steamboat Gothic (Frances Parkinson Keyes), 1952

Steering by a Star (Ruby M. Ayres), 1949

Stella Fregelius (H. Rider Haggard), 1904

Stella Maris (May Wynne), 1932

Stella's Fortune (Charles Garvice), 1912

Step in the Dark, A (Frances Cowen), 1962

Stepdaughter, The (Iris Bromige), 1966

Stepdaughters of War (Evadne Price, as Helen Zenna Smith), 1930

Stephanie (Jane Blackmore), 1972

Stephanie (Anne Eliot, as Caroline Arnett), 1979

Stephen and the Sleeping Saints (Pamela Bennetts), 1977

Stephen Glyn (Annie S. Swan), 1898

Step-Mother, The (Annie S. Swan), 1915

Stepmother of Five (Theresa Charles, as Jan Tempest), 1936

Stepmother's House (Katheryn Kimbrough, as Charlotte Bramwell), 1972

Stepping under Ladders (Maysie Greig), 1938

Steps to the Empty Throne, The (Nigel Tranter), 1969

Stepsons of France (P.C. Wren), 1917

Steven's Wife (Susan Inglis), 1958

Still as the Grave (Mary Linn Roby), 1964

Still Glides the Stream (D.E. Stevenson), 1959

Still She Wishes for Company (Margaret Irwin), 1924

Still Waters (Ruby M. Ayres), 1941

Stinging Nettles (Marjorie Bowen), 1923

Stolen Bride, The (Marjorie Bowen), 1933

Stolen Halo (Barbara Cartland), 1940

Stolen Heart (Mary Burchell), 1952

Stolen Honeymoon (May Edginton), 1942

Stolen March, The (Dornford Yates), 1926

Stone, The (Nigel Tranter), 1958

Stone Bull, The (Phyllis A. Whitney), 1977

Stone Carnation, The (Naomi A. Hintze), 1971

Stone House, The (Dorothy Daniels), 1973

Stone Lily, The (Hester W. Chapman), 1957

Stone Maiden, The (Velda Johnston), 1980

Stone Maiden, The (Anne Rundle, as Alexandra Manners), 1973

Stone of Blood (Juanita Coulson), 1975

Stonewall Brigade (Frank G. Slaughter), 1975

Stony Ground (Lady Miles), 1923

Stop at a Winner (R.F. Delderfield), 1961

Stopover in Paradise (Maysie Greig), 1938

Storrington Papers, The (Dorothy Eden), 1978

Storm Bird, The (Ursula Bloom, as Sheila Burns), 1959

Storm Centre (Charlotte Lamb), 1980

Storm Drift (Ethel M. Dell), 1930

Storm Eagle, The (Rebecca Stratton, as Lucy Gillen), 1980

Storm Flower (Margaret Way), 1975

Storm Haven (Frank G. Slaughter), 1953

Storm Heaven (Anne Maybury), 1949

Storm House (Kathleen Norris), 1929

Storm in a Rain Barrel (Anne Mather), 1971

Storm in the Family (Jane Blackmore), 1956

Storm in the Mountains (Nancy Buckingham), 1967

Storm Music (Dornford Yates), 1934

Storm of Desire (Glenna Finley), 1977

Storm of Wrath, The (Alice Dwyer-Joyce), 1977

Storm over Mandargi (Margaret Way), 1973

Storm over Roseheath (Anne Maybury, as Katherine Troy), 1969

Storm Passage (Kay Thorpe), 1977

Storm Tide (Elisabeth Ogilvie), 1945

Stormcloud and Sunrise (Eleanor Farnes), 1945

Stormy Encounter (Roumelia Lane), 1974

Stormy Haven (Kathryn Blair, as Rosalind Brett), 1952

Stormy Masquerade (Anne Hampson), 1980

Stormy Petrel (Sara Seale), 1941

Stormy Rapture (Margaret Pargeter), 1976

Stormy Surrender (Janet Louise Roberts, as Janette Radcliffe), 1978

Stormy Voyager, A (Annie S. Swan), 1896

Stormy the Way (Anne Hampson), 1973

Story de Luxe (Iris Danbury), 1963

Story Girl, The (L.M. Montgomery), 1911

Story of a Passion (Charles Garvice), 1908

Story of a Whim, The (Grace Livingston Hill), 1903

Story of Andrea Fields, The (Elizabeth Seifert), 1950

Story of Fish and Chips, The (Ruby M. Ayres), 1951

Story of Ivy, The (Marie Belloc Lowndes), 1927

Story of John Willie, The (Ruby M. Ayres), 1948

Story of Julia Page, The (Kathleen Norris), 1915

Story of Julian, The (Susan Ertz), 1931

Story of Marco, The (Eleanor H. Porter), 1911

Story of Rosabelle Shaw, The (D.E. Stevenson), 1937

Story of the Lost Star, The (Grace Livingston Hill), 1932

Story of Veronica, The (Denise Robins), 1946

Strait Gate, The (Annie S. Swan), 1887

Strait-Jacket (Hebe Elsna), 1930

Strand, The (Claire Rayner), 1980

Stranded in Belgium (May Wynne), 1918

Strange as a Dream (Flora Kidd), 1968

Strange Beauty (Maysie Greig), 1938

Strange Bedfellow, The (Evelyn Berckman), 1956

Strange Bedfellow (Janet Dailey), 1979

Strange Beginning (Naomi Jacob), 1961

Strange Bewilderment (Katrina Britt), 1973

Strange Case of Lucile Cléry, The (Marjorie Bowen, as Joseph Shearing), 1941

Strange Case of Miss Annie Spragg, The (Louis Bromfield), 1928

Strange Involvement (Leila Mackinlay), 1972

Strange Journey (Marjorie McEvoy, as Marjorie Harte)

Strange Lady (Robert Hichens), 1950

Strange Love Story, A (Madame Albanesi, as Effie Rowlands), 1919

Strange Loyalties (Jane Arbor), 1949

Strange Loyalty of Dr. Carlisle, The (Elizabeth Seifert), 1952

Strange Marriage (Charles Garvice, as Caroline Hart)

Strange Meeting (Denise Robins), 1952

Strange Paradise (Dorothy Daniels), 1969

Strange Paths (Mary Howard), 1948

Strange Patient for Sister Smith, A (Ursula Bloom, as Mary Essex), 1963

Strange Prodigal, The (Grace Livingston Hill), 1935

Strange Quest of Anne Weston, The (Mary Burchell), 1964

Strange Quest of Nurse Anne, The (Mary Burchell), 1965

Strange Rapture (Denise Robins), 1933

Strange Recompense (Jean S. MacLeod, as Catherine Airlie), 1952

Strange Roads (Maud Diver), 1918

Strange Secrets (Virginia Coffman), 1976

Strange Victory (Rose Franken Meloney), 1939

Strange Visitation of Josiah McNason, The (Marie Corelli), 1904

Strange Visitor (Hebe Elsna), 1956

Strange Waif, The (Violet Winspear), 1962

Stranger at Pembroke (Anne Eliot), 1971

Stranger at the Gate, The (Mary Howard, as Josephine Edgar), 1973

Stranger at the Gates (Evelyn Anthony), 1973

Stranger at Wildings (Madeleine Brent), 1976

Stranger by Night (Margaret Lynn), 1963

Stranger Came By, A (Alanna Knight), 1974

Stranger from the North, The (Lucy Walker), 1959

Stranger in Love (Theresa Charles, as Fay Chandos), 1966

Stranger in My Grave, A (Margaret Millar), 1960

Stranger in the Glen (Flora Kidd), 1975

Stranger in the Night (Charlotte Lamb), 1980

Stranger in Their Midst, The (Jean S. MacLeod), 1953

Stranger on the Beach, The (Anne Betteridge), 1974

Stranger on the Beach (Lilian Peake), 1979

Stranger Prince, The (Margaret Irwin), 1937

Stranger Sweetheart (Maysie Greig, as Jennifer Ames), 1938

Stranger Than Truth (Madame Albanesi, as Effie Rowlands), 1913

Stranger to Love (Theresa Charles, as Jan Tempest), 1960

Stranger Within the Gates (Grace Livingston Hill), 1939

Strangers' Forest (Pamela Hill), 1978

Strangers in Company (Jane Aiken Hodge), 1971

Strangers in Flight (Mignon Eberhart), 1941

Strangers in Love (Viña Delmar), 1951

Strangers in Love (Mary Howard), 1939

Strangers in My House (D.A. Ponsonby), 1948

Strangers into Lovers (Lilian Peake), 1981

Strangers May Kiss (Hettie Grimstead), 1952

Strangers May Marry (Mary Burchell), 1941

Strangers on the Moor (Sylvia Thorpe), 1966

Stranger's Trespass (Jane Arbor), 1968

Strategy of Suzanne, The (Mabel Barnes Grundy), 1929

Stratford Affair, The (Phyllis Hastings), 1978

Strathgallant (Laura Black), 1981

Strathmore (Jessica Stirling), 1975

Stratton Story, The (Elizabeth Cadell), 1967

Straw Crown, The (Jean Stubbs), 1966

Strawberries in the Sea (Elisabeth Ogilvie), 1973

Straws in Amber (Naomi Jacob), 1938

Street Below, The (Ruby M. Ayres), 1922

Street of Gold, The (May Edginton), 1918

Street of Seven Stars, The (Mary Roberts Rinehart), 1914

Street of the City, The (Grace Livingston Hill), 1942

Street of the Five Moons (Barbara Michaels, as Elizabeth Peters), 1978

Street of the Singing Fountain, The (Rona Randall), 1948

Street of the Sun, The (Lance Horner), 1956

Streets, The (Robert Hichens), 1928

String of Silver Beads, A (Patricia Ainsworth), 1972

Strip Girl (Evadne Price), 1934

Strolling Players, The (Alice Dwyer-Joyce), 1975

Strolling Saint, The (Rafael Sabatini), 1913

Strong City, The (Taylor Caldwell), 1942

Strong Hand, The (Warwick Deeping), 1912

Strong Heart, The (Denise Robins), 1965

Strong Hours, The (Maud Diver), 1919

Stronger Passion, The (Ursula Bloom, as Sheila Burns), 1941

Stronger Spell, A (Eleanor Farnes), 1959

Strongest of All Things, The (Madame Albanesi), 1907

Struggle for a Crown (Maureen Peters), 1970

Stuart Sisters, The (Ursula Bloom, as Lozania Prole), 1958

Stuart Stain, The (Willo Davis Roberts), 1978

Stubborn Heart, The (Frank G. Slaughter), 1950

Studies in Love and Terror (Marie Belloc Lowndes), 1913

Studies in Wives (Marie Belloc Lowndes), 1909

Study of Sara (Hebe Elsna), 1930

Subconscious Courtship, The (Berta Ruck), 1922

Substitute Doctor (Elizabeth Seifert), 1957

Substitute for Love (Henrietta Reid), 1967

Substitute for Sherry (Theresa Charles, as Fay Chandos), 1940

Substitute Guest, The (Grace Livingston Hill), 1936

Suburban Young Man, The (E.M. Delafield), 1928

Such a Fine Fellow! (Mabel St. John), 1923

Such Bitter Business (Victoria Holt, as Elbur Ford), 1953

Such Frail Armour (Jane Arbor), 1953

Such Is Love (Mary Burchell), 1939

Such Men Are Dangerous (Elinor Glyn), 1933

Sudden Love (Jean Francis Webb, as Ethel Hamill), 1962

Sudden Sweetheart (Berta Ruck), 1932

Suddenly, In the Air (Betty Beaty, as Karen Campbell), 1969

Suffer to Sing (Countess Barcynska, as Oliver Sandys), 1955

Sugar Candy Cottage (Elizabeth Cadell), 1958

Sugar Cane Harvest (Kay Thorpe), 1975

Sugar in the Morning (Isobel Chace), 1969

Sugar Island (Anne Duffield), 1951

Sugar Island (Jean S. MacLeod), 1964

Sugar Mouse, The (Mary Ann Gibbs), 1965

Suitors of Yvonne, The (Rafael Sabatini), 1902

Summer at Barbazon, A (Kathryn Blair), 1960

Summer at San Milo, The (Nan Asquith), 1965

Summer at Silverwood (Claire Ritchie), 1962

Summer at Willowbank (Ivy Preston), 1980

Summer Change, The (Kate Norway, as Bess Norton), 1961

Summer Comes to Albarosa (Iris Danbury), 1971

Summer Cypress (Pamela Hill, as Sharon Fiske), 1981

Summer Every Day (Jane Arbor), 1966

Summer Fruit (Dornford Yates), 1929

Summer Gone, A (Margaret Maddocks), 1957

Summer House, The (Dorothy Daniels), 1976

Summer in December (Essie Summers), 1970

Summer Island (Jean S. MacLeod), 1968

Summer Magic (Margaret Way), 1971

Summer Mahogany (Janet Dailey), 1978

Summer Morning (May Edginton), 1934

Summer Motley (Eleanor Farnes), 1944

Summer of Sighs (Patricia Gallagher), 1971

Summer of the Dragon (Barbara Michaels, as Elizabeth Peters), 1979

Summer of the Spanish Woman, The (Catherine Gaskin), 1977

Summer People, The (Theresa Charles, as Leslie Lance), 1969

Summer Rain (Jean S. MacLeod), 1938

Summer Season (Rebecca Stratton, as Lucy Gillen), 1971

Summer Song (Hettie Grimstead, as Marsha Manning), 1972

Summer Spell (Sara Seale), 1937

Summer Stock Romance (Adeline McElfresh,

as Elizabeth Wesley), 1961

Summer Story (Mollie Chappell), 1972

Summer Sunday (Dorothy Eden), 1946

Summer to Love, A (Roumelia Lane), 1968

Summer Wife, The (Flora Kidd), 1976

Summerhills (D.E. Stevenson), 1956

Summer-House, The (Rosemary Harris), 1956

Summer's Cloud, A (Jill Tattersall), 1965

Summer's End (Danielle Steel), 1981

Summer's Grace, A (Theresa Charles, as Leslie Lance), 1961

Sun and Candlelight (Betty Neels), 1979

Sun and the Sea, The (Ruby M. Ayres), 1935

Sun in Splendour, The (Juliet Dymoke), 1980

Sun in Splendour, The (Victoria Holt, as Jean Plaidy), 1982

Sun in the Morning, The (Nan Asquith), 1974

Sun Is My Undoing, The (Marguerite Steen), 1941

Sun of Summer, The (Lilian Peake), 1975

Sun on the Mountain (Marion Collin), 1969

Sun on the Sea (Claire Ritchie), 1954

Sun, Sea and Sand (Wynne May), 1970

Sun Still Shines, The (Hebe Elsna, as Laura Conway), 1959

Sun Tower, The (Violet Winspear), 1976

Sun Will Shine, The (May Edginton), 1933

Sunburst (Berta Ruck), 1934

Sunday Evening (Margaret Lynn), 1969

Sunday's Child (Claudette Williams), 1977

Sundial, The (Shirley Jackson), 1958

Sunday Love (Ursula Bloom), 1978

Sundered Hearts (Annie S. Swan), 1886

Sunflower's Look, The (Claire Ritchie), 1958

Sunia (Maud Diver), 1913

Sunlight Beyond (Madame Albanesi, as Effie Rowlands), 1930

Sunlit Hills, The (Madame Albanesi), 1914

Sunlit Seas (Ivy Preston), 1977

Sunlit Way, The (May Edginton), 1928

Sunny Ducrow (Mabel St. John, as Henry St. John Cooper), 1919

Sunny Island, The (Maysie Greig, as Mary Douglas Warren), 1952

Sunrise (Anne Duffield), 1944

Sunrise (Grace Livingston Hill), 1937

Sunrise for Georgie (Ruby M. Ayres), 1941

Sunrise in the West (Edith Pargeter), 1974

Sunset (Christopher Nicole), 1978

Sunset and Dawn (Madame Albanesi, as Effie Rowlands), 1915

Sunset Cloud (Anne Hampson), 1976

Sunset Hour, The (Hebe Elsna, as Vicky Lancaster), 1946

Sunset Is Dawn (Countess Barcynska, as

Marguerite Barclay), 1953

Sunshine-Stealer (Berta Ruck), 1935

Surgeon at Sea (Ursula Bloom, as Sheila Burns), 1969

Surgeon from Holland (Betty Neels), 1970

Surgeon in Charge (Elizabeth Seifert), 1942

Surgeon in Tibet (Irene Roberts), 1970

Surgeon of Distinction (Mary Burchell), 1959

Surgeon on Call (Elizabeth Seifert), 1965

Surgeon, U.S.A. (Frank G. Slaughter), 1966

Surgeon's Call (Elizabeth Harrison), 1973

Surgeon's Choice (Frank G. Slaughter), 1969

Surgeon's Dilemma (Mary Howard), 1961

Surgeon's Marriage, The (Kathryn Blair), 1963

Surgeon's Reputation (Theresa Charles), 1979

Surgeon's Sweetheart, A (Ursula Bloom, as Sheila Burns), 1966

Surgeon's Sweetheart (Theresa Charles), 1982

Surest Bond, The (Madame Albanesi, as Effie Rowlands), 1913

Surly Sullen Bell, The (Russell Kirk), 1962

Surprise (May Edginton), 1948

Surprise Engagement (Berta Ruck), 1946

Surrender, My Love (Glenna Finley), 1974

Survivor of Darkness (Virginia Coffman), 1973

Survivors, The (Anne Edwards), 1968

Survivors of Darkness (Dorothy Daniels), 1969

Susan Crowther (Naomi Jacob), 1945

Susannah and One Elder (Madame Albanesi), 1903

Susannah, The Righteous (Katheryn Kimbrough), 1975

"Susie's" Career (Robert Hichens), 1935

Suspected Four, The (Willo Davis Roberts), 1962

Suspicion (Hebe Elsna, as Vicky Lancaster), 1955

Sussex saga (Phyllis Hastings)

Suvla John (Warwick Deeping), 1924

Suzerain, The (Pamela Bennetts), 1968

Swallow (H. Rider Haggard), 1899

Swallows of San Fedora, The (Betty Beaty), 1970

Swan, The (Marguerite Steen), 1951

Swan House (Baroness von Hutten), 1930

Swan River Story, The (Phyllis Hastings), 1968

Swans and Turtles (Rumer Godden), 1968

Swans' Reach (Margaret Way), 1977

Sweeping Tide, The (Anne Duffield), 1940

Sweet Adventure (Mary Burchell), 1952

Sweet Adventure (Barbara Cartland), 1957

Sweet and Faraway (Lucy Walker), 1955

Sweet and Lovely (Madame Albanesi), 1933

Sweet and Twenty (Joan Smith), 1979

Sweet Are the Ways (Essie Summers), 1965

Sweet as a Rose (Charles Garvice), 1910

Sweet Barbary (Susan Barrie, as Pamela Kent), 1957

Sweet Bloom (Claire Ritchie), 1961

Sweet Cassandra (Denise Robins), 1970

Sweet Cymbeline (Charles Garvice), 1911

Sweet Danger (Maysie Greig), 1935

Sweet Deceiver (Kathryn Blair), 1955

Sweet Enchantress (Barbara Cartland, as Barbara McCorquodale), 1958

Sweet Epitaph (Margaret Lynn), 1971

Sweet Familiarity, A (Daoma Winston), 1981

Sweet Fellows (Countess Barcynska, as Oliver Sandys), 1942

Sweet Friday (Hettie Grimstead, as Marsha Manning), 1972

Sweet Impulse, The (Ursula Bloom, as Sheila Burns), 1956

Sweet Is the Web (Anne Hampson), 1977

Sweet Kate (Rebecca Stratton, as Lucy Gillen), 1971

Sweet Lass of Richmond Hill (Victoria Holt, as Jean Plaidy), 1970

Sweet Lost Years, The (Hebe Elsna), 1955

Sweet Love (Denise Robins), 1934

Sweet Marie-Antoinette (Ursula Bloom, as Lozania Prole), 1969

Sweet Meadows (Mary Burchell), 1963

Sweet Nell (Ursula Bloom, as Lozania Prole), 1965

Sweet Peril (Maysie Greig, as Jennifer Ames), 1935

Sweet Prisoner (Hettie Grimstead), 1961

Sweet Promise (Janet Dailey), 1976

Sweet Punishment (Barbara Cartland), 1931

Sweet Revenge (Anne Mather), 1970

Sweet Rocket (Mary Johnston), 1920

Sweet Roots and Honey (Gwen Westwood), 1974

Sweet Rosemary (Theresa Charles, as Fay Chandos), 1972

Sweet Sanctuary (Charlotte Lamb), 1976

Sweet Savage Love (Rosemary Rogers), 1974

Sweet Shipwreck (Hebe Elsna, as Vicky Lancaster), 1942

Sweet Simplicity (Elizabeth Ashton), 1971

Sweet Sorrel (Irene Roberts), 1963

Sweet Sorrow (Denise Robins), 1940

Sweet Spring of April (Ursula Bloom), 1979

Sweet Stranger (Berta Ruck), 1921

Sweet Sundown (Margaret Way), 1974

Sweet Surrender, The (Rose Burghley), 1959

Sweet Torment (Flora Kidd), 1978

Sweet Waters (Kathryn Blair, as Rosalind Brett), 1955

Sweet William (Madame Albanesi), 1906

Sweet Wind of Morning (Maureen Peters, as Belinda Grey), 1979

Sweet Wine of Youth (Hebe Elsna, as Vicky Lancaster), 1960

Sweetbriar Lane (Countess Barcynska), 1938

Sweeter Unpossessed (Hebe Elsna), 1929

Sweetheart Tree, The (Hettie Grimstead), 1966

Sweethearts Unmet (Berta Ruck), 1919

Swift Water (Emilie Loring), 1929

Swiftest Eagle, The (Alice Dwyer-Joyce), 1979

Swimming Pool, The (Mary Roberts Rinehart), 1952

Swindler, The (Ethel M. Dell), 1914

Swing High, Swing Low (Maysie Greig, as Ann Barclay), 1936

Swing of Youth (Denise Robins), 1930

Sword and Scalpel (Frank G. Slaughter), 1957

Sword and the Cross, The (Warwick Deeping), 1957

Sword and the Shadow, The (Sylvia Thorpe), 1951

Sword and the Swan, The (Roberta Gellis), 1977

Sword Decides!, The (Marjorie Bowen), 1908

Sword in the Sun (Elizabeth Hoy), 1946

Sword of Islam, The (Rafael Sabatini), 1939

Sword of Mithras (Constance Heaven, as Christina Merlin), 1982

Sword of Vengeance (Sylvia Thorpe), 1957

Sword to the Heart, A (Barbara Cartland), 1974

Swordlight (Anne Rundle), 1968

Sycamore Song, The (Isobel Chace, as Elizabeth Hunter), 1975

Sydney (Charles Garvice)

Sylvester (Georgette Heyer), 1957

Sylvia Cary (Frances Parkinson Keyes), 1962

Sylvia Lyndon (Maud Diver), 1940

Sylvia Sorelle (Elizabeth Hoy), 1944

Sympathetic Surgeon, The (Ursula Bloom, as Mary Essex), 1968

Sympathy (May Wynne), 1901

Symphony for Two Players (Maynah Lewis), 1969

Symphony of Bells (Irene Roberts), 1980

Tabitha in Moonlight (Betty Neels), 1972

Table for Two (Maysie Greig), 1946

Tabloid (Louis Bromfield), 1930

Taffy Came to Cairo (Anne Duffield), 1944

Tailor of Vitré, The (May Wynne), 1908

Taint of Tragedy, The (May Wynne), 1917

Taj Mahal, Shrine of Desire (Ursula Bloom, as Lozania Prole), 1972

Take a Chance (Ursula Bloom, as Sheila Burns), 1937

Take a Chance (Theresa Charles, as Leslie Lance), 1940

Take Back Your Love (Katrina Britt), 1975

Take Heed of Loving Me (Hebe Elsna), 1970

Take Love Easy (Elizabeth Hoy), 1941

Take Me with You (Mary Burchell), 1944

Take Pity upon Youth (Hebe Elsna), 1962

Take This Man (Maysie Greig), 1947

Take Three Tenses (Rumer Godden), 1945

Take What You Want (Faith Baldwin), 1970

Take What You Want (Anne Mather), 1975

Take Your Choice, Lady (Maysie Greig, as Jennifer Ames), 1946

Tale of Three Lions, A (H. Rider Haggard), 1887

Tales of Grace and Favour (Doris Leslie), 1956

Tales of the Broad Acres (Naomi Jacob), 1955

Tales of Two People (Anthony Hope), 1907

Talisman, The (Cecily Crowe), 1979

Talisman Ring, The (Georgette Heyer), 1936

Talk of the Town (Joan Smith), 1979

Tall Headlines, The (Audrey Erskine-Lindop), 1950

Tall Man, The (May Edginton), 1950

Tall Pines, The (Kathryn Blair, as Celine Conway), 1956

Tall Stranger, The (D.E. Stevenson), 1957

Tamara (Kathleen Norris), 1935

Tamarind Seed, The (Evelyn Anthony), 1971

Tamarisk (Claire Lorrimer), 1978

Tamarisk (Netta Muskett), 1935

Tamarisk Bay (Kathryn Blair), 1956

Tamarisk in Bloom (Ivy Preston), 1963

Tamberlyn (Audrie Manley-Tucker), 1981

Tamboti Moon (Wynne May), 1969

Taming of Lady Lorinda, The (Barbara Cartland), 1977

Taming of Laura, The (Rachel Lindsay), 1959

Taming of Lisa, The (Flora Kidd), 1972

Taming of Princess Olga (Charles Garvice), 1908

Tangle in Sunshine (Kathryn Blair, as Rosalind Brett), 1957

Tangle of Gold Lace (Irene Roberts), 1963

Tangled Autumn (Betty Neels), 1972

Tangled Fates (May Wynne), 1935

Tangled Harmonies (Eleanor Farnes), 1936

Tangled Love (Kathleen Norris), 1933

Tangled Roots (Iris Bromige), 1948

Tangled Shadows (Flora Kidd), 1979

Tangled Skein, The (Baroness Orczy), 1907

Tangled Tapestry (Anne Mather), 1969

Tangled Threads, The (Eleanor H. Porter), 1919

Tangled Web, A (Eleanor Farnes), 1963

Tangled Web, A (L.M. Montgomery), 1931

Tangled Web, The (Irene Roberts, as Iris Rowland), 1962

Tangled Wood, The (Iris Bromige), 1969

Tansy (Maureen Peters, as Veronica Black), 1975

Tara's Healing (Janice Holt Giles), 1951

Tara's Song (Barbara Ferry Johnson), 1978

Tarnish (Ursula Bloom), 1929

Tarot Spell, The (Willo Davis Roberts), 1970

Tarot's Tower (Gwendoline Butler, as Jennie Melville), 1978

Tarrington Chase (Sylvia Thorpe), 1977

Tartan Ribbon, The (Henrietta Reid), 1976

Tartan Touch, The (Isobel Chace), 1972

Taste for Love, A (Joyce Dingwell), 1967

Taste of Fears (Margaret Millar), 1950

Taste of Wine, A (Chelsea Quinn Yarbro, as Vanessa Pryor), 1982

Tattling Tongues (Mabel St. John), 1922

Tattooed Road, The (Lance Horner), 1960

Tavern, The (Marguerite Steen), 1935

Tavern Knight, The (Rafael Sabatini), 1904

Tawny Are the Leaves (Wynne May), 1968

Tawny Sands (Violet Winspear), 1970

Tea at Gunter's (Pamela Haines), 1974

Tea Is So Intoxicating (Ursula Bloom, as Mary Essex), 1950

Teach Me to Forget (Hebe Elsna, as Laura Conway), 1961

Teach Me to Love (Theresa Charles, as Jan Tempest), 1947

Team, The (Kate Norway, as Hilary Neal), 1965

Team-Up for Ann (Adeline McElfresh), 1959

Tears and Red Roses (Charlotte Lamb, as Laura Hardy), 1982

Tears in Paradise (Jane Blackmore), 1959

Tears of Gold (Laurie McBain), 1979

Tears of Love, The (Barbara Cartland), 1975

Tears of Peace, The (Countess Barcynska), 1944

Tears of Venus, The (Rebecca Stratton), 1979

Technique (May Edginton), 1953

Tell Me My Fortune (Mary Burchell), 1951

Tell Me My Heart (Faith Baldwin), 1950

Temp, The (Anne Betteridge), 1976

Temperamental People (Mary Roberts Rinehart), 1924

Tempest and the Song, The (Claire Ritchie), 1959

Tempestuous April (Betty Neels), 1975

Tempestuous Petticoat, The (Mary Ann Gibbs), 1977

Temple of Dawn (Anne Hampson), 1979

Templeton Memoirs, The (Dorothy Daniels), 1966

Temporal Power (Marie Corelli), 1902

Temporary Address: Reno (Faith Baldwin), 1941

Temporary Boy, The (Phyllis Hastings), 1971

Temporary Wife (Rachel Lindsay, as Roberta Leigh), 1975

Tempt Not This Flesh (Barbara Riefe), 1979

Temptation (Madame Albanesi, as Effie Rowlands), 1912

Temptation (Charlotte Lamb), 1979

Temptation (May Wynne), 1937

Temptation of Mary Barr (Madame Albanesi, as Effie Rowlands)

Temptation of Philip Carr, The (May Wynne), 1905

Temptation of Torilla, The (Barbara Cartland), 1977

Tempted by Love (Madame Albanesi, as Effie Rowlands)

Tempting Fate (Chelsea Quinn Yarbro), 1982

Temptress, The (Rosamond Marshall), 1953

Ten Cent Love (Maysie Greig), 1934

Ten Commandments, The (Warwick Deeping), 1931

Ten Thousand Several Doors (Mary Francis Craig), 1973

Tenant of Binningham Hall (Olga Sinclair), 1970

Tenant of Chesdene Manor (Alice Chetwynd Ley), 1974

Tenant of San Mateo, The (Roumelia Lane), 1976

Ten-Day Queen, The (Ursula Bloom, as Lozania Prole), 1972

Tender Chord, The (Hettie Grimstead), 1967

Tender Conquest (Joyce Dingwell), 1960

Tender Glory, The (Jean S. MacLeod), 1965

Tender Is the Tyrant (Violet Winspear), 1967

Tender Night, The (Lilian Peake), 1975

Tender Only to One (Susan Inglis), 1938

Tender Pilgrim, The (Hettie Grimstead), 1955

Tender Victory (Taylor Caldwell), 1956

Tender Vine, The (Hettie Grimstead), 1974

Tender Winds of Spring, The (Joyce Dingwell), 1978

Tension (E.M. Delafield), 1920

Terminus (Doris Leslie), 1931

Terminus Tehran (Roumelia Lane), 1969

Terms of Surrender (Janet Dailey), 1982

Terracotta Palace, The (Anne Maybury), 1971

Terriford Mystery, The (Marie Belloc Lowndes), 1924

Terror in the Sun (Barbara Cartland), 1979

Terror of the Moor, The (May Wynne), 1928

Terror of the Twin (Dorothy Daniels), 1976

Terror Trap, The (Willo Davis Roberts), 1971

Terror the Black Sheep (May Wynne), 1928

Tesha (Countess Barcynska), 1923

Tessacott Tragedy, The (Charles Garvice), 1913

Testament of Trust (Faith Baldwin), 1960

Testimony of Two Men (Taylor Caldwell), 1968

Tetherstones (Ethel M. Dell), 1923

Thames Camp, A (Mabel Barnes Grundy), 1902

Than This World Dreams Of (Ruby M. Ayres), 1934

Thanesworth House (Katheryn Kimbrough), 1972

Thank Heaven Fasting (E.M. Delafield), 1932

Thankful Rest (Annie S. Swan), 1885

Thanks to Elizabeth (Mary Burchell), 1944

That Awful Scar (Charles Garvice, as Caroline Hart)

That Boston Man (Janet Dailey), 1979

That Carolina Summer (Janet Dailey), 1982

That Enchantress (Doris Leslie), 1950

That Fatal Touch (Mary Linn Roby), 1970

That Girl in Nice (Maysie Greig), 1954

That Girl, Jennifer! (Rona Randall), 1946

That Island Summer (Elizabeth Hoy), 1973

That Man Is Mine! (Faith Baldwin), 1936

That Man Next Door (Rebecca Stratton, as Lucy Gillen), 1971

That Nice Nurse Nevin (Theresa Charles, as Jan Tempest), 1963

That Night (Jane Blackmore), 1963

That None Should Die (Frank G. Slaughter), 1941

That Strange Girl (Charles Garvice), 1911

That Strange Holiday (Petra Sawley), 1972

That Summer at Bacclesea (Mary Ann Gibbs, as Elizabeth Ford), 1956

That Trouble Piece! (Countess Barcynska),

1939

That Which Is Hidden (Robert Hichens), 1939

That Young Person (Sara Seale), 1969

Thawing of Mara, The (Janet Dailey), 1980

Thea (Margaret Maddocks), 1971

Theatre Sister in Love (Ursula Bloom, as Sheila Burns), 1963

Theft of the Heart (Barbara Cartland, as Barbara McCorquodale), 1966

Their Flowers Were Always Black (Phyllis Hastings), 1967

Their Mysterious Patient (Petra Sawley), 1970

Theirs Was the Kingdom (R.F. Delderfield), 1971

Thelma (Marie Corelli), 1887

Theme for Reason, A (Elisabeth Ogilvie), 1970

Theme Song (Leila Mackinlay), 1938

Then Came the Test (Margaret Pedler), 1942

Then Came Two Women (Charlotte Armstrong), 1962

Then Come Kiss Me (Mary Burchell), 1948

That She Fled Me (Sara Seale), 1950

Theodora (Anne Eliot, as Caroline Arnett), 1977

Theodore (May Wynne), 1906

There Are Limits (Denise Robins), 1932

There Are Worse Jungles (Nigel Tranter), 1955

There Came a Tyrant (Anne Hampson), 1972

There Is a Season (Faith Baldwin), 1966

There Is a Tide... (Theresa Charles, as Fay Chandos), 1950

There Is Always Love (Emilie Loring), 1940

There Is But One (Claire Lorrimer, as Patricia Robins), 1965

There Lies Your Love (Gwendoline Butler, as Jennie Melville), 1965

There May Be Heaven (Elisabeth Ogilvie), 1966

There Was a Fair Maid Dwelling (R.F. Delderfield), 1960

There Was a Time (Taylor Caldwell), 1947

There Was Another (Ruby M. Ayres), 1938

There Were Nine Castles (Isobel Chace, as Elizabeth Hunter), 1967

There Were Three Men (Helen Beauclerk), 1949

There Were Three Princes (Joyce Dingwell), 1972

Therefore Must Be Loved (Theresa Charles), 1972

There's Just One Girl (Mabel St. John, as

Henry St. John Cooper), 1919

These Are Our Masters (Annie S. Swan), 1939

These Changing Years (Countess Barcynska), 1961

These Charming People (Michael Arlen), 1923

These Delights (Sara Seale), 1949

These Mortals (Margaret Irwin), 1925

These My Children (Maynah Lewis), 1977

These Old Shades (Georgette Heyer), 1926

These Roots Go Deep (Ursula Bloom), 1939

These White Hands (Warwick Deeping), 1937

They Brought Their Women (Edna Ferber), 1933

They Came to Valeira (Kathryn Blair, as Rosalind Brett), 1950

They Dreamed Too Much (Anne Maybury), 1938

They Found Him Dead (Georgette Heyer), 1937

They Knew Her When (Doris Langley Moore), 1938

They Laugh That Win (Madame Albanesi, as Effie Rowlands), 1899

They Left the Land (Naomi Jacob), 1940

They Lived with Me (Evadne Price, as Helen Zenna Smith), 1934

They Loved in Donegal (Hebe Elsna, as Vicky Lancaster), 1944

They Met in Zanzibar (Kathryn Blair), 1962

They That Go Down (Marguerite Steen), 1930

They That Go Down in Ships (Marguerite Steen), 1931

They Were All in Love (May Edginton), 1938

They Were Not Divided (Hebe Elsna, as Vicky Lancaster), 1952

They Who Love (Faith Baldwin), 1948

Thicket, The (Patricia Gallagher), 1973

Thief of Love, The (Barbara Cartland, as Barbara McCorquodale), 1957

Thieving Magpie, The (Ursula Bloom), 1960

Thine Is My Heart (Mary Burchell), 1942

Thing That Happens to You, A (Evelyn Berckman), 1964

Third Boat, The (Leila Mackinlay), 1967

Third Estate, The (Marjorie Bowen), 1917

Third Eye, The (Elinor Glyn), 1940

Third Generation, The (Annie S. Swan), 1940

Third George, The (Victoria Holt, as Jean Plaidy), 1969

Third Grave, The (David Case), 1981

Third in the House, The (Joyce Dingwell), 1961

Third Love Lucky (Berta Ruck), 1958

Third Miss Chance, The (Elizabeth O. Peter), 1933

Third Miss Wenderby, The (Mabel Barnes Grundy), 1911

Third Richard, The (Pamela Bennetts), 1972

Third Time Lucky (Berta Ruck), 1958

Third Tower, The (Alice Abbott), 1974

Third Uncle, The (Sara Seale), 1964

Third Wife, The (Hebe Elsna), 1928

Thirteen for Luck (May Wynne), 1936

Thirteenth Girl, The (Maysie Greig), 1947

This Alien Heart (Anne Duffield), 1942

This Ancient Evil (Dorothy Daniels), 1966

This Clay Suburb (Hebe Elsna), 1938

This Desirable Bachelor (Maysie Greig), 1941

This Dragon of Desire (Ursula Bloom, as Sheila Burns), 1958

This Errant Heart (Anne Maybury), 1937

This Fearful Paradise (Maysie Greig), 1953

This Flower (Lady Miles), 1933

This Foolish Heart (Susan Inglis), 1940

This Foolish Love (Jean Marsh), 1982

This for Caroline (Doris Leslie), 1964

This Golden Estate (Eleanor Farnes), 1975

This Is Marriage (Ursula Bloom), 1935

This King of Love (Kathryn Blair), 1964

This Land Turns Evil Slowly (Mary Linn Roby), 1971

This Lovely Hour (Anne Maybury), 1937

This Man Her Enemy (Lilian Peake), 1977

This Man Is Not for Marrying (Ursula Bloom, as Mary Essex), 1959

This Merry Bond (Sara Seale), 1938

This Moment in Time (Lilian Peake), 1971

This Much to Give (Jean S. MacLeod), 1945

This Must Be for Ever (Marjorie Lewty), 1962

This One Night (Denise Robins), 1942

This Other Eden (Catherine Gaskin), 1947

This Other Eden (Marilyn Harris), 1977

This Outward Angel (Alanna Knight), 1972

This Passion Called Love (Elinor Glyn), 1925

This Porcelain Clay (Naomi Jacob), 1939

This Publican (Dornford Yates), 1938

This Ravaged Heart (Barbara Riefe), 1977

This Rough Magic (Edith Pargeter), 1953

This Rough Magic (Mary Stewart), 1964

This Second Spring (Jane Arbor), 1948

This Side of Innocence (Taylor Caldwell), 1946

This Side of Paradise (Kay Thorpe), 1979

This Son of Adam (G.B. Burgin), 1910

This Splendid Folly (Margaret Pedler), 1918

This Spring of Love (Denise Robins), 1943

This Strange Adventure (Mary Roberts Rinehart), 1929

This Summer's Rose (Claire Ritchie), 1970

This Time It's Love (Barbara Cartland), 1977

This Time It's Love (Theresa Charles, as Fay Chandos), 1951

This Was a Man (Victoria Holt, as Ellalice Tate), 1961

This Was Tomorrow (Elswyth Thane), 1951

This Way to Happiness (Maysie Greig), 1931

This Wild Enchantment (Hebe Elsna, as Vicky Lancaster), 1938

This Woman to This Man (C.N. and A.M. Williamson), 1917

This Year, Next Year, Sometime— (Berta Ruck), 1932

Thistle and the Rose, The (Victoria Holt, as Jean Plaidy), 1963

Thistle and the Rose, The (Margaret Rome), 1977

Thorn of Arimathea, The (Frank G. Slaughter), 1959

Thorn Tree, The (Henrietta Reid), 1969

Thorn-Apple (Anne Worboys, as Annette Eyre), 1968

Thornwood, The (Doris E. Smith), 1966

Thomas and Sarah (Mollie Hardwick), 1978

Thomas Dryburgh's Dream (Annie S. Swan), 1886

Those Difficult Years (Faith Baldwin), 1925

Those Dominant Hills (Countess Barcynska), 1951

Those Fragile Years (Rose Franken), 1952

Those Who Love (Denise Robins), 1936

Thou Shalt Love Thy Neighbour— (Mabel St. John), 1927

Thou Shalt Not Kill (Marie Belloc Lowndes), 1927

Though I Bid Farewell (Elizabeth Hoy), 1948

Though Worlds Apart (Mary Burchell), 1967

Thousand Candles, A (Joyce Dingwell), 1971

Thousandth Man, The (Ruby M. Ayres), 1939

Three Candles for the Dark (Rosemary Harris), 1976

Three Cedars (Ursula Bloom), 1937

Three Cries of Terror (Katheryn Kimbrough, as Ann Ashton), 1980

Three Crowns, The (Victoria Holt, as Jean Plaidy), 1965

Three Englishment (Gilbert Frankau), 1935

Three Faces of Love (Faith Baldwin), 1957

Three for a Wedding (Betty Neels), 1973

Three Happy Pilgrims (Eleanor Farnes), 1937

Three Latch Keys (Hebe Elsna, as Lyndon Snow), 1943

Three Letters to Pan (Jane Blackmore), 1955

Three Loves (Claire Lorrimer, as Patricia Robins), 1949

Three Marriages (E.M. Delafield), 1939

Three Men and Diana (Kathleen Norris), 1934

Three Men and Jennie (Naomi Jacob), 1960

Three Men in Her Life (Susan Inglis), 1951

Three of Hearts (Berta Ruck), 1917

Three of Us, The (Theresa Charles, as Fay Chandos), 1970

Three Passionate Queens, The (Ursula Bloom, as Lozania Prole), 1964

Three People (Mabel Barnes Grundy), 1926

Three Roads to Heaven (Hebe Elsna, as Vicky Lancaster), 1939

Three Roads to Romance (Theresa Charles, as Fay Chandos), 1945

Three Rooms (Warwick Deeping), 1924

Three Sisters of Briarwick, The (Katheryn Kimbrough), 1973

Three Sons (Ursula Bloom), 1946

Three Strings to a Fortune (Anne Worboys, as Annette Eyre), 1962

Three Weeks (Elinor Glyn), 1907

Three Wise Men of Gotham (Marie Corelli), 1896

Three Women (Faith Baldwin), 1926

Three Women (Kathryn Blair, as Celine Conway), 1955

Three's Company (May Wynne), 1917

Thresholds (Faith Baldwin), 1925

Through All the Years (Essie Summers), 1974

Through a Glass Darkly (Kathleen Norris), 1957

Through Many Waters (Netta Muskett), 1961

Through the Mist (Madame Albanesi), 1934

Through the Postern Gate (Florence L. Barclay), 1912

Through These Fires (Grace Livingston Hill), 1943

Through Weal and Through Woe (Madame Albanesi, as Effie Rowlands), 1913

Throw Away Yesterday (Berta Ruck), 1946

Throw Wide the Door (Emilie Loring), 1962

Throw Your Bouquet (Leila Mackinlay, as Brenda Grey), 1967

Throw-Back, The (G.B. Burgin), 1918

Thunder and the Shouting, The (Christopher Nicole), 1969

Thunder Heights (Irene Roberts), 1969

Thunder Heights (Phyllis A. Whitney), 1960

Thunder of Her Heart (Elisabeth Beresford), 1978

Thunder on Sunday (Betty Beaty, as Karen

Campbell), 1972

Thunder on the Right (Mary Stewart), 1957

Thunderer, The (L. Adams Beck, as E. Barrington), 1927

Thursday's Child (Faith Baldwin), 1976

Thus Doctor Mallory (Elizabeth Seifert), 1940

Thy Bride Am I (Ursula Bloom, as Sheila Burns), 1942

Ticket of Destiny (Ivy Preston), 1969

Ticket-of-Leave Girl, The (Mabel St. John), 1914

Tidal Wave, The (Ethel M. Dell), 1919

Tide at Full, The (Wynne May), 1971

Tide Mill, The (Dorothy Daniels), 1975

Tide of Life, The (Catherine Cookson), 1976

Tides of Love (Patricia Matthews), 1981

Tides of Spring Flow Fast, The (Ursula Bloom), 1956

Tidewater Lover (Janet Dailey), 1978

Tidewrack (Nigel Tranter), 1951

Tie That Binds, The (Eleanor H. Porter), 1919

Tied to Her Apron Strings! (Mabel St. John), 1927

Tiffany's True Love (Florence Stevenson, as Zabrina Faire), 1981

Tiger (Ursula Bloom), 1903

Tiger and the Goat, The (Anne Betteridge), 1978

Tiger Hall (Esther Wyndham), 1954

Tiger in Men, The (Denise Robins), 1937

Tiger Lily (C.N. and A.M. Williamson), 1917

Tiger's Claw, The (G.B. Burgin), 1900

Tiger's Heaven (Phyllis Hastings), 1981

Tightening String, The (Ann Bridge), 1962

Till the End of Time (Lilian Peake), 1973

Till Then, My Love (Maynah Lewis), 1968

Tilly Trotter Trotter series (Catherine Cookson)

Tilly-Make-Haste (Countess Barcynska, as Oliver Sandys), 1924

Tilsit Inheritance, The (Catherine Gaskin), 1963

Tilthammer, The (Charlotte Lamb, as Sheila Lancaster), 1980

Timber Boss (Kay Thorpe), 1978

Timber Man, The (Joyce Dingwell), 1964

Time and the Hour (Faith Baldwin), 1974

Time and the Loving, The (Marjorie Lewty), 1977

Time and the Place, The (Essie Summers), 1958

Time at Tarragon, A (Jill Tattersall), 1969

Time for Happiness, The (Nan Asquith), 1959

Time for Play (Netta Muskett), 1943

Time for Pleasure, A (Phyllis Hastings), 1957

Time for Rejoicing, A (Elizabeth Renier), 1973

Time for Titans, A (Viña Delmar), 1974

Time Is—Time Was (Hebe Elsna), 1960

Time May Change (Nan Asquith), 1961

Time of the Dragon, The (Dorothy Eden), 1975

Time of the Jacaranda, The (Margaret Way), 1970

Time No Longer (Taylor Caldwell, as Max Renier), 1941

Time of Dreaming (Mary Howard, as Josephine Edgar), 1968

Time of Glory (Janice Holt Giles), 1966

Time of Grace (Sara Seale), 1955

Time of the Singing Birds (Grace Livingston Hill), 1945

Time of the Temptress (Violet Winspear), 1977

Time of Their Lives, A (Anne Betteridge), 1974

Time on Her Hands (Leila Mackinlay), 1942

Time Out of Mind (Rachel Field), 1935

Time Piece (Naomi Jacob), 1936

Time Remembered, A (Rebecca Stratton, as Lucy Gillen), 1971

Time Remembered, Time Lost (Rona Randall), 1973

Time Runs Out (Denise Robins, as Julia Kane), 1965

Time Suspended (Jean S. MacLeod), 1974

Time to Heal (Warwick Deeping), 1952

Time to Love, A (Rachel Lindsay, as Janey Scott), 1960

Timed for Love (Glenna Finley), 1979

Timeless Place, A (Jean Stubbs), 1978

Timid Cleopatra, The (Maysie Greig, as Jennifer Ames), 1962

Tinker's Pride (Nigel Tranter), 1945

Tinsel and the Gold, The (Countess Barcynska, as Oliver Sandys), 1959

Tinsel Kisses (Hettie Grimstead), 1958

Tinsel Star (Rachel Lindsay), 1976

Tinted Dream (Maysie Greig, as Jennifer Ames), 1936

Tiptoes (Countess Barcynska, as Oliver Sandys), 1935

Tish series (Mary Roberts Rinehart)

To Be a Bride (Theresa Charles, as Jan Tempest), 1945

To Be a King (Hester W. Chapman), 1934

To Be Beloved (Irene Roberts, as Iris Rowland), 1968

To Bed at Noon (Marjorie Bowen, as Joseph Shearing), 1951

To Burgundy and Back (Dorothy Mackie Low), 1970

To Buy a Bride (Rachel Lindsay, as Roberta Leigh), 1976

To Care Always (Kate Norway), 1970

To Catch a Bride (Glenna Finley), 1977

To Catch a Butterfly (Marjorie Lewty), 1977

To Catch a Dream (Hettie Grimstead, as Marsha Manning), 1970

To Catch a Unicorn (Sara Seale), 1964

To Each Her Dream (Adeline McElfresh), 1961

To Follow the Lead (Annie S. Swan), 1911

To Greet the Morning (Claire Ritchie), 1966

To Have and to Hold (Mary Johnston), 1900

To Journey Together (Mary Burchell), 1956

To Lisa with Love (Irene Roberts, as Iris Rowland), 1975

To Look and Pass (Taylor Caldwell), 1974

To Love a Dark Stranger (Virginia Coffman), 1969

To Love a Stranger (Rosalind Laker, as Barbara Paul), 1979

To Love Again (Denise Robins), 1949

To Love Again (Danielle Steel), 1980

To Love and to Cherish (Madame Albanesi, as Effie Rowlands), 1912

To Love and to Honor (Emilie Loring), 1950

To Love Is to Live (Denise Robins), 1940

To M.L.G. (A.M. Williamson), 1912

To Marry a Tiger (Isobel Chace), 1971

To Meet a Stranger (Victoria Holt, as Eleanor Burford), 1957

To Mend a Heart (Elizabeth Harrison), 1977

To Play with Fire (Flora Kidd), 1977

To Save My Life (Theresa Charles), 1946

To See a Fine Lady (Norah Lofts), 1946

To See a Stranger (Margaret Lynn), 1961

To See Ourselves (Rachel Field), 1937

To See the Glory (Taylor Caldwell), 1963

To Seek a Star (Suzanne Ebel), 1973

To Serve Them All My Days (R.F. Delderfield), 1972

To Sing Me Home (Doris E. Smith), 1969

To Tame a Vixen (Anne Hampson), 1978

To Tell the Truth (Janet Dailey), 1977

To the Hilt (P.C. Wren), 1937

To the Stars (Claire Lorrimer, as Patricia Robins), 1944

To Trust Tomorrow (Nancy John), 1981

To Wear Your Ring (Susan Inglis), 1938

To Wed a Doctor (Elizabeth Seifert), 1968

To Win a Paradise (Elizabeth Hoy), 1947

Toast of the Town, The (Alice Chetwynd Ley), 1969

Toast to Lady Mary, A (Doris Leslie), 1954

Tobias and the Angel (Frank Yerby), 1975

Today Is Mine (Marjorie Bowen), 1941

To-Day Is Ours (Netta Muskett), 1939

Today Is Yours (Emilie Loring), 1938

To-Day We Live (Anne Maybury), 1942

To-Day's Daughter (Berta Ruck), 1929

Today's Virtue (Faith Baldwin), 1931

Together (Maud Diver), 1928

Together Again (Flora Kidd), 1979

Together and Apart (Margaret Kennedy), 1936

Together They Rode (Victoria Holt, as Jean Plaidy), 1945

Toils of Silence (Mabel St. John, as Henry St. John Cooper), 1935

Tolbecken (Samuel Shellabarger), 1956

Told at Monte Carlo (A.M. Williamson), 1926

Toll-Gate, The (Georgette Heyer), 1954

Tom and Some Other Girls (Mrs. George de Horne Vaizey), 1901

Tomalyn's Quest (G.B. Burgin), 1896

Tomboy in Lace (Berta Ruck), 1947

Tomorrow about This Time (Grace Livingston Hill), 1923

Tomorrow Brings Enchantment (Henrietta Reid), 1978

Tomorrow Comes the Sun (Elizabeth Renier), 1969

To-morrow for Apricots (Ursula Bloom), 1929

To-morrow Is Eternal (Ursula Bloom, as Sheila Burns), 1948

Tomorrow Is Theirs (Anne Duffield), 1952

Tomorrow We Marry (Ursula Bloom, as Sheila Burns), 1953

To-morrow's Bargain (Jean S. MacLeod), 1949

To-morrow's Hero (Mary Howard), 1941

Tomorrow's Miracle (Frank G. Slaughter), 1962

To-Morrow's Promise (Hebe Elsna, as Lyndon Snow), 1956

To-morrow's Tangle (Margaret Pedler), 1925

Tongues of Conscience (Robert Hichens), 1900

To-night, Josephine! (Ursula Bloom, as Lozania Prole), 1954

Tontine, The (Thomas B. Costain), 1955

Tony's Memorable Christmas (Annie S. Swan), 1883

Tony's Wife (Madame Albanesi), 1919

Too Common for Him! (Mabel St. John, as Henry St. John Cooper), 1923

Too Few for Drums (R.F. Delderfield), 1964

Too Late for Tears (Maynah Lewis), 1972

Too Many Men (Susan Inglis), 1939

Too Many Women (Maysie Greig, as Jennifer Ames), 1941

Too Much Alone (Maysie Greig, as Jennifer Ames), 1950

Too Much Love of Living (Robert Hichens), 1947

Too Much Together (Ruby M. Ayres), 1936

Too Old for Her Husband! (Mabel St. John), 1924

Too Well Beloved (Hebe Elsna), 1964

Too Wilful for Words! (Mabel St. John), 1915

Too Young to Love (Rachel Lindsay, as Roberta Leigh), 1977

Too Young to Marry (Kathryn Blair, as Rosalind Brett), 1958

Top of the Beanstalk (Theresa Charles, as Jan Tempest), 1940

Top of the Climb, The (Betty Beaty), 1962

Top of the Tree, The (Madame Albanesi, as Effie Rowlands), 1937

Top of the World, The (Ethel M. Dell), 1920

Topaz Charm, The (Janet Louise Roberts, as Janette Radcliffe), 1976

Topaze Island (Claire Lorrimer, as Patricia Robins), 1965

Tormented, The (Dorothy Daniels), 1969

Tormented Lovers (Daoma Winston), 1962

Tormenting Flame (Nancy Buckingham, as Nancy John), 1981

Torrent, The (Henrietta Reid), 1972

Touch Me (Dorothy Daniels, as Suzanne Somers), 1973

Touch Not the Cat (Mary Stewart), 1976

Touch of Glory, A (Frank G. Slaughter), 1945

Touch of Honey, A (Rebecca Stratton, as Lucy Gillen), 1973

Touch of Love, A (Barbara Cartland), 1977

Touch of Magic, A (Isobel Chace, as Elizabeth Hunter), 1981

Touch of Magic, A (Essie Summers), 1973

Touch the Wind (Janet Dailey), 1979

Touching the Clouds (Maysie Greig), 1936

Touchstone, The (Netta Muskett), 1962

Toward the Morning (Hervey Allen), 1948

Towards the Dawn (Jane Arbor), 1956

Towards the Stars (Barbara Cartland), 1971

Towards the Sun (Kathryn Blair, as Rosalind Brett), 1953

Tower, The (Marguerite Steen), 1959

Tower Abbey (Isabelle Holland), 1978

Tower in the Forest (Jean Francis Webb, as Ethel Hamill), 1951

Tower of Dreams (Jean Francis Webb, as Ethel Hamill), 1961

Tower of Kilraven, The (Cecily Crowe), 1965

Tower of the Captive, The (Violet Winspear), 1966

Tower of the Winds, The (Isobel Chace, as Elizabeth Hunter), 1973

Tower Room, The (Dorothy Daniels), 1965

Tower Room, The (Mary Linn Roby), 1974

Towers in the Mist (Elizabeth Goudge), 1938

Town House, The (Norah Lofts), 1959

Town Nurse—Country Nurse (Marjorie Lewty), 1970

Town of Masks, A (Dorothy Salisbury Davis), 1952

Town That Nearly Died, The (Maynah Lewis), 1973

Toy Sword, The (Elizabeth Cadell), 1962

Traceys, The (Iris Bromige), 1946

Trackless Way (Ursula Bloom), 1931

Trader's Cay (Rebecca Stratton), 1980

Tradition of Pride, A (Janet Dailey), 1981

Trailing Glory (Ursula Bloom), 1940

Traitor, The (Baroness Orczy), 1912

Traitor's Road (Dorothy Daniels), 1967

Traitors' Gate (Catherine Gavin), 1976

Traitor's Son (Constance Heaven, as Constance Fecher), 1967

Trampling of the Lilies, The (Rafael Sabatini), 1906

Transformation of Philip Jettan, The (Georgette Heyer, as Stella Martin), 1923

Tranquil Haven, The (Jean S. MacLeod), 1946

Trap, The (Daoma Winston), 1973

Trap for Lovers, A (Jane Blackmore), 1960

Trap for Navarre, A (May Wynne), 1922

Trapped (Mary Linn Roby), 1977

Travellers, The (Jean Stubbs), 1963

Travelling Kind, The (Janet Dailey), 1981

Tread Softly (Lady Miles), 1926

Tread Softly in the Sun (Anne Worboys, as Annette Eyre), 1969

Tread Softly, Nurse (Kate Norway, as Hilary Neal), 1962

Tread Softly on Dreams (Leila Mackinlay, as Brenda Grey), 1970

Treason in November (Juliet Dymoke), 1961

Treasure, The (Kathleen Norris), 1914

Treasure Chest, The (Mary Linn Roby), 1976

Treasure Is Love, The (Barbara Cartland),

1979

Treasure of Heaven, The (Marie Corelli), 1906

Treasure of Ho, The (L. Adams Beck), 1924

Treasure of Pleasant Valley, The (Frank Yerby), 1955

Treasure of the Lake, The (H. Rider Haggard), 1926

Tree Drops a Leaf, The (Ruby M. Ayres), 1938

Tree of Evil (Jean Francis Webb, as Roberta Morrison), 1966

Tree of Idleness, The (Isobel Chace, as Elizabeth Hunter), 1973

Tree of Paradise (Jane Arbor), 1976

Treehaven (Kathleen Norris), 1932

Tregaron's Daughter (Madeleine Brent), 1971

Trellised Walk, The (Anne Rundle, as Joanne Marshall), 1973

Trelawny (Isabelle Holland), 1974

Trelawny's Fell (Isabelle Holland), 1976

Trembling Hills, The (Phyllis A. Whitney), 1956

Trespass (Nigel Tranter), 1937

Trevallion (Sara Seale), 1957

Trial of Conflict, The (Emilie Loring), 1922

Trial and Error (Hebe Elsna, as Lyndon Snow), 1973

Trial Marriage, A (Anne Mather), 1977

Trial of Innocence (Susan Hufford), 1978

Trickster, The (G.B. Burgin), 1909

Tricoleur (Christopher Nicole, as Mark Logan), 1976

Trificante Treasure, The (Daoma Winston), 1968

Tristam of Blent (Anthony Hope), 1901

Triumph (May Edginton), 1923

Triumph of Love, The (Madame Albanesi, as Effie Rowlands), 1911

Triumph of the Rat, The (Denise Robins), 1927

Triumphant Beast, The (Marjorie Bowen), 1934

Tropic Flower (May Edginton), 1932

Tropical Affair, A (Elisabeth Beresford), 1967

Tropical Affairs (Elisabeth Beresford), 1978

Trouble in Thor, The (Charlotte Armstrong, as Jo Valentine), 1953

Trouble with Product X (Joan Aiken), 1966

Troy Chimneys (Margaret Kennedy), 1952

Truant Bride, The (Sara Seale), 1966

Truant Happiness (Madame Albanesi), 1918

Truant Spirit, The (Sara Seale), 1954

Truant Wife, A (Annie S. Swan), 1899

Truce of God, The (Mary Roberts Rinehart), 1920

True Thomas (Nigel Tranter), 1981

True Woman, A (Baroness Orczy), 1911

Trumpets at Rome (Marjorie Bowen), 1936

Trust Betrayed, A (Annie S. Swan), 1939

Trust Emily (May Edginton), 1923

Trust Me, My Love (Theresa Charles), 1975

Truth Game, The (Anne Betteridge), 1966

Truth Game, The (Joyce Dingwell), 1978

Truth in a Circle (Madame Albanesi), 1922

Truxton King (George Barr McCutcheon), 1909

Tryst, The (Grace Livingston Hill), 1921

Tryst (Elswyth Thane), 1939

Trysting Tower, The (Betty Beaty, as Catherine Ross), 1966

Tsar's Woman (Pamela Hill), 1977

Tudor Boy, The (Ursula Bloom, as Lozania Prole), 1960

Tudor Ghosts, The (Pamela Bennetts), 1971

Tudor Rose, The (Julia Fitzgerald, as Julia Watson), 1972

Tudor series (Frances Cowen, as Eleanor Hyde)

Tuesday's Child (Hettie Grimstead), 1973

Tulip Tree, The (Mary Ann Gibbs), 1979

Tulip Tree, The (Kathryn Blair), 1958

Tumult at the Gate, The (Christopher Nicole, as Peter Grange), 1970

Tumult in the North (Marjorie Bowen, as George Preedy), 1931

Tulips for Augusta (Betty Neels), 1971

Tune of Time, The (Ursula Bloom), 1970

Turbulent Messiters, The (Mary Ann Gibbs, as Elizabeth Ford), 1967

Turkish Rondo (Anne Stevenson), 1981

Turn Back the Leaves (E.M. Delafield), 1930

Turn Back the River (W.G. Hardy), 1938

Turn of Life's Road, The (Ursula Bloom), 1976

Turn of the Cards (Mary Linn Roby, as Georgina Grey), 1979

Turn of the Road, The (Hebe Elsna, as Laura Conway), 1960

Turn of the Tide, The (Eleanor H. Porter), 1908

Turn the Page (Nan Asquith), 1970

Turn to the Sun (Anne Duffield), 1944

Turn to the West (Sara Seale), 1953

Turnbulls, The (Taylor Caldwell), 1943

Turning Point, The (Theresa Charles, as Jan Tempest), 1961

Turnstile of Night, The (A.M. Williamson), 1904

Turquoise, The (Anya Seton), 1946

Turquoise Mask, The (Phyllis A. Whitney), 1974

Turret Room, The (Charlotte Armstrong), 1965

Tuxter's Little Maid (G.B. Burgin), 1895

'Twas Love's Fault (Charles Garvice)

Twenty-Four Hours (Louis Bromfield), 1930

Twenty-Four Hours a Day (Faith Baldwin), 1937

Twenty-One (Countess Barcynska), 1924

Twenty-Three and a Half Hours' Leave (Mary Roberts Rinehart), 1918

Twice a Boy (Ruby M. Ayres), 1951

Twice Born (Rose Franken), 1935

Twice Have I Loved (Denise Robins), 1973

Twice Tried (Annie S. Swan)

Twice-Born, The (Cecily Crowe), 1972

Twilight and Dawn (Netta Muskett), 1941

Twilight at the Elms (Dorothy Daniels), 1976

Twilight Moment (Leila Mackinlay), 1976

Twilight of a Tudor (Ursula Bloom), 1952

Twilight on the Floods (Marguerite Steen), 1949

Twilight Return (Katheryn Kimbrough), 1976

Twins of Twineham, The (Mabel St. John), 1911

Twist of Fate (Charlotte Lamb), 1979

Twist in the Silk, A (Dorothy Mackie Low, as Zoe Cass), 1980

Twisted Cameo, The (Katheryn Kimbrough), 1971

Twisted Road, The (Ursula Bloom), 1975

Twisted Road, The (Hettie Grimstead), 1951

Twists and Turns of Love, The (Barbara Cartland), 1978

'Twix Smile and Tear (Charles Garvice)

'Twixt Devil and Deep Sea (A.M. Williamson), 1901

Two Black Sheep (Warwick Deeping), 1933

Two Carnations, The (Marjorie Bowen), 1913

Two Desires, The (May Edginton), 1927

Two Doctors and a Girl (Elizabeth Seifert), 1976

Two Faces of Dr. Collier, The (Elizabeth Seifert), 1974

Two Faces of Love (Countess Barcynska), 1958

Two Fair Daughters (Hebe Elsna, as Laura Conway), 1965

Two Feet from Heaven (P.C. Wren), 1940

Two Flights Up (Mary Roberts Rinehart), 1928

Two for Joy (Audrie Manley-Tucker), 1979

Two Friends (Annie S. Swan), 1898

Two Girls and a Man (Charles Garvice), 1937

Two Good Patriots (Baroness Orczy), 1912

Two Hearts Apart (Elsie Lee, as Jane Gordon), 1973

Two in a Train (Warwick Deeping), 1935

Two in Shadow (Jane Blackmore), 1962

Two in a Tent—and Jane (Mabel Barnes Grundy), 1913

Two Little Rich Girls (Mignon Eberhart), 1972

Two Lost Sheep (May Edginton), 1955

Two Loves (Denise Robins, as Denise Chesterton), 1955

Two Loves for Tamara (Theresa Charles, as Jan Tempest), 1951

Two Loves (Denise Robins), 1975

Two Loves Have I (Mary Burchell), 1976

Two Loves Have I (Mary Howard), 1950

Two Loves in Her Life (Victoria Holt, as Eleanor Burford), 1955

Two Maids and a Man (Charles Garvice), 1912

Two Maids of Rosemarie (May Wynne), 1937

Two Men and a Maid (Mabel St. John, as Henry St. John Cooper), 1920

Two Men and Gwenda (Mabel Barnes Grundy), 1910

Two Miss Speckles, The (Mabel Barnes Grundy), 1946

Two Mrs. Abbotts, The (D.E. Stevenson), 1943

Two Names under the Shore (Susan Ertz), 1947

Two of a Kind (Anne Hampson), 1974

Two of Us, The (Maysie Greig, as Jennifer Ames), 1964

Two Other People (Theresa Charles, as Fay Chandos), 1964

Two Paths (Jean S. MacLeod), 1944

Two Pins in a Fountain (Jane Arbor), 1977

Two Pools in a Field (Ursula Bloom), 1967

Two Queen Annes, The (Ursula Bloom, as Lozania Prole), 1971

Two Saplings, The (Mazo de la Roche), 1942

Two Waifs (Madame Albanesi, as Effie Rowlands), 1914

Two Walk Apart (Hebe Elsna, as Lyndon Snow), 1948

Two Walk Together (Leila Mackinlay), 1945

Two Worlds of Peggy Scott, The (Dorothy Daniels), 1974

Two's Company... (Mabel St. John, as Henry St. John Cooper), 1923

Tycoon for Ann, A (Glenna Finley), 1968

Tzigane (Lady Eleanor Smith), 1935

Ugly Head, The (Ursula Bloom), 1965

Ugly Prince, The (Theresa Charles, as Virginia Storm), 1950

Ukelele Girl, The (Mrs. Patrick MacGill), 1927

Ultimate Surrender, The (Theresa Charles), 1958

Umbrella-Maker's Daughter, The (Janet Caird), 1980

Unbaited Trap, The (Catherine Cookson), 1966

Unbidden Dream (Jean Marsh), 1981

Unbidden Melody (Mary Burchell), 1973

Unborn Tomorrow (Gilbert Frankau), 1953

Unbroken Link, The (Hebe Elsna, as Vicky Lancaster), 1959

Uncertain Flame (Susan Inglis), 1937

Uncertain Heart, The (Denise Robins), 1949

Uncertain Joy, The (Claire Lorrimer, as Patricia Robins), 1966

Uncertain Lover (Hebe Elsna), 1935

Uncertain Summer (Betty Neels), 1972

Uncharted Romance (Mary Howard), 1941

Uncharted Seas (Emilie Loring), 1932

Uncle Jeremy (G.B. Burgin), 1920

Uncle Patterley's Money (G.B. Burgin), 1936

Unconquered (Maud Diver), 1917

Uncrowned King, The (Baroness Orczy), 1935

Undarkening Green (Ursula Bloom), 1959

Undefended Gate, The (Susan Ertz), 1953

Under a Ban (Mabel St. John), 1907

Under False Pretences (Berta Ruck), 1922

Under Gemini (Rosamunde Pilcher), 1976

Under Joint Management (Mary Burchell), 1947

Under Moonglow (Anne Hampson), 1978

Under New Management (Naomi Jacob), 1941

Under the Big Top (Countess Barcynska), 1933

Under the Sky (Claire Lorrimer, as Patricia Robins), 1970

Under the Stars of Paris (Mary Burchell), 1954

Underground Syndicate, The (A.M. Williamson), 1910

Understudy (Berta Ruck), 1933

Undertow (Kathleen Norris), 1917

Undressed Heroine, An (Mabel Barnes Grundy), 1916

Undying Past, The (Hebe Elsna), 1964

Unearthly, The (Dorothy Daniels), 1970

Unearthly, The (Robert Hichens), 1926

Uneasy Conquest (Leila Mackinlay), 1959

Uneasy Freehold (Dorothy Macardle), 1941

Uneducating Mary (Kathleen Norris), 1923

Unexpected Adventure, The (May Wynne), 1939

Unfinished Clue, The (Georgette Heyer), 1934

Unfinished Portrait (Mary Westmacott), 1934

Unforeseen, The (Dorothy Macardle), 1946

Unforgiven, The (Maynah Lewis), 1974

Unforgiving Moment, The (Frances Cowen), 1971

Unforgotten, The (Hebe Elsna, as Laura Conway), 1969

Unforgotten, The (Daoma Winston), 1973

Unforgotten Face, The (Maureen Peters, as Sharon Whitby), 1975

Unframed Portrait, An (Madame Albanesi), 1935

Unfulfilled, The (W.G. Hardy), 1951

Unguarded, The (Dorothy Daniels), 1965

Unguarded Hour, The (Jean S. MacLeod, as Catherine Airlie), 1956

Unhallowed House (D.A. Ponsonby), 1956

Unhappy Bargain (Madame Albanesi, as Effie Rowlands)

Unhappy Parting, The (Elsie Lee), 1973

Unholy Desires (Stephanie Blake), 1981

Unholy Woman, The (Victoria Holt, as Jean Plaidy), 1954

Unicorn (Marguerite Steen), 1931

Unidentified Woman (Mignon Eberhart), 1943

Uninvited, The (Dorothy Macardle), 1942

Uninvited Guest (Theresa Charles, as Jan Tempest), 1939

Unjust Skies, The (R.F. Delderfield), 1962

Unkissed Bride, The (Berta Ruck), 1929

Unknown Ajax, The (Georgette Heyer), 1959

Unknown Eros, The (Doris Langley Moore), 1935

Unknown Heart, The (Barbara Cartland), 1969

Unknown Heart, The (Hettie Grimstead), 1958

Unknown Joy, The (Theresa Charles, as Jan Tempest), 1941

Unknown Lover, An (Mrs. George de Horne Vaizey), 1913

Unknown Mr. Brown, The (Sara Seale), 1972

Unknown Quantity, The (Mignon Eberhart), 1953

Unknown Quantity, The (Ethel M. Dell), 1924

Unknown Quest, The (Katrina Britt), 1971

Unknown Welshman, An (Jean Stubbs), 1972

Unlamented, The (Dorothy Daniels), 1975

Unless Two Be Agreed (Margaret Pedler), 1947

Unlit Fire, The (Denise Robins), 1960

Unlived Year, The (Jean S. MacLeod, as Catherine Airlie), 1962

Unmarried Couple (Maysie Greig), 1940

Unnamed Gentlewoman, An (D.A. Ponsonby), 1976

Unofficial Wife (Ruby M. Ayres), 1937

Unpredictable Bride, The (Barbara Cartland), 1964

Unquiet Spirit, The (Marguerite Steen), 1955

Unrest (Warwick Deeping), 1916

Unseen To-morrow (Jean S. MacLeod), 1943

Unseen Torment (Katheryn Kimbrough), 1974

Unseen Witness, The (May Wynne), 1932

Unshaken Loyalty, The (Denise Robins), 1955

Unsuspected, The (Charlotte Armstrong), 1946

Unsuspected Witness, The (May Wynne), 1945

Untamed Heart, The (Mary Francis Craig, as Alexis Hill), 1980

Untamed Heart, The (Mary Howard), 1940

Until Death (Dorothy Daniels, as Suzanne Somers), 1973

Until I Find Her (Theresa Charles, as Jan Tempest), 1950

Until the Day Break (Louis Bromfield), 1942

Unto Caesar (Baroness Orczy), 1914

Untouched Wife (Rachel Lindsay), 1981

Untrodden Snow, The (Denise Robins), 1958

Unusual Tudor, An (D.A. Ponsonby), 1967

Unwanted Heiress, The (Mabel St. John, as Henry St. John Cooper), 1924

Unwanted Wife (Rachel Lindsay), 1976

Unwary Heart (Anne Hampson), 1969

Unwilling Bride, The (Violet Winspear), 1969

Unwilling Bridegroom, The (Rachel Lindsay, as Roberta Leigh), 1976

Unwilling Guest, An (Grace Livingston Hill), 1902

Unwise Wanderer (Leila Mackinlay), 1952

Up to Val (May Wynne), 1935

Upas Tree, The (Florence L. Barclay), 1912

Uphill Path, The (Leila Mackinlay), 1979

Uphill Road, The (Ruby M. Ayres), 1921

Upon This Rock (Frank G. Slaughter), 1963

Ups and Downs (Annie S. Swan), 1878

Upstairs, Downstairs series (Mollie Hardwick)

Upstart, The (Edison Marshall), 1945

Upturned Palms (Hebe Elsna), 1933

Urbinian, The (Rafael Sabatini), 1924

Ursula Vivian, The Sister-Mother (Annie S. Swan), 1884

Usurper, The (Charles Garvice)

Uther and Igraine (Warwick Deeping), 1903

Utility Husband (Theresa Charles, as Jan Tempest), 1944

Utterly Alone! (Mabel St. John), 1928

Uttermost Farthing, The (Marie Belloc Lowndes), 1908

Vacation for Nurse Dean, A (Claire Ritchie, as Sharon Heath), 1966

Vacillations of Hazel, The (Mabel Barnes Grundy), 1905

Vagabond Daughter (Leila Mackinlay), 1955

Vagabond Harvest (Ursula Bloom), 1925

Vagabond Jess (Mabel St. John, as Henry St. John Cooper), 1919

Vagabond's Daughter, The (Mabel St. John, as Henry St. John Cooper), 1922

Vagabond's Way (Doris Leslie), 1962

Vagrant Dream (Claire Ritchie), 1959

Vagrant Lover (Ursula Bloom, as Sheila Burns), 1945

Vail d'Alvery (Frances Parkinson Keyes), 1947

Vain Delighted (Leila Mackinlay), 1962

Valdez Marriage, The (Violet Winspear), 1978

Valentina (Evelyn Anthony), 1966

Valentine's Day (Sara Seale), 1962

Valerie French (Dornford Yates), 1923

Valiant Dust (P.C. Wren), 1932

Vallette Heritage, The (Janet Louise Roberts, as Louise Bronte), 1979

Valley Deep, Mountain High (Anne Mather), 1976

Village Nurse, The (Ursula Bloom, as Rachel Harvey), 1967

Valley of Aloes, The (Wynne May), 1967

Valley of Bells (Irene Roberts, as Iris Rowland), 1967

Valley of Decision, The (Marcia Davenport), 1942

Valley of Desire, The (Jean S. MacLeod, as Catherine Airlie), 1955

Valley of Flowers (Kathryn Blair), 1957

Valley of Lilacs (Mollie Chappell), 1972

Valley of Night (Jeffery Farnol), 1942

Valley of Nightingales (Elizabeth Renier), 1966

Valley of Palms, The (Jean S. MacLeod), 1950

Valley of Paradise (Margaret Rome), 1975

Valley of Roses, The (Anne Maybury), 1945

Valley of Secrets (Elizabeth Renier), 1970

Valley of Tall Chimneys (Anne Rundle, as

Joanne Marshall), 1975

Valley of the Eagles, The (Eleanor Farnes), 1972

Valley of the Moon (Margaret Way), 1979

Valley of the Ravens (Nancy Buckingham), 1973

Valley of the Reindeer (Rosalind Laker, as Barbara Øvstedal), 1973

Valley of the Shadows (Dorothy Daniels), 1980

Valley of the Vapours (Janet Dailey), 1976

Valley of Yesterday, The (Anne Worboys, as Annette Eyre), 1965

Valour (Warwick Deeping), 1918

Vampire Curse, The (Daoma Winston), 1971

Vampyre of Moura, The (Virginia Coffman), 1970

Van Rhyne Heritage, The (Janet Louise Roberts, as Louisa Bronte), 1980

Vanderlyn's Adventure (Marie Belloc Lowndes), 1931

Vanessa (Catherine Fellows), 1978

Vanish in an Instant (Margaret Millar), 1952

Vanity Box, The (A.M. Williamson, as Alice Stuyvesant), 1911

Vanquished Heart, The (Elizabeth Hoy), 1949

Varick's Legacy (G.B. Burgin), 1912

Varleigh Medallion, The (Sylvia Thorpe), 1979

· Veil of Rushes, A (Irene Roberts, as Iris Rowland), 1967

Veil of Treachery (Dorothy Daniels), 1979

Veil'd Delight, The (Marjorie Bowen), 1933

Veiled Lady, The (May Wynne), 1918

Veils (Robert Hichens), 1943

Velvet Glove, The (Rebecca Stratton), 1978

Velvet Hammer, The (Faith Baldwin), 1969

Velvet Spur, The (Jane Arbor), 1974

Velvet Trap, The (Jane Blackmore), 1969

Venables, The (Kathleen Norris), 1941

Vendetta (Marie Corelli), 1886

Veneer (Ursula Bloom), 1929

Venetia (Georgette Heyer), 1958

Venetian, The (Pamela Bennetts), 1968

Venetian Inheritance (Anne Worboys, as Annette Eyre), 1973

Venetian Lover, The (Ethel Edison Gordon), 1982

Venetian Masque (Rafael Sabatini), 1934

Venetian Rhapsody (Denise Robins), 1954

Vengeance of Love (Charles Garvice, as Caroline Hart)

Vengeful Heart, The (Rachel Lindsay, as Roberta Leigh), 1952

Venice Affair (Joyce Dingwell), 1968

Venus Rising (Julia Fitzgerald), 1982

Venus with Sparrows (Rosemary Harris), 1961

Vera (Elizabeth), 1921

Verdict of the Heart, The (Charles Garvice), 1912

Vermilion (Phyllis A. Whitney), 1981

Veronica (Elisabeth Beresford), 1967

Veronique (Virginia Coffman), 1975

Vertical City, The (Fannie Hurst), 1922

Very House, The (Mazo de la Roche), 1937

Very Naughty Angel, A (Barbara Cartland), 1975

Very Special Man, A (Marjorie Lewty), 1979

Very Special Person, A (Leila Mackinlay, as Brenda Grey), 1967

Vesey Inheritance, The (Gwendoline Butler), 1975

Vexed Inheritance, A (Annie S. Swan), 1890

Vicar of Moura (Virginia Coffman), 1972

Vice Avenged (Lolah Burford), 1971

Vicissitudes of Evangeline, The (Elinor Glyn), 1905

Vicky (Hebe Elsna), 1961

Victim, The (Daoma Winston), 1972

Victim of Love (Nancy Buckingham), 1967

Victoire (Clare Darcy), 1974

Victoria (Evelyn Anthony), 1959

Victoria and Albert (Evelyn Anthony), 1958

Victoria and the Nightingale (Susan Barrie), 1967

Victoria in the Wings (Victoria Holt, as Jean Plaidy), 1972

Victorian Album, The (Evelyn Berckman), 1973

Victorine (Frances Parkinson Keyes), 1958

Victory for Victoria (Betty Neels), 1972

Victory Won, A (Annie S. Swan), 1895

Vienna Summer (Nancy Buckingham), 1979

View of the Sea, A (Margaret Maddocks), 1973

Viking, The (Edison Marshall), 1951

Viking Song (Jean S. MacLeod), 1977

Viking Stranger, The (Violet Winspear), 1966

Villa Faustina, The (Katrina Britt), 1977

Villa Fountains, The (Virginia Coffman), 1968

Village of Fear, The (Frances Cowen), 1974

Villains, The (Charity Blackstock, as Charlotte Keppel), 1980

Vines of Yarrabee, The (Dorothy Eden), 1969

Vineyard Chapel, The (Dorothy Daniels), 1976

Vineyard in a Valley (Gloria Bevan), 1972

Viola Gwyn (George Barr McCutcheon), 1922

Violante (Marjorie Bowen, as George Preedy), 1932

Violet (Charles Garvice), 1911

Violett (Baroness von Hutten), 1904

Violetta (Anne Duffield), 1960

Viper of Milan, The (Marjorie Bowen), 1906

Virgin in Mayfair, A (Barbara Cartland), 1932

Virgin in Paris, A (Barbara Cartland), 1966

Virgin of the Sun, The (H. Rider Haggard), 1922

Virgin Queen, The (Maureen Peters), 1972

Virgin Thorn, The (Ursula Bloom), 1941

Visibility Nil (Mary Elgin), 1963

Vision House (C.N. and A.M. Williamson), 1921

Vision of Balmaine, The (G.B. Burgin), 1911

Vision of Desire, The (Margaret Pedler), 1922

Vision of Stephen, The (Lolah Burford), 1972

Vision Splendid, The (D.K. Broster), 1913

Visit after Dark, A (Daoma Winston), 1975

Visit to Rata Creek (Anne Worboys, as Annette Eyre), 1964

Visit to Rowanbank (Flora Kidd), 1966

Visits of Elizabeth, The (Elinor Glyn), 1900

Vista (Countess Barcynska, as Oliver Sandys), 1928

Vittoria Cottage (D.E. Stevenson), 1949

Vivette on Trial (May Wynne), 1936

Vivian Inheritance, The (Jean Stubbs), 1982

Vixens, The (Frank Yerby), 1947

Vixen's Revenge, The (Charity Blackstock, as Paula Allardyce), 1980

Voice in the Dark, A (Claire Lorrimer), 1967

Voice in the Darkness, A (Pamela Bennetts), 1979

Voice in the Thunder, The (Isobel Chace, as Elizabeth Hunter), 1975

Voice in the Wilderness, A (Grace Livingston Hill), 1916

Voice of Air, The (Evelyn Berckman), 1970

Voice of the Dolls, The (Dorothy Eden), 1950

Voice on the Wind (Dorothy Daniels), 1969

Voices from the Dust (Jeffery Farnol), 1932

Voices in an Empty House (Joan Aiken), 1975

Voices in the Night (Kate Norway), 1973

Voices Long Hushed (Barbara Anne Pauley), 1976

Volunteer Nurse (Anne Duffield), 1942

Voodoo (Samuel Shellabarger, as John Esteven), 1930

Voodoo Widow (Virginia Coffman), 1970

Vote for Love (Barbara Cartland), 1977

Vow on the Heron, The (Victoria Holt, as Jean Plaidy), 1980

Voyage of Destiny (Ivy Preston), 1974

Voyage of Enchantment (Elizabeth Ashton), 1977

Voyage to Cytherea (Rosemary Harris), 1958

Voyage to Santa Fe (Janice Holt Giles), 1962

Voyage Unplanned, The (Frank Yerby), 1974

Wager for Love, A (Caroline Courtney), 1979

Wages of Virtue, The (P.C. Wren), 1916

Wagon to a Star (Maysie Greig), 1952

Waif of the River (Jeffery Farnol), 1952

Waif's Wedding, The (Ruby M. Ayres), 1921

Wait (Evelyn Berckman), 1973

Wait for Night (Frances Cowen), 1980

Wait for Tomorrow (Denise Robins), 1967

Wait for What Will Come (Barbara Michaels), 1978

Waiting at the Church (Charity Blackstock, as Paula Allardyce), 1968

Waiting Darkness, The (Willo Davis Roberts), 1970

Waiting for Willa (Dorothy Eden), 1970

Waiting Room, The (Kate Norway, as Bess Norton), 1961

Waiting Sands, The (Susan Howatch), 1966

Wake the Sleeping Tiger (Margaret Way), 1978

Wakefield Witches, The (Daoma Winston), 1966

Wakefield's Course (Mazo de la Roche), 1941

Walk Around the Square (Daoma Winston), 1975

Walk in the Paradise Garden (Anne Maybury), 1972

Walk into My Parlour (Dorothy Eden), 1947

Walk into My Parlour (Norah Lofts), 1975

Walk into My Parlour (Rona Randall), 1962

Walk into the Wind (Jane Arbor), 1970

Walk Out on Death (Charlotte Armstrong), 1954

Walker in Shadows, The (Barbara Michaels), 1979

Wall, The (Mary Roberts Rinehart), 1938

Wall of Eyes (Margaret Millar), 1943

Wall of Partition, The (Florence L. Barclay), 1914

Wallace, The (Nigel Tranter), 1975

Wallflower (Ruby M. Ayres), 1940

Walls of Gold (Kathleen Norris), 1933

Waltz of Hearts, The (Barbara Cartland), 1980

Waltz-Contest (Berta Ruck), 1941

Wandering Knife, The (Mary Roberts Rinehart), 1952

Wandering Prince, The (Victoria Holt, as Jean Plaidy), 1956

Wanderers, The (Mary Johnston), 1917

Wanderers Eastward, Wanderers West (Kathleen Winsor), 1965

Wanderer's Necklace, The (H. Rider Haggard), 1914

Wanted—Girl Friday (Leila Mackinlay), 1968

Wanted on the Voyage (Berta Ruck), 1930

War and Passion (Christopher Nicole, as Leslie Arlen), 1981

War Changes Everything (Denise Robins), 1943

War Marriage (Denise Robins), 1942

War Surgeon (Frank G. Slaughter), 1967

War to End Wars, The (Mollie Hardwick), 1975

War Wedding, The (C.N. and A.M. Williamson), 1916

Ward of Lucifer (Mary Burchell), 1947

Warfare Accomplished (Edith Pargeter), 1947

Warlock's Daughter, The (Dorothy Daniels, as Angela Gray), 1973

Warm Wind of Farik, The (Rebecca Stratton), 1975

Warner's Chase (Annie S. Swan), 1884

Warrior, The (Frank G. Slaughter), 1956

Warrior King, The (Doris Leslie), 1977

Wartime Beauty (Ursula Bloom), 1943

War-Workers, The (E.M. Delafield), 1918

Warwyck series (Rosalind Laker)

Washington, U.S.A. (Faith Baldwin), 1943

Wasted Love, A (Charles Garvice)

Waster, The (Charles Garvice), 1918

Watch the Wall My Darling (Isobel Chace, as Elizabeth Hunter), 1963

Watch the Wall, My Darling (Jane Aiken Hodge), 1966

Watcher in the Dark, The (Dorothy Daniels, as Angela Gray), 1973

Watchers, The (Willo Davis Roberts), 1971

Watchman's Stone (Rona Randall), 1975

Waterfall (Lucy Walker, as Dorothy Lucie Sanders), 1956

Waterfalls of the Moon, The (Anne Mather), 1973

Waterfront Hospital (Kate Norway), 1961

Waters on a Starry Night (Elisabeth Ogilvie), 1968

Watershed (Nigel Tranter), 1941

Waves of Destiny (Margaret Pedler), 1924

Waves of Fire (Anne Hampson), 1971

Way Beyond, The (Jeffery Farnol), 1933

Way in the Dark, The (Jean S. MacLeod), 1956

Way Men Love, The (Theresa Charles), 1967

Way of a Man, The (Hebe Elsna, as Vicky Lancaster), 1956

Way of a Tyrant, The (Anne Hampson), 1974

Way of Ambition, The (Robert Hichens), 1913

Way of an Eagle, The (Ethel M. Dell), 1911

Way of Compassion, The (Anne Maybury), 1933

Way of Escape, The (Annie S. Swan), 1935

Way of Stars, The (L. Adams Beck), 1925

Way of the Spirit, The (H. Rider Haggard), 1906

Way of the Tamarisk, The (Anne Worboys, as Vicky Maxwell), 1974

Way of Youth, The (Madame Albanesi, as Effie Rowlands), 1925

Way Out, The (G.B. Burgin), 1900

Way the Wind Blows, The (Nan Asquith), 1963

Way Things Are, The (E.M. Delafield), 1927

Way Through the Forest, The (Eleanor Farnes), 1957

Way Through the Maze, A (Hebe Elsna, as Laura Conway), 1963

Way Through the Valley, The (Jean S. MacLeod), 1971

Way to the Lantern, The (Audrey Erskine-Lindop), 1961

Way We Used to Be, The (Theresa Charles, as Jan Tempest), 1965

Ways of Love, The (Jean S. MacLeod, as Catherine Airlie), 1955

Wayside Tavern, A (Norah Lofts), 1980

Wayward as the Swallow (Theresa Charles), 1970

Wayward Love (Hebe Elsna, as Lyndon Snow), 1953

Wayward Madonna, The (Maureen Peters, as Veronica Black), 1970

Wayward Stream, The (Eleanor Farnes), 1949

We All Have Our Secrets (Berta Ruck), 1955

We Are for the Dark (Dorothy Eden), 1944

We Are Ten (Fannie Hurst), 1937

We Are the Pilgrims (Hebe Elsna), 1931

We Have Always Lived in the Castle (Shirley Jackson), 1962

We Lost Our Way (Countess Barcynska), 1948

We Ride the Gale! (Emilie Loring), 1934

We Two Together (Denise Robins), 1959

We Want Our Mummy! (Mabel St. John), 1922

We Women! (Countess Barcynska), 1923

Weak-Eyed, The (Margaret Millar), 1942

Wealth of the Islands, The (Isobel Chace), 1971

Weathercock, The (Margaret Maddocks), 1971

Weave Me a Moonbeam (Irene Roberts), 1982

Weave Me Some Wings (Mary Howard), 1947

Web of Love, The (Elizabeth Hoy), 1952

Web of Passion (Nancy Buckingham, as Nancy John), 1982

Web of Peril, A (Dorothy Daniels), 1974

Web of Silver (Rebecca Stratton, as Lucy Gillen), 1974

Webs (Countess Barcynska), 1922

Wedded—But Alone! (Mabel St. John), 1930

Wedded But Not Wooed (Mabel St. John), 1920

Wedding Bells for Willow (Theresa Charles, as Jan Tempest), 1956

Wedding Day (May Edginton), 1939

Wedding Day, The (C.N. and A.M. Williamson), 1914

Wedding Dress, The (Mary Burchell), 1962

Wedding for Three (Hettie Grimstead), 1963

Wedding March (Berta Ruck), 1938

Wedding of Kitty Barton, The (Annie S. Swan), 1898

Wedding of the Year (Hettie Grimstead, as Marsha Manning), 1974

Wedding Took Place, The (Hebe Elsna), 1939

Wednesday's Children (Joyce Dingwell), 1957

Week by the Sea, A (Mary Ann Gibbs, as Elizabeth Ford), 1962

Week-end Bride (Ursula Bloom, as Sheila Burns), 1939

Weekend in the Garden, A (Lucilla Andrews), 1981

Week-End Marriage (Faith Baldwin), 1932

Week-End Woman (Ruby M. Ayres), 1939

Weep and Know Why (Elisabeth Ogilvie), 1972

Weep Not for Dreams (Ursula Bloom, as Rachel Harvey), 1968

Weeping Ash, The (Joan Aiken), 1980

Weeping Lady, The (Janet Louise Roberts), 1971

Weight Carriers, The (May Edginton), 1909

Weir House, The (Netta Muskett), 1962

Wellington Wendy (Countess Barcynska, as Oliver Sandys), 1941

Wellspring (Janice Holt Giles), 1975

Were Death Denied (Dornford Yates), 1946

Were I Thy Bride (Denise Robins), 1936

We're Not Wanted Now! (Mabel St. John, as Henry St. John Cooper), 1921

Were He a Stranger (Mary Francis Craig), 1978

West of the River (Joyce Dingwell), 1970

West Wind, The (Faith Baldwin), 1962

West Wind Drift (George Barrr McCutcheon), 1920

West with the Vikings (Edison (Marshall), 1961

Western (Frank Yerby), 1982

Westward to My Love (Theresa Charles, as Jan Tempest), 1944

What a Man Wills (Mrs. George de Horne Vaizey), 1915

What a Woman Can Do! (Mabel St. John), 1917

What Became of Anna Bolton (Louis Bromfield), 1944

What Happened Is This (Baroness von Hutten), 1938

What I Found Out in the House of a German Prince (A.M. Williamson), 1915

What Is Love? (E.M. Delafield), 1928

What Matters Most (Denise Robins), 1942

What of the Night? (Marie Belloc Lowndes), 1943

What Really Happened (Marie Belloc Lowndes), 1926

What She Could (Annie S. Swan), 1898

What Shall It Profit? (Annie S. Swan), 1910

What the Heart Says (Evadne Price), 1956

What Then Is Love (Emilie Loring), 1956

What Timmy Did (Marie Belloc Lowndes), 1921

What We're Here For (Kate Norway, as Bess Norton), 1966

What Wild Lie—(Naomi Jacob), 1930

Whatagirl (Countess Barcynska, as Oliver Sandys), 1939

What's-His-Name (George Barr McCutcheon), 1911

Wheat Princess, The (Jean Webster), 1905

Wheel Fortune (Betty Beaty, as Karen Campbell), 1973

Wheels of Chance, The (Jean S. MacLeod, as Catherine Airlie), 1964

Wheels of Fate, The (G.B. Burgin), 1933

Wheels of Time, The (Florence L. Barclay), 1908

When a Girl's Pretty (Mabel St. John), 1914

When a Man Loves (Mabel St. John, as Henry St. John Cooper), 1931

When a Man Marries (Mary Roberts Rinehart), 1909

When a Woman Doctor Loves (Ursula Bloom, as Mary Essex), 1969

When a Woman Loves (Denise Robins, as Denise Chesterton), 1955

When All the World Is Young (Victoria Holt, as Eleanor Burford), 1943

When April Sings (Hettie Grimstead), 1964

When Birds Do Sing (Flora Kidd), 1970

When Clouds Part (Anne Hampson), 1973

When Doctors Disagree (Rose Franken, as Franken Meloney), 1940

When Doctors Love (Ursula Bloom, as Sheila Burns), 1964

When Doctors Marry (Elizabeth Seifert), 1960

When Dreams Come True (G.B. Burgin), 1932

When First I Loved... (Theresa Charles, as Jan Tempest), 1938

When Four Ways Meet (Theresa Charles, as Fay Chandos), 1961

When His Hour Comes (Elinor Glyn), 1915

When I Say Goodbye, I'm Clary Brown (Charity Blackstock, as Charlotte Keppel), 1977

When Hearts Are Light Again (Emilie Loring), 1943

When Love Compels (Mabel St. John, as Henry St. John Cooper), 1933

When Love Is Blind (Mary Burchell), 1967

When Love Is Young (Charles Garvice)

When Love Meets Love (Charles Garvice), 1906

When Love Speaks (Glenna Finley), 1973

When Love's Beginning (Mary Burchell), 1954

When May Follows (Betty Neels), 1980

When Michael Came to Town (Madame Albanesi), 1917

When Next We Meet (Hebe Elsna, as Laura Conway), 1957

When No Man Pursueth (Marie Belloc Lowndes), 1910

When Other Hearts (Victoria Holt, as Eleanor Burford), 1955

When Paris Fell (Ursula Bloom, as Lozania Prole), 1976

When Terror Ruled (May Wynne), 1907

When the Rough Breaks (Anne Hampson), 1970

When the Dream Fades (Elizabeth Hoy), 1980

When the Gallows Is High (Phyllis Hastings), 1971

When the Sun Goes Down (Charity Blackstock), 1965

When the Wind Blows (Marguerite Steen), 1931

When the Witch Is Dead (Mary Linn Roby), 1972

When the World Shook (H. Rider Haggard), 1919

When There's Love at Home (Mabel St. John), 1925

When Three Walk Together (Theresa Charles, as Fay Chandos), 1939

When Time Stands Still (Theresa Charles, as Fay Chandos), 1946

When We Are Married (Victoria Holt, as Eleanor Burford), 1953

When We Two Parted (Theresa Charles, as Fay Chandos), 1940

When Women Love (E.M. Delafield), 1938

When You Have Found Me (Elizabeth Hoy), 1951

Where Are You Going? (Ruby M. Ayres), 1946

Where Beauty Dwells (Emilie Loring), 1941

Where Breezes Falter (Wynne May), 1970

Where Duty Lies (Claire Lorrimer, as Patricia Robins), 1957

Where Eagles Nest (Anne Hampson), 1980

Where Flamingoes Fly (Irene Roberts), 1966

Where Is Love? (Barbara Cartland), 1971

Where Is My Child To-night? (Mabel St. John), 1925

Where Love Leads (Charles Garvice), 1907

Where No Roads Go (Essie Summers), 1963

Where Ratas Twine (Ivy Preston), 1960

Where Satan Dwells (Florence Stevenson), 1971

Where Shall I Wander? (Mary Burchell), 1942

Where Stars May Lead (Ivy Preston), 1978

Where the Cigale Sings (Olga Sinclair), 1976

Where the Dark Streets Go (Dorothy Salisbury Davis), 1969

Where The Heart Is (Theresa Charles, as Jan Tempest), 1955

Where the Lost Aprils Are (Elisabeth Ogilvie), 1975

Where the Moonflower Weaves (Roumelia Lane), 1974

Where the Path Breaks (C.N. and A.M. Williamson, as Captain Charles de Crespigny), 1916

Where the Rivers Meet (Rosemary Ellerbeck, as Nicola Thorne), 1982

Where the Treasure Is (Helen Beauclerk), 1944

Where the Wolf Leads (Jane Arbor), 1980

Where There Are Women (Countess Barcynska, as Marguerite Barclay), 1915

Where There's a Will (Mary Roberts Rinehart), 1912

Where Three Roads Meet (Ethel M. Dell), 1935

Where Two Ways Met (Grace Livingston Hill), 1947

Which Woman? (G.B. Burgin), 1907

While Faith Endures (Madame Albanesi, as Effie Rowlands), 1929

While Murder Waits (Samuel Shellabarger, as John Estevan), 1936

While the Patient Slept (Mignon Eberhart), 1930

Whim of Fate, The (Jean S. MacLeod), 1940

Whisper in the Dark (Anne Maybury, as Katherine Troy), 1961

Whisper of Darkness (Margaret Lynn), 1965

Whisper of Darkness (Anne Mather), 1980

Whisper of Sea-Bells, The (Irene Roberts), 1964

Whisper to the Stars (Hettie Grimstead), 1963

Whispering Palms (Kathryn Blair, as Rosalind Brett), 1954

Whispering Sea, The (Rebecca Stratton, as Lucy Gillen), 1971

Whispers in the Sun (Maysie Greig), 1949

Whistle and I'll Come (Flora Kidd), 1966

Whistle for the Crows (Dorothy Eden), 1962

Whistle in the Wind (Dorothy Daniels), 1976

Whistling Thorn, The (Isobel Chace), 1977

White Abbey (Madame Albanesi, as Effie Rowlands), 1911

White Boy (Christopher Nicole), 1966

White Branches (Madame Albanesi), 1933

White Castello, The (Marjorie McEvoy), 1969

White Christmas (Fannie Hurst), 1942

White Cockade, The (Juliet Dymoke), 1979

White Cockade, The (Jean S. MacLeod), 1960

White Cockatoo, The (Mignon Eberhart), 1933

White Doctor (Kathryn Blair, as Celine Conway), 1961

White Dolphin, The (Rebecca Stratton), 1976

White Dress, The (Mignon Eberhart), 1946

White Flag, The (Gene Stratton Porter), 1923

White Flame (Madame Albanesi), 1930

White Flower, The (Grace Livingston Hill), 1927

White Gate, The (Warwick Deeping), 1913

White Heat (Susan Barrie, as Pamela Kent), 1966

White Hell of Pity (Norah Lofts), 1937

White House of Marisaig, The (Annie S.

Swan), 1938

White Hunter (Elizabeth Hoy), 1951

White in the Black, The (Madame Albanesi), 1926

White Jacket, The (Kate Norway), 1961

White Jade (Willo Davis Roberts), 1975

White Jade (Denise Robins), 1928

White Jasmine (Janet Louise Roberts, as Janette Radcliffe), 1976

White Ladies of Worcester, The (Florence L. Barclay), 1917

White Lady, The (Grace Livingston Hill, as Marcia Macdonald), 1930

White Magic (Faith Baldwin), 1939

White Magnolia (Margaret Way), 1979

White Moths, The (Anne Rundle, as Alexandra Manners), 1979

White Oleander, The (Kathryn Blair), 1953

White Orchids (Grace Livingston Hill), 1935

White Pavilion, the (Velda Johnston), 1973

White Peacock, The (Mary Linn Roby), 1972

White Prophet, The (Hall Caine), 1909

White Rose, The (Alanna Knight), 1973

White Rose of Love (Susan Barrie, as Anita Charles), 1963

White Rose of Winter (Anne Mather), 1973

White Violet, The (Claire Ritchie), 1956

White Witch, The (Elizabeth Goudge), 1958

White Wool (Naomi Jacob), 1944

Whiteoak (Jalna) series (Mazo de la Roche)

Whither? (May Wynne), 1938

Whitton's Folly (Pamela Hill), 1975

Who Are the Heathen? (Annie S. Swan), 1942

Who Can Deny Love? (Barbara Cartland), 1979

Who Goes There? (Dorothy Mackie Low, as Lois Paxton), 1972

Who Knows Sammy Halliday? (Mary Howard), 1974

Who Loses Pays (G.B. Burgin), 1935

Who Love Believes (Elizabeth Hoy), 1955

Who Rides a Tiger (Marie Belloc Lowndes), 1935

Who Rides the Tiger (Anne Mather), 1970

Who Shall Serve? (Annie S. Swan), 1891

Who Walks by Moonlight (Marjorie McEvoy), 1966

Who Was Wendy? (May Wynne), 1932

Who Will Remember? (Margaret Irwin), 1924

Who Would Have Daughters? (Marguerite Steen), 1937

Whole Armor, The (Faith Baldwin), 1951

Whom Love Hath Chosen (Mrs. Patrick MacGill), 1919

Who's Been Sitting in My Chair? (Charlotte

Armstrong), 1962

Who's Calling (Victoria Holt, as Eleanor Burford), 1962

Whoso Diggeth a Pit— (Mabel St. John, as Henry St. John Cooper), 1926

Why It Happened (Marie Belloc Lowndes), 1938

Why Shoot the Butler? (Georgette Heyer), 1933

Why They Married (Marie Belloc Lowndes), 1923

Why Wouldn't He Wait? (Theresa Charles, as Jan Tempest), 1940

Wicked Angel (Taylor Caldwell), 1965

Wicked Cousin (Florence Stevenson, as Zabrina Faire), 1980

Wicked Is My Flesh (Stephanie Blake), 1980

Wicked Loving Lies (Rosemary Rogers), 1976

Wicked Marquis, The (Barbara Cartland), 1973

Wicked Pack of Cards, A (Rosemary Harris), 1969

Wicked Sir Dare (Charles Garvice), 1938

Wicked Wynsleys, The (Alanna Knight), 1977

Wide and Dark (Netta Muskett), 1940

Wide House, The (Taylor Caldwell), 1945

Wide Is the Water (Jane Aiken Hodge), 1981

Wide Pastures (Kathryn Blair, as Celine Conway), 1957

Widening Stream, The (Rachel Lindsay), 1952

Widow, The (Charity Blackstock), 1967

Widow and the Wastrel, The (Janet Dailey), 1977

Widow Jones, The (Mollier Chappell), 1956

Widow of Windsor, The (Victoria Holt, as Jean Plaidy), 1974

Widower's Wife (Theresa Charles), 1963

Widow's Daughters, The (D.A. Ponsonby), 1953

Wife after Work (Theresa Charles, as Jan Tempest), 1943

Wife Apparent (Dornford Yates), 1956

Wife by Arrangement (Mary Burchell), 1946

Wife by Contract (Flora Kidd), 1980

Wife for a Penny (Anne Hampson), 1973

Wife for a Wager (Theresa Charles, as Fay Chandos), 1938

Wife for a Year (Rachel Lindsay, as Roberta Leigh), 1980

Wife for Andrew, A (Rebecca Stratton, as Lucy Gillen), 1969

Wife for Sale (Kathleen Norris), 1933

Wife for the Admiral, A (Mary Ann Gibbs), 1974

Wife—or Housekeeper? (Mabel St. John), 1921

Wife or Maid? (Mabel St. John), 1922

Wife to Christopher (Mary Burchell), 1936

Wife to Order (Lucy Walker), 1961

Wife to Sim (Joyce Dingwell), 1972

Wife vs. Secretary (Faith Baldwin), 1934

Wife Who Dragged Him Down!, The (Mabel St. John), 1920

Wife Who Would Be "Master"!, The (Mabel St. John), 1920

Wife Without Kisses (Violet Winspear), 1961

Wife's Triumph, A (Madame Albanesi, as Effie Rowlands), 1906

Wild and Wonderful (Janet Dailey), 1980

Wild Bird, A (Maud Diver), 1929

Wild Bird, The (Denise Robins), 1932

Wild Boar Wood (Anne Rundle, as Joanne Marshall), 1972

Wild Cat (Laura Black), 1979

Wild Country, The (Louis Bromfield), 1948

Wild Country (Daoma Winston), 1970

Wild Crocus (Kathryn Blair), 1956

Wild Cry of Love, The (Barbara Cartland), 1976

Wild Cry of Love, A (Rosalind Laker, as Barbara Paul), 1978

Wild Daughter, The (Ursula Bloom, as Lozania Prole), 1963

Wild Dream (Olga Sinclair), 1973

Wild Enchantress (Anne Mather), 1976

Wild Fields of Home, The (Jane Arbor), 1975

Wild Fire (Barbara Riefe), 1981

Wild Harp, The (Jacqueline La Tourrette), 1981

Wild Harvest, A (Annie S. Swan), 1929

Wild Heart (Doris E. Smith), 1977

Wild Hunt, The (Jill Tattersall), 1974

Wild Inheritance (Margaret Pargeter), 1978

Wild Is the River (Louis Bromfield), 1941

Wild Land, The (Isobel Chace), 1963

Wild Macraes, The (Jean S. MacLeod, as Catherine Airlie), 1948

Wild Man, The (Margaret Rome), 1980

Wild Memory (Anne Duffield), 1935

Wild Mountain Thyme (Rosamunde Pilcher), 1978

Wild Rose, A (Madame Albanesi, as Effie Rowlands), 1911

Wild Rowan, The (Margaret Pargeter), 1978

Wild Sonata (Susan Barrie), 1968

Wild Summer, The (Irene Roberts, as Iris Rowland), 1970

Wild Swan, The (Margaret Kennedy), 1957

Wild Swan, The (Margaret Way), 1978

Wild, Unwilling Wife, The (Barbara Cartland), 1977

Wild Violets (Theresa Charles, as Fay Chandos), 1959

Wildcatter's Woman (Janet Dailey), 1982

Wildcliffe Bird, The (Constance Heaven), 1981

Wilderling, The (Claire Lorrimer), 1982

Wilderness Inn (Janet Louise Roberts), 1976

Wilderness Trail, The (Kay Thorpe), 1978

Wildest Heart, The (Rosemary Rogers), 1974

Wildfire at Midnight (Mary Stewart), 1956

Wildfire Love (Jane Blackmore), 1980

Wildfire of Love (Glenna Finley), 1979

Wildfire Quest (Jane Arbor), 1972

Wildford's Daughter (Anne Rundle, as Alexandra Manners), 1978

Wild-Fire Nan (Mabel St. John, as Henry St. John Cooper), 1919

Wiles of a Siren, The (Madame Albanesi, as Effie Rowlands), 1906

Wilful Maid, A (Charles Garvice), 1911

Wilful Winnie (Annie S. Swan), 1886

Wilful Woman, A (G.B. Burgin), 1902

...Will Not Now Take Place (Theresa Charles, as Jan Tempest), 1957

Will You Love Me in September (Victoria Holt, as Philippa Carr), 1981

Will You Surrender? (Joyce Dingwell), 1957

Willed to Wed (Leila Mackinlay), 1933

William, By the Grace of God— (Marjorie Bowen), 1916

Williamsburg series (Elsywth Thane)

Willing Hostage, The (Elizabeth Ashton), 1975

Willing Hostage (Marlys Millhiser), 1976

Will-o'-the-Wisp (Baroness Orczy), 1947

Willow Herb, The (Rona Randall), 1965

Willow Maid, The (Maureen Peters), 1974

Willow Weep (Dorothy Daniels), 1970

Willowwood (Mollie Hardwick), 1980

Wind and the Spray, The (Joyce Dingwell), 1961

Wind from the Hill, A (Anne Worboys, as Annette Eyre), 1968

Wind in the Green Trees, The (Mollie Chappell), 1969

Wind of Complication, The (Susan Ertz), 1927

Wind of Death (Mary Linn Roby, as Mary Wilson), 1976

Wind of Fate (Irene Roberts), 1961

Wind off the Small Isles, The (Mary Stewart), 1968

Wind on the Heath (Naomi Jacob), 1956

Wind River (Margaret Way), 1974

Wind Singing, A (Jean S. MacLeod, as Catherine Airlie), 1954

Wind So Gay (Flora Kidd), 1968

Wind Which Moved a Ship (Sophia Cleugh), 1936

Windscreen Weepers, The (Joan Aiken), 1969

Windier Skies (Mary Howard), 1930

Winding Stair, The (Jane Aiken Hodge), 1968

Windmills of Kalakos, The (Iris Danbury), 1976

Window on the Square (Phyllis A. Whitney), 1962

Windows at the White Cat, The (Mary Roberts Rinehart), 1910

Winds from the Sea (Margaret Pargeter), 1975

Winds in the Wilderness (Kathryn Blair, as Rosalind Brett), 1954

Winds of Chance (Jeffery Farnol), 1934

Winds of Desire (May Edginton), 1946

Winds of Desire (Hettie Grimstead), 1954

Winds of Enchantment (Kathryn Blair, as Rosalind Brett), 1949

Winds of Fear (Maysie Greig), 1956

Winds of Fortune (Jeffery Farnol), 1934

Winds of Heaven, The (Margaret Way), 1979

Winds of Night, The (Anne Maybury), 1967

Winds of Spring, The (Anne Maybury), 1948

Winds of the World, The (Ruby M. Ayres), 1918

Windward Crest (Anne Hampson), 1973

Wine, Women, and Waiters (Gilbert Frankau), 1932

Wines of Cyprien (Dorothy Daniels), 1977

Wingarden (Elsie Lee), 1971

Winged Love (Denise Robins), 1941

Wings in the Dust (Netta Muskett), 1933

Wings for Nurse Bennett (Adeline McElfresh), 1960

Wings of Chance (Madame Albanesi, as Effie Rowlands), 1931

Wings of Fear (Mignon Eberhart), 1945

Wings of Love, The (Barbara Cartland), 1962

Wings of Memory, The (Eleanor Farnes), 1953

Wings of the Falcon (Barbara Michaels), 1977

Wings of the Morning (Betty Beaty), 1982

Wings of the Night (Anne Hampson), 1971

Wings on My Heart (Barbara Cartland, as Barbara McCorquodale), 1954

Winifred (Ursula Bloom), 1903

Winner Take All (Ruby M. Ayres), 1937

Winnie Childs, The Shop Girl (C.N. and A.M. Williamson), 1926

Winsome Witch, A (Annie S. Swan), 1933

Winter and Rough Weather (D.E. Stevenson), 1951

Winter at Cray (Rebecca Stratton, as Lucy Gillen), 1971

Winter Bride, The (Carola Salisbury), 1978

Winter Harvest (Norah Lofts), 1955

Winter of Change (Betty Neels), 1973

Winter of Discontents (Gilbert Frankau), 1941

Winter of Fear, A (D.A. Ponsonby, as Sarah Tempest), 1967

Winter of the Witch (Julia Fitzgerald, as Julia Watson), 1972

Winter People, The (Phyllis A. Whitney), 1969

Winter Rose, The (Hettie Grimstead), 1972

Winter Sisters, The (Suzanne Ebel, as Suzanne Goodwin), 1980

Winter Spring, The (Suzanne Ebel, as Suzanne Goodwin), 1978

Winter Wedding (Betty Neels), 1980

Winter's Day (Netta Muskett), 1936

Winter's Passion, A (Doris Langley Moore), 1932

Wintersbride (Sara Seale), 1951

Wintersweet (Mollie Chappell), 1978

Winterwood (Dorothy Eden), 1967

Winthrop Woman, The (Anya Seton), 1958

Wire Blind, The (Netta Muskett), 1944

Wisdom's Daughter (H. Rider Haggard), 1923

Wise and the Foolish Virgins, The (Marguerite Steen), 1932

Wise and the Steadfast, The (Countess Barcynska, as Oliver Sandys), 1961

Wise Forget, The (Mary Howard), 1944

Wise Is the Heart (Anne Duffield), 1947

Wisest Fool, The (Nigel Tranter), 1974

Wish a Day, A (Berta Ruck), 1956

Wish on the Moon (Mary Burchell), 1949

Wish upon a Dream (Hebe Elsna, as Laura Conway), 1958

Wish with the Candles (Betty Neels), 1972

Wishing Star, The (Maysie Greig), 1942

Witch, The (Mary Johnston), 1914

Witch (Barbara Michaels), 1973

Witch Doctor, The (Elisabeth Ogilvie), 1959

Witch from the Sea, The (Victoria Holt, as Philippa Carr), 1975

Witch in Pink, The (Annie S. Swan), 1938

Witches, The (Norah Lofts, as Peter Curtis), 1966

Witches of All Saints, The (Jill Tattersall), 1975

Witches of Conyngton, The (Sylvia Thorpe), 1976

Witches' Sabbath (Charity Blackstock, as Paula Allardyce), 1961

Witch-Finder, The (May Wynne), 1923

Witching Hour, The (Rona Randall), 1970

Witching Hour, The (Florence Stevenson), 1971

Witch's Castle (Dorothy Daniels), 1971

Witch's Crossing (Florence Stevenson), 1975

Witch's Head, The (H. Rider Hagard), 1884

Witch's House, The (Charlotte Armstrong), 1963

Witch's Island (Dorothy Daniels), 1972

Witchstone (Anne Mather), 1974

With a Little Luck (Janet Dailey), 1982

With All Her Heart (Charles Garvice), 1910

With All My Heart (Nan Asquith), 1954

With All My Love (Claire Lorrimer, as Patricia Robins), 1963

With All My Worldly Goods (Mary Burchell), 1938

With Banners (Emilie Loring), 1935

With Every Year (Catherine Gaskin), 1949

With Fire and Flowers (Irene Roberts, as Iris Rowland), 1963

With Fondest Thoughts (Charity Blackstock), 1980

With Heart So True (Madame Albanesi, as Effie Rowlands)

With Murder in Mind (Maureen Peters, as Judith Rothman), 1975

With Somebody Else (Theresa Charles), 1981

With This Ring (Mignon Eberhart), 1941

With This Ring (Emilie Loring), 1960

Withering Fires (Marjorie Bowen), 1931

Within a Year (Faith Baldwin), 1934

Within the Bubble (Marjorie Bowen, as Joseph Shearing), 1950

Within the Gates (G.B. Burgin), 1914

Without a Honeymoon (Theresa Charles, as Jan Tempest), 1952

Witness, The (Grace Livingston Hill), 1917

Witness at Large (Mignon Eberhart), 1966

Wives and Lovers (Margaret Millar), 1954

Wizard, The (H. Rider Haggard), 1896

Wizard's Daughter, The (Barbara Michaels), 1980

Wolf and the Dove, The (Kathleen E. Woodiwiss), 1974

Wolf and the Unicorn, The (Julia Fitzgerald, as Julia Watson), 1971

Wolf in Man's Clothing (Mignon Eberhart), 1942

Wolf of Heimra, The (Jean S. MacLeod), 1965

Wolfe's Cloister (Bentz Plagemann), 1974

Woman Against Her (Madame Albanesi, as Effie Rowlands)

Woman Alive (Susan Ertz), 1935

Woman at the Door, The (Warwick Deeping), 1937

Woman at the Wheel (Leila Mackinlay), 1940

Woman Called Fancy, A (Frank Yerby), 1951

Woman Called Mary, The (Ursula Bloom, as Deborah Mann), 1960

Woman Decides (Charles Garvice), 1908

Woman Doctor, The (Ursula Bloom), 1978

Woman Doctor (Elizabeth Seifert), 1951

Woman from the Sea (Elizabeth Renier), 1971

Woman Hater, The (Ruby M. Ayres), 1920

Woman in Grey, A (A.M. Williamson), 1898

Woman in It, The (Charles Garvice), 1911

Woman in Love (Kathleen Norris), 1935

Woman in Silk and Shadows, A (Dorothy Daniels), 1977

Woman in the Back Seat, The (Marguerite Steen), 1959

Woman in the Firelight, The (Countess Barcynska, as Oliver Sandys), 1911

Woman in the House, The (Robert Hichens), 1945

Woman in the Woods, The (Charity Blackstock, as Lee Blackstock), 1958

Woman Like Us, A (Rosemary Ellerbeck, as Nicola Thorne), 1979

Woman of Experience, A (Countess Barcyṇska), 1931

Woman of Fury (Constance Gluyas), 1978

Woman of Knockaloe, The (Hall Caine), 1923

Woman of Property, A (Maynah Lewis), 1976

Woman of the Family (May Edginton), 1935

Woman of the Horizon, The (Gilbert Frankau), 1917

Woman on Her Own (Faith Baldwin), 1946

Woman on Her Own, A (Jane Blackmore), 1957

Woman on the Roof (Mignon Eberhart), 1968

Woman Scorned, A (Madame Albanesi, as Effie Rowlands), 1899

Woman Thou Gavest Me, The (Hall Caine), 1913

Woman Who Came Between, The (Madame Albanesi, as Effie Rowlands), 1895

Woman Who Came Between (Charles Garvice, as Caroline Hart)

Woman Who Dared, The (A.M. Williamson), 1903

Woman Who Parted Them, The (Mabel St. John, as Henry St. John Cooper), 1926

Woman Who Squandered Men, The (May Edginton), 1927

Woman Who Was Tomorrow, The (Ursula Bloom), 1940

Woman with the Fan, The (Robert Hichens), 1904

Woman Without a Heart, The (G.B. Burgin), 1930

Woman Worth Winning, A (Madame Albanesi, as Effie Rowlands), 1911

Woman Wronged (Charles Garvice, as Caroline Hart)

Woman's Fault, The (Madame Albanesi, as Effie Rowlands), 1915

Woman's Part, The (Annie S. Swan), 1916

Woman's Side of It, The (Denise Robins), 1937

Woman's Soul (Charles Garvice), 1902

Woman's War, A (Warwick Deeping), 1907

Woman's Way, A (G.B. Burgin), 1908

Woman's Way, The (Charles Garvice), 1914

Woman's Way, A (Mabel St. John, as Henry St. John Cooper), 1935

Women Always Forgive (Hebe Elsna), 1934

Women Are Like That (E.M. Delafield), 1929

Women Are So Simple (Theresa Charles, as Fay Chandos), 1941

Women at Work (Margaret Kennedy), 1966

Women Have Hearts (Barbara Cartland), 1980

Women in Love (Hebe Elsna, as Vicky Lancaster), 1957

Women in White (Frank G. Slaughter), 1974

Women Live Too Long (Viña Delmar), 1932

Women Money Buys, The (Maysie Greig), 1931

Women of Eden, The (Marilyn Harris), 1980

Women of the Aftermath (Evadne Price, as Helen Zenna Smith), 1931

Women Who Pass By (Viña Delmar), 1929

Women Who Seek (Denise Robins), 1928

Wonder Cruise (Ursula Bloom), 1933

Wonder of Love, A (Madame Albanesi), 1911

Wonder Trip (Ursula Bloom, as Sheila Burns), 1939

Wondrous To-Morrow, The (Anne Maybury), 1936

Wood and the Trees, The (Mary Elgin), 1967

Wood Is My Pulpit, The (Countess Barcynska), 1942

Woodville Wench, The (Maureen Peters), 1972

Wooing of Rosamond Fayre, The (Berta Ruck), 1915

Wooing of Rose, The (Madame Albanesi, as Effie Rowlands), 1912

Wooing of the Queen, The (L. Adams Beck, as E. Barrington), 1934

Workaday Lady (Maysie Greig), 1936

Working Girl's Honor (Charles Garvice, as Caroline Hart

World Full of Strangers, A (Cynthia Freeman), 1975

World in Spell, A (D.E. Stevenson), 1939

World Is Like That, The (Kathleen Norris), 1940

World of Christy Pembroke, The (Hebe Elsna, as Lyndon Snow), 1978

World of Dreams, A (Madame Albanesi, as Effie Rowlands), 1935

World under Snow (D.K. Broster), 1935

World We Live In, The (Louis Bromfield), 1944

World Well Lost, The (Annie S. Swan), 1935

World Without End (Gilbert Frankau), 1943

World's a Stage, The (Victoria Holt, as Kathleen Kellow), 1960

Worlds Apart (Hester W. Chapman), 1946

World's Desire, The (H. Rider Haggard), 1890

World's Fair Nurse (Dorothy Daniels), 1964

Wormwood (Marie Corelli), 1890

Worse Than Murder (Evelyn Berckman), 1957

Worst Wife in the World, The (Mabel St. John), 1915

Worth Wile (P.C. Wren), 1937

Wounded Heart (Charles Garvice), 1911

Wounded Name, The (D.K. Broster), 1922

Woven of the Wind (Annie S. Swan), 1912

Woven on Fate's Loom (Charles Garvice), 1903

Wreath for Arabella (Doris Leslie), 1948

Wreath of Holly, A (Mollie Chappell), 1959

Wrestler on the Shore, The (May Wynne, as Lester Lurgan), 1912

Write from the Heart (Maysie Greig, as Jennifer Ames), 1972

Writing Man (Countess Barcynska), 1939

Wrong Man, The (Katrina Britt), 1980

Wrong Mr. Right, The (Berta Ruck), 1919

Wrong Woman, The (G.B. Burgin), 1932

Wrongs Righted (Annie S. Swan), 1924

Wych Stone, The (Marjorie McEvoy), 1974

Wychwood (Nicole St. John), 1976

Wyndham's Daughter (Annie S. Swan), 1898

Wynne of Windwhistle (Ruby M. Ayres), 1926

Yankee Pasha (Edison Marshall), 1948

Yankee Stranger (Elswyth Thane), 1944

Year After, The (Ruby M. Ayres), 1916

Year at Coverley, A (Annie S. Swan), 1883

Year of Her Life, A (Hebe Elsna, as Lyndon Snow), 1951

Year of the Dragon (Joyce Dingwell), 1978

Year of the Pageant, The (Mary Ann Gibbs), 1971

Years for Rachel, The (Berta Ruck), 1918

Years of Change, The (Mollie Hardwick), 1974

Yellow Brick Road, The (Elizabeth Cadell), 1960

Yellow God, The (H. Rider Haggard), 1908

Yellow Is for Fear (Dorothy Eden), 1968

Yellow Moon, The (Rebecca Stratton), 1974

Yellow Poppy, The (D.K. Broster), 1920

Yellow Room, The (Mary Roberts Rinehart), 1945

Yesterday and Tomorrow (Hebe Elsna, as Lyndon Snow), 1971

Yesterday Came Suddenly (Maynah Lewis), 1975

Yesterday Is Tomorrow (Countess Barcynska, as Marguerite Barclay), 1950

Yesterday's Evil (Dorothy Daniels), 1979

Yesterday's Harvest (Margaret Pedler), 1926

Yesterday's Lover (Hettie Grimstead, as Marsha Manning), 1969

Yesterday's Madness (Marian Cockrell), 1943

Yesterday's Magic (Jane Arbor), 1957

Yesterday's Mischief (Elizabeth Renier), 1975

Yesterday's Tomorrow (Ursula Bloom), 1968

Yet Love Remains (Mary Burchell), 1938

Yet She Follows (Barbara Cartland), 1944

Yield Not to Temptation! (Mabel St. John, as Henry St. John Cooper), 1923

Yolanda (Naomi Jacob), 1963

Yollop (George Barr McCutcheon), 1922

You Are the One (Berta Ruck), 1945

You Belong to Me (Elizabeth Hoy), 1938

You Can't Escape (Faith Baldwin), 1942

You Can't Have Everything (Kathleen Norris), 1937

You Can't Live Alone (Elizabeth Hoy), 1944

You Can't Lose Yesterday (Elizabeth Hoy), 1940

You Get What You Give (Louis Bromfield), 1951

You Have Chosen (Denise Robins), 1938

You Never Knew (Hebe Elsna), 1933

You Should Have Warned Me (Theresa Charles, as Fay Chandos), 1940

You Took My Heart (Elizabeth Hoy), 1939

You'll Like My Mother (Naomi A. Hintze), 1960

You'll Love Me Yet (Claire Ritchie), 1963

Young Amanda, The (Sara Seale), 1950

Young and Broke (Hebe Elsna), 1943

Young Ann (Mary Ann Gibbs, as Elizabeth Ford), 1973

Young at Heart, The (Ruby M. Ayres), 1942

Young Bar (Rosamunde Pilcher, as Jane Fraser), 1952

Young Barbara (Mar Edginton), 1948

Young Blood (Annie S. Swan), 1917

Young Clementina, The (D.E. Stevenson), 1970

Young Curmudgeon, The (Theresa Charles, as Leslie Lance), 1964

Young Deloraine (G.B. Burgin), 1926

Young Diana, The (Marie Corelli), 1918

Young Doctor (Elizabeth Seifert), 1939

Young Doctor Galahad (Elizabeth Seifert), 1938

Young Doctor Goddard (Elizabeth Harrison), 1978

Young Doctor Kenway (Rona Randall), 1950

Young Doctor Kirkdene (Elizabeth Hoy), 1955

Young Doctor Randall (Adeline McElfresh), 1957

Young Doctors Downstairs, The (Lucilla Andrews), 1963

Young Emmanuel (Naomi Jacob), 1932

Young Green Corn, The (Doris E. Smith), 1971

Young Hearts (Madame Albanesi, as Effie Rowlands), 1924

Young Intruder, The (Eleanor Farnes), 1953

Young Invader, The (Anne Maybury), 1947

Young Is My Love (Ruby M. Ayres), 1941

Young Jonathan (Sophia Cleugh), 1932

Young Kangaroos Prefer Riding (Ursula Bloom, as Mary Essex), 1947

Young Labelle, The (G.B. Burgin), 1924

Young Ladies' Room, The (Mary Ann Gibbs, as Elizabeth Ford), 1945

Young Lady, The (Mary Howard), 1950

Young Lady from Paris, The (Joan Aiken), 1982

Young Lady of Fashion, A (Mary Ann Gibbs), 1978

Young Lady with Red Hair (Mary Ann Gibbs), 1959

Young Love Wakes (Hebe Elsna, as Lyndon Snow), 1940

Young Lucifer (Charity Blackstock), 1960

Young Man Comes to London, A (Michael Arlen), 1931

Young Man from the Country, A (Madame Albanesi), 1906

Young Man with Ideas, A (Mary Ann Gibbs), 1950

Young Man Without Money (Maysie Greig), 1958

Young Man's Slave (Leila Mackinlay), 1936

Young Man's Year, A (Anthony Hope), 1915

Young Men in Love (Michael Arlen), 1927

Young Mrs. Brand (Robert Hichens), 1944

Young Mrs. Savage (D.E. Stevenson), 1948

Young Montrose, The (Nigel Tranter), 1972

Young Mother Hubbard (Kathleen Norris), 1932

Young Ones, The (Mary Howard), 1975

Young Parent (Ursula Bloom), 1934

Young Romantic, The (Iris Bromige), 1964

Young Shoulders (Ruby M. Ayres), 1947

Young Stagers, The (P.C. Wren), 1917

Young Tracy (Kathryn Blair, as Rosalind Brett), 1958

Young Widow, The (Anne Betteridge), 1961

Young Wife, The (Madame Albanesi, as Effie Rowlands), 1911

Young Wives' Tale, A (Doris Leslie), 1971

Younger Brother, The (Annie S. Swan), 1941

Younger Miss Nightingale, The (Hebe Elsna), 1959

Younger Sister, The (Anne Betteridge), 1964

Younger Sister (Kathleen Norris), 1932

Youngest Aunt, The (Ruby M. Ayres), 1952

Youngest Bridesmaid, The (Sara Seale), 1963

Youngest Sister, The (Theresa Charles, as Jan Tempest), 1958

Youngest Venus, The (Berta Ruck), 1928

Your Sins and Mine (Taylor Caldwell), 1955

You're Best Alone (Norah Lofts, as Peter Curtis), 1943

Yours Forever (Maysie Greig), 1948

Yours to Command (Mary Burchell), 1955

Yours with Love (Mary Burchell), 1940

Youth Without Glory (Baroness von Hutten), 1938

Yvonne, The Confident (Katheryn Kimbrough), 1979

Zella Sees Herself (E.M. Delafield), 1917
Zemindar (Valerie Fitzgerald), 1981
Ziska (Marie Corelli), 1897
Zulu Moon (Gwen Westwood), 1980

NOTES
ON
ADVISERS
AND
CONTRIBUTORS

ALTNER, Patricia.   Librarian, U.S. Army Armament Research and Development Command, Dover, New Jersey. Reviewer of historical fiction for *Library Journal*, and Associate Editor, *The Year's Scholarship in Science Fiction, Fantasy, and Horror Literature*.   **Essays:** Pamela Bennetts; Mary Ann Gibbs; Velda Johnston; Alanna Knight; Marjorie McEvoy; Annette Motley; Edith Pargeter; Rona Randall; Rosemary Rogers; Danielle Steel; Chelsea Quinn Yarbro.

ANDERSON, Rachel.   Free-lance writer: children's book reviewer for *Good Housekeeping*. Author of *The Purpled Heart Throbs: The Sub-Literature of Love*, 1974, *Dream Lovers* (autobiography), 1978, and fiction for adults and children.   **Essays:** Madame Albanesi; Ruby M. Ayres; Florence L. Barclay; G.B. Burgin; Hall Caine; Ethel M. Dell; Maud Diver; May Edginton; Maysie Greig; E.M. Hull; Netta Muskett; Margaret Pedler; Berta Ruck.

BAKERMAN, Jane S.   Associate Professor of English, Indiana State University, Terre Haute. Adviser and contributor to *American Women Writers*, 1979, and contributor to *Armchair Detective, Mystery Nook, Writer's Yearbook*, and other periodicals.   **Essays:** Daphne du Maurier; Edna Ferber.

BARGAINNIER, Earl F.   Fuller E. Callaway Professor of English Language and Literature, Wesleyan College, Macon, Georgia; Editor, *Studies in Popular Culture*. Author of *The Gentle Art of Murder: The Detective Fiction of Agatha Christie*, 1980. Editor of *Ten Women of Mystery*, 1981, and *Thirteen Englishmen of Mystery*, forthcoming.   **Essays:** Lance Horner and Kyle Onstott; Edison Marshall; Frank Yerby.

BARNES, Melvyn.   City Librarian, City of Westminster, London. Author of *Best Detective Fiction: A Guide from Godwin to the Present*, 1975, and *Youth Library Work*, 1976 (2nd edition). Editor of the Remploy Deerstalker crime fiction reprints. Adviser and contributor to *Twentieth-Century Crime and Mystery Writers*, 1980, and Contributor to *Novels and Novelists*, 1980.   **Essays:** Evelyn Berckman; Gwendoline Butler; Mignon G. Eberhart; Dornford Yates.

BERNEIS, Susan B.   Free-lance writer. Former librarian.   **Essays:** Laura Black; Madeleine Brent; Cecily Crowe; Naomi A. Hintze; Marlys Millhiser; Elisabeth Ogilvie; Anne Stevenson.

BLEILER, E.F.   Editorial Consultant, Charles Scribner's Sons. Formerly Editor, Dover Publications. Author of *The Checklist of Science-Fiction and Supernatural Fiction*, 1978 (revised edition). Editor of works by Ernest Bramah, R. Austin Freeman, Emile Gaboriau, Robert H. van Gulik, and Roy Vickers, and Dime Novelists and Victorian Sensational Novelists.   **Essays:** Lily Adams Beck; D.K. Broster; Robert Hichens; Dorothy Macardle; Lady Eleanor Smith.

BLOCK, Marylaine.   Assistant Director, St. Ambrose College Library, Davenport, Iowa. Book reviewer for *Library Journal*.   **Essays:** Janet Caird; Marian Cockrell; Catherine Fellows; Rachel Lindsay; Margaret Lynn; Charlotte MacLeod; Joan Smith.

BOUSFIELD, Wendy.   Humanities Librarian, Wichita State University, Kansas. Contributor to *Reference Guide to Science Fiction and Fantasy Magazines*, forthcoming, and reviewer for *Library Journal, American Reference Books Annual, Science Fiction and Fantasy Book Review*, and other periodicals.   **Essay:** Russell Kirk.

BRANCH, Susan.   Librarian, Worthington, Ohio. Reviewer, *Library Journal*.   **Essays:** Joan Aiken; Elizabeth Cadell; Juanita Coulson; Jeffery Farnol.

BUCHANAN, Jean.   Free-lance researcher, editor, and lexicographer. Worked for 6 years on *A Supplement to the Oxford English Dictionary* and *The Pocket Oxford Dictionary* (6th edition). Author of *The History of the English Faculty Library, Oxford*, 1979.   **Essays:** Helen Beauclerk; Marion Collin; Mabel Barnes Grundy; Baroness von Hutten; Norah Lofts; Mrs. Patrick MacGill; Lady Miles.

CADOGAN, Mary.   Secretary of an educational trust; governor of an international school; and free-lance writer. Author of three books on popular literature with Patricia Craig—*You're a Brick, Angela*, 1976, *Women and Children First*, 1978, and *The Lady Investigates*, 1981—and of *The Greyfriars' Characters*, 1975, *The Charles Hamilton Schoolgirls' Album*, 1979, and *The Morcove Companion*, 1981.   **Essays:** Barbara Cartland; Theresa Charles; Jilly Cooper; Frances Cowen; R.F. Delderfield; Valerie Fitzgerald; Cynthia Freeman; Patricia Matthews; L.M. Montgomery; Baroness Orczy; Elizabeth O. Peter; Evadne Price; Mabel St. John; Mrs. George de Horne Vaizey; C.N. and A.M. Williamson; Esther Wyndham; May Wynne.

CARGILL, Jennifer.   Acquisitions Librarian, Miami University, Oxford, Ohio.   **Essay:** Mary Westmacott.

CARTLAND, Barbara.   See her own entry.

CHESTER, Tessa Rose.   Staff member, Renier Collection of Children's Books, Victoria and Albert Museum, London. Reviewer for *Times Educational Supplement* and *Phaedrus*.   **Essays:** Patricia Ainsworth; Elisabeth Beresford; Iris Bromige; Susan Inglis; Denise Robins.

CLEAVER, Pamela.   Free-lance writer. Reviewer for *Children's Book Review, Books and Bookmen*, and *Foundation*, and contributor to *Twentieth-Century Children's Writers*. Author of *The Sparrow Book of Record Breakers* [and *Animal Records*], 2 vols., 1981-82.   **Essays:** Marjorie Bowen, Ann Bridge; Louis Bromfield; Hester W. Chapman; Dorothy Dunnett; Catherine Gavin; H. Rider Haggard; Rosemary Harris; Margaret Irwin; Nigel Tranter.

FRENCH, Warren.   Professor of English and Director of the Center for American Studies, Indiana University-Purdue University, Indianapolis; Member of the Editorial Board, *American Literature* and *Twentieth-Century Literature*; series editor for Twayne publishers. Author of *John Steinbeck*, 1961; *Frank Norris*, 1962; *J.D. Salinger*, 1963 (revised, 1976); *A Companion to "The Grapes of Wrath,"* 1963; *The Social Novel at the End of an Era*, 1966; and a series on American literature, *The Thirties*, 1967, *The Forties*, 1968, *The Fifties*, 1971, and *The Twenties*, 1975.   **Essays:** Warwick Deeping; Frances Parkinson Keyes.

FUCHS, Marcia G.   Reference Librarian and Cataloguer, Guilford Free Library, Connecticut. Reviewer for *Library Journal* and *Reprint Books Bulletin*.   **Essays:** Stephanie Blake; Lolah Burford; David Case; Pamela Hill; Natasha Peters; Nicole St. John.

GOTTSCHALK, Jane.   Professor of English, University of Wisconsin, Oshkosh. Author of essays on detective fiction in *Armchair Detective* and *Twentieth-Century Crime and Mystery Writers*, and on American literature in *Phylon, Wisconsin Review*, and *Renascence*.   **Essays:** Charlotte Armstrong; Mary Roberts Rinehart.

GREY, Elizabeth.   Free-lance writer and broadcaster. Author of 16 books, including biographies of Edith Cavell and Amy Johnson, *The Story of Journalism*, 1968, and *The Noise of Drums and Trumpets*, 1971. Romantic and historical fiction reviewer for *The Times, Good Book Guide*, and *Books and Bookmen*.   **Essays:** Lucilla Andrews; Betty Beaty; Anne Betteridge; Suzanne Ebel; Anna Gilbert; Mollie Hardwick; Elizabeth Harrison; Mary Howard; Rhona Martin; Sarah Neilan; Claire Rayner; Joanna Trollope.

HANSCOM, Marion.   Special Collections/Fine Arts Librarian, State University of New York, Binghamton. Reviewer for *Library Journal*, and editor of two manuscript collections held at her library.   **Essays:** Elizabeth Seifert; Frank G. Slaughter.

HARRIS, Marion R.   Free-lance writer: Editorial Controller, W. Foulsham publishers, Slough, Berkshire. Author of 20 non-fiction books, a historical romance, *Captain of Her Heart*, and 4 Doctor/Nurse romances as Rose Young and Rosemary Young.   **Essays:** Dorothy Mackie Low; Ivy Preston; Irene Roberts; Anne Rundle.

HAYNE, Barrie.   Associate Professor of English and Instructor in Cinema Studies, Innis

College, University of Toronto. Author of articles and reviews on Cooper, Poe, Mrs. Stowe, and numerous papers for the Popular Culture Association. **Essays:** Eleanor H. Porter; Jean Webster.

HAYNE, Joanne Harack. Coordinator, In-House Programs, Ryerson Polytechnical Institute, Toronto. Author of several papers on crime and detective writing for the Popular Culture Association. **Essays:** Susan Ertz; Barbara Michaels; D.E. Stevenson; Jean Stubbs.

HELD, Michael. Free-lance writer. **Essay:** Barbara Riefe.

HEYDUK, Allayne C. Part-time librarian, and free-lance writer. Reviewer for *Library Journal*. **Essays:** Phyllis Hastings; Jessica Stirling.

HINKEMEYER, Joan. Librarian, Denver Public Library; Columnist, *Energy/Environment Newsletter*, Denver. Former English professor, assistant editor, *Colorado Libraries*, and reviewer for *Library Journal* and *Rocky Mountain News*. **Essays:** Sophie Cleugh; Anne Edwards.

JAMES, Louis. Senior Lecturer in English and American Literature, Keynes College, University of Kent, Canterbury. Author of *The Islands in Between*, 1968, and *Fiction for the Working-Class Man 1830-1850*, 1974. **Essays:** Marie Corelli; Anthony Hope.

JENSEN, Margaret. Assistant Professor of Sociology, Hamline University, St. Paul, Minnesota. Author of a Ph.D. dissertation *Women and Romantic Fiction: A Case Study of Harlequin Enterprises, Romances, and Readers*, and articles in *A Room of One's Own* and *Occasional Papers of the McMaster University Sociology of Women Programme*. **Essays:** Mary Burchell; Joyce Dingwell; Anne Hampson; Emilie Loring; Violet Winspear.

KEMP, Barbara. Assistant Head of the Undergraduate Library, University of Michigan, Ann Arbor. Reviewer for *Library Journal* and *American Reference Books Annual*. **Essays:** Robyn Carr; Caroline Courtney; Hebe Elsna; Roberta Gellis; Alice Chetwynd Ley; Laura London; Laurie McBain; Janet Louise Roberts; Mary Linn Roby; Carola Salisbury; Florence Stevenson; Jill Tattersall; Sylvia Thorpe; Patricia Veryan; Sheila Walsh; Claudette Williams.

LANDRUM, Larry N. Associate Professor of English, Michigan State University, East Lansing. Co-Editor, *Dimensions of Detective Fiction*, 1976; contributed "Guide to Detective Fiction" to *Handbook of American Popular Culture*, 1978. **Essays:** Rafael Sabatini; Samuel Shellabarger.

LEETE-HODGE, Lornie. Free-lance writer and editor. Author of many children's books and books on Wiltshire and the Royal Family. **Essays:** Ursula Bloom; Maureen Peters; D.A. Ponsonby.

LOCKHART, Marilyn. Free-lance writer. Former librarian. Reviewer for *Library Journal*. **Essays:** Mary Francis Craig; Anne Eliot; Rosemary Ellerbeck; Rosalind Laker; Jacqueline La Tourrette; Frances Murray; Rosamunde Pilcher; Bentz Plagemann; Jennifer Wade; Anne Worboys.

LONGEST, George C. Associate Professor and Acting Chairman of the English Department, Virginia Commonwealth University, Richmond. Author of *Three Virginia Writers: Mary Johnston, Thomas Nelson Page, and Amélie Rives Troubetzkoy*, 1978, and of many articles and reviews. Editor, annual bibliographies in southern literature for *Mississippi Quarterly*. **Essay:** Mary Johnston.

LYNN, Mary C. Member of the Department of American Studies, Skidmore College, Saratoga Springs, New York. **Essays:** Clare Darcy; Jane Aiken Hodge; Elswyth Thane.

MACDONALD, Gina. Member of the English Department, Loyola University, New

Orleans. Author of articles on Southwestern writers, popular culture, and Shakespearian influences. **Essays:** Alice Abbott; Brian Cleeve; Thomas B. Costain; Susan Hufford; Shirley Jackson; Barbara Ferry Johnson; Barbara Kevern; Marie Belloc Lowndes; Rohan O'Grady; Barbara Anne Pauley.

McGRATH, Joan. Library Consultant, Toronto Board of Education. Contributor to *Twentieth-Century Children's Writers*; columnist for *In Review* and *Emergency Librarian*; reviewer for *Canadian Materials, School Library Journal*, and *Quill and Quire*. **Essays:** Hervey Allen; Evelyn Anthony; Michael Arlen; Marcia Davenport; Mazo de la Roche; Rachel Field; Gilbert Frankau; Rose Franken; Janice Holt Giles; Elizabeth Goudge; W.G. Hardy; Georgette Heyer; Fannie Hurst; Naomi Jacob; Margaret Kennedy; Doris Leslie; Rosamond Marshall; Gene Stratton Porter.

McNALL, Sally Allen. Member of the English Department, University of Kansas, Lawrence. Author of *Who Is in the House? A Psychological Study of Two Centuries of Women's Fiction in America, 1795 to the Present*, 1981. **Essay:** Marilyn Harris.

MELDRUM, P.R. Free-lance writer. Worked in the Public Record Office, London, 11 years. **Essays:** Mollie Chappell; Anne Duffield; Hettie Grimstead; Leila Mackinlay; Kate Norway; Claire Ritchie; Petra Sawley; Olga Sinclair; Annie S. Swan; Daoma Winston.

MOORE, Arlene. Reference and Government Documents Librarian, Missouri Southern State College, Joplin. Author of articles on popular culture and librarianship, and a forthcoming work on the author Bertha M. Clay. Co-Editor, *The North American Union List of Victorian Periodicals*. **Essays:** Jane Arbor; Elizabeth Ashton; Nan Asquith; Susan Barrie; Gloria Bevan; Kathryn Blair; Rose Burghley; Isobel Chace; Eleanor Farnes; Charles Garvice; Elizabeth Hoy; Flora Kidd; Roumelia Lane; Marjorie Lewty; Wynne May; Betty Neels; Margaret Pargeter; Henrietta Reid; Margaret Rome; Sara Seale; Doris E. Smith; Rebecca Stratton; Essie Summers; Lucy Walker; Margaret Way; Gwen Westwood.

MOTTELER, Marilynn. Faculty Assistant, Michigan Technological University, Houghton. **Essays:** Catherine Cookson; Dorothy Eden; Anne Maybury.

MUSSELL, Kay. Director of the American Studies Program, American University, Washington, D.C. Author of *Women's Gothic and Romantic Fiction: A Reference Guide*, 1981. **Essays:** Mary Elgin; Victoria Holt; Charlotte Lamb; Anne Mather; Anya Seton; Mary Stewart; Kay Thorpe.

MUSSER, Necia A. Head of Acquisitions and Collection Development, Western Michigan University Libraries, Kalamazoo. Reviewer for *Library Journal*. **Essays:** Katrina Britt; Iris Danbury; Katheryn Kimbrough; Adeline McElfresh; Lilian Peake.

NEUBERG, Victor. Member of the School of Librarianship, Polytechnic of North London. Author of *Popular Literature: A History and Guide*, 1977.

PAYNTER, Kim. Free-lance writer. **Essays:** Countess Barcynska; Clare Emsley; Jean S. MacLeod.

PIEHL, Kathy. Free-lance writer. Former university teacher. Author of articles on children's writers and on E.L. Doctorow. **Essays:** Rumer Godden; Isabelle Holland; Helen Van Slyke.

POGEL, Nancy H. Associate Professor of American Thought and Language, Michigan State University, East Lansing. Author of an article on Constance Mayfield Rourke in *American Woman Writers*, sections in *Handbook of American Popular Culture*, and a forthcoming book on Woody Allen. **Essay:** George Barr McCutcheon.

RADCLIFFE, Elsa J. Author of *Gothic Novels of the Twentieth Century: An Annotated Bibliography*, 1979.

RADWAY, Janice. Member of the American Civilization Department, University of Pennsylvania, Philadelphia. Author of the forthcoming book *Reading the Romance: Women and Popular Literature*. **Essay:** Kathleen E. Woodiwiss.

REGAN, Nancy. Bookseller and free-lance writer. Author of "A Home of One's Own: Women's Bodies in Recent Women's Fiction" in *Journal of Popular Culture*, 1978. **Essays:** Faith Baldwin; Janet Dailey; Margaret Mitchell; Phyllis A. Whitney; Kathleen Winsor.

ROBERTS, Bette B. Associate Professor of English, Westfield State College, Massachusetts. Author of *The Gothic Romance: Its Appeal to Women Readers and Writers in Late Eighteenth-Century England*, 1980, and articles on gothic writing. **Essays:** Virginia Coffman; Dorothy Daniels.

ROBERTSON, Karen. Member of the English Department, Dutchess Community College, Poughkeepsie, New York. Author of a forthcoming work on women in revenge tragedy. **Essay:** Doris Langley Moore.

ROGERS, Lucy, and **Peggy YORK**. Lucy Rogers is a former teacher, now a free-lance writer. Peggy York has worked in general nursing, then midwifery and district nursing; she is also a short story writer. **Essay:** Audrie Manley-Tucker.

RUGGIERO, Josephine A., and **Louise C. WESTON**. Josephine Ruggiero is Associate Professor of Sociology, Providence College, Rhode Island. Louise Weston is Associate Manager, Marketing Research Department, General Foods Corporation, White Plains, New York. They have collaborated on several articles on women's issues. **Essays:** Susan Howatch; Elsie Lee.

SADLER, Geoffrey. Free-lance writer of western and plantation novels, as Jeff Sadler and Geoffrey Sadler. **Essays:** Dorothy Salisbury Davis; E.M. Delafield; Alice Dwyer-Joyce; Catherine Gaskin; Constance Gluyas; Pamela Haines; Constance Heaven; Claire Lorrimer; Christopher Nicole; Marguerite Steen.

SHIELDS, Anne M. Residential Social Worker at a hostel for homeless persons. **Essays:** Charity Blackstock; Juliet Dymoke.

SHUEY, Andrea Lee. Librarian, Dallas Public Library. Reviewer for *Library Journal*. **Essays:** Viña Delmar; Audrey Erskine-Lindop; Ethel Edison Gordon; Florence Engel Randall; Jean Francis Webb.

STAPLES, Katherine. Instructor in English, University of Texas, Austin, and Part-Time Instructor, Austin Community College. Contributor to *Twentieth-Century Crime and Mystery Writers*, 1980, and *American Women Writers*, 1981; translator of works by Rimbaud, Aragon, and Henri Rousseau. **Essays:** Taylor Caldwell; Elinor Glyn; Margaret Millar.

SUMMERS, Judith. Free-lance writer. **Essays:** Julia Fitzgerald; Maynah Lewis; Margaret Maddocks; Jean Marsh.

TIETZE, Thomas R. Free-lance writer. **Essay:** P.C. Wren.

von ZHAREN, W.M. Free-lance writer currently teaching in Germany. **Essays:** Jane Blackmore; Glenna Finley; Grace Livingston Hill; Elizabeth Renier; Willo Davis Roberts.

WALSH, George. Publisher and free-lance writer. **Essays:** Elizabeth; Patricia Gallagher; Kathleen Norris.

WESTON, Louise C. See the entry for Josephine A. Ruggiero above.

YORK, Peggy. See the entry for Lucy Rogers above.

ZIESELMAN, Paula M.   Professional Assistant to the Executive Director of the Metropolitan Reference and Research Library Agency, New York. Formerly Reference Librarian, New Rochelle Public Library, New York. Editor, *Westchester County Union List of Serials*. Reviewer for *Library Journal*.   **Essay:** Nancy Buckingham.